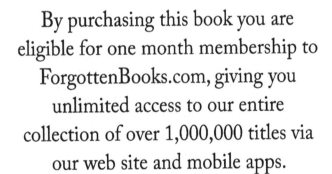

ISBN 978-0-260-16192-5
PIBN 10931753

61ST CONGRESS }   SENATE   { DOCUMENT
2d Session }   { No. 645

REPORT ON CONDITION

OF

WOMAN AND CHILD WAGE-EARNERS IN THE UNITED STATES·

IN 19 VOLUMES

VOLUME XIX: LABOR LAWS AND FACTORY CONDITIONS

Prepared under the direction of

CHAS. P. NEILL

Commissioner of Labor

WASHINGTON
GOVERNMENT PRINTING OFFICE
1912

IN THE SENATE OF THE UNITED STATES,

June 15, 1

Resolved, That the complete report on the condition of wom child wage-earners in the United States, transmitted and to be mitted by the Secretary of Commerce and Labor in response act approved January twenty-ninth, nineteen hundred and entitled "An act to authorize the Secretary of Commerce and to report upon the industrial, social, moral, educational, and p condition of woman and child workers in the United State printed as public document.

CHARLES G. BENNETT,

Secre

2

CONTENTS.

LETTERS OF TRANSMITTAL.

DEPARTMENT OF COMMERCE AND LABOR,
OFFICE OF THE SECRETARY,
Washington, November 23, 1912.

SIR: In partial compliance with the Senate resolution of May 25, 1910, I beg to transmit herewith a report showing the results of an investigation of labor laws and factory conditions in certain States.

This report has just been completed and is the nineteenth volume of the larger report on the investigation carried on in accordance with the act of Congress approved January 29, 1907, which provided "That the Secretary of Commerce and Labor be, and he is hereby, authorized and directed to investigate and report on the industrial, social, moral, educational, and physical condition of woman and child workers in the United States wherever employed, with special reference to their age, hours of labor, term of employment, health, illiteracy, sanitary and other conditions surrounding their occupation, and the means employed for the protection of their health, person, and morals."

Respectfully,   CHARLES NAGEL,
Secretary.

The PRESIDENT OF THE SENATE,
Washington, D. C.

DEPARTMENT OF COMMERCE AND LABOR,
BUREAU OF LABOR,
Washington, November 23, 1912.

SIR: I beg to transmit herewith Volume XIX of the Report on Condition of Woman and Child Wage-Earners in the United States, which relates to labor laws and factory conditions in certain States. This volume forms a part of the report of the general investigation into the condition of woman and child workers in the United States, carried on in compliance with the act of Congress approved January 29, 1907.

The field work of this investigation was carried on by groups of special agents of the bureau under the immediate field supervision of Special Agents Zach C. Elkin, Walter B. Palmer, Frank J. Sheridan, and Ethelbert Stewart. The preparation of this report in its present form, embodying the reports of these agents, is mainly the work of Hugh S. Hanna, Ph. D. The work has been carried on under the general direction and immediate supervision of Charles H. Verrill.

I am, very respectfully,

      .   G. W. W. HANGER,
Acting Commissioner.

The SECRETARY OF COMMERCE AND LABOR,
         Washington, D. C.

INTRODUCTION.

13

INTRODUCTION.

PURPOSE AND METHOD OF THE INVESTIGATION.

This volume presents the results of an investigation into the administration and operation of State labor laws. Phases of this subject have been discussed in preceding volumes of this report. Such discussions, however, covered only certain features of the law and only a very limited number of industries. Moreover, little attempt was made therein to correlate the information for the several States.

Thus the present study may be regarded, from the standpoint of labor legislation, as supplementing and completing the scattered, unrelated data of these earlier volumes. There is, however, little duplication of material. Legal quotations and analyses are necessarily repeated at times, but the investigation proper was conducted entirely independently of the earlier investigations.

Because of the wide range of present day labor legislation in the United States it was found necessary to place definite limits upon the scope of this investigation. With this in view it was decided to restrict the study to such labor laws as were applicable to factories and workshops. Thus mining laws were excluded, as was also special legislation regarding tenement shops and bakeries and occasional laws dealing with conditions of a local or otherwise very limited scope.

A second necessary limitation was upon the number of States to be covered. After a preliminary survey the following 17 were selected: Maine, Massachusetts, Rhode Island, Connecticut, New York, Pennsylvania, New Jersey, Ohio, Illinois, Indiana, Michigan, Wisconsin, Maryland, North Carolina, Georgia, Florida, and Louisiana. This list includes most of the important manufacturing States. It also includes States which are representative of all shades and degrees of labor legislation.

The investigation had two objects: The study and analysis of the labor laws and the gathering of data relative to the actual conditions of labor employment in factories and workshops where women and children are largely employed. The first could be accomplished partly by reference to the printed laws and judicial decisions. In many cases, however, the effective meaning of a law can be understood only in the light of the interpretation placed upon it by the factory inspectors or others enforcing authority. This may be either because the law is obscure and the obscurity has not been removed by judicial opinion, or because the law vests the enforcing authority with broad

15

"discretionary" powers. For these reasons it was desirable to obtain the opinions and working interpretations put upon such laws by factory inspectors and other interested persons.

The second of the mentioned objects, the obtaining of data regarding the conditions of employment in factories and workshops, could be arrived at only by personal investigation in such factories and workshops. For this purpose agents of the Bureau visited such establishments, made the necessary inquiries and examinations, and rendered their reports on prepared schedule forms.

Two kinds of schedules were used in reporting the data for each establishment, the individual slip and the establishment card. The purpose of the individual slip was to obtain personal information concerning the individual employees. It contained inquiries as to the exact work, sex, age, conjugal condition, nativity and race, and also as to the number of hours worked, the money earned during the preceding week, and the rate, whether by piece or time, according to which payment was made. One such slip was to be filled out for each employee. The information thus obtained was used in the preparation of Volume XVIII of this report.

The establishment card contained a long series of inquiries designed to bring out the important facts relative to the conduct of the establishment from the viewpoint of comfort and safety and of the labor law. These inquiries covered such points as the time schedules according to which work was conducted, overtime, safety provisions in case of fire, safeguards against accident from elevators and machinery, conditions of ventilation and sanitation, provisions for the comfort of employees, the posting of time schedules, and the filing of working certificates for children if such filing was required by law. The data thus obtained are presented in this volume.

The list of inquiries on the establishment card was uniform for all establishments visited, but was subject to modification at the discretion of the agent to meet the peculiar conditions of particular industries or particular establishments. Moreover, the agent investigating, in addition to filling out the formal schedule of inquiries, was instructed to render a detailed report of all pertinent information not covered by the schedule.

In an investigation of this character it is impossible so to frame every inquiry as to insure precisely similar understanding thereof in all cases. This is true of that large class of questions involving factory conditions for which there are no accepted standards. Thus, the opinions of two persons as to whether or not a particular workroom is kept in a "reasonably" clean condition might very well differ as there are no accepted standards by which cleanliness may be measured. A similar difference of opinion might arise as to whether a piece of machinery was properly guarded. Such differences may be minimized by a full study of conditions, by a comparison of views, and by agreement on certain fundamental principles. But it is impossible to eliminate entirely the personal equation of the investigator.

. The element of error resulting from this absence of fixed demonstrable standards was perhaps increased in the present investigation by the fact that the field work was necessarily done by a large number of agents acting to some extent independently.

The limit of time and the extent of territory to be covered prevented a uniform inquiry by a single group of agents traveling from State to State. The force of agents employed was divided into four groups, each under the direction of an expert. Each of these groups covered several States. The four State divisions were as follows: (1) Maine, Massachusetts, Rhode Island, North Carolina, Georgia; (2) Connecticut, New York, Maryland, Florida, Louisiana; (3) Pennsylvania, New Jersey, Ohio; (4) Illinois, Indiana, Michigan, Wisconsin.

Within each of these groups the agents acted in close union, visiting the same communities, conferring frequently, "comparing notes." It may be assumed, therefore, that the attitude of such agents in matters involving the personal interpretation of inquiries was in substantial harmony, and that the data obtained for the States of each group may be legitimately compared.

Between the four groups, however, this close, personal touch could not be maintained. And for this reason fair comparison between the States of different groups can not be made on several of the points covered by the investigation.

As the investigation of working conditions was carried on entirely by the method of personal visit, and as the amount of information desired of each visited establishment was large, it was, of course, impossible to cover more than a very small proportion of all the establishments in any State. Selection was necessary and was made with the sole object of obtaining representative industries and establishments.

As regards industries, the choice in each State was of such industries as were of local importance and in which women and children formed a significant factor in the working force. As regards establishments, the choice was for the most part of factories of medium size, although smaller plants were added when the conditions of employment were of special interest. It was the purpose, so far as practicable, to choose in each State and industry at least one very good and one very poor plant from the standpoint of the workers.

EXTENT OF THE INVESTIGATION.

In total the investigation covered 563 establishments, representing 58 more or less clearly separate industries.

The following table classifies the 563 visited establishments by State and by industry:

NUMBER OF ESTABLISHMENTS INVESTIGATED, BY INDUSTRIES AND STATES.

Industries.	Maine.	Massachusetts.	Rhode Island.	Connecticut.	New York.	New Jersey.	Pennsylvania.	Ohio.	Illinois.	Indiana.	Michigan.	Wisconsin.	Maryland.	North Carolina.	Georgia.	Florida.	Louisiana.	Total establishments.
Boots and shoes	4																2	6
Cans, tin					1				2		1		2				2	8
Canning and preserving						1	3				1	1	2					8
Cigar boxes		2					1	2			1	1	3			2	2	14
Cigarettes		3			1									1	1			6
Cigars	2	3	2	2	2	3	9	9	3	5	1		4	1		12	2	60
Clocks and watches				5					1	1								7
Confectionery	3	10	1		4	5	1	6	3	4	2	4	3		3		1	50
Core making							4		5	1								10
Corsets				5			1		1		1							8
Cotton goods					5									8	9		3	25
Crackers and biscuits	1	4				4	8	5	3	3			1		3		3	35
Gloves									3	2								5
Hardware, etc				8					1									9
Hosiery and knit goods	2	7	7	5	7	3	5	6	4	3	3	3		3	7		1	66
Jewelry			5															5
Matches	1					1	2	3	1	1	2	1						12
Nuts and bolts								4			2							6
Paper boxes	6	4	4	2	10	4	3	5	4	5	2		4		1	2	3	59
Pottery						5	2	4		1								12
Shirts									1				4				3	9
Stamped and enamel ware		1			1	1	2	5	2	1		2						15
Tobacco and snuff						1		4	2		2	4	1	8				22
Woolen and worsted goods	7	7	4			4	4	7	3	3	2				4	4		49
All other [1]				8	4	2	1		8	16	2	4	3	1			8	57
Total	26	44	27	35	36	27	50	60	47	47	19	19	28	28	27	14	29	563

[1] Includes industries represented by less than 5 establishments, as follows: Artificial flowers: Illinois, 2. Bags, burlap: Louisiana, 4. Bags, cotton jute, paper: Indiana, 1. Baskets: Indiana, 1. Beer: Indiana, 1; Wisconsin, 1. Binding twine and rope: Illinois, 1. Breakfast food: Michigan, 1. Buggies and surreys: Indiana, 1. Carts, children's: Indiana, 1. Canvas attachments, binder: Illinois, 1. Chairs: Indiana, 1. Chewing gum: Illinois, 2; Louisiana, 1. Coffee packing: Louisiana, 1. Electrical apparatus: Indiana, 3. Fiber boxes and cans: Michigan, 1. Iron beds: Wisconsin, 1. Needles and pins: Connecticut, 3. Optical goods: New York, 1. Paper: Wisconsin, 1. Paper patterns: New York, 1. Pearl buttons: Indiana, 1; Wisconsin, 1. Pencils: New Jersey, 1. Plated tableware: Connecticut, 2; Indiana, 1. Printing and publishing: New York, 1. Rubber goods: Connecticut, 3. Shirt waists: New York, 1. Skirts: Indiana, 1. Soap: New Jersey, 1; Illinois, 1; Indiana, 1. Straw hats: Maryland, 3; Louisiana, 1. Tablets: Illinois, 1. Tin caps and bottle fasteners: Indiana, 1. Tin plate and block iron: Indiana, 1. Tobacco boxes: North Carolina, 1. Toys and novelties: Pennsylvania, 1; Indiana, 1.

The 563 visited establishments employed normally 142,181 persons, distributed by sex and age as follows: Males 16 years of age and over, 64,522; females 16 years and over, 67,522; boys under 16 years, 3,442; girls under 16 years, 6,695. The next table shows the distribution of these employees by States.

NUMBER OF EMPLOYEES OF EACH SEX UNDER 16 YEARS OF AGE AND 16 YEARS AND OVER, IN INDUSTRIES AND ESTABLISHMENTS VISITED, BY STATES.

States.	Establishments.	Industries.	Male employees.		Female employees.		Total employees.
			16 years and over.	Under 16 years.	16 years and over.	Under 16 years.	
Maine	26	8	1,299	36	889	38	2,262
Massachusetts	44	10	2,959	127	3,575	294	6,955
Rhode Island	27	7	2,887	226	2,847	256	6,216
Connecticut	35	9	7,069	196	5,613	299	13,177
New York	36	13	3,968	27	6,023	56	10,074
New Jersey	27	13	3,525	200	5,554	382	9,661
Pennsylvania	50	14	7,783	314	6,521	955	15,573
Ohio	60	12	6,303	81	5,949	302	12,635
Illinois	47	22	4,966	83	6,035	609	11,693
Indiana	47	27	7,042	349	5,776	707	13,874
Michigan	19	12	1,796	181	4,313	399	6,689
Wisconsin	19	10	2,135	110	2,544	336	5,125
Maryland	28	10	2,251	168	4,623	634	7,676
North Carolina	28	8	4,096	793	2,541	553	7,983
Georgia	27	6	2,599	342	1,903	400	5,244
Florida	14	2	2,905	71	1,014	59	4,049
Louisiana	29	15	939	138	1,802	416	3,295
Total	563	58	64,522	3,442	67,522	6,695	142,181

The table which follows makes a further classification of employees by the industries in which they were engaged.

NUMBER OF EMPLOYEES OF EACH SEX UNDER 16 YEARS OF AGE AND 16 YEARS AND OVER, IN ESTABLISHMENTS VISITED, BY INDUSTRIES.

Industries.	Establishments.	Employees.				
		Male.		Female.		Total.
		16 years and over.	Under 16 years.	16 years and over.	Under 16 years.	
Boots and shoes	6	629	24	313	2	968
Cans, tin	8	1,151	95	390	35	1,671
Canning and preserving	8	606	29	831	82	1,548
Cigar boxes	14	418	45	472	47	982
Cigarettes	6	523	26	1,360	76	1,985
Cigars	60	5,062	129	9,698	893	15,782
Clocks and watches	7	2,141	88	980	30	3,239
Confectionery	50	2,326	118	3,341	582	6,367
Core making	10	4,108	3	387		4,498
Corsets	8	726	13	3,698	240	4,677
Cotton goods	25	5,602	629	3,722	512	10,465
Crackers and biscuits	35	1,763	60	2,014	238	4,075
Gloves	5	254	3	1,098	41	1,396
Hardware, etc.	9	3,497	71	1,157	66	4,791
Hosiery and knit goods	66	3,978	435	10,819	1,227	16,459
Jewelry	5	385	10	224	18	637
Matches	12	1,672	112	1,011	168	2,963
Nuts and bolts	6	1,904	48	582	82	2,616
Paper boxes	59	1,290	55	3,647	595	5,587
Pottery	12	1,678	55	602	42	2,377
Shirts	9	582	58	3,217	334	4,191
Stamped and enamel ware	15	4,660	132	1,438	85	6,331
Tobacco and snuff	22	4,442	477	4,744	312	9,975
Woolen and worsted goods	49	6,589	396	5,493	546	13,024
All other [1]	57	8,536	331	6,268	442	15,577
Total	563	64,522	3,442	67,522	6,695	142,181

[1] Including industries represented by less than 5 establishments. See footnote to table on p. 18.

PLAN OF THE REPORT.

In presenting the results of this investigation the topical method has been followed. This is to say, the labor laws and factory conditions are grouped according to similarity under a few main topical or chapter heads. Thus, the third chapter, which treats of hours of labor, comprises such related subjects as limitations on the length of the work day, the posting of time schedules, and the regulation of the meal period. In each such chapter the material is arranged by States, and for each State there is given: First, a summary of the laws regarding the subject treated; second, where desirable and available, comments regarding the interpretation and administration of such laws; and third, a condensed statement, usually in tabular form, of the conditions found in the visited establishments. A full statement of the conditions found in each establishment, as reported on the establishment cards, is given in the general tables at the end of the volume.

In summarizing the laws the effort has been to give all essential points in as brief a space and in as clear a form as possible. Undue condensation, however, has been avoided. Most laws contain little extraneous matter, and the majority of the attempts at condensing labor laws have obtained brevity at the sacrifice of the full truth. Similarly, in seeking to make the present statements of laws as clear as possible, effort has been made to avoid personal readings or interpretation. The language of the law has been preferred in nearly all cases, and especially so when the meaning was at all obscure or ambiguous.

It will be noted, moreover, that in a few cases summaries of legislation are given on subjects in which no investigation of factory conditions was made. This is done for the purpose of making these outline statements of labor legislation as complete as possible. As here offered, they are intended to include all the important laws relative to the conditions of employment in factories and workshops in the 17 States covered.

The field work of the investigation was carried on from December, 1908, to April, 1909. The laws quoted in each case are those which were in force at the time of the field work in the State under consideration. Mention is made in footnotes of all important laws enacted between the time of the field work and January 1, 1910. The laws in force January 1, 1912, relating to the employment of women and children are given in Appendix A, while those relating to the regulation and inspection of factories and workshops are given in Appendix B, at the end of this volume.

CHAPTER I.

SCOPE AND ENFORCEMENT OF THE LAWS.

CHAPTER I.

SCOPE AND ENFORCEMENT OF THE LAWS.

INTRODUCTION.

The 17 States covered by this report varied greatly at the time of this investigation (December, 1908, to April, 1909)[1] in the degree in which they had enacted legislation relative to the employment of women and children and to the comfort, health, and safety of factory workers. In a few of them, notably New York, such legislation was very complete and very carefully drawn. In others, laws upon the subjects referred to were scant and at times obscure. In none of the 17, however, were such laws entirely absent.

By 3 of these 17 States the enforcement of such legislation was left to existing administration and judicial means, i. e., indictment by the grand jury or prosecution by local police officials. These three States were North Carolina, Georgia, and Florida, States in which laws of the character now being considered were few and liberal.

Each of the 14 remaining States has accepted the "factory-inspection" principle—the principle, that is to say, of charging the enforcement of woman and child labor laws and factory laws to officials especially chosen for the purpose.

Not in every case, however, has the principle been carried out fully. Several of the States having an organized factory-inspection force did not vest this force with full jurisdiction in all the legislation commonly regarded as forming part of the woman and child labor and factory laws. The tendency, however, was in that direction, except perhaps in the case of factory laws involving technical matters of building construction in large cities.

Factory inspection, where it exists, is almost always made an immediate function of the State administration. Louisiana alone, among the States covered by this investigation, is peculiar in this respect. In Louisiana, factory inspectors are recognized, and their appointment provided for, by State laws, but the actual appointment of such officers is made by local authorities.

Factory inspection formed a distinct and independent administrative department in about half of the States now being considered. In the

---

[1] For laws in force Jan. 1, 1912, see Appendix A: Laws relating to the employment of women and children, and Appendix B: Laws relating to the regulation and inspection of factories and workshops.

others the duties of factory inspection was made part of the duties of a bureau or department having in total a broader field of labor activities, such as the gathering and publishing of statistics of labor, manufacturing, or agriculture, the conduct of employment bureaus, the collection and diffusion of information relative to economic and industrial conditions. And in one State—Massachusetts—factory inspection is a part of the State police system, while "inspectors of health" under the State Board of Health have certain important duties with reference to sanitation, ventilation, and provisions for the health and comfort of factory workers.

In all of the States being considered the head of the factory-inspection department was appointed by the governor (except Louisiana as above noted), and the assistants or deputies by the governor direct, or, more usually, by the head of the department. In three States—Massachusetts, New York, and Wisconsin—these latter appointments were under civil-service regulations, and in Connecticut the one female deputy must be recommended by an advisory commission. In all the other States these appointments were without any important legal qualifications as to ability or character.

These several points are developed in greater detail in the remaining pages of this chapter, where there is given for each State separately a brief statement of the following points:

1. Scope of the law.
2. Method of enforcing the laws.
3. Organization of the inspection force.
4. Statistical data from the State records, showing the character, amount, etc., of work done during the preceding five years.

The first section—scope of the law—is simply a list of the subjects legislated upon, and does not attempt to summarize the laws themselves. Also, it is to be noted, that the subjects included are limited to those covered by this investigation and discussed in detail in the succeeding chapters of the report. In each case the legislation referred to is as it existed at the time of the field work of the investigation, December, 1908, to April, 1909.

The second section—enforcement of the laws—shows to what authorities the subjects listed under the preceding section were intrusted for enforcement, and the method used in enforcing.

The third section deals with the organization of the inspection force—the number and sex of the inspectors, the salaries paid, the method of appointment, the manner in which the inspection work was carried on, etc.

The fourth section attempts to show the work of the State inspection department as given in the department's own reports, supplemented at times by reference to unpublished records. Whenever possible the data are given for five consecutive years, 1904 to 1908, inclusive.   The information sought, and whenever obtained presented, is chiefly in regard to the following points: The number of inspectors engaged in factory inspection, the number of establishments visited, the number of separate inspections made, the number of orders or warning notices issued, the number of prosecutions begun and of convictions secured, and, in the latter case, the amount of fines and costs imposed, paid, and remitted.   Supplementary information regarding the character of the prosecutions and convictions, the industries in which they occurred, etc., is given in the few cases where obtainable.

These statistical data are presented in tabular form, and as far as possible the tables are uniform.   The State records, however, are by no means•uniform, and are sometimes extremely incomplete.   This rendered the compilation of these tables extremely difficult, and subject at times to a possible margin of error.   Also, for very few States was it possible to obtain all the necessary facts, and for some States a record of the most important facts was entirely lacking.

MAINE.

SCOPE OF THE LAW—SUBJECTS COVERED.[1]

Woman and child labor:

1. Legal age of employment: 14 years, except in establishments using "perishable materials."
2. Prohibited employments for certain classes of persons of legal age: Operation of elevators.
3 Employment certificates: Children 14 to 16 years of age.
4. [Register of child employees: No legislation.]
5. Hours of labor:

> Children under 16 years of age and females 16 years of age and over, 10 hours per day, 60 hours per week. Exceptions: (1) 10-hour day may be extended under certain conditions; (2) 60-hour week may be extended for females 18 years of age and over; and (3) no restrictions in cases of establishments using "perishable materials."
>
> Males 16 to 21 years of age, 10 hours per day, but with broad exceptions.

6. [Night work: No legislation.]
7. Posting of time schedules.
8. [Meal period: No legislation.]

---

[1] The law here referred to is as in force at the time of the investigation, January, 1909.   The text of the laws in force Jan. 1, 1912, is given in the appendixes at the end of the volume.

Factory inspection:
    9. Fire protection:
        Fire escapes.
        Doors opening outward.
        [No legislation as to stairways, exit lights or signs, or fire-
            fighting apparatus.]   •
    10. [Elevators: No legislation.]
    11. [Dangerous machinery: No legislation.]
    12. [Accident reporting: No legislation.]
    13. Provisions for comfort:
        Inspector to remedy "sanitary conditions" injurious to
            health or life.
        [No legislation on specific points.]
    14. Ventilation and sanitation:
        Inspector to remedy injurious "sanitary conditions," etc.
        [No specific requirements.]
    15. [Posting of labor laws: No legislation.]

ENFORCEMENT OF THE LAWS.[1]

With two exceptions the State factory inspector is charged in full
with the enforcement of the factory inspection and the woman and
child labor laws. The exceptions are: (1) The requirement regarding the operation of elevators by children, and (2) the provisions
regarding fire protection. The former requirement is not charged to
any special office for enforcement. The enforcement of the latter
provisions—fire protection—is vested immediately in the local fire
department in places having such department. Elsewhere this duty
devolves upon the factory inspector; and everywhere the factory
inspector has authority to see that the laws regarding fire protection
are enforced.

In case of prosecution the procedure would be this: The factory
inspector would present the alleged violation to the county prosecuting attorney, who, if he considered the offense indictable, would
so advise the grand jury. If an indictment should be found it would
be prosecuted by the county attorney. The trial would be in the
criminal court in Portland, and in the municipal court in any other
city.

The present factory inspector stated (January, 1909) that no cases
of violation of the factory laws or of the woman and child labor laws
had been tried since he was appointed to his present office, March 22,
1905. Also the present State commissioner of labor stated (January,

---

[1] Rev. Stat., 1903, ch. 28, secs. 39 to 44, and ch. 40, secs. 43 to 45. (22d An. Rept.
Com. of Labor, pp. 524–526.)

The law regarding vaccination in paper mills, a subject not covered by this report,
is charged to the local board of health. Idem, ch. 18, secs. 83 to 86.

1909) that he knew of no prosecution under such laws since the establishment of the bureau of industrial and labor statistics in 1887. No such prosecutions are shown in the reports of that bureau from 1887 to 1908, inclusive.

ORGANIZATION OF FACTORY INSPECTION FORCE.

There is only one factory inspector in Maine.   His salary is $1,000.[1] The present incumbent has served approximately four years.

The appointment is made by the governor, with the approval of the council, and is not dependent on any special technical training.

There is no restriction upon the inspector engaging in other work. The present official was in the marble business before his appointment, and still owns a marble-cutting yard, to which he gives more or less attention.

As there is only one inspector, the State is not districted for inspection purposes.   The present inspector has no particular method of covering the State.

There is no record of the number of establishments in the State subject to the inspection laws.

STATISTICAL DATA OF FACTORY INSPECTION.

The published reports of the inspector of factories of Maine for the years 1904 to 1908, inclusive, give no satisfactory information regarding the number of inspections made, etc.   As mentioned above, there have been no prosecutions for violation of the factory laws or woman and child labor laws during the term of the present inspector, and probably not since the establishment of the bureau of industrial and labor statistics in 1887.

MASSACHUSETTS.

SCOPE OF THE LAW—SUBJECTS COVERED.[2]

Woman and child labor:
  1. Legal age of employment: 14 years.
  2. Prohibited employments for certain classes of persons of legal
       age:
           Operation of elevators.
           Manufacture of certain acids.
           In breweries or bottling establishments.

---

[1] Rev. Stat., 1903, ch. 40, sec. 43 (22d An. Rept. Com. of Labor, p. 526).   The law further provides that the governor, if satisfied that the inspector can not perform all the duties required by law, shall appoint a sufficient number of assistant inspectors at $2 a day each.   The present inspector has never called for an assistant.

[2] The law here referred to is as in force at the time of the investigation, December, 1908, to February, 1909.   The text of the laws in force Jan. 1, 1912, is given in the appendixes at the end of this volume.

Woman and child labor—Concluded.

3. Employment certificates: Children 14 to 16 years of age.
4. Register of child employees.
5. Hours of labor: Children under 18 years of age and females 18 years of age and over, 10 hours per day, 58 per week, with exceptions as to 10-hour day.
6. Night work: Prohibited for—
    Minors under 21 years of age and females 21 years of age and over, between 10 p. m. and 6 a. m.
    Children under 18 years of age and females 18 years of age and over, in textile factories, between 6 p. m. and 6 a. m.
7. Posting of time schedule.
8. Meal period: Length and time regulated.

Factory inspection:

9. Fire protection: Fire escapes; there are three sets of provisions, one applicable to whole State, one outside of Boston, and one to Boston only. The general result of these provisions is to require proper means of egress in case of fire, but to leave the determination of details to the inspecting authorities.
10. Elevators:
    Guards on shafts and openings.
    Safety clutches on cars.
    Warning signals on freight elevators.
    [Also many other detailed provisions.]
11. Dangerous machinery:
    Guards on mill gearing and machinery.
    Communication between workroom and engine room.
    Traversing carriages in cotton mills to be located safely.
    Loom guards in textile factories.
    [No legislation regarding friction clutches, belt shifters, or removal of safeguards.]
12. Accident reporting: By employer to factory inspection department.
13. Provisions for comfort:
    Water-closets. [No minimum ratio of accommodations to employees.]
    Seats for females.
    Drinking water.
    [No legislation regarding washing or dressing rooms, except in foundries, and none regarding lunch rooms.]
14. Ventilation and sanitation:
    Factories to be well lighted, ventilated, and kept clean.
    Gases, vapors, dust, etc., to be rendered harmless, as by fans.

Ventilation and sanitation—Concluded.

> Exhaust fans on emery wheels and similar grinding wheels.
>
> Water used for humidifying to be sufficiently pure to prevent odor or injury to health.
>
> Cuspidors to be provided.
>
> [No legislation regarding limewashing or painting.]

15. [Posting of labor laws: No legislation.]

ENFORCEMENT OF THE LAWS.

The responsibility for the enforcement of the factory and woman and child labor laws, as briefed above, is divided among five groups of officers. They are as follows:

1. State factory inspectors (a subdivision of the district police). Laws relating to safeguards for machinery and other means of protection against accident; laws relating to means of egress and other fire protective measures outside of Boston; laws regulating hours of labor of women and children; and laws relating to the employment of minors. ˙

2. State board of health: Laws relating to sanitation, ventilation, and provisions for the health and comfort of factory workers.

3. Local boards of health: Laws relative to pure drinking water, the provision of cuspidors, and (in connection with State board of health), water-closets in factories, and the manufacture of goods in tenement houses.

4. Local building commissioners: Laws relating to the safeguarding of elevators in cities and towns having such commissioners, but the State factory inspectors have concurrent powers and may prohibit the use of elevators they consider unsafe.

5. Building commissioner of Boston: Laws relating to means of egress and other fire-protection devices, and to the construction, guarding, and operation of elevators in the city of Boston.

Prosecutions are conducted by the inspectors in the lower courts. The prosecuting attorney of the district assumes charge in cases of appeal.

Cases are carried first before the police courts, municipal courts, or district courts. Appeals are made to the superior courts.

The courts have been inclined to be lenient toward first offenders. If, however, the evidence shows the offender to have been an habitual violator of the law, the first punishment may be very severe.

The chief inspector stated that in appealed cases the inspectors had been upheld almost invariably and that as a rule the courts had favored a strict enforcement of the law.

ORGANIZATION OF FACTORY-INSPECTION FORCE.

As mentioned above, the enforcement of the labor laws of Massachusetts is divided among several authorities, State and local. The State authorities concerned are the district police and the State board of health. The most important of the local authorities are the Boston building inspectors.

THE DISTRICT POLICE INSPECTORS.

The district police is in charge of a chief, with a salary of $3,000. The inspection work is under the direction of a deputy chief, $2,400, acting with a force of 47 assistant inspectors, each at the salary of $1,500 per year, except one who as chief inspector of boilers receives $2,000, and two female factory inspectors at $1,200 a year. This force is divided as follows: Inspectors of public buildings, 13; inspectors of factories, 14, of whom two are females; inspectors of boilers, 20, including the chief boiler inspector. These three sets of inspectors are separately organized, and their work is usually kept entirely separate, although at times, owing to the lack of a sufficient force, it has been necessary to transfer temporarily inspectors from one division to another. Normally, however, the factory-inspection work is done by the regular factory inspectors, under the immediate direction of the deputy chief, who is chief factory inspector.

The present factory inspectors have served, on the average, about 10 years.

Appointment to the office of factory inspector is under civil-service regulations. Inspectors may not engage in other work during their service with the district police.

For purposes of inspection the State is divided into 9 districts, each containing 1 or more counties. The county of Suffolk, in which is located the city of Boston, is divided, however, into 5 sections and has 5 factory inspectors.

It is the intention of the department that each place of employment subject to inspection should be visited once a year and, in case violations are found, as many additional times as necessary. The chief inspector states, however, that the inspection force is not sufficient to visit each establishment annually.

Each inspector follows his own method of covering his assigned district. As a rule the inspector visits the larger factories first and if it is necessary to omit any the smaller shops are not visited. The textile industry receives special attention.

There is no available record of the number of establishments subject to inspection.

STATE BOARD OF HEALTH INSPECTORS.[1]

There are 15 health inspectors of the State board of health, one for each of the 15 districts into which the State is divided by the board of health. The districts vary in size, population, and number of factories, and because of this the salaries of inspectors are graded. The grading is as follows: $2,500 a year, 1 inspector; $2,400 a year, 1; $2,000 a year, 6; $1,500 a year, 1; $1,200 a year, 5; $600 a year, 1. These salaries are established by the governor, subject to the legal limitation that the total paid shall not exceed a fixed sum.

The system of health inspectors was created by an act of 1907, and all the present inspectors were appointed in July, 1907.

The health inspectors are appointed by the governor. The appointments are not under civil service, but the inspectors must be physicians, and the present appointees were all approved by the State board of health and the Massachusetts Medical Society. While acting as health inspectors the holders of such offices may and do engage in the regular practice of medicine.

No information was obtainable as to the methods by which the health inspectors work, or as to the number of establishments under their jurisdiction.[2]

---

[1] Acts of 1907, ch. 537, secs. 1 to 8 (22d An. Rept. Com. of Labor, pp. 629, 630).
[2] According to a pamphlet, entitled "State Inspectors of Health of Massachusetts: Who they are and what they do," issued by the State board of health in 1911, the powers and duties of the State inspectors of health are as follows:

ADVISORY AUTHORITY.

Health inspection in factories.[1]

The State inspectors of health study the health of persons employed in factories and workshops by—
1. Gathering information concerning—
  (a) The prevalence of tuberculosis and other communicable diseases in factories and workshops.
   Community health is, in a measure, dependent upon the health of persons employed in factories and upon the prevalence of disease in such establishments. The health of persons working in factories is, in turn, to a considerable extent dependent upon conditions in these buildings. In the absence of a law providing for the physical examination of adults in factories, the State inspectors of health, as a regular procedure at the present time, confine such examinations to minors. In the interest of public health, however, they inform employers and employees in certain instances of the desirability of making examinations of adults for the detection of tuberculosis or other communicable diseases.
  (b) The ill health or physical unfitness of minors.
   The work of obtaining information concerning the health of minors employed in factories calls for: (1) A knowledge by the State inspectors of health of the ill health or physical unfitness of the minors, and involves (2) obtaining personal and family histories, recording observations, and, in a considerable proportion of cases, making physical examinations.

---

[1] Acts of 1907, ch. 537; Acts of 1910, chs. 404 and 543; Acts of 1911, ch. 603.

BOSTON BUILDING INSPECTORS.

The enforcement of all provisions relating to precautions against fire, means of egress in case of fire, and safeguards for elevators in the city of Boston is charged to the fire egress inspectors and elevator inspectors, under the direction of the city building commissioner.

There are 4 male elevator inspectors—1 at an annual salary of $1,900, 2 at $1,600, and 1 at $1,000—and three male egress inspectors, 1 at $2,000 a year, and 2 at $1,600.

Both classes of inspectors are appointed under civil-service regulation and are not permitted to engage in other work during the period of service as inspector.

Footnote continued from page 31.
  2. Investigating the effects of occupation on health by considering—
      (a) The existence of occupational diseases in industrial establishments.
          Without some knowledge of community life and conditions it is impossible to understand and weigh accurately the probable effects of occupation on health and their bearing upon the public health.
      (b) The existence of any occupation, process of manufacture, or method which is injurious to the health of adults. In the absence of a law providing for the physical examination of adult workers in factories, State inspectors of Health inform employers and employees in certain instances of the desirability of making examinations for the detection of lead, mercury, or other types of industrial poisoning.
  3. Investigating the employment of minors in occupations, processes of manufacture, or methods that are injurious to health.
      The inquiries do not include those occupations which give rise to or cause physical injuries, or are dangerous to life or limb.
  4. Investigating the lighting of factories and workshops for the purpose of protecting the eyesight of the workers.
      This inquiry, relative to the lighting of factories and workshops in relation to the eye and vision, includes the consideration of light in connection with—
      (a) The kind of work done.
      (b) The acuteness of vision, and the degree of attention required by the work.
      (c) The kind, amount, and distribution of light.
      (d) The frequency with which glasses are worn by the employees.
      (e) The types, frequency, and extent of injuries to the eyes of the employees in certain occupations and processes, and whether—
      (f) Any danger of injury to the eyes that is discovered may be decreased or prevented by any mechanical device or practicable means.
  5. Investigating the effect on health of indoor dampness and excessive heat in factories and workshops.
      This inquiry relates particularly to the regulation of the humidity and temperature in textile factories. Its purpose is to lead to the adoption of such regulations as are practicable to prevent any unnecessary exposure of employees to indoor dampness and extremes of heat.

  *   *   *   *   *   *

EXECUTIVE AUTHORITY.

Health inspection in factories.

The State inspectors of health inspect factories primarily for the purpose of protecting the health and welfare of the persons employed therein. The factory, however, is not an isolated part of the community. In manufacturing centers factory employees mingle freely with persons in other walks of life. The health of the persons who work in factories, therefore, may affect materially the health of the public.

Unlike the consideration of such matters as the means of egress in case of fire—a sort of inspection work complete in itself—the study of the sanitation of factories and its effect upon health is not limited by the factory walls, but involves a knowledge

The inspectors work under the direction of the building commissioner, visiting such streets and buildings as the commissioner directs. Elevators in the main business part of the city are visited as often as three times a year. Egress inspectors inspect all new buildings, but ordinarily do not visit a building a second time unless alterations or additions are made in its construction.

There are about 85,000 buildings in Boston subject to the jurisdiction of the building commissioner.

STATISTICAL DATA OF FACTORY INSPECTION.

The following table presents data compiled from the annual reports of the district police regarding inspections made by the State factory inspectors, prosecutions, convictions, fines imposed, and orders

Footnote continued from page 31.

of the sanitation of each industrial community, including the factory and the home; it includes—

(a) In the factory not merely the inspection of the building but some knowledge of each industrial process and a study of the probable effects of occupation upon the health of the workers at their work, as well as the investigation of the prevalence of communicable and occupational diseases.

(b) In the home some knowledge of the sanitation of home life and surroundings, the habits of the workers, and the prevalence of disease.

In other words, the kind of inspection done by the State inspectors in factories is health inspection rather than factory inspection. The latter signifies work that is confined within the walls of a factory. Health inspection, on the other hand, means the investigation of all influences dangerous to the public health or threatening to affect the same within or without the factory, the school, and the home.

1. The enforcement of factory laws.

The work relative to the sanitation of factories, workshops, and other industrial establishments includes the enforcement of certain laws—

(a) Relative to supplying pure drinking water for employees in manufacturing establishments. (Acts of 1909, ch. 514, sec. 78.)

(b) Relative to the purity and use of water for humidifying purposes in factories and workshops and to the regulation of humidity and temperature of the atmosphere in textile factories. (Acts of 1908, ch. 325; Acts of 1910, ch. 543.)

(c) Relative to the lighting, ventilation, and cleanliness of factories and workshops. (Acts of 1909, ch. 514, sec. 94.)

(d) Relative to providing mechanical ventilating apparatus in factories and workshops. (Acts of 1909, ch. 514, secs. 83–85, inclusive.)

(e) Relative to providing emery wheels and belts and buffing wheels and belts with hoods, suction pipes, and fans or blowers for the protection of employees against dust. (Acts of 1909, ch. 514, secs. 86–90, inclusive.)

(f) Relative to providing seats for women employees. (Acts of 1909, ch. 514, sec. 72.)

(g) Relative to providing foundries with adequate washing facilities and water-closets and to the connection of such buildings with a public sewerage system. (Acts of 1909, ch. 514, sec. 102; R. L., ch. 49, sec. 30.)

(h) Relative to providing proper water-closets for both sexes. (Acts of 1909, ch. 514, secs. 79–82, inclusive, as amended by ch. 259, Acts of 1910.)

(i) Relative to prohibiting the use of suction shuttles in factories. (Acts of 1911, ch. 281.)

2. The exclusion of minors from occupations injurious to health. (Acts of 1910, ch. 404.)

The law relating to the exclusion of minors from occupations injurious to their health may be made applicable to—

(a) A single establishment.

(b) A department in an establishment, or

(c) A single minor.

From an educational point of view it has great value.

issued. Factory inspection in Massachusetts is closely connected with building inspection, there being two sets of inspectors, both under the district police department, and in the published reports of that department the records of the two sets of officials are at times difficult to separate. As far as possible the following table limits itself to the work of the regular factory inspectors, excluding building inspection and also tenement inspection. Elevators are inspected by both building and factory inspectors as a regular part of their work, and on this account no special note is made of elevator inspection in the table.

FACTORY INSPECTIONS, PROSECUTIONS, CONVICTIONS, ETC., BY YEARS, 1904 TO 1908—
MASSACHUSETTS.

[From Reports of District Police: 1904, pp. 45, 46, 51. 52; 1905, pp. 62–64, 65, 69–71; 1906, pp. 72–77; 1907, pp. 7, 24, 58–60; 1908, pp. 70–72.]

	1904	1905	1906	1907	1908
Inspectors [1]...............................	13	14	14	15	14
Inspections [2].............................	8,071	10,008	9,291	[2] 9,683	8,845
Average per inspector......................	621	715	664	646	632
Prosecutions (persons).....................	....	16	48	40	22
Convictions (persons) [4]..................	....	9	40	([5])	([5])
Fines: [6]					
Imposed...............................	....	$402	$595	$783	$365
Paid.................................	....	$402	$595	$783	$365
Remitted.............................	....	....	....	....	....
Orders issued............................	2,663	3,077	3,561	3,318	3,406

[1] Not including chief inspector (work administrative only), building inspectors, or tenement inspectors, but including two women inspectors doing special inspection work.
[2] The reports are not clear as to whether "inspections" represent separate establishments or include second inspections of same establishment. Second inspections, however, were very rare.
[3] Including 1,344 tenement inspections made by regular factory inspectors before that duty was transferred from the district police to the State board of health.
[4] Not including cases pending at end of year, but including cases continued over from preceding year.
[5] Not reported.
[6] Amount of costs not reported.

Footnote continued from page 31.

It insures fair treatment to both the employer and the minor.

The law is not applicable to any factory wherein such special measures are adopted as appear to the State inspector of health to be reasonably practicable and meet the necessities of the case.

3. The provision for devices for preventing eye injuries. (Acts of 1911, ch. 603.)
    The law providing for an investigation of proper lighting conditions of factories and workshops for the purpose of protecting the eyesight of the employees also provides for protection against injury to the eyes by mechanical devices or other practicable means ordered by a State inspector of health with the approval of the State board of health.

Inspection of tenements where clothing is made.[1]

The primary object of the inspection of tenements where clothing is made by the State inspectors of health is to guard the public health against the spread of contagious diseases by means of infected wearing apparel. The work accomplished has resulted in the maintenance of higher sanitary standards in the congested tenement homes. The friendly visits to the homes and the close personal contact with the workers have been a great educational force in the development of higher standards of hygienic living.

Inspection of mercantile establishments.[2]

The State inspectors of health inspect mercantile establishments—
1. To determine whether a sufficient number of seats are provided for women employees and whether there are proper toilet rooms for both sexes in such establishments, and
2. To enforce the statute provisions relating thereto.

[1] Acts of 1909, ch. 514, secs. 106–111, inclusive.
[2] Idem, secs. 72, 79–82, inclusive, as amended by acts of 1910, ch. 259.

The inspection of tenements is done by special factory inspectors, and the data thereupon is not included in the above table.

The industries in which prosecutions and convictions occurred are not shown in the reports of the district police.   In 1904 there were no prosecutions, and the offenses for which convictions were secured are not reported for 1907 and 1908.   In 1905, there were 8 convictions for violations of the woman and child labor laws, and 1 for violation of the moving-picture law.   In 1906 there were 37 convictions for the violation of the woman and child labor laws, 1 for assaulting an inspector, and 1 each for violations- of the weekly payment and the moving-picture laws.

RHODE ISLAND.

SCOPE OF THE LAW—SUBJECTS COVERED.[1]

Woman and child labor:

1. Legal age of employment: 14 years.
2. Prohibited employments for certain classes of persons of legal age:
    Operation of elevators.
    Cleaning of moving machinery, unless approved by factory inspectors.
3. Employment certificates: Children 14 to 16 years of age.
4. [Register of child employees: No legislation.]
5. Hours of labor: Children under 16 years of age and females 16 years of age and over, 10 hours per day, 58 hours per week, with exceptions as to 10-hour day.
6. Night work: Prohibited for children under 16 years of age between 8 p. m. and 6 a. m.
7. Posting of time schedules.
8. [Meal period: No legislation.]

Factory inspection:

9. Fire protection:
    Fire escapes.
    Doors opening outward.
    [No legislation regarding stairways, exit lights or signs, or fire-fighting apparatus.]
10. Elevators:
    Guards on shafts and openings.
    Warning signals.
    [No legislation as to safety clutches on freight elevators.]

---

[1] The law here referred to is as in force at the time of the investigation, December, 1898, to February, 1909.   The text of the laws in force Jan. 1, 1912, is given in the appendixes at the end of this volume.

Factory inspection—Continued.
    11. Dangerous machinery:
        Guards on mill gearing and machinery.
        [No legislation regarding belt shifters, friction clutches,
            communication with engine room, or the removal of
            safeguards.]
    12. Accident reporting: By·employer to factory inspection de-
        partment.
    13. Provisions for comfort:
        Water-closets. [No minimum ratio of accommoda-
            tions to employees.]
        Dressing rooms.
        Seats for females.
        Drinking water.
        [No legislation regarding wash rooms except in foundries,
            and none regarding lunch rooms.]
    14. Ventilation and sanitation: General authority given in-
        spectors to remedy any conditions regarding "heating,
        lighting, ventilation, or sanitary arrangement" injurious
        to health. [No legislation on specific points.]
    15. Posting of labor laws: To be done by inspectors.

ENFORCEMENT OF THE LAWS.

The enforcement of the factory laws and of the woman and child
labor laws is charged in full to the State factory inspection department, with the exception of those upon the four following subjects:

1. *Fire escapes.*—Duty of enforcing rests primarily upon local building inspectors, but factory inspectors have a joint, and what is practically a final, authority in passing upon the sufficiency and character
of means of egress in case of fire.

2. *Elevators.*—Provisions not entirely clear. Local building inspectors are practically responsible, but factory inspectors also have a
broad authority.

3. *Drinking water.*—Enforced by local health authorities.

4. *Toilet facilities in foundries.*—Not charged to any special body
of officials. Factory inspectors assume no responsibility, but do
remind employers of the provisions of the law.

Violations of the law are prosecuted before the district courts. As
prosecutor, the chief factory inspector engages such attorney as he
may choose. Cases are tried before the district courts.

There have been no prosecutions under the factory laws during the
term of the present inspector, who was appointed in 1907. During
that period there have been four prosecutions under the child-labor
laws. These four prosecutions were all in 1907, and all against cotton
mills in Pawtucket for employing children without certificates. The
defendants were found guilty and fined $25 in one case, $15 in one

case, and $10 in each of two cases. As the statutory penalty for such an offense is a fine of not more than $500, the penalties imposed in these cases were very lenient.

In an interview with an agent of the Bureau of Labor, the chief factory inspector stated that he would have preferred to settle these cases without legal action, but that he had resorted to prosecution because the cases had been given wide publication with the charge that he did not dare prosecute large manufacturers. His usual policy, he stated, was to prosecute offenders only as a last resort, as he believed other methods of obtaining results were preferable.

ORGANIZATION OF FACTORY INSPECTION FORCE.[1]

The Rhode Island factory inspection department has a force of three inspectors—a chief, one male assistant inspector, and one female assistant inspector. The annual salary of the chief is $2,000; of each of the assistants, $1,500.

The chief inspector, formerly a newspaper manager, has served 10 years. The male assistant, formerly a mill employee, has served 2 years. The female assistant, formerly a nurse and dressmaker, has served 11 years.

Appointments to the position of inspector are made by the governor, with the consent of the senate, and are entirely political.

Inspectors are not allowed to engage in other work.

The State is not divided into inspection districts, and in performing its work of inspection the department has no fixed method of covering the State. The inspectors confer and the work is assigned as circumstances suggest. Ordinarily the two male inspectors visit the larger establishments, the female inspector covering the mercantile establishments in the city of Providence and the smaller mills. Each establishment is visited at least once a year.

There is no accurate record of the number of establishments subject to inspection. The number visited each year by the inspectors may be accepted, however, as approximately the number subject to inspection. In 1908 this number was 1,913.[2]

STATISTICAL DATA OF FACTORY INSPECTION.

The annual report of the State factory inspector contains a complete list of all establishments inspected during the year, with the following data regarding each: Name of establishment; goods manufactured; number of employees, classified as male and female and as under 16 and 16 and over; sanitary conditions, indicated by the words "excellent," "very good," "good," "fair," and "poor"; recom-

---

[1] For law creating department see Rhode Island Gen. Laws, 1896, ch. 68, sec. 3, as amended by ch. 1215, Acts of 1905 (22d An. Rept. Com. of Labor, p. 1208).

[2] Fifteenth Annual Report of Factory Inspection, Rhode Island, 1908, p. 7.

mendations of orders for changes which the inspector considers to be required by law, and whether such recommendation is complied with. Establishments visited and found not to be in operation are included in this list.

The following table shows in condensed form, for each of the five years 1904 to 1908, inclusive, the more important data presented in these reports regarding inspections, prosecutions, convictions, fines, and orders issued. No statement is made in the reports as to whether or not second inspections were made. It would appear, however, that second inspections were very infrequently, if ever, made.

ESTABLISHMENTS INSPECTED, PROSECUTIONS, CONVICTIONS, ETC., BY YEARS, 1904 TO 1908—RHODE ISLAND.

[Compiled from Annual Reports of Factory Inspection, Rhode Island.]

	1904	1905	1906	1907	1908
Inspectors [1]	2	3	3	3	3
Establishments inspected [2]	653	1,508	1,742	1,899	1,913
Average per inspector	327	503	581	633	638
Prosecutions				4	
Convictions				4	
Fines and costs:					
Imposed				$60	
Paid				$60	
Remitted					
Orders issued [3]	20	61	42	31	19

[1] Including chief inspector, who makes regular inspections.
[2] Including mercantile establishments, laundries, hotels, and bowling alleys, not separately reported; great majority of establishments were factories, however.
[3] With four exceptions each of these orders was to a different establishment.

The four prosecutions and convictions in 1907 were all for violations of the child-labor law.

CONNECTICUT.

SCOPE OF THE LAW—SUBJECTS COVERED.[1]

Woman and child labor:

1. Legal age of employment: 14 years.
2. Prohibited employments for certain classes of persons of legal age:
    Operation of elevators.
    Cleaning of moving machinery if forbidden by inspectors.
3. Employment certificates: Children 14 to 16 years of age.
4. Register of child employees.
5. Hours of labor: Children under 16 years of age and females 16 years of age and over, 10 hours per day, 58 hours per week, with some exceptions as to both day and week.
6. [Night work: No legislation.]
7. Posting of time schedules.
8. [Meal period: No legislation.]

[1] The law here referred to is as in force at the time of the investigation, February, 1909. The text of the laws in force Jan. 1, 1912, is given in the appendixes at the end of this volume.

Factory inspection:
   9. Fire protection:
      Fire escapes.
      [No legislation as to stairways, doors opening outward,
         exit lights or signs, or fire-fighting apparatus.]
  10. Elevators:
      Guards on shafts and floor openings.
      Safety clutches on cars.
  11. Dangerous machinery:
      Guards on mill gearing and machinery.
      [No legislation regarding belt shifters, friction clutches,
         communication with engine room or removal of safe-
         guards.]
  12. [Accident reporting: No legislation.]
  13. Provisions for comfort:
      Water-closets. [No minimum ratio of accommodations
         to employees.]
      Seats for females.
      [No legislation as to washing facilities, except in bakeries
         and foundries, and none as. to dressing rooms, lunch
         rooms, or drinking water.]
  14. Ventilation and sanitation:
      Factories where machinery is used to be well lighted,
         ventilated, and clean.
      Dust-removing appliances.
      [No specific legislation regarding spitting on floors, cus-
         pidors, limewashing, or painting.]
  15. [Posting of labor laws: No legislation.]

ENFORCEMENT OF THE LAWS.

The enforcement of the factory inspection laws, except those relating to fire escapes, rests upon the factory inspection department.[1] The fire-escape provisions are charged to the local officials, but the factory inspectors notify such officials when they consider particular buildings improperly guarded in this respect.   The factory inspectors have no specific authority for enforcing the requirement of seats for females, but they assume the responsibility.

As regards the enforcement of the woman and child labor laws in factories, the factory inspectors have, and assume, very little responsibility.   The laws regarding under-age employment and the use of employment certificates are charged to the State board of education

---

[1] Under law in force at time of investigation. By Acts of 1909, ch. 10, however, the duty of enforcing the fire-escape requirements in the case of factories and workshops was given in full to the State factory inspectors. (Bulletin of the Bureau of Labor, No. 85, p. 523.)

and other school officials. Those regarding hours of labor are not
charged to any special body of officials.[1] It is to be noted, however,
that an act of 1907, providing for a female deputy inspector, directs
such deputy to "inquire into the enforcement of the laws regulating
the employment of women and girls * * * and to report thereon
to the factory inspector." This would seem to impose some obligation upon the factory inspection department in the enforcement of
the woman and child labor laws in so far at least as females are
concerned. In practice the department assumes very little responsibility.

The prosecution of offenders under the factory inspection laws is
by State attorneys, on information and evidence furnished by the
factory inspector. Cases are tried before local magistrates' courts.

The chief factory inspector stated that the courts have upheld the
department in practically every case where he considered the evidence sufficient to warrant a conviction. The real attitude of the
courts at the present time is, however, not a matter of record, as the
factory inspectors have instituted no prosecutions during the past
five years.

The prosecution of violators of the child-labor laws (including the
compulsory attendance laws) is also by the State attorneys. They
are assisted by the truant officers in places having truant officers;
elsewhere by the State compelling agents, who are appointees of the
State board of education.

Cases are heard before local magistrates, and on appeal go to the
superior court of the county.

In the main the attitude of the courts has been favorable to a
strict enforcement of the laws. But the secretary of the State board
of education claims that some of the State attorneys do not do their
full duty in the matter of prosecuting offenders, and advocates making the State compelling agents prosecuting officers in cases of this
kind.

ORGANIZATION OF FACTORY INSPECTION FORCE.[2]

The factory inspection force consists of five members—a chief,
three male deputies, and one female deputy. The chief inspector
receives a salary of $2,500 a year; the deputies are paid $5 per day for
each day actually employed.

---

[1] Under law in force at time of investigation. By Acts of 1909, ch. 220, however,
the factory inspectors are charged with enforcement of the law regarding hours of
labor. (Bulletin of the Bureau of Labor, No. 85, pp. 527, 528.)

[2] For creative law, see Acts of 1903, ch. 97, secs. 1 and 3 (22d An. Rept. Com. of
Labor, p. 245), and Acts of 1907, ch. 241. (Bulletin of the Bureau of Labor, No. 73,
p. 825.)

The chief inspector has served in his present position 14 years. The three male deputies have served, respectively, 9 years, 6 years, and 3 years; the female deputy, 1 year.

The chief inspector is appointed by the governor, with the consent of the senate. The chief appoints the male deputies. None of these appointments are made through civil service. The female deputy is also appointed by the chief, upon the recommendation of an advisory commission of three women. This commission is appointed by the governor. The members serve, respectively, 2, 4, and 6 years, and no two may be residents of the same town.

The inspectors are not allowed to engage in other work.

In performing its duties of inspection the department does not divide the State into regular inspection districts. The work is done by counties, assignments being made by the chief inspector.

There is no record made of the number of establishments subject to the inspection laws.

STATISTICAL DATA OF FACTORY INSPECTION.

The following table shows the number of inspections and number of orders issued by the factory inspectors during each of the five years 1904 to 1908 as completely and as accurately as the published reports permit. There were no prosecutions undertaken by the inspectors during any of the years mentioned.

ESTABLISHMENTS INSPECTED, PROSECUTIONS, CONVICTIONS, ETC., BY YEARS, 1904 TO 1908—CONNECTICUT.

[Compiled from Annual Reports of the Factory Inspector, Connecticut.]

	1904	1905	1906	1907	1908
Inspectors [1]	4	4	4	4	5
Establishments inspected [2]	3,107	2,740	2,816	2,930	3,250
Average per inspector	777	685	704	733	650
Nonfactory inspections: [3]					
Elevators in stores and public buildings	790	445	484	532	548
Mercantile establishments					276
Bakeries	401	383	351	380	403
Separate inspections	(4)	3,548	3,623	3,547	5,325
Average per inspector	(4)	887	906	887	1,065
Prosecutions					
Convictions					
Fines and costs:					
Imposed					
Paid					
Remitted					
Orders issued [5]	518	600	662	829	690

[1] Including chief inspector, who makes regular inspections.
[2] Including nonfactory inspections.
[3] Included in establishments inspected.
[4] Not reported.
[5] Separate orders. In some cases more than one order was issued to same establishment.

NEW YORK.

SCOPE OF THE LAW—SUBJECTS COVERED.[1]

Woman and child labor:

    1. Legal age of employment: 14 years.

    2. Prohibited employments for certain classes of persons of legal age:

        Cleaning of moving machinery.

        Operation of elevators.

        Operation of certain grinding wheels.

        Operation of dangerous machines of any kind.

    3. Employment certificates: Children 14 to 16 years' of age.

    4. Register of child employees.

    5. Hours of labor:

        Children under 16 years of age, 8 hours per day, 48 hours per week.

        Males 16 and 17 years of age and females 16 years of age and over, 10 hours per day, 60 hours per week, with exceptions as to 10-hour day.

    6. Night work prohibited for—

        Children under 16 years of age, between 5 p. m. and 8 a. m.

        Males 16 and 17 years of age, between 12 midnight and 4 a. m.

        Females 16 to 21 years of age, between 9 p. m. and 6 a. m.

    7. Posting of time schedules.

    8. Meal period: Midday and in case of overtime work.

Factory inspection:

    9. Fire protection:

        Fire escapes.

        Stairways, handrailed and screened, and rubber-covered steps.

        Hallways and stairways lighted.

        Doors opening outward and unfastened.

        [No legislation as to fire-fighting apparatus.]

    10. Elevators:

        Guards on shafts and openings.

        Inspection of cables and gearings.

        [No legislation as regards safety clutches.]

---

[1] The law referred to is as in force at the time of the investigation, December, 1908, and January, 1909. The text of the laws in force Jan. 1, 1912, is given in the appendixes at the end of this volume.

Factory inspection—Concluded.

    11. Dangerous machinery:

        Guards on mill gearing and machinery.

        Belt shifters.

        Removal of safeguards forbidden.

        Inspectors may condemn dangerous machines by posting notices.

        Workrooms, halls, and stairs lighted.

        [No legislation as to friction clutches or communication with engine room.]

    12. Accident reporting: By employer to department of labor.

    13. Provisions for comfort:

        Water-closets. [No minimum ratio of accommodations to employees.]

        Wash rooms.

        Dressing rooms, where females are engaged.

        Seats for females.

        [No legislation as to lunch rooms and drinking water.]

    14. Ventilation and sanitation:

        Minimum cubic air space.

        Exhaust fans on emery wheels and other dust-creating machinery.

        Gases, vapors, etc., to be rendered harmless.

        Proper and sufficient means of ventilation.

        Limewashing or painting of walls and ceilings.

        [No legislation regarding general cleanliness of workrooms or as regards spitting on the floor.]

    15. Posting of labor laws.

ENFORCEMENT OF THE LAWS.

The department of labor of New York is charged with the enforcement of all factory laws and all those regarding the employment of women and children.[1] The inspection work is done by two bureaus of this department—the bureau of factory inspection and the bureau of mercantile inspection. The jurisdiction of the former bureau covers all factories and workshops.

The department of labor has its own attorneys for preparing and helping prosecute cases arising in New York City. In the up-State districts prosecutions either are conducted by the district attorneys, aided in each case by the deputy factory inspector who made the complaint, or are heard directly on complaint of the inspector.

Cases are usually heard before a magistrate or similar inferior court, but some cases, especially those involving a jury trial, are heard in the higher courts.

---

[1] The supreme court of the State, however, decided that jurisdiction in the matter of fire escapes in New York City vests solely in local building authorities. See Chapter V of this report, "Safeg ards against fires."

The attitude of the courts toward first-offense cases has not been favorable to the department on the whole. A great many offenders are dismissed with a warning or fined and the fine later suspended. In the opinion of the commissioner of labor and his deputies conditions have much improved in this respect, but they believe that in too many instances magistrates dismiss cases when the evidence is sufficient to warrant the court in imposing the penalty provided by law.

In a newspaper article of December, 1908, the commissioner of labor is quoted as follows: [1]

There is difficulty in obtaining convictions in cases of violations of the labor law for overtime work of women and children.

During the months of September, October, and November officials of the department of labor began action in 165 cases for alleged violation of the labor law. Among the actions instituted 5 were for illegal employment of children in mercantile establishments, 27 for overtime work of women and children, and illegal employment of children in canning factories. In practically every instance these last-mentioned actions were tried before a jury, but in spite of the utmost care on the part of the department officials in the preparation of their cases no convictions were obtained, although it was shown in one instance that a woman worked 17 hours in one day. In another case there was undisputed evidence that a child of 7 years was employed in a "shed" adjoining a canning factory.

A study of the annual reports of the chief factory inspector for a number of years back shows many instances in which the courts failed to support the inspectors. Thus in the report for 1907 it is shown that in about one-half of the cases in which inspectors had secured convictions the court remitted the fine, thus letting the offender off without punishment. In most of the other cases only the minimum fine was imposed.

As the preparation and conduct of a prosecuted case consume a very considerable amount of time, and as the number of cases prosecuted in New York is very large, the time loss of inspectors due to unsuccessful prosecutions is an item of very considerable importance.

ORGANIZATION OF FACTORY INSPECTION FORCE.

The New York department of labor is organized in four main bureaus: (1) Factory inspection; (2) labor statistics; (3) mediation and arbitration; (4) mercantile inspection.[2] The duties of each of these bureaus are indicated roughly in the title.

The bureau of factory inspection is "required to enforce the provisions of the labor law relating to public work; to hours of labor in

---

[1] New York Sun, Dec. 13, 1908.
[2] For organic laws of the department of labor see New York Labor Laws (ch. xxxii of the Gen. Laws), Arts. II, III, V, X, and XIII. Quoted in full in Eighth Annual Report of Commissioner of Labor of New York, 1908, p. I.130 et seq.

brickyards, on street railways, and on steam, surface, and elevated railroads; to hours of work of telegraph operators and signalmen on surface, subway, and elevated railroads; to payment of wages of employees by corporations; to safety of scaffolding used in building construction and repair and methods of floor construction or filling on buildings in cities. It also inspects tenement houses, mines, quarries, and tunnels."[1]

The bureau of mercantile inspection is charged with the enforcement of the provisions of the labor law relating to mercantile establishments. This bureau was created and organized in 1908. Previous to that time the work of mercantile inspection was intrusted to local boards of health.

The bureau of statistics and the bureau of mediation and arbitration do not engage in inspection work of any kind.

The department of labor has at its head a commissioner, who has general direction over the organization and work of the several bureaus.

The personnel of the two inspection bureaus—factory inspection and mercantile inspection—is shown in the following table, the number being classified by position, sex, and salary. Those engaged in strictly clerical work are not included. This table shows conditions as they existed October 1, 1908. During the succeeding year no important changes were made.

NUMBER, SEX, AND SALARIES OF INSPECTORS OF THE DEPARTMENT OF LABOR, OCTOBER 1, 1908—NEW YORK.

[From Eighth Annual Report of the Commissioner of Labor of New York 1908, pp. I.12 to I.14, I.45 to I.49. Ninth Annual Report, 1909, pp. 12, 48–51.]

Titles.	Number.	Sex.	Annual salary.
Commissioner of labor...	1	Male....	$5,000
FACTORY INSPECTION.			
Factory inspector (first deputy commissioner)............................	1	...do.....	3,000
Assistant factory inspector...	1	...do.....	2,400
Do...	1	...do.....	2,000
Superintendent of licenses...	1	...do.....	2,400
Medical inspector..	1	...do.....	2,400
Special agent (legal)..	1	...do.....	1,500
Do...	1	...do.....	1,400
Tunnel inspector..	1	...do.....	1,500
Deputy factory inspectors..	3	...do.....	1,500
Do...	31	...do.....	1,200
Do...	7	...do.....	1,000
Do...	9	Female.	1,200
Do...	1	...do.....	1,000
Total...	59	....	....
MERCANTILE INSPECTION.			
Mercantile inspector (chief)...	1	Male....	2,000
Deputy mercantile inspectors..	7	...do.....	1,000
Do...	1	Female.	1,000
Total...	9	....	....

[1] Ninth Annual Report of Commissioner of Labor of New York, 1909, p. 13.

Special agents of the bureau of statistics may be availed of in case of necessity for field work in the bureau of inspection.

The average number of years of service for the present force of inspectors (with the exception of the mercantile inspectors) is approximately six years. The mercantile force was created in 1908, and all appointments to that force date from October 1, 1908.

The governor appoints the commissioner of labor. The other positions in the department are on the appointment of the commissioner and are all permanent under the civil-service laws except the first deputy (chief factory inspector), one assistant factory inspector, and the mercantile inspector, who may be removed at will by the commissioner.

Members of the department of labor may not engage in other work during their terms of service with the department.

In carrying out the work of inspection the State is divided into inspection districts. New York City comprises more than one-half the total number of districts, and some of the larger cities, such as Buffalo, are also subdivided. Otherwise each district consists of one or more counties.

In New York City the inspectors are assigned to districts which are within street boundaries, and they are supposed to visit and inspect each establishment within that territory. The deputy commissioner, in charge of the branch office in New York City, makes these assignments.

In the "up-State" districts the method of work is the same. One or two inspectors are assigned to a district, which may include one or more counties, and they are expected to visit every establishment therein which is subject to inspection.

Frequently, owing to the lack of sufficient inspectors, it is necessary to shift inspectors from one district to another.

The number of establishments, etc., in New York subject to inspection could not be obtained with any accuracy.

STATISTICAL DATA OF FACTORY INSPECTION.

As noted above, the duties of the factory inspection bureau cover the inspection of factories, workshops, laundries, bakeries, mines and quarries, tunnels, and tenements. There is one inspector for mines and quarries and another for tunnels, each devoting all of his time to the one work. Tenement inspection is done by the regular inspectors. Under a new law, in operation after 1904, tenement buildings are inspected and licensed as units, instead of each workroom being treated separately. This new system reduces materially the work of tenement inspection and also the number of inspections reported to have been made.

The following table shows the activities of the bureau of inspection during each of the five years from 1904 to 1908, inclusive. Owing to the very complete data given in the published reports of the New York Department of Labor, it has been considered desirable to slightly alter the form of the table, as compared with the form used in presenting the data of other States, and to increase the number of subjects treated.

The number of inspectors entered for each year is, as nearly as can be determined from the reports, the average number engaged in active field work.

FACTORY INSPECTIONS, PROSECUTIONS, CONVICTIONS, ETC., BY YEARS, 1904 TO 1908—
NEW YORK.

[From Reports of New York Department of Labor: 1904, pp. I.5, I.6, I.42, III.7 to III.10; 1905, pp. II.7 to II.11, II.14, II.19; 1906, pp. I.27 to I.29, II.7 to II.13; 1907, pp. I.24, II.9 to II.11; 1908, p. I.13, and Factory Inspector's Report, pp. 9 to 18.]

	1904	1905	1906	1907	1908
Inspectors [1]	35	35	38	47	48
Inspections of all kinds [2]	74,201	56,077	60,950	94,207	96,152
Average per inspector	2,120	1,602	1,604	2,004	2,003
Regular factory inspections [3]	27,568	30,094	36,679	35,405	35,334
Average per inspector	788	860	965	753	736
Orders followed up [4]	9,979	8,981	14,145	34,863	32,448
Average per inspector	285	257	372	742	676
Prosecutions	49	202	303	443	815
Convictions:					
Fined	18	59	66	147	222
Sentence suspended	7	62	125	147	201
Fines imposed [5]	$630	$2,510	$1,475	$3,835	$5,146
Orders issued	49,416	39,930	65,337	61,441	69,516
Orders complied with	46,114	34,656	55,039	58,294	65,323

[1] Not including chief inspector, assistants, medical inspector, tunnel inspector, or inspector of mines and quarries, and including only such deputies as were actually engaged in field work.
[2] Inspections, investigations, and visits of all kinds except those made in connection with mines, quarries, and tunnels.
[3] Including only factories and workshops coming under general factory laws.
[4] Revisits made to ascertain if orders had been complied with.
[5] Amounts paid and remitted, not reported.

The number of separate establishments visited does not clearly appear in any of the reports, and therefore can not be given in this table. Inspections are entered under the heads: The number of inspections of all kinds, and the number of "regular" factory inspections. The former title covers all inspections, investigations, and revisits made (except mines and quarries and tunnel inspections), and includes inspections of factories, bakeries, laundries, and workshops, tenement inspections, investigations in connection with the issue of tenement licenses, revisits to see that orders are complied with, and investigations of complaints and accidents—that is to say, every visit paid by an inspector to an establishment. It does not include, however, visits paid to establishments found not in operation or to the "tagging of goods." These entries are valuable as indicating roughly the amount of field work done by the bureau.

The entries under the title "regular factory inspections" are limited strictly to factories and workshops in the narrower sense of the words. They do not include tenement inspections, investigations of complaints, visits to see that orders are complied with, and other special visits, and, on the whole, are preferable for the purposes of comparing one year's work with another.

The number of orders followed up to insure compliance is given, as it illustrates the increasing activity of the bureau in this one direction.

The convictions are reported in two divisions: Those convicted and punished by a fine, and those convicted but fine or sentence remitted. The number of remitted fines warrants this division. Such remission is a continued cause of complaint by the department of labor and the bureau of inspection in their reports.

More detailed data regarding prosecutions and convictions are given in the table which follows.

SUMMARY OF PROSECUTIONS UNDER FACTORY INSPECTION LAWS, BY YEARS, 1904 TO 1908—NEW YORK.

[Compiled from Annual Reports of the Department of Labor, New York: 1904, pp. III.9, III.10; 1905, pp. II.7 to II.11; 1906, pp. II.8 to II.13; 1907, pp. II.9 to II.1?; 1908, Factory Inspector's Report, pp. 9 to 18.]

	1904	1905	1906	1907	1908
Total cases of prosecutions [1]	[2] 49	[3] 202	[3] 303	[4] 443	[5] 815
Acquitted or discharged	24	81	40	61	180
Withdrawn			5	16	29
Pending			67	72	183
Convicted:					
Sentence suspended	7	62	125	147	201
Fined	[6] 18	59	66	147	222
Fines imposed [7]	$630	[8] $2,510	$1,475	$3,835	$5,146

[1] Cases, or instances of violation of factory laws; not number of firms or establishments made defendants. The number of different defendants was—1904, not reported; 1905, not reported; 1906, 205; 1907, 293; 1908, not reported.
[2] Terminated during the year ending Sept. 30.
[3] Including 56 cases carried over from preceding year.
[4] Including 69 cases carried over from preceding year.
[5] Including 72 cases carried over from preceding year.
[6] Including 3 cases in which bail (amounting to $300) was forfeited.
[7] Costs not reported.
[8] Including $1,000 bail forfeited in a "not convicted" case.

The industries in which violations occurred are not shown in the reports. The offenses for which prosecutions were started and those for which convictions were secured are presented in detail in the table which follows.

NUMBER OF VIOLATIONS AND OF CONVICTIONS UNDER FACTORY INSPECTION LAWS, BY NATURE OF OFFENSE AND BY YEARS, 1904 TO 1908—NEW YORK.

Offenses.	1904		1905		1906		1907		1908	
	Violations.	Convictions.	Violations.	Convictions.	Violations.	Convictions.	Violations.	Convictions.	Violations.	Convictions.
Illegal employment of children:										
Under age			9	9	64	34	103	63	146	77
Without certificate	19	9	117	74	137	95	201	145	317	166
In excess of and after legal hours	1		31	20	33	19	70	42	185	128
Prohibited occupations							2	1	1	1
Evidence of age not provided							1			
Obtaining certificates fraudulently					1		1			
Register of children not provided	1		1	1			1		1	
Illegal employment of women and minors:										
In excess of and after legal hours			2	1	13	4	41	33	45	17
Hours of labor not posted									5	2
Addresses of females not kept									1	
Meal period					1		1	1		
General factory laws:										
Posting laws					1	1				
Fire escapes and exits	4	4			1	1			17	5
Dangerous machinery			2	1					5	2
Elevators and hoistways							1			
Ventilation and light	5	1	3	1	8	2	5	2	36	9
Water-closets, dressing and wash rooms	7	3	27	12	40	33	7	3	40	11
Cleaning and whitewashing	2	1	6	1	1	1			4	
Bakery laws	4	3	4	1	1		1	1	3	2
Tenement laws	6	4			1		3	2		
Removal of notice from unsafe scaffold									2	
Interfering with inspector					1	1	5	1	6	2
Weekly payment law									1	1
Total	49	25	202	121	303	191	443	294	815	423

NEW JERSEY.

SCOPE OF THE LAW—SUBJECTS COVERED.[1]

Woman and child labor:

1. Legal age of employment: 14 years.
2. Prohibited employments for certain classes of persons of legal age:
   Cleaning of moving machinery.
   To work between the fixed and traversing parts of machinery in motion.
3. Employment certificates: Optional with employers.
4. Register of children.
5. Hours of labor: Children under 16 years of age, 10 hours per day, 55 hours per week.
6. [Night work: No legislation.]
7. [Posting of time schedules: No legislation.]
8. [Meal period: No legislation.]

---

[1] The law here referred to is as in force at the time of the investigation, December, 1908, and January, 1909. The text of the laws in force Jan. 1, 1912, is given in the appendixes at the end of this volume.

Factory inspection:
  9. Fire protection:
        Fire escapes.
        Doors opening outward.
        [No legislation as to stairways, exit signs, or lights or
            fire-fighting apparatus.]
  10. Elevators:
        Guards on shafts and floor openings.
        [No legislation as to safety clutches.]
  11. Dangerous machinery:
        Guards on mill gearing and machinery.
        Belt shifters.
        Removal of safeguards forbidden.
        Inspectors may condemn dangerous machines by
            posting notices.
        Halls properly lighted.
        [No legislation regarding friction clutches or communi-
            cation with engine room.]
  12. Accident reporting: By employer to factory inspection de-
        partment.
  13. Provisions for comfort:
        Water-closets. [No minimum ratio of accommoda-
            tions to employees.]
        Wash rooms.
        Dressing rooms.
        Seats for females.
        [No legislation regarding lunch rooms or drinking
            water.]
  14. Ventilation and sanitation:
        "Proper and sufficient" ventilation generally.
        An air space standard.
        Exhaust apparatus for certain grinding wheels.
        Limewashing or painting in factories employing wo-
            men and children and carrying on dusty work.
        [No legislation regarding spitting on the floor, cuspi-
            dors, etc.]
  15. Posting of labor laws.

ENFORCEMENT OF THE LAWS.

In New Jersey the department of labor is charged with the enforcement of all the factory laws and all those relative to the employment
of children.

Orders of the inspectors, on appeal, may be tried "in any district
court, recorders' court of cities, and before any justice of the peace

having due jurisdiction or in any other court of competent jurisdiction." [1]

The commissioner institutes prosecutions against alleged violators through the attorney general's office in the higher courts and directly by himself or by one of his deputies in cases tried before justices of the peace.

The attitude of the courts has been favorable to the department in the opinion of the commissioner. A study of the records supports this view.

The department does not place equal emphasis upon all of the provisions of the labor laws. The commissioner explains that "it has been the policy of the department to pay special attention to violation in the order of greatest importance." The order observed is as follows:

1. Child labor.
2. Fire protection.
3. Blower system.
4. Dangerous machinery.
5. Sanitation.
6. Accidents.

That the factory-inspection laws have not received the degree of attention shown in cases of child labor is illustrated by the character of the prosecutions. From 1904 to 1908, inclusive, the commissioner instituted 77 prosecutions for violations of law. All but three of these were against manufacturers, and all but one for the employment of children under legal age. The number of convictions was 70. The single prosecution under other than the child-labor law was against a firm for refusing an inspector admission to its factory. It is not to be inferred from this, however, that the factory laws are unduly neglected. The statement just made was simply to emphasize the fact that the policy of the department has been to place most weight on the child-labor clauses of the law.

ORGANIZATION OF FACTORY INSPECTION FORCE.

The New Jersey Department of Labor, which administers the child-labor and factory-inspection laws, is constituted as follows, office help being excluded:[2]

---

[1] Acts of 1904, ch. 64, sec. 45, as amended by ch. 257, Acts of 1907 (22d An. Rept. Com. of Labor, p. 868).

[2] The law provides for 1 commissioner, 1 assistant, and 13 inspectors, of whom 3 shall be women, and authorizes the commissioner to employ additional inspectors as necessary, at salaries fixed by him. Acts of 1904, ch. 64, sec. 45, as amended by Acts of 1907, ch. 257 (22d An. Rept. Com. of Labor, p. 868), and Acts of 1908, ch. 273 (Bulletin of the Bureau of Labor No. 85, pp. 675, 676).

Titles.	Number.	Sex.	Annual salary.
Commissioner..	1	Male....	$3,500
Assistant commissioner.......................................	1	...do....	2,000
Inspectors...	11	...do....	1,500
Do...	1	...do.....	1,000
Do...	3	Female.	1,500
Total..	15	....	....

The present inspectors have served an average of four years and one month.

The commissioner of labor and the regular inspectors are appointed by the governor. The commissioner, with the approval of the governor, appoints the assistant commissioner, and also appoints special inspectors whenever he considers the work so demands. The appointments are not made under civil service regulations, and, except the requirements that the assistant must be an experienced machinist and the inspectors "suitable persons," the law does not fix the qualifications of appointees.

Inspectors are not permitted to engage in other work during their terms of service.

In carrying on the work of inspection the State is divided by the commissioner of labor into nine districts. From time to time, however, inspectors are assigned to special work without regard to district boundaries.

There is no accurate record of the number of establishments in the State subject to inspection. The number is estimated by the commissioner at about 4,000.

STATISTICAL DATA OF FACTORY INSPECTION.

The following table presents the available data regarding inspections, prosecutions, convictions, and orders issued by the State factory inspection department (department of labor) for the five years 1904 to 1908, inclusive. The data are obtained for the most part from the annual reports of the department of labor. In the matter of prosecutions, convictions, and fines, however, the annual reports are not always full or clear, and the data therein contained upon these points have been supplemented by examination of the original records.

In 1904 the work of inspection was limited to manufacturing establishments. In 1905, bakeries, and in 1907, mercantile establishments were added. The number of mercantile establishments inspected, however, is not shown by the reports and the entries under "inspections" in the table do not include these items.

FACTORY INSPECTIONS, PROSECUTIONS, CONVICTIONS, ETC., BY YEARS, 1904 TO 1908—NEW JERSEY.

Compiled from Annual Reports of the Department of Labor, New Jersey: 1904, pp. 7, 9, 10; 1905, p. 7; 1906, pp. 5, 9; 1907, pp. 4, 9; 1908, pp. 5, 11, 13.]

	1904	1905	1906	1907	1908
Inspectors	6	13	13	13	15
Inspections [1]	2,404	4,174	5,373	6,687	8,363
Average per inspector	401	321	413	514	[3] 616
Prosecutions	23	8	14	27	5
Convictions	[3] 19	8	13	26	4
Fines and costs:					
Imposed	[4]	[4]	[4]	[4]	[4]
Paid [5]	$100	$60	$692	$1,450	$354
Remitted					
Orders issued	272	1,503	1,100	1,578	2,013

[1] Initial inspections only, and not including the many revisits made in following up orders. (Report Department of Labor, 1909, p. 13.) Bakery inspections included as follows: 1905, 721; 1906, 1,168; 1907, 2,203; 1908, 2,589. Inspections of mercantile establishments not included; number not reported during 1907 and 1908.
[2] Computed on basis that of the two new inspectors in 1908, one had served only 5 months and one only 2 months.
[3] Not including 3 cases pending.
[4] Not reported.
[5] Paid during the year specified; may include payments which were due the preceding year.

The reports do not show in what industries prosecutions and convictions occurred. All were for illegally employing children, except a very few for obstructing inspectors in their visits. There were none for violation of the factory laws proper, i. e., for not having fire escapes, etc.

The next table shows the character of the orders issued and also the number of children discharged from factories by inspectors because under legal age. The number of compliances is not given, but in the report for 1908 it is stated that "of the 2,013 orders which have been issued during the past fiscal year to both factories and bakeshops of the State, about 99 per cent of the orders upon which the time limit has expired have been complied with." [1]   Again in the report for 1909 it is stated that "practically all of the orders issued since the creation of the department and upon which the time limit has expired have been performed, and in accomplishing this result it was necessary to institute only one prosecution." [2]

ORDERS ISSUED, AND CHILDREN DISCHARGED AS BEING UNDER LEGAL AGE OF EMPLOYMENT, BY DEPARTMENT OF LABOR, BY YEARS, 1904 TO 1908—NEW JERSEY.

[Compiled from Reports of the Department of Labor, New Jersey: 1904, p. 10; 1905, pp. 5, 7; 1906, p. 9; 1907, p. 9; 1908, p. 13.]

	1904	1905	1906	1907	1908
Orders issued relating to—					
Fire escapes	272	128	62	57	53
Blowers		164	46	49	82
Sanitary betterment		413	339	286	346
Protection against dangerous machinery, etc.		394	215	238	351
Bakeries		404	438	948	1,211
Number of children discharged as under legal age of employment	397	238	361	399	195

[1] Report of the Department of Labor of the State of New Jersey, 1908, p. 13.
[2] Idem. 1909, p. 13.

PENNSYLVANIA.

SCOPE OF THE LAW—SUBJECTS COVERED.[1]

Woman and child labor:

1. Legal age of employment: 14 years.
2. Prohibited employments for certain classes of persons of legal age:

    The cleaning or oiling of moving machinery.

    Operation of elevators.
3. Employment certificates: Children 14 to 16 years of age.
4. Register of child employees.
5. Hours of labor: Children under 16 years of age and females 16 years of age and over, 12 hours per day, 60 hours per week.
6. Night work: Prohibited for children under 16 years of age between 9 p. m. and 6 a. m., except in establishments using "perishable materials."
7. Posting of time schedules.
8. Meal period: Regulated.

Factory inspection:

9. Fire protection: Fire escapes; separate legislation for cities of different classes.
10. Elevators:

    Guards on shafts and openings; separate legislation for cities of different classes.

    [No special legislation as to safety clutches.]
11. Dangerous machinery:

    Guards on mill gearing and machinery.

    Belt shifters.

    Removal of safeguards forbidden.

    Inspectors may condemn dangerous machines by posting notices.

    Overcrowding of machinery.

    [No legislation as to friction clutches or communication with engine room.]
12. Accident reporting: By employer to factory-inspection department.
13. Provisions for comfort:

    Water-closets. [No minimum ratio of accommodations to employees.]

    Wash rooms.

    Dressing rooms.

---

[1] The law here referred to is as in force at the time of the investigation, January to March, 1909. The text of the laws in force Jan. 1, 1912, is given in the appendixes at the end of this volume.

Provisions for comfort—Concluded.
        Seats for females.
        [No legislation as to lunch rooms or drinking water.]
    14. Ventilation and sanitation:
        Minimum cubic air space (250 cubic feet).
        Exhaust fans, etc., for poisonous fumes, gases, and dust.
        Workrooms, halls, etc., to be clean, lighted, and in sanitary condition.
        Inspector may remedy conditions of heating, lighting, ventilation, or sanitation injurious to health.
        [No specific legislation as to limewashing or painting or spitting on floor.]
    15. Posting of labor laws.

ENFORCEMENT OF THE LAWS.

The State factory-inspection department is charged with the enforcement of all the child-labor laws and all the factory-inspection laws, except where regulations regarding fire protection and elevators are made for cities of the first and second classes and enforced by the local building-inspection department thereof.

Prosecutions are conducted by the deputy factory inspectors. Cases are tried before justices of the peace, aldermen, and magistrates.

The chief factory inspector stated that first offenders are never prosecuted. If the offense is repeated, however, prosecution is begun.

The general attitude of the courts has been to sustain the department in cases arising under the factory-inspection laws. In cases involving the child-labor laws, however, the courts have so construed the law as to practically nullify its effect. As a result, the enforcement of these provisions is extremely difficult and not often undertaken.

The chief factory inspector stated that of about 600 cases prosecuted by the department since 1903 for violations of factory laws and woman and child labor laws, not more than 6 had been lost.

ORGANIZATION OF FACTORY INSPECTION FORCE.[1]

The factory inspection department of Pennsylvania is constituted as follows, office help being excluded:

NUMBER, SEX, AND SALARIES OF FACTORY INSPECTORS, 1908—PENNSYLVANIA.

Titles.	Number.	Sex.	Annual salary.
Chief factory inspector	1	Male....	$5,000
Deputy factory inspectors	36	...do ...	1,200
Do	5	Female..	1,200
Total	41		

The present deputies have served in their present offices as follows: Males—18 years, 1; 17 years, 1; 15 years, 3; 13 years, 1; 10 years, 2; 9 years, 3; 8 years, 4; 7 years, 5; 6 years, 2; 5 years, 4; 4 years, 3; 3 years, 2; 2 years, 2; 1 year, 1; less than 1 year, 2. Females—15 years, 1; 14 years, 1; 10 years, 2; 6 years, 1. The average period of service is thus between 7 and 8 years.

The occupations of the deputy inspectors previous to their present service were as follows: Females—housewife, 2; stenographer, 1; milliner, 1; clerk, 1. Males—machinist, 9; clerk, 9; farmer, 3; restaurant keeper, 2; druggist, 2; blacksmith, 1; real estate, 1; veterinary surgeon, 1; member of legislature, 1; clergyman, 1; student, 1; newspaper proprietor, 1; furniture business, 1; bricklayer, 1; county recorder 1; coal operator, 1.

The governor appoints to the office of chief factory inspector, and the chief inspector selects and appoints all the deputies. The appointments are not controlled by civil-service or other regulations.

Inspectors are not permitted to engage in other work during their terms of office.

For inspection purposes the State is divided into 41 districts, to each of which an inspector is assigned. Philadelphia contains 14 of these districts, and Allegheny County, containing the cities of Pittsburgh and Allegheny, 5 districts.[2] Each of the remaining 22 districts is composed of one or more counties, and, with few exceptions, these districts observe county lines as their boundaries.

There is no record of the number of establishments in the State subject to inspection by the factory inspectors.

[1] Acts of 1905, act No. 226, sec. 27. This act provides for a commissioner at $5,000, a chief clerk at $2,000, a statistician at $1,800, an assistant clerk at $1,400, a messenger-typewriter at $1,200, and 39 deputy inspectors at $1,200 each. The number of deputies was increased to 41 by the appropriation act of 1907. (22d An. Rept. Com. of Labor, p. 1180.)

[2] See Nineteenth Annual Report of Factory Inspector, Pennsylvania, 1908, pp. 75, 76.

STATISTICAL DATA OF FACTORY INSPECTION.

The following table compiled from the annual reports of the State factory inspection department shows for each of the five years, 1904 to 1908, the activities of the department as regards inspections, prosecutions, and orders issued. The data are not fully complete, and as the method of presentation in the several reports is not always the same, the entries of the tables can not be used safely for purposes of comparison. The information, however, is suggestive.

The duties of the State factory inspection department include the inspection not only of factories and workshops proper, but also of bakeshops, mercantile establishments, steamboats engaged in inland navigation, and fire escapes, etc., on schools, hospitals, hotels, public halls, and theaters. Prior to 1905, small tenement workshops were also included, but beginning in that year the supervision of such places was charged to the board of health. Boiler inspection is under the general supervision of the chief factory inspector, but the work is not done by the deputy factory inspectors.

ESTABLISHMENTS INSPECTED, PROSECUTIONS, CONVICTIONS, ETC., UNDER FACTORY-INSPECTION LAWS, BY YEARS, 1904 TO 1908—PENNSYLVANIA.

[Compiled from Annual Reports of Factory Inspectors, Pennsylvania: 1904, pp. 3, 5, 9, 10, 12, 13; 1905, pp. 3, 7, 13, 16, 17; 1906, pp. 6, 21, 22, 24, 28; 1907, pp. 15-18; 1908, pp. 13-20.]

	1904	1905	1906	1907	1908
Deputy inspectors	39	39	39	41	41
Establishments inspected [1]	16,589	14,642	13,548	14,231	15,280
Average per inspector	425	375	347	347	373
Separate inspections	48,178	(²)	(²)	(²)	29,473
Average per inspector	1,235				719
Prosecutions (persons)	65	70	100	(²)	32
Convictions (persons)	58	(²)	(²)	³3	⁴31
Fines:					
Imposed ⁵	$971	(²)	(²)	$75	⁶$190
Paid ⁷	$739	$1,362	$3,540	$225	$100
Remitted	$232	(²)	(²)	(²)	(²)
Orders issued	4,020	3,033	(²)	(²)	(²)

[1] Including schools, hospitals, hotels, public halls, theaters, as follows: 1904, 1,516; 1905, not reported; 1906, 1,289; 1907, 499; 1908, 1,664. Also bakeshops, as follows: 1904, 2,116; 1905, 1,927; 1906, 1,020; 1907, 2,100; 1908, 1,638. Also mercantile establishments, as follows: 1904, not reported; 1905, not reported; 1906, 1,739; 1907, 1,364; 1908, 1,433.
[2] Not reported.
[3] Convictions in which fines were not remitted. Total convictions not reported. See Report of Factory Inspector, 1908, p. 14.
[4] Including 3 convictions, appeals pending, and 10 cases in which guilt was acknowledged but prosecution not pressed. Fines were either not imposed or were remitted in 13 of the 19 convictions which were decided and not appealed.
[5] Costs not reported.
[6] Including fines imposed in 2 cases which were appealed.
[7] During course of year and including payments which were due in preceding year.

The industries in which convictions occurred are not shown by the department reports. The offenses for which convictions were secured and also the offenses alleged in the prosecutions are shown in the next table, as far as the information is available. The entries are for numbers of persons convicted and prosecuted, respectively, not individual counts.

NUMBER OF PERSONS PROSECUTED AND CONVICTED UNDER FACTORY INSPECTION LAWS, BY NATURE OF OFFENSE AND BY YEARS, 1904 TO 1908—PENNSYLVANIA.

Offenses.	1904		1905		1906		1907		1908	
	Prosecutions.	Convictions.	Prosecutions.	Convictions.	Prosecutions.	Convictions.	Prosecutions.	Convictions.	Prosecutions.	Convictions.
Employing children illegally:										
Without proper certificates..........			21	(1)	64	(1)	(2)	(2)	4	4
Under age..........................	22	22	10	(1)	14	(1)	(2)	(2)	6	6
Overtime (including women)........			1	(1)	6	(1)	(2)	(2)	1	......
Issuing certificates fraudulently..........	21	14	9	(1)	7	(1)	(2)	(2)	1	1
Obtaining certificates fraudulently......	4	4			......		(2)	(2)	10	10
Elevators and openings................			1	(1)	1	(1)	(2)	(2)	1	1
Mill gearing and machinery.............			*1	(1)	1	(1)	(2)	(2)	......	......
Ventilation and sanitation.............					3	(1)	(2)	(2)	......	......
Closets and dressing rooms..............	2	2	4	(1)	2	(1)	(2)	(2)	......	......
Fire escapes..........................	5	5	19	(1)	1	(1)	(2)	(2)	8	8
Miscellaneous and unclassified..........	11	11	4	(1)	1	(1)	(2)	(2)	1	1
Total......................	65	58	70	(1)	100	(1)	(2)	(2)	32	31

[1] Not reported.
[2] The Nineteenth Annual Report of the Factory Inspector, 1908, pp. 14, 15, simply states that there were 3 convictions in 1907, in which fines were imposed and not remitted. One of these was for employing a child illegally; the 2 other convictions were for maintaining insanitary bakeshops.

OHIO.

SCOPE OF THE LAW—SUBJECTS COVERED.[1]

Woman and child labor:

1. Legal age of employment: 14 years.
2. Prohibited employments for certain classes of persons of legal age: A number of specified occupations including the oiling and cleaning of machinery, operation of elevators, poisonous acids, adjusting belts, etc.
3. Employment certificates: Children 14 to 16 years of age.
4. Register of children.
5. Hours of labor: Children under 16 years of age and females 16 to 18 years of age, 8 hours per day, 48 hours per week.
6. Night work: Prohibited for children under 16 years of age and females 16 to 18 years of age, between 6 p. m. and 7 a. m.
7. Posting of time schedules.
8. Meal period: Length of time regulated.

Factory inspection:

9. Fire protection:
    Fire escapes.
    Life nets.
    Fire extinguishing apparatus.
    Handrails on stairways.

[1] The law here referred to is as in force at the time of the investigation, March, 1909. The text of the laws in force Jan. 1, 1912, is given in the appendixes at the end of this volume.

Factory inspection—Concluded.

  10. Elevators:
- Guards on shafts and openings.
- Inspection of ropes, gears, etc.
- Inspectors may condemn by posting notices.
- [No specific legislation regarding safety clutches.]

  11. Dangerous machinery:
- Guards on mill gearing and machinery.
- Belt shifters.
- Set screws, etc., to be countersunk.
- Devices for stopping individual machines.
- Lighting of hallways and workrooms.
- Inspectors may condemn by posting notices.
- [No legislation as to removal of safeguards or communication with engine room.]

  12. Accident reporting: By employer to factory inspection department.

  13. Provisions for comfort: For females only—
- Water-closets, minimum ratio of one accommodation per 25 females.
- Wash rooms.
- Dressing rooms.
- Seats.
- [No legislation as to lunch rooms or drinking water.]

  14. Sanitation and ventilation:
- General authorization given inspectors to remedy any "heating, lighting or ventilation or sanitary arrangement" that is injurious to health; exhaust fans, etc., on certain grinding machines.
- [No specific legislation regarding spitting on floor, cuspidors, or limewashing or painting.]

  15. [Posting of laws: No legislation.]

ENFORCEMENT OF THE LAWS.[1]

The State factory inspection department is charged with the general enforcement of all factory laws and laws regarding the employment of women and children, as outlined above.

Cases of alleged violation are tried before justices of the peace and in police courts. Prosecutions are conducted by the chief inspector and his deputies. If necessary, cases are carried into the higher courts with the assistance of the attorney general of the State.

The attitude of the courts toward first offenders has been strict in interpreting the law, but inclined to leniency in remitting or

---

[1] Bates' Ann. Stat., 3d ed., Pt. I, Political, sec. 2573a, as amended by act, p. 338, Acts of 1902, and act, p. 530, Acts of 1904 (22d An. Rept. Com. of Labor, p. 998).

suspending fines. On the whole, the general attitude of the courts has been to sustain the factory inspection department.

ORGANIZATION OF FACTORY INSPECTION FORCE.

The following table shows the composition of the factory inspection force, with salaries received, office help being excluded:[1]

NUMBER, SEX, AND SALARIES OF INSPECTORS OF WORKSHOPS AND FACTORIES, 1908—OHIO.

Titles.	Number.	Sex.	Annual salary.
Chief inspector	1	Male....	$2,500
Assistant chief inspector	1	...do.....	2,500
Explosives inspector	1	...do.....	2,000
District inspectors	22	...do.....	1,200
Bakeshop inspectors	2	...do.....	1,200
Women visitors	8	Female .	1,200
Total	35	....	....

The chief inspector has served in his present position 7 years. The office of assistant chief was created by act of the legislature approved April 28, 1908. The terms of service of the other deputies are as follows: Males—12 years, 2; 6 years, 5; 4 years, 2; 3 years, 3; 2 years, 2; less than 1 year, 11. Females—all less than a year, the office of woman visitor having been created February 28, 1908.

Previous to his present office the chief inspector was a sheet and tin-plate worker; the assistant chief an architect. Both the bakery inspectors were formerly bakers. The previous occupations of the other inspectors were as follows: Males—carpenters, 8; machinists, 3; brass worker, 1; ironworker, 1; iron molders, 2; wood workers, 2; oil well and wood worker, 1; elevator builder, 1; pottery worker, 1; bricklayer, 1; painter, 1; electrical worker, 1. Females—school teachers, 2; seamstress, 1; stenographer, 1; forelady in cash-register factory, 1; forelady in glass factory, 1; laundry worker, 1; charity worker, 1.

Factory inspectors are not permitted to engage in other work during their terms of office.

The governor appoints the chief inspector, who, with the approval of the governor, appoints all assistants. There is no civil-service system of selection for any of these offices, but the law requires that all inspectors be "competent and practical mechanics."

For purposes of inspection work the State is divided into 20 districts, arranged in convenient groups of counties. Two district

---

[1] Bates' Ann. Stat., 3d ed., Pt. I, Political, secs. 2573a (as amended by act, p. 338, Acts of 1902, and act, p. 539, Acts of 1904) and 2573a-2 (22d An. Rept. Com. of Labor, pp. 997–999) Acts of 1908, p. 30, sec. 4. (Bulletin of the Bureau of Labor, No. 85, pp. 703, 704.) See also Twenty-fifth Annual Report of the Department of Inspection of the Workshops, Factories, and Public Buildings of Ohio, 1908, pp. 2, 11, 12.

inspectors are assigned to Hamilton County, which includes Cincinnati, and two to Cuyahoga County, in which Cleveland is located. One district inspector is assigned to each of the remaining districts. The two bakery inspectors divide the State for purposes of bakeshop inspections, each covering one-half of the counties. The high-explosive inspector covers factories manufacturing explosives in all parts of the State.

No record is available as to the number of establishments, etc., subject to inspection.

STATISTICAL DATA OF FACTORY INSPECTION.

The inspection duties of the Ohio department of inspection are very broad in their scope. The chief inspector in his report for 1906 comments upon this fact as follows:[1]

During the years since the department was organized, additional duties have, from time to time, been placed upon the department until practically every building in the State, with the exception of private dwellings housing but one or two families, comes within the jurisdiction of this department.

The term "shops and factories" is interpreted by the Ohio law to include manufacturing, mechanical, electrical, mercantile, art and laundrying establishments, printing, telegraph and telephone offices, railroad depots, hotels, memorial buildings, tenement and apartment houses. It is made the duty of the department to inspect these buildings as to their safety, the means of egress, lighting, heating, ventilating and sanitary conditions, and to see that stairways are equipped with handrailings, elevator openings provided with automatic gates or doors, and that every kind and description of machinery, shafting, gearing, elevators and drums are securely guarded, as far as practicable, to protect employees from accidents. Home workshops, or sweatshops as they are termed, are also placed under our jurisdiction, and only such as are used exclusively by the immediate members of the family are exempt. These shops should receive constant attention in order to maintain anything like fair conditions.

Some years ago the legislature passed a law regulating the conditions and surroundings of bakeshops, the product of which is such an important and necessary factor in our lives. This law was also given to the department of factory inspection to enforce.

The manufacture and storage of high explosives in the State attracted the attention of the legislature to such an extent that in 1893 a law was passed to regulate the manufacture, handling and storage of dynamite, powder, nitroglycerine, or their compounds, and the duty of enforcing it was placed upon one of the district inspectors in addition to his other duties. The use of high explosives has so greatly increased since that time, and the requirements of additional laws are such that it would require the entire time and attention of one man to look after the matter properly. It is a great responsibility, as we fully realize, and ample provisions should be made to meet it.

---

[1] Twenty-third Annual Report of the Department of Inspection of the Workshops Factories, and Public Buildings of Ohio, 1906, pp. 17, 18.

The child-labor laws, and those relating to the employment of women in shops and factories, with all their various provisions, are under the jurisdiction of this department, and are sufficient in themselves to keep the department busy the greater part of the year.

In addition to all these diverse duties, the legislature has provided that the department shall inspect all buildings used for the assemblage or betterment of people, which includes opera houses, halls, theaters, churches, schoolhouses, colleges, seminaries, infirmaries, sanitariums, charitable homes, hospitals, and all other buildings used for like purposes. It is the duty of the department to see that these structures are such as will not endanger the lives of those who may assemble therein, and that they are provided with ample means of egress in case of fire or other disaster, and with means to extinguish fire.

This statement of the duties of the inspection department applies with fair accuracy to each of the years 1904 to 1908, covered in the following tables.

The table which follows presents data, obtained from the annual reports of the department of inspection, showing the general activities of the factory inspectors in making inspections, in prosecuting offenders, and in issuing orders for changes. The term "inspections" is here used, as it is in the reports, to include the number of separate inspections made. It does not include revisits to see that orders are complied with, etc. The total inspections made will not correspond to the total establishments inspected because a "building inspection" and a "factory inspection" may be made of a single establishment, and in such case two inspections are credited in this table. The reports do not give complete data as to the number of separate establishments inspected.

INSPECTIONS, PROSECUTIONS, CONVICTIONS, ETC., UNDER FACTORY AND WORK-SHOP LAWS, BY YEARS, 1904 TO 1908—OHIO.

[Compiled from Annual Reports, Department of Inspection, etc., Ohio: 1904, pp. 10, 185, 189–192; 1905, pp. 11, 208, 212–216; 1906, pp. 254–266, 268–272; 1907, pp. 330–342, 348–353; 1908, pp. 10, 173.]

	1904	1905	1906	1907	1908
Inspectors[1]	15	15	15	15	33
Inspections[2]	6,990	7,516	9,807	11,636	12,340
Average per inspector	466	501	654	776	[3] 514
Prosecutions	3	3	313	319	16
Convictions	3	3	[4] 308	[5] 310	16
Fines and costs:					
Imposed	[6] $30	[7] $45	[8] $4,860	[9] $3,085	$213
Paid	$30	$45	$3,269	$2,833	$197
Remitted	(10)	(10)	[11] $1,291	[9] $250	$16
Orders issued	2,215	2,304	2,965	3,753	22,070

[1] Not including chief inspector or the assistant inspector (appointed 1908); work administrative only.
[2] Does not include revisits; does not represent separate establishments in all cases, as a "factory inspection" and a "building inspection" of the same establishment are counted as two inspections. Data not available as to number of separate establishments inspected.
[3] Computed on basis that the 18 new inspectors this year had served only about 6 months each.
[4] Three cases pending; 2 declared not guilty.
[5] Including 32 sentences suspended; 2 cases pending at end of year; 7 cases dismissed.
[6] Fines only, costs not reported; not including amount of fine in one case not given.
[7] Fines only, costs not reported.
[8] Sum of the items shown in report, although total is given as $4,857.
[9] Not including amounts represented by suspended sentences, but including $40 in fines suspended.
[10] Not reported.
[11] Including $119 represented by 6 suspended sentences.

The table following shows the number of each class of inspections made each year. It is to be repeated that each inspection does not represent necessarily a separate establishment. A "building inspection" and a "factory inspection" of the same establishment are entered as two inspections.

NUMBER OF INSPECTIONS MADE BY THE INSPECTION DEPARTMENT, BY KIND OF ESTABLISHMENT OR BUILDING INSPECTED AND BY YEARS, 1904 TO 1908—OHIO.

[Compiled from Annual Reports, Department of Inspection, etc., Ohio: 1904, pp. 189–193; 1905, pp. 212–216; 1906, pp. 268–272; 1907, pp. 348–353; 1908, p. 173.]

Kind of establishments or buildings inspected.	1904	1905	1906	1907	1908
Shops and factories	2,302	2,280	3,060	2,855	2,269
Shop and factory buildings	2,183	2,200	3,002	4,677	2,932
Bakeshops	860	724	801	893	1,128
Bakeshop buildings	860	724	799	885	1,129
Child-labor establishments		979	499	228	1,002
High-explosive establishments	81	104	45	325	119
High-explosive buildings					
Hotel establishments	31	21	301	101	39
Hotel buildings	31	23	303	101	39
Home workshops			154	45	77
Home-workshop buildings			154	41	
Mercantile establishments	11	45	29	67	108
Mercantile buildings	11	40	31	53	110
Schools and colleges	163	176	221	246	1,937
Halls	241	84	138	228	522
Churches	44	25	54	20	484
Opera houses and theaters	119	35	38	48	92
Moving-picture buildings				128	169
Miscellaneous public-assembly buildings	14	21	42	39	143
Tenements	39		84	610	41
Bowling alley and skating rinks—establishments		11	86	23	
Bowling alley and skating rinks—buildings		13	16	23	
Total	6,990	7,516	9,807	11,636	12,340

The industries in which the prosecutions and convictions occurred are not shown in full by the reports. The offenses for which convictions were secured are presented in detail in the table which follows:

NUMBER OF CONVICTIONS SECURED FOR NONCOMPLIANCE WITH LAW BY THE DEPARTMENT OF INSPECTION, BY NATURE OF OFFENSES AND BY YEARS, 1904 TO 1908—OHIO.

Nature of offenses.	1904	1905	1906	1907	1908
Illegal employment of children:					
Under age			43	[1] 45	2
Without certificates			87	[2] 82	2
At night			[3] 176	[3] 169	4
In excess of legal hours				5	3
At prohibited employments			1	1	
Without register				2	
Unclassified	2	3		2	
Total	2	3	[3] 307	[4] 306	11
General factory laws:					
Fire escapes	1				
High explosives			1		
Sanitation, shop				2	
Obstructing aisles in public halls					1
Blower					4
Noncompliance with orders				2	
Total	1		1	4	5
Grand total	3	3	[3] 308	[4] 310	16

[1] 1 prosecution not successful.
[2] 3 prosecutions not successful.
[3] 5 prosecutions not successful.
[4] 9 prosecutions not successful.

ILLINOIS.

SCOPE OF THE LAW—SUBJECTS COVERED.[1]

Woman and child labor:

1. Legal age of employment: 14 years.
2. Prohibited employments for certain classes of persons of legal age: A number of specified occupations, including the oiling and cleaning of machinery, operation of elevators, manufacture of poisonous acids, adjusting belts.
3. Employment certificates: Children 14 to 16 years of age.
4. Register of child employees.
5. Hours of labor: Children under 16 years of age, 8 hours per day, 48 hours per week.
6. Night work: Prohibited for children under 16 years of age between 7 p. m. and 7 a. m.
7. Posting of time schedules.
8. [Meal period: No legislation.]

Factory inspection:

9. Fire protection:
   Fire escapes.
   [No legislation regarding doors opening outward, stairways, exit lights or signs, or fire-fighting apparatus.]
10. [Elevators: No legislation.]
11. [Dangerous machinery: No legislation.]
12. Accident reporting: By employer to State bureau of labor statistics (not factory-inspection department).
13. Provisions for comfort:
    Seats for females.
    [No legislation as to water-closets, wash rooms, dressing rooms, lunch rooms, or drinking water.]
14. Ventilation and sanitation:
    Exhaust fans on certain grinding wheels.
    [No other legislation regarding matters of ventilation or sanitation.]
15. [Posting of labor laws: No legislation.]

ENFORCEMENT OF THE LAWS.

At the time of the field work of this investigation the enforcement of the factory laws and child-labor laws was charged to the factory-inspection department, with the following two exceptions: Requirements relative to fire escapes were intrusted for enforcement to local authorities; accident reporting was required to be made to the bureau of labor statistics, not to the factory-inspection department.

---

[1] The law here referred to is as in force at the time of the investigation, December, 1908, to February, 1909. The text of the laws in force Jan. 1, 1912, is given in the appendixes at the end of this volume.

The factory-inspection department has an office attorney in Chicago, appointed by the governor at a salary of $1,500 per year. It is the duty of this attorney to assume charge of all the legal workings of the office, and prosecute infractions of the law as discovered by the inspectors. The State attorneys in the various counties may be called upon to conduct prosecutions within their respective counties.

In Chicago cases are tried before the municipal court; in other places, before justices of the peace.

The attitude of the courts toward cases brought before them by the factory-inspection department has not been satisfactory to the chief factory inspector. He stated that "the cooperation of the courts is neither hearty nor satisfactory," and that they rarely impose fines in cases of first offense.

Examinations of the records of prosecutions show a very large number of cases dismissed and of fines remitted. Thus the records for 1908 show four child-labor cases dismissed on the ground that "as the defendant did not hire the boy he was not the guilty party," notwithstanding the fact that the boy was employed in defendant's factory and that the law uses the phrase "shall not be employed, permitted, or suffered to work   *   *   *."

In consequence of this construction of the law, a construction shared by several judges, the practice has become rather common of letting by contract a part of the manufacturing when the nature of the work will permit it, the alleged contractors employing the children. That is to say, a man or set of men are paid at piece rates for performing certain operations on a given article or component part of an article. They work in the factory and with the establishment's power and machinery. To their employer they are ordinary pieceworkers, but in addition to this they hire children to help them in certain parts of the work. Thus the real or final employer is enabled to escape the penalty of the child-labor law if it is violated.

ORGANIZATION OF FACTORY INSPECTION FORCE.

The following table shows the personnel of the department of factory inspection with salaries received. Office help is excluded.[1]

NUMBER, SEX, AND SALARIES OF FACTORY INSPECTORS, 1908—ILLINOIS.

Titles.	Number.	Sex.	Annual salary.
Chief inspector	1	Male	$3,000
Assistant chief inspector	1	...do	1,500
Department attorney	1	...do	1,500
Deputy inspectors	22	...do	1,200
Do	3	Female	1,200
Total	28		

[1] Rev. Stat., 1905, sec. 29, as amended by act, p. 310, Acts of 1907 (22d An. Rept. Com. of Labor, p. 341).

About one-fourth of the present force entered the department within the preceding year. The remainder have served from four to six years.

The occupations and trades followed by the inspectors before their present appointment are very diverse. Of the three female deputies, one was formerly a nurse, and another a school teacher. The force of male deputies includes one cigar maker, one motorman, one tailor, one bridge builder, one machinist, several bookkeepers and clerks.

Members of the inspection force are not permitted to engage in other work during their terms of office.

All the members of the factory-inspection department above mentioned are appointed by the governor. The appointments are more or less political in their nature.

For carrying on the work of inspection 11 deputy inspectors are assigned to the city of Chicago and 14 to the counties outside of Chicago.

The method of covering the country districts, as they are called, is as follows: The entire force will start in one county and visit all of the towns in that county where establishments subject to inspection are located. This done, the force for that district then proceeds to another county, and so on, until the district is covered, whereupon they return to their starting point and begin over.

In covering the city of Chicago, each of the force of 11 inspectors assigned to this territory is detailed to one of the 11 districts into which the city is divided, these districts being defined arbitrarily by the chief factory inspector.

It has been the policy of the department to pay particular attention to various trades during their busiest seasons. On the other hand the small number of second inspections reported in the annual reports of the department would indicate that very few places are visited more than once a year.

There is no complete record as to the number of establishments, etc., subject to the inspection laws.

STATISTICAL DATA OF FACTORY INSPECTION.

The more important activities of the Illinois factory-inspection department are exhibited in the following table. The data presented relate to the size of the inspection force, number of inspections made by that force, number of convictions, and the amount of the penalties imposed under such convictions. The information of the published reports is incomplete or lacking as regards other points, such as the number of orders issued. As the report for 1908 is not yet available, the data for that year can not be presented.

INSPECTIONS, PROSECUTIONS, CONVICTIONS, ETC., UNDER FACTORY AND CHILD
LABOR INSPECTION LAWS, BY YEARS, 1904 TO 1907—ILLINOIS.

[Compiled from Annual Reports of Factory Inspectors, Illinois: 1904, pp. V, L, LII; 1905, pp. V, XVIII;
1906, pp. XXI, XXVIII; 1907, pp. 74, 83, 833–837.]

	1904	1905	1906	1907
Inspectors [1]	18	18	18	25
Establishments inspected [2]	45,839	65,207	56,583	49,820
Average per inspector	2,547	3,623	3,144	1,993
Separate inspections [2]	52,181	70,539	62,018	54,886
Average per inspector	2,899	3,919	3,445	2,195
Prosecutions	([3])	([3])	([3])	([3])
Convictions [4]	1,325	1,001	973	320
Fines and costs:				
Imposed	$10,696	$8,508	$7,361	$3,268
Paid	([3])	([3])	([3])	([3])
Remitted	([3])	([3])	([3])	([3])
Orders issued	([3])	([3])	([3])	([3])

[1] Not including chief and assistant chief; work administrative only.
[2] Including a few metal-polishing inspections; remainder are almost entirely child-labor inspections,
except in 1907, when 210 ice cream and butterine establishments and 83 places employing structural iron-
workers are included.
[3] Not reported.
[4] "Counts;" number of defendants in each year was as follows: 1904, 654; 1905, 531; 1906, 434; 1907, 149.

The vast majority of the inspections made were made under the
child-labor laws, factory laws proper being of very limited scope in
Illinois during the years covered by this table. Under the child-labor
laws the inspection service covers a very large number of small
establishments and offices, which employ very few persons. Thus
the report for the first half of the year 1907 shows that 31 architect
offices were inspected, the total number of employees being only
147, none of whom was under 16 years of age and of whom only 9
were women.[1] This system of inspection explains in part the large
number of inspections made per inspector.

The industries in which convictions were obtained are not shown
by the reports with sufficient fullness to reproduce. The offenses
for which convictions were obtained are presented in the next table.

NUMBER OF CONVICTIONS SECURED BY FACTORY INSPECTORS, BY NATURE OF
OFFENSES AND BY YEARS, 1904 TO 1907—ILLINOIS.

[Compiled from Annual Reports of Factory Inspectors, Illinois: 1904, p. LII; 1905, p. XVIII; 1906, p.
XVIII; 1907, pp. 75, 84, 85, 833–837.]

Nature of offenses.	1904	1905	1906	1907
Illegal employment of children:				
Under age	45	35	32	62
Without certificates	582	485	400	129
In excess of legal hours	605	450	426	124
At night	16	21	78	....
In dangerous occupations	6	3	9	3
Where intoxicating liquors are sold	57	....	18	....
Failure to protect metal-polishing wheels	3	1	7	2
Obstructing inspector	5	2	2	....
Failure to post office register	6	....	....	....
Tenement-shop law	....	4	....	....
Failure to provide time-table	....	....	1	....
Total	1,325	1,001	973	320

[1] See Fifteenth Annual Report of Factory Inspectors, Illinois, 1907, pp. 4, 5.

INDIANA.

SCOPE OF THE LAWS—SUBJECTS COVERED.[1]

Woman and child labor:

1. Legal age of employment: 14 years.
2. Prohibited employments for certain classes of persons of legal age:
    Cleaning of moving machinery.
    Operation of elevators.
3. Employment certificates: Children 14 to 16 years of age.
4. Register of child employees.
5. Hours of labor: Children under 16 years of age, and females 16 and 17 years of age, 10 hours per day, 60 hours per week, with exceptions as to 10-hour day.
6. Night work: Prohibited for all females between 10 p. m. and 6 a. m.
7. Posting of time schedules.
8. Meal period: Length of time regulated.

Factory inspection:

9. Fire protection:
    Fire escapes.
    Stairways—handrails and rubber-covered steps.
    Doors opening outward and kept unfastened.
    [No legislation as to exit lights or signs or fire-fighting apparatus.]
10. Elevators:
    Guards on shafts and floor openings.
    Safety clutches on cars.
    Inspection of cables, gears, etc.
11. Dangerous machinery:
    Guards on mill gearing and machinery.
    Belt shifters.
    Communication between workrooms and engine rooms.
    Removal of safeguards.
    Inspector may post condemning notice on dangerous machines.
    [No legislation regarding friction clutches.]
12. Accident reporting: By employer to factory inspection department.
13. Provisions for comfort:
    Water-closets. [Minimum ratio of one accommodation per 25 employees.]
    Wash rooms.

---

[1] The law here referred to is as in force at the time of the investigation, February and March, 1909. The text of the laws in force Jan. 1, 1912, is given in the appendixes at the end of this volume.

Provisions for comfort—Concluded.
> Dressing rooms.
> Seats for females.
> [No legislation as to lunch rooms or drinking water.]

14. Ventilation and sanitation:
> Air space standard—250 cubic feet by day, and 400 by night.
> "Sufficient means of ventilation" in all workrooms.
> Exhaust fans on grindstones and dust-creating machinery.
> Water-closets to be ventilated and kept clean.
> Limewashing or painting.
> Special series of requirements in the case of food-producing establishments.
> [No legislation regarding spitting on floor.]

15. Posting of labor laws.

ENFORCEMENT OF THE LAWS.

The enforcement of all factory laws and of all woman and child labor laws is intrusted in full to the State factory inspection department.

Prosecution before the courts is conducted by the prosecuting attorneys of the several counties.[1] Cases may be carried before any court of competent jurisdiction, and are usually tried before justices or circuit courts.

Few cases, however, are carried into court. In case an inspector's orders are questioned, the procedure is to review the matter carefully with the employer. This results usually in an adjustment satisfactory to all parties. The employment of children without certificates, if a first offense, is not prosecuted, provided the employer fills out and returns to the chief inspector an "Acknowledgment of guilt" form. In any case 20 days are allowed for compliance with an order.

As only flagrant cases of violation are carried into court, the evidence is almost always sufficient to lead to a conviction. It is the policy of the courts to impose the minimum fine and costs upon first offenders.

---

[1] Ann. Stat. of 1894, Rev. of 1901, sec. 7087x (22d An. Rept. Com. of Labor, p. 402).

ORGANIZATION OF FACTORY INSPECTION FORCE.

The personnel of the Indiana Department of Inspection,[1] with the salaries received, is as follows, office help not being included:

NUMBER, SEX, AND SALARIES OF FACTORY INSPECTORS, 1908—INDIANA.

Titles.	Number.	Sex.	Annual salary.
Chief inspector	1	Male	$1,800
Chief deputy inspector	1	...do	1,500
Deputy inspectors	4	...do	1,000
Total	6		

The present force of inspectors has served an average of approximately three years.

Members of the force are not allowed to engage in other work during their term of service as factory inspectors.

The chief factory inspector is appointed by the governor. The chief deputy inspector and the deputy inspectors are appointed by the chief inspector, with the approval of the governor. The appointments are not made under civil-service regulations.

For purposes of carrying out the work of inspection, the State is districted as follows: Marion County constitutes one district. The remainder of the State is divided roughly, as the basis of transportation facilitates, into four districts. One of these four districts is, roughly, the southeast quarter of the State; a second, the southwest quarter, while the north half of the State is divided by an east and west line.

The chief deputy inspects Marion County. The other four deputies are assigned to the remaining districts according to the directions of the chief inspector.

There is no satisfactory record of the number of establishments, etc., subject to the inspection laws.

STATISTICAL DATA OF FACTORY INSPECTION.

The following table summarizes the work of the department of inspection for each of the five years, 1904 to 1908, inclusive, as fully as the reports of the department permit. As the reports and records are not entirely clear upon some of the points covered, and incomplete as regards others, much of the data of the table can be accepted only as fairly approximate.

In addition to the information of factories and workshops under the general factory laws the inspection department is also charged with the subject of fire escapes and means of egress in schools, hotels,

---

[1] For creative act see Ann. Stat. of 1894, Rev. of 1901, sec. 7087s (22d An. Rept. Com. of Labor, p. 401).

and certain other classes of public and semipublic buildings. The inspection of boilers is under the general supervision of the chief inspector, but the actual work of boiler inspection is not done by him or by his deputies.

INSPECTIONS, PROSECUTIONS, CONVICTIONS, ETC., UNDER FACTORY AND CHILD LABOR INSPECTION LAWS, BY YEARS, 1904 TO 1908—INDIANA.

[Compiled from Annual Reports of the Department of Inspection, Indiana: 1904, pp. 6, 7, 11, 12, 13; 1905, pp. 6, 7, 11, 13; 1906, p. 11; 1907, pp. 14, 18, 158, 199; 1908, pp. 12, 19, 24–241.]

	1904	1905	1906	1907	1908
Inspectors [1]	6	6	6	6	6
Establishments inspected [2]	(²)	4,396	4,728	3,893	6,279
Average per inspector		733	788	649	1,047
Separate inspections [4]	4,330	4,501	4,728	3,893	6,348
Average per inspector	722	750	788	649	1,058
Nonfactory inspections: [5]					
Public and semipublic buildings		132	104	158	1,254
Mercantile establishments			(²)	32	72
Bakeries and food-producing establishments		(²)	(²)	(²)	692
Prosecutions	(²)	15	(²)	⁶20	(²)
Convictions	(²)	⁷14	(²)	20	(²)
Fines and costs:					
Imposed	(²)	$218	(²)	$311	(²)
Paid	(²)	(²)	(²)	$311	(²)
Remitted	(²)	(²)	(²)		(²)
Orders issued [8]	2,100	2,400	2,540	2,031	4,192

[1] Including chief inspector, who made some field inspections.
[2] The reports are not always clear as to the distinction between establishments inspected and separate inspections made. This fact renders some of the entries here of doubtful classification.
[3] Not reported.
[4] Including nonfactory inspections.
[5] Included in separate inspections.
[6] For child labor laws only; violations of other laws not reported.
[7] Not including one case; appeal pending.
[8] Not including orders issued for the inspection of steam boilers in 1906, 1907, and 1908.

Of the 14 convictions in 1905, 13 were for violation of the child-labor law and 1 for not reporting accidents. For 1907 only child-labor convictions are reported. The industries in which the convictions for these two years occurred are shown in the following table:

NUMBER OF CONVICTIONS SECURED FOR NONCOMPLIANCE WITH CHILD-LABOR INSPECTION LAWS, BY YEARS, 1905 AND 1907, AND BY INDUSTRIES—INDIANA.

Industries.	1905	1907	Industries.	1905	1907
Glass	6	4	Stoves		1
Bakery	1	1	Wood supply		1
Confectionery	1		Cigars		1
Boxes and baskets	1	4	Engine headlights		1
Scales	1		Wood flooring		2
Printing	1		Trucks	¹1	
Chains	1		Not reported		3
Wheels	1				
Shoes		2	Total	14	20

[1] For not reporting accident.

MICHIGAN.

SCOPE OF THE LAW—SUBJECTS COVERED.[1]

Woman and child labor:
1. Legal age of employment: 14 years.
2. Prohibited employments for certain classes of persons of legal age:
    Cleaning of moving machinery.
    Work dangerous to life or limb.
    Operation of certain grinding wheels by females.
3. Employment certificates: Children 14 to 16 years of age.
4. Register of child employees.
5. Hours of labor: Persons under 18 years of age, and females 18 years of age and over, 10 hours per day, 60 hours per week, with exceptions as to 10-hour day.
6. Night work: Prohibited for children under 16 years of age, between 6 p. m. and 7 a. m.
7. [Posting of time schedules: No legislation.]
8. Meal period: Length of time regulated.
Factory inspection:
9. Fire protection:
    Fire escapes.
    Stairways—handrails and rubber-covered steps.
    Doors opening outward.
    [No legislation as to exit lights or signs or fire-fighting apparatus.]
10. Elevators:
    Guards on shafts and floor openings.
    Inspection of cables, gears.
    [No legislation regarding safety clutches.]
11. Dangerous machinery:
    Guards on mill gearing and machinery.
    Belt shifters.
    [No regulation regarding friction clutches, communication with engine room, or removal of safeguards.]
12. [Accident reporting: No legislation.]
13. Provisions for comfort.
    Water-closets. [Minimum ratio of one accommodation per 25 employees.]
    Wash rooms.
    Dressing rooms.
    Seats for females.
    [No legislation as to lunch rooms or drinking water.]

---

[1] The law here referred to is as in force at the time of the investigation, March, 1909. The text of the laws in force Jan. 1, 1912, is given in the appendixes at the end of this volume.

Factory inspection—Concluded.

   14. Ventilation and sanitation:

           Factories and workshops to be "kept in a cleanly state and free from effluvia * * * from any * * * nuisance."

           Exhaust fans for dust-creating machinery.

           [No legislation regarding limewashing or painting or spitting on floor.]

   15. [Posting of laws: No legislation regarding.]

ENFORCEMENT OF THE LAWS.

The enforcement of all laws relative to factory inspection and to the employment of women and children is charged to the State factory inspection department (known as bureau of labor and industrial statistics).

Inspectors usually institute prosecutions themselves, but, at any time they deem it advisable, may call on the prosecuting attorney of the county, who is required to conduct such prosecutions.[1]

Cases of this character are usually tried before justices of the peace, or police courts. As a rule the courts impose minimum penalties upon first offenders.

Officers of the bureau stated that the attitude of the courts had been very favorable to the inspectors in their enforcement of the laws. The records of prosecuted cases could not be obtained for examination, and the reports of the bureau contain little information upon this point. As far as such information is available, however, it bears out the statement made above that the courts had usually supported the inspection department.

The inspection department, in enforcing the several laws, place special emphasis upon the employment of children under legal age.

ORGANIZATION OF FACTORY INSPECTION FORCE.

Factory inspection in Michigan is under the direction of the bureau of labor and industrial statistics. At the head of this bureau there is a commissioner, with a salary of $2,000 per year, assisted by a deputy commissioner, with a salary of $1,500 per year. The commissioner appoints special agents and factory inspectors, the total number of whom is not determined by law.[2] The number of factory inspectors engaged in field work March 15, 1909, was 14, of whom 12 were males

---

[1] Acts of 1901, act No. 113, sec. 16 (22d An. Rept. Com. of Labor, p. 661).

[2] Comp. Laws 1897, secs. 4597, 4600, as amended by act No. 313, Acts of 1907, and Act No. 113, sec. 1215, Acts of 1901 (22d An. Rept. Com. of Labor, pp. 633, 634). By act No. 285, sec. 4, Acts of 1909, compensation of commissioner was raised to $2,500; that of deputy to $1,800 (Bulletin of the Bureau of Labor, No. 85, pp. 635, 636), and it was enacted that compensation of factory inspectors was not to exceed $1,000 a year.

and 2 females.   There are 2 clerks in charge of the issue of certificates, who rank as inspectors but do no field work.   The salary of an inspector is $3 per day.

The present inspectors have terms of service ranging from 1 to 10 years, an average of about 5 years.

The commissioner is appointed by the governor.   The deputy commissioners, special agents, and factory inspectors are appointed by the commissioner.   Appointments are not made under civil-service regulations, but appointees are required to have a practical knowledge of manufacturing establishments.

Inspectors are not allowed to engage in other work during regular business hours but may do so outside of those hours.

For purposes of inspection the State is divided into 10 districts. Wayne County, including the city of Detroit, is assigned to 6 inspectors.   The law specifies that at least one annual inspection shall be made of all places coming within the jurisdiction of the department. Inspectors make as many extra inspections or visits as conditions demand and time allows.

No accurate record is available as to the number of establishments, etc., subject to inspection.

STATISTICAL DATA OF FACTORY INSPECTION.

Factory inspection in Michigan forms part of the work of the bureau of labor and industrial statistics.   The inspection duties of the factory inspectors cover, in addition to factories and workshops proper, hotels, stores employing 10 or more persons, tenements, foundries (beginning in 1907), and (beginning in 1908) schoolhouses, theaters, and similar public and semipublic buildings as regards means of escape in case of fire.   Also there are special inspections made by women agents into the conditions of employment of women and children.   Stores employing less than 10 persons are inspected upon certain points, but the number of such covered each year is not reported in any degree of fullness and are entirely omitted in the following tabulation.

The published reports regarding the inspection service are very detailed upon certain features of the work, but present other features in a too fragmentary form to be of service in forming a judgment as to the activities of the inspectors.   The number of establishments visited is given, but there is no information regarding second inspections, and the data regarding prosecutions and convictions are too incomplete to be tabulated.

The following table presents for each of the five years, 1904 to 1908, such part of the data referred to as can be summarized with reasonable accuracy.   The number of inspectors entered for each year includes, as nearly as can be computed from the reports, the average number of persons engaged in the actual work of field inspection.   The determination of this number is difficult, particularly for 1908, because of the special inspection system in use and the numerous changes in the force.

ESTABLISHMENTS INSPECTED AND ORDERS ISSUED UNDER THE INSPECTION LAWS, BY YEARS, 1904 TO 1908—MICHIGAN.

[Compiled from Annual Reports of Bureau of Labor and Industrial Statistics, Michigan: 1904, pp. 178, 240, 254, 260, 270; 1905, pp. 176, 246, 259, 266, 282; 1906, pp. 12, 24, 189, 190, 300, 303, 318; 1907, pp. 177, 278, 282, 283, 286–288, 300–303, 314; 1908, pp. 270, 352, 358, 362, 378, 382.]

	1904	1905	1906	1907	1908
Inspectors [1]	12	14	14	14	14
Establishments inspected:					
Factories and workshops	7,168	7,170	7,770	8,335	8,502
Hotels	765	723	946	832	669
Stores, employing 10 or more persons	329	311	359	342	441
Tenements	464	683	810	574	314
Special inspection by women agents	525	837	694	700	727
Schools and other public buildings					882
Total	9,251	9,724	10,579	10,783	11,535
Average per inspector	771	695	756	770	824
Orders issued [2]	2,926	3,444	3,535	3,438	3,700

[1] Including, as nearly as can be determined from the inspection reports, only such inspectors as were engaged in actual field work.
[2] Includes orders issued to all classes of establishments. Number of establishments to which orders issued was: 1904, 1,963; 1905, 2,317; 1906, 2,179; 1907, 1,954; 1908, 2,378.

WISCONSIN.

SCOPE OF THE LAW—SUBJECTS COVERED.[1]

Woman and child labor:

1. Legal age of employment: 14 years. [Exception as to vacation employment does not include factories or workshops.]
2. Prohibited employments for certain classes of persons of legal age: A number of specified employments including (1) oiling and cleaning of moving machinery, (2) operation of elevators, (3) poisonous acids, and (4) adjusting belts.
3. Employment certificates: Children 14 to 16 years of age.
4. Register of child employees.
5. Hours of labor: Children under 16 years of age, 10 hours per day, 55 hours per week, except to save perishable goods from decay.
6. Night work: Prohibited for children under 16 years of age, between 6 p. m. and 7 a. m., except to save perishable goods from decay.
7. [Posting of time schedules: No legislation.]
8. [Meal period: No legislation.]

[1] The law here referred to is as in force at the time of the investigation, March, 1909. The text of the laws in force Jan. 1, 1912, is given in the appendixes at the end of this volume.

Factory inspection:

   9. Fire protection:

      Fire escapes.

      Standpipes or automatic sprinklers.

      Doors opening outward.

      [No legislation regarding stairways or exit lights or signs.]

  10. Elevators:

      Guards on shafts and floor openings.

      Inspectors may condemn, by posting notices.

      [No specific legislation as to safety clutches.]

  11. Dangerous machinery:

      Guards on mill gearing and machinery.

      Communication between workrooms and engine room.

      Removal of safeguards.

      Protection for emery wheels and grindstones.

      [No legislation as to belt shifters or friction clutches.]

  12. Accident reporting: By physicians and surgeons to health officers.

  13. Provisions for comfort:

      Water-closets. [Minimum ratio of 1 accommodation per 20 employees.]

      Dressing rooms.

      Seats for females.

      [No legislation as to washing facilities, except in bakeries and confectioneries, and none as to lunch rooms and drinking water.]

  14. Ventilation and sanitation:

      Overcrowding.

      Exhaust fans, etc., for dust, fumes, and other air impurities; including grinding wheels.

      Factories and workshops to be kept "clean," "free from effluvia arising from any * * * nuisance," "ventilated" and in a "sanitary condition." General authorization for inspectors to remedy bad sanitation.

      Special and elaborate requirements regarding cigar factories, and baking and confectionery establishments.

      [No specific legislation as to spitting on floor in factories generally.]

  15. Posting of labor laws.

ENFORCEMENT OF THE LAWS.

With the exceptions mentioned below, the enforcement of all factory laws and child-labor laws is charged in full to the State factory inspector (bureau of labor and industrial statistics). This statement also applies to the special laws regarding cigar factories and bakery and confectionery establishments. Provision is made for a special bakery inspector, but this official acts under the authority of the chief factory inspector. The exceptions mentioned are as follows:

1. The duty of enforcing the fire-escapes requirements is placed both upon the State factory inspectors and the local fire authorities.

2. The factory inspection department is without authority in the matter of accident reporting.

3. All requirements regarding ventilation and sanitation are charged to the factory inspectors for enforcement, but the local boards of health are to decide in certain cases of dispute when "the laws of health" are being violated.   ·

The law provides that prosecutions shall be conducted by the district attorneys of the several counties, on complaint of the factory inspectors, before any court of competent jurisdiction.[1]

The commissioner of labor stated that the courts as a rule had upheld the department in its efforts to enforce the law. Satisfactory record of prosecutions could not be obtained, but that which was available indicated that the majority of the prosecutions begun by the inspectors had been successful in the courts. Prosecutions for violations of the child labor laws had been numerous—almost 200 in 1907; those for violations of the factory inspection laws, comparatively few.

ORGANIZATION OF FACTORY INSPECTION FORCE.

Factory inspection in Wisconsin is under the jurisdiction of the bureau of labor and industrial statistics. This bureau has at its head a commissioner and a deputy commissioner. The officials more directly concerned with factory inspection proper are a factory inspector and 12 assistants. The titles, number, sex, and salary of these officers are as follows.[2]

---

[1] Ann. Stat. of 1898, Supp. of 1906 Acts of 1907, sec. 1021f (22d An. Rept. Com. of Labor, p. 1407).

[2] Idem, secs. 1021c and 1021d, and Acts of 1907, sec. 170. By the act of 1909, ch. 423, the salary of the commissioner was raised to $3,000 (22d An. Rept. Com. of Labor, pp. 1407 and 1419).

NUMBER, SEX, AND SALARIES OF FACTORY INSPECTORS, 1908—WISCONSIN.

Titles.	Number.	Sex.	Annual salary.
Commissioner.	1	Male....	$2,200
Deputy commissioner.	1	...do....	1,600
Factory inspector.	1	...do....	1,500
Assistant factory inspectors.	10	...do....	1,200
Assistant factory inspector.	1	Female..	1,200
Bakery inspector.	1	Male....	1,200
Total.	13		

As regards the period of service, the force of inspectors is distributed as follows: 8 years, 1; 7 years, 1; 4 years, 1; 3 years, 7; 2 years, 1; 1 year and under, 2. The average is approximately three and a half years.

Inspectors are not allowed to engage in other work during the terms of their service.

The commissioner of the bureau of labor and industrial statistics is appointed by the governor. The other officers of the bureau are appointed by the commissioner. Appointments are made on merit under a civil-service law.

For the purpose of inspection the State is divided into districts, which, however, are not permanent divisions. The districts are arranged on the basis of transportation facilities and are supposed to be of equal importance, so far as the work of inspection is concerned. Each inspector is expected to visit every establishment in his district once a year and to make such additional visits as may be necessary. Revisits are made to places where orders have been issued. The inspectors also investigate the cases of children who are absent at the time of inspection but for whom permits are on file. In the event of special investigations district lines may be disregarded. "In 1908, for example, the entire time of a number of inspectors was devoted for several months to the collection of data concerning accidents."[1]

There is no complete record of the number of establishments subject to inspection.

STATISTICAL DATA OF FACTORY INSPECTION.

The published reports regarding factory inspection in Wisconsin are too incomplete to permit of tabular presentation for a period of years. Reports are made biennially. The data contained in the report for 1907–8[2] may be briefly summarized as follows. The period covered is 21 months.

[1] Thirteenth Biennial Report of the Bureau of Labor and Industrial Statistics, Wisconsin, 1907–8, p. 507.

[2] Idem, pp. 507, 508, 649, 655, 656.

There were 12 inspectors and 7,503 separate establishments inspected, an average of 625 per inspector. Of the establishments inspected, 6,132 were factories and workshops, and 1,371 were hotels, bowling alleys, etc. The number of prosecutions for which "complete reports are at hand" was 63. Of these, 54 were successful, and a total of $570 in fines imposed. The number of orders issued to factories was 6,748, the number issued to other classes of establishments not being reported.

MARYLAND.

SCOPE OF THE LAW—SUBJECTS COVERED.[1]

Woman and child labor:

1. Legal age of employment: 12 years, except in counties from June 1 to October 15.
2. Prohibited employments: Children under 16 years of age in breweries or bottling establishments.
3. Employment certificates for children 12 to 16 years of age, except in counties from June 1 to October 15.
4. Registers of child employees.
5. Hours of labor: Children under 16 years of age, 10 hours per day; hours per week not restricted.
6. [Night work: No legislation.]
7. [Posting of time schedules: No legislation.]
8. [Meal period: No legislation.]

Factory inspecton:

9. Fire protection:
   Fire escapes on sweatshops.
   [No legislation as to stairways, doors opening outward, fire apparatus, or exit signs or lights.]
10. [Elevators: No legislation.]
11. [Dangerous machinery: No legislation.]
12. [Accident reporting: No legislation.]
13. Provisions for comfort:
    Seats for females in factories in Baltimore City.
    [No legislation as to water-closets, wash rooms, dressing rooms, lunch rooms, or drinking water.]
14. Ventilation and sanitation:
    General requirements as regards cleanliness, overcrowding, ventilation, and sanitation.
    Special sanitary regulations applicable only to certain classes of sweatshops, etc.
    [No specific legislation as to limewashing or painting or spitting on floor.]
15. [Posting of labor laws: No legislation.]

---

[1] The law here referred to is as in force at the time of the investigation, January, 1909. The text of the laws in force Jan. 1, 1912, is given in the appendixes at the end of this volume.

ENFORCEMENT OF THE LAWS.

The chief of the bureau of statistics and information is specifically charged with the enforcement of the laws regarding legal age and employment certificates, the law requiring fire escapes on garment-making shops, and with the legal provisions relative to ventilation and sanitation, as far at least as garment-making sweatshops and certain similar establishments are concerned. The legal provisions regarding hours of labor and seats for females are not charged to any specified official or body of officials, and the chief of the bureau of statistics and information assumes no duty in the matter of their enforcement.

Factory inspection cases are given preliminary hearing before a magistrate, and either dismissed forthwith or held for the criminal court of the county. If held for the criminal court the case is presented to the grand jury, and, if an indictment is found, the case is tried before a jury. The prosecution is conducted by the district attorney.

Child-labor cases are tried before magistrates, the inspector conducting the prosecution.

Both the inspection department and the courts favor a minimum penalty in first-offense cases. This is what the department asks for and what the courts usually inflict. Frequently, however, a case is dismissed by the magistrate on payment of costs—usually about $1.70. When a case is dismissed on payment of costs by the judge of the criminal court, the costs alone amount to $17 or $18.

On the whole, however, the attitude of the courts has been favorable to the inspection department.

The department itself does not attempt a very strict enforcement of the child-labor laws. This is clearly indicated in the following statement of the chief, as made in his annual report for 1907:[1]

My duties not only call upon me for the enforcement of the laws, but also the recognition of the fact that the intent of the legislature was, and is, as far as possible, not to disturb the existing business conditions, which might nullify the efforts of our merchants and manufacturers in competing with those States where progressive laws were not enforced, and where employers and employees were left absolutely free to do as they pleased, irrespective of the effect upon the community or its future citizenship.

---

[1] Sixteenth Annual Report of Bureau of Statistics and Information, Maryland, 1907, p. 7.

ORGANIZATION OF FACTORY INSPECTION FORCE.

Factory inspection in Maryland is under the charge of the bureau of statistics and information.[1] The force of this bureau, excluding office help, consists of a chief ($2,500), an assistant chief, 2 "factory inspectors" (acting under the law regarding clothing factories and tenement shops), and 6 child-labor inspectors. In 1908 the factory inspectors and the child-labor inspectors had their duties almost completely consolidated. In total, therefore, there is a field force of 8 inspectors.

Of the 8 inspectors, 7 are males and 1 a female. The salary of the position is $900 per year.

The periods of service of the present force are as follows: 6 years, 1; 3 years, 3; 2 years, 1; 1 year, 1; less than 1 year, 2. The average is approximately two and a half years.

The chief of the bureau of statistics and information is appointed by the governor. The other officers of the bureau are appointed by the chief. The appointments are not made under civil service or other examinations. In an interview with an agent of the Bureau of Labor, the chief stated that two of the inspectors were appointed at the request and upon the recommendation of the Federated Charities Society and that the other six were selected by him personally, with special reference to their qualifications.

The inspectors may not engage in other employment during their terms of office.

The city of Baltimore is divided into seven inspection districts. The rest of the State is not so divided, as practically all the work of inspection is carried on in Baltimore, city and county. The chief of the bureau stated that all establishments employing children to any extent were in Baltimore City or within 10 miles thereof.

There is no record of the number of establishments in Maryland subject to inspection.

STATISTICAL DATA OF FACTORY INSPECTION.

The following table shows the general activity of the factory-inspection department as fully as the information is available in the published reports regarding inspections. In 1904, 1905, and for the greater part of 1906 factory inspection in Maryland was limited to the sanitary and general health conditions of clothing factories and tenement shops. There were two inspectors engaged in this work. In 1906 the supervision of the child-labor law was charged to the

---

[1] Pub. Gen. Laws, Code of 1903, art. 100, sec. 11 (added by ch. 192, Acts of 1906), and art. 27, sec. 242 (22d An. Rept. Com. of Labor, pp. 542 and 551). See also Seventeenth Annual Report of Bureau of Statistics and Information, Maryland, 1908, p. 193.

department, and six child-labor inspectors added (September). As this new work did not become completely organized until the latter part of the year, the data relative thereto are omitted from the table for that year (1906). The regular factory inspectors devoted part of their time to the organization of this new work, however, and as a consequence their regular field work decreased somewhat in its extent. In 1907 the child-labor inspectors (six) and regular factory inspectors (two) worked almost entirely independently, but, for convenience of comparison, the results of their work are combined in the table. In 1908 the two sets of inspectors had their duties more or less completely consolidated, the factory inspectors supervising the child-labor law in places visited by them, the child-labor inspectors carrying out the clothing and tenement law in places visited by them coming under this law.

INSPECTIONS, PROSECUTIONS, CONVICTIONS, ETC., UNDER THE INSPECTION LAWS, BY YEARS, 1904 TO 1908—MARYLAND.

[Compiled from Annual Reports of the Bureau of Statistics and Information, Maryland: 1904, pp. 46, 47; 1905, p. 196; 1906, pp. 55, 56; 1907, pp. 20–22, 73–84; 1908, pp. 195, 196, 207, 248–258.]

	1904	1905	1906	1907	1908
Inspectors...	2	2	2	8	8
Establishments inspected [1]........................	1,336	1,585	1,511	21,399	22,189
Average per inspector........................	668	793	756	2,675	2,774
Separate inspections..............................	(²)	³ 3,585	1,852	22,775	27,001
Average per inspector........................	....	1,793	926	2,847	3,375
Prosecutions......................................	45	19	26	⁴ 70	20
Convictions.......................................	45	18	⁵ 8	⁶ 24	⁷ 10
Fines and costs:					
Imposed......................................	$302	(²)	$57	⁸ $181	⁸ $80
Paid...	(²)	⁹ $400	(²)	(²)	(²)
Remitted.....................................	(²)	(²)	(²)	(²)	(²)
Orders issued.....................................	(²)	(²)	(²)	(²)	(²)

[1] For 1904, 1905, and 1906 includes only clothing factories and tenement shops; for 1907 and 1908 includes also child-labor inspections, distributed as follows: 1907, clothing factories, etc., 774, child labor 20,625; 1908, clothing factories, etc., 2,007, child labor, 20,182. A few child labor inspections in the latter part of 1906 are omitted, as are also the special inspectors who did this work.
[2] Not reported.
[3] Computed from statement in report (p. 196) that duplicate inspections numbered about 2,000.
[4] Not including one case outside of Baltimore City, disposition of which not reported.
[5] Disposition of remaining cases: Dismissed on payment of costs, 2; dismissed with consent of department, 15; lack of evidence, 1.
[6] Disposition of remaining cases: On payment of costs, 13; dismissed on promise to comply with law, 9; bail forfeited, 1; warrant withdrawn, 1; settled, 1; dismissed, 20; no decision, 1.
[7] Disposition of remaining cases: On payment of costs, 4; dismissed, 6.
[8] Fines only, costs not reported.
[9] Report says "upward of $400" was paid the State.

The necessary inspection under the child-labor law was of a very simple character, concerning solely the age of children and the use of certificates. This fact accounts in part for the great number of inspections per inspector. Probably many places visited had no children.

The inspection work under both the clothing and tenement law and the child-labor law was limited almost entirely to the city of Baltimore. The convictions shown in the preceding table were for violations of either the clothing manufacture and tenement law or the child-labor law. The child-labor law became operative in 1907, and of the 24 convictions shown in the preceding table in that year 13 were for noncompliance with its provisions, and 3 of the 10 convictions in 1908 also were for nonconformity to its terms.[1]

The industries in which convictions occurred under the child-labor law are not shown in the reports, but practically all were in the clothing industry.

NORTH CAROLINA.

SCOPE OF THE LAW—SUBJECTS COVERED.[2]

Woman and child labor:

1. Legal age of employment: 12 years.
2. [Prohibited employments: None.]
3. Employment certificates: Age up to which required not specified.
4. [Registers of child employees: No legislation.]
5. Hours of labor: Children and minors under 18 years of age, 66 hours per week, hours per day not restricted.
6. Night work: Prohibited for children under 14 years of age between 8 p. m. and 5 a. m.
7. [Posting of time schedules: No legislation.]
8. [Meal period: No legislation.]

Factory inspection:

9. Fire protection:
   Fire escapes.
   Doors opening outward and unfastened.
   Fire-extinguishing apparatus.
   [No legislation regarding stairways or exit lights or signs.]
10. [Elevators: No legislation.]
11. [Dangerous machinery: No legislation.]
12. [Accident reporting: No legislation.]
13. [Provisions for comfort: No legislation.]
14. [Ventilation and sanitation: No legislation.]
15. [Posting of labor laws: No legislation.]

ENFORCEMENT OF THE LAWS.

There is no factory-inspection system in North Carolina.

The regulations regarding fire protection are charged for enforcement to the insurance commissioner. The child-labor laws are not charged to any special official or body of officials.

---

[1] From Reports of the Bureau of Statistics and Information, Maryland: 1904, pp. 46, 47; 1905, p. 196; 1906, p. 55; 1907, pp. 22, 84; 1908, pp. 207, 258.

[2] The law here referred to is as in force at the time of the investigation, March, 1909. The text of the laws in force Jan. 1, 1912, is given in the appendixes at the end of this volume.

In cases of alleged violation prosecution would be conducted by the district solicitors in the superior courts after indictments had been found by the grand juries.

Inquiries regarding such cases were made in the places visited, but, as far as could be learned, no prosecutions had ever been instituted.

GEORGIA.

SCOPE OF THE LAW—SUBJECTS COVERED.[1]

Woman and child labor:
1. Legal age of employment: 10 years.
2. [Prohibited employments: •None as to factories or work-shops.]
3. Employment certificates: Required, but conditions under which required not entirely clear.
4. [Register of child employees: No legislation.]
5. Hours of labor:
    All employees of cotton or woolen factories, 66 hours per week, with exceptions; hours per day not restricted.
    Persons under 21 years of age in all other factories, sunrise to sunset.
6. Night work: Prohibited for—
    Children under 14 years of age, 7 p. m. to 6 a. m.
    Persons under 21 years of age in all factories other than cotton or woolen mills, sunset to sunrise.
7. [Posting of time schedules: No legislation.]
8. [Meal period: No legislation.]
Factory inspection:
9. Fire protection:
    Fire escapes.
    Doors opening outward.
    Fire-extinguishing apparatus.
    [No legislation regarding stairways or exit lights or signs.]
10. [Elevators: No legislation.]
11. [Dangerous machinery: No legislation.]
12. [Accident reporting: No legislation.]
13. Provisions for comfort:
    Seats for females.
    [No legislation regarding water-closets, wash rooms, dressing rooms, lunch rooms, or drinking water.]
14. [Ventilation and sanitation: No legislation.]
15. [Posting of labor laws: No legislation.]

---

[1] The law here referred to is as in force at the time of the investigation, March, 1909. The text of the laws in force Jan. 1, 1912, is given in the appendixes at the end of this volume.

ENFORCEMENT OF THE LAWS.

There is no factory-inspection service in Georgia.

The fire-escape law is charged to the local authorities for enforcement. The provisions regarding the employment of women and children are not charged to any specific official or body of officials for enforcement. Inquiries regarding such were made in the localities visited during this investigation, but, as far as could be learned, no prosecutions had ever been made.

If a grand jury should bring an indictment for violation of these laws, prosecution would be conducted by the solicitor general in the superior court.

FLORIDA.

SCOPE OF THE LAW—SUBJECTS COVERED.[1]

Woman and child labor:
1. Legal age of employment: 12 years, subject to exceptions (i. e., there is no absolute minimum age in factories or elsewhere).
2. [Prohibited employments: None as to factories or workshops.]
3. Employment certificates: Required only for children working under legal exception, i. e., under 12 years of age.
4. [Register of child employees: No legislation.]
5. Hours of labor: Children under 12 years of age, 9 hours per day, 54 hours per week, with exceptions.
6. Night work: Prohibited for children under 12 years of age between 9 p. m. and 6 a. m., with exceptions.
7. [Posting of time schedules: No legislation.]
8. [Meal period: No legislation.]

Factory inspection:
9. [Fire protection: No legislation.]
10. [Elevators: No legislation.]
11. [Dangerous machinery: No legislation.]
12. [Accident reporting: No legislation.]
13. Provisions for comfort:
    Seats for females in mercantile and "other business pursuits."
    [No legislation as to water-closets, washing facilities, dressing rooms, lunch rooms, or drinking water.]
14. [Ventilation and sanitation: No legislation.]
15. [Posting of labor laws: No legislation.]

---

[1] The law here referred to is as in force at the time of the investigation, March, 1909. The text of the laws in force Jan. 1, 1912, is given in the appendixes at the end of this volume.

ENFORCEMENT OF THE LAWS.

There is no factory-inspection service in Florida.

The duty of enforcing the child-labor laws is charged to the sheriff in the counties and to the city or town marshal or police officers in the several cities and towns. The requirement of seats for females is not charged to any special official or body of officials.

It is the duty of the sheriffs, marshals, and police officers, as above noted, to assist in the prosecution of violators of the child-labor law, the actual prosecutor in each case being the local officer charged with this authority.

In none of the places visited could record be found of any prosecutions under the mentioned laws.

LOUISIANA.

SCOPE OF THE LAW—SUBJECTS COVERED.[1]

Woman and child labor:

1. Legal age of employment: 14 years.
2. Prohibited employments for certain classes of persons of legal age: Cleaning moving machinery.
3. Employment certificates: Children 14 to 16 years of age.
4. Register of child employees.
5. Hours of labor: Persons under 18 years of age and females 18 years of age and over, 10 hours per day, 60 hours per week.
6. Night work: Prohibited for children under 16 years of age and females 16 and 17 years of age between 7 p. m. and 6 a. m.
7. [Posting of time schedules: No legislation.]
8. Meal period: Length of time regulated.

Factory inspection:

9. Fire protection:
    Fire escapes.
    Stairways handrailed.
    Doors opening outward or sliding, and unfastened.
    [No legislation as to exit signs or lights or fire-fighting apparatus.]
10. Elevators:[2]
    Guards on shafts and floor openings.
    [No legislation as to safety clutches.]
11. [Dangerous machinery: No legislation.]
12. Accident reporting:[2] By employer to factory inspector.

---

[1] The law here referred to is as in force at the time of the investigation, March, 1909. The text of the laws in force Jan. 1, 1912, is given in the appendixes at the end of this volume.

[2] Requirements do not apply to establishments employing male adults only.

Factory inspection—Concluded.
    13. Provisions for comfort:[1]
            Water-closets. [Minimum ratio of 1 accommodation
                per 25 persons.]
            Wash rooms.
            Dressing rooms.
            Seats for females.
            [No legislation as to lunch rooms and drinking water.]
    14. Ventilation and sanitation:[1]
            Dust, smoke, and lint, removal of.
            Buildings clean and free from effluvia of drains or other
                nuisances.
            Limewashing or painting.
            [No legislation as to spitting on floor.]
    15. [Posting of labor laws: No legislation.]

ENFORCEMENT OF THE LAWS.

Factory inspection in Louisiana is limited to the city of New Orleans, and in practice many of the factory and woman and child labor laws are limited in their effect to that city.

Within New Orleans the enforcement of nearly all these laws is in the hands of the factory inspector. The only important exception is in the case of the law regarding fire escapes, which is intrusted to the municipal fire authorities for enforcement.

Prosecutions are conducted by the parish attorney.[2]

Cases involving the factory-inspection laws are tried before the superior criminal court, as were also those involving the child-labor laws prior to January 1, 1909. Since that date, however, child-labor cases are tried before the juvenile court.

Prosecutions under the present laws, which are of very recent origin, have been too few in number to indicate accurately the attitude of the courts in general. The inspector stated that the courts were disposed to form a strict observance of the laws, and observation and talks with interested parties support this statement.

ORGANIZATION OF FACTORY INSPECTION FORCE.

There is no State factory inspection in Louisiana, but an act of 1908 requires the city of New Orleans to appoint a factory inspector, and fixes the salary at not more than $750 a year. In the other towns and parishes of the State the appointment of inspectors is optional. At the time of the field work of this investigation none of these other

---

[1] Requirements do not apply to establishments employing male adults only.

[2] Acts of 1908, act No. 301, sec. 3 (Bulletin of the Bureau of Labor, No. 85, p. 597).

places had availed themselves of the permission to appoint an inspector.[1]

The inspector in New Orleans is a female, and is paid a salary of $750 a year. She has served since December, 1906.

The appointment is made by the mayor, with the consent of the city council, and is not subject to civil-service test. The inspector may not engage in other work during the period of service as inspector.

There is no satisfactory record of the number of establishments in New Orleans subject to inspection. But in a city the size of New Orleans, and with the many inspection duties devolving upon her, it is physically impossible for the one woman inspector to cover more than a very small portion of the field in the course of a year.

STATISTICAL DATA OF FACTORY INSPECTION.

The following table shows the number, respectively, of inspectors, inspections, prosecutions, and convictions, and the amount of penalties imposed and paid, for each of the two years, 1907 and 1908. There is no record of the number of orders issued. The data presented refer solely to the city of New Orleans, factory inspection in Louisiana being limited to that one city.

INSPECTIONS, PROSECUTIONS, CONVICTIONS, ETC., UNDER THE INSPECTION LAWS, 1907 AND 1908—LOUISIANA.

	1907	1908
Inspectors	1	1
Inspections [1]	830	(²)
Average per inspector	830	(²)
Prosecutions	2	2
Convictions	³2	³2
Fines and costs:		
Imposed	$50	$100
Paid	$25	$50
Remitted		
Orders issued	(²)	(²)

[1] Whether separate establishments or separate inspections are meant, not reported.
[2] Not reported.
[3] Including one conviction, appeal pending.

The offenses for which the convictions were obtained were: In 1907, for employing children under legal age, 2; in 1908, for employing child under legal age, 1, and for employing child without certificate, 1.

In 1907 one of the convictions occurred in the tin-can industry and one in the mattress industry; in 1908 both convictions occurred in department stores.

---

[1] Acts of 1908, act No. 301, sec. 23, and act No. 155, sec. 3 (Bulletin of the Bureau of Labor, No. 85, pp. 588, 601).

CHAPTER II.

LEGAL AGE, PROHIBITED EMPLOYMENTS, AND WORKING PAPERS.

CHAPTER II.

LEGAL AGE, PROHIBITED EMPLOYMENTS, AND WORKING PAPERS.

. INTRODUCTION.

This chapter covers what may be considered as the fundamental woman and child labor laws—that is to say, those laws which prescribe the personal qualifications which a woman or child must possess in order to be lawfully employed at certain classes of work. The qualifications may relate to age, sex, degree of schooling, physical fitness, etc. The laws referred to are grouped, for convenience of treatment, under three main subject headings: (1) Legal age, (2) prohibited employments, and (3) working papers.[1]

1. LEGAL AGE.—The most familiar and the most significant of child-labor laws is one fixing a minimum age below which children may not be lawfully employed in certain classes of business establishments. The establishments covered usually include all kinds of factories and workshops, very frequently include mercantile establishments, and sometimes include nearly, if not quite, all forms of business activity.

In 12 of the 17 States covered by this investigation the legal age of employment is 14 years in factories and workshops generally. These 12 are Massachusetts, Rhode Island, Connecticut, New York, Pennsylvania, New Jersey, Ohio, Illinois, Indiana, Michigan, Wisconsin, and Louisiana. Maine also has fixed the legal age of employment at 14, but makes a broad exception in favor of all establishments using perishable materials. In North Carolina the legal age is 12 years for all children, and 13 years for all except those working in an apprenticeship capacity. Maryland and Florida fix an ostensible age limit of 12 years, but in both cases important exceptions are made to the law. In Georgia the minimum legal age is 10 years, with an extension to 12 years in the case of those children who are not absolutely dependent on their own earnings for support.

2. PROHIBITED EMPLOYMENTS.—In addition to the fixing of a legal age of employment in certain classes of establishments, most States prohibit the employment of children of immature age at certain occupations recognized as peculiarly dangerous, even although

---

[1] The laws referred to throughout this volume are as in force at the time of the investigation, December, 1908, to April, 1909. The text of the laws in force Jan. 1, 1912, is given in the appendixes at the end of this volume.

such children are of legal age. Not infrequently, indeed, such prohibitions are extended to adult females. The occupations most
usually "prohibited" in this manner are the operation of elevators
and the cleaning of moving machinery. But in a few States—
notably Ohio, Illinois, and Wisconsin—the number of "prohibited
employments" is very large, including the operation of many designated machines, work involving the use of and exposure to poisonous acids, explosives, and alcohol, and, for female children, work
requiring constant standing.[1]

3. WORKING PAPERS.—The term "working papers" is used to
include employment certificates, age and schooling affidavits, employment permits, and similarly named "papers" which children of
legal age but under another specified age must possess as a condition
of lawful employment. In some States these papers serve no purpose but to attest that the child concerned is of legal age. In most
States, however, such papers also certify that the child has received
the amount of schooling prescribed in the school law as a minimum.
Occasionally also the physical fitness of the child must be properly
certified to.

With the exception of New Jersey all of the 13 States having a
legal age limit of 14 years require children of 14 but under 16 years
to be furnished with working papers of some description as a condition of their lawful employment. In New Jersey the use of such
papers is optional with the employer. Maryland, with a 12-year age
limit, requires working papers for children 12 to 16 years of age.
The Georgia law requires children 10 to 12 years of age to have
dependency affidavits, and all minors under 18 to have school certificates. The latter feature of the Georgia law is, however, somewhat
obscure. By the North Carolina law children at work must be
proven to be of legal age by proper papers, but the requirement does
not specify a definite age up to which such papers must be furnished.
In Florida working papers are not required except for children under
12 working during school vacation under legal exception.

In each of the States in which working papers are required of
children the employer is required to keep such papers on file, accessible to the examination of the proper authorities.

Furthermore, in a number of those States which have established
age regulations for the employment of children, the employer is
required to keep a register or wall list of child employees, and sometimes of women employees also.

---

[1] Also in nearly every State there is a general law prohibiting the employment of
children at immoral, indecent, acrobatic and other performances dangerous to life,
limb, health, or morals. As such laws are construed only as applying to acrobatic,
theatrical, and similar performances, and not to the dangers incident to industrial
employments, all reference thereto is omitted from this report.

In the remaining pages of this chapter there are given separately for each of the 17 States covered a summary of the legislation regarding the subjects above mentioned and a statement of the conditions found in the establishments visited.

This latter statement presents in very brief form the information obtained upon legal age, prohibited and dangerous employments, working papers, and the keeping of registers.

The following explanations may be made as to the character of the information given.

The present investigation did not emphasize the subject of legal age. If a child under legal age is employed, it may be either a result of a false statement of age to the employer or due to the use of a false certificate. In either case the truth can be arrived at only by home visits, the study of birth records, etc.; rarely by inquiries made in the establishment where employed. The present investigation was limited almost entirely to the factory itself and to information therein obtainable. Only in very few cases was effort made to verify the ages reported by the child employees. Thus the data on legal age can not be accepted as significant.[1]

In all of the establishments visited information was sought as to the cleaning or oiling of moving machinery by women and children, whether or not the law of the particular State made reference to this subject.

As regards working papers inquiry was limited to finding out the extent to which the papers required by law were on file for all child employees for whom required. Note was made as to whether certificates and affidavits were in proper form and properly worded, but it was not possible to verify the accuracy of the original statements contained therein.

The laws referred to throughout this volume are as in force at the time of the investigation, December, 1908 to April, 1909. The text of the laws in force January 1, 1912, is given in the appendixes at the end of this volume.

---

[1] In the first four volumes of this report the subject of employment under legal age is treated at length, the information presented being the result of home visits and personal inquiries. See Vol. I, Cotton Textile Industry, pp. 147–156, 170–189; Vol. II, Men's Ready-Made Clothing, p. 82; Vol. III, Glass Industry, pp. 212–214; and Vol. IV, Silk Industry, pp. 71–85, 94–101.

MAINE.

SUMMARY OF LAWS.

LEGAL AGE.

The legal age of employment is 14 years in "any manufacturing or mechanical establishment," except establishments "the materials and products of which are perishable and require immediate labor thereon to prevent decay * * * or damage * * *[1]

    Penalty.—For employing child under legal age, $25 to $50.

    Enforcement.—Charged to the State factory-inspection department (i. e., the inspector of factories, workshops, mines and quarries, and his assistants).

PROHIBITED EMPLOYMENTS.[2]

Children under 15, the operation of any elevator.

Persons under 18, the operation of elevators running at a speed of over 200 feet a minute.

    Penalty.—$25 to $100.

    Enforcement.—Enforcement of these requirements is not charged to any special official or officials.

WORKING PAPERS.

A child between 14 and 16 years of age, in order to be legally employed in "any manufacturing or mechanical establishment" (except those using perishable materials, as above, must be able to produce official evidence of its age and receive an employment certificate. The form and method of issue of such certificate are as follows:[3]

    Employment certificates.—The child must present to employer evidence of its age in the form of a copy of the town clerk's record of the birth, a copy of its baptismal record, or its passport. The employer is to retain such evidence and to issue to the child a certificate giving its name and residence, name and residence of parents or guardian, and such other facts as the State factory inspector may

---

[1] Rev. Stat., 1903, ch. 40, secs. 52, 54, and 55, as amended by ch. 46, Acts of 1907 (22d An. Rept. Com. of Labor, pp. 527, 528).

Although establishments using perishable goods are freed from the specific requirements of the child-labor laws, the factory inspector is given a broad authority to supervise the employment of children in such places. This authority, however, seems limited to sanitary and other conditions of work and does not cover the matter of age. Idem, sec. 55 (22d An. Rept. Com. of Labor, p. 528).

[2] Acts of 1907, ch. 4 (22d An. Rept. Com. of Labor, p. 534).

[3] Rev. Stat., 1903, secs. 52 and 53, as amended by ch. 46, Acts of 1907 (22d An. Rept. Com. of Labor, pp. 527, 528).

require. A duplicate of each certificate thus issued is to be furnished the factory inspector immediately upon the issuance of the original, and by him kept on file. Blank certificates are to be furnished by the inspector, in form approved by attorney general.

Filing of age records, etc.—Employer is required to keep birth and baptismal records and passports furnished him by children as evidence of age on file, subject to examination by the factory inspector on demand.[1]

On termination of a child's employment its birth or baptismal record or passport is to be returned to it and the factory inspector notified of the fact and date of the child's leaving employment.

Register of children.—Employers are not required to keep registers or wall lists of child employees.

Penalty.[2]—On employer for employing child in violation of the above provision, $25 to $50.

Enforcement.[2]—It is made the duty of the State factory inspection department to enforce the legal provisions referred to above.

---

[1] Rev. Stat., 1903, ch. 40, sec. 53 as amended by ch. 46, Acts of 1907 (22d An. Rept. Com. of Labor, p. 528).

[2] Idem, secs. 52 and 54, as amended by ch. 46, Acts of 1907 (22d An. Rept. Com. of Labor, p. 528).

Later law: By an act passed shortly after the completion of the field work of this investigation (Acts of 1909, ch. 257, Bulletin of the Bureau of Labor, No. 85, pp. 606–609), the provisions regarding certificates and age proof were radically changed. The more important features of the new law are as follows:

No child under 14 to be employed in any manufacturing or mechanical establishment (except in those using perishable materials or products) and no child 14 to 16 in any such establishment without submitting to employer proof of age (copy of birth record, baptismal record, passport) or age and schooling certificate.

No child under 14 to be employed in a manufacturing, mechanical, mercantile, or other business establishment (except those using perishable materials or products), or in any telegraph or telephone office, or in the transmission of telegraph or telephone messages (during school hours); and no child 14 to 15 to be so employed without submitting to employer an age and schooling certificate.

Employer to receive and file records and passports and age and schooling certificates, and issue to child applicant an employment certificate, of which a duplicate shall be forwarded immediately to factory inspector. On termination of employment copy of record, passport, or age and schooling certificate to be returned to child, or if not claimed by it within 30 days, to the school authorities.

Age and schooling certificates to be issued by school authorities upon satisfactory evidence (1) of age, birth record, baptismal record, passport, or other document; (2) of schooling, i. e., ability to read and write simple sentences in English, and perform simple arithmetic, including division, either by test prepared by school authorities or by signed certificate of teacher in school previously attended. Attendance at evening school may be accepted in lieu of other schooling requirements.

The general form of the age and schooling certificate is prescribed by law, and gives (1) affidavit of parent as to age of child, (2) brief description thereof, (3) schooling ability, and (4) approval and signature of issuing official.

CONDITIONS FOUND.

Each of the 26 establishments visited in Maine employed females 16 years of age and over, but only 14 of them also employed children under 16 years of age. The total number of such children employed by these 14 establishments was 74.

LEGAL AGE.

Individual slips containing inquiries as to age, sex, etc., were made out and signed by most of the children employed in the visited establishments. These age reports were not verified. On one such slip a child reported itself as 13 years of age. This child was a female and was employed in a hosiery mill.

PROHIBITED AND DANGEROUS EMPLOYMENTS.

No children under 16 were reported as operating elevators, and no persons under 18 as operating elevators running at a speed of over 200 feet a minute.

In none of the establishments was it reported that children under 16 cleaned or oiled machinery in motion. In 5 establishments, however, females 16 years of age and over did such work. These establishments with the machines so cleaned or oiled were as follows: One confectionery factory, chocolate enrobers; 2 woolen mills, looms; 1 woolen mill, carder; and 1 woolen mill, looms and spoolers.

WORKING PAPERS.

Of the 14 establishments in which children under 16 were employed, 12 had no proofs of age on file for any of the children employed, and none of them required children to produce such evidences of age as a condition of employment. The other 2 establishments had on file incomplete files of age proofs; in one case for 8 out of 18 children, in the other for 1 out of 6. In each of these cases evidences of age were on file for children who were no longer employed by the establishment.

One establishment claimed that it notified the factory inspector when children under 16 left its employment. The other 13 did not do so.

REGISTERS AND WALL LISTS.

The law does not require the employer to keep a register or wall list of child employees. In none of the establishments visited were such registers or lists on file or posted.

MASSACHUSETTS.

SUMMARY OF LAWS.

LEGAL AGE.[1]

The legal age of employment is 14 years in "any factory, workshop, or mercantile establishment,"[2] and, while public schools are in session, in any other work.

Penalty.[3]—On employer for employing and on parent, etc., for permitting employment of child under legal age, not more than $300, or not more than six months' imprisonment, or both; on employer for each day's additional employment after notification, $20 to $100 or imprisonment not more than six months.

Enforcement.[4]—Charged to the factory-inspection department of the district police. Also truant officers may visit establishments and apprehend children illegally employed.

PROHIBITED EMPLOYMENTS.

Children under 16, the operation of any elevator.

Penalty.—$25 to $100 for each offense.[5]

Children under 18, the operation of elevators running at a speed of over 100 feet a minute.

Penalty.—$25 to $100 for each offense.[5]

Children under 18, in the manufacture of any acid when the State board of health has decided such work dangerous to the health of such persons.

---

[1] Rev. Laws, 1902, ch. 106, sec. 28, as amended by ch. 267, Acts of 1905 (22d An. Rept. Com. of Labor, p. 596).

[2] Definitions: "Factory shall mean any premises where steam, water, or other mechanical power is used in aid of any manufacturing process there carried on."

"Workshop shall mean any premises * * * which is not a factory as above defined wherein manual labor is exercised by way of trade or for purposes of gain in or incidental to a process of making, altering, repairing, ornamenting, finishing, or adapting for sale any article or part of an article, * * * but not to include a private house or private room if majority of persons therein are members of such family."

"Mercantile establishments shall mean any premises used for the purposes of trade in the purchase or sale of any goods or merchandise, and any premises used for the purposes of a restaurant or for publicly providing and serving meals."

Rev. Laws, 1902, ch. 106, sec. 8 (22d An. Rept. Com. of Labor, p. 593).

[3] Acts of 1906, ch. 499, sec. 1 (22d An. Rept. Com. of Labor, p. 622).

[4] Idem, secs. 2, 3, 4, and 5; and Rev. Laws, 1902, ch. 106, sec. 34, and ch. 108, sec. 8, as amended by ch. 413, Acts of 1907 (22d An. Rept. Com. of Labor, pp. 598, 622, 623).

[5] Acts of 1902, ch. 350, secs. 1, 2, and 3 (22d An. Rept. Com. of Labor, p. 613), and Acts of 1907, ch. 550.

Penalty.—$100 for each offense.[1]

Children under 18, in handling intoxicating liquors or packages containing such liquors in a brewery or bottling establishment.

Penalty.—Not less than $50 or imprisonment not less than three months, or both, for each offense. [2]

The law of Massachusetts places no absolute restrictions upon the cleaning or oiling of machinery,[3] but it does authorize the inspectors to prohibit the cleaning of moving machinery, except steam engines, at their discretion.[4]

* * * No machinery, except steam engines in a factory,[5] shall be cleaned while running if objection in writing is made by one of said inspectors * * *.

Penalty.—Not more than $100.

The chief factory inspector stated that the inspection department never used the authority thus given it, as the force of inspectors was too small to give attention to such details.

WORKING PAPERS.

A child of legal age, 14 but under 16, as a condition of lawful employment in "any factory, workshop, or mercantile establishment," must possess an "age and schooling certificate." Also, a minor of 16 years or over must possess a certificate of literacy (i. e., ability to read and write English sufficiently well for admission to fourth grade) from school authorities or be in regular attendance at an evening school unless there is no such evening school in the town or city or unless a physician certifies that such minor is physically unable to both work and attend school.

---

[1] Rev. Laws, 1902, ch. 106, sec. 44 (22d An. Rept. Com. of Labor, pp. 599, 600). By a later law, enacted after the field work of the investigation was completed, the authority thus given the board of health was so broadened as to include the power to prohibit the employment of minors under 18 years of age at any trade, process, or occupation which it may consider dangerous to the health of such persons.—Sec. 1, ch. 404, Acts of 1910 (Bulletin of the Bureau of Labor, No. 91, p. 1073). This authority has been availed of, and the board has issued a list of "dangerous processes." See Report of the Commission to Investigate the Inspection of Factories, etc., Boston, 1911, p. 30.

[2] Idem, ch. 100, sec. 61 (22d An. Rept. Com. of Labor, p. 580).

[3] Idem, ch. 106, sec. 42, prohibits children under 14 years of age cleaning moving machinery in factories, but as ch. 106, sec. 28, as amended by ch. 267, Acts of 1905, prohibits children under 14 being employed in factories, the former prohibition is, from the present standpoint, of little importance (22d An. Rept. Com. of Labor, pp. 596, 599).

[4] Idem, ch. 104, sec. 41, as amended by ch. 503, Acts of 1907, and sec. 56 (22d An. Rept. Com. of Labor, pp. 588, 590).

[5] The term "factory" means "any premises where steam, water, or other mechanical power is used in aid of any manufacturing process there carried on." Idem, ch. 106, sec. 8 (22d An. Rept. Com. of Labor, p. 593).

The legal provisions regarding the contents, issue, etc., of age and schooling certificates, and the keeping of registers by employers are as follows: [1]

Age and schooling certificates.[2]—To be approved only by the local superintendent of schools, by a person authorized by him, or, if there is no superintendent, by the school committee. The conditions under which a certificate is to be issued are these: (1) That child's age is established by certificate of birth or baptism, by register of birth, or, if issuing official is satisfied that such records are not available, by other evidence, under oath, satisfactory to such official; (2) that child is able to read at sight and write legibly simple sentences in English sufficiently well for admission to the fourth grade of the local public schools; [3] (3) that child obtains and presents to issuing official an employment ticket signed by an employer stating that he intends to employ such child when an age and schooling certificate is procured.

A duplicate of each certificate issued to be filled out and kept on file by the school committee.

The form of the age and schooling certificate and that of the employment ticket are prescribed by law. The age and schooling certificate is to contain an affidavit of the parent, guardian, or custodian of child as to the child's age and birthplace, a brief description of the child (height, complexion, color of hair), and certification of issuing official that child can read and write English.

Filing of age and schooling certificates.—Employer to keep on file, accessible to the local truant officer and to the State factory inspector, age and schooling certificates for all children 14 to 16 years of age. [4]

On termination of employment certificate to be returned to child, or, if not demanded by child within 30 days of such time, to be returned to superintendent of schools or school committee.

Register of children.—Employer required to keep two complete lists of all children 14 to 16 years of age employed; one list to be kept

---

[1] General references: Rev. Laws, 1902, ch. 44, sec. 1 (as amended by ch. 320, Acts of 1905, and ch. 383, Acts of 1906); idem, ch. 106, secs. 28 (as amended by ch. 267, Acts of 1905), 29, 30, and 31 (as amended by ch. 213, Acts of 1905, and ch. 224, Acts of 1907), secs. 32, 34, and 35 (as amended by ch. 183, Acts of 1902); idem, ch. 108, sec. 8 (as amended by ch. 413, Acts of 1907); Acts of 1906, ch. 284, sec. 1; Acts of 1906, ch. 499, secs. 1 to 4 (22d An. Rept. Com. of Labor, pp. 578, 595–598, 609, 616, 622, 623).

Later law: By an act passed shortly after the conclusion of the field work of this investigation in Massachusetts the labor laws of the State were consolidated. Acts of 1909, ch. 514 (Bulletin of the Bureau of Labor, No. 85, pp. 618–627). No important changes, however, were thereby made in any of the legal provisions regarding certificates, etc., as summarized in above text.

[2] Rev. Laws, 1902, ch. 106, secs. 29 to 35 (22d An. Rept. Com. of Labor, pp. 596–598).

[3] Acts of 1906, ch. 284, sec. 1 (22d An. Rept. Com. of Labor, p. 616).

[4] Rev. Laws, 1902, ch. 106, secs. 29 and 32 (22d An. Rept. Com. of Labor, pp. 596–598).

on file and one posted conspicuously near the principal entrance of the building in which such children are employed.[1]

Employer must also keep on file one list and send to the superintendent of schools or school committee a similar list of all minors employed who can not read at sight and write legibly simple sentences in English sufficiently well for admission to the fourth grade of the local public schools.[2]

> *Penalties.*[2]—On employer for employing child under 16 in violation of these provisions, not more than $300 or imprisonment not more than 6 months, or both; and for each day's employment after notification by factory inspector or truant officer $20 to $100, or imprisonment not more than 6 months; on employer for retaining certificate, $10 to $100; on parent or guardian for permitting child under 16 to work in violation of these provisions, not more than $300, or imprisonment not more than 6 months, or both; on parent or guardian for permitting illiterate minor 16 to 21 to work in violation of the law, not more than $20; on person signing certificate for knowingly certifying to any materially false statement, not more than $50; on factory inspectors and truant officers for knowingly or willfully neglecting their legal duties, not more than $100.

> *Enforcement.*[3]—The enforcement of the above-quoted provisions is charged to the factory-inspection department of the district police. Truant officers are authorized to visit establishments and ascertain whether children under 16 are illegally employed therein. They shall report cases of illegally employed children to the school committee, the chief of the district police, or the factory inspectors, and may apprehend and take to school without a warrant any such child illegally employed.

CONDITIONS FOUND.

Each of the 44 establishments visited in Massachusetts employed females 16 years of age and over, and 37 of them also employed children under 16 years of age. The total number of children so employed was 421.

---

[1] Rev. Laws, 1902, ch. 106, sec. 29 (22d An. Rept. Com. of Labor, p. 596).

[2] Idem, sec. 32, and Acts of 1906, ch. 499, secs. 1 to 4 (22d An. Rept. Com. of Labor, pp. 598, 622, 623).

[3] Idem, sec. 34; idem, ch. 108, sec. 8 (as amended by ch. 413. Acts of 1907); Acts of 1906, ch. 499, secs. 2, 3, and 4 (22d An. Rept. Com. of Labor, pp. 598, 609, 622).

LEGAL AGE.

Individual slips containing inquiries as to age, sex, etc., were made out and signed by most of the children employed in the visited establishments. In no case did a child signing such slip report itself as under 14 years of age. These age reports were not verified.

PROHIBITED AND DANGEROUS EMPLOYMENTS.

No instances were found of children being engaged in any of the employments forbidden them by law. In two establishments, both woolen and worsted mills, children under 16 were, however, found cleaning or oiling machinery in motion. In both of these cases the machines oiled were carders. In neither of these cases had a factory inspector forbidden children to be so employed. In a third woolen mill the superintendent stated that women occasionally cleaned or oiled looms while in motion.

WORKING PAPERS.

Of the 37 establishments employing children under 16 years of age, 20 had age and schooling certificates on file for all child employees, 7 had no such certificates on file, and 9 had more or less incomplete files. Information was not obtained on this point from 1 establishment.

Lists or registers of child employees were kept on file and in a complete condition by 15 of the 37 establishments, in an incomplete condition by 2 establishments, and were not kept at all by 19, 1 establishment not being reported for on this point. By 6 of the 17 establishments in which such lists were on file, copies thereof were posted conspicuously in the workrooms where children were employed; by 3 such posting was done at the entrance of the factory, but not in the workrooms; and by the remaining 8 lists were nowhere posted.

The Massachusetts law also requires the employer to keep on file a list of all illiterate minors and to forward a list to the school authorities. Such a list was found to be kept by 4 of the 19 establishments from which information upon this point was obtained, and to be forwarded to school authorities by 1 of the 11 establishments from which information was obtained upon this point.

The above figures indicate that the legal provisions regarding filing certificates is more generally observed than the provision regarding the keeping of lists of children and minors. Even where lists are kept there is a tendency to regard one list as sufficient. One employer stated that a factory inspector had told him that, because employees had mutilated the list of minors, he need not keep it posted. Another said that the inspector "will let you off" if certificates are on file, although no list is on file or posted. In several cases lists had not been revised to include children added to the force since the list was originally compiled.

No systematic effort was made to ascertain whether that provision of the law was observed which requires certificates to be returned to the school committee if not called for by the minor when leaving its place of employment. In several establishments, however, it was reported that old certificates were still on file.

RHODE ISLAND.

SUMMARY OF LAWS.

LEGAL AGE.[1]

The legal age of employment is 14 years in any "factory, manufacturing or business establishment," or in any "business" except agricultural and household labor.

> *Penalty.*—For employing, or permitting employment of, child under legal age, not more than $500.
>
> *Enforcement.*—Charged to factory inspection department.

PROHIBITED EMPLOYMENTS.

Children under 18, the operation of passenger elevators.[2]

> *Penalty.*—$5 to $10 per day of such operation.
>
> *Enforcement.*—Charged to local building inspectors where such exist; elsewhere to the State factory inspectors.

This is the only employment absolutely forbidden to children of legal age. There is, however, a legal provision forbidding children under 16 to clean moving machinery unless approved by the factory inspector as not dangerous. (Penalty, not more than $500.) Although this prohibition is not absolute in terms, it is so in practice, as the factory inspectors never approve exceptions of any kind.[3]

---

[1] Gen. Laws, 1896, ch. 68, secs. 1, 3, and 12 (as amended by ch. 1215, enacted 1905) and sec. 2 (as amended by ch. 1458, enacted 1907) (22d An. Rept. Com. of Labor, pp. 1206–1210).

[2] Idem, ch. 108, sec. 16 (as amended by ch. 973, enacted 1902) (22d An. Rept. Com. of Labor, p. 1214).

[3] Idem, ch. 68, secs. 6 and 12 (as amended by ch. 1215, enacted 1905) (22d An. Rept. Com. of Labor, pp. 1209, 1210). The law also prohibits the employment of children under 16 years of age at mendicant or immoral practices or "for or in any business, exhibition, or vocation injurious to the health or morals or dangerous to the life or limb of such child * * *." The context would indicate that the latter clause was not intended to refer to the customary dangers involved in factory and workshop occupations. Gen. Laws, 1896, ch. 115, sec. 4, as amended by ch. 475, enacted 1897 (22d An. Rept. Com. of Labor, p. 1215).

WORKING PAPERS.

A child under 16 years of age, as a condition of employment in any "business" except household and agricultural labor, must obtain an age certificate. The legal provisions regarding the contents, issue, etc., of such certificates and the keeping of registers are, briefly, as follows:

Age certificates.[1]—To be issued under the direction of the local school committee; to show present age, name, and date and place of birth of child, and place of residence of person having control of child. Age given in certificate must be substantiated by duly attested copy of birth record, baptismal record, or passport.

Age certificates to be uniform throughout the State and in substantially the same form as given in the text of the law, as approved by secretary of State board of education.

Issuing official to keep on file a copy of each certificate issued, together with the evidence of age on basis of which certificate was granted.

Filing of certificates.—Employer to possess and keep on file age certificates for all child employees under 16 years of age, and, on demand, to produce such certificates for examination of factory inspector.[1]

On termination of employment certificate to be returned to child, or if not demanded by child within two weeks, to be returned to issuing official.

Register of children.—The law does not require employer to keep a register or wall list of children employed.

Penalties.[2]—For employing, or permitting the employment of, a child under 16 without certificate or making false statement in regard to contents of certificate, not more than $500, except that for refusal to produce certificates on demand of inspector fine to be $10 to $50.

Enforcement.[3]—The legal provisions regarding certificates is charged to the State factory inspection department. If children are found working without certificates, the chief inspector is to report names and addresses of such children to local school committee.

---

[1] Gen. Laws, 1896, ch. 68, sec. 1, as amended by ch. 1215, enacted 1905 (22d An. Rept. Com. of Labor, pp. 1207, 1208).

[2] Idem, secs. 1 and 12, as amended by ch. 1215, enacted 1905 (22d An. Rept., Com. of Labor, pp. 1207, 1210).

[3] Idem, sec. 3, as amended by ch. 1215, enacted 1905 (22d An. Rept. Com. of Labor, p. 1208).

The age certificate in use is of the following form:

{State coat of arms.}   STATE OF RHODE ISLAND.

AGE AND EMPLOYMENT CERTIFICATE.

This certifies that I, living at ...., have control of .... (boy, girl), and that said child was born at ......, and in the county of ...... and State of ......, on ...., and is now .... years and .... months old, as attested to by ....

(Birth certificate, baptismal certificate, or passport.)

....
                                 (Parent or custodian) ....

(The above signature should be made in the presence of the person authorized to issue the certificate.)

I hereby approve the foregoing certificate of above-named child, height .... feet and .... inches, eyes ...... color, complexion ...., hair ......, having no reason to doubt that said child is of the age therein certified, is apparently in sound health, and is physically able to work.

This certificate belongs to the above-named child, and is to be surrendered to said child whenever he leaves the service of the corporation or employer holding the same; but if not claimed by said child within two weeks from such time it shall be returned to the school committee or person authorized to issue the same.

Approved ....

By the authority of the school committee of ....

Dated ...., 190 .

This form is substantially the same as the one given in the law as a model, except that it omits the requirement of a sworn affidavit on the part of the parent. According to Mr. Walter E. Ranger, commissioner of public schools of Rhode Island, the presence of the affidavit requirement was the cause of misunderstanding and was unnecessary. Under the law the age of a child must be proved by a birth certificate, baptismal certificate, or passport. An affidavit is of no value without one of these three forms of proof; with either of them it is superfluous.

CONDITIONS FOUND.

The number of establishments visited in Rhode Island was 27. All of these employed women and 24 employed children under 16 years of age.

LEGAL AGE.

Individual slips containing inquiries as to age, sex, etc., were made out and signed by most of the children employed in the visited establishments. On one such slip a child reported itself as 13 years of age. These age reports were not verified.

PROHIBITED AND DANGEROUS EMPLOYMENTS.

None of the establishments visited possessed passenger elevators, and thus none came within the scope of the law regarding the employment of children under 18 as operators of such elevators.

Women and children were not reported as cleaning moving machinery in any of the establishments. In one establishment, however, women and children oiled looms and spinning frames while in motion, and in a second establishment women oiled moving machinery. In the last-mentioned establishment it is also reported that boys cleaned mule frames while stationary and had frequently been injured by an inadvertent starting of the power.

Of the 24 establishments employing children 14 to 16 years of age, 10 had complete files of age certificates, 2 had no such certificates on file, and the remaining 12 had more or less incomplete files.

In 10 establishments it was not the practice to return certificates to the issuing authorities when children, on terminating their employment, failed to demand their certificates. In each of these cases uncalled-for certificates of old dates were found.

Registers of child employees (a matter not referred to by law) were kept by three establishments.

CONNECTICUT.

SUMMARY OF LAWS.

LEGAL AGE.[1]

The legal age of employment is 14 years in "any mechanical, mercantile, or manufacturing establishment."

> *Penalty.*—For employment of child under legal age, not more than $60, and each week of such employment a separate offense.
>
> *Enforcement.*—Is charged to "the State board of education, and the school visitors, boards of education, and town school committees," and for that purpose the State board of education may employ agents at not more than $5 per working day.

PROHIBITED EMPLOYMENTS.

Children under 16, the operation of elevators.

> *Penalty.*—Not more than $25.
>
> *Enforcement.*—By the factory-inspection department.

This is the only employment absolutely forbidden to children of legal working age. There is, however, a legal provision which directs that—

* * * No machines, other than steam engines, in a factory shall be cleaned while running after notice forbidding the same is given by the inspector to the owners or operators of the factory.[2]

> *Penalty.*—Not more than $50.

---

[1] Gen. Stat., 1902, secs. 4704, 4706, 4707.

Children under 14 are forbidden employment at any kind of work during school term. Idem, sec. 2119 (22d An. Rept. Com. of Labor, pp. 232, 242, 243).

[2] Idem, sec. 4516 and sec. 4522, as amended by ch. 53, Acts of 1903 (22d An. Rept. Com. of Labor, pp. 236, 237).

The chief inspector stated that in exercising its authority under this law the department had no invariable rules of procedure, each condition being judged on its merits. He claimed that as he and all the male inspectors were practical mechanics, with years of experience, they were thoroughly competent to judge of the dangers incident to any machine. He believed, moreover, that the existing law regarding the cleaning of machinery was a model one; that "a law forbidding the cleaning and oiling of all machines while in motion by women and children would be a hardship on the manufacturers."

WORKING •PAPERS.

A child under 16 years of age, as a condition of employment in "any mechanical, mercantile, or manufacturing establishment," must obtain an age certificate. The legal provisions regarding the contents, issue, etc., of such certificates and the keeping of registers are briefly as follows:

Age certificates.—Certificate, stating age of child to be at least 14, to be signed by (1) the registrar of births, marriages, and deaths, or by the town clerk of the town where the child was born, or (2) by a teacher of the school which the child last attended, or (3) by the person having custody of the registry of said school. If child was not born in the United States, the State board of education may, upon investigation of documentary evidence, such as passports, and the taking of testimony of parents or guardian, grant a certificate which shall be accepted as evidence of age.[1]

Schooling.—The issue of an age certificate is not dependent on literacy; but the compulsory education law [2] (1) authorizes the school authorities to forbid the employment at any work of a child 14 to 16 years of age who has not "sufficient schooling" to warrant its leaving school; and (2) requires a child 14 to 16 who can not "read and write," and who is employed in a town having an evening school, to produce monthly a signed certificate of an evening-school teacher showing that it has attended night school 18 consecutive evenings in current month and is a regular attendant.

---

[1] Gen. Stat., 1902, sec. 4705, as amended by ch. 115, Acts of 1905 (22d An. Rept. Com, of Labor. p. 242).

[2] Pub. Acts, 1905, ch. 36, and Gen. Stat., 1902, sec. 2147 (22d An. Rept., Com. of Labor, p. 232). Shortly subsequent to the field work of this investigation, however, a new law, Acts of 1909, ch.123 (approved June 29, 1909), made the ability "to read with facility, to write legibly simple sentences in the English language, and to perform the operations of the fundamental rules of arithmetic up to and including fractions" a precedent to the issue of an age certificate, except that in the case of foreign-born children "an equivalent education in their native language" is accepted. (Bulletin of the Bureau of Labor, No. 85, p. 524.)

Filing of certificates.—Employer to keep on file age certificates for all child employees under 16 years of age, and, on demand, to produce the same, with a list of the names of such children, for examination of agents of State board of education or to agents of the local board of school visitors, town school committee, or board of education.[1]

Register of children.—Employer to keep a list of names of all children under 16 years of age and to produce same for examination of school authorities, as in the case of certificates. (See preceding paragraph.) The law does not require such list of names to be kept posted.[2]

> *Penalties.*—On employer for employing child 14 to 16 without age certificates, not more than $60, and each week of such employment a separate offense; on employer for failure to keep on file age certificates and register of names, not more than $100; on parents for false statements of age, not more than $20; for employing without evening-school certificate, not more than $50.[3]
>
> *Enforcement.*[4]—Is charged to "the State board of education, and the school visitors, board of education, and town school committees;" and for this purpose State board of education may employ agents at not more than $5 per working day.
>
> The factory-inspection department is not charged directly with any responsibility regarding the employment of children under age or without age certificates. But the act of 1907, providing for a female deputy factory inspector, directs such deputy to "inquire into the enforcement of the laws regulating the employment of women and girls * * * and to report thereon to the factory inspector." This would seem to impose some obligation upon the factory-inspection department in the enforcement of these provisions, in so far at least as female children are concerned.[5]

CONDITIONS FOUND.

The number of establishments visited in Connecticut was 35. All of these employed females 16 years of age and over, and 33 of them also employed children under 16 years of age. The total number of such children was 495.

---

[1] Gen. Stat., 1902, sec. 4705, as amended by ch. 115, Acts of 1905 (22d An. Rept. Com. of Labor, p. 242).

[2] Idem.

[3] Idem, secs. 2120, 4705 (as amended by ch. 115, Acts of 1905), and 4706 (22d An. Rept. Com. of Labor, pp. 232, 242, 243).

[4] Idem, sec. 4707 (22d An. Rept. Com. of Labor, p. 243).

[5] Pub. Acts, 1907, ch. 241, sec. 2.

LEGAL AGE.

Individual slips containing inquiries as to age, sex, etc., were made out and signed by most of the children employed in the visited establishments. In no case did a child signing such slip report itself as under 14 years of age. These age reports were not verified.

PROHIBITED AND DANGEROUS EMPLOYMENTS.

No instance was found of a child under 16 years of age operating an elevator.

In 2 of the 33 visited establishments having power-driven machinery it was found that women cleaned or oiled moving machinery. In one of these cases the machinery in question consisted of small watch lathes, in the other of knitting machines. In neither case did it appear that an inspector had issued an order forbidding the cleaning of such machinery by women.

WORKING PAPERS.

Of the 33 establishments employing children 14 to 16 years of age 5 had complete files of age certificates, 4 had no certificates on file, and the remaining 24 had more or less incomplete files.

Registers of children's names were kept in a complete condition by 21 establishments, in an incomplete condition by 4, and were not kept at all by 6. No report upon this point was received from the 2 remaining establishments of the 33 in which children were employed.

NEW YORK.

SUMMARY OF LAWS.[1]

LEGAL AGE.[2]

The legal age of employment in factories is 14 years. The term "factory" is defined to include "also any mill, workshop, or other

---

[1] Special legal regulations regarding employment in mercantile establishments and as newsboys are omitted from this report. (22d An. Rept. Com. of Labor, pp. 925, 928.)

General references: Rev. Stat., 3d ed., 1901, p. 2100, sec. 70 (as amended by ch. 184, Acts of 1903), sec. 71 (as amended by ch. 291, Acts of 1907), sec. 72 (as amended by ch. 184, Acts of 1903), sec. 73 (as amended by ch. 291, Acts of 1907), sec. 75, sec. 76 (as amended by ch. 184, Acts of 1903, and ch. 493, Acts of 1905), and p. 2120, sec. 209 (as amended by ch. 506, Acts of 1907). (22d An. Rept. Com. of Labor, pp. 907–910, 931.)

In 1909, Acts of 1909, the labor laws were consolidated as ch. 31 of the Con. Laws. (Bulletin of the Bureau of Labor No. 85, p. 685.) A few minor changes were made. The only change affecting the legal provisions as quoted above is the substitution of "factory inspector" for "commissioner" as the officer to whom lists of certificates issued are to be sent monthly by officials issuing certificates.

[2] Rev. Stat., 3d ed., 1901, p. 2100, sec. 70 (as amended by ch. 184, Acts of 1903), p. 2120, sec. 209 (as amended by ch. 506, Acts of 1907), and p. 2098, sec. 62 (as amended by ch. 505, Acts of 1907). (22d An. Rept. Com. of Labor, pp. 907, 931.)

manufacturing or business establishment where one or more persons are employed at labor." [1]

> *Penalty.*—First offense, $20 to $50; second offense, $50 to $200 or imprisonment not more than 30 days, or both; third offense, not less than $250 or imprisonment not more than 60 days, or both.
>
> *Enforcement.*—Charged to the factory inspection bureau of the State department of labor.

PROHIBITED EMPLOYMENTS. [2]

Children under 14, all. [3]

Males under 18 and females under 21, the cleaning of machinery in motion. [4]

Children under 15, the operation of elevators. [5]

Children under 18, the operation of any elevator running at a greater speed than 200 feet a minute. [6]

Males under 18 and females all ages, the operation or use of "any emery, tripoli, rouge, corundum, stone, carborundum, or any abrasive or emery polishing or buffing wheel where articles of the baser metals or of iridium are manufactured." [7]

Children under 16, the operation of dangerous machines of any kind.

[No definition of kinds of machines to be considered dangerous.] [8]

> *Penalty.*—For violation of any of the above prohibitions, first offense, $20 to $50; second offense, $50 to $200 or imprisonment not more than 30 days, or both; third offense, not less than $250 or imprisonment not more than 60 days, or both. [9]

---

[1] Rev. Stat., 3d ed., 1901, p. 2089, sec. 2, as amended by ch. 184, Acts of 1903 (22d An. Rept. Com. of Labor, p. 899).

[2] A law of the State forbids the employment of children under 16 years of age in certain acrobatic, mendicant, and immoral practices, and in "any practice or exhibition or place dangerous or injurious to the life, limb, or morals of the child." The quoted clause is very broad in its reading, but the context would indicate that it was not intended to refer to the ordinary occupations of factories and workshops.

[3] Rev. Stat., 3d ed., 1901, p. 2100, sec. 70, as amended by ch. 184, Acts of 1903 (22d An. Rept. Com. of Labor, p. 907).

[4] Idem, p. 2102, sec. 81, as amended by ch. 366, Acts of 1906 (22d An. Rept. Com. of Labor, p. 913).

[5] Idem, p. 2102, sec. 79 (22d An. Rept. Com. of Labor, p. 912).

[6] Idem.

[7] Idem, p. 2102, sec. 92, as amended by ch. 561, Acts of 1903 (22d An. Rept. Com. of Labor, p. 915).

[8] Idem, p. 2102, sec. 81, as amended by ch. 366, Acts of 1906 (22d An. Rept. Com. of Labor, p. 913).

[9] Idem, p. 2120, sec. 209, as amended by ch. 506, Acts of 1907 (22d An. Rept. Com. of Labor, p. 931).

Enforcement.—The above provisions charged to the factory inspection-bureau of the State department of labor.[1]

WORKING PAPERS.

A child 14 to 16 years of age, as a condition of lawful employment in any "factory,"[2] must possess an employment certificate. The legal provisions regarding the contents, issue, etc., of such certificates, and the keeping of registers are briefly as follows.

---

[1] Rev. Stat., 3d ed., 1901, p. 2098, sec. 62, as amended by ch. 505, Acts of 1907 (22d An. Rept. Com. of Labor, p. 907).

Later laws: By a law enacted shortly after the field work of this investigation was completed the number of prohibited employments was greatly expanded. (Acts of 1909, ch. 31, sec. 93, as amended by ch. 299, Acts of 1909.) In force Feb. 17, 1909. The section of the law concerned with this subject is in full as follows, the paragraphing being slightly altered to facilitate reading:

No child under the age of sixteen years shall be employed or permitted to work in operating or assisting in operating any of the following machines: Circular or band saws, wood shapers, wood jointers, planers, sandpaper or wood-polishing machinery; picker machines or machines used in picking wool, cotton, hair, or any upholstery material; paper-lace machines; burnishing machines in any tannery or leather manufactory; job or cylinder printing presses having motive power other than foot; wood turning or boring machinery; stamping machines used in sheet-metal and tinware manufacturing or in washer and nut factories; machines used in making corrugating rolls; steam boilers; dough brakes or cracker machinery of any description; wire or iron straightening machinery; rolling-mill machinery; power punches or shears; washing, grinding, or mixing machinery; calender rolls in rubber manufacturing; or laundering machinery.

No child under the age of sixteen years shall be employed or permitted to work at adjusting or assisting in adjusting any belt to any machinery; oiling or assisting in oiling, wiping, or cleaning machinery; or in any capacity in preparing any composition in which dangerous or poisonous acids are used; or in the manufacture or packing of paints, dry colors, or red or white lead; or in dipping, dyeing [drying], or packing matches; or in the manufacture, packing, or storing of powder, dynamite, nitroglycerine, compounds, fuses, or other explosives; or in or about any distillery, brewery, or any other establishment where malt or alcoholic liquors are manufactured, packed, wrapped, or bottled.

No female under the age of sixteen shall be employed or permitted to work in any capacity where such employment compels her to remain standing constantly.

No child under the age of sixteen years shall be employed or permitted to have the care, custody, or management of or to operate an elevator, either for freight or passengers.

No person under the age of eighteen years shall be employed or permitted to have the care, custody, or management of or to operate an elevator, either for freight or passengers, running at a speed of over two hundred feet a minute.

No male person under eighteen years or woman under twenty-one years of age shall be permitted or directed to clean machinery while in motion.

No male child under the age of eighteen years, nor any female, shall be employed in any factory in this State in operating or using any emery, tripoli, rouge, corundum, stone, carborundum, or any abrasive or emery polishing or buffing wheel where articles of the baser metals or of iridium are manufactured.

[2] The term "factory" is defined to include "also any mill, workshop, or other manufacturing or business establishment where one or more persons are employed at labor." Rev. Stat., 3d ed., 1901, p. 2089, sec. 2, as amended by ch. 184, Acts of 1903 (22d An. Rept. Com. of Labor, p. 899).

Employment certificates.[1]—To be issued by the commissioner of health or by the executive officer of the board or department of health of city, town, or village where child resides or is to be employed, or by such other officer as may be designated by said conmissioner, board, or department, upon application of the person having control of the child.

Certificates shall issue only to children for whom satisfactory evidence of sufficient schooling and of legal age is produced.

Evidence of schooling to be the school record, which shall be furnished on demand, signed by the chief executive officer of the school last attended by child. The record to certify that the child (*a*) has attended school at least 130 days during the 12 months preceding its fourteenth birthday or the time of its application; (*b*) is able to read and write simple sentences in the English language; and (*c*) has received during period mentioned instruction in reading, spelling, writing, English grammar, and geography and is familiar with the fundamental operations of arithmetic up to and including fractions. Such school record shall also give the date of birth and residence of the child as shown on the records of the school, and the name of its parents, guardian, or custodian.

Evidence of legal age to be in one of the following forms: (*a*) Birth certificate (duly attested copy), which shall be conclusive evidence of age; (*b*) certificate of graduation, showing that child is a graduate of a school having a course of study of at least 8 years' duration, provided that record of such school shows child to be at least 14 years of age; (*c*) passport or baptismal certificate; (*d*) other documentary evidence satisfactory to the issuing official and to the local board of health; (*e*) in cities of the first class only, the certificate of examining physicians, designated by the board of health, stating that in their opinion child is at least 14 years of age. The forms of age evidence shall be required in order as enumerated, and no form after the first shall be accepted unless an affidavit of the parent is made showing that none of the preceding forms of evidence can be produced, such affidavit to show age, place and date of birth, and residence of child.

In addition to establishing the child's age and schooling by the forms mentioned, the issuing official is to make an examination of the child, and thereupon sign and file a statement that such child can read and write simple sentences in English, and, in his opinion, is 14

---

[1] Rev. Stat., 3d ed., 1901, p. 2100, sec. 70 (as amended by ch. 184, Acts of 1903), sec. 71 (as amended by ch. 291, Acts of 1907), sec. 72 (as amended by ch. 184, Acts of 1903), sec. 73 (as amended by ch. 291, Acts of 1907), sec. 75, sec. 76 (as amended by ch. 184, Acts of 1903, and ch. 493, Acts of 1905), and p. 2120, sec. 209 (as amended by ch. 506, Acts of 1907). (22d An. Rept. Com. of Labor, pp. 907-910, 931.)

years of age, of normal development, and physically able to perform the work intended. In doubtful cases physical fitness is to be determined by a medical officer of the board of health.

The complete employment certificate is to be signed, in the presence of the issuing official, by the child applicant, and shall contain these facts: Date and place of birth, color of hair and eyes, height and weight, and any distinguishing facial marks, and shall state that the papers evidencing age and schooling have been duly examined, approved, and filed, and that the child has been personally examined by the issuing official.

The issuing officials shall transmit monthly to the office of the factory inspector a list of the names of children to whom certificates have been issued.

Filing of employment certificates.—Employer is required to possess and keep on file in office employment certificates for all children 14 to 16 years of age employed by him, and, on demand, to produce such certificates for examination by the factory inspector.[1]

On termination of a child's employment, such certificate to be surrendered by the employer to the child or to its parent, guardian, or custodian.

Register of children.—Employer is required to keep in office a register showing name, birthplace, age, and place of residence of all children under 16 years of age employed.[1]

> *Penalties.*[2]—Any person violating or failing to comply with the legal provisions above quoted, or who knowingly makes a false statement in relation to an application made for an employment certificate, first offense, $20 to $50; second offense, $50 to $200, or imprisonment not more than 30 days, or both; third offense, not less than $250, or imprisonment not more than 60 days, or both.
>
> *Enforcement.*[3]—The legal provisions regarding certificates, as that of all other factory laws, is charged to the factory inspection bureau of the State department of labor.
>
> In the case of a child apparently under 16 years of age, for whom an employment certificate is not on file, the commissioner of labor may require employer to furnish within 10 days satisfactory evidence that such child is at least 14 years of age, or to cease employing such child.

---

[1] Rev. Stat., 3d ed., 1901, p. 2100, sec. 76, as amended by ch. 184, Acts of 1903, and ch. 493, Acts of 1905 (22d An. Rept. Com. of Labor, p. 410).

[2] Idem, p. 2120, sec. 209, as amended by ch. 506, Acts of 1907 (22d An. Rept. Com. of Labor, p. 931).

[3] Idem, p. 2098 (amended by ch. 505, Acts of 1907), sec. 62, and sec. 76, as amended by ch. 184, Acts of 1903, and ch. 493, Acts of 1905 (22d An. Rept. Com. of Labor, pp. 907, 910).

CONDITIONS FOUND.

The number of establishments visited in New York was 36. All of these employed women, but only 18 employed children under 16 years of age. The total number of children employed was very small, only 83 out of a total of 10,074 employees, an average of less than 3 children per establishment.

LEGAL AGE.

Individual slips containing inquiries as to age, sex, etc., were made out and signed by most of the children employed in the visited establishments. In no case did a child signing such slip report itself as under 14 years of age. These age reports were not verified.

PROHIBITED AND DANGEROUS EMPLOYMENTS.

No women or children under 16 years of age were reported as being employed in operating elevators, cleaning or oiling moving machinery, or in any other occupation forbidden them by law. No information was obtainable as to the employment of males 16 and 17 years of age at cleaning or oiling machinery, operating elevators, or operating polishing 'wheels.

WORKING PAPERS.

Of the 18 establishments employing children 14 to 16 years of age, 9 had complete files of employment certificates, 4 had no such certificates on file, and 5 had more or less incomplete files. In one establishment a few certificates were on file, but not in the names of children employed at the time of investigation.

Registers of children were kept by 10 establishments, and were not kept by 8 establishments. In no case were lists of names, etc., posted in the workrooms.

NEW JERSEY.

SUMMARY OF LAWS.

LEGAL AGE.[1]

The legal age of employment is 14 years in "any factory, workshop, mill, or place where the manufacture of goods of any kind is carried on."

Penalty.—On employer for employing child under legal age, and on person having control of such child for permitting it to be so employed, $50.

Enforcement.—Charged to State factory-inspection department [department of labor.]

---

[1] Acts of 1904, ch. 64, secs. 1 and 5, and sec. 45 (as amended by ch. 257, Acts of 1907) (22d An. Rept. Com. of Labor, pp. 860, 861, 868).

PROHIBITED EMPLOYMENTS.

Children under 16, the cleaning of machinery in motion in any manufacturing establishment.[1]

Children under 16, to work "between the fixed or traversing parts" of any machinery while in motion by the action of mechanical power.[2]

Penalty.—$50 for each offense.

WORKING PAPERS.

Certificates or other proofs of age are not required as a condition of employment for children. The law provides, however, that if an employer, when employing a child, shall furnish himself with proof of the child's age, of a form and in a manner prescribed by law, he shall be absolved from prosecution in case it develops that such child is under legal age.

The commissioner of labor and the factory inspectors may not demand that an employer supply himself with such proofs, but they may require a parent or custodian to submit proof, satisfactory to them, of the age of any child within five days. Also, they may require a medical certificate in the case of children of questionable physical fitness.

The legal provisions regarding the contents, issue, etc., of age certificates and medical certificates are briefly as follows:[2]

Contents and issue of age certificates.[3]—An employer may guard himself against prosecution for employing a child under legal age by filing at the time of employing such child proofs of age of one of the three following forms:

(1) Native-born children: (*a*) An affidavit made and sworn to by parent or custodian, stating following facts regarding child: Name, residence, place and date of birth, names of parents, church attended, school last attended, church where baptized and age of child at baptism; (*b*) a duly attested copy of the birth certificate, or, if birth record is not obtainable, a certified copy of the baptismal record.

(2) Foreign-born children: (*a*) Affidavit as above, with additional statement that child is the same as mentioned in its passport; (*b*) a true copy of the passport.

In each of the above cases, copies of all papers, affidavits, etc., must be mailed to the State department of labor within 24 hours after the same are filed.

(3) In the case of children for whom proofs of age of the above forms can not be secured, the commissioner of labor, upon other proof satis-

---

[1] Acts of 1904, ch. 64, secs. 21 and 30 (22d An. Rept. Com. of Labor, pp. 863, 864).

[2] Idem, (22d An. Rept. Com. of Labor, pp. 860-869).

[3] Idem, sec. 3 (22d An. Rept. Com. of Labor, p. 860).

factory to him, may issue employment permits, which permits shall have same force as age affidavits and certificates.

Medical certificates.[1]—The commissioner, assistant, or any inspector may demand a certificate of physical fitness from a regular physician in the case of children under 16 who, in the judgment of such officer, is physically unfit to do the work for which employed, and may prohibit the employment of such child until such certificate is produced.

Filing of certificates.[2]—Employer, upon demand, to produce all certificates, transcripts, passports, and affidavits which he may possess for the inspection of the commissioner, his assistant, or any inspector, and also for the inspection of truant officers if such are acting under written authority from the commissioner.

Register of children.[3]—Employer to keep a register, showing names, residences, and time of employment of children under 16 years of age, working under certificates, transcripts, passports, and affidavits. Such registers, upon demand, to be produced for inspection of the commissioner, his assistant, or the inspectors, and also of the truant officers when such officers are authorized in writing by the commissioner.

Penalties.[4]—On employer for refusing to produce certificates, registers, etc., for inspection, $50; on employer for employing child after notice of commissioner that parent or custodian has not produced proofs of age, $50; on employer for continuing to employ a child after commissioner or inspector has demanded a medical certificate and before such certificate has been obtained, $25; on any person for making false statement regarding certificates or passports, $50.

Enforcement.[5]—Enforcement of the above-quoted legal provisions is intrusted to the State department of labor.

The commissioner, his assistant, or any inspector is empowered to demand of parent, parents, or custodian, proof of the age of any child found at work. If such proof is not presented within five days, the employer to discharge such child upon written notice from commissioner.

CONDITIONS FOUND.

The number of establishments visited in New Jersey was 27. All of these employed females 16 years of age and over, and 25 employed children under 16 years of age. The number of such children was 582.

---

[1] Acts of 1904, ch. 64, sec. 7 (22d An. Rept. Com. of Labor, p. 861).

[2] Idem, sec. 8 (22d An. Rept. Com. of Labor, p. 861.).

[3] Idem.

[4] Idem, secs. 5, 6, 7, 8 (22d An. Rept. Com. of Labor, pp. 860, 861).

[5] Idem, sec. 5 and sec. 45 (as amended by ch. 257, Acts of 1907) (22d An. Rept. Com. of Labor, pp. 861, 868).

LEGAL AGE.

Individual slips containing inquiries as to age, sex, etc., were made out and signed by most of the children employed in the visited establishments. In no case did a child signing such slip report itself as under 14 years of age. These age reports were not verified.

PROHIBITED AND DANGEROUS EMPLOYMENTS.

No cases were reported of women or children either cleaning or oiling machinery while in motion.

WORKING PAPERS.

Of the 25 establishments employing children under 16 years of age, 13 had complete files of age certificates, 6 had no such certificates on file, and 4 had incomplete files; no report upon the point was received from the remaining 2 establishments. In total, therefore, 17 of the 23 establishments reported upon this point had more or less complete files of age certificates.

Registers of children employed were kept by 12 of these 17 establishments and were not kept by 5. In none of the 6 establishments in which certificates were entirely absent were registers kept.

In one establishment a large number of certificates were on file, but the names thereon did not correspond in most cases with the names of the children there employed.

In three of the establishments having certificates on file no copies thereof had been sent to the office of the State department, as the law requires, in order to make the certificate a valid defense in case of prosecution.

PENNSYLVANIA.

SUMMARY OF LAWS.

LEGAL AGE.[1]

The legal age of employment is 14 years in any "establishment" (i. e., any place where men, women, and children are employed for compensation, with the exception of coal mining, farm labor, and domestic labor [2].)

> *Penalty.*[3]—For violating the above provision in any way, $25 to $500, or imprisonment 10 to 60 days.
>
> *Enforcement.*[4]—Charged to the State factory inspection department.

---

[1] Acts of 1905, ch. 226, secs. 1, 2, 23, 25, 27 (22d An. Rept. Com. of Labor, pp. 1175, 1180).

[2] Idem, sec. 1 (22d An. Rept. Com. of Labor, p. 1175). There is a separate child-labor law for the coal-mining industry.

[3] Idem, sec. 23 (22d An. Rept. Com. of Labor, p. 1180).

[4] Idem, secs. 25, 27 (22d An. Rept. Com. of Labor, pp. 1180, 1181).

PROHIBITED EMPLOYMENTS.[1]

Children under 16,[2] the cleaning or oiling of machinery in motion and the operation of elevators or lifts.

Penalty.—$25 to $500, or imprisonment 10 to 60 days.

Enforcement.—Charged to State factory inspection department.

WORKING PAPERS.

Children of legal age, 14, but under 16, may not be employed lawfully in any establishment (definition as above, in section on legal age), unless an employment certificate is first obtained.

---

[1] The State law also prohibits the employment of children under 15 years of age at acrobatic performances or "any vocation injurious to the health or dangerous to the life or limb of such child." The context of this statute would indicate that the quoted clause was not intended to refer to the customary dangers of factory or workshop employment. Brightly's Purdon's Digest, 12th ed., 1895, p. 1015, sec. 11 (22d An. Rept. Com. of Labor, p. 1084.)

[2] Acts of 1905, act No. 226, secs. 4, 23, 25, 27 (22d An. Rept. Com. of Labor, pp. 1176, 1180.)

An act passed subsequent to the field work of this investigation increased very considerably the number of prohibited occupations, although most of these occupations are not related to the work of factories or workshops. Acts of 1909, act No. 182, in effect Jan. 1, 1910 (Bulletin of the Bureau of Labor No. 85, pp. 748–751.) This later law contains two sections relative to the subject now being considered.

The first is an absolute prohibition against the employment of persons under 18 years of age at any of the following kinds of work: "In or about blast furnaces, tanneries, docks, wharves, quarries; in the outside erection and repair of electric wires; in the running or management of elevators, lifts, or hoisting machines; in oiling hazardous and dangerous machinery in motion; at switch tending, gate tending, track repairing; as brakemen, firemen, engineers, motormen, conductors upon railroads; as pilots, firemen, or engineers upon boats or vessels engaged in the transportation of passengers or merchandise; in or about establishments wherein nitroglycerine, dynamite, dualin, guncotton, gunpowder, or other high or dangerous explosive, is manufactured, compounded, or stored."

The second section is a conditional prohibition against the employment of children 16 years of age in "establishments for the manufacture or preparation of white lead, red lead, paints, phosphorus, phosphorus matches, poisonous acids, or for the manufacture or stripping of tobacco or cigars." The condition referred to is that the prohibition does not hold if it is "proved to the satisfaction of the chief factory inspector that the danger or menace to the health or safety of minors * * * has been removed * * *."

Penalty, first offense, $10 to $25, or imprisonment 10 days, or both; second offense, not more than $50, and 90 days' imprisonment, or both.

Contrasting this later law concerning prohibited occupations with the earlier law, as given in the text above, three points may be noted: (1) The prohibited age for operating elevators is raised to 18 years and the penalty for violation reduced; (2) the oiling of "dangerous machinery" in motion is forbidden for persons under 18 by the new law, whereas the old law, while dealing only with children under 16, flatly forbade such persons to oil any machinery in motion; (3) the new law does not refer to the subject of cleaning moving machinery, thus apparently leaving in force the restriction of the old law as quoted in the text.

Owing to judicial decisions relative to the constitutionality of certain portions of the child-labor act of 1905, the form and method of issue of certificate had undergone considerable changes during the period between the passage of the original act and the time of the field work of this investigation (January 18 to March 9, 1909). The following summary of the legal provisions concerning certificates, registers, etc., gives as nearly as can be determined the legal interpretations accepted at the time of this investigation.[1]

Employment certificates.—To be issued by any person authorized to administer oaths on forms prepared by chief factory inspector. The conditions of issue are: (1) That child is able to read and write English on examination of issuing official; (2) that child has attended school according to law; and (3) that an affidavit of parent or guardian is made stating age, date and place of birth of child; if there is no parent or guardian, the affidavit may be made by the child.

Filing of certificates.—Employer is required to keep on file employment certificates for all children between 14 and 16 years of age, and to produce such certificates for examination of factory inspectors.

Certificate is to be returned to the child when employment ceases.

Register of children.—Employer is required to keep posted in every room where children under 16 years of age are employed a list of their names with their ages.

Penalties.[2]—Any person for violating any of the above-quoted legal provisions, $25 to $500, or imprisonment 10 to 60 days.

Enforcement.—The State factory inspection department is charged with the enforcement of the above-quoted provisions.

---

[1] Acts of 1905, act No. 226 (22d An. Rept. Com. of Labor, pp. 1175–1181); and Acts of 1901, act No. 206 (Bulletin of the Bureau of Labor, No. 43, pp. 1304–1306).

Later law: By an act in force shortly subsequent to the field work of this investigation in Pennsylvania, the child-labor provisions were radically altered. Acts of 1909, ch. 182, in force Jan. 1, 1910 (Bulletin of the Bureau of Labor No. 85, pp. 748–751.) The more important of the new provisions relating to certificates and registers are these: Certificates to be issued only by designated school authorities, upon evidence of age. Forms of age evidence to be accepted in the following order: (1) Birth certificate, baptismal certificate, passport, or other official record; (2) school register; (3) affidavit of parent, guardian, or other person. Employment certificate is to state age of child, complexion, color of hair, ability to read and write English, and list of establishments in which child may be legally employed. Employer to keep "two complete lists of all minors under the age of 16 years employed in or for his or her establishment; one of said lists to be kept on file in the office of the employer, and one to be conspicuously posted in each of the several departments in or for which minors are employed."

For a full discussion of the Pennsylvania law and the difficulties of its interpretation, see Silk Industry, Vol. IV, this report, pp. 85–92.

[2] As given in laws of 1905 (22d An. Rept. Com. of Labor, p. 1180).

CONDITIONS FOUND.

Of the 50 establishments visited, all employed females 16 years of age and over, and 42 also employed children under 16 years of age. The number of such children employed was 1,269.

LEGAL AGE.

Individual slips containing inquiries as to age, sex, etc., were made out and signed by most of the children employed in the visited establishments. In no case did a child signing such slip report itself as under 14 years of age. These age reports were not verified.

PROHIBITED AND DANGEROUS EMPLOYMENTS.

In one of the 41 establishments having machinery and employing children, children were reported as cleaning or oiling moving machinery. The establishment manufactured hosiery and knit goods, and the machines referred to were knitting machines. In another factory, making cakes, crackers, and candy, females 16 years of age and over oiled or cleaned chocolate-dipping machines in motion.

No cases were found of elevators being operated by children under 16.

WORKING PAPERS.

Of the 42 establishments employing children under 16 years of age, 27 had employment certificates on file for all children, 1 had no such certificates for any of the children employed, and 14 had more or less incomplete files.

REGISTERS.

Registers, showing names and ages of child employees, were kept in a complete condition by 26 of the 42 establishments employing children under 16, in an incomplete condition by 2, and were not kept at all by 14. In 25 of the 28 establishments keeping registers, such registers were posted in the workrooms where such children were employed, and were not so posted in 3.

OHIO.

SUMMARY OF LAWS.

LEGAL AGE.[1]

The legal age of employment is 14 years, in any "factory, workshop, business office, * * * mercantile or other establishment."[2]

---

[1] Acts of 1908, p. 30, secs. 1 to 4 (amending secs. 6986–7, 6986–8, 6986–9, and 6986–10 of Ann. Stat.). (Bulletin of the Bureau of Labor, No. 85, pp. 701–704.)

[2] The full list is "Factory, workshop, business office, telephone or telegraph office, restaurant, bakery, hotel, apartment house, mercantile or other establishment * * * nor in the distribution or transmission of merchandise or messages."

Penalty.—For employing or permitting employment of a child under legal age, $25 to $50.

Enforcement.—As regards factories, workshops, and mercantile establishments, by State factory inspection department.

PROHIBITED EMPLOYMENTS.

Children under 16, any of the following employments: [1]

Sewing-machine belts;

Adjusting belts to machinery;

Oiling, or assisting in oiling, wiping, or cleaning machinery;

Operating—

Circular or band saws, wood shapers, wood jointers, planers, sandpaper or wood-polishing machinery;

Job or cylinder printing presses operated by power other than foot;

Emery or polishing wheels used for polishing metal;

Wood-turning or boring machinery;

Stamping machines used in sheet metal or tinware manufacturing;

Stamping machines in washer and nut factories;

Corrugating rolls, such as are used in roofing and washboard factories;

Steam boilers, steam machinery, or other steam-generating apparatus;

Dough brakes or cracker machinery of any description;

Wire or iron straightening machinery;

Rolling-mill machinery, punches, or shears;

Washing, grinding, or mixing mills;

Calender rolls in rubber manufacturing;

Laundering machinery;

Passenger or freight elevators;

In any capacity in preparing any composition in which dangerous or poisonous acids are used;

Manufacture of paints, colors, or white lead;

Dipping, dyeing (drying), or packing matches;

Manufacturing, packing, or storing powder, dynamite, nitroglycerin, compounds, fuses, or other explosives;

Manufacture of goods for immoral purposes;

As pin boys in bowling alleys;

In or about any distillery, brewery, or any other establishment where malt or alcoholic liquors are manufactured, packed, wrapped, or bottled;

---

[1] Acts of 1908, p. 30, secs. 2, 3, and 4 (Bulletin of the Bureau of Labor, No. 85, pp. 702–704).

In any hotel, theater, concert hall, drug store, saloon, or place of amusement wherein intoxicating liquors are sold;

Nor in any other employment that may be considered dangerous to their lives and limbs, or where their health may be injured or morals depraved.

For females under 16, any work requiring constant standing, or in assorting, manufacturing, or packing tobacco.

Penalty.—For employing, or permitting employment, of child in above-mentioned employments, $25 to $50.

Enforcement.—As regards factories, workshops, and mercantile establishments, by State factory inspection department.

It is to be noted that in the above list of employments prohibited to children under 16 there occurs the clause "nor in any other employment that may be considered dangerous to their lives and limbs, or where their health may be injured." The effect of this would seem to be to invest the inspection department with authority to increase the number of prohibited employments to include at least such employments as it may develop are no less dangerous than those specifically mentioned.

WORKING PAPERS.[1]

A child of legal age, 14, but under 16 years of age, as a condition of lawful employment in, or in connection with, a "factory, workshop, business office * * * mercantile, or other establishment,"[2] must possess an "age and schooling" certificate. Also the factory inspectors may demand medical certificates in cases where children appear to be of questionable physical fitness. The legal provisions regarding the contents, issue, etc., of such certificates and the keeping of registers by employers are as follows:

Age and schooling certificates.[3]—Form prepared by State commissioner of common schools. Certificates to be approved only by superintendent of schools, or by a person authorized by him, in cities or districts having such superintendents, and elsewhere by the clerk of the local board of education. To be issued upon proof satisfactory to said officials that child is of legal age and can read and write legibly the English language.

---

[1] Bates' Ann. Stat., 3d ed., Pt. II, Civ., sec. 4022-2 (as amended by act p. 615, Acts of 1902, and act p. 334, Acts of 1904), sec. 4022-3 (as amended by act p. 615, Acts of 1902), and sec. 4022-5 (22d An. Rept. Com. of Labor. pp. 1006, 1007, 1025, 1026); and Acts of 1908, p. 30, secs. 1 to 4 (amending secs. 6986-7, 6986-8, 6986-9, and 6986-10 of Anno. Stat.) (Bulletin of the Bureau of Labor, No. 85, pp. 701-704).

[2] For full list see ante, footnote 2 under the head Legal Age.

[3] Bates' Ann. Stat., 3d ed., Pt. II, Civ., sec. 4022-2 (as amended by act p. 615, Acts of 1902, and act p. 334, Acts of 1904) (22d An. Rept. Com. of Labor, pp. 1006, 1007).

Medical certificates.[1]—If a factory inspector is in doubt as to the physical fitness of a boy under 16 or of a girl under 18 years of age found working in, or in connection with, any of the establishments enumerated above, he shall require a certificate signed by a medical officer of board of health that such child is physically able to perform the work for which employed. Such certificate to be signed by the child in the presence of the officer issuing the same.

Filing of age and schooling certificates.[2]—Employer to keep on file age and schooling certificates for each child employee 14 to 16 years of age and to be produced for inspection upon request of the chief or district factory inspector or of a truant officer.

On termination of employment of child the certificate of said child to be returned forthwith by employer to person who issued it.

Register of children.[3]—Employer to keep a correct record, stating name, birthplace, date of birth, and place of residence of boys 14 to 16 years of age and of girls 14 to 18 years of age.

Penalties.[4]—On any person for employing, or permitting employment of, a child in violation of the above provisions, $25 to $50.

Enforcement.[5]—The State factory inspection service is charged with the general enforcement of the above-quoted provisions. Eight women visitors are added to the department to aid in the special work of enforcing the woman and child labor laws. Truant officers, also, are vested with authority to enter factories and see that children under 16 unable to read and write are not employed in violation of the law.

Inspectors are instructed to conduct forthwith to the office of the judge of the juvenile or probate court for examination any child working in, or in connection with, any of the above-mentioned establishments who may appear to be under legal age or who refuses to give to the inspector his or her name, age, and place of residence.

CONDITIONS FOUND.

Of the 60 establishments visited, all employed females 16 years of age and over and 31 employed children under 16 years of age. The number of such children employed was 383.

---

[1] Acts of 1908, p. 30, sec. 1 (Bulletin of the Bureau of Labor, No. 85, p. 702).

[2] Idem (Bulletin of the Bureau of Labor, No. 85, p. 701).

[3] Idem (Bulletin of the Bureau of Labor, No. 85, p. 702).

[4] Idem, sec. 3 (Bulletin of the Bureau of Labor, No. 85, p. 703).

[5] Idem, secs. 1 and 4 (Bulletin of the Bureau of Labor, No. 85, pp. 702–704) and Bates' Ann. Stat., 3d ed., Pt. II, Civ., sec. 4022–5 (22d An. Rept. Com. of Labor, p. 1007).

LEGAL AGE.

Individual slips containing inquiries as to age, sex, etc., were made out and signed by most of the children employed in the visited establishments.   In no case did a child signing such slip report itself as under 14 years of age.   These age reports were not verified.

PROHIBITED AND DANGEROUS EMPLOYMENTS.

In 3 of the 13 tobacco and cigar factories scheduled, females under 16 were found in "assorting, manufacturing, or packing tobacco."

In none of the factories visited were children reported as oiling or cleaning moving machines or as operating elevators.   In one, women (females 16 years of age and over) were reported as cleaning or oiling machinery in motion.

Females under 16 years of age were engaged at work requiring constant standing in a number of establishments, but complete data on this point were not obtained.

WORKING PAPERS.

Of the 31 establishments employing children under 16 years of age, 20 had age and schooling certificates on file for all children, 4 had no such certificates for any of the children employed, and 7 had more or less incomplete files.

REGISTERS.

Registers of children under 16 years of age were kept in a complete condition by 11 establishments, in an incomplete condition by 1, and were not kept at all by 19.   In 2 of the 12 cases where registers were kept, such registers or wall lists of names were posted in the workrooms.   The law requires the names of females 16 and 17 to be recorded in registers the same as for children under 16.   The information obtained did not cover this latter point except for 1 establishment, for which it was reported that the register included all females up to 18 years of age.

ILLINOIS.

SUMMARY OF LAWS.

LEGAL AGE.[1]

The legal age of employment is 14 years in any factory, workshop, mercantile establishment, office, etc.,[2] and no child under 14 may be employed legally at any gainful occupation during term of local public schools.

---

[1] Hurd's Rev. Stat., 1905, ch. 48, sec. 20 (22d An. Rept. Com. of Labor, p. 335).

[2] The full list of places to which this law applies is "Any theater, concert hall, or place of amusement where intoxicating liquors are sold, or in any mercantile institution, store, office, hotel, laundry, manufacturing establishment, bowling alley, passenger or freight elevator, factory or workshop or as a messenger or driver therefor."

Penalty.[1]—On person having control of child for permitting it to work under legal age, $5 to $25; on employer for employing child under legal age, $5 to $100.

Enforcement.[2]—Charged to State factory inspection department.

PROHIBITED EMPLOYMENTS.

Children under 16,[3] any of the following employments:

Sewing belts.

Adjusting belts to machinery.

Oiling, or assisting in oiling, wiping, or cleaning machinery.

Operating, or assisting in operating—

> Circular or band saws, wood shapers, wood jointers, planers, sandpaper or wood-polishing machinery.
>
> Emery or polishing wheels used for polishing metal.
>
> Wood turning or boring machinery.
>
> Stamping machines in sheet-metal and tinware manufacturing.
>
> Stamping machines in washer and nut factories.
>
> Corrugating rolls, such as are used in roofing factories.
>
> Passenger or freight elevators.
>
> Steam boiler, steam machinery, or other steam-generating apparatus.
>
> Dough brakes, or cracker machinery of any description.
>
> Wire or iron straightening machinery.
>
> Rolling-mill machinery, punches, or shears.
>
> Washing, grinding, or mixing mill or calender rolls in rubber manufacturing.
>
> Laundry machinery.

As pin boys in bowling alleys.

Preparing any composition in which dangerous or poisonous acids are used.

In the manufacture of paints, colors, or white lead.

In the manufacture of goods for immoral purposes.

In any employment dangerous to their lives or limbs, or where their health may be injured or their morals depraved.

In any theater, concert hall, or place of amusement, wherein intoxicating liquors are sold.

For females under 16,[4] any work requiring constant standing.

---

[1] Hurd's Rev. Stat., 1905, ch. 48, sec. 20m (22d An. Rept. Com of Labor, p. 339).

[2] Idem, sec. 20l (22d An. Rept. Com. of Labor, p. 339).

[3] Idem, sec. 20j (22d An. Rept. Com. of Labor, pp. 338, 339).

[4] Idem, sec. 20j (22d An. Rept. Com. of Labor, p. 338).

Penalties.[1]—On employer, $5 to $100; on person having control of child, $5 to $25.

Enforcement.[2]—Charged to State factory inspection department.

It is to be noted that in the above list of employments prohibited to children under 16 there occurs the clause "or any other employment that may be considered dangerous to their lives or limbs." This vests the inspection department with authority to increase the number of prohibited employments to include at least such other employments as it may develop are no less dangerous than those specifically mentioned.

WORKING PAPERS.[3]

A child between 14 and 16 years of age, in order to be legally employed in a factory, workshop, mercantile establishment, office, etc.,[4] must possess an "age and school certificate," certifying to its age and to either its ability to read and write or its attendance at evening school. The legal provisions regarding the contents, issue, etc., of such certificates and the keeping of registers by employers are as follows:

Contents and issue of age and school certificates.[5]—To be issued only by the superintendent of schools, or by a person authorized by him in writing, or where there is no such superintendent, by a person authorized by school board, or by superintendent or principal of a parochial school.

Such certificate not to be issued unless satisfactory evidence of age and schooling is presented. Evidence of age: (1) School census; (2) certificate of birth or baptism; (3) town or city register of birth; (4) records of public or parochial schools; (5) in cases where these are not available, the juvenile or county court, on oath of parent or guardian, may issue an age certificate. Evidence of schooling: (1) A school certificate, signed by parent, teacher, and principal, certifying as to grade in school, ability to read and write simple sentences, and age, date, and place of birth according to school records; (2) an evening school attendance certificate, signed by parent, teacher, and principal, certifying as to registration and regular attendance of child, and age, date, and place of birth according to school records.

---

[1] Hurd's Rev. Stat., 1905, ch. 48, sec. 20m (22d An. Rept. Com. of Labor, p. 339).

[2] Idem, sec. 201 (22d An. Rept. Com. of Labor, p. 339).

[3] Idem, secs. 20a to 20m, and idem, ch. 122, sec. 313 (as amended by act p. 520, Acts of 1907 (22d An. Rept. Com. of Labor, pp. 335–339, 374).

[4] The full list of places to which certificate law applies is the same as that to which the law regarding under-age employment applies (see ante, footnote 2 under the head Legal Age), with the omission of the words "where intoxicating liquors are sold" after the words "place of amusement." Idem, sec. 20c (22d An. Rept. Com. of Labor, p. 336).

[5] Hurd's Rev. Stat., ch. 48, secs. 20c to 20g (22d An. Rept. Com. of Labor, pp. 336–338).

In places where there are no evening schools and at times when such schools are not in session, age and school certificate not to be approved unless child can "read at sight and write legibly simple sentences." The certificate of a principal of a public or parochial school to be prima facie evidence as to the literacy of a child.

The parent or guardian must make oath as to the truth of the facts set forth in the age and school certificate.

Filing of certificates.[1]—Certificate is issued in duplicate, the copy being forwarded to State factory inspector and the original given to child and by the child surrendered to employer during term of employment.

Employer to keep age and school certificates on file and accessible to the members of the State factory inspection department. If child leaves employment and does not reclaim certificate within 30 days, employer to return same to school authorities.

Register of children.—(1) Employer to keep a register recording the names, ages, and places of residence of all child employees 14 to 16 years of age.[2]

(2) Employer to post and keep posted a list of the names, ages, and places of residence of children under 16 in every workroom where such children are employed.[3]

(3) Employer to keep a complete and correct list of all illiterate children under 16, unless such children are attending night school.[4]

Penalties.[5]—On parent, etc., for permitting child under 16 to work in violation of above provisions, $5 to $25; on employer, for failure to produce certificates, registers, and lists, $5 to $50; for noncompliance with above provisions, or obstructing inspectors, $5 to $100; on persons signing certificates, for any materially false statement, $5 to $100.

Enforcement.[6]—State factory inspection department charged with enforcement of these provisions. Inspectors to visit as often as possible all establishments and places enumerated above where minors are or may be employed and ascertain whether law is complied with.

Inspectors may require age and school certificates and lists of children to be produced.

---

[1] Hurd's Rev. Stat., 1905, ch. 48, secs. 20c to 20g (22d An. Rept. Com. of Labor, pp. 336–338).

[2] Idem, sec. 20a (22d An. Rept. Com. of Labor, pp. 335, 336).

[3] Idem, sec. 20b and sec. 26 (22d An. Rept. Com. of Labor, pp. 336, 340).

[4] Idem, sec. 20c (22d An. Rept. Com. of Labor, p. 336).

[5] Idem, sec. 20m (22d An. Rept. Com. of Labor, p. 339).

[6] Idem, secs. 20h and 20l (22d An. Rept. Com. of Labor, pp. 338, 339.)

On written complaint to school authorities that a child is anywhere employed contrary to this act, said authorities must report complaint to State inspector of factories.

CONDITIONS FOUND.

The number of establishments visited was 47. All of these employed women, but only 30 employed children under 16 years of age. The total number of such children was 692.

LEGAL AGE.

Individual slips containing inquiries as to age, sex, etc., were made out and signed by most of the children employed in the visited establishments. In no case did a child signing such slip report itself as under 14 years of age. These age reports were not verified.

PROHIBITED AND DANGEROUS EMPLOYMENTS.

In none of the factories visited were children under 16 found to clean or oil machinery in motion. In two, however, children were reported as cleaning machinery while stationary, and in three females 16 years of age and over were accustomed to cleaning and oiling machinery while such machinery was moving, the machines so oiled or cleaned being looms in two woolen mills and a wrapping machine in a chewing-gum factory. In the latter case the work was done by a forewoman only.

In a number of the establishments visited females under 16 were engaged in occupations requiring constant standing, but no complete data were obtained upon this subject.

With the exceptions noted above no children under 16 were found to be engaged at any of the employments mentioned in the law quoted above. In a number of cases, however, children were found working at machines which, although evidently dangerous, are not specifically included by law among prohibited occupations. Among such dangerous machines may be mentioned squaring shears, embossing press, creasing and cutting press, corner cutter, ender, stayer, and punch presses.

WORKING PAPERS.

Of the 30 establishments employing children under 16 years of age, 22 had complete files of age and school certificates, 1 had no such certificates on file, and 7 had more or less incomplete files.

Registers of children, fully complete, were kept by 18 of these 30 establishments, in incomplete condition by 3, and not kept at all by 9. In 20 of the 21 establishments in which registers were kept, such registers were posted in the workroom where children were employed.

INDIANA.

SUMMARY OF LAWS.

LEGAL AGE.[1]

The legal age of employment is 14 years in "any manufacturing or mercantile establishment, mine, quarry, laundry, renovating works, bakery, or printing office." [2]

> *Penalty.*—For employing or permitting the employment of child under legal age, first offense, not more than $50; second offense, not more than $100, to which may be added not more than 10 days' imprisonment; third offense, not less than $250 and not more than 30 days' imprisonment.

Enforcement.—Charged to the factory inspection department.

PROHIBITED EMPLOYMENTS.[3]

Males under 16 and females under 18, the cleaning of machinery in motion.

Persons under 18, the operation of elevators.

> *Penalty.*—First offense, not more than $50; second offense, not more than $100, to which may be added imprisonment for not more than 10 days; third offense, not less than $250, and not more than 30 days' imprisonment.

Enforcement.—By the State factory inspection department.

---

[1] Ann. Stats. of 1894, Rev. of 1901, secs. 7087b, 7087v, and 7087y (22d An. Rept. Com. of Labor, pp. 397, 402).

[2] Defined more fully by law as "any mill, factory, workshop, store, place of trade, or other establishment where goods, wares, or merchandise are manufactured or offered for sale, or any mine or quarry where coal and stone are mined and quarried for the market, and persons are employed for hire. Idem, sec. 7087r (22d An. Rept. Com. of Labor, p. 401).

[3] Ann. Stat. of 1894, Rev. of 1901, secs. 7087d, 7087i, 7087r, 7087v, and 7087y (22d An. Rept. Com. of Labor, pp. 398, 399, 401, 402).

The employment of children is prohibited at acrobatic, mendicant, and immoral practices, or in "any vocation injurious to the health or dangerous to the life and limb." The context of this section of the law would indicate that the prohibition contained in the clause quoted was not intended to refer to the customary dangers involved in factory and workshop occupations. Idem, secs. 2241, 2242, and 2243 (22d An. Rept. Com. of Labor, pp. 380, 381).

WORKING PAPERS.

Children under 16 years of age may not be employed in any of the mentioned establishments (1) unless an affidavit certifying to the age of such child is provided; (2) unless, if the chief factory inspector demands, a medical certificate of physical ability to perform the work is obtained; and (3) except during the vacation of the public schools, unless such child can "read and write simple sentences in the English language."

The legal provisions regarding the contents, issue, etc., of such certificates and the keeping of registers are condensed below.

Age certificates.[1]—Required for children 14 to 16 employed in manufacturing establishments, etc. (as enumerated in preceding section). Affidavit (certificate) to be made by parent or guardian to state the age, date, and place of birth of child; if child has no parent or guardian affidavit to be made by child itself.

Medical certificates.[2]—The chief factory inspector may demand a certificate of physical fitness from some regular physician in the case of children who may seem physically unable to perform the work at which employed, and may prohibit the employment of any child who can not obtain such a certificate.

Filing of age certificates.[3]—Employer required to keep age certificates on file, and produce the same on demand of the factory inspector.

The duty of obtaining a certificate devolves absolutely upon the employer, and the parents' failure to inform him of the age of a child unlawfully employed is no excuse.[4]

Register of children.[5]—(1) Employer to keep a register of children under 16, showing name, birthplace, age, and place of residence of each such child, and to produce said register on demand of factory inspector.

(2) Employer to keep posted conspicuously in every room where children under 16 are employed a list of their names, with their ages.

Penalties.[6]—Any person failing to comply with the above-quoted provisions: First offense, not more than $50; second offense, not more than $100, to which may be added not more than 10 days' imprisonment; third offense, not less than $250 and not more than 30 days' imprisonment.

---

[1] Ann. Stat. of 1894, Rev. of 1901, sec. 7087b (22d An. Rept. Com. of Labor, p. 397).

[2] Idem, sec. 7087b (22d An. Rept. Com. of Labor, p. 398).

[3] Idem, sec. 7087b (22d An. Rept. Com. of Labor, pp. 397, 398).

[4] 71 N. E. Rep. 922 (22d An. Rept. Com. of Labor, p. 398).

[5] Ann. Stat. of 1894, Rev. of 1901, sec. 7087b (22d An. Rept. Com. of Labor, pp. 397, 398).

[6] Idem, sec. 7087y (22d An. Rept. Com. of Labor, p. 402).

Enforcement.[1]—The State factory inspection department is instructed to enforce the above-quoted provisions.

CONDITIONS FOUND.

The number of establishments visited in Indiana was 47. Of these, 46 employed females 16 years of age and over, and 40 employed children under 16 years of age. The total number of such children was 1,056.

LEGAL AGE.

Individual slips containing inquiries as to age, sex, etc., were made out and signed by most of the children employed in the visited establishments. In no case did a child signing such slip report itself as under 14 years of age. These age reports were not verified.

PROHIBITED AND DANGEROUS EMPLOYMENTS.

No instance was found of a child under 18 years of age operating an elevator.

In 3 of the 41 establishments having power-driven machinery it was found that cleaning or oiling of moving machinery was done by women and children, in 1 by women but not by children, and in 1 by children but not by women. The machines cleaned or oiled were sewing machines, circular knitters, knitting machines, joining machines, and cold rolls.

WORKING PAPERS.

Of the 40 establishments employing children 14 to 16 years of age, 19 had complete files of age certificates, 6 had no certificates on file, and the remaining 15 had more or less incomplete files. In 1 establishment 2 children under 16 years of age were employed who could not read or write.

REGISTERS.

Registers of children were kept in a complete condition by 15 of the 40 establishments in which children were employed, in an incomplete condition by one other, and were not kept at all in 24 establishments. In 9 of the 16 cases in which registers were kept, wall lists of names were kept posted in workrooms where children were at work. No wall lists were posted in the 31 remaining establishments in which children were employed.

The affidavit system is greatly abused throughout the State, so abused, in fact, that with little or no difficulty a child of any age may secure an affidavit. Frequently the notaries make no effort to secure proof of age, and it has been stated that many notaries, when exe-

---

[1] Ann. Stat. of 1894, Rev. of 1901, sec. 7087v (22d An. Rept. Com. of Labor, p. 402).

cuting an affidavit, begin with the age given by the child and from this supply the date of birth. The practice of falsifying ages is so general as to be spoken of everywhere. Blank certificates are kept in stock by many firms. Often the bookkeeper or other official of the company is the notary who fills out the blanks for the children employed. In one of the establishments visited several children were found to be working without certificates, and when the fact was called to the attention of the bookkeeper she replied, "I am a notary, so execute all affidavits for the children employed. I'll just fill them out and have them taken home to be signed to-night." When asked whether she did not require the parents to appear before her and take oath as to the age given, she said in a surprised tone, "Is that necessary?"

MICHIGAN.

SUMMARY OF LAWS.

LEGAL AGE.[1]

The legal age of employment is 14 years in "any mercantile institution, store, office, hotel, laundry, manufacturing establishment, passenger or freight elevator, factory or workshop, telegraph or messenger service." [2]

> *Penalty.*—For employing, or permitting employment of child under legal age, $5 to $100, or imprisonment 10 to 90 days, or both.
>
> *Enforcement.*—Charged to State factory inspection department.

PROHIBITED EMPLOYMENTS.

Males under 18 and females under 21, the cleaning of machinery in motion, or at any work whereby life or limb is endangered or health likely to be injured or morals depraved.

> *Penalty,* $5 to $100, or imprisonment 10 to 90 days, or both.[3]

---

[1] Acts of 1901, act No. 113, sec. 2 (as amended by act No. 169, Acts of 1907), sec. 12 and sec. 18. (22d An. Rept. Com. of Labor, pp. 658, 660, 662.)

[2] Within the meaning of the terms herein used are "all places where goods, wares, or products are manufactured, repaired, cleaned, or sorted." Idem, sec. 14 (as amended by act No. 46, Acts of 1903).

Later law: By the consolidating act of 1909, act No. 285, sec. 10, the legal age limit of 14 was made to apply also to bowling alleys, mines, and theaters. (Bulletin of the Bureau of Labor, No. 85, p. 636.)

[3] Acts of 1901, act No. 113, sec. 3 (as amended by act No. 169, Acts of 1907), and sec. 18 (22d An. Rept. Com. of Labor, pp. 659, 662). By the consolidated labor law of 1909, act No. 285 (Bulletin of the Bureau of Labor, No. 85, p. 640), the minimum fine for violation was increased to $10. Also by this law the employment of such persons was specifically forbidden in distilleries, breweries, or other places where malt or alcoholic liquors are manufactured, packed, wrapped, or bottled; and it was directed that females should not be "unnecessarily required in any employment to remain standing constantly."

Females, all ages, the operation of "wheels or emery belts of any description, either leather, leather covered, felt, canvas, paper, cotton, or wheels or belts rolled or coated with emery or corundum, or cotton wheels used as buffs."

Penalty.—$25 to $100, or imprisonment 30 to 90 days, or both.[1]

The prohibition against emery-wheel grinding by females is specific, and as it applies to all females, should involve no difficulty in its enforcement. The prohibition against cleaning moving machinery is also specific, but, as it applies only to males under 18 and females under 21, involves, in its enforcement, the difficulty of determining when persons are of these ages, as the law makes no provision for legally establishing the ages of persons over 16 years of age.

The prohibition that no males under 18 and no females under 21 shall be employed at any work in which "his or her life or limb is endangered" clearly applies, as shown by its context, to the dangers incident to machinery. The precise employments to be considered dangerous, however, are not specified. The determination thereof is presumably left to the inspection department.

Enforcement.[2]—The factory inspection department is charged with enforcing the above prohibitions relative to cleaning moving machinery and employments dangerous to life and limb.

The prohibition against the employment of females at emery belts and grinding wheels is to be enforced by factory inspectors, sheriffs, constables, and county prosecuting attorneys, who, on complaint, are to investigate, and if law is violated are to notify justice of peace or police magistrate, the latter to issue warrant, prosecuting to be done by prosecuting attorney.

WORKING PAPERS.

A child of 14 but under 16 years of age must have its age and literacy established by sworn statement before it may be lawfully employed in a manufacturing establishment, factory, workshop, store, etc. (as listed in full in section on "Legal age," above). Also, in cases of doubtful physical fitness, a medical certificate may be demanded by a factory inspector.

---

[1] Acts of 1899, act No. 202, sec. 7 (added by act No. 172, Acts of 1905) and sec. 6 (22d An. Rept. Com. of Labor, pp. 653, 654). By the consolidated labor law of 1909, act No. 285, the penalty for violating this act was changed to $10 to $100, or imprisonment 10 to 90 days, or both.

[2] Acts of 1901, act No. 113, sec. 12, and Acts of 1899, act No. 202, sec. 5 (22d An. Rept. Com. of Labor, pp. 654, 660).

The legal provisions regarding the character of such sworn statements, etc., and the keeping of registers by employers are briefly as follows:[1]

Contents and issue of permits (sworn statements).[2]—The sworn statement (which serves as an employment permit) is to be made by the parent or guardian, to state age and date and place of birth of child and that the child is able to read and write English. In the case of a foreign-born child, resident of the United States for less than three years, a permit for employment to be issued to it on proof that it can read and write. Finally, if child has no parent or guardian, the statement referred to is to be made by the child itself. In Detroit and Grand Rapids all sworn statements must be made before a deputy factory inspector.

Medical certificates.[3]—Any factory inspector may demand a certificate of physical fitness from the county physician in the case of any child under 16 who seems to him physically incapable of performing the work for which employed, and may prohibit employment of any child that can not obtain such a certificate.

Filing of permits (statements).[4]—Employer to keep sworn statements (permits) for all children employed on file, subject to examination of factory inspector on demand.

---

[1] By an act of 1909, act No. 285, the requirements relative to working papers for children were very considerably changed in the direction of making them more stringent. (See Bulletin of the Bureau of Labor, No. 85, pp. 636–638.) The following is a brief synopsis of the new law:

Employment permit to be issued only by (1) superintendent of schools, or some one duly authorized by him; (2) a State employment bureau; (3) probate judge in county, or (4) judge of juvenile court in city.

The permit to be issued only on proof of satisfactory schooling and age. Proof of schooling to consist of school record, certifying regular attendance of 100 days during year previous to 14th birthday or to application for permit, ability to read and write simple sentences in English, instruction in reading, writing, spelling, English grammar, and geography, and is familiar with fundamental operations of arithmetic up to and including fractions. Such school record to be signed by chief executive officer of the school, and to give age and residence of child as given on records of school, and name of parent, guardian, or custodian. Proof of age to consist of passport or duly attested transcript of record of birth, or if no such official proof is obtainable, the affidavit of parent or guardian (or child itself if it has no parent or guardian) as to date and place of birth of child, accompanied, if possible, by certificate of physician or midwife attending at such birth. Also, there must be a statement of issuing official that he has examined the child and believes it can read and write English, is 14 years of age or upward, is normally developed, is able to perform the work intended, and that its working.is "essential to the support of itself or its parents." In doubtful cases, physical fitness to be determined by medical officer of board of health.

[2] Acts of 1901, act No. 113, sec. 2 (as amended by act No. 169, Acts of 1907) (22d An. Rept. Com. of Labor, pp. 658, 659).

[3] Idem, sec. 4 (22d An. Rept. Com. of Labor, p. 659).

[4] Idem, sec. 2 (as amended by act No. 169, acts of 1907) (22d An. Rept. Com. of Labor, pp. 658, 659).

Register of children.[1]—Employer to keep a register, recording the name, birthplace, age, and place of residence of every child under 16 years of age. Said register to be subject to examination of factory inspector on demand.

    Penalty.[2]—For employing or permitting the employment of a child in violation of the above-mentioned provisions, $5 to $100, or imprisonment 10 to 90 days, or both.

    Enforcement.[3]—Rests upon the factory inspection department.

CONDITIONS FOUND.

All of the 19 establishments visited in Michigan employed females 16 years of age and over, and 14 also employed children under 16 years of age. The number of such children was 580.

LEGAL AGE.

Individual slips containing inquiries as to age, sex, etc., were made out and signed by most of the children employed in the visited establishments. In no case did a child signing such slip report itself as under 14 years of age. These age reports were not verified.

PROHIBITED AND DANGEROUS EMPLOYMENTS.

In none of the establishments visited were children under 16 or women found to clean or oil machinery in motion. No information was obtained as to whether males 16 to 18 engaged in such work.

No instance was found of a female operating grinding wheels of any kind.

WORKING PAPERS.

Sworn statements of age, etc. (which serve as employment permits), were on file for all children under 16 years of age in 5 of the 14 establishments where children were employed. Each of the other 9 establishments had incomplete files of such statements.

In one establishment several of the age statements on file were acknowledged before the secretary of the company; some of these were made in pencil and were lacking in date, notarial seal, etc.

In one establishment in which age statements were on file for only one of three child employees, the other two children stated that they had such statements at home, but had never been directed to bring them to the office.

In a third establishment in which statements were reported as on file for 42 of 63 children, the head bookkeeper stated that statements for the remaining 21 children had been obtained and were in the office, but could not be found at the time.

---

[1] Acts of 1901, act No. 113, sec. 2 (as amended by act No. 169, acts of 1907) (22d An. Rept. Com. of Labor, pp. 658, 659).

[2] Idem, sec. 18 (22d An. Rept. Com. of Labor, p. 662).

[3] Idem, sec. 12 (22d An. Rept. Com. of Labor, p. 660).

REGISTERS.

Registers showing name, etc., of all child employees were on file in 4 of the 14 establishments where children were employed and were not on file in the remaining 10. In none of the 4 establishments where registers were kept were such registers posted in the workrooms.

WISCONSIN.

SUMMARY OF LAWS.

LEGAL AGE.

Children under 14 years of age are forbidden employment "in any factory, workshop, bowling alley, or in or about any mine." Also, such children may not be employed lawfully at any other "gainful occupation," except that, during the vacations of the public schools, children 12 years of age and under 14, if they obtain vacation permits, may be employed "in any store, office, hotel, mercantile establishment, telegraph, telephone, or public messenger service." None of these restrictions, however, are to apply to "farming or other outdoor occupations not dangerous to life or limb." [1]

> *Penalty.*[2]—On parent or guardian, $5 to $25, or not more than 30 days' imprisonment; on employer, $25 to $100, or not more than 30 days' imprisonment.
>
> *Enforcement.*[3]—Charged to State factory inspection department.

PROHIBITED EMPLOYMENTS.

Children under 16, any of the following:[4]
> Sewing belts.
> Adjusting belts.
> Oiling, or assisting in oiling, wiping, or cleaning machinery in motion.
> Operating, or assisting in operating—
>> Circular or band saws, wood shaper, wood jointer, planer, sandpaper, or wood-polishing machinery.
>> Picker machine or machines used in picking wool, cotton, hair, or any upholstering material.
>> Paper-lacing machine.
>> Leather-burnishing machine.

---

[1] Ann. Stat., 1898, Supp. of 1906, Acts of 1907, secs. 1728a—3 and 1728a—4 (22d An. Rept. Com. of Labor, pp. 1426, 1427).

[2] Idem, secs. 1728h and 1728i (22d An. Rept. Com. of Labor, p. 1428).

[3] Idem, sec. 1728d (22d An. Rept. Com. of Labor, p. 1428). For street trades see Acts of 1909, secs. 1728p to 1728–Z-a (Bulletin of the Bureau of Labor, No. 85, pp. 806-808.)

[4] Idem, sec. 1728a—2 (22d An. Rept. Com. of Labor, p 1426).

Dough brakes or cracker machinery of any description.

Laundry machinery.

Emery or polishing wheel for polishing metal.

Wood turning machine.

Stamping machine in sheet metal and tinware manufacturing.

Stamping machine in washer and nut factories.

Stamping machine in lace paper and leather manufacturing.

Corrugating rolls in roofing factories.

Burnishing machines in any tannery or leather manufactory.

Wire or iron straightening machinery.

Rolling mill machinery, punches, or shears.

Washing, grinding, or mixing mill.

Calendar rolls in rubber manufacturing.

In the manufacture of paints, colors, or white lead.

In the manufacture of any composition in which dangerous or poisonous acids are used.

In the manufacture of any goods for immoral purposes.

In any tobacco warehouse, cigar, or other factory where tobacco is manufactured or prepared.

In any place where intoxicating liquors are made, given away, or sold.

In any theater or concert hall.

In operating any passenger or freight elevator, steam boiler, or steam generating apparatus.

Or in any other employment dangerous to life or limb, injurious to the health or depraving of the morals of such child.

Females under 16, any work requiring constant standing.

Penalty.[1]—On parent or guardian, $5 to $25, or imprisonment not more than 30 days; on employer, $25 to $100, or imprisonment not more than 30 days.

Enforcement.—Charged to State factory inspection department.[2]

The full force of the last clause of the above list referring to all children under 16, "or in any other employment dangerous to life or limb, etc.," can not be determined in advance. Such a clause, however, would seem to vest the factory inspection department with sufficient authority to prohibit the employment of children at such other occupations as experience may demonstrate are as dangerous as any of those mentioned by name in the list.

---

[1] Ann. Stat. of 1898, Supp. of 1906, Acts of 1907, sec. 1728h and 1728i (22d An. Rept. Com. of Labor, p. 1428).

[2] Idem, sec. 1728d (22d An. Rept. Com. of Labor, p. 1428).

WORKING PAPERS.

Children 14 years of age, but under 16, must possess a work permit or certificate in order to be employed lawfully in "any factory or workshop, bowling alley, or in or about any mine," or (with certain exceptions as regards vacation work as noted above in section on legal age) in any "store, hotel, mercantile establishment, laundry, telegraph, telephone, or public messenger service."

The legal provisions regarding the contents, issue, etc., of such certificates, and the keeping of registers by employers, are summarized below:[1]

Contents and issue of work permits.—Authority to issue permits (both regular work and vacation permits) is given to the following persons: Commissioner of labor, State factory inspector, assistant factory inspectors, judge of county court, judge of municipal court, judge of juvenile court, and register of probate of the city, town, or district where the child applicant resides. The power of granting permits may not be delegated. No work permit may be granted to any child "unable to read and write simple sentences in the English language or the language of his native country."[1]

When the issuing official has reason to doubt the age of a child applicant, proof of age may be demanded—baptismal certificate or birth certificate; in absence thereof, the record of first school enrollment; and if none of these data are available "such other proof as may be satisfactory" to the issuing official.[1]

Permit to be revoked when it appears that it has been obtained by false statement as to age.[2]

The commissioner of labor, the factory inspector, or assistant factory inspector may refuse to grant permits in the case of children

---

[1] Ann. Stat. of 1898, Supp. of 1906, Acts of 1907, sec. 1728 to 1728j (22d An. Rept. Com. of Labor, pp. 1425–1429). By an act in force shortly after the close of the field work of this investigation in Wisconsin (Acts of 1909, approved June 10, 1909 (Bulletin of the Bureau of Labor, No. 85, pp. 805, 806), some brief but important changes are made in the law as quoted in the text above. These are as follows:

1. Regular work permits are required in all "gainful occupations."

2. A written and signed recommendation of the school principal where the child attended school, or of the clerk of the board of education if there is no principal, is required before a work permit can be issued.

3. Authority to issue permits is withdrawn from the "register of probate."

4. The exception as regards the employment of children 12 to 14 in "farming or other outdoor occupation not dangerous to life or limb" is amended by striking out all after the word "farming."

5. Truant officers are authorized to visit factories, inspect registers, etc., and factory inspectors are given the power of truant officers to enforce laws regarding school attendance. This group of officials—factory inspectors and truant officers—is charged with the enforcement of all State statutes relative to child labor.

[2] Idem, secs. 1728a—1 and 1728a—6 (22d An. Rept. Com. of Labor, pp. 1426, 1427).

who may seem physically unable to perform the labor at which they are employed.[1]

Officials issuing work permits must keep a record thereof, showing name, date, and place of birth and place of school attended by any such child, and the county, municipal, and juvenile judges and registers of probate must report number of permits issued by them, when so requested by the commissioner of labor or factory inspector.[2]

Filing of permits.[3]—Employer must provide and keep on file permits for all children employed under 16 years of age.

Register of children.[4]—Employer of children under 16 in any of the earlier enumerated employments (except "farming and other outdoor occupations") to keep a register showing name, age, date of birth, and residence of all such children, and to produce said register on demand of factory inspectors.

Penalties.[5]—On parent or guardian for permitting a child to be employed in violation of the above legal provisions, $5 to $25, or imprisonment not more than 30 days; on employer, for violating these provisions or obstructing factory inspectors, $25 to $100, or not more than 30 days' imprisonment.

Enforcement.[6]—All the above-mentioned legal provisions are charged in full to the State factory inspection department. Truant officers are given authority to visit places of employment, investigate violations of the child labor laws, and report same to the local school authorities and to the State factory inspection department.

CONDITIONS FOUND.

All of the 19 establishments visited in Wisconsin employed females 16 years of age and over, and 12 of them also employed children under 16 years of age. The total number of such children was 446.

LEGAL AGE.

Individual slips containing inquiries as to age, sex, etc., were made out and signed by most of the children employed in the visited establishments. In no case did a child signing such slip report itself as under 14 years of age. These age reports were not verified.

[1] Ann. Stat. of 1898, Supp. of 1906, Acts of 1907, sec. 1728e (22d An. Rept. Com. of Labor, p. 1428).

[2] Idem, sec. 1728a5 (22d An. Rept. Com. of Labor, p. 1427).

[3] Idem, sec. 1428b2 (22d An. Rept. Com. of Labor, pp. 1427, 1428).

[4] Idem, sec. 1428b1 (22d An. Rept. Com. of Labor, p. 1427).

[5] Idem, sec. 1728h and 1728i (22d An. Rept. Com. of Labor, p. 1428).

[6] Idem, secs. 439ca, 1728d (22d An. Rept. Com. of Labor, pp. 1402, 1428).

PROHIBITED AND DANGEROUS EMPLOYMENTS.

In none of the establishments visited were children under 16 found cleaning or oiling moving machinery, or operating elevators. In one females 16 and over did clean or oil moving machinery. This was a button factory and the machines in question were grinding machines and countersinking machines.

In 10 of the 12 establishments in which female children under 16 were employed, such children were employed in occupations requiring practically constant standing.

WORKING PAPERS.

Work permits were on file for all child employees in 11 of the 12 establishments employing children. In the one remaining establishment the file was incomplete.

REGISTERS.

Registers showing names, residences, etc., of child employees were kept on file by only one of the 12 establishments employing children. In this case the register was kept in the office.

MARYLAND.

SUMMARY OF LAWS.

LEGAL AGE.[1]

The legal age of employment is 12 years in "any mill, factory, workshop, office, restaurant, hotel, apartment house, store, telephone or telegraph office, or other establishment or business," except in the counties, from June 1 to October 15.

> *Penalty.*—On employer, for employing child under legal age, and on person having control of child under legal age for permitting it to work, $5 to $50; on employer for continuing such employment after notification, $5 to $20 per day.
>
> *Enforcement.*—Charged to the chief of the State bureau of statistics and information, acting through child labor inspectors, and to the attendance officers of the public schools.

PROHIBITED EMPLOYMENTS.

Children under 16,[2] in handling intoxicating liquors or packages containing such liquors, in breweries or bottling establishments.

> *Penalty*, $10 to $100.

---

[1] Pub. Gen. Laws, Code of 1903, art. 100, sec. 4, as amended by ch. 192, Acts of 1906, and secs. 9, 10, and 11, added by ch. 192, Acts of 1906 (22d An. Rept. Com. of Labor, pp. 549, 551, 552).

[2] Idem, art. 27, secs. 311, 312 (22d An. Rept. Com. of Labor, p. 542).

The law does not cover the subject of cleaning or oiling machinery.

WORKING PAPERS.

A child of 12 but under 16 years of age, in order to be employed lawfully in "any mill, factory, workshop, office, restaurant, hotel, apartment house, store, telephone or telegraph office, or other establishment or business" (except in the counties from June 1 to October 15) must possess an employment permit. The legal provisions regarding the contents, issue, etc., of such permits, and the keeping of registers by employers are briefly as follows:

Contents and issue of employment permits.[1]—To be issued, for employment in Baltimore City, by the State bureau of statistics and information; for employment outside of Baltimore City, by the board of health or principal health officer of the city or county.

Certificate shall not be issued unless satisfactory evidence of age is furnished. Evidence to consist of duly attested transcript of the certificate of birth or baptism, or other religious records, or the register of birth. In the absence of such record of birth the affidavit of the person having control of child is to be accepted, provided absence of such record is certified to by the proper authorities.

The form of the employment permit is prescribed by law. It provides for a statement of name, age, date and place of birth of child, and is to be sworn to by the person having control of child. Also, it is to be signed by the issuing official, with a statement of the child's height, color of eyes, complexion, color of hair, and that it can read at sight and write legibly simple sentences in English, is of normal development, of sound health, and physically able to perform the work intended.

The birth certificate, or a certificate from proper authorities that there is no birth record, to be attached to each certificate.

A duplicate of each employment permit is to be filled out and kept on file by the issuing official.

Filing of permits.[2]—Employer of children 12 to 16 years of age in establishments mentioned above is required to keep an employment permit for each such child on file and accessible to the child labor inspectors and the attendance officers.

The permit is the property of the child, and if not demanded by it within 30 days of termination of its employment shall be returned by employer to office of issue.

---

[1] Pub. Gen. Laws, Code of 1903, art. 100, secs. 5 to 8, added by ch. 192, Acts of 1906 (22d An. Rept. Com. of Labor, pp. 550, 551).

[2] Idem (22d An. Rept. Com. of Labor, p. 550).

Register of children.[1]—Employer of children 12 to 16 in establishments mentioned above to keep a complete list (register) of all such children on file, and in the case of children employed in factories, workshops, mills, or messenger service, a duplicate of such list to be conspicuously posted near the principal entrance of building in which such children are employed.

> *Penalty.*[2]—On employer for employing child in violation of the above provisions, or on person having control of child for permitting it to so work, $5 to $50; on employer for continuing to employ child after notified by an inspector or attendance officer not to do so, $5 to $20 per day; on employer for retaining a permit in violation of the law, $10; on any person for knowingly certifying to any materially false statement in a permit, not more than $50.

> *Enforcement.*[3]—Charged to the chief of the State bureau of statistics and information, acting through child-labor inspectors, and to the attendance officers of the public schools.

CONDITIONS FOUND.

The number of establishments visited was 28. Each of these employed both females 16 years of age and over and children under 16 years of age. The total number of such children was 802.

LEGAL AGE.

Individual slips containing inquiries as to age, sex, etc., were made out and signed by most of the children employed in the visited establishments. In no case did a child signing such slip report itself as under 12 years of age. These age reports were not verified.

PROHIBITED AND DANGEROUS EMPLOYMENTS.

No breweries or bottling establishments were visited in Maryland, and thus no data obtained as to the employment of children therein.

The law does not prohibit women or children to clean or oil moving machinery, but no cases were found of children under 16 being so employed, and in only one establishment were females 16 years of age and over found to be so employed. This was a shirt-making establishment, in which a woman was found cleaning a collar-ironing machine in motion.

---

[1] Pub. Gen. Laws, Code of 1903, art. 100, sec. 5, added by ch. 192, Acts of 1906 (22d An. Rept. Com. of Labor, p. 550).

[2] Idem, sec. 9 (as added by ch. 192, acts of 1906) (22d An. Rept. Com. of Labor, p. 551).

[3] Idem, secs. 10 and 11 (as added by ch. 192, Acts of 1906) (22d An. Rept. Com. of Labor, pp. 551, 552).

WORKING PAPERS.

Of the 28 establishments visited, all of which employed children 12 to 16 years of age, 8 had complete files of employment certificates, 4 had no such certificates on file, and 16 had more or less incomplete files.

REGISTERS.

Registers of such children were kept by 18 establishments and not kept by 10. Of the 18 in which registers were kept, such registers (or wall lists) were posted in the workrooms where children were employed in 4 cases and were not posted in 13; in the remaining establishments information was not secured upon this point. Also, no information was secured as to whether or not registers were kept conspicuously posted near the principal entrance, as required by law in the case of all factories.

NORTH CAROLINA.

SUMMARY OF LAWS.

LEGAL AGE.[1]

The legal age of employment is 12 years in any "factory or manufacturing establishment;" except that children of 12 but under 13 years of age may be employed as apprentices if they have had four months' school attendance during the preceding year.

> *Penalty.*—On employer who "knowingly or willfully" violates the above provision, as for a misdemeanor, at the discretion of the court.

PROHIBITED EMPLOYMENTS.

There are no employments prohibited to children of legal age.

WORKING PAPERS.[2]

As regards this subject the law provides simply that—

All parents, or persons standing in relation of parent, upon hiring their children to any factory or manufacturing establishment, shall furnish such establishment a written statement of the age of such child or children being so hired, and certificate as to school attendance. * * *

---

[1] Acts of 1907, ch. 463, secs. 1 and 3 (22d An. Rept. Com. of Labor, pp. 970, 971). This act seems to supersede former act (Rev. of 1905, sec. 3362 (22d An. Rept. Com. of Labor, p. 962), which differs from it as regards legal age only in that it excepts "oyster canning and packing manufactories where * * * opening or shucking oysters" is paid for "by the gallon or bushel."

[2] Idem, sec. 3. Also see Rev. of 1905, sec. 3364, for a substantially similar law, which was apparently superseded, although not specifically repealed, by the one quoted in the text. (22d An. Rept. Com. of Labor, pp. 962, 971.)

Penalty.—On parent for misstatement of age òr school attendance in such statement; and on employer for "knowingly or willfully" violating any provision "of this act," as for a misdemeanor, at the discretion of the court.

A reading of the above provision shows that while age and school attendance proofs are required as a condition of employment, the law omits to state up to what age such proofs are to be necessary. If the term "children" is construed to mean persons under 21, the law on this one point is unusually stringent. However, it is so construed very rarely—only by one of the several establishments visited during this investigation. Usually it is interpreted simply as requiring age statements for children under 13 years, and when this is done the requirement is reduced to little more than one of having age statements for children of the specific age of 12 employed as apprentices.

The law does not specifically require employers to keep age statements, once obtained, on file, although this requirement may possibly be inferred.

Registers or lists of the names, etc., of child employees are not required to be kept.

CONDITIONS FOUND.

UNDER-AGE EMPLOYMENT.

As noted above, the law prohibits the employment of children under 12 years of age absolutely, and of children under 13 except when employed in an apprenticeship capacity.

In 17 of the 28 establishments visited a total of 116 children under 13 was found employed. Forty-nine of these children, representing 8 establishments, were under 12 years of age. The other 67 children, representing 15 establishments, were between 12 and 13 years of age. Most of the children under 12 years of age, and many of those of 12, were "helpers"—i. e., working for their parents or other relatives, not on the company's books and not paid by company. None of the establishments reported such "helpers" as employees, but most of them facilitated the agents of the Bureau in the effort to obtain information regarding such children. The opinion was general that the establishment kept within the pale of the law by keeping the names of helpers off the pay rolls and ignoring their presence in the factory. Some of the helpers worked regularly full time; others worked only before and after school hours and on Saturday.

The employment of children 12 years of age but under 13, of whom 47 were found in this investigation, introduces the question of apprenticeship.

Under the North Carolina statute governing apprenticeship, an apprentice is an infant under 21 years of age, without means of support, bound out for a term of not less than 3 years to learn a trade or handicraft; the master agreeing to teach such trade or craft, to provide food, clothes, lodging, and medical attendance, to teach the child, if ignorant thereof, reading, writing, and the rules of arithmetic to the double rule of three, etc.[1]

In none of the establishments employing children 13 years of age did the employer claim that such children were apprentices within the meaning of this statute. A few—3 cotton mills and 1 woolen mill—held that as the children were beginners they were apprentices in a secondary meaning of the word. The others stated that such children could not properly be considered as apprentices. Several considered the apprenticeship clause of the law as absurd on its face, and as being only a cloak to evade the 12-year limit, and one expressed an opinion that there were no real apprentices in either the tobacco or cotton industries, and no place for apprentices in tobacco or cotton factories except in the machine repairing shops.

PROHIBITED AND DANGEROUS EMPLOYMENTS.

There are, as noted above, no employments prohibited to children of legal age.

In 2 of the establishments visited children under 16 oiled or cleaned moving machinery. One of these cases was that of a boy oiling spinning frames in a cotton mill. The other was that of a boy oiling knitting machines in a knit-goods establishment.

The legal provisions forbidding the employment of children without written age statements by parents or those standing in the place of parents does not specify up to what age such statements are to be required.

Nearly all the employers visited construed the law as applying only to children under 13 years of age. That is to say, if a child applying for work appeared to be not more than 13 years old an age statement should be required; that, if such statement showed child to be under 12 years of age, it should be dismissed; and that if statement showed child to be 12 years of age it might be employed under the apprenticeship clause.

A very few of the establishments extended the requirement to all young children under, say, 16 years of age; but most of them made such requirement only in case of children whose appearance might indicate they were under 13. One factory claimed that it demanded age statements of employees up to 21 years old, but on examination this proved to have been done partly at least in order to have every employee sign away back pay in case he or she should leave the mill without due notice.

---

[1] Revisal of 1905, ch. 4 (22d An. Rept. Com. of Labor, p. 27).

Of the 28 establishments visited, 18 did and 10 did not require age statements for child applicants. Of the 10 that did not require statements, 7 were employing children under 13 at the time of investigation. Of the 18 that did require statements, 10 were employing children under 13.

Of the 15 establishments employing children of 12 years of age and under 13 (which under the usual construction of the law is legal), 8 required age statements, and 7 did not make such requirement.

The law regarding age statements requires such statements to contain also a certificate of school attendance. The amount of school attendance required is not specified, but the position of this clause in the body of the law would suggest that it refers to the 4 months' school attendance required of apprentices 12 years old.

Investigation on this point was limited, therefore, to the 15 establishments employing children of 12 but under 13 years of age. It developed that only 1 of these 15 establishments had such school attendance certificates on file. One other had such certificates for some but not all of its child employees, and one claimed to obey the spirit of the law by maintaining a free school for 4 months of the year. The other 12 establishments did not give any attention to the school-certificate feature of the law.

GEORGIA.

SUMMARY OF LAWS.

LEGAL AGE AND WORKING PAPERS.

Children under 10 years of age are unconditionally forbidden to be employed in factories of manufacturing establishments. Children under 12 years may not be so employed unless they are orphans without other means of support, or are the children of widowed mothers or of aged or disabled fathers dependent on them for support.[1]

These provisions of the law are clear, but otherwise the legal provisions relating to the employment of children are obscure and subjected to many widely different interpretations. Because of this, the

---

[1] Acts of 1906, p. 98, secs. 1 to 7 (22d An. Rept. Com. of Labor, pp. 297, 298). There are no special prohibited employments for children except (1) children under 12 may not be employed in any acrobatic, immoral, or mendicant employment, and (2) minors may not be employed in barrooms, etc. See Code of 1895, Vol. III, Pen., secs. 445 and 706 (L. L. 294).

By a court decision it was held that the employment of a child under the prescribed age is negligence per se, and if such child is injured by reason of his employment he has, as a matter of law, a cause of action against his employer. The failure to obtain a certificate, where a child is of proper age for employment, is criminal, but entails no liability to the child in case of his injury. 60 S. E. Rep. 1068, Acts of 1906, p. 98, secs. 1, 2, 4, 5, 6, 7. (22d An. Rept. Com. of Labor, p. 298).

present discussion divides the law into its constituent sections, and, quoting each section separately, gives under each head the more important legal interpretations, together with the facts developed in this investigation.[1]

SECTION 1. No child under 10 years of age shall be employed or allowed to labor in or about any factory or manufacturing establishment * * * under any circumstances.[2] .

> *Penalty.*—On employer, parent, or person standing in place of parent, as for a misdemeanor, i. e., fine not to exceed $1,000, imprisonment not to exceed six months, or chain gang not to exceed 12 months, or any two or all three of these punishments.

This provision clearly prohibits not only the employment of any child under 10, but also the working of a child as a "helper," even although such child is not directly employed by the establishment.

In 3 of the 27 establishments visited children under 10 years of age were found working as "helpers," the total number of such children being 8.

SEC. 2. No child under 12 years of age shall be so employed, or allowed to labor (i. e., in factory or manufacturing establishment) unless such child be an orphan and has no other means of support, or unless a widowed mother or an aged or disabled father is dependent upon the labor of such child.

In which event, before putting such child at such labor, such father shall produce and file in the office of such factory or manufacturing establishment, a certificate from the ordinary of the county, * * * certifying under his seal of office to the facts required to be shown as herein prescribed: *Provided*, That no ordinary shall issue any such certificate except upon strict proof in writing and under oath, clearly showing the necessary facts; *And provided further*, That no such certificate shall be granted for longer than one year, nor accepted by any employer after one year from the date of such certificate.

> *Penalty.*—As above (sec. 1).

In 8 of the 27 establishments visited 32 children between 10 and 12 years of age were found working. Two of these were "helpers." The other 30 were employed directly.

Of these 32 children, 11 were neither orphans nor the children of widows or of aged or disabled fathers, and their employment was thus without legal sanction.

Of the 21 children who were either orphans or children of aged or disabled fathers, 2, children of disabled fathers, were working with improper certificates (i. e., with certificates issued by notaries pub-

---

[1] Acts of 1906, p. 98, secs. 1, 2, 4, 5, 6, 7 (22d An. Rept. Com. of Labor, pp. 297, 298).

[2] Code of 1895, Vol. III, Pen., sec. 1039 (22d An. Rept. Com. of Labor, p. 294).

lic instead of by county ordinaries), and 6, children of widows, were working when, as inquiry developed, their earnings were not necessary to the support of themselves or of their mothers.

The clause of the above provision relative to certificates seems plainly to indicate that such certificates are required only in the case of aged or disabled fathers.   More than one-half of the employers interviewed, however, held the opinion that an ordinary's certificate was necessary also for children of widows, although some who held this opinion did not act upon it in all cases.   A few employers, moreover, considered that such certificates were necessary for children of these three classes up to the age of 18.   One of the notaries interviewed also held to this interpretation.

The law requires exception certificates to be issued by county ordinaries and does not seem to contemplate that notaries have such power.   Several establishments, however, accept a simple affidavit issued by a notary public as sufficient.   Thus, one of the hosiery mills visited had accepted the affidavits of notaries in the case of 4 children of widows or of aged or disabled fathers.

Section 4 of the law includes in its scope two groups of children— those under 14, and those 14 to 18 years of age—for which the legal requirements are not entirely the same.   Therefore, for purposes of convenient discussion, this section is here subdivided.

Section 4 A. No child, except as heretofore provided (i. e., orphans, etc., with exception certificates), under 14 years of age shall be employed or allowed to labor in or about any factory or manufacturing establishment * * *, unless he or she can write his or her name and simple sentences, and shall have attended school for 12 weeks of the preceding year, 6 weeks of which school attendance shall be consecutive; * * * and at the end of each year, until such child shall have passed the public-school age, an affidavit certifying to such attendance, as is required by this section, shall be furnished to the employer by the parent, guardian, or person sustaining parental relation to such child.

Penalty.—As above (sec. 1).

In interpreting this provision two questions arise: Whether attendance at night school is sufficient? and What is meant by the term "preceding year?"   As these questions also arise in connection with the next provision considered, discussion thereof will be postponed to that place.

In 18 of the 27 establishments visited children under 14, not included in the exception clauses of the law, were found working. In 9 of these 18 establishments some such children were found who were unable to write their names and simple sentences.   In 6, some such children had not attended school 12 weeks during the preceding year, or, if so, had not attended 6 weeks consecutively.   In 7, some such children were employed without affidavits of school attendance. The total number of such children found without school-attendance certificates was 92.   •

SECTION 4 B. No * * * child * * * between the ages of 14 and 18 years shall be so employed [i. e., in factory or manufacturing establishment] unless such child shall have attended school for 12 weeks of the preceding year, 6 weeks of which school attendance shall be consecutive;

And at the end of each year, until such child shall have passed the public-school age, an affidavit certifying to such attendance, as is required by this section, shall be furnished to the employer by the parent or guardian or person sustaining parental relation to such child.

The provisions of this section shall apply only to children entering such employment at the age of 14 years or less.

Penalty.—As above (sec. 1).

The attorney general, in an official opinion on the child-labor law, construes the phrase "at the age of 14 or less" to refer to children who have not reached "the age of 15 years."

The requirement that school-attendance affidavits be furnished to employers at the end of each year was frankly declared by some establishments to be a dead letter so far as it relates to children 15 to 18 years of age. Everywhere, indeed, this requirement was regarded as unreasonable, if not absurd.

Also the provision quoted is very obscure on certain points and is subjected to widely varying interpretations. Some of these unsettled points are as follows:

First. Does the phrase "12 weeks' school attendance in the preceding year" mean from January to December, or did it mean the preceding school year (say, from September to June), or does it mean the 12 months immediately previous to the time the child applies for work? The first construction would seem the correct one, but the last one is generally accepted when children apply for work.

Second. May night-school attendance be substituted for day-school attendance? Several establishments thought it might, and one woolen mill maintained a 3 months' night school in order to meet the law. The attorney general, however, held in an official opinion that night-school attendance was not contemplated by the law.

Third. Must the employer have on file annual affidavits of school attendance only for the 14 to 18 year old children who entered his own employ before their fifteenth birthday, or must he have such affidavits for children who had entered any manufacturing employment before that age?

This point is discussed by the attorney general in an official opinion on the child-labor law, but the opinion is not entirely clear as to which of the two possible interpretations he therein points out is the one he accepts. A manufacturer, interviewed by an agent of the Bureau, referred to this clause of the law as a "joker," inserted in the act with the purpose of practically nullifying the law.

Five establishments which had set for themselves a high standard in all matters of child labor required such annual affidavits of school attendance from all 14 to 18 year old children who had worked in any manufacturing establishment before they were 14 years of age.

One establishment made the same requirements for those under 16 years of age.

Five other establishments asked school affidavits of those 14 to 18 years of age only when such persons had first done manufacturing work in their own establishments; and one made this requirement only for those under 16 years of age.

The remaining 15 establishments paid no attention to this feature of the law.

SECTION 5. It shall be unlawful for * * * any factory or manufacturing establishment to hire or employ any child unless there is first provided and placed on file in the office of * * * employer an affidavit signed by the parent, guardian, or person standing in parental relation thereto, certifying to the age and date of birth of such child, and other facts required in this act.

Penalty.—As above (sec. 1). To extend also to persons making false statements as to contents of affidavit, etc.

An examination of this section shows that the law omits to mention the age up to which age certificates are required.

CONDITIONS FOUND.

Of the 27 establishments visited (some of which were not employing children at the precise time of this investigation), 11 did not require age certificates under any circumstances. Fifteen had set for themselves varying age limits in this respect—2 at 12, 1 at 13, 5 at 14, 1 at 16, and 6 at 18. For the remaining establishments no report was secured on this point.

The 15 establishments which had established age limits of some character did not always observe their standards. In total these 15 establishments employed 524 children under the age limits set up by themselves as the limits up to which all employees were to furnish age affidavits; 95 of these children had no such affidavits on file.

SECTION 6. The affidavit and certificates required in this act shall be open to inspection by the grand juries of any county where such factory or manufacturing establishments are located.

The requirement of this section is simply that all working papers shall be open to the inspection of the grand jury. It does not require actual inspection. Impliedly, however, it does require that all working papers be kept on file.

One of the establishments visited reported that their affidavits and certificates had been once inspected by the grand jury. The others reported that no such inspection had ever been made.

The law does not require that employers keep registers or lists of child employees.

The legal provisions relative to the employment of children, as above quoted, are not charged to any special office or officer for enforcement. There is no factory inspection service in Georgia.

FLORIDA.

SUMMARY OF LAWS.

LEGAL AGE.[1]

The legal age of employment is 12 years in "any factory or work-shop, bowling alley, barroom, beer garden, place of amusement where intoxicating liquors are sold, or in or about any mine or quarry." Also, children under 12 may not be employed at any other gainful occupation, except (1) that during school vacation such children may be employed in any "reputable place of work" not expressly forbidden in the above clause, and (2) that none of these legal limitations shall apply to household or agricultural work. Also, nothing in the law is to "abridge the right of a parent or guardian to require work from his child in his own vocation and under his supervision and direction."

> *Penalty.*—On employer, not more than $1,000, or imprisonment not more than 6 months, or both; on parent, or person standing in place of parent, not more than $500, or imprisonment not more than 90 days, or both. One day's illegal employment to constitute a violation.

> *Enforcement.*—Charged to sheriffs in the counties, and to the city or town marshals or police officers in the cities or towns.

PROHIBITED EMPLOYMENTS.[2]

There are no employments prohibited to children of legal age, except that certain occupations of a mendicant, acrobatic, and immoral nature are forbidden to children under 14.

---

[1] Acts of 1907, ch. 5686, secs. 1, 2, 5, 6, 7, 8, 9 (22d An. Rept. Com. of Labor, pp. 285, 286).

[2] Gen. Stats., 1906, sec. 3237 (22d An. Rept. Com. of Labor, pp. 281, 282).

This section of the law contains a clause which reads "or in any business, exhibition, or vocation injurious to the health or dangerous to the life or limbs." This prohibition is a broad one in terms, but the context indicates that it is intended to apply only to acrobatic and similar employments, not to the usual machine dangers of a factory or workshop.

The law also prohibits the employment of a child under 15 years for more than 60 days without consent of person having legal control of the child. Penalty: Not more than 60 days, or not more than $20. Gen. Stats., 1906, sec. 3728 (22d An. Rept. Com. of Labor, p. 283).

WORKING PAPERS.[1]

Affidavits or certificates are required only in the case of children under 12 years working during school vacation.

Contents and issue of vacation certificates.—Vacation certificates are to be issued by county or municipal judges.   To be issued only upon affidavit of parent or person standing in place of parent, stating age and date of birth of child, that there is no free public school then in session in the district, city, or town, and a certificate from a practicing physician that child is physically able to perform the work intended.

Filing of certificates.—Employer is to keep on file a register of all employment certificates, together with copies of the affidavit of parent or guardian and physician's certificate.   To be subject to the inspection of any city, county, or State officer of the county, or of the city or town marshal or any member of the police force in the juris-diction of which the establishment is located.

Registers.—There is no requirement as to keeping of registers or lists of names of children over legal age.

> *Penalties.*—On employer, for violation of any of these provisions, or hindering an officer, not more than $1,000, or imprisonment not more than 6 months, or both; on parent, or person stand-ing in place of parent, for violating any of these provisions, or making misstatement of material facts, not more than $500, or imprisonment not more than 90 days, or both.   One day's illegal employment to constitute a violation.

> *Enforcement.*—Charged to the sheriffs in the counties, and to the city or town marshal or police officers in the cities or towns.

Two points in the law as above condensed are to be emphasized. The first is that the legal limit of 12 years does not apply to children acting as "helpers" to their parents or guardians.   This exception is of much importance in Florida, as the cigar and tobacco industries generally offer considerable opportunity for the employment of "helpers."   The second point to be emphasized is that the only working papers mentioned by law are vacation permits, and that these are required only in the case of certain children under 12 years of age.

CONDITIONS FOUND.

None of the children directly employed by the establishments vis-ited was reported as under 12 years of age.   In a number of cases, however, children under 12 were found working as "helpers" to their parents or guardians.   Such children were not paid by the establish-ments in which they worked, nor was their time of working regu-lated by the establishment.   This being so, they were regarded as

---

[1] Acts of 1907, ch. 5686, secs. 1 to 9 (22d An. Rept. Com. of Labor, pp. 285, 286).

coming under the legal exception which permits children under 12 to work during vacation and under the supervision of their parents or guardians. No special effort was made to discover the total number of children so working.

As the investigation in Florida was limited to factories, the subject of vacation permits did not come under observation.

The law does not require registers of children's names to be kept, and none were kept in any of the 14 establishments visited.

In none of the establishments visited were children under 16 found to clean or oil moving machinery.

LOUISIANA.

SUMMARY OF LAWS.

LEGAL AGE.[1]

The legal age of employment is 14 years in "any mill, factory, mine, packing house, manufacturing establishment, workshop, laundry, millinery or dressmaking store or mercantile establishment in which more than five persons are employed, or in any theater, concert hall, or in or about any place of amusement where intoxicating liquors are made or sold, or in any bowling alley, bootblacking establishment, freight or passenger elevator, or in the transmission or distribution of messages, either telegraph or telephone, or any other messages, or merchandise, or in any other occupation not herein enumerated which may be deemed unhealthful or dangerous." Agricultural and domestic industries, however, are specifically excepted.

Penalty.—$25 to $50, or imprisonment 10 days to 6 months, or both.

Enforcement.—Charged to the commissioner of labor and industrial statistics, his deputies, and factory inspectors, locally appointed.

PROHIBITED EMPLOYMENTS.

Females, all ages, and males under 21[2] to clean machinery in motion.

Penalty.—$25 to $50, or imprisonment 10 to 30 days, or both.

Enforcement.—Charged to the commissioner of labor and industrial statistics, his deputies, and factory inspectors, locally appointed.

WORKING PAPERS.[3]

Children 14 to 16 years of age, as a condition of lawful employment in any of the establishments or occupations enumerated above (see

[1] Acts of 1908, act No. 301, secs. 1 and 3 (Bulletin of the Bureau of Labor, No. 85, pp. 596, 597).

[2] Idem, secs. 3 and 17 (Bulletin of the Bureau of Labor, No. 85, pp. 597, 600).

[3] Idem, (Bulletin of the Bureau of Labor, No. 85, pp. 596–601).

section on "Legal age"), must have an age certificate.[1] Provided that a child may be employed without certificate if employer immediately notifies the factory inspector and procures an age certificate from child within five days.[1] Also, factory inspector may demand a certificate of physical fitness if child appears to inspector to be under legal age.[2]

The legal provisions regarding the issue, contents, etc., of age certificates and the keeping of registers are as follows:

Contents and issue of age certificates.[3]—To be issued by State factory inspectors or factory inspectors appointed locally. To issue upon following proof of age: Certificate of birth or baptism, official register of birth, records of public or parochial schools, or certified copy of passport; provided, however, that if such evidence is not obtainable the parent, guardian, or custodian may, on oath made before factory inspector or juvenile court, receive age certificate from that authority.

A duplicate of each age certificate issued to be forwarded to office of State factory inspector, who is to furnish printed forms of age certificates to issuing authorities. The exact form of the age certificate is prescribed by law. It provides for the signed statement of the parent, guardian, or custodian as to age, etc., of child, and for the declaration of issuing authority that, having no reason to doubt that the child is of the age certified to, he approves of the certificate. A brief description of the child—weight, height, complexion, and color of hair—is given.

Certificate belongs to child, and to be returned to it on termination of employment; if not claimed by child within 30 days of such time, certificate must be returned to office of State factory inspector.

Filing of certificates.—Employer to have and keep on file age certificates for all children under 16 years of age. Certificates to "be subject to review" by the State or any other factory inspector, and may be canceled by such inspector if he or she finds that such certificates were obtained fraudulently.[4]

Registers.—Every employer employing five or more children under 18 in any of the places enumerated above must post and keep posted in every room where such persons are employed, a list containing the name, age, and place of residence of every person under 18 years of age.[5]

---

[1] Acts of 1908, act No. 301, sec. 6 (Bulletin of the Bureau of Labor, No. 85, p. 598).
[2] Idem, sec. 8 (Bulletin of the Bureau of Labor, No. 85, p. 599).
[3] Idem, sec. 2 (Bulletin of the Bureau of Labor, No. 85, p. 596).
[4] Idem, secs. 2 and 6 (Bulletin of the Bureau of Labor, No. 85, p. 598).
[5] Idem, sec. 6 (Bulletin of the Bureau of Labor, No. 85, p. 598).

Penalties.[1]—On employer for failure to procure and keep on file age certificates, and failure to post registers of names, $25 to $50, or imprisonment 10 days to 6 months, or both; on parent, guardian, or custodian, for making false statement as to age of a child, $10 to $25, or imprisonment 10 to 30 days, or both; on anyone for obtaining or assisting to obtain a certificate by fraud, $10 to $50.

Enforcement.[2]—Charged to "the commissioner of labor and industrial statistics," his deputies, and factory inspectors, locally appointed.

CONDITIONS FOUND.

All of the 29 establishments visited employed females 16 years of age and over, and 26 also employed children under 16 years of age. The number of such children was 554.

LEGAL AGE.

Individual slips containing inquiries as to age, sex, etc., were made out and signed by most of the children employed in the visited establishments. These age reports were not verified.

In a cracker factory a boy working regularly 60 hours a week reported himself as 13 years of age. In an oyster canning establishment a number of children working in the capacity of "helpers" reported themselves as under 14 years of age. The field write-up in this plant makes the following statements:

The ———— Company imports all of its oyster shuckers from Baltimore, shipping them down in the fall and back again in the spring. It employs only heads of families, the purpose being to get families, so that the men can work in the boats and docks and the women and children at shucking and packing oysters. It is on this ground that the company claims that no children are employees of the firm. It deals only with the heads of the families, but the children are paid directly for the work they do.

Children who are just learning to walk are often brought into the factory by the mothers and left in the oyster carts to keep them from crawling away. Children 4, 5, and 6 years stand with their mothers and often try to shuck a few oysters. Children 7 and 8 years and upward can and do shuck, usually at the same carts at which their mothers stand.

The employer has posted the following notice in front of the factory at a little-used entrance: "According to the new law of the State of Louisiana, no child under the age of 14 will be allowed to work in any factory. The parents of such children will hereafter govern

---

[1] Acts of 1908, act No. 301, secs. 2, 6, and 7 (Bulletin of the Bureau of Labor, No. 85, pp. 596, 598).

[2] Idem, sec. 3 (Bulletin of the Bureau of Labor, No. 85, p. 597).

their conduct accordingly." This sign is written in English. Only a very small percentage of the employees can either speak or read English.

PROHIBITED AND DANGEROUS EMPLOYMENTS.

No women or children were found cleaning or oiling moving machinery or mill gearing, and no children were reported as being employed operating elevators.

The factory inspector of New Orleans, however, reports that in her inspections she frequently found boys oiling and cleaning moving machinery, although not required to do so by the management.

WORKING PAPERS.

Age certificates for all child employees were on file in 6 of the 26 establishments employing children under 16; in 14 others the files were incomplete; and in the remaining 6 there were no such certificates on file.

REGISTERS.

Lists of child employees under 18 were posted in workrooms where such persons were employed in 2 of the 23 establishments employing at least 5 children under 18; were on file in the offices or at the entrances in 7 other establishments, and were not on file at all in the remaining 14.

CHAPTER III.

OF LABOR, NIGHT WORK, POSTING OF TIME SCHEDULES, MEAL PERIOD.

157

CHAPTER III.

HOURS OF LABOR, NIGHT WORK, POSTING OF TIME SCHEDULES, MEAL PERIOD.

INTRODUCTION.

This chapter covers the following subjects: Daily and weekly working hours, night work, the posting of time schedules of daily working hours, and the length of the meal period allowed employees.

The legislation upon the subject of hours of labor varies so much, in major as well as in minor matters, among the 17 States covered by this report that it is impossible to give even a fairly complete summary statement of these laws. The summary given in the following six paragraphs is, therefore, not an attempt to summarize the laws themselves, but is intended simply to show to what extent the subjects considered in this chapter had or had not been made subjects of legislation in the States covered. No note is made therein regarding laws affecting males 16 years of age and over, and the laws mentioned are limited to those affecting factories and workshops.[1]

Nine of the 17 States forbid night work for all children under 16 years of age; that is, forbid employment between specified hours of the evening and morning. These 9 States are Massachusetts, Rhode Island, New York, Pennsylvania (except for factories using perishable materials), Ohio, Illinois, Michigan, Wisconsin, and Louisiana. A similar prohibition in Indiana applies only to female children. North Carolina and Georgia prohibit night work for children under 14 years of age, and Florida for children under 12 years of age. Georgia also has an old law limiting the working hours of many classes of labor to the period between sunrise and sunset, but this law was generally regarded as "dead." The other four States—Maine, Connecticut, New Jersey, and Maryland—do not limit in any way the employment of children at night.

Laws establishing a maximum legal day and legal week for children under 16 years of age are in force in all the States covered except 4, the exceptions being Maryland, North Carolina, Georgia, and Florida. Maryland has established a legal day for such children but not a legal week, while Georgia (for cotton and woolen mills) and North

---

[1] The laws referred to throughout this volume are as in force at the time of the investigation Dec., 1908, to April, 1909. The text of the laws in force Jan. 1, 1912, is given in the appendixes at the end of this volume.

Carolina fix a maximum week but not a maximum day. Florida restricts the hours of labor only in the case of children under 12 years of age.

The restriction of night work for adult females (i. e., females 16 years of age and over) is much less frequent than is that for children. Only 2 States—Massachusetts and Indiana—forbid the employment of all females of 16 years of age and over at night. A New York law with a restriction of this character has been declared unconstitutional as regards females of 21 years of age, but is apparently left intact as regards females 16 years of age and under 21 years of age. Also, Ohio and Louisiana extend the prohibition of night work for female children to include those under 18 years of age. None of the other 12 States—Maine, Rhode Island, Connecticut, Pennsylvania, New Jersey, Illinois, Michigan, Wisconsin, Maryland, North Carolina, Georgia, or Florida—offer any legal opposition to the employment of females 16 years of age and over at night.

The length of the working-day and of the working week is limited for all females 16 years of age and over in 8 States—Maine, Massachusetts, Rhode Island, Connecticut, New York, Pennsylvania, Michigan, and Louisiana. In 3 other States—Ohio, Indiana, and North Carolina—a restriction of this character is made for females up to the age of 18 years, but not for those over that age. In the remaining 6 States of the 17 covered—New Jersey, Illinois, Wisconsin, Maryland, Georgia,[1] and Florida—there is no limitation of any kind upon the working hours of females 16 years of age and over.

The posting of time schedules is a subject of legislation in 9 of the 17 States covered. These States are Maine, Massachusetts, Rhode Island, Connecticut, New York, Pennsylvania, Ohio, Illinois, and Indiana. One of these—Pennsylvania—requires such posting to be done for all employees. Two—Ohio and Indiana—require it to be done only for children and females under 18 years of age. The other 6 make the requirement for children under 16 or 18 years of age and for all females.

The length of the meal period is a matter of legislation in 7 of the 17 States covered. These 7 States are Massachusetts, New York, Pennsylvania, Ohio, Indiana, Michigan, and Louisiana. In each of these the law provides that the midday meal period, of certain classes of employees at least, shall be of a specified length, one hour in the majority of instances. But in each of these laws a second provision is made that the specified period may be shortened under certain conditions, usually with the written consent of the factory inspection department.

This brief statement of the extent of legislation upon the hours of labor, etc., of women and children is, to repeat, only very roughly

---

[1] Except the "sunrise-to-sunset" law referred to above.

accurate. It takes no account of many legal exceptions and omits all reference to several significant points.

Below is given for each of the States covered an account of the public laws upon the subject of hours of labor in its several phases, and a statement of the conditions found in the visited establishments, so far at least as they affected women and children.

1. The regular hours of labor of women and children are shown in tabular form. This table gives a list of all the time schedules met with and the number of women and children working under each schedule, and the number of establishments in which each schedule was observed. It was found that in several instances there was more than one time schedule in force in the same establishment. Therefore, in the tables for some of the States the same establishment may be entered more than once in the same column.

The time schedules given are, as nearly as could be ascertained, those according to which the establishments normally operated, those recognized by the management itself as normal. At times there was difficulty in ascertaining the true facts. Thus, in an establishment employing pieceworkers, such pieceworkers not infrequently worked more or less irregularly. Such cases as these were decided each on its own merits, the minimum hours of labor being accepted in cases of doubt.

Sometimes, also, an establishment operates fewer hours in one season of the year, as in summer, than during the rest of the year. The present investigation was conducted in the winter season, when nearly all establishments were operating according to their longest schedules. Therefore, as a rule, the winter schedule is entered in the table, with a footnote of explanation in each case where a seasonal change was made.

2. Particularly difficult was the obtaining of reliable data regarding overtime work. The information sought was the amount of overtime work done by each establishment during the preceding year. Usually such information could be readily ascertained as regards the gross amount of overtime; but almost always there was great difficulty in finding out what classes of persons had so worked; that is to say, whether women and children had worked overtime as well as men, and, if so, the number of women and children so working and whether they had worked the full amount of overtime on each occasion.

As an example, the following may be cited. An establishment, whose regular working time is 55 hours a week, is located in a State which fixes the legal work for males under 16 years of age and for females under 18 years of age at 60 hours. This establishment reports, or its books show, that during the preceding year it had, on occasion, worked as much as 7 hours a week overtime. Such overtime, however, had been worked by only a portion of the plant. The question then arises whether males under 16 years of age and females under 18 years of age had been among those working this overtime. As pay rolls rarely ever show the ages of employees, this may be an impossible question to answer. Even if it can be answered, the further question arises whether such persons had worked the full 7 hours overtime reported as the maximum. They need not have done so necessarily, as very frequently some of the overtime workers work longer hours than others. And, under the conditions supposed in this example, males under 16 years of age and females under 18 years of age may have worked as much as 5 hours a week overtime without exceeding the legal limit established by law.

Because of these and similar difficulties, the obtained information regarding overtime work as a cause of unlawful employment is very incomplete, and the data regarding such overtime, as given in the following pages, can be accepted only as examples, and not as representative of full conditions.

3. The requirement that time schedules be posted has a two-fold object: First, to inform the employees of their rights and duties in the matter of working hours, and thus avoid misunderstandings due to verbal contracts; and, second, to enable the factory inspectors to enforce the laws more readily. The latter point may be of much importance, provided that the times of beginning and stopping work are given in the schedule, as well as the bare number of hours.

Suppose, for example, a factory with a regular working day of 10 hours in a State which fixes the legal day of women and children also at 10 hours. If there is a posted time schedule in the factory showing the precise times of beginning and stopping work, the employment of women and children at any other time of the day is necessarily unlawful. This greatly reduces the difficulty of enforcing the law, as in case of violation it is necessary to establish simply that work was being done by women or children either before or after the posted hours. In the absence of such posted schedule it is necessary to find out, in order to prove a legal violation, the time of beginning work, the time of stopping, the time allowed for meals, any time lost by breakdown of machinery, etc.—a proceeding which at times is a matter of great difficulty.

As indicated by the preceding remarks, a posted time schedule, in order to be of any considerable service, must show the exact times of beginning and stopping work each day and the time allowed for lunch. A schedule which shows simply the number of hours worked per day loses much of its value; and a schedule showing simply the number of hours required per week has very little value of any kind. Therefore, in the presentation below of data regarding the posting of time schedules in the several establishments visited, no account is taken of schedules which show nothing more than the total hours of labor per week.

4. Little comment is necessary regarding the tables showing the length of the meal period in the visited establishments. Unless otherwise stated, the meal period referred to is in each case that occuring at or about noon on the regular day shift. As far as possible variations in the length of the meal period allowed different classes of employees, or different departments in the same factory, are noted, but in some cases variations affecting only adult males were not reported.

The laws referred to throughout this volume are as in force at the time of the investigation, December, 1908, to April, 1909. The text of the laws in force January 1, 1912, is given in the appendixes at the end of this volume.

MAINE.

SUMMARY OF LAWS.

Hours of labor:[1]

> Children under 16 years of age and females 16 years of age and over in "any manufacturing or mechanical establishment," except those using perishable materials, requiring immediate labor to prevent decay or damage:[2] Legal day, 10 hours; legal week, 60 hours.
>
>> *Exceptions:* 1. The 10-hour day, but not the 60-hour week, may be increased (a) to make repairs to prevent interruption of ordinary running of machinery; (b) to make a shorter workday on one day of week; (c) to make up time lost on a previous day of same week because of stopping of machinery on which person concerned was dependent for employment.
>>
>> 2. A female 18 years of age and over may contract for a longer day than 10 hours, but such excess not to be more than 6 hours in any one week, or 60 hours in any one year, and provided that additional payment is made for such excess, and that, during minority, consent of parent or guardian is obtained.

---

[1] Rev. Stat. 1903, ch. 40, sec. 48. The exception designated 1 (c) occurs in sec. 49 (22d An. Rept. Com. of Labor, p. 527).

By a law enacted shortly after the field work of this investigation was completed the hours of labor per week for women and children were reduced to 58. Acts of 1909, ch. 70 (Bulletin of the Bureau of Labor, No. 85, p. 601).

[2] For this exception see Rev. Stat. 1903, ch. 40, secs. 55 and 56 (22d An. Rept. Com. of Labor, p. 528).

In these excepted industries no legal restrictions are placed upon the hours of labor, but it is provided that the factory inspector, on complaint, and in conjunction with the municipal authorities, may prohibit the employment of children working under what he considers detrimental conditions as regards hours of labor, sanitation, etc.

Males 16 to 21 years of age, in any of the establishments above
enumerated: Legal day, 10 hours, unless such minor contracts
voluntarily, and with consent of parent or guardian, and
receives additional payment therefor.

Night work: Not restricted by law for any class of employees.

Posting of time schedules: Required in the case of children under 16
years of age and females 16 years of age and over in places
enumerated above. Schedule to show the number of working hours
each day of week and the precise hours when work and dinner
period begins and stops. To be printed in plain, large type, the
form to be supplied by the inspector of factories after approval by
the attorney general, and to be posted conspicuously in every room
where such persons are employed. Employment in any day for a
longer period than stated on schedule a legal violation, except for
the purpose of making up for time lost on a previous day of the
same week because of stopping of machinery on which person concerned was dependent for employment.[1]

Meal period: Not regulated by law.

Penalty.—On employer for violating any of the above legal provisions, and on parent or guardian for permitting a minor to
be so employed, $25 to $50.[2]

Enforcement.—Charged to the State factory inspector.[3]

The State factory inspector in his report for 1907 points out how a
violation may readily occur under that provision of the law which
permits the 10-hour day to be exceeded in order to make up for time
lost because of stopping of machinery.[4]

* * * There will be a section of the plant shut down representing one-quarter of the department. When this lost time is made
up, instead of this one-quarter running to make up the lost time, the
whole department will be run to the required time to keep up its
work.

The State factory inspector stated that he did not see much advantage in the law requiring the posting of time schedules, but that it did
enable him to observe more easily whether factories exceeded their
regular running time.

CONDITIONS FOUND.

The number of establishments visited was 26. All of these employed females 16 years of age and over and 14 of them also employed
children under 16 years of age.

---

[1] Rev. Stat. 1903, ch. 40, sec. 49 (22d An. Rept. Com. of Labor, p. 527).

[2] Idem, sec. 50 (22d An. Rept. Com. of Labor, p. 527).

[3] Idem, sec. 43 (22d An. Rept. Com. of Labor, p. 526).

[4] "Report of inspector of factories, workshops, mines, and quarries," in Report
of the Bureau of Industrial and Labor Statistics, 1907, p. 500.

HOURS OF LABOR.

In none of the establishments were women or children employed at Sunday work or on a night shift.

The following table shows the regular hours of labor of women and children in the several establishments. The table gives, for women and children separately, the number of persons working according to each time schedule met with and the number of establishments represented in each case.

HOURS OF LABOR OF WOMEN AND CHILDREN—MAINE.

Hours of labor.			Females 16 years of age and over.		Children under 16 years of age.	
Per week.	Per day.		Number working specified hours.	Establishments represented.	Number working specified hours.	Establishments represented.
	Monday to Friday.	Saturday.				
24	4	4	....	....	1	1
47	8	7	19	2	....	....
54	9	9	9	1	....	....
55	10	5	53	1	12	1
56	9½	8½	31	1	....	....
¹57	9½	9½	15	1	....	....
59	10	9	381	9	32	5
60	10	10	104	5	7	3
60	10⅘	5⅘	157	5	12	3
60	11	5	120	1	10	1
Total.	....	....	889	26	74	14

¹ Winter schedule; summer (June, July, and August) 4½ hours less.

Examination of this table shows that in none of the establishments did the regular time schedules of women and children exceed the legal maximum of 60 hours a week. In several instances the daily hours exceeded 10, but when such was the case it was for the purpose of reducing the length of the work period on Saturday.

Overtime work, i. e., in excess of the regular hours of labor listed in the above table, was reported as having been done during the preceding year by 14 of the 26 establishments. In one of these such overtime work had been done only by men. The occasions on which overtime had been worked varied among the other 13, from 2 to 60 times a year, averaging about 20; the average number of overtime hours per week similarly varied from 2½ to 15, averaging about 8.

No entirely satisfactory data were obtained as to whether children under 16 years of age or females under 18 years of age had been employed at the overtime work mentioned. In at least 4 cases, however, females 18 years of age and over had worked sufficient overtime to make their total hours per week exceed the maximum of 66 permitted to such workers. Details of these four cases are as follows:

Establishment 16, paper boxes.—Regular hours of labor 59 per week. Females 18 years of age and over here employed had worked 10 hours a week overtime for several weeks, a total of 69 hours per week.

Establishment 14, paper boxes.—Regular hours 60 per week. Females 18 years of age and over had on occasion worked 8¾ hours a week overtime, a total of 68¾ hours per week.

Establishment 8, confectionery.—Regular hours for females 57 per week. Females 18 years of age and over had worked overtime as much as 12 hours a week on several occasions, a total of 69 hours a week.

Establishment 22, woolens.—Regular hours per week 60. Females 18 years of age and over had worked overtime as much as 15 hours per week, making a total of 75 hours per week when working overtime.

No information was obtained as to the working of those portions of the law requiring females 18 years of age and over and male minors (i. e., under 21 years of age) to have specific contracts in order to be lawfully employed more than 60 hours a week.

POSTING OF TIME SCHEDULES.

The time schedules showing daily hours of labor for women and children (if both were employed) were posted conspicuously and very generally in the rooms where such persons worked in 7 of the 26 establishments visited. In none of the other 19 establishments was such posting done.

MEAL PERIOD.

The length of the midday meal period was 60 minutes for all employees in each of the 26 establishments visited.

MASSACHUSETTS.

SUMMARY OF LAWS.

Hours of labor:[1]

Children under 18 years of age and females 18 years of age and over in "manufacturing or mechanical" establishments: Legal day, 10 hours; legal week, 58 hours.

---

[1] Rev. Laws 1902, ch. 106, sec. 24, as amended by ch. 435, Acts of 1902 (22d An. Rept. Com. of Labor, p. 595). For mercantile establishments the legal week is also fixed at 58 hours, but the working day is not restricted for such establishments. Rev. Laws 1902, ch. 106, sec. 23, as amended by ch. 397, Acts of 1904 (22d An. Rept. Com. of Labor, p. 595). By a law passed shortly after the field work of this investigation was completed, it was enacted that from and after Jan. 1, 1910, no child under 18 and no females 18 and over are to be employed in a manufacturing establishment more than 56 hours per week, except that when the employment is by seasons the number of hours per week may exceed 56 but not 58, provided that the average for a year is not more than 56 hours per week. Acts of 1909, ch. 514, sec. 48 (Bulletin of the Bureau of Labor, No. 85, pp. 622, 623).

Exceptions.—None as to 58-hour week, but 10-hour day may be extended (*a*) to make a shorter workday one day in the week; (*b*) to make up time lost on a previous day of the same week because of stopping of machinery on which person concerned was dependent for employment, if such stopping was for at least 30 consecutive minutes.

Night work:[1] Prohibited for—

All minors (i. e., under 21 years of age) and females 21 years of age and over in "manufacturing" of any kind, between 10 p. m. and 6 a. m.

Children under 18 years of age and females 18 years of age and over in the "manufacture of textile goods," between 6 p. m. and 6 a. m.

Posting of time schedules: Required in the case of children under 18 years of age and females 18 years of age and over employed in "manufacturing or mechanical" establishments. Schedule to show number of working hours each day, and precise hours when work and meal periods begin and end. To be in printed form, furnished by factory inspection department, after approval by attorney general, and to be posted conspicuously in every room in which such persons are employed. Employment at any time other than stated on schedule a legal violation, except to make up time lost on a previous day of the same week because of stopping of machinery on which person concerned was dependent for employment, if such stopping was for at least 30 consecutive minutes, and then only after a written report of the time of occurrence and duration of such overtime employment is sent to the factory inspection department.[2]

Meal period:

(*a*) When five or more children under 18 years of age or females 18 years of age and over are employed in the same factory, they shall have their meal times at the same hour if they begin work at the same hour, and in no case shall any such persons be employed during the regular meal hour at performing other work than their own.

(*b*) When five or more such persons are employed in a factory or workshop, they shall not be employed more than six consecutive hours without an interval of at least half an hour for a meal, except that employment may continue 6½ hours, if all

---

[1] Rev. Laws 1902, ch. 106, sec. 27, as amended by ch. 267, Acts of 1907 (22d An. Rept. Com. of Labor, p. 596).

[2] Idem, sec. 24, as amended by ch. 435, Acts of 1902 (22d An. Rept. Com. of Labor, p. 595). A similar requirement as to the posting of time schedules is made for mercantile establishments. Rev. Laws 1902, ch. 106, sec. 23, as amended by ch. 397, Acts of 1904 (22d An. Rept. Com. of Labor, p. 595).

work ceases not later than 1 o'clock p. m., or 7½ hours, if work ends not later than 2 p. m. and opportunity for eating lunch while at work is given.

Exceptions.—None of these provisions regarding meal periods apply to iron works, glass works, paper mills, letterpress establishments, print works, bleaching works or dyeing works, and the chief factory inspector (chief of district police), with the approval of the governor, may grant an exemption certificate to any other class of factories or workshops if it is proven to his satisfaction that such exemption is necessary because of the nature of the work and that it can be made without injury to the health of the persons concerned.[1]

Penalty.[2]—On employees for violating provisions regarding hours of labor, posting of time schedules, and meal periods, $50 to $100; and for violating provision regarding night work, $20 to $50. On parent or guardian for permitting a minor to work more than legal number of hours per day and week, $50 to $100 for each offense.

Enforcement.—Charged to the State factory inspection service (a department of the district police).[3]

The chief factory inspector regarded the law requiring the posting of time schedules as an excellent one. He stated that before such posting was required an inspector often had to watch a factory for a week or more to find if an employee was working overtime. The employer would almost invariably become suspicious and dismiss the employee for half a day or longer. Conviction was practically impossible. Now, however, an inspector can determine at once whether an employee is working overtime, because any work except during scheduled time is overtime work.

CONDITIONS FOUND.

The number of establishments visited was 44. All of these employed females 16 years of age and over, and 37 of them also employed children under 16 years of age.

---

[1] Rev. Laws 1902, ch. 106, secs. 36, 37, and 38. Employer is free from blame if work is done during meal hours without orders, provided the time schedule is posted. Rev. Laws 1902, ch. 106, sec. 39.

[2] Idem, secs. 25 and 27 (as amended by ch. 267, Acts of 1907), and sec. 40 (22d An. Rept. Com. of Labor, pp. 596, 599).

[3] Acts of 1906, ch. 499, sec. 2, and Rev. Laws 1902, ch. 108, sec. 8 (as amended by ch. 413, Acts of 1907) (22d An. Rept. Com. of Labor, pp. 609, 622).

HOURS OF LABOR.

In none of the establishments visited were women or children employed on Sunday or on a night shift.

The following table shows the regular hours of labor of women and children in the several establishments. It gives, for women and children separately, the number of persons working according to each time schedule met with and the number of establishments represented in each case.

HOURS OF LABOR OF WOMEN AND CHILDREN—MASSACHUSETTS.

Hours of labor.			Females 16 years of age and over.		Children under 16 years of age.	
Per week.	Per day. Monday to Friday.	Per day. Saturday.	Number working specified hours.	Establishments represented.	Number working specified hours.	Establishments represented.
45	8	5	38	3	2	1
46	8	6	10	1	....	....
49½	9	4½	8	1	1	1
50	9	5½	248	5	53	5
50½	9	5	9	1	1	1
51¾	8¾	8	150	1	....	....
52	9½	4½	39	1	3	1
53	9	8	52	2	8	2
53	9½	5½	424	3	60	3
[1] 54	9¼	7¾	214	1	11	1
54 1/12	9 11/12	4½	25	1	2	1
55	10	5	14	1	4	1
55⅙	9⅚	6	46	2	19	2
56	10	6	182	2	9	2
57	10	7	45	1	....	....
57	10¼	5¾	19	1	1	1
57½	9⅔	9⅙	55	1	3	1
57½	10	7½	67	1	6	1
58	9⅔	9⅔	41	1	9	1
58	10	8	187	1	37	2
58	10¼	6¾	20	1	....	....
58	10 7/12	5 1/12	26	1	3	1
58	10 23/36	5⅚	50	1	6	1
58	10½	5½	1,571	9	182	8
59	10	9	35	1	1	1
Total..	....	....	3,575	44	421	[2] 37

[1] Winter schedule; summer, 9⅞ hours Monday to Friday, 4⅝ hours Saturday, 54 hours per week.
[2] Actual number of establishments. The total can not be found by simple addition of the column, as some establishments work on more than one time schedule.

An examination of this table shows that 1 establishment, employing 35 women and 1 child, worked regularly 59 hours a week, i. e., in excess of the maximum legal week. In none of the other establishments did the regular hours of labor exceed 58 a week, nor, except to make a shorter workday on Saturday, exceed 10 hours a day.

Overtime work, i. e., in excess of the regular working schedules as entered in the above table, was reported as having been done during the previous year in 18 of the 44 establishments. In 3 of these 18, men only had worked overtime; in 9 others the amount of overtime reported was not sufficient on the average to make the total hours per week of women or children exceed the legal maximum of

58 hours a week. In each of the remaining 6 establishments the overtime plus the regular hours was in excess of the maximum legal hours, and in each of these establishments women and minors under 18 were employed and worked overtime when the factory so worked. Whether children under 16 years of age so worked was not ascertained.

The 6 establishments referred to, with the amount of overtime reported for each, were as follows: A confectionery factory, regular hours 55¼ a week, overtime on 15 occasions, averaging 3½ hours a week; a confectionery establishment, regular hours 55¼, overtime on 4 occasions, averaging 3½ hours a week; a hosiery factory, regular hours 56 per week, averaged 4 hours a week overtime, number of occasions not reported; an enamel-ware factory, regular hours 55 per week, overtime on 36 occasions, averaging 5 hours a week; and two woolen mills, regular hours per week 58, each worked overtime on about 45 occasions, averaging 6 hours a week in one case and 12 hours in the other.

In 16 establishments minors under 18 years of age and women worked at other hours than those stated in the posted time schedules.

POSTING OF TIME SCHEDULES.

Time schedules, showing daily working hours of women and children (if both were employed), were conspicuously and very generally posted in workrooms where such persons were employed by 34 of the 44 establishments; were posted in halls but not in workrooms in 2 establishments; were posted for children but not for women by 2 establishments; and in the remaining 6 establishments, in all of which women and in 5 of which children were employed, no posting of any kind had been done.

MEAL PERIOD.

The following table classifies the 44 visited establishments according to the length of the midday meal period in each:

LENGTH OF MIDDAY MEAL PERIOD—MASSACHUSETTS.

Length of meal period (in minutes).	Establishments having meal period of specified length.	
	Number.	Per cent.
30	14	32
40	3	7
45	[1] 7	16
60	[2] 20	45

[1] Including 1 establishment in which meal period is 60 minutes in summer.
[2] Including 1 establishment in which a few employees are allowed 80 minutes.

In none of the establishments visited were minors under 18 years of age or women reported as working during the lunch period.

RHODE ISLAND.

SUMMARY OF LAWS.

Hours of labor:[1]

> Children under 16 years of age and females 16 years of age and over in "any manufacturing or mechanical establishment": Legal day, 10 hours; legal week, 58 hours.
>
> > *Exceptions:* None as to the 58-hour week, but the 10-hour day may be increased (a) to make repairs necessary to prevent the interruption of the ordinary running of machinery; (b) to make a shorter workday one day in the week.

Night work:[2] Prohibited for—

> Children under 16 years of age in "any factory or manufacturing or business establishment," between 8 p. m. and 6 a. m.

Posting of time schedules:[3] Required in case of children under 16 years of age and women 16 and over in places enumerated above. Schedule to show number of hours to be worked each day; to be in printed form, and posted conspicuously in every room where such persons are employed. Employment for a longer time than stated on schedule is a legal violation, unless for the purpose of making up time lost on a previous day of same week in consequence of the stopping of machinery upon which person concerned was dependent for employment. [The law does not require that the schedule show the precise times of beginning and stopping work, nor that the schedule form be supplied by the State.]

---

[1] Gen. Laws, 1896, ch. 198, sec. 22, as amended by ch. 994, enacted 1902 (22d An. Rept. Com. of Labor, pp. 1216, 1217).

Later law: By ch. 384, Acts of 1909, passed subsequent to the field work of this investigation, the legal week was reduced to 56 hours (Bulletin of the Bureau of Labor, No. 85, p. 763).

[2] Idem, ch. 68, sec. 1, as amended by ch. 1215, enacted 1905 (22d An. Rept. Com. of Labor, pp. 1206, 1207).

Mercantile establishments are exempted from the night work prohibition on Saturdays and on either of the four days immediately preceding Christmas.

[3] Idem, ch. 198, sec. 22, as amended by ch. 994, enacted 1902 (22d An. Rept. Com. of Labor, pp. 1216, 1217).

Meal period: There is no legal provision regarding the length of the meal period.

> *Penalty.*[1]—For violation of provisions regarding hours of labor and posting of time schedules, not exceeding $20; for violation of provision regarding night work, not exceeding $500.
>
> *Enforcement.*[2]—Charged to factory-inspection department.

The factory-inspection department does not attempt to enforce to the letter the requirement that a time schedule be posted in every workroom in which women and children are employed. In the case of communicating rooms, where employees pass frequently from one to the other, it is not considered necessary that a schedule be posted in each room. It is regarded as sufficient if a schedule is posted in a room through which all the employees concerned must pass. On the other hand, if rooms on the same floor have separate entrances, it is held that a schedule should be posted in each room. Furthermore, the chief inspector does not believe that the law requiring time schedules was intended to apply to small establishments. It seems to him unnecessary that small stores, for instance, should keep a schedule of hours posted, and in such cases he does not require such posting.

CONDITIONS FOUND.

The number of establishments visited was 27. All of these employed women (females 16 years of age and over) and 24 employed children under 16 years of age.

HOURS OF LABOR.

In none of the establishments visited was night work or Sunday work performed.

The regular hours of labor of women and children in the 27 establishments are presented in the following table. This table shows for women and children separately the number of such persons working according to each time schedule met with and the number of establishments represented in each case.

---

[1] Gen. Laws, 1896, ch. 198, sec. 23; and idem, ch. 68, sec. 12 (as amended by ch. 1215, enacted 1905) (22d An. Rept. Com of Labor, pp. 1210, 1217).

[2] Idem, ch. 68, sec. 3 (as amended by ch. 1215, enacted 1905) and as added to by ch. 708, enacted 1899 (22d An. Rept. Com of Labor, pp. 1208, 1210).

HOURS OF LABOR OF WOMEN AND CHILDREN—RHODE ISLAND.

Hours of labor.			Females 16 years of age and over.		Children under 16 years of age.	
Per week.	Per day.		Number working specified hours.	Establishments represented.	Number working specified hours.	Establishments represented.
	Monday to Friday.	Saturday.				
44	8	4	35	1	....	....
48	8	8	3	1	....	....
49	9	4	40	1	3	1
54	9	9	5	1	....	....
55	10	5	126	2	15	2
1 56	9½	8½	130	3	7	3
57	10	7	27	1	2	1
58	10¾	4½	35	1	8	1
58	10½	5½	2,133	14	425	13
58	10	8	250	1	8	1
59	10	9	37	2	6	2
60	10	10	26	1	8	1
Total..	....	....	2,847	2 27	482	2 24

1 In summer 1 establishment with 80 women and 2 children worked 4 hours less, the reduction being made on Saturday.
2 Actual number of establishments. The total number can not be found by simple addition of the column, as some establishments work on more than one time schedule.

An examination of this table shows that in 3 establishments the regular working period for women exceeded 58 hours and in 3 establishments the regular weekly working period for children exceeded 58 hours.

Overtime work during the previous year was reported as having been done in 14 establishments, in all of which women and in all but 1 of which children were employed. The occasions on which such overtime work was done varied among the establishments concerned from 7 to 60 and the average amount per week from 2½ to 15 hours. In 3 of these establishments men only engaged in overtime work; in 4 women and in 3 children, whose regular time schedules were not more than 58 hours, worked sufficient overtime on occasion to make their weekly work periods exceed 58 hours; in the remaining 7 establishments information was not obtained as to the sex and age of those working overtime.

Details regarding the overtime work of women and children in the 4 establishments in which such is reported are as follows:

Establishment 23, paper boxes.—Rush season from September to January; women engaged in the more responsible employments work overtime at such season; children and women doing simpler work are not employed overtime, as their work can be done by new hands taken on at the time. Regular hours of women, 56 per week; overtime work averages 9 hours per week.

Establishment 24, woolen and worsted goods.—The wool-spinning and carding departments are the ones most frequently operated overtime.

Regular hours of work for women and children, 58 per week; overtime usually 3 or 4 times a week, from 6 to 9 p. m.

Establishment 26, woolen and worsted goods.—Superintendent stated that it had never been customary to run the factory overtime, but that they "were doing it at present (i. e. at time of agent's visit) one hour a day to make up time lost in January in putting hood on the engine." Regular hours of women and children, 58 per week. This one hour of overtime was done after regular closing time—5.50 to 6.50 p. m. On the two occasions of agent's visit to factory it was observed that lunch period was cut short 5 minutes, which would add another half hour per week.

Establishment 27, woolen and worsted goods.—A small amount of overtime work was being done at time of agent's visit in the combing and drawing rooms. Regular hours of women and children, 58 per week. Examination of pay roll showed that during week ending January 30, 1909, 53 females 16 years of age and over and 6 children under 16 years of age (2 girls, 4 boys) worked from 61 to 73 hours, the majority working 69 hours.

POSTING OF TIME SCHEDULES.

In one of the establishments visited time schedules, showing daily working hours of women and children, were conspicuously posted in all workrooms in which such persons were employed; in 3 such posting was in a number of workrooms but not in all; in 1 a schedule was posted in the office but not in the factory rooms; in the remaining 22 establishments, in all of which women, and in 19 of which children were employed, time schedules were nowhere posted.

MEAL PERIOD.

The following table classifies the 27 establishments visited according to the length of the midday meal period in each:

LENGTH OF MIDDAY MEAL PERIOD—RHODE ISLAND.

Length of meal period (in minutes).	Establishments having meal period of specified length.	
	Number.	Per cent.
30	2	7
45	7	26
50	1	4
60	17	63

CONNECTICUT.

SUMMARY OF LAWS.

Hours of labor:

Children under 16 years of age [1] and females 16 years of age and over in "any manufacturing, mechanical, or mercantile establishment:" Legal day, 10 hours; legal week, 58 hours.

Exceptions: The 10-hour day may be extended (*a*) to make repairs to prevent interruption of the ordinary running of machinery; (*b*) to make a shorter workday on one day in the week; (*c*) to make up time lost on a previous day of same week because of the stopping of machinery on which person concerned was dependent for employment. The 58-hour week may be extended to 60 hours from September to May, inclusive, if it is reduced to 55 hours during June, July, and August, and if notice to the employees of the change is posted by January 1 of the year concerned.[2]

Night work:[3] Not restricted by law for any class of employees.

Posting of time schedules:[4] Required in the case of children under 16 years of age and females 16 years of age and over in places enumerated above. Schedule to show the number of hours' work required each day of the week, and to be posted conspicuously in every room where such persons are employed. Employment for a longer period than stated on schedule is a legal violation, except to make up time lost on a previous day of the same week because of stopping of machinery on which person concerned was dependent for employment. [The law does not require that the schedule show the precise times of beginning and stopping work, nor that the schedule form be supplied by the State.]

Meal period: There is no legal provision regarding the length of the meal period.

Penalty.[5]—On employer for violating any of the provisions mentioned above, and on parent or guardian for permitting a minor to be employed in violation of such provisions, not more than $20 for each offense.

---

[1] Acts of 1907, ch. 251, sec. 1 (22d An. Rept. Com. of Labor, p. 250).

[2] By a law approved Aug. 12, 1909 (Acts of 1909, ch. 220, sec. 2), mercantile establishments are exempted from the restriction regarding hours from Dec. 17 to 25, provided not less than 7 holidays with pay are given during the year. (Bulletin of the Bureau of Labor, No. 85, p. 527).

[3] By a law approved Aug. 12, 1909 (Acts of 1909, ch. 220, sec. 3) children under 16 and women may not be employed "after 10 o'clock in the evening of any day," unless two shifts of workers are employed, in which case no one shift shall be employed more than 10 hours per day (Bulletin of the Bureau of Labor No. 85, p. 527).

[4] Acts of 1907, ch. 251, sec. 1 (22d An. Rept. Com. of Labor, p. 250).

[5] Idem, sec. 2 (22d An. Rept. Com. of Labor, pp. 250, 251).

Enforcement.—The law regarding hours of labor, above quoted, is part of the general law of the State, and is not charged to the factory inspection department for enforcement. The act of 1907, providing for a female deputy factory inspector, directs such deputy to "inquire into the enforcement of the laws regulating the employment of women and girls * * * and report thereon to the factory inspector."[1] This would seem to impose some obligation upon the department in the enforcement of these provisions, in so far at least as females are concerned.[2]

The factory inspectors stated that they were not in favor of the law requiring the posting of time schedules; that they could see no real advantage in it; and that the whole law was weakened by having portions which were useless and difficult of enforcement. The chief factory inspector also stated that the law regarding hours of labor was abused by certain mercantile establishments which gave their employees certain hours off during part of the week in order to work late on Saturday night.

CONDITIONS FOUND.

The number of establishments visited was 35. All of these employed women (females 16 years of age and over), and 33 also employed children under 16 years of age.

HOURS OF LABOR.

In none of the establishments visited was night work or Sunday work performed.

The regular hours of labor of women and children in the several establishments are presented in the following table. This table shows for women and children separately the number of such persons working according to each time schedule met with, and the number of establishments represented in each case. The hours shown represent the "winter" schedule; that is, from September to May. Several establishments avail themselves of the law which permits of a longer working schedule during these months, provided not more than 55 hours per week are worked during June, July, and August.

---

[1] Pub. Acts, 1907, ch. 241, sec. 2.

[2] The act of 1909, which repeats the provisions regarding hours of labor as quoted in the text and adds the restriction regarding night work mentioned in note 3, previous page, specifically vests the factory inspection department with its enforcement. Acts of 1909, ch. 220, sec. 4 (Bulletin of the Bureau of Labor, No. 85, p. 528).

HOURS OF LABOR OF WOMEN AND CHILDREN—CONNECTICUT.

Hours of labor.			Females 16 years of age and over.		Children under 16 years of age.	
Per week.	Per day.		Number working specified hours.	Establishments represented.	Number working specified hours.	Establishments represented.
	Monday to Friday.	Saturday.				
45	8	5	43	2	4	1
52	9½	4½	620	2	20	2
53¼	9	8¼	86	1	11	1
54	9	9	....	....	1	1
55	10	5	1,624	5	48	5
56	9½	8½	27	1	5	1
57½	10½	5	180	1	6	1
58	10	8	222	2	28	2
58	10½	5½	292	2	23	2
58½	10₇₁₀	5¼	86	2	8	2
59	10	9	1,143	9	198	9
60	10	10	1,290	8	143	8
Total..	....	....	5,613	35	495	[1] 33

[1] Actual number of establishments. The total number can not be found by simple addition of the column as some establishments work on more than one time schedule.

An examination of the above table shows that in 19 establishments the regular working week for women exceeded 58 hours, and in 19 establishments also the regular working week for children exceeded 58 hours, the total number of establishments represented in those two groups being 20.   In none of these cases did the working week exceed 60 hours.   The Connecticut law, as noted, permits of a 60-hour week for women and children from September to May, provided not more than 55 hours a week are worked during June, July, and August, and provided a notice to that effect is posted by January 1 of the year concerned.   The present investigation was made in the month of February.   Eleven of the 20 establishments visited, whose hours of labor for women or children, or both, exceeded 58, were reported as reducing such hours to 55 in June, July, and August; 1 had given no notice of any such reduction; and information upon this point was not obtained from the remaining 8.

Overtime work,'i. e., in excess of the regular hours as given in the preceding table, was reported as not having been done during the preceding year in 29 of the 35 establishments visited, and as having been done in 6.   In each of these 6 establishments in which overtime was done, women and children were employed; in 2 it was ascertained that men only had worked overtime; in the remaining 4 no satisfactory information was obtained on this point.

POSTING OF TIME SCHEDULES.

Time schedules for women and children were posted in all rooms in which such persons worked in 2 of the establishments visited, and in 1 such complete posting was done for children but not for women. In 3 others weekly time schedules were posted in the respective offices of the companies, but not in the workrooms. In the remaining 29 establishments, in all of which women, and in all but 2 of which children were employed, time schedules were nowhere posted.

MEAL PERIOD.

The following table classifies the 35 visited establishments according to the length of the midday meal period in each:

LENGTH OF MIDDAY MEAL PERIOD—CONNECTICUT.

Length of meal period (in minutes).	Establishments having meal period of specified length.	
	Number.	Per cent.
30	1	3
45	4	11
60	30	86

NEW YORK.

SUMMARY OF LAWS.

Hours of labor:[1]

Children under 16 years of age in "any factory" (defined as including "also any mill, workshop, or other manufacturing or business establishment where one or more persons are employed at labor"):[2] Legal day, 8 hours; legal week, 48 hours in 6 days. If employed in two or more factories in same day or week the total time of employment not to exceed that allowed in a single factory.

Exceptions: None.

Females 16 years of age and over and males 16 and 17 years of age in "any factory" (as defined above): Legal day, 10 hours; legal week, 60 hours in 6 days. If employed in two or more factories in same day or week the total time of employment not to exceed that allowed in a single factory.

---

[1] Rev. Stat., 3d ed., 1901, p. 2100, sec. 77 (as amended by ch. 507, Acts of 1907), subdivisions 1, 2, 3, and 6, and sec. 78 (as amended by ch. 507, Acts of 1907) (22d An. Rept. Com. of Labor, p. 910).

For regulations regarding hours of labor and night work in mercantile establishments, business offices, etc., see Rev. Stat., 3d ed., 1901, p. 2114, sec. 161 (as amended by ch. 490, Acts of 1906) and idem, p. 2100, sec. 77 (as amended by ch. 507, Acts of 1907). subdivision 6. (22d An. Rept. Com. of Labor, pp. 925, 926.)

[2] Idem, p. 2089, sec. 2, as amended by ch. 550, Acts of 1904 (22d An. Rept. Com. of Labor, p. 899).

Exceptions: None as to 60-hour week, but the 10-hour day may be extended, not to exceed 12 hours, (*a*) regularly in not to exceed 5 days a week in order to make a short workday on one day in week; (*b*) irregularly in not to exceed 3 days a week, provided, in both cases, that the requirements as to posting of time schedules (as detailed below) be complied with.

Night work:[1] Prohibited for—

Children under 16 years of age in "any factory" (as defined above): Between 5 p. m. and 8 a. m.

Exceptions: None.

Males 16 and 17 years of age in "any factory" (as defined above): Between 12 midnight and 4 a. m.

Exceptions: None.

Females 16 to 21 years of age in "any factory" (as defined above): Between 9 p. m. and 6 a. m.

Exceptions: None.

Posting of time schedules:[2] Required in case of all persons subject to the legislation regarding hours of labor described above. Schedule to show number of working hours each day and time when work begins and ends. To be printed, in a form furnished by the commissioner of labor, and posted conspicuously in every room in which such persons are employed. The terms of the schedule shall not be changed after beginning of labor on first day of week without consent of commissioner of labor. Employment before or after hours stated in schedule is a legal violation, and the presence of such persons in a factory outside of these hours, or if no notice is posted, between 6 p. m. and 7 a. m. constitutes prima facie evidence of violation. When nature of work prevents the fixing of the hours of labor weekly in advance, the commissioner of labor may grant a permit exempting such factory from requirements as to posting time schedule, provided that the daily hours of labor be posted, and that a time book be kept showing names and addresses of all female employees and the hours worked by each of them each day, and be exhibited to representatives of the department of labor on demand. Such

---

[1] Rev. Stat., 3d ed., 1901, p. 2100, sec. 77, as amended by ch. 507, Acts of 1907, subdivisions 1, 2, and 3 (22d An. Rept. Com. of Labor, p. 910).

The original law contained a prohibition against night work by any female, but this was declared unconstitutional as regards adult females. People *v.* Williams, 81 N. E. Rep. 778 (decided by court of appeals, June 14, 1907). For full discussion of this decision see Seventh Annual Report of Commissioner of Labor of New York, 1907, pp. I. 47 to I. 51.

[2] Idem, subdivisions 4 and 5 (22d An. Rept. Com. of Labor, p. 911).

permit to be kept posted in place designated by commissioner of labor, and may be revoked by him on failure to comply with above requirements.

Meal period:[1] In factories to be at least 60 minutes long for regular noon-day meal, unless the factory inspector shall permit a shorter time. Such permit to be in writing and conspicuously posted in the main entrance of the factory, and may be revoked at any time. When overtime is worked for more than one hour after 6 p. m., at least 20 minutes shall be allowed for lunch before beginning overtime work.

Penalty:[2] On any person who violates any of the above quoted legal provisions; first offense, $20 to $50; second offense, $50 to $200, or not more than 30 days' imprisonment, or both; third offense, not less than $250 or not more than 60 days' imprisonment, or both.

Enforcement:[3] All legal provisions regarding hours of labor and night work is charged to the State bureau of factory inspection (a bureau of the State department of labor).

Factory inspectors, in interviews with agents of the Bureau, expressed themselves generally as in favor of the principle of posted time schedules, but thought that the strict enforcement of the law regarding this point took up time that could be more advantageously employed in enforcing more important laws. This attitude is well expressed in the following excerpt from the report of the chief factory inspector for 1905 (p. 14).

The orders enumerated in Division I of this table are unimportant, as the subjects covered do not affect the conditions of employment or welfare of employees. The posting of laws, schedule of hours and noonday permits do not add one iota to the respect in which the law is held by the average manufacturer, neither does compliance with the inspectors' orders to properly post them add to the comfort or safety of employees; nevertheless, the statute directs that they shall be pos e in every factory and shop, and, as will be seen, these trivial orders constitute more than 50 per cent of the total given in this table.

CONDITIONS FOUND.

The number of establishments visited was 36. All of them employed females 16 years of age and over, and 18 employed children under 16 years of age.

In none of the establishments visited was night work or Sunday work done by women (i. e., females 16 years of age and over) or by children.

---

[1] Rev. Stat., 3d ed., 1901, p. 2102, sec. 89 (22d An. Rept. Com. of Labor, p. 914).

[2] Idem, p. 2120, sec. 209, as amended by ch. 506, Acts of 1907 (22d An. Rept. Com. of Labor, p. 931).

[3] Idem, p. 2098, as amended by ch. 505, Acts of 1907, sec. 62, subdivision 4 (22d An. Rept. Com. of Labor, p. 907).

HOURS OF LABOR.

The regular hours of labor of women and children in these establishments are presented in the following table. This table shows for women and children separately the number of such persons working according to each time schedule met with, and the number of establishments represented in each case.

HOURS OF LABOR OF WOMEN AND CHILDREN—NEW YORK.

Hours of labor.			Females 16 years of age and over.		Children under 16 years of age.	
Per week.	Per day. Monday to Friday.	Per day. Saturday.	Number working specified hours.	Establishments represented.	Number working specified hours.	Establishments represented.
40	8				4	1
43½	8	3½			13	1
45	8	5			8	1
45¼	8	5¼			3	1
47¼	8	7¼			2	1
48	8	8	152	1	27	6
49	8	9			10	1
52½	10½		153	1		
53	9	8	260	2	1	1
53½	9	8½	387	1		
54	9	9	632	4		
54	9¾	5¼	193	2		
55	9½	7½	56	1	1	1
55	10	5	429	1		
55½	9½	8	26	1	1	1
56	9½	8½	6	1	1	1
56	9¾	7¼	155	1		
57	9½	9½	12	1		
57	10¼	5¾	962	1	4	1
57½	10½	5	40	1		
58	10	8	36	1	1	1
59	10	9	1,571	7	7	2
60	[1] 9½	9½	125	1		
60	10	10	104	4		
60	10¼	8¾	149	1		
60	11	5	575	3		
Total..			6,023	36	83	[2] 18

[1] Except Tuesday and Thursday, 11 hours.
[2] Actual number of establishments. The total number can not be found by simple addition of the column, as some establishments work on more than one time schedule.

Examination of this table shows that the regular time schedules of children exceeded 48 hours a week and 8 hours a day for 26 children employed in (allowing for duplication) 7 establishments. In no case did the regular working week of women exceed the legal limit of 60 hours.

Overtime work, i. e., in excess of the regular time schedules as given in the above table, was reported as having been done during the previous year in 14 establishments. In one of these, men only had engaged in such work. As regards the remaining 13, no information was obtainable as to the ages and sex of persons working overtime. As, however, women were employed in all 13, and as in more than half they formed a majority of the total employees and almost completely monopolized important occupations, it is probable that when overtime work was done women in many cases worked the additional time as well as men. If they did so work, the amount of overtime was on the average sufficient in 8 of the 13 establishments to cause the weekly hours of women to exceed 60.

As regards children, no such supposition can be made as was just made in the case of women. Only 6 of the 13 establishments referred to employed children under 16 years of age, and in each of these cases the number of children was proportionately very small and their services easily dispensed with.

As regards males 16 and 17 years of age, for whom the law establishes a 60-hour week as for women, no information regarding overtime work was obtained.

POSTING OF TIME SCHEDULES.

In 20 of the 36 establishments visited time schedules showing daily working hours of women and children (if both were employed) were conspicuously and very generally posted in the workroom where such persons were employed. In 1 establishment such posting was done for women but not for children, and in 3 for children but not for women. In the remaining 12 establishments, in all of which women, and in 9 of which children were employed, the hours of labor were either not posted at all, or were posted in only a very few of the workrooms where such persons were employed.

MEAL PERIOD.

The following table classifies the 36 visited establishments according to the length of the midday meal period in each:

LENGTH OF MIDDAY MEAL PERIOD—NEW YORK.

Length of meal period (in minutes).	Establishments having meal period of specified length.	
	Number.	Per cent.
30	[1] 19	53
45	1	3
50	2	6
60	14	39

[1] Including 1 in which males had 60 minutes; and 1 in which some of the employees had 60 minutes.

From this table is seen that in 22 of the 36 establishments the meal period for all or some of the employees was under 60 minutes. In such case the law requires a permit from the factory inspectors to be obtained and conspicuously posted in the main entrance of the factory. Such permits were posted in 19 of these 22 establishments; in the other 3 there were no posted permits.

NEW JERSEY.

SUMMARY OF LAWS.

Hours of labor: [1]

    Children under 16 years of age, in "any factory, workshop, mill, or place where the manufacture of goods of any kind is carried on:" Legal day, 10 hours; legal week, 55 hours.

        Exceptions: None.

Night work: Not restricted by law for any class of employees.

Posting of time schedules: Not required by law.

Meal period: Not regulated by law.

    Penalty.[2]—On employer for violating law quoted above regarding hours of labor of children—$50 for each offense.

    Enforcement.[3]—Charged to factory inspection department (department of labor).

CONDITIONS FOUND.

The number of establishments visited was 27. All of these employed women (females 16 years of age and over) and 25 also employed children under 16 years of age.

HOURS OF LABOR.

In none of the establishments visited was Sunday work performed. In none was night work done by children, but in one 157 females 16 years of age and over worked on a night shift, their working hours being 11 per night from Monday to Friday, a total of 55 hours per week.

The regular hours of labor of all the women and children in the several establishments visited are presented in the following table. This table shows for women and children separately the number of such persons working according to each time schedule met with, and the number of establishments represented in each case.

---

  [1] Acts of 1904, ch. 64, sec. 9 (22d An. Rept. Com. of Labor, p. 861). For legislation regarding hours of labor and night work in mercantile establishments see Acts of 1907, ch. 229, sec. 1; and in bakeries, Acts of 1905, ch. 102, secs. 2 and 9 (22d An. Rept. Com. of Labor, pp. 869, 870, 875).

  [2] Idem (22d An. Rept. Com. of Labor, p. 861).

  [3] Idem, sec. 45 (as amended by ch. 257, Acts of 1907) (22d An. Rept. Com. of Labor, p. 868).

HOURS OF LABOR OF WOMEN AND CHILDREN—NEW JERSEY.

Hours of labor.			Females 16 years of age and over.		Children under 16 years of age.	
Per week.	Per day.		Number working specified hours.	Establishments represented.	Number working specified hours.	Establishments represented.
	Monday to Friday.	Saturday.				
46¼	8¼	5	215	1	....	....
50	10	....	38	1	....	....
52	9	7	98	2	25	2
53	9½	5½	....	....	5	1
54	[illegible]	9	187	2	32	3
55	10	5	1,057	7	237	8
55½	10	5½	45	1	19	1
56	10	6	687	2	58	2
57½	9¾	8¾	273	1	15	1
57½	10	7½	17	1	....	....
57½	10½	5	70	1	23	1
58	10½	5½	953	3	93	3
58½	10½	6	98	1	....	....
59	10	9	1,059	4	75	3
[1] 55	11	....	157	1	....	....
Total..	....	....	5,554	[2] 27	582	25

[1] Night work.
[2] Actual number of establishments. The total number can not be found by simple addition of the column, as some establishments work on more than one time schedule.

An examination of this table shows that in 11 establishments the regular working hours for children under 16 years of age exceeded 55 hours a week, and that in 4 establishments such working hours exceeded 10 hours a day.

Overtime, i. e., work in excess of the regular hours as given in the above table, was reported as not having been done during the preceding year in 17 establishments, and as having been done in 10. In one of these 10 establishments it was reported that boys whose regular hours per week were 57½ frequently worked overtime; in the remaining 9 establishments in which overtime was done, information regarding the ages and sex of the persons working overtime could not be obtained.

POSTING OF TIME SCHEDULES.

Daily time schedules for women and children (a matter not referred to by law) were posted in one establishment, and for children only in 3 other establishments. In the remaining 23 establishments, in all of which women, and in all but 2 of which children were employed, time schedules were nowhere posted.

MEAL PERIOD.

Information in regard to the length of the midday meal period was obtained for 26 of the 27 establishments visited. The following table classifies these 26 establishments on this point.

LENGTH OF MIDDAY MEAL PERIOD.—NEW JERSEY.

Length of meal period (in minutes).	Establishments having meal period of specified length.	
	Number.	Per cent.
30	8	31
45	1 1	4
60	17	65

1 Including 1 in which males, including a few children, were allowed only 30 minutes.

In the one establishment where night work was done by women, the midnight meal period was 30 minutes in length.

PENNSYLVANIA.

SUMMARY OF LAWS.[1]

Hours of labor:[2]

Children under 16 years of age and females 16 years of age and over, in "any establishment," i. e., any place where men, women, or children are employed for compensation, with the exception of coal mining, farm labor, and domestic labor:[3] Legal day, 12 hours; legal week, 60 hours.

Exceptions: None.

Night work:[4] Prohibited for—

Children under 16 years of age, in "any establishment" (as above defined) between 9 p. m. and 6 a. m.

---

[1] Shortly after the completion of the field work of this investigation, Pennsylvania enacted a new law regarding the hours of labor of children in factories, workshops, and several other classes of establishments. The distinguishing points of this law are as follows:

Males under 16 and females under 18 may not be employed more than 10 hours a day, except to make a shorter workday one day in week, and in no case more than 58 hours a week. Night work is prohibited for such persons between 9 p. m. and 6 a. m., but the exception regarding the employment of males 14 to 16 at night in establishments requiring continuous operation remains substantially unaltered. A meal period of 45 minutes for such persons, subject to no exceptions, is also provided for. The penalties for violation are: First offense, $10 to $25 or 10 days' imprisonment, or both; second offense, not more than $50 or 90 days' imprisonment, or both. The new law went into effect Jan. 1, 1910. Acts of 1909, act No. 182, secs. 5, 6, and 11 (Bulletin of the Bureau of Labor, No. 85, pp. 749, 750).

[2] Acts of 1905, act No. 226, sec. 3 (22d An. Rept. Com. of Labor, p. 1175).

[3] Idem, sec. 1 (22d An. Rept. Com. of Labor, p. 1175).

[4] Idem, sec. 3 (22d An. Rept. Com. of Labor, pp. 1175, 1176). Retail mercantile establishments are exempt from the night work restriction on Saturday and for the 20 days from Dec. 5 to Dec. 25, provided in latter case that working hours do not exceed 10 hours a day or 60 hours a week.

Exceptions: When the business of an establishment requires continuous operation to prevent waste of material, male children 14 to 16 years of age may be employed after 9 p. m. if they have not been employed between 6 a. m. and 9 p. m.; also, if such an establishment operates two shifts of workers, male children 14 to 16 years may be employed partly by day and partly by night. But in no case shall the consecutive hours of labor of children working after 9 p. m. be more than 9.

Posting of time schedules:[1] Required in the case of all employees, men, women, or children, in any establishment (as above defined). Schedule to show the number of hours per day for each day of week. To be printed and to be posted conspicuously in every room where such persons are employed. [The law does not require that schedule show precise hours of beginning and stopping work, nor that schedule form be supplied by State.]

Meal period:[2] In any establishment (as above defined), not less than one hour to be allowed for the noonday meal, but the chief factory inspector, for good cause, may reduce the meal time in establishments where the other provisions of the factory inspection law are observed.

Penalty:[3] On anyone for violating any of the legal provisions above quoted, $25 to $500, or imprisonment 10 to 60 days, for each offense.

Enforcement:[4] By State factory inspection department.

CONDITIONS FOUND.

The number of establishments visited was 50. All of these employed females 16 years of age and over and 42 of them also employed children under 16 years of age.

HOURS OF LABOR.

In none of these establishments did the regular hours of labor of women and children include Sunday work. Regular work on a night shift, however, was done by 110 females over 16 years of age in 2 establishments, one an enameling plant, the other a worsted mill, and by 67 children under 16 years of age in 1 establishment, a worsted mill. In each of these cases the hours worked were 12 per night from Monday to Friday, a total of 60 hours a week.

---

[1] Acts of 1905, ch. 226, sec. 10 (22d An. Rept. Com. of Labor, p. 1177).
[2] Idem, sec. 9 (22d An. Rept. Com. of Labor, p. 1177.)
[3] Idem, sec. 23 (22d An. Rept. Com. of Labor, p. 1180).
[4] Idem, secs. 25 and 27 (22d An. Rept. Com. of Labor, p. 1180).

The regular hours of labor of all the women and children in the several establishments visited are presented in the following table. The table shows for women and children separately the number of such persons working according to each time schedule met with, and the number of establishments represented in each case.

HOURS OF LABOR OF WOMEN AND CHILDREN—PENNSYLVANIA.

Hours of labor.			Females 16 years of age and over.		Children under 16 years of age.	
Per week.	Per day. Monday to Friday.	Per day. Saturday.	Number working specified hours.	Establishments represented.	Number working specified hours.	Establishments represented.
48	8	8	103	2	1	1
50	9	5	7	2	....	....
50	10	....	64	1	5	1
51½	9½	4	129	1	4	1
52¼	9½	4¾	36	1	10	1
52½	9½	5	58	1	1	1
54½	10	4½	137	2	27	2
55	9½	7½	136	2	28	2
55	10	5	380	4	94	3
55½	9½	8	17	1	....	....
55½	10	5½	44	1	5	1
57	10	7	308	2	25	2
57	10¼	5¾	179	1	7	1
57¼	10¼	6	94	1	18	1
57½	10	7½	228	2	90	3
57½	10½	5	109	3	22	2
58	10	8	174	1	15	1
58⅓	10⅔	5	508	1	33	1
58½	10	8½	151	2	....	....
58½	10½	6	120	2	16	2
59	10	9	86	1	10	1
59	10½	8 7/12	8	1	....	....
59½	10	9½	94	1	7	1
59½	10⅙	8⅔	52	1	19	1
59¾	10¾	6	268	1	59	1
60	10	10	37	1	7	1
60	10⅙	9⅙	411	1	32	1
60	10¼	8¾	215	1	99	1
60	10½	7½	782	5	99	5
60	10¾	6¼	1,195	3	416	3
60	11	5	281	1	53	1
[1] 60	12	....	110	2	67	1
Total...	....	....	6,521	[2] 50	1,269	[2] 42

[1] Night work.
[2] Actual number of establishments. The total number can not be found by simple addition of the column, as some establishments work on more than one time schedule.

An examination of this table shows that while the great majority of the women and children employed worked 60 hours a week and at least 10 hours a day, the maximum legal working day (12 hours) and working week (60 hours) were not exceeded (except as already noted, by children working on a night shift).

Overtime work, i. e., in excess of the regular working schedules as entered in the above table, was reported as being done during the preceding year in 13 of the 47 establishments from which information on this point was received. In 3 of the 13 in which overtime was done, the amount of overtime worked by women was not sufficient to make their average working week exceed the legal 60 hours.

All of the remaining 10 establishments employed women, and 9 also employed children. In each, women worked overtime when the establishment so worked, and in several the children also worked the same overtime as the women and men, although completely satisfactory information upon this point was not obtained. The number of occasions during the year on which overtime had been worked varied among these 10 establishments from 4 to 65, averaging about 32, one establishment not being reported for on this point. The average amount of overtime per week similarly varied from 2 to 12 hours, averaging about 7 hours. In every case the average amount done was sufficient to make the total hours of labor of women or children so working exceed 60 hours a week.

POSTING OF TIME SCHEDULES.

Time schedules, showing the daily hours of labor of women and children (if both were employed), were conspicuously and very generally posted in the workroom where such persons were employed in 31 of the 50 establishments visited. In 1 establishment such posting had been done for women but not for children. In the remaining 18, in all of which women and in 12 of which children were employed, such posting had not been done for either class of employees.

The Pennsylvania law regarding the posting of hours of labor is peculiar among the States covered in that it requires such posting to be done for all employees. The degree in which it had been done for women and children in the establishments visited is shown above. For males over 16 years of age it had been done in 33 of the 50 establishments visited, all of which employed such males.

MEAL PERIOD.

The following table classifies the 50 visited establishments according to the length of the meal period in each:

LENGTH OF MIDDAY MEAL PERIOD—PENNSYLVANIA.

Length of meal period (in minutes).	Establishments having meal period of specified length.	
	Number.	Per cent.
25	1	2
30	28	56
35	3	6
40	2	4
45	7	14
50	1	2
60	8	16

In so far as information was obtained upon this point, a permit from the factory inspector for shortening the meal period was on file, as required by law, in those factories in which the meal period was less than 60 minutes.

OHIO.

SUMMARY OF LAWS.

Hours of labor:[1]

> Children under 16 years of age and females 16 and 17 years of age in "factory, workshop, business office, telephone or telegraph office, restaurant, bakery, hotel, apartment house, mercantile or other establishment * * *, nor in the distribution or transmission of merchandise or messages:" Legal day, 8 hours; legal week, 48 hours
>
> *Exceptions:* None.

Night work:[1] Prohibited for—

> Children under 16 years of age and females 16 and 17 years of age in establishments and occupations above mentioned between 6 p. m. and 7 a. m.
>
> *Exceptions:* None.

Posting of time schedules:[1] Is required in the case of children under 16 years of age and females 16 and 17 years of age in establishments above mentioned. Schedule to show the maximum number of working hours per day and per week. To be in printed form, furnished upon application by the factory inspection department after approval by attorney general, and posted conspicuously in every room where such persons are employed. [The law does not require that schedule show precise hours of beginning and stopping work.]

Meal period:[2] At least 30 minutes to be allowed children under 16 years of age and females 16 and 17 years of age employed in establishments and occupations mentioned above.

> *Penalty.*[3]—On employer for violating any of the legal provisions enumerated, $25 to $50.

Enforcement.[4]—As regards shops, factories, and mercantile establishments to be by the factory-inspection department.

CONDITIONS FOUND.

Of the 60 establishments visited all employed females 16 years of age and over, and 31 employed children under 16 years of age.

---

[1] Acts of 1908, p. 30, sec. 1 (Bulletin of the Bureau of Labor, No. 85, pp. 701, 702).
[2] Idem (Bulletin of the Bureau of Labor, No. 85, p. 702).
[3] Idem, sec. 3 (Bulletin of the Bureau of Labor, No. 85, p. 703).
[4] Idem, sec. 4 (Bulletin of the Bureau of Labor, No. 85, p. 703).

HOURS OF LABOR.

In none of the visited establishments did the regular working hours of women or children include work on Sunday or on a night shift.

The following table shows the regular hours of labor of women and children in these establishments, giving separately for children under 16 years of age, females 16 years of age and over, and females of the precise ages of 16 and 17 years of age, the number of such persons working according to each time schedule met with, and the number of establishments represented in each case. Data are given for the special class of females 16 and 17 years of age because of the fact that the Ohio law puts such females, as regards hours of labor, in the same category as children under 16 years of age. Information regarding females 16 and 17 years of age, however, is incomplete, as in many establishments it was impossible to obtain the correct ages of females over 16 years of age.

HOURS OF LABOR OF WOMEN AND CHILDREN—OHIO.

Hours of labor.			Females 16 years of age and over.		Children under 16 years of age.		Females 16 and 17 years of age.	
	Per day.		Number working specified hours.	Establishments represented.	Number working specified hours.	Establishments represented.	Number working specified hours.	Establishments represented.
Per week.	Monday to Friday.	Saturday.						
44	8	4	9	1	......	......	163	......
45	8	5	163	3	16	3	163	3
46	8	6	96	2	......	......	96	2
48	8	8	308	18	132	15	265	18
48	8¼	7	......	......	13	1	......	......
48	8½	5	......	......	174	2	......	......
48½	8½	6	224	2	......	......	......	......
49	9	4	45	1	......	......	......	......
50	9	5	15	1	......	......	......	......
52½	9	7½	43	1	......	......	......	......
53	9	8	258	3	18	3	......	......
54	9	9	31	2	2	1	......	......
55	9½	7½	68	1	......	......	......	......
55	10	5	2,678	19	4	3	25	4
56	9½	8½	19	1	......	......	......	......
57	10	7	162	2	......	......	......	......
57⁷⁄₁₂	10¼	6¾	97	1	......	......	......	......
58½	10	8½	310	2	16	2	60	2
59	10	9	260	3	2	1	6	1
59	10⅔	5⅝	84	1	3	1	......	......
60	10	10	799	17	......	......	42	3
60	10¼	9¼	181	1	3	1	......	......
60	10½	8½	99	1	......	......	7	1
Total	......	......	5,949	¹ 60	383	¹ 31	654	¹ 33

¹ Actual number of establishments. The total number can not be found by simple addition of the column as some establishments work on more than one time schedule.

The Ohio law, as noted above, fixes a flat 8-hour day and 48-hour week for children under 16 years of age and also for females 16 and 17 years of age. Examination of the above table shows that of the 383 children under 16 years of age employed the regular working schedules of 48, representing 12 different establishments, exceeded 48 hours a week; and that the working schedules of 187 other children, representing 3 different establishments, although not exceeding 48 hours a week, did exceed 8 hours a day from Monday to Friday.   In the case of females 16 and 17, 140 of the 654 reported as of these ages worked, according to regular time schedules, exceeding 48 hours a week.

In 2 of the establishments in which children under 16 years of age worked more than 8 hours a day, but not more than 48 hours a week, it was stated that the State factory-inspection department had consented to the working schedule in force.

Overtime work, i. e., in excess of the regular time schedules given in the above table, was reported as having been done during the preceding year by 21 of the 60 establishments' visited.   In 2 of these 21 establishments it was reported that such overtime work was limited to male employees over 16 years of age; in 1 women and children also worked overtime.   In the remaining 18 establishments no precise information was obtained as to whether or not children under 16 years of age and females 16 and 17 years of age worked overtime along with the rest of the force.   An examination of the pay roll in 1 establishment showed that 1 girl, 16 years of age, whose scheduled hours were 48 a week, had worked 115 hours during the pay-roll period of two weeks.

The number of occasions on which overtime work had been done varied among the 21 establishments which had so worked from 8 to 78, averaging about 43, no report on this point being received for 3 establishments.   The average hours per week of overtime work in these cases also varied from $1\frac{1}{2}$ to 9, averaging about 4, no report on this point being received from 1 establishment.

POSTING OF TIME SCHEDULES.

Time schedules showing daily working hours of women and children (if both were employed) were conspicuously and very generally posted in the workrooms where such persons were employed in 34 of the 56 establishments for which information on this point was obtained.   In 2 such posting was done for children but not for women. In the remaining 20, in all of which women, and in 6 of which children were employed, no such posting had been done.   In at least 7 of the 20 establishments in which posting was not done females 16 and 17 years of age were employed, and it is probable that such persons were also employed in the other 13, although in these latter the precise ages of females 16 years of age and over were not obtained.

In 1 establishment blank time schedules were posted, but the hours of labor had not been entered thereon.

MEAL PERIOD.

The following table classifies the 60 visited establishments according to the length of the meal period in each:

LENGTH OF MIDDAY MEAL PERIOD—OHIO.

Length of meal period (in minutes).	Establishments having meal period of specified length.	
	Number.	Per cent.
30	[1] 29	48
35	1	2
45	8	13
50	3	5
60	19	32

[1] Including 1 in which adult males are allowed 15 minutes.

ILLINOIS.

SUMMARY OF LAWS.[1]

Hours of labor:[2]

Children under 16 years of age in "any gainful occupation": Legal day, 8 hours; legal week, 48 hours.

Exceptions: None.

Night work:[2] Prohibited for—

Children under 16 years of age in "any gainful occupation": Between 7 p. m. and 7 a. m.

Exceptions: None.

Posting of time schedules: Required in the case of—

Children under 16[2] years of age in "any gainful occupation." Schedule to show number of hours of work each day of the week and precise hours when work and meal periods begin and end. To be in printed form, furnished by State factory inspector, and to be posted conspicuously in every room where such children are employed. Employment of child at other times than stated on schedule is a legal violation.

---

[1] By an act passed shortly after the field work of this investigation was completed, a legal day of 10 hours was established for all females in mechanical establishments, factories, and laundries. Acts of 1909, p. 212, secs. 1, 2, and 3. Approved June 15, 1909. (Bulletin of the Bureau of Labor, No. 85, p. 553.) This law was upheld by the State supreme court as constitutional. Ritchie *v.* Wayman, 91 N. E. Rep., 695 (Bulletin of the Bureau of Labor, No. 89, pp. 428–430).

[2] Hurd's Rev. Stat., 1905, ch. 48, sec. 20i (22d An. Rept. Com. of Labor, p. 338).

Females 16 years of age and over[1] in "any manufacturing establishment, factory, or workshop." Schedule to show "the hours for each day of the week between which work is required." To be printed and posted conspicuously in every room where such persons are employed. [This law does not require schedule form to be furnished by State.]

Meal period: No legal provision regarding the length of the meal period.

Penalty.[2]—On employer for violating above-quoted provisions, $5 to $100 for each offense; on persons having control of a child under 16 years of age for permitting it to work in violation of these provisions, $5 to $25 for each offense.

Enforcement.[3]—Charged to the State factory inspection department.

The factory inspector expressed himself as favorable toward the law regarding the posting of time schedules, but believed there should be a requirement that the schedules should be in the various languages of the employees concerned.

CONDITIONS FOUND.

The number of establishments visited was 47. All of these employed women (females 16 years of age and over), and 30 employed children under 16 years of age.

HOURS OF LABOR.

In none of these establishments did the regular working schedules call for Sunday work on the part of women or children, or for night work by children. In two establishments, however, women worked on regular night shifts; in 1 case 15 women working 9 hours per night Monday to Friday, a total of 45 hours per week; in the other 30 women working 10 hours per night Monday to Friday, a total of 50 hours per week.

The following table shows for women and children separately the number of such persons working according to each time schedule met with, and the number of establishments represented in each case. The working hours given represent the regular "winter schedule"; that is, for the whole year, except 2 or 3 months in summer.

---

[1] Hurd's Rev. Stat., 1905, ch. 48, sec. 26 (22d An. Rept. Com. of Labor, p. 340).

[2] Idem, sec. 20m (22d An. Rept. Com. of Labor, p. 339).

[3] Idem, sec. 20l (22d An. Rept. Com. of Labor, p. 339).

HOURS OF LABOR OF WOMEN AND CHILDREN—ILLINOIS.

Hours of labor.			Females 16 years of age and over.		Children under 16 years of age.	
Per week.	Per day. Monday to Friday.	Per day. Saturday.	Number working specified hours.	Establishments represented.	Number working specified hours.	Establishments represented.
44	8	4	....	....	1	1
44½	8	4½	....	....	1	1
46½	8½	4	73	1	....	....
47	8½	4½	13	1	....	....
47½	8	7½	....	....	59	1
47½	8½	5	7	1	....	....
48	8	8	328	2	621	25
49	9	4	[illegible]5	1	....	....
51	9½	4½	120	1	....	....
51⅛	9¼	4⅞	13	1	....	....
52	8¾	8¼	110	1	....	....
52	9½	4½	74	1	....	....
52½	9½	5	3	1	....	....
52⅚	9⅔	4½	21	1	....	....
53	9	8	291	2	....	....
54	9	9	318	4	....	....
54	9⅞	4⅝	96	1	....	....
54	10	5	88	3	....	....
54½	9¼	8¼	257	1	....	....
55	9½	7½	220	1	....	....
55	10	5	58	2	5	1
55½	10	5½	140	1	....	....
56	9½	8½	544	4	....	....
56	10	6	35	1	....	....
56½	9½	9	50	1	....	....
57	9½	9½	221	3	2	1
58	10	8	342	1	....	....
58½	10	8½	431	2	....	....
59	10	9	789	4	....	....
60	10	10	1,264	6	....	....
60	10⅛	9⅜	16	1	....	....
60	10⅞	5⅝	33	1	3	1
[1] 45	9	....	15	1	....	....
[1] 50	10	....	30	1	....	....
Total..	....	....	6,035	[2] 47	692	[2] 30

[1] Night work.
[2] Actual number of establishments. The total number can not be found by simple addition of the column, as some establishments work on more than one time schedule.

NOTE.—In 3 establishments, shorter working hours in summer were reported, as follows, the reduction in each case being made on Saturday: Establishment 11: 210 women, 89 children; winter, women, 60, children, 48; summer (July 1–Sept. 1), 55 and 45, respectively; establishment 13: 170 women, 25 children; winter, women, 54, children, 48: summer (June 1–Sept. 1), 49½ and 44½, respectively; establishment 25: 48 women, 9 children; winter, women, 54, children, 48; summer (May 15–Sept. 16), 50 and 45, respectively.

As noted above, the laws of Illinois in force at the time of this investigation did not limit the hours of labor of women. In the case of children, however, the legal day was fixed at 8 hours, and the legal week at 48 hours. Examination of the above table shows that 10 children under 16 years of age, working in 3 different establishments, were regularly employed for more than 8 hours a day and 48 hours a week.

Overtime work, i. e., in excess of the regular working hours listed in above table, was reported as having been done during the previous year by 27 of the 47 establishments. The number of occasions on which overtime was worked varied from 6 to 150 per year, averaging about 35. The amount of overtime work per week varied from 1 hour to 20 hours, averaging about 9 hours. In each of the 27 establishments working overtime women were employed, and in most cases worked such overtime as well as the men.   In 20 of these 27 establishments children were employed.   Satisfactory information as to whether or not such children worked overtime when the factory so worked was not obtained.   In four cases, however, an examination of the pay rolls showed that children under 16 years of age, whose regular hours were reported as 48 per week, had exceeded this amount, in one such case as much as 60 hours per week having been worked.

POSTING OF TIME SCHEDULES.

In 9 of the 47 establishments visited time schedules showing daily working hours of women and children (if both were employed) were conspicuously and very generally posted in the workrooms where such persons were employed.   In 15 such posting was done for children but not for women.   In the remaining 23 establishments, in all of which women and in 10 of which children were employed, the daily working hours were either not posted at all or were posted in only a very small proportion of the workrooms where women and children were employed.

MEAL PERIOD.

No report was received from one establishment as to the number of minutes allowed employees for meals.   The following table classifies the remaining 46 establishments according to the length of the midday meal period in each:

LENGTH OF MIDDAY MEAL PERIOD—ILLINOIS.

Length of meal period (in minutes).	Establishments having meal period of specified length.	
	Number.	Per cent.
30	[1] 31	67
45	[2] 1	2
50	1	2
55	1	2
60	[3] 12	26

[1] Including 1 in which some adult males were allowed 60 minutes.
[2] Including 1, in which adult males were allowed 30 minutes.
[3] Including 1 in which a few employees were allowed 30 minutes, and 1 in which pieceworkers fix own meal period.

INDIANA.

SUMMARY OF LAWS.

Hours of labor:[1]

Children under 16 years of age and females 16 and 17 years of age in "any manufacturing or mercantile establishment, laundry, renovating works, bakery, or printing office:"[2] Legal day, 10 hours; legal week, 60 hours.

Exceptions: None as to the 60-hour week, but 10-hour day may be increased in order to make a shorter day on one day in the week, provided that the days of work do not average more than 10 hours each.

Night work:[3] Prohibited for—

All females in any "manufacturing" capacity: Between 10 p. m. and 6 a. m.

Exceptions: None.

Posting of time schedules:[1] Required in the case of children under 16 years of age and females 16 and 17 years of age employed in establishments enumerated in above section on "hours of labor." Schedule to show number of working hours per day for each day of the week and time of beginning and stopping work. To be in printed form, and posted conspicuously in every room in which such persons are employed. Employment for longer than the hours stated in the schedule is a violation. [The law does not require that the schedule form be supplied by State.]

Meal period.[4]—All employees of any "manufacturing or mercantile establishment, mine, quarry, laundry, renovating works, bakery, or printing office" to have at least 60 minutes for the noonday meal; but the chief inspector, for good cause shown, may grant permits, exempting special establishments from this requirement, such permit to be conspicuously posted in the main entrance of the establishment, and may be revoked by chief inspector at discretion.

Penalty.[5]—On any person for violating, or for permitting a child or young person to work in violation of any of the above provisions—first offense, not more than $50; second offense, not more than $100, to which may be added not more than 10 days' imprisonment; third offense, not less than $250 and not more than 30 days' imprisonment.

---

[1] Ann. Stat. of 1894, Rev. of 1901, sec. 7087a (22d An. Rept. Com. of Labor, p. 397).

[2] For complete definition of these terms see footnote, p. 128.

[3] Ann. Stat. of 1894, Rev. of 1901, sec. 7087c (22d An. Rept. Com. of Labor, p. 398).

[4] Idem, sec. 7087k (22d An. Rept. Com. of Labor, pp. 399, 400).

[5] Idem, sec. 7087y (22d An. Rept. Com. of Labor, p. 402).

Enforcement.[1]—All above provisions intrusted to the State factory inspection department.

CONDITIONS FOUND.

The number of establishments visited was 47. Of these 46 employed females 16 years of age and over and 40 employed children under 16 years of age.

HOURS OF LABOR.

In none of the establishments visited was Sunday work performed by women or children. In none was night work done by females, but in one there were 10 boys under 16 years of age who worked regularly on a night shift 8 hours a night, 6 nights a week, a total of 48 hours a week.

The regular hours of labor of women and children in the several establishments visited are presented in the following table. This table shows for women and children separately the number of such persons working according to each time schedule met with and the number of establishments represented in each case:

HOURS OF LABOR OF WOMEN AND CHILDEN—INDIANA.

Hours of labor.			Females 16 years of age and over.		Children under 16 years of age.	
Per week.	Per day. Monday to Friday.	Per day. Saturday.	Number working specified hours.	Establishments represented.	Number working specified hours.	Establishments represented.
44	8	4	200	1	32	1
47	8½	4½	67	1	2	1
48	8	8	....	....	15	1
49½	9	4½	700	1	40	1
52	9	7	16	1	....	....
54	9	9	32	2	3	1
54½	10	4½	....	....	10	1
55	9⅚	5⅚	180	1	29	1
55	10	5	1,556	8	344	4
56	9½	8½	67	1	....	....
56½	9½	9	70	1	14	1
57	9½	9½	35	1	10	1
57	9⅔	8⅔	65	1	20	1
57½	10½	5	19	1	....	....
58	10	8	1,113	6	203	6
58½	10	8½	36	1	4	1
59	10	9	840	8	147	9
59½	10	9½	44	1	10	1
60	10	10	198	4	77	5
60	10⅙	9⅙	365	4	64	4
60	10¼	8¾	136	1	14	1
60	10⅓	7⅓	12	1	2	1
60	10⅔	5⅔	25	1	6	1
[2] 48	8	8	....	....	10	1
Total..	....	....	5,776	[3] 46	1,056	[3] 40

[1] Ann. Stat. of 1894, Rev. of 1901, sec. 7087v (22d Ann. Rept. Com. of Labor, p. 402).
[2] Night work.
[3] Actual number of establishments. The total number can not be found by simple addition of the column, as some establishments work on more than one time schedule.

As shown by this table, the regular hours of work for children and for women in no case exceeded 60 per week. In several instances, however, the performance of overtime work made the working week of such persons exceed the legal 60 hours. In total, overtime work was reported as having been done during the previous year by 23 establishments. The occasions on which overtime work was done varied among the establishments concerned from 6 to 150, and the average amount per week from 2 to 20 hours. In 7 of these establishments men only engaged in overtime work; in 7 women and children and in 3 women worked sufficient overtime on several occasions to make their weekly work periods exceed 60 hours; in 3 establishments overtime work was done, but not in sufficient amount on the average to make the working week for women and children exceed 60 hours. In the 3 establishments remaining of those mentioned as working overtime no satisfactory information was obtainable as to the age and sex of the persons so working.

The above remarks concerning overtime work by women relate to all females 16 years of age and over. It was impossible to obtain any information as to how many of the women reported on in each case specifically were 16 and 17 years of age.

POSTING OF TIME SCHEDULES.

Daily time schedules for women and children were posted conspicuously in 19 establishments. In the remaining 28 establishments, in each of which either women or children or both were employed, such schedules were either not posted at all or posted in only a very few of the workrooms in which such persons were employed.

MEAL PERIOD.

The following table classifies the 47 establishments visited according to the length of the midday meal period in each:

LENGTH OF MIDDAY MEAL PERIOD—INDIANA.

Length of meal period (in minutes).	Establishments having meal period of specified length.	
	Number.	Per cent.
30	8	17
40	3	6
45	2	4
50	2	4
60	32	68

In 7 of the 15 cases in which this table shows the meal period to have been less than 60 minutes in length, permits for the shortening of such period were posted as required by law. In the other 8 cases no permits were posted.

MICHIGAN.

SUMMARY OF LAWS.[1]

Hours of labor:[2]

Children under 16 years of age, females 16 years of age and over, and males 16 and 17 years of age in "any manufacturing establishment" (i. e., in "all places were goods, wares, or products are manufactured, repaired, cleaned, or sorted, in whole or in part)":[3] Legal day, 10 hours; legal week, 60 hours.

Exceptions: The 60-hour week may be increased only for the purpose of making machine repairs necessary to prevent interruption of the ordinary running of the establishment. The 10-hour day may be increased to make a shorter workday on the last day of the week.

Night work:[4] Prohibited for—

Children under 16 years of age in "any manufacturing establishment or workshop" [as defined above] between 6 p. m. and 7 a. m.

Posting of time schedules: Not required by law.

Meal periods:[5] In "any manufacturing establishment" the noonday meal period to be not less than 45 minutes, except that a factory inspector, for good cause shown, may issue a written permit allowing a shorter period, such permit to be conspicuously posted in the main entrance of the establishment, and to be revoked by inspectors at discretion.

Penalty.[6]—On any person for violating, or for permitting a child to be employed in violation of, any of the legal provisions quoted above, $5 to $100, or 10 to 90 days' imprisonment, or both.

---

[1] Shortly after the completion of the field work of this investigation a new law was passed in Michigan concerning hours of labor and night work. The distinguishing features of this law as regards manufacturing establishments are as follows: Legal day for males under 18 and all females, 10 hours a day; legal week, 54 hours, and not more than an average of 9 hours a day in any work:

Except that these provisions are not to apply to any person engaged in preserving perishable goods in fruit and vegetable canning establishments. Night work forbidden to children under 16 and females 16 to 18 between 6 p. m. and 6. a. m. (Bulletin 85, p. 636; Acts of 1909, act No. 285, sec. 9.)

[2] Acts of 1901, act No. 113, sec. 1, as amended by act No. 169, Acts of 1907 (22d An. Rept. Com. of Labor, p. 658). In stores employing more than 10 persons, legal week for males under 18 and for all females is not to exceed 60 hours.

[3] Idem, sec. 14, as amended by act No. 46, Acts of 1903 (22d An. Rept. Com. of Labor, p. 661).

[4] Idem, sec. 2, as amended by act No. 169, Acts of 1907 (22d An. Rept. Com. of Labor, p. 658).

[5] Idem, sec. 11 (22d An. Rept. Com. of Labor, p. 660).

[6] Idem, sec. 18 (22d An. Rept. Com. of Labor, p. 662).

Enforcement.[1]—Charged to the State factory-inspection department (bureau of labor and industrial statistics).

CONDITIONS FOUND.

All of the 19 establishments visited employed females 16 years of age and over, and 14 of them also employed children under 16 years of age.

HOURS OF LABOR.

In none of the establishments visited were children reported as working on Sunday. In one some of the women employees worked on Sunday about seven times a year, but when so working were given some other day in the week as holiday.

Work on a night shift was reported as being done by one child, and by no women. The child referred to was a boy 15 years of age. His employment at night was only temporary, during a rush season.

The regular hours of labor of all the women and children in the several establishments visited are presented in the following table. The table shows, for women and children separately, the number of such persons working according to each time schedule met with and the number of establishments represented in each case.

HOURS OF LABOR OF WOMEN AND CHILDREN—MICHIGAN.

Hours of labor.			Females 16 years of age and over.		Children under 16 years of age.	
Per week.	Per day. Monday to Friday.	Per day. Saturday.	Number working specified hours.	Establishments represented.	Number working specified hours.	Establishments represented.
[2] 52½	9½	5	[2] 1,000	1	[2] 121	1
54	9¾	5¼	705	1	63	1
54½	9½	7	70	1	13	1
55	9½	7½	200	1	15	1
55	10	5	962	3	101	3
55½	9½	8	60	1	20	1
58½	10	8½	28	1	15	1
[3] 59	10	9	[3] 332	3	72	1
59	10½	6½	108	1	56	1
60	10	10	220	2	3	1
60	10¼	8¾	50	1	3	1
60	10⅓	8⅓	360	1	27	1
60	10½	7½	218	2	70	1
[4] 60	12	....	....	....	1	1
Total ..	....	....	4,313	19	580	[5] 14

[1] Acts of 1901, act No. 113, secs. 12, 15, and 16 (22d An. Rept. Com. of Labor, pp. 660, 661).

[2] Including an unreported number of strippers and banders who worked 10 hours Monday to Friday, 5 hours Saturday, 55 hours week.

[3] Seven Sundays during the year some employees of one establishment worked 8 hours and were given some other day off during the week.

[4] Night work.

[5] Actual number of establishments. The total number can not be found by simple addition of the column, as some establishments work on more than one time schedule.

Examination of this table shows that in none of the several establishments did the regular hours of labor of women or children exceed the legal maximum of 60 a week, or, except when compensated for by a shorter Saturday, 10 per day.

Overtime work was reported as having been done during the previous year by 11 of the 19 visited establishments. In one of these cases men only worked overtime. The number of occasions on which overtime was worked varied among the other 10 establishments from 10 to 26, averaging about 17. The average number of overtime hours per week similarly varied from 4 to 9, averaging 6½.

Complete information was not obtained as to whether women and children worked overtime in all these cases, but a brief examination of the pay rolls showed that such persons had so worked in at least 2 establishments. It is probable, moreover, that women if not children had so worked in all the establishments referred to, as in all of them women were engaged in essential manufacturing processes.

The pay roll examination mentioned showed that in 1 establishment a boy under 16 years of age had worked 69 hours, and a girl under 16 years of age 63 hours during the week preceding the date of visit. In a second instance women were shown to have worked occasionally as much as 67 hours a week.

POSTING OF TIME SCHEDULES.

Time schedules showing daily hours of labor were posted in the office of 1 of the 19 establishments visited. In none of the other establishments were time schedules anywhere posted, but in 1 each employee was given a copy of the factory rules and these included a statement of the hours of labor.

MEAL PERIOD.

The following table classifies the 19 visited establishments according to the length of the midday meal period in each:

LENGTH OF MIDDAY MEAL PERIOD—MICHIGAN.

Length of meal period (in minutes).	Establishments having meal period of specified length.	
	Number.	Per cent.
30	8	42
45	4	21
50	1	5
60	6	32

As seen in this table, 8 establishments had a meal period of less than 45 minutes, and thus under the law required a special permit from a factory inspector. No such permit was posted in 7 of these 8 establishments, and information on this point was not received from the other one.

WISCONSIN.

SUMMARY OF LAWS.

Hours of labor:[1]

Children under 16 years of age, in "any gainful occupation:" Legal day, 10 hours; legal week, a total of 55 hours in 6 days.

Exception: To save perishable goods from serious damage.

No other exceptions applicable to factories or workshops.[2]

Night work:[1] Prohibited for—

Children under 16 years of age in "any gainful occupation:" Between 6 p. m. and 7 a. m.

Exception: To save perishable goods from serious damage.

No other exceptions applicable to factories or workshops.[2]

Posting of time schedules: Not required by law.

Meal period: Not regulated by law.

Penalty.[3]—On employer for violating above quoted provisions, $25 to $100, or not more than 30 days' imprisonment for each offense; on parent or guardian for permitting a child to work in violation of those provisions, $5 to $25 or not more than 30 days' imprisonment.

Enforcement.[4]—Charged to factory inspection department (bureau of labor and industrial statistics).

CONDITIONS FOUND.

All of the 19 establishments visited employed females 16 years of age and over, and 12 of them also employed children under 16 years of age.

---

[1] Ann. Stat. of 1898, Supp. of 1906, Acts of 1907, sec. 1728c (22d An. Rept. Com. of Labor, p. 1428).

Special legislation regarding cigar factories provides that no person under 18 shall work at "manufacturing cigars" more than 8 hours a day or 48 hours a week. Idem, sec. 1636–106 (22d An. Rept. Com. of Labor, p. 1424).

[2] The complete exceptions to the quoted laws are (a) children carrying newspapers between 4 and 6 a. m. and 4 and 8 p. m., who obey the laws concerning school attendance, are exempt from legal restrictions regarding hours of labor and night work; (b) children between 14 and 16 in stores may work as late as 9 p. m., but not more than 10 hours a day and not more than 55 hours or 6 days a week.

[3] Ann. Stat. of 1898, Supp. of 1906, Acts of 1907, secs. 1728h and 1728i (22d An. Rept. Com. of Labor, p. 1428).

[4] Idem, sec. 1728d (22d An. Rept. Com. of Labor, p. 1428).

HOURS OF LABOR.

In none of the establishments visited did the ~gular time schedules of women or children call for Sunday work or for work on a night shift.

The following table shows for women and children separately the number of such persons working according to each of the time schedules met with, and the number of establishments represented in each case.

HOURS OF LABOR OF WOMEN AND CHILDREN—WISCONSIN.

Hours of labor.			Females 16 years of age and over.		Children under 16 years of age.	
Per week.	Per day.		Number working specified hours.	Estab- lish- ments repre- sented.	Number working specified hours.	Estab- lish- ments repre- sented.
	Monday to Friday.	Saturday.				
45	9	....	61	1	2	1
53	9	8	70	1	5	1
54	9	9	17	1	....	
55	9½	7½	400	1	75	1
55	10	5	463	4	309	8
¹ 59	10	9	796	3	....	
60	10	10	² 737	² 10	55	² 2
Total...	....	....	2,544	³ 19	446	³ 12

¹ In 2 establishments 4 hours less on Saturdays from May to September, inclusive.
² Includes 3 establishments, with 187 women, but no children, in which pieceworkers, number not sep- arately reported, work from 3 to 8 hours per week less.
³ Actual number of establishments. The total number can not be found by simple addition of the column, as some establishments work on more than one time schedule.

Examination of this table shows that in 2 establishments children under 16 years of age worked regularly in excess of the legal 55-hour week. In neither of these cases could such excess be attributed to the necessity of "saving perishable goods from serious damage."

Overtime work was reported as having been done during the previous year by 8 of the 19 establishments. The number of occasions on which such overtime had been worked varied among these 8 establishments from 7 to 100, averaging about 57. The average number of overtime hours per week similarly varied from 8 to 18, averaging about 15.

In at least 4 of these establishments the women had worked overtime as well as the men. Whether or not children had so worked was not ascertained.

POSTING OF TIME SCHEDULES.

Time schedules showing daily hours of women or children were not posted in any of the 19 establishments visited.

MEAL PERIOD.

The following table classifies the 19 visited establishments according to the length of the midday meal period in each:

LENGTH OF MIDDAY MEAL PERIOD—WISCONSIN.

Length of meal period (in minutes).	Establishments having meal period of specified length.	
	Number.	Per cent.
30	5	26
60	14	74

MARYLAND.

SUMMARY OF LAWS.

Hours of labor:

Children under 16 years of age [1] in "any manufacturing business or factory established in any part of the State or in any mercantile business in the city of Baltimore": Legal day, 10 hours; legal week not restricted by law.

Exceptions: None.

All employees [2] of companies engaged in manufacturing certain classes of cotton and woolen goods are subject to a legal day of 10 hours. As the meaning and effect of this law and its exceptions are not entirely clear, the law is reproduced here in full:

SECTION 1. No corporation or manufacturing company engaged in manufacturing either cotton or woolens yarns, fabrics, or domestics of any kind, incorporated under the laws of this State, and no officer, agent, or servant of such named corporation or manufacturing company, and no person or firm owning or operating such corporation or manufacturing company within the limits of this State, and no agent or servant of such firm or person shall require, permit, or suffer its, his, or their employees in its, his, or their service, or under his, its, or· their control, to work for more than 10 hours during each or any day of 24 hours for one full day's work and shall make no contract or agreement with such employees or any of them: *Provided,* That they or he shall (sic) work for more than 10 hours for 1 day's work during each or any day of 24 hours, and said 10 hours shall constitute 1 full day's work.

SEC. 2. Any such named corporation or manufacturing company within the limits of this State shall be allowed, under the provisions of this section, the privilege of working male employees, over the age of 21 years, over the limit of 10 hours for the express purpose only of making repairs and improvements and getting fires made, steam up, and the machinery

---

[1] Pub. Gen. Laws, Code of 1903, art. 27, sec. 217 (22d An. Rept. Com. of Labor, p. 539).

[2] Idem, art. 100, secs. 1 and 2 (22d An. Rept. Com. of Labor, p. 549).

ready for use in their works, which can not be done during the limits of the 10 hours; the extra compensation for all such work to be settled between such corporation and manufacturing companies and the employees: *Provided,* That nothing in this article shall be so construed as to prohibit any employer from making a contract with his male employees, over the age of 21 years, to work by the hour for such time as may be agreed upon.

Night work: Not restricted for any class of employees.

Posting of time schedules: Not required by law.

Meal period: Not regulated by law.

> *Penalty.*[1]—The employment of a child under 16 years of age more than 10 hours a day or permitting such employment is considered as a misdemeanor. The penalty for violating the law regarding hours of labor in cotton and woolen mills not less than $100 for each offense.

> *Enforcement.*—Not charged to any special body. The factory inspection department (the bureau of statistics and information) makes no attempt to enforce these provisions.

The chief factory inspector, in an interview with an agent of the United States Bureau of Labor, stated that he did not think laws regulating hours of labor in factories were necessary or advisable; that such matters can best be settled by employers themselves. In support of this view, he pointed out that the reports of his department for the past five years indicate a gradual reduction of hours in factories. The chief factory inspector also expressed himself as being unable to see any advantage to be gained by having the hours of labor posted, and as not being in favor of a law upon the subject.

The investigation in Maryland did not cover establishments manufacturing cotton or woolen goods.

CONDITIONS FOUND.

The number of establishments visited was 28. Each of them employed both females 16 years of age and over and children under 16.

HOURS OF LABOR.

In none of these establishments was Sunday work regularly done by women or children. In none was night work done by children, but in one a woman was employed on a night shift, working 10 hours a night, 6 nights a week, a total of 60 hours a week.

The regular hours of labor for women and children in the 28 establishments referred to are presented in the following table. This table shows for women and children separately the number of such persons working according to each time schedule met with, and the number of establishments represented in each case.

---

[1] Pub. Gen. Laws, Code of 1903, art. 27, sec. 218. Idem, art. 100, sec. 3 (22d An. Rept. Com. of Labor, pp. 539, 549).

HOURS OF LABOR OF WOMEN AND CHILDREN—MARYLAND.

Hours of labor.			Females 16 years of age and over.		Children under 16 years of age.	
Per week.	Per day. Monday to Friday.	Per day. Saturday.	Number working specified hours.	Establishments represented.	Number working specified hours.	Establishments represented.
50	9	5	760	1	62	1
52½	8¾	8¾	440	1	39	1
54	9	9	159	1	29	1
54	9⅛	8⅜	198	1	10	1
54½	9¼	8¼	20	1	12	1
55	10	5	717	2	58	2
55½	9½	8	44	1	49	1
55¾	10	5¾	....	....	125	1
56	10	6	196	1	13	1
56½	9½	9	150	1	25	1
56¾	10¼	5½	509	1	78	1
57	10¼	5¾	545	1	....	....
57½	9¾	8¾	....	....	1	1
58	10	8	456	2	95	2
58½	10	8½	25	1	9	2
59	10	9	58	2	21	2
59½	10	9½	24	1	25	2
60	10	10	264	7	136	8
60	[1] 10½	9½	16	1	4	1
60	10⅛	9⅜	....	....	6	1
60	10¼	8¾	19	1	3	1
62	10½	9½	22	1	2	1
[2] 60	10	10	1	1	....	....
Total..	....	....	4,623	[3] 28	802	[3] 28

[1] Except Friday, 10⅛ hours.
[2] Night force.
[3] Actual number of establishments. The total number can not be found by simple addition of the column, as some establishments work on more than one time schedule.

As noted in the summary of the law given above, the only legal restriction upon the hours of labor is that children under 16 years of age may not be employed more than 10 hours a day. Examination of this table shows that 93 such children, employed in 5 different establishments, worked on a regular time schedule exceeding 10 hours a day for 5 days of the week. In one of these establishments, moreover, 2 children and 22 women worked regularly more than 60 hours a week. In the 1 case of regular night work reported only 1 woman was so employed.

Overtime work, i. e., work in excess of the time schedules as entered in the preceding table, was reported as having been done during the preceding year by 17 of the 28 establishments visited. The number of occasions on which such overtime had been done varied among the several establishments from 3 to 60, averaging about 28; the average number of hours overtime per week varied similarly from 2 to 18, averaging about 9. In 1 of the 17 establishments mentioned as working overtime, no children under 16 years of age had so worked. As regards the other 16 establishments no precise information was obtained as to the ages and sex of persons working overtime. As, however, with 2 exceptions these establishments were engaged in work in which females filled essential manufacturing processes, it is highly probable that women did work overtime when the factory so worked.

POSTING OF TIME SCHEDULES.

Time schedules showing daily hours of work for women and children were posted in the workrooms where such persons were employed, in 3 of the 28 establishments visited. In 23 no such posting was done, and in the remaining 2 no information upon this point was obtained. In 1 establishment a schedule of hours together with a copy of the factory regulations was furnished each employee personally.

MEAL PERIOD.

The following table classifies the 28 establishments visited according to the length of the midday meal period in each:

LENGTH OF MIDDAY MEAL PERIOD—MARYLAND.

Length of meal period (in minutes).	Establishments having meal period of specified length.	
	Number.	Per cent.
20	1	4
30	1 22	79
45	2	7
60	3	11

1 Including 1 in which a few males are allowed 50 minutes.

NORTH CAROLINA.

SUMMARY OF LAWS.

Hours of labor:[1]

Children under 16 years of age, females 16 and 17 years of age, males 16 and 17 years of age, in a "factory or manufacturing establishment:" Legal day, not restricted; legal week, 66 hours.

Exceptions: None as to legal week, but the following persons are exempt from the application of the law: Engineers, firemen, machinists, superintendents, overseers, section and yard hands, office men, watchmen and repairers of breakdowns.

Night work:[2] Prohibited for—

Children under 14 years of age in "a factory" between 8 p. m. and 5 a. m.

Posting of time schedules: Not required by law.

Meal period: Not regulated by law.

[1] Rev. of 1905, sec. 3363, and also Acts of 1907, ch. 463, sec. 2 (22d An. Rept. Com. of Labor, pp. 962, 971).

[2] Acts of 1907, ch. 463, sec. 4 (22d An. Rept. Com. of Labor, p. 971),

Penalty.—For "knowingly and willfully" requiring persons under 18 years of age to work more than 66 hours a week, as for a misdemeanor, at the direction of the court; for working children under 14 at night, not specified.[1]

Enforcement.—Not charged to any special body. The State has no factory inspection system.

CONDITIONS FOUND.

Twenty-six of the 28 establishments visited employed females 16 years of age and over, and each of the 28 establishments employed children under 16 years of age. The total number of such children employed was 1,346, an average of about 48 per establishment.

HOURS OF LABOR.

In none of the visited establishments did the regular time schedules of women or children call for Sunday work. In 1, however, women and children worked at night (i. e., between 8 p. m. and 5 a. m.). Some of the children so working were under 14 years of age.

The following table shows the regular hours of labor of women and children in the 28 establishments. It gives for women and children separately the number of such persons working according to each time schedule met with, and the number of establishments represented in each case.

HOURS OF LABOR OF WOMEN AND CHILDREN—NORTH CAROLINA.

Hours of labor.			Females 16 years of age and over.		Children under 16 years of age.	
Per week.	Per day. Monday to Friday.	Per day. Saturday.	Number working specified hours.	Establishments represented.	Number working specified hours.	Establishments represented.
[2] 55	10	[2] 5	698	2	383	2
58	10	8	680	5	245	6
59	10	9	112	2	62	3
59	10⅙	8⅙	77	1	32	1
59½	10¼	8¼	52	2	18	2
59¾	10⅓	8 1/12	35	1	32	1
60	10⅓	8⅓	55	1	29	1
60	10½	7½	115	2	60	2
60½	10 5/12	8 5/12	21	1	15	1
61	10½	8½	143	1	37	1
66	11 5/12	8 11/12	393	6	355	6
66	11½	8½	106	1	48	1
66¼	11 7/12	8⅓	50	1	22	1
[3] 56⅔	11⅓	....	4	1	8	1
Total ..	....	....	2,541	[4] 26	1,346	[4] 28

[1] Rev. of 1905, sec. 3363, and also Acts of 1907, ch. 463, sec. 3 (22d An. Rept. Com. of Labor, pp. 962, 971).

[2] Except for about 75 employees in picking department of 1 establishment, 4 hours more.

[3] Night work.

[4] Actual number of establishments. The total number can not be found by simple addition of the column, as some establishments work on more than one time schedule.

Examination of this table shows that in 1 establishment, employing 50 women (several of whom were under 18 years of age) and 22 children, the regular hours exceed 60 a week, which is the legal maximum for persons under 18 years of age. In this case the machinery of the establishment was stopped at the completion of 66 hours, but employees were required to remain 15 minutes to "clean up."

Overtime work was reported as having been done during the preceding year by 10 of the 28 establishments. In 1 of these 10 cases men only had worked overtime, and in 2 only a portion of the establishment had so worked. In the remaining 7 establishments of those referred to, the factory generally had run overtime, including women and children as well as men. In 4 of these cases such overtime, plus the regular hours, made a working week in excess of 66 hours, which is the legal maximum for persons under 18 years of age. The full hours per week, when working overtime, in these 4 establishments, were 76, 71½, 70½, and 72, respectively.

POSTING OF TIME SCHEDULES.

In 1 of the establishments visited daily time schedules for women and children were posted in all rooms in which such persons were employed. In none of the other 27 establishments were the hours of labor posted.

MEAL PERIOD.

The following table classifies the 28 establishments visited according to the length of the midday meal period in each:

LENGTH OF MIDDAY MEAL PERIOD—NORTH CAROLINA.

Length of meal period (in minutes).	Establishments having meal period of specified length.	
	Number.	Per cent.
30	1	4
40	1	4
45	11	39
60	15	54

In the 2 establishments in which night work was done, the time allowed for the midnight lunch was 15 minutes. Of the 10 establishments in which overtime work had been done, the time allowed for lunch before beginning overtime work was 60 minutes in 1 and 30 minutes in 5, while in the other 4 establishments no lunch period was allowed at such time.

GEORGIA.

SUMMARY OF LAWS.

Hours of labor:

All employees [1] of "cotton or woolen manufacturing establishments:" Legal day, not limited; [2] legal week, 66 hours.

> *Exceptions:* (a) The 66-hour week may be extended in order "to make up lost time, not to exceed 10 days, caused by accidents or other unavoidable circumstances;" (b) the law does not apply to engineers, firemen, watchmen, mechanics, teamsters, yard employees, clerical force, and all help needed "to clean up and make necessary repairs or changes in or of machinery."

Females under 21 years of age and males under 21 years of age [3] in "all other manufacturing establishments or machine shops" (i. e., other than cotton or woolen mills): Legal day, from sunrise to sunset, "the usual and customary time for males being allowed from the same;" legal week, not limited.

> *Exceptions:* None.

Night work: Prohibited for—

Children under 14 years of age [4] "in or about any factory or manufacturing establishment," between 7 p. m. and 6 a. m.

Females under 21 years of age and males under 21 years of age [5] in all manufacturing establishments, other than cotton or woolen factories, between sunset and sunrise.

Posting of time schedules: Not required by law.

Meal period: Not regulated by law.

> *Penalties:* (a) On a cotton or woolen manufacturing establishment making or enforcing a contract in violation of the law establishing a 66-hour week in such establishments, $25 to $500 for each offense; [6] (b) on employer for employing children under 14 years of age between 7 p. m. and 6 a. m., and on parent or guardian for hiring or placing a child under 14 years of age to work under such conditions, the same as for a misdemeanor; [7] (c) for violating law limiting hours of labor to the time between sunrise and sunset, penalty not specified.

> *Enforcement.*—Not charged to any specific body. There is no factory-inspection system in Georgia.

---

[1] Code, 1895, sec. 2615 (22d An. Rept. Com. of Labor, p. 289).

[2] The law verbally establishes a legal day of 11 hours, but the further provision that employees may arrange otherwise, so long as the number of hours per week does not exceed 66, effectively nullifies the 11-hour day provision.

[3] Code, 1895, sec. 2619 (22d An. Rept. Com. of Labor, p. 289).

[4] Acts of 1906, p. 98, sec. 3 (22d An. Rept. Com. of Labor, p. 298).

[5] Code, 1895, sec. 2619 (22d An. Rept. Com. of Labor, p. 289).

[6] Idem, sec. 2617 (22d An. Rept. Com. of Labor, p. 289).

[7] Acts of 1906, p. 98, sec. 7 (22d An. Rept. Com. of Labor, p. 298).

CONDITIONS FOUND.

Each of the 27 establishments visited employed females 16 years of age and over, and 26 also employed children under 16 years of age.

HOURS OF LABOR.

In none of these establishments was night work (i. e., work on a regular night shift) done, and in none did women and children work on Sunday.

The following table shows the regular hours of labor of women and children in the 27 establishments referred to.

The time schedules given are those observed in that part of the year, usually winter, when the working hours were longest. Three establishments reduced their working week by 4 or 5 hours in summer, and 1 made a similar reduction during the winter months. Also 2 other factories—a box factory, regular hours 60 per week, and a confectionery establishment, regular hours 56 per week—frequently worked only a half day on Saturday, although such reduction was not made at scheduled times.

It is to be noted also that the table does not include occasional instances in which school children worked in a factory a few hours per day before and after school. Thus in a hosiery factory 12 children were reported as so working about 4 hours a day.

HOURS OF LABOR OF WOMEN AND CHILDREN—GEORGIA.

Hours of labor.			Females 16 years of age and over.		Children under 16 years of age.	
Per week.	Per day. Monday to Friday.	Per day. Saturday.	Number working specified hours.	Establishments represented.	Number working specified hours.	Establishments represented.
55	11⅓	....	205	3	156	3
56	9½	8½	53	1	12	1
56⅔	10⅓	5	86	1	66	1
[1] 59	10	9	107	3	25	3
59	10¼	7¾	60	1	6	1
59	10½	6½	123	1	75	1
[2] 59¼	10¾	5½	71	1	41	1
59½	10¾	5¾	38	1	9	1
[3] 60	10	10	33	2	14	2
[4] 60	10⅛	9⅜	68	2	2	1
60	10⅞	5⅝	711	4	139	4
60	$10\frac{11}{12}$	$5\frac{5}{12}$	37	1	25	1
60½	10¾	6¾	38	1	9	1
60⅔	11	5⅔	22	1	7	1
62¼	11¼	6	50	1	35	1
64	11½	6½	76	1	65	1
66	11⅓	9⅓	11	1	4	1
66	11½	8½	37	1	16	1
66⅓	$11\frac{5}{12}$	9¼	77	1	36	1
Total..	....	....	1,903	[5] 27	742	[5] 26

[1] Winter schedule for 2 establishments; summer schedule, about 6 months, 4 hours less.
[2] Summer schedule; winter schedule, Oct. 1 to Mar. 31, 30 minutes less per day, 3 hours less per week.
[3] Winter schedule for 1 establishment; summer schedule, about 6 months, 5 hours less.
[4] Winter schedule for 1 establishment; summer schedule, about 6 months, 4 hours less.
[5] Actual number of establishments. The total number can not be found by simple addition of the column, as some establishments work on more than 1 time schedule.

Examination of this table shows that in 1 establishment the regular time schedule for women and children exceeded 66 hours a week. This was a woolen mill, to which the 66-hour limit of the law applied.

Overtime work during the preceding year had been done by 10 of the 27 establishments. In 6 of these the overtime, plus the regular working period, made a working week in excess of 66 hours. Only 1 of these 6 establishments, however, was a woolen or cotton mill and thus within the legal restriction of 66 hours per week. In this factory, with regular hours 66 per week, overtime had been worked about 30 times during the year, the average amount per week when so working being 12½ hours. Women as well as men had here worked overtime, but children had not.

Practically all of the factories other than cotton and woolen mills were operated during some part of the year either before sunrise or after sunset, or both. This investigation in Georgia, however, developed that the sunrise to sunset clause of the law was practically a dead letter. No factory paid attention to it and there was no apparent effort to enforce it.

POSTING OF TIME SCHEDULES.

The law of Georgia does not require that time schedules be posted.

In 1 of the 27 establishments visited, time schedules showing the daily hours of labor for minors and women were posted in all workrooms. In 2 others time schedules showing weekly working hours were similarly posted. In the remaining 24 establishments such posting was nowhere done.

MEAL PERIOD.

The following table classifies the 27 establishments visited according to the length of the midday meal period in each:

LENGTH OF MIDDAY MEAL PERIOD—GEORGIA.

Length of meal period (in minutes).	Establishments having meal period of specified length.	
	Number.	Per cent.
30	1 11	41
35	1	4
40	6	22
45	3	11
60	6	22

1 Including 1 establishment in which some women and children had 35 minutes; and 1, in which a few hands had 60 minutes.

In the 10 establishments doing overtime work, the time allowed for lunch before overtime work began was 20 minutes in 1 establishment and 30 minutes in 3, while in 6 no time was allowed for lunch before overtime work commenced.

It was reported that in 1 of the cotton mills the machinery was never stopped and that employees could work during the meal period if they wished to do so.

FLORIDA.

SUMMARY OF LAWS.

Hours of labor and night work:[1]

Children under 12 years of age in "gainful occupations:" Legal day, 9 hours; legal week, 6 days; night work prohibited between 9 p. m. and 6 a. m. Subject to the following conditions: (a) No child under 12 years of age, unless working for in the vocation of, and under the supervision and direction of, parent or guardian, shall be employed at any time in a factory, workshop, mine, quarry, bowling alley, barroom, beer garden, or place of amusement·where intoxicating liquors are sold, or, during the session of the public schools, in any other occupation for gain. (b) Household and agricultural work are exempt from the above quoted legal restrictions regarding hours of labor and night work.

Posting of time schedules: Not required by law.

Meal period: Not regulated by law.

Penalties.[2]—On employer for violating above legal provisions regarding hours of labor and night work of children, not more than $1,000, or imprisonment of not more than 6 months, or both; on parent or guardian for permitting child under 12 years of age to be employed in violation of such provisions, not more than $500 or imprisonment of not more than 90 days, or both.

Enforcement.[3]—Charged to the sheriff, the city or town marshal or police officers, within whose jurisdiction the place of employment may be located. There is no factory inspection department in Florida.

CONDITIONS FOUND.

Each of the 14 establishments visited employed females 16 years of age and over, and 13 of the 14 also employed children under 16 years of age.

HOURS OF LABOR.

Nearly all the establishments visited in Florida were cigar factories. Most of the employees therein were pieceworkers, who very seldom worked according to fixed time schedules. Therefore, the following table, giving the time schedules of women and children in the several factories, is only approximately accurate. It gives in

---

[1] Acts of 1907, ch. 5686, secs. 2, 3, and 9 (22d An. Rept. Com. of Labor, pp. 285, 286).

[2] Idem, secs. 6 and 7 (22d An. Rept. Com. of Labor, pp. 285, 286).

[3] Idem, sec. 5 (22d An. Rept. Com. of Labor, p. 285).

the case of each establishment the time schedule of the time workers, or that considered by the establishment as its regular schedule. In no case did employees regularly exceed such schedule, but in many cases pieceworkers failed to equal it. No detailed information was sought in this matter, as there was no law limiting the hours of labor of any person 12 years of age or over, or even of children under 12 years of age if acting as "helpers" and not directly employed by the factory in question.

Also, it is to be repeated that the children covered by this table include only regular employees and do not include "helpers."

HOURS OF LABOR OF WOMEN AND CHILDREN—FLORIDA.

Hours of labor.			Females 16 years of age and over.		Children under 16 years of age.	
Per week.	Per day.		Number working specified hours.	Establishments represented.	Number working specified hours.	Establishments represented.
	Monday to Friday.	Saturday.				
52	6	7	48	1	10	1
54	9	9	127	2	27	2
57	10	7	80	2	17	1
58	10	8	143	2	14	2
60	10	10	351	3	35	3
60	10½	7½	265	4	27	4
Total ..	....	....	1,014	14	130	13

No Sunday work and no night work was done by any of these establishments.

Overtime work during the preceding year was reported as having been done in only one establishment. This was a cigar-box factory, which had worked overtime on 45 occasions during the year, averaging when so working 10 hours overtime per week.

POSTING OF TIME SCHEDULES.

Time schedules showing hours of labor of women or children were not posted in any of the establishments visited.

MEAL PERIOD.

The following table classifies the 14 establishments visited according to the length of the midday meal period in each:

LENGTH OF MIDDAY MEAL PERIOD—FLORIDA.

Length of meal period (in minutes).	Establishments having meal period of specified length.	
	Number.	Per cent.
30	[1] 4	29
60	9	64
75	1	7

[1] Including 1 establishment in which part of force had 60 minutes.

LOUISIANA.

SUMMARY OF LAWS.

Hours of labor:[1]

Children under 16 years of age, females 16 years of age and over, and males 16 and 17 years of age in factories, workshops, mines, mercantile establishments (in which more than 5 persons are employed), etc.:[2] Legal day, 10 hours; legal week, 60 hours.

> *Exceptions:* Limitations on working-day and working week not to apply to mercantile establishments on Saturday night or 20 days before Christmas. No exceptions as regards factories and workshops.

Night work:[3] Prohibited for—

Children under 16 years of age and females 16 and 17 years of age in establishments and occupations enumerated above; between 7 p. m. and 6 a. m.

> *Exceptions:* Limitation on working week not to apply to mercantile establishments on Saturday night or during 20 days before Christmas. No exceptions as regards factories and workshops.

Posting of time schedules: Not required by law.

Meal period:[3] One hour to be "allowed each day for dinner" in all establishments and occupations enumerated above, but at the desire of two-thirds of the employees this period may be reduced to not less than 30 minutes.

> *Exception:* Does not apply to stores and mercantile establishments on Saturday or 20 days before Christmas.

> *Penalties:* For violation of provision regarding hours of labor and meal period, $25 to $50, or imprisonment of 10 days to 6 months, or both;[3] for violation of provision regarding night work, $25 to $100, or imprisonment of 10 days to 6 months, or both.[4]

---

[1] Acts of 1908, act No. 301, sec. 4 (Bulletin of the Bureau of Labor, No. 85, pp. 597, 598).

[2] The full list of places and occupations to which the law applies is as follows: "Mill, factory, mine, packing house, manufacturing establishment, workshop, laundry, millinery or dressmaking store or mercantile establishment in which more than five persons are employed, or in any theater, concert hall, or in or about any place of amusement where intoxicating liquors are made or sold, or in any bowling alley, bootblacking establishment, freight or passenger elevator, or in the transmission or distribution of messages, either telegraph or telephone, or any other messages, or merchandise, or in any other occupation not herein enumerated which may be deemed unhealthful or dangerous." But all agricultural and domestic industries are specifically excluded from the operation of the law. Acts of 1908, act No. 301, sec. 1 (Bulletin of the Bureau of Labor, No. 85, p. 596).

[3] Acts of 1908, act No. 301, sec. 4 (Bulletin of the Bureau of Labor, No. 85, p. 598).

Enforcement:[1] " It shall be the duty of the commissioner of labor and industrial statistics and his deputies, and such factory inspectors as will be appointed in incorporated cities and towns by the mayor or with the consent of the council, and in parishes, by the police jury * * * to enforce the provisions of this act."

CONDITIONS FOUND.

All of the 29 establishments visited employed females 16 years of age and over, and 26 of them also employed children under 16 years of age. No information was obtained as regards males 16 and 17 years of age, who under the law relating to hours of labor are classed with children.

HOURS OF LABOR.

In none of the 29 establishments did the regular working hours of women or children include Sunday work or work on a night shift.

The following table shows, separately for women and children, the number of such persons working according to each time schedule met with, and the number of establishments represented in each case.

HOURS OF LABOR OF WOMEN AND CHILDREN.—LOUISIANA.

Hours of labor.			Females 16 years of age and over.		Children under 16 years of age.	
Per week.	Per day.		Number working specified hours.	Establishments represented.	Number working specified hours.	Establishments represented.
	Monday to Friday.	Saturday.				
48	8	8	6	1	....	....
50	9	5	249	2	57	2
50½	8½	8	17	1	4	1
52	9	7	54	2	16	2
52	9½	4½	352	1	108	1
53	9½	5½	65	1	12	1
54	9	9	....	....	5	1
55	10	5	64	3	25	2
56	9½	8½	304	1	34	1
56½	9½	9	16	1	23	1
56½	10	6½	9	1	1	1
57	9½	9½	....	....	8	1
57	10	7	39	1	2	1
58	10	8	32	1	14	2
59	10	9	39	2	7	2
59½	10	9½	....	....	1	1
60	10	10	405	10	142	8
60	10½	7½	151	1	95	1
Total ..	....	....	1,802	29	554	[2] 26

[1] Acts of 1908, Act No. 301, sec. 3. See also idem, sec. 23, and Acts of 1906, act No. 34, sec. 6. (Bulletin of the Bureau of Labor, No. 85, pp. 598, 601, and 22d An. Rept. Com. of Labor, p. 523.)

[2] Actual number of establishments. The total number can not be found by simple addition of the column, as some establishments work on more than one time schedule.

Examination of this table shows that in none of these establishments did the regular hours of women or children exceed the legal maximum of 60 a week. In 1, however, 151 women and 95 children worked in excess of the maximum legal day of 10 hours.

Overtime work was reported as having been done during the preceding year by 9 establishments. In the case of 1 of these establishments such overtime was so frequent as to almost constitute part of the regular working hours. This was an oyster canning factory situated outside of New Orleans. The regular hours were reported as 10 per day, 60 per week. On busy days, however, i. e., days when the oysters were coming in fast, women and children began shucking frequently at 4.30 or 5 o'clock in the morning and worked as much as 15 hours per day.

Overtime work by the other 8 establishments reported as so working varied as to number of occasions from 3 to 50, averaging about 16, and as to the average number of overtime hours per week from 3 to 18, averaging about 8. Complete information was not obtained as to whether women and children worked overtime on all these occasions. It was developed, however, that in most of these factories women had worked overtime as well as the men, and that in a few of them at least children also had so worked.

POSTING OF TIME SCHEDULES.

Time schedules for women and children were posted in none of the 29 establishments visited.

MEAL PERIOD.

The following table classifies the 29 establishments visited according to the length of the midday meal period in each:

LENGTH OF MIDDAY MEAL PERIOD—LOUISIANA.

Length of meal period (in minutes).	Establishments having meal period of specified length.	
	Number.	Per cent.
30	20	69
60	9	31

Although information upon this point was difficult to obtain, it did not appear that in any instance where the meal period was less than one hour such reduction was without the consent of at least two-thirds of the employees.

CHAPTER IV.

POSTING OF LABOR LAWS.

CHAPTER IV.

POSTING OF LABOR LAWS.

INTRODUCTION.

For the purpose of informing employees and keeping them informed of the laws under which they work, the method is sometimes followed of posting copies of the labor laws, or of portions thereof, in conspicuous places in the factory workrooms.

This is a matter of legislation in 6 of the 17 States covered by the investigation. These 6 States are Rhode Island, New York, Pennsylvania, New Jersey, Indiana, and Wisconsin. In 3 of these, New York, Pennsylvania, and Indiana, it is specifically required that the employer shall post a copy of the factory and woman and child labor laws, or of the significant portions thereof, in a conspicuous manner. In Rhode Island it is required that the factory inspectors, not the employers, shall do such posting. The New Jersey provision orders the commissioner of labor to furnish copies of the labor laws for posting, on request of the employer; it does not compel the employer to make such request. Finally, the Wisconsin law on this subject is simply that the factory inspectors are authorized to post copies of the labor laws if they consider such procedure desirable.

In none of the other 11 States is legislation upon this subject in force. Several of these States, however, do require time schedules to be posted, and in a few instances an abstract of the labor laws is printed on the form used for the time schedule, and this results in such abstract being posted.

The laws referred to throughout this volume are as in force at the time of the investigation, December, 1908, to April, 1909. The text of the laws in force January 1, 1912, is given in the appendixes at the end of this volume.

MAINE.

There is no legal requirement that the factory laws or woman and child labor laws be posted.

In 3 establishments the woman and child labor laws were posted in some of the workrooms, and in another establishment a copy of the Maine school laws was hung. In none of the remaining 22 establishments were any of the laws referred to posted.

MASSACHUSETTS.

There is no legal reference in the legislation of Massachusetts to the posting of any of the labor laws. There is, however, a requirement that time schedules for women and children be posted, and the forms used for these schedules contain a printed copy of those sections of the law relating to the subject of hours of labor.

Therefore, the sections of the law referred to (secs. 24 and 25, ch. 106) may be considered as being posted wherever the time schedules are posted. (See section on "Posting of time schedule," pp. 167 and 170 of this report.) As regards the posting of all the labor laws, information was not obtained.

RHODE ISLAND.

The posting of the factory and woman and child labor laws is required by the following legal provision:[1]

A printed copy of this chapter shall be posted by the inspectors in each workroom of every factory, manufacturing or mercantile establishment where persons are employed who are affected by the provisions of this chapter.

The chapter here referred to includes the child labor and factory inspection laws of the State.

It will be observed that, as the legal provision reads, a copy of the law is to be posted in every workroom where persons affected thereby are employed, but that the posting is to be done by the factory inspectors. This latter provision would seem to absolve employers from responsibility in the matter further than to see that copies of the law once posted are kept posted.

The factory inspection department does not attempt to carry out to the letter the requirement that a copy of the law be posted in every workroom in which persons affected by the law are employed. In the case of communicating rooms, where employees pass frequently from one to the other, it is not considered necessary that posting be done in each room. It is regarded as sufficient if a copy of the law is posted in a room through which all the employees concerned must pass. On the other hand, if rooms on the same floor have separate entrances, it is held that posting should be done in each room. Furthermore, the chief inspector does not believe that the requirement as to the posting of the law was intended to apply to all establishments; such, for instance, as small stores.

The present investigation developed that in 11 of the 27 establishments visited copies of the woman and child labor laws and of the factory inspection laws were very generally posted in all workrooms where women and children were employed. In 13

---

[1] Gen. Laws, 1896, ch. 68, sec. 13 (22d An. Rept. Com. of Labor, p. 1210).

establishments copies of the law were nowhere posted, and in the remaining 3 such posting was too scattered or to inconspicuous to be of any practical service.

CONNECTICUT.

There is no State law regarding the posting of copies of the woman and child labor or factory laws.

In 3 of the 35 establishments visited copies of the law were very generally posted in workrooms where women and children were employed. In the remaining 32 establishments no such posting was anywhere done.

NEW YORK.

The law of New York requires all labor laws to be posted. The requirement in full is as follows: [1]

A copy or abstract of the provisions of this chapter applicable thereto, to be prepared and furnished by the commissioner of labor, shall be kept posted by the employer in a conspicuous place on each floor of every factory where persons are employed who are affected by the provisions thereof.

The term "factory" includes also "any mill, workshop, or other manufacturing establishment where one or more persons are employed at labor." [2]

The chapter here referred to includes all of the laws of New York State bearing upon matters of labor or factory inspection.

Penalty.—First offense, $20 to $50; second offense, $50 to $200, or imprisonment not more than 30 days, or both; third offense, not less than $250, or imprisonment not more than 60 days, or both.

Thus, in New York the labor laws are to be posted, in full or in abstract form, upon each floor of a factory, not, as in Rhode Island, in each workroom. The limitation that posting is only to be done on floors where persons affected by the laws are employed is of little importance, as a portion at least of the State labor laws applies to every class of employees. The State is to furnish the copies of the laws to be posted but the employer is responsible for the proper posting thereof.

Factory inspectors interviewed by agents of the Bureau expressed themselves generally as in favor of the principle of labor-law posting, but thought that the strict inforcement of the law upon this point took up time that could be employed more advantageously in inforc-

---

[1] Rev. Stat., 3d ed., 1901, p. 2098, sec. 68, as amended by ch. 505, Acts of 1907, and p. 2120, sec. 209, as amended by ch. 506, Acts of 1907 (22d An. Rept. Com. of Labor, pp. 907, 931).

[2] Idem, p. 2089, sec. 2, as amended by ch. 550, Acts of 1904.

ing more important laws. This attitude is well expressed in the following excerpt from the report of the chief factory inspector for 1905 (p. 14):

The orders enumerated in Division I of this table are unimportant, as the subjects covered do not affect the conditions of employment or welfare of employees. The posting of laws, schedule of hours, and noonday permits do not add one iota to the respect in which the law is held by the average manufacturer, neither does compliance with the inspectors' orders to properly post them add to the comfort or safety of employees; nevertheless, the statute directs that they shall be posted in every factory and shop, and, as will be seen, these trivial orders constitute more than 50 per cent of the total given in this table.

Copies of the labor laws were posted on all floors of 28 of the 36 establishments visited, and were nowhere posted in 6. Information upon this point was not reported for the other 2 establishments.

NEW JERSEY.

A section of chapter 64 of the Acts of 1904, which contains practically all the child labor and factory laws, provides that: [1]

An abstract of this law shall be prepared and furnished upon request by the commissioner to every corporation, firm, or person in this State who is affected thereby, and every manufacturer to whom a copy of such abstract is sent or delivered shall post such abstract of this law and keep it posted in plain view in such place that it can be easily read by the employees or operatives in coming in or going out from said factory, workshop, or mill.

This law covers in its scope all factories, workshops, mills, or other places where the manufacture of goods of any kind is carried on.[2]

There is no specific penalty attached for the violation of this provision, and the provision itself is not mandatory as regards the posting of the factory laws. The State commissioner of labor is ordered to prepare abstracts of the factory laws and to furnish employers therewith on request. The employer, however, is under no legal obligation to make such request. As regards the place of posting the abstract, the law provides merely that it be done once, at the entrance of the factory, and in such manner that it may be conveniently read by the employees.

Copies of the law referred to in the above-quoted statute were conspicuously posted in 7 of the 27 establishments visited, and in 1 other establishment such posting was done in the office only. In the remaining 19 establishments copies of the law were nowhere posted.

---

[1] Acts of 1904, ch. 64, sec. 25 (22d An. Rept. Com. of Labor, p. 864).
[2] Idem, sec. 1 (22d An. Rept. Com. of Labor, p. 860).

PENNSYLVANIA.

The Pennsylvania law regarding the posting of labor laws is as follows: [1]

Every person, firm, or corporation employing men, women, or children in any establishment shall post and keep posted in a conspicuous place, in every room where such help is employed, a printed copy of the factory laws * * *.

The term "establishment" in this law means any place where men, women, or children are employed for money, with the exception of domestic service, coal mining, and farm labor.[2]

Penalty.—$25 to $500, or imprisonment 10 to 60 days.

This law is specific in its directions, leaving little or no room for the exercise of personal judgment. Under it it becomes the duty of every employer to post in every workroom where anyone is employed for a money return a printed copy of the factory laws.

The chief factory inspector stated that he favors and enforces the above law, but was doubtful as to its effectiveness.

Copies of the factory laws were conspicuously and very generally posted in workrooms containing women and children (if both were employed) in 39 of the 50 establishments visited; and were not so posted in 11 establishments.

OHIO.

There is no specific legal requirement that copies of the labor laws be posted. The factory-inspection department, however, prepares printed posters containing the factory laws and supplies them for posting.

Copies of the woman and child labor laws were found to be conspicuously posted in the workrooms where such persons worked in 47 of the 60 establishments visited, were posted in only a few of several workrooms in 2 establishments, and were nowhere posted in the remaining 11.

ILLINOIS.

The Illinois law makes no provision for the posting of factory laws or laws relating to woman and child labor. There is, however, a legal requirement that for minors a time schedule and register of names be posted in every room where such minors are employed,[3] and the blank forms of these schedules and registers contain a printed copy of the laws relating to these particular subjects.

---

[1] Acts of 1905, act No. 226, secs. 10 and 23 (22d An. Rept. Com. of Labor, pp. 1177, 1180).

[2] Idem, sec 1 (22d An. Rept. Com. of Labor, p. 1175).

[3] Hurd's Rev. Stat., 1905, ch. 48, secs. 20*b* and 20*i* (22d An. Rept. Com. of Labor, pp. 336, 338).

The chief factory inspector thinks that all laws, schedules, etc., posted for the information of employees, should be in the various languages of the employees, and not merely in English, which many factory workers do not understand.

Copies of the woman and child labor laws were posted in the workrooms where women and children were employed in 15 of the 47 establishments visited. In the remaining 32 establishments, in all of which women, and in 15 of which children, were employed, such posting was nowhere done.

INDIANA.

The Indiana law makes the following provision regarding the posting of labor and factory laws: [1]

It shall be the duty of the chief inspector   *   *   *   to furnish copies of this act, which shall be conspicuously posted or hung, and kept posted or hung, in each workroom of every manufacturing or other establishment to which it relates   *   *   *   by the proprietor or occupant thereof.

The act referred to contains the factory and woman and child labor laws of the State and relates to ·· manufacturing or mercantile establishments, mine, quarry, laundry renovating works bakery. or printing office.'' [2]

> *Penalty.*—First offense, not more than $50; second offense, not more than $100, to which may be added imprisonment for not more than 10 days; third offense, not less than $250 and imprisonment for not more than 30 days.

A duty is thus placed upon every factory employer to post a copy of the factory and woman and child labor laws in every workroom of his establishment.

Printed copies of the laws are supplied by the chief factory inspector on request. They are printed on large sheets of white paper, which are easily torn down and destroyed. This fact probably accounts for many of the cases of noncompliance with the law.

Women or children or both were found employed in all of the 47 establishments visited. The present investigation developed that in 19 of these 47 copies of the woman and child labor and factory laws were very generally posted in all workrooms where such persons were employed. In the remaining 28 establishments such posting was either not done at all or was done too inconspicuously to be of practical service.

---

[1] Ann. Stat. of 1894, Rev. of 1901, secs. 7087w and 7087y (22d An. Rept. Com. of Labor, p. 402).

[2] Idem, sec. 7087r (22d An. Rept. Com. of Labor, p. 401).

MICHIGAN.

There is no law in Michigan regarding the posting of the labor laws or any portion thereof.

In 3 of the 19 establishments visited copies of the woman and child labor laws were posted in the workrooms where such persons were employed. In none of the other 16 establishments was there any posting of the laws.

WISCONSIN.

The law of Wisconsin does not require factory and labor laws to be posted, but it authorizes the inspector to do so. The legal provision upon this point is as follows: [1]

Any officer of the bureau of labor and industrial statistics may post in any factory or workshop examined by him the laws relating to the employment of children therein, hours of labor, fire escapes, or other matters pertaining to the health and safety of artisans; any person who shall remove or mutilate such laws so posted shall be fined $50 for each offense.

Under this provision the duty devolves upon an employer to see that laws once posted by an inspector are not removed or destroyed, but he is not responsible for the original posting. The posting is entirely at the discretion of the several inspectors, who are under no legal obligation in the matter. Nor does the law specify where posting is to be done.

Copies of the factory laws and the woman and child labor laws were found posted in one of the 19 establishments. In this instance such posting had been done in 4 of the 18 workrooms. In none of the other 18 establishments was any portion of the labor laws anywhere posted.

MARYLAND.

The law of Maryland does not require copies of the labor laws to be posted.

In 2 of the 28 establishments visited the more important labor laws were posted. No such posting was done by the other 26 establishments.

NORTH CAROLINA.

There is no legal requirement relative to the posting of the labor laws.

In 7 of the 28 establishments visited copies of the woman and child labor laws were posted in about half of the workrooms. In the other 21 establishments no such posting was anywhere done.

---

[1] Ann. Stat. of 1898, Supp. of 1906, Acts of 1907, sec. 1021*h* (22d An. Rept. Com. of Labor, p. 1408).

GEORGIA.

There is no legal requirement relative to the posting of the labor laws.

In 3 of the 27 establishments visited copies of the laws relative to labor were posted conspicuously in the workrooms.   No such posting was done in any of the other 24 establishments.

FLORIDA.

There are no legal requirements relative to the posting of the labor laws.

In none of the 14 establishments visited were copies of the labor laws, or of any portion thereof, anywhere posted.

LOUISIANA.

There is no legal requirement in Louisiana that copies of any of the labor laws be posted in any class of establishments.

In none of the 29 establishments visited were copies of the labor laws, or any portion thereof, anywhere posted.

CHAPTER V.

SAFEGUARDS AGAINST FIRE.

CHAPTER V.

SAFEGUARDS AGAINST FIRE.

INTRODUCTION.

Fire risks, both to property and person, are of such an evident character as to call for no comment. Such risks are extremely pertinent to modern factory buildings, but not peculiarly so. Other classes of buildings, such as theaters, hotels, and hospitals, are subject to fire dangers of as significant a character as are factories.

As a result, laws regarding fire protection are usually very broad in their scope and are frequently regarded as not forming part of the so-called labor laws. The enforcement of such laws, for instance, although sometimes intrusted to the regular factory inspection department, is frequently charged to other special authorities, such as local building inspectors or local fire departments. This is particularly the case in many of the larger cities, where the fire laws are very often contained in the municipal building codes and municipal ordinances, and the enforcement thereof is made a local matter. In less than half of the States covered by this investigation were the important laws regarding fire protection State laws and wholly under the jurisdiction of the State factory inspection department.[1]

Because of this and because of the further fact that fire protection is in considerable part a highly technical subject, the present investigation did not attempt a thorough study of this subject. All that was attempted was to obtain information upon a few significant points, the determination of which did not involve technical matters of a disputed character.

Safeguards against fire may be grouped under four main heads: (1) Fire prevention; (2) fire-resisting construction; (3) fire escapes; and (4) fire extinction.[2] The present investigation was limited almost entirely to safeguards falling under the latter two groups. It is to be noted, however, that it is the safeguards within these two groups that most frequently are made subjects of legislation. The information obtained, therefore, although insufficient in many cases to show whether particular buildings were or were not "safe," is sufficient to

---

[1] The laws referred to throughout this volume are as in force at the time of the investigation, December, 1908, to April, 1909. The text of the laws in force Jan. 1, 1912, is given in the appendixes at the end of this volume.

[2] This classification is made by Calder, The Prevention of Factory Accidents, p. 248.

indicate roughly the success of certain laws and the degree in which the several establishments had sought to safeguard their employees from the risks of fire.

To cite an extreme example, the fact that a 4-story frame factory building has one or more fire escapes does not necessarily render the employees therein safe from fire risks. But the fact that such a building has no fire escapes, or that the fire escapes provided are themselves combustible, does indicate a marked disregard for the safety of such employees.

Below is given for each State separately a statement of the laws relative to safeguards against fire and a tabular summary of the obtained data regarding existing conditions.

The table used separates the buildings of the several establishments into two main divisions, according as the material of construction is or is not frame. The buildings of each of these divisions are grouped according to height, and the table shows for each group the number of buildings having specified safeguards against the dangers due to fire. The safeguards specified are these: Fire escapes, doors opening outward, stairways lighted and handrailed, fire-fighting apparatus of various kinds, exit signs or lights, and fire drills.

The following explanatory remarks may be made as to the use of terms in this table, etc.:

1. *Fire escapes.*—The term "fire escape" includes any form of emergency stairway exit, whether of the ordinary outside fire-escape type, or inclosed inside stairway, or the so-called "tower fire escape," provided that such escapes are of fireproof construction. In a number of instances buildings were equipped with so-called "fire escapes" partly or wholly of wood. Buildings having no other escapes than these are classed as not having fire escapes. In some cases adequate fire escapes were rendered much less useful by obstructions to the entrances. The number of buildings in which escapes were so obstructed in any degree is shown in the table.

2. *Exit doors.*—The table shows the number of buildings in which all exit doors opened outward, and also the number in which exit doors were obstructed by locking, furniture, etc. No distinction is here made between hall doors and external doors.

3. *Stairways.*—The proper lighting and handrailing of stairways is of importance in preventing accident even when the question of fire does not enter. In a period of excitement due to fire, however, these precautions are of increased importance. The law sometimes accepts the inclosing of a stairway with walls in lieu of handrails, but in this table such inclosing is not regarded as a satisfactory alternative.

4. *Fire apparatus.*—The forms of fire-extinguishing apparatus included in the table are: (a) Fire extinguishers, (b) fire hose, (c) the

sprinkler system, (d) standpipes, and (e) fire buckets. Fire hose is considered as being provided only when inside the building, and special note is made of those buildings where such hose is on all floors. Also fire buckets are not considered as being provided unless they are kept full of water.

5. *Exit lights or signs.*—Lights and signs are alternative methods of indicating exits either to stairways or to fire escapes or to main doors.

6. *Fire drills.*—A fire drill is considered as being effective only when it includes all employees, or at least a large portion thereof, and when the drilling is sufficiently frequent to render the employees familiar therewith.

Finally, it is to be noted that except in the matter of fire drills the entries in the table represent buildings. In case an establishment had more than one building and the several buildings were not uniform as regards fire protection, the principal building was selected for tabulation.

The laws referred to throughout this volume are as in force at the time of the investigation, December, 1908, to April, 1909. The text of the laws in force January 1, 1912, is given in the appendixes at the end of this volume.

MAINE.

SUMMARY OF LEGISLATION.

The Maine law provides for the outward opening of doors in all buildings intended for public use, and for "suitable and sufficient fire escapes" on all factories and business buildings employing persons above the first floor, the suitability and sufficiency thereof to be determined by local authorities. The law upon these points reads as follows:[1]

Every building intended temporarily or permanently for public use * * * shall have all inner doors intended for egress open outward. The outer doors of all such buildings shall be kept open when the same are used by the public unless they open outward; but fly doors opening both ways may be kept closed.

* * * Every building in which any trade, manufacture, or business is carried on, requiring the presence of workmen above the first story, * * * shall at all times be provided with suitable and

---

[1] Rev. Stat., 1903, ch. 28, secs. 37 to 44 (22d An. Rept. Com. of Labor, pp. 524, 525). By an act in force subsequent to the field work of this investigation in Maine, Acts of 1909, ch. 194, approved Apr. 1, 1909 (Bulletin of the Bureau of Labor, No. 85, p. 602), the second paragraph of the law as quoted above is amended to read as follows: "Every building in which any trade, manufacture, or business is carried on, requiring the presence of workmen above the first story, * * * shall at all times be provided with proper egresses or other means of escape from fire sufficient for the use of all persons * * * employed * * * therein. These egresses and means of escape shall be kept unobstructed, in good repair, and ready for use, the sufficiency thereof to be determined as provided in the following section."

sufficient fire escapes, outside stairs, or ladders from each story or gallery above the level of the ground, easily accessible to all inmates in case of fire or of an alarm of fire; the sufficiency thereof to be determined as provided in the following section.

[The board of fire engineers in localities where such exist, and elsewhere the municipal authorities] shall annually make careful inspection of the precautions and safeguards provided in compliance with the foregoing requirements, and pass upon their sufficiency * * *, and upon their state of repair; and direct such alterations, additions, and repairs as they adjudge necessary.

[The law further provides that whenver such officers find conditions of a building satisfactory they shall issue to the occupant a certificate to that effect, which certificate shall be valid for one year, and must be kept posted in the building.]

> *Penalties.*—On occupant for failure to procure and keep posted a certificate, $10 per week; on owner or occupant for failure to comply with order as to alterations, etc., $50, and $5 for each day's continuance of failure, and also, if the authorities order such building not to be used until orders regarding fire protection are complied with, a further fine of $20 to $50 for using such building contrary to the order; on municipal officer or fire engineer for failure to perform the duties imposed by this act, a fine of $50.

In these sections, as quoted, the local authorities are charged with full discretion and responsibility in the matter of fire protection. By another section of the law, however, it is directed that the factory inspector "shall enforce the due observance of * * * sections * * * [of the law] relating to the swinging of doors, and fire escapes in factories and workshops."[1] The authority thus given the factory inspector is not accepted by him as complete. In an interview with an agent of this Bureau, the State factory inspector said that he considered it the duty of the local officers to enforce the law in regard to fire escapes, but that if, in the course of his work, he noticed that such provisions in a factory were inadequate and that the occupant had no certificate of inspection, he would give a warning notice and require that a certificate be procured.

In the administration of the law regarding fire escapes a very liberal construction has usually been put upon the phrase "sufficient and satisfactory fire escapes, outside stairs or ladders." In practice, the law is not construed to mean that special equipment of fire escapes is absolutely required. If the ordinary stairways and passageways are considered sufficient a building may be approved. Thus the State factory inspector, in an interview with an agent of this Bureau, stated that he understood the law to mean that fire escapes should

---

[1] Rev. Stats., 1903, ch. 40, sec. 45 (22d An. Rept. Com. of Labor, p. 526).

be required only when a building was dangerous without them, not if the building had other sufficient means of egress.

As suggestive of the attitude of the local authorities toward this law, the following summary is presented of a statement made by the chief of the fire engineers of one of the factory towns visited.

The chief engineer stated that the board of engineers was aware that all the fire escapes on the woolen mills of the town were simple wooden ladders, but, considering that the mill workers, male and female, are of a class used to taking care of themselves, the board felt that no such elaborate escapes were necessary as in the case of the town hall, school buildings, and certain business blocks where old people and children were likely to congregate.

The chief considered absurd the idea of enforcing in Maine's winter climate the legal requirement that outside doors which open inward shall be kept open when the building is in use by the public. He further stated that the board had never made written requirements of any owner of a building; as everyone in the town·knew everyone else the chief was able to visit owners personally and tell them his opinions of their buildings. In this way the board had required fire escapes to be built on four schoolhouses, the town hall, and two business blocks. These were soon to be completed, but as there was only one man in the town who could build fire escapes properly, and as he could not do the full amount of the work in 60 days, the board had paid no attention to the 60 days' limit set by law.

CONDITIONS FOUND.

Five of the 26 establishments visited had buildings 2 stories in height, 3 being constructed of frame and 2 of brick. None of these 5 had incombustible fire escapes, but their regular stairs, halls, etc., were sufficient to serve as exits in case of fire.

The other 21 establishments had buildings 3 or more stories in height. Ten of these were partly or wholly of frame; the other 11 were of brick or concrete.

The following table classifies the buildings of these several establishments by height and character of construction, and shows the number in each group having certain more important means of fire protection.

KIND OF FIRE PROTECTION, BY HEIGHT AND CHARACTER OF CONSTRUCTION OF BUILDINGS—MAINE.

[Each entry represents 1 building. When an establishment has more than 1 building and the several buildings are not uniform as regards fire protection, the principal building has been selected as representative. A building constructed partly of wood is classed in the table as a frame building. Figures for fire escapes wholly or partly of wood are not shown in the table.]

Kind of fire protection.	Establishments having specified fire protection.					
	Construction other than frame.		Frame.			Total.
	3-story.	4-story.	3-story.	4-story.	5-story.	
Number of establishments	7	4	6	3	1	21
Fire escapes:						
Incombustible	3	2	....	2	1	8
Obstructed	....	....	....	1	1	2
Exit doors:						
All opening outward	1	....	....	....	....	1
Some obstructed	2	....	2	2	....	¹ 6
Stairways:						
Properly lighted	3	1	....	3	1	8
With handrails	6	1	1	1	1	10
Fire apparatus:						
Fire extinguishers	5	1	5	2	1	14
Fire hose—						
Inside building	3	1	4	1	....	9
On all floors	1	....	1	1	....	3
Sprinkler system	4	1	2	3	1	11
Standpipes	3	....	1	1	1	6
Fire buckets (kept full)	3	2	....	3	1	9
Exit lights or signs	....	....	....	....	....	....
Fire drills	....	....	....	....	....	....

¹ Not including 7 establishments, not reported as to construction.

In each of 3 establishments one exit or hall door was kept locked during working hours.

In 1 establishment there was an iron ladder fire escape, but the platforms thereof were without rails.

In none of the 23 establishments listed in the table were fire inspection certificates posted, although in 6 cases such certificates had been issued. Four establishments reported that inspections by fire officials were made frequently; 4 that such inspections were made regularly once a year; 1 that it had been inspected about 3 years previously; and 5 that such inspection had never been made. No reports on this point were received from the remaining establishments.

MASSACHUSETTS.

SUMMARY OF LEGISLATION.

There are three series of requirements in the State law relative to the subject of fire protection on factories, etc. One of these applies to the whole State; one applies to all places outside of Boston, and one applies only to the city of Boston, being part of the building code of that city. These three series of legal provisions are presented below in slightly condensed form:[1]

[1] Rev. Laws, 1902, ch. 104, secs. 40 and 47 (22d An. Rept. Com. of Labor, pp. 588, 589), and acts of 1905, ch. 347.

A. Provisions applicable to whole State.

(a) No outside or inside doors of any building in which operatives are employed shall be so locked, bolted, or otherwise fastened during the hours of labor as to prevent free egress.

Penalty.—Not more than $100.

(b) Explosives or inflammable compounds shall not be used in any factory in such place or manner as to obstruct or render hazardous the egress of operatives in case of fire.

Penalty.—Not more than $100.

(c) Any article or thing placed upon a fire escape or an outside means of egress of any building is hereby declared a common nuisance.

Penalty.—Not more than $100 on owner, occupant, etc., if such article or thing remains more than 20 minutes.

(d) Every stairway of every building shall be kept free and unobstructed.

Penalty.—Not more than $500.[1]

Enforcement.—Charged to the factory inspection department of the district police.[2]

B. Provisions applicable outside of Boston.[3]

I. (a) No building * * * more than 2 stories in height which is designed to be used above the second story * * * as a factory, workshop, or mercantile or other establishment and has accommodations for 10 or more persons above said story, * * * shall be erected until a copy of the plans thereof has been deposited with the [State] inspector of factories and public buildings for the district in which it is to be erected * * *.

Such building shall not be erected without sufficient egresses and other means of escape from fire, properly located and constructed.

The certificate of the inspector, indorsed with the approval of the district police, shall be conclusive evidence of a compliance with the provisions of this chapter.

(b) The inspectors of factories and public buildings shall * * * examine all buildings within their respective districts which are subject to the provisions of this chapter. If, in the judgment of any such inspector, such building conforms to the requirements of this chapter, he shall issue to the owner, lessee, or occupant * * * a certificate to that effect.

Such certificate shall not continue in force for more than 5 years * * *, but * * * [while] in force it shall be conclusive evidence of a compliance * * * with the pro-

---

[1] Acts of 1905, ch. 347.

[2] Rev. Laws, 1902, ch. 108, sec. 8, as amended by ch. 413, Acts of 1907 (22d An. Rept. Com. of Labor, p. 609).

[3] Idem, ch. 104, secs. 15 and 22, sec. 25 (as amended by ch. 503, Acts of 1907), and secs. 26, 50, 53, and 55 (22d An. Rept. Com. of Labor, pp. 585–590).

visions of this chapter. * * * A copy of * * * certificate shall be kept posted in a conspicuous place upon each story of such building * * *. [Certificate void if character of building, work, etc., is changed.]

II. [A factory, workshop, mercantile or other establishment] * * * in which 10 or more persons are employed above the second floor * * * [or to which a factory inspector deems the requirement applicable] * * *—

(a) Shall be provided with proper egresses or other means of escape from fire sufficient for the use of all persons * * * employed * * * therein; but no owner, lessee, or occupant * * * shall be deemed to have violated this provision unless he has been notified in writing by such inspector what additional egresses or means of escape * * * are necessary and has neglected or refused to supply the same.

(b) The egresses and means of escape shall be kept unobstructed, in good repair, and ready for use, and every such egress shall be provided with a sign having on it the word "Exit," in letters not less than 5 inches in height and so as plainly to indicate to persons within the building the location of such egresses.

(c) Stairways on the outside * * * shall have suitable railed landings at each story above the first, accessible at each story from doors or windows, and such landings, doors, and windows shall be kept clear of ice, snow, and other obstructions. * * *

(d) If the inspector so directs in writing, women or children shall not be employed in * * * [any such building] in a room above the second story from which there is only one egress.

(e) And all doors and windows in any building which is subject to the provisions of this section shall open outwardly.

(f) And every room above the second story in any such building * * * shall be provided with more than one egress by stairways or by such other way or device, approved in writing by the inspector, as the owner may elect, on the inside or outside of the building, placed as near as practicable at each end of the room.

(g) The certificate of the inspector shall be conclusive evidence of a compliance with such [i. e., all the above-mentioned] requirements.

(h) Each story above the second story of a building * * * [used as above-mentioned] shall be supplied with means of extinguishing fire, consisting of pails of water or other portable apparatus or of a hose attached to a suitable water supply and capable of reaching any part of such story; and such appliances shall be kept at all times ready for use and in good condition.

Penalty.[1]—For violation of any of the above provisions, $50 to $1,000. The owner, lessee, or occupant to be liable for all

---

[1] Rev. Laws, 1902, ch. 104, secs. 50 and 55 (22d An. Rept. Com. of Labor, pp. 589, 590).

personal injuries caused by a violation. No criminal prosecution to be commenced until after four weeks' notice, in writing, by a factory inspector of changes necessary, with opportunity to comply with the law.

Enforcement.—Charged to factory-inspection department of district police.[1]

C. Provisions applicable to Boston city only.[2]

(a) Every building shall have, with reference to its height, condition, construction, surroundings, character of occupation, and number of occupants, reasonable means of egress in case of fire satisfactory to the [local] building commissioner.

Except that in all factories or workshops, hereafter built or altered, of second-class construction, where 10 or more persons are employed above the second floor, one exit shall consist of a fireproof stairway inclosed in incombustible material.

[A second-class building is one of which the external and party walls only are fireproof.]

(b) Every permanent building more than 20 feet high having a flat roof shall have permanent means of access to the roof from the inside by an opening not less than 2 by 3 feet, with a fixed stepladder.

Penalty.—Not exceeding $100.

Enforcement.—Charged to building department of Boston, which department is under the charge of a building commissioner appointed by the mayor.

Reviewing the provisions quoted above, the following points may be noted:

1. The law provides that inspectors may issue certificates of compliance for factories, etc., outside of Boston in which 10 or more persons are employed above the second floor (B. I. a.) Nineteen such factories were visited. A certificate of the character mentioned was found in only 1 of these 19. Most manufacturers were unaware of this feature of the law.

2. The law (B. II. d.) provides that in factories of the class mentioned above an inspector may prohibit the employment of women and children in a room above the second story which has only one egress. The chief inspector stated that no fixed rule had been made in this matter, as many rooms with only one egress are entirely safe.

3. Stairways on the outside of a building (of the class above described) must have suitable railed landings accessible and unobstructed (B. II. c.) But the law makes no such provision if fixed ladders are used instead of stairways, nor does it prohibit the use of such ladders.

---

[1] Rev. Laws, 1902, ch. 108, sec. 8, as amended by ch. 413, Acts of 1907 (22d An. Rept. Com. of Labor, p. 609).

[2] Acts of 1907, ch. 550, secs. 1, 11, 12, and 132.

4. The requirement that in buildings outside of Boston doors open outward; that egresses and means of escape be kept unobstructed, in good repair, ready for use, and marked "Exit" in large letters; that landings of fire escapes be kept free of ice and snow and other obstructions; and that fire apparatus be provided are mandatory and leave little to the discretion of the inspector.

Aside from these requirements the law makes no provision concerning the character of the egresses in buildings outside of Boston and already erected except that they must be "proper" and "sufficient for the use of all persons * * * employed * * * therein." Therefore, either inside or outside exits may be maintained. If inside, they may be incombustible or otherwise; if outside, they may be ladders or fire escapes, wooden or metallic; and in any case there is no violation of the law unless the inspector gives written notice stating what additional means of escape are necessary and the owner, lessee, or occupant refuses or neglects to supply the same.

CONDITIONS FOUND.

Of the 44 establishments visited in Massachusetts, 37 had buildings 3 or more stories in height. Eighteen of these were in Boston and 19 outside of Boston. The following table classifies the buildings of the several establishments by height and shows the number in each height group having certain more important means of fire protection. Also, as the laws governing fire protection make important distinctions between Boston and the rest of the State, the table makes this separation. None of the 18 buildings in Boston entered in this table was of frame construction and 2 were "fireproofed", i. e., of reinforced concrete, etc. Of the 19 entered as "outside of Boston," 5 were wholly or partly of frame construction, and 1 was fireproofed.

KIND OF FIRE PROTECTION, BY HEIGHT AND CHARACTER OF CONSTRUCTION OF BUILDINGS—MASSACHUSETTS.

[Each entry represents 1 building. When an establishment has more than 1 building and the several buildings are not uniform as regards fire protection, the principal building has been selected as representative. A building constructed partly of wood is classed in the table as a frame building. Figures for fire escapes wholly or partly of wood are not shown in the table.]

Kind of fire protection.	Establishments having specified fire protection.					
	Boston (no frame construction).					
	3-story.	4-story.	5-story.	6-story.	7-story.	Total, Boston.
Number of establishments	3	6	2	6	1	18
Fire escapes:						
Incombustible	3	5	2	6	1	17
Obstructed		2	1	1	1	5
Exit doors:						
All opening outward		1				1
Some obstructed		1				¹1
Stairways:						
Properly lighted	3	3	1	5		12
With handrails	3	4	2	6	1	16
Fire apparatus:						
Fire extinguishers	1		1	4	1	7
Fire hose—						
Inside building	2			1		²3
On all floors	2			1		²3
Sprinkler system		2		2		4
Standpipes	1	1		2		4
Fire buckets (kept full)	2	5	2	3	1	13
Exit lights or signs	1		1			2

Kind of fire protection.	Establishments having specified fire protection.							
	Outside of Boston.							
	Construction other than frame.				Frame.		Total, outside Boston.	Total, State.
	3-story.	4-story.	5-story.	6-story.	3-story.	4-story.		
Number of establishments	6	4	3	1	4	1	19	37
Fire escapes:								
Incombustible	1	4	3	1		1	10	27
Obstructed		2	1				3	8
Exit doors:								
All opening outward	2			1	1		²4	²5
Some obstructed			1				³1	⁴2
Stairways:								
Properly lighted	5	3	1	1	3		13	25
With handrails	4	3	1		3		11	27
Fire apparatus:								
Fire extinguishers	2	3	3	1	4	1	14	21
Fire hose—								
Inside building	3	1	2	1	1	1	9	²12
On all floors	3	1	2	1	1		8	²11
Sprinkler system	4	3	3	1	1	1	13	17
Standpipes	2	1	3	1	1	1	9	13
Fire buckets (kept full)	5	3	2	1	1		12	25
Exit lights or signs	1		1	1		1	4	6
Fire drills		1	2			1	²5	²5

¹ Not including 17 establishments, not reported as to construction.
² Not including 1 establishment, not reported as to construction.
³ Not including 16 establishments, not reported as to construction.
⁴ Not including 33 establishments, not reported as to construction.

In several of the establishments visited straight iron ladders served as fire escapes. These are entered in the above table, but the value of straight iron ladders in case of fire is questionable. Four establishments, 1 of which was a 4-story building, had outside fire escapes of "wood." These were merely fixed wooden ladders, some with and some without wooden landings.

RHODE ISLAND.

SUMMARY OF LEGISLATION.

The law of Rhode Island requires that certain classes of buildings, including factories employing persons above the second floor, shall have outside metallic fire escapes or inside incombustible stairways. It also provides that in factories employing 25 or more persons the exit and hall doors shall open outward. The law is not entirely clear as to what officials are to enforce these provisions as regards factories. Primarily it would appear that this duty devolves upon local building inspectors, where such exist. In the section of the law establishing State factory inspectors and prescribing their duties it is provided, however, that such factory inspectors shall enforce the requirements of the factory law relating to "means of egress in case of fire." This authority is a broad one, and invests the factory inspectors with power to issue orders regarding fire escapes even though the local building inspectors have approved of the means of escape already provided.

The following is an abridgement of the several sections of the law dealing with the subject of fire protection in factories and workshops as referred to above:

(A) Fire escapes.[1]

> (1) Every building three or more stories in height, * * * used * * * as a seminary, college, academy, schoolhouse, hospital, asylum, hotel, lodging house, * * * factory or workshop in which employees are usually working in the third or any higher story thereof, and every building used for office purposes three or more stories in height, shall be provided * * *
> (2) Either with proper and sufficient, strong, and durable, metallic fire escapes upon the external walls, sufficient in number, which fire escapes shall extend from the highest occupied story to the top of the first story of said building;
> (3) Or with proper and sufficient incombustible stairs and stairways at opposite ends of the building, extending from the highest occupied story to the ground;
> (4) Said stairs and stairways shall be connected by open passageways of suitable width;
> (5) Said fire escapes, stairs, and stairways to be suitable and sufficient to afford to persons within said building proper

[1] Gen. Laws, 1896, ch. 108, secs. 1 to 14 (22d An. Rept. Com. of Labor, pp. 1211-1214).

egress * * * in case of fire therein, and to be kept in
repair * * *;

(6) It shall be the duty of the inspectors of buildings of the
* * * cities and towns, from time to time * * * to
make * * * inspection of all buildings in the city or
town * * * which in their opinion might * * * be
specially dangerous to persons therein in case of conflagration.

(7) Said inspectors of buildings shall have power * * * to
exempt by a written certificate * * * any building from
the provisions of this chapter, whenever in the opinion of said
inspector said building, by reason of location * * * or for
any other reason does not require said fire escapes * * *
stairs, and stairways.

(8) Whenever the inspector of buildings * * * shall * * *
be satisfied that any building * * * is provided with fire
escapes or with stairs and stairways, in accordance with the
provisions of this chapter, he shall upon request * * *
give to * * * owner a certificate to that effect. Such
certificate * * * shall exempt the owners * * * from
all civil and criminal liability under this chapter * * *.

Penalty.—$100 to $500.

(B) Doors opening outward.[1]

(1) All buildings used as factories, laundries, or workshops
* * *, in which * * * 25 or more persons are employed,
shall have the doors or windows of or to any exit or fire escape
so arranged as to swing outward. [The rooms of such build-
ings] * * * where the entrance * * * is from a corridor or hallway * * * shall have the doors of entrance
thereto so arranged as to swing outward.

(2) If any such door or window of such * * * room shall
be locked or fastened during working hours the lock or fastening shall be such, and kept in such condition, that the same
can be easily and quickly unlocked or unfastened * * *
from the inside.

(3) It shall be the duty of the inspector of buildings of each city
or town to enforce * * * this act. In any city or town
where there is no such inspector it shall be the duty of each
of the factory inspectors, and such person or persons as may be
appointed for the purpose by any city or town council, to
enforce the same.

Penalty.—$100, and each day of failure to constitute a
separate offense.

(C) Means of egress.[2]

If the factory inspectors, or either one of them, find that * * *
the means of egress in case of fire or other disaster is not sufficient, or in accordance with all the requirements of law,
* * * either or both shall notify the proprietor of such
factory or workshop to make the alterations or additions
necessary within 90 days.

---

[1] Acts of 1908, ch. 1536, secs. 7 to 11 (Bulletin of the Bureau of Labor, No. 85, p. 762).
[2] Gen. Laws, 1896, ch. 68, sec. 9 (22d An. Rept. Com. of Labor, p. 1209).

There are no provisions in the State law regarding fire apparatus, exit signs or lights, or lighting of halls and stairways.

CONDITIONS FOUND.

Of the 27 establishments visited, 21 had buildings 3 or more stories in height. One of these 21 was of simple frame construction; the remaining 20 had external and dividing walls of brick, concrete, or other incombustible material, although in most cases floors, partitions, doors, etc., were of wood.

The following table classifies the 21 establishments mentioned by height and material of construction, and shows the number of each group having certain more important means of fire protection:

KIND OF FIRE PROTECTION, BY HEIGHT AND CHARACTER OF CONSTRUCTION OF BUILDINGS—RHODE ISLAND.

[Each entry represents 1 building. When an establishment has more than 1 building and the several buildings are not uniform as regards fire protection, the principal building has been selected as representative. A building constructed partly of wood is classed in the table as a frame building. Figures for fire escapes wholly or partly of wood are not shown in the table.]

| Kind of fire protection. | Establishments having specified fire protection. | | | | | | Total. |
| | Construction other than frame. | | | | | Frame. | |
	3-story.	4-story.	5-story.	6-story.	7-story.	3-story	
Number of establishments	6	6	4	2	2	1	21
Fire escapes:							
Incombustible	3	5	4	2	2		16
Obstructed		2		1			3
Exit doors:							
All opening outward	4	2	1		2		9
Some obstructed	3	2					1 5
Stairways:							
Properly lighted	3	3	4	1	2	1	14
With handrails	2	2	3	1	2	1	11
Fire apparatus:							
Fire extinguishers	3	2	3	2	1	1	12
Fire hose—							
Inside building	.	4			1		7
On all floors	1	4			1		6
Sprinkler system	3	6	3	2	2		16
Stand pipes	3	3	2	2	1		11
Fire buckets (kept full)	5	1 1	3	2	1	1	1 13
Exit lights or signs							
Fire drills	1	1					2

1 Not including 1 establishment, not reported as to construction.

CONNECTICUT.

SUMMARY OF LEGISLATION.

The Connecticut law requires, at the discretion of the inspecting authorities, outside fire escapes on all buildings used as factories, etc., which are more than 2 stories in height and in which more than 20 persons are employed above the first floor. The number of fire escapes required is proportioned to the length of the building, one for each 150 feet of length.[1]

If any * * * workshop, manufactory, * * * or other building * * * in which more than 20 persons shall be employed above the first story, shall be more than 2 stories in height, it shall be provided with at least one fire escape, of iron or other incombustible material, on the outside of said building; unless, in the opinion of the authority inspecting the same, such building is sufficiently supplied with safe and proper means of egress.

And if such building shall be more than 150 feet in length it shall be provided with one such fire escape for every 150 feet, or fractional part thereof exceeding 50 feet, and such fire escapes shall be conveniently accessible from each story of said building.

> *Penalty.*—On owner, for failure to provide fire escapes within 3 months after notice from proper authority, not more than $500 or imprisonment not more than 6 months, or both.
>
> *Enforcement.*—Charged to local authorities—the building inspectors where such exist, elsewhere the borough wardens and the town selectmen.[2] The factory inspectors, however, notify the local building inspectors when, in their opinion, a building has not sufficient protection against fire.

CONDITIONS FOUND.

Of the 35 establishments visited, 31 had buildings 3 or more stories in height. Five of these 31 were in whole or in considerable part of frame construction; the remaining 26 had external and dividing walls of brick, concrete, or other incombustible material, although in most cases floors, partitions, doors, etc., were of wood. The following table classifies the 31 establishments mentioned by height and material of construction, and shows the number of each group having certain important means of fire protection.

---

[1] Gen. Stat., 1902, secs. 2629, 2630, and 2631 (22d An. Rept. Com. of Labor, pp. 233, 234).

[2] Idem, sec. 2631 (22d An. Rept. Com. of Labor, p. 234).

By an act approved almost immediately after the completion of the field work of this investigation the State factory inspector is given authority to enforce this law so far as concerns factories and workshops. Acts of 1909, ch. 10, approved Apr. 12, 1909 (Bulletin of the Bureau of Labor, No. 85, p. 523).

KIND OF FIRE PROTECTION, BY HEIGHT AND CHARACTER OF CONSTRUCTION OF
BUILDINGS—CONNECTICUT.

[Each entry represents 1 building. When an establishment has more than 1 building and the several buildings are not uniform as regards fire protection, the principal building has been selected as representative. A building constructed partly of wood is classed in the table as a frame building. Figures for fire escapes wholly or partly of wood are not shown in the table.]

| Kind of fire protection. | Establishments having specified fire protection. | | | | | | Total. |
| | Construction other than frame. | | | | Frame. | | |
	3-story.	4-story.	5-story.	6-story.	3-story.	4-story.	
Number of establishments...................	10	9	4	3	2	3	31
Fire escapes:							
Incombustible...........................	4	5	2	2	....	....	13
Obstructed.............................	....	1	....	....	... ...	....	1
Exit doors:							
All opening outward....................	1	2	....	1	1	....	5
Some obstructed........................	3	1	....	1	....	....	1 5
Stairways:							
Properly lighted.......................	9	8	4	3	2	3	29
With handrails.........................	7	8	3	3	2	3	26
Fire apparatus:							
Fire extinguishers.....................	7	4	3	3	1	1	19
Fire hose—							
Inside building.....................	3	3	2	3	1	3	15
On all floors.......................	3	2	1	3	1	3	13
Sprinkler system....................	5	8	3	3	1	3	23
Standpipes..........................	....	3	1	3	1	2	10
Fire buckets (kept full)	9	8	4	3	1	3	28
Exit lights or signs.......................	....	....	....	....	....	1	1
Fire drills................................	1	1	....	1	....	....	3

1 Not including 1 establishment, not reported as to construction.

NEW YORK.

SUMMARY OF LEGISLATION.

The law of New York requires outside fire escapes on all factories 3 or more stories high. The number and character of escapes to be provided in individual cases is left largely to the discretion of the factory inspector. Stairways must have proper handrails and be properly screened, and the factory inspector may require steps to be covered with rubber. Doors leading in or to all factories must open outwardly where practicable and must not be fastened during working hours. Exit signs or lights are not specifically required, but in the section of the factory law dealing with safeguards against machine dangers, it is provided that the commissioner may order workrooms, halls, and stairs to be properly lighted, "such light to be independent of the motive power" of the factory.

The enforcement of these several legal provisions is intrusted by the provisions themselves to the State factory inspection department. By an important decision of the supreme court of the State, however, it was decided that jurisdiction over the subject of fire escapes in New York City (boroughs of the Bronx, Manhattan, and Brooklyn) is vested exclusively in the local superintendents of buildings.[1]

1 City of New York v. Trustees Sailors' Snug Harbor, 85 App. Div. 355; affirmed 180 N. Y. 527 (mem.). See also opinion of the Attorney General, Jan. 16, 1904. (These references are quoted in Third General Report of New York Department of Labor, 1903, p. 121.)

The several legal provisions referred to above are in full as follows:
Fire escapes.[1]

> Such fire escapes as may be deemed necessary by the factory inspector shall be provided on the outside of every factory in this State consisting of 3 or more stories in height.
>
> Each escape shall connect with each floor above the first, and shall be of sufficient strength, well fastened and secured, and shall have landings or balconies not less than 6 feet in length and 3 feet in width, guarded by iron railings not less than 3 feet in height, embracing at least 2 windows at each story and connected with the interior by easily accessible and unobstructed openings.
>
> The balconies or landings shall be connected by iron stairs, not less than 18 inches wide, with steps of not less than 6 inches tread, placed at a proper slant and protected by a well-secured handrail on both sides, and shall have a drop ladder not less than 12 inches wide reaching from the lower platform to the ground.
>
> The windows or doors to the landing or balcony of each fire escape shall be of sufficient size and located as far as possible, consistent with accessibility, from the stairways and elevator hatchways or openings, and a ladder from such fire escape shall extend to the roof.
>
> Stationary stairs or ladders shall be provided on the inside of every factory from the upper story to the roof, as a means of escape in case of fire.
>
> Any other plan or style of fire escape shall be sufficient if approved in writing by the factory inspector.[2]
>
> If there is no fire escape, or the fire escape in use is not approved by the factory inspector, he may, by a written order served upon the owner, proprietor, or lessee of any factory, or the agent or superintendent thereof, or either of them, require one or more fire escapes to be provided therefor, at such location and of such plan and style as shall be specified in such order.
>
> Within 20 days after the service of such order, the number of fire escapes required therein shall be provided, each of which shall be of the plan and style specified in the order, or of the plan and style described in the preceding section [i. e., the previous paragraphs quoted above].

Stairways.[3]

> Proper and substantial handrails shall be provided on all stairways in factories. The steps of such stairs shall be covered with rubber, securely fastened thereon, if in the opinion of the

---

[1] Rev. Stat., 3d ed., 1901, p. 2102, secs. 82 and 83 (22d An. Rept. Com. of Labor, p. 913).

[2] By judicial decision it has also been determined that where the statutory fire escape has not been provided, if the jury finds that an escape equally safe and convenient has been provided, the employer has performed his duty under the statute. 51 N. Y. St., 248 (22d An. Rept. Com. of Labor, p. 913).

[3] Rev. Stat., 3d ed., 1901, p. 2102, sec. 80 (22d An. Rept. Com. of Labor, p. 912).

factory inspector the safety of employees would be promoted thereby. The stairs shall be properly screened at the sides and bottom.

Doors opening outward.[1]

All doors leading in or to any such factory shall be so constructed as to open outwardly where practicable, and shall not be locked, bolted, or fastened during working hours.

Lights in hallways, etc.[2]

When in the opinion of the commissioner of labor it is necessary, the workrooms, halls, and stairs leading to the workrooms shall be properly lighted, and in cities of the first class, if deemed necessary by the commissioner of labor, a proper light shall be kept burning by the owner or lessee in the public hallways near the stairs upon the entrance floor and upon the other floors on every workday in the year, from the time when the building is opened for use in the morning until it is closed in the evening, except at times when the influx of natural light shall make artificial light unnecessary. Such lights to be independent of the motive power of such factory.

Penalty.—For violation of any of the above-quoted provisions: First offense, $20 to $50; second offense, $50 to $200, or imprisonment not more than 30 days, or both; third offense, not less than $250, or imprisonment not more than 60 days, or both.[3]

CONDITIONS FOUND.

All of the 36 establishments visited in New York had buildings 3 or more stories in height. None of these buildings was of frame construction, and a few of the higher ones were entirely "fireproofed."

The following table classifies the buildings of these 36 establishments by height, and shows the number in each group having certain important means of fire protection:

---

[1] Rev. Stat., 3d ed., 1901, p. 2102, sec. 80 (22d An. Rept. Com. of Labor, p. 912).

[2] Idem, sec. 81, as amended by ch. 366, Acts of 1906 (22d An. Rept. Com. of Labor, p. 912).

[3] Idem, p. 2120, sec. 209, as amended by ch. 506, Acts of 1907 (22d An. Rept. Com. of Labor, p. 931).

KIND OF FIRE PROTECTION, BY HEIGHT AND CHARACTER OF CONSTRUCTION OF BUILDINGS—NEW YORK.

[Each entry represents 1 building. When an establishment has more than 1 building and the several buildings are not uniform as regards fire protection, the principal building has been selected as representative. Figures for fire escapes wholly or partly of wood are not shown in the table.]

Kind of fire protection.	Establishments having specified fire protection.								
	Construction other than frame.								Total.
	3-story.	4-story.	5-story.	6-story.	7-story.	8-story.	9-story.	15-story.	
Number of establishments.............	5	10	5	7	4	1	3	1	36
Fire escapes·									
Incombustible.....................	2	9	5	7	4	1	3	1	32
Obstructed........................		4	3		2				9
Exit doors:									
All opening outward...............	3	2	3	2	1	1	2	1	15
Some obstructed..................				1					1 1
Stairways:									
Properly lighted...................	4	6	4	6	4	1	3	1	29
With handrails	5	9	5	7	4	1	2	1	34
Fire apparatus:									
Fire extinguishers.................	3	5	3	3	1		2	1	18
Fire hose—									
Inside building...............	2	3	2	1	2		2	1	13
On all floors..................	2	1	2	1	2		2	1	11
Sprinkler system..................	2	3	3	5	1	1	3	1	19
Standpipes........................	2	4		3	2	1	1	1	14
Fire buckets (kept full)...........	5	8	4	7	4	1	3		32
Exit lights or signs..................	2		1	2	1		1	1	8
Fire drills..........................									

1 Not including 28 establishments, not reported as to construction.

NEW JERSEY.

SUMMARY OF LEGISLATION.

The law of New Jersey provides that buildings used for manufacturing purposes must have external fire escapes or fire towers. The construction of the fire escapes is prescribed by the law in great detail, leaving little or no discretion to the enforcing authority in this matter. The legal provisions are as follows:[1]

Every factory, workshop, mill, or place where the manufacture of goods * * * is carried on * * * which is 3 or more stories in height and in which 25 or more * * * employees shall be at work on or above the third floor shall be provided with outside iron fire escapes as hereinafter provided; the fire escapes shall be located at such places on the said building as may be best suited for the purpose intended or as the commissioner may designate in writing, and shall take in one or more windows on each floor above the first floor; fire escapes may project into the public highway to a distance not greater than 4 feet beyond the building line.

Here follows several sections which prescribe in great detail the construction and care of fire escapes to be erected under this law.

1 Acts of 1904, ch. 64, secs. 34 to 45, as amended by ch. 257, Acts of 1907 (22d An. Rept. Com. of Labor, pp. 865–869).

The more important of these requirements are briefly summarized below:

Fire escapes to consist of outside iron balconies and stairways at each floor above the first, connecting said balconies to the ground.

The slope of the stairway to be no greater than a ratio of 1 horizontal to 1¼ vertical.

The balconies to be not less than 3 feet wide, taking in at each story at least 1 window of each part of the building separated by inside walls in which 25 or more employees may be at work.

A landing, not less than 24 inches square, to be at head and foot of each stairway.

Openings upon each balcony to be easy of access and kept unobstructed.

Floors of balconies to be of wrought iron or steel slats at least 1¼ by three-eighths of an inch, placed not more than 1¼ inches apart.

Openings for stairways to be at least 21 by 42 inches and to have no covers.

Platforms to be able safely to sustain a load of at least 80 pounds per square foot.

The outside top rail of balconies to be at least 3 feet high, to extend around the entire platform, and of a specified size, strength, and method of riveting.

Stairways to be capable of sustaining a safe load of at least 100 pounds in all its parts and the treads a concentrated load of 200 pounds.

Treads to be not less than 7 inches wide and the rise not more than 9 inches.

Stairs to be not less than 20 inches wide between inside of strings, and there shall be a clear passage between stairway and wall of building of not less than 14 inches.

Stairways to have a handrail of not less than three-fourths inch round wrought iron rod or pipe, not less than 30 or more than 42 inches above steps.

Brackets supporting balconies to be of a specified size and character and riveted to wall in a specified manner.

There shall be a drop ladder from lower balcony to ground, instead of fixed stairway, when the fire escape is over a highway. If such balcony is more than 16 feet above the ground an intermediate landing balcony shall be provided not more than 10 feet from ground. Drop ladder to be at least 15 inches wide, and constructed as specified in detail.

A gooseneck ladder to be provided from top balcony to roof; to be securely fastened to wall of building and extend at least 30 inches above the roof. There shall be a space of at least 14 inches between such ladder and the outer rail of balcony.

All parts of such fire escapes shall receive not less than two coats of paint at time of erection, and thereafter shall be painted as necessary.

The commissioner [of labor] shall have power to make and have served an order in writing * * * ordering that a fire escape shall be erected * * * or ordering that a fire escape already erected shall be changed and altered in such manner as he shall * * * designate; such fire escapes must conform to the provisions of this act: *Provided*, That fire towers, when approved by the commissioner, shall be legal protection the same as iron fire escapes as hereinbefore provided.

Penalty.—For failure to comply with said orders within the time therein limited, a fine of $100 and an additional fine of $10 per day for each additional day of noncompliance.

As regards the outward opening of doors the law directs that—

All the main doors, both inside and outside, of places coming under the provisions of this act [i. e. factory, workshop, mill, or place where the manufacture of goods of any kind is carried on], shall open outwardly or be sliding doors, and shall be kept unbolted and unlocked during the hours of employment.

Penalty.—$50.[1]

There is no legal provision regarding exit signs and lights, but in the section of law dealing with dangerous machinery it is enacted that—

When in the opinion of the commissioner it is necessary, the halls leading to workrooms shall be provided with proper lighting facilities.

Penalty.—$50.[1]

Enforcement.—Charged to the State department of labor.[2]

CONDITIONS FOUND.

Information regarding fire protection was not obtained in the case of one of the 27 establishments visited. Of the remaining 26, 20 had buildings 3 or more stories in height, the material of construction being brick in all cases except one where the building was of brick and concrete.

---

[1] Acts of 1904, ch. 64, secs. 12, 13, and 30 (22d An. Rept. Com. of Labor, pp. 862, 864).

[2] Idem, sec. 45, as amended by ch. 257, Acts of 1907 (22d An. Rept. Com. of Labor, p. 868).

The following table classifies the 20 establishments mentioned by height, and shows the number of each group having certain important means of fire protection:

KIND OF FIRE PROTECTION, BY HEIGHT AND CHARACTER OF CONSTRUCTION OF BUILDINGS—NEW JERSEY.

[Each entry represents 1 building. When an establishment has more than 1 building and the several buildings are not uniform as regards fire protection, the principal building has been selected as representative. Figures for fire escapes wholly or partly of wood are not shown in the table.]

Kind of fire protection.	Establishments having specified fire protection.					
	Construction other than frame.					Total.
	3-story.	4-story.	5-story.	6-story.	8-story.	
Number of establishments	5	10	3	1	1	20
Fire escapes:						
Incombustible	1	8	1	1	1	12
Obstructed	1	2				3
Exit doors:						
All opening outward	1	3	1		1	6
Some obstructed						
Stairways:						
Properly lighted	5	10	3	1	1	20
With handrails	4	9	2	1	1	17
Fire apparatus:						
Fire extinguishers	2	5	2	1		10
Fire hose—						
Inside building	1	4	3	1	1	10
On all floors		3	3	1	1	8
Sprinkler system	1	6	2	1	1	11
Standpipes		4	1	1	1	7
Fire buckets (kept full)	5	8	3	1	1	18
Exit lights or signs	1	2		1		4
Fire drills	1	2		1		4

PENNSYLVANIA.

SUMMARY OF LEGISLATION.

The subject of fire escapes and means of protection against fire is under the jurisdiction of the State factory inspection department in only such places as have less than 100,000 population. For cities of the first class (population 1,000,000 or more) and cities of the second class (population 100,000 to 1,000,000) there are special "municipal corporations" acts which prescribe building regulations and place the supervision thereof in the hands of the local authorities.

All but 6 of the 50 establishments visited in Pennsylvania and all but 1 of the 41 having buildings three or more stories high were in cities of the first or second classes, and others not within the jurisdiction of the State factory inspection department. Because of this fact and because the building regulations for these cities, as prescribed in the "municipal acts," are extremely full such regulations are not reproduced here. It is sufficient for the present purpose to note that under those regulations all buildings three or more stories high in cities of the first and second classes are required to maintain a high standard of safety against fire risks.

The more important of the State laws relative to fire escapes in places not of the character mentioned, and thus under the jurisdiction of the State factory inspection department, are given below in somewhat condensed form.[1]

Fire escapes.

> SECTION 10. * * * Every storehouse, factory, manufactory, or workshop of any kind in which employees * * * are usually employed * * * in the third or any higher story * * * shall be provided with a permanent, safe external means of escape therefrom in case of fire, independent of all internal stairways, the number and location of such escapes to be governed by the size of the building and the number of its inmates and arranged in such a way as to make them readily accessible, safe, and adequate * * *.
>
> SEC. 11. Such escapes to consist of outside open iron stairways of not more than 45 degrees slant, with steps not less than 6 inches in width and 24 inches in length.
>
> SEC. 12. And all of said buildings, capable of accommodating from 100 to 500 or more persons as operatives .* * * shall be provided with 2 such stairways, and more than 2 stairways if such be necessary * * *.
>
> SEC. 13. And it shall be the duty of the owner or owners * * * to provide and cause to be securely affixed outside of every such building such permanent, external, uninclosed fire escape.
>
> SEC. 14. Nothing herein contained shall prohibit any person * * * from * * * erecting any other and different device, design, or instrument being a permanent, safe, external means of escape, subject to the inspection and approval of the constituted authorities * * *.
>
> *Penalty.*—Not exceeding $300 and imprisonment 1 to 2 months, and in case of fire liability for damages for personal injuries and to imprisonment 6 to 12 months.

Ropes, etc.

> SECTION 1. * * * It shall be the duty of the owner or owners * * * of every building * * * more than 2 stories high * * * and used * * * as a hotel, factory, manufactory, workshop * * * to provide and cause to be securely affixed to a bolt through the wall over the window head, inside of at least 1 window in each room on the third * * * and * * * each higher floor * * * a chain at least 10 feet in length, with a rope at least 1 inch in diameter, securely attached thereto, of sufficient length to extend to the ground, or such other appliances as may be approved by * * * [specified local authorities].

---

[1] Brightly's Purdon's Digest, 12th ed., 1895, p. 914, secs. 1 to 16, with amendments by act No. 204, Acts of 1897 (22d An. Rept. Com. of Labor, pp. 1081–1083).

Later law.—By a law of 1909, act No. 233 (Bulletin of the Bureau of Labor, No. 85, pp. 753, 754), fire-escape requirements in cities of the first and second classes were made clearer and more stringent and the power of inspectors extended.

[Sections 2 and 3 require more than 1 rope per window in case of very large rooms, and section 4 requires such ropes to be kept in a convenient place.]

Penalty.—Not exceeding $300 and imprisonment 1 to 12 months, and in case of fire, liability for damages for personal injuries.

Specified local authorities are given power to examine such means of escape, and if satisfied therewith to issue certificates of compliance. The possession of such a certificate relieves the owner from the liability of fines, damages, and imprisonment.

By a subsequent law the enforcement of all provisions, State or local, relative to fire protection, except in cities of the first and second classes, is intrusted to the State factory inspection department.[1]

Wherever the law makes it the duty of the owner, lessee, or other person * * * to erect and maintain fire escapes or appliances for the extinguishment of fire, or for proper and sufficient exits in case of fire or panic, the chief factory inspector or his deputy shall inspect all said buildings * * * and notify the owners, lessee, or other persons in charge of same to comply with said law.

And all fire escapes, exits, and fire extinguishing appliances shall be provided and located by order of the chief factory inspector or his deputy and shall be subject to * * * [their] approval * * *

Provided, That the provisions of this section shall not apply to cities of the first and second classes.

CONDITIONS FOUND.

Of the 50 establishments visited in Pennsylvania 41 had buildings 3 or more stories in height. Twenty-five of these 41 were in Philadelphia (the only city of the first class), 15 were in cities of the second class, and 1 was in a city of the third class. None of the buildings was of frame construction, and 5 (all in cities of the first and second classes) were "fireproofed."

The following table groups the buildings of the 41 establishments by height and by character of place where located, and shows the number in each group having certain important means of fire protection:

---

[1] Acts of 1905, act No. 226, sec. 22 (22d An. Rept. Com. of Labor, p. 1180).

KIND OF FIRE PROTECTION, BY HEIGHT AND CHARACTER OF CONSTRUCTION OF BUILDINGS—PENNSYLVANIA.

[Each entry represents 1 building. When an establishment has more than 1 building and the several buildings are not uniform as regards fire protection, the principal building has been selected as representative. Figures for fire escapes wholly or partly of wood are not shown in the table.]

Kind of fire protection.	Establishments having specified fire protection.										Cities of third class.	Grand total.
	Cities of first class.					Cities of second class.						
	3-story.	4-story.	5-story.	6-story.	Total.	3-story.	4-story.	5-story.	6-story.	Total.	4-story.	
Number of establishments.	3	7	10	5	25	6	1	5	3	15	1	41
Fire escapes:												
Incombustible	2	7	9	5	23	3	1	5	3	12	1	36
Obstructed	1	2	2	1	6	.....	1	1	.....	2	.....	8
Exit doors:												
All opening outward	1	1	7	2	11	1	.....	1	2	4	1	16
Some obstructed	.....	1	.....	.....	1	1	.....	.....	.....	1	.....	2
Stairways:												
Properly lighted	1	6	9	4	20	5	1	5	3	14	1	35
With handrails	2	7	10	5	24	6	1	5	2	14	1	39
Fire apparatus:												
Fire extinguishers	1	4	3	2	10	4	1	2	1	8	.....	18
Fire hose—												
Inside building	1	3	6	2	12	2	1	3	2	8	1	21
On all floors	.....	1	4	2	7	2	1	3	2	8	1	16
Sprinkler system	.....	4	7	3	14	1	1	2	2	6	1	21
Standpipes	.....	4	7	2	13	2	1	2	2	7	1	21
Fire buckets (kept full)	2	7	7	4	20	6	1	3	.....	10	.....	30
Exit lights or signs	.....	4	8	3	15	1	.....	.....	2	3	.....	18
Fire drills	1	3	1	1	6	.....	1	1	.....	2	.....	8

OHIO.

SUMMARY OF LEGISLATION.

The laws of Ohio vest the factory-inspection department with a very considerable authority to insist upon satisfactory means of egress in case of fire.

The legal provisions relating to fire escapes and means of egress are as follows:

It shall be the duty of any owner * * * of any factory, workshop, tenement house, inn, or public house, if * * * more than 2 stories high, to provide convenient exits from the different upper stories * * * which shall be easily accessible in case of fire.

And it shall be the duty of any owner * * * [of any such building] * * * more than 3 stories high, in addition to the provisions governing 3-story buildings, to provide a life-saving device, or net, which shall be approved by the fire chief of the city, or village, * * * or if * * * outside of the city or village * * * by the State inspector of workshops and factories; and said life-saving device, or net, shall be kept on the first floor at or near the entrance of * * * [the building].[1]

---

[1] Acts of 1908, p. 83, sec. 2573, amending same section of Revised Statutes (Bulletin of the Bureau of Labor, No. 85, p. 705).

It shall be their duty [i. e., inspectors of workshops and factories] to visit all shops and factories [1] in their respective districts as often as possible to see that all the provisions * * * of this act are strictly * * * carried out; * * * and it shall be their duty to examine * * * as to the means of exit from all such places in case of fire or other disaster * * *.[2]

Said inspectors, if they find upon such inspection * * * that the means of egress in case of fire or other disaster is not sufficient, or that efficient means for extinguishing fire is not provided on each floor * * * shall notify the owners, proprietors, or agents of such shops or factories * * * to make the alterations or additions necessary without delay: *Provided, however,* That for such of the alterations * * * as may be of such nature as to make it impossible to comply with immediately, the chief inspector may grant from 15 to 30 days' time * * *.[3]

> *Penalty.*—For failure to make alterations, etc., within time granted—$50 to $500; after conviction $10 per day until alterations are made.[2]

A special section of the law requires stairways to be handrailed, and prescribes minutely the method of railing to be followed:[4]

> All stairs or stairways for ingress or egress to and from all tenement houses, apartments, manufactories, mills, shops, stores * * * shall be provided * * * with a good, substantial handrail extending from the top to the bottom of said stairs or stairway, and the same shall be firmly fastened * * * to the wall or other support * * * and such handrail shall be constructed or made of wood not less than $1\frac{1}{2}$ inches wide and $2\frac{1}{2}$ inches thick; or iron not less than $1\frac{1}{2}$ inches in diameter and shall be put up and maintained along all the said stairs and in all the said stairways in the said buildings * * *.

> *Penalty.*—$10 to $100.

> *Enforcement.*—Charged to State factory inspectors.

CONDITIONS FOUND.

Of the 60 establishments visited in Ohio, 54 had buildings 3 or more stories in height. None of these was of frame construction, and 6 were "fireproofed;" i. e., of reenforced concrete or brick and concrete.

---

[1] Term "shops" and "factories" includes the following: Manufacturing, mechanical, electrical, mercantile, art and laundering establishments, printing, telegraph and telephone offices, railroad depots, hotels, memorial buildings, tenement and apartment houses. Bates's Ann. Stat., 3d ed., Pt. I, Political, sec. 2573d (22d An. Rept. Com. of Labor, p. 999).

[2] Bates' Ann. Stat., 3d ed., Pt. I, Political, sec. 2573a-3, as amended by act, p. 338, Acts of 1902, and act, p. 530, Acts of 1904 (22d An. Rept. Com. of Labor, p. 998).

[3] Idem, sec. 2573c, as amended by act, p. 530, Acts of 1904 (22d An. Rept. Com. of Labor, pp. 998, 999).

[4] Idem, Pt. II, Civ., secs. 4238-15 and 4238-16 (22d An. Rept. Com. of Labor, pp. 1007, 1008).

The following table classifies the buildings of the 54 establishments referred to by height, and shows the number in each height group having certain important means of fire protection.

KIND OF FIRE PROTECTION, BY HEIGHT AND CHARACTER OF CONSTRUCTION OF BUILDINGS—OHIO.

[Each entry represents 1 building. When an establishment has more than 1 building and the several buildings are not uniform as regards fire protection, the principal building has been selected as representative. Figures for fire escapes wholly or partly of wood are not shown in the table.]

	Establishments having specified fire protection.					
Kind of fire protection.	Construction other than frame.					Total.
	3-story.	4-story.	5-story.	6-story.	8-story.	
Number of establishments	17	23	4	9	1	54
Fire escapes:						
Incombustible	10	19	3	9	1	42
Obstructed		1		2		3
Exit doors:						
All opening outward	10	12	2	3		27
Some obstructed				1		[1] 1
Stairways:						
Properly lighted	16	23	4	9	1	53
With handrails	16	23	4	9	1	53
Fire apparatus:						
Fire extinguishers	8	11	2	6	1	28
Fire hose—						
Inside building	15	14	2	3	1	35
On all floors	12	10	1	2	1	[2] 26
Sprinkler system	11	11	2	2		26
Standpipes	12	7		3		22
Fire buckets (kept full)	12	14	2	7		35
Exit lights or signs	5	12	1	3	1	22
Fire drills	3	1		1		5

[1] Not including 1 establishment, not reported as to construction.
[2] Not including 3 establishments, not reported as to construction.

In one of the 3-story buildings entered in this table as not having an incombustible fire escape, no employees worked above the second floor. Also, in one of the 4-story buildings entered as not having a fire escape, there was a continuous stairway in the middle of the building leading from the roof to the ground, and there was an adjoining roof accessible from the upper stories. On this account the superintendent stated that no special fire escape was necessary.

ILLINOIS.

SUMMARY OF LEGISLATION.

The law of Illinois regarding fire escapes, in force at the time of the field work of this investigation, makes the following provisions:[1]

'All buildings * * * which are 4 or more stories in height, excepting such as are used for private residences exclusively, but including flats and apartment buildings, shall be provided with 1 or more metallic ladder or stair fire escapes attached to the outer walls thereof and extending from, or suitably near the ground, to the uppermost story thereof, and provided with platforms of such forms and dimensions, and in such proximity to 1 or more windows of each story above the first, as to render access to such ladder or stairs from each such story easy and safe.

The number, location, material, and construction of such escapes to be subject to the approval of [the county authorities in counties and of the corporate authorities in organized villages, towns, and cities].

Provided, however, That all buildings more than 2 stories in height, used for manufacturing purposes or for hotels, dormitories, schools, seminaries, hospitals, or asylums, shall have at least 1 such fire escape for every 50 persons for which working, sleeping, or living accommodations are provided above the second stories of said buildings. * * *

All buildings of the number of stories and used for the purposes set forth in section one (1) [i. e., all the preceding quotation] of this act, which shall be hereafter erected * * *, shall upon or before their completion each be provided with fire escapes of the kind and number, and in the manner set forth in said section 1 of this act.

Penalty.—$25 to $200, and $50 for each additional week of failure to comply with legal notice within 30 days. On enforcing officials, for failure to carry out law, $5 to $100.

---

[1] Hurd's Rev. Stat., 1905, ch. 55a, secs. 1 to 6 (22d An. Rept. Com. of Labor, pp. 347, 348).

Later law.—By an act passed shortly after the completion of this investigation, Acts of 1909, p. 202, secs. 14 to 17 (Bulletin of the Bureau of Labor, No. 85, p. 549), the provisions regarding fire escapes were increased in scope and their enforcement charged in full to the factory inspection department.

The more significant provisions of the new law are these: All factories, mills, workshops, and mercantile establishments to have—

1. "Sufficient and reasonable" means of escape in case of fire, by more than one means of egress, to be kept unobstructed, in good repair, ready for use, and plainly marked.

2. Doors opening outward, slide or roll, and so constructed as to open easily and quickly from within.

3. "Proper and substantial handrails" provided on all stairways, treads to be so constructed as to offer a firm foothold.

4. Proper lights kept burning in hallways and stairways, and in front of elevators, except during period when natural light is sufficient.

There are no legal provisions regarding fire-fighting apparatus, the outward opening of doors, exit lights, the construction of stairways, or the lighting of halls and stairways.

The enforcement of the law, as quoted above, is charged to county and municipal authorities. The State factory inspection department is given no authority and is charged with no responsibility in this matter.

CONDITIONS FOUND.

Of the 47 establishments visited, 44 had buildings 3 or more stories in height. Two of these 44 were constructed partly of brick and partly of frame; the remaining 42 had external and dividing walls of brick, concrete, or other incombustible material, although in most cases floors, partitions, doors, etc., were of wood; 4 of these latter were reported as being "fireproofed."

The following table classifies the 44 establishments 3 stories or more in height by height and material of construction, and shows the number of each group having certain important means of fire protection:

KIND OF FIRE PROTECTION, BY HEIGHT AND CHARACTER OF CONSTRUCTION OF BUILDINGS—ILLINOIS.

[Each entry represents 1 building. When an establishment has more than 1 building and the several buildings are not uniform as regards fire protection, the principal building has been selected as representative. A building constructed partly of wood is classified in the table as a frame building. Figures for fire escapes wholly or partly of wood are not shown in the table.]

	Establishments having specified fire protection.						
Kind of fire protection.	Construction other than frame.					Frame.	Total.
	3-story.	4-story.	5-story.	6-story.	7-story.	3-story.	
Number of establishments...................	9	11	12	7	3	2	44
Fire escapes:							
Incombustible.............................	7	9	12	7	3	1	39
Obstructed...............................	1	1	3	....	1	....	6
Exit doors:							
All opening outward......................	3	3	6	....	....	....	12
Some obstructed.........................	2	....	1	....	....	....	¹ 3
Stairways:							
Properly lighted.........................	² 5	9	10	6	2	....	² 32
With handrails	² 4	11	10	7	3	1	² 36
Fire apparatus:							
Fire extinguishers.......................	4	10	9	5	....	....	28
Fire hose—							
Inside building......................	3	4	4	3	1	1	16
On all floors........................	2	4	4	2	....	1	13
Sprinkler system.........................	4	9	7	2	3	1	26
Standpipes...............................	3	3	7	4	2	1	20
Fire buckets (kept full)...................	5	9	8	3	1	1	27
Exit lights or signs.........................	....	4	7	4	3	....	18
Fire drills.................................	1	2	1	....	....	....	4

¹ Not including 14 establishments, not reported as to construction.
² Not including 2 establishments, not reported as to construction.

This table shows that with two exceptions each of the scheduled buildings 4 or more stories in height had at least 1 incombustible fire escape, thus fulfilling in substance the first section of the law as quoted above. The exceptions were two 4-story buildings, 1 of which had no fire escape, and 1 a "fire escape" of wood. The second section of the law requires at least 1 fire escape for each 50 persons employed above the second floor of buildings used for manufacturing purposes. Information upon this point was obtained in only a very few cases, and the only definite statement that can be made is that in 4 instances at least the proportion of 1 fire escape to each 50 employees was not observed. Details as to these 4 instances are as follows:

Establishment 24.—Occupies fourth floor of a 4-story building; 78 employees; only 1 fire escape.

Establishment 33.—Occupies whole of a 5-story building; 290 employees above second floor, 118 of whom are girls under 16; 2 fire escapes; a proportion of 145 employees per fire escape.

Establishment 34.—Occupies third and fourth stories of a 4-story building; 100 employees; 1 fire escape.

Establishment 37.—Occupies 5 upper stories of a 7-story building; 455 employees; 6 fire escapes; a proportion of 76 employees per fire escape.

INDIANA.

SUMMARY OF LEGISLATION.

The State law relating to fire escapes on factories and other establishments is very complete as regards the subjects referred to and very detailed in many of its requirements. In its enforcement it places a broad discretionary power in the hands of the department of inspection of factories, workshops, etc. The more important provisions of the law are as follows:[1]

SECTION 1. Every building in which persons are employed above the second story in a factory, workshop, or mercantile or other establishment * * * and every [such building] * * * of more than two stories in height shall be provided with proper ways of egress or means of escape from fire, sufficient for the use of all persons * * * in such building.

And such ways of egress * * * shall be kept free from obstruction, in good repair, and ready for use at all times.

And all rooms above the second story * * * shall be provided with more than one way of egress or escape from fire, placed as near as practicable at opposite ends of the room and leading to fire escapes on the outside of such buildings or to stairways on the inside, provided with proper railings.

---

[1] Acts of 1903, ch. 222, secs. 1, 2, 3, 6, and 7 (22d An. Rept. Com. of Labor, pp. 406–408). A new fire-escape law was passed and approved a few days before the field work of this investigation was completed in Indiana. Acts of 1909, ch. 118. Approved Mar. 6, 1909 (Bulletin of the Bureau of Labor, No. 85, pp. 567, 568).

This new law does not change materially any of the provisions of the former law as quoted above, except that it substitutes local fire chiefs in place of the State factory inspector in sections 1 and 2 of the law—i. e., the sections relating to the issue of exemption certificates, etc. The State department of inspection, however, is still required to see that the provisions of the act are everywhere enforced.

All external doors * * * shall open outward, and all windows open outward or upward.

The certificate of the chief inspector of the department of inspection of the State shall be prima facie evidence of a compliance with such requirements.

SEC. 2. In addition to the foregoing means of escape from fire, all such buildings * * * as are more than 2 stories in height shall have 1 or more fire escapes on the outside * * * as may be directed by the chief inspector aforesaid, except in such cases as the said chief inspector may deem such fire escapes to be unnecessary * * * and in such cases of exemption the said chief inspector shall give * * * a written certificate to that effect and his reason therefor.

And such fire escapes as are provided for in this section shall be constructed according to specifications issued or approved by the department of inspection and shall be connected with each floor above the first, well-fastened and secured, and of sufficient strength; * * * shall have landings or balconies guarded by iron railings not less than 3 feet in height, and embracing 1 or more windows at each story, and connecting with the interior by easily accessible and unobstructed openings; and the balconies or landings shall be connected by iron stairs, placed at a slant of not more than 45 degrees, protected by a well-secured handrail on both sides, with a 12-inch-wide drop ladder from the lower platform, reaching to the ground; except in cases of school buildings, iron stairs shall extend to a ground landing, and no telegraph, telephone, electric-light poles or wires, signs or other obstructions shall interfere with the construction and use of any fire escape.

SEC. 3. Any other plan or style of fire escape shall be sufficient, if approved by the chief inspector. * * *

The windows or doors to each fire escape shall be of sufficient size and be located, as far as possible, consistent with accessibility from the stairways and elevator hatchways or openings, and the ladder thereof shall extend to the roof.

Stationary stairs or ladders shall be provided on the inside of such establishment from the upper story to the roof * * *.

Penalty.—For neglect or refusal to comply with any of these provisions, not exceeding $200 and imprisonment 1 to 2 months; and also additional penalties in cases of a fire occurring in absence of such escapes as provided by law.

In addition to the fire-escape law referred to above there are specific legal requirements as to the provisions of handrails on stairways, the screening of such stairs, the outward opening of doors and the fastening of doors. These requirements are in full as follows:[1]

Proper and substantial handrails shall be provided on all stairways in all establishments above enumerated [i. e., manufacturing or mercantile establishment, laundry, renovating works, bakery, or printing office].

---

[1] Ann. Stat. of 1894, Rev. of 1901, secs. 7087f and 7087g (22d An. Rept. Com. of Labor, pp. 398, 402).

And where in the opinion of the chief inspector it is necessary, the steps of said stairs * * * shall be substantially covered with rubber, securely fastened thereon. * * *

The stairs shall be properly screened at the sides and bottom.

All doors leading in or to such establishments aforesaid shall be so constructed as to open outwardly where practicable, and shall be neither locked, bolted, nor fastened during working hours.

Penalty.—First offense, not more than $50; second offense, not more than $100, to which may be added not more than 10 days' imprisonment; third offense, not less than $250, and not more than 30 days' imprisonment.

The enforcement of all the provisions quoted above—regarding fire escapes, stairways, doors, etc.—is charged in full to the State department of inspection of factories, workshops, etc.[1]

CONDITIONS FOUND.

Of the 47 establishments visited in Indiana, 36 had buildings 3 or more stories in height, the material of construction being brick, with inside floors, doors, etc., usually of wood.

The following table classifies the buildings of these 36 establishments by height, and shows the number in each group having certain important means of fire protection.

KIND OF FIRE PROTECTION, BY HEIGHT AND CHARACTER OF CONSTRUCTION OF BUILDINGS—INDIANA.

[Each entry represents 1 building. When an establishment has more than 1 building and the several buildings are not uniform as regards fire protection, the principal building has been selected as representative. Figures for fire escapes wholly or partly of wood are not shown in the table."]

Kind of fire protection.	Establishments having specified fire protection.				
	Construction other than frame—				Total.
	3-story.	4-story.	5-story.	6-story.	
Number of establishments	22	12	1	1	36
Fire escapes:					
Incombustible	12	[2]7	1	1	[1]21
Obstructed	1	(²)			[1]1
Exit doors:					
All opening outward	3	1			4
Some obstructed	2	1			3
Stairways:					
Properly lighted	20	12	1	1	34
With handrails	20	11	1	1	33
Fire apparatus:					
Fire extinguishers	14	9	1	1	25
Fire hose—					
Inside building	12	7	1	1	21
On all floors	8	6	1	1	16
Sprinkler system	8	8		1	17
Standpipes	6	7	1	1	15
Fire buckets (kept full)[3]	14	7		1	22
Exit lights or signs	1	2	1	1	5
Fire drills	1	1		1	3

[1] Acts of 1903, ch. 222, sec. 7, and Ann. Stat. of 1894, Rev. of 1901, sec. 7087v (22d An. Rept. Com. of Labor, pp. 402, 408).
[2] Data not reported for 1 establishment.
[3] In 3 cases the water was kept in barrels, with buckets close by.

Examination of this table shows that in 14 of the 36 buildings 3 stories or more in height, no incombustible fire escapes were provided; no report being received from 1 establishment. In 3 of these cases no persons were regularly employed above the second floor. In each of the remaining 11 buildings, 7 of which were 3 stories and 4 four stories in height, it was reported that persons worked above the second floor. The law authorizes the chief inspector to exempt by written certificate any building from the requirement of outside fire escapes if he considers the other means of escape sufficient. In none of the 11 cases cited were exemption permits on file.

Fire escapes constructed of wood were found in 2 establishments.

MICHIGAN.

SUMMARY OF LEGISLATION.

The Michigan law requires fire escapes on factories, etc., when the State factory inspectors regard such escapes as necessary. The kind of fire escape to be used is also left to the discretion of the inspectors. The law reads:[1]

Fire escapes shall be provided for all manufacturing establishments, hotels, stores, theaters, schools, halls, apartment houses, and public buildings 2 or more stories in height, if in the opinion of the factory inspector it is necessary to insure the safety of persons in such places.

Said fire escapes or means of egress, or as many thereof as may be deemed sufficient by the inspector, shall be provided, and where it is necessary to provide fire escapes on the outside of such buildings, they shall consist of landings and balconies at each floor above the first, to be built according to specifications provided by the factory inspector.

Factory inspectors shall, in writing, notify the owner, agent, or lessee of such [buildings] * * * of the required location and specifications of such fire escapes as may be ordered.

Penalty.—$5 to $100, or imprisonment 10 to 90 days, or both.

The law also contains certain provisions regarding the construction of stairways and the outward opening or sliding of doors. These provisions are as follows:[2]

Stairways with substantial handrails shall be provided in manufacturing establishments, and where in the opinion of the factory inspector it is necessary the steps of such stairs * * * shall be substantially covered with rubber, securely fastened thereon, for the better safety of persons employed * * *.

---

[1] Acts of 1901, act No. 113, sec. 6, as amended by act No. 140, Acts of 1907, and idem, sec. 18 (22d An. Rept. Com. of Labor, pp. 659, 662). The act of 1909, act No. 285, which consolidates and revises the labor laws, does not make any changes in the sections regarding fire escapes (Bulletin of the Bureau of Labor, No. 85, p. 658).

[2] Idem, sec. 7; and idem, sec. 18 (22d An. Rept. Com. of Labor, pp. 660, 662).

The stairs shall be properly screened at sides and bottom where females are employed, and where practicable the doors of such establishments shall swing outwardly or slide, as ordered by said factory inspector, and shall be neither locked, bolted, nor fastened during working hours.

Penalty.—$5 to $100, or imprisonment 10 to 90 days, or both.

Enforcement.—Rests upon the State factory inspection department.[1]

There are no legal provisions regarding fire fighting apparatus, or exit lights and signs.

CONDITIONS FOUND.

All of the 19 establishments visited had buildings 2 or more stories in height, and thus, at the discretion of the factory inspector, might be required to have fire escapes. In 4 of these establishments there were no buildings over 2 stories in height; none of these had fire escapes, but in all 4 the means of exit in case of fire seemed sufficient.

Each of the remaining 15 establishments had buildings 3 or more stories high. The following table classifies the main buildings of these establishments by height, and shows the number in each height group having certain important means of fire protection. One of these 15 buildings was of frame construction; one was "fireproofed;" the others were of brick with interior wood millwork.

KIND OF FIRE PROTECTION, BY HEIGHT AND CHARACTER OF CONSTRUCTION OF BUILDINGS—MICHIGAN.

[Each entry represents 1 building. When an establishment has more than 1 building and the several buildings are not uniform as regards fire protection, the principal building has been selected as representative. A building constructed partly of wood is classed in the table as a frame building. Figures for fire escapes wholly or partly of wood are not shown in the table.]

	Establishments having specified fire protection.						
Kind of fire protection.	Construction other than frame.					Frame.	Total.
	3-story.	4-story.	5-story.	6-story.	7-story.	3-story.	
Number of establishments...................	3	4	5	1	1	1	15
Fire escapes:							
Incombustible........................	2	4	4	1	1	1	13
Obstructed............................							
Exit doors:							
All opening outward.................		2	1				3
Some obstructed.....................	1						1
Stairways:							
Properly lighted.....................	3	4	4	1	1	1	14
With handrails.......................	3	4	4	1	1	1	14
Fire apparatus:							
Fire extinguishers...................	3	2	4	1			10
Fire hose—							
Inside building...................		4	3	1	1		9
On all floors.....................		4	3	1			8
Sprinkler system....................	1	3	2			1	7
Standpipes..........................	1	3	1	1		1	7
Fire buckets (kept full).............	2	3	3	1	1	1	11
Exit lights or signs......................		3	1		1		5
Fire drills..............................					1		1

[1] Acts of 1901, act No. 113, secs. 12 to 15 (22d An. Rept. Com. of Labor, pp. 660, 661).

WISCONSIN.

SUMMARY OF LEGISLATION.

The laws of Wisconsin contain two series of provisions regarding fire escapes and fire apparatus on factories and workshops. The two series are similar in reading and meaning, the chief difference being in the penalty imposed for violation. One of these series relates to public and semipublic buildings generally, including buildings containing workrooms; the second series seems to relate more specifically to manufacturing establishments. The latter series of provisions is as follows: [1]

Every person or corporation owning, occupying, or controlling any factory, workshop, or structure 3 or more stories high * * * in which 25 or more persons are employed at any kind of labor, shall provide and keep connected with the same one or more good and substantial metallic or fireproof ladders, stairs, or stairways, ready for use at all times, reaching from the cornice to the top of the first story, and placed on the outside thereof in such position and number as may be designated by the chief of the fire department or fire marshal of the city or village * * * or by the State factory inspector.

And at each story above the first a wrought-iron balcony in connection with such ladder, such balcony to be substantially attached to the structure, and of such length as to permit of access to it from 2 or more windows on each story, and of sufficient size to furnish reasonable means of escape to the persons employed therein from each and every floor or story above the first.

And in all cities and villages where there is a water supply * * * there shall be attached to such fire escape, except on structures equipped with automatic sprinklers, a 3-inch wrought-iron standpipe extending from a point within 5 feet from the ground to a point 3 feet above the roof or cornice, and on the roof shall be attached a 2½-inch angle hose valve * * *.

> *Penalty.*—For failure to provide fire escapes and hose within 3 months after written order of fire chief, marshal or inspector, a fine not exceeding $100.

> *Enforcement.*—Charged to the local fire authorities and also, specifically, to the State factory inspectors. [2]

---

[1] Ann. Stat. of 1898, Supp. of 1906 (with Acts of 1907 inserted), sec. 1636–4 (22d An. Rept. Com. of Labor, pp. 1410, 1411); this is the general law referred to in the text. Idem., sec. 4390a (22d An. Rept. Com. of Labor, p. 1439); this is the law which relates primarily to factories and workshops.

Later law.—An act in force subsequent to the field work of this investigation, Acts of 1909, amends the earlier act in several of its details and the penalty imposed, but leaves its substance unchanged (Bulletin of the Bureau of Labor, No. 85, p. 804).

[2] Ann. Stat., sec. 1021f, and references in preceding footnote (22d An. Rept. Com. of Labor, p. 1407).

As regards the outward opening of doors the law provides that: [1]

Every building, now or hereafter used, in whole or in part, as a * * * factory or workshop * * * must be provided with outer doors that shall open or swing outwardly, and when storm doors are used at the entrance, * * * either inside or outside, said storm doors shall have a glass therein not less than 15 inches square, which glass shall be not less than 4 feet from the floor or approach, unless the commissioner of labor and industrial statistics, the factory inspector or assistant factory inspector in his judgment shall deem it otherwise.

Penalty.—Not exceeding $500 or imprisonment not exceeding 90 days.

The State factory inspectors are instructed to enforce this requirement.

There are no requirements of the State law regarding exit lights and signs, or regarding the construction of stairways.[2]

CONDITIONS FOUND.

Twelve of the 19 establishments visited had buildings 3 or more stories in height. The following table classifies the main buildings of these 12 establishments by height, and shows the number in each height group having certain important means of fire protection. None of these buildings were of frame construction, and 2 were "fireproofed."

---

[1] Ann. Stat., sec. 4390 (22d An. Rept. Com. of Labor, p. 1438). Amended by an act passed subsequent to the field work of this investigation, Acts of 1909 (Bulletin of the Bureau of Labor, No. 85, p. 810).

[2] The municipal building code of Milwaukee provides that all stairways in buildings occupied as factories above the second floor must be inclosed, and that every building over 3 stories in height shall be provided with two ways of egress, "inclosed in walls of incombustible material with no interior openings from apartments, but accessible from all apartments on each floor." Each section in a building having fireproof partitions is for this purpose considered as a separate building.

KIND OF FIRE PROTECTION, BY HEIGHT AND CHARACTER OF CONSTRUCTION OF
BUILDINGS—WISCONSIN.

[Each entry represents 1 building. When an establishment has more than 1 building and the severa
buildings are not uniform as regards fire protection, the principal building has been selected as representative. Figures for fire escapes wholly or partly of wood are not shown in the table.]

Kind of fire protection.	Establishments having specified fire protection.					
	Construction other than frame.					Total.
	3-story.	4-story.	5-story.	6-story.	7-story.	
Number of establishments.................................	3	4	3	1	1	12
Fire escapes:						
Incombustible...............................	1	2	3	1	1	8
Obstructed.......................			1			1
Exit doors:						
All opening outward...........................	1	1	1	1	1	5
Some obstructed.......................						(¹)
Stairways:						
Properly lighted..............................	3	3	3	1	1	11
With handrails.............................	3	4	3	1	1	12
Fire apparatus:						
Fire extinguishers...........................	3	2			1	6
Fire hose—						
Inside building............................	2	3	2	1	1	9
On all floors.............................	1	2	2		1	6
Sprinkler system............................	1	2	3	1		7
Standpipes.................................	1	2	3	1	1	8
Fire buckets (kept full).....................	2	3	2			7
Exit lights or signs.................................						
Fire drills..		1				1

¹ Three not reported as to construction.

All of the establishments covered in this table were in communities
having a public water supply, and thus, under the law, were required
to have standpipes.

MARYLAND.

SUMMARY OF LEGISLATION.

The fire-escape law of Maryland applies only to garment-working
factories (sweatshops) in the city of Baltimore. The legal provisions, which are few and simple, are in full as follows:[1]

The owner or owners of any * * * house or building used
as a sweatshop or factory where 4 or more persons are employed as
garment workers, on other than the first floor of such house or building, shall provide fire escapes for the same.

Penalty.—On owner for failure to provide fire escape. $200, or
imprisonment 60 days, or both.

The enforcement of this law does not seem to be charged to any
special administrative body, but the State factory inspector has
authority to enforce it. He says that he exercises this authority
by withholding the permit required of sweatshops until proper
fire escapes, approved by the city building department, have been
provided.

[1] Pub. Local Laws, Code of 1888, art. 4, sec. 280, Rev. of 1898, ch. 123, Acts of 1898
(22d An. Rept. Com. of Labor, p. 562).

In the case of establishments other than sweatshops the State factory inspector has no authority as regards fire escapes or fire-fighting equipment.

There is no State legislation regarding fire-fighting apparatus, the outward opening of doors, exit signs and lights, or the construction and guarding of stairways.

CONDITIONS FOUND.

Of the 28 establishments visited, 24 had buildings 3 or more stories in height. None of these buildings was of frame construction, and a few of the higher ones were "fireproofed." The following table classifies the buildings of these 24 establishments by height, and shows the number of each group having certain important means of fire protection

KIND OF FIRE PROTECTION, BY HEIGHT AND CHARACTER OF CONSTRUCTION OF BUILDINGS—MARYLAND.

[Each entry represents 1 building. When an establishment has more than 1 building and the several buildings are not uniform as regards fire protection, the principal building has been selected as representative. Figures for fire escapes wholly or partly of wood are not shown in the table.]

Kind of fire protection.	Establishments having specified fire protection.						Total.
	Construction other than frame.						
	3-story.	4-story.	5-story.	6-story.	7-story.	9-story.	
Number of establishments	5	3	4	8	2	2	24
Fire escapes:							
Incombustible	3	3	2	8	2	2	20
Obstructed		1			1		2
Exit doors:							
All opening outward	1	1	1	1	1	1	6
Some obstructed							(1)
Stairways:							
Properly lighted	5	1	3	7	2	2	20
With handrails	2	3	3	6	1	2	17
Fire apparatus:							
Fire extinguishers	2	2	1	5			10
Fire hose—							
Inside building	1	2		5		2	10
On all floors	1	1		5		2	9
Sprinkler system	1	2		6	1	2	12
Standpipes		2		6	1	2	11
Fire buckets (kept full)	4	3	4	8	2	2	23
Exit lights or signs	1	1	1	1	2	1	7
Fire drills				1		2	3

[1] Fifteen not reported as to construction.

In one of the establishments the fire-fighting equipment was unusually complete. The following are extracts from the data on this plant furnished by the agent in the field:

This establishment maintains a fully equipped fire department among its employees. The establishment has a number of hose reels and system of fire-alarm boxes on each floor, which are connected with the engine room. When an alarm is sounded from a certain floor, the engineer blows the factory whistle to correspond to the number of the floor the fire is on. When the whistle blows an alarm from any floor, the female employees at each end of the building form a line and proceed to the stairways located at each end of the building, and march downstairs to the street, while those employed in the middle part of the floor proceed in line to the spiral fire escape and get in, and the chute carries them to the street, where they are taken from the spiral fire escape by two male employees who are detailed at that point.

The male employees on each floor, when an alarm is sounded, proceed to their proper places in each room or section where the hose is constantly attached to standpipe. The hose is unwound, or, if it is on racks, taken down and straightened out. If it is what is called a "wet drill," the water is turned on and the stream of water is directed into the areaway or on top of the building.

In the winter months the establishment has what are called "dry drills" in which the employees do not go out of the building, nor is the water turned on, but the employees form in line at the designated sections.

The drills are held at least once a month, and the alarm is sounded from any different floor. There is no set time for holding the drills.

NORTH CAROLINA.

SUMMARY OF LEGISLATION.

A fire-protection law affecting manufacturing establishments generally was passed and ratified shortly before the field work of this investigation in North Carolina was begun, and was legally in full effect at that time.[1] As, however, this law was so new, and as previously there had been no State legislation regarding the subject, the results of this investigation can not be accepted as measuring the effect of the law.

As the law referred to is in many respects very broad in its scope and very detailed in its requirements, it is quoted below almost in its entirety:

SECTION 3. All doors for ingress and egress * * * of all * * * factories with more than 20 employees shall be so hung as to open outwardly from the * * * workshops * * *.

SEC. 4. All factories, manufactories, establishments, or workshops of three or more stories in height, in which thirty or more people are employed above the first floor * * * , shall be provided with one or (if the proper officials shall deem necessary) more outside fire escapes, not less than 6 feet in length and 3 feet in width, properly and safely constructed, guarded by iron railings not less than 3 feet in length and taking in at least 1 door and 1 window or 2 windows at each story and connected with the interior by easily accessible and unobstructed openings;

And the said fire escapes shall connect by iron stairs not less than 24 inches wide, the steps to be not less than 6 inches tread, placed at

---

[1] Acts of 1909, ch. 637, secs. 3 to 6, inclusive. Ratified Mar. 6, 1909. (Bulletin of the Bureau of Labor, No. 85, p. 695.) Investigation conducted in North Carolina from Mar. 18 to Apr. 2, 1909.

not more than an angle of 45° slant and protected by a well-secured hand rail on both sides, with a 12-inch-wide drop ladder from the lowest platform reaching to the ground;

That no outside fire escapes shall be required where there are already sufficient inside stairways;

That for every 20 people employed on any floor above the second * * * there shall be one rope or portable fire escape, and that each story shall be amply supplied with means for extinguishing fires;

That all the main doors, both inside and outside, in factories, except fire doors, shall open outwardly when the proper official shall so direct, and that no outside or inside door of any building wherein operatives are employed shall be so locked, bolted, or otherwise fastened during the hours of labor as to prevent egress.

SEC. 5. Every building in which 20 or more persons are employed above the second story in a factory, workshop, or mercantile or other establishment, the owner or agent * * * of which * * * is notified in writing by the insurance commissioner * * * , shall be provided with proper ways of egress or other means of escape from fire sufficient for the use of all persons * * * employed * * * and such ways of egress and means of escape shall be kept free from obstructions, in good repair and ready for use.

Every room above the second story in any such building in which 20 or more persons are employed shall be provided with more than one way of egress by stairways on the inside or outside of the building.

All doors in any building, subject to the provisions of this act, shall open outwardly, if the insurance commissioner or one of his deputies shall direct in writing.

> Penalty.—On owner, for failure "to comply with the provisions of this act in accordance with the orders of the authorities," $10 to $50 for each day's neglect.

The insurance commissioner is charged with the enforcement of the above-quoted provisions. There is no State factory inspection service in North Carolina.

CONDITIONS FOUND.

Eighteen of the 28 establishments visited had buildings 3 or more stories in height. None of these buildings was of frame.

The following table classifies the buildings of these 18 establishments by height, and shows the number in each group having certain important means of fire protection.

KIND OF FIRE PROTECTION, BY HEIGHT AND CHARACTER OF CONSTRUCTION OF BUILDINGS—NORTH CAROLINA.

[Each entry represents 1 building. When an establishment has more than 1 building and the several buildings are not uniform as regards fire protection, the principal building has been selected as representative. Figures for fire escapes wholly or partly of wood are not shown in the table.]

Kind of fire protection.	Establishments having specified fire protection.			
	Construction other than frame.			Total.
	3-story.	4-story.	5-story.	
Number of establishments..................................	9	7	2	18
Fire escapes:				
Incombustible.....................................	3	5	2	10
Obstructed..				
Exit doors:				
All opening outward.............................		1		1
Some obstructed.................................	3	2	1	6
Stairways:				
Properly lighted.................................	4	3	1	1 8
With handrails...................................	3		1	1 4
Fire apparatus:				
Fire extinguishers...............................	3	1		4
Fire hose—				
Inside building...............................		7		7
On all floors.................................		7		7
Sprinkler system.................................	7	6	1	14
Standpipes.......................................	3	5	1	9
Fire buckets (kept full).........................	9	7	2	18
Exit lights or signs..................................		3		3
Fire drills...		5		5

[1] Not including 1 establishment, not reported as to construction.

GEORGIA.

SUMMARY OF LEGISLATION.

The law of Georgia requires every factory building more than 2 stories high to have more than one means of egress by stairways, to have all main doors open outwardly, and to be supplied with fire-extinguishing apparatus on each floor. The law reads as follows:[1]

Owners of every building more than 2 stories in height, not including the basement, used in the third or higher stories, in whole or in part, as factory or workshop, shall provide more than one way of egress from each story of said building, above the second story, by stairways, on the inside or outside of said building, and such stairways shall be, as nearly as may be practicable, at opposite ends of each story and so constructed that, in case of fire, the ground can be readily reached from the third and higher stories.

Stairways on the outside of said buildings shall have suitable railed landings at each story above the first, and shall connect with each of said stories by doors or windows, opening outwardly, and such doors, windows, and landings shall be kept at all times clear of obstructions.

All the main doors of such ouildings, both inside and outside, shall open outwardly, and each story shall be amply supplied with means for extinguishing fires.

[1] Code, 1895, Vol. II, Civ. Code, secs. 2622, 2623, and 2625 (22d An. Rept. Com. of Labor, pp. 289, 290).

Penalty.—On owner, for failure to comply with the law or with written orders of the enforcing authorities, as for a misdemeanor, fine not to exceed $1,000, imprisonment not to exceed 6 months, or chain gang not to exceed 12 months, or any 2 or all 3 of these punishments.[1]

Enforcement.—Charged to the local authorities of the municipality or county where the building is situated. There is no State factory inspection service in Georgia.

CONDITIONS FOUND.

Twelve of the 27 establishments visited in Georgia had buildings 3 or more stories in height. None of these buildings were of frame construction.

The following table classifies the buildings of these 12 establishments by height, and shows for each height group the number having certain important means of fire protection.

KIND OF FIRE PROTECTION, BY HEIGHT AND CHARACTER OF CONSTRUCTION OF BUILDINGS—GEORGIA.

[Each entry represents 1 building. When an establishment has more than 1 building and the several buildings are not uniform as regards fire protection, the principal building has been selected as representative. Figures for fire escapes wholly or partly of wood are not shown in the table.]

Kind of fire protection.	Establishments having specified fire protection.			
	Construction other than frame.			Total.
	3-story.	4-story.	5-story.	
Number of establishments	5	6	1	12
Fire escapes:				
Incombustible		5	1	6
Obstructed		3		3
Exit doors:				
All opening outward	1			1
Some obstructed	1	2		[1] 3
Stairways:				
Properly lighted	3	4	1	8
With handrails	2	3	1	[2] 6
Fire apparatus:				
Fire extinguishers	2			2
Fire hose—				
Inside building	3	1	1	5
On all floors	2	1	1	4
Sprinkler system	2	5	1	8
Standpipes	3	1		4
Fire buckets (kept full)	2	5	1	8
Exit lights or signs				
Fire drills				

[1] Not including 2 establishments, not reported as to construction.
[2] Not including 1 establishment, not reported as to construction.

FLORIDA.

SUMMARY OF LEGISLATION.

There are no legal provisions relative to the subject of fire escapes or fire protection.

[1] Code, 1895, Vol. III, Pen. Code, secs. 510 and 1039 (22d An. Rept. Com. of Labor, p. 294).

CONDITIONS FOUND.

Nine of the 14 establishments visited had buildings 3 or more stories in height. Four of these 9 were of frame construction; the other 5 were of brick or concrete.

The following table classifies these several buildings by height and by material of construction and shows for each group the number having certain important means of fire protection.

KIND OF FIRE PROTECTION, BY HEIGHT AND CHARACTER OF CONSTRUCTION OF BUILDINGS—FLORIDA.

[Each entry represents 1 building. When an establishment has more than 1 building and the several buildings are not uniform as regards fire protection, the principal building has been selected as representative. A building constructed partly of wood is classed in the table as a frame building. Figures for fire escapes wholly or partly of wood are not shown in the table.]

Kind of fire protection.	Establishments having specified fire protection.				
	Construction other than frame.		Frame.		Total.
	3-story.	4-story.	3-story.	4-story.	
Number of establishments	3	2	3	1	9
Fire escapes:					
Incombustible	1	2			3
Obstructed					
Exit doors:					
All opening outward					
Some obstructed					
Stairways:					
Properly lighted	3	2	3	1	9
With handrails	2	1	2	1	6
Fire apparatus:					
Fire extinguishers	3	2	2	1	8
Fire hose—					
Inside building	1	1	1		3
On all floors	1	1	1		3
Sprinkler system	1				1
Standpipes			1		1
Fire buckets (kept full)		1	2	1	4
Exit lights or signs					
Fire drills		2			2

LOUISIANA.

SUMMARY OF LEGISLATION.

Louisiana legislation requires outside metallic fire escapes on all buildings, not private residences, 4 or more stories in height, in the city of New Orleans. In the special case of factories it requires that all buildings used for manufacturing purposes, more than 2 stories in height, shall have 1 outside metallic fire escape for every 25 persons employed above the second floor. The text of the law is as follows:[1]

All buildings, except such as are used for private residences exclusively, in the city of New Orleans, of 4 or more stories in height, shall be provided with 1 or more metallic ladders or metallic fire escapes,

---

[1] Rev. Laws, 1897, p. 754, act No. 97, Acts of 1888, secs. 1, 2, and 3 (22d An. Rept. Com. of Labor, p. 515).

including from the first story to the upper stories of such buildings, and above the roof and on the outer walls thereof, in such location and numbers and of such material and construction as the mayor, chief engineer of the fire department of their respective districts, the city surveyor and chairman of the fire committee of the city council and commissioner of public buildings, or a majority of them may from time to time determine.

After such determination * * * • the chief engineer * * * may * * * by a notice in writing * * * require such owner or agent to cause such metallic ladder or fire escape to be placed upon such building, within 30 days after the service of such notice:

Provided, however, That all buildings more than 2 stories in height, used for manufacturing purposes, shall have 1 metallic ladder for every 25 persons, or less, employed above the second story.

> *Penalty.*—For failure to comply with written notice within 30 days, $25 to $250, and also $25 for each week of neglect.

The law also requires that stairways in factories have substantial handrails and that doors therein shall open outwardly or slide, and be kept unfastened during working hours :[1]

Stairways with substantial handrails shall be provided in factories, mills, and manufacturing establishments for the better safety of persons employed in said establishments.

The doors of such establishments shall swing outwardly or slide, as ordered by the factory inspector and it shall be neither locked, bolted or fastened during working hours.

> *Penalty.*—$25 to $50, or imprisonment 10 to 30 days, or both.

The enforcement of the statute regarding stairways and doors is charged to the factory inspectors.[2] Factory inspectors are locally appointed in Louisiana, and at the time of the field work of this investigation, the only inspector in the State was in the city of New Orleans.

The statute regarding fire escapes is not charged to the factory inspectors, its enforcement being the duty of other municipal authorities. The New Orleans factory inspector, although having no power to enforce the fire escape requirements, reports cases of defective or absent fire escapes to the chief of the fire department. The chief of the fire department, in an interview with an agent of this Bureau, made the following statement:

The enforcement of the fire-escape law is done by this department. No systematic inspection of houses is made to see whether or not the fire-escape law is obeyed. The factory inspector, employees, or other persons may report the need of fire escapes on certain * * * buildings; or the firemen, in pursuit of their usual duties, may find buildings with insufficient fire escapes. Such cases are investigated by the fire department, and if found necessary, fire escapes are ordered to be provided; and the department sees that its orders are carried out.

---

[1] Acts of 1908, act No. 301, sec. 15 (Bulletin of the Bureau of Labor, No. 85, p. 600).
[2] Idem, sec. 23 (22d An. Rept. Com. of Labor, p. 601).

The enforcement of the law takes a year or two. No report is kept or made.

The requirement of 1 fire escape for every 25 employees is very stringent, and is rarely observed in large establishments. Thus, 1 factory scheduled, with a 5-story building and 750 employees, had 3 large fire escapes. Under the law it should have had 30 fire escapes, for which there was probably not room on the outside of the building.

CONDITIONS FOUND.

Twenty-three of the 29 establishments had buildings 3 or more stories in height. None of these buildings are frame.

The following table classifies the buildings of these 23 establishments by height, and shows for each height group the number having certain important means of fire protection:

KIND OF FIRE PROTECTION, BY HEIGHT AND CHARACTER OF CONSTRUCTION OF BUILDINGS—LOUISIANA.

[Each entry represents 1 building. When an establishment has more than 1 building and the several buildings are not uniform as regards fire protection, the principal building has been selected as representative. Figures for fire escapes wholly or partly of wood are not shown in the table.]

Kind of fire protection.	Establishments having specified fire protection.			
	Construction other than frame.			Total.
	3-story.	4-story.	5-story.	
Number of establishments	13	8	2	23
Fire escapes:				
Incombustible	2	4	2	8
Obstructed		1		1
Exit doors:				
All opening outward	1	4	2	7
Some obstructed				
Stairways:				
Properly lighted	7	6	2	15
With handrails	13	7	2	22
Fire apparatus:				
Fire extinguishers	4	2	2	8
Fire hose—				
Inside building	4	3	2	9
On all floors	1	3	2	6
Sprinkler system	3	3	2	8
Standpipes	4	3		7
Fire buckets (kept full)	7	7	2	16
Exit lights or signs		1	2	3
Fire drills	2			2

CHAPTER VI.

SAFEGUARDING OF MACHINERY.

277

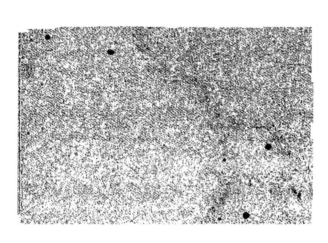

CHAPTER VI.

SAFEGUARDING OF MACHINERY.

INTRODUCTION.

The term "machinery" is here used to include not only manufacturing machines proper, such as rolling machines, punch presses, wood shapers, but also all forms of power-driven mechanism, such as shafting, belting, gearing, and a few stationary structures not usually classified as machinery, such as open vats filled with hot or dangerous liquids. Elevators fall within the meaning of the term, but because of the distinct character and special importance of this topic it is considered in a separate chapter. This seems desirable because the character of the accidents incident to elevators, and the laws relating to their safeguarding, can be easily distinguished from the corresponding facts regarding other forms of machinery.

Broadly speaking, all power-driven machinery is in some degree dangerous to personal safety. If it is not directly menacing, as are low uninclosed belts, unguarded punch presses, etc., it becomes so under certain conditions, as in the attempt to clean when in motion. With machinery as it is, it is practically impossible to remove all these risks. A moment's carelessness may undo the best protective measures so far devised. Nevertheless, by the intelligent use of protective measures of proven efficiency, the danger incident to machinery may be reduced to an almost negligible minimum.

DANGERS OF MACHINERY, AND PROTECTIVE MEASURES.

Before proceeding to a detailed presentation of laws and conditions by States, it seems desirable to offer a brief preliminary outline of the more common dangers connected with machinery and the possible protective measures against such dangers. This is necessary to a proper understanding of the several laws, of the evils they seek to remedy, and of the difficulties and intricacies connected with their proper framing and with their proper administration. The points touched upon in this outline are those of which State laws most frequently take cognizance.

Factory machinery, excluding elevators, fall into three main classes: Prime movers—steam engines, electric motors, etc.; power transmitters (or mill gearing)—shafting, belting, gearing; and individual manufacturing machines.

The present discussion will limit itself almost entirely to the second and third of these classes of machinery. The prime mover is a frequent source of accident, but in nearly all factories the dangers incident thereto are limited to a very small number of adult male employees—engineers, firemen, etc.—at work in a special room, engine room or power room. Moreover, the most dangerous feature of any prime mover is perhaps the boiler of the steam engine, and although in many States such boilers are subjected to legal restrictions and public inspection, such restrictions and inspection are usually considered as being separate from ordinary factory inspection. If, indeed, boiler inspection is provided for by law, it is usually intrusted to a force of inspectors with special technical equipment. For these reasons the present investigation paid little attention to the subject of prime movers, and in consequence little attention will be given it in this report.

From the standpoint of safety against accident, the most satisfactory power system yet devised is that of electricity, operating by means of individual motors adjacent and connected with each manufacturing machine used in the plant. This avoids all shafting, belting, and gearing, which in many factories occupy such a large space and are such a constant menace to the safety of employees. The individual motor also has another important advantage. One of the most important safety provisions in a factory is some device for quickly stopping a machine. If, for instance, a man's hand is caught in the cog gearing of a rolling machine, the seriousness of the accident may be greatly diminished, and a fatal issue perhaps avoided, by a quick stopping of the machine. The individual motor is adapted to such quick stopping. The pressing of a button or the moving of a lever, which can be done probably by the victim himself, will immediately cut off the power and bring the moving parts to an almost instantaneous stop.

The individual motor system, therefore, itself supplants many safeguards required for safety's sake by the older system of a central power plant with numerous cumbrous power transmitters. With it, the only important safety provision needed in the factory, except with especially dangerous machines, is the inclosing of exposed moving parts of the motor and machine, either by close-fitting guards or by fences, as the circumstances may direct.

The system of the individual motor is of comparatively recent introduction, and, while it is rapidly extending its field, it is as yet existent in only a comparatively small proportion of manufacturing establishments. The great majority of such establishments are equipped with some form of centrally located prime mover, from which the power is transmitted to the various parts of the factory and to the individual machines by means of shafting, belting, and gearing. This is the system which most State legislatures in enacting laws upon the subject of machinery protection have had in view.

POWER TRANSMITTERS.

It is an accepted principle of safety that every part of the power transmission system, so located as to permit anyone coming into personal contact with it or near enough to have the clothing caught therein, should be fully guarded. Thus, for example, if overhead shafts or pulleys are not within, say, 7 feet of the floor, special guarding is rarely necessary. In practice, however, it is seldom possible to locate all the transmitting mechanism at such a safe height. Even if the main parts are overhead, the subordinate parts connecting with the individual machines are necessarily low. In many factories, moreover, where little care has been taken in the original installation of the transmission system, even the main shafts and belts are low down, sometimes at the floor level and even in open troughs below the floor level.

The danger of personal injury to employees under these circumstances is evident, and even the most reasonable considerations of safety require fencing, or other suitable guarding, to be placed at all exposed mill gearing of this character. Broadly speaking, moreover, such safeguarding should not be limited to places which are dangerous because necessarily frequented by employees. It has been repeatedly demonstrated that it is unsafe to leave unguarded any dangerous condition in a factory because located in a place supposedly never used by anyone as a passageway.

The exact character of the guarding devices which should be employed with exposed power transmitters can not be determined, of course, in advance. Conditions differ widely and there are consequent differences in the proper methods of treatment. Certain general principles, however, may be laid down. Thus, main shafts, belts, and pulleys, when overhead but not sufficiently high above the floor to be out of reach of passers-by, may be protected by troughs suspended underneath, so arranged as to prevent the body or clothing of a person from coming in contact with the moving mechanism itself. Gearing near or on the floor level may be protected by a fence sufficiently high to prevent a person from falling against the moving parts, and not so close to such moving parts as to permit clothing or parts of the body being caught when brushing by the fence. Vertical shafts and belting passing through floors are particularly dangerous because of the necessary floor openings and, in consequence, should be fenced with particular care.

SUBORDINATE TRANSMITTERS.

With subordinate transmitters; that is to say, belts, shafts, or gearing leading from the main transmitters to the manufacturing machinery, or from one to another part of this machinery, the attendant dangers are of the same general character as with the main transmitters. The possibility of accident, however, is perhaps even greater in the case of the subordinate moving parts of a machine than with the more prominent transmitters, the very prominence of which act in some degree as a warning. Unguarded cogs, wheels, or other moving parts of machines are dangerous not only to the operatives themselves, but also to other employees who pass near such machines, for in a factory workroom machines are almost necessarily arranged in series with passageways, or at least passage room, on one or more sides.

Almost always such dangerous parts can be protected by guards so arranged that the wheels or cogs are shielded at the point where a person's body or clothing may be caught most readily. To provide such guards upon completed machines is usually more difficult than to make such provisions at the time the machine is built, and much of the machinery manufactured at present is fully equipped with protecting devices before it is offered for sale. Nevertheless, there are comparatively few cases in which unprotected gearing on completed machinery can not be rendered comparatively harmless by means of simple safeguards, relatively inexpensive and of established merit, and this without interfering with the operation of the machine.

SET SCREWS.

One of the major sources of accident in connection with transmission shafting is the projecting set screws. The set screw is a small screw placed on the collar of shafting in order to hold the collar to the axle. Frequently its head is square and projecting, and revolving rapidly with the shafting it may easily attract and entangle any loose material coming within its reach. The clothing of anyone coming near to it may be readily caught and if the clothing does not part under the strain, its wearer will be dragged to the shaft and injured.

The set screw may be guarded efficiently and cheaply in any one of three general ways. It may be countersunk below the surface of the collar and worked with a box key or screw driver, or it may be made in hollow form and adjusted by means of a square key, or, finally, the projecting screw head may be protected by means of an additional wooden collar fitting around the original metal collar and with a hole in it to fit over the screw head. By this means a completely smooth surface is attained. The first and second of the enumerated methods require a special form of collar and screw. The third method, however, is adaptable to any existing condition without any change in the metal parts.

BELT SHIFTERS.

It is at present a very general, although not universal, practice in factories to operate all belts on the tight-and-loose-pulley system.

This system, as the name indicates, consists in having a pair of pulleys for every belt connection, one of these pulleys being firmly fastened to the shaft, the other revolving freely on the shaft. When it is desired to put the belt in use, it is swung on to the fixed pulley, and when it is desired to put it out of use it is transferred to the loose pulley, which, swinging freely on the shaft, stops all motion in the belt. The purpose of this is to avoid the primitive and dangerous system of unshipping a belt by simply pushing it off the pulley and either letting it dangle from the shaft or hanging the loose end on a hook. The danger of the "dangling" belt is very great, as an unevenness or a fold in the belt may cause it to catch in the shaft. Such a method of unshipping is rarely employed now except in the case of machines employing a very slow motive power, such as stamping presses, where it is claimed loose pulleys are often impracticable.

The shipping or shifting of belts by hand is extremely dangerous and is rarely if ever necessary. For shifting belts when tight and loose pulleys are used there are numerous mechanical appliances. These are controlled by a lever or cord and permit a belt to be shifted from the one pulley to the other without imposing any danger upon the person doing the shifting. If only a single pulley is used, the shipping and unshipping may be done by properly constructed poles without danger. To do this with an ordinary stick is dangerous as the stick may catch between the pulleys and belt and be thrown or twisted in such a way as to injure the person doing the work.

POWER-CONTROL DEVICES.

From the standpoint of safeguarding against accident, it is of great and evident importance to have some method of rapidly stopping the mill gearing and machinery. Thus, in the event of a workman having a part of his clothes or body caught in a moving belt, the immediate stopping of such belt might prevent a serious accident, whereas a delay of even several seconds might be fatal. The imperative need of power-control devices, therefore, can not be too greatly emphasized. All authorities agree upon their importance, and in several States the law requires their provision. Such devices do not take the place of the fencing, railing, and other guarding devices earlier mentioned, but they offer an invaluable supplement thereto. They are the final resort when other safeguards are impracticable or, even if provided, for some reason fail to fulfill their functions.

As has already been pointed out, the most satisfactory method of quick power control is that offered by the system of having an individual motor for each machine. The individual motor obviates all main transmitting shafts, belts, and pulleys and thus avoids a considerable proportion of the usual machinery accidents. It does not obviate the need of proper guards around the exposed moving parts of the machine, but it does offer a very efficient method of power control in case of accident. The simple pressing of a button or the pulling of a lever is sufficient to cut off the current and bring the moving part to immediate rest.

As yet, however, only a comparatively small percentage of factories are equipped with the individual motor system. These may be omitted from further consideration, therefore, and attention directed to the question of power control in factories employing a centrally located power system, with shafts and other transmitters to carry the power to the various parts of the factory.·

For such factories as these, and they are in the great majority, power-control devices are of three general forms, each aiming to control the power at a different point.

(a) Devices for stopping the power at its source. The most primitive method of doing this is by establishing means of communication between the several working parts of the factory and the power room, whereby the engineer or other attendant may be quickly informed of the need of shutting off the power. Such a system of communication may employ speaking tubes, electric lights, or bells. Its weakness is that it depends for effectiveness upon the constant presence of the attendant, a condition which experience has shown to be unreliable. Of greater effectiveness is a mechanical device for stopping the engine, such device being controlled either by electric button or cord pulls easily accessible to each group of employees. On the whole, however, the automatic control of the prime mover is not satisfactory. Usually the mechanical device is seldom used, easily gets out of order, and often fails to work when needed. Moreover, in the case of steam engines, the shutting off of the steam power is frequently not sufficient for the purpose intended, as the flywheel may keep the machinery in motion for a considerable time after the engine power is shut off. It is generally recognized, therefore, that to be most efficient power devices should operate by stopping the power transmitters or the individual machines rather than the prime mover.

(b) Devices for stopping the power transmitters in sections. The purpose here is to stop the power in a particular room or section of a factory without stopping it in the other parts. A system of tight and loose pulleys is not a sufficient safeguard in itself to meet many important dangerous conditions, such a condition, for instance, as arises when a belt breaks, entangles itself upon a shaft, and sweeps a large section of the working space with its loose whirling ends. To meet such contingencies friction clutches and other similar appliances are used. These operate directly on the transmission shaft and are so constructed that the simple movement of a lever or the pulling of a cord will disconnect a section of the shafting from the adjacent section and thereby cut off the power.

(c) Devices for stopping the individual machines without stopping the main shafting.   There are several methods of accomplishing this purpose.   The most common and the one most frequently mentioned in the State laws is the system of a tight and loose pulley with a mechanical belt shifter attached.   When it is desired to stop the machine, the lever or cord controlling the shifting device is pulled; thereby the belt running from the main shaft to the machine is shifted from the fixed pulley to one which has a loose axis, and the power cut off from the machine.   The importance of such a device is that if properly constructed it can be operated by the employee at the machine in case of accident to himself, such an accident, for instance, as having a hand caught between rollers or cogs.

In summary of this discussion of power-control devices it may be concluded that the second of the mentioned forms, for disconnecting the power transmission by sections, is of the greatest single value, as it most efficiently attains the desired object of guarding against machine accidents.   The third form, for stopping individual machines quickly, is a valuable supplement to the one just described.   Means of quick communication with the engine room is less satisfactory and is not necessary if the other devices are used.

MACHINES ESPECIALLY DANGEROUS.

While, as has been previously stated, all power-driven machines are dangerous in greater or less degree to any one coming in contact with their moving parts, there are some which subject the persons operating them to especial dangers.   This class is not well defined, but it is sufficiently distinct to lead to the frequent use of the term "dangerous machinery" in the industrial world and in the laws of certain States.   The class, moreover, is quite large.   For present purposes, however, it will be sufficient to consider briefly three important types.   These selected types are: The punch press or stamping machine used for stamping out such things as jar caps and metal tags; the roll-feed machine used in laundry ironing, rubber works, and many other industries; and the grinding or polishing wheel, of stone or emery.

(a) The punch press machine consists essentially of a die and an overhanging plunger or punch.   The article to be stamped is placed upon the die, whereupon the punch descends with sufficient force to stamp the article into the shape of the prepared die.   The operator feeds blanks to the machine and removes the stamped articles. The danger incurred is that of having the hand or fingers crushed between the punch and the die.   The degree of danger depends somewhat upon whether or not the machine operates automatically, by means of a foot treadle, or by means of a hand lever.   With a hand lever the danger is minimized, as an operator must remove his hand from the die before starting the punch. The automatic press is most dangerous, as the operator must then feed the machine with automatic regularity, and in a moment of forgetfulness may be too late in withdrawing his hand.

Various devices are possible for lessening the danger incurred by a punch-press operator. Sometimes sticks or other implements are used to remove and place the article, but this method is not always practicable. Nearly always, however, it is possible to equip the machine with some form of guard which will warn or push away the hand before the punch reaches it. It may also be remarked at this place that the corner-staying machine used in making paper boxes involves a very similar risk to that involved in the punch press. With the corner-staying machines, hard metal finger caps offer valuable and efficient protection. Mechanical guards similar to those just mentioned in connection with punch presses are also possible [1] but are not often used.

(b) The roll-feed machine, as illustrated by the ordinary ironing machine used in factories, has of course a very evident danger. Usually the hands of the operator must be placed close to the rolls in feeding or adjusting the articles to be ironed, and the slightest inadvertence will result in a hand being caught and pulled in between the revolving heavy metal rolls. To prevent such injuries simple safeguards are possible and efficient, such, for instance, as a strip of wood placed in front of the feed roll at just sufficient height to permit the articles to be fed under it. Variations of this device may be applied to almost any form of roll-feed machinery.

(c) The greatest danger involved in the use of grindstones and emery wheels is that of their bursting. Careful selection of the wheels before mounting is extremely desirable, and in addition to this both grindstones and emery wheels may be inclosed as much as possible by hoods strong enough to withstand the strain of a bursting wheel. On mechanically operated grindstones there is also the danger of a workman's hand slipping and being caught between the stone and the rest, and thus being seriously injured. Such an accident can be guarded against by the use of a releasing rest.[2]

VATS AND PANS.

Open vats and pans containing molten or hot liquids are the subject of legislation in a number of States, and may be conveniently considered as coming under a discussion of machine dangers. The

---

[1] The Prevention of Industrial Accidents: No. 1, General, p. 152. Published by the Fidelity and Casualty Co. of New York.

[2] Van Schaack, Safeguards for the Prevention of Industrial Accidents, p. 19. Ætna Life Insurance Co.; also The Prevention of Industrial Accidents: No. 1, General, p. 145 et seq. Published by the Fidelity and Casualty Co. of New York.

danger arising from such vats and pans is a serious one, although receptacles of this character occur only in a limited number of establishments, such, for instance, as paint, color, oil, paper, soap, and starch factories.[1] When such vats can not be kept constantly covered, the safest method of guarding is probably to so build them that they are at least 3 feet above the standing level.[1] In any case, they should be effectively fenced.

TRAVERSING CARRIAGES.

The so-called traversing carriage is found in only a limited number of machines, its chief example in the textile industry. It consists of a moving carriage which is an integral part of the machine, but which in part of its course extends beyond the fixed parts of the machine. The danger to be apprehended is that a person might be caught between the carriage on its outward course and some fixed structure. The more serious risk of such a situation can be avoided by providing that there shall be a space of, say, not less than 18 inches between a traversing carriage when farthest out and the nearest fixed structure. In two of the States covered, Massachusetts and New Jersey, the danger of the traversing carriage is recognized by law.

WARNING NOTICES POSTED BY EMPLOYERS.

Although rarely required by law, it is the practice in many establishments to post conspicuous warning notices upon dangerous machinery or at dangerous places. Warning notices, of course, should never be used in place of mechanical safeguards, but when such safeguards are impracticable, and very often as an additional means of safety even when other guards are present, they are of very considerable value.

CONDEMNATION NOTICES POSTED BY INSPECTORS.

In a number of States the law giving an inspector authority to order safeguards upon machinery is supplemented by a special provision authorizing him to condemn such machinery by placing upon it a notice absolutely forbidding its use until specified safety measures have been taken, and attaching a penalty for the premature removal of the notice. The purpose of a posted notice of this kind is to act as a visible warning to employer and employees, and, in practice, it has frequently proved of much greater force than a simple order given or sent to the employer at his office.

REMOVAL OF SAFEGUARDS.

As far as possible all safeguards should be securely fixed in place so that they can not be easily removed or deranged. This, however, is not always possible. Often, for instance, it is necessary to make

---

[1] Calder, The Prevention of Factory Accidents, pp. 242 and 243.

guards around gearing easily removable in order that oiling, cleaning, and repairing may be conveniently done. When such is the case the mere installation of safeguards is not sufficient to prevent accident. It is also vitally necessary to keep such safeguards in place and in good order when the machinery is in operation. The employer can not be held entirely responsible for carelessness on the part of the employees in this matter. The law in several States recognizes this fact and provides a punishment for employees who are careless in the removal of provided safeguards from moving machinery or who operate such machinery when safeguards are not in place.[1]

CONDITIONS FOUND.

Seventeen States are covered by the present report. In seven of these States, at the time the field work of this investigation was in progress, no legislation upon the subject of machine accidents or machine safeguarding, in any of the phases commented upon above, was in force. These 7 States are: Maine,[2] Illinois, Maryland,[3] North Carolina, Georgia, Florida, and Louisiana. Each of the remaining 10 States has laws of greater or less stringency upon one or more of the mentioned points. These 10 States are: Massachusetts, Connecticut, Rhode Island, New York, Pennsylvania, New Jersey, Ohio, Indiana, Michigan, and Wisconsin.

In the pages which follow are given, separately for each of the States, a statement of the legal provisions, if any, relative to machinery safeguarding, and a tabular showing of the conditions found existing in the establishments visited. This table covers but a few of the more important points. It attempts, simply, to show in what degree the several establishments had sought—First, to prevent accident by (a) guarding dangerous shafts, belts, gears, and machines; (b) by forbidding employees to remove safeguards once provided; and (c) by posting warning notices on dangerous machines and at dangerous places; and, second, to reduce the severity of injury in case of accident by providing methods for quickly stopping the machinery in case of accident. These methods are grouped as of five kinds: (a) Means for direct control of power from workrooms, such as is supplied by individual motors; (b) belt shifters; (c) friction

---

[1] The law referred to throughout this volume is as in force at the time of the investigation, December, 1908, to April, 1909. The text of the laws in force Jan. 1, 1912, is given in the appendixes at the end of this volume.

[2] Except as regards steam-boiler inspection. (22d An. Rept. Com. of Labor, p. 524.)

[3] Except special legislation regarding blowers for stone mills in a single county (Carroll). (22d An. Rept. Com. of Labor, p. 570.)

clutches; (*d*) means of quick communication with engine room, such as electric bells; and (*e*) special apparatus applicable to only a few machines.

This classification, while sufficiently accurate for the purpose of presenting briefly the information obtained, is necessarily somewhat rough. Thus, belt shifters not only offer a means for stopping machinery in case of accident, but, in themselves, prevent accidents by doing away with belt shifting by hand.

Also, it is to be especially noted that in some cases the provisions listed are mutually exclusive. Thus, if a machine is supplied with satisfactory and substantial mechanical safeguards, the posting of a warning notice may be superfluous. Again, if the power is supplied by means of individual motors, there may be no main shafting and thus no possibility of friction clutches or even, at times, of belt shifters. These conditions are allowed for in the table by giving in each case not only the number of establishments reported on, but also the number to which the specified provision applies. It follows, therefore, that an entry in the table showing the lack of a specified provision in certain factories indicates not only that such provision was lacking but that it was applicable and desirable.

An establishment is entered in the table as having or not having a specified provision according to the general practice of the whole establishment. Thus, if belt shifters are very generally provided where necessary, the establishment is credited with having such devices, although in a few cases belt shifters may be absent.[1]

A full statement of the conditions found in each establishment is given in Chapter XI, General Tables, of this volume.

MAINE.

The laws of Maine, at the time of this investigation, made no regulations concerning the safeguarding of machinery or mill gearing, with the single exception of steam boilers.[2]

CONDITIONS FOUND.

Of the 26 establishments visited 23 had power-driven machinery of a sufficiently dangerous character to require safeguarding. The table following shows to what ex*ent necessary safeguarding devices had been provided by these 23 establishments.

---

[1] The presence of the column showing the number of establishments reported on is necessitated by the unsatisfactory character of some of the reports.

[2] The law here referred to is as in force at the time of the investigation, January, 1909. The text of the laws in force Jan. 1, 1912, is given in the appendixes at the end of this volume.

ESTABLISHMENTS VISITED HAVING AND NOT HAVING SPECIFIED SAFETY DEVICES FOR GUARDING AGAINST ACCIDENT FROM MILL GEARING OR MACHINERY—MAINE.

Devices.	Establishments—			
	Reporting on specified device.	With provision of specified device applicable.	With specified device—	
			Provided.	Not provided.
For preventing accidents:				
Proper guarding on mill gearing and machinery.............	23	23	9	14
Rule against removal of safeguards........................	18	16	2	14
Warning notices posted on dangerous machines.............	23	23	1	22
For stopping machinery in case of accident:				
Direct control of power from workroom....................	23	23	[1] 13	10
Belt shifters...	23	22	16	6
Friction clutches..	23	17	10	7
Means of quick communication with engine room..........	23	10	[2] 2	8
Other special apparatus..................................	23	....	[3] 3	....

[1] All operated by electric power, control devices being electric cut-offs or switches.
[2] One by telephone; 1 by push button.
[3] Two have hand brakes on machines; 1 has both hand and foot brakes.

MASSACHUSETTS.

SUMMARY OF LEGISLATION.[1]

As regards the subject of safeguarding mill gearing and machinery, there are two legal provisions of general application, and two which are limited to a single industry, the manufacture of textiles. The general provisions are these:

(A) The belting, shafting, gearing, and drums of all factories, if so placed as, in the opinion of the inspectors of factories and public buildings, to be dangerous to employees therein while engaged in their ordinary duties, shall be as far as practicable securely guarded.

Penalty.—A fine of not more than $100.[2]

(B) In every manufacturing establishment in which the machinery is propelled by steam, communication shall be provided between each room in which such machinery is placed and the room in which the engineer is stationed by means of speaking tubes, electric bells, or appliances to control the motive power, or such other means as shall be satisfactory to the inspectors of factories and public buildings, if in the opinion of the inspectors such communication is necessary.

Penalty.—A fine of not less than $25 nor more than $100.[3]

The two provisions applicable solely to the textile industry are these:

(C) The owner of a cotton factory which shall have been erected subsequent to the 28th day of May, in the year 1896, who permits the

---

[1] The law here referred to is as in force at the time of the investigation, December, 1908, to February, 1909. The text of the laws in force Jan. 1, 1912, is given in the appendixes at the end of this volume.

[2] Rev. Laws, 1902, ch. 104, sec. 41, as amended by ch. 503, Acts of 1907, and sec. 56 (22d An. Rept. Com. of Labor, pp. 588, 590).

[3] Idem, sec. 38 (22d An. Rept. Com. of Labor, p. 588).

traversing carriage of a self-acting mule in such factory to travel within 12 inches of any pillar, column, pier, or fixed structure shall be punished by a fine of not less than $20 nor more than $50 for each offense.[1]

(D) It shall be the duty of all persons owning, managing, or operating factories in this Commonwealth, in which looms are employed, to equip the looms with such guards or other devices as will prevent injury to employees from shuttles falling or being thrown from the looms. Such guards or other devices shall be made of such material and placed in such manner as shall be approved by the inspection department of the district police. * * * .

Penalty.—Fine of not more than $100 for each week violation continues.[2]

The legislation of Massachusetts upon the subject of machine guarding is thus seen to be brief and, except for the two requirements regarding textile factories only (C and D), rather indefinite. Under the first-quoted provision (A) the inspector may insist upon a considerable degree of care being used in guarding belting, shafting, and gearing, but it would not appear that his authority under the law would be sufficient to allow him to require friction clutches, loose pulleys, or other means of quickly cutting off the power by sections or by machines. Nor is he given specific power to condemn, by posting a notice, dangerous machines or dangerous places. Nor are employees forbidden to remove safeguards once provided.

The authority of the inspectors as regards the establishment of means of communication between workrooms and engine rooms in factories using steam power extends to the determination of the necessity of such communication as well as to the choice of means.

The enforcement of the legal provisions as quoted is entirely in the hands of the State factory inspection department (the district police).

CONDITIONS FOUND.

Of the 44 establishments visited, 40 had power-driven machinery of sufficiently dangerous character to require safeguarding. The following table shows to what extent necessary safeguarding devices had been provided by these 40 establishments.

---

[1] Rev. Laws, 1902, ch. 104, sec. 42 (22d An. Rept. Com. of Labor, p. 589).

[2] Acts of 1904, ch. 347, secs. 1, 2, and 3 (22d An. Rept. Com. of Labor, p. 615).

ESTABLISHMENTS VISITED HAVING AND NOT HAVING SPECIFIED SAFETY DEVICES FOR GUARDING AGAINST ACCIDENT FROM MILL GEARING OR MACHINERY— MASSACHUSETTS.

Devices.	Establishments—			
	Reporting on specified device.	With provision of specified device applicable.	With specified device—	
			Provided.	Not provided.
For preventing accident:				
Proper guarding on mill gearing and machinery............	40	40	19	21
Rule against removal of safeguards.......................	2	2	2	....
Warning notices posted on dangerous machines.............	37	28	1	27
For stopping machinery in case of accident:				
Direct control of power from workroom...................	38	38	[1] 12	26
Belt shifters..	40	38	32	6
Friction clutches..	37	31	19	12
Means of quick communication with engine room..........	40	28	[2] 12	16
Other special apparatus.................................	40	....	[3]	....

[1] In 10 establishments, electric power, method of control being electric cut-offs or switches; method of control not reported in 2 establishments.
[2] In 3, by telephone; in 2, by bell pull; in 2, by press button; in 2, by electric bell; in 2, by both telephone and signal bell; in 1, by telephone and electric gong.
[3] In 1 establishment, automatic stops on machines; in 1, kind of apparatus not reported.

RHODE ISLAND.

SUMMARY OF LEGISLATION.[1]

In the matter of safeguarding mill gearing and machinery two provisions are made by law. They are as follows: [2]

(A) All belting and gearing shall be provided with proper safeguards.

(B) If the factory inspectors, or either one of them, find that * * * the belting, shafting, gearing, elevators, drums, and machinery in shops and factories are located so as to be dangerous to employees, and not sufficiently guarded, or that the vats, pans, or structures filled with molten metal or hot liquid are not surrounded with proper safeguards for preventing accident or injury to those employed at or near them, either or both shall notify the proprie or of such factory or workshop to make the alterations or additions necessary within ninety days; * * *

Penalty.—A fine of not more than $500.

The authority of these provisions is sufficient to enable the inspectors to insist upon all power transmitters, machinery, and open vats being properly safeguarded against accident. The law does not specifically require belt shifters, friction clutches, or other appliances for stopping machines quickly, nor does it require the provision of quick means of communication between workrooms and engine rooms. There is, moreover, no prohibition against employees removing safeguards from machinery, and no requirement that warning

[1] The law here referred to is as in force at the time of the investigation, December, 1908, to February, 1909. The text of the laws in force Jan. 1, 1912, is given in the appendixes at the end of this volume.
[2] Gen. Laws of 1896, ch. 68, secs. 6, 9, and 12, as amended by ch. 1215, enacted 1905 (22d An. Rept. Com. of Labor, pp. 1209, 1210).

notices shall be posted upon dangerous machines. And, finally, the inspector is not authorized to condemn a dangerous machine by forbidding its use until properly altered or safeguarded.

The first of these two quoted provisions (A), that requiring "all belting and gearing" to be equipped with proper safeguards, is apparently mandatory. But the second (B), which repeats and enlarges upon the first, is enforceable only as the inspectors may determine, and, as in any case no standards of proper safeguarding are erected or even suggested, the inspector's discretion is necessarily very complete.

The State factory inspection department is charged in full with the enforcement of all legislation, as above quoted, regarding protection against machine accidents.[1]

In an interview with an agent of the Bureau of Labor, the chief inspector stated that the factory inspection department had given the question of guarding machinery very careful consideration; that, at the department's suggestion, the manufacturers had made rules against the wearing of loose clothing by employees and rules forbidding women and girls to work with their hair hanging loose or in braids, and that, under the regulations of the department no machinery could be cleaned while in motion if the inspector considered it to be dangerous. The chief inspector believed as a result of this care the number of accidents in the State had been greatly reduced.

CONDITIONS FOUND.

Twenty-five of the 27 establishments visited had power-driven machinery of a sufficiently dangerous character to require safeguarding.

The following table shows to what extent necessary safeguarding devices had been provided by these 25 establishments:

ESTABLISHMENTS VISITED HAVING AND NOT HAVING SPECIFIED SAFETY DEVICES FOR GUARDING AGAINST ACCIDENT FROM MILL GEARING OR MACHINERY—RHODE ISLAND.

Devices.	Establishments—			
	Reporting on specified device.	With provision of specified device applicable.	With specified device—	
			Provided.	Not provided.
For preventing accidents:				
Proper guards on mill gearing and machinery	25	25	15	10
Rule against removal of safeguards	24	24	8	16
Warning notices posted on dangerous machines	25	21	4	17
For stopping machinery in case of accident:				
Direct control of power from place of work	24	24	[1]12	12
Belt shifters	25	25	22	3
Friction clutches	24	17	12	5
Means of quick communication with engine room	24	12	[2]6	6
Other special apparatus	25			

[1] Gen. Laws of 1896, ch. 68, sec. 3, as amended by ch. 1215, enacted 1905 (22d An. Rept. Com. of Labor, p. 1208).
[1] These 12 are all operated by electric power and the control devices are electric cut-offs or switches.
[2] One by telephone; 5 by electric bells or push buttons.

CONNECTICUT.

SUMMARY OF LEGISLATION.[1]

The legal requirements concerning machinery safeguarding are contained in one section, which reads in part as follows:[2]

The belting, shafting, gearing, machinery, and drums of all factories and buildings where machinery is used, when so placed as, in the opinion of the inspector, to be dangerous to the persons employed therein while engaged in their ordinary duties, shall, as far as practicable, be securely guarded. * * *

Penalty.—A fine of not more than $50.

No standards of safeguarding are erected or suggested, and there are no mandatory requirements. The inspector is to decide, at his discretion, when guarding is necessary, and, subject of course to judicial appeal, to decide what particular kinds of safeguards will fulfill the intention of the law. Moreover, the specified dangers need be guarded against only in so far as they affect employees engaged in their ordinary duties.

The law makes no specific mention of other dangerous situations or remedies. It does not require appliances for quickly stopping machines, means of quick communication between workrooms and engine room, or warning notices to be placed upon dangerous machines. The inspector is not given authority to condemn dangerous machinery by forbidding its use until properly altered or safeguarded, and employees are not forbidden by law to remove safeguards once installed.

The factory inspection department is charged in full with the enforcement of the above requirements.

In an interview with an agent of the Bureau of Labor, the chief inspector was asked his opinion of possible laws making employees responsible for such acts as removing safeguards from machinery, and requiring warning notices upon dangerous machines. In reply he stated his belief that a law upon the former subject would be of some benefit, but he did not think it necessary to have warning notices placed on dangerous machines, although, of course, there was no objection thereto.

CONDITIONS FOUND.

Thirty-three of the 35 visited establishments had power-driven machinery of a sufficiently dangerous character to require safeguarding.

---

[1] The law here referred to is as in force at the time of the investigation, February, 1909. The text of the laws in force Jan. 1, 1912, is given in the appendixes at the end of this volume.

[2] Gen. Stat., 1902, sec. 4516 and sec. 4522, as amended by ch. 53, Acts of 1903 (22d An. Rept. Com. of Labor, pp. 236, 237).

The following table shows to what extent necessary safeguarding devices had been provided by these 33 establishments:

ESTABLISHMENTS VISITED HAVING AND NOT HAVING SPECIFIED SAFETY DEVICES FOR GUARDING AGAINST ACCIDENT FROM MILL GEARING OR MACHINERY—CONNECTICUT.

Devices.	Establishments—			
	Reporting on specified device.	With provision of specified device applicable.	With specified device—	
			Provided.	Not provided.
For preventing accidents:				
Proper guards on mill gearing and machinery..............	33	33	17	16
Rule against removal of safeguards........................	33	33	24	9
Warning notices posted on dangerous machines............	33	32	....	32
For stopping machinery in case of accident:				
Direct control of power from place of work.................	33	33	[1] 12	21
Belt shifters...	33	33	33	....
Friction clutches..	33	33	32	1
Means of quick communication with engine room..........	33	21	[2] 12	9
Other special apparatus..................................	33	....	[3] 1	....

[1] Of these, 8 are operated by electric power and the control devices are electric cut-offs or switches; 4 are operated by steam power, and the control devices are push buttons which automatically stop engine.
[2] Ten by telephone; 1 by electric bell or push button; 1 by telephone and electric bell.
[3] Automatic shut-off.

NEW YORK.

SUMMARY OF LEGISLATION.[1]

As regards the subject of safeguarding dangerous machinery the legislation of New York is, in comparison with the legislation of most of the other States covered by this report, very complete. That is to say, it covers, with more or less fullness and precision, nearly all of the points regarding machinery protection which any of those States have embodied in their laws. The New York legislation consists of the following five provisions:[2]

(A) The owner or person in charge of a factory where machinery is used shall provide, in the discretion of the commissioner of labor, belt shifters or other mechanical contrivances for the purpose of throwing on or off belts on pulleys. Whenever practicable, all machinery shall be provided with loose pulleys.

(B) All vats, pans, saws, planers, cogs, gearing, belting, shafting, set screws, and machinery of every description shall be properly guarded.

(C) No person shall remove or make ineffective any safeguard around or attached to machinery, vats, or pans while the same are in use unless for the purpose of immediately making repairs thereto, and all such safeguards so removed shall be promptly replaced. * * *

[1] The law here referred to is as in force at the time of the investigation, December, 1908, and January, 1909. The text of the laws in force Jan. 1, 1912, is given in the appendixes at the end of this volume.

[2] Rev. Stat., 3d ed., 1901, p. 2102, sec. 81, as amended by ch. 366, Acts of 1906, and idem, sec. 209, as amended by ch. 506, Acts of 1907 (22d An. Rept. Com. of Labor, pp. 912, 913, 931).

(D) If a machine or any part thereof is in a dangerous condition or is not properly guarded the use thereof may be prohibited by the commissioner of labor, and a notice to that effect shall be attached thereto. Such notice shall not be removed until the machine is made safe * * * and in the meantime such unsafe or dangerous machinery shall not be used.

(E) When, in the opinion of the commissioner of labor it is necessary, the workrooms, halls, and stairs leading to the workrooms shall be properly lighted, * * * such lights to be independent of the motive power of such factory.

> *Penalty.*—For the first offense, a fine of not less than $20 nor more than $50; second offense, $50 to $200, or imprisonment not more than 30 days, or both; third offense, not less than $250, or imprisonment not more than 60 days, or both.

Reviewing these provisions the following points may be emphasized. Under the first provision (A) the inspection department may order belt shifting appliances to be installed whenever it thinks such appliances necessary, and also loose pulleys whenever such pulleys are practicable. As mentioned in an earlier discussion, nearly all satisfactory mechanical belt shifts involve the use of the loose pulley.

The second provision (B) requires in mandatory terms that all power transmitters and machinery of every description, including vats, pans, saws, and planers shall be securely guarded. No discretion is given the inspection department in these matters, further than in such degree as the department may be called upon to decide when safeguards are "proper."

The fourth provision (D) supplements the second by authorizing the inspection department to condemn, in its discretion, any machine which it may consider to be dangerous. The effect of such condemnation is greatly strengthened by the use of the condemnation notice, posted upon the condemned machine, which may not be used nor may the notice be removed, under penalty, until the machine has been made safe to the satisfaction of the department.

The third provision (C) makes the employee responsible for properly maintaining safeguards once provided. The requirement is mandatory and clear.

The final one of the quoted provisions (E) concerns the proper lighting of halls and workrooms. Such a requirement occurs in the laws of several States, and usually its primary object is to insure safety in case of fire. In the New York law, however, this requirement is part of a section dealing solely with machinery protection, and is apparently intended as a safeguard against machine accidents as well as against fire danger. Its importance might be considerable at times, as in many factories the danger of machine accidents is much increased by improper lighting.

The enforcement of all the laws of New York regarding machinery protection, as quoted above, is intrusted fully to the State factory inspection department.

The attitude of the State commissioner of labor toward the laws regarding machinery protection is clearly exhibited in the following excerpts from the report of that officer for the year 1907: [1]

In practice the deputy factory inspectors are not accustomed to classify their powers under the different provisions above referred to, but rather to examine all the machinery and appurtenances of each factory and to require everything that is unnecessarily dangerous to be properly safeguarded. Many things essential to factories are necessarily dangerous and accidents from them can be absolutely prevented only by abolishing them altogether; but no provisions of the law can have such an absurd intent. Therefore section 87 must be construed to give the factory inspector authority to require only what is practicable, and section 81 to give him authority to require only such safeguards for machinery as will be useful and practicable and to prohibit the use of such machines only as are worn, broken, defective, improperly erected or put together, etc., or are of a style generally abandoned because admitted to be unsafe. But while the factory inspector can not order that all machinery be new, of the safest style and in the most perfect condition, nor that older styles, methods, or processes be immediately abandoned in favor of what he considers to be the newest and safest, yet his deputies can and always should point out and explain all possible improvements with which they are acquainted, and urge their adoption when opportunity offers.

Orders relative to safety are issued from the department's office, usually in the general terms of the statute, e. g., "properly guard rip saw"; but the inspectors are expected to understand how all orders they recommend can be properly carried out and to explain how to the persons in charge of the factories. Every order issued is accompanied by a notice that an appeal therefrom to the head of the department (or bureau) will be given proper consideration. When such an appeal is received, that can not be disposed of conclusively upon the records or by correspondence, the inspector available with the greatest knowledge or experience in the line of the particular question raised is sent to review the decision of the original inspector. Such appeals result in revoking, suspending, modifying, or extending the time in some orders; in others in modifying the advice as to methods of compliance without changing the orders; and in others in sustaining the original orders and advice but in explaining the methods of correction more successfully to the satisfaction of the manufacturers. The proportion of cases where orders to safeguard machinery have to be insisted upon against the continued protests of proprietors is comparatively small, and rarely are prosecutions necessary. In other words, this function of factory inspection in the better class of factories has become largely advisory and supervisory, with all reference to compulsion habitually avoided, and is accepted by proprietors in a spirit of sympathy and cooperation. And it is

[1] Seventh Annual Report of the Commissioner of Labor of New York, 1907, Vol. I, pp. I.36, I.37, I.38.

noticeable that this spirit of mutual consideration increases in proportion to the competency and ability of the inspectors to explain and to convince proprietors of the usefulness and practicability of their requirements. This happy condition, most conducive to procuring the maximum of improvements, is due to the fact that the provisions of our factory laws relative to safety, therein differing from some of their provisions relative *to* health, require nothing arbitrary or vexatious and nothing either absolutely or comparatively useless. Thereby all reasonable opposition and any waste of time in enforcing changes that are of no benefit are avoided.

As to the need of technical, scientific advice in the matter of machinery safeguards the commissioner makes the following suggestive remarks:[1]

As appears from what has just been said, it is my opinion that the staff of the bureau of factory inspection is peculiarly competent to carry out the safety provisions of the factory laws. The majority of the inspectors are versed in mechanics, and in the examination of many thousands of factories they have acquired an experience and knowledge in this subject that few other persons can equal. But it is most desirable that the staff should be competent on all points, and that it now is not. There is no engineer in the bureau, and one is needed, not only to pass upon certain difficult questions that occasionally arise which need technical education to determine, but also to advise and instruct the deputy inspectors in the use of such scientific formulas and information as may expedite and improve their work. * * * The bureau also needs an electrician. The rapid increase in the use of motors and electric equipment calls for at least one officer who is an expert on this subject. The English factory department has long had an electric inspector.

Some means are needed for instructing new inspectors in the causes of accidents and the devices or methods of guarding against them other than the slow school of experience. The more advanced countries of Europe have museums of safety devices. We should have at least a laboratory of photographs or drawings of such devices, and should be enabled to issue illustrated handbooks of instruction and advice on this subject for the use and guidance of our inspectors.

CONDITIONS FOUND.

Thirty-three of the 36 establishments visited had power-driven machinery of a sufficiently dangerous character to require safeguarding.

The following table shows to what extent necessary safeguarding devices had been provided by these 33 establishments:

---

[1] Seventh Annual Report of the Commissioner of Labor of New York, 1907, Vol. I, pp. I.39 and I.40.

ESTABLISHMENTS VISITED HAVING AND NOT HAVING SPECIFIED SAFETY DEVICES FOR GUARDING AGAINST ACCIDENT FROM MILL GEARING OR MACHINERY—NEW YORK.

Devices.	Report-ing on specified device.	With pro-vision of specified device appli-cable.	With specified device—	
			Provided.	Not provided.
For preventing accidents:				
Proper guarding on mill gearing and machinery.............	32	32	6	26
Rule against removal of safeguards........................	6	5	5	....
Warning notices posted on dangerous machines.............	31	26	2	24
For stopping machinery in case of accident:				
Direct control of power from workroom.....................	32	32	[1] 10	22
Belt shifters..	33	33	30	3
Friction clutches...	33	31	31	....
Means of quick communication with engine room...........	33	24	[2] 13	11
Other special apparatus...................................	33	....	[3] 1	....

[1] These 10 are all operated by electric power (one of which has some other power in part of plant), the control devices being electric cut-offs or switches.
[2] Six by telephones; 2 by electric bells; 4 by speaking tubes; 1 by electric gong and speaking tube.
[3] Automatic stops on machines.

NEW JERSEY.

SUMMARY OF LEGISLATION.[1]

The legislation of New Jersey upon the subject of machinery safeguards resembles closely the legislation of New York and Pennsylvania already described.   The legal provisions are as follows: [2]

(A) The owner or person in charge of any of the places coming under the provisions of this act [i. e. as prescribed in section 1, "factory, workshop, mill, or place where the manufacture of goods of any kind is carried on."] where machinery is used, shall provide, in the discretion of the commissioner, belt shifters or other mechanical contrivances for the purpose of throwing on or off belts or pulleys; whenever practicable, all machinery shall be provided with loose pulleys.

(B) All vats, pans, saws, planers, cogs, gearing, belting, shafting, set screws, drums, and machinery of every description shall be properly guarded.

(C) No person shall remove or make ineffective any safeguard around or attached to such machinery, vats, or pans while the same are in use, unless for the purpose of immediately making repairs thereto, and all such safeguards so removed shall be promptly replaced.

(D) If the machinery, or any part thereof, or any vat, pan, or vessel containing molten metal or hot liquid is in a dangerous condition or is not properly guarded, the use thereof may be prohibited by the commissioner, and a notice to that effect shall be attached thereto; such notice shall not be removed until the machinery is made safe * * *; and in the meantime such unsafe or dangerous machinery * * * shall not be used.

[1] The law here referred to is as in force at the time of the investigation, December, 1908, and January, 1909.   The text of the laws in force Jan. 1, 1912, is given in the appendixes at the end of this volume.
[2] Acts of 1904, ch. 64, secs. 13 and 30 (22d An. Rept. Com. of Labor, pp. 862, 864).

(E) When, in the opinion of the commissioner, it is necessary, the halls leading to workrooms shall be provided with proper lighting facilities.

Penalty.—$50 for each offense.

As these several provisions are so closely similar to those of New York and Pennsylvania upon the same topics, comment upon the meanings and purposes of such provisions need not be repeated. The differences are in minor points which require no special emphasis.

The State factory inspection department [department of labor] is charged with the enforcement of all the provisions and requirements relating to safeguards on machinery.[1]

CONDITIONS FOUND.

Twenty-five of the 27 visited establishments had power-driven machinery of a sufficiently dangerous character to require safeguarding.

The following table shows to what extent proper and necessary safeguarding devices were provided in these 25 establishments:

ESTABLISHMENTS VISITED HAVING AND NOT HAVING SPECIFIED SAFETY DEVICES FOR GUARDING AGAINST ACCIDENT FROM MILL GEARING OR MACHINERY—NEW JERSEY.

Devices.	Reporting on specified device.	With provision of specified device applicable.	With specified device—	
			Provided.	Not provided.
For preventing accidents:				
Proper guarding on mill gearing and machinery	25	25	17	8
Rule against removal of safeguards	20	20	19	1
Warning notices posted on dangerous machines	25	5	2	3
For stopping machinery in case of accidents:				
Direct control of power from workroom	24	24	[1] 11	13
Belt shifters	24	22	18	4
Friction clutches	25	21	19	2
Means of quick communication with engine-room	25	14	[2] 1	13
Other special apparatus	25		[3] 1	

[1] Of these, 7 are operated by electric power, the control devices being electric cut-offs or switches; 1 is operated by steam power, the method of control being by a push button which stops engine; 3, method of control not reported.
[2] By electric push button.
[3] Automatic stops on all machines.

PENNSYLVANIA.

SUMMARY OF LEGISLATION.[2]

As regards the safeguarding of machinery against accidents the legal provisions of Pennsylvania are, for the most part, closely similar to those of New York. The provisions are as follows:[3]

[1] Acts of 1904, ch. 64, sec. 45, as amended by ch. 257, Acts of 1907 (22d An. Rept. Com. of Labor, p. 868).

[2] The law here referred to is as in force at the time of the investigation, January to March, 1909. The text of the laws in force Jan. 1, 1912, is given in the appendixes at the end of this volume.

[3] Acts of 1905, act No. 226, secs. 11 and 23 (22d An. Rept. Com. of Labor, pp. 1177, 1180).

(A) The owner or person in charge of an establishment where machinery is used shall provide belt shifters or other mechanical contrivances for the purpose of throwing on or off belts or pulleys. Whenever practicable, all machinery shall be provided with loose pulleys.

(B) All vats, pans, saws, planes, cogs, gearing, belting, shafting, set screws, grindstones, emery wheels, flywheels, and machinery of every description shall be properly guarded.

(C) No person shall remove or make ineffective any safeguard around or attached to machinery, vats, or pans while the same are in use, except for the purpose of immediately making repairs thereto, and all such safeguards so removed shall be properly replaced * * *.

(D) If a machine or any part thereof is in a dangerous condition, or is not properly guarded, the use thereof may be prohibited by the chief factory inspector or by his deputy, and a notice to that effect shall be attached thereto. Such notice shall not be removed until the machinery is made safe * * *, and in the meantime such unsafe or dangerous machinery shall not be used.

(E) The floor space of no working room in any establishment shall be so crowded with machinery as thereby to cause risk to the life or limb of an employee; nor shall there be in any establishment machinery in excess of the sustaining power of the floors and walls thereof.

> *Penalty.*—A fine of not less than $25 nor more than $500, or an imprisonment in the county jail not less than 10 days nor more than 60 days.

The close similarity, even as to the wording, between the first four of these provisions (A, B, C, and D) and the corresponding provisions of the New York law as quoted on pages 295, 296 is evident on comparison. The only important difference is in the first provision. In the New York law the requirement of belt-shifting appliances is not absolute, but it is discretionary with the inspection department. In the Pennsylvania law this requirement is made mandatory.

The last of the above quoted provisions of the Pennsylvania law (E)—regarding the overcrowding of the workrooms with machinery— is peculiar to Pennsylvania among the States considered in this report. The requirement is important as enabling certain dangerous conditions to be prevented which could not be legally reached, perhaps, by other provisions of the law. Thus, it might easily happen that machines otherwise sufficiently guarded and obeying all the requirements of the law in the matter of safeguards might impose serious danger upon employees by being too closely crowded.

The State factory inspection department is apparently charged with the carrying out of all the legal provisions regarding dangerous machinery above enumerated.[1]

---

[1] Acts of 1905, act No. 226, sec. 27 (22d An. Rept. Com. of Labor, p. 1180).

The chief factory inspector states that great improvements have been effected in the safeguarding of machinery, and mentions particularly that all projecting set screws within possible reach of employees are now countersunk.

CONDITIONS FOUND.

Of the 50 establishments visited, 41 had power-driven machinery of a sufficiently dangerous character to require safeguarding.

The following table shows to what extent necessary and proper safeguarding devices had been provided:

ESTABLISHMENTS VISITED HAVING AND NOT HAVING SPECIFIED SAFETY DEVICES FOR GUARDING AGAINST ACCIDENT FROM MILL GEARING OR MACHINERY—PENNSYLVANIA.

Devices.	Reporting on specified device.	With provision of specified device applicable.	With specified device—	
			Provided.	Not provided.
For preventing accidents:				
Proper guarding on mill gearing and machinery............	41	41	32	9
Rule against removal of safeguards.....................	40	37	35	2
Warning notices posted on dangerous machines............	32	12	6	6
For stopping machinery in case of accident:				
Direct control of power from workroom....................	41	41	[1]18	23
Belt shifters.......................................	41	39	37	2
Friction clutches...................................	41	36	35	1
Means of quick communication with engine room..........	41	23	[2]4	19
Other special apparatus.............................	40			

[1] All electric power, control devices being electric cut-offs or switches.
[2] Two by telephones; 1 by steam whistle; 1 by signal bell on each floor.

For 1 establishment it was reported that, although all machinery was guarded, there was an undue crowding of the various machines.

OHIO.

SUMMARY OF LEGISLATION.[1]

Upon the subject of safeguarding mill gearing and machinery the Ohio law has 3 important sections, certain features of which differ materially from the laws of any of the other States covered by this report. The 3 sections are as follows:[2]

(A) * * * It shall be their duty [i. e., the factory inspectors] to examine * * * all belting, shafting, gearing, elevators, drums, and machinery of every kind and description in and about such shops

---

[1] The law here referred to is as in force at the time of the investigation, March, 1909. The text of the laws in force Jan. 1, 1912, is given in the appendixes at the end of this volume.

[2] Bates' Ann. Stat., 3d ed., Pt. I, Political, sec. 2573a (as amended by act, p. 338, Acts of 1902, and act, p. 530, Acts of 1904), and sec. 2573c (as amended by act, p. 530, Acts of 1904); Idem, Pt. II, Civ., sec. 4364–89c, 4364–89d, 4364–89e, and 4364–89f (22d An. Rept. Com. of Labor, pp. 998, 1014, 1015).

and factories,[1] and see that the same are not located so as to be dangerous to employees when engaged in their ordinary duties, and that the same, so far as practicable, are securely guarded, and that every vat, pan, or structure filled with molten metal or hot liquid shall be surrounded with proper safeguards for preventing accident or injury to those employed at or near them * * *.

[If said inspectors find conditions otherwise, they shall order necessary changes to be made without delay, but the chief inspector may allow 15 to 30 days to make such changes.]

Penalty.—A fine of not less than $50 nor more than $500, and $10 for each additional day of failure or negligence after conviction.

(B) The owners and operators of factories and workshops * * * and all places where machinery of any kind is used or operated, shall take ordinary care, and make such suitable provisions as to prevent injury to persons who may come in contact with any such machinery, or any part thereof;

And such ordinary care and suitable provisions shall include:

(1) The casing or boxing of all shafting when operating * * * near floors, or * * * between, from or through floors, or * * * near passageway, or directly over the heads of employees;

(2) The inclosure of all exposed cogwheels, flywheels, band wheels, all main belts transmitting power from engine to dynamo, or other kind of machinery, and all openings through floors, through, or in which such wheels or belts may operate, with substantial railing;

(3) The covering, cutting off, or countersinking of keys, bolts, set screws, and all parts of wheels, shafting, or other revolving machinery, projecting unevenly * * *;

(4) The lighting of hallways, rooms * * * and other places wherein sufficient daylight is not obtainable;

(5) The guarding of all saws and other woodcutting and wood shaping machinery;

(6) Providing shifters for shifting belts, and poles and other appliances for removing and replacing belts on single pulleys, and

(7) Adjusting runways and staging used for oiling and other purposes more than 5 feet from floors with hand railing;

(8) And providing countershafting with tight and loose pulleys or such other suitable appliances in each room, separate from the engine room, for disconnecting machinery from other machinery when in operation.

Penalty.—First offense, a fine not exceeding $100; each subsequent offense, not less than $50 nor more than $500.

(C) * * * Any * * * inspector of workshops and factories who shall obtain knowledge of violation of * * * [provision B above] is hereby authorized, whenever he may deem it advisable, to paste upon any machine, device, elevator, utensil, struc-

---

[1] The term "shops and factories" includes: "Manufacturing, mechanical, electrical, mercantile, art, and laundering establishments, printing, telegraph and telephone offices, railroad depots, hotels, memorial buildings, tenement and apartment houses." Bates' Ann. Stat., 3d ed., Pt. I, Political, sec. 2573d. (22d An. Rept. Com. of Labor, p. 999.)

ture, or machinery, or part of machinery of any kind, a notice stating that * * * operatives or employees are liable to injury by its use or operation, and such notice shall designate and describe the alteration * * * necessary to be made * * * and the time to be allowed for such alteration * * * and no such machine * * * shall be used or operated after such notice is posted thereon until such change or alteration is made to the satisfaction of the inspector * * *.

Penalty.—First offense, a fine of not less than $25 nor more than $100; each subsequent offense, $50 to $500.

Reviewing this legislation, it is to be emphasized that the Ohio law is unusually specific in its demands. Not only does it order all dangerous machinery, including open vats, to be securely guarded, it mentions precisely certain things and conditions which are to be considered as dangerous. Thus, all exposed shafts, belts, gearing, machines, etc., are to be surrounded with reasonable guards; set screws and similar projecting parts of revolving machinery are to be countersunk or otherwise rendered harmless; the shifting of belts by hand is forbidden, although the use of ordinary shifting poles is recognized as legal; staging for oiling is to be fenced, although its use is not obligatory; countershafting is to be provided with suitable appliances for quickly stopping individual machines; rooms and hallways are to be sufficiently lighted.

Most of these requirements are sufficiently clear to leave little room for the personal opinion of inspectors or employers in their application. In addition, moreover, the inspectors are given a broad authority to insist upon proper safeguarding, and to this end they may absolutely condemn any machinery they consider dangerous and forbid its use until it is rendered safe to their satisfaction.

The law makes no reference to the subject of quick communication with the engine room; to the use of friction clutches or similar devices for quickly stopping large sections of the power system, including main shafts and belts as well as subordinate shafting and individual machines; to the use of warning notices by employers, or to the removal of safeguards by employees.

The State factory inspection department is charged in full with the duty and responsibility of enforcing all the State legislation regarding machinery protection, as above quoted.[1]

---

[1] Bates' Ann. Stat., 3d ed., Pt. I, Political, sec. 2573a (as amended by act, p. 338, Acts of 1902); Idem, Pt. II, Civ., sec. 4364–89g, Acts of 1908, p. 30, sec. 4 (22d An. Rept. Com. of Labor, pp. 997, 998, 1013, 1015, and Bulletin of the Bureau of Labor, No. 85, pp. 703, 704).

CONDITIONS FOUND.

Fifty of the 60 establishments visited had power-driven machinery of a sufficiently dangerous character to require safeguarding.

The following table shows to what extent proper and necessary safeguards had been provided by these 50 establishments:

ESTABLISHMENTS VISITED HAVING AND NOT HAVING SPECIFIED SAFETY DEVICES FOR GUARDING AGAINST ACCIDENT FROM MILL GEARING OR MACHINERY— OHIO.

| | Establishments— | | | |
| Devices. | Reporting on specified device. | With provision of specified device applicable. | With specified device— | |
			Provided.	Not provided.
For preventing accidents:				
Proper guarding on mill gearing and machinery	50	50	42	8
Rule against removal of safeguards	48	47	35	12
Warning notices posted on dangerous machines	37	· 10	4	6
For stopping machines in case of accident:				
Direct control of power from workroom	47	47	[1] 26	21
Belt shifters	50	50	50	....
Friction clutches	50	50	47	3
Means of quick communication with engine room	47	20	[2] 2	18
Other special apparatus	50	....	[3] 1	....

[1] All operated by electric power, control devices being electric cut-offs or switches.
[2] Electric bells in both cases; in 1 establishment engine is in workroom.
[3] Separate stops on all machines.

ILLINOIS.

At the time of the field work of this investigation[1] the Illinois law made no provision for the guarding of mill gearing or machinery or for otherwise preventing accidents due to shafts, belts, gearing, machinery, vats, etc.[2]

CONDITIONS FOUND.

Thirty-nine of the 47 establishments visited had power-driven machinery of a sufficiently dangerous character to require safeguarding.

The following table shows to what extent proper and necessary safeguards had been provided by these 39 establishments.

[1] December, 1908, to February, 1909. The text of the laws in force Jan. 1, 1912, is given in the appendixes at the end of this volume.

[2] Shortly after the field work of this investigation was completed, however, legislation upon this subject was enacted, which legislation is in many respects the most complete as yet enacted by any American State. Acts of 1909, p. 202 (Bulletin of the Bureau of Labor, No. 85, pp. 545–547).

ESTABLISHMENTS VISITED HAVING AND NOT HAVING SPECIFIED SAFETY DEVICES FOR GUARDING AGAINST ACCIDENT FROM MILL GEARING OR MACHINERY— ILLINOIS.

Devices.	Establishments—			
	Reporting on specified device.	With provision of specified device applicable.	With specified device—	
			Provided.	Not provided.
For preventing accidents:				
Proper guarding on mill gearing and machinery............	39	39	15	24
Rule against removal of safeguards........................	16	15	13	2
Warning notices posted on dangerous machines............	35	32	4	28
For stopping machines in case of accident:				
Direct control of power from workroom....................●	37	37	1 24	13
Belt shifters..	39	38	28	10
Friction clutches...	39	28	20	8
Means of quick communication with engine room..........	39	16	2 6	10
Other special apparatus....................................	38	....	3 4	....

1 Twenty-three operated by electric power, control devices being electric cut-offs or switches; 1, method of control not reported.
2 Two by electric bell; 4 by telephone.
3 Brakes on machines in 2 cases; stop levers in 1; transmitter in 1.

INDIANA.

SUMMARY OF LEGISLATION.[1]

The legislation of Indiana regarding machinery safeguarding consists of the following five provisions:[2]

(A) It shall be the duty of the owner of any aforesaid establishment, or his agent, superintendent, or other person in charge of the same, to furnish and supply, or cause to be furnished and supplied therein, in the discretion of the chief inspector, where machinery is used, belt shifters or other safe mechanical contrivances for the purpose of throwing on or off belts or pulleys; and whenever possible, machinery therein shall be provided with loose pulleys;

(B) All vats, pans, saws, planers, cogs, gearing, belting, shafting, set screws, and machinery of every description therein shall be properly guarded; and

(C) No person shall remove or make ineffective any safeguard around or attached to any planer, saw, belting, shafting, or other machinery, or around any vat or pan, while the same is in use, unless for the purpose of immediately making repairs thereto, and all such safeguards shall be promptly replaced.

(D) By attaching thereto a notice to that effect the use of any machinery may be prohibited by the chief inspector should such machinery be regarded as dangerous. Such notice * * * shall only be removed after the required safeguards are provided, and the unsafe or dangerous machinery shall not be used in the meantime.

(E) In every manufacturing or other establishment, * * * where the machinery used is propelled by steam, communication shall be provided between each room where such machinery is placed and

[1] The law here referred to is as in force at the time of the investigation, February and March, 1909. The text of the laws in force Jan. 1, 1912, is given in the appendixes at the end of this volume.
[2] Ann. Stat. of 1894, Rev. of 1901, secs. 7087i, 7087g, and 7087y (22d An. Rept. Com. of Labor, pp. 398, 399, 402).

the room where the engineer is stationed by means of speaking tubes, electric bells, or appliances that may control the motive power, or such other means as shall be satisfactory to the chief inspector: *Provided*, That in the opinion of the inspector such communication is necessary.

Penalty.—For the first offense a fine of not more than $50; second offense, not more than $100, to which may be added imprisonment for not more than 10 days; third offense, not less than $250 and not more than 30 days' imprisonment.

The last of these five provisions (E)—that relating to means of communication between workrooms and engine room—is found in the laws of only two of the other States covered by this report—Massachusetts and Wisconsin. The other four provisions, as quoted (A, B, C, and D), are closely similar to corresponding provisions of New York, Pennsylvania, and New Jersey (pp. 295, 299, 301) and need not be again commented upon. There is no legal requirement of friction clutches or similar devices for shutting off the power in sections. Nor is there any requirement that employers shall post warning notices on dangerous machines or in dangerous places.

The enforcement of all legal provisions regarding dangerous machinery, as quoted above, is intrusted in full to the State factory-inspection department.[1]

CONDITIONS FOUND.

Forty-one of the 47 visited establishments had power-driven machinery of a sufficiently dangerous character to require safeguarding.

The following table shows to what extent proper and necessary safeguarding devices were provided by these 41 establishments:

ESTABLISHMENTS VISITED HAVING AND NOT HAVING SPECIFIED SAFETY DEVICES FOR GUARDING AGAINST ACCIDENT FROM MILL GEARING OR MACHINERY—INDIANA.

Devices.	Establishments [1]—			
	Reporting on specified device.	With provision of specified device applicable.	With specified device—	
			Provided.	Not provided.
For preventing accidents:				
Proper guarding on mill gearing and machinery	41	41	22	19
Rule against removal of safeguards	41	39	23	16
Warning notices posted on dangerous machines	39	31	6	25
For stopping machinery in case of accident:				
Direct control of power from workroom	41	41	[3] 21	20
Belt shifters	41	40	37	3
Friction clutches	41	36	33	3
Means of quick communication with engine room	41	18	[4] 6	12
Other special apparatus	41	....	[5] 1	....

[1] Ann. Stat. of 1894, Rev. of 1901, sec. 7087v (22d An. Rept. Com. of Labor, p. 402).
[2] Two establishments (Nos. 38 and 44) had more than 1 engine room with separate power equipment. In these cases the table contains data for only 1 of these separate equipments—the 1 in the building or department which had the greater number of employees.
[3] These 21 are all operated by electric power, the control devices being electric cut-offs or switches.
[4] Two by telephone; 1 by telephone and bell; 1 by telephone and whistle; 1 by bell; 1 by gong.
[5] Foot levers on machines.

MICHIGAN.

SUMMARY OF LEGISLATION.[1]

Upon the subject of machinery safeguarding Michigan has the three following legal provisions:[2]

(A) It shall also be the duty of the owner of any factory, or his agent, superintendent or other person in charge of the same, to furnish or supply, or cause to be furnished or supplied, in the discretion of the factory inspector, where machinery is in use, proper shifters or other mechanical contrivances for the purpose of throwing belts on or off pulleys.

(B) All gearing or belting shall be provided with proper safeguards, and wherever possible machinery shall be provided with loose pulleys.

(C) All vats, saws, pans, planers, cogs, set screws, gearing, and machinery of every description, shall be properly guarded when deemed necessary by the factory inspector.

Penalty.—A fine of not less than $5 nor more than $100, or imprisonment of not less than 10 days nor more than 90 days, or both.

The first of these provisions (A) regarding belt shifters or other mechanical appliances of the same purpose is enforceable only at the inspector's discretion. The third provision (C), relating to a general safeguarding of all gearing and machinery is of the same character as to its enforcement. The second provision (B), regarding the guarding of belting and gearing is, however, mandatory and remains so notwithstanding the fact that otherwise its meaning is substantially repeated in the third provision.[3]

The more important points covered by law in one or more other States, but not touched upon in the legislation of Michigan are: Prohibition against the removal of safeguards by employees; authorizing of the factory inspector to condemn dangerous machinery by forbidding its use; requiring means of communication between workrooms and engine room; requiring employers to post warning notices upon dangerous machinery and at dangerous places. There is no requirement of such devices as friction clutches for cutting off the mill gearing in sections, although the need of being able to stop machinery quickly is recognized in the requirement that "wherever possible machinery shall be provided with loose pulleys" (provision B).

The State factory inspection department is made responsible for the enforcement of all legislation upon the subject of machinery protection, as above quoted.[4]

---

[1] The law here referred to is as in force at the time of the investigation, March, 1909. The text of the laws in force Jan. 1, 1912, is given in the appendixes at the end of this volume.

[2] Acts of 1901, act No. 113, secs. 8 and 18 (22d An. Rept. Com. of Labor, pp. 660, 662).

[3] 111 N. W. Rep., 110 (22d An. Rept. Com. of Labor, p. 660).

[4] Acts of 1901, act No. 113, sec. 12 (22d An. Rept. Com. of Labor, p. 660).

CONDITIONS FOUND.

Each of the 19 establishments had machinery of a sufficiently dangerous character to require safeguarding. The following table shows to what extent proper and necessary safeguarding devices had been provided:

ESTABLISHMENTS VISITED HAVING AND NOT HAVING SPECIFIED SAFETY DEVICES FOR GUARDING AGAINST ACCIDENT FROM MILL GEARING OR MACHINERY—MICHIGAN.

	Establishments—			
Devices.	Reporting on specified device.	With provision of specified device applicable.	With specified device—	
			Provided.	Not provided.
For preventing accidents:				
Proper guarding on mill gearing and machinery............	19	19	10	9
Rule against removal of safeguards..........................	19	18	12	6
Warning notices posted on dangerous machines.............	19	17	2	15
For stopping machinery in case of accident:				
Direct control of power from workroom....................	19	19	[1] 14	5
Belt shifters...	19	19	19	....
Friction clutches...	19	17	17	....
Means of quick communication with engine room..........	19	5	[2] 2	3
Other special apparatus....................................	19	....	....	....

[1] All 14 operated by electric power, method of control being cut-offs or switches.
[2] One by speaking tube; 1 by telephone.

WISCONSIN.

SUMMARY OF LEGISLATION.[1]

The legislation of Wisconsin upon the subject of machine safeguarding is presented below in the form of six main provisions. These provisions do not follow the order in which they appear in the original law, but are rearranged to facilitate comparison with the laws of other States:

(A) All belting, shafting, gearing, hoists, fly wheels, elevators, and drums therein [i. e., in any place where persons are employed to perform labor] which are so located as to be dangerous to employees in the discharge of their duty shall be securely guarded or fenced.

Penalty.—A fine of not more than $25 for each offense, each day's negligence after conviction to constitute a separate offense.[2]

(B) The owner or manager of every place where persons are employed to perform labor shall surround every stationary vat, pan, or other vessel into which molten metal or hot liquids are poured or kept with proper safeguards for the protection of his employees. * * *

---

[1] The law here referred to is as in force at the time of the investigation, March, 1909. The text of the laws in force Jan. 1, 1912, is given in the appendixes at the end of this volume.

[2] Ann. Stat. of 1898, Supp. of 1906, Acts of 1907, sec. 1636J (22d An. Rept. Com. of Labor, p. 1410).

Penalty.—A fine of not more than $25 for each offense, each day's negligence after conviction to constitute a separate offense.[1]

(C) Any such officer [of the bureau of labor and industrial statistics] * * * may order bull wheels, flywheels, tumbling rods, elevator wells, stairways, shafting, or dangerous machinery of any kind to be enclosed or otherwise guarded so as to protect workmen or others. * * *

Penalty.—For refusal to obey written order of such officer, $50 for each offense.[2]

(D) Any person who shall remove any guard or other safety device from bull wheels, flywheels, tumbling rods, elevator wells, stairways, shafting, or dangerous machinery, while such * * * is in motion or use, and shall neglect or fail to replace such safety device before permitting such * * * to be put in motion or use shall be fined not less than $5 nor more than $50, or by imprisonment in the county jail not to exceed 30 days, or both, for each such offense.[3] * * *

(E) It is also the duty of such officers [of the bureau of labor and industrial statistics], when in their judgment it may be necessary, to see that in every manufacturing establishment, the machinery in which is propelled by steam or other power, communication, by means of speaking tubes or electric bells, shall be provided between each room in which machinery so operated is placed and the room in which the engineer is stationed.[3]

Penalty.—A fine of not less than $10 nor more than $50 for each offense.

(F) No emery wheels or grindstone in any factory, mill, or workshop shall be used when the same is known to the person using the same to be cracked or otherwise defective, nor operated at a greater speed than indicated or guaranteed by the manufacturer.[3]

Penalty.—A fine of not less than $25 nor more than $100 for each offense.

The first two of these six provisions (A and B) are mandatory requirements that dangerous mill gearing and all open vats of hot metals or liquids be safeguarded. It is to be noted, however, that the requirement as to guarding mill gearing does not extend to every place which might be dangerous, but only to such as are actually dangerous to employees in the discharge of their duties.[4]

The third provision (C) is simply a broad authorization enabling the inspector, in his judgment, to require safeguards upon mill gearing and machinery; to enforce, that is to say, the provisions of the preceding two provisions. It does not, however, remove the mandatory character of those requirements.

---

[1] Ann. Stat. of 1898, Supp. of 1906, Acts of 1907, sec. 1636j (22d An. Rept. Com. of Labor, p. 1410).

[2] Idem, sec. 1021h (22d An. Rept. Com. of Labor, p. 1408).

[3] Idem, sec. 1636-40 (22d An. Rept. Com. of Labor, p. 1416).

[4] 86 N. W. Rep., 153 (22d An. Rept. Com. of Labor, p. 1410).

Provision (D) is a mandatory requirement against employees removing safeguards once provided, the wording of the law upon this point being very similar to that used by the laws of several other of the States now being considered.

In authorizing the inspectors to require quick means of communication to be provided between engine room and workroom of any factory (provision E) the Wisconsin law touches upon a subject which only two other of the States covered by this report—Massachusetts and Indiana—have embodied in their laws.

The last of the provisions above listed (F) aims to lessen the danger inherent in grindstones and emery wheels. Many States direct that proper blowers and other devices for carrying off the dust of such wheels shall be provided, but Wisconsin alone among the States covered attempts to safeguard against accidents due to the explosion of such wheels.

The most important provision regarding safeguarding of machinery not mentioned in the Wisconsin law is that requiring devices for shutting off the mill gearing in sections and for quickly stopping individual machines. There is also no requirement that employers shall post warning notices on dangerous machines, and none authorizing the inspectors to condemn dangerous machinery by prohibiting its use until necessary changes are made to render it safe.

The enforcement of all legislation, as above quoted, regarding protection against machine dangers is charged to the State factory inspection department, bureau of labor and industrial statistics.

CONDITIONS FOUND.

Seventeen of the 19 establishments visited had power-driven machinery of a sufficiently dangerous character to require safeguarding.

The following table shows to what extent proper and necessary safeguarding devices had been provided by these 17 establishments:

ESTABLISHMENTS VISITED HAVING AND NOT HAVING SPECIFIED SAFETY DEVICES FOR GUARDING AGAINST ACCIDENT FROM MILL GEARING OR MACHINERY—WISCONSIN.

Devices.	Reporting on specified device.	With provision of specified device applicable.	With specified device—	
			Provided.	Not provided.
For preventing accidents:				
Proper guarding on mill gearing and machinery............	17	17	15	2
Rule against removal of safeguards.......................	17	17	17	0
Warning notices posted on dangerous machines............	16	16	5	11
For stopping machinery in case of accident:				
Direct control of power from workrooms...................	16	16	[1]6	10
Belt shifters..	17	17	17	0
Friction clutches..	17	16	14	2
Means of quick communication with engine room..........	17	11	[2]7	4
Other special apparatus..................................	17	....	[3]1	....

[1] All operated by electric power, the control devices being cut-offs or switches.
[2] Three by telephone; 3 by electric bell; 1 by method not reported.
[3] Stop motions on knitting machines in 1 establishment.

MARYLAND.

SUMMARY OF LEGISLATION.

The laws of Maryland, at the time of this investigation, January, 1909, made no provision for the guarding of mill gearing or machinery, or for otherwise preventing accidents due to shafting, belts, gearing, machinery, vats, etc.,[1] except special legislation regarding blowers for stone mills in a single county (Carroll).

The chief factory inspector in an interview with an agent of the Bureau stated that he had never advocated a law requiring manufacturers to guard machinery. He did not believe such a law necessary. "Employees ought to refuse to work at dangerous machines," he said, and "employers can not compel employees to endanger their lives or operate machines that are dangerous if the employees do not want to do it."

CONDITIONS FOUND.

Twenty-four of the 28 establishments visited had power-driven machinery of a sufficiently dangerous character to require safeguarding.

The following table shows to what extent proper and necessary safeguarding devices had been provided by these 24 establishments:

ESTABLISHMENTS VISITED HAVING AND NOT HAVING SPECIFIED SAFETY DEVICES FOR GUARDING AGAINST ACCIDENT FROM MILL GEARING OR MACHINERY—MARYLAND.

Devices.	Reporting on specified device.	With provision of specified device applicable.	With specified device—	
			Provided.	Not provided.
For preventing accidents:				
Proper guarding on mill gearing and machinery............	24	24	13	11
Rule against removal of safeguards........................	9	8	6	2
Warning notices posted on dangerous machines............	24	21	3	18
For stopping machines in case of accidents:				
Direct control of power from workroom....................	24	24	[1] 7	17
Belt shifters...	24	24	21	3
Friction clutches..	24	23	18	5
Means of quick communication with engine room..........	24	17	[2] 7	10
Other special apparatus..................................	24			

[1] These 7 are all operated by electric power, the control devices being electric cut-offs or switches.
[2] Two by telephone; 3 by electric bells; 1 by telephone and push button; 1 by speaking tube and gong.

NORTH CAROLINA.

There were, at the time of this investigation, no legal provisions relating to the safeguarding of dangerous machinery.[2]

---

[1] Acts of 1894, ch. 202 (22d An. Rept. Com. of Labor, p. 570).

[2] The law here referred to is as in force at the time of the investigation, March, 1909. The text of the laws in force Jan. 1, 1912, is given in the appendixes at the end of this volume.

CONDITIONS FOUND.

In each of the 28 establishments visited there was power-driven machinery of a sufficiently dangerous character to require safeguarding. The following table shows to what extent proper and necessary safeguarding devices had been provided:

ESTABLISHMENTS VISITED HAVING AND NOT HAVING SPECIFIED SAFETY DEVICES FOR GUARDING AGAINST ACCIDENT FROM MILL GEARING OR MACHINERY—NORTH CAROLINA.

Devices.	Reporting on specified device.	With provision of specified device applicable.	With specified device—	
			Provided.	Not provided.
For preventing accidents:				
Proper guarding on mill gearing and machinery	28	28	18	10
Rule against removal of safeguards	28	26	8	18
Warning notices posted on dangerous machines	28	24	1	23
For stopping machinery in case of accidents:				
Direct control of power from workrooms	28	28	[1] 13	15
Belt shifters	27	26	15	11
Friction clutches	27	21	11	10
Means of quick communication with engine room	28	15	[2] 4	11
Other special apparatus	28	....	[3] 1	....

[1] All operated by electric power, control devices being electric cut-offs or switches.
[2] One by speaking tube; 1 by electric bell; 2 by telephone.
[3] Foot lever on lumping machine in one establishment.

GEORGIA.

The laws of Georgia contained no legal provisions relative to the safeguarding of dangerous machinery at the time of this investigation.[1]

CONDITIONS FOUND.

Each of the 27 establishments had machinery of a sufficiently dangerous character to require safeguarding. The table following shows to what extent proper and necessary safeguards had been provided.

[1] The law here referred to is as in force at the time of the investigation, March, 1909. The text of the laws in force Jan. 1, 1912, is given in the appendixes at the end of this volume.

ESTABLISHMENTS VISITED HAVING AND NOT HAVING SPECIFIED SAFETY DEVICES FOR GUARDING AGAINST ACCIDENT FROM MILL GEARING OR MACHINERY—GEORGIA.

Devices.	Establishments—			
	Reporting on specified device.	With provision of specified device applicable.	With specified device—	
			Provided.	Not provided.
For preventing accidents:				
Proper guarding on mill gearing and machinery............	27	27	17	10
Rule against removal of safeguards......................	23	22	4	18
Warning notices posted on dangerous machines...........	27	27	2	25
For stopping machinery in case of accidents:				
Direct control of power from workrooms............●......	27	27	[1] 11	16
Belt shifters..	27	27	23	4
Friction clutches......................................	27	20	7	13
Means of quick communication with engine room	27	16	[2] 3	13
Other special apparatus................................	27			

[1] Ten operated by electric power, control devices being electric cut-offs or switches; 1 operated by steam power, control device a wire pull which stops engine.
[2] Two by electric bell; 1 by telephone.

Of one woolen mill it is reported: "The fact that pickers, spinning frames, slubbers, twisters, and spoolers are here safely guarded demonstrates the practicability of doing so."

FLORIDA.

There were, at the time of this investigation, no legal provisions relative to the safeguarding of mill gearing or machinery.[1]

CONDITIONS FOUND.

In only 2 of the 14 establishments visited was there power-driven machinery of a sufficiently dangerous character to require special safeguarding.

The following table shows to what extent proper and necessary safeguarding devices had been provided by these 2 establishments:

ESTABLISHMENTS VISITED HAVING AND NOT HAVING SPECIFIED SAFETY DEVICES FOR GUARDING AGAINST ACCIDENT FROM MILL GEARING OR MACHINERY—FLORIDA.

Devices.	Establishments—			
	Reporting on specified device.	With provision of specified device applicable.	With specified device—	
			Provided.	Not provided.
For preventing accidents:				
Proper guarding on mill gearing and machinery............	2	2	....	2
Rule against removal of safeguards......................	2	2	1	1
Warning notices posted on dangerous machines...........	2	2	....	2
For stopping machinery in case of accident:				
Direct control of power from workroom....................	2	2	[2] 1	1
Belt shifters..	2	2	2	....
Friction clutches......................................	2	2	2	....
Means of quick communication with engine room...........	2	1	....	1
Other special apparatus................................	2			

[1] The law here referred to is as in force at time of the investigation, March, 1909. The text of the laws in force Jan. 1, 1912, is given in the appendixes at the end of this volume.
[2] Operated by electric power, control device being electric cut-off or switch.

LOUISIANA.

There was, at the time of this investigation, no legislation in Louisiana requiring machinery safeguarding.[1]

CONDITIONS FOUND.

In 26 of the 29 visited establishments there was power-driven machinery of a sufficiently dangerous character to require safeguarding.

The following table shows to what extent proper and necessary safeguarding devices had been provided by these 26 establishments:

ESTABLISHMENTS VISITED HAVING AND NOT HAVING SPECIFIED SAFETY DEVICES FOR GUARDING AGAINST ACCIDENT FROM MILL GEARING OR MACHINERY— LOUISIANA.

Devices.	Establishments—			
	Reporting on specified device.	With provision of specified device applicable.	With specified device—	
			Provided.	Not provided.
For preventing accidents:				
Proper guarding on mill gearing and machinery............	26	26	12	14
Rule against removal of safeguards.........................	26	25	16	9
Warning notices posted on dangerous machines............	26	20	1	19
For stopping machinery in case of accident:				
Direct control of power from workroom.....................	26	26	[2] 14	12
Belt shifters...	26	26	21	5
Friction clutches..	26	23	21	2
Means of quick communication with engine room..........	26	11	[3] 1	10
Other special apparatus...................................	26			

[1] The law here referred to is as in force at the time of this investigation, March, 1909. The text of the laws in force Jan. 1, 1912, is given in the appendixes at the end of this volume.
[2] All operated by electric power, control devices being electric cut-offs or switches.
[3] By telephone.

CHAPTER VII.

SAFEGUARDING OF ELEVATORS.

.

CHAPTER VII.

THE SAFEGUARDING OF ELEVATORS.

INTRODUCTION.

As this report deals solely with factories and workshops, it is concerned primarily with freight elevators and very little with passenger elevators. Very few manufacturing establishments are provided with special passenger elevators, and almost none of those visited during this investigation were so provided. A freight elevator of some sort is, however, present in practically all factories of more than one story in height. In some instances such elevator is of very crude construction, but this fact does not lessen its interest from the standpoint of safeguarding. For, broadly speaking, the cruder the type of elevator the greater the chance of accident. In the present chapter, therefore, the term elevator is used to cover every form of permanently installed hoisting apparatus.

A large number of elevator accidents are due to a degree of negligence on the part of the injured persons which no reasonable mechanical safeguards can prevent.[1] The remainder, certainly as numerous, can, however, be guarded against by purely mechanical means of proven merit. And it is not improbable that a number of accidents due to so-called negligence could be prevented by indirect measures, such as a more complete system of warning notices, a greater discrimination in the character of the persons interested with the operation of elevators, and a more thorough instruction of such persons in the handling of elevators.

The present chapter covers the subject of mechanical safeguards on elevators and of accidents due directly to elevator shafts and cars.

A full statement of the conditions found in each establishment is given in Chapter XI, General Tables, of this volume.

The fireproofing of elevator shafts is a part of the broad subject of fire protection and is not considered here.

The requirement of some State laws that children under a specified age shall not be permitted to operate elevators has a twofold aim— to prevent injury to passengers by unskilled handling of elevators,

---

[1] Van Schaack, Safeguards for the Prevention of Industrial Accidents, p. 105, Ætna Life Insurance Co. "About 50 per cent of the elevator accidents are caused by carelessness on the part of either the operators or the injured parties; about 25 per cent are due to unguarded conditions of the hoistways and the entrance; and the remainder to falling or runaway cars."

and to guard immature persons from unduly dangerous employments. The latter aim is the one most usually emphasized, and thus the subject of the operation of elevators by children has been considered in the chapter dealing with prohibited and dangerous employments (see pp. 89–155 of this report) rather than in the present chapter.

DANGERS CONNECTED WITH ELEVATORS, AND PROTECTIVE MEASURES.

Before proceeding to a detailed discussion of the State laws relative to elevator protection and of the conditions found in the establishments visited, a brief review is made of the more common elevator dangers and of some of the safeguards devised to prevent their occurrence.

The more prevalent forms of elevator accidents may be classified in five large groups, according as they are due to—

1. Improperly guarded hoistway;
2. Improperly guarded gates or doors;
3. Improperly guarded car;
4. Falling of elevator car; or
5. Falling of overhead parts upon the car.

IMPROPERLY GUARDED HOISTWAYS.

One of the most common elevator accidents is that of a person falling down an elevator shaft. Passenger elevators are almost always completely inclosed by walls running from the floor to the ceiling on all sides except that used for entrance to the car, and this entrance side is usually so inclosed that when the door is shut there is no opening in any part of the shafting surface. Frequently, however, freight elevators are not thus tightly inclosed. Usually they have guarding devices of some kind, but these may vary from a solid or mesh wall several feet high to a simple fencing consisting of nothing but a single line of rail, one or more sides of which is pivoted so that it may be unshipped for loading or unloading the car.

When hoistways are not fully inclosed, trapdoors or hatches are frequently employed to keep persons from falling into the well opening. Such hatches are usually automatic or semiautomatic, opening and closing as the elevator approaches and leaves a floor, although the self-acting principle is by no means universally employed. Hatches or traps such as these, when closed, are, of course, an excellent protection against the danger of falling through the floor opening. When, moreover, the opening and closing are automatic, the danger mentioned is almost completely guarded against. On the other hand, the automatic trap, especially if employed without other safeguards, introduces its own element of danger—that of crossing or being on the trap when it is raised, and thereby being thrown and possibly being caught between the opening door and the elevator runway, wall, or other near-by vertical surface.[1]

Fencing composed simply of a low single railing, such as is frequently used, is sufficient to guard against the danger just mentioned, that of preventing injury due to falling down an elevator opening or to crossing an automatic trapdoor. But the low rail or fence is not sufficient to guard against another very common form of accident— that of a person allowing part of the body to project over the shaft opening and thus being caught by the descending car. There are several makeshift devices for preventing this kind of accident, but the only really satisfactory safeguard is the use of a high fencing with no openings large enough to permit the insertion of any part of the body.

Finally, there may be mentioned the danger due to leaving the bottom of a shaft unguarded. If the lower end of the shaft is flush with the flooring and is uninclosed, there is always the possibility of such space being used as a passageway and of a person so passing being caught and crushed beneath the descending car. Proper shafting walls or guardrails may prevent such accidents, and an additional safeguard is to leave a clear space of several feet below the lowest point reached by the car in its descent.[1]

IMPROPERLY GUARDED GATES OR DOORS.

As the gate or door is an integral part of the elevator shafting, many of the remarks already made as to the danger of improper guardrails or fences apply here with equal force. In addition, however, the gate possesses certain dangers of its own. The most important of these dangers is that of leaving the gate open when the car is not at the floor. A gate, even though it entirely protects the entrance to the car, is generally regarded as dangerous if it is not automatic or at least semiautomatic, opening and closing as the car arrives and departs. Another accepted principle is that the gate should not open outward, but should lift or slide, and if the elevator is entirely closed should not be capable of being unfastened from the outside. The not infrequent use of a simple sliding rail for closing the entrance to an elevator shaft is dangerous, among other reasons because it can be so easily opened and left open.

IMPROPERLY GUARDED CARS.

A frequent injury in connection with freight elevators is the result of the operator or a passenger allowing some portion of his body to extend beyond the car and having it caught in some projecting part

---

[1] The Prevention of Industrial Accidents: No. 1, General, p. 103. Published by the Fidelity & Casualty Co. of New York.

of the shaft, such as sills, beams, and tops of window recesses.[1] This risk can be avoided by inclosing the car itself with some form of fencing, including a railing or fencing at the entrance or entrances. This method, however, is sometimes difficult, as it interferes with the use of all sides of the car for shipping and unshipping goods. But even in the case of absolutely unprotected cars, much of the danger can be avoided by having all projections beveled with sloping surfaces so as to push any projecting portion of the body back into the car instead of crushing it. Also, in the case of inclosed cars, this may be done with the side or sides of the shaft opposite the door or doors of the car.

FALLING OF THE CAR.

For the prevention of accidents from falling elevator cars, two devices are in use. These are usually known, respectively, as the "speed-governor safety device" and the "breaking safety device." The latter mechanism is a safety clutch attached to the elevator and so constructed that when the cables break the clutch is thrown, stopping the car immediately. Its weakness is that the fall of a car may be due to other causes than breaking cables. Thus if, because of a break in the gearing, the winding drum is released, the cables unroll rapidly, and the car falls. In such case the tension of the cables is often sufficient to keep the ordinary breaking safety device from working. To meet an emergency such as this, the speed governor safety device has been constructed. This is a safety clutch, much like the one just described, with the important difference that it is controlled by a speedometer and acts as soon as the car in falling exceeds a certain fixed speed. This device also has the advantage of the other device in that it operates not only when the car falls, but also when, owing to some derangement of the machinery, the car runs away upward.

FALLING OF OVERHEAD PARTS.

Passenger elevators are sometimes raised and lowered by means of hydraulic pressure acting underneath the car. But more frequently in the case of passenger elevators, and almost always with freight elevators, the lifting is done by hoisting cables. This method of hoisting requires a system of pulleys, beams, etc., at the top of the shaft and more or less immediately over the car. Serious accidents are not infrequently caused by some of these overhead parts becoming detached and crashing down upon the car. As a preventive measure against this kind of accident, a strong grating may be placed at the top of the shaft just under the working parts referred to.

---

[1] The Prevention of Industrial Accidents: No. 1, General, p. 100. Published by the Fidelity & Casualty Co. of New York.

The above discussion of elevator risks and safeguards is not intended to be exhaustive. It aims simply to point out and emphasize those dangers which experience has shown to be most prevalent and to have serious results most frequently. Its purpose is to make more intelligible the following presentation and discussion of State laws upon this subject.

Of the 17 States covered by this report, 6 have no laws dealing with elevator protection.[1] These 6 States are: Maine, Illinois, Maryland, North Carolina, Georgia, and Florida. Each of the remaining 11 States—Massachusetts, Rhode Island, Connecticut, New York, Pennsylvania, New Jersey, Ohio, Indiana, Michigan, Wisconsin, and Louisiana—has legislation of some character on this subject.[2]

A comparison of the legislation of these several States shows important uniformities as well as important differences. The point most deserving of emphasis, however, is that of the degree in which the laws were mandatory upon employers or enforceable only at the discretion of the inspecting authorities. As is the case with so many factory laws in the States covered, the legislation regarding elevators usually places a wide discretionary power in the hands of the inspectors. This discretion frequently extends so as to include the determination of what safeguards shall be provided in a particular case as well as whether any safeguards are necessary. As the question of the significance of thus vesting factory inspectors with such broad discretion has been discussed in full in another chapter, it need not be repeated here.[3]

In the remaining pages of this chapter there are given, for each State separately, a statement of the law, if any, relative to elevator safeguarding, and a brief tabular statement of the conditions found existing in the establishments visited. This table shows the respective numbers of establishments having and not having (1) all elevator shafts and openings properly guarded by gates, doors, walls, etc.; (2) elevator cars provided with safety clutches or other satisfactory devices for preventing the car from falling in case of accident to the hoisting apparatus; and (3) both of the mentioned safeguarding provisions.

The information thus given, although far from offering an exhaustive view of the subject, is sufficient to show to what extent the several establishments had sought to render their elevators reasonably safe, both for the operators thereof and for the other employees.

---

[1] In Illinois an elevator law was enacted shortly after the completion of the field work in that State. Acts of 1909, p. 202, sec. 4 (Bulletin of the Bureau of Labor, No. 85, pp. 546, 547).

[2] The law here referred to is as in force at the time of the investigation, December, 1908, to April, 1909. The text of the laws in force Jan. 1, 1912, is given in the appendixes at the end of this volume.

[3] See Chapter X, Ventilation and Sanitation, pp. 435–503 of this volume.

In considering the effectiveness of a law regarding elevator protection, it is desirable to bear in mind that there are other factors than the law tending to make employers guard their elevators. One of them is, of course, the fear of damage suits. Another, and more important one perhaps, is the elevator inspector. Many employers carry elevator insurance, and in such cases the insuring company is interested in having the insured elevator put and kept in as safe condition as possible.

MAINE.

. There was, at the time of this investigation,[1] no State law regarding the subject of elevator protection.

CONDITIONS FOUND.

Twenty-two of the 26 establishments visited had freight elevators. None had passenger elevators, and as a rule employees were not allowed to use the freight elevators to carry themselves up and down stairs. The following table shows the completeness of elevator protection in the 22 establishments referred to:

ESTABLISHMENTS HAVING AND NOT HAVING SPECIFIED SAFEGUARDS ON ALL ELEVATORS—MAINE.

	Establishments—		
Safeguards.	Reported on.	With specified safeguards on all elevators—	
		Provided.	Not provided.
Shafts and openings with proper guards	22	11	11
Cars with safety stopping devices	22	17	5
Both shafts and cars guarded	22	7	15

On one of the elevators entered in the above table as not having proper safety clutches, clutches had been provided but were out of order and would probably have failed to work properly in case of need.

In 2 establishments women were allowed to operate the elevators.

In 3 establishments the operator of the elevator had to lean into shaft to start and stop the car.

Of the 22 establishments that had elevators, 2 reported that their elevators had been inspected by the State factory inspector; and the other 20 that no such inspection had been made.

[1] January, 1909. The text of the laws in force Jan. 1, 1912, is given in the appendixes at the end of this volume.

MASSACHUSETTS.

SUMMARY OF LEGISLATION.[1]

There are two series of requirements in the State law relative to the safeguarding of elevators. One series occurs in the general law of the State and applies to all establishments within the State, except as special exception is made. The second forms part of the building code of Boston and applies only to that city. The two series of legal provisions are presented below in a slightly condensed form.

A. LAWS RELATING TO STATE.[2]

(1) Elevator * * * cars, whether used for freight or passengers shall be provided with a suitable mechanical device by which they will be securely held in the event of an accident to the shipper rope or hoisting machinery, or any similar accident,

(2) And they shall be guarded and equipped with some * * * device * * * which shall prevent any person from being caught between the floor of the * * * car and the floor of the building while attempting to enter or leave the elevator.   • .

(3) Elevators used for carrying freight shall be equipped with a suitable device which shall act as a danger signal to warn people of the approach of the elevator.

(4) Elevator wells hereafter built shall be so constructed that that part of the inside surface of the well which comes in front of the opening or door of * * * car shall be flush with the * * * car,

(5) And the door opening from * * * elevator well into the building shall be placed not more than 2 inches back from the face of * * * well, so as to allow no space for a foothold between the car and well door * * * .

(6) All the above construction work and devices shall be approved by the [State] inspectors of factories and public buildings, except that in the city of Boston they shall be approved by the building commissioner, and in other cities by the inspector of buildings; but upon the approval of said * * * [officials] any elevator may be used without any or all of such appliances or devices if the nature of the business is such that the necessity for the same will not warrant the expense.

(7) The openings of all hoistways, hatchways, elevators, and wellholes upon every floor of a factory or mercantile or public building shall be protected by sufficient trapdoor or self-closing hatches and safety catches or such other safeguards as the inspectors of factories and public buildings direct; and due diligence shall be used to keep such trapdoors closed at all times, except when in actual use by the occupant of the building who has the use and control of the same.

(8) If an elevator * * * used for freight or passengers is, in the judgment of the inspector of factories and public buildings,

---

[1] The law here referred to is as in force at the time of the investigation, December, 1908, to February, 1909. The text of the laws in force Jan. 1, 1912, is given in the appendixes at the end of this volume.

[2] Rev. Laws, 1902, ch. 104, secs. 27, 28, 43 (22d An. Rept. Com. of Labor, pp. 587–589).

unsafe or dangerous to use or has not been constructed in the manner required by law, said inspector shall immediately post conspicuously upon the entrance to or door of the * * * car * * * a notice of its dangerous condition and shall prohibit its use until made safe to his satisfaction. No person shall * * * remove such notice or operate such elevator while the notice is posted * * * . The provisions of this section [8] shall not apply to the city of Boston.

Penalty.[1]—A fine of not more than $100.

Enforcement of the above provisions is charged in general to the factory inspection department [of the district police] but with the important proviso that the authority to approve safety devices and construction work belongs to the local inspectors of buildings. [Decision of the attorney general.] The State factory inspectors, however, may ignore the approval of the local inspectors by placarding the elevator with a condemning notice, as provided for in the law as quoted above.

The second requirement of the law as quoted above—devices to prevent persons from being caught between floor of car and floor of building—is peculiar to Massachusetts among the States covered. The chief factory inspector in an interview with an agent of the Bureau stated that when the law was enacted a certain company claimed to manufacture a device which would meet the requirement. No such device is obtainable, however, and as a result this provision of the law is not fully complied with.

The law as quoted authorizes the State or local inspectors to permit the use of elevators without safety clutches, etc., if the nature of the business does not warrant the expense. The chief inspector stated that the State inspectors never make exceptions of this character.

B. LAWS RELATING TO BOSTON.[2]

(1) Shaft openings to be protected by self-closing gates, rails, trapdoors or equivalent devices, and closed when not in use.

(2) Every elevator to be provided with a safety attachment to prevent car from falling.

(3) Passenger elevators hereafter built, operated by drum and cables, to have overspeed governor to prevent car from descending at overspeed. And all elevators to have a slack-cable device to stop machinery in case car is held up or cables part.

(4) Freight elevators to have suitable danger signals to give warning of car's approach.

(5) The machinery over an elevator to have an underneath grille to catch falling material.

(6) Elevator cables hereafter installed that pass through beveled sockets, the ends returning and refitting into the same, shall have in addition lead or babbitt metal poured into the ends of the socket, to prevent the possibility of the cables slipping.

---

[1] Rev. Laws, 1902, ch. 104, sec. 56 (22d An. Rept., Com. of Labor, p. 590).

[2] Acts of 1907, ch. 550, sec. 38.

(7) The space between the car and door of each elevator landing to be not more than 2 inches.

(8) All elevators hereafter installed to be so located as to give easy and safe access to all principal parts of the machinery.

(9) Freight elevators hereafter built on the line of an external wall to be so constructed that there shall be no recess in the outer wall and that there may be not more than 4 inches space between platform of car and outer wall. Side of platform and line of doorway to be flush with well way, and the door openings from well into building to be placed at least 6 inches back from face of well, so as to allow space for self-closing gates.

Outside openings to freight elevators to be protected by self-closing slatted gates, "vertical," with spaces not wider than 2 inches between the slats.

(10) Elevator shafts to be of fireproof material. All shaft openings, except in the case of passenger elevators, to have fireproof doors and iron thresholds. Wire-glass panels may be used in such doors. Outside windows or openings of elevator shafts to have three vertical iron rods, painted red, equally spaced off.

(11) The commissioner shall post a conspicuous warning and notice at each entrance of an elevator which is not constructed or furnished according to law, or which has become unsafe. Penal offence to remove such notice or operate elevator until new permit is given.

(12) The commissioner may require such additional safeguards on an elevator as, in his judgment, the condition, use, or surroundings of the elevator may demand.

(13) No elevator to be used until the same is approved by the commissioner in writing; and no elevator to be hereafter installed without a permit therefor.

(14) Manufacturers of elevators must test, in the presence of an inspector, the safety devices of such elevators before turning the same over to the owners for use. An inspector may at any time require a test of the safety devices of an elevator, if he thinks desirable.

(15) If an accident occur to any elevator, causing personal injury or damaging the machinery or running parts of the elevator, report thereof shall be made to the commissioner before any repairs are made or elevator operated again, so that cause of accident, etc., may be investigated.

Penalty.[1]—A fine of not more than $500.

Enforcement of these regulations is made to devolve upon the building department of Boston, which department is under the charge of a building commissioner appointed by the mayor.[2]

CONDITIONS FOUND.

Of the 44 establishments visited, 37 had elevators, all of which were freight elevators. The following table shows the completeness of elevator protection in these 37 establishments.

---

[1] Acts of 1907, ch. 550, sec. 132.   [2] Idem, sec. 1.

ESTABLISHMENTS HAVING AND NOT HAVING SPECIFIED SAFEGUARDS ON ALL
ELEVATORS—MASSACHUSETTS.

Safeguards.	Establishments—		
	Reported on.	With specified safeguards on all elevators—	
		Provided.	Not provided
Shafts and openings properly guarded....................................	37	27	10
Cars with safety stopping devices..	37	36	1
Both shafts and cars guarded..	37	27	10

In 2 establishments the only elevator guards were chains and ropes,
hooked in center. In 2 others gates and guard rails were provided,
but in several cases were tied or wedged open; and in 1 of these
establishments the operator had to lean far into shaft in order to
start car.

In 8 establishments the elevators were without danger signals,
which are required by law, and in 1 other the signal did not work.

RHODE ISLAND.

SUMMARY OF LEGISLATION.[1]

The legislation of Rhode Island upon the subject of elevator safeguarding consists of two series of legal provisions. As the interpretation and mutual relation of these two series of laws are not entirely
clear it is necessary to reproduce them in full. The first series, A, is
as follows:[2]

SERIES A.

1. It shall be the duty of the owner, agent, or lessee of any such
factory, manufacturing or mercantile establishment [i. e., employing
5 or more persons or 1 child under 16], where hoisting shafts or wellholes are used, to cause the same to be properly and substantially
inclosed or secured if, in the opinion of the inspectors, it is necessary
to protect the life or limbs of those employed in such establishments.

2. It shall be the duty of the owner, agent, or lessee to provide or
cause to be provided such proper trap or automatic doors, so fastened
in or at all elevator ways as to form substantial surfaces when closed,
and so constructed as to open and close by the action of the elevator
in its passage either ascending or descending, if so directed by said
factory inspectors or either one of them.

3. If the factory inspectors, or either one of them, find that * * *
the elevators * * * in shops or factories are located so as to be
dangerous to employees, and not sufficiently guarded, * * *

---

[1] The law here referred to is as in force at the time of the investigation, December,
1908, to February, 1909. The text of the laws in force Jan. 1, 1912, is given in the
appendixes at the end of this volume.

[2] Gen. Laws, 1896, ch. 68, secs. 5 and 9, and sec. 12, as amended by ch. 1215, enacted
1905 (22d An. Rept. Com. of Labor, pp. 1209, 1210).

either or both shall notify the proprietor of such factory or workshop to make the alterations or additions necessary within 90 days; * * *

Penalty.—A fine of not more than $500.

The enforcement of the protective measures referred to in these provisions is specifically charged, it will be noted, to the State factory inspectors. When such inspectors think necessary, elevator shafts are to be guarded (A 1), automatic trapdoors are to be provided (A 2), and any dangerous condition or location of elevators is to be corrected (A 3). In total, therefore, these provisions would seem to vest the State factory inspectors with a very broad authority to insist upon elevator safeguarding.

The second series of legal provisions is as follows: [1]

SERIES B.

1. Every elevator used for conveying persons or goods from one story to another of any building, the well of which elevator is not so protected as to be inaccessible from without while the elevator is moving, shall have attached to it some suitable appliance which shall give automatically, at all times, on every floor of said building which it approaches, a distinct, audible warning signal that said elevator is in motion.

2. All hoistway and elevator openings through floors where there is no shaft shall be protected by sufficient railings, gates, trapdoors, or other mechanical devices equivalent thereto, and the same shall be kept closed in the nighttime or when not in use.

3. Every passenger elevator, except plunger elevators, shall be provided with some safety arrangement to prevent falling.

4. And every passenger elevator shall be fitted with some suitable device to prevent the elevator car from being started until the door or doors opening into the elevator shaft are closed; * * *

. 5. It shall be the duty of every inspector of buildings * * * to inspect all elevators in every building within his jurisdiction; and it shall be the duty of the factory inspectors * * * to inspect all elevators in every building within their jurisdiction in any city or town where there is no inspector of building[s]. [Said building and factory inspector to require compliance with above provisions.]

Penalty.—A fine of $5 to $10 per day for each day elevator is operated contrary to the law and to the orders of the inspectors.

The third and fourth of these provisions (B 3 and B 4) are very important, requiring as they do safety clutches to prevent the elevator car from falling and devices to prevent the car from starting while the door is open. As, however, these two requirements refer solely to passenger elevators, which rarely exist in factories, they are of little significance in the present discussion. The first and second provisions (B 1 and B 2), however, refer to freight elevators as well

---

[1] Gen. Laws, 1896, ch. 108, secs. 15 and 16, as amended by ch. 973, enacted 1902 (22d An. Rept. Com. of Labor, pp. 1214, 1215).

as to those used only for passengers. They require, respectively, that elevators with unclosed shafts shall be equipped with warning signals to notify persons of the approach of the car, and that elevators with unclosed shafts shall have their floor openings provided with railings, gates, traps or similar devices, which shall be kept closed when the elevator is not in use.

The provisions of the second group (B) differ from those of the first (A) in that they are completely mandatory in form. They also differ in that they are enforceable by the State inspection department only in such places as have no local building inspectors.

From the point of view of the present administrative practice in Rhode Island, the most significant of the several provisions quoted above is the one regarding warning signals (B 1). This provision, by requiring warning signals on unclosed shafts, assumes the existence of open shafts. The inspection department accepts this view. It favors inclosed elevator shafts, and does not sanction trapdoors or self-closing hatches as the sole means of protection.[1] It believes the warning signal highly unsatisfactory, adding as it does but another noise to the many other noises of most factories. If, however, the warning signal has been provided, the department does not regard the law as giving it authority to force an employer to install gates or railings.

CONDITIONS FOUND.

Of the 27 establishments visited 22 had freight elevators; none had passenger elevators. The following table shows the completeness of elevator protection in the 22 establishments referred to:

ESTABLISHMENTS HAVING AND NOT HAVING SPECIFIED SAFEGUARDS ON ALL
ELEVATORS—RHODE ISLAND.

Safeguards.	Establishments—		
	Reported on.	With specified safeguards on all elevators—	
		Provided.	Not provided.
Shafts and openings properly guarded	22	12	10
Cars with safety stopping devices	22	1 20	1
Both shafts and cars guarded	22	1 11	10

1 In one case elevator was of block-and-tackle type, carrying no passengers, and thus not requiring safety devices.

In one case it was reported that while the elevator shaft was properly guarded, the operator of the car had to lean into the shaft when

---

[1] These trapdoors were for the most part installed by the mill owners before the passage of the factory act, for the purpose of lessening fire risks and thereby reducing insurance rates. J. K. Towles in Factory Legislation of Rhode Island, p. 112.

starting the car, thus placing himself in considerable danger of accident.

Of the 22 establishments having elevators, 16 reported that their elevators had been regularly inspected by the State factory inspectors; 1 that its elevator had been regularly inspected by an insurance company inspector; 1 that its elevator had never been inspected; 1 that its factory was new and, consequently, that elevator inspection had not been necessary; and in the case of 3 establishments no report was received upon this point. Of the 16 establishments whose elevators were reported as having been regularly inspected by the State factory inspectors, 5 had certificates on file and 11 did not have such certificates.

CÓNNECTICUT.

SUMMARY OF LEGISLATION.[1]

The requirements of law in Connecticut upon the subject of elevator safeguarding are as follows:[2]

(A) The inspector [i. e. the State factory inspector] shall examine all elevators, whether in factories, mercantile establishments, storehouses, workhouses, dwellings, or other buildings, and may order hoistways, hatchways, elevator wells, and wellholes to be protected by trapdoors, self-closing hatches, safety catches, or other safeguards as will insure the safety of all persons therein.

(B) Due diligence shall be used to keep such trapdoors closed at all times, except when in actual use by an occupant of the building having the use and control of the same.

(C) All elevator cabs or cars, whether used for freight or passengers, shall be provided with some suitable mechanical device, if considered necessary by said inspector, whereby the cab or car will be securely held in the event of accident to the shipper rope or hoisting machinery, or from any similar cause, and said mechanical device shall at all times be kept in good working order.

> *Penalty.*—The penalty for violation is not given in the chapter containing the above provisions. It is probable, however, that the penalty of "not more than $50" mentioned in General Statutes, section 4522 (as amended by ch. 53, Acts of 1903) applies here.

The factory inspector is thus made the judge as to when any of the enumerated protective measures are necessary. If he considers remedies are called for, he may order hoistways and wellholes to be protected, and may require elevator cars to be provided with mechanical devices to prevent falling. The latter provision does not leave much room for the choice of means; there are comparatively

---

[1] The law here referred to is as in force at the time of the investigation, February, 1909. The text of the laws in force Jan. 1, 1912, is given in the appendixes at the end of this volume.

[2] Acts of 1903, ch. 97, sec. 2, and Gen. Stat., 1902, sec. 4522 (as amended by ch. 53, Acts of 1903.) (22d An. Rept. Com. of Labor, pp. 237, 245.)

few devices of the kind referred to. As regards the choice of measures by which hoistways and openings are to be guarded there is room for broad discretion. The law permits the use of any kind of safeguard that "will insure the safety" of persons within the building.

The responsibility for the carrying out of the intention of the above-quoted legal provisions rests entirely upon the factory inspection department.

CONDITIONS FOUND.

Of the 35 establishments visited, 34 had freight elevators; none had passenger elevators. The following table shows the completeness of elevator protection in the 34 establishments referred to:

ESTABLISHMENTS HAVING AND NOT HAVING SPECIFIED SAFEGUARDS ON ALL ELEVATORS—CONNECTICUT.

		Establishments—	
Safeguards.	Reported on.	With specified safeguards on all elevators—	
		Provided.	Not provided.
Shafts and openings with proper guards	34	31	3
Cars with safety stopping devices	34	34	
Both shafts and cars guarded	34	31	3

NEW YORK.

SUMMARY OF LEGISLATION.[1]

The legislation of New York State upon the subject of elevator safeguarding is as follows:[2]

1. If, in the opinion of the factory inspector, it is necessary to protect the life or limbs of factory[3] employees, the owner, agent, or lessee of such factory where an elevator, hoisting shafts, or wellhole is used,

2. Shall cause, upon written notice from the factory inspector, the same to be properly and substantially inclosed, secured, or guarded,

3. And shall provide such proper traps or automatic doors so fastened in or at all elevator ways, except passenger elevators enclosed on all sides, as to form a substantial surface when closed and so constructed as to open and close by action of the elevator in its passage either ascending or descending.

---

[1] The law here referred to is as in force at the time of the investigation, December, 1908, and January, 1909. The text of the laws in force Jan. 1, 1912, is given in the appendixes at the end of this volume.

[2] Rev. Stat., 3d ed., 1901, p. 2102, sec. 79, and p. 2120, sec. 209 (as amended by ch. 506, Acts of 1907). (22d An. Rept. Com. of Labor, pp. 911, 912.)

[3] The term "factory" as used in the New York law includes "also any mill, workshop, or other manufacturing or business establishment where one or more persons are employed at labor." Rev. Stat., 3d ed., 1901, p. 2089, sec. 2 (as amended by ch. 550, Acts of 1904). (22d An. Rept. Com. of Labor, p. 899.)

4. The factory inspector may inspect the cable, gearing, or other apparatus of elevators in factories and require them to be kept in a safe condition.

Penalty.—For the first offense, a fine of not less than $20 nor more than $50; second offense, not less than $50 nor more than $200, or imprisonment not more than 30 days, or both; third offense, not less than $250, or imprisonment not less than 60 days, or both.

The enforcement of the several provisions of this law, it will be noted, is dependent entirely upon the desire and the activity of the factory-inspection department. No absolute duty devolves upon the owner of a building to safeguard elevators contained therein until so ordered by the factory inspector. The authority of the inspection department in the matter is, however, amply sufficient to enable it to insist upon the maintenance of excellent conditions.

The law recognizes the necessity of guarding elevator shafts, of providing automatic trapdoors, and of keeping the cables, gears, etc., in a safe condition. Apparently, however, it does not recognize the desirability of safety clutches or other devices to keep elevator cars from falling. Whether or not the inspectors have authority to order such devices is not clear.

CONDITIONS FOUND.

Of the 36 establishments visited, 35 had elevators. The following table shows the completeness of elevator protection in these 35 establishments:

ESTABLISHMENTS HAVING AND NOT HAVING SPECIFIED SAFEGUARDS ON ALL ELEVATORS—NEW YORK.

Safeguards.	Establishments—		
	Reported on.	With specified safeguards on all elevators—	
		Provided.	Not provided.
Shafts and openings with proper guards	35	29	6
Cars with safety stopping devices	35	32	3
Both shafts and cars guarded	35	27	8

In two of the cases where the elevator shafts were reported as improperly guarded, doors or gates leading to the shafts were provided, but were not kept closed. In another case the door used as the elevator outlet to the yard of the factory was also used as a common passageway by the employees, who in doing so walked beneath the elevator car.

NEW JERSEY.

SUMMARY OF LEGISLATION.[1]

The provision of the New Jersey law regarding elevator safeguarding is in full as follows:[2]

The openings of all hoistways, hatchways, elevators, and wellholes upon every floor of any place coming under the provisions of this act,[3] shall be protected by good and sufficient trapdoors or self-closing hatches and safety catches, or strong guard rails at least 3 feet high, and shall be kept closed and protected at all times except when in actual use by the occupant of the building having the use and control of the same.

Penalty.—$50 for each offense.

These requirements concern but a single point—the protection of floor openings. Alternative methods of protection are permitted—simple trapdoors, "self-closing hatches and safety catches," or guard rails at least 3 feet high. If one method is used, the others need not be. No mention is made of safety devices to keep elevator cars from falling or of safeguard against bad cables, gears, etc.

The requirements, as quoted, are all mandatory in form. The duty of supervising and enforcing the law is charged to the State factory, inspection department.[4]

CONDITIONS FOUND.

Of the 27 establishments visited, 24 had elevators. The following table shows the completeness of elevator protection in these 24 establishments:

ESTABLISHMENTS HAVING AND NOT HAVING SPECIFIED SAFEGUARDS ON ALL
ELEVATORS—NEW JERSEY.

Safeguards.	Establishments—		
	Reported on.	With specified safeguards on all elevators—	
		Provided.	Not provided.
Shafts and openings, with proper guards..	24	23	1
Cars, with safety stopping devices....................................	24	19	5
Both shafts and cars guarded..	24	19	5

[1] The law here referred to is as in force at the time of the investigation, December 1908, and January, 1909. The text of the laws in force Jan. 1, 1912, is given in the appendixes at the end of this volume.
[2] Acts of 1904, ch. 64, secs. 11 and 30 (22d An. Rept. Com. Labor, pp. 861, 862, 864).
[3] The places coming under this act are factories, workshops, mills, or places where the manufacture of goods of any kind is carried on. Acts of 1904, ch. 64, sec. 1 (22d An. Rept. Com. of Labor, p. 860).
[4] Acts of 1904, ch. 64, secs. 30 and 45, as amended by ch. 257, Acts of 1907 (22d An. Rept. Com. of Labor, pp. 864, 868, 869).

In the case of 1 establishment it was reported that although the shafts of the elevator were properly guarded the swinging gate on one floor was kept unlatched whether or not the car was at that floor.

PENNSYLVANIA.

SUMMARY OF LEGISLATION.[1]

As in the case of fire escapes (see p. 252), cities of the first and second classes (i. e., population of 100,000 or over) have special regulations as to elevator protection, enforceable by local authorities, while in other places similar provisions are enforced by the State factory inspection department. Only 6 of the 50 establishments visited were not in cities of the first or second classes.

The several sets of laws referred to are alike in requiring elevator shafts and openings in all classes of establishments to be securely guarded. None of the State laws, however, make a specific requirement of safety clutches or similar devices for stopping car from falling in case of accident.

The text of the law applicable to establishments in all places other than cities of the first and second classes is as follows:[2]

1. The owner, * * * or other person having charge * * * of any establishment * * * or other building where elevators, hoisting shafts, lifts, or wellholes are used, shall cause the same to be properly and substantially inclosed, secured, or guarded; and shall provide such proper traps or automatic doors, so fastened in or at all elevator ways, except elevators inclosed on all sides, as to form a substantial surface when closed, and so constructed as to open and close by action of the elevator in its passage, either ascending or descending.

2. The cable, gearing, or other apparatus of elevators, hoisters, or lifts shall be kept in a safe condition.

3. *Provided*, That the provisions of this section shall not apply to cities of the first and second classes.

> *Penalty.*—A fine of not less than $25 nor more than $500 or imprisonment 10 to 60 days.

---

[1] The law here referred to is as in force at the time of the investigation, January to March, 1909. The text of the laws in force Jan. 1, 1912, is given in the appendixes at the end of this volume.

[2] Acts of 1905, act No. 226, sec. 12 (22d An. Rept. Com. of Labor, p. 1178).

CONDITIONS FOUND.

Of the 50 visited establishments, 42 had elevators. The following table classifies these 42 establishments by the character of the community where located and shows for those of each class the completeness of elevator protection:

ESTABLISHMENTS HAVING AND NOT HAVING SPECIFIED SAFEGUARDS ON ALL ELEVATORS—PENNSYLVANIA.

Safeguards and classes of cities.	Establishments—		
	Reported on.	With specified safeguards on all elevators—	
		Provided.	Not provided.
Shafts and openings with proper guards:			
Cities of first class	25	21	4
Cities of second class	15	13	2
Cities of third class	2	2	....
Total	42	36	6
Cars with safety stopping devices:			
Cities of first class	25	25	....
Cities of second class	15	13	2
Cities of third class	2	2	....
Total	42	40	2
Both shafts and cars guarded:			
Cities of first class	25	21	4
Cities of second class	15	11	4
Cities of third class	2	2	....
Total	42	34	8

In 1 establishment entered in the table as having elevator shafts guarded the guards were frequently out of place. In 2 other establishments the space between the top of the gate and the ceiling was unguarded, with consequent danger to those riding on the car. In 1 of these 2 establishments a boy had been killed because of the condition just mentioned.

OHIO.

SUMMARY OF LEGISLATION.[1]

The legislation secured in Ohio upon elevator safeguarding is as follows:

(A) * * * It shall be their duty [i. e., the factory inspectors] * * * to examine * * * elevators, * * * and machinery of every kind and description in and about such shops and factories [2] and see that the same are not located so as to be dangerous

---

[1] The law here referred to is as in force at the time of the investigation, March, 1909. The text of the laws in force Jan. 1, 1912, is given in the appendixes at the end of this volume.

[2] The term "shops and factories" includes manufacturing, mechanical, electrical, mercantile, art and laundering establishments, printing, telegraph and telephone offices, railroad depots, hotels, memorial buildings, tenement and apartment houses. Bates' Ann. Stat., 3d ed., Pt. I, Political, sec. 2573d (22d An. Rept. Com. of Labor, p. 999).

to employees when engaged in their ordinary duties and that the same, so far as practicable, are securely guarded   *   *   *.

If the factory inspectors find conditions otherwise, they shall order necessary changes to be made without delay, but chief inspector may allow 15 to 30 days for such changes.

> *Penalty.*—Not less than $50 and not more than $500, and $10 per day for each additional day of failure or negligence after conviction.[1]

(B) The owners and operators of factories and workshops   *   *   * and all places where machinery of any kind is used or operated shall take ordinary care and make such suitable provisions as to prevent injury to persons who may come in contact with any such machinery or any part thereof, and such ordinary care and such suitable provisions shall include   *   *   *   the railing in all unused elevator openings, the placing of automatic gates or floor doors, and the keeping of same in good condition on each floor from which and where on each side or sides of elevator openings, entrance to the elevator carriage is obtained, [and] the frequent examination and keeping in sound condition of ropes, gearing, and other parts of elevators   *   *   *.

> *Penalty.*—For the first offense to be fined not more than $100; for every subsequent offense not less than $50 nor more than $500.[2]

(C)   *   *   * any   *   *   * inspector of workshops and factories who shall obtain knowledge of violation of   *   *   * [provision (B) above] is hereby authorized' whenever he may deem it advisable to paste upon any   *   *   * elevator   *   *   * or machinery   *   *   * a notice stating   *   *   * that operatives or employees are liable to injury by its use or operation, and such notice shall designate and describe the alteration   *   *   * necessary to be made   *   *   * and the time allowed for such alteration   *   *   * and no such   *   *   * elevator   *   *   * or machinery of any kind shall be used or operated after such notice is posted thereon, until such change or alteration is made to the satisfaction of the inspector   *   *   *.

> *Penalty.*—For the first offense to be fined not less than $25 nor more than $100, and for every subsequent offense not less than $50 nor more than $500.[3]

Briefly summarized, these several legal provisions are of the following effect: The employer is directed to exercise all ordinary care in guarding elevators, and it is specifically provided that such care shall include the placing of automatic gates or floor doors and the keeping of ropes, gears, and other parts in safe condition. The fac-

---

[1] Bates' Ann. Stat., 3d ed., Pt. I, Political, sec. 2573a (as amended by act, p. 338, Acts of 1902, and Act, p. 530, acts of 1904) and sec. 2573c (as amended by act, p. 530, Acts of 1904). (22d An. Rept. Com. of Labor, pp. 998, 999.)

[2] Idem, Civ., secs. 4364–89c and 4364–89d (22d An. Rept. Com. of Labor, pp. 1014, 1015).

[3] Idem, secs. 4364–89c and 4364–89f (22d An. Rept. Com. of Labor, p. 1015).

tory inspectors are ordered to make inspections of all elevators, and if they find conditions which, in their opinion, are dangerous to employees when engaged in ordinary duties they are authorized to require the necessary remedies. And, finally, the inspectors are given a broad discretionary authority to condemn forthwith and forbid the use of any elevator which for any reason they may consider unsafe or dangerous to operate. •

Full responsibility for the enforcement of the laws regarding elevator safeguarding rests upon the State factory inspection department.[1]

CONDITIONS FOUND.

Of the 60 establishments visited 58 had elevators. In each of these 58 establishments all elevator cars were provided with safety clutches to prevent car from falling in case of accident to the hoisting apparatus, and in the 55 cases in which information upon this point was reported the elevator shafts and openings were satisfactorily guarded.

ILLINOIS.

The laws[2] of Illinois in force at the time of the field work of this investigation made no provision for the guarding of elevators or elevator cars.[3]

CONDITIONS FOUND.

Of the 47 establishments visited 39 had elevators. The following table shows the completeness of elevator protection in these 39 establishments:

ESTABLISHMENTS HAVING AND NOT HAVING SPECIFIED SAFEGUARDS ON ALL ELEVATORS—ILLINOIS.

Safeguards.	Establishments—		
	Reported on.	With specified safeguards on all elevators—	
		Provided.	Not provided.
Shafts and openings with proper guards	39	35	4
Cars with safety-stopping devices	39	36	3
Both shafts and cars guarded	39	34	5

[1] Bates' Ann. Stat., 3d ed., Pt. I, Civ., sec. 4364–89g (22d An. Rept. Com. of Labor, p. 1015), and also reference in footnotes above.

[2] December, 1908, to February, 1909. The text of the laws in force Jan. 1, 1912, is given in the appendixes at the end of this volume.

[3] By a law passed subsequent to the field work of this investigation, however, the guarding of elevator shafts and cars is required. Acts of 1909, p. 202, sec. 4 (Bulletin of the Bureau of Labor, No. 85, pp. 546, 547). The requirements are that in all factories, mercantile establishments, mills, and workshops (1) elevator openings shall be "securely fenced, inclosed, or otherwise safely protected" and "due diligence" be used to keep such means of protection closed when not in use; (2) elevator cabs or cars, whether freight or passenger, shall be provided with "some device whereby the car or cab may be held in the event of accident to the shipper rope or hoisting machinery or controlling apparatus."

In one of the cases in which the elevator shafts were reported as not being properly guarded, guards were provided but the rails were not kept closed when elevator car was away.

INDIANA.

SUMMARY OF LEGISLATION.[1]

The Indiana law upon elevator safeguarding is very complete in its scope. It provides as follows:[2]

(A) It shall be the duty of the owner or lessee of any manufacturing or mercantile establishment, laundry, renovating works, bakery, or printing office, where there is an elevator, hoisting shaft, or well-hole, to cause the same to be properly and substantially inclosed or secured, if in the opinion of the chief inspector it is necessary to protect the lives or limbs of those employed in such establishments.

(B) It shall also be the duty of the owner, agent, or lessee of each of such establishments to provide, or cause to be provided, if in the opinion of the chief inspector, the safety of persons in or about the premises should require it, such proper trap or automatic doors so fastened in or at all elevator ways as to form a substantial surface when closed, and so constructed as to open and close by the action of the elevator in its passage, either ascending or descending, but the requirements of this section shall not apply to passenger elevators that are closed on all sides.

(C) The chief inspector shall inspect the cables, gearing, or other apparatus of elevators in the establishments above enumerated and require that the same be kept in safe condition.

(D) With proper safety devices whereby the cabs or cars will be securely held in event of accident to the cable or rope or hoisting machinery, or from any similar cause.

Penalty.—To be fined not more than $50 for the first offense; for the second offense, not more than $100, to which may be added imprisonment for not more than 10 days; and for the third offense, not less than $250 and not more than 30 days' imprisonment.

The factory inspector is thus made the judge as to when the protective measures referred to by the law are necessary. Until orders are received from the inspection department failure to provide guards is not negligence.[3]

The authority of the department to correct unsafe conditions is very broad. It may require (A) that hoisting shafts be inclosed or secured, (B) that automatic trapdoors be provided at all floor openings, (C) that cables, gearings, etc., be in safe condition, and (D) that elevator cars be equipped with safety devices to prevent falling.

---

[1] The law here referred to is as in force at the time of the investigation, February and March, 1909. The text of the laws in force Jan. 1, 1912, is given in the appendixes at the end of this volume.

[2] Ann. Stat. of 1894, Rev. of 1901, secs. 7087e and 7087g (22d An. Rept. Com. of Labor, pp. 398, 402).

[3] 82 N. E. Rep. 114 (22d An. Rept. Com. of Labor, p. 398).

The first three provisions (A, B, and C), it may be observed, are almost identical in their wording with the New York statute (p. 332). The only difference of importance is that the Indiana law directs (provision C) that the inspector "shall" inspect cables, etc., and require such to be in safe condition, whereas the New York statute merely authorizes, and does not positively require, the inspecting department to perform such action. The authority given the inspector to order safety devices on elevator cars to prevent falling (provision D) does not occur in the New York law.

The full responsibility for the enforcement of all the legal provisions regarding elevator protection, as quoted above, rests upon the State factory inspection department.[1] •

<h2 style="text-align:center">CONDITIONS FOUND.</h2>

Of the 47 establishments visited, 40 had elevators. The following table shows the completeness of elevator protection in these 40 establishments:

ESTABLISHMENTS HAVING AND NOT HAVING SPECIFIED SAFEGUARDS ON ALL ELEVATORS—INDIANA.

Safeguards.	Establishments—		
	Reported on.	With specified safeguards on all elevators—	
		Provided.	Not provided.
Shafts and openings with proper guards	40	37	3
Cars with safety stopping devices	40	38	2
Both shafts and cars guarded	40	36	4

<h2 style="text-align:center">MICHIGAN.</h2>
<h3 style="text-align:center">SUMMARY OF LEGISLATION.[2]</h3>

The following provision represents the legislation of Michigan upon the subject of elevator guarding:[3]

(A) It shall be the duty of the owner, agent or lessee of any manufacturing establishment where hoisting shafts or wellholes are used, to cause the same to be properly inclosed and secured.

(B) It shall also be the duty of the owner, agent, or lessee to provide or cause to be provided at all elevator openings in any manufacturing establishment, workshop, hotel, or store, such proper trap or automatic doors or automatic gates, so constructed as to open or close by the action of elevators either ascending or descending.

[1] Ann. Stat. of 1894, Rev. of 1901, sec. 7087v (22d An. Rept. Com. of Labor, p. 402).

[2] The law here referred to is as in force at the time of the investigation, March, 1909. The text of the laws in force Jan. 1, 1912, is given in the appendixes at the end of this volume.

[3] Acts of 1901, act No. 113, secs. 5 and 18 (22d An. Rept. Com. of Labor, pp. 659, 662).

(C) The factory inspector, assistant factory inspector, or deputy factory inspector shall inspect the cables, gearing, or other apparatus of elevators in manufacturing establishments, workshops, hotels, and stores at least once in each year, and more frequently if necessary, and require that the same be kept in a safe condition.

Penalty.—Fine of not less than $5 nor more than $100, or imprisonment not less than 10 days nor more than 90 days, or both.[1]

As regards subject matter this law is closely similar to the New York statute (see pp. 332, 333). Both provide for the guarding of elevator shafts, for the provision of automatic gates or doors at floor openings, and for the inspection of cables, gearing, etc. They differ chiefly in the extent to which the factory inspection department is vested with discretionary authority in enforcing the several requirements. The New York law is entirely "discretionary"—that is to say, no duty devolves upon the owner of a factory to provide elevator safeguards until he is specifically ordered to do so by the factory inspector. The Michigan law, on the other hand, is mandatory as regards the first two requirements—the guarding of elevator shafts and the provision of automatic trap doors—and as regards the third requirement—the inspection of cables, gearing, etc., by the factory inspectors—it makes such inspection a duty on the part of the inspectors instead of merely giving the inspectors discretionary authority in the matter, as does the New York law. It is also to be noted that the Michigan law requires that the inspection of the cables, gearing, etc., shall take place at least once each year.

The State factory inspection department of Michigan is specifically charged with the duty of enforcing all of the above quoted provisions.[2]

CONDITIONS FOUND.

Eighteen of the 19 establishments visited had freight elevators. The following table shows the completeness of elevator protection in these 18 establishments:

ESTABLISHMENTS HAVING AND NOT HAVING SPECIFIED SAFEGUARDS ON ALL ELEVATORS—MICHIGAN.

Safeguards.	Establishments—		
	Reported on.	With specified safeguards on all elevators—	
		Provided.	Not provided.
Shafts and openings with proper guards	18	17	1
Cars with safety stopping devices	18	18	....
Both shafts and cars guarded	18	17	1

[1] By Acts of 1909, act 285, sec. 54 (Bulletin of the Bureau of Labor, No. 85, p. 640), the minimum fine was raised to $10.
[2] Acts of 1901, act No. 113, sec. 12 (22d An. Rep. Com. of Labor, p. 660).

WISCONSIN.

SUMMARY OF LEGISLATION.[1]

The statutes of Wisconsin contain the following provisions relative to the safeguarding of elevators:[2] ·

(A) * * * [Elevators in any] place where persons are employed to perform labor * * * which are so located as to be dangerous to employees in the discharge of their duty shall be securely guarded or fenced.

> *Penalty.*—$25 for each offense, and each day's neglect of failure, after conviction, to constitute a separate offense.[3]

(B) Any such officer [i. e., State inspector] may order * * * elevator wells * * * or dangerous machinery of any kind to be inclosed or otherwise guarded so as to protect workmen or others.

> *Penalty.*—$50 for each refusal to obey written order.[4]

(C) [No] person * * * shall remove any guard or other safety device from * * * elevator wells * * * shafting or dangerous machinery, while such * * * is in motion or use * * *.

> *Penalty.*—$5 to $50, or imprisonment not more than 30 days, or both.[4]

(D) It shall be the duty of such officers [i. e., the State inspectors] to examine freight and passenger elevators and to condemn those found to be defective and unsafe by serving written notice * * * or by posting such notice on the walls or cab of any elevator found to be in an unsafe condition.

[After condemnation operation of elevator without proper repairs renders owner liable, civilly and criminally, for each physical injury, whether or not such injury results in death.][4]

The first of these three provisions—requiring elevators to be "securely guarded or fenced"—is mandatory upon employers. Failure to guard an elevator dangerous to an employee engaged in his ordinary duties is a legal violation and is negligence per se,[5] the jury determining when the location of an elevator is dangerous. It is to be noted, however, that the requirement is not that every place be guarded which might possibly cause injury, but only such places as are dangerous to employees engaged in the discharge of their duties.[6] This latter point may be of considerable importance as

---

[1] The law here referred to is as in force at the time of the investigation, March, 1909. The text of the laws in force January 1, 1912, is given in the appendixes at the end of this volume.

[2] The provisions quoted here do not include a law regarding the fireproofing of walls and casings and passenger elevators. Ann. Stat. of 1898, Supp. of 1906, Acts of 1907, sec. 1636–5 (22d An. Rept. Com. of Labor, p. 1411).

[3] Ann. Stat. of 1898, Supp. of 1906, Acts of 1907, sec. 1636j (22d An. Rept. Com. of Labor, p. 1410).

[4] Idem, sec. 1021h (22d An. Rept. Com. of Labor, p. 1408).

[5] 73 N. W. Rep., 563 (22d An. Rept. Com. of Labor, p. 1410).

[6] 86 N. W. Rep., 153 (22d An. Rept. Com. of Labor, p. 1410).

many accidents occur where the persons affected are not technically engaged in the discharge of any duty, but without negligence or even undue carelessness on their part.

The second and fourth of the quoted provisions confer a broad authority upon the factory inspectors to order elevators to be protected—the second by authorizing such officials to require elevator wells to be inclosed or otherwise guarded, the fourth by directing them to inspect all elevators and to condemn such as are dangerous. The power given the inspectors by the latter provision is extremely broad. Its wording is such that the authority to condemn might include any kind of defect in the elevator car or shafting, but the probable intention was that it should cover only those defects which threatened the safety of passengers and operators.

The enforcement of the several provisions regarding elevator protection, as quoted above, rests with the State factory inspection department.

CONDITIONS FOUND.

Fifteen of the 19 establishments visited had elevators. The following table shows the completeness of elevator protection in these 15 establishments:

ESTABLISHMENTS HAVING AND NOT HAVING SPECIFIED SAFEGUARDS ON ALL ELEVATORS—WISCONSIN.

		Establishments—	
Safeguards.	Reported on.	With specified safeguards on all elevators—	
		Provided.	Not provided.
Shafts and openings properly guarded	15	15	....
Cars with safety stopping devices	15	14	1
Both shafts and cars guarded	15	14	1

MARYLAND.

The laws of Maryland, at the time of this investigation, made no provision for protection against elevator accidents.[1]

The chief factory inspector stated that he paid no attention to the matter of elevator safety in factories or elsewhere.

---

[1] The law here referred to is as in force at the time of the investigation, January, 1909. The text of the laws in force Jan. 1, 1912, is given in the appendixes at the end of this volume.

CONDITIONS FOUND.

Of the 28 establishments visited, 26 had elevators. The following table shows the completeness of elevator protection in these 26 establishments:

ESTABLISHMENTS HAVING AND NOT HAVING SPECIFIED SAFEGUARDS ON ALL ELEVATORS—MARYLAND.

Safeguards.	Establishments—		
	Reported on.	With specified safeguards on all elevators—	
		Provided.	Not provided.
Shafts and openings with proper guards................................	26	24	2
Cars with safety stopping devices..	25	22	3
Both shafts and cars guarded...	25	20	5

In one case it was reported that, in addition to the elevator shafts, etc., not being properly guarded, it was necessary for the operator to lean into the shaft in starting and stopping car.

NORTH CAROLINA.

There were at the time of the investigation no legal provisions relative to the safeguarding of elevators.[1]

CONDITIONS FOUND.

Twenty-two of the 28 establishments visited had freight elevators. None had passenger elevators.

The following table shows the degree of elevator protection existing in these 22 establishments:

ESTABLISHMENTS HAVING AND NOT HAVING SPECIFIED SAFEGUARDS ON ALL ELEVATORS—NORTH CAROLINA.

Safeguards.	Establishments—		
	Reported on.	With specified safeguards on all elevators—	
		Provided.	Not provided.
Shafts and openings properly guarded....................................	22	13	9
Cars with safety stopping devices...	22	20	2
Both shafts and cars guarded...	22	13	9

In the case of 1 elevator enumerated in the table as having shafting improperly guarded, swinging gates had been provided, but these were usually left open.

[1] The law here referred to is as in force at the time of the investigation, March, 1909. The text of the laws in force Jan. 1, 1912, is given in the appendixes at the end of this volume.

GEORGIA.

There were at the time of this investigation no legal provisions relative to the safeguarding of elevators.[1]

CONDITIONS FOUND.

Twenty-two of the 27 establishments visited had freight elevators. None had passenger elevators.

The following table shows the completeness of elevator protection in these 22 establishments:

ESTABLISHMENTS HAVING AND NOT HAVING SPECIFIED SAFEGUARDS ON ALL ELEVATORS—GEORGIA.

Safeguards.	Establishments—		
	Reported on.	With specified safeguards on all elevators—	
		Provided.	Not provided.
Shafts and openings properly guarded	22	14	8
Cars with safety stopping devices	22	18	4
Both shafts and cars guarded	22	12	10

FLORIDA.

There were at the time of this investigation no legal provisions relative to the safeguarding of elevators.[1]

CONDITIONS FOUND.

Eleven of the 14 establishments visited had freight elevators. None had passenger elevators.

The following table shows the extent of elevator protection in these 11 establishments:

ESTABLISHMENTS HAVING AND NOT HAVING SPECIFIED SAFEGUARDS ON ALL ELEVATORS—FLORIDA.

Safeguards.	Establishments—		
	Reported on.	With specified safeguards on all elevators—	
		Provided.	Not provided.
Shafts and openings properly guarded	11	11	0
Cars with safety stopping devices	11	8	3
Both shafts and cars guarded	11	8	3

[1] The law here referred to is as in force at the time of the investigation, March, 1909. The text of the laws in force Jan. 1, 1912, is given in the appendixes at the end of this volume.

LOUISIANA.

SUMMARY OF LEGISLATION.[1]

The legislation of Louisiana regarding elevator protection consists of the following provision: [2]

The openings of all hatchways, elevators, and wellholes upon every floor of every manufacturing, mechanical, or mercantile or public buildings where women or children are employed in this State shall be protected by good and sufficient trapdoors of [or] self-closing hatches or safety catches or good strong guardrails at least three feet high.

Penalty.—$25 to $50, or imprisonment 10 to 30 days, or both.

This law, it will be noted, applies only to such establishments as employ women or children. The actual requirements of the law are few and concern themselves solely with one subject—the protection of elevator floor openings.

The requirements are mandatory, although the simplicity of the law's wording leaves a considerable latitude for the exercise of personal judgment in determining when the protective devices supplied are "good and sufficient." The enforcing authorities are the factory inspectors, who, under the Louisiana practice, are local, not State, appointees.[3]

CONDITIONS FOUND.

Twenty of the twenty-nine establishments visited had elevators. The following table shows the completeness of elevator safeguarding in these 20 establishments:

ESTABLISHMENTS HAVING AND NOT HAVING SPECIFIED SAFEGUARDS ON ALL ELEVATORS—LOUISIANA.

Safeguards.	Establishments—		
	Reported on.	With specified safeguards on all elevators—	
		Provided.	Not provided.
Shafts and openings properly guarded....................................	20	16	4
Cars with safety stopping devices...	20	19	1
Both shafts and cars guarded.................	20	16	4

[1] The law here referred to is as in force at the time of the investigation, March, 1909. The text of the laws in force Jan. 1, 1912, is given in the appendixes at the end of this volume.
[2] Acts of 1908, act No. 301, sec. 18 (Bulletin of the Bureau of Labor, No. 85, p. 600).
[3] Ac s of 1906, act No. 34, sec. 6, and (Bulletin of the Bureau of Labor, No. 85, p. 601) Acts of 1908, act 301, sec. 23.

CHAPTER VIII

REPORTING OF ACCIDENTS.

CHAPTER VIII.

REPORTING OF ACCIDENTS.

INTRODUCTION.

Accurate and full information of the character and causes of factory accidents is the material sought by legislators and factory inspectors in their efforts to prevent such accidents. Without such information intelligent and pertinent laws can not be framed nor can the inspection department exercise its influence and authority in the most direct and effective ways.

With this end in view, 10 of the 17 States covered by this report provide by law for the public reporting of factory accidents. These 10 are: Massachusetts, Rhode Island, New York, New Jersey, Pennsylvania, Ohio, Illinois, Indiana, Wisconsin, and Louisiana.[1] In 1 of these, Louisiana, the law applies only to establishments employing children under 18 years of age, or women. In the remaining States—Maine, Michigan, Maryland, North Carolina, Georgia, and Florida—no such reporting is required.[2]

Important differences exist among the accident-reporting requirements of the 10 States having such requirements. These differences may be shown by a brief consideration of the several legal provisions upon the following points: (1) By whom and to whom reports are to be made; (2) kinds of accidents to be reported; and (3) period within which reports are to be forwarded.

Upon the first of these points the laws of 9 of the 10 States considered are alike in requiring accidents to be reported by the individual employer to the State factory inspector or other official with analogous functions. The 1 State which is exceptional in this respect is Wisconsin. Here the law does not require accident reports from employers, but orders simply that every physician and surgeon in the State shall report to the local registrar of vital statistics accidents to persons whom they are called upon professionally to treat.

As regards the second point—kinds of accidents to be reported—the laws of the 10 States under consideration agree in directing that all fatal accidents be reported. But they do not agree as to accidents resulting in injuries not of a fatal character. The object of an

---

[1] Connecticut was added to this list shortly after the field work was completed in that State. See p. 365.

[2] The law here referred to is as in force at the time of the investigation, December, 1908, to April, 1909. The text of the laws in force Jan. 1, 1912, is given in the appendixes at the end of this volume.

accident-reporting law is fulfilled when all accidents causing injuries of a reasonably serious nature are reported. Difficulty arises, however, when an attempt is made to define the terms "serious" or "reasonably serious." To avoid this difficulty 2 States—New York and Indiana—require all accidents, however slight the resulting injuries, to be reported. The Pennsylvania law orders "serious" accidents to be reported, leaving the definition of the term "serious" to the factory inspection department, and Ohio places a similar responsibility upon the factory inspector by the use of the phrase "serious accident resulting in bodily injury." Each of the remaining 6 States under review measures the seriousness of an injury by the period of incapacitation, and provides that only those accidents shall be reported which either have a fatal result or cause the sufferer to be incapacitated from work for a certain period. Illinois fixes this period at 30 days; Rhode Island, New Jersey, Louisiana, and Wisconsin at 2 weeks; and Massachusetts at 4 days.

Of even less uniformity are the laws of the 10 States under review as regards the third of the mentioned points—the period in which accidents are to be reported. The Massachusetts law requires reports to be made "forthwith." Pennsylvania allows 24 hours, and New York and Indiana 48 hours for all reports to be made. New Jersey requires fatal accidents to be reported within 24 hours, but allows 4 weeks and a day for nonfatal accidents. In similar manner, Rhode Island orders fatal accidents to be reported within 48 hours, but allows 3 weeks for those of a nonfatal character, and in Ohio 7 days are allowed for the reporting of fatal accidents and 30 for those of a nonfatal character. In Illinois and Wisconsin no reports need be made in less than 30 days, and the Louisiana law requires semiannual reports only.

In the following pages of this chapter are given for each of the 17 States covered, first, a statement of the law, if any, regarding accident reporting; second, a condensed statement of such information regarding the frequency and character of accidents as is available in the reports and records of the State; and, third, a statement of such data regarding accidents and accident reporting as were obtained by personal visits to the several establishments.

The information of the last of the three-mentioned classes is very incomplete. Effort was made in each of the visited establishments to ascertain the number of accidents resulting in injuries to employees that had occurred during the preceding year, and, if the establishment was in a State in which accident reporting was required, the extent to which such accidents had been reported. Many establishments, however, had no records of accidents, and in others the records were incomplete or unreliable. The information obtained is, therefore, too incomplete to be of much value.

A full statement of the conditions found in each establishment is given in Chapter XI, General Tables, of this volume.

MAINE.

There 'was, at the time of this investigation, no law of Maine requiring the reporting of accidents to the State.[1] The commissioner of industrial and labor statistics favors such a law. In his report for 1908 he says:

We recommend the enactment of a law requiring a report of all accidents, fatal or otherwise, to employees in any industrial or other establishment where labor may be employed, be made to the bureau of industrial and labor statistics, the same to be tabulated and made a part of the annual report of the labor department.[2]

CONDITIONS FOUND.

Accidents causing injury to employees were recorded as having occurred during the year previous by 6 of the 26 establishments visited, the total number of such accidents being 12.

MASSACHUSETTS.

SUMMARY OF LEGISLATION.[1]

By the law of Massachusetts all accidents causing death or four days' loss of time must be reported to the factory-inspection department [the district police]. The provision in detail is as follows:[3]

All manufacturers, manufacturing corporations, and proprietors of mercantile establishments shall forthwith send to the chief of the district police a written notice of any accident to an employee while at work in any * * * establishment operated by them, if the accident results in * * * death * * * or in such bodily injury as to prevent * * * returning to his work within four days thereafter. The chief of the district police shall * * * [acknowledge receipt of notice] and he shall keep a record of all accidents so reported to him, of the name of the person injured, of the city or town in which the accident occurred and the cause thereof, and shall include an abstract of said record in his annual report. * * *

Penalty.—Not more than $20.

The following table shows for the years 1905, 1906, 1907, and 1908 the number of accidents, fatal and not fatal, and the principal causes of such accidents, as reported to the district police and as presented in the annual reports of that department. The report for 1908 covers only 11 months, December 1, 1907, to November 1, 1908. The industries in which the accidents occurred are not shown in these reports.

---

[1] The law here referred to is as in force at the time of the investigation, January, 1909, in Maine, and December, 1908, to February, 1909, in Massachusetts, The text of the laws in force Jan. 1, 1912, is given in the appendixes at the end of this volume.

[2] Twenty-second Annual Report of the Bureau of Industrial and Labor Statistics, Maine, 1908, p. vii.

[3] Rev. Laws, 1902, ch. 106, sec. 17 (22d An. Rept. Com. of Labor, p. 594).

NUMBER OF INDUSTRIAL ACCIDENTS REPORTED TO THE DISTRICT POLICE OF MASSACHUSETTS, BY CAUSES, 1905 TO 1908.

[Compiled from Annual Reports of the Chief of the Massachusetts District Police: 1905 pp. 95, 96, 99, 100; 1906, pp. 107, 108, 113, 114; 1907, pp. 109, 110, 115, 116; 1908, p. 152.]

Cause of accidents.	1905		1906		1907		1908 [1]	
	Fatal.	Other.	Fatal.	Other.	Fatal.	Other.	Fatal.	Other.
Machinery in cotton, woolen, and paper mills and shoe factories............................	......	1,097	4	1,115	2	1,082	2	815
Machinery in planing or saw mills, ironworks, or other mechanical works.................	3	352	3	456	1	457	7	274
Shafting, belting, or pulleys.................	10	75	7	63	7	83	7	133
Elevators, or while working about the same, the majority being caught between car and flooring......................................	11	64	15	75	7	79	7	52
Falling into elevator wells....................	6	5	7	20	7	9	5	9
Falling of elevator cars.......................	1	......	1	8	1	7	......	6
Scalds and burns..............................	3	94	10	108	4	142	1	94
Receiving electric shock......................	4	......	......	2	1	5	4	2	1
Bursting of pulley............................	......	......	......	2	......	......	......	......
Bursting of stone wheel.......................	......	......	1	1	......	......	......	......
Bursting of emery wheel......................	......	......	1	1	......	3	......	......
Breaking of a heeling machine................	......	......	......	1	......	......	......	......
Falling, principally from staging.............	......	69	......	88	......	83	2	188
Falling, other................................	5	95	1	134	5	149	(2)	(2)
Being struck by heavy weights...............	......	71	......	105	1	86	1	165
Flying steel, etc.............................	2	27	4	44	5	26	......	14
Splinters, etc., all being slight in nature.....	......	73	......	70	......	86	......	71
Struck by railroad cars or engines............	......	......	......	......	......	6	......	......
Explosions....................................	1	......	2	......	3	......	......	......
Suffocated....................................	......	......	......	......	3	......	......	......
Miscellaneous................................	......	629	......	827	7	919	8	186
Total......................	46	2,651	58	3,119	64	3,215	42	2,008

[1] Eleven months only.   [2] Probably included under preceding cause.

The report for 1908 explains that of the 2,050 accidents occurring during the 11 months reported upon, "42 were fatal, 470 were serious in their nature, and 1,538 were classified as 'slight injuries.'"[1] This distribution between serious and slight injuries is not shown in the earlier reports.

The report for 1908 also makes the following statement:

Of the total number [of accidents], there were 731 arising from causes other than in the operation of machinery, constituting more than 35 per cent of the entire number reported, and it is assumed that such cases are not of the class to which the law applies. * * * The fact that such accidents * * * are so promptly reported by manufacturers and others, although there would seem to be no legal requirements for so reporting them, would seem to show a desire and intent on the part of those interested to observe the provisions of the law in its broadest sense rather than in any degree to violate any of such provisions.

The chief of the district police explains his attitude toward the investigation of reported accidents as follows:

An investigation is made by an inspector of this department in each case of fatal accident reported, as well as in each case where such an investigation is deemed necessary by the nature and condition reported, in order to ascertain if more adequate means of protection can be

[1] Report of the Chief of the Massachusetts District Police for the year ending Dec. 31, 1908, p. 149.

applied to insure against the possibility of the recurrence of such accidents.[1]

CONDITIONS FOUND.

In 18 of the 44 establishments visited, accidents causing injury to employees were recorded as having occurred during the preceding year, the total number of such accidents being 238. In 2 of these 18 establishments none of the accidents, 4 in total, had caused as much as 4 days' loss of time, and thus reporting to the State was not necessary. By 5 of the remaining 16 establishments such reporting to the State had been done, and had not been done by 2, satisfactory information on this point not being obtained from the other 9.

RHODE ISLAND.

SUMMARY OF LEGISLATION.[2]

The law of Rhode Island requires fatal accidents and those incapacitating the injured party for two weeks or more to be reported to the factory inspector. The provision in full is as follows:[3]

It shall be the duty of the owner or superintendent [of establishments employing 5 or more persons or any child under 16 years of age] to report in writing to the factory inspectors all fatal accidents within 48 hours after their occurrence; all accidents which prevent the injured person or persons from returning to work within 2 weeks after the injury shall, within 1 week after the expiration of such 2 weeks, be reported in writing by the person in charge of such establishment or place to the said inspectors, stating as fully as possible the cause of such accidents.

Penalty.—Not more than $500.

The form used by the factory-inspection department for accident reports is as follows:

STATE OF RHODE ISLAND.

REPORT OF ACCIDENT TO FACTORY INSPECTORS.

(In accordance with Sec. 7, Chap. 1278, Public Laws.)

1. Name and address of establishment...
2. Name and age of person injured..
3. Date of accident...
4. Machine, etc., on which accident occurred....................................
5. Nature and extent of injuries sustained......................................
6. {Time at which accident occurred: } ....
   {Forenoon or afternoon.   }
7. Cause: Carelessness or misfortune?..
   Date.., 19....

---

[1] Report of the Chief of the Massachusetts District Police for the year ending Dec. 31, 1908, pp. 151, 152.

[2] The law here referred to is as in force at the time of the investigation, December, 1908, to February, 1909. The text of the laws in force Jan. 1, 1912, is given in the appendixes at the end of this volume.

[3] Gen. Laws 1896, ch. 68, secs. 7 and 12, as amended by ch. 1215, enacted 1905 (22d An. Rept. Com. of Labor, p. 1209). And see sec. 2 for establishments affected by law.

The chief factory inspector, in an interview with a special agent of the Bureau, stated that fatal accidents are promptly reported, but that there was some difficulty in securing reports of other accidents. However, as the State is small and as the newspapers enable him to trace accidents that may not be officially reported, he believes that few, if any, accidents are not brought to his attention. He maintained that Rhode Island has fewer serious accidents in proportion to the number of employees than any other State. This favorable condition he attributed to four causes: (1) The proper arrangement of factories; (2) the careful guarding of machinery; (3) an intelligent class of employees; and (4) the attention paid to the matter by the inspectors.

The following table shows the number of accidents reported to the State factory-inspection department for the years 1905, 1906, 1907, and 1908, as presented in the annual reports of that department for those years.

In the reports fatal accidents are separately classified, and also serious accidents are distinguished from those of a minor nature. No formal definition or explanation is given of the word "serious" as thus used, but from the accidents listed as serious it would appear that the word is interpreted with considerable strictness.

NUMBER OF INDUSTRIAL ACCIDENTS REPORTED TO THE FACTORY-INSPECTION DEPARTMENT OF RHODE ISLAND, 1905 TO 1908.

[Compiled from Annual Reports of Factory Inspection, Rhode Island: 1905, pp. 14–16; 1906, pp. 14–16; 1907, pp. 14–18; 1908, pp. 15–17.]

Year.	Accidents reported.			
	Fatal.	Serious.	Other.	Total.
1905	2	5	73	80
1906	2	14	70	86
1907	3	28	100	131
1908	2	14	81	97

The industries in which these accidents occurred are not stated in the printed reports except for those accidents which are classified as fatal or serious. For them the following classification has been made:

NUMBER OF FATAL AND SERIOUS INDUSTRIAL ACCIDENTS REPORTED TO THE FACTORY-INSPECTION DEPARTMENT OF RHODE ISLAND, BY INDUSTRIES, 1905 TO 1908.

[Compiled from Annual Reports of Factory Inspection, Rhode Island: 1905, pp. 14–16; 1906, pp. 14–16; 1907, pp. 14–18; 1908, pp. 15–17.]

Industry.	1905		1906		1907		1908	
	Fatal.	Serious.	Fatal.	Serious.	Fatal.	Serious.	Fatal.	Serious.
Cotton textiles	1	4	1	8	3	17		6
Woolen textiles						2	1	1
Worsted textiles			1	1		1	1	2
Dyeing cotton and wool						2		1
Foundry and machine shops	1			2		5		2
Jewelry				1				
Wire works				1				
Electric works				1				
Laundry						1		
Rubber shoes								1
Bakery								1
Total	2	5	2	14	3	28	2	14

CONDITIONS FOUND.

In 14 of the 27 establishments visited accidents resulting in injuries to employees were recorded as having occurred during the preceding year, the number of such accidents being 62. In 9 of these14 establishments none of the injuries received had caused incapacitation from work for as much as two weeks' time. In the remaining 5 establishments accidents causing at least two weeks' loss of time had occurred and, under the law, required reporting to the State factory-inspection department. Such reporting had been done by 4 establishments and had not been done by 1.

CONNECTICUT.

At the time of the field work of this investigation there was no law [1] in Connecticut regarding the reporting of accidents.[2]

---

[1] The law here referred to is as in force at the time of the investigation, February, 1909. The text of the laws in force Jan. 1, 1912, is given in the appendixes at the end of this volume.

[2] By an act passed shortly subsequent to this investigation, however, accident reporting was required. Acts of 1909, ch. 150. (Bulletin of the Bureau of Labor, No. 85, p. 525.) The important features of this law are as follows: Manufacturing and mercantile establishments to report to the State factory inspection department, within 15 days, all accidents causing death or loss of 1 week's time. Report to state name of injured, time of accident, nature of injury, and, if a machine accident, location and character of machine. Reports to be confidential and inspectors not to be witnesses in cases resulting from such accidents unless they are present at the time of the accident. Penalty for not reporting after having received forms for such reports is a fine of not more than $20.

CONDITIONS FOUND.

Accidents resulting in injury to employees and occurring during the preceding year were recorded by 19 of the 35 establishments visited. The total number of such accidents was 718.

NEW YORK.

SUMMARY OF LEGISLATION.[1]

The New York law regarding accident reporting is as follows:[2]

The person in charge of any factory[3] shall report in writing to the commissioner of labor all deaths, accidents, or injuries sustained by any person therein or on the premises, within 48 hours after the time of the accident, death, or injury, stating as fully as possible the cause of the death or the extent and cause of the injury, and the place where the injured person has been sent, with such other or further information relative thereto as may be required by the said commissioner, who may investigate the causes thereof and require such precautions to be taken as will prevent the recurrence of similar happenings. No statement contained in any such report shall be admissible in evidence in any action arising out of the death or accident therein reported.

Penalty.—First offense, $20 to $50; second offense, $50 to $200, or imprisonment not more than 30 days, or both; third offense, not less than $250, or imprisonment not more than 60 days, or both.

This law, it may be observed, is very strict in its requirements. All accidents are to be reported; reports must be made within 48 hours; and all persons in the factory premises, whether employees or not, are to be considered as coming within the scope of the law. The commissioner of labor has modified the strictness of the first requirement—that all accidents be reported—by an administrative order, under which accidents causing less than 5 hours' loss of time need not be reported.

The final provision of the law as quoted—that statements contained in reports of accidents shall not be admissible as evidence in damage suits—was added to the statute in 1907, a number of years after the adoption of the original statute. Its purpose was to increase the fullness and accuracy of accident reports by freeing the employer of the fear that his signed reports might be used against him in suits

---

[1] The law here referred to is as in force at the time of the investigation, December, 1908, and January, 1909. The text of the laws in force Jan. 1, 1912, is given in the appendixes at the end of this volume.

[2] Rev. Stat., 3d ed., 1901, p. 2102, sec. 87 (as amended by ch. 216, Acts of 1906), and p. 2120, sec. 209 (as amended by ch. 506, Acts of 1907). (22d An. Rept. Com. of Labor, p. 914.)

[3] The term "factory" as used in the New York law includes "also any mill, workshop, or other manufacturing or business establishment where one or more persons are employed at labor." Rev. Stat., 3d ed., 1901, p. 2089, sec. 2 (as amended by ch. 550, Acts of 1904).

arising out of the accident. The amendment apparently has been very successful in attaining its object.

The following table shows the number and severity of the accidents occurring in New York State during each of the years 1905, 1906, 1907, and 1908, as reported to the State department of labor. The data of the table are taken from the annual reports of that department for the years mentioned. As the New York law requires accidents to be reported within 48 hours of their occurrence, it is evident that in some cases the person reporting is unable to state with certainty whether a given injury will result ultimately in death or permanent disability, or whether it will be entirely recovered from. Therefore, the division of injuries into those of a temporary character and those of a permanent character is necessarily subject to some degree of error. To meet this difficulty in part the system of classification used in the reports, beginning with that for 1907, introduces an intermediate class of accidents—to include those injuries which are of such a serious nature as to lead to the presumption that they will be permanent in their effects. The table here presented follows the classification used by the reports referred to, but arranges the data in somewhat different form in order to make comparison more convenient.

NUMBER OF INDUSTRIAL ACCIDENTS REPORTED TO THE NEW YORK DEPARTMENT OF LABOR, BY NATURE OF INJURIES, 1905 TO 1908.

[Compiled from Reports of the Bureau of Factory Inspection, New York: 1905, pp. II.12, II.13; 1906, pp. II.216 to II.219; 1907, pp. II.70 to II.73; 1908, pp. 102 to 105.]

Nature of injuries.	1905	1906	1907	1908
Temporary injuries:				
Lacerations	1,570	2,542	3,283	2,401
Burns	518	1,134	1,347	1,030
Cuts	1,454	2,024	2,310	1,730
Bruises	1,055	2,749	3,252	2,445
Sprains (and dislocations, 1905)	336	526	696	690
Fractures	462	576	665	485
Plural injuries	(1)	874	1,679	1,229
Other	404	820	1,066	790
Total	5,799	11,245	14,298	10,800
Serious injuries, probably permanent	(1)	(1)	2,053	1,649
Permanent injuries (not fatal), involving loss of—				
One or more limbs	32	42	54	37
One or both hands or feet	43	44	58	36
One or more fingers	(2)	(2)	1,909	1,168
One or both eyes	27	48	90	57
Internal	62	83	174	114
All other	1,413	1,777	448	337
Total	1,577	1,994	2,733	1,749
Fatal	167	259	344	257
Not reported	20	7	3	....
Grand total	7,563	13,505	19,431	14,455

1 Not reported separately.
2 Not reported separately. Included, probably, under "Other permanent injuries."

Since 1905 the published reports of the New York Bureau of Factory Inspection do not classify by industries the accidents reported except in the case of fatal accidents. The classification as made for fatal accidents in 1908 is presented below:

NUMBER OF PERSONS OF SPECIFIED AGE AND MARITAL CONDITION FATALLY INJURED BY INDUSTRIAL ACCIDENTS, BY INDUSTRIES, 1908—NEW YORK.

[From Report of Bureau of Factory Inspection, New York, 1908, pp. 120, 121.]

Industries.	Age.					Marital condition.		
	Under 16 years	16 and under 18 years.	18 years and over.	Not reported.	Total.	Single.	Married.	Not reported.
Stone, clay and glass products:								
Stone			17	1	18	7	11	
Miscellaneous mineral products..			1		1	1		
Cement and lime			5		5	1	3	1
Brick, tile, and pottery			1		1	1		
Metals, machines, and conveyances:								
Copper, lead, zinc, etc		1	8		9	4	5	
Iron and steel products (including mines)	[1]1	1	[2]51		53	[3]8	43	2
Electrical apparatus			2		2	2		
Vehicles			29		29	7	19	3
Boat and ship building			[4]5		5	2	2	1
Agricultural implements			4		4	1	3	
Wood manufactures	[4]2		15		17	8	9	
Leather and rubber goods	[1]1	1	7		9	4	5	
Chemicals, oils, paints, etc			[2]25		25	[3]7	16	2
Paper and pulp			16		16	6	10	
Printing and paper goods	[1]1		4		5	2	2	1
Textiles		1	9		10	6	3	1
Foods, liquors, and tobacco:								
Cereals, fruit, and groceries			7		7	4	3	
Provisions			1		1	1		
Dairy products	[1]1				1	1		
Bakery products, confectionery, etc			4		4	2	2	
Breweries			2		2	[3]1	.1	
Water, light, and power			11		11	1	8	2
Tunnels			20		20	6	10	4
Transportation and communication..		1	1		2	1	1	
Total	6	5	245	1	257	81	159	17

[1] Not an employee.
[2] Two not employees.
[3] Including one widower.
[4] One not an employee.

The next table shows the accidents reported for the year 1908, classified according to the cause and severity of each. The table is slightly condensed from a similar table in the report of the State bureau of factory inspection.

NUMBER OF ACCIDENTS IN FACTORIES, QUARRIES, AND TUNNEL CONSTRUCTION RESULTING IN INJURIES, BY CAUSE AND NATURE OF INJURIES, 1908—NEW YORK.

[From Report of Bureau of Factory Inspection, New York, 1908, pp. 102–104.]

Cause.	Temporary injuries.	Serious injuries (probably permanent).	Permanent injuries (not fatal).	Fatal.	Total.
MECHANICAL POWER.					
Transmission of power:					
Motors (engines, dynamos, flywheels, etc.)	75	16	¹29	2	122
Air fans, steam pumps, etc	22	7	9	....	38
Gearing	149	56	96	1	302
Set screws	29	2	9	1	41
Shafting	46	6	9	¹8	69
Belts and pulleys	226	28	35	¹15	304
Conveying and hoisting machinery:					
Elevators and lifts	¹166	32	26	¹28	252
Cranes (steam, electric, portable, etc.)	45	14	13	3	75
Hoisting and conveying apparatus, not elsewhere specified	581	92	85	15	773
Locomotives and trains	137	31	27	28	223
Woodworking machines:					
Saws	219	80	179	6	484
Planers	50	18	47	....	¹115
Joiners	21	4	45	....	70
Shapers	27	8	16	....	51
Lathes	8	....	1	....	9
Heading machines	3	1	4	....	8
Other woodworking machines	75	17	26	....	118
Paper and printing machinery:					
Barkers	10	11	14	....	35
Calenders and other paper-making machines	134	46	38	3	221
Paper cutting, stitching, and staying machines	109	47	43	....	199
Printing presses	52	18	31	1	102
Textile machinery:					
Picking machines	14	7	11	....	32
Carding machines	19	6	5	....	30
Spinning machines	29	5	5	....	39
Looms	95	12	9	....	116
Formers, knitting machines, and other textile machinery	93	12	21	2	128
Sewing machines, etc	53	4	7	....	64
Laundry machines	12	2	5	....	19
Leather-working machinery	36	20	24	1	81
Metal-working machinery:					
Stamping machines	133	145	234	....	512
Drilling and milling machines	157	29	40	....	226
Screw machines	16	3	....	....	19
Lathes	92	14	12	....	118
Drop and other power hammers	64	31	17	1	113
Shears	52	8	30	....	90
Rollers	60	12	12	1	85
Other	190	62	50	1	303
Polishing machines:					
Contact with grindstones, emery wheels, etc	45	21	17	....	83
Struck by fragments of polishing wheels	122	17	6	4	149
Other	72	24	11	....	107
Machines used in bakeries, confectionery establishments, etc	14	11	18	1	44
Machines not otherwise specified	235	33	52	4	324
Total	3,787	1,012	1,368	126	6,293
HEAT AND ELECTRICITY.					
Explosives (powder, dynamite, etc.)	¹47	14	13	16	90
Explosion and ignition of gases or dust	84	10	2	5	101
Explosion of boilers, steam pipes, and other machines	37	7	3	¹8	55
Other injuries from steam and hot liquids	184	13	3	....	200
Caustics	83	13	5	....	101
Explosion of molten metals	52	14	2	1	69
Other accidents from molten metals	151	26	3	....	180
Vats, pans, etc. (containing hot liquids or caustics)	40	3	....	8	51
Electricity	209	19	....	13	241
Fire and heat, not elsewhere specified	203	8	3	6	220
Total	1,090	127	34	57	1,308
FALL OF PERSON.					
Fall from ladder, scaffold, platform, etc	258	16	19	10	303
Fall from machinery, trucks, engines, etc	166	7	12	3	188
Fall caused by collapse of support	201	18	10	2	231

¹ One not an employee.

NUMBER OF ACCIDENTS IN FACTORIES, QUARRIES, AND TUNNEL CONSTRUCTION RESULTING IN INJURIES, BY CAUSE AND NATURE OF INJURIES, 1908—NEW YORK—Concluded.

Cause.	Temporary injuries.	Serious injuries (probably permanent).	Permanent injuries (not fatal).	Fatal.	Total.
FALL OF PERSON—concluded.					
Fall through opening in floor, etc.	97	5	5	2	109
Fall in hoistway, shaft, etc.	1 41	3	2	2 13	59
Fall on stairs, etc.	59	4			63
Fall on level by slipping.	107	4	5		116
Fall on level by tripping.	105	3	3		111
All other.	139	13	8	1	161
Total.	1,173	73	64	31	1,341
INJURED BY WEIGHTS.					
Falling rock and earth (quarrying, excavating, etc.).	163	16	10	13	202
Falling pile of material (lumber, coal, cement, etc.).	124	4	7	4	139
Falling walls, doors, and other objects.	679	34	29	4	746
Tools or weights dropped by person injured.	134	7	2		143
Falling objects dropped by other persons.	59	3	4	2	68
Heavy material or parts on which injured persons were at work.	313	34	28		375
Machinery being moved.	90	9	14		113
Falling of material from trucks in transit.	109	5	7		121
Handling of castings, flasks, etc.	342	34	22		398
Handling of stone, ore, etc.	59	10	3	1	73
Handling of lumber, paper, and other material.	251	16	24		291
Loading and unloading.	293	14	19	1	327
Cause insufficiently described for classification.	130	16	17		163
Total.	2,746	202	186	25	3,159
FLYING OBJECTS.					
Struck in eye by piece of metal, glass, etc.	348	77	35		460
Other injuries from flying objects.	125	10	5		140
Total.	473	87	40		600
Vehicles, and accidents caused by animals.	213	34	16	3	266
MISCELLANEOUS.					
Hand tools (hammers, knives, wrenches, files, etc.).	408	39	11		458
Tools in hands of fellow workmen.	89	16	10		115
Injured while fitting and assembling, not elsewhere specified.	89	9	4		102
Caught on nail, wire, sharp projection, etc.	278	23	9		310
Cut on glass.	54	2	3		59
Injured by stepping on nail, sliver, etc.	216	5			221
Inhalation of poisonous gases.	28	1		5	34
All other causes.	156	19	4	10	189
Total.	1,318	114	41	15	1,488
Grand total.	10,800	1,649	1,749	257	14,455

1 One not an employee.   2 Two not employees.

CONDITIONS FOUND.

In 17 of the 36 establishments visited accidents resulting in injuries to employees were recorded as having occurred during the preceding year, the total number of such accidents being 110. In 6 of these 17 establishments all such accidents had been reported to the State department of labor; in 2 only such accidents as the employer regarded as "serious" has been reported; and in 1 where 10 accidents had been recorded none had been reported to the State. In the remaining 8 establishments satisfactory information on this point was not obtained.

NEW JERSEY.

SUMMARY OF LEGISLATION.[1]

On the subject of accident reporting the law of New Jersey provides that:

All accidents that prevent the injured person or persons from returning to work within 2 weeks, or which result in death, shall be reported in writing to the department [of labor] * * * within 24 hours after the expiration of 4 weeks or after the death of such person injured, as the same may be.[2]

Penalty.—$50 for each offense.

The published reports of the State department of labor for 1906 and 1907 give no information regarding the accidents reported during those years. The reports for 1905 and 1908 give the number of accident reports received by the department during each of those years (350 in 1905, 508 in 1908), but give no further information regarding these accidents.[3]

That the reporting of accidents was incomplete and that the department previously had placed no emphasis upon the enforcement of the law regarding accident reporting is recognized in a circular letter addressed to manufacturers by the department under date of November 10, 1908. This letter, after calling attention to the legal requirements in the matter of accident reporting, concludes as follows: "We trust that the manufacturers of the State will more thoroughly cooperate with the department in this respect, but we are writing this circular letter as a notification of the fact that in the future the department will insist upon a strict compliance with the provisions of the law enunciated in this communication, and will, in the event of noncompliance, feel justified in enforcing the penalty provided by law."

The annual report of the department following the issue of this letter states that reports had been received of 1,134 as against 508 during the preceding year. Again, however, no details regarding accidents are given.[4]

CONDITIONS FOUND.

In 9 of the 27 establishments visited accidents resulting in injuries to employees were recorded as having occurred during the preceding year, the number of such accidents being 90. In 4 of these 9 establishments none of the injured persons had been incapacitated from work for as much as two weeks' time. In the remaining 5 establishments, as the injured persons had been incapacitated for at least

---

[1] The law here referred to is as in force at the time of the investigation, December, 1908, and January, 1909. The text of the laws in force Jan. 1, 1912, is given in the appendixes at the end of this volume.

[2] Acts of 1904, ch. 64, secs. 28 and 30 (22d An. Rept. Com. of Labor, p. 864).

[3] Report of Department of Labor, New Jersey, 1908, p. 9.

[4] Idem, 1909, p. 8.

2 weeks, the reporting of these accidents to the State department of labor was required by law. In none of these cases, however, was information upon this point obtained.

PENNSYLVANIA.

SUMMARY OF LEGISLATION.[1]

The Pennsylvania requirement regarding accident reporting is as follows:[2]

It shall be the duty of the owner or superintendent of any establishment to report, in writing, to the chief factory inspector every serious accident or serious injury done to any person in his or her employ, where such accident or serious injury occurred in or about the premises where employed, within 24 hours after the accident or injury occurs, stating as fully as possible the cause of such accident or injury; and in all fatal and serious accidents the chief factory inspector or his deputy may subpoena witnesses, administer oaths, and do whatever may be necessary in order to make a thorough and complete investigation of the same: *Provided. however.* That the provisions of this section shall not be construed as interfering with the duties of coroners under existing laws.

Penalty.—$25 to $500, or 10 to 60 days' imprisonment, for each offense.

The law thus calls for the reporting of all accidents causing serious injury. It does not define the word "serious." The factory inspection department issued specific instructions to manufacturers not to report accidents such as cuts and bruises not of a serious nature. This lack of precision in determining what accidents are to be reported has led, it is believed, to considerable indifference toward the law on the part of manufacturers.

The following table shows the number of accidents reported to the department of factory inspection during each of the years 1905, 1906, 1907, and 1908. The table is compiled from the data published in the annual reports of the chief inspector. As the data are not given in the same form in each of these reports, and as, in some cases, the explanation of the meaning of the data is not clear, the table is necessarily incomplete. The chief factory inspector states that although the law calls for accident reports from "any establishment" he has no jurisdiction regarding the prevention of accidents except those occurring in or about "machinery, elevators, flywheels, boilers, pits, vats, etc." (as mentioned in the law relating to the safeguarding of machinery).[3] As a result, his annual reports are concerned

[1] The law here referred to is as in force at the time of the investigation, January to March, 1909. The text of the laws in force Jan. 1, 1912, is given in the appendixes at the end of this volume.

[2] Acts of 1905, act No. 226, secs. 20 and 23, also Brightly's Purdon's Digest, 12th ed., 1895, p. 865, sec. 18 (22d An. Rept. Com. of Labor, pp. 1079, 1179).

[3] See Annual Reports of Factory Inspector, Pennsylvania, 1905, p. 4; 1906, p. 5; and 1908, p. 6.

almost solely with accidents occurring in connection with places or things over which he has such jurisdiction. In the reports for 1906 and 1907 all accidents reported to the department are listed, whether or not they come within what the chief inspector considers to be its jurisdiction. For 1905 and 1908, however, it would appear that the accidents listed in the annual reports are only such as come "within the jurisdiction of the department." In no case, however, do these reports include accidents in mines or on railroads.

NUMBER OF ACCIDENTS REPORTED TO THE CHIEF FACTORY INSPECTOR OF PENN-
SYLVANIA, 1905 TO 1908.

From Annual Reports of the Factory Inspector, Pennsylvania: 1905, pp. 3, 4; 1906, p. 26; 1907, pp. 16, 17;
1908, pp. 18, 19.]

Year.	Within jurisdiction of factory inspector.			Not within jurisdiction of factory inspector.			Total.		
	Fatal.	Non-fatal.	All.	Fatal.	Non-fatal.	All.	Fatal.	Non-fatal.	All.
1905........................	162	923	1,085	(¹)	(¹)	(¹)	162	923	1,085
1906........................	60	844	904	171	1,295	1,466	231	2,139	² 2,370
1907........................	59	589	648	236	1,775	2,011	295	2,364	² 2,659
1908........................	114	³ 1,256	1,370	(¹)	(¹)	(¹)	114	1,256	1,370

¹ Data not given in factory inspector's report.
² In the report the items sum up differently from the totals shown, but in this table the items have been assumed to be correct in preference to the totals.
³ Of these, 336 are reported as "serious" and 920 as "slight."

For the years 1905, 1906, and 1907 accidents are classified simply as fatal and nonfatal. For the year 1908, however, a separation of the 1,256 nonfatal accidents is made into serious, 336 in number, and slight, 920 in number.

Commenting upon the accident returns in the report of 1906, the chief factory inspector says: "Of the seriously injured at least 20 per cent of the number could, with propriety, have been reported among the killed, the nature of their injuries precluding the possibility of any recovery."[1]

The next table classifies the fatal and serious accidents reported in 1908, by cause of accident.

---

[1] Annual Report of the Factory Inspector, Pennsylvania, 1906, p. 5.

NUMBER OF ACCIDENTS REPORTED TO THE CHIEF FACTORY INSPECTOR OF PENN-
SYLVANIA, BY CAUSES, 1908.

[From Annual Report of the Factory Inspector, Pennsylvania, 1908, pp. 18, 19.]

Causes.	Fatal.	Serious.
Belting, pulleys, and shafting..	9	16
Burns..	1	14
Cranes and hoisting chains..	15	40
Engines and cars in or about establishments................................	14	11
Elevators..	6	9
Electric wires..	2	1
Explosions...	15	25
Falls from ladders, etc., and tripping during employment.....................	16	52
Falling substances, injuring men during employment........................	13	43
Flying substances, injuring men during employment........................	4	3
Fire escapes, jumping from...	4	13
Gearing...	3	75
Molding machines..	1	....
Saws..	2	14
Set screws...	2	10
Shapers, joiners, and planers..	3	10
Suffocations..	4	....
Total...	114	336

CONDITIONS FOUND.

In 12 of the 50 establishments accidents causing injuries to employees were recorded as having occurred during the preceding year,
the total number of such accidents being 77. In 3 of these 12 establishments all such accidents had been reported to the State factory
inspection department. For the other 9 no satisfactory information
on this point was obtained.

OHIO.

SUMMARY OF LEGISLATION.[1]

The requirements of the Ohio law regarding accident reporting are
very detailed. The law reads as follows: [2]

It shall be the duty of all manufacturers [3] * * * to forward by
mail to the chief inspector of workshops and factories * * * a
report of each and every serious accident, resulting in bodily injury
to any person, which may occur in their establishment, giving particulars of the same as fully as can be ascertained, upon blanks which
shall be furnished by the chief inspector * * *. If death shall
result to any employee from any such accident, said report shall contain the age, name, sex, and employment of the deceased, whether

---

[1] The law here referred to is as in force at the time of the investigation, March, 1909.
The text of the laws in force Jan. 1, 1912, is given in the appendixes at the end of this
volume.

[2] Bates' Ann. Stat., 3d ed., Pt. I, Political, secs. 2573–1, 2573–2 (22d An. Rept.
Com. of Labor, pp. 999, 1000).

[3] "The term manufacturer * * * shall be held to mean any person who * * *
[in any capacity] makes or causes to be made, or who deals in any kind of goods or
merchandise, or who owns, controls, or operates any street railway or laundering establishment, or is engaged in the construction of buildings, bridges, or structures, or in
loading or unloading vessels or cars, or moving heavy materials, or operating dangerous machinery, or in the manufacture or use of explosives." Bates' Ann. Stat.,
3d ed., Pt. I, Political, sec. 2573–2 (22d An. Rept. Com. of Labor, p. 1000).

married, the number of persons, if any, deprived of support in consequence thereof, and the cause of the accident, if known. If the accident has caused bodily injury of such a nature as to prevent the person injured from returning to his or her employment within six or more days after the occurrence of the accident, then the report shall contain the age, name, sex, and employment of the disabled, the nature and extent of the injury received, how caused, if known, how long continuously disabled, loss of time and wages therefrom, and if possible the expenses thereby incurred in full.

Any manufacturer who shall fail to comply with the requirements of this act in each case of death by accident within 7 days thereafter, and in each case of injury by accident within 30 days thereafter, shall be deemed guilty of a misdemeanor, and on conviction thereof * * * shall be fined in any sum not less than $10 nor more than $50.

The expression "serious accident resulting in bodily injury" is interpreted strictly by the factory-inspection department and, in practice, all accidents, including even those of comparatively minor nature, are subject to reporting. The law specifies in detail the form in which the reports are to be made out and directs the chief inspector to supply manufacturers with blanks prepared according to this form. The blank form in use is as follows:

ACCIDENT BLANK.

Accident causing death must be reported within SEVEN days after death ensues; accident causing injury must be reported within THIRTY days after injury, or as soon thereafter as the questions on blank can be accurately answered.

Name of manufacturer, firm, company, or contractor, ...

City or town, ... Street and number, ...

County, ...

ACCIDENT RESULTING FATALLY.

Name, ... Sex, ... Age, ... years. Married or single, ...

Time of day deceased began work, ... Time of accident, ...

Date of accident, ... Date of death, ...

Cause of accident, ...

At what employed, ...

Number of persons deprived of support in consequence of accident, ...

ACCIDENT PREVENTING RETURN TO WORK IN SIX OR MORE DAYS.

Name, ... Sex, ... Age, ... years. Married or single, ...

Address of injured person, ...

Time of day injured began work, ... Time of accident, ...

Date of injury, ... Cause of accident (on what kind of machinery or how injured), ...

At what employed, ...

Was injured person familiar with work at which engaged and machinery which he was operating? ....

Was machinery in good order and guarded so as to prevent accident under ordinary circumstances? ....

If not guarded, why? ....

Nature and extent of injury (description): ....

Number of persons deprived of support in consequence of accident, ...
How long continuously disabled on account of accident, ...
Amount of expense incurred to injured person on account of accident, whether paid
  by injured or other person, ... $.......
Loss of time to injured person, ... working days. Loss of wages, $.......

GENERAL REMARKS.

[Describe how accident occurred.]

It will be noted that the data called for by the form cover not only the physical aspect of the injury but also what may be called its social aspect. Thus information is required as to the number of persons deprived of support in consequence of accident, and, when the injury is not fatal, the money loss in wages and the expense incurred by the injured person as a result of the accident.

The summary statements of accidents prepared from the reports received by the department and published in its annual reports are made in considerable detail. The following table, compiled from these statements, shows the number of accidents reported in each of the four years 1905, 1906, 1907, and 1908, classified by severity. The classification is into three classes—fatal, serious, and minor. The department does not state the exact interpretation placed by it upon the word "serious."

NUMBER OF INDUSTRIAL ACCIDENTS REPORTED TO THE DEPARTMENT OF INSPEC-
TION OF WORKSHOPS, FACTORIES, AND PUBLIC BUILDINGS OF OHIO, 1905 TO 1908.

[Compiled from Annual Reports of the Department of Inspection of Workshops, Factories, and Public
  Buildings, Ohio: 1905, pp. 209-211; 1906, p. 267; 1907, pp. 343-347; 1908, pp. 168, 169.]

	1905	1906	1907	1908
Fatal	59	103	252	105
Serious	253	332	485	397
Minor	957	1,433	1,290	752
Total	1,269	1,868	2,027	1,254

The next table, slightly condensed from a corresponding table in the department's report for 1908, classifies the reported accidents for that year by industries and by severity of injury.

NUMBER OF INDUSTRIAL ACCIDENTS REPORTED TO THE DEPARTMENT OF INSPECTION OF WORKSHOPS, FACTORIES, AND PUBLIC BUILDINGS OF OHIO, BY INDUSTRIES AND SEVERITY OF INJURY, 1908.

[From Report of Department of Inspection of Workshops, etc., Ohio, 1908, pp. 168, 169.]

Industry.	Fatal.	Serious.	Minor.	Total.
Iron industry:				
Blast furnaces, steel and bar mills	30	174	129	333
Boiler making	2	2	4	8
Can factories		7	6	13
Foundries	5	26	29	60
Manufacturing machinery	4	24	36	64
Miscellaneous iron industries	3	6	20	29
Sheet and tin plate mills	5	9	10	24
Shovel and plow making		7	13	20
Stamping and enameling	4	5	12	21
Automobiles, wagons, buggies, and metal wheels		7	13	20
Bridge and ship building	2	6	6	14
Car building and repairing	5	42	370	417
Chemicals, oils, and drugs	2	8	5	15
Clay and mineral products		11	8	19
Clothing and millinery			1	1
Contractors	9	3	1	13
Food products and confections	9	3	7	19
Glass	2	4	6	12
High explosives	6	1	2	9
Laundries		1	1	2
Leather and rubber goods	1	7	6	14
Mercantile establishments and hotels	1	1	2	4
Miscellaneous industries	2	9	7	18
Musical instruments			1	1
Paper, jute, and strawboard		5	5	10
Power houses and lighting plants	7	9	8	24
Printing and lithographing	2	3	2	7
Textiles	1	4	1	6
Tobacco and liquors	1	2	7	10
Woodworking industries	2	11	34	47
Total	105	397	752	1,254

The causes of these 1,254 accidents, as shown in the same report, were as follows:

NUMBER OF INDUSTRIAL ACCIDENTS REPORTED TO THE DEPARTMENT OF INSPECTION OF WORKSHOPS, FACTORIES, AND PUBLIC BUILDINGS OF OHIO, BY CAUSES AND SEVERITY, 1908.

[From Report of Department of Inspection of Workshops, etc., Ohio, 1908, pp. 168, 169.]

Causes.	Fatal.	Serious and minor.
Elevators	4	18
Explosions	8	20
Woodworking machines	1	55
Machines other than woodworking	6	149
Cranes, hoists, conveyors	5	25
Belts, shafts, pulleys, and set screws	12	38
Handling iron and steel products	5	169
Hit and falling	36	213
Wheels and presses	3	47
Working around cars	1	92
Furnaces and molten metal	3	39
Slivers, chippings, scales		53
Hand tools		86
Electric wires and dynamos	5	5
High explosives	5	1
Handling lumber	1	32
Steam pipes		10
Unclassified or other causes	10	97
Total	105	1,149

CONDITIONS FOUND.

In 13 of the 60 establishments visited accidents resulting in injuries to employees were recorded as having occurred during the preceding year, the total number of such accidents being 54. In each of these cases a report of the accident had been made to the State factory inspection department. •

ILLINOIS.

SUMMARY OF LEGISLATION.[1]

By an act which became operative July 1, 1907, the State of Illinois provided for accident reporting in the following terms: [2]

It shall be the duty of every person, firm, or corporation employing laborers, artisans, mechanics, miners, clerks, or any other servants or employees of any character to make a report to the State bureau of labor statistics of every serious injury entailing a loss of 30 or more days' time, injury or death of every employee caused by accident while in the performance of any duty or service for such employer within 30 days from the date of such injury or death. Such report shall give the name of the employer, character of business of such employer, where located, date of injury or death, name of person killed or injured, character of employment of service, and cause of such injury or death, and when injury alone, then the character and extent of such injury, residence, nativity, and age of the person injured or killed, whether married or single, and, if known, how many persons are dependent upon such employee.

It shall be the duty of the State bureau of labor statistics to cause such reports to be made and to enforce the provisions of this act and shall cause all of such accidents or deaths by accidents to be classified into trades or kinds of employment, and shall cause the same to be published at least once each year on or before January 1.

Penalty.—$25 to $200.

The distinctive points to be noted in this law are, first, that reports are to be made only for fatal accidents or those causing loss of 30 days' time; and, second, that the reports are to be sent to the bureau of labor statistics, which bureau is entirely separate from the factory inspection department.

The act just quoted was in force at the time the field work of this investigation in Illinois was being done (December, 1908, to February, 1909), but was superseded shortly thereafter (June, 1909) by an act which in many respects was of a radically different character. Thus, under the later act, accident reports are to be made to the factory inspection department instead of to the bureau of labor as formerly provided, and accidents causing a loss of 15 days' time are to be reported and not merely those causing a loss of 30 days. The

---

[1] The law here referred to is as in force at the time of the investigation, December, 1908, to February, 1909. The text of the laws in force Jan. 1, 1912, is given in the appendixes at the end of this volume.

[2] Acts of 1907, p. 308, secs. 1, 2, and 3 (22d An. Rept. Com. of Labor, p. 375).

later act also contains a provision, absent from the earlier act, by which no statement contained in an accident report is admissible in any damage suit arising out of the accident.

Section 24 of the act is as follows:[1]

It shall be the duty of the owner or lessee or superintendent or person in charge of any factory, mercantile establishment, mill, or workshop in this State to send to the chief State factory inspector, in writing, an immediate report of all accidents or injuries resulting in death. It shall also be the duty of the person in charge of such factory, mercantile establishment, mill, or workshop to report between the 15th and 25th of each month all accidents or injuries occurring during the previous calendar month, which entailed a loss to the person injured of 15 consecutive days' time or more. All reports shall state the cause and character of the injury, character of employment, and the age and sex of the person injured. No statement contained in any such report shall be admissible in evidence in any action arising out of the death or accident therein reported: *Provided*, That any such employer who shall make the reports of accidents, required by this act, shall not be required to make such reports to any other State officer, board, or commission.

The report of the State bureau of labor statistics for 1908 gives a full tabular presentation of the accidents reported to it under the act of 1907. The data are for the latter six months of the year only, and because of the newness of the law the records are recognized by the bureau as being "presumably incomplete." [2] The following table is from the report referred to. It gives a summary statement of the accident reports received, classified as fatal and nonfatal, by industries, and by number of causes and number of reporting employers. As only such accidents were reported as caused a loss of at least 30 days' time,[3] all the accidents here listed as nonfatal may reasonably be assumed to have been of a serious nature.

---

[1] Acts of 1909, p. 202, sec. 24 (Bulletin of the Bureau of Labor, No. 85, p. 550).
[2] Fifteenth Biennial Report of Bureau of Labor Statistics, Illinois, 1908, p. 6.
[3] Idem, p. 14.

FATAL AND NONFATAL ACCIDENTS IN SPECIFIED INDUSTRIES, PERSONS KILLED AND INJURED, WITH NUMBER OF CAUSES, OCCUPATIONS, AND EMPLOYERS, JULY 1 TO DECEMBER 31, 1907—ILLINOIS.

[From Fifteenth Biennial Report of Bureau of Labor Statistics, Illinois, 1908, p. 13.]

Industries.	Fatal accidents.				Nonfatal accidents.			
	Persons killed.	Number of causes.	Number of occupations.	Number of employers.	Persons injured.	Number of causes.	Number of occupations.	Number of employers.
Beef packing.........	5	3	2	3	17	14	6	4
Coal mining.........	100	16	14	59	287	30	31	67
Contracting.........	6	5	3	4	10	6	4	7
Manufacturing.......	37	30	16	22	302	63	78	76
Total...........	148	54	35	88	616	113	119	154
Railroading:								
Elevated.........					4	3	4	2
Interurban.......	3	3	2		8	5	3	5
Steam...........	129	38	26	33	412	78	39	47
Street...........	8	7	4	3	22	12	9	2
Underground....	1	1	1	1	10	7	7	1
Total..........	141	49	33	39	456	105	62	57
Stone quarrying......	3	3	2	2	7	27	2	1
Miscellaneous........	6	6	6	6	15	10	10	9
Grand total....	298	112	76	135	1,094	255	193	221

The form provided by the bureau of labor statistics for the reporting of accidents was as follows:[1]

STATE BUREAU OF LABOR STATISTICS.

SPRINGFIELD, ILLINOIS.

(Date of reporting accident) ......, .., 19...

Employer, name of...

Kind of business...

Where located..

Date of injury or death...

Name of person injured or killed..

Kind of employment..

Cause of injury or death..

If injury alone, character and extent of...

....

Probable period of disability..

(Please state as near as possible about how long this person will be disabled.)

Residence..

Nativity............. Age......... Married............. Single..............

How many persons dependent upon such employee...............................

NOTE.—Each accident must be reported on a separate blank. Do not report any nonfatal injury until the expiration of thirty (30) days. This form can be used in reporting either fatal or nonfatal accidents by erasing the word "injured" or "killed" in accordance with the facts in the respective cases.

For copy of the law see other side of this sheet.

Address to

SECRETARY BUREAU OF LABOR STATISTICS.

SPRINGFIELD, ILLINOIS.

Report received....... .. 19...

[1] Fifteenth Biennial Report of the Bureau of Labor Statistics, Illinois, 1908, pp. 7, 8.

CONDITIONS FOUND.

In 23 of the 47 establishments visited accidents resulting in injuries to employees were recorded as having occurred during the preceding year, the total number of accidents being 822. By 4 of these 23 establishments reports of such accidents had been made to the State authorities; by 2 no such report had been made; by 2 it was stated that as none of the accidents recorded has caused as much as 30 days' loss of time, reporting to the State was not required by law; in the remaining 15 establishments information upon this point was not secured.

INDIANA.

SUMMARY OF LEGISLATION.[1]

The Indiana law regarding accident reporting directs that:[2]

It shall be the duty of the owner, agent, superintendent, or other person having charge of any manufacturing or mercantile establishment, mine, quarry, laundry, renovating works, bakery, or printing office within this State, or of any floor or part thereof, to report in writing to the chief inspector all accidents or injury done to any person in such premises within 48 hours of the time of the accident, stating as fully as possible the extent and cause of such injury, and the place where the injured person is sent, with such other information relative thereto as may be required by the chief inspector.

The chief inspector is hereby authorized and empowered to fully investigate the causes of such accident, and to require such reasonable precautions to be taken as will, in his judgment, prevent the recurrence of similar accidents.

Penalty.—First offense, not more than $50; second offense, not more than $100; to which may be added imprisonment for not more than 10 days; third offense, not less than $250 and not more than 30 days' imprisonment.

The law thus requires all accidents to be reported. The inspection department, however, in order not to overburden the records, informed employers that reports were desired only in the case of accidents of a serious nature. No standard was suggested as to what constitutes a "serious" accident, and as a result a wide diversity of practice exists. It was found in the course of this investigation that some factories reported all accidents requiring medical attention, that others reported only those causing a loss of at least two weeks' time, while one establishment stated that its practice was to report only such accidents as caused death or permanent disability.

---

[1] The law here referred to is as in force at the time of the investigation, February and March, 1909. The text of the laws in force Jan. 1, 1912, is given in the appendixes at the end of this volume.

[2] Ann. Stat. of 1894, Rev. of 1901, sec. 7087h and 7087y (22d An. Rept. Com. of Labor, pp. 399, 402).

The law specifies certain data which each accident report must contain, and in addition it authorizes the chief inspector to require such additional information as he may consider desirable. The form used by the inspection department is in blank, as follows:

DEPARTMENT OF INSPECTION, STATE OF INDIANA.

ACCIDENT REPORT.

Name of establishment...

City or town........................... Street and number....................

Kind of business or output..

Name of person injured....................... Age........ Sex...........

Married........ Residence................. Street and number...............

Date of injury..................... Time, ...a. m................p. m.

Does he speak English......................... Piece or day worker.............

Nature and extent of injury..

....

Fatal......................... Serious.................... Slight...............

Probable length of disability..

Where injured person was sent..

Physician employed............................. At whose expense............

At what employed when injured..

Cause (by what kind of machinery, or otherwise, and how done)...................

Was machine or other cause guarded............. If not, why..................

Was injured person regularly employed on such machine..........................

Had injured person worked on similar machinery prior to this employment.........

How can such accidents be guarded against or prevented..........................

....

    Date of reporting......................

....
[Signature of firm or person reporting.]

The following table shows the number of accidents reported for the years 1905, 1906, 1907, and 1908, classified according to seriousness. The data of this table are derived from the annual reports of the State factory inspection department for the years named.

NUMBER OF ACCIDENTS REPORTED TO THE DEPARTMENT OF INSPECTION OF INDIANA, BY SEVERITY OF INJURY, 1905 TO 1908.

[Compiled from Annual Reports of the Department of Inspection, Indiana,: 1905, p. 8; 1906, p. 12; 1907, p. 10; 1909, p. 8.]

	Accidents reported in the year—			
	1905	1906	1907	1908
Fatal......	47	39	62	69
Serious, i. e., loss of 25 days or more...............	(1)	(1)	454	364
Slight, i. e., loss of from 5 to 25 days............	(1)	(1)	455	442
Very slight, i. e., loss of under 5 days................	(1)	(1)	1,316	773
All accidents reported.................	1,250	2,087	2,287	1,648

¹ Not shown in annual report.

The next table classifies the fatal, serious, and slight accidents reported for the year 1908, by the industrial divisions in which they occurred. The table is condensed from a table given in the report of the State inspection department for that year. The slight discrepancies in the figures here given for serious and slight accidents as compared with the totals given in the preceding table occur in the original report.

ACCIDENTS RESULTING IN FATAL, SERIOUS, OR SLIGHT INJURIES REPORTED TO THE DEPARTMENT OF INSPECTION OF INDIANA, BY INDUSTRIES, 1908.

[From Twelfth Annual Report of the Department of Inspection, Indiana, 1908, pp. 244–248.]

Industries.	Fatal.	Serious.	Slight.
Clay and mineral industries	6	28	31
Corn and malt products		6	5
Explosives	31	25	2
Food products	1	4	13
Garments and wearing apparel		1	4
Glass industries	1	1	11
Leather industries			3
Metal industries	13	150	214
Musical instruments			1
Paints, oils, varnish, japans, and glue		3	2
Paper, jute, box, and strawboard		13	14
Printing, binding, lithographing, stencils		5	3
Public utilities	2	6	3
Rubber industries		2	2
Textile industries		10	7
Woodworking industries	3	90	93
Buggies, carriages, and wagons	1	7	13
Miscellaneous and unclassified	11	17	19
Total	69	368	440

CONDITIONS FOUND.

In 25 of the 47 establishments visited accidents resulting in injuries to employees were recorded as having occurred during the preceding year, the total number of such accidents being 491. In 17 of these 25 establishments all such accidents had been reported to the State factory inspection department; in 1 in which 15 accidents were recorded, only those causing more than one week's disability were reported; and in the remaining 7 establishments none of the accidents had been reported. In 1 of these latter establishments, in which 15 accidents were recorded as having occurred during the preceding year, it was stated that only such accidents as caused permanent disability were ever reported. The authority of a factory inspector was claimed for this interpretation of the law.

MICHIGAN.

There was, at the time of this investigation,[1] no law requiring accidents to be reported to the State. The State factory inspectors, however, are instructed by the chief of the bureau to obtain at every visit to a factory a list of the accidents that have occurred since the

[1] March, 1909. The text of the laws in force Jan. 1, 1912, is given in the appendixes at the end of this volume.

last visit. The data thus obtained, recognized as very incomplete, are published in the annual reports of the bureau of labor and industrial statistics.

CONDITIONS FOUND.

Accidents causing injuries to employees, and occurring during the year preceding, were recorded by 12 of the 19 visited establishments. The total of accidents so recorded was 97. None of these accidents was fatal, but at least 1 was of a very serious character. This occurred in a confectionery establishment. A girl, stooping to pick up paper from the floor, had her hair caught in the rod of an enrobing machine and a part of her scalp was torn off.

WISCONSIN.

SUMMARY OF LEGISLATION.[1]

The State of Wisconsin has the following legal provisions regarding accident reporting:[2]

It shall be the duty of all physicians and surgeons practicing in this State to report within 30 days to the local registrar of vital statistics of the district, any accident to any person whom they are called upon to care for professionally when such person is thereby incapacitated from pursuing his usual vocation for a period of 2 weeks or more, using such form of certificate as may be provided by the State bureau of vital statistics.

Penalty.—Not specified.

The system of accident reporting provided for by this law is, it will be noted, peculiar to Wisconsin among the States covered by this investigation. Its distinguishing points are three: First, accidents are to be reported by physicians and surgeons, not by employers; second, reports are to be made to public health officials, not to the bureau in charge of labor and factory inspection matters; and, third, physicians and surgeons are to report all accidents arising in the course of their respective practices and not merely such accidents as are specifically of an industrial character.

Although, as has been noted, the State bureau of labor and industrial statistics has nothing to do with the collection of accident statistics, it tabulates the returns made under the law above quoted and publishes the results of such tabulation as part of its regular duties. In these published reports the accident data is presented in very considerable detail. The accuracy of the original data, however, is seriously questioned by the State bureau. The criticism concerns the system of accident reporting by physicians and surgeons.

---

[1] The law here referred to is as in force at the time of the investigation, March, 1909. The text of the laws in force Jan. 1, 1912, is given in the appendixes at the end of this volume.

[2] Ann. Stat. of 1898, Supp. of 1906, Acts of 1907, secs. 1022–1053 (22d An. Rept. Com. of Labor, p. 1409).

In the report of the bureau for 1907–8 it is said: [1]

It is very probable that these records are far from complete. In order to throw some light upon this matter all the physicians whose names appear on the accidents certificates for Milwaukee County for one year were counted. All of the accidents were reported by 162 physicians, which is about 40 per cent of the total number of the physicians in that county. It is improbable that the other 60 per cent could have been without accident cases. The same conclusion is indicated by examining a list of the establishments in Milwaukee County from which the accidents were reported, and also a list of the more prominent concerns from which no accidents were reported. This incompleteness, however, probably does not exist for the fatal accidents in Milwaukee County, because the coroner was active in reporting these when a physician did not do so. On the whole, we may say that the Wisconsin method of reporting accidents, although it yields a useful body of statistics, has not resulted in a complete enumeration of accidents and will not do so until considerable effort has been expended in educating the physicians of the State. It is one argument in favor of a system of compensation for all accidents to workingmen while employed that it would result in an automatic reporting of accidents. But, still, the reports by physicians have the advantage that they tell us something about all classes of accidents. The nonindustrial accidents are not far from being as numerous as the industrial accidents. Accidents present a broad social problem and not merely one phase of the relation between master and servant.

And again in the report for 1909–10: [2]

That the physicians do not report nearly all of the accidents was pointed out in the previous report. As further evidence on this point, we may compare the physicians' returns of railroad accidents with the reports to the Wisconsin Railroad Commission.

The railroad companies apparently report only the accidents from the operation of trains, and not those happening to employees in shops. The physicians report both kinds, as they are supposed to report all accidents that happen. If we eliminate from the physicians' returns of railroad accidents those happening to machinists, carpenters, etc., in shops, so as to make them compare with the railroad commission's figures, we find that in the same months (October 1, 1907, to October 1, 1908) the railroad commission received reports of 1,528 accidents as against 765 reported by physicians, that is, the physicians reported one-half as many. If this same incompleteness exists for all classes of accidents, the total number of accidents to employees while at work in Wisconsin was about 10,000 in 1907–8. A further evidence of the incompleteness of physicians' reports is shown by the fact that at least 50 fatal cases were noted in a Milwaukee newspaper in one year which were not reported by physicians.

---

[1] Thirteenth Biennial Report of the Bureau of Labor and Industrial Statistics, Wisconsin, 1907–8, pp. 10, 11.

[2] Fourteenth Biennial Report of the Bureau of Labor and Industrial Statistics, Wisconsin, 1909-10, Pt. II, Industrial Accidents in Wisconsin, pp. 72, 73.

The legal provision regarding accident reporting, as above described, went into effect in 1905. Data regarding accident reports made under this provision are available for the years 1906, 1907, and 1908 (year ending October 1 in each case).

The following table shows, for each of these three years, the total number of accidents reported, and for 1907 and 1908 the number of such accidents which were of an industrial character. For 1906 the latter information is not given in the published reports.

ACCIDENTS REPORTED TO PUBLIC HEALTH OFFICIALS BY PHYSICIANS AND SUR-
GEONS, 1906 TO 1908—WISCONSIN.

[Compiled from Biennial Reports of Bureau of Labor and Industrial Statistics, Wisconsin: 1907-1908, pp.
6, 7; 1909-1910, Pt. II, p. 71.]

Year ending October 1—	All.	Indus-trial.	Per cent indus-trial of all.
1906.	11,481	(1)	....
1907.	13,572	7,186	53.0
1908.	10,392	5,003	48.0

1 Information not available.

The next table classifies the industrial accidents reported according as the resulting injury caused death, permanent disability, or tempo-rary disability. The distinction between the two latter classes rep-resents in each case simply the prognosis of the physician made at the time the report was sent in.

INDUSTRIAL ACCIDENTS REPORTED TO PUBLIC HEALTH OFFICIALS BY PHYSICIANS
AND SURGEONS, BY RESULT OF INJURY, 1907 AND 1908—WISCONSIN.

[Compiled from Biennial Reports of the Bureau of Labor and Industrial Statistics, Wisconsin: 1907-1908,
p. 15; 1909-1910, Pt. II, p. 75.]

Result of injury.	Accidents reported for the year ending October 1—			
	1907		1908	
	Number.	Per cent.	Number.	Per cent.
Fatal.	204	2.8	135	2.7
Permanent disability.	1,037	14.4	574	11.5
Temporary disability.	5,815	80.9	4,141	82.8
Not stated.	130	1.8	153	3.0
Total.	7,186	99.9	5,003	100.0

The distribution of the 5,003 industrial accidents reported for the year ending October 1, 1908, by the industries in which they occurred is shown in the succeeding table.

INDUSTRIAL ACCIDENTS REPORTED TO PUBLIC HEALTH OFFICIALS BY PHYSICIANS AND SURGEONS, BY INDUSTRIES AND SEVERITY OF INJURIES, 1908—WISCONSIN.

[From Fourteenth Biennial Report of the Bureau of Labor and Industrial Statistics, Wisconsin, 1909-10, Pt. II, p. 79.]

Industries.	Industrial accidents resulting in injuries which were—					
	Fatal.	Serious.	Severe.	Slight.	Not stated.	Total.
Agriculture...	3	41	117	16	1	178
Lumbering...	4	60	155	49	6	274
Mining..	11	24	93	50	2	180
Quarrying..		20	11	2	....	33
Personal and domestic service (laundries, hotels, and households)..	2	12	33	10	2	59
Manufactures:						
Bakeries and confectionery............................	....	6	18	1	....	25
Barrels and cooperage.................................	....	....	10	2	....	12
Boxes, paper...	1	1	39	2	1	44
Boxes, wood, and excelsior...........................	....	21	30	4	....	55
Beet sugar..	....	....	3	....	....	3
Boots, shoes, and gloves..............................	....	2	30	8	....	40
Breweries..	3	28	251	58	4	344
Dye works, chemicals, and glue	....	4	9	1	....	14
Flour and feed..	2	2	27	1	....	32
Food preparations.....................................	....	8	18	2	....	28
Furniture...	1	15	98	33	2	149
Iron, steel, and brass, not structural..................	9	62	374	60	5	510
Knitting, textile and clothing.........................	....	6	17	2	....	25
Meat...	....	4	25	5	....	34
Paper and pulp.......................................	3	19	60	9	1	92
Printing, publishing, engraving, and binding..........	....	2	40	4	1	47
Saw and planing......................................	6	52	175	49	4	286
Stone and marble cutting.............................	....	3	8	3	....	14
Shipbuilding..	....	2	46	16	1	65
Tanning and leather..................................	2	6	83	10	....	101
Tile and brick..	1	2	5	....	....	8
Tinware and sheet metal..............................	1	11	65	12	2	91
Wagons and carriages.................................	....	1	22	15	....	38
Woodenware..	....	3	21	21	....	45
Powder...	3	1	1	6	....	11
Automobiles..	....	....	32	2	....	34
Agricultural implements...............................	....	3	67	8	3	81
Total...	32	264	1,574	334	24	2,228
Other mechanical:						
Building..	4	19	61	4	1	89
Sewers, ditches, and roads............................	4	4	12	3	1	24
Ice...	3	3	23	2	....	31
Structural iron.......................................	1	3	7	1	....	12
Dredging and dam construction.......................	....	3	17	2	....	22
Total...	12	32	120	12	2	178
Trades and mercantile:						
Fuel dealers..	7	13	127	18	3	168
Mercantile...	6	18	122	10	2	158
Plumbing, painting, etc..............................	3	1	38	4	....	46
Total...	16	32	287	32	5	372
Transportation:						
Steam rail..	31	86	833	72	17	1,039
Street and interurban.................................	2	7	33	72	2	116
Lake transportation...................................	4	6	62	12	5	89
Total...	37	99	928	156	24	1,244
Public utilities:						
Gas and electric......................................	5	6	42	1	3	57
Water..	....	1	4	....	....	5
Telephone and telegraph..............................	1	2	6	1	....	10
Total...	6	9	52	2	3	72
Public Service: Police and fire department and other public servants.......................................	5	7	43	8	2	65
Industry not stated......................................	7	21	76	12	4	120
Grand total.......................................	135	621	3,489	683	75	5,003

CONDITIONS FOUND.

Accidents causing injury to employees and happening during the preceding year were recorded by 6 of the 19 establishments visited, the total number of such accidents being 157.

MARYLAND.

The law of Maryland, at the time of this investigation (January, 1909),[1] made no requirement for the reporting of accidents to the State bureau of statistics and information or to any other State official.

The chief of the bureau stated ·that he was in favor of such a law and was recommending it in his present report.

CONDITIONS FOUND.

In 12 of the 28 establishments visited accidents causing injury to employees were recorded as having occurred during the previous year, the total number of accidents so recorded being 109. In 14 establishments no accidents have been recorded; and from the remaining 2 no information was secured on this point.

NORTH CAROLINA.

There was, at the time of this investigation (March, 1909),[1] no law requiring the reporting of accidents to the State.

CONDITIONS FOUND.

Accidents causing injury to employees and occurring during the preceding year were recorded by 17 of the 28 establishments visited, the total number of such accidents being 205.

GEORGIA.

There was, at the time of this investigation (March, 1909), no legal requirement that accidents be reported to the State.[1]

CONDITIONS FOUND.

Accidents causing injury to employees and occurring during the preceding year were recorded by 15 of the 27 establishments visited. The total number of accidents so recorded was 69.

FLORIDA.

There was, at the time of this investigation (March, 1909),[1] no law requiring the reporting of accidents to the State.

---

[1] The text of the laws in force Jan. 1, 1912, is given in the appendixes at the end of this volume.

CONDITIONS FOUND.

Accidents causing injury to employees and occurring during the preceding year were recorded by 2 of the 14 establishments visited. The total number of accidents so recorded was 5. Both of the establishments referred to were cigar-box factories. In each of them employees had lost fingers on saws which were used for cutting up the material for the boxes. In 1 of the establishments, also, an employee had fallen through a trapdoor and injured himself.

LOUISIANA.

SUMMARY OF LEGISLATION.[1]

The Louisiana law requires accidents causing disability of at least two weeks to be reported, but only in the case of establishments employing women, young persons (under 18 years), or children. Section 20 of the law is as follows: [2]

All accidents in manufacturing, mechanical, or other establishments or places within the State where children, young persons, or women are employed which prevent the injured person or persons from returning to work within two weeks after the injury or which result in death shall be reported semiannually by the person in charge of such establishment or place to the inspector. * * *

> *Penalty.*—$5 to $10, or imprisonment 24 hours to 10 days, or both.

The provision that reports shall be made semiannually is peculiar to the law of this State. The weakness of such a provision is that it permits such a long period to elapse between an accident and its report that an investigation of its causes and proper remedies is rendered difficult.

The law requiring accident reporting, as above quoted, was approved July 9, 1908. As the field work of this investigation in Louisiana was done within nine months of that date, the effect and result of the law could not be satisfactorily studied.

CONDITIONS FOUND.

Accidents causing injury to employees and occurring during the preceding year were recorded by 13 establishments of the 29 visited. The total number of accidents recorded was 49. In 1 of these establishments, in which 3 accidents were recorded, none had caused as much as 2 weeks' loss of time, and thus did not require reporting to the State. Of the other 12 establishments 9 had reported accidents to the State and 3 had made no such reports.

---

[1] The law here referred to is as in force at the time of the investigation, March, 1909. The text of the laws in force Jan. 1, 1912, is given in the appendixes at the end of this volume.

[2] Acts of 1908, act No. 301, sec. 20 (Bulletin of the Bureau of Labor, No. 85, pp. 600, 601).

CHAPTER IX.

PROVISIONS FOR THE COMFORT OF EMPLOYEES.

CHAPTER IX.

PROVISIONS FOR THE COMFORT OF EMPLOYEES.

INTRODUCTION.

The present chapter, under the rather general title of "Provisions for comfort," covers the following topics: Water-closets, washing facilities, dressing rooms, lunch rooms, rest rooms, and seats for female employees. Related topics—such as cleanliness, dust, fumes—are considered in a separate chapter under the heading "Ventilation and sanitation." This method of selection is somewhat arbitrary, but it observes a more or less accepted use of terms and is convenient for purposes of treatment.

The several States covered by the investigation differ widely in the degree in which the comfort of factory workers has been made a matter of public law.[1]

Of the topics listed above, the one that has been most frequently legislated upon is that of seats for female employees. Only 2 of the 17 States covered, Maine and North Carolina, have no specific legal requirement upon this point.

The subject upon which the next largest number of States has legislated is that of water-closet accommodations. Eleven of the 17 States have legal provisions upon this point, although in some cases such provisions are incomplete. In only 5 of the 11 States with such provisions is a standard of sufficiency provided in the law itself. Indiana, Michigan, and Louisiana require at least 1 seat for each 25 employees; Ohio makes the same requirement in the case of females, but not of males; and Wisconsin requires 1 seat for each 20 employees. The 6 States devoid of legislation upon the subject of water-closets are Maine, Illinois, Maryland, North Carolina, Georgia, and Florida.

Dressing rooms in factories form a matter of legislation in 9 of the 17 States, and wash rooms in 7 of the 17. In several of these cases, however, the legal provision is not a requirement but simply an authorization for the factory inspector to make a requirement if he considers it necessary, and in Ohio the law applies only to females. Maine, Massachusetts, Connecticut, Illinois, Maryland, North Carolina, Georgia, and Florida have no legal references to either wash

---

[1] The law here referred to is as in force at the time of the investigation, December, 1908, to April, 1909. The text of the laws in force Jan. 1, 1912, is given in the appendixes at the end of this volume.

rooms or dressing rooms in factories. In Rhode Island and Wisconsin legislation is limited to dressing rooms and does not cover wash rooms.

In only 2 States, Massachusetts and Rhode Island, is the subject of the drinking water supply referred to by law. And in none of the 17 States covered are lunch rooms or rest rooms a matter of State legislation.

Below is given for each State an account of the public laws upon the several topics here considered, and a tabular statement of the conditions as found in the several establishments visited. The statement of conditions is in the form of two tables. One of these is limited to the subject of water-closet accommodations. The second covers the remaining topics considered. The contents of these tables are, in full, as follows:

The first table shows the respective numbers of establishments having and not having water-closets (1) separate for the sexes, (2) with approaches private, (3) in a cleanly condition, (4) so located and cared for that the air of the workrooms is unaffected, and (5) in sufficient number for the satisfactory accommodation of the employees of both sexes. On this latter point of sufficiency there might well arise differences of opinions as to any single standard. The proper measure of sufficiency is, of course, by means of a ratio between the number of employees and the number of accommodations, but no one ratio has met with universal acceptance. So far, however, as State laws and municipal ordinances have prescribed a fixed ratio of this character, such ratio has in few, if any, cases been more stringent than 20 persons per seat, and rarely less stringent than 30 persons per seat. Therefore, in the present table a classification is made according to each of three ratios—20 to 1, 25 to 1, and 30 to 1. And for the sake of easy comparison this threefold classification has been made in the case of States having legally prescribed ratios as well as in the case of States having no such legal standards.

The second table shows the respective numbers of establishments in which the following provisions were sufficient, insufficient, or entirely absent: Washing facilities, dressing rooms, rest rooms for females, lunch rooms, seats for females, and good drinking water. In the case of dressing rooms classification is made, by sexes, for all the establishments visited, and also for the smaller group of establishments in which the nature of the work was such as to make it more or less imperative, for the sake of comfort and decency, that employees change from street to working clothes within the factory. In this latter case dressing rooms may be considered as necessary, and the table so considers them, except where the number of persons changing their clothes is very small.

In the matter of seats for females the table classifies the establishments according to whether the seats provided were sufficient or insufficient. No establishment was visited in which there was a total absence of seats, although in a number of cases seats were provided only for those whose work was of a sedentary character. The term "provided" here refers solely to provision by the employer. No account is taken of a few cases where employees supply their own seats.

Owing to the general lack of accepted standards there is often considerable difficulty in determining, in particular instances, whether a wash room, dressing room, rest room, or lunch room is to be called satisfactory. In such an investigation as the present, therefore, it was necessary to leave all final decisions to the judgment of the agents in the field. General instructions, however, were issued to the agents, and these instructions would tend to make the replies approximately uniform. The following is a condensed statement of some of the more important points covered by these instructions:

By dressing room is meant a room where workers will have an opportunity, with reasonable privacy, to make necessary changes of clothing and to properly care for hats, wraps, etc. It does not mean a pretense of such a room, such as is sometimes obtained by hanging curtains or piling boxes in the workrooms, unless such arrangement assures more or less permanent privacy. Nor does it mean a simple wash room.

A large wash room, however, may also be entered as a dressing room if it is sufficient in size and has the necessary equipment of hooks, etc. Moreover, if such a room contains couches and chairs properly screened off, it may also be entered as a rest room.

On the same principle a lunch room is to be considered as such when it consists of a room set aside for the purpose and not used as a workroom. If, however, a room is properly equipped with chairs and tables and is sufficiently large for the purpose, the fact that it is also used for dressing or even as a wash room does not disqualify it as a lunch room.

Similarly, in regard to water-closets the instructions were as follows:

The determination of whether or not closets are separate should be based upon fact, not name. If the management permits promiscuous use, closets are not separate even though so labeled. If not marked for the sexes, but agent finds that they are separately used, they are to be regarded as separate.

The presence of leakage of any sort, dampness of floors or seats, any bad odor, any failure of the plumbing, or filth constitutes uncleanliness. Mere disorder, as paper litter, is not uncleanliness. Reasonable privacy of approach is secured when the approach is through another room, as a wash or dressing room, when it is reached from a passageway which effectually separates it from the workroom, or when the entrance is effectually screened. Also, a closet might have reasonable privacy of approach under some conditions other than those enumerated. The agent must be the judge in particular cases, but in no case is reasonable privacy secured when the closet opens directly from a workroom where both sexes are employed, or where the closets for males and females have a single approach.

The air of a workroom is to be regarded as affected if the odor from a closet is noticeable in any part of the workroom, even although it can not be detected in all parts.

A full statement of the conditions found in each establishment is given in Chapter XI, General Tables, of this volume.

MAINE.

SUMMARY OF LEGISLATION.[1]

The laws of Maine make no specific requirements as regards any of the subjects considered in this chapter—i. e., water-closets, wash rooms, dressing rooms, lunch rooms, rest rooms, seats for female employees, or drinking water. The sole legislation bearing upon any of these points is a general authorization given the factory inspector to remedy certain bad sanitary conditions. The law reads:[2]

He [the State factory inspector] shall also examine into the sanitary conditions of factories, workshops, mines and quarries, and when any condition or thing is found that in his opinion endangers the health or lives of the employees he shall notify and direct the employer to rectify the same; and if said employer shall neglect or refuse so to do within a reasonable time, said inspector may cause the same to be done at the expense of the employer.

The order thus given the inspector to remedy bad conditions is, of course, a narrow one. The law practically defines the term "bad sanitary condition" as one which "endangers the health or lives of employees," and it is difficult, if not impossible, in many instances to establish that a given condition is positively dangerous to health, although it may be clearly and seriously unfavorable to .comfort. Thus, while wash rooms and dressing rooms in factories, at least in factories of a certain class, are generally recognized as highly desirable, it can rarely be established that the absence of such conveniences is injurious to health. As a result the above-quoted law can be accepted, apparently, as applying only to conditions of drainage, etc., which are grossly bad.

The State factory inspector is of the belief that the question of toilet conveniences solves itself in individual establishments. In an interview with an agent of the Bureau of Labor, he stated that there was no demand for a law requiring factories to furnish seats for female employees; that every factory he knew of permitted its' female employees to sit, the chief trouble being that females who are

---

[1] The law here referred to is as in force at the time of the investigation, January, 1909. The text of the laws in force Jan. 1, 1912, is given in the appendixes at the end of this volume.

[2] Rev. Stat., 1903, ch. 40, sec. 44, as amended by ch. 77, Acts of 1907 (22d An. Rept. Com. of Labor, p. 526).

working by the piece and who are, consequently, anxious to work as much as possible, do not avail themselves of their opportunities to sit.

In the annual report of the State bureau of industrial statistics for 1908 there is a special report on the industrial conditions surrounding women and children employed in the textile mills of Lewiston, Auburn, Biddeford, and Saco. The following excerpts from this special report are concerned with the subject of toilet facilities in the mills at Lewiston and Auburn:[1]

The toilet rooms in some of the mills are in the towers, or corridors, but in others they are in the workroom where the air at best is difficult to breathe. In a weave room in one of the largest mills, where there are about 90 people, there are 3 closets built close together at the side of the room, not far from the looms. Two are labeled "Ladies" and one "Men." They are provided with the flush closet, inclosed nearly to the ceiling, but have no covering over the top. It is, of course, a difficult thing to keep conditions of this kind ideal in a place where so many are employed, but several of the workers in this room say that at times when the steam is at high pressure, causing the air to be particularly enervating, the conditions of these closets make matters very much worse. They also speak of the bad condition noticed when coming into the room in the morning. Closets could and should be arranged to give a greater degree of privacy. "Why don't you complain to the overseer?" was asked of several. "It will do no good, and we are afraid of losing our jobs if we find fault."

The women do not all wear their street dresses while at work, but change them for gowns of thinner material. In some rooms there are individual wardrobes or lockers, as in some of the cloth halls and other places. Boxes are provided for the weavers to keep their wraps and other clothing in, placed beside the machines. It is necessary to fold the garments, as the boxes are not constructed in such a way as to allow of their being suspended. Others hang their wraps on a convenient post, covering them with a piece of the cotton cloth they have assisted in weaving. There are wash rooms in some of the mills, but there appear to be no general robing and disrobing places for the women. As observed in one weave room, when time for the noon hour comes, the women take a wooden pail which they keep beside their machines, fill it with water at the sink, and bring it back again. They have soap, cloth, and towel, and perform their toilet while watching their machines, even to taking down curl papers, combing their hair, changing shoes or waist if they wish, donning skirt, hat, and coat while work is going on, the only privacy being the shelter of the machinery. The power is shut off at 12 and at 6, and there is little time lost by the operatives in reaching the outer world.

This question of the sanitary conditions in our large mills and workshops I find a hard one to enforce, as in most or all cases the help are largely responsible for the conditions, and nothing but constant care and attention on the part of the employer will keep the conditions healthy. A very few of our mills still hold to the old

[1] Twenty-second Annual Report of Bureau of Industrial and Labor Statistics, Maine, 1908, pp. 20, 21, 442.

system of sewerage and closets, and from these we have some trouble. There is at the present time an effort being made to have this corrected and more modern and up-to-date systems adopted.

CONDITIONS FOUND.

The two following tables summarize the conditions found in the 26 visited establishments as regards water-closet accommodations, washing facilities, etc.

WATER-CLOSET ACCOMMODATIONS—MAINE.

Character of water-closet accommodations.	Establishments—	
	Having specified provisions.	Not having specified provisions.
Separate for sexes.................	19	7
Private approaches for—		
Males.................	14	12
Females.................	10	16
Clean for—		
Males.................	19	7
Females.................	23	3
Air of workroom unaffected.................	24	2
Separate for sexes, with one seat for each—		
20 males or less.................	14	5
20 females or less.................	12	7
25 males or less.................	16	3
25 females or less.................	14	5
30 males or less.................	18	1
30 females or less.................	15	4
Not separate for sexes, with one seat for each—		
20 persons or less.................	5	2
25 persons or less.................	5	2
30 persons or less.................	7	....

WASH ROOM, DRESSING ROOM, REST ROOM, LUNCH ROOM, ETC., ACCOMMODATIONS—MAINE.

Character of accommodations.	Establishments—		
	Having specified provisions.		Not having specified provisions.
	Sufficient.	Not sufficient.	
Wash rooms:			
Facilities for washing...........................	14	9	3
Separate wash rooms......................	2	1	23
Towels...........................	9	....	17
Soap...........................	10	....	16
Towels and soap...........................	9	....	17
Dressing rooms:			
Separate for males...........................	6	....	20
Separate for males in work requiring change of clothing.....	4	....	....
Separate for females...........................	13	....	13
Separate for females in work requiring change of clothing...	11	....	1
Rest rooms for females...........................	....	....	26
Lunch rooms...........................	....	1	25
Seats for females...........................	12	14	....
Good drinking water...........................	20	....	6

A paper-box establishment reported that formerly it had a modern marble-finished lavatory for females, but that the girls spent so much time in it the more attractive features were removed.

MASSACHUSETTS.

SUMMARY OF LEGISLATION.[1]

The laws of Massachusetts require in manufacturing establishments generally water-closets, seats for females, and pure drinking water. Wash rooms and dressing rooms are required only in the single case of foundries employing 10 or more men.   Lunch rooms and rest rooms are not referred to by law.[2]

The legal provisions regarding water-closets, excluding special legislation concerning foundries only, are as follows, separation into paragraphs being made for convenience of reference:[3]

Every factory in which 5 or more persons are employed, and every factory, workshop, mercantile or other establishment or office in which 2 or more children under 18 years of age or women are employed—

(a) Shall be kept clean and free from effluvia arising from any drain, privy, or nuisance; and

(b) Shall be provided, within reasonable access, with a sufficient number of proper water-closets, earth closets, or privies; and

(c) Wherever 2 or more males and 2 or more females are employed together, a sufficient number of separate water-closets, earth closets, or privies shall be provided for the use of each sex, and plainly so designated; and

(d) No person shall be allowed to use a closet or privy which is provided for persons of the other sex.

(e) If it appears * * * that any act, neglect, or fault in relation to any drain, water-closet, earth closet, privy * * * is punishable or remediable under * * * any other law relative to the preservation of the public health, but not under the provisions * * * [quoted above] * * * [the State board of health] shall give notice in writing thereof to the board of health of the city or town in which such factory or workshop is situated, and such [local] board of health shall thereupon inquire into the subject of the notice and enforce the laws relative thereto.

Penalty.[4]— For violating any of the above provisions, not more than $100.

In reviewing these provisions it will be observed that while the requirements are mandatory in form, the exercise of personal judgment is necessary in determining what is a "sufficient number" of closets, and when they are "within reasonable access."   No stand-

---

[1] The law here referred to is as in force at the time of the investigation, December, 1908, to February, 1909.   The text of the laws in force Jan. 1, 1912, is given in the appendixes at the end of this volume.

[2] There is also special legislation regarding toilet conveniences, etc., in bakeries, but this does not extend to confectioneries or other food-producing establishments. Rev. Laws, 1902, ch. 75, sec. 28 (22d An. Rept. Com. of Labor, p. 579).   For tenement shop laws, see Rev. Laws, 1902, ch. 106, sec. 56, as amended by ch. 238, Acts of 1905 (22d An. Rept. Com. of Labor, pp. 601, 602).

[3] Rev. Laws, 1902, ch. 106, secs. 47 and 49, and Acts of 1907, ch. 537, sec. 5 (22d An. Rept. Com. of Labor, pp. 600, 629).

[4] Idem, sec. 70 (22d An. Rept. Com. of Labor, p. 604).

ards are erected by the law and the State board of health, which is charged with the enforcement of these provisions, has erected no fixed standards of its own.[1] The building law of Boston, however, provides that every building in that city shall have at least 1 closet accommodation for every 20 persons employed, with separate accommodations for the sexes, and also that every inclosure containing 1 or more water-closets shall have adequate ventilation to the outer air either by window or by suitable light shaft.[1]

As each of the establishments covered by this investigation employed at least 2 children under 18 years of age or 2 women, all of them were subject to the requirements just quoted.

As regards seats for female employees the law directs as follows:[2]

A person who employs females in any manufacturing, mechanical, or mercantile establishment shall provide suitable seats for their use and shall permit the use of such seats by them when they are not necessarily engaged in the active duties of their employment.

Penalty.—$10 to $30 for each offense.

The intention of this law is clear. The fulfilling of the intention, however, involves a very considerable exercise of personal judgment. In the first place, it is necessary in each case to determine what number of seats and what character of seats are "suitable." In the second place, the direction that the use of such seats shall be permitted to such employees when not necessarily engaged in their active duties is difficult to enforce without the active cooperation of the employees. Inspectors, on their visits, may be able to decide with considerable justice whether or not the seats provided in a particular establishment are suitable in character and sufficient in number. But it is very difficult for such inspectors to ascertain whether, at other times, the employees are allowed to use such seats freely. The methods by which the spirit of the law in this particular may be evaded are numerous.

The requirement that pure drinking water shall be furnished employees is mandatory, clear, and not difficult of enforcement. It reads:[3]

All manufacturing establishments in this Commonwealth shall provide fresh and pure drinking water, to which their employees shall have access during working hours.

Penalty.—$100 for each offense.

In the case of foundries, but of no other establishments, washing and dressing facilities must be provided; and in this case, also, additional requirements are made as to water-closets. The law reads:[4]

---

[1] Acts of 1907, ch. 550, sec. 12.

[2] Rev. Laws, 1902, ch. 106, sec. 41 (22d An. Rept. Com. of Labor, p. 599).

[3] Acts of 1902, ch. 322, secs. 1 and 2 (22d An. Rept. Com. of Labor, pp. 612, 613).

[4] Acts of 1906, ch. 250, secs. 1 and 2 (22d An. Rept. Com. of Labor, pp. 615, 616).

Every foundry engaged in the casting of iron * * * or other metal, and employing 10 or more men, shall establish and maintain, except in * * * the absence of public or private sewerage or of any running-water system, toilet room of suitable size and condition for the men to change their clothes therein, and provided with wash-bowls, sinks, or other suitable set appliances connected with running hot and cold water, and also a water-closet connected with running water and separated from the . said toilet room.   The said water-closet and toilet room shall be connected directly with the foundry building, properly heated, ventilated and protected, so far as may be reasonably practicable, from the dust of the foundry.

Penalty.—Not more than $50 for each offense.

The legal demands of this provision are full and precise.   It is to be emphasized, however, that this law applies solely to foundries, and that women and children are seldom employed in such establishments.

The enforcement of all the legal provisions quoted above, except in so far as such enforcement requires structural alterations in buildings, is entrusted to the State board of health, those which were previously under the supervision of the factory inspection department of the district police having been transferred thereto in 1907.   When the proper enforcement of the laws requires structural changes in buildings, the necessity thereof must be reported by the board of health to the factory inspection department of the district police.[1]

CONDITIONS FOUND.

The 2 following tables summarize the conditions found in the 44 establishments visited, as regards water-closet accommodations, washing facilities, etc.

WATER-CLOSET ACCOMMODATIONS—MASSACHUSETTS.

Character of water-closet accommodations.	Establishments—	
	Having specified provisions.	Not having specified provisions.
Separate for sexes	42	2
Private approaches for—		
Males	25	19
Females	26	18
Clean for—		
Males	37	7
Females	41	3
Air of workroom unaffected	43	1
Separate for sexes,[2] with one seat for each—		
20 males or less	33	8
20 females or less	30	11
25 males or less	34	7
25 females or less	34	7
30 males or less	39	2
30 females or less	36	5
Not separate for sexes, with one seat for each—		
20 persons or less		2
25 persons or less	1	1
30 persons or less	2	

[1] Acts of 1907, ch. 537, sec. 5 (22d An. Rept. Com. of Labor, p. 629).
[2] One establishment not reported.

WASH ROOM, DRESSING ROOM, REST ROOM, LUNCH ROOM, ETC., ACCOMMODATIONS—
MASSACHUSETTS.

	Establishments—		
Character of accommodations.	Having specified provisions—		Not having specified provisions.
	Sufficient.	Not sufficient.	
Wash rooms:			
Facilities for washing	29	13	2
Separate wash rooms	6	[1] 2	36
Towels	18	1	25
Soap	24	1	19
Towels and soap	18	1	25
Dressing rooms:			
Separate for males	11	1	32
Separate for males in work requiring change of clothing	9	1	5
Separate for females	16	3	25
Separate for females in work requiring change of clothing	12	3	4
Rest rooms for females	1		43
Lunch rooms	8		36
Seats for females	32	12	
Good drinking water	40		4

[1] For females only, in 1 establishment.

In one of the confectionery factories the lunch room was unusually large and comfortable and contained a piano for the use of the employees. In a paper-box factory there was no lunch room, but coffee was served at noon at 2 cents a cup.

RHODE ISLAND.

SUMMARY OF LEGISLATION.[1]

Rhode Island has legislation in regard to four of the topics covered by this chapter: Water-closets, dressing rooms, seats for female employees, and pure drinking water. Wash rooms are required only in the special case of foundries, and lunch rooms and rest rooms are nowhere referred to by law.[2]

The full legal provisions upon the points mentioned are as follows: [3]

(a) Water-closets, earth closets, or privies shall be provided in all places where women and children are employed, in such manner as shall, in the judgment of said (factory) inspectors, meet the demands of health and propriety.

(b) Separate dressing rooms for women and girls shall be provided in all establishments where such are deemed a necessity by said factory inspectors;

---

[1] The law here referred to is as in force at the time of the investigation, December, 1908, to February, 1909. The text of the laws in force Jan. 1, 1912, is given in the appendixes at the end of this volume.

[2] There is no special legislation regarding tenement shops, and there was none regarding bakeries or confectioneries at the time of the field work of this investigation. A law of 1910, however, makes certain regulations regarding toilet facilities in bakeries, confectioneries, and ice-cream factories. Acts of 1910, ch. 549 (Bulletin of the Bureau of Labor, No. 91, pp. 1149–1151).

[3] Gen. Laws, 1896, ch. 68, sec. 8 (22d An. Rept. Com. of Labor, p. 1209).

(c) And in every manufacturing, mechanical, or mercantile establishment in which women and girls are employed, there shall be provided, conveniently located, seats for such women and girls, and they shall be permitted to use them when their duties do not require their standing.

Penalty.—Not more than $500.[1]

(d) All manufacturing establishments in this State shall provide fresh drinking water of good quality, to which their employees shall have access during working hours.[2]

Penalty.—$100 for each offense.

(e) Every foundry in this State employing 10 or more men shall provide suitable toilet rooms, containing washbowls or sinks, provided with water, water-closets, and a room wherein the men may change their clothes, said rooms to be within the building used for said foundry, and shall be protected from the weather, heated, and ventilated.[3]

Penalty.—$50 to $100.

In reviewing these provisions the following points may be noted: The requirement of water-closets (a) is mandatory, but no standard of sufficiency is declared, and no legal demand made that such closets be convenient of access, private in their approaches or even that they be separate for the sexes. These points are left to the discretion of the inspectors, and in practice no standards, such as that of a minimum ratio of accommodations to persons, have been adopted.

In the case of dressing rooms (b) the discretion allowed is even greater; not only are the factory inspectors to determine what kind of room is satisfactory, but also they are to determine in each establishment whether any dressing accommodation is necessary. The chief factory inspector stated that employers provide dressing rooms, where such are necessary, on their own initiative; that in no case had he been compelled to insist upon such provision; and that he would not go into the matter in particular cases unless complaints should be made.

The requirement of seats for female employees (c) is mandatory in form, but the determination of what seats are satisfactory and when sufficient is left to the factory-inspection department. In practice, the department requires no particular kind of seats, but the chief inspector expressed himself as opposed to the use of three-legged stools. He considered such stools dangerous, because easily upset, one or two serious accidents having resulted from their use. He considered that waste boxes, if conveniently located, were seats within the meaning of the law, being more serviceable and less dangerous than stools.

---

[1] Gen. Laws, 1896, ch. 68, sec. 12 (22d An. Rept. Com. of Labor, p. 1210).

[2] Acts of 1907, ch. 1429, secs. 1 and 2 (22d An. Rept. Com. of Labor, p. 1224).

[3] Acts of 1904, ch. 1142, secs. 1 and 2 (22d An. Rept. Com. of Labor, p. 1223).

The legal provisions regarding toilet accommodations in foundries (e) is very detailed in its requirements and precise in the terms used. Foundries, however, rarely employ women or children and none were covered by this investigation in Rhode Island.

All of the above-quoted legal provisions, except those regarding foundries and drinking water, are charged to the factory-inspection department for enforcement.[1] The law relating to pure drinking water is enforceable by the local authorities.[2] The legislation regarding foundries is not placed under the supervision of any special body, but the inspection department, while assuming no responsibility for its enforcement, reminds foundry owners of its existence and requirements.

CONDITIONS FOUND.

The 2 following tables summarize the conditions found in the 27 visited establishments as regards water-closet accommodations, washing facilities, etc.

WATER-CLOSET ACCOMMODATIONS—RHODE ISLAND.

Character of water-closet accommodations.	Establishments—	
	Having specified provisions.	Not having specified provisions.
Separate for sexes..........	25	2
Private approaches for—		
Males..........	15	12
Females..........	15	12
Clean for—		
Males..........	20	7
Females..........	22	5
Air of workroom unaffected..........	23	4
Separate for sexes, with one seat for each—		
20 males or less..........	16	9
20 females or less..........	11	14
25 males or less..........	20	5
25 females or less..........	16	9
30 males or less..........	20	5
30 females or less..........	18	7
Not separate for sexes, with one seat for each—		
20 or less..........	2	....

---

[1] Gen. Laws, 1896, ch. 68, sec. 3, as amended by ch. 1215, enacted 1905 (22d An. Rept. Com. of Labor. p. 1208).
[2] Acts of 1907, ch. 1429, sec. 2 (22d An. Rept. Com. of Labor, p. 1224).

WASH ROOM, DRESSING ROOM, REST ROOM, LUNCH ROOM, ETC., ACCOMMODA-
TIONS—RHODE ISLAND.

Character of accommodations.	Establishments—		
	Having specified provisions—		Not having specified provisions.
	Sufficient.	Not sufficient.	
Wash rooms:			
Facilities for washing..	20	7	....
Separate wash rooms..	....	....	27
Towels...	6	....	21
Soap..	10	....	[1] 17
Towels and soap...	4	....	[1] 23
Dressing rooms:			
Separate for males...	4	....	23
Separate for males, in work requiring change of clothing....	3	....	....
Separate for females...	6	....	21
Separate for females, in work requiring change of clothing...	5	....	1
Rest rooms for females...	....	....	27
Lunch rooms..	1	....	26
Seats for females...	16	11	....
Good drinking water..	27	....	....

[1] In 1 establishment use of soap is prohibited for trade reasons.

CONNECTICUT.

SUMMARY OF LEGISLATION.[1]

Water-closets and seats for females are required in factories generally. Washing facilities are not required in any class of establishments except bakeries, and when so ordered by the factory inspector, in foundries. Dressing rooms, rest rooms, lunch rooms, and drinking water are not referred to by law.[2]

Upon the subject of water-closets the law reads:[3]

Every * * * factory, * * * or * * * any other building where more than five persons are employed, shall provide and keep in good sanitary condition suitable water-closet accommodations for the use of the persons employed.

Penalty.—Not more than $50.

The determination of whether or not the closets provided are "suitable" is left to the discretion of the inspecting department. No standard as to the number of persons per closet accommodation is erected by law, but the chief factory inspector has set up an official standard of 1 closet to each 25 persons employed. There is no specific legal requirement that the closets should have privacy of approach or even that there should be separate closets for the sexes.

---

[1] The law here referred to is as in force at the time of the investigation, February, 1909. The text of the laws in force Jan. 1, 1912, is given in the appendixes at the end of this volume.

[2] The tenement-shop legislation does not cover specifically any of the subjects considered in this chapter. Gen. Stat., 1902, secs. 4527 to 4530 (22d An. Rept. Com. of Labor, pp. 237, 238).

[3] Gen. Stat., 1902, sec. 4519 and sec. 4522, as amended by ch. 53, Acts of 1903 (22d An. Rept. Com. of Labor, p. 236).

Both of these requirements, however, may be assumed to have been intended by the law in directing that closets should be "suitable." The chief factory inspector stated that his department requires separate closets for the sexes, but does not insist upon privacy of approach.

Seats for females are required in the following terms: [1]

Every person, partnership, or corporåtion employing females in any mercantile, mechanical, or manufacturing establishment shall furnish and provide suitable seats for the use of all females so employed, and shall permit the use of such seats by said females when they are not necessarily engaged in the active duties for which they are employed.

Penalty.—Not more than $50.

This requirement, it is to be observed, is closely similar to corresponding requirements of several other States—Massachusetts, Rhode Island, etc.

Washing facilities, as has been noted, may be required by the factory inspector in the case of foundries: [2]

The factory inspector shall have power and authority by order to that effect to require the proprietor of any foundry in this State in which 10 or more men are employed, and situated in a locality where there is such system for the disposal of sewage as to make such order practicable, to provide for the use of such employees a toilet room of such suitable dimensions as such inspector may determine, containing washbowls or sinks connected with running water, with facilities for heating the same, such room to be directly connected with such foundry building, properly heated, ventilated, and protected from the dust of said foundry.

Penalty.—Not more than $50.

This provision regarding washing facilities in foundries is similar to the corresponding provisions of the laws of Massachusetts and Rhode Island (pp. 391, 393) except that in each of these last-mentioned States the requirement is mandatory, whereas in Connecticut the necessity of wash rooms in foundries is left to the inspector's discretion. Women and children, to repeat what has been stated earlier, are rarely employed in foundries, and no such establishment was covered by this investigation.

The legal provisions quoted above, with the exception of the one regarding seats for females, are specifically charged to the State factory-inspection department for enforcement. [3] The requirement of seats for females is not charged to any special body for enforcement,

---

[1] Gen. Stat., 1902, sec. 4703 (22d An. Rept. Com. of Labor, p. 242).

[2] Acts of 1905, ch. 140, secs. 1 and 2 (22d An. Rept. Com. of Labor, p. 248).

For requirement of wash rooms in bakeries see Gen. Stat. 1902, sec. 2569, as amended by ch. 13, Acts of 1905 (22d An. Rept. Com. of Labor, p. 232). Since the field work of this investigation was completed the requirement as to bakeries has been extended to all factories engaged in the preparation of foodstuffs, tobacco, and cigars. Acts of 1909, ch. 120, sec. 14 (Bulletin of the Bureau of Labor, No. 85, p. 524).

[3] Gen. Stat., 1902, sec. 4519 (22d An. Rept. Com. of Labor, p. 236).

but the chief factory inspector stated that his department assumes the responsibility for its enforcement although he did not believe he had any real authority in the matter.   He expressed himself as unfavorable toward the enactment of legislation requiring wash rooms, dressing rooms, lunch rooms, or rest rooms in factories.   He believed that manufacturers were inclined to furnish, and did voluntarily furnish, such conveniences when necessary.

CONDITIONS FOUND.

The 2 following tables summarize the conditions found in the 35 visited establishments as regards water-closet accommodations, washing facilities, etc.

It was noted above that, while the State law does not provide a standard of sufficiency in the matter of water-closets, the chief factory inspector has set up an administrative standard of one accommodation to each 25 persons employed.   It was found, however, that the standards used by the various local health officials differed in many cases from that erected by the factory inspector, with considerable resultant confusion.

WATER-CLOSET ACCOMMODATIONS—CONNECTICUT.

Character of water-closet accommodations.	Establishments—	
	Having specified provisions.	Not having specified provisions.
Separate for sexes.	35	....
Private approaches for—		
Males [1].	30	4
Females.	32	1
Clean for—		
Males [1].	32	3
Females.	34	2
Air of workroom unaffected.	35	....
Separate for sexes, with one seat for each—		
20 males or less [1].	25	9
20 females or less.	24	11
25 males or less [1].	27	7
25 females or less.	28	7
30 males or less [1].	32	2
30 females or less.	30	5

[1] One not reported.

WASH ROOM, DRESSING ROOM, REST ROOM, LUNCH ROOM, ETC., ACCOMMODATIONS—
CONNECTICUT.

Character of accommodations.	Establishments—		
	Having specified provisions—		Not having specified provisions.
	Sufficient.	Not sufficient.	
Wash rooms:			
Facilities for washing..	27	8	....
Separate wash rooms..	7	....	28
Towels..	4	....	31
Soap..	9	....	26
Towels and soap..	4	....	31
Dressing rooms:			
Separate for males	7	....	28
Separate for males, in work requiring change of clothing.....	5	....	6
Separate for females..	7	4	24
Separate for females, in work requiring change of clothing...	3	....	2
Rest rooms for females..	1	....	34
Lunch rooms..	....	....	35
Seats for females..	35	....	....
Good drinking water..	35	....	....

NEW YORK.

SUMMARY OF LEGISLATION.[1]

Water-closets, wash rooms, and seats for female employees are required in factories generally. Dressing rooms are not required unconditionally, but the inspection department, at its discretion, may order dressing rooms to be provided in establishments employing women and girls. Lunch rooms, rest rooms, and drinking water are not referred to in the State law.[2]

The legal provisions regarding water-closets, wash rooms and dressing rooms are as follows, the sequence in which the provisions occur in the law being slightly changed in order to facilitate reference:[3]

(a) Every factory[4] shall contain a suitable, convenient, and separate water-closet or water-closets for each sex, which shall be properly

---

[1] The law here referred to is as in force at the time of the investigation, December, 1908, and January, 1909. The text of the laws in force Jan. 1, 1912, is given in the appendixes at the end of this volume.

[2] Bakeries and confectionery establishments are considered as factories as regards the requirements of water-closets, etc. Rev. Stat., 3d ed., 1901, p. 2108, sec. 114, as amended by ch. 401, Acts of 1906 (22d An. Rept. Com. of Labor, p. 921).

For special legislation regarding mercantile establishments see Rev. Stat., 3d ed., 1901, p. 2114, secs. 168, 169, 170; tenement shops, see idem, p. 2102, sec. 94 (added by ch. 178, Acts of 1906). (22d An. Rept. Com. of Labor, pp. 915, 916, 927, 928.) This special legislation is quite similar to that quoted in the text for factories proper.

[3] Rev. Stat., 3d ed., 1901, p. 2102, sec. 88, as amended by ch. 485, Acts of 1907, and p. 2120, sec. 209, as amended by ch. 506, Acts of 1907 (22d An. Rept. Com. of Labor, pp. 914, 931).

[4] The term "factory" as used in the New York law includes "also any mill, workshop, or other manufacturing or business establishment where one or more persons are employed at labor." Idem, p. 2089, sec. 2, as amended by ch. 550, Acts of 1904 (22d An. Rept. Com. of Labor, p. 899).

screened, ventilated, and kept clean and free from all obscene writing or marking.   *   *   *   The water-closets used by women shall have separate approaches.   Inside closets shall be maintained whenever practicable, and in all cases when required by the commissioner of labor.

(b)   *   *   *   A suitable and convenient wash room (shall be contained in every factory).

(c) When women or girls are employed, a dressing room shall be provided for them, when required by the commissioner of labor.

Penalty.—First offense, $20 to $50; second offense, $50 to $200, or by imprisonment of not more than 30 days, or both; third offense, not less than $250, or imprisonment of not more than 60 days, or both.

And in the special case of foundries it is further enacted that:

(d) In all brass and iron foundries there shall be provided and maintained for the use of employees, suitable wash rooms with proper water service, and suitable provision for drying of the working clothes of persons using the same.

Penalty.—Same as for violation of provisions (a), (b), and (c) quoted above.

The requirement as to seats for females is that:[1]

(e) Every person employing females in a factory or as waitresses in a hotel or restaurant, shall provide and maintain suitable seats for the use of such female employees, and permit the use thereof by such employees to such an extent as may be reasonable for the preservation of their health.

Penalty.—Same as for violation of provisions (a) to (d) quoted above.

---

[1] Rev. Stat., 3d ed., 1901, p. 2092, sec. 17, and also idem, p. 2120, sec. 207 (22d An. Rept. Com. of Labor, pp. 903, 931).

Seats for female employees as required in mercantile establishments by a law which is much more detailed and specific in character than the one for factories quoted above.

By a law passed since the field work of this investigation was completed females under 16 are forbidden to work in any employment requiring constant standing. Con. Laws, 1909, ch. 31, sec. 93, as amended by ch. 299, Acts of 1909 (Bulletin of the Bureau of Labor, No. 85, p. 686).

In reviewing these provisions the following points may be noted:
(1) The requirement of water-closets is very complete, except in the
one matter of sufficiency. Closets must be suitable, convenient, separate for the sexes, with separate approaches, and are to be inside the
building when practicable and in all cases when ordered by the commissioner of labor. No standard of adequacy is erected by the law,
but the inspection department has set up the following administrative
standard:

WATER-CLOSET ACCOMMODATIONS REQUIRED FOR MALE AND FEMALE EMPLOY-
EES—NEW YORK.[1]

For females.		• For males.	
Total number employed.	One closet accommo- dation for each—	Total number employed.	One closet accommo- dation for each—
100 or less.............................	25	100 or less...........................	25
100 to 200.............................	30	100 to 500.........,.................	40
200 to 1,000...........................	40	500 or over...........................	50
1,000 or more..........................	50		

[1] In calculating the number of closets required, any odd number of persons, less than is specified above,
if equal to 20 per cent of these figures, is to be reckoned as full quota.

(2) The requirement as to wash rooms is mandatory in that a wash
room must be provided in every factory. It leaves full discretion to
the inspection department, however, in determining what kind of
washing facilities shall be accepted as "suitable and convenient."
The commissioner of labor stated that he did not consider ordinary
sinks as being wash rooms within the meaning of the law.

(3) The requirement of dressing rooms is entirely optional with the
factory inspection department. The intention is, of course, that the
department shall exercise this discretion by ordering dressing rooms
in factories where the nature of the work renders it necessary or
desirable that employees should change their clothes when coming to
and leaving the factory.

(4) The requirement of seats for females differs from the corresponding requirements of the States already considered—Massachusetts, Rhode Island, and Connecticut—in that it directs that females
shall be allowed to sit as much "as may be reasonable for the preservation of their health." In the absence of authoritative medical
decision, this leaves room for a wide variation of personal judgment.
It is the practice of the inspection department not to press any fixed
idea on the subject, when a manufacturer is apparently trying to do
all that the nature of the employment of his female help will allow.

The enforcement of the legal provisions quoted above is intrusted
in full to the factory inspection bureau of the State department of
labor.[1]

[1] Rev. Stat., 3d ed., 1901, p. 2098, amended by ch. 505, Acts of 1907, sec. 62 (22d
An. Rept. Com. of Labor, p. 907).

CONDITIONS FOUND.

The 2 following tables summarize the conditions found in the 36 visited establishments as regards water-closet accommodations, washing facilities, etc.

WATER-CLOSET ACCOMMODATIONS—NEW YORK.

Character of water-closet accommodations.	Establishments—	
	Having specified provisions.	Not having specified provisions.
Separate for sexes	36	....
Private approaches for—		
Males	27	9
Females	28	8
Clean for—		
Males	33	3
Females	35	1
Air of workrooms unaffected	36	....
Separate for sexes, with one seat for each [1]—		
20 males or less	32	
20 females or less	28	
25 males or less	34	
25 females or less	31	
30 males or less	34	
30 females or less	31	

[1] Accommodations in 1 establishment not reported.

WASH ROOM, DRESSING ROOM, REST ROOM, LUNCH ROOM, ETC., ACCOMMODATIONS—NEW YORK.

Character of accommodations.	Establishments—		
	Having specified provisions—		Not having specified provisions.
	Sufficient.	Not sufficient.	
Wash rooms:			
Facilities for washing	26	10	....
Separate wash rooms	10	....	26
Towels	17	....	19
Soap	15	....	21
Towels and soap	15	....	21
Dressing rooms:			
Separate for males	9	4	22
Separate for males, in work requiring change of clothing	6	2	8
Separate for females	20	6	10
Separate for females, in work requiring change of clothing	4	2	1
Rest rooms for females	3	....	33
Lunch rooms	6	....	30
Seats for females	36	....	....
Good drinking water	36	....	....

In one establishment the lunch room was provided with a stove and cooking utensils for use of employees.

NEW JERSEY.

SUMMARY OF LEGISLATION.[1]

Water-closets and wash rooms are required in all factories and workshops, as also are dressing rooms, if such are considered necessary and ordered by the commissioner of labor. Seats for female employees are required under an old statute, which has never been specifically repealed, but which is not considered by the factory-inspection department as being still in effect. Lunch rooms, rest rooms, and drinking water are not referred to by law.[2]

The legal provisions regarding water-closets, wash rooms, and dressing rooms are, in full, as follows, the order in which the paragraphs occur in the original law being slightly changed in order to facilitate reference:[3]

(a) Every factory, workshop, or mill shall contain sufficient, suitable, convenient, and separate water-closets for each sex, which shall be properly screened, ventilated, and kept clean. * * * The water-closets used by women shall have separate approaches.

(b) A suitable and convenient wash room [shall be contained in each such establishment].

(c) If women or girls are employed, a dressing room shall be provided for them when ordered by the commissioner.

Penalty.—$50.

These provisions, it will be observed, are almost precisely similar to the corresponding provisions of New York State. The only important difference is that the New York statute has a requirement that, under certain conditions, closets shall be inside the establishment concerned—a requirement which the New Jersey law does not have. Otherwise the similarity is so close that the remarks regarding the New York law may be applied here and need not be repeated.

The New Jersey law, like the New York law, does not establish a standard as to the ratio of closet accommodations to employees, nor

---

[1] The law here referred to is as in force at the time of the investigation, December, 1908, and January, 1909. The text of the laws in force Jan. 1, 1912, is given in the appendixes at the end of this volume.

[2] By ch. 102, Acts of 1905 (22d An. Rept. Com. of Labor, pp. 869–871), bakeries and confectioneries are declared to be within the provisions applicable to factories, etc., as quoted in this chapter. The only additional requirement of this law of interest here is one forbidding water-closets to be within or to communicate with the workrooms of bakeries or confectioneries. By a law enacted subsequent to the field work of this investigation the legislation regarding bakeries and confectioneries was elaborated and made to apply to all places used for the "production, manufacture, preparation, packing, storage, or distribution" of food products. Acts of 1909, ch. 231 (Bulletin of the Bureau of Labor, No. 85, pp. 679–681).

The tenement-house legislation of New Jersey does not refer specifically to water-closets, etc. Acts of 1904, ch. 64, secs. 31 and 32 (22d An. Rept. Com. of Labor, pp. 864, 865).

There is no legislation regarding mercantile establishments.

[3] Acts of 1904, ch. 64, secs. 23 and 30 (22d An. Rept. Com. of Labor, p. 863).

has the State factory-inspection department established any standard of its own for administrative purposes.

In the matter of wash rooms the department makes no attempt to enforce the law literally. It is satisfied if there are washing facilities, such as sinks in the workrooms, and does not require a separate "room."

As regards dressing rooms the commissioner stated that, under the discretionary authority allowed him by the law, he required dressing rooms to be provided in establishments where the nature of the work required women and girls to change their clothing. In the silk industry, for example, the street attire is not changed, while in tobacco and cigar factories such a change is usually made.

The law regarding seats for females directs that:[1]

Every person or corporation employing female employees in any manufacturing, mechanical, or mercantile establishment in this State shall provide suitable seats for the use of the female employees so employed and shall permit the use of such seats by them when they are not necessarily engaged in the active duties for which they are employed.

Penalty.—$50 for each offense.

As mentioned above, this law has not been specifically repealed; but it is not included in the compilation of laws of the factory-inspection department, 1907, and the department does not consider the law as being in effect.

The enforcement of all the legal provisions quoted above except the one relating to seats for females is intrusted to the factory-inspection department.[2]

---

[1] Gen. Stat., 1895, p. 1675, secs. 217 and 218, as amended by ch. 192, acts of 1898 (22d An. Rept. Com. of Labor, pp. 845, 846).

[2] Acts of 1904, ch. 64, sec. 30 (22d An. Rept. Com. of Labor, p. 864).

CONDITIONS FOUND.

The 2 following tables show, in summary form, the conditions found in the 27 establishments visited as regards water-closet accommodations, washing facilities, etc.:

WATER-CLOSET ACCOMMODATIONS—NEW JERSEY.

Character of water-closet accommodations.	Establishments—	
	Having specified provisions.	Not having specified provisions.
Separate for sexes	27	
Private approaches for—		
Males	27	6
Females	19	8
Clean for—		
Males	17	10
Females	24	3
Air of workroom unaffected	21	6
Separate for sexes, with one seat for each—		
20 males or less	19	8
20 females or less	16	11
25 males or less	21	6
25 females or less	18	9
30 males or less	23	4
30 females or less	23	4

WASH ROOM, DRESSING ROOM, REST ROOM, LUNCH ROOM, ETC., ACCOMMODATIONS—NEW JERSEY.

Character of accommodations.	Establishments—		
	Having specified provisions—		Not having specified provisions.
	Sufficient.	Not sufficient.	
Wash rooms:			
Facilities for washing	18	9	
Separate wash rooms	11		16
Towels	9		18
Soap	11		16
Towels and soap	9		18
Dressing rooms:			
Separate for males	5		22
Separate for males, in work requiring change of clothing	3		1
Separate for females	16	2	9
Separate for females, in work requiring change of clothing	10		5
Rest rooms for females	6		21
Lunch rooms	9		18
Seats for females	18	9	
Good drinking water	27		

PENNSYLVANIA.

SUMMARY OF LEGISLATION.[1]

Water-closets, wash rooms, dressing rooms, and seats for female employees are required in all kinds of establishments, whether manu-

---

[1] The law here referred to is as in force at the time of the investigation, January to March, 1909. The text of the laws in force Jan. 1, 1912, is given in the appendixes at the end of this volume.

facturing or not.[1] Lunch rooms, rest rooms, and drinking water are not referred to by law.

The legal provision regarding water-closets, wash rooms, and dressing rooms is as follows:[2]

(a) Every person, firm, or corporation employing males and females in the same establishment shall provide for such employees suitable and proper wash and dressing rooms, and water-closets for males and females; and

(b) The water-closets, wash and dressing rooms used by females shall not adjoin those used by males, but shall be built entirely away from them, and shall be properly screened and ventilated;

(c) And all water-closets shall at all times be kept in a clean and sanitary condition.

Penalty.—$25 to $500, or imprisonment 10 to 60 days, for each offense.

The Pennsylvania law thus subjects water-closets, wash rooms, and dressing rooms to the same requirements. These requirements are very stringent as regards the number of establishments affected, separation of the sexes, and privacy. The matter of privacy is particularly insisted upon, the law directing that the toilet accommodations for the females "shall not adjoin those used by the males, but shall be built entirely away from them, and shall be properly screened." These directions are so clear and mandatory that there is little room for the exercise of personal judgment.

As regards the sufficiency and character of the accommodations offered there is, however, wide latitude of personal judgment. The law erects no standards of number as regards water-closets, and no standards of capacity as regards wash rooms and dressing rooms. It is directed that such accommodations shall be "suitable and proper," and the factory inspection department determines what conditions fulfill these requirements.

As regards seats for females the law provides in terms similar to those used in the laws of several other States:[3]

Every person, firm, or corporation employing girls or adult women in any establishment shall provide suitable seats for their use, and shall permit such use when the employees are not necessarily engaged in active duties.

---

[1] Special legislation regarding bakeries does not apply to confectionery establishments. Brightly's Digest, 1893–1903, p. 62, secs. 14 and 15; and Acts of 1905, act No. 226, sec. 17 (22d An. Rept. Com. of Labor, pp. 1145,1179).

For special legislation regarding tenement shops, see Brightly's Digest, 1893–1903, p. 825, sec. 2; and Acts of 1905, act No. 226, sec. 14 (22d An. Rept. Com. of Labor, pp. 1163, 1178).

[2] Acts of 1905, act No. 226, secs. 8 and 23 (22d An. Rept. Com. of Labor, pp. 1177, 1179, 1180).

[3] Idem, secs. 7 and 23 (22d An. Rept. Com. of Labor, pp. 1177, 1180).

Penalty.—$25 to $500, or imprisonment 10 to 60 days for each offense.

The legal provisions quoted above are all charged to the State factory inspection department for enforcement.[1]

CONDITIONS FOUND.

The following 2 tables summarize the conditions found in the 50 visited establishments as regards water-closet accommodations, washing facilities, etc.

WATER-CLOSET ACCOMMODATIONS—PENNSYLVANIA.

Character of water-closet accommodations.	Establishments—	
	Having specified provisions.	Not having specified provisions.
Separate for sexes....................	49	1
Private approaches for—		
Males [2]...................	46	1
Females.................	48	2
Clean for—		
Males [2]...................	42	5
Females.................	49	1
Air of workroom unaffected..............	46	4
Separate for sexes, with one seat for each [1]—		
20 males or less................	33	3
20 females or less..............	33	15
25 males or less................	36	5
25 females or less..............	35	13
30 males or less................	39	2
30 females or less..............	38	10
Not separate for sexes, with one seat for each—		
25 persons or less..............	1	....

WASH ROOM, DRESSING ROOM, REST ROOM, LUNCH ROOM, ETC., ACCOMMODATIONS—PENNSYLVANIA.

Character of accommodations.	Establishments—		
	Having specified provisions—		Not having specified provisions.
	Sufficient.	Not sufficient.	
Wash rooms:			
Facilities for washing................	50	....	....
Separate wash rooms................	[4] 35	....	15
Towels..........................	23	....	27
Soap............................	31	....	19
Towels and soap.................	23	....	27
Dressing rooms:			
Separate for males................	27	1	22
Separate for males, in work requiring change of clothing...	20	1	9
Separate for females.............	42	....	8
Separate for females, in work requiring change of clothing..	33	....	4
Rest rooms for females................	[5] 12	....	38
Lunch rooms.........................	14	....	36
Seats for females....................	42	8	....
Good drinking water................	50	....	....

[1] Acts of 1905, act No. 226, secs. 25, 26, and 27 (22d An. Rept. Com. of Labor, p. 1180).
[2] Three establishments not reported.
[3] Accommodations not reported for males in 8 establishments, for females in 1.
[4] For females only in 5 establishments.
[5] Including 1, sufficiency not reported.

In 1 establishment a dressing room for females, sufficient in size, was provided, but had been rendered useless by having the door removed.

In several cases the toilet and wash rooms were combined, and in 1 establishment the men's room was a combination closet, washing and dressing room.

OHIO.

SUMMARY OF LEGISLATION.[1]

Legislation regarding toilet conveniences in factories and workshops concerns females only. For such persons it is required that water-closets, wash rooms, dressing rooms, and seats shall be provided in all manufacturing and mercantile establishments. There is no legislation regarding lunch rooms, rest rooms, or drinking water.[2]

The legal provisions regarding water-closets, wash rooms, and dressing rooms are as follows:[3]

(a) The owner of the building [i. e., manufacturing, mechanical, or mercantile establishment] shall provide, on the same floor, or floor immediately above or below, of the building wherein any female persons are employed,

Suitable and separate toilet and dressing rooms and water-closets for the exclusive use of such female employees,

(b) And, where possible, such dressing rooms and water-closets shall be situated together,

(c) With 1 water-closet for every 25 females or less, and where there are more than 25 there shall be provided an additional water-closet, up to the number of 50, and above that number in the same ratio. *Provided*, That no such closet * * * be placed in a basement or cellar, unless such basement or cellar is used for manufacturing, mechanical, or mercantile purposes, and females are employed therein. *And provided further*, That such closets, in the same ratio as above mentioned, shall be placed on the outside of such building, at a distance not to exceed 20 feet in such cities, towns, and villages as are not provided with a system of waterworks, unless such building is provided with a dry-closet system, such closets to be kept in good sanitary condition at all times.

Penalty.—$10 to $25.

Seats for females are required in the following terms:

(d) Every person or corporation employing female employees in any manufacturing, mechanical, or mercantile establishments in this State shall provide a suitable seat for the use of each female employee so employed.

---

[1] The law here referred to is as in force at the time of the investigation, March, 1909. The text of the laws in force Jan. 1, 1912, is given in the appendixes at the end of this volume.

[2] For special legislation regarding tenement shops see Bates' Ann. Stat., 3d ed., Pt. II, Civ., secs. 4364–4380 to 4364–4385; and for that regarding bakeries, idem, secs. 4364–4371 to 4364–4379 (22d An. Rept. Com. of Labor, pp. 1011–1013).

[3] Bates' Ann. Stat., 3d ed., Pt. II, Civ., secs. 4364–4369 and 4364–4370 (22d An. Rept. Com. of Labor, p. 1010).

And shall permit the use of such by them when they are not necessarily engaged in the active duties for which they are employed.

And shall permit the use of such seats at all times when such use would not actually and necessarily interfere with the proper discharge of the duties of such employees.

And such seat shall be constructed or adjusted where practicable so as to be a fixture and not obstruct such female when actually engaged in the performance of such duties when such seat can not be used.[1]

Penalty.—$10 to $25.

These several provisions relate, it may be repeated, solely to female employees, the comfort of male employees not being directly considered by the law. Subject to this limitation, however, the legislation of Ohio upon the subjects now being considered is, as compared with most of the other States covered by this report, unusually precise. A considerable latitude is left to the discretion of the inspectors in determining when wash rooms, dressing rooms, and closets are "suitable," but many important conditions are so far standardized that there is little opportunity for abuse within the law. Four points in the quoted provisions may be commented upon in this connection.

(*a*) The law directs that the toilet and dressing rooms and water-closets are to be on the same floor as, or on the neighboring floor to, the one on which are located the employees whom they are to serve. This requirement aims to avoid the not infrequent evils arising from such conditions as that of having closets on only one floor of a tall building, and that of placing the closets in only one of a group of buildings.

(*b*) It is required that, where possible, the dressing rooms and water-closets shall be situated together. The advisability of such an arrangement is evident.

(*c*) The law establishes a standard ratio of not less than 1 closet accommodation to each 25 female employees. This ratio of 1 to 25 is generally recognized as a satisfactory one. The importance of such a fixed standard was commented upon in the early part of this chapter.

(*d*) As regards the subject of seats for females, the Ohio law is notable in that it provides that the females concerned may use such seats when "such use would not actually and necessarily interfere with the proper discharge of the duties of such employees." Such a provision, if properly enforced, may have quite a different effect than that of the usual provision, which directs simply that permission to use seats shall be granted when the employees concerned are "not necessarily engaged in the active duties of their employment."

---

[1] Bates' Ann. Stat., 3d ed., Pt. II, Civ., secs. 4364-69 and 4364-70 (22d An. Rept. Com. of Labor, p. 1010).

The former clause recognizes the possibility of work being done while sitting, and in such cases the right of the employees to sit. The latter clause usually results, in practice, in making the employer the judge of whether or not his female employees shall ever be permitted to sit. Of importance also is the provision of the Ohio law which provides that seats for females shall be so constructed as to be fixtures but not so as to interfere with the work when the seats are not in use.[1]

Finally, it may be observed that, while it is required that closets shall be separate for the sexes, there is no requirement as to privacy of location or approach.

The enforcement of the provisions quoted above is intrusted in full to the State factory inspection department.[2]

The chief factory inspector, in his report for the year 1907, makes the following statement regarding seats and water-closets:[3]

It is true we have a law which requires that suitable and separate dressing rooms and closets shall be provided for the exclusive use of females, and that a seat shall be provided for the use of every female employed, the use of which shall be permitted when it does not interfere with her duties. We find, however, that too often it is merely the letter of the law that has been complied with and not the spirit. Seats are provided, but I am afraid the women are frequently given to understand they are not to be used at any time. In our inspections we have found deplorable conditions surrounding the sanitary facilities; such, for instance, as closets for both sexes located side by side with wooden partitions, and, where women were employed at night, we found closets located at the rear of the lot some distance from the building. This, too, not because of the lack of sewer facilities, but because it was claimed the room could not be spared in the factory building.

---

[1] Under the child-labor law of 1908, Acts of 1908, p. 30, sec. 2 (Bulletin of the Bureau of Labor, No. 85, p. 703), females under 16 years of age are forbidden to be employed in any work requiring them to stand constantly.

[2] Bates' Ann. Stat., 3d ed., sec. 4364–69.

[3] Twenty-fourth Annual Report of the Department of Inspection of Workshops, Factories, and Public Buildings, Ohio, 1907, p. 10.

CONDITIONS FOUND.

The following 2 tables summarize the conditions found in 60 establishments visited as regards water-closet accommodations, washing facilities, etc.:

WATER-CLOSET ACCOMMODATIONS—OHIO.

Character of water-closet accommodations.	Establishments—	
	Having specified provisions.	Not having specified provisions.
Separate for sexes..	60	....
Private approaches for—		
Males [1]...	57	2
Females..	58	2
Clean for—		
Males [1]...	55	4
Females..	60	....
Air of workroom unaffected...................................	59	1
Separate for sexes, with one seat for each [2]—		
20 males or less..	48	10
20 females or less..	40	18
25 males or less..	55	3
25 females or less..	47	11
30 males or less..	55	3
30 females or less..	50	8

[1] No males in 1 establishment.
[2] No males in 1 establishment; number closets for females not reported in 2 establishments and for males in 1.

WASH ROOM, DRESSING ROOM, REST ROOM, LUNCH ROOM, ETC., ACCOMMODATIONS—OHIO.

Character of accommodations.	Establishments—		
	Having specified provisions—		Not having specified provisions.
	Sufficient.	Not sufficient.	
Wash rooms:			
Facilities for washing.......................................	57	1	2
Separate wash rooms......................................	27	[1] 3	30
Towels..	27	1	32
Soap..	31	1	28
Towels and soap..	25	1	34
Dressing rooms:			
Separate for males..	31	....	28
Separate for males, in work requiring change of clothing....	22	....	8
Separate for females.......................................	50	....	10
Separate for females, in work requiring change of clothing...	34	....	1
Rest rooms for females...	7	....	53
Lunch rooms..	11	1	48
Seats for females..	57	3	....
Good drinking water..	60	....	....

[1] In 3 establishments separate wash rooms for females only.

Examination of the first table shows that of the 58 establishments reporting on this point, 11 had more than 25 female employees per closet accommodation, thereby disregarding the legal requirement as above quoted.

ILLINOIS.

SUMMARY OF LEGISLATION.[1]

Seats for females are required in manufacturing, mercantile, and commercial establishments. The other subjects covered by this chapter—water-closets, wash rooms, dressing rooms, lunch rooms, rest rooms, and drinking water—are not referred to by the State law as it existed at the time the field work of this investigation was completed.[2]

The legal provision regarding seats for females is as follows:[3]

All establishments subject to factory inspection [i. e., factories, mercantile establishments, mills, workshops, and commercial institutions], where girls and women are employed, shall provide suitable seats for the use of the girls and women, and they shall be permitted the use of such seats when not necessarily engaged in their active duties.

Penalty.—$25–$100.

This requirement is quite similar to the corresponding ones for several of the States already reviewed, and in consequence needs no additional comment. Its enforcement is charged to the factory-inspection department.[4]

---

[1] The law here referred to is as in force at the time of the investigation, December, 1908, to February, 1909. The text of the laws in force Jan. 1, 1912, is given in the appendixes at the end of this volume.

[2] An Act approved June 4, 1909 (Bulletin of the Bureau of Labor, No. 85, pp. 547, 549, 550), however, covers the subject of water-closets, wash rooms, dressing rooms, and seats for females in factories in a very complete manner.

Special legislation regarding butterine and ice cream factories, Acts of 1907, p. 309, secs. 1 to 5 (22d An. Rept. Com. of Labor, pp. 375, 376), does not cover confectioneries or other food-producing establishments.

For special legislation regarding tenement shops see Hurd's Rev. Stat., 1905, ch. 48, secs. 21 to 28 (22d An. Rept. Com. of Labor, pp. 340, 341).

A city ordinance of Chicago, in effect at the time of this investigation, required that "sufficient and separate water-closets shall be provided for male and female employees, and such water-closets shall be properly ventilated."

[3] Hurd's Rev. Stat., 1905, ch. 48, secs. 36 and 48. Females under 16 years of age are forbidden to be employed at any work requiring constant standing. Idem., sec. 20j (22d An. Rept., Com. of Labor, pp. 339, 342, 343).

[4] Idem, sec. 29, as amended by act, p. 310, Acts of 1907 (22d An. Rept. Com. of Labor, p. 341).

CONDITIONS FOUND.

The following 2 tables summarize the conditions found in the 47 establishments visited as regards water-closet accommodations, washing facilities, etc.

WATER-CLOSET ACCOMMODATIONS—ILLINOIS.

Character of water-closet accommodations.	Establishments—	
	Having specified provisions.	Not having specified provisions.
Separate for sexes	47	....
Private approaches for—		
Males	31	16
Females	30	17
Clean for—		
Males	35	12
Females	41	6
Air of workroom unaffected	43	4
Separate for sexes, with one seat for each [1]—		
20 males or less	35	7
20 females or less	40	6
25 males or less	38	4
25 females or less	43	3
30 males or less	40	2
30 females or less	44	2

[1] Closet accommodations not reported in 5 cases for males and in 1 case for females.

WASH ROOM, DRESSING ROOM, REST ROOM, LUNCH ROOM, ETC., ACCOMMODATIONS— ILLINOIS.

Character of accommodations.	Establishments—		
	Having specified provisions—		Not having specified provisions.
	Sufficient.	Not sufficient.	
Wash rooms:			
Facilities for washing	24	23	....
Separate wash rooms	17	1	29
Towels [1]	19	1	26
Soap [1]	21	1	24
Towels and soap [1]	18	1	27
Dressing rooms:			
Separate for males	15	1	31
Separate for males, in work requiring change of clothing	8	....	10
Separate for females	23	7	17
Separate for females, in work requiring change of clothing	10	3	1
Rest rooms for females	4	2	41
Lunch rooms	10	....	37
Seats for females	37	10	....
Good drinking water	47	....	....

[1] 1 not reported.

Water-closets are reported, and are listed in the above table, as being separate for the sexes in all of the establishments visited. In one woolen and worsted factory, however, males and females were found to use the same closet on one floor, although separate closets were provided on other floors.

One establishment, manufacturing hosiery and knit goods, reported that several years previously it had provided rest and lunch rooms, but that as so little use was made of them they had been discontinued. In the case of a match factory it was reported that employees ate lunch in the workrooms. In this same establishment the dressing room for females formed the exit for men and women leaving the factory. A tinware factory, although having no rest room, did have a room fitted up for the emergency treatment of accident cases.

INDIANA.

SUMMARY OF LEGISLATION.[1]

Water-closets, wash rooms, and seats for female employees are required in manufacturing and mercantile establishments. Dressing rooms for females may be required by the chief factory inspector when he thinks such conveniences necessary. There is no legal reference to the subjects of lunch rooms, rest rooms, or drinking water.[2]

The legal provisions as to wash rooms, water-closets, dressing rooms, and seats for females are as follows:[3]

(a) and (b) A suitable and proper wash room and water-closets shall be provided by the owner, agent, or lessee in each establishment above enumerated (i. e., manufacturing or mercantile establishments, laundry, renovating works, bakery, or printing office), and such water-closets shall be properly screened and ventilated, and kept at all times in a clean condition.

With not less than 1 seat for each 25 persons, and 1 seat for each fraction thereof above 10, employed in such establishment.

And if women and girls are employed in any such establishment, the water-closets used by them shall have separate approaches and be separated and apart from those used by the men.

All water-closets shall be kept free of obscene writing and marking.

(c) A dressing room shall be provided for women and girls, when required by the chief inspector, in any establishment aforesaid in which women and girls are employed.

---

[1] The law here referred to is as in force at the time of the investigation, February and March, 1909. The text of the laws in force Jan. 1, 1912, is given in the appendixes at the end of this volume.

[2] Special legislation exists in regard to water-closets and wash rooms in bakeries and confectioneries. The requirement, however, is simply that such conveniences shall be provided and that they shall be separate from the rooms where the manufacturing processes are conducted. Ann. Stat., 1894, Rev. of 1901, sec. 6725h.(22d An. Rept. Com. of Labor, p. 385). By a law enacted after the field work of this investigation was completed, more stringent regulations are made as regards toilet conveniences in all food-producing establishments. Acts of 1909, ch. 163, sec. 5 (Bulletin of the Bureau of Labor, No. 85, p. 571).

Special legislation regarding tenement shops does not cover directly the subjects of water-closets, etc.

[3] Ann. Stat. of 1894, Rev. of 1901, sec. 7087j and 7087y (22d An. Rept. Com. of Labor, pp. 399, 402).

(*d*) And the employer of such women and girls shall provide a suitable seat for the use of each female employee placed conveniently where she works, and shall permit the use of the same when she is not necessarily engaged in the active duties for which she is employed, and such seats shall be constructed or adjusted where practicable so as to be a fixture and not obstruct such female when actually engaged in the performance of such duties when such seat can not be used.

Penalty.—First offense, not more than $50; second offense, not more than $100, to which may be added imprisonment for not more than 10 days; third offense, not less than $250, and not more than 30 days' imprisonment.

Reviewing these provisions, it will be observed (*a*) that as regards wash rooms the legal requirement is very general. It is simply ordered that a "suitable and proper" wash room shall be provided, the inspector being at liberty to exercise full discretion in determining when a wash room fulfills those conditions. It would appear, however, that the law requires a distinct wash room of some character in every establishment, and that the mere presence of running water or water pails in a workroom would not be sufficient to fulfill the legal command. (*b*) In the matter of water-closets the law is more specific than in the case of wash rooms. It requires that closets shall be "suitable and proper," that they shall be separate for the sexes, that the approaches to the closets shall be separate for the sexes, and, of very great importance, it requires that there shall be one accommodation for each 25 persons or fraction thereof above 10. This standard of one accommodation to 25 persons is the same adopted by the law of Ohio. The Ohio law regarding water-closets, however, refers to females only, whereas the Indiana law covers both males and females. The Indiana law, on the other hand, makes no specific reference to the location of closets. (*c*) Dressing room for females are not absolutely required by the law, but the inspector is given authority to order such conveniences when he considers such an order necessary. It is the probable intention of the law that the inspector should order dressing rooms where the nature of the work renders it necessary or desirable for the female employees to make a change of clothing in the factory. (*d*) As regards seats for females the Indiana law is like that of Ohio in requiring that the seats shall be so constructed as to be permanent fixtures. It differs from the Ohio law, however, in that it does not order that females shall be allowed the use of the seats when the work is not thereby interfered with.

All of the above-quoted legal provisions are charged to the State factory inspection department for enforcement.[1]

---

[1] Ann. Stat., 1894, Rev. of 1901, sec. 7087v (22d An. Rept. Com. of Labor, p. 402).

CONDITIONS FOUND.

The 2 following tables summarize the conditions found in the 47 visited establishments as regards water-closet accommodations, washing facilities, etc.:

WATER-CLOSET ACCOMMODATIONS—INDIANA.

Character of water-closet accommodations.	Establishments—	
	Having specified provisions.	Not having specified provisions.
Separate for sexes..	47	....
Private approaches for—		
Males..	44	3
Females...	40	6
Clean for—		
Males..	37	10
Females [1]..	43	3
Air of workroom unaffected..	47	....
Separate for sexes, with one seat for each [2]—		
20 males or less...	36	9
20 females or less...	18	28
25 males or less...	40	5
25 females or less...	30	16
30 males or less...	41	4
30 females or less...	35	11

[1] No females in 1 establishment.
[2] No females in 1 establishment; and number of closets for males not reported in 2 establishments.

WASH ROOM, DRESSING ROOM, REST ROOM, LUNCH ROOM, ETC., ACCOMMODATIONS—INDIANA.

Character of accommodations.	Establishments—		
	Having specified provisions—		Not having specified provisions.
	Sufficient.	Not sufficient.	
Wash rooms:			
Facilities for washing...	23	23	1
Separate wash rooms [1]..	10	[2] 5	31
Towels...	23	....	24
Soap...	26	....	21
Towels and soap..	22	....	25
Dressing rooms:			
Separate for males..	17	1	29
Separate for males, in work requiring change of clothing....	6	....	4
Separate for females [3]..	18	7	21
Separate for females, in work requiring change of clothing ...	5	....	2
Rest rooms for females [3]...	3	....	43
Lunch rooms..	7	[4] 2	38
Seats for females [3]..	36	10	....
Good drinking water..	46	....	1

[1] Not reported, 1 establishment.   [3] No females in 1 establishment.
[2] Three for females only.   [4] One for males only.

As noted above, the State law prescribes a standard of at least 1 seat for each 25 persons employed. Examination of the first table shows that this standard was not observed by 5 out of 45 establishments in the case of males, and by 16 out of 46 in the case of females.

In 1 establishment, a bag factory, provisions for the comfort of employees were especially good. Separate wash rooms with towels and soap, a dressing room for females, a lunch room, and a rest room were provided, and in each instance the provision was sufficient. The rest room was in connection with the dressing room, had 2 cots and a supply of first-aid remedies. A matron was in charge. Ten minutes extra were allowed for lunch between 9 and 10 a. m. At noon coffee with cream and sugar was furnished free in the lunch rooms. An entertainment was given weekly at noon by the local Y. W. C. A. The room was provided with an organ. The water-closets were clean, had privacy of approach, with 1 seat for each 9 males and 1 seat for each 26 females.

On the other hand, in several of the establishments visited, provisions for the comfort of employees were very inadequate. In 1 cigar factory with 686 employees—30 males and 656 females—the washing facilities were limited to 5 ordinary sinks and spigots; and in 1 woolen mill with 210 employees—67 males and 143 females—there were no washing facilities at all. In another woolen mill where the female workers get so dirty from grease and lint as to make it necessary for them to comb their hair and change their clothing before going into the street, there were no dressing rooms. Large pieces of burlap, behind which the girls crouched while dressing, hung in the corners and bits of mirrors were placed on the window sills.

This factory with 143 employees—66 males and 77 females—had neither rest rooms, dressing rooms, wash rooms, nor lunch rooms; no place, in fact, for the employees to get away from the workrooms.

In 1 establishment sanitary drinking fountains were provided.

MICHIGAN.

SUMMARY OF LEGISLATION.[1]

Water-closets, wash rooms, dressing rooms, and seats for females are required in manufacturing and mercantile establishments generally. There are no legal requirements as to lunch rooms, rest rooms, or drinking water. Foundries are subject to special legislation regarding the supplying of hot water for washing purposes and the provision of some means for drying clothes.[2]

---

[1] The law here referred to is as in force at the time of the investigation, March, 1909. The text of the laws in force Jan. 1, 1912, is given in the appendixes at the end of this volume.

[2] Tenement-shop legislation does not refer directly to the subject of toilet facilities. Acts of 1901, act No. 113, sec. 17, as amended by act No. 169, Acts of 1907 (22d An. Rept. Com. of Labor, pp. 661, 662).

There is no special legislation regarding bakeries.

Excluding, for the moment, the special legislation regarding foundries, the legal provisions as to water-closets, wash rooms, and dressing rooms are as follows:[1]

Every manufacturing establishment, workshop, hotel, or store in which 5 or more persons are employed, and every institution in which 2 or more children, young persons, or women are employed, (a) and (b) shall be supplied with proper wash and dressing rooms, and kept in a cleanly state and free from effluvia arising from any drain, privy, or other nuisance.

(c) And shall be provided within reasonable access with a sufficient number of water-closets, earth closets, or privies for the reasonable use of persons employed therein, at least 1 of such closets for each 25 persons employed.

And wherever 2 or more persons and 1 or more female persons are employed as aforesaid, a sufficient number of separate and distinct water-closets, earth closets, or privies shall be provided for the use of each sex, and plainly so designated, and no person shall be allowed to use any such closet or privy assigned to persons of the other sex.

Penalty.—$5 to $100 or imprisonment 10 to 90 days or both.

These provisions apply only to establishments employing more than a minimum number of persons, but this minimum is so low that practically all factories and workshops are included within the scope of the law.

Examining the provisions in detail, it may be observed that while the requirements concerning water-closets are elaborate and on some points very precise, those concerning wash rooms and dressing rooms are few in number and general in character. As regards wash and dressing rooms it is provided merely that they shall be "proper." In practice the inspection department is free to determine what kind and number of rooms are within the meaning of the term "proper." It is probably not imperative under the law that the washing and dressing facilities shall be in entirely distinct rooms, but the law is clear in demanding that at least one wash and dressing room shall be provided in each establishment. It is not specifically required that such rooms shall be separate for the sexes, but this may be assumed from the requirement that they shall be "proper."

As regards water-closets the most significant requirement is that there shall be at least 1 closet accommodation for each 25 persons. This ratio, it will be remembered, is the same as that provided for in the laws of Ohio and Indiana. It is also directed that closets shall be within "reasonable access," and "separate and distinct" for the sexes. The interpretation of these terms is subject to con-

---

[1] Acts of 1901, act No. 113, secs. 10 (as amended by act No. 169, Acts of 1907) and 18 (22d An. Rept. Com. of Labor, pp. 660, 662).

siderable latitude of personal judgment, but they are specific enough to enable the enforcing authority to insist upon closets being conveniently located and, as between the sexes, private in their approaches.

Seats for female employees are required by law in the following terms:[1]

(d) All persons who employ females, in stores, shops, offices, or manufactories, as clerks, assistants, operatives, or helpers in any business, trade, or occupation carried on or operated by them, shall be required to procure and provide proper and suitable seats for all such females, and shall permit the use of such seats, rests, or stools as may be necessary, and shall not make any rules, regulations, or orders preventing the use of such stools or seats, when such female employees are not actively imployed in their work in such business or employment.

Penalty.—Not to exceed $25.

One clause of this provision deserves comment—"shall permit the use of such seats * * * as may be necessary." If "necessary" here means "necessary to health," the effect of this law would be similar to that of the law of New York, which in the same connection uses the phrase "as may be reasonable for the preservation of their health" (see p. 399). In the absence of definite medical authority on this subject, and in the absence of medically trained inspectors, the effect of such a clause may not be great, but it provides an opening for an effective administration of the spirit of the law regarding seats for females.

In the case of foundries, the law makes two special provisions:[2]

Hot water shall be kept available for washing purposes during the season in which artificial heating is necessary.

When it is thought necessary and advisable by a State factory inspector, facilities shall be provided for drying the clothing of persons employed therein.

Penalty.—$5 to $100, or imprisonment 10 days to 3 months, or both.

Foundries rarely employ women or children and no such establishment was visited during the course of this investigation.

The State factory inspection department [bureau of labor and industrial statistics] is charged with the supervision and enforcement of all the provisions above quoted.[3]

---

[1] Comp. Laws 1897, secs. 5373, 5374 (22d An. Rept. Com. of Labor, p. 636).

[2] Acts of 1907, act No. 152, secs. 4 and 9 (22d An. Rept. Com. of Labor, p. 667).

[3] Acts of 1901, act No. 113, sec. 15; Acts of 1907, act No. 152, sec. 7 (22d An. Rept. Com. of Labor, pp. 661, 668).

CONDITIONS FOUND.

The following tables summarize the conditions found in the 19 visited establishments as regards water-closet accommodations, washing facilities, etc.:

WATER-CLOSET ACCOMMODATIONS—MICHIGAN.

Character of water-closet accommodations.	Establishments—	
	Having specified provisions.	Not having specified provisions.
Separate for sexes........	19	....
Private approaches for—		
Males........	14	5
Females........	14	5
Clean for—		
Males........	14	5
Females........	14	5
Air of workroom unaffected........	15	4
Separate for sexes, with one seat for each—		
20 males or less........	15	4
20 females or less........	11	8
25 males or less........	18	1
25 females or less........	14	5
30 males or less........	18	1
30 females or less........	16	3

WASH ROOM, DRESSING ROOM, REST ROOM, LUNCH ROOM, ETC., ACCOMMODATIONS— MICHIGAN.

Character of accommodations.	Establishments—		
	Having specified provisions—		Not having specified provisions.
	Sufficient.	Not sufficient.	
Wash rooms:			
Facilities for washing........	11	8	....
Separate wash rooms........	4	3	12
Towels........	11	....	8
Soap........	12	....	7
Towels and soap........	10	....	9
Dressing rooms:			
Separate for males........	11	1	7
Separate for males, in work requiring change of clothing....	3	....	2
Separate for females........	10	3	6
Separate for females, in work requiring change of clothing...	1	....	1
Rest rooms for females........	1	....	18
Lunch rooms........	5	....	14
Seats for females........	18	1	....
Good drinking water........	19	....	....

The Michigan law, as noted above, prescribes a standard of not less than 1 water-closet seat for each 25 persons employed. Examination of the first table shows that this standard was not observed by 1 of the 19 establishments in the case of males, and by 5 of the 19 in the case of females.

A large cigar factory provides a dressing room, with attendant, where hats and wraps are checked; and a large lunch room, with a woman attendant.   Lunch was served free at one time, but now cost prices are charged.   Employees are not permitted to take their own lunches into the workrooms.

A tobacco and snuff factory contains an ample lunch room with chairs and tables, and serves coffee and tea free to employees.   No lunching is allowed at the worktables. •

A match factory serves free coffee in a large lunch room, with one attendant.

A confectionery establishment furnishes late books and magazines in the girls' rest room, and has a smoking room for men where similar literature is supplied.   •

Sanitary drinking fountains are provided in a woolen mill.

WISCONSIN.

SUMMARY OF LEGISLATION.[1]

Water-closets are required in all manufacturing and mercantile establishments where 8 or more persons are employed, and seats for females in all such establishments, irrespective of the number of employees.[2]   Dressing rooms are not required unconditionally, but may be ordered by the members of the inspection department in places where the nature of the work is such as to make change of clothing necessary or desirable.   Washing facilities are not required in any class of establishments except bakeries and confectioneries; and lunch rooms, rest rooms and drinking water are not referred to in the State law.

In addition to the general provisions regarding water-closets, etc., in manufacturing and mercantile establishments generally, there are a few special regulations regarding cigar factories and bakery and confectionery establishments.

Excluding the special legislation regarding cigar and confectionery establishments, the legal provisions regarding water-closets, dressing rooms, and seats for females are as follows:[3]

(a) Every factory, mill, or workshop, mercantile or mechanical establishment, or other building where 8 or more persons are employed shall be provided within reasonable access with a sufficient number of water-closets, earth closets, or privies for the reasonable use of the persons employed therein.

And whenever male and female persons are employed as aforesaid together, water-closets, earth closets, or privies separate and apart

---

[1] The law here referred to is as in force at the time of the investigation, March, 1909. The text of the laws in force Jan. 1, 1912, is given in the appendixes at the end of this volume.

[2] The tenement-shop laws make some special requirements regarding water-closets in such establishments.   Ann. Stat. of 1898, Supp. of 1906, Acts of 1907, secs. 1636–73 (22d An. Rept. Com. of Labor, p. 1421).

[3] Ann. Stat. of 1898, Supp. of 1906, Acts of 1907, secs. 1636–31, 1636–32, 1636–35, and 1728l (22d An. Rept. Com. of Labor, pp. 1415, 1429).

shall be provided for the use of each sex and plainly so designated, and no person shall be allowed to use such closet or privy assigned to the other sex.

Such closet shall be proper inclosed and ventilated and at all times kept in a clean and good sanitary condition.

When the number employed is more than 20 of either sex, there shall be provided an additional closet for such sex up to the number of 40, and above that number in the same ratio.

The commissioner of labor or any factory inspector may require such changes in the placing of such closets as he may deem necessary and may require other changes which may serve the best interest of morals and sanitation.

(b) In factories, mills, or workshops, mercantile or mechanical establishments, or other places where the labor performed by the operator is of such a character that it becomes desirable or necessary to change the clothing, wholly or in part, before leaving the building at the close of the day's work, separate dressing rooms shall be provided for females whenever so required by the commissioner of labor or any factory inspector.

Penalty.—$10 to $100.

(c) Every person or corporation employing females in any manufacturing, mechanical, or mercantile establishment in the State of Wisconsin shall provide suitable seats for the females so employed, and shall permit the use of such seats by them when they are not necessarily engaged in the active duties for which they are employed.[1]

Penalty.—$10 to $30 for each offense.

In reviewing these provisions it will be observed that while the provisions regarding dressing rooms and seats for females apply to establishments irrespective of the number of their employees, those regarding water-closets apply only to establishments having at least eight employees. Each of the establishments in Wisconsin covered by this investigation had more than eight employees, and were thus subject to the requirements of this law.

(a) The legal provisions regarding water-closets, while leaving many details to the discretion of the factory inspectors, are unmistakable upon most points. Thus, it is ordered that closets shall be separate and separately located for the sexes; privacy of approach and convenience of access are clearly implied; and a ratio is established between the number of employees and the number of seats. This ratio is fixed at 1 accommodation for each 20 persons—a more stringent standard than that of Ohio, Indiana, Michigan, and Louisiana, in which the ratio is 1 to 25, and which are the only other States of those covered having standards of this character fixed by law. Finally, it should be especially noted that the Wisconsin law specifically authorizes the inspection department to order whatever

---

[1] The law of Wisconsin also forbids the employment of females under 16 years of age at any work requiring constant standing. Ann. Stat. of 1898, Supp. of 1906, Acts of 1907, sec. 1728-1 (22d An. Rept. Com. of Labor, p. 1426).

additional changes in the location or character of closets it may think necessary in the interest of morals and sanitation. This is a broad authority, under which the inspection department may insist upon excellent water-closet conditions.

In the matter of dressing rooms the law is not mandatory. It leaves to the inspection department the discretion of determining when dressing rooms are necessary, and if so, the character of such rooms.

The requirement regarding seats for females is quite similar to that of several other of the States already reviewed upon this point and need not be again commented upon.

The special legislation regarding cigar factories refers briefly to two subjects—dressing rooms and water-closets. The legal provision is as follows:[1]

Where men and women are employed [in manufacturing cigars] there shall be separate dressing rooms and water-closets for the different sexes.

Penalty.—First offense, $10 to $25; second offense, $25 to $50.

In cigar factories, therefore, dressing rooms are unconditionally required for each of the sexes in establishments employing both males and females. This is in contrast with the previously quoted provision regarding dressing rooms in other classes of establishments, dressing rooms in such cases being required only when ordered by the inspection department. As regards water-closets, the special law concerning cigar factories adds nothing to the general law requiring closets separate for the sexes in manufacturing establishments generally.

The special legislation regarding bakeries and confectioneries requires washing facilities and dressing rooms in unconditional terms. The law reads:[2]

All bakeries and confectioneries shall be provided with ample toilet facilities apart from the utensils used in the preparation of said foods to enable the workmen employed therein to keep their persons clean.

Said bakeries and confectioneries shall also be provided with a separate dressing room to enable the workmen to change their clothes and keep the same in a proper condition.

No water-closet, earth closet, privy, or ash pit shall be within or communicate directly with the bake room or any other room used in the manufacture of bread or other food products in any bakery or confectionery establishment.

The chief purpose of these special requirements is, of course, to insure a pure product and not to guard the health or increase the comforts of the worker.

---

[1] Ann. Stat. of 1898, Supp. of 1906, Acts of 1907, secs. 1636–107 and 1636–108 (22d An. Rept. Com. of Labor, p. 1424).

[2] Idem, sec. 1636–62 (22d An. Rept. Com. Labor, p. 1418).

All of the above-quoted provisions are charged to the State factory inspection department [bureau of labor statistics] for enforcement.[1] To aid in enforcing the separate regulations regarding bakeries and confectioneries a special officer, known as the bakery inspector, is provided for by law, but this officer is under the direction of the commissioner of labor, who is at the head of the factory inspection service.

CONDITIONS FOUND.

The following tables summarize the conditions found in the 19 visited establishments as regards water-closet accommodations, washing facilities, etc.

WATER-CLOSET ACCOMMODATIONS—WISCONSIN.

Character of water-closet accommodations.	Establishments—	
	Having specified provisions.	Not having specified provisions.
Separate for sexes	19	
Private approaches for—		
Males	17	2
Females	18	1
Clean for—		
Males	18	1
Females	19	
Air of workroom unaffected	19	
Separate for sexes, with one seat for each [1]—		
20 males or less [2]	17	1
20 females or less	12	7
25 males or less [2]	18	
25 females or less	16	3
30 males or less [2]	18	
30 females or less	17	2

WASH ROOM, DRESSING ROOM, REST ROOM, LUNCH ROOM, ETC., ACCOMMODATIONS—WISCONSIN.

Character of accommodations.	Establishments—		
	Having specified provisions—		Not having specified provisions.
	Sufficient.	Not sufficient.	
Wash rooms:			
Facilities for washing	13	1	5
Separate wash rooms	7		12
Towels	8	1	10
Soap	10		9
Towels and soap	8	1	10
Dressing rooms:			
Separate for males	7		12
Separate for males, in work requiring change of clothing	3		2
Separate for females	13	1	5
Separate for females, in work requiring change of clothing	5	1	
Rest rooms for females	1		18
Lunch rooms	2		17
Seats for females	13	6	
Good drinking water	19		

[1] Ann. Stat., 1898, Supp. of 1906, Acts of 1907, secs. 1636–66, 1636–71, 1636–109 (22d An. Rept. Com. of Labor, pp. 1419, 1424).
[2] One establishment not reported.

As noted above, the Wisconsin law prescribes a maximum ratio of not less than 1 closet accommodation for every 20 persons employed. Examination of the first table shows that this standard was not observed by 1 of 18 establishments in the case of males, and by 7 of 19 in the case of females.

A tobacco factory employed a woman attendant to look after dressing room and keep workrooms cleán.

A match factory contained a large lunch room where employees ate in two sections. Soup and coffee were served free.

The above tables include 4 confectionery establishments, which, as noted in the legal summary abóve, are subject to especial regulations as regards toilet facilities.* Two of these 4 confectionery establishments had sufficient and separate wash. rooms, furnished with soap and towels; sufficient dressing rooms, separate for the sexes; and water-closets clean, private, and with less than 20 persons per accommodation. The third of the 4 confectionery establishments had equally satisfactory conditions, except that it did not furnish towels to its employees. The fourth confectionery establishment on the other hand, although amply and satisfactorily supplied with dressing rooms and water-closets, had no washing facilities of any kind for the use of its employees.

MARYLAND.

SUMMARY OF LEGISLATION.[1]

A public general law of Maryland requires seats for females in all mercantile establishments within the State, and a public local law requires seats for females in mercantile and manufacturing establishments in Baltimore City.[2] There are no legal requirements regarding water-closets, wash rooms, dressing rooms, lunch rooms, rest rooms, or drinking water.[3]

The legal provision regarding seats for females in Baltimore City is as follows:[4]

Every employer of females and mercantile or manufacturing establishment in the city of Baltimore must provide and maintain suit-

---

[1] The law here referred to is as in force at the time of the investigation, January, 1909. The text of the laws in force Jan. 1, 1912, is given in the appendixes at the end of this volume.

[2] Pub. Gen. Laws, Code of 1903, art. 27, sec. 230, as amended by ch. 287, Acts of 1904 (22d An. Rept. Com. of Labor, pp. 539, 540). Pub. Local Laws, Code of 1888, art. 4, sec. 505, as amended by ch. 589, Acts of 1900 (22d An. Rept. Com. of Labor, p. 564).

[3] The legislation regarding tenement shops does not refer specifically to the subjects of water-closets, wash rooms, etc. There is no special State legislation regarding bakeries.

[4] Pub. Local Laws, Code of 1888, art. 4, sec. 505, as amended by ch. 589, Acts of 1900, and sec. 506, Rev. of 1898, ch. 123, Acts of 1898 (22d An. Rept. Com. of Labor, p. 564).

able seats for the use of such employees. A person is deemed not to maintain suitable seats for the use of female employees unless he permits the use thereof by such employees to such extent as may be reasonable for the preservation of health and proper rest, and the question of what is thus reasonable is one for determination by the jury or the court acting as a jury in any prosecution hereunder.

Penalty.—$150.

This requirement applies, as noted above, only to the city of Baltimore; but as approximately four-fifths of the female factory employees of Maryland are within that city the scope of the requirement is nevertheless very broad.[1] Its enforcement is not charged to the State factory inspection department, which assumes no responsibility or authority in the matter.

While, as has been mentioned, there are no legal requirements regarding toilet facilities of any kind, there is a provision of the factory inspection law which bears indirectly upon the subject of water-closets. The provision referred to is as follows:[2]

All factories, manufacturing establishments, or workshops in this State shall be kept in a cleanly condition and free from effluvia arising from any drain, privy, or other nuisance.

The factory inspection department, however, does not construe this provision as vesting it with any authority in the matter of water-closets. If in the course of his inspection duty a factory inspector finds a water-closet in bad condition, he notifies the local board of health, but does not take the initiative in remedying such bad condition.

In an interview with the chief factory inspector that official stated his belief that factories should be compelled to furnish suitable wash rooms, but that he had never advocated a law on the subject because he did not think it of sufficient importance in view of the fact that other more important changes in the law were being sought. As regards dressing rooms and lunch rooms, he did not believe there was any necessity for special legislation; that employers would furnish voluntarily such conveniences when necessary.

CONDITIONS FOUND.

The 2 following tables summarize the conditions found in the 28 establishments visited as regards water-closet accommodations, washing facilities, etc.

---

[1] Twelfth Census of the United States, 1900, Vol. VIII, Manufactures, Pt. II, pp. 336, 337.

[2] Pub. Gen. Laws, Code of 1903, art. 27, sec. 234 (22d An. Rept. Com. of Labor, p. 540).

WATER-CLOSET ACCOMMODATIONS—MARYLAND.

Character of water-closet accommodations.	Establishments—	
	Having specified provisions.	Not having specified provisions.
Separate for sexes..	28	....
Private approaches for—		
Males..	27	1
Females..	27	1
Clean for—		
Males..	27	1
Females..	27	1
Air of workroom unaffected................................	28	....
Separate for sexes, with one seat for each—		
20 males or less.......................................	25	3
20 females or less.....................................	14	14
25 males or less.......................................	26	2
25 females or less.....................................	16	12
30 males or less.......................................	26	2
30 females or less.....................................	21	7

WASH ROOM, DRESSING ROOM, REST ROOM, LUNCH ROOM, ETC., ACCOMMODATIONS— MARYLAND.

Character of accommodations.	Establishments—		
	Having specified provisions—		Not having specified provisions.
	Sufficient.	Not sufficient.	
Wash rooms:			
Facilities for washing...............................	25	3	....
Separate wash rooms.............................	3	....	25
Towels...	4	....	24
Soap..	7	....	21
Towels and soap...................................	4	....	22
Dressing rooms:			
Separate for males..................................	13	....	15
Separate for males, in work requiring change of clothing....	10	2	16
Separate for females................................	24	....	4
Separate for females, in work requiring change of clothing..	15	....	13
Rest rooms for females.................................	4	2	22
Lunch rooms...	2	....	26
Seats for females......................................	26	2	....
Good drinking water...................................	28	....	....

In 1 of the establishments reported as not having a lunch room, provision was made by which employees could obtain coffee at 2 cents a cup and ham sandwiches at 3 cents apiece.

NORTH CAROLINA.

There was, at the time of this investigation, no State legislation [1] in North Carolina upon any of the subjects considered in this chapter—water-closets, wash rooms, dressing rooms, lunch rooms, rest rooms, seats for female employees, or drinking water.[2] Nor any factory-inspection service.

[1] The law here referred to is as in force at the time of the investigation, March, 1909. The text of the laws in force Jan. 1, 1912, is given in the appendixes at the end of this volume.

[2] An act ratified shortly after the field work of this investigation was completed requires seats for females in manufacturing and mercantile establishments. Acts of 1909, ch. 857, secs. 1 and 2 (Bulletin of the Bureau of Labor, No. 85, p. 696).

CONDITIONS FOUND.

The 2 following tables summarize the conditions found in the 28 visited establishments as regards water-closet accommodations, washing facilities, etc. In 2 establishments no females were employed.

In several tobacco factories both colored and white persons were employed, and when this was the case, separate closets were provided for the races. Also, in all the cases of this kind met with, the number of employees per accommodation was more favorable to the colored than to the white. Therefore, in the first of the following tables the information upon the point of closet sufficiency is given in most cases for the white employees only.

WATER-CLOSET ACCOMMODATIONS—NORTH CAROLINA.

Character of water-closet accommodations.	Establishments—	
	Having specified provisions.	Not having specified provisions.
Separate for sexes [1]	27	1
Private approaches for—		
Males	15	13
Females [2]	13	13
Clean for—		
Males	20	8
Females [2]	20	6
Air of workroom unaffected	26	2
Separate for sexes, with one seat for each [3]—		
20 males or less	12	15
20 females or less [2]	13	12
25 males or less	15	12
25 females or less [2]	16	9
30 males or less	20	7
30 females or less [2]	18	7

[1] In 1 establishment separate closets for colored and white and for sexes provided, but closets for colored employees used promiscuously at times by the sexes.
[2] No females in 2 establishments.
[3] Excluding 1 establishment in which closets were not separate for sexes, data not reported.

WASH ROOM, DRESSING ROOM, REST ROOM, LUNCH ROOM, ETC., ACCOMMODATIONS—NORTH CAROLINA.

Character of accommodations.	Establishments—		
	Having specified provisions—		Not having specified provisions.
	Sufficient.	Not sufficient.	
Wash rooms:			
Facilities for washing	17	8	3
Separate wash rooms	2	1	25
Towels	1	1	26
Soap	3	1	24
Towels and soap	1	1	26
Dressing rooms:			
Separate for males	2		26
Separate for males, in work requiring change of clothing			
Separate for females [1]	3		23
Separate for females, in work requiring change of clothing			
Rest rooms for females [2]	1		24
Lunch rooms	1		27
Seats for females [1]	5	21	
Good drinking water	26		2

[1] No females in 2 establishments.
[2] One establishment not reported; 2, no females.

As shown by the first table, separate closets were not provided for the sexes in 1 of the 26 establishments employing both sexes. In one, while separate closets were provided for the sexes and for the two races, those for the colored employees were used promiscuously at times.

GEORGIA.

SUMMARY OF LEGISLATION.[1]

The law of Georgia requires seats for females in all manufacturing and mercantile establishments. There is no legislation regarding the other subjects covered in this chapter—water-closets, wash rooms, dressing rooms, lunch rooms, rest rooms, or drinking water.

The law regarding seats for females is as follows:[2]

All persons and corporations employing females in manufacturing, mechanical, or mercantile establishments must provide suitable seats, and permit their use by such females when not necessarily engaged in the active duties for which they were employed.

Penalty.—Same as for a misdemeanor (i. e., fine not to exceed $1,000, imprisonment not to exceed 6 months, a chain gang not to exceed 12 months, or any two or all three penalties).

The enforcement of this requirement is not charged to any specific official or set of officials. There is no factory inspection department or service in Georgia.

CONDITIONS FOUND.

The 2 following tables summarize the conditions found in the 27 visited establishments as regards water-closet accommodations, washing facilities, etc.

WATER-CLOSET ACCOMMODATIONS—GEORGIA.

Character of water-closet accommodations.	Establishments—	
	Having specified provisions.	Not having specified provisions.
Separate for sexes	27	....
Private approaches for—		
Males	18	9
Females	15	12
Clean for—		
Males	17	10
Females	18	9
Air of workroom unaffected	24	3
Separate for sexes, with one seat for each [1]—		
20 males or less	21	6
20 females or less	17	10
25 males or less	23	4
25 females or less	23	4
30 males or less	25	2
30 females or less	25	2

[1] The law here referred to is as in force at the time of investigation, March, 1909. The text of the laws in force Jan. 1, 1912, is given in the appendixes at the end of this volume.
[2] Code, 1895, Vol. III, Pen. Code, sec 127 (22d An. Rept. Com. of Labor, p. 293).

WASH ROOM, DRESSING ROOM, REST ROOM, LUNCH ROOM, ETC., ACCOMMODA-
TIONS—GEORGIA.

Character of accommodations.	Establishments—		
	Having specified provisions—		Not having specified provisions.
	Sufficient.	Not sufficient.	
Wash rooms:			
Facilities for washing.	20	4	3
Separate wash rooms.	8		19
Towels.	14		13
Soap.	12		15
Towels and soap.	12		15
Dressing rooms:			
Separate for males.	8		19
Separate for males, in work requiring change of clothing.	7		
Separate for females.	10	1	16
Separate for females, in work requiring change of clothing.	8		
Rest rooms for females.			27
Lunch rooms.			27
Seats for females.	8	19	
Good drinking water.	25		2

As shown by the table, none of the 27 establishments had lunch rooms. Two factories, both under the same management, served hot soup and crackers at noon from a kettle in the hall, and were planning to have regular lunch rooms installed. In most of the other establishments the employees went home for meals, but in 2 factories, a candy and a cracker factory, respectively, the employees brought their lunches to the factory and ate at their work places, on the stairways, and at other places.

One establishment provided ice water during 8 months of the year.

FLORIDA.

SUMMARY OF LEGISLATION.[1]

Seats for female employees are required in mercantile and "other business pursuits." There is no legislation regarding any of the other topics covered in this chapter—water-closets, wash rooms, dressing rooms, lunch rooms, rest rooms, or drinking water.

The requirement of seats for females is in the following terms:[2]

If any merchant, storekeeper, employer of male or female clerks, salesmen, cash boys or cash girls, or other assistants in mercantile or other business pursuits requiring such employees to stand or walk during their active duties neglect to furnish, at their own cost or expense, suitable chairs, stools, or sliding seats attached to the counters or walls for the use of such employees when not engaged in their active work and not required to be on their feet in the proper performance of their several duties, or refuse to permit their said employees to make reasonable use of said seats during business hours

[1] The law here referred to is as in force at the time of the investigation, March, 1909. The text of the laws in force Jan. 1, 1912, is given in the appendixes at the end of this volume.

[2] Gen. Stat., 1906, sec. 3235 (22d An. Rept. Com. of Labor, p. 281).

for the purposes of necessary rest and where such use will not interfere with humane or reasonable requirements of their employment, he shall, upon conviction thereof, be punished by a fine of not more than $100 or imprisonment not exceeding 60 days.

This provision is generally supposed to have been aimed at the department stores, and no officials make any attempt to enforce it in the case of manufacturing establishments. It would appear, however, that the phrase "other business pursuits," which occurs in the enumeration of places to which the law is to apply is sufficiently broad in its meaning to include factories and workshops.

The law regarding seats for females is not charged to any special body for enforcement. There is no organized factory-inspection service in the State.

CONDITIONS FOUND.

The following tables summarize the conditions found in the 14 establishments visited as regards water-closet accommodations, washing facilities, etc. Twelve of the 14 establishments were cigar factories. As most of these cigar factories were located in residential districts, with the employees living near by, the demand for certain conveniences in the factory, such as lunch rooms, was limited.

WATER-CLOSET ACCOMMODATIONS—FLORIDA.

	Establishments—	
Character of water-closet accommodations.	Having specified provisions.	Not having specified provisions.
Separate for sexes..	14	....
Private approaches for—		
Males..	12	2
Females..	13	1
Clean for—		
Males..	8	6
Females..	10	4
Air of workroom unaffected..	12	2
Separate for sexes, with one seat for each—		
20 males or less..	6	8
20 females or less..	10	4
25 males or less..	6	8
25 females or less..	10	4
30 males or less..	7	7
30 females or less..	11	3

WASH ROOM, DRESSING ROOM, REST ROOM, LUNCH ROOM, ETC., ACCOMMODATIONS—
FLORIDA.

	Establishments—		
Character of accommodations.	Having specified provisions—		Not having specified provisions.
	Sufficient.	Not sufficient.	
Wash rooms:			
Facilities for washing	9	5	....
Separate wash rooms	9	1	
Towels	3	....	11
Soap	4	....	10
Towels and soap	3	....	11
Dressing rooms:			
Separate for males			14
Separate for males, in work requiring change of clothing	....	....	....
Separate for females			14
Separate for females, in work requiring change of clothing	....		
Rest rooms for females	2		12
Lunch rooms	2		12
Seats for females	14	....	....
Good drinking water	14	....	....

LOUISIANA.

SUMMARY OF LEGISLATION.[1]

Water closets, wash rooms, and dressing rooms are required in manufacturing and mercantile establishments in which 5 or more young persons or women are employed. Seats for females are required in all manufacturing and mercantile establishments. Lunch rooms, rest rooms, and drinking water are not referred to in the State law.[2]

The legal provisions regarding water-closets, wash rooms, and dressing rooms are as follows:[3]

Every factory, mill, manufacturing establishment, workshop, warehouse, mercantile establishment * * * [packing house, etc.] in which 5 or more young persons or women are employed and every such institution in which 2 or more children, young persons, or women are employed—

Shall be supplied with proper wash and dressing rooms,

And kept in a cleanly state and free from effluvia arising from any drain, privy, or other nuisance,

And shall be provided, within reasonable access, with a sufficient number of proper water-closets or privies for the reasonable use of the persons employed,

And at least 1 of such closets shall be provided for each 25 persons employed,

---

[1] The law here referred to is as in force at the time of the investigation, March, 1909. The text of the laws in force Jan. 1, 1912, is given in the appendixes at the end of this volume.

[2] There is no special legislation regarding tenement shops or bakeries or other food-producing establishments.

[3] Acts of 1908, act No. 301, sec. 14 (Bulletin of the Bureau of Labor, No. 85, pp. 599, 600). See also Acts of 1906, act No. 34, sec. 4 (22d An. Rept. Com. of Labor, p. 522).

And wherever 2 or more persons and 1 or more female persons are employed as aforesaid, a sufficient number of separate and distinct water-closets, earth closets, or privies shall be provided for the use of each sex and plainly so designated,

And no person shall be allowed to use any such closet or privy assigned to persons of the other sex,

And said closets or privies shall not be locked during working hours.

Penalty.—$25 to $50, or imprisonment 10 to 30 days, or both.

Thus, as regards wash rooms and dressing rooms, the law says simply that they must be "proper." The factory inspector of New Orleans does not require wash rooms to be "rooms" as such, but accepts sinks and similar facilities located in the workrooms as fulfilling the intention of the law, if such facilities are sufficient in number. In the matter of dressing rooms, however, the inspector insists that they be separated from the workrooms by substantial partitions. No information upon these subjects is available for the remainder of the State, as, at the time of this investigation, the organized factory inspection service was limited to the city of New Orleans.

The legislation regarding water-closets is much more specific than that regarding wash rooms and dressing rooms. It is required broadly that water-closets shall be "proper"; but in addition it is specified that closets shall be reasonable of access, separate for the sexes, with a plain designation to that effect, and of sufficient number to allow at least 1 accommodation for each 25 persons. Among the States now being considered the further requirement that closets shall not be locked during working hours is peculiar to the law of Louisiana.

The factory inspector of New Orleans stated that the law regarding water-closets was not being strictly enforced at the present time, as a new underground sewer system was being installed in the city, and it would be inconsiderate to ask manufacturers to improve toilet arrangements until they were able to make connections with the new sewer system.

The legal provision concerning seats for females is that [1]—

Every person who shall employ any female in any factory, mill, warehouse, manufacturing establishment, workshop, or store * * * [packing house, etc.] shall provide suitable seats, chairs, or benches for the use of the females so employed, which shall be so placed as to be accessible to said employees,

And shall permit the use of such seats, chairs, or benches by them when they are not necessarily engaged in the active duties for which they are employed,

And there shall be provided at least 1 chair to every 3 females.

Penalty.—$25 to $50, or 10 to 30 days' imprisonment, or both.

The distinctive feature of this law is the requirement that there shall be at least 1 seat for each 3 females employed. As applied to all

---

[1] Acts of 1908, act No. 301, sec. 13 (Bulletin of the Bureau of Labor, No. 85, p. 599). See also Acts of 1900, act No. 55, sec. 1; and Acts of 1906, act No. 34, sec. 3 (22d An. Rept. Com. of Labor, pp. 518, 522).

classes of establishments, the ratio of 1 seat to 3 persons is, of course, entirely arbitrary. It is interesting, however, as being, among the States now being considered, the only attempt to establish such a standard by law.

The enforcement of the factory-inspection laws of Louisiana is intrusted to locally appointed factory inspectors. [1]

CONDITIONS FOUND.

The two following tables summarize the conditions found in the 29 visited establishments as regards water-closet accommodations, washing facilities, etc.:

WATER-CLOSET ACCOMMODATIONS—LOUISIANA.

Character of water-closet accommodations.	Establishments—	
	Having specified provisions.	Not having specified provisions.
Separate for sexes	29	
Private approaches for—		
Males	24	5
Females	25	4
Clean for—		
Males [2]	23	5
Females	27	2
Air of workroom unaffected	27	2
Separate for sexes, with one seat for each—		
20 males or less [2]	23	5
20 females or less [2]	17	12
25 males or less [2]	27	1
25 females or less	24	5
30 males or less [2]	27	1
30 females or less	27	2

WASH ROOM, DRESSING ROOM, REST ROOM, LUNCH ROOM, ETC., ACCOMMODATIONS—
LOUISIANA.

Character of accommodations.	Establishments—		
	Having specified provisions—		Not having specified provisions.
	Sufficient.	Not sufficient.	
Wash rooms:			
Facilities for washing	22	6	1
Separate wash rooms	18	[2] 2	9
Towels	11		18
Soap	11		18
Towels and soap	11		18
Dressing rooms:			
Separate for males	18	3	8
Separate for males, in work requiring change of clothing	14	2	3
Separate for females	23	2	4
Separate for females, in work requiring change of clothing	17	2	1
Rest rooms for females	1		28
Lunch rooms	6		23
Seats for females	26	3	
Good drinking water	27		2

[1] Acts of 1906, act No. 34, sec. 6 (22d An. Rept. Com. of Labor, p. 523), and Acts of 1908, act No. 301, sec. 23 (Bulletin of the Bureau of Labor, No. 85, p. 601).
[2] One establishment not reported.
[2] For females only, in one establishment.

As above noted, the Louisiana law prescribes a standard of at least 1 closet accommodation for every 25 persons employed. The first table shows that this standard was not observed by 1 of 28 establishments in the case of males and by 2 of 29 in the case of females.

Also, the law requires the closets for the sexes to be so designated. In 20 establishments such designation had not been made.

One establishment having a lunch room furnished free tea and coffee with milk and sugar.

Two establishments, both having lunch rooms, furnished lunch at approximately cost prices—one at 40 cents a week, the other at 35 cents a week.

FIRST AID TO THE INJURED AND SICK—MASSACHUSETTS AND MICHIGAN.

A law of Massachusetts requires that factories using machinery shall provide proper medicine and surgical appliances for the prompt treatment of injured or sick employees. Michigan has a similar requirement in the special case of foundries.[1]

The Massachusetts law referred to reads as follows:[2]

Every ` * * * factory or shop in which machinery is used for any manufacturing purpose, or for any other purpose except for elevators, or for heating or hoisting apparatus, shall at all times keep and maintain, free of expense to the employees, such a medical and surgical chest as shall be required by the local board of health * * * containing plasters, bandages, absorbent cotton, gauze, and all other necessary medicines, instruments, and other appliances for the treatment of persons injured or taken ill upon the premises.

Penalty.—$5 to $500 per week.

Of the 44 establishments visited in Massachusetts, 40 had machinery used for manufacturing purposes. Information regarding the presence or absence of the medical appliances mentioned was obtained for 38 of these 40 establishments. Such appliances were provided by 28 of these 38 establishments and were not provided by the other 10. Also, 1 establishment which was not equipped with machinery was provided with a medical and surgical chest.

The Michigan law, applicable solely to foundries, is as follows:[3]

There shall be kept on hand at all times in every foundry a reasonable supply of limewater, sweet oil, vaseline, bandages, and absorbent cotton for use of the workmen in case of burns or accident.

Penalty.—$5 to $100, or imprisonment 10 days to 3 months, or both.

Enforcement.—By State factory inspection department.

As foundries were not covered by this investigation, no information regarding the effect of the above law was obtained.

---

[1] Three other States require similar emergency outfits in the special case of mines: Ill. Rev. Stat., ch. 93, sec. 30; Ind. Acts of 1905, ch. 50, sec. 13; Ohio, Acts of 1904, p. 63 (22d An. Rept. Com. of Labor, pp. 367, 414, 1031).

[2] Acts of 1907, ch. 164, secs. 1 and 2 (22d An. Rept. Com. of Labor, p. 624).

[3] Acts of 1907, act No. 152, secs. 6, 7, 8, and 9 (22d An. Rept. Com. of Labor, p. 668).

CHAPTER X.

VENTILATION AND SANITATION.

CHAPTER X.

VENTILATION AND SANITATION.

INTRODUCTION.

Under the general heading "Ventilation and sanitation" this chapter considers the following topics: [1]

1. Ventilation (i. e., the renewal of the breathing air).
2. The removal of dust, fumes, and gases due to special manufacturing processes.
3. Cleanliness of floors, walls, ceilings, etc., of workrooms.
4. Expectoration on workroom floors and measures to prevent such practice.

The consideration is limited to factories and workshops, except when otherwise specifically mentioned.

All factories and workshops are, of course, confronted in greater or less degree with the problem of proper ventilation. In large buildings and rooms, with proportionately few workpeople and no dust or fume generating processes, the matter is not a serious one. Normal care in the opening of windows and doors is usually sufficient to insure a reasonably pure breathing atmosphere. In many factories, however, the working force is so large in proportion to the working space that special and constant attention must be given to the subject if proper health conditions are to be maintained. This necessity is greatly increased in some establishments by the existence of manufacturing processes which produce dust or fumes—such processes, for instance, as lacquering, enameling glassware, emery wheel grinding, and those requiring the use of alcohol, phosphorus, sulphur, hydrofluoric acid and other dangerous chemicals and acids.

Legislation regarding the subject has rarely attempted the establishment of standards by which good or bad conditions of ventilation may be precisely determined. Nor, as a rule, does the law specify definite methods by which a pure breathing atmosphere is to be maintained. [2] A recent statute of Illinois (1909) is exceptional in both of these particulars. This statute seeks to solve the problem at issue by providing that in all workrooms where the cubic feet of air space per person is not above an established minimum, placed very high, there

---

[1] Allied health topics, such as heating, lighting, vaccination in certain classes of mills, etc., were not covered in this investigation.

[2] The law here referred to is as in force at the beginning of 1909. The text of the laws in force Jan. 1, 1912, is given in the appendixes at the end of this volume.

shall be artificial means of supplying fresh air of a specified amount per person per hour. This law was passed after the field work of this investigation was completed. Its importance, however, warrants its reproduction here, if not as a model, at least as a measure by which the laws of the other States may be tested.

In every room or apartment of any factory, mercantile establishment, mill or workshop, where 1 or more persons are employed, at least 500 cubic feet of air space shall be provided for each and every person employed therein, and fresh air, to the amount specified in this act, shall be supplied in such a manner as not to create injurious drafts, nor cause the temperature of any such room or apartment to fall materially below the average temperature maintained: *Provided*, Where lights are used which do not consume oxygen, 250 cubic feet of air space shall be deemed sufficient. All rooms or apartments of any factory, mercantile establishment, mill or workshop, having at least 2,000 cubic feet of air space for each and every person employed in each room or apartment, and having outside windows and doors whose area is at least one-eighth of the total floor area, shall not be required to have artificial means of ventilation; but all such rooms or apartments shall be properly aired before beginning work for the day and during the meal hours. All such rooms, or apartments having less than 2,000 cubic feet of air space, but more than 500 cubic feet of air space for each and every person employed therein, and which have outside windows and doors whose area is at least one-eighth of the floor area, shall be provided with artificial means of ventilation, which shall be in operation when the outside temperature requires the windows to be kept closed, and which shall supply during each working hour at least 1,500 cubic feet of fresh air for each and every person employed therein. All such rooms or apartments having less than 500 cubic feet of air space for each and every person employed therein, all rooms or apartments having no outside windows or doors, and all rooms or apartments having less than 2,000 cubic feet of air space for each and every person employed therein, and in which the outside window and door area is less than one-eighth of the floor area, shall be provided with artificial means of ventilation, which will supply during each working hour throughout the year at least 1,800 cubic feet of fresh air for each and every person employed therein: *Provided*, That the provisions of the preceding portions of this section shall not apply to storage rooms or vaults: *And provided further*, That the preceding portions of this section shall not apply to those rooms or apartments in which manufacturing processes are carried on which from their peculiar nature would be materially interfered with by the provisions of this section. No part of the fresh-air supply required by this section shall be taken from any cellar or basement.

The following terms of this section shall be interpreted to mean: The air space available for each person is the total interior volume of a room, expressed in cubic feet, without any deductions for machinery contained therein, divided by the average number of persons employed therein.

Outside windows and doors are those connecting directly with the outside air; the window and door area is the total area of the windows and doors of all outside openings; and the floor area is the total floor area of each room.

All factories, mercantile establishments, mills, or workshops shall be kept free from gas or effluvia arising from any sewer, drain, privy, or other nuisance on the premises. All poisonous or noxious fumes or gases arising from any process, and all dust of a character injurious to the health of the persons employed, which is created in the course of a manufacturing process, within such factory, mill, or workshop shall be removed as far as practicable by either ventilating or exhaust devices.[1]

A reading of this law shows it to be very complete. A fixed hourly supply of fresh air, such as it contemplates, is an excellent assurance of a good breathing atmosphere within a factory, provided, of course, that the supply is sufficient in amount and that the work carried on does not produce an excessive amount of fumes, gases, dust, etc. It avoids, moreover, the difficulties of determining air purity by personal judgment or even by air tests. It requires some degree of medical or chemical knowledge to ascertain the purity of the air in a given room; but a skilled mechanic, and many factory inspectors are of this class, is well able to test a mechanical ventilating system and to determine whether or not it is in proper working condition.

The above law exempts from the requirement of artificial ventilating devices a workroom containing at least 2,000 cubic feet of air space per person and having outside windows and doors whose area is at least one-eighth of the total floor area. The requirements for exceptions, however, are here placed so high that there is little danger of abuse.

As before mentioned, the law of Illinois as just quoted was enacted subsequent to the field work of this investigation. At that time neither Illinois nor any other of the States covered had a law of this character. A few of the States had a legal requirement of a minimum cubic air space per person, but none of them demanded a continuous supply of fresh air, and in most cases the minimum air space required was extremely small. Upon the value of the air space standard by itself and the inefficiency of natural means of ventilation under most conditions, the New York Medical Inspector of Factories makes the following statement:

Natural means of ventilation in factories are inefficient, and compliance with a legal requirement establishing a minimum cubic air space per person is not a reliable guarantee of proper or sufficient ventilation. In many places [in New York State] where air tests were made, the results showed a larger percentage of CO_2 where the room was large and the workers few than in others where the conditions were reversed.[2]

---

[1] Illinois, Acts of 1909, p. 202, secs. 11 and 12 (Bulletin of the Bureau of Labor, No. 85, pp. 547, 548).

[2] Annual Report of Bureau of Factory Inspection, New York, 1907, p. 26.

This criticism of the air space standard of ventilation is accepted generally as a valid one. Nevertheless, it is to be observed that in the absence of a better system such a requirement is not without a certain value, provided, of course, that the air space established as a minimum is reasonably large. It has, moreover, the merit of being enforceable with comparative ease.

The problem of factory ventilation is, of course, greatly complicated by the presence of dust or fume producing processes. In such cases it is not sufficient to provide means for refreshing the air of the workrooms. It is necessary to prevent the dust and fumes from originally escaping into the air. To accomplish this, hoods with suction pipes or similar protective apparatus may be supplied for each machine or process causing such dust or fumes. In the case of grinding by emery wheels and other wheels of similar character, this is specifically recognized by several State laws. Less frequently such recognition extends to all grinding machines or even to all dust and fume producing processes.

As regards matters of factory sanitation, State legislation is usually even less specific than it is as regards matters of ventilation. Most frequently the law makes no more than a broad, rather indefinite requirement, such as that factories shall be kept in "good, sanitary condition," or that the factory inspectors shall see to it that the "heating, lighting, ventilation, and sanitary conditions" are good and proper.

A legal provision of this character is usually not very effective, except in remedying grossly bad conditions. This is almost necessarily so. Such a provision is generally accepted as meaning only that sanitary conditions shall not be so bad as to be injurious to health. Factory inspectors as a class have not the necessary medical knowledge to enable them to decide, and, if so, to prove to the satisfaction of a court that a condition is positively injurious to health, as distinguished from being merely unpleasant to view or smell.

As illustrating clearly the importance of expert medical assistance in enforcing, as also in properly framing laws regarding health matters, the following quotation from the report of the commissioner of labor of New York is of pertinent interest. The passage was written in 1907, after a medical inspector had been provided for by law, but before one had been appointed.

Turning now to the other question, whether the staff of the bureau of factory inspection has been proper and sufficient to carry out the existing health provisions, the answer seems obvious. The majority of the inspectors are mechanics; some have had a legal education, and a few have studied elementary sanitation. But although half of the factory laws relate to disease and sanitation, there has never been a single medical officer in the department. The deputy factory inspectors are competent to discover insufficient ventilation, where odors or extreme oppressiveness betray it; they can see breaks in plumbing, have more than the ordinary layman's ability to detect disease, and are perfectly competent to cope with obvious filth. Therefore, in dealing with grossly insanitary conditions they are fully competent and have done splendid work, especially in tenant factories and tenement houses (which subjects are explained separately hereafter). But when higher standards or more difficult questions of sanitation are reached, medical judgment, direction, and support is wanted. Courts that will accept a mechanic inspector's description of overcrowding or filth as evidence of insanitary conditions will hardly enforce his unsupported opinion as to defective ventilation, etc. And the proprietors of the better classes of factories, who acquiesce readily in the advice or orders of such inspectors in regard to machinery or safety, can not be expected to accept his decisions upon doubtful questions of sanitation. Therefore 'all orders of a mechanic inspector relative to sanitation, to which there is any objection, should be reviewed and affirmed by a medical expert before a dissatisfied proprietor should be expected to comply with them or before they should be enforced by legal process. Moreover there must be many points in sanitation as to which our inspections could be improved if the present staff had proper technical instruction and direction. And, assuming that it is a proper function of factory inspection to advise whatever is reasonably necessary for health, whether required by law or not, and that the majority of proprietors of factories proper would comply with such advice if convincingly explained regardless of legal obligations, it is obvious that many improvements might be induced by expert sanitary inspections. And to perceive the defects of existing laws as they are disclosed in operation and to devise proper measures to correct them requires medical cooperation and investigations. Finally, it is a question for medical investigation whether the existing regulations relative to the labor of women, minors, and children can not be improved so as to make them more beneficial and effective as regards such persons and yet at the same time more easily enforceable and less embarrassing to industry. I have therefore always insisted that the need of medical advice in the bureau of factory inspection is imperative; and the last legislature accordingly provided for one medical inspector of factories. This one official will be sufficient for a time, to blaze the way; but after a while one or two more will doubtless prove to be necessary.[1]

Most of the legislation regarding matters of ventilation and sanitation is "discretionary" in character—that is to say, it leaves much to the judgment and discretion of the inspection department or of the individual inspector. The laws in force are constantly modified by such terms as "proper," "sufficient," "in the judgment of the inspector;" and while this is also true in regard to other factory laws it is especially noticeable in connection with the laws regarding the subjects now being considered. The recent Illinois law in regard to the supplying of workrooms with fresh air is absolute in its force and

---

[1] Seventh Annual Report of the Commissioner of Labor, New York, 1907, pp. 131 to 133.

definite in its instructions. So also are the provisions of certain State laws regarding dust-removing devices, minimum air space, lime-washing of walls, and a few other points. On the whole, however, the discretion allowed the inspectors in the matters now being considered, and especially in those of general sanitation, is extremely broad.

That unsatisfactory results are frequently obtained by thus vesting the inspectors with such broad discretionary authority has already been suggested. It is due simply to the fact that in most States the factory-inspection department is not equipped with proper technical knowledge in the difficult subjects of ventilation and sanitation. Nevertheless, in the present state of knowledge upon these subjects and with the inspection systems in operation in most States there is frequently no alternative method. Satisfactory standards are so uncommon that to make precise and invariable requirements would frequently render the law's enforcement unjust if not impossible.

Two methods have been suggested for meeting these difficulties. One method is to leave the laws regarding ventilation and sanitation general in their character, and to vest the inspectors with broad discretionary authority in their enforcement; and, as a corollary, to have, as inspectors, men with the necessary technical equipment. Such men could decide each individual case on its merits, and in case of dispute could speak as authorities, a thing the ordinary inspector can not do in these matters. The other method is to have the subject of factory ventilation and sanitation studied by experts, whose duty would be to frame simple standards that the ordinary inspector, a mechanic perhaps but not a physician, would be able to enforce.

At the time of the field work of this investigation only two of the States covered had made any serious attempt to make the suggested relation between expert medical knowledge and factory inspection. These two States are Massachusetts and New York.[1]

In New York State the office of medical inspector of factories was created in 1907, the office being regarded as an integral part of the State factory inspection department. The duty of the medical inspector is to study factory conditions bearing on the health of employees, and, when possible, to frame remedial standards.

In Massachusetts a similar end is sought by vesting the State board of health with enforcing authority in the case of laws relating to questions of ventilation and sanitation. The board acts in this matter through a corps of 15 health inspectors, all practicing physicians. The State is districted and a health inspector is assigned each district. The duties of this organization are not only to enforce existing laws, but also to study the general subject of health conditions in factories, with a view to further legislation.

---

[1] Both Illinois and Wisconsin now (1912) have medical inspectors of factories.

In this connection there may be mentioned also a provision of the law of Louisiana relative to the removal of dust, smoke, and lint. The law authorizes the inspector to order proper removing devices in such cases, "*Provided*, That two mechanical engineers, one chosen by the inspector and the other by the owner or owners of the establishment, shall agree as to the necessity of such * * * contrivance * * * . Upon the failure of said two mechanical engineers to agree a third * * * shall be chosen to arbitrate."[1] This represents in a measure the system of expert advice in technical matters. The advice provided for, however, is simply that of temporary arbitrators.

The present report covers 17 States. At the time of the field work of this investigation no laws regarding the subjects covered in this chapter had been enacted by 3 States—North Carolina, Georgia, and Florida. Each of the remaining 14 States had legislated on some or all of these subjects. The widely varying character of this legislation forbids a general summary of its contents.

Below is given, for each of the States covered, an outline of the legislation, if any, upon matters of ventilation and sanitation. This is followed in each case by a brief statement of the conditions found in the course of the investigation.

This statement covers the following points:

1. *Cleanliness of workrooms.*—The information upon this subject is given in a short table, which shows the number of establishments in which the floors, walls, and ceilings of the workrooms were in a clean condition at the time of the visit. As there is no accepted standard by which cleanliness can be measured with exactness, the data obtained represent necessarily the personal opinions of the agents making the visits. The agents were instructed, however, to report as unclean only such conditions as were unnecessarily bad. That is to say, the ordinary litter of the day's work, which is not insanitary and which is removed every day, was not considered as in itself warranting the classing of a workroom as unclean. But the presence of any filth, grime, accumulated dirt, grease, or refuse, the existence of which was unwholesome or unnecessary, was considered as a sufficient reason for reporting a workroom as not in clean condition.

2. *Spitting on the floor and the provision of cuspidors.*—A tabular presentation is here made of the respective numbers of establishments in which habitual spitting on the floor was or was not done, in which such free spitting was or was not prohibited by factory rules, and in which cuspidors were or were not provided. A factory rule, as the term is here used, means either a posted rule or a definite verbal order which there is at least some effort made to enforce. Cuspidors were regarded as being provided when they were present in the

---

[1] Acts of 1908, act No. 301, sec. 19 (Bulletin of the Bureau of Labor, No. 85, p. 600).

workrooms, whether they were supplied by the employers or by the employees.

3. *General ventilation and the removal of dust and fumes.*—In obtaining information upon these subjects it was impossible to determine in a given workroom whether the condition of the air was absolutely good or bad. The difficulty of deciding when a condition is really injurious and not merely unpleasant has already been mentioned. To have established the full facts in this investigation would have required a more complete technical equipment than was available. All that could be attempted was to ascertain and report certain evident facts, which while not conclusive in themselves, are suggestive of the conditions existing.

These facts are presented in the form of two tables. The first groups the several establishments according to the amount of air space per person in the most crowded workroom, and shows for each of these groups the respective numbers of establishments having and not having special ventilating appliances in addition to the doors and windows.

The second of these two tables classifies the establishments according to the presence or absence in the workrooms of irritating or injurious dust or fumes, and, if present, whether or not special devices for removing such dust or fumes had been provided. All dust or fumes irritating to the nose or throat are here reported. For reasons above mentioned, no attempt was made to ascertain whether such dust or fumes were of a character or in sufficient quantity to be positively injurious.

In these tables, as in most of the other tables of this report, it is to be emphasized that when an unsatisfactory condition is credited to an establishment it means that such condition existed in one or more workrooms, not necessarily in the whole establishment.

A full statement of the conditions found in each establishment is given in Chapter XI, General Tables, of this volume.

MAINE.

SUMMARY OF LEGISLATION. [1]

Legislation upon the subjects considered in this chapter is limited to a single and very general provision, which directs that: [2]

He [the factory inspector] shall also examine into the sanitary condition of factories, workshops, mines and quarries, and when any condition or thing is found that, in his opinion, endangers the health or lives of the employees, he shall notify and direct the employer

---

[1] The law here referred to is as in force at the beginning of 1909. The text of the laws in force Jan. 1, 1912, is given in the appendixes at the end of this volume.

[2] Rev. Stat., 1903, ch. 40, sec. 44, as amended by ch. 77, Acts of 1907 (22d An. Rept. Com. of Labor, p. 526).

to rectify the same; and if said employer shall neglect or refuse so to do within a reasonable time, said inspector may cause the same to be done at the expense of the employer.

The possible scope of such a provision as this is not entirely clear. The inspector is authorized to remedy any bad sanitary condition, but as the law then proceeds to define a bad sanitary condition as one which "endangers the health or lives of employees," it would seem probable that the law is to be interpreted in a narrow sense, as referring, that is to say, only to the grosser evils of drainage, plumbing, cleanliness, etc. This is apparently the interpretation followed by the State factory inspector, who states that in enforcing the quoted requirement he has erected no fixed standards, but insists that the sanitary arrangements of a factory shall be kept reasonably clean.

CONDITIONS FOUND.

CLEANLINESS OF WORKROOMS.

The conditions as regards general cleanliness of the workrooms of the 26 establishments visited is shown in the following table:

CLEANLINESS OF WORKROOMS—MAINE.

All workrooms clean?		Establishments.
Floors.	Walls and ceilings.	
Yes......	Yes.......	13
Yes......	No........	2
No........	Yes.......	5
No........	No........	6

SPITTING ON THE FLOOR AND THE PROVISION OF CUSPIDORS.

Habitual spitting on the floor by employees was reported in 12 of the 26 establishments; in 13 there were factory rules against such spitting; and in 11 cuspidors were provided.

The relation between spitting on the floor and the presence of cuspidors and of rules against spitting is shown in the next table:

CONDITIONS AS TO SPITTING ON THE FLOOR—MAINE.

	Total establishments.	Establishments in which spitting on floor is done.
Cuspidors:		
Provided......................	11	1
Not provided.................	15	11
Spitting on floor:		
Prohibited....................	13	3
Not prohibited...............	13	9
Provisions both for cuspidors and against spitting on floor........	8	1

GENERAL VENTILATION AND THE REMOVAL OF DUST AND FUMES.

The two following tables present briefly the conditions found in the several establishments visited as regards the general subject of ventilation and the special topic of dust and fumes.

CONDITIONS AS TO VENTILATION—MAINE.

Air space per person in most crowded room.	Establishments.		
	Total.	Special ventilating appliances—	
		Provided.	Not provided.
Under 250 cubic feet....................			
250 and under 500 cubic feet..........	6	1	5
500 and under 1,000 cubic feet........	4	1	3
1,000 and under 2,000 cubic feet......	9	3	6
2,000 and under 3,000 cubic feet......	7		7
3,000 cubic feet and over.............			
Total.........................	26	5	21

CONDITIONS AS TO DUST OR FUMES IN WORKROOMS—MAINE.

Injurious or irritating dust or fumes in workrooms.	Establishments.	
Not noticeable......................	......	6
Noticeable:		
Removal devices provided.......	7	
Removal devices not provided...	13	
		20
Total establishments............	......	26

MASSACHUSETTS.

SUMMARY OF LEGISLATION.[1]

Massachusetts possesses a very considerable body of legislation regarding the ventilation and sanitary conditions of factories and workshops. A feature of this legislation peculiar to Massachusetts, among the States covered by this report, is that its enforcement is confided, not to the State factory inspection department, but to the State board of health, with its own force of inspectors.[2]

Of the legal provisions concerning ventilation and sanitation the one of most general scope reads as follows.[3]

---

[1] The law here referred to is as in force at the beginning of 1909. The text of the laws in force Jan. 1, 1912, is given in the appendixes at the end of this volume.

[2] There is also special legislation regarding certain matters of ventilation and sanitation in bakeries, but this does not apply to confectioneries or other food-producing establishments. Rev. Laws, 1902, ch. 75, secs. 28 to 34, as amended by ch. 403, Acts of 1902 (22d An. Rept. Com. of Labor, p. 579). For special legislation regarding tenement shops, Rev. Laws, 1902, ch. 106, sec. 56, as amended by ch. 238, Acts of 1905, to sec. 61, inclusive (22d An. Rept. Com. of Labor, pp. 601, 602).

[3] Rev. Laws, 1902, ch. 104, sec. 41 (as amended by ch. 503, Acts of 1907) and sec. 56 (22d An. Rept. Com. of Labor, pp. 588, 590).

(a) All factories and workshops shall be well lighted, well ventilated, and kept clean.

Penalty.—Not more than $100.

This requirement is broad but indefinite. It is supplemented, however, by other provisions, which, while frequently leaving much to the discretion of the enforcing authority, are more detailed and definite in their contents. Such of these other provisions as relate specifically to the subject of ventilation may be classified as follows:

(b) A factory in which 5 or more persons and a workshop in which 5 or more women or young persons are employed shall, while work is carried on therein, be so ventilated that the air shall not become so impure as to be injurious to the health of the persons employed therein and so that all gases, vapors, dust, or other impurities injurious to health, which are generated in the course of the manufacturing process or handicraft carried on therein shall, so far as practicable, be rendered harmless.[1]

Penalty.—Not more than $100.

(c) If, in a workshop or factory * * * [such as described in preceding paragraph], any process is carried on by which dust is caused which may be inhaled to an injurious extent by the persons employed therein, and it appears to an inspector * * * that such inhalation would be substantially diminished without unreasonable expense by the use of a fan or by other mechanical means, such fan or other mechanical means, if he so directs, shall be provided, maintained, and used.[2]

Penalty.—Not more than $100.

(d) Any persons, firm, or corporation operating a factory or workshop in which emery wheels or belts or buffing wheels or belts injurious to the health of employees are used shall * * * provide such wheels and belts with a hood or hopper connected with suction pipes, and with fans or blowers, in accordance with the provisions hereinafter contained, which apparatus shall be placed and operated in such a manner as to protect any person or persons using any such wheel or belt from the particles or dust produced by the operation thereof, and to convey the said particles or dust either outside of the building or to some receptacle so placed as to receive and confine the said particles or dust. [Here follows a detailed description of the character of blowers, fans, suction pipes, etc., required.]

This act shall not apply to grinding machines upon which water is used * * *, nor to solid emery wheels used in * * * woodworking establishments, nor to any emery wheel 6 inches and under in diameter used in establishments when the principal business is not emery wheel grinding.[3]

Penalty.—First offense, $25 to $100; second offense, $25 to $100, or imprisonment not more than 60 days, or both.

---

[1] Rev. Laws, 1902, ch. 106, secs. 51 and 70 (22d An. Rept. Com. of Labor, pp. 601, 604).

[2] Idem, secs. 52 and 70 (22d An. Rept. Com. of Labor, pp. 601, 604).

[3] Acts of 1903, ch. 475, secs. 1 to 6 (22d An. Rept. Com. of Labor, pp. 613, 614).

(e) Every factory in which 5 or more persons are employed, and every factory, workshop, mercantile or other establishment or office in which 2 or more children, under 18 years of age, or women are employed, shall be kept clean and free from effluvia arising from any drain, privy, or nuisance * * *.[1]

Penalty.—Not more than $100.

(f) The water used for humidifying purposes by any person, firm, or corporation operating a factory or workshop, shall be of such a degree of purity as not to give rise to any impure or foul odors, and shall be so used as not to be injurious to the health of persons employed in such factories or workshops.[2]

Penalty.—$10 to $1,000.

In reviewing these several legal provisions regarding ventilation it will be observed that the law is very full in its description of the bad conditions to be avoided. The method of remedying such bad conditions, however, except in the case of emery grinding, is left to the discretion of the enforcing authority. Thus, no standards by which good ventilation is to be judged are established, and, except in the case of emery dust, no legal violation attaches to an employer for not using fans or other mechanical apparatus for removing dust, unless such mechanical apparatus has been ordered by an inspector. Again, the law regarding water used for humidifying purposes leaves it to the inspecting authority to establish standards of purity and to decide when the use of such water becomes injurious. In the special case of emery wheels, buffing wheels, etc. (d), however, the requirements as to dust removal are extremely full, the law not only ordering the use of suction fans, etc., but describing in detail the kind of apparatus that is to be installed.

The Massachusetts law is less full and specific in regard to matters of general sanitation in factories than it is in regard to matters of ventilation. It is provided—as already quoted in provisions (a) and (e)—that factories and workshops shall be kept "clean." No interpretation of the word "clean" is given, however, and no specific requirements are made in the matter of cleanliness, except the following two regarding the providing of cuspidors and as to free expectoration, respectively:

Suitable receptacles for expectoration shall be provided in all factories and workshops by the proprietors thereof, the same to be of such form and construction and of such number as shall be satisfactory to the board of health of the city or town in which the factory or workshop is situated.[3]

Penalty.—Not more than $100.

---

[1] Rev. Laws, 1902, ch. 106, secs. 47 and 70 (22d An. Rept. Com. of Labor, p. 600).

[2] Acts of 1908, ch. 325, secs. 1 and 2 (Bulletin of the Bureau of Labor, No. 85, p. 613).

[3] Rev. Laws, 1902, ch. 104, sec. 41 (as amended by ch. 503, Acts of 1907) and sec. 56 (22d An. Rept. Com. of Labor, pp. 588–590).

No person shall expectorate or spit * * *, except in receptacles provided for the purpose, in or upon any part of * * * any
mill or factory * * *.[1]

Penalty.—Not more than $20.

Thus, except as regards free expectoration and the provision of
cuspidors, the whole matter of factory cleanliness is left to the discretion of the health inspecting department, acting under authority
of the general provision that factories and workshops must be "clean."
To what extent this discretionary power might be used in ordering
particular things—such as the limewashing of walls—is, of course,
dependent on judicial interpretation. It would seem clear, however,
that the intention of the legal provisions regarding sanitation, is also
of those regarding ventilation, is such as to warrant the inspectors in
establishing high standards and insisting upon efficient remedies.

The fact has already been noted that in Massachusetts the enforcement of the laws concerning ventilation and sanitation is not confined, as it is in most of the States covered by this report, to the
State factory-inspection department. Prior to 1907 the factory-
inspection department (a division of the district police in Massachusetts) did have this duty in regard to all such laws except the
one regarding cuspidors, the enforcement of which was intrusted to
the local boards of health. In the year named, however, the authority of the factory-inspection department in all matters of ventilation and sanitation was discontinued, and placed in the hands of the
State board of health, acting through a force of health inspectors,
each of whom is a physician.[2]

The reason for this transfer of authority was the belief that, as
ventilation and sanitation were matters involving medical knowledge, physicians acting as health inspectors would be better equipped
to supervise laws dealing with such subjects than were the regular
factory inspectors, who were not expected to be, and rarely were,
equipped with a medical training.

On the other hand, two criticisms have been made concerning the
present system. One of these is of a general character: That,
although a man may be an excellent physician, he is not thereby
necessarily qualified as an inspector; that it is not enough to be able
to detect bad conditions; the inspectors must also know how to order
structural or mechanical changes necessary to remedy such bad conditions. The second criticism is of the particular system in force in

---

[1] Acts of 1906, ch. 165, secs. 1 and 2 (as amended by Acts of 1907, ch. 410, sec. 1,
and Acts of 1908, ch. 150).

[2] Acts of 1907, ch. 537, secs. 1 to 8, and also Rev. Laws, 1902, ch. 106, sec. 49 (22d
An. Rept. Com. of Labor, pp. 600, 629).

Massachusetts, and is to the effect that the existence of two sets of inspectors, mutually irresponsible, visiting the same establishments, but without coordinating their visits or results, is not conducive to efficient administration.[1]

In the exercise of its authority in matters of ventilation and sanitation, the State board of health has followed the plan of having each case dealt with individually and independently by the inspector of health under whose jurisdiction it comes. No comprehensive standards have been established for the guidance of the separate inspectors. The chief factory inspector stated that when the laws concerning ventilation and sanitation were under the jurisdiction of his department it had established a ventilation standard of 30 cubic feet of fresh air per minute per person; but that this standard had been abandoned by the board of health and none other had been established in its place.

CONDITIONS FOUND.

CLEANLINESS OF WORKROOMS.

The condition as regards general cleanliness of the workrooms in the 44 establishments visited are shown in the following table:

CLEANLINESS OF WORKROOMS—MASSACHUSETTS.

All workrooms clean?		Estab-lishments.
Floors.	Walls and ceilings.	
Yes......	Yes......	22
Yes......	No.:......	8
No.......	Yes......	8
No.......	No........	6

SPITTING ON THE FLOOR AND THE PROVISION OF CUSPIDORS.

Spitting on the floor was reported as being done habitually in 15 of the 44 establishments visited; in 26 there were factory rules against such free spitting; in 21 cuspidors had been provided.

The relation between spitting on the floor and the provision of cuspidors and of rules against spitting is shown in the following table.

---

[1] Report of the commission to investigate the inspection of factories, etc. Boston, 1911 (State document).

CONDITIONS AS TO SPITTING ON THE FLOOR—MASSACHUSETTS.

	Total establishments.	Establishments in which spitting on floor is done.
Cuspidors:		
Provided...................	21	5
Not provided.................	23	10
Spitting on floor:		
Prohibited...................	26	6
Not prohibited...............	18	9
Provisions both for cuspidors and against spitting on floor..	18	5

GENERAL VENTILATION AND THE REMOVAL OF DUST AND FUMES.

The two following tables present briefly the conditions found in the several visited establishments as regards the general subject of ventilation and the special topic of dust and fumes:

CONDITIONS AS TO VENTILATION—MASSACHUSETTS.

Air space per person in most crowded room.	Establishments.		
	Total.	Special ventilating appliances—	
		Provided.	Not provided.
Under 250 cubic feet.................	4	....	4
250 and under 500 cubic feet.......	12	5	7
500 and under 1,000 cubic feet.......	11	3	8
1,000 and under 2,000 cubic feet......	12	4	8
2,000 and under 3,000 cubic feet......	2	....	2
3,000 cubic feet and over.............	3	....	3
Total...........................	44	12	32

CONDITIONS AS TO DUST OR FUMES IN WORKROOMS—MASSACHUSETTS.

Injurious or irritating dust or fumes in workrooms.	Establishments
Not noticeable...........................	11
Noticeable:	
Removal devices provided........	8
Removal devices not provided....	24
	[1] 33
Total establishments............	44

[1] Including one not reported as to removal devices.

RHODE ISLAND.

SUMMARY OF LEGISLATION.[1]

The legislation of Rhode Island upon the subjects of ventilation and sanitation is contained in a single provision—a general authoriza-

[1] The law here referred to is as in force at the beginning of 1909. The text of the laws in force Jan. 1, 1912, is given in the appendixes at the end of this volume.

tion given the State factory inspectors to remedy conditions injurious to the health of employees. The legal provision is in full as follows:[1]

If the factory inspectors, or either one of them, find that the heating, lighting, ventilation or sanitary arrangement. of any shop or factory is such as to be injurious to the health of the persons employed therein, * * * either or both shall notify the proprietor of such factory or workshop• to make the. alterations or additions necessary within 90 days * * *.

Penalty.—Not more than $500.

The factory inspectors are thus directed to remedy conditions which are injurious to the health of employees. Presumably, they are to be the judges of what conditions are injurious. Such a position, as has already been pointed out, is a difficult one. A given condition may be palpably bad, but that it is positively injurious to health may not be susceptible of easy proof, especially by inspectors who are untrained in medicine. Also, it is to be noted, that the form of the law is such that full responsibility attaches to the inspectors. No legal blame rests upon an employer for maintaining even the most grossly harmful conditions until an inspector has decided that such conditions are injurious and has ordered a remedy.

The factory inspectors recognize the difficulty of establishing standards of ventilation, and in many matters, involving a knowledge of medicine and sanitary engineering, do not feel competent to pass judgment. The chief inspector believes that the State board of health should be authorized to establish standards in matters of ventilation, such standards to be enforced by the factory inspection department.

Under date of January 6, 1909, the chief factory inspector issued the following letter to the "Manufacturers of Rhode Island."

PROVIDENCE, R. I., *January 6, 1909.*

To the Manufacturers of Rhode Island:

GENTLEMEN: I am aware that you are interested in the movement to prevent the spread of tuberculosis. The most eminent authorities maintain that a habit of spitting on the floor in factories is a prolific source of danger in spreading the disease. I would suggest that if you could be prevailed upon to take such measures as circumstances will permit to prevent this practice in your factories much good might be accomplished. Paper spittoons that will hold water for several days can be procured at a very small cost, and if placed in convenient places throughout your factories I think the help could easily be induced to use them. As often as necessary they could be replaced with new ones and taken away and thrown under the boilers and burned without entailing a very serious expense. I would further suggest that in water-closets, wash rooms and in all corners where spitting is more liable to be done, the disease germs can be effectually destroyed by brushing the floors of those places with a mixture of corrosive sublimate, muriate of ammonia and water, put together in the following ratio

Corrosive sublimate... ½ pound.
Muriate ammonia.. ½ pound.
Water..:................... 1 barrel.

The Brown & Sharpe Manufacturing Co. are using the above and have great faith in its efficiency. I trust the foregoing suggestions will receive your kind consideration.

J. ELLERY HUDSON,
Chief Factory Inspector.

---

[1] Gen. Laws 1896, ch. 68, secs. 9 and 12, as amended by ch. 1215, enacted 1905 (22d An. Rept. Com. of Labor, p. 1209).

CONDITIONS FOUND.

CLEANLINESS OF WORKROOMS.

The conditions as regards general cleanliness of the workrooms of the 27 visited establishments are shown in the next table:

CLEANLINESS OF WORKROOMS—RHODE ISLAND.

All workrooms clean?		Estab- lishments.
Floors.	Walls and ceilings.	
Yes......	Yes.......	20
No.......	Yes.......	2
No.......	No........	5

SPITTING ON THE FLOOR AND THE PROVISION OF CUSPIDORS.

Habitual spitting on factory floors by employees was done in 9 of the 27 establishments; in 20 there was a rule against such spitting; and in 12 cuspidors were provided.

The relation between spitting on the floor and the provision of cuspidors and the existence of rules against spitting is shown in the following table:

CONDITIONS AS TO SPITTING ON THE FLOOR—RHODE ISLAND.

	Total establish- ments.	Establish- ments in which spitting on floor is done.
Cuspidors:		
Provided.....................	12	3
Not provided................	15	6
Spitting on floor:		
Prohibited...................	20	5
Not prohibited..............	7	4
Provisions both for cuspidors and		
against spitting on floor........	9	2

GENERAL VENTILATION AND THE REMOVAL OF DUST AND F

The two following tables show briefly the conditions found
several visited establishments as regards the general subj
ventilation and the special topic of dust and fumes:

CONDITIONS AS TO VENTILATION—RHODE ISLAND.

Air space per person in most crowded room.	Establishments.		
	Total.	Special ventilating appliances—	
		Provided.	Not provided.
Under 250 cubic feet.....................	....	....	....
250 and under 500 cubic feet.........	4	....	4
500 and under 1,000 cubic feet........	8	7	1
1,000 and under 2,000 cubic feet......	1 10	7	2
2,000 and under 3,000 cubic feet......	3	....	3
3,000 cubic feet and over..............	1	1	....
Not reported..........................	1	1	....
Total.......................	27	16	10

[1] Including 1 establishment not reported as to special ventilating appliance.

CONDITIONS AS TO DUST OR FUMES IN WORKROOMS—RHODE ISLAN

Injurious or irritating dust or fumes in workrooms.	Establishments.
Not noticeable.........................	7
Noticeable:	
Removal devices provided........	1 12
Removal devices not provided....	8
	20
Total establishments...........	27

[1] Removal devices in 1 establishment not in good working order.

CONNECTICUT.

SUMMARY OF LEGISLATION.[1]

The law of Connecticut contains two legal provisions regarding ventilation and sanitation in factories, etc.[2] One of these is very general in its terms and scope; the other applies to the matter of dust removal. The provisions referred to are as follows:[3]

(a) All factories and buildings where machinery is used shall be well lighted, ventilated, and kept as clean as the nature of the business will permit.

Penalty.—Not more than $50.

(b) Wherever the inspector, on complaint of any person, shall find it necessary, for the preservation of the health of the employees in any manufacturing establishment, factory, or mill in which is carried on the business of buffing, polishing, or grinding metals, or any operations in which an excessive amount of dust is generated, that such dust should be removed from the atmosphere of the rooms or apartments used for that purpose, he shall, in writing, direct the person, or corporation owning, occupying, or carrying on business in such premises, within three months from the date of such order, to introduce and operate such appliances or devices as may be necessary to remove, so far as the nature of the business will permit, such excessive dust or foreign matter: *Provided,* That such appliances or devices do not restrict or interfere with the aforesaid business or operations.

Penalty.—Not more than $50.

The first of the above-quoted provisions is very general in its terms, but would seem to vest the inspection department with a very considerable discretionary authority. It directs that factories using machinery shall be well ventilated and kept as clean as the nature of the business will permit. It differs from the somewhat similar provisions of the Rhode Island law: First, in that legal responsibility attaches to an employer originally, and not merely after an inspector has made an order; and second, in that the requirement is that con-

---

[1] The law here referred to is as in force at the beginning of 1909. The text of the laws in force Jan. 1, 1912, is given in the appendixes at the end of this volume.

[2] Excluding special legislation regarding tenement shops (Gen. Stat., 1902, sec. 4529, 22d An. Rept. Com. of Labor, p. 237) and bakeries (Gen. Stat. 1902, sec. 2569, as amended by ch. 13, Acts of 1905, 22d An. Rept. Com. of Labor, p. 232). By a law passed subsequent to the field work of this investigation the regulations regarding bakeries were extended to cover food-preparing establishments generally, Acts of 1909, ch. 120, sec. 14 (Bulletin of the Bureau of Labor, No. 85, p. 524).

Connecticut also has legal provisions concerning two matters allied to those considered in this chapter. One of these provisions is a prohibition against the use of "stained, painted, or corrugated glass in factory windows, where the same is injurious to the eyes of the workmen therein." (Gen. Stat., 1902, sec. 4518, 22d An. Rept. Com. of Labor, p. 236). The other is a requirement that employees of paper mills be vaccinated. (Gen. Stat., 1902, sec. 4693, 22d An. Rept. Com. of Labor, p. 241.)

[3] Gen. Stat., 1902, secs. 4516, 4520, 4521, and sec. 4522, as amended by ch. 53, Acts of 1903 (22d An. Rept. Com. of Labor, pp. 236, 237).

ditions shall be good and not merely that they shall not be "injurious to health." These two points would seem to be of considerable importance in determining the efficiency of a law. It is to be noted, however, that the legal provision of Connecticut just considered applies only to establishments using machinery, and not to workshops in which there is no machinery.   •

The factory inspecting department has enacted no fixed standards of ventilation or cleanliness to be followed in administering the law, but decides each case on its merits. The department accepts the law as sufficient to enable it to insist upon limewashing when necessary, but not as giving it authority to prohibit spitting on the floor or to require cuspidors. The chief inspector expressed himself as being in favor of a definite law upon these latter points.

The second of the two quoted provisions applies to the subject of dust removal. It does not cover the removal of fumes and gases, but it does apply to all forms of dust, and not merely to the one form of emery dust, as is the case in some State laws upon the subject. The provision is in considerable detail, but most of this detail weakens rather than strengthens its force. It authorizes the inspector to order the installation of mechanical devices for removing dust but it restricts this authority by several conditioning clauses. Thus the inspector is authorized presumably to act only on complaint made; the dust must be sufficiently excessive to be dangerous to health, a point which, as has been earlier noted, is often difficult to establish; and, finally, the inspector may not order mechanical appliances to be installed if such appliances "restrict or interfere with" the business or operation concerned.

CONDITIONS FOUND.

CLEANLINESS OF WORKROOMS.

The workrooms of the 35 establishments visited are classified in the following table as regards cleanliness:

CLEANLINESS OF WORKROOMS—CONNECTICUT.

All workrooms clean?		Estab-lishments.
Floors.	Walls and ceilings.	
Yes......	Yes......	29
Yes......	No.......	1
No........	Yes......	1
No........	No........	4

SPITTING ON THE FLOOR AND THE PROVISION OF CUSPIDORS.

Habitual spitting on factory floors by employees was reported in 13 of the 35 establishments; in 16 there was a rule against such practice; and in 19 cuspidors were provided.

The relation between spitting on the floor and the provision of cuspidor and the existence of rules against spitting is shown in the next table.

CONDITIONS AS TO SPITTING ON THE FLOOR—CONNECTICUT.

	Total establish- ments.	Establish- ments in which spitting on floor is done.
Cuspidors:		
Provided....................	19	1
Not provided................	16	12
Spitting on floor:		
Prohibited..................	16	3
Not prohibited..............	19	10
Provisions both for cuspidors and against spitting on floor........	11	....

GENERAL VENTILATION AND THE REMOVAL OF DUST AND FUMES.

The two following tables show briefly the conditions found as regards the general subject of ventilation and the special topic of dust and fumes.

CONDITIONS AS TO VENTILATION—CONNECTICUT.

Air space per person in most crowded room.	Establishments.		
	Total.	Special ventilating appliances—	
		Provided.	Not provided.
Under 250 cubic feet..................	....	....	....
250 and under 500 cubic feet.........	9	2	7
500 and under 1,000 cubic feet.......	12	7	5
1,000 and under 2,000 cubic feet......	11	2	9
2,000 and under 3,000 cubic feet......	2	....	2
3,000 cubic feet and over.............	1	....	1
Total......................	35	11	24

CONDITIONS AS TO DUST OR FUMES IN WORKROOMS—CONNECTICUT.

Injurious or irritating dust or fumes in workrooms.	Estab- lishments.
Not noticeable...........................	21
Noticeable:	
Removal devices provided........	[1] 11
Removal devices not provided....	2
	13
Not reported............................	1
Total establishments............	35

[1] Removal devices in 2 establishments not in good working order.

NEW YORK.

SUMMARY OF LEGISLATION.[1]

The legislation of New York covers the subject of ventilation and dust removal with considerable fullness, but as regards matters of cleanliness and general sanitation it is limited, for manufacturing establishments as a class, to a single provision regarding limewashing and painting.[2]

The legal provisions are, in full, as follows:

(a) No more employees shall be required or permitted to work in a room in a factory [3] between the hours of 6 o'clock in the morning and 6 o'clock in the evening than will allow to each of such employees not less than 250 cubic feet of air space; and, unless by a written permit of the factory inspector, not less than 400 cubic feet for each employee so employed between the hours of 6 o'clock in the evening and 6 o'clock in the morning, provided such room is lighted by electricity at all times during such hours while persons are employed therein.[4]

(b) The owner, agent, or lessee of a factory shall provide in each workroom thereof proper and sufficient means of ventilation and shall maintain proper and sufficient ventilation.

(c) If excessive heat be created or if steam, gases, vapors, dust, or other impurities that may be injurious to health be generated in the course of the manufacturing process carried on therein, the room must be ventilated in such a manner as to render them harmless, so far as is practicable.

In case of failure, the commissioner of labor shall order such ventilation to be provided. Such owner, agent, or lessee shall provide such ventilation within 20 days after the service upon him of such order * * * .[5]

(d) Exhaust fans of sufficient power shall be provided for the purpose of carrying off dust from emery wheels, grindstones, and other machinery creating dust; except where in case of woodworking machinery, the commissioner of labor, after first making and filing

---

[1] The law here referred to is as in force at the beginning of 1909. The text of the laws in force Jan. 1, 1912, is given in the appendixes at the end of this volume.

[2] For special legislation regarding tenement shops see Rev. Stat., 3d ed., 1901, p. 2102, secs. 94 and 95 (added by ch. 178, Acts of 1906), sec. 100 (as amended by ch. 129, Acts of 1906) (22d An. Rept. Com. of Labor, pp. 915-920). For mercantile establishments see idem, p. 2114, secs. 168 to 171 (22d An. Rept. Com. of Labor, pp. 927, 928).

[3] The term "factory," as used in the New York law, includes "also any mill, workshop, or other manufacturing or business establishment where one or more persons are employed at labor." Rev. Stat., 3d ed., 1901, p. 2089, sec. 2, as amended by ch. 550, Acts of 1904 (22d An. Rept. Com. of Labor, p. 899).

[4] Rev. Stat., 3d ed., 1901, p. 2102, sec. 85, and p. 2120, sec. 209 (as amended by ch. 506, Acts of 1907) (22d An. Rept. Com. of Labor, pp. 914, 931).

[5] Idem, sec. 86, as amended by ch. 490, Acts of 1907 (22d An. Rept. Com. of Labor, p. 914).

in the public records of his office a written statement of the reasons therefor, shall decide that it is unnecessary for the health and welfare of the operatives.[1]

(e) The walls and ceilings of each workroom in a factory shall be limewashed or painted when, in the opinion of the factory inspector, it will be conducive to the health or cleanliness of the persons working therein.[2]

Penalty.—For provision (c) above, $10 per day for each day of failure after said 20 days. For other provisions (a), (b), (d), (e), first offense, $20 to $50; second offense, $50 to $200, or imprisonment not more than 30 days, or both; third offense, not less than $250, or imprisonment not more than 60 days, or both.

The importance of certain of the points contained in these provisions may be emphasized: The first provision establishes an airspace standard—a minimum of 250 cubic feet in the day and a minimum of 400 cubic feet at night. The air-space standard, as has already been noted, is at best an unreliable guaranty of good ventilation, and this is especially the case when the minimum requirements are as low as in this law. The second provision requires not only that sufficient means of ventilation be maintained, but also that they be properly used. This distinction is of much importance. The aim of this requirement is elaborated upon by the third provision, which directs that all air impurities such as steam, gases, vapors, and dust, generated in the course of the work and which may be injurious to health, shall be so handled as to be rendered harmless. In the special case of dust arising from grinding processes, moreover, the law, as shown in the fourth provision above, specifically orders the use of exhaust fans. The fifth provision authorizes the inspection department to require limewashing or painting but does not make such limewashing or painting mandatory.

The enforcement of these several provisions is charged to the State factory inspection department. The discretion given the department in the matter of determining when conditions need correcting is very broad. The air-space requirement is specific. So also is the requirement that exhaust fans be provided for grindstones. In all other matters referred to by the law, as, for instance, the determination of when air impurities are "injurious to health," when means of ventilation are "proper and sufficient," when limewashing or painting is necessary—the inspection department establishes its own rules.

---

[1] Rev. Stat., 3d ed., p. 2102, sec. 81, as amended by ch. 366, Acts of 1906, and p. 2120, sec. 209, as amended by ch. 506, Acts of 1907 (22d An. Rept. Com. of Labor, pp. 912, 931).

[2] Idem, sec. 84 and p. 2120, sec. 209, as amended by ch. 506, Acts of 1907 (22d An. Rept. Com. of Labor, pp. 914, 931).

Under the New York law, bakeries and confectionery establishments are to be regarded as factories, and thus subjected to all the legal provisions regarding ventilation and sanitation, as above quoted. In addition, bakeries and confectionery establishments are subjected to the following special regulations: [1]

(f) They shall be kept at all times in a clean and sanitary condition. If, on inspection, the commissioner of labor finds any bakery or confectionery to be so unclean, ill drained, or ill ventilated as to be unsanitary he may, after not less than 48 hours' notice in writing * * * , order the person found in charge thereof immediately to cease operating it until it be properly cleaned, drained, or ventilated. [If this order is not observed the commissioner may seal up the ovens, etc., such seal to be removed only by him.]

In considering the laws regarding ventilation it is of much importance to note that since the year 1907 the State of New York has had a medical inspector as an integral part of its regular inspection department. Much of the work of this officer has been the study of problems of ventilation, and in large part such a study means a search for proper and easily applied standards of ventilation. [2]

The general character of the New York law as it existed at the time of the field work of this investigation is clearly and pertinently considered in the following excerpt from the report of the State commissioner of labor: [3]

The health provisions of the factory laws are both ill balanced and defective.

There is nothing in them that requires proper heating. This omission is supplied in some local ordinances, but elsewhere its want is sometimes serious.

They do not require that proper drinking water be supplied. The lack of it is a frequent cause of hardship and ill health in lower grade factories. Under section 94 the factory inspectors can require that a sufficient water supply for washing and toilets be provided in tenant factories and that water tanks in such buildings be kept clean; but their authority ends there.

They do not regulate "humidity." This is one of the most important subjects of regulation abroad. As it is an unknown subject to our inspectors it can not be affirmed that it needs regulating here, but there is a fair presumption that it does.

There is nothing in them to require that workrooms shall be kept clean, except those special provisions that relate to bakeries, laundries, tenements, and certain kinds of shops in tenant factories, and section 84, which prescribes that walls and ceilings shall be painted and white-

---

[1] Rev. Stat., 3d ed., 1901, p. 2108, sec. 114, as amended by ch. 401, Acts of 1906 (22d. An. Rept. Com. of Labor, p. 921). There are several requirements regarding bakeries alone, but the above seems to be the only one including confectioneries also.

[2] See report of medical inspector of factories in Annual Report of the Bureau of Factory Inspection, New York, 1908, p. 24.

[3] Seventh Annual Report of the Commissioner of Labor, New York, 1907, pp. I 29 and I 30.

washed when required. The special provisions referred to cover the classes of workshops in which alone filth is at all common, but even in the better kinds of factories, left unregulated in this particular, injurious dust, waste, and dirty matter are often allowed to accumulate. Pressrooms, even of some of the most reputable newspapers, are very bad in this respect, and show high rates of mortality and sickness. The more complete codes of European countries deal with this subject fully and prescribe frequent wet cleanings. Our code needs similar provisions, and also some special regulation to counteract the evil results from spitting.

Our law as to ventilation has been very imperfect. Section 85 limits the number of persons who may be employed in a workroom according to the cubic air space, but that is of little value unless there also be sufficient ventilation. Section 86 requires that all workrooms shall have proper and sufficient means of ventilation, but until the amendment of this year it did not require that they be kept ventilated. Section 81 requires exhaust systems for metal-polishing wheels and other dust-producing machinery, but it is defective in not applying to machinery or processes creating injurious gases, fumes, heat, etc. Therefore section 86 was amended by chapter 490, Laws of 1907, to prescribe that workrooms shall be kept properly ventilated, and that "if excessive heat be created, or if steam, gases, vapors, dust, or other impurities that may be injurious to health be generated * * * the room must be ventilated in such a manner as to render them harmless so far as practicable."

The provision of section 81 requiring exhaust fans upon all metal-polishing or grinding wheels without exception is too rigid, and both causes hardship and is often unenforceable. Exhaust fans with the necessary connections are very expensive, and should not be required where unnecessary or useless. Where one or two wheels only are used in uncrowded and especially well-ventilated rooms other and cheaper methods of keeping the dust away from the workmen are equally effective and should be permitted. And where the wheels are in tool or machine shops for only occasional use, to require an exhaust fan is nothing but a vexatious handicap upon industry. Referring to the sanitary question involved in the use of such wheels, the English Departmental Report of 1907 on "Compensation for industrial diseases" says: "It must be understood that men whose employment is that of engineers, but who occasionally and for comparatively short periods use a grindstone to sharpen their tools or to file down a piece of metal to be fitted, can not be considered as especially liable to disease." In the very cases where the application of this provision is most useless it is hardest to enforce, for it then meets with reasonable opposition. And one of the worst consequences of such arbitrary provisions is that they reduce the total benefits of factory inspection by occupying the time of inspectors in forcing changes of no benefit to anyone.

CONDITIONS FOUND.

CLEANLINESS OF WORKROOMS.

The workrooms of the 36 establishments visited are classified in the following table according to the degree of cleanliness existing therein.

CLEANLINESS OF WORKROOMS—NEW YORK.

All workrooms clean?		Estab- lishments.
Floors.	Walls and ceilings.	
Yes......	Yes......	29
Yes......	No........	1
No........	Yes......	2
No........	No........	4

SPITTING ON THE FLOOR AND THE PROVISION OF CUSPIDORS.

Habitual spitting on the floor by employees was done in 15 of the 36 establishments visited; in 19 there was a rule against such spitting; and in 18 cuspidors were provided.

The relation between spitting on the floor and the provision of cuspidors and the existence of rules against spitting is shown in the following table:

CONDITIONS AS TO SPITTING ON THE FLOOR—NEW YORK.

	Total establish- ments.	Establish- ments in which spitting on floor is done.
Cuspidors:		
Provided.....................	18	3
Not provided................	18	12
Spitting on floor:		
Prohibited...................	19	1
Not prohibited..............	17	14
Provisions both for cuspidors and against spitting on floor........	15	1

GENERAL VENTILATION AND THE REMOVAL OF DUST AND FUMES.

The two following tables show briefly the conditions found in the several visited establishments as regards the general subject of ventilation and the special topic of dust and fumes.

CONDITIONS AS TO VENTILATION—NEW YORK.

Air space per person in most crowded room.	Establishments.		
	Total.	Special ventilating appliances—	
		Provided.	Not provided.
Under 250 cubic feet.....................	1	....	1
250 and under 500 cubic feet.........	7	....	7
500 and under 1,000 cubic feet........	15	3	12
1,000 and under 2,000 cubic feet......	8	2	6
2,000 and under 3,000 cubic feet......	2	....	2
3,000 cubic feet and over.............	3	1	2
Total.....................	26	6	30

CONDITIONS AS TO DUST OR FUMES IN WORKROOMS—NEW YORK.

Injurious or irritating dust or fumes in workrooms.	Establishments.	
Not noticeable..........................	......	27
Noticeable:		
Removal devices provided........	2	
Removal devices not provided....	7	
		9
Total establishments............	......	36

NEW JERSEY.

SUMMARY OF LEGISLATION.[1]

New Jersey legislation upon matters of ventilation and sanitation consists of four main provisions. These provisions require, respectively, "proper and sufficient" ventilation generally, the observance of an air-space standard, the use of mechanical devices for removing dust due to grinding, and, in certain classes of establishments, the limewashing of walls and ceilings.[2]

---

[1] The law here referred to is as in force at the beginning of 1909. The text of the laws in force Jan. 1, 1912, is given in the appendixes at the end of this volume.

[2] By ch. 102, Acts of 1905 (22d An. Rept. Com. of Labor, pp. 869–871), bakeries and confectioneries are declared to be within the provisions applicable to factories, etc. Additional requirements as to ventilation and sanitation are made as follows: Drainage and plumbing shall be such as will conduce to a proper and healthful sanitary condition; there shall be air shafts, windows, or ventilating pipes sufficient to insure ventilation; shall at all times be kept in a clean and sanitary condition; the commissioner of labor may order a bakery closed at once if he finds it unclean, ill-drained, or ill-ventilated.

By a law enacted subsequent to the field work of this investigation the legislation regarding bakeries and confectioneries was elaborated and made to apply to all places used for the "production, manufacture, preparation, packing, storage, or distribution" of food or food products. Acts of 1909, ch. 231 (Bulletin of the Bureau of Labor, No. 85, pp. 679–681).

The tenement-house legislation of New Jersey does not refer specifically to ventilation and sanitary conditions. Acts of 1904, ch. 64, secs. 31 and 32 (22d An. Rept. Com. of Labor, pp. 864, 865).

The first three provisions referred to, dealing specifically with the subject of good breathing air, are as follows:

(a) The owner, agent, or lessee of a place coming under the provisions of this act [i. e., factory, workshop, mill, or place where the manufacture of goods of any kind is carried on], or employer, shall provide in each workroom thereof proper and sufficient means of ventilation; in case of failure the commissioner [of labor] shall order such ventilation to be provided.[1]

> Penalty.—$10 per day for each day's noncompliance with commissioner's order, after expiration of time given by such order to make the change.

(b) Not less than 250 cubic feet of air space shall be provided for each employee or operative at work in a room in a place within the meaning of this act [i. e., factory, workshop, etc., as in preceding paragraph] between the hours of 6 o'clock in the morning and 6 o'clock in the evening, and not less than 400 cubic feet of air space for each employee so employed between the hours of 6 o'clock in the evening and 6 o'clock in the morning: Provided, In all cases where the amount of air space provided does not exceed the amount above fixed, that such room is lighted by electricity during all hours that artificial lights are necessary and persons are employed therein, unless a written permit shall be obtained from the commissioner.[2]

> Penalty.—$50 for each offense.

(c) All corporations, firms, or persons conducting a manufacturing business in any of the places coming under the provisions of this act [i. e., factory, workshop, etc., as in preceding paragraph], where emery wheels or emery belts of any description are used, either solid emery, leather, leather covered, felt, canvas, linen, paper, cotton, or wheels or belts rolled or coated with emery or corundum, or cotton wheels used as buffs, shall provide the same with blowers or similar apparatus, which shall be placed over, beside, or under wheels or belts in such a manner as to protect the person or persons using the same from the particles of the dust produced and caused thereby, and to carry away the dust arising from or thrown off by such wheels or belts while in operation, directly to the outside of the building, or to some receptacle placed so as to receive and confine such dust: Provided, That grinding machines upon which water is used * * *· and small emery wheels that are used temporarily for tool grinding in small shops employing not more than three persons at such work, shall be exempt from the provisions of this section if so ordered by the commissioner [of labor]. [Here follows a detailed description of the character of blowers, fans, suction pipes, etc., required.][3]

> Penalty.—$50.

The first of these provisions directs, in general terms, that "proper and sufficient means of ventilation" shall be provided. The factory

---

[1] Acts of 1904, ch. 64, sec. 20 (22d An. Rept. Com. of Labor, p. 863).

[2] Idem, secs. 19 and 30 (22d An. Rept. Com. of Labor, pp. 863, 864).

[3] Idem, secs. 14 and 30 (22d An. Rept. Com. of Labor, pp. 862, 864).

inspection department is made the judge of when these conditions are complied with, and the employer is legally blameless until an order has been issued by the department directing him to make specified changes.

The second and third provisions are supplemental to the one preceding. They are precise in character, giving specific rules to be observed in order to make ventilation "proper." The second provision establishes an air-space standard—250 cubic feet during the day and 400 cubic feet during the night—but makes certain exemptions in the case of establishments using electricity as an illuminant. The merits of the air-space standard are its precision and its ease of enforcement. Its weaknesses, as earlier pointed out, are: First, that an air-space requirement by itself is not a satisfactory standard of ventilation; and, second, that a minimum as low as that of the New Jersey law is inadequate to correct serious overcrowding.

The requirement contained in the third-quoted provision—regarding the removal of dust due to emery grinding—closely resembles in its wording similar requirements of several of the other States covered by this report. It is very precise in its statement of its object and of the means of attaining that object. In obeying and in enforcing this provision very little room is left for the exercise of personal judgment. It is to be emphasized, however, that the law refers solely to the removal of dust due to grinding. Other kinds of dust, and fumes and gases of all kinds, are not covered by any specific legal requirements.

As regards matters of sanitation and cleanliness the New Jersey law makes but the single provision that:

(d) Factories and workshops in which women and children are employed, and where dusty work is carried on, shall be limewashed or painted at least once in every 12 months.[1]

Penalty.—$50.

This requirement, it will be noted, is closely limited, applying only to factories and workshops in which women and children are employed and where the work done is dust producing.

The enforcement of all the above-quoted provisions regarding ventilation and sanitation is intrusted in full to the factory-inspection department.[2]

---

[1] Acts of 1904, ch. 64,, secs. 24 and 30 (22d An. Rept. Com. of Labor, p. 863).

[2] Idem, secs. 18 and 30 (22d An. Rept. Com. of Labor, pp. 863, 864).

CONDITIONS FOUND.

CLEANLINESS OF WORKROOMS.

The following table classifies the workrooms of the 27 visited establishments according to the general cleanliness thereof.

CLEANLINESS OF WORKROOMS—NEW JERSEY.

All workrooms clean?		Estab- lishments.
Floors.	Walls and ceilings.	
Yes......	Yes.......	19
Yes......	No........	3
No........	Yes.......	1
No........	No........	4

SPITTING ON THE FLOOR AND THE PROVISION OF CUSPIDORS.

Habitual spitting on the factory floors by employees was done in 16 of the 27 establishments; in 14 there was a rule against such spitting; and in 9 cuspidors were provided.

The relation between spitting on the floor and the provision of cuspidors and the existence of rules against spitting is shown in the following table:

CONDITIONS AS TO SPITTING ON THE FLOOR—NEW JERSEY.

	Total establish- ments.	Establish- ments in which spitting on floor is done.
Cuspidors:		
Provided....................	9	1
Not provided................	18	15
Spitting on floor:		
Prohibited...................	14	3
Not prohibited..............	13	13
Provisions both for cuspidors and against spitting on floor........	9	1

GENERAL VENTILATION AND THE REMOVAL OF DUST AND FUMES.

The two following tables show briefly the conditions found in the several establishments visited as regards the general subject of ventilation and the special topic of dust and fumes:

CONDITIONS AS TO VENTILATION—NEW JERSEY.

Air space per person in most crowded workroom.	Establishments.		
	Total.	Special ventilating appliances—	
		Provided.	Not provided.
Under 250 cubic feet................	1	....	1
250 and under 500 cubic feet..........	3	1	2
500 and under 1,000 cubic feet........	7	2	5
1,000 and under 2,000 cubic feet......	10	....	10
2,000 and under 3,000 cubic feet......	1	1	....
3,000 cubic feet and over.............	5	4	1
Total........................	27	8	19

CONDITIONS AS TO DUST OR FUMES IN WORKROOMS—NEW JERSEY.

Injurious or irritating dust or fumes in workrooms.	Establishments.
Not noticeable.......................	13
Noticeable:	
Removal devices provided........ 3	
Removal devices not provided.... 10	
	13
Not reported.......................	1
Total establishments...........	27

PENNSYLVANIA.

SUMMARY OF LEGISLATION.[1]

The legislation of Pennsylvania contains the following provisions regarding the ventilation and sanitation of factories and workshops:[2]

(a) If the inspector of factories finds that the heating, lighting, ventilation or sanitary arrangements of any shop, or factory, is such as to be injurious to the health of persons employed therein * * * he shall notify the proprietor of such factory or workshop to make the alterations or additions necessary within 60 days. * * *[3]

Penalty.—Not more than $500.

---

[1] The law here referred to is as in force at the beginning of 1909. The text of the laws in force Jan. 1, 1912, is given in the appendixes at the end of this volume.

[2] For special legislation regarding the sanitation of bakeries, not including confectioneries, see Brightly's Digest, 1893–1903, p. 62, secs. 14 and 15, and Acts of 1905, act No. 226, sec. 17 (22d An. Rept. Com. of Labor, pp. 1145, 1179).

For special legislation regarding tenement shops, see Brightly's Digest, 1893–1903, p. 825, sec. 2, and Acts of 1905, act No. 226, sec. 14 (22d An. Rept. Com. of Labor, pp. 1163, 1178).

[3] Brightly's Purdon's Digest, 12th ed. 1895, p. 865, secs. 21 and 26 (22d An. Rept. Com. of Labor, p. 1080).

(b) The owner, agent, lessee, or other person having charge or managerial control of any establishment, shall provide or cause to be provided not less than 250 cubic feet of air space for each and every person in every workroom in said establishment, where persons are employed.

(c) And shall provide that all workrooms, halls, and stairways in said establishment be kept in a clean and sanitary condition and properly lighted.[1]

Penalty.—$25 to $500 or 10 to 60 days' imprisonment for each offense.

(d) Exhaust fans of sufficient power, or other sufficient devices, shall be provided for the purpose of carrying off poisonous fumes and gasses, and dust from emery wheels, grindstones and other machinery creating dust.[2]

Penalty.—$25 to $500, or 10 to 60 days' imprisonment for each offense.

The first of these provisions is very general in character and is weak in that, first, it authorizes the inspector to order remedies only when conditions are injurious to health, a point which, as has already been commented upon, is frequently difficult to establish, and, second, it does not place the employer under an obligation to maintain good conditions in the absence of a specific order from the inspector.

In practice, however, this provision is superseded by provisions (b) and (c), which although limited in scope, are now more positive in their requirements. Provision (b) demands that there shall be not less than 250 cubic feet of air space for each employee. The weaknesses of the air-space standard have already been pointed out. Its value is especially small when the standard is fixed as low as 250 cubic feet per person. Its merit is that it is precise in its demands and easily enforceable.

Provision (c) requires that factories, etc., shall be kept in a "clean and sanitary condition." No interpretation is given to the phrase "clean and sanitary" and no test standards of any kind are established. As a result the inspector is vested with a very broad discretionary power. On the other hand, the provision is mandatory in form, placing an obligation immediately upon every employee to maintain good conditions.

The fourth provision provides for the general removal of all poisonous fumes, gases, and dust. The chief difficulty in the strict enforcement of such a requirement is, probably, the determination of what gases, fumes, and dust are poisonous. The law does not provide how standards in this matter are to be obtained.

---

[1] Acts of 1905, act No. 226, secs. 13 and 23 (22d An. Rept. Com. of Labor, p. 1178).
[2] Idem, secs. 11 and 23 (22d An. Rept. Com. of Labor, p. 1177).

Summarizing opinions on all of the quoted provisions it would appear that, while the requirements are indefinite upon many points, they are sufficiently thorough to enable the inspecting department to insist upon the correction of all seriously bad conditions.

The State factory inspection department is charged with the enforcement of all the legal provisions regarding sanitation and ventilation.

CONDITIONS FOUND.

CLEANLINESS OF WORKROOMS.

The conditions as regards general cleanliness of the workrooms of the 50 establishments visited are shown in the following table:

CLEANLINESS OF WORKROOMS—PENNSYLVANIA.

All workrooms clean?		Estab-lishments.
Floors.	Walls and ceilings.	
Yes......	Yes.......	41
Yes......	No........	5
No........	Yes.......	2
No........	No........	2

SPITTING ON THE FLOOR AND THE PROVISION OF CUSPIDORS.

Spitting on the floor was reported as being habitually done by employees in 22 of the 50 establishments. Such spitting was prohibited in 37, and in 21 cuspidors were furnished.

The following table shows the relation between spitting on the floor and the provision of cuspidors and the existence of factory rules against spitting.

CONDITIONS AS TO SPITTING ON THE FLOOR—PENNSYLVANIA.

	Total establish-ments.	Establish-ments in which spitting on floor is done.
Cuspidors:		
Provided......................	21	4
Not provided.................	29	18
Spitting on floor:		
Prohibited....................	37	10
Not prohibited...............	13	12
Provisions both for cuspidors and against spitting on floor........	21	4

GENERAL VENTILATION AND THE REMOVAL OF DUST AND FUMES.

The two following tables show briefly the conditions found in the several establishments visited as regards the general subject of ventilation and the special topic of dust and fumes.

CONDITIONS AS TO VENTILATION—PENNSYLVANIA.

Air space per person in most crowded room.	Establishments.		
	Total.	Special ventilating appliances—	
		Provided.	Not provided.
Under 250 cubic feet................	....	....	....
250 and under 500 cubic feet........	3	1	2
500 and under 1,000 cubic feet.......	¹16	....	15
1,000 and under 2,000 cubic feet......	24	8	16
2,000 and under 3,000 cubic feet......	4	4	....
3,000 cubic feet and over............	1	1	....
Not reported.......................	2	....	2
Total........................	¹50	14	35

¹ Including 1 establishment not reported as to ventilating apparatus.

CONDITION AS TO DUST OR FUMES IN WORKROOMS—PENNSYLVANIA.

Injurious or irritating dust or fumes in workrooms.	Establishments.
Not noticeable.........................	30
Noticeable:	
Removal devices provided........ 10	
Removal devices not provided.... 10	
	20
Total establishments.............	50

OHIO.

SUMMARY OF LEGISLATION.[1]

The legislation of Ohio in regard to matters of ventilation and sanitation consists (1) of a general authorization given factory inspectors to correct such conditions of "heating, lighting, ventilation or sanitary arrangement" as seem to them "injurious to health," and (2) a specific requirement that dust-removing appliances be provided with certain grinding machines.[2]

The legal provisions referred to above are in full as follows:

(a) It shall be their duty [i. e., of the chief inspector and district inspectors] to visit all shops and factories[3] in their respective dis-

---

[1] The law here referred to is as in force at the beginning of 1909. The text of the laws in force Jan. 1, 1912, is given in the appendixes at the end of this volume.

[2] For special legislation regarding sweatshops see Bates' Ann. Stat., 3d ed., Part II, Civil, secs. 4364–80 and 4364–81 (22d An. Rept. Com. of Labor, pp. 1012, 1013). Special legislation also exists for bakeries, but not for confectioneries and other food-producing establishments. Idem, secs. 4364–71 to 4364–79 (22d An. Rept. Com. of Labor, p. 1011). Also note that tenement houses are included in the law as "shops and factories." See footnote below.

[3] The term "shops and factories" shall be held to include the following: Manufacturing, mechanical, electrical, mercantile, art and laundering establishments,

tricts as often as possible, to see that all the provisions and requirements of this act are strictly observed and carried out; they shall carefully inspect the sanitary condition of the same, and it shall be their duty to examine the system of sewerage in connection with said shops and factories, the situation and conditions of water-closets or urinals in and about such shops and factories and also the system of heating, lighting and ventilating all rooms in such shops and factories where persons are employed at daily labor.

Said inspectors, if they find upon such inspection that the heating, lighting, ventilation, or sanitary arrangement of any shop or factory is such as to be injurious to the health of persons employed or residing therein * * *, shall notify the owners, proprietors, or agents of such shops or factories * * * to make the alterations or additions necessary without delay. [Chief inspector may allow 15 to 30 days for compliance.]

> *Penalty.*—$50 to $500, and $10 per day for each day after conviction and until changes ordered are made.[1]

(*b*) All persons, companies, or corporations operating any factory or workshop, where emery wheels or emery belts of any description are used, either solid emery, leather, leather covered, felt, canvas, linen, paper, cotton, or wheels or belts rolled or coated with emery or corundum, or cotton wheels used as buffs, shall provide the same with blowers, or similar apparatus, which shall be placed over, beside, or under such wheels or belts in such a manner as to protect the person or persons using the same from the particles of the dust produced and caused thereby, and to carry away the dust arising from or thrown off by such wheels or belts while in operation, directly to the outside of the building, or to some receptacle placed so as to receive and confine such dust: *Provided*, That grinding machines upon which water is used * * * and small emery wheels that are used temporarily for tool grinding and small shops employing not more than one man at such work and do not create dust enough in the opinion of the inspector to be injurious to the operator, shall be exempt from the provisions of this act.

[Here follows a detailed description of character of blowers, fans, suction pipes, etc., required.]

It shall be the duty of the chief inspector * * * to cause his district inspectors to inspect such workshops and factories * * *

---

printing, telegraph, and telephone offices, railroad depots, hotels, memorial buildings, tenement and apartment houses." Bates's Ann. Stat., 3d ed., Part I, Political, sec. 2573*d* (22d An. Rept. Com. of Labor, p. 999).

[1] Idem, secs. 2573*a* and 2573*c*, as amended by act, p. 338, Acts of 1902, and act, p. 530, Acts of 1904 (22d An. Rept. Com. of Labor, pp. 997–999).

By an act of 1908, providing for women visitors to investigate, etc., the conditions of labor in establishments employing women and children, such visitors are authorized to examine into the conditions of ventilation and sanitation in factories and workshops. The wording of this later law is quite similar to that used in the older law regarding factory inspectors, as quoted above, with the difference, however, that the women visitors are given no authority to compel compliance. They report to the chief inspector any bad conditions they may discover, and the chief inspector issues the necessary notices. Acts of 1908, p. 30, sec. 4. (Bulletin of the Bureau of Labor, No. 85, p. 703).

having and using such machinery as is named in this act   *   *   *;
and the chief inspector shall notify the person or persons, company, or corporation operating such workshop or factory to comply
with the provisions of this act within 30 days after date of issuing
order   *   *   *.

Penalty.—For each offense, $50 to $100, or imprisonment not
    less than 30 days, or both.[1]   •

The second of these provisions—regarding the removal of dust due
to grinding—is quite the same as that contained in the laws of several
of the other States covered by this report.   It not only requires that
dust-removing appliances be provided but describes in detail the kind
of appliances which alone will satisfy the law.

The first provision, on the other hand, is very indefinite in its terms.
It directs simply that the factory inspectors shall order remedied any
conditions of ventilation and sanitation which appear to them injurious
to health.   No standards or tests are provided by law.   The inspectors are given full authority to act according to their best judgment.
The extreme difficulty of determining with certainty when certain
conditions are positively injurious to health has already been commented upon.   It is recognized by the chief factory inspector in the
following statement:

It is my sincere belief that provision should be made for the appointment of at least one person connected with the medical profession in order that reliable and scientific investigation might be made
of the sanitation and ventilation of our shops and factories   *   *   *.[2]

The State factory inspection department is intrusted with the
supervision and enforcement of all legal provisions dealing with
ventilation or sanitation in factories and workshops.

CONDITIONS FOUND.

CLEANLINESS OF WORKROOMS.

The next table classifies the workrooms of the 60 visited establishments according to the general conditions of cleanliness existing
therein.

CLEANLINESS OF WORKROOMS—OHIO.

All workrooms clean?		Estab-lishments.
Floors.	Walls and ceilings.	
Yes......	Yes.......	56
Yes......	No........	1
No........	Yes.......	1
No........	No........	2

[1] Bates' Ann. Stat., 3d ed., Part II, Civil, secs. 4364–86 to 4364–89a and 4364–89b (22d An. Rept. Com.
of Labor, pp. 1013, 1014).
[2] Twenty-fourth Annual Report of the Department of Inspection of Workshops, Factories, and Public
Buildings, 1907, p. 13.

SPITTING ON THE FLOOR AND THE PROVISION OF CUSPIDORS.

Habitual spitting on the floor by employees was reported as being done in 19 of the 60 establishments visited; in 48 there was a rule against such spitting; and in 30 cuspidors were provided, 1 establishment not being reported for on this last point.

The relation between spitting on the floor and the provision of cuspidors and the existence of rules against spitting is shown in the following table:

CONDITIONS AS TO SPITTING ON THE FLOOR—OHIO.

	Total establishments.	Establishments in which spitting on floor is done.
Cuspidors:[1]		
Provided...................	30	3
Not provided................	29	16
Spitting on floor:		
Prohibited................	48	11
Not prohibited.............	12	8
Provisions both for cuspidors and against spitting on floor.......	28	3

[1] One establishment not reported.

GENERAL VENTILATION AND THE REMOVAL OF DUST AND FUMES.

The two following tables show briefly the conditions found in the several establishments visited as regards the general subject of ventilation and the special topic of dust and fumes:

CONDITIONS AS TO VENTILATION—OHIO.

Air space per person in most crowded room.	Establishments.		
	Total.	Special ventilating appliances—	
		Provided.	Not provided.
Under 250 cubic feet..................	1	....	1
250 and under 500 cubic feet.........	2	1	1
500 and under 1,000 cubic feet........	18	2	16
1,000 and under 2,000 cubic feet......	34	10	24
2,000 and under 3,000 cubic feet......	4	1	3
3,000 cubic feet and over.............	1	....	1
Total.....................	60	14	46

CONDITIONS AS TO DUST OR FUMES IN WORKROOMS—OHIO.

Injurious or irritating dust or fumes in workrooms.	Establishments.
Not noticeable........................	43
Noticeable:	
Removal devices provided.........	[1] 7
Removal devices not provided....	10
	17
Total establishments............	60

[1] Removal devices in one establishment not in good working order.

ILLINOIS.

SUMMARY OF LEGISLATION.[1]

At the time of the field work of this investigation Illinois legislation regarding topics covered by this chapter was limited to a requirement for the removal of dust due to certain kinds of grinding and to special provisions applicable to tenement shops and butterine and ice cream factories only.[2]

The provision regarding the removing of dust caused by emery grinding is substantially the same as that found in the laws of several of the other States covered by this investigation. It relates solely to the one class of dust producers. Its wording is as follows:[3]

All persons, companies, or corporations operating any factory or workshop where emery wheels or emery belts of any description are used, either solid emery, leather, leather covered, felt, canvas, linen, paper, cotton, or wheels or belts rolled or coated with emery or corundum, or cotton wheels used as buffs, shall provide the same with blowers, or similar apparatus, which shall be placed over, beside or under such wheels or belts in such a manner as to protect the person or persons using the same from the particles of the dust produced and caused thereby, and to carry away the dust arising from or thrown off by such wheels or belts while in operation, directly to the outside of the building, or to some receptacle placed so as to receive and confine such dust: *Provided*, That grinding machines upon which water is used * * * shall be exempt from the provisions of this act, * * * [and also] small shops employing not more than one man in such work.

[Here follows a detailed description of the character of the blowers, fans, suction pipes, etc., required.]

The factory inspector is instructed to enforce the above provision, on complaint.

Penalty.—$25 to $100.

---

[1] The law here referred to is as in force at the beginning of 1909. The text of the laws in force Jan. 1, 1912, is given in the appendixes at the end of this volume.

[2] By an act approved June 4, 1909, however, very comprehensive legislation regarding the ventilation and sanitation of factories was put in force. The thorough and well considered character of this legislation has already been considered (pp. 437–439). In many respects it is the most important legislation upon these subjects as yet enacted in any American State. Acts of 1909, p. 202, secs. 10 to 13 (Bulletin of the Bureau of Labor, No. 85, pp. 547–549).

Special legislation regarding butterine and ice cream factories does not cover confectionery or other food-producing establishments. Acts of 1907, p. 309, secs. 1 to 5 (22d An. Rept. Com. of Labor, pp. 375, 376).

For special legislation regarding tenement shops, see Hurd's Rev. Stat., 1905, ch: 48, secs. 21 to 28 (22d An. Rept. Com. of Labor, pp. 340, 341).

[3] Hurd's Rev. Stat., 1905, ch. 48, secs. 43 to 48 (22d An. Rept. Com. of Labor, pp. 342, 343).

CONDITIONS FOUND.

CLEANLINESS OF WORKROOMS.

The following table groups the workrooms of the 47 establishments visited according to the general conditions of cleanliness found therein:

CLEANLINESS OF WORKROOMS—ILLINOIS.

All workrooms clean?		Estab-lishments.
Floors.	Walls and ceilings.	
Yes......	Yes......	35
Yes......	No.......	6
No........	Yes......	3
No........	No.......	3

SPITTING ON THE FLOOR AND THE PROVISION OF CUSPIDORS.

Habitual spitting on factory floors by employees was reported as being done in 26 of the 47 establishments visited; in 23 such spitting was prohibited by factory rule; and in 16 cuspidors were provided.

The relation between spitting on the floor and the provision of cuspidors and the existence of rules against spitting is shown in the following table:

CONDITIONS AS TO SPITTING ON THE FLOOR—ILLINOIS.

	Total establish-ments.	Establish-ments in which spitting on floor is done.
Cuspidors:		
Provided.....................	16	5
Not provided....................	31	21
Spitting on floor:		
Prohibited.....................	23	7
Not prohibited.................	24	19
Provisions both for cuspidors and against spitting on floor...........	13	3

The present investigation did not cover ice cream and butterine factories, for which there is a special series of sanitary regulations.

GENERAL VENTILATION AND THE REMOVAL OF DUST AND FUMES.

The two following tables show briefly the conditions found in the several establishments visited as regards the general subject of ventilation and the special topic of dust and fumes.

CONDITIONS AS TO VENTILATION—ILLINOIS.

Air space per person in most crowded room.	Establishments.		
	Total.	Special ventilating appliances—	
		Provided.	Not provided.
Under 250 cubic feet..................	1	....	1
250 and under 500 cubic feet.........	8	3	5
500 and under 1,000 cubic feet.......	16	4	12
1,000 and under 2,000 cubic feet......	17	4	13
2,000 and under 3,000 cubic feet......	3	2	1
3,000 cubic feet and over............	1	....	1
Not reported [1].....................	1	....	1
Total......................	47	13	34

[1] But over 1,000 cubic feet.

CONDITIONS AS TO DUST OR FUMES IN WORKROOMS—ILLINOIS.

Injurious or irritating dust or fumes in workrooms.	Establishments.
Not noticeable........................	16
Noticeable:	
Removal devices provided........ 8	
Removal devices not provided... 23	
	31
Total establishments............	47

INDIAN.

SUMMARY OF LEGISLATION.[1]

Indiana legislation establishes an air-space standard of ventilation; requires sufficient "means" of ventilation; requires dust-creating machinery to be provided with exhaust fans; orders water-closets to be kept clean; authorizes the factory inspector to order the lime-washing of walls and ceilings; and for food manufacturing establishments provides a special series of sanitary regulations.[2]

The text of the three legal provisions regarding ventilation of workrooms and dust removal is as follows:[3]

---

[1] The law here referred to is as in force at the beginning of 1909. The text of the laws in force Jan. 1, 1912, is given in the appendixes at the end of this volume.

[2] Special legislation regarding tenement shops makes no specific regulations as regards subjects considered in this chapter. Ann. Stat. of 1894, Rev. of 1901, sec. 7087n (22d An. Rept. Com. of Labor, p. 400).

[3] Ann. Stat. of 1894, Rev. of 1901, secs. 7087i, 7087o, and 7087y (22d An. Rept. Com. of Labor, pp. 399, 400, 402).

(a) No less than 250 cubic feet of air space shall be allowed for each person in any workroom where persons are employed during the hours between 6 o'clock in the morning and 6 o'clock in the evening, and not less than 400 cubic feet of air space shall be provided for each person in any workroom where persons are employed between 6 o'clock in the evening and 6 o'clock in the morning. By a written permit the chief inspector may allow persons to be employed in a room where there are less than 400 cubic feet but not less than 250 cubic feet of air space for each person employed between 6 o'clock in the evening and 6 o'clock in the morning: *Provided*, Such room is lighted by electricity at all times during such hours while persons are employed therein.

(b) There shall be sufficient means of ventilation provided in each workroom of every manufacturing or mercantile establishment, laundry, renovating works, bakery, or printing office within this State, and the chief inspector shall. notify the owner in writing to provide, or cause to be provided, ample and proper means of ventilation for such workroom, and shall prosecute such owner, agent, or lessee if such notification be not complied with within 20 days of the service of such notice.

(c) Exhaust fans of sufficient power shall be provided for the purpose of carrying off dust from emery wheels and grindstones and dust-creating machinery from establishments where used.

> *Penalty.*—First offense, not more than $50; second offense, not more than $100, to which may be added imprisonment for not more than 10 days; third offense, not less than $250 and not more than 30 days' imprisonment.

The first of these provisions—establishing an air-space standard—is almost the same in wording and quite the same in meaning as the corresponding provisions of the New York and New Jersey laws (see pp. 458, 464). The merits and weaknesses of such an air-space standard have already been commented upon. On the one hand, it is precise in its terms, mandatory, and easily enforceable. On the other hand, the air-space standard, by its very nature, can not be a very satisfactory test of pure air, and is especially ineffective where the minimum requirement is as low as it is in the Indiana law—250 cubic feet per person by day and 400 cubic feet per person by night.

Under the second of the above quoted provisions the inspector is authorized to insist upon sufficient "means" of ventilation, and this would appear to free him from being absolutely bound by the air-space standard. Then, if the inspector finds the air conditions very bad in an establishment, he is justified in ordering the means of ventilation to be improved, even although the air-space standard is observed.

The third of the quoted provisions relates to the use of exhaust fans for the removal of dust. It will be observed that the requirement is absolutely mandatory and applies to all kinds of dust-producing grindstones or machinery, not merely to grindstones, as is the case in the laws of several of the other States.

As regards matters of sanitation and general cleanliness, the
Indiana law provides that water-closets shall be kept clean and well
ventilated and that, if the inspector considers it desirable, walls and
ceilings shall be limewashed or painted.   The exact legal provisions
upon these points are as follows: [1]

(*d*) Water-closets shall be properly * * * ventilated and kept
at all times in a clean condition.

(*e*) The walls and ceilings of each room in every establishment
aforesaid (i. e., manufacturing or mercantile establishment * * *
laundry, renovating works, bakery, or printing office) shall be limewashed or painted, when in the opinion of the chief inspector it shall
be conducive to the health or cleanliness of the persons working
therein.

Penalty.—First offense, not more than $50; second offense, not
more than $100, to which may be added imprisonment for not more
than 10 days; third offense, not less than $250 and not more than 30
days' imprisonment.

Establishments engaged in the manufacture of food products are
subjected by the Indiana laws to an extensive and important series
of special regulations regarding ventilation and sanitation.   The
primary purpose of these requirements is to insure purity of product;
the protection of the health of the employees is only a secondary
effect.   Several of the regulations, however, do have this secondary
effect in an important degree.   The regulations referred to are as
follows: [2]

(*f*) (1) Every building, room, basement, or cellar occupied or used
as a bakery or confectionery, canning, packing, pickling or preserving
establishment, or for the manufacture (for sale) of any food product
shall be properly heated, lighted, drained, plumbed and ventilated
and conducted with a strict regard to the health of the operatives
and the purity and wholesomeness of the food articles produced.

(2) The floors, side walls, ceilings, fixtures, furniture, and utensils
of every establishment or place where food products are manufactured or stored shall at all times be kept in a clean, healthful, and
sanitary condition.

(3) The side walls and ceilings of every bake room or confectionery
shall be well plastered, wainscoted, or ceiled with metal or lumber.

(4) Plastered walls and ceilings shall be oil painted or kept well
limewashed, and all interior woodwork in every bakery or confectionery shall be kept well oiled or painted with oil paint and kept
washed clean with soap and water.

(5) And every building, room, basement, or cellar occupied or
used for the manufacture of any food products shall have, if deemed

---

[1] Ann. Stat. of 1894, Rev. of 1901, secs. 7087j, 7087l, and 7087y (22d An. Rept.
Com. of Labor, pp. 399, 400, 402).

[2] Idem, secs. 6725a to 6725i (22d An. Rept. Com. of Labor, pp. 385, 386).   By a
law enacted after the field work of this investigation was completed the requirements
regarding food-producing establishments were elaborated.   Acts of 1909, ch. 163 (Bulletin of the Bureau of Labor, No. 85, pp. 570–572).

necessary by the chief inspector, an impermeable floor, made of cement or tile laid in cement.

(6) The sleeping place or places for the persons employed in a bakeshop shall be separate and apart from the bake room; and no person shall be allowed to sleep in a bake room or place where flour or meal or the products thereof are stored.

(7) No employer shall knowingly require, permit, or suffer any person to work in a bakery or confectionery who is affected with consumption of the lungs, or with scrofula, or with any venereal disease, or with any communicable skin disease.

(8) Cuspidors shall be provided by the owner or operator for each workroom of every bakery or confectionery, and no employee or other person shall expectorate on the floor or side walls of any bakery or confectionery or place where the manufacure of any food product is conducted.

(9) Plain notices shall be posted in every place where food products of any kind are produced forbidding all persons expectorating on the floors of such establishment.

(10) The door and window openings of every food-producing establishment during fly season shall be fitted with self-closing, wire-screen doors and top outward-tipping wire window screens.

(11) Every bakery and confectionery shall be provided with wash room and water-closet or closets, but separate and apart from the bake room or rooms where the manufacture of any food products is conducted.

Penalty.—First offense, $10 to $50; second offense, $50 to $100; third offense, not less than $200 or imprisonment for not more than 60 days, or both.

The State factory inspection department is charged with the enforcement of all legislation regarding sanitation and ventilation.[1]

CONDITIONS FOUND.

CLEANLINESS OF WORKROOMS.

The condition as regards general cleanliness in the workrooms of the 47 visited establishments is shown in the following table:

CLEANLINESS OF WORKROOMS—INDIANA.

All workrooms clean?		Establish- ments.
Floors.	Walls and ceilings.	
Yes......	Yes.......	39
Yes......	No.........	3
No........	Yes.......	3
No........	No........	2

Four of the 8 food-producing establishments visited were among those in which the floors or walls and ceilings were not kept in a clean condition.

---

[1] Ann. Stat. of 1894, Rev. of 1901, secs. 6725c and 7087v (22d An. Rept. Com. of Labor, pp. 385, 402).

SPITTING ON THE FLOOR AND THE PROVISION OF CUSPIDORS.

Habitual spitting on factory floors by employees was done in 22
of the 47 establishments visited; in 23 there was a rule against such
spitting; and in 17 cuspidors were provided.

The relation between spitting on the floor and the provision of
cuspidors and the existence of rules against spitting is shown in the
following table:

CONDITIONS AS TO SPITTING ON THE FLOOR—INDIANA.

	Total establishments.	Establishments in which spitting on floor is done.
Cuspidors:		
Provided	17	4
Not provided	30	18
Spitting on floor:		
Prohibited	23	7
Not prohibited	24	15
Provisions both for cuspidors and against spitting on floor	16	4

Of the 8 food-producing establishments which are subjected to
special regulations regarding promiscuous spitting, cuspidors were
provided in 3; there were rules against free spitting in 6; and spitting
on the floor was habitual in 1.

GENERAL VENTILATION AND THE REMOVAL OF DUST AND FUMES.

The two following tables show briefly the conditions found in the
several visited establishments as regards the general subject of ventilation and the special topic of dust and fumes:

CONDITIONS AS TO VENTILATION—INDIANA.

Air space per person in most crowded room.	Establishments.		
	Total.	Special ventilating appliances—	
		Provided.	Not provided.
Under 250 cubic feet			
250 and under 500 cubic feet	10	2	8
500 and under 1,000 cubic feet	25	6	19
1,000 and under 2,000 cubic feet	10	2	8
2,000 and under 3,000 cubic feet	1	1	
3,000 cubic feet and over	1		1
Total	47	11	36

CONDITIONS AS TO DUST OR FUMES IN WORKROOMS—INDIANA.

Injurious or irritating dust or fumes in workrooms.	Establishments.
Not noticeable..........................	 18
Noticeable:	
Removal devices provided........	[1] 14
Removal devices not provided....	15
	29
Total establishments...........	 47

[1] In 2 establishments devices not in good working order.

MICHIGAN.

SUMMARY OF LEGISLATION.[1]

Legislation in Michigan concerning matters of ventilation and sanitation is limited to three main provisions. One of these provides for the removal of dust due to certain kinds of grinding; the second enlarges upon the first by requiring, at the discretion of the inspector, the use of exhaust fans for all kinds of machine dust; the third provides in general terms that factories and workshops shall be kept in a cleanly condition.[2]

The first two of the three mentioned provisions are as follows:

(a) All persons, companies or corporations, operating any factory or workshop, where wheels or emery belts of any description are in general use, either leather, leather covered, felt, canvas paper, cotton or wheels or belts rolled or coated with emery or corundum, or cotton, wheels used as buffs, shall provide the same with fans or blowers, or similar apparatus, when ordered by the commissioner of labor, which shall be placed in such a position or manner as to protest [protect] the person or persons using the same from the particles of the dust produced and caused thereby, and to carry away the dust arising from, or thrown off by such wheels or belts, while in operation, directly to the outside of the building or to some other receptacle placed so as to receive and confine such dust. * * * *Provided*, That grinding machines upon which water is used * * * shall be exempt from the conditions of this act * * * [and also] solid emery wheels used in sawmills or planing mills or other woodworking establishments.

[1] The law here referred to is as in force at the beginning of 1909. The text of the laws in force Jan. 1, 1912, is given in the appendixes at the end of this volume.

[2] Special legislation upon one or more points of ventilation and sanitation exists; for foundries, as regards the removal of various fumes and gases, Acts of 1907, act No. 152, sec. 3; for mattress factories, as regards the removal of dust, Acts of 1907, act No. 252, sec. 1; and for tenement shops in considerable detail, Acts of 1901, act No. 113, sec. 17 (as amended by act No. 169, Acts of 1907). (See 22d An. Rept. Com. of Labor, pp. 661, 662, 667, 668.)

The city of Detroit has a 500-cubic-foot-air-space standard in factories, etc.

[Here follows a detailed description of character of blowers, fans, suction pipes, etc., required.] [1]

No person shall be employed to operate any of the wheels, buffers, or belts mentioned * * * (above) in any basement so called, or any room lying wholly or partly beneath the surface of the ground, unless such workrooms shall be provided with sufficient means of light, heat, and ventilation as shall be prescribed by the State factory inspector.[2]

It shall be the duty of any factory inspector, sheriff, constable, or prosecuting attorney * * * upon receiving notice in writing, signed by any person or persons having knowledge of such facts, that * * * [a] factory or workshop is not provided with such appliances as herein provided for to visit * * * such factory or workshop * * * and upon ascertaining * * * that the proprietors * * * have failed to comply with * * * this act * * * [to begin prosecution].

Penalty.—$25 to $100, or imprisonment 30 to 90 days, or both.[3]

(b) Exhaust fans shall be provided for the purpose of carrying off dust from emery wheels and grindstones, and dust creating machinery, wherever deemed necessary by the factory inspector.[4]

Penalty.—$5 to $100, or imprisonment 10 to 90 days, or both.

Provision (a), it will be noted, is almost precisely the same as corresponding provisions in the laws of several of the States covered by this report. The only important difference is the added clause of the Michigan law, which prohibits persons to be employed at emery wheels or belts in rooms below the ground level unless the conditions of heat, light, and ventilation therein shall meet with the approval of the factory inspector. The provision as a whole is precise and so detailed in its description of the kinds of blowers, fans, etc., to be used that there is little room for the exercise of personal judgment. Its requirements, however, are not mandatory until a specific order is issued by the factory inspection department.

Provision (b), dealing with the same subject of dust removal as does provision (a), is somewhat broader in scope in that it requires exhaust fans for all dust-creating machinery, but is less precise in wording. It is not mandatory in form, its requirements being invocable only when the factory inspector thinks necessary; and it does not describe the kinds of fans to be used or otherwise establish any guides for the employer or inspector. Under its authority,

---

[1] Acts of 1899, act No. 202, secs. 1 to 7, as added to by act No. 193, Acts of 1903, and act No. 172, Acts of 1905 (22d An. Rept. Com. of Labor, pp. 653, 654).

[2] Idem, sec. 5a, added by act No. 193, Acts of 1903 (22d An. Rept. Com. of Labor, p. 654).

[3] Idem, sec. 6 (22d An. Rept. Com. of Labor, p. 654).

[4] Acts of 1901, act No. 113, secs. 9 and 18 (22d An. Rept. Com. of Labor, p. 660).

however, the inspection department may insist upon mechanical appliances for removing machine-made dust.

These two provisions, it may be emphasized, relate solely to the matter of dust removal. There is no legislation regarding the removal of fumes and gases or the establishment of good ventilation systems generally.

As regards cleanliness and general conditions of sanitation the Michigan law provides simply that—

(c) Every manufacturing establishment, workshop, hotel, or store in which 5 or more persons are employed, and every institution in which 2 or more children, young persons, or women are employed, shall be * * * kept in a cleanly state and free from effluvia arising from any drain, privy, or other nuisance * * *.[1]

Penalty.—$5 to $100, or imprisonment 10 to 90 days, or both.

This requirement is mandatory in form, but, in the absence of standards of cleanliness, its enforcement necessarily involves a wide use of the inspector's discretion.

The factory inspection department is charged with the enforcement of all the legal provisions regarding ventilation and sanitation.

CONDITIONS FOUND.

CLEANLINESS OF WORKROOMS.

Conditions regarding cleanliness of workrooms in the 19 visited establishments are shown in the following table:

CLEANLINESS OF WORKROOMS—MICHIGAN.

All workrooms clean?		Estab-lishments.
Floors.	Walls and ceilings.	
Yes......	Yes.......	16
No........	Yes.......	1
No........	No........	2

SPITTING ON THE FLOOR AND THE PROVISION OF CUSPIDORS.

Spitting on the floor was reported as being habitual among employees in 8 of the 19 establishments; by 14 such spitting was forbidden by factory rules; and by 9 cuspidors were provided.

[1] Acts of 1901, act No. 113, sec. 10, as amended by act No. 169 and sec. 18, Acts of 1907 (22d An. Rept. Com. of Labor, p. 660).

The following table shows the relation between spitting on the floor and the provision of cuspidors and rules against spitting:

CONDITIONS AS TO SPITTING ON THE FLOOR—MICHIGAN.

	Total establish-ments.	Establish-ments in which spitting on floor is done.
Cuspidors:		
Provided	9	2
Not provided	10	6
Spitting on floor:		
Prohibited	14	5
Not prohibited	5	3
Provisions both for cuspidors and against spitting on floor	8	2

GENERAL VENTILATION AND THE REMOVAL OF DUST AND FUMES.

The two following tables show briefly the conditions found in the several establishments visited as regards the general subject of ventilation and the special topic of dust and fumes:

CONDITIONS AS TO VENTILATION—MICHIGAN.

Air space per person in most crowded room.	Establishments.		
	Total.	Special ventilating appliances—	
		Provided.	Not provided.
Under 250 cubic feet			
250 and under 500 cubic feet	4	2	2
500 and under 1,000 cubic feet	6	1	5
1,000 and under 2,000 cubic feet	1	1	
2,000 and under 3,000 cubic feet			
3,000 cubic feet and over			
Over 1,000 cubic feet	8	2	6
Total	19	6	13

CONDITIONS AS TO DUST OR FUMES IN WORKROOMS—MICHIGAN.

Injurious or irritating dust or fumes in workrooms.	Establish-ments.
Not noticeable	4
Noticeable:	
Removal devices provided	8
Removal devices not provided	7
	15
Total establishments	19

WISCONSIN.

SUMMARY OF LEGISLATION.[1]

The legislation of Wisconsin regarding ventilation and sanitation may be conveniently considered in three divisions, according as it relates to business establishments generally, to cigar factories, or to bakery and confectionery establishments.[2]

The legal provisions relating to business establishments generally are six in number:

(a) No person or corporation shall employ and put to work in any factory, workshop, or other place where labor is performed, or in any part of any such place, a larger number of persons than can be kept at work there without doing violence to the laws of health. The local board of health shall have power to determine any question arising under this provision, and its written determination shall be conclusive upon all parties to any action or proceeding under the same.

Penalty.—Not more than $25 for each offense, and each day's negligence or failure after a conviction to be a separate offense.[3]

(b) If in any of the aforesaid places [i. e., factory, mill, workshop, mercantile establishment, or other building where 8 or more persons are employed] any process is carried on by which dust or fumes is caused, which may be inhaled by the persons employed therein, or if the air should become exhausted or impure, there shall be provided a fan or such other mechanical device as will substantially carry away all such dust or fumes or other impurities.[4]

Penalty.—$10 to $100.

(c) All persons, companies, or corporations operating any factory or workshop where grinding machines or grinding wheels, emery wheels or emery belts of any description * * * either solid emery, leather, leather covered, felt, canvas, linen, paper, cotton, or wheels or belts rolled or coated with emery or corundum, or cotton wheels used as buffs, shall, when deemed necessary by the factory inspector, assistant factory inspector, or any officer of the bureau of labor, provide such wheels or belts with blower or similar apparatus, which shall be placed over, beside, or under such wheels or belts in such manner as to protect the person or persons using the same from the particles of the dust produced and caused thereby, and to carry away the dust arising from or thrown off by such wheels or belts while in operation, directly to the outside of the building or to some receptacle placed so as to receive and confine such dust: *Provided,* That grinding machines upon which water is used * * * and

---

[1] The law here referred to is as in force at the beginning of 1909. The text of the laws in force Jan. 1, 1912, is given in the appendixes at the end of this volume.

[2] For special legislation regarding tenement shops, see Ann. Stat. of 1898, Supp. of 1906, Acts of 1907, secs. 1636–71 to 1636–77 (22d An. Rept. Com. of Labor, pp. 1419–1422).

[3] Ann. Stat. of 1898, Supp. of 1906, Acts of 1907, sec. 1636j (22d An. Rept. Com. of Labor, p. 1410).

[4] Idem, secs. 1636–33 and 1636–35 (22d An. Rept. Com. of Labor, p. 1415).

other wheels used for tool grinding be exempt from the provisions of this act.

[Here follows a detailed description of the character of fans, blowers, suction pipes, etc., required, but appliances in use at the time of the passage of this act, and which have proven satisfactory, need not be changed.][1]

Penalty.—$25 to $100.

(*d*) All of the aforesaid places [i. e., factory, mill, workshop, mercantile or mechanical establishment or other building where 8 or more persons are employed] shall be kept clean and free from effluvia arising from any drain, privy, or nuisance, and shall be ventilated and kept in a sanitary condition. •

(*e*) The commissioner of labor or any factory inspector may require such changes or additions to be made in any of the aforesaid places as will promote the best measures of sanitation.

Penalty.—$10 to $100.[2]

(*f*) Water-closets * * * shall be properly * * * ventilated and at all times kept in a clean and good sanitary condition.

Penalty.—$10 to $100.[3]

Reviewing these provisions, it will be observed that the subject of ventilation and pure air is covered in considerable detail. The first provision forbids overcrowding; the second requires exhaust fans where there are any manufacturing processes causing dust, fumes, or other air impurities; the third provides that, where deemed necessary by the factory inspector, grinding machines and grinding wheels of any description shall have dust-removing appliances, the precise character of which is prescribed by law; the fourth, in general terms, requires workrooms to be ventilated and kept free from effluvia due to bad drainage; the sixth is a special requirement that water-closets shall be ventilated; and the fifth is a broad authorization given the factory inspection department to order any "changes or additions" that will, in its opinion, promote the best measures of sanitation, the word sanitation being here used probably in a broad sense to include matters of ventilation also.

The law, however, erects no standards by which good and bad conditions of ventilation may be judged. Except as the first provision, regarding overcrowding, directs otherwise, this duty is apparently left to the factory inspection department, which at the time of the field work of this investigation had provided itself with no general administrative standards in this matter. The provision regarding

---

[1] Ann. Stat. of 1898, Supp. of 1906, Acts of 1907, secs. 1636–39 to 1636–46 (22d An. Rept. Com. of Labor, pp. 1416, 1417).

[2] Idem, secs. 1636–34 and 1636–35 (22d An. Rept. Com. of Labor, p. 1415).

[3] Idem, secs. 1636–31 and 1636–35 (22d An. Rept. Com. of Labor, pp. 1415).

overcrowding [provision (a)] is peculiar in that it directs that the local boards of health shall have the final determination.   The law forbids the crowding of employees beyond the point where "the laws of health" are violated.   The factory inspection department is charged with the enforcement of the law, but the local board of health is to decide in cases of dispute when "the laws of health" are being violated.   The several local·boards are apparently free to give different interpretations to similar conditions.

As regards matters of general sanitation and cleanliness, as distinguished from those concerning pure air, the law, as presented in the above-quoted legal provisions, requires that factories, workshops, etc., shall be "kept clean" and "in a sanitary condition" [provision (d)]; that water-closets especially shall be kept "in a clean and good sanitary condition" [provision (f)], and vests the factory inspection department with a broad authority to order any "changes or additions" that, in its opinion, will "promote the best measures of sanitation" [provision (e)].   These directions do not specify exact conditions or exact remedies, but it would seem that under their combined authority the inspection department would have sufficient power to insist upon reasonably high standards of cleanliness.

The commissioner of labor, in an interview, stated that the law regarding overcrowding gives much trouble.   There are no standards. The inspectors decide individual cases according to their individual judgments, the decisions being subject to reversal by the local boards of health.   In one case of apparently serious overcrowding the board of health ruled against the factory-inspection department.

He also stated that the injuriousness of dust and fumes is also an extremely difficult matter for the inspectors to deal with.   Usually an inspector determines a case "according as he thinks the dust and fumes would be, or would not be, clearly harmful to himself or to the average person."   No apparatus is used to detect, test, or measure the injuriousness of fumes or dust, and in test cases the harmfulness of particular substances is difficult to prove.

Cigar factories and bakery and confectionery establishments are subject to special regulations regarding ventilation and sanitation. These regulations are designed primarily to insure purity of product, but their secondary effect upon the health and comfort of employees is of much importance.   In reproducing here the regulations referred to, a few provisions which have no bearing upon this latter aspect of the subject are omitted.

The legal provisions applicable to cigar factories are as follows:[1]

(a) No shop or place wherein cigars are manufactured shall be located below the ground floor.

---

[1] Ann. Stat. of 1898, Supp. of 1906, Acts of 1907, secs. 1636–101 to 1636–109 (22d An. Rept. Com. of Labor, p. 1424).

(b) Each employee in any shop or place wherein cigars are manufactured, shall, while actually employed, be allowed to use 20 square feet of surface space, unobstructed to the ceiling.

(c) Every room wherein cigars are manufactured shall contain at least 700 cubic feet of air space. It shall in every part be not less than 8 feet in height, from floor to ceiling, every window shall have not less than 12 square feet in superficial area, and the entire area of window surface shall be not less than 12 per cent of the floor space of such room.

(d) Every room in which cigars are manufactured while work is carried on shall be so ventilated that the air shall not become impure and injurious to the health of the persons employed therein, and it shall wherever necessary, by the means of air shafts or other ventilation, be so changed as to render harmless all gases, dust, and other impurities generated in the process of manufacturing cigars. All windows are to be kept open for 30 minutes before working hours and for 30 minutes after working hours.

(e) Every such shop or place in which 1 or more persons are employed and every such factory in which 5 or more persons are employed, shall be kept clean. The dust must be removed from work tables and floors once every day, the floors scrubbed at least once a week and 1 cuspidor provided for every 2 employees.

Penalty.—First offense, $10 to $25; second offense, $25 to $50.

The legal provisions regarding bakery and confectionery establishments are in such very considerable detail that they are given here only in summary form:[1]

Bakery and confectionery establishments:

(a) Shall be well drained and all plumbing therein shall be constructed in accordance with well-established sanitary principles and of good workmanship.

(b) Shall be light, airy, and dry.

(c) The air * * * shall at all times be kept pure and free from harmful odors and noxious gases.

(d) Floors and side walls so constructed as to exclude rats, mice, and other vermin, * * * be free from moisture and kept in a good state of repair. Said floors shall have a smooth surface and be impermeable, and may be constructed of wood, cement, or tile laid in cement.

(e) No floor shall be constructed in a room * * * where the floor of said room is more than 8 feet below the level of the street, sidewalk, or adjacent ground. [The meaning of this is apparently that no establishment in existence at time of passage of this law shall have a floor more than 8 feet below ground. See requirement (m) as regards establishments built after passage of this law.]

(f) Walls and ceiling * * * shall be whitewashed at least as often as once in 6 months.

(g) And the floors, utensils, and furniture * * * and wagons used for the delivery of * * * food products shall at all times be kept in a sanitary, clean condition.

---

[1] Ann. Stat. of 1898, Supp. of 1906, Acts of 1907, secs. 1636–61 to 1636–67 (22d An. Rept. Com. of Labor, pp. 1417–1419).

(*h*) The furniture and utensils * * * shall also be so arranged so that the same can be easily and perfectly cleaned.

(*i*) No food shall be prepared in any unclean manner or near any filthy object * * * or by any person wearing filthy clothing, nor by any person afflicted with a loathsome disease.

(*j*) No water-closet, earth closet, privy, or ash pit shall be within or communicate directly with * * * any * * * room used in the manufacture of * * * food products.

(*k*) Sleeping places for workmen * * * shall be separate and distinct from the places used in the manufacture of * * * food products.

(*l*) While engaged in the manufacture of * * *. food products workmen * * * shall provide themselves with caps and slippers or shoes and an external suit of coarse linen * * * and these garments shall * * * be kept in a clean condition.

(*m*) After the passage of this act no new * * * establishment shall be established or operated in a room the floor of which is more than 5 feet below the level of the street, sidewalk, or adjacent ground, nor in any room the ceiling of which is less than 8 feet high from the floor.

(*n*) No building, room, or apartment shall be used for the purpose of establishing a bakery or confectionery establishment * * * unless a license is secured. [License to be issued by the commissioner of labor after examining the premises and finding that they are in clean and sanitary condition and otherwise conform to all the provisions of this act.]

Penalty.—$20 to $100, or imprisonment for not more than 90 days, or both.[1]

All the legal provisions regarding sanitation and ventilation, as above quoted, are enforceable by the factory inspection department. In addition the boards of health, both State and local, are instructed to see that the requirements regarding bakery and confectionery establishments are observed. A special bakery inspector is also provided for, but such official is to act under the direction of the head of the regular inspection department.[2]

---

[1] An act of 1909 amends the above act by striking out the prohibition as to the construction of a floor in establishments more than 8 feet below the level of the ground; painting once in 2 years and scrubbing once in 6 months is directed as an alternative to whitewashing the walls and ceiling once in 6 months; and the handling of, caring for, and preparation of food in an unclean manner is prohibited. Acts of 1909, amendment to sec. 1636–61 (Bulletin of the Bureau of Labor, No. 85, p. 804).

[2] Ann. Stat. of 1898, Supp. of 1906, Acts of 1907, secs. 1636–45, 1636–66, 1636–109 (22d An. Rept. Com. of Labor, pp. 1417, 1419, 1424).

CONDITIONS FOUND.

CLEANLINESS OF WORKROOMS.

The table below shows the conditions existing in the workrooms of the 19 visited establishments as regards general cleanliness:

CLEANLINESS OF WORKROOMS—WISCONSIN.

All workrooms clean?		Establish-ments.
Floors.	Walls and ceilings.	
Yes......	Yes.......	18
Yes......	No........	1

The one establishment in which the workrooms were not all in clean condition was a writing-paper factory. Here it was reported that the walls in the rag-making room were unnecessarily dirty, being covered with dust accumulations.

A confectionery establishment was in unusually good condition. Its management stated that it was the endeavor of the firm to provide model accommodations for its employees, and that the results had been indorsed by the board of health and by the factory inspector.

SPITTING ON THE FLOOR AND THE PROVISION OF CUSPIDORS.

Spitting on the floor was reported as habitual among employees in 5 of the 19 establishments; in 8 such spitting was prohibited by factory rules; and in 6 cuspidors were provided.

The relation between spitting on the floor and the provision of cuspidors and of rules against spitting is shown in the next table:

CONDITIONS AS TO SPITTING ON THE FLOOR—WISCONSIN.

	Total establish-ments.	Establish-ments in which spitting on floor is done.
Cuspidors:		
Provided.....................	6	....
Not provided................	13	5
Spitting on floor:		
Prohibited...................	8	....
Not prohibited..............	11	5
Provisions both for cuspidors and against spitting on the floor.....	3	....

GENERAL VENTILATION AND THE REMOVAL OF DUST AND FUMES.

The two following tables show briefly the conditions found in the several visited establishments as regards the general subject of ventilation and the special topic of dust and fumes:

CONDITIONS AS TO VENTILATION—WISCONSIN.

Air space per person in most crowded room.	Establishments.		
	Total.	Special ventilating appliances—	
		Provided.	Not provided.
Under 250 cubic feet................			
250 and under 500 cubic feet.........	8	1	7
500 and under 1,000 cubic feet........	6	2	4
1,000 and under 2,000 cubic feet......	5	4	1
2,000 and under 3,000 cubic feet......			
3,000 cubic feet and over............			
Total...........................	19	7	12

CONDITIONS AS TO DUST OR FUMES IN WORKROOMS—WISCONSIN.

Injurious or irritating dust or fumes in workrooms.	Establishments.
Not noticeable.........................	14
Noticeable:	
Removal devices provided........ 1	
Removal devices not provided ... 4	
	5
Total establishments.............	19

MARYLAND.

SUMMARY OF LEGISLATION.[1]

Maryland legislation upon the subject of ventilation and sanitation falls into two classes, according as it applies to (1) all factories and workshops, or (2) only such places as manufacture clothing or other articles by which disease may be transmitted.[2]

Legal provisions of the first class, i. e., applicable to all factories and workshops, are as follows:

(A) All factories, manufacturing establishments, or workshops in the State shall be kept in a cleanly condition and free from effluvia arising from any drain, privy, or other nuisance;

(B) And no factory, manufacturing establishment, or workshop shall be so overcrowded while work is carried on therein as to be injurious to the health of the persons employed therein;

---

[1] The law here referred to is as in force at the beginning of 1909. The text of the laws in force Jan. 1, 1912, is given in the appendixes at the end of this volume.

[2] This is also a public local law requiring dust-removing appliances on stone grinders in a single county—Carroll. See Acts of 1894, ch. 202, secs. 1 to 3 (22d An. Rept. Com. of Labor, p. 570).

(C) And every such factory, manufacturing establishment, or workshop shall be well and sufficiently lighted and ventilated in such a manner as to render harmless, as far as practicable, all the gases, vapors, dust, or other impurities generated in the course of the manufacturing process or handicraft carried on therein, which may be injurious to health.

Penalty.—$150 for each offense.[1] •

By these provisions factories and workshops are required to be clean, free from overcrowding, and kept free from dust, fumes, gases, or other air impurities resulting from the work carried on. The requirements are all mandatory in form, but, as the terms of the law are very general, the determination of what are satisfactory conditions of ventilation and cleanliness leaves wide latitude for the exercise of personal judgment.

The second class of legislation referred to—that regarding the manufacture of clothing, etc.—is aimed primarily at the correction of the usual "sweat shop" evils. As a whole, however, it is too broad in its scope to be treated simply as "sweat shop" legislation. Its important provisions are as follows: [2]

(D) (a) If any individual or body corporate engaged in the manufacture or sale of clothing or of any other article whereby disease may be transmitted shall with reasonable means of knowledge * * *, directly or indirectly cause or permit any garments, or such other articles as aforesaid, to be manufactured or made up * * * or any work to be done thereupon * * * in a place or under circumstances involving danger to the public health, such individual or corporation, upon conviction * * * shall be fined not less than $10 nor more than $100 for each garment manufactured, made up or worked upon.

The term "a place or under circumstances involving danger to the public health," as employed above, is defined as—[3]

(b) Any room or apartment (1) which shall not contain at least 400 cubic feet of clear space for each person * * * or (2) wherein the thermometer shall habitually stand, during the hours of labor at or above 80° F., before the 1st day of May or after the 1st day of October of any year, or (3) wherein any person suffering from a contagious, infectious, or otherwise dangerous disease or malady, shall sleep, labor, or remain, or (4) wherein, if of less superficial area than 500 square feet, any artificial light shall be habitually used between the hours of 8 a. m. and 4 p. m., or (5) from which the débris of manufacture and all other dirt or rubbish shall not be removed at least once in every 24 hours, or (6) which shall be pronounced ill ventilated,

---

[1] Pub. Gen. Laws, Code of 1903, art. 27, secs. 234, 235 (22d An. Rept. Com. of Labor, p. 540).

[2] Idem, sec. 236 (22d An. Rept. Com. of Labor, p. 540).

[3] Idem, sec. 238 (22d An. Rept. Com. of Labor, pp. 540, 541).

or otherwise unhealthy by any officer or board having legal authority so to do.

Penalty.—60 days to 1 year, and may be fined not exceeding $1,000.

The remaining provisions of this class of legislation, later as to time of enactment, amplify the preceding provisions by making additional regulations in the case of 24 enumerated articles, particularly likely to become disease transmitters: [1]

(c) No room or apartment in any tenement or dwelling house shall be used except by the immediate members of the family living therein * * * for the manufacture of coats, vests, trousers, knee pants, overalls, cloaks, hats, caps, suspenders, jerseys, blouses, waists, waist bands, underwear, neckwear, furs, fur trimmings, fur garments, shirts, purses, feathers, artificial flowers, cigarettes, or cigars. No [such] room or apartment * * * shall be used by any family[,] * * * [and] no person, firm, or corporation shall work in, or hire or employ any person to work * * * in any building, rear building, or building in the rear of a tenement or dwelling house, at making * * * any of the articles mentioned in this section, without first obtaining a written permit from the chief of the bureau of industrial statistics, stating the maximum number of persons allowed to be employed therein. Such permit shall not be granted until an inspection of such premises has been made by the factory inspector * * * and such permit may be revoked by the chief of the bureau * * * at any time the health of the community or of those so employed may require it. [Permit to be obtained annually, and posted in a conspicuous place.]

Penalty.—$5 to $100, or imprisonment 10 days to 1 year, or both.

As regards the enforcement of the legal requirements regarding sanitation and ventilation, as above quoted, the law is not entirely clear. The legal provisions upon this point are as follows: [2]

The chief of the bureau of industrial statistics, or his assistant, or any inspector shall have authority to enter any room in any tenement or dwelling house, workshop, manufacturing establishment, mill, factory, or place where any goods are manufactured, for the purpose of inspection.

The person, firm, or corporation owning or controlling or managing such places shall furnish access to and information in regard to such places to the said chief of the bureau of industrial statistics or his deputies at any and all reasonable times while work is being carried on. The chief of the bureau of industrial statistics shall appoint two deputies as assistants, whose duty it shall be to make such inspections of the tenements, dwelling houses, factories, workshops, mills, and such other places as he may designate and to do such other work as the said chief of the bureau of industrial statistics shall designate.

---

[1] Pub. Gen. Laws, Code of 1903, art. 27, secs. 240, 243 (22d An. Rept. Com. of Labor, p. 541).

[2] Idem, secs. 241 and 242 (22d An. Rept. Com. of Labor, pp. 541, 542).

These provisions would seem to vest the bureau of industrial statistics with the authority, if not the duty, to enforce all the laws regarding ventilation and sanitation. The bureau, however, interprets this authority as extending only to the special classes of factories and workshops mentioned above in provision (D) (c).[1]

CONDITIONS FOUND.

CLEANLINESS OF WORKROOMS.

The following table shows the conditions found in the workrooms of the 28 visited establishments as regards general cleanliness:

CLEANLINESS OF WORKROOMS—MARYLAND.

All workrooms clean?		Establish-ments.
Floors.	Walls and ceilings.	
Yes......	Yes.......	18
Yes......	No........	3
No........	Yes.......	4
No........	No........	3

The 10 establishments in which workrooms were not clean were as follows: Two canning factories, 3 cigar factories, and 1 each of confectionery, cracker, paper-box, shirt, and tobacco factories.

SPITTING ON THE FLOOR AND THE PROVISION OF CUSPIDORS.

Habitual spitting on the floor by employees was done in 9 of the 28 establishments visited; in 19 there was a rule against such spitting; and in 16 cuspidors were provided.

The relation between spitting on the floor and the provision of cuspidors and the existence of rules against such spitting is shown in the following table:

CONDITIONS AS TO SPITTING ON THE FLOOR—MARYLAND.

	Total establishments.	Establishments in which spitting on floor is done.
Cuspidors:		
Provided......................	16	3
Not provided..................	12	6
Spitting on floor:		
Prohibited....................	19	3
Not prohibited...............	9	6
Provisions both for cuspidors and against spitting on floor........	15	3

[1] See Sixteenth Annual Report of Bureau of Statistics and Information of Maryland, 1907, p. 71 et seq.

GENERAL VENTILATION AND THE REMOVAL OF DUST AND FUMES.

The two following tables show briefly the conditions found in the several visited establishments as regards the general subject of ventilation and the special topic of dust and fumes.

CONDITIONS AS TO VENTILATION—MARYLAND.

Air space per person in most crowded room.	Establishments.		
	Total.	Special ventilating appliances—	
		Provided.	Not provided.
Under 250 cubic feet....................			
250 and under 500 cubic feet.........	8	6	2
500 and under 1,000 cubic feet.......	13	7	6
1,000 and under 2,000 cubic feet......	4	1	3
2,000 and under 3,000 cubic feet......	2	1	1
3,000 cubic feet and over.............	1		1
Total......................	28	15	13

CONDITIONS AS TO DUST OR FUMES IN WORKROOMS—MARYLAND.

Injurious or irritating dust or fumes in workrooms.	Establishments.
Not noticeable.........................	21
Noticeable:	
Removal devices provided........ 5	
Removal devices not provided.... 2	7
Total establishments...........	28

NORTH CAROLINA.

There were, at the time of this investigation, no legal provisions relative to the sanitation or ventilation of any class of establishments.[1]

CONDITIONS FOUND.

CLEANLINESS OF WORKROOMS.

The conditions of the workrooms of the 28 visited establishments as regards cleanliness is shown in the following table:

CLEANLINESS OF WORKROOMS—NORTH CAROLINA.

Workrooms clean?		Establishments.
Floors.	Walls and ceilings.	
Yes......	Yes.......	12
Yes......	No........	1
No.......	Yes.......	5
No.......	No........	10

[1] The law here referred to is as in force at the beginning of 1909. The text of the laws in force Jan. 1, 1912, is given in the appendixes at the end of this volume.

SPITTING ON THE FLOOR AND THE PROVISION OF CUSPIDORS.

Spitting on the floor by employees was reported as habitual in 20 of the 28 establishments; in 18 such spitting was prohibited; and in 18 cuspidors were provided.

The following table shows the relation between spitting on the floor and the provision of cuspidors and the prohibition of such spitting:

CONDITIONS AS TO SPITTING ON THE FLOOR—NORTH CAROLINA.

	Total establishments.	Establishments in which spitting on floor is done.
Cuspidors:		
Provided.....................	18	10
Not provided................	10	10
Spitting on floor:		
Prohibited..................	18	10
Not prohibited.............	10	10
Provisions both for cuspidors and against spitting on the floor...	16	8

GENERAL VENTILATION AND THE REMOVAL OF DUST AND FUMES.

The two following tables show briefly the conditions found in the several visited establishments as regards the general subject of ventilation and the special topic of dust and fumes:

CONDITIONS AS TO VENTILATION—NORTH CAROLINA.

Air space per person in most crowded room.	Establishments.		
	Total.	Special ventilating appliances—	
		Provided.	Not provided.
Under 250 cubic feet.................	1	....	1
250 and under 500 cubic feet..........	3	....	3
500 and under 1,000 cubic feet........	5	1	4
1,000 and under 2,000 cubic feet......	10	3	7
2,000 and under 3,000 cubic feet......	6	4	2
3,000 cubic feet and over.............	2	1	1
Not reported.........................	1	1	....
Total...........................	28	10	18

CONDITIONS AS TO DUST OR FUMES IN WORKROOMS—NORTH CAROLINA.

Injurious or irritating dust or fumes in workrooms.	Establishments.
Not noticeable........................	3
Noticeable:	
Removal devices provided........	9
Removal devices not provided....	15
	24
Not reported.........................	1
Total establishments............	28

GEORGIA.

There were, at the time of this investigation, no legal provisions relative to matters of sanitation or ventilation.[1]

CONDITIONS FOUND.

CLEANLINESS OF WORKROOMS.

The following table shows the conditions of the workrooms in the 27 visited establishments as regards cleanliness:

CLEANLINESS OF WORKROOMS—GEORGIA.

All workrooms clean?		Estab- lishments.
Floors.	Walls and ceilings.	
Yes......	Yes.......	13
Yes......	No........	4
No........	Yes.......	3
No.......	No........	7

SPITTING ON THE FLOOR AND THE PROVISION OF CUSPIDORS.

Habitual spitting on the floor by employees was reported as done in 21 of the 26 establishments from which information on this point was obtained. In 16 of these 26 establishments cuspidors were provided and in 9 spitting on the floor was forbidden by factory rules.

The following table shows the relation between spitting on the floor and the provision of cuspidors and of rules against spitting:

CONDITIONS AS TO SPITTING ON THE FLOOR—GEORGIA.

	Total establish- ments.	Establish- ments in which spitting on floor is done.
Cuspidors: [2]		
Provided....................	16	11
Not provided..............	10	10
Spitting on floor: [2]		
Prohibited..................	9	8
Not prohibited.............	17	13
Provisions both for cuspidors and against spitting on floor [1]......	7	6

[1] The law here referred to is as in force at the beginning of 1909. The text of the laws in force Jan. 1, 1912, is given in the appendixes at the end of this volume.
[2] One establishment not reported.

GENERAL VENTILATION AND THE REMOVAL OF DUST AND FUMES.

The following tables show briefly the conditions found in the several visited establishments as regards the general subject of ventilation and the special topic of dust and fumes:

CONDITIONS AS TO VENTILATION—GEORGIA.

Air space per person in most crowded room.	Establishments.		
	Total.	Special ventilating appliances—	
		Provided.	Not provided.
Under 250 cubic feet.....................	....	....	....
250 and under 500 cubic feet.........	1	1	....
500 and under 1,000 cubic feet........	7	5	2
1,000 and under 2,000 cubic feet......	11	6	5
2,000 and under 3,000 cubic feet......	3	2	1
3,000 cubic feet and over..............	5	2	3
Total...........................	27	16	11

CONDITIONS AS TO DUST OR FUMES IN WORKROOMS—GEORGIA.

Injurious or irritating dust or fumes in workrooms.	Establishments.
Not noticeable.........................	 5
Noticeable:	
Removal devices provided........	8
Removal devices not provided....	14 ── 22
Total establishments...........	 27

FLORIDA.

There were, at the time of this investigation, no legal provisions of the State law relative to matters of ventilation or sanitation.[1]

CONDITIONS FOUND.

CLEANLINESS OF WORKROOMS.

The conditions regarding cleanliness of workrooms as found in the 14 establishments visited are presented in the table following:

CLEANLINESS OF WORKROOMS—FLORIDA.

All workrooms clean?		Establishments.
Floors.	Walls and ceilings.	
Yes......	Yes......	9
No........	Yes......	3
No........	No........	2

[1] The law here referred to is as in force at the beginning of 1909. The text of the laws in force Jan. 1, 1912, is given in the appendixes at the end of this volume.

SPITTING ON THE FLOOR AND THE PROVISION OF CUSPIDORS.

Habitual spitting on the floor by employees was reported as being done in 9 of the 14 establishments; in 8 such spitting was forbidden by factory rules; and in 12 cuspidors were provided.

The following table shows the relation between spitting on the floor and the provision of cuspidors and the existence of factory rules against free spitting:

CONDITIONS AS TO SPITTING ON THE FLOOR—FLORIDA.

	Total establishments.	Establishments in which spitting on floor is done.
Cuspidors:		
Provided....................	12	7
Not provided................	2	2
Spitting on floor:		
Prohibited....................	8	3
Not prohibited...............	6	6
Provisions both for cuspidors and against spitting on floor.......	8	3

GENERAL VENTILATION AND THE REMOVAL OF DUST AND FUMES.

The two following tables show briefly the conditions found in the several visited establishments as regards the general subject of ventilation and the special topic of dust and fumes:

CONDITIONS AS TO VENTILATION—FLORIDA.

	Establishments.		
Air space per person in most crowded room.	Total.	Special ventilating appliances—	
		Provided.	Not provided.
Under 250 cubic feet..................	1	....	1
250 and under 500 cubic feet.........	6	....	6
500 and under 1,000 cubic feet........	4	....	4
1,000 and under 2,000 cubic feet......	1	....	1
2,000 and under 3,000 cubic feet......	1	....	1
3,000 cubic feet and over.............	1	....	1
Total............................	14	....	14

CONDITIONS AS TO DUST OR FUMES IN WORKROOMS—FLORIDA.

Injurious or irritating dust or fumes in workrooms.	Establishments.
Not noticeable...........................	12
Noticeable:	
Removal devices provided.........	2
Removal devices not provided....	
	2
Total establishments.............	14

LOUISIANA.

SUMMARY OF LEGISLATION.[1]

The legislation of Louisiana contains three provisions regarding matters of ventilation and sanitation. One of these relates to the removal of dust, smoke, and lint; a second is a requirement, general in its character, that factories, etc., shall be kept clean; the third vests the factory inspector with the authority to order limewashing or painting.[2]

These three legal provisions read as follows:

(a) In all establishments in the State wherein children, young persons [i. e., 14 to 18 years of age] or women are employed where any process is carried on by which dust or smoke or lint is generated the inspector shall have the power and authority to order that a fan or fans or some other dust or smoke or lint removing or consuming contrivance or contrivances be so placed as to prevent the inhalation of such dust or smoke or lint by the employees: *Provided*, That 2 mechanical engineers, 1 chosen by the inspector and the other by the owner or owners of the establishment, shall agree as to the necessity of such fan or fans or other dust or smoke or lint removing contrivance or contrivances. Upon the failure of said 2 mechanical engineers to agree, a third mechanical engineer shall be chosen to arbitrate.

Penalty.—$25 to $50, or imprisonment 10 days to 6 months, or both.[3]

(b) Every factory, mill, manufacturing establishment, workshop, warehouse, mercantile establishment or store, and all other occupations and establishments hereinabove mentioned [4] in which 5 or more young persons or women are employed, and every such institution in which 2 or more children, young persons, or women are employed shall be * * * kept in a cleanly state and free from effluvia arising from any drain, privy, or other nuisance * * *.

Penalty.—$25 to $50, or imprisonment 10 days to 30 days, or both.[5]

---

[1] The law here referred to is as in force at the beginning of 1909. The text of the laws in force Jan. 1, 1912, is given in the appendixes at the end of this volume.

[2] There is no special legislation regarding sweat shops or food-producing establishments.

[3] Acts of 1908, act No. 301, sec. 19 (Bulletin of the Bureau of Labor, No. 85, p. 600).

[4] The "occupations and establishments" referred to are given in section 1 of the act as follows: "In any mill, factory, mine, packing house, manufacturing establishment, workshop, laundry, millinery or dressmaking store, or mercantile establishment, in which more than 5 persons are employed, or in any theater, concert hall, or in or about any place of amusement where intoxicating liquors are made or sold, or in any bowling alley, boot blacking establishment, freight or passenger elevator, or in the transmission or distributing of messages, either telegraph or telephone, or any other messages, or merchandise, or in any other occupation not herein enumerated which may be deemed unhealthful or dangerous."

[5] Acts of 1908, act No. 301, sec. 14, and Acts of 1906, act No. 34, sec. 4 (Bulletin of the Bureau of Labor, No. 85, p. 599, and 22d An. Rept. Com. of Labor, p. 522).

(c) Every factory, mill, or workshop in the State where women and children are employed shall be limewashed or painted when deemed necessary and ordered by the health authorities.

Penalty.—$25 to $50, or imprisonment 10 to 30 days, or both.[1]

As regards ventilation, it will be observed that the subject is referred to only in so far as it relates to the presence of dust, smoke, or lint in the breathing atmosphere, and then only to establishments in which women or children under 18 are employed. Where such a condition exists the inspector is authorized to order the installation of fans or other dust-removing contrivances, subject, however, to the important provisions that a consulting board of mechanical engineers agree upon the necessity of such removal. This method of determining such matters is peculiar to the legislation of Louisiana, among the States now being considered. At the time of the field work of this investigation the law referred to was too recent to have established its value.

The second and third of the above-quoted provisions relate to matters of sanitation and cleanliness. The second provision requires manufacturing establishments generally, in which more than a fixed number of young persons and women are employed, to be kept in a clean condition and free from effluvia due to bad drainage. The requirement is mandatory, but, because of the general character of its wording, leaves a broad discretion to the judgment of the enforcing authority. The third provision, regarding limewashing and painting, is specific in its directions and applies to all manufacturing establishments employing women and children. It becomes a requirement, however, only when the health authorities have issued a definite order to that effect.

The enforcement of the legal provisions above quoted is specifically charged to the factory inspection department.[2] This seems antagonistic, however, to the clause in the third provision which directs that the health authorities shall make the necessary orders regarding limewashing and painting.

The only factory inspector in Louisiana at the time of the field work of this investigation was in the city of New Orleans.

The factory inspector of New Orleans, in an interview, stated that while the factories of the city were not in the best possible sanitary condition, things were gradually getting into shape. The law was new and she believed she had to be conservative in enforcing it at the start. She stated that her orders regarding the cleaning up of workrooms were generally obeyed. If they were not she reported the case to the board of health.

---

[1] Acts of 1908, act No. 301, sec. 16 (Bulletin of the Bureau of Labor, No. 85, p. 600).

[2] Idem, sec. 3, and Acts of 1906, act No. 34, sec. 6 (Bulletin of the Bureau of Labor, No. 85, p. 597, and 22d An. Rept. Com. of Labor, p. 523).

The secretary of the city board of health of New Orleans, in an interview, stated that a house-to-house inspection is made once or twice a year, and orders given to improve insanitary conditions. Factories, mills, etc., are included in these general inspections. Moreover, if the factory inspector, an employee, or anyone else reports the existence of insanitary conditions to the board, an investigation is made, and, if necessary, orders for improvement are given. No record of these inspections is kept.

CONDITIONS FOUND.

CLEANLINESS OF WORKROOMS.

The conditions of the workrooms of the 29 visited establishments as regards cleanliness is shown in the following table:

CLEANLINESS OF WORKROOMS—LOUISIANA.

All workrooms clean?		Establishments.
Floors.	Walls and ceiling.	
Yes......	Yes........	20
Yes......	No.........	2
No........	Yes........	5
No........	No.........	2

SPITTING ON THE FLOOR AND THE PROVISION OF CUSPIDORS.

Spitting on the floor by employees was reported as being done in 16 of the 29 establishments. In 6 such spitting was forbidden by factory rules, and in 3 cuspidors were provided.

The next table shows the relation between spitting on the floor and the provision of cuspidors and of rules against such spitting.

CONDITIONS AS TO SPITTING ON THE FLOOR—LOUISIANA.

	Total establishments.	Establishments in which spitting on floor is done.
Cuspidors:		
Provided.....................	3	1
Not provided................	26	15
Spitting on floor:		
Prohibited...................	6	....
Not prohibited..............	23	16
Provisions both for cuspidors and against spitting on floor...	2	....

GENERAL VENTILATION AND THE REMOVAL OF DUST AND FUMES.

The two following tables show briefly the conditions found in the several establishments visited as regards the general subject of ventilation and the special topic of dust and fumes.

CONDITIONS AS TO VENTILATION—LOUISIANA.

Air space per person in most crowded room.	Establishments.		
	Total	Special ventilation appliances—	
		Provided.	Not provided.
Under 250 cubic feet.................	1	....	1
250 and under 500 cubic feet..........	2	1	1
500 and under 1,000 cubic feet........	7	4	3
1,000 and under 2,000 cubic feet......	11	2	9
2,000 and under 3,000 cubic feet......	3	1	2
3,000 cubic feet and over.............	2	....	2
Not reported.........................	3	2	1
Total.........................	29	10	19

CONDITIONS AS TO DUST OR FUMES IN WORKROOMS—LOUISIANA.

Injurious or irritating dust or fumes in workrooms.	Establishments.
Not noticeable.......................	24
Noticeable:	
Removal devices provided.........	
Removal devices not provided....	5
	5
Total establishments...........	29

CHAPTER XI.

GENERAL TABLES.

Table I.—NUMBER OF EMPLOYEES, BY SEX AND BY AGE GROUPS, HOURS OF LABOR, LUNCH PERIOD, AND OVERTIME WORK.

MAINE.

Establishment number.	Industry.	Number of employees.					Hours of labor.				Time allowed for lunch (minutes).	Overtime work.	
		Male.		Female.			Per day.						
		Under 16 yrs. of age.	16 years of age and over.	Under 16 yrs. of age.	16 years of age and over.	Total.	Monday to Friday.	Saturday.	Sunday.	Total per week.		Times required during year.	Average hours per week when worked.
1	Boots and shoes		50		17	67	10	9		59	60	¹52	3
2	....do	1	84		36	121	10	9		59	60		
3	....do		50		30	80	10	9		59	60		
4	....do	17	336	1	191	545	10	9		59	60		
5	Cigars	{	19			19	8	8		48	} 60		
					9	9	8	7		47			
6	....do	{	19			19	8	8		48	} 60		
					10	10	8	7		47			
7	Confectionery	2	22	2	35	61	10	9		59	60	2	12½
8	...do	{	3			3	10	²10		²60	} 60	24	12
					15	15	9½	²9½		²57			
9	....do	1	5	1	8	15	10	10		60	60	24	6
10	Crackers and biscuits	1	17		13	31	10	10		60	60	15	5
11	Hosiery and knit goods		1	6	6	13	10	9		59	60	5	2½
12	....do		10		10	20	10	9		59	60		
13	Matches	{	75			75	10	10		60	} 60		
				12	53	65	10	5		55			
14	Paper boxes	1	4	3	10	18	10	10		60	60	10	8½
15	...do		8		32	40	10	10		60	60		
16	...do		14	3	48	65	10	9		59	60	30	10
17	...do	{ 1	5		9	14	9	9		54	} 60	6	6
						1	4	4		24			
18	...do		8		31	39	9½	8½		56	60	12	8½
19	do		4		8	12	10	9		59	60	6	3
20	Woolen and worsted goods		60		18	78	10¼	5½		60	60		
21	...do	2	37	2	34	75	10¼	5½		60	60	60	6
22	...do	2	35		21	58	10¼	5½		60	60	31	15
23	...do		64		41	105	10	10		60	60		
24	...do		62		46	108	10¼	5½		60	60		
25	...do	5	170	5	120	300	11	5		60	60		
26	...do	{ ³3	³99	³3	³38	³143	10¼	5½		60	} 60	31	7½
			⁴38			⁴38	11½			57½			
	Total	36	1,299	38	889	2,262							

MASSACHUSETTS.

1	Cigar boxes	1	49	3	32	85	9	8		53	60		
2	....do	3	18	1	20	42	9	8		53	30		
3	Cigarettes	1	16		8	25	9	4½		49½	30		
4	....do		13		10	23	8	6		46	30		
5	....do		14	4	27	45	9	5		50	60		
6	Cigars		56	2	17	75	8	5		45	60		
7	....do		41		14	55	8	5		45	60		
8	....do		17		7	24	8	5		45	60		
9	Confectionery		14	6	50	70	9	5		50	30	36	8
10	....do	{	15			15	9½	5½		53	} 30	40	6
				10	50	60	9	5		50			
11	....do	{	355			355	10	6		56	30	15	4
		3		50	371	424	9½	5½		53	30	15	4½
12	....do	{	15			15	10	6		56	} 30		
				5	35	40	9½	5½		53			
13	....do	{	7			7	10	6		56	} 30		
				2	18	20	9½	5½		53			

¹ Men only.
² Winter schedule; summer, 4½ hours less (during June, July, and August).
³ Day force.
⁴ Night force.

TABLE I.—NUMBER OF EMPLOYEES, BY SEX AND BY AGE GROUPS, HOURS OF LABOR, LUNCH PERIOD, AND OVERTIME WORK—Contd.

MASSACHUSETTS—Concluded.

Establishment number.	Industry.	Number of employees. Male. Under 16 yrs. of age.	Male. 16 years of age and over.	Female. Under 16 yrs. of age.	Female. 16 years of age and over.	Total.	Hours of labor. Per day. Monday to Friday.	Saturday.	Sunday.	Total per week.	Time allowed for lunch (minutes).	Overtime work. Times required during year.	Average hours per week when worked.
14	Confectionery	....	12	....	......	12	10	5	.....	55	30	84	6¼
		....	......	9	66	75	9	5	.....	50	30	84	8
15	....do	2	33	14	26	75	9⅚	6	.....	55⅙	40	15	[1] 3½
16	....do	1	19	2	20	42	9⅚	6	.....	55⅙	40	4	[2] 3½
17	....do	....	65	....	......	65	9½	5½	.....	53	30	28	8
		4	......	20	55	79	9	5	.....	50			
18	....do	....	4	....	......	4	9½	6	.....	53½	60	3	3
		....	......	1	9	10	9	5½	.....	50½			
19	Cotton goods	7	207	12	189	415	10½	5½	.....	58	45	......	......
20	....do	47	459	37	426	969	10½	5½	.....	58	[3] 45	......	......
21	....do	8	395	10	417	830	10½	5½	.....	58	60	......	......
22	Crackers and biscuits	1	28	2	6	37	10½	5½	.....	58	60	([4])	([4])
23	....do	1	11	8	41	61	9⅔	9⅔	.....	58	[5] 60	......	......
24	....do	8	204	27	187	426	10	8	.....	58	60	......	......
25	....do	....	52	1	35	88	10	9	.....	59	60	......	......
26	Hosiery and knit goods	....	5	....	150	155	8¾	8	.....	51¾	60	......	......
27	....do	....	4	....	45	49	10	7	.....	57	30	......	......
28	....do	....	12	1	19	32	10¼	5¾	.....	57	45	......	......
29	....do	2	51	6	144	203	10	6	.....	56	60	([6])	[7] 4
30	....do	....	5	1	38	44	10	6	.....	56	60	......	......
31	....do	9	18	21	279	327	10½	5½	.....	58	30	......	......
32	....do	....	2	3	55	60	9⅝	9⅜	.....	57½	30	......	......
33	Paper boxes	1	50	10	214	275	[8] 9¼	[8] 7¾	.....	[8] 54	60	84	4
34	....do	....	7	2	25	34	9 11/12	4½	.....	54 1/12	30	4	3½
35	....do	2	12	....	......	14	10	8	.....	58	60	12	1
		....	......	3	39	42	9½	4½	.....	52	60	12	3
36	....do	2	14	4	67	87	10	7½	.....	57½	60	[9] 20	18
37	Stamped and enameled ware	3	93	1	14	111	10	5	.....	55	60	36	5
38	Woolen and worsted goods	....	47	....	......	47	10⅞	5⅝	.....	60	45	......	......
		6	......	5	38	49	10½	5½	.....	58			
39	....do	....	12	1	21	34	10½	5½	.....	58	45	45	6
40	....do	....	123	....	47	170	10½	5½	.....	58	60	......	......
41	....do	7	215	9	148	379	10½	5½	.....	58	60	45	12
42	....do	....	17	....	20	37	10¼	6¾	.....	58	45	[9] 30	10
43	....do	....	100	....	......	100	10⅞	5⅝	.....	60	45	......	......
		5	......	1	50	56	10 19/40	5⅝	.....	58			
44	....do	3	53	....	26	82	10 7/12	5 1/12	.....	58	40	......	......
	Total	127	2,959	294	3,575	6,955	.....	.....	.....	.....	......	......	......

RHODE ISLAND.

Establishment number.	Industry.	Male. Under 16 yrs. of age.	Male. 16 years of age and over.	Female. Under 16 yrs. of age.	Female. 16 years of age and over.	Total.	Monday to Friday.	Saturday.	Sunday.	Total per week.	Time allowed for lunch (minutes).	Times required during year.	Average hours per week when worked.
1	Cigars	....	21	....	3	24	8	8	.....	48	60	......	......
		....	1	....	5	6	9	9	.....	54			
2	....do	....	72	....	......	72	8	8	.....	48	60	......	......
		....	3	....	......	3	9	9	.....	54			
		....	......	2	27	29	10	7	.....	57			
3	Confectionery	2	14	6	8	30	10½	5½	.....	58	30	......	......
4	Cotton goods	11	257	7	132	407	10½	5½	.....	58	45	12	2½

[1] Women; men average 8 hours a week.
[2] Women; men average 4 hours a week.
[3] In winter; in summer, 60 minutes.
[4] Not reported; only men worked overtime.
[5] For some; 80 minutes for some.
[6] Not reported.
[7] For 1 month only; data for rest of year not reported.
[8] Winter schedule; summer, 9⅝ hours Monday to Friday; 4⅞ hours Saturday; 54 hours per week.
[9] Men only.

TABLE I.—NUMBER OF EMPLOYEES, BY SEX AND BY AGE GROUPS, HOURS OF LABOR, LUNCH PERIOD, AND OVERTIME WORK—Contd.

RHODE ISLAND—Concluded.

Establishment number.	Industry.	Number of employees. Male. Under 16 yrs. of age.	Male. 16 years of age and over.	Female. Under 16 yrs. of age.	Female. 16 years of age and over.	Total.	Hours of labor. Per day. Monday to Friday.	Per day. Saturday.	Per day. Sunday.	Total per week.	Time allowed for lunch (minutes).	Overtime work. Times required during year.	Overtime work. Average hours per week when worked.
5	Cotton goods	16	178	3	189	386	10½	5½	.....	58	60	......	......
6	.....do	31	271	19	201	522	10½	5½	.....	58	50	......	......
7	.....do	55	618	36	431	1,140	10½	5½	.....	58	60	......	......
8	Hosiery and knit goods	5	24	8	83	120	10½	5½	.....	58	45	[1] 25	10
9	.....do	7	30	19	229	285	10½	5½	.....	58	60	......	......
10	.....do	3	25	19	160	207	10½	5½	.....	58	45	......	......
11	.....do	.....	13	11	89	113	10½	5½	.....	58	30	[1] 30	2½
12	.....do	1	31	7	250	289	10	8	.....	58	60	......	......
13	.....do	.....	3	.....	18	21	10½	5½	.....	58	60	......	......
14	.....do	.....	28	8	35	71	10¾	4¼	.....	58	45	......	......
15	Jewelry	.....	12	5	28	45	10	9	.....	59	60	60	10
16	.....do	.....	50	.....	9	59	10	9	.....	59	60	12	15
17	.....do	.....	......	.....	35	35	8	4	.....	44	60	20	15
		4	136	4	67	211	10	5	.....	55			
18	.....do	2	142	5	59	208	10	5	.....	55	60	......	......
19	.....do	4	45	4	26	79	10	10	.....	60	60	50	2½
20	Paper boxes	.....	......	3	40	43	9	4	.....	49	60	......	......
		.....	13	.....	......	13	10	5	.....	55			
21	.....do	.....	......	2	80	82	9½	[2] 8½	.....	[2] 56	60	20	10
		.....	22	.....	......	22	10	[2] 9	.....	[2] 59			
22	.....do	.....	......	1	8	9	9½	8½	.....	56	60	7	4
		.....	3	.....	......	3	10	9	.....	59			
23	.....do	.....	......	4	42	46	9½	8½	.....	56	60	30	9
		1	9	.....	......	10	10	9	.....	59			
24	Woolen and worsted goods	29	430	59	203	721	10½	5½	.....	58	60	31	10½
25	.....do	1	98	.....	72	171	10½	5½	.....	58	45	[1] 45	3
26	.....do	24	246	15	172	457	10½	5½	.....	58	45	(3)	5
27	.....do	30	92	9	146	277	10½	5½	.....	58	45	(4)	(4)
	Total	226	2,887	256	2,847	6,216	.....	.....	.....	.....	.....	......	......

CONNECTICUT.

Establishment number.	Industry.	Male. Under 16 yrs. of age.	Male. 16 years of age and over.	Female. Under 16 yrs. of age.	Female. 16 years of age and over.	Total.	Monday to Friday.	Saturday.	Sunday.	Total per week.	Time allowed for lunch (minutes).	Times required during year.	Average hours per week when worked.
1	Cigars	.....	85	.....	......	85	8	8	.....	48	60	......	......
		1	......	.....	......	1	10	9	.....	[5] 59			
		.....	......	4	26	30	8	5	.....	45			
2	.....do	.....	51	.....	......	51	8	8	.....	48	60	......	......
		.....	......	.....	17	17	8	5	.....	45			
3	Clocks and watches	57	832	15	296	1,200	10	9	.....	[5] 59	60	180	10
4	.....do	6	179	.....	16	201	10	5	.....	55	60	......	......
5	.....do	3	111	1	139	254	10	5	.....	55	60	......	......
6	.....do	3	119	1	26	149	10	5	.....	55	60	......	......
7	.....do	9	312	6	76	403	10½	5½	.....	58	60	[1] 91	(3)
8	Corsets	.....	60	8	441	509	9½	4½	.....	52	60	......	......
9	.....do	3	369	26	1,369	1,767	10	5	.....	55	60	45	8
10	.....do	.....	17	12	179	208	9½	4½	.....	52	60	9	2½
11	.....do	.....	35	36	371	442	10	9	.....	[6] 59	60	......	......
12	.....do	.....	23	.....	18	41	10	9	.....	[6] 59	60	......	......
13	Hardware and metal specialties	3	118	.....	17	138	10	10	.....	[7] 60	60	......	......
14	.....do	27	788	9	113	937	[8] 10	[8] 9	.....	[8] 59	[8] 60	......	......
15	.....do	8	84	2	17	111	10	10	.....	[7] 60	60	......	......

[1] Men only.
[2] Winter schedule; in summer 4 hours less.
[3] Not reported.
[4] Some overtime work done; amount not reported.
[5] Information as to shortening hours of labor in June, July, and August not reported.
[6] No notice posted regarding 55-hour week during June, July, and August.
[7] Winter schedule; during June, July, and August, 55 hours per week.
[8] Except men in one department working night or day shift, 12 hours per day, 72 hours per week, time for lunch irregular; establishment operates 55 hours per week during June, July, and August.

TABLE I.—NUMBER OF EMPLOYEES, BY SEX AND BY AGE GROUPS, HOURS OF LABOR, LUNCH PERIOD, AND OVERTIME WORK—Contd.

CONNECTICUT—Concluded.

Establishment number.	Industry.	Number of employees.					Hours of labor.				Time allowed for lunch (minutes).	Overtime work.	
		Male.		Female.		Total.	Per day.			Total per week.		Times required during year.	Average hours per week when worked.
		Under 16 yrs. of age.	16 years of age and over.	Under 16 yrs. of age.	16 years of age and over.		Monday to Friday.	Saturday	Sunday.				
16	Hardware, etc.	.....	559	1	165	725	10	10	.....	[1] 60	60	......	......
17	.....do.	16	792	21	424	1,253	10	10	.....	[1] 60	60	......	......
18	.....do.	2	175	18	169	364	10	9	.....	[1] 59	60	......	......
19	.....do.	1	198	1	12	212	10	8	.....	58	60	......	......
20	.....do.	13	400	13	210	636	10	8	.....	58	60	......	......
21	Hosiery and knit goods.	2	12	26	80	120	10	9	.....	[2] 59	45	......	......
22	.....do.	2	42	1	50	95	10 7/12	5 1/6	.....	[2] 58 1/12	45	......	......
23	.....do.	.....	37	5	36	78	10 7/12	5 1/6	.....	[2] 58 1/12	45	......	......
24	.....do.	3	86	5	216	310	10½	5½	.....	58	60	......	......
25	.....do.	.....	85	.....	......	85	11	5	.....	60	60	......	......
		1	......	5	180	186	10½	5	.....	57½			
26	Needles and pins.	4	359	12	181	556	10	10	.....	[1] 60	30	......	......
27	.....do.	24	378	42	305	749	10	10	.....	[1] 60	60	......	......
28	.....do.	.....	57	.....	......	57	10	9½	.....	59½	45	......	......
		.....	......	11	86	97	9	8¼	.....	53¼			
29	Paper boxes.	.....	8	3	43	54	10	10	.....	[1] 60	60	......	......
30	.....do.	.....	4	.....	......	4	10	9	.....	59	60	......	......
		.....	......	5	27	32	9½	8½	.....	56			
31	Plated tableware	1	89	.....	22	112	10	9	.....	[2] 59	60	......	......
32	.....do.	1	25	.....	12	38	10	9	.....	[2] 59	60	4	2
		.....	......	1	......	1	9	9	.....	54			
33	Rubber goods.	.....	32	3	62	97	10	9	.....	[1] 59	60	......	......
34	.....do.	2	441	3	74	520	10	5	.....	55	60	[3] 96	15
35	.....do.	4	107	3	138	252	10	10	.....	[1] 60	60	......	......
	Total.	196	7,069	299	5,613	13,177	......	......	......	......	......	......	......

NEW YORK.

Establishment number.	Industry.	Male under 16	Male 16 and over	Female under 16	Female 16 and over	Total.	Monday to Friday.	Saturday	Sunday.	Total per week.	Time allowed for lunch (minutes).	Times required during year.	Average hours per week when worked.
1	Cans, tin.	.....	220	.....	40	260	10½	5	.....	57½	[4] 30	25	3
2	Cigarettes.	.....	269	4	962	1,235	10¼	5¾	.....	57	[4] 30	......	......
3	Cigars.	1	89	4	227	321	10	9	.....	59	60	......	......
4	.....do.	.....	114	.....	155	269	9¾	7¼	.....	56	[4] 45	......	......
		1	......	1	......	2	8	7½	.....	47½			
5	Confectionery.	.....	17	.....	20	37	10	10	.....	60	[4] 30	7	15
6	.....do.	.....	108	.....	125	233	[5] 9½	9½	.....	60	[4] 30	......	......
7	.....do.	.....	239	.....	272	511	10	9	.....	59	([6])	24	5
		1	......	9	......	10	8	9	.....	49			
8	.....do.	.....	5	.....	12	17	9½	9½	.....	57	[4] 30	21	2½
9	.....do.	.....	45	.....	76	121	10	9	.....	59	60	20	7
		.....	......	5	......	5	8	8	.....	48			
10	Cotton goods.	.....	73	.....	94	167	11	5	.....	60	60	......	......
11	Crackers and biscuits.	.....	[7] 39	.....	[7] 50	[7] 89	10	10	.....	60	[4] 30	6	6
		.....	[8] 1	.....	......	[8] 1	10	.....	10	60			
12	.....do.	.....	26	.....	18	44	10	10	.....	60	[4] 30	......	......
13	.....do.	.....	100	.....	194	294	10	9	.....	59	[4] 50	......	......
14	.....do.	.....	81	.....	144	225	10	9	.....	59	[4] 50	......	......
15	Hosiery and knit goods.	.....	63	.....	429	492	10	5	.....	55	60	......	......
		.....	......	8	......	8	8	5	.....	45			
16	.....do.	.....	47	.....	533	580	10	9	.....	59	60	[3] 120	9
17	.....do.	.....	[7] 137	.....	[7] 235	[7] 372	11	5	.....	60	60	......	......
		.....	[8] 48	.....	......	[8] 48	10	.....	.....	50			
18	.....do.	.....	192	.....	153	345	10½	.....	.....	52½	60	......	......
		3	......	1	......	4	8	.....	.....	40			
19	.....do.	.....	127	.....	246	373	11	5	.....	60	60	......	......
		2	......	11	......	13	8	3½	.....	43½			

[1] Winter schedule; during June, July, and August, 55 hours per week.
[2] Information as to shortening hours of labor in June, July, and August not reported.
[3] Men only.
[4] Special permit from factory inspector for shortening lunch period.
[5] Except Tuesday and Thursday, 11 hours.
[6] Males, 60 minutes; females, 30 minutes, by special permit.
[7] Day force.
[8] Night force.

TABLE I.—NUMBER OF EMPLOYEES, BY SEX AND BY AGE GROUPS, HOURS OF LABOR, LUNCH PERIOD, AND OVERTIME WORK—Contd.

NEW YORK—Concluded.

Establishment number.	Industry.	Number of employees.					Hours of labor.				Time allowed for lunch (minutes).	Overtime work.	
		Male.		Female.		Total.	Per day.			Total per week.		Times required during year.	Average hours per week when worked.
		Under 16 yrs. of age.	16 years of age and over.	Under 16 yrs. of age.	16 years of age and over.		Monday to Friday.	Saturday.	Sunday.				
20	Hosiery and knit goods	....	4	....	36	40	10	8	....	58	[1] 30	......	......
21	.....do	....	68	....	149	217	10¼	8¾	....	60	60	......	......
		2	......	3	......	5	8	8	....	48			
22	Optical goods	....	960	....	387	1,347	9	8½	....	53½	60	......	......
		9	......	1	......	10	8	8	....	48			
23	Paper boxes	....	18	....	80	98	9	9	....	54	[1] 30	......	......
		1	......	....	......	1	8	8	....	48			
24	.....do	....	58	2	125	185	10	9	....	59	30	30	2
25	.....do	1	26	....	......	27	10	8	....	58	[1] 30	......	......
		....	......	1	56	57	9½	7½	....	55			
26	.....do	....	4	....	......	4	10	9	....	59	30	50	7
		....	......	....	6	6	9½	8½	....	56			
27	.....do	1	45	....	......	46	9½	8½	....	56	[1] 30	7	2
		....	......	1	94	95	9	8	....	53			
28	.....do	....	16	....	......	16	10	8	....	58	30	......	......
		....	......	1	26	27	9½	8	....	55½			
29	.....do	....	75	....	75	150	9¾	5¼	....	54	[1] 30	12	3
30	.....do	....	22	....	118	140	9¾	5¼	....	54	[1] 30	14	6
		1	......	2	......	3	8	5¼	....	45¼			
31	.....do	....	5	....	16	21	9	9	....	54	60	......	......
		....	......	1	......	1	8	8	....	48			
32	.....do	....	14	....	91	105	9	9	....	54	60	......	......
33	Paper patterns	....	28	....	445	473	9	9	....	54	60	......	......
34	Printing and publishing	[2] 4	[2] 401	[2] 1	[2] 152	[2] 558	8	8	....	48	60	43	10
		....	[3] 73	....	......	[3] 73	8	8	....	48			
35	Shirt waists	....	14	....	166	180	9	8	....	53	[4] 60	......	......
36	Stamped and enameled ware	....	97	....	16	113	10	10	....	60	[1] 30	30	6
	Total	27	3,968	56	6,023	10,074	....	....	....	....	....	......	......

NEW JERSEY.

Establishment number.	Industry.	Male under 16 yrs. of age.	Male 16 years of age and over.	Female under 16 yrs. of age.	Female 16 years of age and over.	Total.	Monday to Friday.	Saturday.	Sunday.	Total per week.	Time allowed for lunch (minutes).	Times required during year.	Average hours per week when worked.
1	Canning and preserving	....	[2] 121	....	[2] 98	[2] 219	10½		....	58½	30	......	......
		....	[3] 20	....	......	[3] 20	11		....	60			
2	Cigars	29	176	3	708	916	10		....	55	30	24	3
3	.....do	5	28	33	620	686	10½	½	....	58	([5])	......	......
4	.....do	2	16	35	313	366	10½	6½	....	58	30	24	10
5	Confectionery	....	29	13	12	54	10	9	....	59	60	......	......
6	Corsets	2	19	13	273	307	9¾	8¾	....	57½	60	......	......
7	Hosiery and knit goods	5	103	11	197	316	10		....	55	60	......	......
8	.....do	16	235	25	207	483	10		....	59	60	27	9
9	.....do	3	28	3	26	60	10		....	55	60	35	15
10	Matches	5	34	13	20	72	10½	5½	....	58	30	......	......
11	Paper boxes	2	60	15	129	206	9	9	....	54	60	......	......
12	.....do	....	51	21	153	225	10	9	....	59	30	2	6
13	.....do	....	20	....	......	20	10½	6	....	58½	30	3	8
		2	......	17	45	64	10	5½	....	55½			
14	.....do	....	9	3	24	36	10	5	....	55	60	......	......
15	Pencils	30	77	59	177	343	10	5	....	55	60	......	......
16	Pottery	....	152	....	......	152	9	9	....	54	60	......	......
		8	......	15	87	110	9	7	....	52			
17	.....do	....	145	....	......	145	[6] 9½	[6] 5	....	[6] 52½	30	12	3
		8	......	15	70	93	10½	5	....	57½			

[1] Special permit from factory inspector for shortening lunch period.
[2] Day force.
[3] Night force.
[4] Thirty minutes for some, permit for shortening lunch period on file.
[5] Not reported.
[6] Except machinists, 8 hours per day, 48 hours per week.

TABLE I.—NUMBER OF EMPLOYEES, BY SEX AND BY AGE GROUPS, HOURS OF LABOR, LUNCH PERIOD, AND OVERTIME WORK—Contd.

NEW JERSEY—Concluded.

Establishment number.	Industry.	Number of employees. Male. Under 16 yrs. of age.	Male. 16 years of age and over.	Female. Under 16 yrs. of age.	Female. 16 years of age and over.	Total.	Hours of labor. Per day. Monday to Friday.	Per day. Saturday.	Per day. Sunday.	Total per week.	Time allowed for lunch (minutes).	Overtime work. Times required during year.	Average hours per week when worked.
18	Pottery	8	82	1	58	149	9	9		54	60		
19	....do		132	2	11	145	9	7		52	60		
20	....do	6	108			114	9	9		54	60	12	3
					17	17	10	7½		57½			
21	Soap	5	50			55	9½	5½		53	30		
					215	215	8¼	5		46¼	45		
22	Stamped and enameled ware	[1] 26	[1] 588	[1] 14	[1] 109	[1] 737	10	5		55	30		
			[2] 28			[2] 28	12			60			
23	Tobacco and snuff		186		687	873	10	9		59	60		
		4		36		40	10	5		55			
24	Woolen and worsted goods	26	459	17	277	779	10	6		56	60		
25	....do	[1] 4	[1] 133	[1] 7	[1] 416	[1] 560	10	5		55	60	208	21
			[2] 100		[2] 157	[2] 257	11			55	30		
26	....do	4	230	11	410	655	10	6		56	60	212	10
27	....do		106		38	144	10			50	60		
	Total	200	3,525	382	5,554	9,661							

PENNSYLVANIA.

Establishment number.	Industry.	Male. Under 16 yrs. of age.	Male. 16 years of age and over.	Female. Under 16 yrs. of age.	Female. 16 years of age and over.	Total.	Monday to Friday.	Saturday.	Sunday.	Total per week.	Time allowed for lunch (minutes).	Times required during year.	Average hours per week when worked.
1	Canning and preserving	2	134	30	411	577	10⅙	9⅙		60	[3] 30	30	12
2	....do		72	10	86	168	10	9		59	[3] 30	25	6
3	....do		30	5	44	79	10	5½		55½	[4] 30	30	12
4	Cigar boxes	1	31	1	27	60	10½	5		57½	[3] 30		
5	Cigars	2	10	70	620	702	10½	7½		60	[4] 30		
6	....do	1	24	3	129	157	9½	4		51½	60		
7	....do		13	2	96	111	10	5		55	[4] 45		
8	....do		1	1	50	52	10	4½		54½	[4] 30		
9	....do		97	44	190	331	10	5		55	60		
10	....do	2	55	22	285	364	10	7		57	[4] 30		
11	....do		10	15	174	199	10	8		58	[3] 30		
12	....do	1	51	4	64	120	10			50	60		
13	....do		36	1	65	102	8	8		48	60		
14	Confectionery		124		148	272	10	8½		58½	[4] 30		
		14		41		55	10	7½		57½			
15	....do		33	7	94	134	10	9½		59½	[4] 30	([5])	2
16	....do		21	2	68	91	10½	6		58½	[4] 30	20	1
17	....do	1	12	5	44	62	9½	7½		55	[4] 30	24	1
18	Core making		[6] 1,500			[6] 1,500	([5])	([5])	([5])	([5])	([5])	([5])	([5])
					4	4	9	5		50	60		
19	....do		[6] 800			[6] 800	([5])	([5])	([5])	([5])	([5])	([5])	([5])
					38	38	8	8		48	[4] 30		
20	....do		[1] 198			[1] 198	10	9		59	[4] 30		
					[1] 17	[1] 17	9½	8		55½			
			[2] 57			[2] 57	12			60			
21	....do		[6] 1,500			[6] 1,500	([5])	([5])	([5])	([5])	([5])	([5])	([5])
					8	8	10 1/12	8 1/12		59	[3] 25	35	9
22	Crackers and biscuits	7	113	20	143	283	10	7½		57½	60		
23	....do	6	48	42	90	186	10	5		55	[4] 35	([5])	3
24	....do		40	8	85	133	10	7½		57½	[4] 30		
25	....do		77	1	50	128	10½	7½		60	[4] 30		
26	....do		53	18	54	125	10½	7½		60	[4] 30		
27	....do	4	33	10	52	99	10½	6		58½	[4] 35		

[1] Day force.
[2] Night force.
[3] Permit for shortening lunch period on file.
[4] Permit for shortening lunch period not reported.
[5] Not reported.
[6] Total male force; schedules taken only for departments employing women.

TABLE I.—NUMBER OF EMPLOYEES, BY SEX AND BY AGE GROUPS, HOURS OF LABOR, LUNCH PERIOD, AND OVERTIME WORK—Contd.

PENNSYLVANIA—Concluded.

Establishment number.	Industry.	Number of employees.					Hours of labor.				Time allowed for lunch (minutes).	Overtime work.	
		Male.		Female.		Total.	Per day.			Total per week.		Times required during year.	Average hours per week when worked.
		Under 16 yrs. of age.	16 years of age and over.	Under 16 yrs. of age.	16 years of age and over.		Monday to Friday.	Saturday.	Sunday.				
28	Crackers and biscuits	.....	44	1	34	79	10½	7½	.....	60	[1] 30	40	5
29	.....do	1	18	6	24	49	10½	7½	.....	60	60	......	......
30	Hosiery and knit goods	50	252	210	823	1,335	10¾	6¼	.....	60	[1] 45	18	2½
31	.....do	3	33	30	508	574	10⅔	5	.....	58⅓	[2] 40	4	4
32	.....do	17	74	42	268	401	10¾	6	.....	59¾	[1] 30	......	......
33	.....do	1	46	11	139	197	10¾	6¼	.....	60	[1] 30	......	......
34	.....do	.....	39	1	23	63	10	7	.....	57	[1] 30	40	10
35	Matches	4	52	3	37	96	10	10	.....	60	[2] 50	......	......
36	.....do	.....	10	.....	4	14	10	5	.....	55	[2] 30	......	......
37	Nuts and bolts	9	356	11	24	400	10½	5	.....	57½	[1] 30	......	......
38	.....do	36	273	63	215	587	10¼	8¾	.....	60	[2] 45	......	......
39	Paper boxes	....	32	.....	......	32	10½	7½	.....	60	[1] 30	......	......
		....	......	22	92	114	9½	7½	.....	55			
40	.....do	....	32	.....	......	32	10½	5	.....	57½	[1] 30	......	......
		2	......	24	87	113	10	4½	.....	54½			
41	.....do	....	5	.....	......	5	10¼	5¾	.....	57	[1] 30	......	......
		....	......	1	58	59	9½	5	.....	52½			
42	Pottery	.....	18	.....	3	21	9	5	.....	50	60	......	......
43	.....do	.....	52	.....	3	55	10	8½	.....	58½	[1] 30	......	......
44	Stamped and enameled ware	[3] 14	[3] 188	[3] 5	[3] 52	[3] 259	10⅙	8⅔	.....	59½	[2] 35	......	......
		....	[4] 16	.....	[4] 8	[4] 24	12	.....	.....	60			
45	.....do	[3] 9	[3] 42	[3] 1	[3] 36	[3] 88	9½	4¾	.....	52¼	[2] 30	......	......
		....	[4] 5	.....	......	[4] 5	12	.....	.....	60			
46	Toys and novelties	7	345	11	94	457	10¼	6	.....	57¼	[2] 45	......	......
47	Woolen and worsted goods	[3] 63	[3] 171	[3] 81	[3] 233	[3] 548	10¾	6¼	.....	60	[2] 45	......	......
		41	[4] 77	[4] 26	[4] 102	[4] 246	12	.....	.....	60			
48	.....do	15	279	38	281	613	11	5	.....	60	[2] 45	......	......
49	.....do	1	87	6	179	273	10¼	5¾	.....	57	[2] 45	65	5
50	.....do	.....	64	.....	58	122	10½	5	.....	57½	[2] 40	......	......
	Total	314	7,783	955	6,521	15,573	.....	.....	.....	......	......	......	......

[1] Permit for shortening lunch period on file.
[2] Permit for shortening lunch period not reported.
[3] Day force.
[4] Night force.

TABLE I.—NUMBER OF EMPLOYEES, BY SEX AND BY AGE GROUPS, HOURS OF LABOR, LUNCH PERIOD, AND OVERTIME WORK—Contd.

OHIO.

Establishment number	Industry	Male Under 16 yrs. of age	Male 16 years of age and over	Female Under 16 yrs. of age	Female 16 and 17 yrs. of age	Female 18 years of age and over	Total	Per day Mon. to Fri.	Sat.	Sun.	Total per week	Time allowed for lunch (min.)	Times required during year	Average hours per week when worked
1	Cigar boxes		23			32	55	10	10		60	45		
		4		1	6		11	8	8		48			
2	....do		27			14	41	10	10		60	30		
					1		1	8	8		48			
3	Cigars		18			207	225	8½	6		48½	45		
					94		94	8	6		46			
4	....do	1	18			86	105	10	5		55	60		
				2	24		26	8	5		45			
5	....do		14			302	316	10	5		55	60		
				1	63		64	8	5		45			
6	....do		73		5	43	121	8	8		48	60		
7	....do					45	45	9	4		49	45		
8	....do		33			9	42	8	4		44	30		
9	....do		26		14	78	118	10	5		55	30		
10	....do		43			15	58	9	5		50	60		
					9		9	8	8		48			
11	....do		11			6	17	9	9		54	60		
					15		15	8	8		48			
12	Confectionery		62		6	35	103	10	10		60	30	78	3
				1			1	8	8		48			
13	....do		46			41	87	10	10		60	30		
				4	11		15	8	8		48			
14	....do		36			22	58	10	10		60	30	78	1½
				5	12		17	8	8		48			
15	....do		14		3	14	31	10	10		60	45	78	2½
				2			2	8	8		48			
16	....do		45			19	64	10	10		60	30	78	4
				1	1		2	10	5		55			
				41	41		82	8	8		48			
17	....do		24			38	62	10	10		60	30	78	3
				12	35		47	8	8		48			
18	Crackers and biscuits		47			54	101	10	5		55	45	12	3
				1	14		15	8	8		48			
19	....do		48			42	90	10	10		60	60		
					4		4	8	8		48			
20	....do		67			15	82	10	5		55	30	(1)	3
			20			18	38	10	10		60			
21	....do	1		6	8		15	8	8		48	30		
22	....do		23		(2)	[2]19	42	9½	8½		56		[8]36	9
23	Hosiery and knit goods	2	66	11	52	197	328	10	8½		58½	30	26	6
24	....do		39		6	126	171	10	9½		59	30	48	6
25	....do		9			43	52	9	7½		52½	60		
		3					3	8	8		48			
26	....do		11	1		39	52	10	9		59	30		
27	....do	1	29	2		181	213	10¼	9¼		60	60	54	7½
28	....do		28			97	125	10¼	6¾		57 7/12	60	20	4
29	Matches		472		(4)	[4]178	650	10	5		55	45		
30	....do		187		(4)	[4]122	309	10	5		55	60		
31	....do		18		(5)	[5]22	40	10	5		55	60		
32	Nuts and bolts		400			102	502	10	10		60	30		
						30	30	8	8		48			
33	....do		500	2	9	12	523	10	5		55	30	(6)	(6)

[1] One period; time not reported.
[2] Females 16 and 17 not separately reported.
[3] Men only.
[4] Females 16 and 17 not separately reported; worked 8 hours Monday to Friday, 5 hours Saturday, 45 hours per week.
[5] Females 16 and 17 not separately reported; worked 8 hours Monday to Saturday, 48 hours per week.
[6] Exact data not reported; women and children worked as much as 10 hours per week overtime.

TABLE **I.**—NUMBER OF EMPLOYEES, BY SEX AND BY AGE GROUPS, HOURS OF LABOR, LUNCH PERIOD, AND OVERTIME WORK—Contd.

OHIO—Concluded.

Establishment number.	Industry.	Number of employees.					Hours of labor.				Overtime.	
		Male.		Female.			Per day.					
					16 years of age and over.						Time allowed for lunch (minutes).	Times required during year.	Average hours per week when worked.
		Under 16 yrs. of age.	16 years of age and over.	Under 16 yrs. of age.	16 and 17 yrs. of age.	18 years of age and over.	Total.	Monday to Friday.	Saturday.	Sunday.	Total per week.			
34	Nuts and bolts.	... 3	300	 6	 23	154	454 32	10 8	10 8	....	60 43	} 30	....	....
35	....do	.....	75	.....	1	12	88	10	5	.....	55	30	....	....
36	Paper boxes....	.....	16	 25	 16	39	55 41	10 8	5 8	....	55 48	} 30	....	....
37	....do	.....	25	.....	33	48	106	10	10	.....	60	30	78	2½
38	....do	.....	14	 3	 13	41	55 16	10 8	10 8	....	60 48	} 30	(1)	3
39	....do	.....	24	 9	 16	57	81 25	10 8	10 8	....	60 48	} 30	15	2
40	....do	.....	16	 5	 6	68	84 11	9½ 8	7½ 8	....	55 48	} 30	....	....
41	Pottery	.....	159	1	.....	75	235	9	8	.....	53	60	....	....
42	....do	10	147	.....	.....	66	223	9	8	.....	53	60	....	....
43	....do	2	92	.....	.....	25	119	9	9	.....	54	60	....	....
44	....do	5	366	2	.....	117	490	9	8	.....	53	60	....	....
45	Stamped and enameled ware	² 2	² 135 ³ 12	² 1	....	² 84	² 222 ³ 12	10½ 8	5¾	 8	59½ 43	} 50	⁴ 8	6
46	....do	....	² 91 ³ 11	....	....	² 58	² 149 ³ 11	10 8	5	 8	55 48	} 50	....	....
47	....do	....	160 ³ 15	....	² 7	² 92	² 259 ³ 15	10½ 10	8½	 10	60 60	} 50	36	6
48	....do	....	² 238 ³ 15	....	....	² 89	² 327 ³ 15	10 9	9	 9	59 54	} 30	30	9
49	....do	² 3	² 121 ³ 14	....	² 8	² 53	² 185 ³ 14	10 9	8½	....	58½ 45	} 60	....	....
50	Tobacco and snuff	.....	40	.....	.....	220	260	10	5	.....	55	30	....	....
51	....do	.....	7	.....	.....	24	31	10	5	.....	55	30	....	....
52	....do	....	7	....	 2	17	24 2	8 8	8½ 6	....	48½ 46	} 35	....	....
53	....do	 12	914	 1	 76	612	1,526 89	10 8	5 5	....	55 45	} 60	10	2
54	Woolen and worsted goods	 26	332	 146	..... (⁶)	⁵ 654	986 172	10 8½	5 5	....	55 48	} 45	....	....
55	....do	....	84	 2	..... (⁶)	⁵ 153	237 2	10 8½	5 5	....	55 48	} 60	....	....
56	....do	.....	147	.....	.....	69	216	10	10	.....	60	30	12	5
57	....do	 5	26	 8	....	132	158 13	10 8½	7 7	....	57 48	} 30	....	....
58	....do	.....	108	.....	.....	30	138	10	7	.....	57	(7)	....	....
59	....do	.....	80	.....	.....	11	91	10	10	.....	60	45	....	....
60	....do	.....	35	.....	.....	12	47	10	5	.....	55	30	....	....
	Total....	81	6,303	302	664	5,285	12,635	.....	.....	.....	.....	.....	.....	.....

¹ One period; time not reported.
² Day force.
³ Night force.
⁴ Men only.
⁵ Including females 16 and 17 working 48 hours per week.
⁶ Included in females 18 and over.
⁷ Males, 15 minutes; females, 30 minutes.

TABLE I.—NUMBER OF EMPLOYEES, BY SEX AND BY AGE GROUPS, HOURS OF LABOR, LUNCH PERIOD, AND OVERTIME WORK—Contd.

ILLINOIS.

Establishment number.	Industry.	Number of employees. Male. Under 16 yrs. of age.	Male. 16 years of age and over.	Female. Under 16 yrs. of age.	Female. 16 years of age and over.	Total.	Hours of labor. Per day. Monday to Friday.	Saturday.	Sunday.	Total per week.	Time allowed for lunch (minutes).	Overtime work. Times required during year.	Average hours per week when worked.
1	Artificial flowers....	....	3	....	24	27	9½	9½	....	57	30	18	15
		....	......	1	......	1	8	8	....	48			
2	....do..............	....	8	....	50	58	9½	9½	....	57	30	......	......
		1	......	2	......	3	8	8	....	48			
3	Binding twine and rope............	....	174	....	393	567	10	8½	....	58½	30	......	......
4	Cans, tin..........	....	210	....	140	350	10	5½	....	55½	30	......	......
5	....do..............	....	190	....	40	230	10	5	....	55	30	10	6
6	Canvas attachments binder....	....	4	....	38	42	10	8½	....	58½	30	......	......
7	Chewing gum.......	....	......	1	......	1	8	4½	....	44½	60	......	......
		....	6	....	13	19	8½	4½	....	47	60		
		....	......	....	13	13	9⅓	4½	....	51⅙	40		
		....	......	....	21	21	9⅔	4½	....	52⅚	20		
8	....do..............	....	[1] 31	....	......	[1] 31	10	5	....	55	30	......	......
		....	......	....	[1] 74	[1] 74	9½	4½	....	52			
		....	......	....	[1] 73	[1] 73	8½	4	....	46½			
		....	[2] 4	....	[2] 30	[2] 34	10	......	....	50			
9	Cigars............	....	102	2	30	134	8	8	....	48	60	6	6
10	....do..............	....	309	....	243	552	9½	8½	....	56	30	40	2
		....	......	4	......	4	8	8	....	48			
11	....do..............	....	6	....	3	9	9½	5	....	52½	30	12	14
		....	19	....	7	26	8½	5	....	47½	60		
12	Clocks and watches.	....	409	....	298	707	8	8	....	48	60	......	......
13	Confectionery.......	....	115	....	210	325	10	[3] 10	....	[3] 60	30	40	12
		6	......	83	......	89	8	[4] 8	....	[4] 48			
14	....do..............	....	45	2	147	194	9½	9½	....	57	30	30	15
15	....do..............	....	120	....	170	290	9	[5] 9	....	[5] 54	30	30	15
		....	......	25	......	25	8	[6] 8	....	[6] 48			
16	Core making........	....	12	....	96	108	9⅚	4⅚	....	54	30	......	......
17	....do..............	....	1	....	23	24	[7] 10	5	....	54	30	8	5
18	....do..............	....	......	....	120	120	9½	4½	....	51	45	......	......
		....	11	....	......	11	[7] 10	5	....	54	30		
19	....do..............	....	1	....	42	43	[7] 10	5	....	54	30	......	......
20	....do..............	....	1	....	23	24	[7] 10	5	....	54	30	6	5
21	Corsets............	....	58	....	342	400	10	8	....	58	30	15	1
		8	......	82	......	90	8	8	....	48			
		....	10	....	......	10	9½	5½	....	53	60		
22	Crackers and biscuits............	....	83	....	141	224	9	8	....	53	60	......	......
23	....do..............	....	40	....	39	79	9	9	....	54	60	......	......
		....	......	13	......	13	8	8	....	48			
24	....do..............	....	[1] 36	....	[1] 61	[1] 97	9	9	....	54	60	12	6
		[1] 7	......	[1] 2	......	[1] 9	8	8	....	48			
		....	[2] 20	....	[2] 15	[2] 35	9	......	....	45			
25	Gloves............	....	130	....	241	371	10	9	....	59	30	......	......
		....	......	11	......	11	8	8	....	48			
26	....do..............	....	25	....	......	25	10	9½	....	59½	30	......	......
		....	......	....	50	50	9½	9	....	56½			
		2	......	1	......	3	8	8	....	48			
27	....do..............	....	21	....	48	69	9	[8] 9	....	[8] 54	30	......	......
		1	......	8	......	9	8	[9] 8	....	[9] 48			
28	Hardware and metal specialties..	....	[1] 259	....	[1] 30	[1] 289	10	10	....	60	30	......	......
		[1] 1	......	[1] 1	......	[1] 2	8	8	....	48			
		....	[2] 124	....	......	[2] 124	12	......	....	60			
29	Hosiery and knit goods............	....	24	....	257	281	9¼	8¼	....	54½	30	30	6
		....	......	19	......	19	8	8	....	48			

[1] Day force.
[2] Night force.
[3] July 1 to Sept. 1, 5 hours on Saturday, 55 per week.
[4] July 1 to Sept. 1, 5 hours on Saturday, 45 per week.
[5] June 1 to Sept. 1, 4½ hours on Saturday, 49½ per week.
[6] June 1 to Sept. 1, 4½ hours on Saturday, 44½ per week.
[7] Except Friday, 1 hour less.
[8] May 15 to Sept. 16, 5 hours on Saturday, 50 per week.
[9] May 15 to Sept. 16, 5 hours on Saturday, 45 per week.

Table I.—NUMBER OF EMPLOYEES, BY SEX AND BY AGE GROUPS, HOURS OF LABOR, LUNCH PERIOD, AND OVERTIME WORK—Contd.

ILLINOIS—Concluded.

Establishment number.	Industry.	Male Under 16 yrs. of age.	Male 16 years of age and over.	Female Under 16 yrs. of age.	Female 16 years of age and over.	Total.	Monday to Friday.	Saturday.	Sunday.	Total per week.	Time allowed for lunch (minutes).	Times required during year.	Average hours per week when worked.
30	Hosiery and knit goods	....	3	....	35	38	9	4	.....	49	30	48	9
		....	....	1	.....	1	8	4	.....	44			
31	....do	...	175	....	225	400	10	10	.....	60	60	......	....
		5	....	5	.....	10	8	8	.....	48			
32	....do	....	[1]85	.....	[1]200	[1]285	10	10	.....	60	60	......	....
		[1]5	[1]60	....	....	[1]60	11	11	.....	66			
		....	....	[1]12	....	[1]17	8	8	.....	48			
		....	[2]40	....	.....	[2]40	13	....	.....	65			
33	Matches	....	80	....	60	140	10	10	.....	60	30	......	....
		....	30	....	.....	30	10	9	.....	59			
34	Paper boxes	....	....	....	80	80	9½	8½	.....	56	30	40	12
		1	....	24	.....	25	8	8	.....	48			
35	....do	...	38	....	207	245	10	9	.....	59	30	150	10
		1	....	118	.....	119	8	8	.....	48			
		....	4	.....	.....	4	10	9	.....	59			
36	....do	....	....	....	26	26	9½	8½	.....	56	30	15	7
		....	....	70	.....	70	8	8	.....	48			
		....	65	....	.....	65	10	8	.....	58			
37	....do	....	....	....	220	220	9½	7½	.....	55	30	60	5
		9	....	59	....	9	8	8	.....	48			
		....	....	59	.....	59	8	7½	.....	47½			
38	Shirts	....	16	....	195	211	9½	8½	.....	56	60	16	18
		....	....	10	....	10	8	8	.....	48			
		....	[1]300	.....	....	[1]300	9¾	9¼	.....	58			
		[1]8	....	....	[1]110	[1]110	8¾	8¼	.....	52			
39	Soap	[1]8	[2]10	....	[1]30	[1]38	8	8	.....	48	30	150	6
		....	[2]10	.....	....	[2]10	12	12	.....	72			
		....	[1]7	.....	....	[1]7	11	11	11	77			
		....	[2]7	.....	....	[2]7	13	13	13	91			
		....	[1]650	.....	[1]225	[1]875	10	9	.....	59			
40	Stamped and enameled ware	[1]20	[1]80	[1]8	....	[1]108	8	8	.....	48	30	50	6
		....	[1]40	....	....	[2]40	8	8	....	48			
		....	[1]15	.....	....	[1]15	12	12	12	84			
		....	[2]10	.....	....	[2]10	12	12	12	84			
		[1]5	[1]88	....	[1]18	[1]111	10	5	.....	55			
41	....do	....	[1]10	....	....	[1]10	8	8	.....	48	30	40	8
		....	[2]8	.....	....	[2]8	11	....	.....	55			
		....	[2]10	.....	....	[2]10	8	8	.....	48			
42	Tablets	1	92	....	116	208	10	9	.....	59	60	......	......
		....	....	3	....	4	8	8	.....	48			
43	Tobacco and snuff	....	200	....	539	739	10	10	.....	60	([3])	40	4½
		....	....	11	....	11	8	8	.....	48			
44	....do	....	75	....	150	225	9	8	.....	53	30	30	3
45	Woolen and worsted goods	....	65	....	35	100	10	6	.....	56	60	15	10
46	....do	....	18	....	16.	34	10½	9½	.....	60	50	30	20
47	....do	2	74	1	33	110	10½	5¾	.....	60	55	8	10
	Total	83	4,966	609	6,035	11,693	....	....	....	....	....	....	....

INDIANA.

Establishment number.	Industry.	Male Under 16 yrs. of age.	Male 16 years of age and over.	Female Under 16 yrs. of age.	Female 16 years of age and over.	Total.	Monday to Friday.	Saturday.	Sunday.	Total per week.	Time allowed for lunch (minutes).	Times required during year.	Average hours per week when worked.
1	Bags (cotton, jute, and paper)	4	43	25	180	252	9¾	5½	.....	55	[4]40	......	......
2	Baskets	15	100	10	35	160	10	9	.....	59	[4]30	60	6
3	Beer	3	58	....	7	68	9	9	.....	54	60	15	2
4	Buggies and surreys	35	375	5	65	480	10	10	.....	60	60	[5]35	;

[1] Day force.
[2] Night force.
[3] Not reported.
[4] No permit on file for shortening lunch period.
[5] Men only.

TABLE I.—NUMBER OF EMPLOYEES, BY SEX AND BY AGE GROUPS, HOURS OF LABOR, LUNCH PERIOD, AND OVERTIME WORK—Contd.

INDIANA—Continued.

Establishment number.	Industry.	Number of employees. Male. Under 16 yrs. of age.	Male. 16 years of age and over.	Female. Under 16 yrs. of age.	Female. 16 years of age and over.	Total.	Hours of labor. Per day. Monday to Friday.	Per day. Saturday.	Per day. Sunday.	Total per week.	Time allowed for lunch (minutes).	Overtime work. Times required during year.	Average hours per week when worked.
5	Carts (children's)	1	90	6	78	175	10	9	.....	59	60	150	10
6	Chains	.....	143	.....	67	210	9½	[1] 8½	.....	[1] 56	[2] 30	[3] 40	16
7	Cigars	.....	30	144	512	686	10	8	.....	58	60	12	3
8	do	.....	1	3	120	124	10	8	.....	58	60	.....	.....
9	do	.....	2	15	50	67	10	8	.....	58	60	.....	.....
10	do	.....	6	2	67	75	8½	4½	.....	47	60	.....	.....
11	do	.....	4	32	200	236	8	4	.....	44	60	.....	.....
12	Clocks and watches	10	179	7	129	325	10	9	.....	59	60	[3] 20	10
13	Confectionery	.....	6	.....	25	31	9	9	.....	54	60	30	10
14	do	.....	20	2	33	55	10	10	.....	60	60	32	9
15	do	.....	15	8	52	75	10	10	.....	60	[2] 30	25	20
16	do	5	40	15	50	110	10	9	.....	59	[2] 30	50	15
17	Core making	3	27	.....	.....	30	10	9	.....	59	60	.....	.....
		.....	.....	.....	16	16	9	7	.....	52			
18	Crackers and biscuits	.....	22	3	37	62	10	9	.....	59	60	.....	.....
19	do	6	75	1	19	101	10⅙	9⅙	.....	60	60	.....	.....
20	do	[4] 1	[4] 50	[4] 5	[4] 25	[4] 81	[5] 10⅔	5⅔	.....	60	[7] 40	[8] 26	5
		.....	[4] 4	[4] 2	[4] 12	[4] 18	[5] 10⅓	7⅓	.....	60			
		.....	[6] 1	.....	.....	[6] 1	10	10	.....	60			
21	Electrical apparatus	.....	218	.....	135	353	10	5	.....	55	60	.....	.....
22	do	.....	170	.....	80	250	10	5	.....	55	60	[3] 18	12
23	do	.....	45	.....	100	145	10	5	.....	55	60	.....	.....
24	Gloves	.....	5	6	80	91	10	9	.....	59	60	.....	.....
25	do	.....	10	15	250	275	10	5	.....	55	60	[8] 6	10
26	Hosiery and knit goods	100	600	200	800	1,700	10	5	.....	55	60	17	2½
27	do	3	23	15	109	150	10	[9] 5	.....	55	[7] 40	.....	.....
28	do	.....	49	8	193	250	10⅛	9⅜	.....	60	60	100	10
29	Matches	20	90	25	80	215	10⅛	9⅜	.....	60	[7] 50	.....	.....
30	Paper boxes	1	14	9	44	68	10	9½	.....	59½	60	.....	.....
31	do	5	25	5	50	85	10	9	.....	59	60	18	9
32	do	.....	14	.....	19	33	10½	5	.....	57½	[2] 30	.....	.....
33	do	1	20	3	36	60	10	8½	.....	58½	[7] 30	.....	.....
34	do	.....	40	11	55	106	10	5	.....	55	60	36	5
35	Pearl buttons	.....	19	.....	27	46	10	5	.....	55	[7] 45	.....	.....
36	Plated table ware	.....	175	1	36	212	10	8	.....	58	60	.....	.....
37	Pottery	8	225	6	70	309	9½	[10] 9	.....	[10] 56½	60	.....	.....
38	Shirts	10	45	.....	.....	55	10	4½	.....	54½	60	.....	.....
		.....	.....	40	700	740	9	4½	.....	49½			
39	Skirts	.....	1	2	48	51	10	10	.....	60	60	84	12
40	Soap	.....	25	10	35	70	9½	9½	.....	57	60	.....	.....
41	Stamped and enameled ware	[4] 15	[4] 650	[4] 10	[4] 275	[4] 950	10	8	.....	58	60	[8] 45	8
		.....	[4] 75	.....	.....	[4] 75	10½	10½	.....	63			
		.....	[4] 15	.....	.....	[4] 15	12	12	12	84			
		.....	[6] 75	.....	.....	[6] 75	12½	12½	.....	75			
		.....	[6] 15	.....	.....	[6] 15	12	12	12	84			
42	Tin caps and bottle fasteners	.....	20	.....	.....	20	9¾	8¼	.....	58	60	.....	.....
		.....	.....	20	65	85	9⅔	8⅓	.....	57			
43	Tin plate and black iron	[4] 15	[4] 550	.....	[4] 120	[4] 685	10	8	.....	58	[7] 30	.....	.....
		[4] 15	[4] 450	.....	.....	[4] 465	8	8	.....	48			
		.....	[4] 40	.....	.....	[4] 40	12	12	12	84			
		10	[6] 450	.....	.....	[6] 460	8	8	.....	48			
		.....	[6] 40	.....	.....	[6] 40	12	12	12	84			

[1] Except during summer months, when establishment closes at noon on Saturday.
[2] Permit on file for shortening lunch period.
[3] Men only.
[4] Day force.
[5] Except Friday, 1 hour more.
[6] Night force.
[7] No permit on file for shortening lunch period.
[8] Overtime work is done only in certain occupations, which include women and children.
[9] On account of depression in business this plant had not operated on Saturdays during previous year.
[10] Alternate weeks ½ hour less.

TABLE I.—NUMBER OF EMPLOYEES, BY SEX AND BY AGE GROUPS, HOURS OF LABOR, LUNCH PERIOD, AND OVERTIME WORK—Contd.

INDIANA—Concluded.

Establishment number.	Industry.	Number of employees.					Hours of labor.				Time allowed for lunch (minutes).	Overtime work.	
		Male.		Female.		Total.	Per day.			Total per week.		Times required during year.	Average hours per week when worked.
		Under 16 yrs. of age.	16 years of age and over.	Under 16 yrs. of age.	16 years of age and over.		Monday to Friday.	Saturday.	Sunday.				
44	Toys and novelties..	25	167	.....	......	192	10	10	.....	[1] 60	[2] 30	....	....
45	Woolen and worsted goods........	7	60	7	136	210	10½	8¾	.....	[1] 60	45	60	10
46	.....do.............	[3] 31	[3] 1,216	[3] 25	[3] 381	[3] 1,653	10	9	.....	59	60	([6])	([6])
		....	[4] 19	.....	......	[4] 19	11	11	.....	66			
		....	[5] 20	.....	......	[5] 20	8	8	.....	48			
		....	[4] 10	.....	......	[4] 10	12	12	12	84			
47	.....do.............	....	66	4	73	143	10⅛	9⅛	.....	[1] 60	50	15	10
	Total.........	349	7,042	707	5,776	13,874	.....	.....	.....	......	......	....	....

MICHIGAN.

Establishment number.	Industry.	Male under 16 yrs. of age.	Male 16 years of age and over.	Female under 16 yrs. of age.	Female 16 years of age and over.	Total.	Monday to Friday.	Saturday.	Sunday.	Total per week.	Time allowed for lunch (minutes).	Times required during year.	Average hours per week when worked.
1	Breakfast foods.....	.....	96	.....	204	300	10	9	([7])	59	60	....	....
2	Cans, tin...........	[3] 59	[3] 200	[3] 13	[3] 84	[3] 356	10	9	.....	59	[8] 30	15	4
		[4] 1	[4] 41	.....	......	[4] 42	12	.....	.....	60			
3	Cigar boxes.........	15	40	.....	......	55	10	8½	.....	58½	60	10	6
		.....	....	20	60	80	9½	8	.....	55½			
4	Cigars..............	1	19	120	1,000	1,140	9½	5	.....	52½	45	20	8
		([9])	([9])	([9])	([9])	([9])	10	5	.....	55			
5	Confectionery......	.....	50	.....	150	200	10	10	.....	60	60	26	9
6	.....do.............	.....	50	3	70	123	10	10	.....	60	[8] 30	24	9
7	Corsets.............	.....	135	63	705	903	9¾	5¼	.....	54	45	12	6
8	Fiber boxes and cans............	28	160	28	108	324	10½	6½	.....	59	[8] 30	20	6
9	Hosiery and knit goods............	.....	8	15	[10] 200	223	9½	7½	.....	55	[8] 30	12	5
10	.....do.............	.....	5	.....	28	33	10	8½	.....	58½	60	....	....
11	.....do.............	1	76	26	[10] 360	463	10¼	8⅓	.....	60	50	....	....
12	Matches............	[3] 40	[3] 250	[3] 30	[3] 175	[3] 495	10½	7½	.....	60	[8] 30	....	....
		....	[3] 30	.....	......	[3] 30	10½	10	.....	62½			
		....	[3] 12	.....	......	[3] 12	12	10½	.....	70½			
		...	[3] 10	.....	......	[2] 10	12	12	12	84			
		....	[4] 4	.....	......	[4] 4	12	12	12	84			
13	.....do.............	3	20	10	70	103	9½	7	.....	54½	[8] 30	....	....
14	Paper boxes........	.....	100	.....	44	144	10	9	.....	59	60	....	....
15	.....do.............	1	70	12	250	333	10	5	.....	55	[11] 30	....	....
16	Tobacco and snuff..	10	121	18	247	396	10	5	.....	55	[8] 30	[12] 300	15
17	.....do.............	20	199	40	465	724	10	5	.....	55	45	....	....
18	Woolen and worsted goods........	.....	88	.....	43	131	10½	7½	.....	60	60	12	4
19	.....do.............	2	12	1	50	65	10¼	8¾	.....	60	45	20	8
	Total.........	181	1,796	399	4,313	6,689	.....	.....	.....	......	......	....	....

[1] On account of depression in business this plant had operated only 8 hours per day, 5 days a week, during previous year.
[2] Permit on file for shortening lunch period.
[3] Day force.
[4] Night force.
[5] Work from 3 a. m. to 12 noon.
[6] Men only; 48 worked 12 times during year an average of 2 hours a week; 943 worked 40 times during year an average of 10 hours a week.
[7] Seven Sundays during the year some employees worked 8 hours and were given some other day off during the week.
[8] No permit on file for shortening lunch period.
[9] Strippers and banders; number not separately reported.
[10] Not including home finishers.
[11] Permit for shortening lunch period not reported.
[12] For men in one department only.

TABLE I.—NUMBER OF EMPLOYEES, BY SEX AND BY AGE GROUPS, HOURS OF LABOR, LUNCH PERIOD, AND OVERTIME WORK—Contd.

WISCONSIN.

Establishment number.	Industry.	Male Under 16 yrs. of age.	Male 16 years of age and over.	Female Under 16 yrs. of age.	Female 16 years of age and over.	Total.	Per day Monday to Friday.	Per day Saturday.	Per day Sunday.	Total per week.	Time allowed for lunch (minutes).	Overtime times required during year.	Overtime average hours per week when worked.
1	Beer		26			26	10	10		60	60		
					17	17	9	9		54			
2	Cigar boxes	2	10		8	20	10	5		55	30	30	8
				2	61	63	9			45			
3	Confectionery		15		29	44	10	10		60	60	78	18
				5		5	10	5		55			
4	....do.		35		50	85	10	10		60	60	78	18
		2		3		5	10	5		55			
5	....do.		27		100	127	10	10		60	60	78	18
		2		12		14	10	5		55			
6	....do.		70[1]		110[1]	180[1]	10	10		60	60	70	18
		20[1]		54[1]		74[1]	10	5		55			
7	Hosiery and knit goods		25		95	120	10	9[2]		59[2]	60		
8	....do.		25	75	400	500	9½	7½		55	30	18	12
9	....do.		240		656	896	10	9[2]		59[2]	60		
10	Iron beds	4			50	54	10	5		55	60	100	12
		5	45	10	110	170	10	10		60			
		40[3]	300[3]	75[3]	190[3]	605[3]	10	5		55			
11	Matches		20[3]			20[3]	12	12	12	84	30		
			8[4]			8[4]	12	12	12	84			
12	Paper	(5)	(5)		65	65[5]	10	5		55	60		
				5	70	75	9	8		53			
13	Pearl buttons		57		45	102[6]	10	9		59	60		
14	Stamped and enameled ware	10[3]	230[3]	30[3]	110[3]	380[3]	10	10		60			
			30[3]			30[3]	12	12		72			
			5[3]			5[3]	12	12	12	84	30		
			30[4]			30[4]	12	12		72			
			5[4]			5[4]	12	12	12	84			
15	....do.	25	750	15	200	990	10	5		55	30		
16	Tobacco and snuff		47		23	70	10[7]	10[7]		60[7]	60	7	18
							9[8]	9[8]		54[8]			
17	....do.		35		71	106	10[7]	10[7]		60[7]	60		
							9[8]	7[8]		52[8]			
18	....do.		80		87	167	10[7]	10[7]		60[7]	60		
							9½[8]	9½[8]		57[8]			
19	....do.		20		47	67	10	10		60	60		
	Total	110	2,153	336	2,544	5,125							

MARYLAND.

Establishment number.	Industry.	Male Under 16 yrs. of age.	Male 16 years of age and over.	Female Under 16 yrs. of age.	Female 16 years of age and over.	Total.	Per day Monday to Friday.	Per day Saturday.	Per day Sunday.	Total per week.	Time allowed for lunch (minutes).	Overtime times required during year.	Overtime average hours per week when worked.
1	Canning and preserving		47	1	28	76	10	10		60	30	12	12
2	....do.	2	25		64	91	10	10		60	30	52	12
3	....do.	5	82	6	65	158	10	10		60	30		
4	Cans, tin	3	97	5	20	125	10	8¼		60	20	6	12
5	....do.	3	80		19	102	10½	8¼		60	45	12	4
6	Cigar boxes	1	4	1	10	16	10	9		59	30		
7	....do.	1	15	3	25	44	10	8½		58½	30	60	12
8	....do.	4	11		16	31	10½[9]	9½		60	30		
9	Cigars	1	30	1	22	54	10½[9]	9½			30		

[1] During October, November, and December an additional force of approximately 110 men and 120 women is employed.
[2] Four hours less on Saturdays from May to September, inclusive
[3] Day force.
[4] Night force.
[5] Number of males not reported.
[6] Not including home workers.
[7] For time workers.
[8] For pieceworkers.
[9] Except Friday, 10½ hours.

TABLE I.—NUMBER OF EMPLOYEES, BY SEX AND BY AGE GROUPS, HOURS OF LABOR, LUNCH PERIOD, AND OVERTIME WORK—Contd.

MARYLAND—Concluded.

Establishment number.	Industry.	Number of employees.					Hours of labor.				Time allowed for lunch (minutes).	Overtime work.	
		Male.		Female.			Per day.						
		Under 16 yrs. of age.	16 years of age and over.	Under 16 yrs. of age.	16 years of age and over.	Total.	Monday to Friday.	Saturday.	Sunday.	Total per week.		Times required during year.	Average hours per week when worked.
10	Cigars	2	83	27	159	271	9	9	.....	54	30	[1] 24	7
11	....do	4	91	9	244	348	10	5	.....	55	30	60	15
12	....do	{[2] 2	[2] 101	[2] 76	[2] 509	[2] 688	10½	5½	.....	56¾ }	30		
		.....	[3] 3	.....	.....	[3] 3	13	13	13	91			
13	Confectionery	2	43	9	24	78	10	10	.....	60	30	24	15
		{[2] 5	[2] 38	.....	.....	[2] 43	10	8½	.....	58½ }			
14	....do	.....	[2] 49	[2] 44	[2] 93	9½	8	.....	55½	30	18	2
		.....	[3] 1	.....	.....	[3] 1	13	13	13	91			
		.....	.....	.....	[3] 1	[3] 1	10	10	.....	60			
15	....do	38	90	13	17	158	10	10	.....	60	30	10	15
16	Crackers and biscuits	9	46	29	46	130	10	10	.....	60	30	.....	.....
17	Paper boxes	.....	11	12	47	70	10	8	.....	58	30	50	9
18	....do	{1	5	.....	.....	6	9½	8¾	.....	57½ }	45	3	6
		.....	.....	12	20	32	9½	8½	.....	54½			
19	....do	2	15	13	24	54	10	9½	.....	59½	30	.....	.....
20	....do	2	17	17	48	84	10	9	.....	59	30	.....	.....
21	Shirts	5	129	57	760	951	9	5	.....	50	30	.....	.....
22	....do	5	46	40	473	564	10	5	.....	55	30	.....	.....
23	....do	27	258	56	409	750	10	8	.....	58	30	54	2
		.....	75	.....	.....	75	10½	6	.....	58½			
24	....do	{10	.....	115	.....	125	10	5¾	.....	55¾ }	30	15	18
		.....	.....	.....	545	545	10½	5½	.....	57			
25	Straw hats	{10	320	.....	.....	330	10	9½	.....	59½ }	60	32	3
		.....	.....	25	150	175	9½	9	.....	56½			
26	....do	14	245	.....	.....	259	10	10	.....	60	60	18	3
		.....	.....	39	440	470	8¾	8¾	.....	52½			
27	....do	{6	98	.....	.....	104	10½	9½	.....	60 }	50	24	3
		.....	.....	10	198	208	9½	8½	.....	54	30		
28	Tobacco and snuff	4	145	9	196	354	10	6	.....	56	30	.....	.....
	Total	168	2,251	634	4,623	7,676	.....	.....	.....	......	.....	.....	.....

NORTH CAROLINA.

1	Cigarettes	17	166	24	186	393	10	8	.....	58	60	15	5
2	Cigars	8	38	29	143	218	10½	8½	.....	61	30	37	15
3	Cotton goods	54	260	52	92	458	11¹⁄₁₂	8¹¹⁄₁₂	.....	66	45	26	5¼
4	....do	12	80	10	50	152	11⁷⁄₁₂	8¼	.....	66½	40	.....	.....
5	....do	30	137	18	106	291	11½	8½	.....	66	45	.....	.....
6	....do	{[2] 29	[2] 176	[2] 27	[2] 74	[2] 306	11⅓	8¹¹⁄₁₂	.....	66	45 }	.....	.....
		[3] 6	[3] 21	[3] 2	[3] 4	[3] 33	11¼	.....	.....	56¾	15		
7	....do	{[2] 19	[2] 39	[2] 19	[2] 35	[2] 112	11¼	8¹¹⁄₁₂	.....	66	45 }	[4] 104	7
		.....	[3] 19	.....	.....	[3] 19	11¼	.....	.....	56¾	15		
8	....do	46	198	50	99	393	11½	8¹¹⁄₁₂	.....	66	45	.....	.....
9	....do	29	158	19	76	282	11½	8¹¹⁄₁₂	.....	66	45	.....	.....
10	....do	21	82	18	54	175	10½	7½	.....	60	60	[5] 25	2½
11	....do	15	68	6	61	150	10½	7½	.....	60	60	[5] 52	2½
12	Hosiery and knit goods	22	14	10	35	81	10½	8¹⁄₁₂	.....	59¼	60	18	2
13	....do	10	34	22	77	143	10½	8¼	.....	59	60	.....	.....
14	....do	9	23	20	55	107	10½	8¼	.....	60	45	.....	.....
15	Paper boxes	2	10	.....	23	35	10	8	.....	58	60	15	5
16	Tobacco and snuff	110	404	5	68	587	10	8	.....	58	60	.....	.....
17	....do	33	367	.....	.....	400	10	8	.....	58	60	.....	.....
18	....do	10	123	3	85	221	10	8	.....	58	60	90	12¼
19	....do	10	187	31	318	546	10	8	.....	58	60	.....	.....
20	....do	32	172	15	135	354	10	5	.....	55	60	.....	.....
21	....do	7	72	5	49	133	10	9	.....	59	60	.....	.....

[1] Employees over 16 only.
[2] Day force.
[3] Night force.
[4] For 20 per cent of men employees.
[5] For some departments only.

TABLE I.—NUMBER OF EMPLOYEES, BY SEX AND BY AGE GROUPS, HOURS OF LABOR, LUNCH PERIOD, AND OVERTIME WORK—Contd.

NORTH CAROLINA—Concluded.

Establishment number.	Industry.	Number of employees. Male. Under 16 yrs. of age.	Male. 16 years of age and over.	Female. Under 16 yrs. of age.	Female. 16 years of age and over.	Total.	Hours of labor. Per day. Monday to Friday.	Per day. Saturday.	Per day. Sunday.	Total per week.	Time allowed for lunch (minutes).	Overtime work. Times required during year.	Overtime work. Average hours per week when worked.
22	Tobacco and snuff	204	958	132	563	1,857	10	[1] 5	.....	[1] 55	60	......	......
23	....do	21	83	6	63	173	10	9	.....	59	60	......	......
24	Tobacco boxes, wood and tin	23	31	.....	.....	54	10	9	.....	59	60	......	......
25	Woolen and worsted goods	5	60	9	39	113	10¼	8¼	.....	59½	45	40	12½
26	....do	2	32	13	21	68	10 5/12	8 7/12	.....	60½	45	......	......
27	....do	5	58	6	17	86	11 5/12	8 11/12	.....	66	45	......	......
28	....do	2	26	2	13	43	10¼	8¼	.....	59½	45	......	......
	Total	793	4,096	553	2,541	7,983	.....	.....	.....	......	......	......	......

GEORGIA.

Establishment number.	Industry.	Male. Under 16 yrs. of age.	Male. 16 years of age and over.	Female. Under 16 yrs. of age.	Female. 16 years of age and over.	Total.	Monday to Friday.	Saturday.	Sunday.	Total per week.	Time allowed for lunch (minutes).	Times required during year.	Average hours per week when worked.
1	Confectionery	.....	28	2	37	67	10⅙	[2] 9⅙	.....	[2] 60	30	30	10
2	....do	.....	16	12	53	81	9½	[3] 8½	.....	[3] 56	60	30	6⅔
3	....do	6	42	5	37	90	10	[2] 9	.....	[2] 59	30	40	10
4	Cotton goods	32	515	18	352	917	10⅞	5⅝	.....	60	40	......	......
5	....do	19	458	24	267	768	10⅞	5⅝	.....	60	60	......	......
6	....do	16	239	11	65	331	10⅞	5⅝	.....	60	30	([4])	4½
7	....do	12	53	7	27	99	10⅞	5⅝	.....	60	60	......	......
8	....do	32	163	22	78	295	[5] 11⅓	.....	.....	[6] 55	40	......	......
9	....do	29	143	27	55	254	[5] 11⅓	.....	.....	[6] 55	40	......	......
10	....do	21	157	25	72	275	[5] 11⅓	.....	.....	55	40	......	......
11	....do	32	178	33	76	319	11½	6½	.....	64	40	......	......
12	Crackers and biscuits	.....	31	8	29	68	10	[2] 9	.....	[2] 59	[7] 30	40	10
13	....do	.....	24	3	16	43	10	[8] 10	.....	[8] 60	60	[9] 6	5
14	....do	.....	18	.....	31	49	10⅙	9⅙	.....	60	30	30	10
15	Hosiery and knit goods	10	18	15	37	80	10 11/12	5 5/12	.....	60	30	......	......
16	....do	7	32	.....	22	61	11	5⅔	.....	60⅔	35	......	......
		14	35	52	86	187	10⅓	5	.....	56⅔	30		
17	....do	[10] 35	[11] 69	[10] 40	[11] 123	[11] 267	10½	6½	.....	59	30	......	......
		....	[12] 4	.....	......	[12] 4	10½	17½	.....	70			
		....	[13] 5	.....	......	[13] 5	13	.....	5½	70½			
18	....do	16	36	19	50	121	11¼	6	.....	62¼	45	......	......
19	....do	14	46	27	71	158	[14] 10¾	[14] 5¾	.....	[14] 59½	45	......	......
20	....do	3	13	6	38	60	10¾	6¾	.....	60½	60	......	......
21	....do	2	8	4	60	74	10¼	7¾	.....	[15] 59	60	......	......
22	Paper boxes	4	7	7	17	35	10	[3] 10	.....	[3] 60	30	25	2½
23	....do	.....	12	6	41	59	10	9	.....	59	30	40	15
24	Woolen and worsted goods	23	111	13	77	224	11 5/12	9¼	.....	66⅓	35	......	......
25	....do	1	8	3	11	23	11⅓	9⅓	.....	66	40	......	......
26	....do	5	88	4	38	135	10¾	5¾	.....	59½	45	......	......
27	....do	9	42	7	37	95	11½	8½	.....	66	30	30	12½
	Total	342	2,599	400	1,903	5,244	.....	.....	.....	......	......	......	......

[1] Except some in picking department, and cleaners, about 75 employees, 4 hours more.
[2] Winter schedule; summer schedule, about 6 months, 4 hours less.
[3] Frequently work only half day on Saturday.
[4] Nearly every week.
[5] Except Friday, 9⅔ hours.
[6] When running normally, operate 66 hours per week.
[7] Except hands in bake room, who have 60.
[8] Winter schedule; summer schedule, about 6 months, 5 hours less.
[9] Part of force, but includes females.
[10] Day force; not including 12 children under 16 (sex not reported), working in the mill before and after school about 4 hours per day.
[11] Day force.
[12] Day hands, males over 16, work 11 hours overtime every Saturday.
[13] Night force.
[14] Summer schedule; winter schedule, Oct. 1 to Mar. 31, 30 minutes less Monday to Saturday, 3 hours less per week.
[15] When running normally, operate 62 hours per week.

TABLE I.—NUMBER OF EMPLOYEES, BY SEX AND BY AGE GROUPS, HOURS OF LABOR, LUNCH PERIOD, AND OVERTIME WORK—Concld.

FLORIDA.

[Hours of labor as given for cigar factories show the hours of time-workers or those recognized by the establishments as the regular working hours. Pieceworkers in most of these factories work irregularly, and usually less than the time schedules given.]

Establishment number.	Industry.	Number of employees.					Hours of labor.				Time allowed for lunch (minutes).	Overtime work.	
		Male.		Female.		Total.	Per day.			Total per week.		Times required during year.	Average hours per week when worked.
		Under 16 yrs. of age.	16 years of age and over.	Under 16 yrs. of age.	16 years of age and over.		Monday to Friday.	Saturday.	Sunday.				
1	Cigar boxes	9	139	14	101	263	9	9	.....	54	[1]30	45	10
2	....do	3	31	1	26	61	9	9		54	30		
3	Cigars	4	130	6	48	188	9	7		52	60		
4	....do	3	414		73	490	10	8		58	60		
5	....do	8	172	3	70	253	10	8		58	60		
6	....do	14	335	3	66	418	10	7		57	60		
7	....do		56		14	70	10	7		57	30		
8	....do	6	196	9	174	385	10	10		60	30		
9	....do	3	402	3	66	474	10	10		60	60		
10	....do	4	70	3	36	113	10½	7½		60	60		
11	....do		240	5	128	373	10½	7½		60	60		
12	....do	1	51	1	17	70	10½	7½		60	60		
13	....do	9	269	4	84	366	10½	7½		60	75		
14	....do	7	400	7	111	525	10	10		60	60		
	Total	71	2,905	59	1,014	4,049							

LOUISIANA.

Establishment number.	Industry.	Male Under 16	Male 16 and over	Female Under 16	Female 16 and over	Total.	Mon. to Fri.	Sat.	Sun.	Total per week.	Lunch (min.).	Times required.	Avg. hours.
1	Bags, burlap	8	34	14	65	121	10	10		60	30		
2	....do		25		23	48	10	10		60	30		
3	....do	1	53	25	94	173	10	10		60	30		
4	....do	2	31	11	32	76	10	8		58	30		
5	Boots and shoes	5	61	1	21	88	10	9		59	30		
6	....do	1	48		18	67	10	9		59	30		
7	Canning and preserving	20	75	30	35	160	10	10		60	60	(²)	(²)
8	Cans, tin	15	30	8	16	69	9½	9		56½	30	50	10
9	....do	14	83	9	31	137	10	5		55	30	10	6
10	Chewing gum	1	6	11	65	83	9½	5½		53	30		
11	Cigar boxes		15		27	42	10	5	..:.	55	60		
12	....do {	1	5			6	10	8		58	60		
					6	6	8	8		48			
13	Cigarettes and tobacco {	8	45			53	9½	9½		57	60		
				44	167	211	9	5		50			
14	Cigars	3	117	31	304	455	9½	8½		52	60		
15	....do	3	25	105	352	485	9½	4½		52	30		
16	Coffee packing		7		12	19	10	10		60	30	3	4½
17	....do		37		15	60	10	10		60	30		
18	Confectionery {	1	17			18	10	9½		59½	30	24	18
				4	17	21	8½	8		50½			
19	Crackers and biscuits	2	35	8	55	100	10	10		60	60	30	6
20	....do {	[3]1	[3]39	[3]8	[3]28	[3]76	10	10		60	60	6	5
			[4]9			[4]9	10	10		60			
21	....do	4	40	5	66	115	10	10		60	60	5	8
22	Hosiery and knit goods	31	64	64	151	310	10½	7½		60	30		
23	Paper boxes		2	1	9	12	10	6½		56½	30		
24	....do	2	3	6	12	23	10	10		60	30		
25	....do {	5	16			21	9	9		54	30		
				14	40	54	9	7		52			
26	Shirts		10	13	82	105	9	5		50	30	3	3
27	....do			2	14	16	9	7		52	30		
28	....do	1	3	1	39	44	10	7		57	30		
29	Straw hats	2	4		6	12	10	5		55	60		
	Total	138	939	416	1,802	3,295							

[1] Except in cedar mill, 60 minutes.   [3] Day force.
[2] Overtime frequent, exact amount not reported.   [4] Night force.

TABLE II.—POSTING OF SCHEDULE OF HOURS OF LABOR, POSTING OF LAWS, AND REGISTERS OF CHILDREN, ETC.

MAINE.

Establishment number.	Schedule posted showing daily hours of work of— Women.	Children.	Laws posted.	Register of children. Register on file.	Register posted in workrooms.	Working papers on file for how many children.
1	Yes..	(1)	No..	(1)	......	(1)
2	No..	No..	No..	No..	No...	None.
3	Yes..	(1)	No..	(1)	......	(1)
4	Yes..	Yes..	No..	No...	No...	8 of 18.
5	No..	(1)	No..	(1)	......	(1)
6	No..	(1)	No..	(1)	......	(1)
7	No..	No..	No..	No...	No...	None.
8	No..	(1)	No..	(1)	......	(1)
9	No..	No..	No..	No...	No...	None.
10	No..	No..	No..	No...	No...	None.
11	No..	No..	No..	No...	No...	1 of 6.
12	No..	(1)	No..	(1)	......	(1)
13	Yes..	Yes..	No..	No...	No...	None.
14	No..	No..	No..	No..	No...	None.
15	No..	(1)	No..	(1)	......	(1)
16	Yes..	Yes..	No..	No...	No...	None.
17	No..	No..	No..	No...	No...	None.
18	No..	(1)	No..	(1)	......	(1)
19	No..	(1)	No..	(1)	......	(1)
20	Yes..	(1)	Yes..	(1)	......	(1)
21	Yes..	Yes..	Yes..	No...	No...	None.
22	No..	No..	No..	No...	No...	None.
23	No..	(1)	No..	(1)	......	(1)
24	No..	(1)	No..	(1)	......	(1)
25	No..	No..	Yes..	No...	No...	None.
26	No..	No..	No..	No...	No...	None.

MASSACHUSETTS.

Establishment number.	Schedule posted showing daily hours of work of— Women.	Children.	Laws posted.	Register of children. Register on file.	Register posted in workrooms.	Working papers on file for how many children.
1	Yes..	Yes..	(2)	No..	No...	None.
2	No..	No..	(2)	No...	No...	All.
3	No..	No..	(2)	No..	No...	None.
4	Yes..	(1)	(2)	(1)	......	(1)
5	Yes..	Yes..	(2)	Yes..	No..	All.
6	Yes..	Yes..	(2)	No..	No...	All.
7	Yes..	(1)	(2)	(1)	......	(1)
8	Yes..	(1)	(2)	(1)	......	(1)
9	Yes..	Yes..	(2)	Yes..	Yes..	All.
10	No..	Yes..	(1)	Yes (3).	No...	All.
11	Yes..	Yes..	(2)	Yes..	No (4)..	All.
12	Yes..	Yes..	(2)	No...	No...	All.
13	Yes..	Yes..	(2)	No...	No...	All.
14	Yes..	Yes..	(2)	Yes..	Yes..	8 of 9.
15	Yes..	Yes..	(2)	No..	No...	10 of 16.
16	Yes..	Yes..	(2)	No...	No...	All.
17	No..	No..	(2)	No...	No...	23 of 24.
18	Yes..	Yes..	(2)	No...	No...	None.
19	Yes..	Yes..	(2)	Yes..	Yes..	All.
20	Yes..	Yes..	(2)	Yes..	Yes..	75 of 84.
21	Yes..	Yes..	(2)	Yes..	Yes..	All.
22	Yes..	Yes..	(2)	Yes..	No...	All.
23	Yes..	Yes..	(2)	Yes..	No...	All.
24	Yes..	Yes..	(2)	Yes..	No...	All.
25	No..	Yes..	(2)	Yes..	No...	All.
26	No..	(1)	(2)	(1)	......	(1)
27	Yes..	(1)	(2)	(1)	......	(1)
28	Yes..	Yes..	(2)	No...	No...	None.
29	No (4).	No (4)	(2)	No...	No...	3 of 8.
30	No (4).	No (4)	(2)	No...	No...	None.
31	Yes..	Yes..	(2)	No...	No...	20 of 30.
32	Yes..	Yes..	(2)	No...	No...	None.
33	Yes..	Yes..	(2)	No...	No...	All.
34	Yes..	Yes..	(2)	No...	No...	All.
35	Yes..	Yes..	(2)	Yes..	No...	All.
36	Yes..	Yes..	(2)	No...	No (4)..	4 of 6.
37	Yes..	Yes..	(2)	Yes..	No (4)..	All.
38	Yes..	Yes..	(2)	Yes (3).	Yes..	Some.
39	Yes..	Yes..	(2)	No...	No...	None.
40	Yes..	No (4).	(2)	(1)	......	(1)
41	Yes..	Yes..	(2)	Yes..	No (4)..	All.
42	Yes..	(1)	(2)	(1)	......	(1)
43	No..	No..	(2)	No...	No...	2 of 6.
44	No..	No..	(2)	(2)	(2)	(2)

RHODE ISLAND.

Establishment number.	Schedule posted showing daily hours of work of— Women.	Children.	Laws posted.	Register of children. Register on file.	Register posted in workrooms.	Working papers on file for how many children.
1	No..	(1)	No..	(1)	......	(1)
2	No..	No..	No..	No...	No...	None.
3	No..	No..	No..	No...	No...	3 of 8.
4	No..	No..	No..	Yes..	No...	All.
5	No (6).	No (6).	Yes..	Yes..	No...	All.
6	Yes .	Yes..	No..	No...	No...	30 of 50.
7	No..	No..	No..	No...	No...	61 of 91.
8	Yes (7).	Yes (7)	No..	No...	No...	8 of 13.
9	No..	No..	Yes..	No...	No...	21 of 26.
10	No..	No..	Yes..	No...	No...	14 of 22.
11	No..	No..	No..	No...	No...	All.
12	No..	No..	No..	No...	No...	4 of 8.
13	No..	(1)	No..	(1)	......	(1)
14	No..	No..	No..	No...	No...	All.
15	No..	No..	No..	No..	No...	All.
16	No..	(1)	No..	(1)	......	(1)
17	No..	No..	No..	No...	No...	All.
18	Yes..	No..	Yes..	No...	No...	All.
19	No..	No..	No..	No...	No...	All.
20	No..	No..	No..	No...	No...	1 of 3.
21	No..	No..	Yes..	No...	No...	All.
22	No..	No..	Yes..	No...	No...	All.
23	No..	No..	Yes..	No...	No...	4 of 5.
24	Yes..	No..	Yes..	No...	No...	22 of 33.
25	No..	No..	Yes..	No...	No...	None.
26	No..	No..	Yes..	No...	No...	28 of 39.
27	No..	No..	Yes..	No...	No...	28 of 39.

1 No children employed.
2 Not reported.
3 Register not complete.
4 Posted in halls, but not in rooms.
5 Posted near entrance.
6 In office only.
7 Typewritten form.

TABLE II.—POSTING OF SCHEDULE OF HOURS OF LABOR, POSTING OF LAWS, AND REGISTERS OF CHILDREN, ETC.—Continued.

CONNECTICUT.

Establishment number.	Schedule posted showing daily hours of work of— Women.	Children.	Laws posted.	Register of children. Register on file.	Register posted in work-rooms.	Working papers on file for how many children.
1	No..	No..	No..	Yes..	No...	30 of 36.
2	No..	No..	No..	No...	No...	None.
3	No..	(1)	No..	(1)	......	(1)
4	No..	No..	No..	Yes..	No...	67 of 72.
5	No..	No..	No..	Yes..	No...	4 of 6.
6	No..	No..	No..	Yes..	No...	3 of 4.
7	No..	No..	Yes.	Yes..	No...	2 of 4.
8	Yes..	Yes..	No..	Yes..	No...	12 of 15.
9	No..	No..	No..	(2)	No...	None.
10	No..	No..	No..	(2)	No...	Some.
11	No..	No..	No..	Yes..	No...	Some.
12	No..	No..	No..	Yes 3.	No...	Some.
13	No..	(1)	No..	(1)	......	(1)
14	No 4.	No 4.	No..	Yes..	No...	1 of 3.
15	No 4.	No 4.	No..	Yes..	No...	7 of 10.
16	No..	No..	No..	Yes..	No...	All.
17	No..	No..	No..	Yes 3.	No...	10 of 37.
18	No..	No..	No..	No...	No...	19 of 20.
19	No..	No..	No..	Yes..	No...	None.
20	No..	No..	No..	Yes 4.	No...	18 of 26.
21	No..	No..	No..	No...	No...	20 of 28.
22	No..	No..	No..	Yes..	No...	All.
23	No..	No..	No..	No...	No...	2 of 5.
24	No..	No..	No..	Yes..	No...	6 of 8.
25	No..	No..	No..	Yes..	No...	Some.
26	No..	No..	No..	Yes..	No...	15 of 16.
27	No 4.	No 4.	No..	Yes..	No...	50 of 66.
28	No..	No..	No..	Yes..	No...	7 of 11.
29	No..	No..	No..	Yes..	No...	All.
30	No..	No..	Yes.	Yes 3.	No...	4 of 5.
31	No..	No..	No..	No...	No...	None.
32	No..	No..	No..	No...	No...	All.
33	No..	No..	No..	Yes..	No...	All.
34	No..	No..	Yes.	No...	No...	3 of 5.
35	Yes..	Yes..	Yes.	Yes..	No...	5 of 7.

NEW YORK.

Establishment number.	Schedule posted showing daily hours of work of— Women.	Children.	Laws posted.	Register of children. Register on file.	Register posted in work-rooms.	Working papers on file for how many children.
1	Yes..	(1)	Yes.	(1)	......	(1)
2	Yes..	(1)	Yes.	(1)	......	(1)
3	No..	No..	No..	No...	No...	None.
4	Yes..	Yes.	Yes.	No...	No...	1 of 5.
5	No..	No..	(2)	No...	No...	1 of 2.
6	Yes..	(1)	Yes.	(1)	......	(1)
7	Yes..	(1)	Yes.	(1)	......	(1)
8	No..	Yes.	No..	Yes..	No...	Some.
9	Yes..	(1)	Yes.	(1)	......	(1)
10	No..	Yes.	Yes.	Yes..	No...	3 of 5.
11	No..	(1)	No..	(1)	......	(1)
12	Yes..	(1)	Yes.	(1)	......	(1)
13	Yes..	(1)	Yes.	(1)	......	(1)
14	Yes..	(1)	Yes.	(1)	......	(1)
15	Yes..	(1)	Yes.	(1)	......	(1)
16	No..	Yes.	Yes.	Yes..	No...	All.
17	Yes..	(1)	Yes.	(1)	......	(1)
18	Yes..	(1)	Yes.	(1)	......	(1)
19	No..	No..	Yes.	No...	No...	All.
20	No..	No..	Yes.	Yes..	No...	All.
21	No..	(1)	Yes.	(1)	......	(1)
22	Yes..	Yes.	Yes.	Yes..	No...	None.
23	No..	No..	No..	Yes..	No...	All.
24	Yes..	Yes.	Yes.	Yes..	No...	All.
25	No..	No..	Yes.	Yes..	No...	All.
26	No..	No..	Yes.	No...	No...	None.
27	No..	(1)	No..	(1)	......	(1)
28	No..	No..	(2)	No...	No...	None.
29	No..	No..	No..	No...	No...	All.
30	Yes..	(1)	Yes.	(1)	......	(1)
31	Yes..	Yes.	Yes.	Yes..	No...	All.
32	Yes..	No..	Yes.	No...	No...	All.
33	No..	(1)	Yes.	(1)	......	(1)
34	Yes..	(1)	Yes.	(1)	......	(1)
35	Yes..	Yes.	Yes.	Yes..	......	3 of 5.
36	Yes..	(1)	Yes.	(1)	......	(1)

NEW JERSEY.

Establishment number.	Schedule posted showing daily hours of work of— Women.	Children.	Laws posted.	Register of children. Register on file.	Register posted in work-rooms.	Working papers on file for how many children.
1	No..	(1)	No..	(1)	......	(1)
2	No..	No..	No 4.	Yes..	(2)	All.
3	No..	No..	No..	Yes..	No...	All.
4	No..	No..	No..	Yes..	(2)	33 of 37.
5	No..	No..	No..	No...	No...	3 of 13.
6	No..	No..	No..	No...	No...	9 of 15.
7	No..	No..	No..	Yes..	No...	All.
8	No..	No..	No..	No...	No...	(2)
9	No..	No..	No..	No...	No...	(2)
10	No..	No..	No..	Yes..	No...	All.
11	No..	No..	No..	No...	No...	All.
12	No..	No..	No..	No...	No...	All.
13	No..	No..	No..	No...	No...	All.
14	No..	No..	No..	No...	No...	None.
15	Yes	Yes.	Yes.	Yes..	No...	All.
16	No..	No..	No..	No...	No...	None.
17	No..	No..	No..	No...	No...	None.
18	No..	No..	No..	No...	No...	None.
19	No..	No..	No..	No...	No...	None.
20	No..	No..	No..	No...	No...	All.
21	No..	No..	No..	Yes..	No...	All.
22	No..	No..	Yes.	No...	No...	28 of 40.
23	No..	No..	Yes.	Yes..	No...	All.
24	No..	Yes.	Yes.	Yes..	No...	All.
25	No..	Yes.	Yes.	Yes..	No...	All.
26	No..	Yes.	Yes.	Yes..	No...	All.
27	No..	(4)	Yes.	(1)	......	(1)

1 No children employed. 3 Not reported. 4 Register not complete. 4 In office only.

TABLE **II.**—POSTING OF SCHEDULE OF HOURS OF LABOR, POSTING OF LAWS, AND REGISTERS OF CHILDREN, ETC.—Continued.

PENNSYLVANIA.

Establishment number.	Schedule posted showing daily hours of work of— Women.	Children.	Laws posted.	Register of children. Register on file.	Register posted in workrooms.	Working papers on file for how many children.
1	Yes..	Yes.	Yes.	Yes..	Yes..	All.
2	Yes..	Yes.	Yes.	Yes..	Yes..	7 of 10.
3	No..	No..	Yes.	No...	No...	All.
4	Yes..	Yes.	Yes.	Yes..	Yes..	All.
5	Yes..	Yes.	Yes.	Yes[1].	Yes[1].	62 of 72.
6	No..	No..	No..	No...	No ..	None.
7	Yes..	Yes.	Yes.	No...	No ..	All.
8	Yes..	Yes.	Yes.	No...	No ..	All.
9	Yes..	Yes.	Yes.	No...	No ..	39 of 44.
10	Yes..	Yes.	Yes.	Yes..	Yes..	All.
11	Yes..	Yes.	Yes.	Yes..	Yes..	All.
12	No..	No..	Yes.	No...	No ..	1 of 4
13	Yes..	Yes.	Yes.	No...	No ..	All.
14	Yes..	Yes.	Yes.	Yes..	Yes..	All.
15	No..	No..	No..	Yes..	Yes..	All.
16	Yes..	Yes.	Yes.	Yes..	Yes..	All.
17	Yes..	Yes.	Yes.	Yes..	Yes..	All.
18	No..	[2]	No..	[2]	....	[2]
19	No..	[2]	Yes.	[2]	....	[2]
20	No..	[2]	Yes.	[2]	....	[2]
21	No..	[2]	Yes.	[2]	....	[2]
22	No..	No..	No..	Yes..	No...	All.
23	Yes..	Yes.	Yes.	Yes..	Yes..	45 of 48.
24	No..	No..	No..	No...	No...	6 of 8.
25	Yes..	Yes.	Yes.	Yes..	Yes..	All.
26	No..	No..	No..	No...	No...	All.
27	Yes..	Yes.	Yes.	Yes..	Yes..	13 of 14.
28	Yes..	No..	Yes.	Yes..	Yes..	All.
29	No..	No..	No..	No...	No...	4 of 7.
30	Yes..	Yes.	Yes.	Yes..	Yes..	259 of 260.
31	Yes..	Yes.	Yes.	Yes..	Yes..	All.
32	Yes..	Yes.	Yes.	Yes..	Yes..	55 of 59.
33	Yes..	Yes.	Yes.	Yes..	Yes..	10 of 12.
34	No..	No..	No..	No...	No...	All.
35	Yes..	Yes.	Yes.	Yes..	No...	All.
36	Yes..	[2]	Yes.	[2]	....	[2]
37	No..	No..	Yes.	No...	No...	All.
38	Yes..	Yes.	Yes.	Yes..	No...	All.
39	Yes..	Yes.	No..	Yes..	Yes..	21 of 22.
40	Yes..	Yes.	Yes.	Yes[1].	Yes[1].	23 of 24.
41	Yes..	Yes.	Yes.	No...	No...	All.
42	No..	[2]	Yes.	[2]	....	[2]
43	No..	[2]	No..	[2]	....	[2]
44	No..	Yes.	Yes.	Yes..	No...	All.
45	No..	No..	Yes.	No...	No...	1 of 10.
46	No..	No..	No..	Yes..	No...	All.
47	Yes..	Yes.	Yes.	Yes..	Yes..	All.
48	Yes..	Yes.	Yes.	Yes..	Yes..	All.
49	Yes..	Yes.	Yes.	Yes..	Yes..	All.
50	Yes..	[2]	Yes.	[2]	....	[2]

OHIO.

Establishment number.	Schedule posted showing daily hours of work of— Women.	Children.	Laws posted.	Register of children. Register on file.	Register posted in workrooms.	Working papers on file for how many children.
1	Yes..	Yes.	Yes.	No...	No...	All.
2	No..	[2]	No..	[2]	....	[2]
3	[2]	[2]	Yes.	[2]	....	[2]
4	No..	Yes.	Yes.	Yes..	No...	All.
5	Yes..	Yes.	Yes.	Yes..	No...	All.
6	No..	[2]	No..	[2]	....	[2]
7	No..	[2]	No..	[2]	......	[2]
8	No..	[2]	No..	[2]	....	[2]
9	Yes..	[2]	Yes.	[2]	....	[2]
10	No..	[2]	No..	[2]	....	[2]
11	No..	[2]	No..	[2]	....	[2]
12	[3]	[2]	Yes.	Yes..	No...	All.
13	Yes..	Yes.	Yes.	No...	No...	3 of 4.
14	Yes..	Yes.	Yes.	No...	No...	All.
15	Yes..	Yes.	Yes.	No...	No...	1 of 2.
16	Yes..	Yes.	Yes.	No...	No...	37 of 42.
17	Yes..	Yes.	Yes.	Yes[1].	No...	6 of 12.
18	Yes..	Yes.	Yes.	Yes..	No...	All.
19	Yes..	[2]	Yes.	[2]	....	[2]
20	Yes..	[2]	Yes.	[2]	....	[2]
21	Yes..	Yes.	Yes.	No...	No...	All.
22	No..	[2]	No..	[2]	....	[2]
23	Yes..	Yes.	Yes.	No...	....	5 of 13.
24	Yes..	[2]	Yes.	[2]	....	[2]
25	No..	No..	Yes.	No...	No...	All.
26	No..	No..	No..	No...	No...	All.
27	No..	No..	No..	Yes..	No...	None.
28	Yes..	[2]	Yes.	[2]	....	[2]
29	Yes..	[2]	Yes.	[2]	....	[2]
30	No..	[2]	No..	[2]	....	[2]
31	Yes..	[2]	Yes.	[2]	....	[2]
32	Yes..	[2]	Yes.	[4]	....	[2]
33	Yes..	Yes.	Yes.	No...	No...	All.
34	Yes..	Yes.	Yes.	No...	No...	All.
35	Yes..	[2]	Yes.	[2]	....	[2]
36	Yes..	Yes.	Yes.	No...	No...	24 of 25.
37	Yes..	[2]	Yes.	[2]	....	[2]
38	Yes..	Yes.	Yes.	No...	No...	All.
39	Yes..	Yes.	Yes.	Yes..	No...	All.
40	Yes..	Yes.	Yes.	No...	No...	3 of 5.
41	No..	No..	Yes.	No...	No...	All.
42	Yes..	Yes.	Yes.	No...	No...	None.
43	Yes..	Yes.	Yes.	No...	No...	All.
44	No..	No..	Yes.	Yes..	No...	All.
45	No..	No..	Yes.	No...	No...	None.
46	No..	[2]	Yes.	[2]	....	[2]
47	No..	[2]	Yes.	[2]	....	[2]
48	No..	[2]	Yes.	[2]	....	[2]
49	Yes..	Yes.	Yes.	No...	No...	None.
50	Yes..	[2]	Yes.	[2]	....	[2]
51	[4]	[2]	Yes.	[2]	....	[2]
52	Yes..	[2]	Yes.	[2]	....	[2]
53	Yes..	Yes.	Yes.	Yes..	No...	All.
54	Yes..	Yes.	Yes.	Yes..	No...	All.
55	Yes..	Yes.	Yes.	Yes..	No...	All.
56	No..	[2]	No..	[2]	....	[2]
57	Yes..	Yes.	Yes.	Yes..	No...	All.
58	No..	[2]	Yes.	[2]	....	[2]
59	No..	[2]	No..	[2]	....	[2]
60	No..	[2]	No..	[2]	....	[2]

[1] Register not complete.   [2] No children employed.   [3] Not reported.

TABLE **II.**—POSTING OF SCHEDULE OF HOURS OF LABOR, POSTING OF LAWS, AND REGISTERS OF CHILDREN, ETC.—Continued.

ILLINOIS.

Establishment number.	Schedule posted showing daily hours of work of— Women.	Children.	Laws posted.	Register of children. Register on file.	Register posted in work-rooms.	Working papers on file for how many children.	Establishment number.	Schedule posted showing daily hours of work of— Women.	Children.	Laws posted.	Register of children. Register on file.	Register posted in work-rooms.	Working papers on file for how many children.
1	No..	No..	No..	No...	No...	All.	25	No..	Yes.	Yes.	Yes..	Yes..	All.
2	No..	No..	No..	No...	No...	All.	26	Yes..	Yes.	Yes.	Yes..	Yes..	All
3	No..	(1)	No..	(1)	......	(1)	27	Yes..	Yes.	No..	Yes..	Yes..	All.
4	No..	(1)	No..	(1)	......	(1)	28	No..	Yes.	Yes.	Yes..	Yes..	All.
5	No..	Yes.	Yes.	Yes..	Yes.	All.	29	No..	No..	No..	No..	No..	All.
6	No..	(1)	No..	(1)	......	(1)	30	No..	No..	No..	No..	No..	All.
7	No..	No..	No..	No...	No...	None.	31	No..	(1)	No..	(1)	......	(1)
8	No..	Yes.	No..	Yes..	Yes.	All.	32	No..	Yes.	Yes.	Yes..	Yes..	All.
9	No..	(1)	No..	(1)	......	(1)	33	Yes..	Yes.	Yes.	Yes..	Yes..	All.
10	No..	(1)	No..	(1)	....	(1)	34	No..	Yes.	Yes.	Yes..	Yes..	All.
11	No..	Yes.	Yes.	Yes.[2]	Yes..	82 of 89.	35	Yes..	Yes.	Yes.	Yes..	Yes..	All.
12	No..	No..	No..	No..	No...	1 of 2.	36	No..	Yes.	Yes.	Yes..	Yes..	All.
13	No..	No..	No..	Yes..	Yes.	21 of 25.	37	No..	Yes.	Yes.	Yes..	No..	All.
14	No..	(1)	No..	(1)	......	(1)	38	Yes..	Yes.	No..	Yes.[2]	Yes..	Some.
15	Yes..	(1)	No..	(1)	......	(1)	39	No..	No..	No..	No..	No..	Some.
16	Yes..	(1)	No..	(1)	......	(1)	40	No..	(1)	No..	(1)	......	(1)
17	Yes..	(1)	No..	(1)	......	(1)	41	No..	(1)	No..	(1)	......	(1)
18	Yes..	(1)	No..	(1)	......	(1)	42	No..	No..	No..	No...	No...	All.
19	No..	Yes.	No..	Yes..	Yes.	87 of 90.	43	No..	Yes.	No..	Yes..	Yes..	All.
20	No..	(1)	No..	(1)	......	(1)	44	No..	(1)	No..	(1)	......	(1)
21	No..	Yes.	Yes.	Yes..	Yes..	All.	45	No..	(1)	No..	(1)	......	(1)
22	No..	Yes.	Yes.	Yes..	Yes..	Some.	46	No..	(1)	No..	(1)	......	(1)
23	No..	Yes.	Yes.	Yes..	Yes..	All.	47	No..	No..	No..	No...	No...	All.
24	No..	Yes.	Yes.	Yes.[2]	Yes..	All.							

INDIANA.

Establishment number.	Schedule Women.	Children.	Laws posted.	Register on file.	Register posted in work-rooms.	Working papers.	Establishment number.	Schedule Women.	Children.	Laws posted.	Register on file.	Register posted in work-rooms.	Working papers.
1	No..	No..	No..	No...	No...	All.	25	No..	No..	No..	Yes..	Yes..	All.
2	No..	No..	No..	No...	No...	Some.	26	Yes .	Yes.	No..	No...	No...	Some.
3	Yes .	Yes.	Yes.	No...	No...	All.	27	No..	No..	No..	Yes..	No...	All.
4	No..	No..	No..	No...	No...	All.	28	No..	No..	No..	No..	No...	All.
5	No..	No..	No..	No...	No...	All.	29	No..	No..	Yes.	No..	No...	Some.
6	No..	(1)	No..	(1)	......	(1)	30	No..	No..	No..	Yes..	No...	All.
7	Yes .	Yes.	Yes.	Yes..	No...	All.	31	No..	Yes.	No..	No..	No...	All.
8	No..	No..	No..	No...	No...	None.	32	Yes .	(1)	Yes.	(1)	......	(1)
9	Yes .	Yes.	Yes.	Yes..	Yes..	All.	33	No..	No..	No..	No...	No...	Some.
10	No..	No..	No..	No...	No...	None.	34	No..	No..	No..	Yes..	Yes..	All.
11	No..	No..	No..	Yes..	No...	All.	35	No..	(1)	No..	(1)	......	(1)
12	Yes .	Yes.	Yes.	No...	No...	11 of 17.	36	Yes .	Yes.	Yes.	No...	No...	None.
13	No..	(1)	No..	(1)	......	(1)	37	Yes .	Yes.	Yes.	Yes..	Yes..	Some.
14	No..	No..	No..	No...	No...	None.	38	No..	No..	No..	No..	No...	Some.
15	Yes .	Yes.	Yes.	Yes..	Yes..	All.	39	No..	No..	No..	No..	No...	None.
16	Yes .	Yes.	Yes.	Yes..	Yes..	All.	40	No..	No..	No..	No..	No...	None.
17	Yes .	Yes.	Yes.	No...	No...	1 of 3.	41	Yes .	Yes.	Yes.	No..	No...	Some.
18	No..	No..	No..	No...	No...	1 of 3.	42	No..	No..	No..	No..	No...	All.
19	No..	No..	Yes.	Yes..	No...	All.	43	No..	No..	No..	No..	No...	Some.
20	No..	No..	No..	Yes..	No...	4 of 8.	44	(1)	Yes.	Yes.	No..	No...	23 of 25.
21	Yes .	(1)	Yes.	(1)	......	(1)	45	Yes .	Yes.	Yes.	No..	No...	Some.
22	No..	(1)	No..	(1)	......	(1)	46	Yes .	Yes.	Yes.	No..	No...	All.
23	No..	(1)	Yes.	(1)	......	(1)	47	Yes .	Yes.	No..	No..	No...	2 of 4.
24	Yes .	Yes.	Yes.	Yes.[2]	Yes..	All.							

MICHIGAN.

Establishment number.	Schedule Women.	Children.	Laws posted.	Register on file.	Register posted in work-rooms.	Working papers.	Establishment number.	Schedule Women.	Children.	Laws posted.	Register on file.	Register posted in work-rooms.	Working papers.
1	No..	(1)	No..	(1)	......	(1)	11	No..	No..	No..	Yes..	No...	All.
2	No..	No..	No..	Yes..	No..	All.	12	No..	No..	Yes.	No..	No...	Some.
3	No..	No..	No..	No...	No...	33 of 35.	13	No..	No..	Yes.	No..	No...	Some.
4	No..	No..	Yes.	Yes..	No...	85 of 121.	14	No..	(1)	No..	(1)	......	(1)
5	No..	(1)	No..	(1)	......	(1)	15	No..	No..	No..	No..	No...	All.
6	No..	No..	No..	No...	No...	All.	16	No..	No..	No..	No..	No...	All.
7	No..	No..	No..	Yes..	No..	42 of 63.	17	No..[4]	No..[4]	No..	No..	No...	48 of 60.
8	No..	No..	No..	No...	No...	50 of 56.	18	No..	(1)	No..	(1)	......	(1)
9	No..	No..	No..	No..	No...	5 of 15.	19	No..	No..	No..	No..	No...	1 of 3.
10	No..	(1)	No..	(1)	......	(1)							

[1] No children employed. [2] Register not complete. [3] No women employed. [4] In office only.

TABLE **II.**—POSTING OF SCHEDULE OF HOURS OF LABOR, POSTING OF LAWS, AND REGISTERS OF CHILDREN, ETC.—Continued.

WISCONSIN.

Establishment number.	Schedule posted showing daily hours of work of—		Laws posted.	Register of children.		Working papers on file for how many children.	Establishment number.	Schedule posted showing daily hours of work of—		Laws posted.	Register of children.		Working papers on file for how many children.
	Women.	Children.		Register on file.	Register posted in workrooms.			Women.	Children.		Register on file.	Register posted in workrooms.	
1	No..	(1)	No..	(1)	....	(1)	11	No..	No..	Yes.	No...	No...	Some.
2	No..	No..	No...	No...	No...	All.	12	No..	No..	No..	No...	No...	All.
3	No..	No..	No...	No...	No...	All.	13	No..	(1)	No..	(1)	....	(1)
4	No..	No..	No...	No...	No...	All.	14	No..	No..	No...	No...	No...	All.
5	No..	No..	No...	No...	No...	All.	15	No..	No..	No...	No...	No...	All.
6	No..	No..	No...	No...	No...	All.	16	No..	(1)	No..	(1)	....	(1)
7	No..	(1)	No..	(1)	....	(1)	17	No..	(1)	No..	(1)	....	(1)
8	No..	No..	No...	No...	....	All.	18	No..	(1)	No..	(1)	....	(1)
9	No..	No..	No...	Yes..	No...	All.	19	No..	(1)	No..	(1)	....	(1)
10	No..	No..	No...	No...	No...	All.							

MARYLAND.

Establishment number.	Women.	Children.	Laws posted.	Register on file.	Register posted in workrooms.	Working papers on file for how many children.	Establishment number.	Women.	Children.	Laws posted.	Register on file.	Register posted in workrooms.	Working papers on file for how many children.
1	No..	No..	No..	No..	No...	All.	15	No..	No..	No..	No...	No...	49 of 51.
2	No..	No..	No..	No..	No...	None.	16	No..	No..	No..	Yes..	No...	27 of 38.
3	No..	No..	No..	No..	No...	None.	17	No..	No..	Yes.	Yes..	No...	All.
4	No..	No..	No..	Yes..	No...	All.	18	No..	No..	No..	Yes..	No...	12 of 13.
5	No..	No..	No..	Yes..	No...	All.	19	No..	No..	No..	Yes..	No...	14 of 15.
6	No..	No..	No..	No..	No...	All.	20	No..	No..	No..	Yes..	No...	17 of 19.
7	No..	No..	No..	No..	No...	None.	21	No..	No..	No..	Yes..	No...	44 of 62.
8	No..	No..	No..	Yes..	(2)	None.	22	No..	No..	No..	Yes..	No...	27 of 36.
9	No..	No..	No..	No..	No...	All.	23	Yes..	Yes..	No..	Yes..	No...	76 of 83.
10	No..	No..	No..	Yes..	No...	22 of 29.	24	Yes..	Yes..	No..	Yes..	No...	112 of 125.
11	No..	No..	No..	Yes..	Yes..	12 of 13.	25	Yes..	Yes..	No..	Yes..	No...	33 of 35.
12	No..	No..	No..	Yes..	Yes..	76 of 78.	26	(2)	(2)	No..	Yes..	Yes..	48 of 53.
13	No..	No..	No..	Yes..	No...	All.	27	No..	No..	No..	Yes..	No...	15 of 16.
14	(2)	(2)	Yes.	No...	No...	All.	28	No..	No..	No..	Yes..	Yes..	6 of 13.

NORTH CAROLINA.

[Tabulation relating to registers and working papers for children is omitted for this State. For explanation, see section of text dealing with these subjects.]

Establishment number.	Women.	Children.	Laws posted.	Establishment number.	Women.	Children.	Laws posted.
1	No..	No..	No..	15	No..	No..	No..
2	No..	No..	No..	16	No..	No..	No..
3	No..	No..	Yes.	17	(2)	No..	No..
4	Yes .	Yes..	Yes.	18	No..	No..	No..
5	No..	No..	No..	19	No..	No..	No..
6	No..	No..	Yes.	20	No..	No..	No..
7	No..	No..	Yes.	21	No..	No..	No..
8	No..	No..	Yes.	22	No..	No..	No..
9	No..	No..	Yes.	23	No..	No..	No..
10	No..	No..	No..	24	(3)	No..	No..
11	No..	No..	No..	25	No..	No..	No..
12	No..	No..	No..	26	No..	No..	No..
13	No..	No..	No..	27	No..	No..	Yes.
14	No..	No..	No..	28	No..	No..	No..

¹ No children employed.   ² Not reported.   ³ No women employed.

TABLE **II.**—POSTING OF SCHEDULE OF HOURS OF LABOR, POSTING OF LAWS, AND REGISTERS OF CHILDREN, ETC.—Concluded.

GEORGIA.

[Tabulation relating to registers and working papers for children is omitted for this State. For explanation, see section of text dealing with these subjects.]

Establishment number.	Schedule posted showing daily hours of work of—		Laws posted.	Register of children.		Working papers on file for how many children.	Establishment number.	Schedule posted showing daily hours of work of—		Laws posted.	Register of children.		Working papers on file for how many children.
	Women.	Children.		Register on file.	Register posted in workrooms.			Women.	Children.		Register on file.	Register posted in workrooms.	
1	No..	No..	No..		'		15	No..	No..	No..			
2	No..	No..	No..				16	No..	No..	Yes.			
3	No..	No..	No..	.			17	No..	No..	No..			
4	No..	No..	No..				18	No..	No..	No..			
5	No..	No..	No..				19	No..	No..	No..			
6	No..	No..	Yes.				20	No..	No..	No..			
7	No..	No..	No..				21	No..	No..	No..			
8	No..	No..	No..				22	No..	No..	No..			
9	No..	No..	Yes.				23	Yes .	Yes.	No..			
10	No..	No..	No..	.			24	No..	No..	No..			
11	No..	No..	No..				25	No..	No..	No..		.	
12	No..	No..	No..				26	No..	No..	No..			
13	No..	No..	No..				27	No..	No..	No..			
14	No..	(1)	No..										

FLORIDA.

[Tabulation relating to registers and working papers for children is omitted for this State. For explanation, see section of text dealing with these subjects.]

1	No..	No..	No..				8	No..	No..	No..			
2	No..	No..	No..				9	No..	No..	No..			
3	No..	No..	No..				10	No..	No..	No..			
4	No..	No..	No..				11	No..	No..	No..			
5	No..	No..	No..				12	No..	No..	No..			
6	No..	No..	No..				13	No..	No..	No..			
7	No..	(1)	No..				14	No..	No..	No..			

LOUISIANA.

1	No..	No..	No..	Yes..	No...	8 of 22.	16	No..	No..	No..	Yes..	No...	All.
2	No..	(1)	No..	(1)	....	(1)	17	No..	No..	No..	No...	No...	3 of 5.
3	No..	No..	No..	Yes..	Yes..	All.	18	No..	No..	No..	No...	No...	5 of 10.
4	No..	No..	No..	Yes..	No...	All.	19	No..	No..	No..	Yes..	Yes..	6 of 9.
5	No..	No..	No..	No...	No...	1 of 6.	20	No..	No..	No..	No...	No...	None.
6	No..	No..	No..	No...	No...	None.	21	No..	No..	No..	Yes..	No...	All.
7	No..	No..	No..	No...	No...	None.	22	No..	No..	No..	No...	No...	All.
8	No..	No..	No..	No...	No...	19 of 23.	23	No..	No..	No..	No...	No...	2 of 8.
9	No..	No..	No..	No...	No...	All.	24	No..	No..	No..	No...	No...	12 of 19.
10	No..	No..	No..	No...	No...	8 of 12.	25	No..	No..	No..	No...	No...	4 of 13.
11	No..	(1)	No..	(1)	....	(1)	26	No..	No..	No..	No...	No...	None.
12	No..	No..	No..	No...	No...	None.	27	No..	No..	No..	No...	No...	1 of 2.
13	No..	No..	No..	Yes..	No...	27 of 34.	28	No..	No..	No..	No...	No...	None.
14	No..	No..	No..	Yes..	No...	104 of 108.	29	No..	No..	No..	Yes..	No...	46 of 52.
15	No..	(1)	No..	(1)	....	(1)							

[1] No children employed.

TABLE **III.**—SAFEGUARDING AGAINST FIRE: CHARACTER OF

MAINE.

Establishment number.	Building.			Fire escapes.				
	Construction material.	Number of stories.	Stories occupied by this establishment.	Outside of building.			Inside of building (and incombustible).	
				Number.	Material.	Obstructions.	Number.	Obstructions.
1	Brick............	4	All......	1	Iron and wood.	Tables in front of windows.	None.	....
2	.....do............	3	All......	None.		..........,	[2]1	None....
3	Frame............	4	All......	1	Iron.........	None............	None.	....
4	.....do............	4	All......	2	.....do.........	Board in front of window.	None.	....
5	Brick............	4	All......	None.			None.	
6	.....do............	3	2d, 3d ...	None.			None.	
7	{Frame (metal sheathed).	3	All......	None.			None.	
8	Brick............	4	All......	1	Iron.........	None............	None.	
9	.....do............	3	All......	None.			None.	
10	Frame..........	3	All......	None.			None.	
11	.....do............	2	All......	None.			None.	
12	Brick............	4	3d, 4th...	1	Iron.........	None............	None.	
13	.....do............	2	All......	None.			None.	
14	.....do............	2	All......	None.			None.	
15	.....do............	3	All......	None.			None.	
16	.....do............	3	All......	2	Iron.........	None............	None.	
17	Frame............	.2	All......	None.			None.	
18	.....do............	2,3	All......	None.		.......,...	None.	
19	.....do............	3	All......	None.			None.	
20	Concrete and frame.	4	All......	[5]1	Wood ladder.	One approach obstructed.	None.	
21	Frame............	2,3	All......	2	.....do.........	None............	None.	
22	Brick and concrete.	2,3	All......	1	.....do.........	.....do............	None.	
23	Brick............	3	All......	[5]2	Iron ladder....	.....do............	None.	
24	Brick and frame.	5	All......	2	Iron.........	1 locked window; 1 exit obstructed.	None.	....
25	Frame............	2	All......	None.			None.	
26	Frame and brick.	3, 3½	All......	[5]2	Wood ladders	None............	None.	

MASSACHUSETTS.

1	Brick............	2	All......	None.			None.	....
2	.....do............	3	All......	None.			None.	....
3	.....do............	4	2d, 3d...	None.			None.	....
4	.....do............	4	3d, 4th...	1	Iron.........	None............	None.	....
5	.....do............	3	All......	1	.....do.........	.....do............	None.	....
6	.....do............	5	2d, 3d, 4th, 5th.	1	.....do.........	.....do............	None.	....
7	.....do............	6	4th, 5th .	1	.....do.........	.....do............	None.	....
8	.....do............	4	3d.........	1	.....do.........	.....do............	None.	....
9	.....do............	5	2d, 3d, 4th, 5th.	1	.....do.........	Packages in front of window.	None.	....

[1] Stairway inclosed.
[2] Wood stairs inclosed in fireproof walls.
[3] Door locked during working hours.
[4] Also each match wrapper has a saucer filled with water and a sponge to extinguish incipient fires.
[5] Sliding.
[6] Not reported.
[7] One door kept locked during working hours.

BUILDING, MEANS OF ESCAPE, AND FIRE-FIGHTING APPARATUS.

MAINE.

Other facilities for escape.								Fire-fighting apparatus.						
Exit doors.			Stairway.				Exit lights or signs provided.	Number of fire extinguishers.	Fire hose on what floors.	Sprinkler system.	Standpipes.	Fire buckets.		Establishment. number.
Not opening outward.		Obstructed.	Properly lighted.	Provided with hand rails.	Fire drills held.							Provided.	Kept full of water.	
External.	Hall.													
2	1	None.	Yes...	No [1]...	No..	No..	None.	None..	Yes.	No..	Yes.	Yes.	1
1	8	None.	Yes...	Yes...	No..	No..	None.	None..	Yes.	Yes..	Yes.	Yes.	2
None.	1	[5] 1	Yes...	No [1]..	No..	No..	5	None..	Yes.	No...	Yes.	Yes.	3
1	1	[5] 1	Yes...	No [1]..	No..	No..	None.	None..	Yes.	Yes..	Yes.	Yes.	4
1	1	None.	{1 yes.. 2 no...}	Yes...	No..	No..	None.	None..	No..	No...	No..	....	5
1	3	None.	No....	Yes...	No..	No..	None.	None..	No..	No...	No..	....	6
1	None.	None.	{1 yes.. 1 no...}	{1 yes.. 1 no...}	No..	No..	None.	None..	No..	No...	Yes.	No..	7
3	4	None.	{1 yes.. 2 no...}	{1 yes.. 2 no...}	No..	No..	4	4th....	No..	No...	Yes.	Yes.	8
2	None.	2	{3 yes.. 2 no...}	{4 yes.. 1 no...}	No..	No..	3	None..	No..	Yes..	No..	....	9
3	None.	4	{4 yes.. 2 no...}	{4 yes.. 2 no...}	No..	No..	11	1st, 2d.	No..	Yes..	No..	....	10
None.	None.	None.	Yes....	No....	No..	No..	None.	1st....	No..	No...	Yes.	Yes.	11
1	1	None.	No.....	No [1]..	No..	No..	None.	None..	No..	No...	No..	....	12
2	None.	None.	Yes....	Yes....	No..	No..	[4] 12	All....	Yes.	Yes..	Yes.	Yes.	13
2	None.	None.	No.....	Yes....	No..	No..	None.	None..	No..	No...	No..	....	14
1	[5] 1	1	Yes....	Yes....	No..	No..	1	1st....	No..	No...	Yes.	Yes.	15
1	None.	None.	Yes....	Yes....	No..	No..	12	None..	Yes.	No...	No..	....	16
None.	None.	None.	No.....	Yes....	No..	No..	3	None..	Yes.	No...	Yes.	Yes.	17
1	None.	([6])	{2 yes.. 2 no...}	{2 yes.. 2 no...}	No..	No..	30	Cellar.	No..	No...	No..	...:...	18
3	None.	[7] 2	No.....	Yes....	No..	No..	1	None..	No..	No...	No..	....	19
5	5	([6])	Yes....	Yes....	No..	No..	4	All [9]..	Yes.	No...	Yes.	Yes.	20
4	None.	([6])	No.....	No [1]..	No..	No..	1	All....	Yes.	No...	No..	....	21
None.	None.	([6])	No.....	Yes....	No..	No..	5	1st [10]..	Yes.	No...	No..	....	22
None.	([11])	([6])	No.....	Yes....	No..	No..	18	All....	Yes.	Yes..	Yes.	Yes.	23
2	1	([6])	Yes....	Yes....	No..	No..	6	None [12]	Yes.	Yes..	Yes.	Yes.	24
1	1	([6])	No.....	No [1]..	No..	No..	([13])	1st....	Yes.	No...	Yes.	Yes.	25
4	5	([6])	No.....	{2 no [1].. 3 yes..}	No..	No..	12	1st, 2d.	Yes.	No...	Yes.	No..	26

MASSACHUSETTS.

1	3	([6])	Yes...	Yes...	No..	No..	4	None .	No..	No...	No..	....	1
5	[5] 6	([6])	Yes...	Yes...	No..	No..	None.	None .	No..	No...	Yes.	Yes.	2
1	None.	[14] 1	Yes...	Yes...	No..	No..	None.	None .	No..	No...	No..	....	3
1	2	([6])	No....	No [1] ..	No..	No..	None.	None .	No..	No...	Yes.	Yes.	4
1	4	([6])	Yes...	Yes...	No..	No..	None.	All....	No..	No...	No..	....	5
1	None.	([6])	Yes...	Yes...	No..	No..	None.	None..	No..	No...	Yes.	Yes.	6
1	2	([6])	Yes...	Yes...	No..	No..	None.	None .	No..	No...	No..	....	7
None.	None.	([6])	Yes...	Yes...	No..	No..	None.	None .	No..	No...	Yes.	Yes.	8
1	3	([6])	No....	Yes...	No..	Yes.	4	None .	No..	No...	Yes.	Yes.	9

[5] Platforms not railed.
[9] Not connected with water, but there are 4 or 5 outside high-pressure water plugs.
[10] In pump room and outside shed.
[11] Some sliding.
[12] Outside hose connections will reach any part of the building.
[13] Extinguishers present, number not reported.
[14] Hall door, second floor, kept locked.

TABLE **III.**—SAFEGUARDING AGAINST FIRE: CHARACTER OF
MASSACHUSETTS—Concluded.

Establishment number.	Building.			Fire escapes.				
				Outside of building.			Inside of building (and incombustible).	
	Construction material.	Number of stories.	Stories occupied by this establishment.	Number.	Material.	Obstructions.	Number.	Obstructions.
10	Brick	4	All......	1	Iron........	10-gallon tin cans on escape; cases in front of one entrance.	None.	....
11	.....do...........	³ 6	All......	6	.....do........	None............	6	None....
12	.....do...........	6	All......	None.	....	....	1	...do....
13	.....do...........	4	4th......	3	Iron..........	Counters in front of window.	None.	....
14	.....do...........	4,6	2d, 3d, 4th.	1	.....do......	None............	⁴ 1	None....
15	.....do...........	4	All......	2	.....do......	Boxes in front of escapes.	None.	....
16	Frame..........	3	All......	None.	....	....	None.	....
17	Concrete and steel.	5	All......	None.	....	....	2	None....
18	Brick...........	7	7th......	1	Iron..........	High bench......	None.	....
19	Stone..........	3	All......	1	.....do......	None............	⁵ 3	None....
20	4 brick, 3 stone...	⁶ 2–5	All......	10	...do......	...do..........	1	...do....
21	3 stone, 1 brick...	³ 3–6	All......	18	...do......	...do..........	⁵ 15	...do....
22	Frame..........	3	All......	None.	....	....	None.	....
23	Brick..........	3	All......	None.	....	....	None.	....
24	Brick and concrete.	6	All......	None.	....	....	4	None ..
25	Brick..........	2	All......	None.	....	....	None.	....
26	.....do...........	3	All......	2	Iron..........	None............	1	None ...
27	Frame..........	2	All......	None.	....	....	1	...do....
28	.....do...........	2	All......	None.	....	....	None.	....
29	.....do...........	4	All......	5	4 wood,1 steel	3 of wood obstructed by tables; storm window.	None.	....
30	.....do...........	3	All......	2	Wood........	Windows do not open outward; table; snow and ice on landing.	None.	....
31	Brick..........	3	All......	3	Iron..........	None............	None.	....
32	.....do...........	4	4th......	1	.....do......	...do..........	None.	....
33	.....do...........	4	All......	2	.....do......	...do..........	3	None....
34	Reenforced concrete.	6	4th......	2	.....do......	...do..........	1	Machines and goods.
35	Frame..........	2	All......	None.	....	....	None.	....
36	.....do...........	3	All......	None.	....	....	None.	....
37	3 brick, 2 frame	⁶ 1,2,3	All......	None.	....	....	None.	....
38	Brick..........	4	All......	1	Iron..........	None............	None.	....
39	Frame..........	2	All......	None.	....	....	None.	....
40	Brick..........	3,4	All......	1	Iron..........	2 landings obstructed by a belt guard box and locked window.	None.	....
41	.....do...........	3,5	All......	6	.....do......	Approach to 1 landing locked.	2	None...
42	Frame..........	2½	All......	1	Wood........	1 landing obstructed by a locked window.	None.	....
43	Brick..........	3	All......	1	.....do......	None............	None.	....
44	.....do...........	3	All......	None.	....	....	None.	....

¹ Not reported.
² Several connected buildings, highest part 6 stories.
³ Sliding.
⁴ From fourth to third floors.
⁵ Wood stairs inclosed in fireproof walls.
⁶ Seven buildings; three 2 stories, one 3, one 4, two 5.

BUILDING, MEANS OF ESCAPE, AND FIRE-FIGHTING APPARATUS—Con.

MASSACHUSETTS—Concluded.

Other facilities for escape.							Fire-fighting apparatus.						
Exit doors.			Stairway.		Fire drills held.	Exit lights or signs provided.	Number of fire extinguishers.	Fire hose on what floors.	Sprinkler system.	Standpipes.	Fire buckets.		Establishment number.
No opening outward.		Obstructed.	Properly lighted.	Provided with hand rails.							Provided.	Kept full of water.	
External.	Hall.												
3	3	(¹)	No....	Yes...	No..	No..	None.	None .	No..	No...	Yes.	Yes.	10
18	None.	(¹)	Yes...	Yes...	No..	No..	42	None .	Yes.	Yes..	Yes.	Yes.	11
2	All [8].	(¹)	Yes...	Yes...	No..	No..	None.	None .	No..	No..	Yes.	Yes.	12
2	2	(¹)	No....	No....	No..	No..	None.	None .	Yes.	No...	Yes.	Yes.	13
1	3	(¹)	No....	Yes...	No..	No..	3	(¹)	No..	No...	Yes.	Yes.	14
2	None.	(¹)	Yes...	Yes...	No..	No..	8	None .	No..	No..	No..	......	15
3	None.	(¹)	Yes...	Yes...	(¹)	No..	4	None .	No..	No...	Yes.	Yes.	16
4	None.	(¹)	Yes...	Yes...	No..	No..	14	None .	Yes.	Yes.	No..	......	17
1	1	(¹)	No....	Yes...	No..	No..	2	None .	No..	No...	Yes.	Yes.	18
None.	None.	None.	Yes...	Yes...	No..	No..	None.	All....	Yes.	Yes.	Yes.	Yes.	19
4	None.	[7]1	{3 no.. 23 yes.}	{3 no.. 23 yes.}	Yes.	No..	100	All....	Yes.	Yes.	Yes.	Yes.	20
None.	None.	None.	Yes...	No[9]..	No..	Yes.	16	All....	Yes.	Yes.	Yes.	Yes.	21
None.	None.	(¹)	Yes...	Yes...	No..	No..	4	None .	No..	No..	No..	......	22
None.	None.	(¹)	Yes...	Yes...	No..	No..	9	All....	No..	Yes.	Yes.	Yes.	23
[8]25	[8]28	(¹)	Yes...	Yes...	No..	No..	30	All....	Yes.	Yes..	No..	......	24
1	2	(¹)	Yes...	Yes...	No..	Yes.	4	None .	Yes.	Yes.	Yes.	Yes.	25
3	7.	(¹)	Yes...	Yes...	No..	No..	None.	All....	No..	Yes.	Yes.	Yes.	26
2	1	(¹)	{1 yes.. 1 no...}	No....	No..	No..	4	None .	No..	No...	Yes.	Yes.	27
3	4	(¹)	{2 yes.. 1 no...}	No[9] .	No..	No..	8	None .	No..	No..	.Yes.	Yes.	28
None.	1	(¹)	{2 yes.. 1 no...}	Yes.	Yes.	Yes.	8	{1st, 2d. 3d.}	Yes.	Yes..	No..	......	29
None.	1	(¹)	Yes...	{1 yes.. 1 no...}	Yes.	No..	9	All....	Yes.	Yes..	No..	......	30
[8]1	None.	(¹)	Yes...	Yes...	No..	Yes.	10	None .	No..	No..	Yes.	Yes.	31
None.	3	(¹)	Yes...	Yes...	No..	No..	None.	None .	No..	Yes.	Yes.	Yes.	32
None.	[8]10	(¹)	Yes...	Yes...	Yes.	No..	8	None .	Yes.	No..	Yes.	Yes.	33
None.	2	(¹)	Yes...	Yes...	No..	No..	2	None .	No..	No..	No..	......	34
1	None.	(¹)	No....	Yes...	No..	No..	None.	None .	Yes.	No..	No..	......	35
1	None.	(¹)	No....	Yes...	No..	No..	9	None .	No..	No..	No..	......	36
(¹)	None.	(¹)	Yes...	{5 no [10] 4 yes..}	No..	No..	None.	None .	Yes.	No..	Yes.	Yes.	37
3	4	(¹)	Yes...	Yes...	No..	No..	1	None .	Yes.	No..	Yes.	Yes.	38
7	None.	(¹)	Yes...	Yes...	No..	No..	2	1st,2d.	Yes.	No..	Yes.	Yes.	39
1	1	(¹)	{2 yes.. 3 no..}	{1 no [10] 4 yes..}	No..	No..	None.	All....	Yes.	Yes.	Yes.	Yes.	40
11	34	(¹)	{8 yes.. 2 no...}	{1 yes[10] 9 no...}	Yes.	Yes.	32	All....	Yes.	Yes.	Yes.	Yes.	41
5	1	(¹)	No....	No [10]..	No..	No..	34	None .	Yes.	Yes.	Yes.	No..	42
3	3	(¹)	Yes...	Yes...	No..	No..	None.	None[11]	Yes.	No..	Yes.	Yes.	43
5	[8]9	(¹)	No....	No [10]..	No..	No..	1	All....	Yes.	No..	No..	......	44

[7] Locked.
[8] Four buildings; two 6 stories, one 5, one 3.
[9] Five buildings; two 1 story, two 2 story, one 3 stories.
[10] Stairways inclosed.
[11] Fire hose on outside of building and connection there and on 2 floors with city mains.

TABLE **III.**—SAFEGUARDING AGAINST FIRE: CHARACTER OF

RHODE ISLAND.

Establishment number.	Building.			Fire escapes.				
	Construction material.	Number of stories.	Stories occupied by this establishment.	Outside of building.			Inside of building (and incombustible).	
				Number.	Material.	Obstructions.	Number.	Obstructions.
1	Frame............	2	All......	None.	....	....	None.	....
2	Brick............	3	All [2].....	None.	....	....	None.	....
3	....do............	5	([3])	1	Iron..........	None............	None.	....
4	....do............	3	All......	None.	....	....	[4] 2	None....
5	....do............	4	All......	2	Iron..........	None............	[4] 3	...do....
6	Stone............	5	All......	5	....do........	....do..........	None.	....
7	Brick............	3	All......	2	....do........	....do..........	None.	....
8	Frame............	2	All......	None.	....	....	None.	....
9	Brick............	4	All......	2	{1 iron, 1 iron and wood.	{In some cases windows open with difficulty.	None.	....
10	....do............	3,4	All......	1	Iron..........	None............	None.	....
11	....do............	1	All......	None.	....	....	None.	....
12	....do............	3,6	1st,2d,3d	2	Iron..........	{Knitting machine; table.	None.	....
13	Frame............	3	All [2].....	None.	....	....	None.	....
14	Brick............	2	All......	None.	....	....	None.	....
15	....do............	5	3d......	1	Iron..........	None............	None.	....
16	....do............	6	3d......	2	....do........	....do..........	None.	....
17	....do............	5	3d, 4th, 5th.	2	....do........	....do..........	None.	....
18	....do............	7	4th,5th.	2	....do........	....do..........	None.	....
19	....do............	7	6th......	1	....do........	....do..........	None.	....
20	....do............	3	All......	None.	....	....	None.	....
21	....do............	1	All......	None.	....	....	None	
22	....do............	3	All......	None.	....	....	None.	....
23	....do............	2	All......	None	....	....	None.	....
24	Stone............	[12] 1–4	All......	4	2 iron, 2 wood	None............	None.	....
25	....do............	4	All......	3	2 iron, 1 wood	{Several exits locked.	None.	....
26	Brick............	2,3	All......	1	Iron..........	None............	None.	....
27	Stone............	4	All......	5	Wood........	{Windows locked; machinery.	None	....

[1] Stairway inclosed.
[2] Third story not used for workroom.
[3] Not reported.
[4] Wood stairs inclosed in fireproof walls.
[5] In hose house.
[6] Locked.
[7] In card room and in hose house.
[8] One sliding.

BUILDING, MEANS OF ESCAPE, AND FIRE-FIGHTING APPARATUS—Con.

RHODE ISLAND.

Other facilities for escape.							Fire-fighting apparatus.						Establishment number.
Exit doors.			Stairway.		Fire drills held.	Exit lights or signs provided.	Number of fire extinguishers.	Fire hose on what floors.	Sprinkler system.	Standpipes.	Fire buckets.		
Not opening outward.		Obstructed.	Properly lighted.	Provided with hand rails.							Provided.	Kept full of water.	
External.	Hall.												
4	6	None.	Yes	No[1]	No	No	None.	None	No	No	No	......	1
None.	None.	None.	Yes	No[1]	No	No	8	None	No	No	Yes	Yes	2
2	None.	None.	Yes	No	No	No	1	None	Yes	No	Yes	Yes	3
None.	None.	1	Yes	Yes	No	No	None.	None	Yes	Yes	Yes	Yes	4
None.	None.	None.	Yes	{1 no[1], 2 yes}	No	No	None.	All	Yes	Yes	Yes	Yes	5
None.	None.	None.	Yes	Yes	No	No	None.	None[5]	Yes	Yes	Yes	Yes	6
None.	None.	[6]2	Yes	{3 no[1], 6 yes}	No	No	None.	(7)	Yes	Yes	Yes	Yes	7
3	1	None.	Yes	Yes	No	No	6	None	Yes	No	Yes	Yes	8
1	[8]11	None.	Yes	{1 no[1], 5 yes}	No	No	8	None	Yes	No	No	......	9
None.	None.	[6]1	Yes	Yes	No	No	None.	All	Yes	No	No	......	10
[6]2	None.	1	Yes[9]	No[1]	No	No	None.	None	Yes	No	Yes	Yes	11
[8]1	3	None.	{3 yes, 3 no}	No[1]	No	No	6	None	Yes	Yes	Yes	Yes	12
3	2	None.	Yes	Yes	No	No	6	None	No	No	Yes	Yes	13
2	None.	None.	Yes	Yes	No	No	None.	None	No	No	Yes	No	14
1	2	None.	Yes	Yes	No	No	1	None	Yes	Yes	No	......	15
None.	1	None.	Yes	Yes	No	No	2	None	Yes	Yes	Yes[10]	Yes	16
None.	7	None.	Yes	Yes	No	No	8	None	No	No	Yes	Yes	17
None.	None.	None.	Yes	Yes	No	No	None.	All	Yes	No	No	......	18
None.	None.	None.	Yes	Yes	No	No	[11]7	None	Yes	Yes	Yes	Yes	19
None.	None.	(2)	{3 yes, 1 no}	{3 yes, 1 no}	No	No	8	None	No	No	Yes	Yes	20
1	None.	None.	Yes[9]	{1 yes[9], 1 no[9]}	No	No	None.	None	Yes	No	Yes	Yes	21
1	1	None.	No	Yes	No	No	2	None	No	No	No	......	22
2	None.	None.	Yes	Yes	No	No	6	None	Yes	No	Yes	Yes	23
1	8	None.	{4 yes, 3 no}	Yes[13]	No	No	None.	None	Yes	Yes	No	......	24
[14]8	1	3	No	No[15]	No	No	None.	All	Yes	No	Yes	No	25
2	2	1	No	{1 yes, 3 no[1]}	Yes[13]	No	None.	All	Yes	No	Yes	Yes	26
3	8	None.	No	No[1]	No	No	5	All	Yes	Yes	Yes	(2)	27

[9] Stairway to basement.
[10] Two 52-gallon tanks kept full of water.
[11] In building; 1 on floor where this shop is located.
[12] Nine buildings, from 1 to 4 stories.
[13] All operators do not drill, but there is an organized fire company.
[14] Sliding.
[15] Four stairways inclosed; 1 not inclosed.

TABLE III.—SAFEGUARDING AGAINST FIRE: CHARACTER OF CONNECTICUT.

Establishment number.	Building.			Fire escapes.				
	Construction material.	Number of stories.	Stories occupied by this establishment.	Outside of building.			Inside of building (and incombustible).	
				Number.	Material.	Obstructions.	Number.	Obstructions.
1	Brick..........	[1]1,3,4	All......	[2]2	Iron........	None; but location almost inaccessible.	None.	....
2	....do..........	4	All......	2	....do.......	Box at window..	None.	....
3	Brick and stone..	3	All......	1	....do.......	None...........	None.	....
4	Brick..........	[4]2,4,5	All......	[5]4	....do.......	....do.........	None.	....
5	Frame..........	3	All......	None.	....	....	None.	....
6	....do..........	4	All......	None.	....	....	None.	....
7	Brick and frame..	[7]3,4	All......	[8]1	Wood........	None[9]	None.	....
8	Brick..........	5	All......	5	Steel........	....do.........	None.	....
9	....do..........	3	All......	None.	....	....	None.	....
10	....do..........	3	All......	2	Iron........	None...........	None.	....
11	....do..........	3	All......	None.	....	....	None.	....
12	....do..........	3	All......	None.	....	....	None.	....
13	....do..........	3	All......	None.	....	....	None.	....
14	....do..........	1	All......	None.	....	....	None.	....
15	Brick and frame..	2	All......	None.	....	....	None.	....
16	Brick..........	6	All......	8	Iron and wood.	None...........	None.	....
17	....do..........	6	All......	7	5 steel, 2 steel and wood.	....do.........	None.	....
18	....do..........	6	All......	6	Iron........	....do.........	1	None....
19	....do..........	[11]1,2	All......	None.	....	....	None.	....
20	....do..........	[12]4,5,6	All......	[13]6	Steel........	None...........	None.	....
21	....do..........	3	All......	1	Iron........	....do.........	None.	....
22	....do..........	3	All......	1	Wood........	....do.........	None.	....
23	Brick and stone.	4	All......	1	Iron and wood.	....do.........	None.	....
24	Brick and frame.	4	All......	None.	....	....	None.	....
25	Brick..........	4	All......	None.	....	....	None.	....
26	....do..........	4	All......	5	Steel........	None...........	None.	....
27	....do..........	4	All......	None.	....	....	None.	....
28	....do..........	5	All......	None.	....	....	None.	....
29	Brick and frame.	3	All......	1	Steel and wood.	None...........	None.	....
30	Brick..........	4	3d	None.	....	....	None.	....
31	....do..........	3	All......	None.	....	....	None.	....
32	....do..........	5	All......	2	Iron........	None...........	None.	....
33	....do..........	2	All......	1	Wood........	....do.........	None.	....
34	....do..........	[15]3	All......	1	Iron........	....do.........	None.	....
35	....do..........	5	All......	None.	....	....	None.	....

[1] Three buildings; one 1, one 3, and one 4 stories.
[2] On 4-story building.
[3] Fire hose on first floor in two buildings; outside for the 4-story building.
[4] Three buildings; one 2, one 4, and one 5 stories.
[5] On 5-story building.
[6] In main building; in other buildings, yes.
[7] Two buildings; one 3, and one 4 stories.
[8] On 4-story building.
[9] Accessible from one floor only.

BUILDING, MEANS OF ESCAPE, AND FIRE-FIGHTING APPARATUS—Con.

CONNECTICUT.

Exit doors. Not opening outward. External.	Hall.	Obstructed.	Stairway. Properly lighted.	Provided with hand rails.	Fire drills held.	Exit lights or signs provided.	Number of fire extinguishers.	Fire hose on what floors.	Sprinkler system.	Standpipes.	Fire buckets. Provided.	Kept full of water.	Establishment number.
15	11	10	Yes...	Yes...	No..	No..	7	(⁸)	Yes.	No...	Yes.	Yes.	1
1	None.	None.	Yes...	Yes...	No..	No..	None.	None .	No..	No...	No..	......	2
1	4	None.	Yes...	Yes...	No..	No..	None.	None.	No..	No...	No..	......	3
1	None.	None.	No⁶...	Yes...	No..	No..	59	All....	Yes.	No...	Yes.	Yes.	4
None.	None.	None.	Yes...	Yes...	No..	No..	None.	All....	Yes.	Yes.	Yes.	Yes.	5
None.	None.	None.	Yes...	Yes...	No..	No..	None.	All....	Yes.	Yes.	Yes.	Yes.	6
7	3	None.	Yes...	Yes...	No..	No..	None.	All....	Yes.	No...	Yes.	Yes.	7
7	None.	None.	Yes...	Yes...	No..	No..	20	All....	Yes.	No...	Yes.	Yes.	8
3	4	None.	Yes...	Yes...	No..	No..	14	All....	Yes.	No...	Yes.	Yes.	9
None.	None.	5	Yes...	Yes...	No..	No..	18	None .	No..	No...	Yes.	Yes.	10
2	None.	None.	Yes...	Yes...	No..	No..	3	None .	No..	No...	Yes.	Yes.	11
5	2	1	Yes...	Yes...	No..	No..	24	All....	No..	No...	Yes.	Yes.	12
2	None.	¹⁰2	Yes...	Yes...	No..	No..	8	None .	No..	No...	Yes.	Yes.	13
None.	None.	None.	......	......	No..	No..	None.	All....	Yes.	No...	Yes.	Yes.	14
7	None.	None.	Yes...	No....	No..	No..	None.	1st....	No..	No...	Yes.	Yes.	15
None.	None.	None.	Yes...	Yes...	Yes.	No..	12	All....	Yes.	Yes.	Yes.	Yes	16
2	None.	9	Yes...	Yes...	No..	No..	30	All....	Yes.	Yes.	Yes.	Yes.	17
2	3	None.	Yes...	Yes...	No..	No..	36	All....	Yes.	Yes.	Yes.	Yes.	18
3	None.	None.	Yes...	Yes...	No..	No..	None.	1st....	Yes.	No...	Yes.	Yes.	19
5	None.	None.	Yes...	Yes...	Yes.	No..	8	All....	Yes.	No...	Yes.	Yes.	20
5	None.	None.	Yes...	Yes...	No..	No..	5	None .	Yes.	No...	Yes.	Yes.	21
6	None.·	None.	No....	No....	No..	No..	None.	None .	Yes.	No...	Yes.	Yes.	22
1	None.	None.	Yes...	Yes...	No..	No..	None.	None .	Yes.	Yes.	Yes.	Yes.	23
2	10	None.	Yes...	Yes...	No..	Yes.	36	All....	Yes.	No...	Yes.	Yes.	24
9	12	None.	Yes...	Yes...	No..	No..	None.	2d, 3d, 4th.	Yes.	No...	Yes.	Yes.	25
4	7	None.	Yes...	No....	No..	No..	None.	None¹⁴	Yes.	No...	Yes.	Yes.	26
None.	None.	None.	Yes...	Yes...	No..	No..	65	None¹⁴	Yes.	Yes.	Yes.	Yes.	27
4	25	None.	Yes...	Yes...	No..	No..	None.	1st....	Yes.	No...	Yes.	Yes.	28
2	1	None.	Yes...	Yes...	No..	No..	18	None .	No..	No...	No..	......	29
2	2	None.	Yes...	Yes...	No..	No..	None.	None .	Yes.	No...	Yes.	Yes.	30
6	None.	None.	Yes...	No....	No..	No..	None.	None .	Yes.	No...	Yes.	Yes.	31
2	None.	None.	Yes...	Yes...	No..	No..	6	None .	No..	No...	Yes.	Yes.	32
3	None.	3	Yes...	Yes...	No..	No..	6	None .	No..	No...	Yes.	Yes.	33
9	None.	None.	Yes...	No⁶...	Yes.	No..	72	All¹⁶ .	Yes.	No...	Yes.	Yes.	34
10	20	(¹⁷)	Yes...	No⁶...	No..	No..	75	None .	Yes.	Yes.	Yes.	Yes.	35

¹⁰ Locked.
¹¹ Two buildings; one 1-story, and one 2 stories.
¹² Three buildings; one 4 stories, one 5, and one 6.
¹³ Two on each building.
¹⁴ Hose in yard.
¹⁵ Two buildings, 3 stories each.
¹⁶ Main building; other building, no fire hose.
¹⁷ Not reported.

TABLE III.—SAFEGUARDING AGAINST FIRE: CHARACTER OF

NEW YORK.

Establishment number.	Building.			Fire escapes.				
	Construction material.	Number of stories.	Stories occupied by this establishment.	Outside of building.			Inside of building (and incombustible).	
				Number.	Material.	Obstructions.	Number.	Obstructions.
1	Brick............	4	All......	None.	....	....	None.	....
2	.....do...........	4	All......	2	Steel.........	None............	None.	....
3	.....do...........	²5,6	All......	6	Iron...........	.....do.......	None.	....
4	.....do...........	6	All......	2	.....do.........	.....do............	None.	....
5	.....do...........	5	All......	2	.....do.........	Doors and windows locked; tables nailed across windows.	None.	....
6	.....do...........	3	All......	None.	....	....	None.	....
7	.....do...........	5	2d, 3d, 4th, 5th.	2	Iron...........	Boxes piled everywhere.	None.	....
8	.....do...........	9	All......	2	.....do.........	None............	1	None....
9	.....do...........	3	All......	None.	....	....	None.	....
10	.....do...........	4	All......	1	Steel.........	Benches........	None.	....
11	.....do...........	4	All......	3	Iron...........	None............	None.	....
12	.....do...........	4	All......	1	Steel.........	Trolley on 2d floor	None.	....
13	.....do...........	3	All......	None.	....	....	None.	....
14	Brick, tile, and steel.	6	All......	None.	....	....	2	None....
15	.....do...........	8	All......	None.	....	....	2	...do.....
16	Brick............	3	All......	2	Iron...........	None............	None.	....
17	.....do...........	4	All......	2	.....do.........	.....do............	None.	....
18	.....do...........	4	All......	2	.....do.........	.....do............	1	None....
19	.....do...........	6,9	All......	2	.....do.........	.....do............	None.	....
20	.....do...........	5	All......	1	.....do.........	.....do............	None.	....
21	.....do...........	7	(¹)	3	.....do.........	.....do............	None.	....
22	.....do...........	3	All......	1	.....do.........	.....do............	None.	....
23	Brick and concrete.	³3,4,5	All......	⁴3	2 iron, 1 wood	Benches and tools across windows.	⁴4	None....
24	Brick............	6	3d......	5	Steel.........	None............	None.	....
25	.....do...........	6	All......	2	.....do.........	.....do............	None.	....
26	.....do...........	5	All......	1	.....do.........	.....do............	None.	....
27	.....do...........	4	3d......	1	.....do.........	.....do............	None.	....
28	.....do...........	7	(¹)	2	.....do.........	Bench and finished work.	None.	....
29	Brick and stone.	4	All......	1	.....do.........	Platform scales; boxes.	None.	....
30	Concrete and steel.	9	4th, 5th.	None.	....	....	4	None....
31	Brick............	6	4th, 5th, 6th.	2	Steel.........	None............	None.	....
32	.....do...........	7	5th......	2	.....do.........	Benches and machinery.	None.	....
33	.....do...........	4	All......	3	.....do.........	Benches........	None.	....
34	Brick and stone..	15	All......	5	Iron...........	None............	3	None....
35	Brick............	7	All......	4	.....do.........	.....do............	None.	....
36	.....do...........	6	All......	2	Steel.........	.....do............	None.	....

¹ Not reported.
² Two buildings; one 5, and one 6 stories.

BUILDING, MEANS OF ESCAPE, AND FIRE-FIGHTING APPARATUS—Con.

NEW YORK.

Other facilities for escape.							Fire-fighting apparatus.						
Exit doors.			Stairway.								Fire buckets.		
Not opening outward.		Ob-struct-ed.	Prop-erly lighted.	Pro-vided with hand rails.	Fire drills held.	Exit lights or signs pro-vid-ed.	Num-ber of fire extin-guish-ers.	Fire hose on what floors.	Sprin-kler sys-tem.	Stand-pipes.	Pro-vid-ed.	Kept full of wa-ter.	Es-tab-lish-ment num-ber.
Exter-nal.	Hall.												
2	None.	(¹)	No....	Yes...	No..	No..	None.	None..	No..	No...	Yes.	Yes.	1
1	None.	(¹)	Yes...	Yes...	No..	No..	12	None..	No..	No...	Yes.	Yes.	2
None.	None.	(¹)	Yes...	Yes...	No..	No..	None.	All....	Yes.	No...	Yes.	Yes.	3
1	None.	None.	Yes...	Yes...	No..	Yes.	None.	None..	No..	No...	Yes.	Yes.	4
None.	None.	(¹)	Yes...	Yes...	No..	No..	None.	None..	No..	No...	Yes.	Yes.	5
2	None.	(¹)	No....	Yes...	No..	No..	None.	None..	No..	No...	Yes.	Yes.	6
None.	None.	(¹)	No....	Yes...	No..	Yes.	8	None..	Yes.	No...	Yes.	Yes.	7
None.	None.	(¹)	Yes...	Yes...	No..	No..	None.	All....	Yes.	No...	Yes.	Yes.	8
2	3	(¹)	Yes...	Yes...	No..	No..	None.	None..	No..	No...	Yes.	Yes.	9
3	None.	(¹)	Yes...	Yes...	No..	No..	15	None..	No..	No...	Yes.	Yes.	10
1	1	(¹) {1 yes.. 1 no...}	{1 yes.. 1 no...}		No..	No..	8	3d, 4th	Yes.	Yes..	Yes.	Yes.	11
None.	None.	(¹)	Yes...	Yes...	No..	No..	5	All....	No..	Yes..	Yes.	Yes.	12
None.	None.	(¹)	Yes...	Yes...	No..	No..	3	All....	No..	Yes..	Yes.	Yes.	13
None.	None.	None.	Yes...	Yes...	No..	No..	8	None..	Yes.	Yes..	Yes.	Yes.	14
None.	None.	(¹)	Yes...	Yes...	No..	No..	None.	None..	Yes.	Yes..	Yes.	Yes.	15
None.	None.	(¹)	Yes...	Yes...	No..	No..	12	All....	Yes.	Yes..	Yes.	Yes.	16
None.	None.	None.	Yes...	Yes...	No..	No..	None.	None..	Yes.	Yes..	Yes.	Yes.	17
1	None.	(¹) {1 yes.. 1 no.}	Yes...		No..	No..	7	{2d,3d, 4th.}	Yes.	Yes..	No........		18
None.	None.	None.	Yes...	No...	No..	No..	25	All....	Yes.	Yes..	Yes.	Yes.	19
2	None.	None.	Yes...	Yes...	No..	No..	12	All....	Yes.	No..	No....		20
None.	None.	(¹)	Yes...	Yes...	No..	No..	None.	None..	No..	No..	Yes.	Yes.	21
None.	None.	None.	Yes...	Yes...	No..	Yes.	30	None..	Yes.	No..	Yes.	Yes.	22
None.	None.	(¹)	Yes...	Yes...	No..	No..	None.	All....	Yes.	No..	Yes.	Yes.	23
1	3	(¹)	No....	Yes...	No..	No..	16	None..	Yes.	No..	Yes.	Yes.	24
3	None.	(¹)	Yes...	Yes...	No..	No..	None.	None..	No..	No..	Yes.	Yes.	25
2	None.	(¹)	Yes...	Yes...	No..	No..	1	None..	No..	No..	Yes.	Yes.	26
1	1	(¹)	Yes...	Yes...	No..	No..	None.	None..	No..	No..	No........		27
2	None.	(¹)	Yes...	Yes...	No..	No..	None.	None..	No..	No..	Yes.	Yes.	28
1	None.	(¹)	No....	Yes...	No..	No..	None.	None..	No..	No..	Yes.	Yes.	29
1	None.	(¹)	Yes...	Yes...	No..	No..	18	None..	Yes.	None	Yes.	Yes.	30
1	None.	(¹)	Yes...	Yes...	No..	No..	6	None..	Yes.	Yes..	Yes.	Yes.	31
2	14	(¹)	Yes...	Yes...	No..	No..	None.	All....	No..	Yes..	Yes.	Yes.	32
4	None.	(¹)	Yes...	Yes...	No..	No..	None.	None..	No..	No...	Yes.	Yes.	33
None.	None.	(¹)	Yes...	Yes...	No..	Yes.	60	All....	Yes.	No..	No........		34
1	None.	None.	Yes...	Yes...	No..	Yes.	60	All....	Yes.	Yes..	Yes.	Yes.	35
3	6	1	Yes...	Yes...	No..	Yes.	None.	None..	Yes.	Yes..	Yes.	Yes.	36

¹ Five buildings; two 3 stories, two 4 stories, one 5 stories.
⁴ None on the two 4-story buildings.

TABLE **III.**—SAFEGUARDING AGAINST FIRE: CHARACTER OF

NEW JERSEY.

Establishment number.	Building.			Fire escapes.				
				Outside of building.			Inside of building (and incombustible).	
	Construction material.	Number of stories.	Stories occupied by this establishment.	Number.	Material.	Obstructions.	Number.	Obstructions.
1	Brick............	4	All......	1	Iron.........	None............	None.	....
2	.....do............	6	All......	6	2 iron, 4 iron and wood.	.....do............	None.	....
3	.....do............	4	All......	5	Iron.........	One exit obstructed by locked room; one by benches and table.	None.	....
4	.....do............	3	All......	4	.....do......	One exit obstructed by packing table.	None.	....
5	.....do............	4	All......	1	.....do......	Approaches obstructed by furniture.	None.	....
6	.....do............	4	All......	3	.....do......	None............	1	None....
7	.....do............	5	All......	None.			None.	....
8	.....do............	4	All......	1	Iron.........	None............	1	None....
9	.....do............	1	All......	None.			None.	....
10	.....do............	1	All......	None.			None.	....
11	.....do............	5	All......	6	Iron.........	None............	None.	....
12	.....do............	2	All......	None.			None.	....
13	.....do............	3	All......	None.			None.	....
14	.....do............	4	3d, 4th,.	1	Iron.........	None......	None.	....
15	.....do............	4	All......	4	.....do......	.....do......	None.	....
16	.....do............	4	All......	None.			None.	....
17	.....do............	2	All......	None.			None.	....
18	.....do............	3	All......	None.			None.	....
19	.....do............	4	All......	None.			None.	....
20	.....do............	3	All......	None.			None.	....
21	Brick and concrete.	8	All......	4	3 iron, 1 iron and concrete.	None............	6	None....
22	Brick............	2	All......	None.			None.	....
23	.....do............	4,5	All......	7	Iron and wood.	None............	None.	....
24	.....do............	4	All......	(1)	Steel.........	None............	1	None....
25	.....do............	1,3	All......	None.			None.	....
26	.....do............	(2)	(2)	(2)	(2)	(2)	(2)	(2)
27	.....do............	2	All......	None.			None.	

[1] Fire escapes provided, but number not reported.

BUILDING, MEANS OF ESCAPE, AND FIRE-FIGHTING APPARATUS--Con.

NEW JERSEY.

Exit doors. Not opening outward. External.	Exit doors. Not opening outward. Hall.	Exit doors. Obstructed.	Stairway. Properly lighted.	Stairway. Provided with hand rails.	Fire drills held.	Exit lights or signs provided.	Number of fire extinguishers.	Fire hose on what floors.	Sprinkler system.	Standpipes.	Fire buckets. Provided.	Fire buckets. Kept full of water.	Establishment number.
2	None.	None.	Yes...	Yes...	Yes.	No..	13	All....	Yes.	Yes..	Yes.	Yes.	1
21	2	None.	Yes...	Yes...	Yes.	Yes.	25	All....	Yes.	Yes..	Yes.	Yes.	2
2	None.	None.	Yes...	Yes...	No..	No..	15	None .	No..	No...	Yes.	No..	3
1	None.	None.	Yes...	Yes...	No..	No..	None.	None .	No..	No...	Yes.	Yes.	4
1	None.	None.	Yes...	Yes...	No..	No..	None.	None .	No..	No...	Yes.	Yes.	5
None.	None.	None.	Yes...	Yes...	No..	Yes.	None.	All....	Yes.	No...	Yes.	Yes.	6
None.	None.	None.	Yes...	Yes...	No..	No..	1	All....	Yes.	No...	Yes.	Yes.	7
5	2	None.	Yes...	Yes...	No..	No..	70	None .	Yes.	Yes..	No..		8
2	1	None.	....	....	No..	No..	8	All....	No..	No...	Yes.	No..	9
None.	None.	None.	....	....	No..	No..	2	All....	Yes.	No...	Yes.	Yes.	10
1	None.	None.	Yes...	{12 no. 4 yes.}	No..	No..	None.	All....	No..	No...	Yes.	Yes.	11
1	1	1	Yes...	Yes...	No..	No..	25	None..	No..	No...	Yes.	Yes.	12
2	1.	None.	Yes...	No...	No..	No..	None.	None..	No..	No...	Yes.	Yes.	13
1	1	None.	Yes...	No...	No..	No..	None.	None..	No..	No...	Yes.	Yes.	14
None.	None.	None.	Yes...	Yes...	No..	No..	None.	None..	Yes.	No...	Yes.	Yes.	15
2	None.	None.	Yes...	Yes...	No..	No..	8	None..	No..	No...	Yes.	Yes.	16
None.	None.	None.	Yes...	Yes...	No..	No..	30	All....	No..	No...	No..		17
4	None.	None.	Yes...	Yes...	No..	No..	6	None..	No..	No...	Yes.	Yes.	18
1	1	None.	Yes...	Yes...	No..	No..	None.	All....	Yes.	No...	Yes.	Yes.	19
None.	1	None.	Yes...	Yes...	No..	No..	None.	None..	No..	No...	Yes.	Yes.	20
None.	None.	None.	Yes...	Yes...	No..	No..	None.	All....	Yes.	Yes..	Yes.	Yes.	21
None.	None.	None.	Yes...	Yes...	No..	No..	None.	None..	No..	No...	Yes.	Yes.	22
9	None.	None.	Yes...	Yes...	No..	No..	75	All....	Yes.	Yes..	Yes.	Yes.	23
None.	None.	None.	Yes...	Yes...	Yes.	Yes.	500	1st....	Yes.	Yes..	Yes.	Yes.	24
None.	None.	None.	Yes...	Yes...	Yes.	Yes.	4,000	Hose room.	Yes.	No...	Yes.	Yes.	25
(1)	(1)	(1)	(1)	(1)	(1)	(1)	(1)	(1)	(1)	(1)	(1)	(1)	26
None.	None.	None.	Yes...	Yes...	No..	Yes.	7	All....	Yes.	No...	Yes.	Yes.	27

1 Not reported.

TABLE **III.**—SAFEGUARDING AGAINST FIRE: CHARACTER OF
PENNSYLVANIA.

[Establishments 4, 5, 6, 7, 8, 14, 15, 16, 17, 18, 22, 25, 26, 28, 29, 31, 32, 33, 34, 39, 40, 41, 42, 43 46, 47, 48, 49, 13, 21, 23, 24, 27, 37, 38, and 45 are in cities of the second class (population 100,000 to 1,000,000). Estab

Establishment number.	Building.			Fire escapes.				
	Construction material.	Number of stories.	Stories occupied by this establishment.	Outside of building.			Inside of building (and incombustible).	
				Number.	Material.	Obstructions.	Number.	Obstructions.
1	Brick............	5	All......	16	12 wood, 4 steel.	Two barrels in stairway to fire escape.	None.	....
2	....do............	5	All......	1	Iron..........	None............	None.	....
3	....do............	3	All......	2	....do..........	....do	None.	....
4	....do............	4	All......	3	....do..........	Work benches, machinery on 4th floor.	None.	....
5	Brick and concrete.	5	All......	None.	....	....	2	None....
6	Brick............	6	(¹)	1	Iron..........	None............	None.	....
7	....do............	5	(¹)	1	....do..........	Work table at window.	1	None....
8	....do............	4	All......	1	....do..........	None............	None.	....
9	....do............	6	All......	2	....do..........	....do...........	None.	....
10	....do............	5	All......	2	....do..........	....do...........	None.	....
11	....do............	5	All......	1	....do..........	....do...........	(²)	None....
12	....do............	3	All......	1	....do..........	....do...........	None.	....
13	....do............	3	All......	None.	....	....	None.	....
14	....do............	5	All......	3	Steel..........	None...........	None.	....
15	....do............	6	All......	2	....do..........	....do...........	1	None....
16	Brick and stone³.	....	....					
17	Brick............	5	All......	2	Steel..........	None...........	2	None....
18	Brick and steel..	1	All......	None.	....	....	None.	....
19	Steel............	1	All......	None.	....	....	None.	....
20	Frame (metal sheathed).	1	All......	None.	....	....	None.	....
21	Brick and steel..	4	All......	2	Iron..........	Machinery.......	None.	....
22	....do............	5	All......	1	....do..........	None............	²2	None....
23	Brick............	6	All......	2	....do..........	....do...........	None.	....
24	....do............	6	All......	2	....do..........	....do...........	None.	....
25	....do............	4	All......	1	....do..........	....do...........	None.	....
26	....do............	4	All......	None.	....	....	2	(⁶)
27	....do............	5	All......	1	Iron..........	None............	1	None....
28	Brick and cement.	3	All......	1	....do..........	....do...........	None.	....
29	Brick............	5	All......	None.	....	....	1	(⁶)
30	....do............	3,4	All......	None.	....	....	⁷7	None....
31	....do............	6	All......	None.	....	....	²2	...do....
32	....do............	4	All......	None.	....	....	²3	...do....
33	....do............	4	All......	2	Iron..........	None............	²1	...do....
34	....do............	6	2d, 3d, 4th.	1	....do..........	Boxes in front of windows.	None.	....
35	....do............	1	All......	1	....do..........	None...........	None.	....
36	....do............	1	All......	None.	....	....	None.	....
37	....do³..........	3	All......	None.	....	....	None.	....
38	Brick, concrete, steel.	3	All......	3	Iron..........	None...........	None.	....
39	Brick............	6	All......	1	....do..........	....do...........	1	None....
40	....do............	5	All......	None.	....	....	²2	...do....
41	....do............	5	4th, 5th.	None.	....	....	1	...do....
42	....do............	2,3	All......	None.	....	....	None.	....
43	....do............	3	All......	None.	....	....	²1	(⁹)
44	Brick, iron, frame.¹⁰	2	All......	None.	....	....	None.	....
45	Brick iron......	¹¹1,3	All......	2	Wood..........	None...........	None.	.........,..
46	Brick............	2	All......	4	Iron..........	....do...........	None.	....
47	....do............	¹²5	All......	None.	....	....	None	....
48	Brick and stone	¹³1,2	All......	1	Steel..........	None...........	1	None....
49	Brick............	4	All......	6	....do..........	....do...........	3	...do....
50	....do............	5	All......	2	....do..........	....do...........	2	...do....

¹ Not reported.
² Wood stairs inclosed in fireproof walls.
³ Factory occupies basement only; data for building not reported.
⁴ On 3 floors, not specified.
⁵ Work table.
⁶ One door nailed; another obstructed by pile of material.
⁷ Stairways to basement.

BUILDING, MEANS OF ESCAPE, AND FIRE-FIGHTING APPARATUS—Con.

PENNSYLVANIA.

and 50 are in cities of the first class (population 1,000,000 or over). Establishments 1, 2, 3, 9, 10, 11, 12, lishments 19, 20, 30, 35, 36, and 44 are in communities of less than 100,000 population.]

Other facilities for escape.							Fire-fighting apparatus.						
Exit doors.			Stairway.				Number of fire extinguishers.	Fire hose on what floors.	Sprinkler system.	Standpipes.	Fire buckets.		Establishment number.
Not opening outward.		Obstructed.	Properly lighted.	Provided with hand rails.	Fire drills held.	Exit lights or signs provided.					Provided.	Kept full of water.	
External.	Hall.												
None.	None.	None.	Yes...	Yes...	Yes.	Yes.	50	All....	Yes.	Yes..	Yes.	Yes.	1
1	None.	None.	Yes...	Yes...	No..	No..	None.	2	None..	Yes.	No...	Yes.	Yes.	2
5	None.	1	Yes...	Yes...	No..	No..	None.	2	None..	No..	No...	Yes.	Yes.	3
1	1	None.	Yes...	Yes...	No..	Yes.	12	2d, 3d, 4th.	Yes.	Yes..	Yes.	Yes.	4
None.	None.	None.	Yes...	Yes...	No..	Yes.	None.	All....	Yes.	Yes..	No..	....	5
1	5	None.	Yes...	Yes...	No..	No..	None.	None..	No..	No...	Yes.	Yes.	6
None.	5	None.	No....	Yes...	No..	Yes.	None.	None..	No..	No...	Yes.	Yes.	7
1	None.	None.	No....	Yes...	No..	No..	None.	None..	No..	No...	Yes.	Yes.	8
None.	None.	None.	Yes...	Yes...	No..	No..	28	All....	No..	Yes..	Yes.	No..	9
1	None.	None.	Yes...	Yes...	No..	No..	9	None..	No..	No...	Yes.	Yes.	10
1	None.	None.	Yes...	Yes...	No..	No..	None.	All....	No..	No...	No..	....	11
None.	None.	None.	No....	Yes...	No..	No..	None.	None..	No..	No...	Yes.	Yes.	12
1	None.	None.	Yes...	Yes...	No..	No..	None.	None..	No..	No...	Yes.	Yes.	13
None.	None.	None.	Yes...	Yes...	No..	No..	12	None..	Yes.	Yes..	Yes.	Yes.	14
None.	None.	None.	Yes...	Yes...	No..	Yes.	None.	All....	Yes.	Yes..	Yes.	Yes.	15
....													16
None.	None.	None.	Yes...	Yes...	No..	Yes.	None.	(4)	Yes.	Yes..	Yes.	Yes.	17
None.	None.	None.	....	....	No..	Yes.	None.	All....	No..	No...	Yes.	Yes.	18
7	None.	None.	....	....	No..	No..	1	All....	No..	No...	Yes.	Yes.	19
None.	None	None.	....	....	No..	No..	2	None.	No..	No...	No..	....	20
6	1	None.	Yes...	Yes...	Yes.	No..	16	All....	Yes.	Yes..	Yes.	Yes.	21
None.	None.	None.	Yes...	Yes...	No..	Yes.	2	1st....	Yes.	Yes..	Yes.	Yes.	22
None.	None.	None.	Yes...	Yes...	No.:	No..	None.	None..	Yes.	No...	No..	....	23
1	None.	None.	Yes...	No....	No..	No..	None.	All....	Yes.	Yes..	Yes.	Yes.	24
1	None.	1	Yes...	Yes...	No..	No..	3	1st....	No..	No...	Yes.	Yes.	25
1	1	None.	Yes...	Yes...	No..	No..	None.	None..	No..	No...	Yes.	Yes.	26
1	None.	None.	Yes...	Yes...	No..	No..	None.	All....	No..	Yes..	No..	....	27
None.	None.	None.	Yes...	Yes...	Yes.	No..	3	None..	No..	No...	Yes.	Yes.	28
None.	1	None.	Yes...	Yes...	No..	No..	None.	All....	No..	No...	Yes.	No..	29
None.	None.	None.	Yes...	Yes...	No..	No..	None.	All....	No..	Yes..	No..	....	30
None.	None.	None.	Yes...	Yes...	Yes.	Yes.	3	All....	Yes.	No...	No..	....	31
1	1	None.	Yes...	Yes...	Yes.	No..	24	None..	Yes.	Yes..	Yes.	Yes.	32
1	1	None.	Yes...	Yes...	No..	Yes.	6	None.	Yes.	Yes..	Yes.	Yes.	33
1	None.	None.	No....	Yes...	No..	No..	None.	None..	No..	No...	Yes.	Yes.	34
None.	None.	None.	....	....	No..	No..	12	All....	Yes.	No...	No..	....	35
1	None.	1	Yes?..	Yes?..	No..	No..	None.	All....	No..	No...	No..	....	36
1	1	None.	Yes...	Yes...	No..	No..	4	All....	Yes.	Yes..	Yes.	Yes.	37
2	None.	None.	Yes...	Yes...	No..	No..	143	All....	No..	Yes..	Yes.	Yes.	38
1	None.	None.	Yes...	Yes...	No..	No..	1	None.	Yes.	Yes..	Yes.	Yes.	39
None.	None.	None.	Yes...	Yes...	Yes.	Yes.	8	None.	Yes.	Yes..	Yes.	No..	40
1	1	None.	Yes...	Yes...	No..	Yes.	None.	None	No..	No...	Yes.	Yes.	41
4	2	None.	No....	Yes...	No..	No..	None.	1st, 2d	No..	No...	Yes.	Yes.	42
1	1	None.	No....	No....	No..	No..	None.	None	No..	No...	No..	....	43
1	None.	None.	Yes...	Yes...	Yes.	No..	40	All....	Yes.	Yes..	Yes.	Yes.	44
3	None.	None.	Yes...	Yes...	No..	No..	15	None	No..	No...	Yes.	Yes.	45
12	None.	None.	Yes...	Yes...	No..	No..	None.	All....	No..	No...	Yes.	Yes.	46
None.	None.	None.	Yes...	Yes...	No..	Yes.	None.	All....	Yes.	Yes..	Yes.	Yes.	47
None.	All....	None.	Yes...	No....	Yes.	Yes.	None.	1st...	Yes.	Yes..	Yes.	Yes.	48
None.	None.	None.	Yes...	Yes...	Yes.	No..	None.	All....	Yes.	Yes..	Yes.	Yes.	49
None.	None.	None.	Yes...	Yes...	Yes.	No..	None.	All....	Yes.	Yes..	Yes.	Yes.	50

[8] Data for this establishment refer only to building where women are employed.
[9] Door hard to open; steps covered with rubbish.
[10] Three buildings; 1 brick, 1 iron, 1 frame.
[11] Two buildings; one 1-story, one 3-story.
[12] Four buildings, each 5 stories.
[13] Two buildings, each 2 stories; several buildings, 1 story each.

Table III.—SAFEGUARDING AGAINST FIRE: CHARACTER OF

OHIO.

Establishment number.	Building.			Fire escapes.				
				Outside of building.			Inside of building (and incombustible).	
	Construction material.	Number of stories.	Stories occupied by this establishment.	Number.	Material.	Obstructions.	Number.	Obstructions.
1	Brick............	4	All......	1	Iron.........	None............	None.	....
2	.....do..........	5	All......	1	.....do......	.....do..........	None.	....
3	.....do..........	6	All......	1	.....do......	On 1 floor partition with door between window and workroom; on 3 floors, work tables in way.	None.	
4	.....do..........	4	All......	1	.....do......	None............	None.	....
5	.....do..........	4	All......	2	.....do......	.....do..........	2	None....
6	.....do..........	4	All......	1	.....do......	.....do..........	None.	....
7	.....do..........	3	All......	1	.....do......	.....do..........	None.	....
8	.....do..........	4	All......	1	.....do......	Work benches obstruct one entrance.	None.	....
9	.....do..........	4	All......	2	.....do......	None............	None.	....
10	.....do..........	4	All......	1	.....do......	.....do..........	None.	....
11	Brick and concrete.	3	All......	1	Concrete and wood.	.....do..........	None.	....
12	Brick............	5,6	All......	1	Iron.........	On 1 floor table against window.	None.	....
13	.....do..........	5	All......	2	.....do......	None............	None.	....
14	.....do..........	6	All......	1	.....do......	.....do..........	None.	....
15	.....do..........	4	All......	None.			None.	....
16	.....do..........	4	All......	1	Iron.........	None............	None.	....
17	.....do..........	4	All......	1	.....do......	.....do..........	None.	....
18	.....do..........	6	All......	1	.....do......	.....do..........	1	None....
19	.....do..........	4	All......	1	.....do......	.....do..........	None.	....
20	Concrete.........	2,3	All......	None.			1	None....
21	Brick............	3	All......	1	Iron.........	None............	None.	....
22	.....do..........	3	All......	2	.....do......	.....do..........	None.	....
23	.....do..........	4	All......	None.			²3	None....
24	.....do..........	6	All......	1	Iron.........	None............	None.	....
25	Brick and concrete.	6	4th, 5th, 6th. (¹)	1	.....do......	.....do..........	1	None....
26	Brick............	6	(¹)	1	.....do......	.....do..........	None.	....
27	.....do..........	3	All......	None.			²1	None....
28	.....do..........	2,3	All......	None.			None.	....
29	.....do..........	4	All......	1	Iron.........	None............	6	None....
30	.....do..........	2	All......	None.			7	..do....
31	.....do..........	2	All......	None.			None.	....
32	.....do..........	2	All......	None.			None.	....
33	.....do..........	4	All......	1	Iron.........	None............	None.	....
34	.....do..........	4	All......	1	.....do......	.....do..........	None.	....
35	.....do..........	4	All......	1	.....do......	.....do..........	None.	....
36	.....do..........	4	All......	2	.....do......	.....do..........	None.	....
37	.....do..........	6	All......	1	.....do......	.....do..........	None.	....
38	.....do..........	5	All......	1	.....do......	.....do..........	None.	....
39	.....do..........	4	All......	2	.....do......	.....do..........	None.	....
40	.....do..........	4	All......	1	.....do......	.....do..........	None.	....
41	.....do..........	⁴2,3,4	All......	None.			None.	....
42	.....do..........	⁵3,4	All......	None.			None.	....
43	.....do..........	3	All......	3	Wood........	None............	None.	....
44	.....do..........	3	All......	None.			None.	....
45	Brick (metal sheathed).	⁷1,3	All......	None.			None.	....
46	Brick............	⁸1,2,3	All......	None.			None.	....
47	Brick (metal sheathed).	⁹1,2,3	All......	None.			None.	....

¹ Not reported.
² Wood stairs inclosed in fireproof walls.
³ Location not reported.
⁴ Two buildings; one, 2 stories; one, part 3 and part 4 stories.
⁵ Four buildings; three 3 stories, one 4 stories.

BUILDING, MEANS OF ESCAPE, AND FIRE-FIGHTING APPARATUS—Con.

OHIO.

Other facilities for escape.							Fire-fighting apparatus.						Establishment number.
Exit doors.			Stairway.		Fire drills held.	Exit lights or signs provided.	Number of fire extinguishers.	Fire hose on what floors.	Sprinkler system.	Standpipes.	Fire buckets.		
Not opening outward.		Obstructed.	Properly lighted.	Provided with hand rails.							Provided.	Kept full of water.	
External.	Hall.												
1	None.	None.	Yes...	Yes...	No..	No..	None.	1st....	Yes.	No...	No		1
None.	None.	None.	Yes...	Yes...	No..	No..	None.	None .	No..	No...	Yes.	Yes.	2
2	None.	None.	Yes...	Yes...	No..	No..	None.	None .	No..	No...	Yes.	Yes.	3
1	None.	None.	Yes..	Yes...	No..	No..	None.	None .	No..	No...	Yes.	Yes.	4
2	None.	None.	Yes...	Yes...	Yes.	Yes.	None.	All....	No..	No...	Yes.	Yes.	5
None.	None.	None.	Yes...	Yes...	No..	No..	12	None .	No..	No...	No..		6
None.	None.	None.	Yes...	Yes...	No..	No..	None.	None .	No..	No...	No..		7
None.	None.	None.	Yes...	Yes...	No..	No..	None.	None .	No..	No...	No..		8
None.	None.	None.	Yes...	Yes...	No..	No..	4	All....	No..	No...	No..		9
1	None.	None.	Yes...	Yes...	No..	Yes.	5	None .	No..	No...	No..		10
None.	None.	None.	Yes...	Yes...	No..	No..	None.	None .	No..	No...	No..		11
1	None.	None.	Yes...	Yes...	No..	No..	None.	None .	No..	No...	Yes.	Yes.	12
1	None.	None.	Yes...	Yes...	No..	No..	16	None .	Yes.	No...	No..		13
1	None.	None.	Yes...	Yes...	No..	No..	2	None .	No..	No...	Yes.	Yes.	14
1	None.	None.	Yes...	Yes...	No..	No..	None.	None .	No..	No...	No..		15
None.	1	None.	Yes...	Yes...	No..	Yes.	72	None .	No..	No...	Yes.	Yes.	16
1	None.	None.	Yes...	Yes...	No..	Yes.	12	None .	Yes.	No...	Yes.	Yes.	17
1	None.	None.	Yes...	Yes...	Yes.	No..	27	None .	No..	No...	No..		18
None.	None.	None.	Yes..	Yes...	Yes.	No..	3	All....	No..	No...	Yes.	Yes.	19
None.	None.	None.	Yes...	Yes...	Yes.	No..	40	All....	No..	No...	No..		20
None.	None.	None.	Yes...	Yes...	No..	No..	12	All....	No..	No...	No..		21
1	None.	(1)	Yes...	Yes...	No..	No..	None.	1st....	Yes.	Yes.	Yes.	Yes.	22
None.	None.	None.	Yes...	Yes...	No..	No..	None.	None .	Yes.	Yes.	Yes.	Yes.	23
None.	None.	None.	Yes...	Yes...	No..	Yes.	12	All....	No..	Yes.	Yes.	Yes.	24
None.	None.	1	Yes...	Yes...	No..	No..	9	None .	No..	No...	No..		25
1	None.	None.	Yes...	Yes...	No..	No..	None.	Yes[8].	Yes.	Yes.	Yes.	Yes.	26
4	1	None.	Yes...	Yes...	No..	No..	None.	All....	Yes.	Yes.	Yes.	Yes.	27
6	None.	None.	Yes...	Yes...	No..	No..	2	All....	Yes.	Yes.	Yes.	Yes.	28
47	None.	None.	Yes...	Yes...	No..	Yes.	25	All....	Yes.	No...	Yes.	Yes.	29
10	None.	None.	Yes...	Yes...	Yes.	No..	25	All....	No..	No...	Yes.	Yes.	30
1	None.	None.	Yes...	Yes...	No..	No..	12	All....	Yes.	No...	Yes.	Yes.	31
None.	None.	None.	Yes...	Yes...	No..	No..	40	All....	Yes.	No...	Yes.	Yes.	32
None.	None.	None.	Yes...	Yes...	No..	Yes.	None.	1st....	Yes.	No...	No..		33
None.	None.	None.	Yes...	Yes...	No..	Yes.	40	Yes[8].	Yes.	No...	Yes.	Yes.	34
None.	1	None.	Yes...	Yes...	No..	Yes.	8	All....	Yes.	Yes.	No...		35
1	None.	None.	Yes...	Yes...	No..	Yes.	None.	None .	No..	No...	Yes.	Yes.	36
1	None.	None.	Yes...	Yes...	No..	Yes.	13	None .	No..	No...	Yes.	Yes.	37
1	None.	None.	Yes...	Yes...	No..	Yes.	6	Yes[8].	No..	No...	Yes.	Yes.	38
1	None.	None.	Yes...	Yes...	No..	Yes.	None.	All....	No..	Yes.	Yes.	Yes.	39
None.	None.	None.	Yes...	Yes...	No..	Yes.	None.	All....	No..	No...	Yes.	Yes.	40
None.	None.	None.	Yes...	Yes...	No..	No..	None.	All....	Yes.	No...	Yes.	Yes.	41
None.	None.	None.	Yes...	Yes...	No..	No..	10	1st....	Yes.	No...	Yes.	No..	42
15	None.	None.	Yes...	Yes...	No..	No..	6	All....	Yes.	No...	Yes.	Yes.	43
6 40	None.	None.	No....	No....	No..	No..	None.	All....	No..	Yes.	No...		44
None.	None.	None.	Yes...	Yes...	No..	No..	None.	All....	No..	Yes.	Yes.	Yes.	45
1	None.	None.	Yes...	Yes...	Yes.	No..	None.	1st....	No..	Yes.	Yes.	Yes.	46
10	None.	None.	Yes...	Yes...	No..	No..	None.	(10)	Yes.	Yes.	Yes.	Yes.	47

[6] Sliding.
[7] Eight buildings; one 3 stories, seven 1 story.
[8] Four buildings; one 3 stories, one 2 stories, two 1 story.
[9] Seven buildings; three 3 stories, two 2 stories, two 1 story.
[10] Reels for 4 buildings.

TABLE **III.**—SAFEGUARDING AGAINST FIRE: CHARACTER OF

OHIO—Concluded.

Es-tab-lish-ment num-ber.	Building.			Fire escapes.				
	Construction material.	Num-ber of sto-ries.	Stories occupied by this estab-lish-ment.	Outside of building.			Inside of building (and incom-bustible).	
				Num-ber.	Material.	Obstructions.	Num-ber.	Obstruc-tions.
48	Brick........	[1] 1,4	All......	None.			None.	
49	....do..........	[2] 1	All......	None.			None.	
50	Concrete........	8	All......	None.			1	None....
51	Brick....	2	All......	None.			None.	
52	....do..........	2	All......	None.			None.	
53	....do..........	5	All......	None.			None.	
54	Brick and steel..	6	All......	20	Steel	None...........	7	None....
55	Brick...........	1,2,3	All......	4	....do.......	....do......	None.	
56	....do..........	3	All......	2	....do.......	....do......	[3] 2	None....
57	....do..........	3	All......	2	....do.......	....do......	None.	
58	....do..........	4	All......	1	....do.......	....do......	None.	
59	....do..........	1,3	All......	1	....do.......	....do......	None.	
60	B r i c k a n d cement.	3	All [4]....	None.			None.	

ILLINOIS.

1	Brick...........	3	1st......	1	Iron..........	None...........	None.	
2	....do..........	6	5th......	2	....do.......	....do......	None.	
3	....do..........	4	All......	13	....do.......	....do......	None.	
4	....do..........	4	2d.......	2	1 iron, 1 wood.	....do......	None.	
5	....do..........	4	All......	1	Iron..........	....do......	None.	
6	....do..........	5	All......	2	....do.......	....do......	None.	
7	....do..........	3	1st......	1	....do.......	....do......	None.	
8	....do..........	5	All......	2	....do.......	....do......	None.	
9	....do..........	3	All......	1	....do.......	....do......	None.	
10	....do..........	3, 4	All......	4	....do.......	Work benches....	None.	
11	....do..........	5	All......	4	....do.......	None...........	None.	
12	....do..........	7	All......	2	....do.......	....do......	None.	
13	....do..........	5	All......	2	....do.......	Boxes in front of exits; machine on 4th floor.	None.	
14	....do..........	6	All [5]....	3	....do.......	None...........	None.	
15	....do..........	3	All [5]....	1	....do.......	....do......	None.	
16	....do..........	3	All [5]....	2	....do.......	....do......	None.	
17	....do..........	5	All [5]....	2	....do.......	....do......	None.	
18	....do..........	4	All [5]....	1	Wood	....do......	None.	
19	Stone...........	5	2d, 3d, 4th, 5th	1	Iron..........	On 5th floor, window fasten-ed and machine in front of it.	None.	
20	Brick and steel..	5	All......	None.			1	None....
21	Brick...........	5	All......	2	Iron..........	None...........	None.	
22	....do..........	6	All......	2	....do.......	....do......	None.	
23	....do..........	5	All......	8	....do.......	....do......	None.	
24	....do..........	4	4th......	1	....do.......	....do......	None.	
25	....do..........	6	3d.......	3	....do.......	....do......	None.	
26	....do..........	3	All......	None.			None.	
27	....do..........	4	All......	1	Iron..........	None...........	2	None....
28	....do..........	7	6th......	6	....do.......	....do......	None.	
29	....do..........	4	All......	None.			None.	
30	B r i c k a n d cement.	[10] 4	All......	None.			1	None....

[1] Two buildings; one 1 story, one 4 stories.
[2] Three buildings, 1 story each.
[3] Wood stairs inclosed in fireproof walls.
[4] All employees on second floor.
[5] Not reported.
[6] All sliding.

BUILDING, MEANS OF ESCAPE, AND FIRE-FIGHTING APPARATUS—Con.

OHIO—Concluded.

Not opening outward — External	Not opening outward — Hall	Obstructed	Properly lighted	Provided with hand rails	Fire drills held	Exit lights or signs provided	Number of fire extinguishers	Fire hose on what floors	Sprinkler system	Standpipes	Fire buckets — Provided	Fire buckets — Kept full of water	Establishment number
None.	None.	None.	Yes...	Yes...	No..	No..	12	All....	No..	Yes.	Yes.	Yes.	48
None.	None.	None.	......	......	No..	No..	1	All....	No..	Yes.	Yes.	Yes.	49
2	None.	None.	Yes..	Yes..	No..	Yes.	25	All....	No..	No..	No..	......	50
None.	None.	None.	Yes..	Yes..	No..	No..	None.	1st..	No..	No..	No..	......	51
3	None.	None.	Yes..	Yes..	No..	No..	3	1st..	No..	No..	No..	......	52
None.	None.	None.	Yes..	Yes..	No..	No..	None.	All....	Yes.	No..	No..	......	53
None.	None.	None.	Yes..	Yes..	No..	Yes.	1,000	All....	Yes.	Yes.	Yes.	Yes.	54
None.	None.	None.	Yes..	Yes..	No..	Yes.	215	All....	Yes.	Yes.	Yes.	Yes.	55
None.	None.	None.	Yes..	Yes..	No..	Yes.	50	All....	Yes.	Yes.	Yes.	Yes.	56
None.	None.	None.	Yes..	Yes..	No..	Yes.	None.	All....	Yes.	Yes.	Yes.	Yes.	57
None.	None.	None.	Yes..	Yes..	No..	Yes.	None.	All....	Yes.	Yes.	Yes.	Yes.	58
None.	None.	None.	Yes..	Yes..	No..	No..	30	All....	Yes.	Yes.	Yes.	Yes.	59
None.	None.	None.	Yes..	Yes..	No..	No..	6	All....	Yes.	Yes.	Yes.	Yes.	60

ILLINOIS.

Not opening outward — External	Not opening outward — Hall	Obstructed	Properly lighted	Provided with hand rails	Fire drills held	Exit lights or signs provided	Number of fire extinguishers	Fire hose on what floors	Sprinkler system	Standpipes	Fire buckets — Provided	Fire buckets — Kept full of water	Establishment number
2	None.	1	([8])	([8])	No..	No..	None.	None .	No..	No...	No...	......	1
None.	1	None.	Yes..	Yes..	No..	No..	None.	None .	No..	No...	No...	......	2
([8])	None.	None.	Yes..	Yes..	Yes.	Yes.	100	All....	Yes.	Yes..	Yes.	Yes.	3
None.	None.	None.	Yes..	Yes..	No..	Yes.	2	None .	Yes.	No..	Yes.	Yes.	4
4	None.	None.	Yes..	Yes..	No..	No..	60	None .	Yes.	No..	Yes.	Yes.	5
None.	None.	3	Yes..	Yes..	No..	No..	24	None .	Yes.	No..	No...	......	6
3	None.	2	([8])	([8])	No..	No..	None.	None .	No..	No...	No...	......	7
None.	None.	([8])	Yes..	Yes..	No..	No..	12	None .	No..	Yes..	Yes.	Yes.	8
2	None.	([8])	Yes..	No[7]..	No..	No..	None.	None .	No..	No...	No...	......	9
3	None.	None.	Yes..	Yes..	No..	No..	12	None .	Yes.	No..	No[8].	......	10
None.	4	([8])	No...	No[7]..	No..	Yes.	None.	None .	Yes.	No..	No...	......	11
4	4	([8])	Yes..	Yes..	No..	Yes.	None.	None .	Yes.	No..	No...	......	12
2	None.	([8])	Yes..	No[7]..	No..	Yes.	None.	All....	No..	Yes..	Yes.	Yes.	13
1	None.	None.	Yes..	Yes..	No..	No..	3	3d,6th	Yes.	Yes..	Yes.	Yes.	14
1	None.	None.	Yes..	Yes..	No..	No..	1	3d.....	Yes.	Yes..	Yes.	Yes.	15
None.	None.	None.	Yes..	Yes..	No..	No..	2	None .	Yes.	Yes..	Yes.	Yes.	16
None.	None.	None.	Yes..	Yes..	No..	No..	1	All....	Yes.	Yes..	Yes.	Yes.	17
None.	None.	None.	Yes..	Yes..	No..	No..	1	All....	Yes.	Yes..	Yes.	Yes.	18
None.	None.	None.	Yes..	Yes..	No..	Yes.	4	None .	Yes.	No..	Yes.	Yes.	19
None.	None.	([8])	Yes..	Yes..	No..	No..	16	None .	Yes.	Yes..	Yes.	Yes.	20
2	[10]10	None.	Yes..	Yes..	No..	Yes.	10	None .	No..	No...	Yes.	Yes.	21
2	6	None.	No...	Yes..	No..	No..	None.	None .	No..	No...	No...	......	22
None.	None.	None.	Yes..	Yes..	Yes.	Yes.	None.	All....	No..	Yes..	Yes.		23
None.	11	None.	Yes..	Yes..	No..	Yes.	12	All....	No..	No...	No...	......	24
None.	[10]2	None.	Yes..	Yes..	No..	Yes.	5	None .	Yes.	No...	No...	......	25
20	None.	None.	Yes..	Yes..	Yes.	No..	100	All....	Yes.	Yes..	Yes.	Yes.	26
None.	None.	([8])	Yes..	Yes..	No..	No..	36	None .	Yes.	Yes..	Yes.	Yes.	27
None.	1	None.	Yes..	Yes..	No..	Yes.	None.	None .	Yes.	Yes..	No...	......	28
4	12	None.	Yes..	Yes..	No..	No..	None.	All....	Yes.	No...	Yes.	Yes.	29
4	[11]14	None.	No....	Yes..	No..	No..	10	None .	Yes.	No...	Yes.	Yes.	30

[7] Stairway inclosed.
[8] Sand and blankets in flat steel room for extinguishing fire.
[9] Whole establishment, but only those departments employing females were scheduled.
[10] Two buildings, 4 stories each.
[11] Some sliding.

TABLE **III.**—SAFEGUARDING AGAINST FIRE: CHARACTER OF

ILLINOIS—Concluded.

Establishment number.	Building.			Fire escapes.				
	Construction material.	Number of stories.	Stories occupied by this establishment.	Outside of building.			Inside of building (and incombustible).	
				Number.	Material.	Obstructions.	Number.	Obstructions.
31	Brick............	1	All......	None.	....	....	None.	....
32	.....do............	5	All......	1	Iron..........	On 4th floor, piles of cardboard.	None.	....
33	.....do............	5	All......	2	.....do......	None.............	None.	....
34	.....do............	4	3d, 4th..	1	.....do......	.....do.......	None.	....
35	.....do............	6	All......	2	.....do......	.....do.......	⁴1	None....
36	.....do............	3	All......	1	.....do......	No rope on pulley of sliding door to fire escape.	None.	....
37	.....do............	7	3d, 4th, 5th, 6th, 7th.	6	Iron..........	Soap frames close to window.	None.	....
38	Brick and frame.	⁵1, 2, 3	All......	⁵5	.....do......	None.............	None.	....
39	Brick............	1	All......	None.	....	....	None.	....
40	.....do............	6	All......	4	Iron..........	None.............	None.	....
41	.....do............	5	All......	2	.....do......	.....do.......	None.	....
42	.....do............	3	All......	3	.....do......	.....do.......	None.	....
43	.....do............	6	All......	6	.....do......	.....do.......	None.	....
44	Brick and concrete.	4	All......	None.	....	....	3	None....
45	Brick............	3 and loft.	All......	None.	....	....	None.	....
46	Brick and frame.	3	All......,	None.	....	....	None.	....
47	Brick and concrete.	1	All......	None.	....	....	None.	....

INDIANA.

Establishment number.	Construction material.	Number of stories.	Stories occupied.	Number.	Material.	Obstructions.	Number.	Obstructions.
1	Brick............	4	All......	1	Iron..........	None.............	None.	....
2	Frame............	2	All......	None.	....	....	None.	....
3	Brick............	1 and loft.	All......	None.	....	....	None.	....
4	.....do............	3	All......	5	Iron..........	None.............	None.	....
5	.....do............	1,2	All......	None.	....	....	None.	....
6	.....do............	2,4	All......	1	Iron..........	None.............	None.	....
7	.....do............	5	All......	2	.....do......	.....do.......	None.	....
8	.....do............	4	All......	1	.....do......	.....do.......	None.	....
9	.....do............	3	3d.......	1	.....do......	.....do.......	None.	....
10	.....do............	3	2d.......	1	.....do......	.....do.......	None.	....
11	.....do............	3	All......	2	.....do......	.....do.......	None.	....
12	.....do............	3	All......	2	.....do......	.....do.......	None.	....
13	.....do............	3	All......	None.	....	....	None.	....
14	.....do............	4	All......	1	Iron..........	None.............	None.	....
15	.....do............	4	All......	1	.....do......	.....do.......	None.	....
16	.....do............	4	All......	3	.....do......	.....do.......	None.	....
17	.....do............	1	All......	None.	....	....	None.	....
18	.....do............	3	All......	None.	....	....	None.	....
19	.....do............	4	All......	1	Iron..........	None.............	None.	....
20	.....do............	3	All......	1	.....do......	Exit through locked storage room.	None.	....

¹ Some sliding.
² Not reported.
³ Sliding.
⁴ Wood stairs inclosed in fireproof walls.
⁵ Three buildings; one 1 story, one 2 stories, one 3 stories.
⁶ On 3-story building.

BUILDING, MEANS OF ESCAPE, AND FIRE-FIGHTING APPARATUS—Con.

ILLINOIS—Concluded.

| Other facilities for escape. | | | | | | | Fire-fighting apparatus. | | | | | | |
Exit doors. Not opening outward. External.	Hall.	Stairway. Obstructed.	Properly lighted.	Provided with hand rails.	Fire drills held.	Exit lights or signs provided.	Number of fire extinguishers.	Fire hose on what floors.	Sprinkler system.	Standpipes.	Fire buckets. Provided.	Kept full of water.	Establishment number.
[1]8	[1]6	(2)	......	....	No..	No..	None.	All....	Yes.	No...	Yes.	Yes.	31
[3]2	None.	(2)	Yes...	Yes...	No..	Yes.	12	None .	No..	Yes..	No..	......	32
3	8	None.	Yes...	Yes...	No..	Yes.	15	None .	Yes.	Yes..	Yes.	Yes.	33
2	None.	None.	Yes...	Yes...	Yes.	No..	8	None .	No..	No...	Yes.	Yes.	34
[1]7	15	(2)	Yes...	Yes...	No..	Yes.	8	All....	No..	Yes..	No..	......	35
None.	None.	None.	Yes...	Yes...	No..	No..	None.	None .	No..	No...	Yes.	Yes.	36
4	30	None.	No....	Yes...	No..	Yes.	None.	1st....	Yes.	Yes..	Yes.	Yes.	37
All.	(7)	None.	No....	Yes...	No..	No..	None.	All ...	Yes.	Yes..	Yes.	Yes.	38
3	8	(2)	......	....	No..	No..	6	All ...	No..	No...	No..	......	39
[1]5	[1]18	None.	Yes...	Yes...	No..	No..	14	All ...	No..	Yes..	Yes.	Yes.	40
2	3	(2)	No....	Yes...	No..	No..	10	All ...	No..	No...	Yes.	No..	41
None.	None.	None.	No....	No....	No..	No..	None.	None .	No..	No...	No..	......	42
5	None.	(2)	Yes...	Yes...	No..	No..	54	None .	No..	Yes..	Yes.	Yes.	43
3	10	(2)	Yes...	Yes...	No..	Yes.	12	None .	Yes.	No...	Yes.	Yes.	44
5	None.	(2)	No....	No....	No..	No..	12	All ...	Yes.	No...	Yes.	Yes.	45
3	None.	(2)	No....	No....	No..	No..	None.	None .	No..	No...	No..	......	46
8	None.	(2)	......	....	No..	No..	6	All ...	No..	No...	Yes.	Yes.	47

INDIANA.

External.	Hall.	Obstructed.	Properly lighted.	Provided with hand rails.	Fire drills held.	Exit lights or signs provided.	Number of fire extinguishers.	Fire hose on what floors.	Sprinkler system.	Standpipes.	Provided.	Kept full of water.	Establishment number.
None.	None.	None.	Yes...	Yes...	No..	No..	12	1st...	Yes.	No...	Yes.	Yes.	1
3	None.	None.	No....	Yes...	No..	No..	None.	None .	No..	No...	No..	......	2
[3]8	None.		....	....	No..	No..	5	None .	No..	No...	No..	......	3
[1]24	18	None.	No....	Yes...	Yes.	No..	24	All ...	Yes.	No...	Yes.	Yes.	4
6	None.	5	Yes...	Yes...	No..	No..	None.	None .	Yes.	Yes..	No..	......	5
[1]10	None.	None.	Yes...	Yes...	No..	No..	163	All ...	Yes.	Yes..	Yes.	Yes.	6
None.	2	None.	Yes...	Yes...	No..	Yes.	24	All ...	No..	Yes..	No..	......	7
3	None.	2	Yes...	No....	No..	Yes.	6	None .	No..	No...	No..	......	8
None.	None.	1	Yes...	Yes...	No..	No..	None.	None .	No..	No...	No..	......	9
1	None.	None.	Yes...	No....	No..	No..	None.	None .	No..	No...	Yes.	(8)	10
2	4	None.	Yes...	Yes...	No..	No..	None.	Basement.	Yes.	Yes..	Yes.	Yes.	11
5	None.	None.	Yes...	Yes...	No..	No..	12	None[9].	Yes.	No...	Yes.	(10)	12
2	None.	None.	Yes...	Yes...	No..	No..	None.	2 floors	No..	No...	No..	......	13
[1]3	1	None.	Yes...	Yes...	No..	No..	4	All ...	Yes.	Yes..	No..	......	14
3	8	None.	Yes...	Yes...	No..	No..	None.	None .	No..	No...	Yes.	Yes.	15
[1]3	1	None.	Yes...	Yes...	No..	No..	24	None .	Yes.	Yes..	Yes[11]	Yes.	16
4	None.	None.	......	....	No..	No..	2	All ...	No..	No...	No..	......	17
3	None.	None.	Yes...	Yes...	No..	No..	6	1st ...	Yes.	No...	No..	......	18
1	None.	None.	Yes...	Yes...	No..	No..	9	All...	Yes.	No...	No..	......	19
5	None.	None.	Yes...	Yes...	No..	No..	None.	None.	No..	No...	Yes.	Yes.	20

7 Several do not open outward; exact number not reported.
8 Water in barrel near by.
9 Hose in outside hose house.
10 Water in barrels; sand is provided for smothering benzine fires.
11 In attic only.

TABLE III.—SAFEGUARDING AGAINST FIRE: CHARACTER OF
INDIANA—Concluded.

Establishment number.	Building.			Fire escapes.				
	Construction material.	Number of stories.	Stories occupied by this establishment.	Outside of building.			Inside of building (and incombustible).	
				Number.	Material.	Obstructions.	Number.	Obstructions.
21	Brick............	[1] 2,3	All......	[2] 6	Iron..........	None............	None.	....
22	....do...........	3	All......	None.	....	....	2	None....
23	....do...........	3	All [3].....	None.	....	....	None.	....
24	Frame..........	2	All......	None.	....	....	None.	....
25	Brick..........	2	All......	None.	....	....	None.	....
26	....do...........	3	All......	None.	....	....	None.	....
27	....do...........	3	All......	None.	....	....	None.	....
28	....do...........	[6] 2,3	All......	[7] 2	Iron..........	None............	None.	....
29	....do...........	1	All......	None.	....	....	None.	....
30	....do...........	3	All [3].....	None.	....	....	None.	....
31	....do...........	4	All......	None.	....	....	None.	....
32	....do...........	4	1st and basement.	([8])	([8])	([8])	([8])	([8])
33	....do...........	3	All......	1	Iron..........	None............	None.	....
34	....do...........	4	All......	None.	....	....	None.	....
35	....do...........	1 and basement.	All......	None.	....	....	None.	
36	....do...........	1,2	All......	None.	....	....	None.	....
37	....do...........	2,3	All......	None.	....	....	None.	....
38	....do...........	3	All......	None.	....	....	None.	....
39	....do...........	3	2d......	None.	....	....	None.	....
40	{....do...........	3	All......	None.	....	....	None.	....
	{Frame..........	2	All......	None.	....	....	None.	....
41	Brick..........	1,4	All......	None.	....	....	None.	....
42	Brick and frame.	1,2	All......	None.	....	....	None.	....
43	Brick and frame (metal sheathed).	1	All......	None.	....	....	None.	....
44	Brick..........	2,3	All......	3	2 iron,1 wood.	None............	None.	....
45	....do...........	[13] 3,4	All......	1	Wood..........	....do.........	None.	....
46	{....do...........	4	All......	4	Iron..........	....do.........	None.	....
	{....do...........	5	All......	4	....do.........	....do.........	None.	....
	{....do...........	6	All......	2	....do.........	....do.........	None.	....
47	....do...........	[14] 3	All......	[15] 2	....do.........	....do.........	None.	....

[1] Four buildings; one 2 stories, three 3 stories.
[2] Three on one 3-story building; one on each of other buildings.
[3] Third floor used for storage only.
[4] Locked during working hours.
[5] On one side only; needed on both sides.
[6] Three principal buildings; one 2 stories, two 3 stories.
[7] One on each of the 3-story buildings.
[8] Not reported.

BUILDING, MEANS OF ESCAPE, AND FIRE-FIGHTING APPARATUS—Con.

INDIANA—Concluded.

Other facilities for escape.							Fire-fighting apparatus.						Establishment number.
Exit doors.			Stairway.		Fire drills held.	Exit lights or signs provided.	Number of fire extinguishers.	Fire hose on what floors.	Sprinkler system.	Standpipes.	Fire buckets.		
Not opening outward.		Obstructed.	Properly lighted.	Provided with hand rails.							Provided.	Kept full of water.	
External.	Hall.												
None.	None.	None.	Yes...	Yes...	No..	Yes.	None.	All....	Yes.	No...	Yes.	Yes.	21
13	None.	None.	Yes...	Yes...	No..	No..	40	All....	No..	Yes..	Yes.	Yes.	22
2	None.	[4]1	Yes...	Yes...	No..	No..	48	All....	No..	No..	No..		23
3	None.	None.	Yes...	Yes...	No..	No..	None.	All....	No..	No..	Yes.	Yes.	24
3	1	None.	No....	Yes[5]..	No..	No..	None.	All....	No..	No..	No..		25
None.	None.	None.	Yes...	Yes...	No..	No..	16	All....	Yes.	No..	Yes.	Yes.	26
2	....	None.	Yes...	Yes...	No..	No..	None.	2d, 3d.	No..	Yes..	Yes.	Yes.	27
11	None.	None.	Yes...	Yes...	No..	No..	19	None.	Yes.	Yes..	Yes.	Yes.	28
12	6	None.	....	....	No..	No..	10	All....	Yes.	No..	Yes.	Yes.	29
5	None.	None.	Yes...	Yes...	No..	No..	24	None.	No..	No..	Yes.	Yes.	30
2	1	None.	Yes...	Yes...	No..	No..	6	All....	No..	Yes.	Yes.	Yes.	31
4	None.	None.	Yes...	Yes...	No..	No..	8	None.	Yes.	Yes..	No..	......	32
4	None.	None.	Yes...	Yes...	No..	No..	13	None.	No..	No..	No..	......	33
4	None.	None.	Yes...	Yes...	No..	No..	25	None.	Yes.	Yes..	Yes.	Yes.	34
1	2	None.	Yes...	Yes...	No..	No..	None.	None.	No..	No..	No..	......	35
2	None.	None.	Yes...	Yes...	Yes.	No..	100	All....	Yes.	Yes..	Yes.	Yes.	36
[9]13	1	None.	No....	Yes...	No..	No..	15	None[10]	No..	No..	No..	......	37
4	None.	None.	Yes...	Yes...	No..	No..	55	None[10]	Yes.	No..	Yes.	Yes.	38
1	None.	None.	Yes...	No....	No..	No..	None.	None.	No..	No..	No..	......	39
1	None.	None.	Yes...	Yes...	No..	No..	8	All....	No..	No..	No..		} 40
None.	None.	None.	Yes...	Yes...	No..	No..	4	None.	No..	No..	No..		
All.[9]	(9)	None.	Yes...	Yes...	Yes.	No..	None.	All....	Yes.	No..	Yes.	Yes.	41
10	3	None.	No....	No....	No..	No..	3	None.	No..	No..	No..		42
(9)	4	None.	....	....	Yes.	No..	None.	All....	Yes.	No..	Yes.	Yes.	43
3	None.	None.	Yes...	Yes...	No..	No..	24	All....	No..	Yes.	Yes.	Yes[11]	44
7	None.	None.	Yes...	Yes...	No..	No..	None.	All....	No..	Yes.	Yes.	No..	45
10	2	None.	Yes...	Yes...	Yes.	Yes.	15	All....	Yes.	Yes.	No[13]	......	
[9]13	None.	None.	Yes...	Yes...	Yes.	Yes.	6	3d....	Yes.	Yes.	No..		} 46
10	10	None.	Yes...	Yes...	No..	No..	44	All....	No..	Yes.	Yes.	Yes.	
8	(9)	None.	Yes...	Yes...	No..	No..	54	All....	No..	Yes.	Yes.	Yes.	47

9 Some sliding.
10 Hose in outside hose house.
11 Water in barrels; buckets of sand also provided.
12 Two buildings; one 3 stories, one 4 stories.
13 Buckets filled with sand in cement room.
14 Two buildings, 3 stories each.
15 On each building.

TABLE III.—SAFEGUARDING AGAINST FIRE: CHARACTER OF

MICHIGAN.

Establishment number.	Building.			Fire escapes.				
	Construction material.	Number of stories.	Stories occupied by this establishment.	Outside of building.			Inside of building (and incombustible).	
				Number.	Material.	Obstructions.	Number.	Obstructions.
1	Brick..........	4	All......	2	Iron.........	None...........	None.	....
	Frame..........	3	All......	None.			None.	
	....do..........	2	All......	None.			None.	
2	Brick..........	3	All......	None.			¹2	None....
3	....do..........	3	All......	None.			None.	
4	....do..........	7	All......	4	Iron.........	None...........	None.	....
5	....do..........	5	All......	None.			None.	....
6	....do..........	5	All......	2	Iron.........	None...........	None.	
7	....do..........	5	All......	None.			¹3	None....
8	....do..........	2	All......	None.			None.	
9	....do..........	3	All......	2	Iron.........	None...........	None.	
10	....do..........	2	All......	None.			None.	
11	....do..........	4	All......	1	Iron.........	None...........	¹2	None....
12	Brick and cement	4	All......	None.			3	None....
13	Brick..........	2	All......	None.			None.	
14	....do..........	2	All......	None.			None.	
15	....do..........	6	All......	1	Iron.........	None...........	¹2	None....
16	....do..........	5	All......	2	....do........	....do........	None.	
	Brick and frame.	4	All......	2	....do........	....do........	None.	
17	Brick..........	5	All......	2	....do........	....do........	None.	
	....do..........	4	All......	1	....do........	....do........	None.	
	....do..........	5	All......	3	....do........	....do........	None.	
18	....do..........	4	All......	3	....do........	....do........	¹2	None....
19	Frame..........	3	All......	3	1 iron, 2 wood	....do........	None.	....

WISCONSIN.

Establishment number.	Building.			Fire escapes.				
	Construction material.	Number of stories.	Stories occupied by this establishment.	Outside of building.			Inside of building (and incombustible).	
				Number.	Material.	Obstructions.	Number.	Obstructions.
1	Brick..........	2	All......	None.			None.	
2	....do..........	4	All......	None.			None.	
3	....do..........	3	All......	None.			None.	
4	Brick and stone..	2	All......	None.			None.	
5	Brick..........	4	All......	1	Iron.........	None...........	None.	
6	Brick and concrete.	7	All......	2	....do........	....do........	None.	
7	Brick..........	3	All......	None.			None.	
8	....do..........	5	All......	2	Iron.........	Entrances (windows) 3 feet from floor; workbench obstructs 1 entrance.	None.	
9	....do..........	3	All......	5	2 iron, 3 wood.	None...........	None.	
10	....do..........	6	All......	4	Iron.........	....do........	None.	None....
11	Brick and concrete.	1,4	All......	None.			2	None....
12	Brick..........	5	2d, 3d, 5th.	2	Iron.........	None...........	None.	
13	Stone..........	2	All......	None.			None.	
14	Brick..........	¹⁰1,4	1st, 2d¹¹.	None.			None.	
15	....do..........	5	All......	8	Iron.........	None...........	None.	
16	....do..........	1	All......	None.			None.	
17	....do..........	2	All......	None.			None.	
18	....do..........	1	All......	None.			None.	
19	....do..........	1	All......	None.			None.	

¹ Wood stairways inclosed in fireproof walls.
² Sliding.
³ Basement and seventh.
⁴ Men are instructed how to proceed in case of fire.
⁵ Some sliding.
⁶ Except stairway leading to basement.

BUILDING, MEANS OF ESCAPE, AND FIRE-FIGHTING APPARATUS—Con.

MICHIGAN.

Exit doors: Not opening outward — External	Hall	Obstructed	Properly lighted	Stairway: Provided with hand rails	Fire drills held	Exit lights or signs provided	Number of fire extinguishers	Fire hose on what floors	Sprinkler system	Standpipes	Fire buckets — Provided	Fire buckets — Kept full of water	Establishment number
None.	None.	None.	Yes...	Yes...	No..	Yes.	4	All....	No..	No..	No..		
None.	None.	None.	Yes...	Yes...	No..	No..	4	All....	No..	No..	Yes.	Yes.	1
None.	None.	None.	Yes...	Yes...	No..	No..	4	All....	No..	No..	Yes.	Yes.	
[2]4	None.	None.	Yes...	Yes...	No..	No..	20	None.	Yes.	Yes..	Yes.	Yes.	2
2	8	1	Yes...	Yes...	No..	No..	14	None..	No..	No..	No..		3
1	None.	None.	Yes...	Yes...	Yes.	Yes.	None.	([5])	No..	No..	Yes.	Yes.	4
None.	None.	None.	Yes...	No...	No..	No..	None.	All....	No..	No..	Yes.	Yes.	5
4	4	None.	No....	Yes...	No..	Yes.	5	None.	Yes.	No..	No..		6
1	None.	None.	Yes...	Yes...	No..	No..	12	All....	Yes.	Yes..	Yes.	Yes.	7
[2]6	None.	None.	Yes...	Yes...	No..	No..	8	All....	Yes.	Yes..	Yes.	No..	8
1	2	None.	Yes...	Yes...	No..	No..	7	None..	No..	No..	Yes.	Yes.	9
4	None.	None.	Yes...	Yes...	Yes.	No..	6	All....	No..	Yes..	Yes.	Yes.	10
None.	None.	None.	Yes...	Yes...	No[4].	Yes.	25	All....	Yes.	Yes..	Yes.	Yes.	11
10	All.[2]	None.	Yes...	Yes...	No..	No..	None.	All....	Yes.	Yes..	Yes.	Yes.	12
5	3	None.	Yes...	Yes...	No..	No..	None.	1st..	Yes.	No..	Yes.	Yes.	13
None.	None.	None.	Yes...	Yes...	No..	No..	None.	All....	No..	No..	Yes.	Yes.	14
[6]5	None.	None.	Yes...	Yes...	No..	No..	24	All....	No..	Yes..	Yes.	Yes.	15
5	None.	None.	Yes...	Yes...	No..	No..	10	None..	No..	No..	No..		
8	1	None.	Yes[4].	Yes...	No..	No..	None.	All....	No..	No..	No..		16
None.	5	None.	Yes...	Yes...	No..	No..	10	All....	No..	No..	Yes.	Yes.	
[2]3	None.	None.	Yes...	Yes...	No..	No..	10	All....	No..	No..	Yes.	Yes.	
[2]2	5	None.	Yes...	Yes...	No..	No..	10	All....	No..	No..	Yes.	Yes.	17
[6]12	None.	None.	Yes...	Yes...	No..	Yes.	None.	All....	Yes.	Yes..	Yes.	([7])	18
2	None.	None.	Yes...	Yes...	No..	No..	None.	None..	Yes.	Yes..	Yes.	([7])	19

WISCONSIN.

Exit doors: Not opening outward — External	Hall	Obstructed	Properly lighted	Stairway: Provided with hand rails	Fire drills held	Exit lights or signs provided	Number of fire extinguishers	Fire hose on what floors	Sprinkler system	Standpipes	Fire buckets — Provided	Fire buckets — Kept full of water	Establishment number
2	None.	([8])	Yes...	Yes...	No..	No..	5	All....	No..	No..	Yes.	Yes.	1
None.	None.	None.	Yes...	Yes...	No..	No..	None.	None..	No..	No..	Yes.	Yes[7]	2
1	None.	([8])	Yes...	Yes...	No..	No..	7	None..	No..	No..	No..		3
4	None.	([8])	Yes...	Yes...	No..	No..	None.	None..	No..	No..	No..		4
1	None.	([8])	Yes...	Yes...	No..	No..	24	All....	Yes.	Yes..	No..		5
None.	None.	([8])	Yes...	Yes...	No..	No..	16	All....	No..	Yes..	Yes.	No..	6
None.	None.	None.	Yes...	Yes...	No..	No..	12	1st,2d.	No..	No...	Yes.	Yes.	7
None.	None.	None.	Yes...	Yes...	No..	No..	None.	None..	Yes.	Yes..	Yes.	Yes.	8
6	None.	None.	Yes...	Yes...	No..	No..	12	All....	Yes.	Yes..	Yes.	Yes.	9
None.	None.	None.	Yes...	Yes...	No..	No..	None.	1st...	Yes.	Yes..	No..		10
8	All.[2]	None.	Yes...	Yes...	Yes.	No..	None.	All....	Yes.	Yes..	Yes.	Yes.	11
3	None.	None.	Yes...	Yes...	No..	No..	None.	All....	Yes.	Yes..	No[9]	Yes[7]	12
None.	None.	([8])	Yes...	Yes...	No..	No..	None.	All....	No..	No..	Yes.	Yes.	13
16	([8])	None.	No....	Yes...	No..	No..	20	Main..	No..	No..	Yes.	Yes.	14
4	All.[2]	None.	Yes...	Yes...	No..	No..	None.	All....	Yes.	Yes..	Yes.	Yes.	15
3	None.	([8])	....	....	No..	No..	36	None..	No..	No..	No..		16
2	2	([8])	Yes...	Yes...	No..	No..	8	None..	No..	No..	Yes.	Yes[7]	17
1	5	([8])	....	....	No..	No..	30	All....	No..	No..	No..		18
2	None.	([8])	....	....	No..	No..	12	None..	No..	No..	No..		19

[7] Water in barrels.
[8] Not reported.
[9] On 1 floor only.
[10] Two buildings; one 4 stories, one 1 story.
[11] Only second floor of the 4-story building.

TABLE III.—SAFEGUARDING AGAINST FIRE: CHARACTER OF

MARYLAND.

Establishment number.	Building.			Fire escapes.				
				Outside of building.			Inside of building (and incombustible).	
	Construction material.	Number of stories.	Stories occupied by this establishment.	Number.	Material.	Obstructions.	Number.	Obstructions.
1	Brick............	2	All......	None.			None.	....
2	....do...........	1	All......	None.	....	....	None.	....
3	Frame...........	1	All......	None.	....	....	None.	....
4	Brick............	4	All......	1	Steel..........	None............	None.	....
5	....do...........	2	All......	None.	....	....	None.	....
6	....do...........	3	All......	None.	....	....	None.	....
7	....do...........	3	All......	1	Iron...........	None............	None.	....
8	....do...........	3	All......	1	....do.........	....do.........	None.	....
9	....do...........	5	All......	1	....do.........	....do.........	None.	....
10	....do...........	4,6	All......	1	....do.........	....do.........	None.	....
11	....do...........	4,5	All......	None.	....	....	None.	....
12	Brick and iron...	9	All......	1	Steel..........	None............	None.	....
13	Brick............	3	All......	2	Wrought iron.	....do.........	None.	....
14	Brick and iron...	4	All......	2	....do.........	....do.........	1	None....
15	Brick............	6	All......	1	....do.........	....do.........	None.	....
16	....do...........	5	All......	1	Iron...........	....do.........	None.	....
17	Concrete........	5	All......	None.	....	....	None.	....
18	Brick............	4	All......	1	Steel..........	Toilet and dressing rooms in front of windows leading to escape.	None.	....
19	....do...........	3	All......	None.	....	....	None.	....
20	....do...........	7	All......	1	Iron...........	None............	None.	....
21	....do...........	[4]6,7	All......	[5]2	Steel..........	Counter across room on 5th floor of 1 building.	[5]5	None....
22	....do...........	6	All......	2	Iron...........	None............	None.	....
23	....do...........	[7]6	All......	[5]2	Steel..........	....do..........	[5]2	None....
24	....do...........	6	All......	None.	....	....	2	...do.....
25	....do...........	6	All......	None.	....	....	2	...do.....
26	....do...........	6	All......	1	Steel..........	None............	2	...do.....
27	....do...........	6	All......	1	....do.........	....do..........	1	...do.....
28	....do...........	8,9	All......	None.	....	....	1	...do.....

[1] Not reported.
[2] For some.
[3] Also 2 small chemical fire engines are available.
[4] One building 7 stories, one 6 stories.
[5] One on each building.

BUILDING, MEANS OF ESCAPE, AND FIRE-FIGHTING APPARATUS—Con.

MARYLAND.

Other facilities for escape.							Fire-fighting apparatus.						
Exit doors.			Stairway.		Fire drills held.	Exit lights or signs provided.	Number of fire extinguishers.	Fire hose on what floors.	Sprinkler system.	Standpipes.	Fire buckets.		Establishment number.
Not opening outward.		Obstructed.	Properly lighted.	Provided with hand rails.							Provided.	Kept full of water.	
External.	Hall.												
16	None.	None.	Yes...	Yes...	No..	No..	None.	All....	No..	No...	Yes.	Yes.	1
None.	None.	None.	......	......	No..	No..	None.	All....	No..	No...	Yes.	Yes.	2
None.	None.	None.	......	......	No..	No..	30	All....	No..	No...	Yes.	Yes.	3
1	None.	(1)	No....	Yes...	No..	No..	12	All....	Yes.	Yes..	Yes.	Yes.	4
None.	None.	(1)	Yes...	Yes...	Yes [2]	No..	28	All....	Yes.	Yes..	Yes.	Yes.	5
None.	None.	(1)	Yes...	No....	No..	No..	None.	None..	No..	No...	No..	......	6
3	None.	(1)	Yes...	No....	No..	No..	None.	None..	No..	No...	Yes.	Yes.	7
3	None.	(1)	Yes...	No....	No..	No..	12	None..	No..	No...	Yes.	Yes.	8
1	None.	(1)	No....	Yes...	No..	No..	None.	None..	No..	No...	Yes.	Yes.	9
4	None.	(1)	No....	{1 yes../3 no..}	No..	No..	None.	None..	No..	No...	Yes.	Yes.	10
8	None.	(1)	Yes...	Yes...	No..	No..	None.	None..	No..	No...	Yes.	Yes.	11
None.	None.	(1)	Yes...	Yes...	Yes.	No..	None.	All....	Yes.	Yes..	Yes.	Yes.	12
5	1	(1)	Yes...	Yes...	No..	Yes.	3	All....	Yes.	Yes..	Yes.	Yes.	13
None.	None.	(1)	Yes...	Yes...	No..	Yes.	10	None..	Yes.	Yes..	Yes.	Yes.	14
1	None.	(1)	Yes...	No....	No..	No..	24	All....	Yes.	Yes..	Yes.	Yes.	15
None.	None.	None.	Yes...	{2 yes../2 no..}	No..	Yes.	[3]8	None..	No..	No...	Yes.	Yes.	16
4	None.	(1)	Yes...	Yes...	No..	No..	None.	None..	No..	No...	Yes.	Yes.	17
4	None.	(1)	No....	Yes...	No..	No..	None.	1st....	No..	No...	Yes.	Yes.	18
2	None.	None.	Yes...	Yes...	No..	No..	None.	None..	No..	No...	Yes.	Yes.	19
4	None.	(1)	Yes...	No....	No..	No..	None.	None..	No..	No...	Yes.	Yes.	20
None.	None.	(1)	Yes...	Yes...	No..	Yes.	None.	None..	Yes.	Yes..	Yes.	Yes.	21
None.	None.	None.	Yes...	Yes...	No..	No..	20	None..	No..	No...	Yes.	Yes.	22
6	9	None.	Yes...	Yes...	No..	No..	35	(9)	(10)	Yes...	Yes.	Yes.	23
2	None.	None.	Yes...	Yes...	No..	No..	20	All....	Yes.	Yes..	Yes.	Yes.	24
4	None.	None.	Yes...	Yes...	No..	No..	None.	All....	Yes.	Yes..	Yes.	Yes.	25
3	None.	None.	Yes...	Yes...	Yes.	No..	30	All....	Yes.	Yes..	Yes.	Yes.	26
2	None.	None.	Yes...	Yes...	No..	No..	None.	None..	Yes.	Yes..	Yes.	Yes.	27
None.	1	None.	Yes...	Yes...	Yes.	Yes.	None.	All....	Yes.	Yes..	Yes.	Yes.	28

[6] Three on 1 building, two on other.
[7] Two buildings, 6 stories each.
[8] Wood stairs inclosed in fireproof walls; both on main building.
[9] Main building all; other, none.
[10] Main building, no; other, yes.

TABLE **III.**—SAFEGUARDING AGAINST FIRE: CHARACTER OF

NORTH CAROLINA.

Estab-lish-ment num-ber.	Building.			Fire escapes.				
	Construction material.	Num-ber of sto-ries.	Stories occupied by this estab-lish-ment.	Outside of building.			Inside of building (and incom-bustible).	
				Num-ber.	Material.	Obstructions.	Num-ber.	Obstruc-tions.
1	Brick...........	4	All......	1	Iron..........	None............	None.	None....
2	.....do...........	5	All......	None.			1	None....
3	.....do...........	1	All......	None.			None.	
4	.....do...........	1	All......	None.			None.	
5	.....do...........	2	All......	1	Iron..........	None............	None.	
6	.....do...........	[4] 3	All......	None.			None.	
7	.....do...........	3	All......	None.			None.	
8	.....do...........	[4] 3	All......	None.			[7] 1	None....
9	.....do...........	2	All......	None.			None.	
10	.....do...........	1	All......	None.			None.	
11	.....do...........	1,3	All......	1	Iron..........	None............	None.	
12	Frame...........	2	All......	None.			None.	
13	Brick...........	3	All......	None.			None.	
14	.....do...........	1	All......	None.			None.	
15	.....do...........	4	4th....	1	Iron..........	None............	None	
16	.....do...........	4	All......	2	....do..........	....do..........	None.	
17	.....do...........	4	All......	4	....do..........	....do..........	None.	
18	.....do...........	1	All......	None.			None.	
19	.....do...........	4	All......	1	Iron..........	None............	None.	
20	.....do...........	4	All [5].....	None.			None.	
21	.....do...........	3	All......	None.			None.	
22	.....do...........	[11] 3,5	All......	1	Wood........	None............	3	None....
23	.....do...........	4	All......	None.			None.	
24	.....do...........	3	1st.....	None.			None.	
25	.....do...........	2	All......	None.			None.	
26	.....do...........	3	All......	None.			None.	
27	.....do...........	2	All......	None.			None.	
28	.....do...........	3	1st, 2d...	1	Wood........	None............	(?)	None....

[1] Sliding.
[2] Stairway inclosed.
[3] Some sliding.
[4] Sealed fire buckets containing fire extinguishing liquid.
[5] Fire hose outside.
[6] Main building only; women and children not employed in other buildings.
[7] Wood stairs inclosed in fireproof walls.

BUILDING, MEANS OF ESCAPE, AND FIRE-FIGHTING APPARATUS—Con.

NORTH CAROLINA.

Other facilities for escape.							Fire-fighting apparatus.						
Exit doors.			Stairway.								Fire buckets.		
Not opening outward.		Obstructed.	Properly lighted.	Provided with hand rails.	Fire drills held.	Exit lights or signs provided.	Number of fire extinguishers.	Fire hose on what floors.	Sprinkler system.	Standpipes.	Provided.	Kept full of water.	Establishment number.
External.	Hall.												
6	¹2	None.	Yes...	No³...	Yes.	Yes.	None.	All....	Yes.	Yes.	Yes.	Yes.	1
3	²14	1	No....	No³...	No..	No.	None.	None.	No..	No...	Yes.	Yes⁴	2
None.	None.	None.	....	....	Yes.	No.	26	None⁵	Yes.	No...	Yes.	Yes.	3
8	¹1	4	....	....	Yes.	No.	None.	None⁶	Yes.	Yes..	Yes.	Yes.	4
7	⁸7	1	Yes...	Yes...	No..	No.	None.	None⁶	Yes.	Yes..	Yes.	Yes.	5
13	None.	None.	Yes...	Yes...	No..	No.	None.	None⁶	Yes.	No...	Yes.	Yes.	6
6	None.	1	{2 yes.. {1 no...	{2 yes.. {1 no...	}No..	No.	None.	None⁶	Yes.	No...	Yes.	Yes.	7
10	3	None.	No....	{3 yes.. {2 no...	}No..	No.	6	None⁶	Yes.	Yes..	Yes.	Yes.	8
7	None.	None.	No....	Yes...	No..	No.	4	None⁶	Yes.	No...	Yes.	Yes.	9
7	None.	None.	No....	No³...	No..	No.	None.	None⁶	Yes.	Yes..	Yes.	Yes.	10
None.	3	None.	Yes...	No³...	No..	No.	None.	None⁶	Yes.	Yes..	Yes.	Yes.	11
None.	2	None.	Yes...	No....	No..	No.	10	All....	Yes.	Yes..	Yes.	Yes.	12
2	None.	1	Yes...	{Yes 1. {No 2..	}No..	No.	6	None..	No..	No...	Yes.	Yes.	13
3	1	None.	Yes...	No³...	No..	No.	None.	All....	Yes⁸	Yes.	Yes.	Yes.	14
6	¹1	None.	Yes...	No³...	Yes.	Yes.	None.	All....	Yes.	Yes.	Yes.	Yes.	15
⁸4	²38	1	No....	No¹...	Yes.	No.	43	All....	Yes.	No...	Yes.	Yes.	16
5	²10	2	No....	No¹...	Yes.	No.	None.	All....	Yes.	No...	Yes.	Yes.	17
¹10	None.	None.	....	....	No..	No.	8	All....	Yes.	Yes..	No....	......	18
None.	None.	None.	Yes...	No³...	Yes.	Yes.	None.	All....	Yes.	Yes.	Yes.	Yes.	19
²3	3	None.	No....	No³...	No..	No.	None.	All....	Yes.	Yes.	Yes.	Yes.	20
2	2	None.	{1 yes.. {1 no...	}Yes...	No..	No.	None.	None.	No..	No...	Yes.	Yes¹⁰	21
2	16	None.	Yes...	Yes...	No¹¹.	No.	None.	None⁶	Yes.	Yes..	Yes.	Yes.	22
4	1	None.	No....	No....	No..	No.	None.	All....	No..	Yes..	Yes.	Yes¹⁰	23
1	None.	None.	(¹²)	(¹²)	No..	No.	None.	None..	Yes.	Yes..	Yes.	Yes.	24
10	¹4	1	{1 yes.. {2 no...	{1 yes.. {2 no...	}Yes.	No.	36	None⁵	Yes.	No...	Yes.	Yes.	25
7	1	None.	Yes...	Yes...	No..	No.	10	None⁶	Yes.	No...	Yes.	Yes.	26
5	1	None.	Yes...	No....	No..	No.	None.	None⁶	Yes.	No...	Yes.	Yes.	27
5	¹8	1	{2 yes.. {2 no...	{2 yes.. {2 no...	}No..	No.	None.	None⁶	Yes.	No...	Yes.	Yes.	28

⁸ In part of factory only.
⁹ No employees above third floor.
¹⁰ Water in casks.
¹¹ Two buildings; one 3 stories, one 5.
¹² But there is a fire department composed of certain employees.
¹³ Not reported.

TABLE III.—SAFEGUARDING AGAINST FIRE: CHARACTER OF

GEORGIA.

Establishment number.	Building.			Fire escapes.				
	Construction material.	Number of stories.	Stories occupied by this establishment.	Outside of building.			Inside of building (and incombustible).	
				Number.	Material.	Obstructions.	Number.	Obstructions.
1	Brick...........	4	All......	2	Iron.........	2 windows stuck..	None.	....
2	....do..........	4	All......	2	....do.......	None...........	None.	....
3	....do..........	2	All......	None.			None.	....
4	....do..........	[2] 4	All......	[3] 4	Iron.........	2 windows fastened.	[4] 8	None....
5	....do..........	5	All......	2	....do.......	None...........	[1]	....
6	....do..........	3	All......	None.			[1]	....
7	....do..........	2	All......	None.			None.	....
8	....do..........	2	All......	None.			None.	....
9	....do..........	2	All......	None.			None.	....
10	....do..........	2	All......	None.			None.	....
11	Brick and stone..	2	All......	[10] 2	Wood........	None...........	None.	....
12	Brick...........	2	All......	None.			None.	....
13	....do..........	4	All......	1	Iron.........	Window openings too small on one floor; packing table in front of window.	None.	....
14	....do..........	4	All......	2	....do.......	None...........	None.	....
15	....do..........	[12] 1,2	All......	None.			None.	....
16	....do..........	[12] 1,2	All......	None.			None.	....
17	....do..........	2	All......	None.			None.	....
18	....do..........	1,2	All......	None.			None.	....
19	Frame	1	All......	None.			None.	....
20	Brick...........	2	All......	None.			None.	....
21	....do..........	1,2	All......	None.			None.	....
22	....do..........	3	All......	None.			None.	....
23	Brick and stone .	3	All......	None.			None.	....
24	Brick...........	4	All......	None.			None.	....
25	Stone...........	3	All......	None.			None.	....
26	Brick...........	1,2	All......	None.			None.	....
27	Stone...........	3	All......	None.			None.	....

[1] Not reported.
[2] Four buildings, 4 stories each.
[3] One on each building.
[4] Wood stairs inclosed in fireproof walls.
[5] Hose connected with city water; also force pump available.
[6] Sliding.
[7] And outside.
[8] Some sliding.

BUILDING, MEANS OF ESCAPE, AND FIRE-FIGHTING APPARATUS—Con.

GEORGIA.

Other facilities for escape.							Fire-fighting apparatus.						
Exit doors.			Stairway.								Fire buckets.		Estab-lish-ment num-ber.
Not opening outward.		Ob-struct-ed.	Prop-erly lighted.	Pro-vided with hand rails.	Fire drills held.	Exit lights or signs pro-vid-ed.	Num-ber of fire extin-guish-ers.	Fire hose on what floors.	Sprin-kler sys-tem.	Stand-pipes.	Pro-vid-ed.	Kept full of wa-ter.	
Exter-nal.	Hall.												
1	1	(1)	Yes...	No....	No..	No..	None.	None..	Yes.	No...	Yes.	Yes.	1
1	None.	1	Yes...	Yes...	No..	No..	None.	None..	No..	No...	Yes.	Yes.	2
2	None.	None.	Yes...	No....	No..	No..	None.	None..	Yes.	Yes..	Yes.	Yes.	3
8	None.	None.	Yes...	Yes...	No..	No..	None.	All....	Yes.	Yes..	Yes.	Yes.	4
3	None.	None.	Yes...	Yes...	No..	No..	None.	All....	Yes.	No[5]..	Yes.	Yes.	5
None.	None.	None.	Yes...	Yes...	No..	No..	None.	All....	Yes.	Yes..	Yes.	Yes.	6
None.	None.	None.	Yes...	No....	No..	No..	None.	2d....	Yes.	No...	Yes.	Yes.	7
5	[6]2	None.	Yes...	Yes...	No..	No..	None.	2d[7]....	Yes.	Yes..	Yes.	Yes.	8
5	[6]4	None.	Yes...	Yes...	No..	No..	4	2d[7]....	Yes.	Yes..	Yes.	Yes.	9
[8]7	[6]4	None.	Yes...	Yes...	No..	No..	40	None[9].	Yes.	Yes..	Yes.	Yes.	10
5	[8]10	None.	{2 yes../2 no...} Yes...	No..	No..	None.	None[9].	Yes.	Yes..	Yes.	Yes.	11
1	None.	None.	Yes...	No....	No..	No..	None.	None..	Yes.	Yes..	Yes.	Yes.	12
2	None.	1	No....	Yes...	No..	No..	None.	None..	Yes.	No...	Yes.	(11)	13
1	1	(1)	Yes...	No....	No..	No..	None.	None..	Yes.	No...	Yes.	Yes.	14
4	None.	None.	(1)	(1)	No..	No..	2	None..	Yes.	No...	Yes.	Yes.	15
3	None.	(1)	Yes...	Yes...	No..	No..	2	1st....	Yes.	Yes..	Yes.	Yes.	16
2	[6]2	(1)	Yes...	Yes...	No..	No..	2	None[9].	Yes.	Yes..	Yes.	Yes.	17
[8]7	None.	(1)	No....	Yes...	No..	No..	3	None[9].	Yes.	Yes..	Yes.	Yes.	18
20	None.	(1)	......	......	No..	No..	3	None[9].	Yes.	Yes..	Yes.	Yes.	19
5	1	(1)	Yes...	Yes...	No..	No..	None.	All....	No..	No...	Yes.	Yes.	20
5	1	(1)	Yes...	No[13]..	No..	No..	None.	1st....	Yes.	Yes..	Yes.	Yes.	21
[8]3	1	None.	{2 yes../1 no..} {2 yes../1 no..}	No..	No..	None.	None..	No..	No...	Yes.	No..	22
7	None.	[14]6	Yes...	No....	No..	No..	None.	All....	No..	No...	Yes.	Yes.	23
[8]5	1	None.	{3 yes../4 no..} (1)	No..	No..	None.	None[9].	Yes.	No...	Yes.	Yes.	24
3	1	None.	No....	No....	No..	No..	2	2d....	No..	Yes[15]	No..	......	25
8	[6]7	6	No....	No[13]..	No..	No..	None.	None[9].	Yes.	Yes..	Yes.	Yes.	26
1	None.	None.	Yes...	Yes...	No..	No..	39	None[9].	Yes.	Yes[15]	Yes.	No..	27

[9] Fire hose outside.
[10] Sloping platforms from second floor to ground.
[11] In winter; not in summer.
[12] Two buildings; one 1-story, one 2-story.
[13] Stairways inclosed.
[14] Five locked during working hours.
[15] Not on building, but serving it.

TABLE III.—SAFEGUARDING AGAINST FIRE: CHARACTER OF

FLORIDA.

Estab-lish-ment num-ber.	Building.			Fire escapes.				
	Construction material.	Num-ber of sto-ries.	Stories occupied by this estab-lish-ment.	Outside of building.			Inside of building (and incom-bustible).	
				Num-ber.	Material.	Obstructions.	Num-ber.	Obstruc-tions.
1	Concrete blocks..	1	All......	None.			None.	
2	Brick...........	1	All......	None.			None..	
3	Concrete and frame.	2½	All......	None.			None.	
4	Concrete........	4	All......	2	Iron..........	None..............	None.	
5	Frame...........	3	All......	None.			None.	
6	.....do..........	2½	All......	None.			None.	
7	Brick...........	3	All......	None.			None.	
8	Frame...........	4	All......	None.			None.	
9	Brick...........	3	All......	4	Steel and wood.	None..............	None.	
10	Frame	2½	All......	None.			None.	
11	.....do..........	3	All......	None.			None.	
12	.....do..........	3	All......	None.			None.	
13	Brick...........	4	All......	None.			1	None....
14	.....do..........	3	All......	None.			None.	

LOUISIANA.

Estab-lish-ment num-ber.	Construction material.	Num-ber of sto-ries.	Stories occupied	Num-ber.	Material.	Obstructions.	Num-ber.	Obstruc-tions.
1	Brick............	1	All......	None.			None.	
2	.....do..........	1	All......	None.			None.	
3	Brick and con-crete.	4	All......	1	Iron..........	None..............	None.	
4	Brick...........	4	All......	None.			None.	
5	.....do..........	4	All......	1	Iron..........	None..............	None.	
6	.....do..........	3	All......	None.			None.	
7	Frame (metal sheathed).	1	All......	None.			None.	
8	.....do..........	1	All......	None.			None.	
9	Brick and steel..	2,3	All......	1	Iron..........	None..............	[2]3	None ...
10	Brick...........	3	All......	None.			None.	
11	.....do..........	4	All......	None.			None.	
12	.....do..........	3	2d, 3d...	None.			None.	
13	.....do..........	5	(4)	3	Steel [1]........	None..............	None.	
14	.....do..........	5	All......	3	Steel and wood.	.....do.........	None.	
15	.....do..........	3	2d, 3d...	None.			None.	
16	.....do..........	1	All......	None.			None.	
17	.....do..........	4	All......	1	Iron..........	Table at window.	None.	
18	.....do..........	3	All......	None.			None.	
19	.....do..........	3	All......	None.			None.	
20	.....do..........	3	All......	None.			None.	
21	Brick and gal-vanized iron.	3	All......	3	Iron..........	None..............	None.	
22	Brick...........	4	All......	None.			None.	
23	.....do..........	3½	All......	None.			None.	
24	Frame and sheet metal.	2	All......	None.			None.	
25	Brick...........	3	All......	None.			None.	
26	.....do..........	3	3d.......	None.			None.	
27	.....do..........	3	All......	None.			None.	
28	.....do..........	4	All......	None.			None.	
29	.....do..........	4	All......	2	Steel..........	None..............	None.	

[1] Water in barrels.
[2] Wood stairs inclosed in fireproof walls.
[3] Fire hose outside.
[4] Not reported.

BUILDING, MEANS OF ESCAPE, AND FIRE-FIGHTING APPARATUS—Con.

FLORIDA.

Other facilities for escape.							Fire-fighting apparatus.						
Exit doors.			Stairway.								Fire buckets.		
Not opening outward.		Obstructed.	Properly lighted.	Provided with hand rails.	Fir drills held.	Exit lights or signs provided.	Number of fire extinguishers.	Fire hose on what floors.	Sprinkler system.	Standpipes.	Provided.	Kept full of water.	Establishment number.
External.	Hall.												
7	None.	None.	......	......	No..	No..	8	All....	No..	No...	Yes.	Yes.	1
2	None.	None.	......	......	No..	No..	3	None..	No..	No...	No..	......	2
2	3	None.	No....	Yes...	No..	No..	None.	All....	No..	Yes..	Yes.	No..	3
1	None.	None.	Yes...	Yes...	Yes..	No..	15	All....	No..	Yes..	Yes.	Yes.	4
2	None.	None.	Yes...	Yes...	No..	No..	2	None..	No..	No..	Yes.	No..	5
4	2	None.	Yes...	Yes...	No..	No..	None.	None..	No..	No...	Yes.	Yes.	6
3	None.	None.	Yes...	No....	No..	No..	6	None..	No..	No..	No..	No..	7
2	None.	None.	Yes...	Yes...	No..	No..	20	None..	No..	No..	Yes.	Yes.	8
1	None.	None.	Yes...	Yes...	No..	No..	21	None..	Yes.	No..	No..	......	9
2	2	None.	Yes...	Yes...	No..	No..	None.	All....	No..	No..	Yes.	Yes.	10
3	None.	None.	Yes...	Yes...	No..	No..	15	All....	No..	Yes..	Yes.	Yes.	11
1	None.	None.	Yes...	No....	No..	No..	None.	None..	No..	No..	Yes.	Yes.	12
1	None.	None.	Yes...	No....	Yes..	No..	18	None..	No..	No..	No..	......	13
2	None.	None.	Yes...	Yes...	No..	No..	20	All....	No..	No...	No..	......	14

LOUISIANA.

None.	None.	None.	...·..	......	No..	No..	None.	None..	No..	No...	Yes.	Yes[1]	1
None.	None.	None.	......	......	No..	No..	None.	None..	No..	No...	Yes.	Yes[1]	2
None.	None.	None.	Yes...	Yes...	No..	No..	11	All....	Yes.	Yes..	Yes.	Yes[1]	3
1	None.	None.	Yes...	No....	No..	No..	25	None..	No..	No...	Yes.	Yes.	4
1	None.	None.	Yes...	Yes...	No..	No..	None.	None..	No..	No...	Yes.	Yes[1]	5
2	1	None.	Yes...	Yes...	No..	No..	None.	None..	No..	No...	Yes.	Yes[1]	6
None.	None.	None.	......	......	No..	No..	None.	All....	No..	No...	Yes.	Yes.	7
3	None.	None.	......	......	No..	No..	12	All....	No..	No..	Yes.	Yes[1]	8
2	None.	None.	Yes...	Yes...	Yes..	No..	19	None[3]..	Yes.	No..	No..	......	9
1	None.	None.	Yes...	Yes...	Yes..	No..	1	All....	No..	Yes..	No..	......	10
None.	None.	None.	Yes...	Yes...	No..	No..	None.	All....	Yes.	Yes..	Yes.	Yes[1]	11
1	None.	None.	No....	Yes...	No..	No..	None.	None..	No..	No..	Yes.	Yes[1]	12
None.	None.	None.	Yes...	Yes...	No..	Yes.	1	All....	Yes.	No..	Yes.	Yes[1]	13
None.	None.	None.	Yes...	Yes...	No..	Yes.	1	All....	Yes.	No..	Yes.	Yes[1]	14
1	None.	None.	Yes...	Yes...	No..	No..	2	3d.....	No..	No..	Yes.	Yes[1]	15
None.	None.	None.	No....	......	No..	No..	None.	None..	No..	No..	Yes.	Yes[1]	16
None.	None.	None.	No....	Yes...	No..	No..	None.	None..	No..	No..	Yes.	No..	17
2	None.	None.	Yes...	Yes...	No..	No..	None.	None..	No..	No..	Yes.	No..	18
None.	None.	None.	Yes...	Yes...	No..	No..	None.	1st....	Yes.	No..	No..	......	19
4	None.	None.	Yes...	Yes...	No..	No..	None.	None..	No..	Yes..	No..	......	20
1	None.	None.	Yes...	Yes...	No..	No..	None.	1st....	Yes.	Yes..	Yes.	Yes[1]	21
1	2	None.	No....	Yes...	No..	No..	None.	None..	No..	No...	No[6]	Yes[6]	22
1	None.	None.	......	......	No..	No..	4	None..	No..	No..	Yes.	Yes[1]	23
5	None.	None.	Yes...	Yes...	No..	No..	25	None..	No..	No..	Yes.	Yes[1]	24
8	4	None.	No....	Yes...	No..	No..	None[7]	None..	No..	No...	Yes.	Yes.	25
1	None.	None.	No....	Yes...	No..	No..	None.	None..	No..	No..	No..	No..	26
5	None.	None.	No....	Yes...	No..	No..	None.	None..	No..	No..	Yes.	Yes.	27
2	None.	None.	Yes...	Yes...	No..	No..	None.	None..	No..	No..	Yes.	Yes.	28
None.	None.	None.	Yes...	Yes...	No..	Yes.	None.	All....	Yes.	Yes..	Yes.	Yes[1]	29

[6] One wood platform.
[6] Each girl is provided with pail of water used in her work.
[7] But have automatic alarm system.

TABLE **IV.**—ACCIDENT SAFEGUARDING AND

MAINE.

Es-tab-lish-ment num-ber.	Mill gearing and machinery unguarded or improperly guarded.	Machinery.				
			Devices for stopping machinery.			
		Direct control of source of power in work-room.	For notifying en-gine room.	Belt shifters.	Friction clutches.	Other special appa-ratus.
1	None unguarded...........................	Yes [1]..	([2])	Yes..	([2])........	No....
2	4 machine belts...........................	Yes [1]..	([2])	Yes...	([2])........	No....
3	Few belts through floor....................	Yes [1]..	([2])	Yes...	([2])........	No....
4	8 belts on cutting machines; 2 main belts..	Yes [1]..	([2])	([2])....	([2])........	No....
5	No machinery..............................					
6	.....do...................................					
7	1 mixer; 2 kettles; 1 depositor; 1 molding and 1 cutting machine.	No....	No....	No....	No......	No....
8	No machinery..............................					
9	None unguarded...........................	Yes [1]..	([2])	Yes...	Yes....	No....
10	.....do...................................	Yes [1]..	([3])	Yes...	Yes....	No....
11	Shafting under looper table; set screws; knitting machines.	No....	No..................	Yes...	No....	No....
12	Shafting under sewing-machine table....	Yes [1]..	([2])	No [8]...	Yes....	No....
13	None unguarded...........................	No....	No..................	Yes...	Yes....	No....
14	.....do...................................	Yes [1]..	([2])	No....	Yes....	No....
15	.....do...................................	Yes [1]..	([2])	No....	Yes....	No....
16	.....do...................................	Yes [1]..	([3])	Yes...	Yes....	No....
17	.....do...................................	No....	Telephone........	Yes...	No......	Yes [11].
18	.....do...................................	Yes [1]..	([2])	Yes...	([2])........	Yes [13].
19	Staying machines.........................	Yes [1]..	([2])...............	Yes...	([2])........	Yes [13].
20	Carders; pickers; looms; presses; shears; shafting on 2 floors; set screws.	No....	No..................	Yes...	Yes....	No....
21	Looms; carders; presses; pickers; main belts generally.	No....	No..................	No [8]...	No [8]...	No....
22	Looms; carders; mixers; duster; shears; rotary press; main belts and shafting generally.	No....	Push button.......	No [8]...	No [8]...	No....
23	Looms; carders; presses; mules; dye-house machinery; several main belts.	No....	No..................	Yes...	No [8]...	No....
24	Looms; mules; carders; presses; shears; washers; pickers; extractors; some main belts.	No....	No..................	Yes...	Yes....	No....
25	Looms; carders; washers; dressers; mules; low belting; set screws.	Yes [1]..	([2])	Yes...	Yes....	No....
26	Looms; pickers; carders; shears; presses; dressers; some low belting and shafting.	No....	No..................	Yes...	No [8]...	No....

[1] Electric power.
[2] Not necessary.
[3] Not reported.
[4] No children employed.
[5] Operator must lean into shaft to start car.
[6] No elevators in building.
[7] Clean chocolate enrober.
[8] Some, but not all cases.
[9] Report to State not required.
[10] Not applicable; guards not removable.

ACCIDENTS: MACHINERY AND ELEVATORS.

MAINE.

| Machinery. | | | | | Elevators. | | Accidents recorded by establishment during past year. | | Establishment number. |
| Safeguards. | | Warnings posted on dangerous machines. | Machinery cleaned or oiled, while in motion, by— | | Shafts and openings properly guarded. | Safety clutches or other proper safety devices provided. | | | |
Removed by employees.	Removal by employees forbidden.		Women.	Children.			Number.	Reported to State as required by law.	
(3)	(3)	No	No	(4)	No	Yes [5]	None.		1
No	No	No	No	No	Yes	Yes	None.		2
No	No	No	No	(4)	No	Yes [5]	None.		3
No	No	No	No	No	No	Yes [5]	None.		4
					(6)		None.		5
					(6)		None.		6
(3)	(3)	No	Yes [7]	No	Yes	Yes	None.		7
					No	Yes	None.		8
No	No	No	No	No	Yes	No	None.		9
No	No	No	No	No	Yes	No	None.		10
No	No	No	No	No	(6)		None.		11
No	(3)	No	No	(4)	(6)		None.		12
No	Yes	No	No	No	Yes	Yes	4	(9)	13
(10)	(10)	No	No	No	Yes	Yes	2	(9)	14
Yes	No	No	No	(4)	Yes	Yes	None.		15
Yes	No	No	No	No	Yes	Yes	2	(9)	16
Yes	Yes	Yes	No	No	No	Yes	None.		17
No	No	No	No	(4)	Yes	No	1	(9)	18
(10)	(10)	No	No	(4)	Yes	No	2	(9)	19
No	(3)	No	No	(4)	Yes [12]	Yes	None.		20
No	No	No	Yes [14]	No	No	No [15]	None.		21
No	No	No	No	No	No	Yes	None.		22
No	No	No [8]	Yes [16]	(4)	No	Yes	None.		23
No	No	No	Yes [16]	(4)	No [13]	Yes	None.		24
No	No	No	No	No	No	Yes	1	(9)	25
(3)	(3)	No	Yes [17]	No	No	Yes	None.		26

[11] Foot and hand brakes on machines.
[12] Hand brakes on machines.
[13] Women allowed to operate elevator.
[14] Looms.
[15] Clutches provided, but do not work properly.
[16] Carders.
[17] Looms and spoolers.

TABLE **IV.**—ACCIDENT SAFEGUARDING AND

MASSACHUSETTS.

Establishment number.	Mill gearing and machinery unguarded or improperly guarded.	Machinery.				
		Devices for stopping machinery.				
		Direct control of source of power in workroom.	For notifying engine room.	Belt shifters.	Friction clutches.	Other special apparatus.
1	Belting on sawing. and paper cutting machines.	No....	Press button.......	Yes...	No......	No....
2	4 belts on sawing and trimming machines.	Yes[2].	([3]).................	Yes..	([3])......	No....
3	None unguarded................	Yes[2].	([3]).................	Yes..	([3])......	No....
4	....do....................	Yes[2].	([3]).................	Yes..	([3])......	No....
5	....do....................	No....	No.............	Yes..	No......	No....
6	No machinery.................					
7	....do.................					
8	....do.................					
9	None unguarded............	Yes[2].	([2]).................	Yes..	([2])......	No....
10	Belting in 2 rooms low............	No....	No.............	Yes..	Yes....	No....
11	Cream-molding machine............	Yes[2].	Telephone a n d speaking tube.[3]	Yes..	Yes....	No....
12	None unguarded............	Yes[2].	Telephone[3].......	Yes..	Yes....	No....
13	....do............	No....	No.............	Yes..	Yes....	No....
14	....do............	Yes[2].	([3]).............	Yes..	No......	No....
15	....do............	No....	Telephone and signal bell.	Yes..	([1])......	No....
16	....do............	No....	Electric bell.......	Yes..	([1])......	No....
17	....do............	Yes[2].	Telephone[3].......	Yes..	([2])......	No....
18	....do............	No....	Telephone.........	Yes..	([1])......	No....
19	Combers; speeders; slubbers; some belts..	No....	Electric gong and telephone.	Yes..	Yes....	Yes[9].
20	None unguarded.....	Yes[10]	([2]).................	Yes..	Yes....	No....
21	Looms; speeders; belts.................	([1])....	No.............	Yes..	Yes....	No....
22	None unguarded.................	No....	Bell pull.........	Yes..	No......	No....
23	....do..................	No....	No.............	Yes..	No......	No[1]...
24	....do..................	No....	Te ephone.........	Yes..	Yes....	No....
25	Cake mixers; spindle mixers; buffers; belting in nailing machine.	No....	Electric bell.......	Yes..	Yes....	No....
26	Shafting under sewing-machine tables...	No....	No.............	Yes..	Yes....	No....
27	None unguarded............	No....	No.............	Yes..	Yes....	No....
28	Winder (belt); knitting machine (handle); shafting; and belts under tables.	No....	Telephone.........	Yes..	No......	No....
29	3 main belts; 2 winders (belts)...........	([1]).....	No.............	Yes..	Yes....	Yes[11].
30	No machinery.................					
31	Footing machines (handles).............	No....	Electric push button.	Yes..	No......	No....
32	Winders (belts); footing machines (handles).	No....	No.............	Yes..	Yes....	No....
33	None unguarded.................	Yes[3].	([3]).................	([3])....	([3])......	No....
34	....do..................	Yes[2].	([3]).................	([3])....	([3])......	No....
35	Papering machines.................	No....	No.............	No....	Yes....	No....
36	None unguarded.................	No....	No.............	No....	Yes....	No....
37	Stamping machines.................	No....	Bell pull.........	Yes..	No......	No....
38	Looms; carders; some main belts passing through floor.	No....	No.............	No....	No......	No....
39	Carders; looms; mules; pickers.........	No....	No.............	Yes..	Yes....	No....
40	Looms; carders; and machine belts in finishing room.	No....	No.............	Yes..	No......	No....
41	Looms; carders; belts; gearing generally..	Yes[14]	Electric bells and telephones.[3]	Yes[12]	Yes[13]...	No....
42	Looms; carders; and main belts........	No....	No.............	No....	No......	No....
43	Looms; carders; main belts; gearing generally.	No....	Bell system and telephones.	No....	No......	No....
44	Looms; carders; pickers; main belting and shafting; set screws.	No....	No.............	No....	Yes....	No....

[1] Not reported.
[2] Electric power.
[3] Not necessary.
[4] No children employed.
[5] No elevators in building.
[6] No dangerous machine.
[7] Data not obtainable.
[8] None caused as much as 4 days' loss of time; therefore did not require reporting to State.
[9] Automatic stops on machines.

ACCIDENTS: MACHINERY AND ELEVATORS—Continued.

MASSACHUSETTS.

Machinery.					Elevators.		Accidents recorded by establishment during past year.		Establishment number.
Safeguards.			Machinery cleaned or oiled, while in motion, by—		Shafts and openings properly guarded.	Safety clutches or other proper safety devices provided.			
Removed by employees.	Removal by employees forbidden.	Warnings posted on dangerous machines.	Women.	Children.			Number.	Reported to State as required by law.	
(¹)........	(¹)........	No.......	No.......	No.......	Yes.....	Yes.....	None.	....	1
(¹)........	(¹)........	No.......	No.......	No.......	No.......	Yes.....	None.	....	2
(¹)........	(¹)........	No.......	No.......	No.......	Yes.....	Yes.....	None.	....	3
(¹)........	(¹)........	No.......	No.......	(⁴).......	(⁵).......		None.	....	4
(¹)........	(¹)........	No.......	No.......	No.......	Yes.....	Yes.....	None.	....	5
....	....	....	....	....	Yes.....	Yes.....	None.	....	6
....	....	....	....	....	Yes.....	Yes.....	None.	....	7
(¹)........	(¹)........	No.......	No.......	No.......	Yes.....	Yes.....	None.	....	8
(¹)........	(¹)........	No.......	No.......	No.......	Yes.....	Yes.....	None.	....	9
(¹)........	(¹)........	(⁶).......	No.......	No.......	Yes.....	Yes.....	5	(⁷).	10
(¹)........	(¹)........	(⁶).......	No.......	No.......	Yes.....	Yes.....	36	(⁷).......	11
(¹)........	(¹)........	(⁶).......	No.......	No.......	Yes.....	Yes.....	None.		12
(¹)........	(¹)........	(⁶).......	No.......	No.......	Yes.....	Yes.....	None.		13
(¹)........	(¹)........	(⁶).......	No.......	No.......	Yes.....	Yes.....	1	(⁸)	14
(¹)........	(¹)........	(¹).......	No.......	No.......	Yes.....	Yes.....	25	(⁷)	15
(¹)........	(¹)........	(⁶).......	No.......	No.......	Yes.....	Yes.....	1	(⁷)	16
(¹)........	(¹)........	(⁶).......	No.......	No.......	Yes.....	Yes.....	None.		17
(¹)........	(¹)........	(⁶).......	No.......	No.......	Yes.....	Yes.....	None.		18
No.......	(¹)........	No.......	No.......	No.......	Yes.....	Yes.....	26	Yes.....	19
No.......	Yes.....	Yes......	No.......	No.......	Yes.....	Yes.....	37	Yes.....	20
Yes.....	Yes.....	No......	No.......	No.......	No.......	Yes.....	37	(⁷).......	21
(¹)........	(¹)........	No......	No.......	No.......	No.......	Yes.....	3	(⁷).....	22
(¹)........	(¹).:.....	No......	No.......	No.......	Yes.....	Yes.....	None.	(⁷).......	23
(¹)........	(¹)........	(⁸)......	No.......	No.......	Yes.....	Yes.....	20	(⁷).......	24
(¹)........	(¹)........	(¹)......	No.......	No.......	Yes.....	Yes.....	23	Yes.....	25
(¹)........	(¹)........	No.......	No.......	(⁴).......	Yes.....	Yes.....	None.	....	26
(¹)........	(¹)........	No.......	No.......	(⁵).......	(⁵).......		None.	....	27
(¹)........	(¹)........	No.......	No.......	No.......	(⁵).......		None.	....	28
(¹)........	(¹)........	No.......	No.......	No.......	No.......	Yes.....	None.	....	29
....	....	....	....	....	(⁶).......		None.	....	30
(¹)........	(¹)........	No.......	No.......	No.......	Yes.....	Yes.....	3	No......	31
(¹)........	(¹)........	(¹).......	No.......	No.......	Yes.....	Yes.....	None.		32
(¹)........	(¹)........	No.......	No.......	No.......	Yes.....	Yes.....	8	(⁷).......	33
(¹)........	(¹)........	No.......	No.......	No.......	Yes.....	Yes.....	None.	....	34
(¹)........	(¹)........	No.......	No.......	No.......	No.......	No.......	None.	....	35
(¹)........	(¹)........	No.......	No.......	No.......	No.......	Yes.....	3	(⁸).......	36
(¹)........	(¹)........	No.......	No.......	No.......	No.......	Yes.....	None.	....	37
(¹)........	(¹)........	No.......	No.......	Yes¹³....	(⁵).......		2	No......	38
(¹)........	(¹)........	No.......	No.......	No.......	(⁵).......		None.	....	39
(¹)........	(¹)........	No.......	(¹).......	(⁴).......	No.......	Yes.....	None.	....	40
(¹)........	(¹)........	No.......	No.......	Yes¹⁵....	No.......	Yes.....	3	Yes.....	41
(¹)........	(¹)........	No.......	No.......	(⁴).......	(⁶).......		None.	....	42
(¹)........	(¹)........	No.......	No.......	No.......	No.......	Yes.....	3	(⁷).......	43
(¹)........	(¹)........	No.......	Yes¹⁶....	No.......	Yes.....	Yes.....	2	Yes.....	44

¹⁰ Method of control not reported.
¹¹ Kind of apparatus not reported.
¹⁷ Carders.
¹³ In most, but not all cases.

¹⁴ For most of factory; method of control not reported.
¹⁵ Four boys oil bearings on carders.
¹⁶ Looms.

TABLE **IV.**—ACCIDENT SAFEGUARDING AND

RHODE ISLAND.

Establishment number.	Mill gearing and machinery unguarded or improperly guarded.	Machinery.				
			Devices for stopping machinery.			
		Direct control of source of power in workroom.	For notifying engine room.	Belt shifters.	Friction clutches.	Other special apparatus.
1	No machinery............................	....	....	....	....	....
2	....do....					
3	None unguarded........................	Yes [3]..	([4])................	Yes...	([4]).......	No....
4	....do............................	No....	No..............	Yes...	Yes.....	No....
5	....do............................	No....	Telephone.........	Yes...	Yes.....	No....
6	Drawing frames (belts)..............	No....	Electric bell......	Yes...	No......	No....
7	None unguarded........................	No....	Electric bell......	Yes...	No......	No....
8	Belts on carders......................	Yes [3]..	([4])................	Yes...	([4]).......	No....
9	None unguarded........................	No....	Press button.....	Yes...	No......	No....
10	....do....	No....	Press button.....	Yes...	([5]).......	No....
11	Shafting under sewing tables; winders (belts).	No....	No................	Yes...	No......	No....
12	Several machines in paper-box department.	Yes [3]..	([4])................	Yes...	([4]).......	No....
13	2 belts................................	Yes [3]..	([4])................	Yes...	([4]).......	No....
14	Belts from shafting to knitting machines.	([5])....	No................	Yes...	Yes.....	No....
15	None unguarded........................	No....	No................	Yes...	No......	No....
16	....do............................	Yes [3]..	([4])................	Yes...	([4]).......	No....
17	....do............................	No....	No................	Yes...	Yes.....	No....
18	....do............................	Yes [3]..	([4])................	Yes...	([4]).......	No....
19	....do............................	Yes [3]..	([4])................	Yes...	([4]).......	No....
20	....do............................	Yes [3]..	([4])................	Yes...	Yes.....	No....
21	....do............................	Yes [3]..	([4])................	No....	Yes.....	No....
22	....do............................	Yes [3]..	([4])................	No....	Yes.....	No....
23	Staying machines......................	Yes [3]..	([4])................	No....	Yes.....	No....
24	{Looms; shears; cards; presses; washers; twisters; spinning frames; etc.	}No....	Press button......	Yes...	Yes.....	No....
25	Looms; shears; presses; washers; low belting; shafting; some set screws.	No....	No................	Yes...	Yes.....	No....
26	None unguarded........................	No....	([5])..............	Yes...	Yes.....	No....
27	Combs; gilling boxes; twisters; spinning frames; cards; shafting; belting.	Yes [3]..	([4])................	Yes...	Yes.....	No....

[1] No elevator in building.
[2] None caused as much as 2 weeks' loss of time; therefore did not require reporting to State
[3] Electric power
[4] Not necessary.
[5] Not reported.
[6] Plunger type.
[7] Name of machines not specified.
[8] Boys in habit of cleaning mule frames not in motion, and many accidents caused by inadvertently starting the frame while being cleaned.

ACCIDENTS: MACHINERY AND ELEVATORS—Continued.

RHODE ISLAND.

Machinery					Elevators		Accidents recorded by establishment during past year.		Establishment number.
Safeguards.			Machinery cleaned or oiled, while in motion, by—		Shafts and openings properly guarded.	Safety clutches or other proper safety devices provided.	Number.	Reported to State as required by law.	
Removed by employees.	Removal by employees forbidden.	Warnings posted on dangerous machines.	Women.	Children.					
....	....	....	....	....	(¹)......	....	None.	....	1
....	....	....	....	....	(¹)......	....	1	(²)......	2
No......	(⁵)......	No......	No......	No......	Yes.....	Yes⁶....	None.	....	3
No......	Yes.....	No......	Yes⁷....	No⁸.....	{1 yes... / 1 no...	Yes....	14	Yes....	4
No......	No......	No......	No......	No......	No......	Yes....	6	Yes....	5
No......	No......	No......	Yes⁹....	Yes¹⁰...	{1 yes... / 3 no...	Yes....	2	Yes....	6
No......	Yes.....	No......	No......	No......	No......	Yes....	None.	....	7
No......	No......	No......	No......	No......	Yes.....	Yes....	None.	....	8
No......	No......	No......	No......	No......	Yes.....	Yes....	None.	....	9
No......	No......	No......	No......	No......	No.....	Yes....	1	No......	10
No......	No......	No......	No......	No......	Yes.....	Yes....	None.	....	11
No......	No......	No......	No......	No......	Yes¹¹...	Yes....	10	(²)......	12
No......	No......	No......	No......	(¹²).....	No......	No......	None.	....	13
No......	No......	No......	No......	No......	(¹)......	....	1	(²)......	14
No......	Yes.....	(¹³).....	No......	No......	Yes.....	....	1	(⁴)......	15
No......	No......	(¹³).....	No......	(¹²).....	Yes.....	Yes....	None.	....	16
No......	Yes.....	(¹³).....	No......	No......	Yes.....	Yes....	None.	....	17
No......	Yes.....	No......	No......	No......	Yes.....	Yes....	2	(²)......	18
No......	Yes.....	(¹³).....	No......	No......	Yes.....	Yes....	4	(²)......	19
No......	Yes.....	No......	No......	No......	No.....	Yes....	2	(²)......	20
Yes.....	No......	No......	No......	No......	(¹⁴).....	....	10	(²)......	21
Yes.....	No......	Yes.....	No......	No......	Yes.....	(¹⁵).....	None.	....	22
Yes.....	No......	No......	No......	No......	(¹⁴).....	....	6	(²)......	23
No......	No......	Yes.....	No......	No......	{1 yes... / 3 no...	Yes....	2	Yes....	24
No......	No......	No......	No......	No......	Yes.....	Yes....	None.	....	25
No......	Yes.....	Yes.....	No......	No......	No......	Yes....	None.	....	26
No......	No......	Yes.....	No......	No......	No......	Yes....	None.	....	27

⁹ Looms; spinning frames.
¹⁰ Spindles.
¹¹ Operator must lean into shaft.
¹² No children employed.
¹³ No dangerous machines.
¹⁴ No elevator in building.
¹⁵ Not necessary; block and tackle hoist; no passengers.

TABLE **IV.**—ACCIDENT SAFEGUARDING AND

CONNECTICUT.

Establishment number.	Mill gearing and machinery unguarded or improperly guarded.	Machinery.				
			Devices for stopping machinery.			
		Direct control of source of power in work-room.	For notifying engine room.	Belt shifters.	Friction clutches.	Other special apparatus.
1	One belt; a few presses	No	Bells and annunciators.	Yes	Yes	No
2	No machinery					
3	....do					
4	None unguarded	Yes[2]	(3)	Yes	Yes	No
5	Saws	No	Telephone	Yes	Yes	No
6	Fly wheels on presses	No	...do	Yes	Yes	No
7	Belts; a few presses	No	...do	Yes	Yes	No
8	None unguarded	No	...do	Yes	Yes	No
9	Sewing and lace stringing machines	No	No	Yes	Yes	No
10	Several each of sewing, shaping, stamping, corner staying and scoring machines and desk presses; 60 foot presses; 8 wire, 8 stud, and 9 desk machines.	Yes[2]	Electric signal bell[3]	Yes	Yes	No
11	Sewing-machine shafts	Yes[1]	(3)	Yes	Yes	No
12	1 cloth cutter; 6 strip winding machines; all shafts on sewing machines.	No	No	Yes	No	No
13	6 covering and 7 hook machines; 7 stud presses; 6 cutting presses.	No	No	Yes	Yes	No
14	None unguarded	No	Telephone	Yes	Yes	No
15	....do	No	...do	Yes	Yes	No
16	Several belts through floor; a few presses	Yes[5]	(3)	Yes	Yes	No
17	None unguarded	Yes[5]	(3)	Yes	Yes	No
18	A few presses; several belts	Yes[5]	(3)	Yes	Yes	No
19	None unguarded	Yes[5]	(3)	Yes	Yes	No
20	Most of presses; one main belt	Yes[5]	(5)	Yes	Yes	No
21	None unguarded	Yes[5]	(3)	Yes	Yes	No
22	....do	No	No	Yes	Yes	No
23	....do	No	No	Yes	Yes	No
24	....do	No	Telephone	Yes	Yes	No
25	Belts and pulleys on all picker machines	No	...do	Yes	Yes	No
26	None unguarded	No	Telephone and electric bells.	Yes	Yes	No
27	....do	No	Telephone	Yes	Yes	No
28	Belts and pulleys on pin machines	No	...do	Yes	Yes	No
29	Some belts through floors	Yes[5]	(3)	Yes	Yes	No
30	None unguarded	No	No	Yes	Yes	No
31	....do	No	No	Yes	Yes	No
32	....do	No	No	Yes	Yes	Yes[13]
33	4 mixing machines; calender machine; 8 presses; sewing machines; belting.	No	No	Yes	Yes	No
34	None unguarded	Yes[5]	(3)	Yes	Yes	No
35	....do	Yes[5]	(3)	Yes	Yes	No

[1] Report to State not required.
[2] Electric power.
[3] Not necessary.
[4] Small watch lathes.
[5] Doors not automatic; insufficiently guarded and left open.
[6] No children employed.
[7] No elevator in building.

ACCIDENTS: MACHINERY AND ELEVATORS—Continued.

CONNECTICUT.

Machinery.					Elevators.		Accidents recorded by establishment during past year.		
Safeguards.		Warnings posted on dangerous machines.	Machinery cleaned or oiled, while in motion, by—		Shafts and openings properly guarded.	Safety clutches or other proper safety devices provided.			Establishment number.
Removed by employees.	Removal by employees forbidden.		Women.	Children.			Number.	Reported to State as required by law.	
No	Yes	No	No	No	Yes	Yes	134	(1)	1
					Yes	Yes	None.		2
					Yes	Yes	None.		3
No	Yes	No	No	No	Yes	Yes	30	(1)	4
No	Yes	No	No	No	Yes	Yes	None.		5
No	Yes	No	Yes⁴	No	Yes	Yes	None.		6
No	No	No	No	No	Yes	Yes	None.		7
No	Yes	No	No	No	Yes	Yes	3	(1)	8
No	Yes	No	No	No	Yes	Yes	3	(1)	9
Yes	No	No	No	No	Yes	Yes	86	(1)	10
No	Yes	No	No	No	Yes	Yes	None.		11
No	Yes	No	No	No	No⁹	Yes	3	(1)	12
No	Yes	No	No	(⁶)	Yes	Yes	2	(1)	13
No	Yes	No	No	No	(⁷)		3	(1)	14
No	Yes	No	No	No	Yes	Yes	None.		15
Yes	Yes	No	No	No	Yes	Yes	86	(1)	16
No	No	No	No	No	Yes⁹	Yes	29	(1)	17
No	No	No	No	No	Yes	Yes	None.		18
No	No	No	No	No	Yes	Yes	None.		19
No	No	No	No	No	Yes	Yes	None.		20
No	Yes	(10)	No	No	Yes	Yes	None.		21
No	Yes	No	No	No	Yes	Yes	2	(1)	22
No	Yes	No	No	No	Yes	Yes	None.		23
No	No	No	Yes¹¹	No	No	Yes	2	(1)	24
No	Yes	No	No	No	Yes	Yes	None.		25
No	Yes	No	No	No	Yes	Yes	19	(1)	26
No	No	No	No	No	Yes	Yes	10	(1)	27
No	No	No	No	No	Yes	Yes	None.		28
(12)	Yes	No	No	No	Yes	Yes	None.		29
Yes	Yes	No	No	No	Yes	Yes	1	(1)	30
No	Yes	No	No	No	No	Yes	3	(1)	31
No	Yes	No	No	No	Yes	Yes	1	(1)	32
No	Yes	No	No	No	Yes	Yes	3	(1)	33
No	Yes	No	No	No	Yes	Yes	298	(1)	34
No	Yes	No	No	No	Yes	Yes	None.		35

⁸ Push button which automatically stops engine.
⁹ Except on one floor.
¹⁰ No dangerous machine.
¹¹ Knitting machines.
¹² From staying machines only.
¹³ Automatic stops on some machines.

TABLE IV.—ACCIDENT SAFEGUARDING AND

NEW YORK.

Establishment number.	Mill gearing and machinery unguarded or improperly guarded.	Machinery.				
			Devices for stopping machinery.			
		Direct control of source of power in workroom.	For notifying engine room.	Belt shifters.	Friction clutches.	Other special apparatus.
1	Presses; buffing wheels; a few belts	No	No	Yes	Yes	No
2	A few belts; several punch presses	Yes⁴	(²)	Yes	Yes	No
3	Several corner cutting, stripping, and staying machines.	No	Electric bell signal.	Yes	Yes	No
4	No machinery					
5	...do					
6	Belts; mixing machines (gearing)	No	No	Yes	Yes	No
7	Belts on molding machines; candy cutters.	No	Speaking tubes	Yes	Yes	No
8	Revolving kettles; nougat cutter; casting machines; can filler; starch buck; belting in general.	Yes⁴	(²)	Yes	(⁵)	No
9	Belting through floor in several instances.	No	Speaking tube	Yes	Yes	No
10	Belting in several instances	Yes⁸	Speaking tubes	Yes	Yes	No
11	None unguarded	No	Telephone	Yes	Yes	No
12	Several belts; cracker or cake machine	Yes⁴	(⁵)	Yes	Yes	No
13	None unguarded	No	Speaking tubes	No	Yes	No
14	1 sprocket on labeling machine; 3 belts from line shaft to machines.	Yes⁴	(⁵)	Yes	Yes	No
15	Mixing machines (gearing); quadrant cog on cutting machines; belt.	Yes⁴	(⁵)	Yes	Yes	No
16	None unguarded	No	Telephone	Yes	Yes	No
17	Knitting and winding machines on one floor.	Yes⁴	(⁵)	Yes	(⁵)	No
18	Cutting machines	No	Telephone	Yes	Yes	Yes¹¹
19	Machines in picking and carding room	No	do	Yes	Yes	No
20	Spinning mules; lapping and carding machines.	No	No	No	Yes	No
21	Belting on knitting machines	No	No	No	Yes	No
22	None unguarded	No	No	No	Yes	No
23	(²)	No	Telephone	Yes	Yes	No
24	A few belts; 1 saw	No	No	Yes	Yes	No
25	A few belts; staying machine; 1 saw	No	No	Yes	Yes	No
26	A few belts	No	No	Yes	Yes	No
27	No machinery					
28	Staying machines; a few belts	No	No	Yes	Yes	No
29	2 belts; 1 shear; setting-up machines	(¹)	No	Yes	Yes	(¹)
30	A few folding and pasting machines	Yes⁴	(⁵)	Yes	Yes	No
31	Belts; a few folding and pasting machines	Yes⁴	(⁵)	Yes	Yes	No
32	Some presses, staying machines, and belts.	Yes⁴	(⁵)	Yes	Yes	No
33	Some belts	No	No	Yes	Yes	No
34	None unguarded	No	Electric gong and speaking tube.	Yes	Yes	No
35	Flywheels on large presses	No	Telephone	Yes	Yes	No
36	None unguarded	No	Electric bells	Yes	Yes	No

¹ Not reported.
² No children employed.
³ Bottom of shaft used as passageway under elevator.
⁴ Electric power.
⁵ Not necessary.
⁶ Data not obtainable.

ACCIDENTS: MACHINERY AND ELEVATORS—Continued.

NEW YORK.

Machinery					Elevators.		Accidents recorded by establishment during past year.		Establishment number.
Safeguards.			Machinery cleaned or oiled, while in motion, by—		Shafts and openings properly guarded.	Safety clutches or other proper safety devices provided.			
Removed by employees.	Removal by employees forbidden.	Warnings posted on dangerous machines.	Women.	Children.			Number.	Reported to State as required by law.	
(1)........	(1)........	No.......	No.......	(2)........	{2 no 1.... / 5 yes....} Yes....	Yes....	6	Yes....	1
(1)........	(1)........	No.......	No.......	(2)........	Yes....	Yes....	7	(6).......	2
(1)........	(1)........	No.......	No.......	No.......	{1 no.... / 4 yes....} Yes....	Yes....	None.	....	3
....	....	....	....	....	Yes....	Yes....	None.	....	4
....	....	....	....	....	Yes....	No......	None.	....	5
(1)........	(1)........	No.......	No.......	(2)........	Yes....	Yes....	None.	....	6
(1)........	(1)........	No.......	No.......	(2)........	Yes....	Yes....	9	(6).......	7
(1)........	(1)........	No.......	No.......	No.......	Yes....	Yes....	10	No......	8
(1)........	(1)........	(7)........	No.......	(2)........	Yes....	Yes....	None.	....	9
(1)........	(1)........	(7)........	No.......	No......	Yes....	Yes....	6	(6).......	10
(1)........	(1)........	No.......	No.......	(2)........	Yes....	Yes....	None.	....	11
(1)........	(1)........	No.......	No.......	(2)........	Yes....	Yes....	None.	....	12
(1)........	(1)........	(7)........	No.......	(2)........	Yes....	Yes....	None.	....	13
No.......	Yes......	(1)........	No.......	(2)........	Yes....	Yes....	4	Yes 9....	14
(1)........	(1)........	(1)........	No.......	(2)........	Yes....	Yes....	9	Yes 9....	15
(1)........	(1)........	Yes......	No.......	No.......	(10).......	....	3	(6).......	16
(1)........	(1)........	(7)........	No.......	(2)........	Yes....	Yes....	2	Yes.....	17
(1)........	(1)........	No.......	No.......	(2)........	Yes....	Yes....	2	(6).......	18
No.......	Yes......	No.......	No.......	No......	Yes....	Yes....	2	Yes.....	19
(12)........	(12)........	No.......	No.......	No......	No......	Yes....	17	Yes.....	20
(1)........	(1)........	No.......	No.......	(2)........	Yes....	No......	None.	....	21
No.......	Yes......	No.......	No.......	No......	Yes....	Yes....	None.	....	22
(1)........	(1)........	No.......	No.......	No......	Yes....	Yes....	6	(6).......	23
(1)........	(1)........	No.......	No.......	No......	Yes....	Yes....	None.	....	24
(1)........	(1)........	No.......	No.......	No......	Yes....	Yes....	None.	....	25
(1)........	(1)........	No.......	No.......	No......	No......	Yes....	11	(6).......	26
....	....	....	....	....	No......	No......	None.	....	27
(1)........	(1)........	No.......	No.......	No......	Yes....	Yes....	None.	....	28
(1)........	(1)........	No.......	No.......	No......	No......	Yes....	None.	....	29
(1)........	(1)........	No.......	No.......	(2)........	Yes....	Yes....	2	(6).......	30
(1)........	(1)........	No.......	No.......	No......	Yes....	Yes....	None.	....	31
(1)........	(1)........	No.......	No.......	No......	Yes....	Yes....	None.	....	32
Yes......	(1)........	No.......	No.......	(2)........	Yes....	Yes....	None.	....	33
(1)........	(1)........	Yes......	No.......	(2)........	Yes....	Yes....	1	Yes....	34
No.......	Yes......	No.......	No.......	No......	Yes....	Yes....	13	Yes....	35
No.......	Yes......	(7)........	No.......	(2)........	Yes....	Yes....	None.	....	36

1 No dangerous machine.
8 Electric power in part of plant.
9 Only serious accidents are reported.
10 No elevator in building.
11 Automatic stops on machines.
12 Not applicable; guards not removable.

TABLE **IV.**—ACCIDENT SAFEGUARDING AND

NEW JERSEY.

Es-tab-lish-ment num-ber.	Mill gearing and machinery unguarded or improperly guarded.	Machinery.				
			Devices for stopping machinery.			
		Direct control of source of power in work-room.	For notifying en-gine room.	Belt shifters.	Friction clutches.	Other special appa-ratus.
1	None unguarded........................	Yes¹..	(²).............	Yes...	Yes.....	No....
2	....do........	Yes¹..	Telephone².......	Yes...	Yes.....	Yes⁴..
3	No machinery...........................					
4	....do..					
5	None unguarded........................	No....	No.............	Yes...	Yes.....	No....
6	....do..	No....	No.............	Yes...	Yes.....	No....
7	Lopping and carding machines; dyeing apparatus.	Yes⁵..	(²).............	(¹⁰)...	Yes.....	No....
8	None unguarded........................	Yes¹..	(²).............	Yes...	(²)......	No....
9	....do..	No....	No.............	Yes...	Yes.....	No....
10	....do..	No....	No.............	Yes...	No.....	No....
11	1 each of staying, corner cutting, lining, scoring, and slitting machines.	No....	No.............	Yes...	Yes.....	No....
12	Staying machines......................	No....	No.............	Yes...	Yes.....	No....
13	....do.........................	(¹⁰)..	No.............	No....	Yes.....	No....
14	....do..	No....	No.............	No....	Yes.....	No....
15	None unguarded......................	Yes¹..	(²).............	Yes...	Yes.....	No....
16	Clay-mixing machinery; lithographing press.	No....	No.............	No....	Yes.....	No....
17	Die-making machines..................	Yes¹³..	(⁸).............	Yes...	Yes¹³..	No....
18	None unguarded......................	No....	No.............	Yes...	Yes.....	No....
19	....do..	No....	No.............	Yes...	No.....	No....
20	Clay-mixing machinery..................	No....	No.............	No....	Yes.....	No....
21	None unguarded......................	Yes¹..	(²).............	Yes...	(²)......	No....
22	....do..	No....	No.............	Yes...	Yes.....	No....
23	....do..	Yes¹..	(²).............	Yes...	(²)......	No....
24	....do..	Yes¹..	(²).............	Yes...	Yes.....	No....
25	....do..	Yes¹²..	Electric bell¹...	(²).....	Yes.....	No....
26	....do..	Yes¹³..	.....do.¹.........	(²).....	Yes.....	No....
27	....do..	No....	Electric button....	Yes...	Yes.....	No....

PENNSYLVANIA.

[Establishments 4, 5, 6, 7, 8, 14, 15, 16, 17, 18, 22, 25, 26, 28, 29, 31, 32, 33, 34, 39, 40, 41, 42, 43, 46, 47, 48, 49, 21, 23, 24, 27, 37, 38, and 45 are in cities of the second class (population 100,000 to 1,000,000).]

1	None unguarded........................	Yes¹..	(²).............	Yes...	(²).....	No....
2	....do........	Yes¹..	(²).............	Yes...	Yes.....	No....
3	....do........	Yes¹..	(²).............	No....	(²).....	No....
4	....do........	No....	Signal bells on each floor.	Yes...	Yes.....	No....
5	No machinery¹³.........................					
6	No machinery					
7	....do........					
8	....do..					
9	....do..					
10	None unguarded......................	Yes¹..	(²).............	(²).....	(²)......	No....
11	....do..	Yes¹..	(²).............	(²).....	(²)......	No....
12	No machinery..........................					
13	....do..					

¹ Electric power.
² Not necessary.
³ No dangerous machine.
⁴ No children employed.
⁵ Causing less than 2 weeks' loss of time; therefore reporting was not required.
⁶ Automatic stops on all machines.
⁷ One swing gate unlatched.

ACCIDENTS: MACHINERY AND ELEVATORS—Continued.

NEW JERSEY.

Safeguards.		Warnings posted on dangerous machines.	Machinery cleaned or oiled, while in motion, by—		Shafts and openings properly guarded.	Safety clutches or other proper safety devices provided.	Accidents recorded by establishment during past year.		Establishment number.
Removed by employees.	Removal by employees forbidden.		Women.	Children.			Number.	Reported to State as required by law.	
No......	Yes......	(³)........	No......	(⁴)........	Yes....	Yes....	2	(⁵)......	1
No......	Yes......	(⁵)........	No......	No........	Yes....	Yes....	40	(⁵)......	2
....	....	....	....	....	Yes ⁷..	Yes....	1	(⁸)......	3
....	....	....	....	....	Yes....	Yes....	None.	....	4
No......	Yes......	(³)........	No......	No........	Yes....	Yes....	None.	....	5
No......	Yes......	(³)........	No......	No........	Yes....	Yes....	None.	....	6
No......	Yes......	(³)........	No......	No........	Yes....	Yes....	None.	....	7
No......	Yes......	(³)........	No......	No........	Yes....	Yes....	None.	....	8
No......	No......	(⁵)........	No......	No........	(¹¹)....	....	None.	....	9
No......	Yes......	(³)........	No......	No........	(¹¹)....	....	None.	....	10
No......	Yes......	(³)........	No......	No........	Yes....	Yes....	8	(⁸)......	11
No......	Yes......	Yes......	No......	No........	Yes....	Yes....	33	(⁸)......	12
(¹⁰)....	(¹⁰)....	(³)........	No......	No........	{1 no.. / 2 yes.	}No......	1	(⁵)......	13
(¹⁰)....	(¹⁰)....	(³)........	No......	No........	Yes....	No......	1	(⁵)......	14
No......	Yes......	(³)........	No......	No........	Yes....	Yes....	None.	....	15
(¹⁰)....	(¹⁰)....	(³)........	No......	No........	Yes....	No......	None.	....	16
(¹⁰)....	(¹⁰)....	(³)........	No......	No........	(¹¹)....	....	None.	....	17
No......	Yes......	(³)........	No......	No........	Yes....	No......	None.	....	18
No......	Yes:....	(³)........	No......	No........	Yes....	Yes....	None.	....	19
(¹⁰)....	(¹⁰)....	(³)........	No......	No........	Yes....	No......	None.	....	20
No......	Yes......	(³)........	No......	No........	Yes....	Yes....	None.	....	21
No......	Yes......	(³)........	No......	No........	Yes....	Yes....	None.	....	22
No......	Yes......	(⁵)........	No......	No........	Yes....	Yes....	3	(⁸)......	23
No......	Yes......	Yes......	No......	No........	Yes....	Yes....	1	(⁸)......	24
No......	Yes......	No......	No......	No........	Yes....	Yes....	None.	....	25
No......	Yes......	No......	No......	No........	Yes....	Yes....	None.	....	26
No......	Yes......	No......	No......	(⁴)........	Yes....	Yes....	None.	....	27

PENNSYLVANIA.

and 50 are in cities of the first class (population 1,000,000 or over). Establishments 1, 2, 3, 9, 10, 11, 12, 13, Establishments 19, 20, 30, 35, 36, and 44 are in communities of less than 100,000 population.]

No......	Yes......	(²)........	No......	No......	Yes....	Yes....	6	Yes.....	1
No......	Yes......	(³)........	No......	No......	Yes....	Yes....	None.	....	2
No......	Yes......	(³)........	No......	No......	Yes....	Yes....	None.	....	3
No......	Yes......	(¹⁰)......	No......	No......	Yes....	Yes....	3	(⁵)......	4
....	....	....	....	....	Yes....	Yes....	None.	....	5
....	....	....	....	....	Yes....	Yes....	None.	....	6
....	....	....	....	....	Yes....	Yes....	None.	....	7
....	....	....	....	....	(¹¹)....	....	None.	....	8
....	....	....	....	....	Yes....	Yes....	None.	....	9
(¹⁴)....	(¹⁴)....	(³)........	No......	No......	Yes....	Yes....	None.	....	10
(¹⁴)....	(¹⁴)....	(⁵)........	No......	No......	Yes....	Yes....	None.	....	11
....	....	....	....	....	Yes....	No......	None.	....	12
....	....	....	....	....	Yes....	Yes....	None.	....	13

⁸ Data not obtainable.
⁹ Push button which automatically stops engine.
¹⁰ Not reported.
¹¹ No elevator in building.
¹² Method of control not reported.
¹³ There is 1 power-driven machine, but it is very simple and in no way dangerous.
¹⁴ Not applicable; guards not removable.

TABLE **IV.**—ACCIDENT SAFEGUARDING AND

PENNSYLVANIA—Concluded.

Establishment number.	Mill gearing and machinery unguarded or improperly guarded.	Machinery.				
			Devices for stopping machinery.			
		Direct control of source of power in workroom.	For notifying engine room.	Belt shifters.	Friction clutches.	Other special apparatus.
14	None unguarded........................	Yes [1]..	([2]).................	Yes...	Yes.....	No....
15	....do..................................	Yes [1]..	([2]).................	Yes...	Yes.....	No....
16	....do..................................	No....	No.................	Yes...	No.....	No....
17	....do..................................	No....	No.................	Yes...	Yes.....	No....
18	No machinery [5]........................					
19	None unguarded........................	No....	No.................	Yes...	Yes.....	No....
20	No machinery [3]........................					
21	None unguarded........................	No....	No.................	Yes...	Yes.....	No....
22	Gearing on 2 mixers and 1 wire cake-cutting machine; belts on 16 mixers, 24 nailing machines, and 1 sugar mill; rollers on 6 brakes.	Yes [1]..	([2]).................	Yes...	Yes.....	No....
23	None unguarded........................	Yes [1]..	([2]).................	Yes..	Yes.....	No....
24	....do..................................	No....	No.................	Yes...	Yes.....	No....
25	....do..................................	Yes [1]..	([2]).................	Yes...	Yes.....	No....
26	....do..................................	No....	No.................	Yes...	Yes.....	No....
27	....do..................................	Yes [1]..	([2]).................	Yes...	Yes.....	No....
28	....do..................................	No....	No.................	Yes...	([2]).....	No....
29	....do..................................	No....	No.................	Yes...	Yes.....	No....
30	Corner-staying machine, box department.	Yes [1]..	([2]).................	Yes...	Yes.....	No....
31	None unguarded........................	Yes [1]..	([2]).................	Yes...	Yes.....	No....
32	....do..................................	Yes [1]..	([2]).................	Yes...	Yes.....	No....
33	Winding, knitting, and finishing machines.	No....	No.................	Yes...	Yes.....	No....
34	Winding machine........................	No....	No.................	Yes...	Yes.....	No....
35	None unguarded........................	No....	Steam whistles....	Yes...	Yes.....	No....
36	....do..................................	No....	No.................	Yes...	Yes.....	No....
37	Belting in men's department...........	No....	No.................	Yes...	Yes.....	No....
38	None unguarded........................	Yes [1]..	([2]).................	Yes...	Yes.....	No....
39	Corner-staying machines................	No....	No.................	Yes...	Yes.....	No....
40	....do..................................	Yes [1]..	([7]).................	Yes...	Yes.....	No....
41	....do..................................	No....	No.................	Yes...	Yes.....	No....
42	None unguarded........................	No....	No.................	No...	Yes.....	No....
43	Belting on clay-making machinery [15]....	No....	No.................	Yes...	Yes.....	No....
44	None unguarded	No....	No.................	Yes...	Yes.....	No....
45	....do..................................	No....	No.................	Yes...	Yes.....	No....
46	....do..................................	Yes [1]..	([2]).................	Yes...	Yes.....	No....
47	....do..................................	Yes [1]..	([2]).................	Yes...	Yes.....	([7])....
48	....do..................................	No....	No.................	Yes...	Yes.....	No....
49	....do..................................	No....	Telephone........	Yes...	Yes.....	No....
50	....do..................................	No....	....do............	Yes...	Yes.....	No....

[1] Electric power.
[2] Not necessary.
[3] No dangerous machine.
[4] No elevator in building.
[5] Data obtained only for departments where females were employed.
[6] Data obtained for females only.
[7] Not reported.
[8] No children employed.

ACCIDENTS: MACHINERY AND ELEVATORS—Continued.

PENNSYLVANIA—Concluded.

Machinery.					Elevators.		Accidents recorded by establishment during past year.		Establishment number.
Safeguards.		Warnings posted on dangerous machines.	Machinery cleaned or oiled, while in motion, by—		Shafts and openings properly guarded.	Safety clutches or other proper safety devices provided.	Number.	Reported to State as required by law.	
Removed by employees.	Removal by employees forbidden.		Women.	Children.					
No	Yes	(³)	No	No	Yes	Yes	None		14
No	Yes	(³)	No	No	Yes	Yes	None		15
No	Yes	(³)	No	No	(⁴)		None		16
No	Yes	(³)	No	No	Yes	Yes	None		17
					(⁴)		None⁶		18
No	Yes	(⁷)	No	(⁸)	(⁴)		None⁶		19
					(⁴)		None⁶		20
No	Yes	(⁷)	No	(⁸)	No	Yes	None		21
No	Yes	Yes	No	No	Yes	Yes	8	Yes⁹	22
No	Yes	(³)	No	No	Yes	Yes	None		23
No	Yes	(³)	Yes¹⁰	No	Yes	Yes	None		24
No	Yes	Yes	No	No	Yes	Yes	None		25
No	Yes	(³)	No	No	Yes	Yes	None		26
No	Yes	(³)	No	No	Yes	Yes	None		27
No	Yes	(³)	No	No	Yes	Yes	1	(¹¹)	28
No	Yes	(³)	No	No	Yes	Yes	None		29
Yes	No	No	No	Yes¹²	Yes	Yes	None		30
No	Yes	(⁷)	No	No	Yes	Yes	None		31
No	Yes	(⁷)	No	No	Yes	Yes	None		32
No	No	No	No	No	Yes	Yes	None		33
(¹³)		No	No	No	No	Yes	None		34
No	Yes	(³)	No	No	(⁴)		1	(¹¹)	35
No	Yes	(³)	No	(⁸)	(⁴)		None		36
No	Yes	(⁷)	No	No	Yes	Yes	None		37
No	Yes	Yes	No	No	Yes	No	3	(¹⁴)	38
Yes	Yes	No	No	No	No	Yes	2	(¹⁴)	39
Yes	No	Yes	No	No	No	Yes	2	(¹⁴)	40
Yes	Yes	No	No	No	Yes	Yes	None		41
No	(⁷)	(⁷)	No	(⁸)	Yes	Yes	None		42
No	Yes	No	No	(⁸)	No	Yes	None		43
No	Yes	(⁷)	No	No	Yes	Yes	11	(¹⁴)	44
No	Yes	(⁷)	No	No	No	Yes	12	(¹⁴)	45
No	Yes	(³)	No	No	(⁴)		18	Yes	46
No	Yes	Yes	No	No	Yes	Yes	None		47
No	Yes	(³)	No	No	Yes	Yes	None		48
No	Yes	Yes	No	No	Yes	Yes	10	(¹¹)	49
No	Yes	(³)	No	(⁸)	Yes	Yes	None		50

⁹ Only serious accidents.
¹⁰ Chocolate dipping machines.
¹¹ Report not required; minor accident.
¹² Knitting machine.
¹³ No safeguard.
¹⁴ Data not obtainable.
¹⁵ Only men are required to pass dangerous machinery.

TABLE **IV.**—ACCIDENT SAFEGUARDING AND

OHIO.

Establishment number.	Mill gearing and machinery unguarded or improperly guarded.	Machinery.				
			Devices for stopping machinery.			
		Direct control of source of power in workroom.	For notifying engine room.	Belt shifters.	Friction clutches.	Other special apparatus.
1	None unguarded.	No...	No...	Yes...	Yes...	No...
2	....do.	Yes[1].	(³).	Yes...	Yes...	No...
3	No machinery					
4	....do.					
5	....do.					
6	....do.					
7	....do.					
8	....do.					
9	....do.					
10	....do.					
11	....do.					
12	None unguarded	Yes[2].	(³).	Yes...	Yes...	No...
13	....do.	No...	No...	Yes...	Yes...	No...
14	....do.	Yes[2].	(³).	Yes...	Yes...	No...
15	....do.	Yes[2].	(³).	Yes...	Yes...	No...
16	....do.	Yes[2].	(³).	Yes...	Yes...	No...
17	....do.	Yes[2].	(³).	Yes...	Yes...	No...
18	....do.	Yes[2].	(³).	Yes...	Yes...	No...
19	....do.	No...	No...	Yes...	Yes...	No...
20	....do.	Yes[2].	(³).	Yes...	Yes...	No...
21	....do.	Yes[2].	(³).	Yes...	Yes...	No...
22	Buffer: 2 packing tables, rollers on breakers, some belting.	No...	Bell.	Yes...	Yes...	No...
23	None unguarded	Yes[2].	(³).	Yes...	Yes...	No...
24	....do.	Yes[2].	(³).	Yes...	Yes...	No...
25	....do.	Yes[2].	(³).	Yes...	Yes...	No...
26	....do.	Yes[2].	(³).	Yes...	Yes...	No...
27	....do.	No...	Electric bell.	Yes...	Yes...	No...
28	....do.	No...	No...	Yes...	Yes...	No...
29	....do.	(⁵).	(⁵).	Yes...	Yes...	Yes[5].
30	....do.	Yes[2].	(³).	Yes...	Yes...	No...
31	....do.	No...	No...	Yes...	Yes...	No...
32	Threading machines.	Yes[2].	(³).	Yes...	Yes...	No...
33	No machinery					
34	Threading machines.	No...	No...	Yes...	Yes...	No...
35	None unguarded	No...	No...	Yes...	Yes...	No...
36	Corner-staying machine.	Yes[2].	(³).	Yes...	Yes...	No...
37	Corner-staying machine.	Yes[2].	(³).	Yes...	Yes...	No...
38	....do.	Yes[2].	(³).	Yes...	Yes...	No...
39	....do.	No...	No...	Yes...	Yes...	No...
40	Corner staying and stitching machines.	Yes[2].	(³).	Yes...	Yes...	No...
41	None unguarded	No...	No...	Yes...	Yes...	No...
42	....do.	No...	No...	Yes...	Yes...	No...
43	....do.	(⁶).	(⁶).	Yes...	Yes...	No...
44	....do.	(⁶).	(⁶).	Yes...	Yes...	No...
45	....do.	No...	No...	Yes...	Yes...	No...
46	....do.	No...	No...	Yes...	Yes...	No...
47	....do.	No...	No...	Yes...	Yes...	No...
48	....do.	Yes[2].	(³).	Yes...	Yes...	No...
49	....do.	No...	Engine in work-room.³	Yes...	Yes...	No...
50	....do.	Yes[2].	(³).	Yes...	Yes...	No...
51	....do.	No...	No...	Yes...	Yes...	No...
52	....do.	No...	No...	Yes...	No...	No...
53	....do.	Yes[2].	Speaking tube³.	Yes...	Yes...	No...
54	....do.	Yes[2].	(³).	Yes...	Yes...	No...
55	....do.	No...	No...	Yes...	Yes...	No...
56	....do.	No...	No...	Yes...	No...	No...
57	....do.	Yes[2].	(³).	Yes...	Yes...	No...
58	....do.	Yes[2].	(³).	Yes...	Yes...	No...
59	....do.	No...	No...	Yes...	No...	No...
60	....do.	Yes[2].	(³).	Yes...	Yes...	No...

[1] No dangerous machine. [3] Not necessary. [5] No elevator in building.
[2] Electric power [4] No children employed [6] Not reported.

ACCIDENTS: MACHINERY AND ELEVATORS—Continued.

OHIO.

Machinery.					Elevators.		Accidents recorded by establishment during past year.		Establishment number.
Safeguards.		Warnings posted on dangerous machines.	Machinery cleaned or oiled, while in motion, by—		Shafts and openings properly guarded.	Safety clutches or other proper safety devices provided.			
Removed by employees.	Removal by employees forbidden.		Women.	Children.			Number.	Reported to State as required by law.	
No	Yes	(1)	No	No	Yes	Yes	None.		1
No	Yes	(1)	No	(4)	Yes	Yes	None.		2
					Yes	Yes	None.		3
					Yes	Yes	None.		4
					Yes	Yes	None.		5
					Yes	Yes	None.		6
					Yes	Yes	None.		7
					(5)		None.		8
					Yes	Yes	None.		9
					Yes	Yes	None.		10
					Yes	Yes	None.		11
No	Yes	(1)	No	No	Yes	Yes	None.		12
No	Yes	(1)	No	No	Yes	Yes	None.		13
No	Yes	(1)	No	No	Yes	Yes	None		14
No	Yes	(1)	No	No	Yes	Yes	None		15
No	Yes	(1)	No	No	(6)	Yes	None.		16
No	Yes	(1)	No	No	(6)	Yes	None.		17
No	Yes	(1)	No	No	Yes	Yes	1	Yes	18
(6)	(6)	(1)	No	(4)	Yes	Yes	None.		19
No	Yes	(1)	No	(4)	Yes	Yes	None		20
No	Yes	(1)	No	No	Yes	Yes	None.		21
(6)	(6)	(1)	No	(4)	Yes	Yes	None		22
No	No	(6)	No	No	Yes	Yes	None.		23
No	No	(6)	No	(4)	Yes	Yes	4	Yes	24
(7)	(7)	(6)	No	No	Yes	Yes	None.		25
No	No	(6)	No	No	Yes	Yes	2	Yes	26
No	No	(6)	Yes	No	Yes	Yes	4	Yes	27
No	No	(6)	No	(4)	Yes	Yes	None		28
No	Yes	Yes	No	(4)	Yes	Yes	None.		29
No	Yes	No	No	(4)	Yes	Yes	None.		30
No	Yes	(1)	No	(4)	Yes	Yes	1	Yes	31
No	Yes	(1)	No	(4)	(6)	Yes	None		32
					Yes	Yes	None.		33
No	Yes	(1)	No	No	Yes	Yes	None.		34
No	Yes	(1)	No	(4)	Yes	Yes	None.		35
No	Yes	(1)	No	No	Yes	Yes	None.		36
No	Yes	(1)	No	(4)	Yes	Yes	None.		37
No	Yes	Yes	No	No	Yes	Yes	None.		38
Yes	No	(1)	No	No	Yes	Yes	None.		39
No	Yes	(1)	No	No	Yes	Yes	None.		40
No	Yes	(6)	No	No	Yes	Yes	None.		41
No	No	(6)	No	No	Yes	Yes	None.		42
No	No	(9)	No	No	Yes	Yes	None.		43
No	No	(9)	No	No	Yes	Yes			44
No	No	(9)	No	No	Yes	Yes	4	Yes	45
No	No	(9)	No	(4)	Yes	Yes	None.		46
No	Yes	Yes	No	(4)	Yes	Yes	2	Yes	47
No	No	(6)	No	(4)	Yes	Yes	12	Yes	48
No	Yes	(1)	No	No	(9)		2	Yes	49
No	Yes	(1)	No	(4)	Yes	Yes	None.		50
No	Yes	(1)	No	(4)	Yes	Yes	None.		51
No	Yes	(1)	No	(4)	Yes	Yes	None.		52
No	Yes	(1)	No	No	Yes	Yes	None.		53
No	Yes	No	No	No	Yes	Yes	12	Yes	54
No	Yes	Yes	No	No	Yes	Yes	None.		55
No	Yes	No	No	(4)	Yes	Yes	5	Yes	56
No	Yes	No	No	No	Yes	Yes	2	Yes	57
No	Yes	No	No	(4)	Yes	Yes	3	Yes	58
No	Yes	(1)	No	No	Yes	Yes	None.		59
No	Yes	No	No	(4)	Yes	Yes	None.		60

[1] Not applicable; guards not removable.
[8] Separate stops on all machines.
[9] Electric cut-off.

TABLE **IV.**—ACCIDENT SAFEGUARDING AND

ILLINOIS.

Establishment number.	Mill gearing and machinery unguarded or improperly guarded.	Machinery.				
			Devices for stopping machinery.			
		Direct control of source of power in workroom.	For notifying engine room.	Belt shifters.	Friction clutches.	Other special apparatus.
1	No machinery					
2	....do					
3	None unguarded	No....	Telephone	Yes....	Yes....	Yes [3].
4	....do	Yes [4]..	([5])	Yes....	([5])	Yes [6]..
5	....do	Yes [4]..	([5])	Yes....	([5])	No....
6	....do	Yes [4]..	([5])	Yes....	([5])	No....
7	No machinery					
8	None unguarded	No....	No	Yes....	Yes....	No....
9	No machinery					
10	None unguarded	Yes [4]..	([5])	Yes....	Yes....	No....
11	Candy machines, etc.[11]	Yes [4]..	Telephone [5]	Yes....	Yes....	No....
12	Chocolate-dipping machine (belts)	No....	Telephone	Yes....	No....	No....
13	Candy machines; candy cutters; mixer; equalizer.	Yes [4]..	Telephone [5]	Yes....	([5])	No....
14	None unguarded	Yes [4]..	([5])	Yes....	([5])	No....
15	No machinery					
16	....do					
17	....do					
18	....do					
19	Cutter; tipper; riveter; stamper; eyeleter.	Yes [4]..	([5])	Yes....	([5])	No....
20	Dough break	No....	No	Yes....	Yes....	No....
21	1 roller	Yes [4]..	Telephone [5]	Yes....	Yes....	No....
22	Conveyor	Yes [4]..	Telephone [5]	Yes....	Yes....	No....
23	None unguarded	([7])	Electric bell	Yes....	Yes....	([7])
24	....do	([7])	Telephone	No....	No....	Yes [13]
25	....do	Yes [4]..	Electric bell [5]	([5])	([5])	No....
26	All in barbed wire department	Yes [14]	Telephone	No [15]	Yes....	No....
27	None unguarded	Yes [4]..	([5])	Yes....	([5])	No....
28	Knitting machines	Yes [4]..	([5])	Yes....	Yes....	No....
29	None unguarded	No....	No	Yes....	No....	No....
30	Knitting and dye machines	Yes [4]..	([5])	Yes....	Yes....	No....
31	Saw; peeling machine; match machines	No....	No	No....	No....	No....
32	Paper cutter; corner cutter; corner stayer. ender.	Yes [4]..	([5])	No....	Yes....	No....
33	Corner stayer; paper slitter; tube cutter; cutting machine.	Yes [4]..	([5])	No....	Yes....	No....
34	Paper slitter	Yes [4]..	([5])	No....	Yes....	No....
35	1 each of papering, ending, staying, and wrapping machines.	Yes [4]..	([5])	No....	Yes....	No....
36	None unguarded	Yes [4]..	([5])	Yes..	([5])	No....
37	1 each of staying, soap-pressing, and soap-wrapping machines.	No....	No	Yes..	Yes....	No....
38	Cutting and drawing presses; saws	No....	No	Yes....	Yes....	No....
39	Punch presses; trimming, beading, and bulging machines.	No....	No	No....	No....	No....
40	Bumping machines; low belting	No....	Electric bell	Yes....	Yes....	No....
41	Bumping, notching, and punching machines; squaring shears.	Yes [4]..	([5])	Yes..	Yes....	Yes [17].
42	None unguarded	Yes [4]..	Telephone [5]	Yes..	Yes....	No....
43	Main belts	Yes [4]..	Telephone [5]	Yes..	([5])	No....
44	None unguarded	Yes [4]..	Telephone [5]	Yes..	([5])	No....
45	Drier; brush picker; cards; looms; brush; press.	No....	No	Yes....	No....	No....
46	Pickers; carders; looms; presser	No....	No	No [15]	No....	No....
47	Mule spinners; warper; press; cards; pickers; looms; fullers.	No....	No	No [15]	No....	No.

[1] No elevator in building.
[2] Brakes in all practical cases.
[3] No children employed.
[4] Electric power.
[5] Not necessary.

[6] Safety brakes.
[7] Not reported.
[8] Wrapping machine.
[9] Data not obtainable.
[10] No dangerous machine.

ACCIDENTS: MACHINERY AND ELEVATORS—Continued.

ILLINOIS.

Machinery.					Elevators.		Accidents recorded by establishment during past year.		Establishment number.
Safeguards.			Machinery cleaned or oiled, while in motion, by—		Shafts and openings properly guarded.	Safety clutches or other proper safety devices provided.			
Removed by employees.	Removal by employees forbidden.	Warnings posted on dangerous machines.	Women.	Children.			Number.	Reported to State as required by law.	
					(1)		None.		1
					Yes	Yes	None.		2
No	Yes	Yes	No	(3)	Yes	Yes	268	Yes	3
No	Yes	No	No	(3)	(1)		9	Yes	4
(7)	(7)	No	Yes [8]	No	Yes	Yes	None.		5
(7)	(7)	(7)	No	(2)	Yes	Yes	4	(9)	6
					(1)		None.		7
(7)	(7)	(7)	No	No	Yes	Yes	None.		8
					Yes	No	None.		9
No	Yes	(10)	No	(3)	(1)		None.		10
(7)	(7)	No	No	No	Yes	Yes	None.		11
(7)	(7)	No	No	No	Yes	Yes	None.		12
(7)	(7)	No	No	No	Yes	Yes	None.		13
No	Yes	Yes	No	(3)	Yes	Yes	27	(12)	14
					Yes	Yes	None.		15
					Yes	Yes	4	(9)	16
					Yes	Yes	None.		17
					Yes	Yes	None.		18
No	Yes	No	No	No	Yes	Yes	4	Yes	19
(7)	(7)	No	No	(3)	Yes	Yes	21	(9)	20
(7)	(7)	No	No	No	Yes	Yes	None.		21
No	Yes	No	No	No	1 no, 1 yes	1 no, 1 yes	None.		22
No	Yes	(10)	No	No	Yes	Yes	None.		23
(7)	(7)	(7)	No	No	Yes	Yes	3	(12)	24
No	No	(7)	No	No	Yes	Yes	None.		25
No	Yes	No	No	No	Yes	Yes	50	(9)	26
(7)	(7)	No	No	No	Yes	Yes	5	(9)	27
(16)		No	No	No	Yes	Yes	1	(9)	28
(7)	(7)	No	No	No	1 no, 1 yes	Yes	4	(9)	29
No	(7)	(10)	No	No	Yes	Yes	None.		30
(7)	(7)	No	No	(2)	(1)		4	(9)	31
(7)	(7)	No	No	No	Yes	Yes	None.		32
(7)	(7)	No	No	No	Yes	Yes	24	(9)	33
No	Yes	No	No	No	Yes	Yes	9	(9)	34
(7)	(7)	No	No	No	Yes	Yes	15	No	35
No	Yes	No	No	No	Yes	Yes	None.		36
Yes	No	No	No	No	No	Yes	138	Yes	37
No	Yes	No	No	No	Yes	Yes	86	No	38
(7)	(7)	No	No	No	(1)		6	(9)	39
No	Yes	Yes	No	(3)	Yes	Yes	38	(9)	40
(7)	(7)	No	No	(3)	Yes	Yes	94	(9)	41
No	Yes	Yes	No	No	No	No	None.		42
(7)	(7)	No	No	No	Yes	Yes	None.		43
(7)	(7)	No	No	(3)	Yes	Yes	None.		44
(7)	(7)	No	Yes [18]	(3)	Yes	Yes	6	(9)	45
(7)	(7)	No	No	(2)	(1)		None.		46
(7)	(7)	No	Yes [18]	No	(1)		2	(9)	47

11 All machines run by women and children are guarded.
12 Report not required; no accident causing as much as 30 days' loss of time.
13 Transmitter.
14 Method not reported.
15 Some, but not all cases.
16 No safeguard.
17 Stop levers.
18 Looms.

TABLE IV.—ACCIDENT SAFEGUARDING AND

INDIANA.

Establishment number.	Mill gearing and machinery unguarded or improperly guarded.	Machinery.				
		Devices for stopping machinery.				
		Direct control of source of power in workroom.	For notifying engine room.	Belt shifters.	Friction clutches.	Other special apparatus.
1	None unguarded	Yes¹	(²)	Yes	Yes	No
2	Circular and band saws; stapling machines.	No	Engine room adjacent to workroom.	Yes	No	No
3	Bottler.	Yes¹	(²)	Yes	(²)	No
4	Drills; tire-cutting machines; emery wheels.	No	No	Yes	Yes	No
5	Drill presses.	Yes¹	Telephone²	Yes	Yes	No
6	Beveling, punching, reaming, and milling machines.	Yes¹	(²)	Yes	Yes	No
7	No machinery.					
8	....do....					
9	....do....					
10	....do....					
11	....do....					
12	None unguarded	Yes¹	(²)	Yes	(²)	No
13	....do....	Yes¹	(²)	(²)	(²)	No
14	Chocolate-coating machines.	No	No	Yes	Yes	No
15	None unguarded	Yes¹	(²)	Yes	Yes	No
16	....do....	Yes¹	Speaking tube²	Yes	Yes	No
17	No machinery.					
18	None unguarded	No	No	Yes	No	No
19	....do....	No	Bell; telephone	Yes	Yes	No
20	....do....	No	No	Yes	Yes	No
21	Armature machines (belts)	Yes¹	Telephone³	Yes	Yes	No
22	None unguarded	Yes¹	(²)	Yes	Yes	No
23	....do....	No	Engine in workroom.	Yes	Yes	No
24	....do....	Yes¹	(²)	No	Yes	No
25	Cutting machines (belts)	Yes¹	(²)	Yes	Yes	No
26	None unguarded	No	Telephone	Yes	Yes	No
27	....do....	No	No	Yes	Yes	No
28	Low shafting.	No	No	Yes	Yes	No
29	Veneering machine.	No	No	Yes	Yes	No
30	Ender; staying machine.	No	No	Yes	Yes	No
31	Creasing press; Gordon press; corner cutter; metal stayer.	Yes¹	(²)	Yes	Yes	No
32	None unguarded	Yes¹	(²)	Yes	Yes	No
33	Printing, cutting, and creasing presses; ender.	No	Telephone	Yes	Yes	No
34	Ending machine.	Yes¹	Telephone³	Yes	Yes	No
35	Grinder; button machine.	Yes¹	(²)	No	(²)	No
36	None unguarded	Yes¹	(²)	Yes	Yes	No
37	....do....	No	No	Yes	Yes	No
38	....do....	Yes¹	Telephone³	Yes	Yes	Yes ¹⁴
39	....do....	Yes¹	(²)	No	(²)	No
40	....do....	Yes¹	(²)	Yes	(²)	No
	....do....	No	No	Yes	Yes	No
41	Punch and draw presses; belts on machines generally.	Yes¹	(²)	Yes	Yes	No
42	Belting and fly wheels on all machines.	No	No	Yes	Yes	No
43	Cold rolls; slitters and squaring shears.	Yes¹	(²)	Yes	Yes	No
44	None unguarded	No	Gong	Yes	No	No
45	Looms; spoolers; spinning machines.	No	Bell	Yes	Yes	No
46	None unguarded (wool department).	Yes¹	(²)	Yes	(²)	No
	None unguarded (rubber department)¹⁷	No	Whistle; telephone.	Yes	Yes	No
47	None unguarded	No	No	Yes	Yes	No

¹ Electric power.
² Not necessary.
³ Reported to State only accidents causing permanent disability; none such past year.
⁴ No elevator in building.
⁵ Not reported.
⁶ No children employed.
⁷ No dangerous machine.
⁸ Report to State only such accidents as cause loss of over one week's time; one reported past year.

ACCIDENTS: MACHINERY AND ELEVATORS—Continued.

INDIANA.

| Machinery. | | | | | | Elevators. | Accidents recorded by establishment during past year. | | Establishment number. |
| Safeguards. | | | Machinery cleaned or oiled, while in motion, by— | | Shafts and openings properly guarded. | Safety clutches or other proper safety devices provided. | | | |
Removed by employees.	Removal by employees forbidden.	Warnings posted on dangerous machines.	Women.	Children.			Number.	Reported to State as required by law.	
No	Yes	No	No	No	Yes	Yes	1	Yes	1
No	No	No	No	No	Yes	Yes	12	No	2
No	No	No	No	No	Yes	Yes	150	(3)	3
No	Yes	No	No	No	Yes	Yes	85	Yes	4
No	No	No	No	No	(4)		None.		5
No	No	(5)	No	(5)	Yes	Yes	3	Yes	6
					Yes	Yes	None.		7
					Yes	Yes	None.		8
					No	No	None.		9
					Yes	Yes	None.		10
					Yes	Yes	1	Yes	11
No	Yes	(7)	No	No	(4)		None.		12
No	No	(6)	No	(6)	Yes	Yes	None.		13
No	No	No	No	No	Yes	Yes	None.		14
No	Yes	No	No	No	Yes	Yes	None.		15
No	Yes	(7)	No	No	Yes	Yes	3	Yes	16
					(4)		None.		17
No	Yes	No	No	No	Yes	Yes	None.		18
No	Yes	No	No	No	Yes	Yes	4	Yes	19
No	Yes	No	No	No	Yes	Yes	None.		20
No	No	(7)	No	(6)	Yes	Yes	15	(8)	21
No	Yes	Yes	No	(6)	Yes	Yes	3	Yes	22
No	Yes	No	No	(6)	No	Yes	None.		23
No	Yes	Yes	Yes[9]	Yes[9]	Yes	No	15	No	24
No	No	(7)	No	No	Yes	Yes	None.		25
No	Yes	Yes	Yes[10]	Yes[10]	Yes	Yes	None.		26
No	Yes	(7)	Yes[11]	Yes[11]	Yes	Yes	1	No	27
No	No	Yes	No	No	Yes	Yes	2	Yes	28
No	No	(7)	No	No	(4)		3	Yes	29
No	No	No	No	No	Yes	Yes	2	No	30
Yes	Yes	No	Yes[11]	No	Yes	Yes	2	Yes	31
No	Yes	No	No	(6)	Yes	Yes	1	Yes	32
Yes	No	No	No	No	Yes	Yes	None.		33
Yes	No	No	No	No	Yes	Yes	3	Yes	34
(13)	(13)	No	No	(6)	(4)		None.		35
No	Yes	No	No	No	Yes	Yes	5	Yes	36
No	No	(7)	No	No	Yes	Yes	None.		37
No	No	No	No	No	Yes	Yes	None.		38
(13)	(13)	No	No	No	(4)		None.		39
No	Yes	No	No	No	}No	Yes	None.		40
No	Yes	No	No	No	Yes	Yes	89	No	41
No	Yes	No	No	No	Yes	Yes	4	No	42
No	Yes	No	No	Yes[14]	(4)	Yes	33	Yes	43
No	No	No	(16)	No	Yes	Yes	6	Yes	44
No	No	No	No	No	Yes	Yes	6	Yes	45
No	Yes	Yes	No	No	}Yes	Yes	42	Yes	46
No	Yes	Yes	No	No	Yes	Yes	None.		47

9 Sewing machines.
10 Oiling sewing machines and circular knitters.
11 Knitting machines.
13 Joining machine.
13 Not applicable; guards not removable.

14 Foot levers on machines.
15 Cold rolls.
16 No women employed.
17 No machinery in warehouse.

TABLE **IV.**—ACCIDENT SAFEGUARDING AND

MICHIGAN.

Establishment number.	Mill gearing and machinery unguarded or improperly guarded.	Machinery.				
		Devices for stopping machinery.				
		Direct control of source of power in workroom.	For notifying engine room.	Belt shifters.	Friction clutches.	Other special apparatus.
1	None unguarded	Yes [1]	([2])	Yes	Yes	No
2	....do	Yes [1]	([2])	Yes	Yes	No
3	Paper cutter; punch press	No	Speaking tube	Yes	Yes	No
4	None unguarded	Yes [1]	([2])	Yes	([2])	No
5	Enrober (belt and gearing); chocolate kettle (belt).	Yes [1]	([2])	Yes	([5])	No
6	Chocolated dipper (belt)	Yes [1]	Telephone [3]	Yes	Yes	No
7	None unguarded	Yes [1]	([3])	Yes	Yes	No
8	Presses	No	No	Yes	Yes	No
9	None unguarded	Yes [1]	Telephone [3]	Yes	Yes	No
10	....do	Yes [1]	([3])	Yes	Yes	No
11	Corner-cutting machine	Yes [1]	Alarm system; telephone.[3]	Yes	Yes	No
12	Saws	Yes [1]	([2])	Yes	Yes	No
13	Block machines (gearing); belts	No	No	Yes	Yes	No
14	None unguarded	Yes [1]	Telephone [3]	Yes	Yes	No
15	Creasing press; printing press; ender; shears.	Yes [1]	Speaking tube [3]	Yes	Yes	No
16	Drier (belts)	Yes [1]	Telephone [3]	Yes	Yes	No
17	None unguarded	Yes [1]	Telephone [2]	Yes	Yes	No
18	....do	No	Telephone	Yes	Yes	No
19	....do	No	No	Yes	Yes	No

WISCONSIN.

1	None unguarded	No	Yes [3]	Yes	No	No
2	....do	No	Telephone	Yes	Yes	No
3	....do	No	Electric bell	Yes	No	No
4	....do	No	Electric bell	Yes	Yes	No
5	....do	No	Electric bell	Yes	Yes	No
6	....do	Yes [1]	([2])	Yes	Yes	No
7	....do	No	Telephone	Yes	Yes	Yes [10]
8	....do	Yes [1]	Telephone [2]	Yes	Yes	No
9	....do	Yes [1]	Telephone [3]	Yes	Yes	No
10	....do	No	Telephone	Yes	Yes	No
11	....do	([3])	No	Yes	Yes	No
12	....do	No	No	Yes	Yes	No
13	....do	Yes [1]	([2])	Yes	Yes	No
14	Punch presses; trimming and beading machines.	No	No	Yes	Yes	No
15	Punch and bumping presses	No	No	Yes	Yes	No
16	None unguarded	Yes [1]	([2])	Yes	Yes	No
17	No machinery					
18	None unguarded	Yes [1]	([3])	Yes	([5])	No
19	No machinery					

[1] Electric power.
[2] Not necessary.
[3] No children employed.
[4] Report to State not required.
[5] No dangerous machine.
[6] Not applicable; guards not removable.

ACCIDENTS: MACHINERY AND ELEVATORS—Continued.

MICHIGAN.

	Machinery.				Elevators.				
Safeguards.		Warnings posted on dangerous machines.	Machinery cleaned or oiled, while in motion, by—		Shafts and openings properly guarded.	Safety clutches or other proper safety devices provided.	Accidents recorded by establishment during past year.		Establishment number.
Removed by employees.	Removal by employees forbidden.		Women.	Children.			Number.	Reported to State as required by law.	
No......	No......	No......	No......	(³)......	Yes......	Yes.....	None.	....	1
No......	Yes......	No......	No......	No......	No......	Yes.....	26	(⁴)......	2
No......	Yes......	No......	No......	No......	Yes.....	Yes.....	6	(⁴)......	3
No......	No......	No......	No......	No......	Yes.....	Yes.....	None.	....	4
No......	No......	No......	No......	(³)......	Yes.....	Yes.....	4	(⁴)......	5
No......	No......	No......	No......	No......	Yes.....	Yes.....	None.	....	6
No......	Yes......	No......	No......	No......	Yes.....	Yes.....	5	(⁴)......	7
No......	Yes......	No......	No......	No......	Yes.....	Yes.....	12	(⁴)......	8
No......	Yes......	(⁶)......	No......	No......	Yes.....	Yes.....	4	(⁴)......	9
No......	Yes......	(⁶)......	No......	(³)......	Yes.....	Yes.....	None.	....	10
Yes......	Yes......	No......	No......	No......	Yes.....	Yes.....	10	(⁴)......	11
Yes......	Yes......	No......	No......	No......	Yes.....	Yes.....	17	(⁴)......	12
(⁶)......	(⁶)......	No......	No......	No......	Yes.....	Yes.....	2	(⁴)......	13
No......	No......	No......	No......	(³)......	Yes.....	Yes.....	None.	....	14
Yes......	Yes......	Yes......	No......	No......	Yes.....	Yes.....	None.	....	15
No......	Yes......	No......	No......	No......	Yes.....	Yes.....	4	(⁴)......	16
No......	No......	Yes......	No......	No......	Yes.....	Yes.....	4	(⁴)......	17
No......	Yes......	No......	No......	(³)......	Yes.....	Yes.....	3	(⁴)......	18
No......	Yes......	No......	No......	No......	(⁷)......		None.	....	19

WISCONSIN.

No......	Yes......	No......	No......	(³)......	Yes.....	No......	None.	....	1
No......	Yes......	Yes......	No......	No......	Yes.....	Yes.....	None.	....	2
No......	Yes......	No......	No......	No......	Yes.....	Yes.....	None.	..:......	3
No......	Yes......	(⁹)......	No......	No......	Yes.....	Yes.....	2	(⁴)......	4
No......	Yes......	No......	No......	No......	Yes.....	Yes.....	None.	....	5
No......	Yes......	No......	No......	No......	Yes.....	Yes.....	1	(⁴)......	6
No......	Yes......	No......	No......	(³)......	(⁷)......		None.	....	7
No......	Yes......	No......	No......	No......	Yes.....	Yes.....	None.	....	8
No......	Yes......	Yes......	No......	No......	Yes.....	Yes.....	None.	....	9
No......	Yes......	Yes......	No......	No......	Yes.....	Yes.....	None.	....	10
No......	Yes......	Yes......	No......	No......	Yes.....	Yes.....	43	(⁴)......	11
No......	Yes......	Yes......	No......	No......	Yes.....	Yes.....	4	(⁴)......	12
No......	Yes......	No......	Yes ¹¹...	(³)......	Yes.....	Yes.....	None.	....	13
No......	Yes......	No......	No......	No......	Yes.....	Yes.....	61	(⁴)......	14
No......	Yes......	No......	No......	No......	Yes.....	Yes.....	46	(⁴)......	15
No......	Yes......	No......	No......	(³)......	(⁷)......		None.	....	16
....	....	....	....	....	Yes.....	Yes	None.	....	17
No......	Yes......	No......	No......	(³)......	(⁷)......		None.	....	18
....	....	....	....	....	(⁷)......		None.	....	19

⁷ No elevator in building.　　　　　¹⁰ Stop motions on knitting machines.
⁸ Method not reported.　　　　　　　¹¹ Grinding and counter sinking machines.
⁹ Not reported.

TABLE **IV.**—ACCIDENT SAFEGUARDING AND

MARYLAND.

Establishment number.	Mill gearing and machinery unguarded or improperly guarded.	Machinery.				
			Devices for stopping machinery.			
		Direct control of source of power in • workroom.	For notifying engine room.	Belt shifters.	Friction clutches.	Other special apparatus.
1	No machinery.................					
2	....do..					
3	None unguarded.............	No....	No................	Yes...	Yes....	No....
4	Hanging belts; bead roller (gearing)......	No....	No................	Yes...	Yes....	No....
5	1 belt passing through floor............	No....	No................	Yes...	No.....	No....
6	None unguarded.	No....	No................	Yes...	No.....	No....
7	....do..	No....	No................	Yes...	No.....	No....
8	....do..	No....	No................	Yes...	No.....	No....
9	No machinery..					
10	None unguarded.........................	No....	No................	Yes...	Yes....	No....
11	No machinery...					
12	None unguarded.............	No....	Telephone.........	Yes...	Yes....	No....
13	....do..	No....	Electric bell.....	Yes...	Yes....	No....
14	....do..	No....	Electric bell.....	Yes...	Yes....	No....
15	....do..	No....	Electric bell.....	Yes...	Yes....	No....
16	Mixers and cutters and conveyors	No....	Speaking tube and gong.	Yes...	Yes....	No....
17	Lacing, staying, and corner-cutting machines.	Yes [5]..	([6])	No....	Yes....	No....
18	Staying machines.......................	No....	No................	No....	Yes....	No....
19	Lace machine......................	No....	No................	Yes...	Yes....	No....
20	None unguarded....................	No....	No................	Yes...	No.....	No....
21	Dampening machine (gearing)............	Yes [5]..	([6])	Yes...	Yes....	No....
22	Sewing machines......................	No....	Telephone.........	No....	No.....	No....
23	Sewing tables............	Yes [5]..	Electric bells [4]...	Yes...	Yes....	No....
24	Sewing machine; dangling belt..........	Yes [5]..	Telephone [4].......	Yes...	([6]).....	No....
25	None unguarded..............	Yes [5]..	([6])...............	Yes...	Yes....	No....
26	....do..	Yes [5]..	([6])...............	Yes...	Yes....	No....
27	....do..	Yes [5]..	([6])...............	Yes...	Yes....	No....
28	Granulator and cutting knives..........	No....	Telephone; push button.	Yes...	Yes....	No....

NORTH CAROLINA.

1	None unguarded..................	Yes [5]..	([6])...............	Yes...	Yes....	No....
2	....do..	Yes [5]..	([6])...............	Yes...	Yes....	No....
3	....do..	No....	No................	No [10]..	Yes....	No....
4	Cards.......................	Yes [5]..	([6])...............	Yes...	Yes....	No....
5	Cards; main belts............	No....	No................	No....	Yes....	No....
6	None unguarded..............	No....	No................	No [10]..	No [10]..	No....
7	....do..	No....	No................	No [10]..	Yes....	No....
8	....do..	No....	Electric bell......	Yes...	Yes....	No....
9	....do..	No....	No................	No [10]..	No [10]..	No....
10	Drawing frames (belts)................	Yes [5]..	([6])...............	Yes...	([6]).....	No....
11	Drawing frames and speeders (belts).....	Yes [5]..	([6])	Yes...	([6])......	No....
12	None unguarded.............	No....	No................	Yes...	No.....	No....
13	Shafting under sewing machines..........	Yes [5]..	([6])...............	Yes...	([6])......	No....
14	None unguarded...............	No....	No................	Yes...	No......	No....

[1] No elevator in building.
[2] Not reported.
[3] Data not obtainable.
[4] Report to State not required.
[5] Electric power.
[6] Not necessary.
[7] No safeguard.
[8] No dangerous machine.

ACCIDENTS: MACHINERY AND ELEVATORS—Continued.

MARYLAND.

Machinery					Elevators		Accidents recorded by establishment during past year.		Establishment number.
Safeguards.		Warnings posted on dangerous machines.	Machinery cleaned or oiled, while in motion, by—		Shafts and openings properly guarded.	Safety clutches or other proper safety devices provided.			
Removed by employees.	Removal by employees forbidden.		Women.	Children.			Number.	Reported to State as required by law.	
					Yes....	Yes....	None.	....	1
					(1)		None.	....	2
No......	Yes......	No......	No......	No......	(1)		None.	....	3
(2)	(2)	Yes......	No......	No......	Yes....	Yes....	(3)	....	4
(2)	(2)	Yes......	No......	No......	Yes....	Yes....	None.	....	5
(2)	(2)	No......	No......	No......	Yes....	No......	None.	....	6
(2)	(2)	No......	No......	No......	Yes....	(2)	None.	....	7
(2)	(2)	No......	No......	No......	Yes....	Yes....	None.	....	8
					No......	Yes....	None.	....	9
(8)	(2)	No......	No......	No......	Yes....	Yes....	None.	....	10
					Yes....	No......	None.	....	11
(2)	(2)	No......	No......	No......	Yes....	Yes....	60	(4)	12
(2)	(2)	No......	No......	No......	Yes....	Yes....	None.	(4)	13
(2)	(2)	No......	No......	No......	Yes....	Yes....	1	(4)	14
(2)	(2)	No......	No......	No......	Yes....	Yes....	1	(4)	15
No......	No......	No......	No......	No......	Yes....	Yes....	7	(4)	16
(2)	(2)	No......	No......	No......	Yes....	Yes....	6	(4)	17
(2)	(2)	No......	No......	No......	No......	Yes....	None.	....	18
Yes......	(2)	No......	No......	No......	Yes....	Yes....	3	(4)	19
(2)	(2)	No......	No......	No......	Yes....	Yes....	10	(4)	20
(2)	(2)	No......	No......	No......	Yes....	Yes....	4	(4)	21
(7)		(8)	No......	No......	Yes....	No......	(2)	....	22
Yes......	Yes......	No......	No......	No......	Yes....	Yes....	None.	....	23
No......	Yes......	(8)	Yes.9	No......	Yes....	Yes....	2	(4)	24
No......	No......	No......	No......	No......	Yes....	Yes....	None.	....	25
No......	Yes......	No......	No......	No......	Yes....	Yes....	1	(4)	26
No......	Yes......	(8)	No......	No......	Yes....	Yes....	2	(4)	27
No......	Yes......	Yes......	No......	No......	Yes....	Yes....	12	(4)	28

NORTH CAROLINA.

Removed by employees.	Removal by employees forbidden.	Warnings	Women.	Children.	Shafts and openings.	Safety clutches.	Number.	Reported.	Est. no.
No......	Yes......	(8)	No......	No......	Yes....	Yes....	87	(4)	1
No......	No......	No......	No......	No......	Yes....	Yes....	None.	....	2
(11)	(11)	Yes......	No......	No......	(1)		12	(4)	3
No......	No......	No......	No......	No......	(1)		None.	....	4
No......	Yes......	No......	No......	No......	No......	No......	None.	....	5
No......	No......	No......	No......	No......	Yes....	Yes....	12	(4)	6
No......	No......	No......	No......	No......	Yes....	Yes....	4	(4)	7
No......	Yes......	No......	No......	No......	Yes....	Yes....	9	(4)	8
(11)	(11)	No......	No......	No......	Yes....	Yes....	4	(4)	9
No......	No......	No......	No......	No......	Yes....	Yes....	2	(4)	10
No......	No......	No......	No......	Yes.12	{1 no, 1 yes} Yes....		1	(4)	11
No......	No......	No......	No......	No......	No......	Yes....	None.	....	12
No......	No......	No......	No......	No......	No......	Yes....	None.	....	13
No......	No......	No......	No......	Yes.13	Yes....	Yes....	1	(4)	14

9 Ironing machine.
10 Some, but not all cases.
11 Not applicable; guards not removable.
13 One boy oils spinning frames.
14 Boys oil knitting machines.

TABLE **IV.**—ACCIDENT SAFEGUARDING AND

NORTH CAROLINA—Concluded.

Establishment number.	Mill gearing and machinery unguarded or improperly guarded.	Machinery.				
			Devices for stopping machinery.			
		Direct control of source of power in workroom.	For notifying engine room.	Belt shifters.	Friction clutches.	Other special apparatus.
15	None unguarded	Yes[1]	(²)	Yes	Yes	No
16	....do	Yes[1]	(²)	(²)	Yes	No
17	....do	Yes[1]	(²)	No[5]	Yes	No
18	....do	Yes[1]	(²)	No	(²)	No
19	....do	Yes[1]	(²)	Yes	(²)	No
20	....do	No	Telephone	No	Yes	No
21	....do	No	Speaking tube	Yes	No	No
22	....do	Yes[1]	Telephone[²]	No	Yes	No
23	Belts and presses on lumping machines	No	Telephones	(⁶)	(⁶)	Yes[⁹]
24	Folding and bending machines	Yes[1]	(²)	Yes	(²)	No
25	Looms; mule-spinning frames; garnett machine.	No	No	Yes	No[5]	No
26	Looms (gearing and shuttle guards)	No	No	No[5]	No[5]	No
27	Looms; shuttle guards	No	No	No[5]	No[5]	No
28	None unguarded	No	No	Yes	No[5]	No

GEORGIA.

1	Dipping machine; low shafting	Yes[1]	(²)	Yes	(²)	No
2	None unguarded	Yes[1]	(²)	Yes	Yes	No
3	....do	No	No	Yes	No[5]	No
4	....do	No	No	Yes	No[5]	No
5	....do	No	No	No	No	No
6	....do	No	Telephone	Yes	Yes	No
7	A few looms; cards	No	No	No	No[5]	No
8	None unguarded	No	No	Yes	No	No
9	....do	No	Electric bells	Yes	No	No
10	....do	No	Electric bells	Yes	Yes	No
11	....do	No	No	Yes	Yes	No
12	....do	No	No	Yes	No[5]	No
13	Conveyor; mixing and cracker machines	Yes[1]	(²)	Yes	(²)	No
14	Gearing generally	Yes[1]	(²)	Yes	(²)	No
15	None unguarded	Yes[1]	(²)	Yes	(²)	No
16	Belts; cards; drawing frames; knitting machines (handles).	Yes[1]	(²)	Yes	(²)	No
17	None unguarded	Yes[1]	(²)	Yes	(²)	No
18	Shafting under sewing table	Yes[14]	(²)	Yes	No	No
19	None unguarded	No	No	Yes	No	No
20	....do	No	No	Yes	No	No
21	....do	No	No	Yes	No	No
22	....do	Yes[1]	(²)	No	Yes	No
23	....do	Yes[1]	(²)	Yes	Yes	No
24	Looms; mules; cards	No	No	Yes	Yes	No
25	Pickers; cards; presses; looms	No[16]	No	Yes	No[5]	No
26	Cards; looms; mules; extractor; dryers	Yes[1]	(²)	Yes	(²)	No
27	Mules; looms; cards; presses; pickers; belts.	No[16]	No	No[5]	No[5]	No

[1] Electric power.
[²] Not necessary.
[³] No dangerous machine.
[⁴] Report to State not required.

[⁵] Some, but not all cases.
[⁶] No women employed.
[⁷] No elevator in building.
[⁸] Not reported.

ACCIDENTS: MACHINERY AND ELEVATORS—Continued.

NORTH CAROLINA—Concluded.

Machinery.					Elevators.		Accidents recorded by establishment during past year.		Establishment number.
Safeguards.		Warnings posted on dangerous machines.	Machinery cleaned or oiled, while in motion, by—		Shafts and openings properly guarded.	Safety clutches or other proper safety devices provided.	Number.	Reported to State as required by law.	
Removed by employees.	Removal by employees forbidden.		Women.	Children.					
No	Yes	(²)	No	No	Yes...	Yes	9	(⁴)	15
No	No	No	No	No	No	Yes	None		16
No	No	No	(⁶)	No	No	Yes	None		17
No	No	(³)	No	No	(⁷)		10	(⁴)	18
No	No	(²)	No	No	Yes	Yes	12	(⁴)	19
No	No	No	No	No	Yes	Yes	4	(⁴)	20
No	No	No	No	No	No	Yes	None		21
No	Yes	No	No	No	{1 no / 3 yes}	{1 no / 3 yes}	31	(⁴)	22
No	No	No	No	No	Yes	Yes	None		23
No	Yes	No	(⁶)	No	(⁷)		3	(⁴)	24
No	No	No	No	No	No	Yes	1	(⁴)	25
No	Yes	No	No	No	(⁷)		None		26
No	No	No	No	No	(⁷)		3	(⁴)	27
No	Yes	No	No	No	Yes	Yes	None		28

GEORGIA.

Machinery.					Elevators.		Accidents recorded.		No.
(⁸)	(⁸)	No	No	No	Yes	Yes	4	(⁴)	1
No	No	No	No	No	Yes	Yes	1	(⁴)	2
No	(⁸)	No	No	No	Yes	Yes	None		3
No	Yes	No	Yes ¹⁰	No	Yes	Yes	16	(⁴)	4
No	No	No	No	No	Yes	Yes	5	(⁴)	5
No	No	No	No	No	Yes	Yes	4	(⁴)	6
No	No	No	No	No	(⁷)		None		7
No	Yes	No	No	No	Yes	Yes	6	(⁴)	8
No	Yes	No	No	No	Yes	Yes	7	(⁴)	9
No	Yes	No	No	No	Yes	Yes	11	(⁴)	10
No	No	No	No	Yes ¹¹	No	No	None		11
No	(⁸)	No	No	No	No	Yes	1	(⁴)	12
(¹²)	(¹²)	No	No	No	No	Yes	None		13
(⁸)	(⁸)	No	No	(¹²)	Yes	Yes	2	(⁴)	14
No	No	No	No	No	Yes	Yes	1	(⁴)	15
No	No	No	No	No	Yes	Yes	4	(⁴)	16
No	No	No	No	No	Yes	No	3	(⁴)	17
No	No	No	No	No	Yes	Yes	1	(⁴)	18
No	No	No	No	No	(⁷)		None		19
No	No	No	No	No	Yes	No	None		20
No	No	No	No	No	(⁷)		None		21
Yes	No	No	No	No	No	Yes	3	(⁴)	22
Yes	No	No	No	No	No	Yes	None		23
No	No:	Yes	Yes ¹⁵	Yes ¹⁵	No	Yes	None		24
No	No	No	No	No	(⁷)		None		25
No	No	Yes	No	No	No	No	None		26
No	No	No	No	No	(⁷)		None		27

⁹ Foot lever on lumping machine.
¹⁰ Looms.
¹¹ Two boys oil spindles.
¹² Not applicable; guards not removable.
¹³ No children employed.
¹⁴ Wire pull to stop engine, in all workrooms.
¹⁵ Clean spinning frames.
¹⁶ Water power.

TABLE **IV.**—ACCIDENT SAFEGUARDING AND

FLORIDA.

Establishment number.	Mill gearing and machinery unguarded or improperly guarded.	Machinery.				
			Devices for stopping machinery.			
		Direct control of source of power in ● workroom.	For notifying engine room.	Belt shifters.	Friction clutches.	Other special apparatus.
1	Some saws; several belts.................	Yes [1]..	(²)..............	Yes...	Yes.....	No....
2	Saws, several belts, and pulleys..........	No....	No................	Yes...	Yes.....	No....
3	No machinery.............................	......	....	......	....	....
4	.....do..................................	......	....	......	....	....
5	.....do..................................	......	....	......	....	....
6	.....do..................................	......	....	......	....	....
7	.....do..................................	......	....	......	....	....
8	.....do..................................	......	....	......	....	....
9	.....do..................................	......	....	......	....	....
10	.....do..................................	......	....	......	....	....
11	.....do..................................	......	....	......	....	....
12	.....do..................................	......	....	......	....	....
13	.....do..................................	......	....	......	....	....
14	.....do..................................	......	....	......	....	●

LOUISIANA.

1	None unguarded.........................	Yes [1]..	(²)..............	Yes...	Yes.....	No....
2	No machinery............................	......	....	......	....	....
3	None unguarded.........................	Yes [1]..	(²)...........	Yes...	Yes.....	No....
4	....do..................................	Yes [1]..	(²)	Yes...	Yes.....	No....
5	....do..................................	No....	No.	Yes...	Yes.....	No....
6	....do..................................	Yes [1]..	(²)	Yes...	Yes.....	No....
7	Soldering machine (belt)................	No....	No.............	Yes...	Yes.....	No....
8	Coating and punching presses; line folder; belts.	No....	Engine in workroom.²	Yes...	Yes.....	No....
9	A few presses..........................	Yes [1]..	(²)............	Yes...	Yes.....	No....
10	None unguarded........................	No....	No.............	Yes...	Yes.....	No....
11	2 saws.................................	No....	No.	Yes...	Yes.....	No....
12	Belts..................................	Yes [1]..	(²)..............	No....	Yes.....	No....
13	None unguarded........................	No....	Telephone........	Yes...	Yes.....	No....
14	No machinery...........................	......	....	......	....	....
15	None unguarded........................	Yes [1]..	(²)	Yes...	(²)....	No....
16	Several belts..........................	Yes [1]..	(²)	Yes...	(²)....	No....
17	None unguarded........................	No....	No.	Yes...	No....	No....
18	Brake; packing tables; 5 mixers.........	No....	No.	Yes...	Yes.....	No....
19	1 brake; 6 mixers......................	No....	No.	Yes...	Yes.....	No....
20	Rolling and cutting machines...........	No....	No.	Yes...	No....	No....
21	None unguarded........................	Yes [1]..	Telephone ²....	Yes...	Yes.....	No....
22	....do..................................	Yes [1]..	(²)	No....	(²)....	No....
23	Staying machine; 2 belts through floor...	No....	No.	Yes...	Yes.....	No....
24	2 belts through floor..................	No....	No.	Yes...	Yes.....	No....
25	Several belts..........................	Yes [1]..	(²)	No....	Yes.....	No....
26	None unguarded........................	Yes [1]..	(²)	No....	Yes.....	No....
27	Sewing tables..........................	Yes [1]..	(²)	No....	Yes.....	No....
28	No machinery...........................	......	....	......	....	....
29	Cutting machines......................	No....	No.	Yes...	Yes.....	No....

[1] Electric power.
[2] Not necessary.
[3] No elevator in building.
[4] Report to State not required.

ACCIDENTS: MACHINERY AND ELEVATORS—Concluded.

FLORIDA.

| Machinery | | | | | Elevators | | Accidents recorded by establishment during past year. | | Establishment number. |
| Safeguards. | | Warnings posted on dangerous machines. | Machinery cleaned or oiled, while in motion, by— | | Shafts and openings properly guarded. | Safety clutches or other proper safety devices provided. | | | |
Removed by employees.	Removal by employees forbidden.		Women.	Children.			Number.	Reported to State as required by law.	
No......	Yes......	No......	No......	No......	(³)......	....	4	(⁴)	1
No......	No......	No......	No......	No......	(³)......	....	1	(⁴)	2
....	....	....	....	....	Yes......	Yes......	None.	....	3
....	....	....	....	....	Yes......	Yes......	None.	....	4
....	....	....	....	....	Yes......	Yes......	None.	....	5
....	....	....	....	....	(³)......	....	None.	....	6
....	....	....	....	(⁵)......	Yes......	No......	None.	....	7
....	....	....	....	....	Yes......	No......	None.	....	8
....	....	....	....	....	Yes......	No......	None.	....	9
....	....	....	....	....	Yes......	Yes......	None.	....	10
....	....	....	....	....	Yes......	Yes......	None.	....	11
....	....	....	....	....	Yes......	Yes'......	None.	....	12
....	....	....	....	....	Yes......	Yes......	None.	....	13
....	....	....	....	....	Yes......	Yes......	None.	....	14

LOUISIANA.

Removed by employees.	Removal by employees forbidden.	Warnings posted on dangerous machines.	Women.	Children.	Shafts and openings properly guarded.	Safety clutches or other proper safety devices provided.	Number.	Reported to State as required by law.	Establishment number.
No......	No......	No......	No......	No......	(³)......	....	2	Yes......	1
....	....	....	....	....	(³)......	....	1	Yes......	2
No......	Yes......	(⁶)......	No......	No......	No......	Yes......	2	Yes......	3
No......	Yes......	No......	No......	No......	Yes......	Yes......	1	Yes......	4
No......	Yes......	No......	No......	No......	Yes......	Yes......	2	Yes......	5
No......	Yes......	No......	No......	No......	No......	No......	3	Yes......	6
No......	Yes......	No......	No......	No......	(³)......	....	1	No......	7
No......	Yes......	No......	No......	No......	(²)......	....	3	(⁷)	8
No......	No......	Yes......	No......	No......	Yes......	Yes......	None.	....	9
No......	No......	No......	No......	No......	Yes......	Yes......	None.	....	10
No......	Yes......	No......	No......	(⁵)......	Yes......	Yes......	2	Yes......	11
No......	No......	No......	No......	No......	(³)......	....	None.	....	12
No......	Yes......	No......	No......	No......	Yes......	Yes......	None.	....	13
....	....	....	....	....	Yes......	Yes......	None.	....	14
No......	No......	(⁶)......	No......	(⁵)......	No......	Yes......	None.	....	15
No......	No......	(⁶)......	No......	No......	(²)......	....	4	No......	16
No......	Yes......	No......	No......	No......	Yes......	Yes......	None.	....	17
No......	Yes......	No......	No......	No......	Yes......	Yes......	None.	....	18
No......	Yes......	No......	No......	No......	Yes......	Yes......	1	No......	19
(⁸)......	(⁸)......	No......	No......	No......	Yes......	Yes......	None.	....	20
No......	Yes......	No......	No......	No......	Yes......	Yes......	7	Yes......	21
Yes......	Yes......	No......	No......	No......	(³)......	....	None.	....	22
No......	No......	No......	No......	No......	(³)......	....	None.	....	23
No......	Yes......	No......	No......	No......	Yes......	....	None.	....	24
No......	Yes......	(⁶)......	No......	No......	No......	Yes......	None.	....	25
No......	No......	(⁶)......	No......	No......	Yes......	Yes......	None.	....	26
No......	No......	(⁶)......	No......	No......	(³)......	....	None.	....	27
....	....	....	....	....	Yes......	Yes......	None.	....	28
No......	No......	No......	No......	No......	Yes......	Yes......	20	Yes......	29

⁵ No children employed.
⁶ No dangerous machine.
⁷ Report not required; accidents caused less than 2 weeks' loss of time.
⁸ Not applicable; guards not removable.

TABLE **V.**—PROVISIONS FOR COMFORT OF EMPLOYEES: WASH ROOM
LUNCH ROOMS, AND

MAINE.

Establishment number.	Facilities for washing.			Establishments furnish—		Dressings rooms provided.				Nature of work requires change of clothing for—	
	Separate wash rooms.	Other.	Sufficient.	Towels.	Soap.	Separate for— Males.	Females.	Sufficient for— Males.	Females.	Males.	Females.
1	No	Sinks	Yes	No	No	No	No			No	No
2	Yes	Bowls	Yes	No	No	No	No			No	No
3	No	Sinks	Yes	No	No	No	Yes		Yes	No	No
4	No	do	No	No	No	No	Yes		Yes	No	No
5	Yes	(¹)	No	Yes	Yes	No	No			No	Yes²
6	No	Sink	No	Yes	Yes	Yes	Yes	Yes	Yes	No	Yes²
7	No	Sinks	Yes	No	No	Yes	Yes	Yes	Yes	Yes	Yes
8	No	do	Yes	Yes	Yes	Yes	Yes	Yes	Yes	Yes	Yes
9	No	do	Yes	Yes	Yes	Yes	Yes	Yes	Yes	Yes	Yes
10	No	do	Yes	Yes	Yes	Yes	Yes	Yes	Yes	Yes	Yes
11	No	None	No	No	No	No	No			No	No
12	No	Sink	No	No	Yes	No	No			No	No
13	Yes	do	Yes	Yes	Yes	No	No			No	No
14	No	do	Yes	No	No	No	Yes		Yes	No	Yes
15	No	Sinks	Yes	Yes	Yes	No	Yes		Yes	No	Yes
16	No	do	Yes	Yes	Yes	No	Yes		Yes	No	Yes
17	No	do	Yes	Yes	Yes	No	Yes		Yes	No	Yes
18	No	do	Yes	No	No	Yes	Yes	Yes	Yes	No	Yes
19	No	do	Yes	No	No	No	Yes		Yes	No	Yes
20	No	None	No	No	No	No	No			No	No
21	No	Buckets¹¹	No	No	No	No	No			No	No
22	No	None	No	No	No	No	No			No	No
23	No	Sinks	No	No	No	No	No			No	No
24	No	do	No	No	No	No	No			No	No
25	No	do	No	No	No	No	No			No	No
26	No	do	No	No	No	No	No			No	No

MASSACHUSETTS.

Establishment number.	Separate wash rooms.	Other.	Sufficient.	Towels.	Soap.	Separate Males.	Separate Females.	Sufficient Males.	Sufficient Females.	Change Males.	Change Females.
1	No	Sink	Yes	Yes	Yes	No	Yes		Yes	No	No
2	No	Sinks	Yes	Yes	Yes	No	Yes		Yes	No	No
3	No	do	Yes	Yes	Yes	No	No			No	Yes
4	No	Sink	No	Yes	Yes	No	No		Yes	No	Yes
5	No	do	No	Yes	Yes	No	No			No	No
6	No	Sinks	Yes	No	No	No	Yes		Yes	No	Yes
7	No	do	Yes	No	No	No	Yes		No	No	Yes
8	No	do	Yes	No	No	Yes	Yes	Yes	Yes	No	Yes
9	Yes	do	Yes	Yes	Yes	Yes	Yes	Yes	Yes	Yes	Yes
10	No	Sink	No	Yes	Yes	Yes	Yes	Yes	Yes	Yes	Yes
11	Yes	Sinks	Yes	Yes	Yes	Yes	Yes	Yes	Yes	Yes	Yes
12	Yes	Sink	Yes	Yes	Yes	Yes	Yes	Yes	Yes	Yes	Yes
13	No	Sinks	Yes	Yes	Yes	No	No		Yes	Yes	Yes
14	No	Sink	No	No	Yes	Yes	Yes	No	No	Yes	Yes
15	No	do	No	No	Yes	Yes	Yes	No	No	Yes	Yes
16	No	do	Yes	No	Yes	Yes	No			Yes	Yes
17	Yes	Sinks	Yes	Yes	Yes	Yes	Yes	Yes	Yes	Yes	Yes
18	No	Sink	Yes	Yes	Yes	No	No			Yes	Yes
19	Yes	None	Yes	No	No	No	No			No	No
20	No	Sinks	Yes	No	No	Yes	Yes	Yes	Yes	Yes	Yes
21	No	do	No	No	No	No	No			No	No
22	Yes³	do	No	No	Yes	Yes	No	No		Yes	No

¹ No urinals.
² Not reported.
³ A few women change skirts.
⁴ Not separate for sexes; 19 males, 9 females, 1 seat; average, 28 persons per seat.
⁵ Not separate for sexes; 19 males, 10 females, 1 seat; average, 29 persons per seat.
⁶ Not separate for sexes; 3 males, 15 females, 2 seats; average, 9 persons per seat.
⁷ Not separate for sexes; 1 male, 12 females, 1 seat; average, 13 persons per seat.

FACILITIES, DRESSING ROOMS, REST-ROOMS, SEATS FOR FEMALES, WATER-CLOSETS.

MAINE.

| Rest rooms for females. | | Sufficient seats provided for females. | Lunch rooms provided. | Water-closets. | | | | | | | | Air of workrooms affected by water-closets. | Establishment number. |
| Provided. | Sufficient. | | | Separate for the sexes. | Privacy of approach for— | | Number of male employees per urinal. | Number of employees per seat. | | Clean for— | | | |
					Males.	Females.		Males.	Females.	Males.	Females.		
No...		Yes..	No...	Yes..	Yes...	Yes...	13	6	4	Yes..	Yes..	No...	1
No...		Yes..	No...	Yes..	Yes...	Yes...	21	21	9	Yes..	Yes..	No...	2
No...		Yes..	.No...	Yes..	Yes...	Yes...	[1]	13	15	Yes..	Yes..	No...	3
No...		Yes..	No...	Yes..	Yes...	Yes...	[1]	44	38	Yes..	Yes..	No...	4
No...		Yes..	No...	No...	No...	No...	[1]	[4]	[4]	Yes..	Yes..	No...	5
No...		Yes..	No...	No...	No...	No...	[1]	[5]	[5]	Yes..	Yes..	No...	6
No...		Yes..	No...	Yes..	No...	No...	[1]	24	37	Yes..	Yes..	Yes..	7
No...		No...	No...	No...	No...	No...	[1]	[6]	[6]	Yes..	Yes..	No...	8
No...		No...	No...	Yes..	Yes...	No...	[1]	6	5	Yes..	Yes..	No...	9
No...		No...	No...	Yes..	Yes..	No...	[1]	6	7	Yes..	Yes..	No...	10
No...		Yes..	No...	No...	No...	No...	[1]	[7]	[7]	No...	No...	No...	11
No...		No...	No...	No...	No...	No...	[1]	[8]	[8]	No...	No...	No...	12
No...		No...	Yes9.	Yes..	Yes...	Yes...	[1]	19	22	Yes..	Yes..	No...	13
No...		No...	No...	Yes..	Yes...	Yes...	[1]	5	13	Yes..	Yes..	No...	14
No...		Yes..	No...	Yes..	Yes...	Yes...	[1]	8	16	Yes..	Yes..	No...	15
No...		Yes..	No...	Yes..	Yes...	Yes...	[1]	7	26	Yes..	Yes..	No...	16
No...		No...	No...	No...	No...	No...	[1]	[10]	[10]	Yes..	Yes..	No...	17
No...		No...	No...	Yes..	Yes...	Yes...	[1]	4	16	Yes..	Yes..	No...	18
No...		No...	No...	Yes..	Yes...	Yes...	[1]	2	8	Yes..	Yes..	No...	19
No...		No...	No...	Yes..	Yes...	No....	[1]	30	18	{1 yes.. / 1 no...}	Yes..	No...	20
No...		No...	No...	Yes..	No...	No....	[1]	20	36	No...	No...	[12]	21
No...		No...	No...	Yes..	Yes...	No....	[1]	12	21	{2 yes. / 1 no.}	Yes..	No...	22
No...		Yes..	No...	No...	No...	No....	[1]	[13]	[13]	Yes..	Yes..	No...	23
No.,..		Yes..	No...	Yes..	No.,..	No....	[1]	12	15	{3 yes. / 2 no.}	Yes..	No...	24
No...		No...	No...	Yes..	Yes...	No....	[1]	29	42	Yes..	Yes..	No...	25
No...		No...	No...	Yes..	No...	No....	[1]	17	10	{4 yes. / 2 no.}	Yes .	No...	26

MASSACHUSETTS.

Provided.	Sufficient.	Suff. seats	Lunch	Separate	Males.	Females.	No. male per urinal	Males.	Females.	Males.	Females.	Air	Est.
No...		Yes..	No...	Yes..	{1 yes.. / 1 no...}	Yes...	25	25	12	Yes..	Yes..	No...	1
No...		Yes..	No...	Yes..	No...	No....	7	7	11	Yes..	Yes..	No...	2
No...		Yes..	No...	Yes..	No...	Yes....	[1]	9	8	Yes..	Yes..	No...	3
No...		Yes..	No..	No...	No...	Yes....	[1]	[14]	[14]	Yes..	Yes..	No...	4
No...		Yes..	Yes..	Yes..	Yes...	Yes....	5	2	5	Yes..	Yes..	No...	5
No...		Yes..	No...	Yes..	No...	Yes....	56	28	19	Yes..	Yes..	No...	6
No...		Yes..	No...	Yes..	No...	Yes....	21	41	14	Yes..	Yes..	No...	7
No...		Yes..	No...	Yes..	No...	No....	[1]	9	7	Yes..	Yes..	No...	8
No...		Yes..	No...	Yes..	Yes...	No....	[1]	7	14	Yes..	Yes..	No...	9
No...		No...	Yes..	Yes..	No...	No....	[1]	5	20	Yes..	Yes..	No...	10
Yes..	Yes..	Yes..	Yes..	Yes..	No...	No....	[1]	6	10	Yes..	Yes..	No...	11
No...		Yes..	Yes..	Yes..	No...	No....	[1]	3	20	Yes..	Yes..	No...	12
No...		Yes..	No...	Yes..	No...	No....	[1]	7	20	Yes..	Yes..	No...	13
No...		Yes..	No...	Yes..	Yes...	Yes....	[1]	12	38	Yes..	Yes..	No...	14
No...		No...	No...	Yes..	No...	No....	[1]	12	20	Yes..	Yes..	No...	15
No...		Yes..	No...	Yes..	No...	No....	[1]	10	11	Yes..	Yes..	No...	16
No...		No...	Yes..	Yes..	Yes...	Yes....	17	6	5	Yes..	Yes..	No...	17
No...		Yes..	No...	Yes..	Yes...	Yes....	[1]	4	10	Yes..	Yes..	No...	18
No...		Yes..	No...	Yes..	Yes...	Yes....	[1]	18	17	Yes..	Yes..	No...	19
No...		No...	No...	Yes..	Yes...	No....	[1]	16	17	Yes..	Yes..	No...	20
No...		Yes..	No...	Yes..	No...	No....	[1]	10	11	No...	No...	Yes..	21
No...		Yes..	No...	Yes..	Yes...	Yes....	[1]	29	8	Yes..	Yes..	No...	22

8 Not separate for sexes; 10 males, 10 females, 1 seat; average, 20 persons per seat.
9 For females only.
10 Not separate for sexes; 6 males, 9 females, 1 seat; average, 15 persons per seat.
11 A bucketful of water, unchanged for each washer.
12 No. 3 floors; yes, 1 floor.
13 Not separate for sexes; 64 males, 41 females, 7 seats; average, 15 persons per seat.
14 Not separate for sexes; 13 males, 10 females, 1 seat; average, 23 persons per seat.

TABLE **V.**—PROVISIONS FOR COMFORT OF EMPLOYEES: WASH ROOM LUNCH ROOMS, AND

MASSACHUSETTS—Concluded.

Establishment number.	Facilities for washing.					Dressing rooms provided.				Nature of work requires change of clothing for—	
	Separate wash rooms.	Other.	Sufficient.	Establishments furnish—		Separate for—		Sufficient for—			
				Towels.	Soap.	Males.	Females.	Males.	Females.	Males.	Females.
23	No...	20-foot trough	No...	No...	No...	Yes..	Yes..	Yes..	Yes..	Yes..	Yes..
24	No...	Sinks	Yes.	Yes.	Yes.	No...	Yes..		Yes.	Yes..	No...
25	Yes.	Sink	Yes.	Yes.	Yes.	Yes.	Yes..	Yes..	Yes.	Yes..	Yes..
26	No...	Sinks	Yes.	No...	No...	No...	No...			No...	No...
27	No...	...do	Yes.	No...	Yes.	No...	No...			No...	No...
28	No...	...do	Yes.	No...	No...	No...	No...			No...	No...
29	No...	Bowl; sinks	Yes.	Yes.	Yes.	No...	No...			No...	No...
30	No...	Sinks	Yes.	Yes.	Yes.	No...	No...			No...	No...
31	No...	...do	Yes.	No...	No...	No...	No...			No...	No...
32	No...	Sink	Yes.	No...	No...	No...	No...			No...	No...
33	No...	Sinks	Yes.	Yes.	Yes.	No...	No...			No...	No...
34	No...	Sink	Yes.	Yes.	Yes.	Yes.	Yes..	Yes..	Yes..	No...	No...
35	No...	Sinks	Yes.	No...	Yes.	No...	No...			No...	No...
36	No...	...do	No...	No...	No...	No...	No...			No...	No...
37	Yes..	...do	No...	No...	No...	No...	Yes..		Yes..	No...	Yes..
38	No...	...do	No...	No...	No...	No...	No...			No...	No...
39	No...	None	No...	No...	No...	No...	No...			No...	No...
40	No...	Sinks	No...	No...	No...	No...	No...			No...	No...
41	No...	Washstands and sinks	Yes.	Yes 4.	Yes 4.	No...	No...			No...	No...
42	No...	None	No...	No...	No...	No...	No...			No...	No...
43	No...	Sink	No...	No...	No...	No...	No...			No...	No...
44	No...	Sinks	No...	No...	No...	No...	No...			No...	No...

RHODE ISLAND.

Establishment number.	Separate wash rooms.	Other.	Sufficient.	Towels.	Soap.	Males.	Females.	Males.	Females.	Males.	Females.
1	No...	Sinks	Yes..	Yes..	No...	No...	No...			No...	No...
2	No...	...do	Yes..	Yes..	No 5.	No...	Yes..		Yes.	No...	Yes..
3	No...	...do	Yes..	Yes..	Yes..	Yes..	Yes..	Yes..	Yes..	Yes..	Yes..
4	No...	...do	Yes..	No...	No...	No...	No...			No...	No...
5	No...	...do	Yes..	No...	No...	No...	No...			No...	No...
6	No...	...do	No...	No...	No...	No...	No...			No...	No...
7	No...	...do	No...	No...	No...	No...	No...			No...	No...
8	No...	...do	Yes..	No...	No...	No...	No...			No...	No...
9	No...	...do	Yes..	No...	No...	No...	No...			No...	No...
10	No...	...do	Yes..	No...	No...	No...	Yes..		Yes..	No...	No...
11	No...	...do	Yes..	No...	No...	No...	No...			No...	No...
12	No...	...do	Yes..	No...	No...	No...	No...			No...	No...
13	No...	...do	Yes..	No...	Yes..	No...	No...			No...	No...
14	No...	...do	Yes..	No...	No...	No...	No...			No...	No...
15	No...	...do	No...	No...	Yes..	No...	No...			No...	No...
16	No...	Sinks	Yes..	No...	Yes..	No...	No...			No...	No...
17	No...	...do	Yes..	Yes..	Yes..	Yes..	No...	Yes..		Yes..	No...
18	No...	...do	Yes..	No...	Yes..	No...	No...			No...	No...
19	No...	Sinks and basins	Yes..	No...	Yes..	No...	No...			No...	No...
20	No...	Sinks	Yes..	No...	Yes..	No...	Yes..		Yes.	No...	Yes..
21	Yes..	...do	Yes..	No 7.	No 7.	Yes..	Yes..	Yes..	Yes..	Yes..	Yes..
22	No...	Sink	Yes..	Yes..	Yes..	No...	No...			No...	No...
23	No...	Sinks and basins	Yes..	Yes..	Yes..	Yes..	Yes..	Yes..	Yes..	No...	Yes..
24	No...	...do	No...	No...	No...	No...	No...			No...	No...
25	No...	Sinks	No...	No...	No...	No...	No...			No...	No...
26	No...	...do	No...	No...	No...	No...	No...			No...	No...
27	No...	...do	No...	No...	No...	No...	No...			No...	No...

[1] No urinals.
[2] Not separate for sexes; 2 males, 58 females, 2 seats; average, 30 persons per seat.
[3] Not reported.
[4] Provided for a small proportion of employees only.

FACILITIES, DRESSING ROOMS, REST ROOMS, SEATS FOR FEMALES, WATER-CLOSETS—Continued.

MASSACHUSETTS—Concluded.

| Rest rooms for females. | | Sufficient seats provided for females. | Lunch rooms provided. | Water-closets. | | | | | | | | Air of workrooms affected by water-closets. | Establishment number. |
| Provided. | Sufficient. | | | Separate for the sexes. | Privacy of approach for— | | Number of male employees per urinal. | Number of employees per seat. | | Clean for— | | | |
					Males.	Females.		Males.	Females.	Males.	Females.		
No...		Yes..	No...	Yes..	Yes...	Yes...	(1)	3	10	Yes..	Yes..	No...	23
No...		No...	Yes..	Yes..	Yes...	Yes...	(1)	8	10	Yes..	Yes..	No...	24
No...		No...	No...	Yes..	Yes...	Yes...	52	10	7	Yes..	Yes..	No...	25
No...		Yes..	No...	Yes..	Yes...	Yes...	(1)	5	25	Yes..	Yes..	No...	26
No...		Yes..	No...	Yes..	No....	No....	(1)	4	45	Yes..	Yes..	No...	27
No...		No...	No...	Yes..	Yes...	No....	(1)	12	20	No...	Yes..	No...	28
No...		No...	No...	Yes..	No....	No....	(1)	18	38	Yes..	Yes..	No...	29
No...		Yes..	No...	Yes..	Yes...	Yes...	(1)	2	13	Yes..	Yes..	No...	30
No...		No...	Yes..	Yes..	Yes...	Yes...	(1)	27	33	Yes..	Yes..	No...	31
No...		Yes..	No...	No...	No....	No....	(1)	(2)	(3)	Yes..	Yes..	No...	32
No...		Yes..	No...	Yes..	Yes...	Yes...	(1)	(3)	(3)	Yes..	Yes..	No...	33
No...		Yes..	No...	Yes..	Yes...	Yes...	(1)	7	27	Yes..	Yes..	No...	34
No...		Yes..	No...	Yes..	Yes...	Yes...	(1)	14	42	Yes..	Yes..	No...	35
No...		Yes..	No...	Yes..	Yes...	Yes...	(1)	16	18	Yes..	Yes..	No...	36
No...		Yes..	No...	Yes..	Yes...	Yes...	32	12	8	Yes..	Yes..	No...	37
No...		Yes..	No...	Yes..	Yes...	No....	(1)	27	22	No...	Yes..	No...	38
No...		Yes..	No...	Yes..	Yes...	No....	(1)	6	22	No...	Yes..	No...	39
No...		No...	No...	Yes..	No....	No....	(1)	41	24	No...	No...	No...	40
No...		Yes..	Yes..	Yes..	No....	No....	74	9	9	Yes..	No...	No...	41
No...		Yes..	No...	Yes..	Yes...	No....	(1)	9	20	No...	No...	No...	42
No...		No...	No...	Yes..	No....	No....	(1)	26	26	No...	No...	No...	43
No...		No...	No...	Yes..	Yes...	Yes...	28	9	13	Yes..	Yes..	No...	44

RHODE ISLAND.

| Rest rooms for females. | | Sufficient seats provided for females. | Lunch rooms provided. | Water-closets. | | | | | | | | Air of workrooms affected by water-closets. | Establishment number. |
Provided.	Sufficient.			Separate for the sexes.	Males.	Females.	Number of male employees per urinal.	Males.	Females.	Males.	Females.		
No...		Yes..	No...	Yes..	Yes...	Yes...	(1)	11	8	No...	Yes..	No...	1
No...		Yes..	No...	Yes..	Yes...	Yes...	38	38	29	Yes..	No...	No...	2
No...		No...	No...	Yes..	{3 yes.. / 1 no..}	No....	(1)	4	14	Yes..	Yes..	No...	3
No...		Yes..	No...	Yes..	No....	No....	(1)	22	12	Yes..	Yes..	No...	4
No...		Yes..	No...	Yes..	Yes...	Yes...	(1)	19	19	No...	No...	No...	5
No...		Yes..	No...	Yes..	Yes...	Yes...	25	25	18	{8 yes. / 4 no..}	{8 yes. / 4 no..}	}Yes..	6
No...		No...	No...	Yes..	Yes...	Yes...	224	56	39	Yes..	Yes..	No...	7
No...		No...	No...	No...	No....	No....	(1)	15	23	Yes..	Yes..	No...	8
No...		Yes..	No...	Yes..	No....	No....	(1)	12	41	Yes..	Yes..	No...	9
No...		Yes..	No...	Yes..	No....	No....	(1)	5	13	Yes..	Yes..	No...	10
No...		Yes..	No...	Yes..	Yes...	Yes...	(1)	13	25	Yes..	Yes..	No...	11
No...		Yes..	No...	Yes..	Yes...	Yes...	(1)	8	23	Yes..	Yes..	No...	12
No...		Yes..	No...	No...	No....	No....	(1)	(6)	(6)	Yes..	Yes..	No...	13
No...		Yes..	No...	Yes..	Yes...	Yes...	(1)	14	22	Yes..	Yes..	No...	14
No...		Yes..	No...	Yes..	No....	No....	(1)	12	33	No...	No...	Yes..	15
No...		Yes..	No...	Yes..	Yes...	Yes...	50	17	5	Yes..	Yes..	No...	16
No...		Yes..	No...	Yes..	Yes...	Yes...	47	20	27	Yes..	Yes..	No...	17
No...		Yes..	No...	Yes..	Yes...	Yes...	(1)	24	16	Yes..	Yes..	No...	18
No...		Yes..	No...	Yes..	Yes...	Yes...	(1)	16	10	Yes..	Yes..	No...	19
No...		No...	No...	Yes..	Yes...	Yes...	(1)	7	43	Yes..	Yes..	No...	20
No...		No...	Yes..	Yes..	{1 no.. / 1 yes..}	No....	(1)	11	41	Yes..	Yes..	No...	21
No...		No...	No...	No...	Yes...	No....	(1)	(6)	(6)	Yes..	Yes..	Yes..	22
No...		No...	No...	Yes..	Yes...	Yes...	(1)	2	8	Yes..	Yes..	No...	23
No...		No...	No...	Yes..	Yes...	No....	66	21	10	Yes..	Yes..	No...	24
No...		No...	No...	Yes..	No....	No....	99	33	24	No...	Yes..	No...	25
No...		No...	No...	Yes..	No....	No....	(1)	45	62	No...	No...	No...	26
No...		No...	No...	Yes..	No....	No....	(1)	41	31	No...	No...	No...	27

5 Use of soap prohibited for trade reasons.
6 Not separate for sexes; 3 males, 18 females, 2 seats; average, 11 persons per seat.
7 Soap and towels furnished by employees.
8 Not separate for sexes; 3 males, 9 females, 1 seat; average, 12 persons per seat.

Table **V.**—PROVISIONS FOR COMFORT OF EMPLOYEES: WASH ROOM
LUNCH ROOMS, AND

CONNECTICUT.

Establishment number.	Facilities for washing.			Establishments furnish—		Dressing rooms provided.				Nature of work requires change of clothing for—	
	Separate wash rooms.	Other.	Sufficient.			Separate for—		Sufficient for—			
				Towels.	Soap.	Males.	Females.	Males.	Females.	Males.	Females.
1	Yes..	Sinks and pails........	No...	No...	No...	Yes..	Yes..	Yes..	No...	Yes..	No...
2	No...	Sinks................	Yes..	No...	No...	No...	Yes..		Yes..	No...	No...
3	No...	......do.............	Yes..	No...	No...	No...	No...			No...	No...
4	No...	......do.............	Yes..	No...	No...	Yes..	Yes..	Yes..	Yes..	Yes..	No...
5	No...	Sink................	Yes..	No...	No...	No...	No...			No...	No...
6	No...	Sinks................	Yes..	No...	No...	No...	No...			No...	No...
7	No...	......do.............	Yes..	No...	No...	No...	No...			Yes..	No...
8	No...	......do.............	Yes..	No...	No...	No...	No...			Yes..	No...
9	No...	Sink................	No...	Yes..	Yes..	No...	No...			No...	No...
10	Yes..	None................	No...	Yes..	Yes..	No...	No...			No...	No...
11	No...	Sink................	No...	Yes..	Yes..	No...	No...			No...	No...
12	No...	......do.............	No...	No...	No...	No...	No...			No...	No...
13	No...	......do.............	No...	No...	No...	No...	Yes..		No...	No...	No...
14	No...	......do.............	Yes..	No...	No...	No...	No...			No...	No...
15	No...	Sinks................	Yes..	No...	No...	No...	No...			No...	Yes..
16	No...	......do.............	Yes..	No...	No...	No...	Yes..		Yes..	No...	Yes..
17	No...	......do.............	Yes..	No...	No...	No...	No...			Yes..	Yes..
18	No...	......do.............	Yes..	No...	No...	No...	No...			Yes..	No...
19	No...	......do.............	Yes..	No...	No...	No...	No...			Yes..	No...
20	No...	......do.............	Yes..	No...	No...	No...	No...			No...	No...
21	No...	Sanitary basins.......	Yes..	Yes..	Yes..	Yes..	Yes..	Yes..	Yes..	No...	No...
22	No...	Sinks................	Yes..	No...	No...	No...	No...			No...	No...
23	No...	......do.............	Yes..	No...	No...	No...	No...			Yes..	No...
24	Yes..	None................	Yes..	No...	Yes..	No...	No...			No...	No...
25	Yes..	Sinks................	Yes..	No...	Yes..	No...	No...			No...	No...
26	No⁴..	......do.............	Yes..	No...	Yes..	Yes..	No...	Yes..		Yes..	No...
27	Yes..	None................	Yes..	No...	No...	No...	No...			No...	No...
28	No...	Sinks................	Yes..	No...	No...	No...	No...			No...	No...
29	No...	......do.............	Yes..	No...	No...	No...	No...			No...	No...
30	No...	......do.............	Yes..	No...	No...	No...	Yes..		No...	No...	Yes..
31	Yes..	......do.............	Yes..	No...	Yes..	Yes..	Yes..	Yes..	Yes..	Yes..	No...
32	No...	......do.............	Yes..	No...	No...	Yes..	Yes..	Yes..	Yes..	Yes..	Yes..
33	No...	Sink................	No...	No...	No...	No...	Yes..		No...	No...	No...
34	Yes..	Sinks................	(¹)...	No...	Yes..	Yes..	Yes..	Yes..	Yes..	No...	No...
35	No...	Sinks and basins......	Yes..	No...	No...	No...	No...			No...	Yes..

¹ No urinals.
² Not reported.
³ In 2 buildings, yes; in 1 building, no.

FACILITIES, DRESSING ROOMS, REST ROOMS, SEATS FOR FEMALES, WATER-CLOSETS—Continued.

CONNECTICUT.

Rest rooms for females.		Sufficient seats provided for females.	Lunch rooms provided.	Water-closets.								Air of work-rooms affected by water-closets.	Establishment number.
Provided.	Sufficient.			Separate for the sexes.	Privacy of approach for—		Number of male employees per urinal.	Number of employees per seat.		Clean for—			
					Males.	Females.		Males.	Females.	Males.	Females.		
No...	....	Yes..	No...	Yes..	No....	Yes...	68	19	9	Yes..	Yes..	No...	1
No...	....	Yes..	No...	Yes..	Yes...	Yes...	43	43	30	Yes..	Yes..	No...	2
No...	....	Yes..	No...	Yes..	Yes...	Yes...	51	26	17	Yes..	Yes..	No...	3
No...	....	Yes..	No...	Yes..	Yes...	Yes...	68	19	9	Yes..	Yes..	No...	4
No...	....	Yes..	No...	Yes..	Yes...	Yes...	(1)	10	3	Yes..	Yes..	No...	5
No...	....	Yes..	No...	Yes..	Yes...	Yes...	29	4	7	Yes..	Yes..	No...	6
No...	....	Yes..	No...	Yes..	Yes...	Yes...	15	11	5	Yes..	Yes..	No...	7
No...	....	Yes..	No...	Yes..	Yes...	Yes...	40	8	8	Yes..	Yes..	No...	8
No...	....	Yes..	No...	Yes..	No....	Yes...	(1)	30	50	Yes..	Yes..	No...	9
No...	....	Yes..	No...	Yes..	Yes...	Yes...	93	29	42	Yes..	Yes..	No...	10
No...	....	Yes..	No...	Yes..	(2)....	Yes...	(2)	(2)	64	(2)....	Yes..	No...	11
No...	....	Yes..	No...	Yes..	Yes...	Yes...	35	18	34	No...	Yes..	No...	12
No...	....	Yes..	No...	Yes..	Yes...	Yes...	(1)	12	9	Yes..	Yes..	No...	13
No...	....	Yes..	No...	Yes..	Yes...	Yes...	15	15	3	Yes..	Yes..	No...	14
No...	....	Yes..	No...	Yes..	Yes...	Yes...	46	31	19	Yes..	Yes..	No...	15
No...	....	Yes..	No...	Yes..	Yes...	Yes...	23	5	2	Yes..	Yes..	No...	16
No...	....	Yes..	No...	Yes..	Yes...	Yes...	40	12	12	Yes..	Yes..	No...	17
No...	....	Yes..	No...	Yes..	No....	No....	59	13	21	Yes..	Yes..	No...	18
No...	....	Yes..	No...	Yes..	Yes...	Yes....	199	14	7	Yes..	Yes..	No...	19
No...	....	Yes..	No...	Yes..	(3)....	(4)	83	20	14	Yes..	Yes..	No...	20
No...	....	Yes..	No...	Yes..	Yes...	Yes....	(1)	5	12	Yes..	Yes..	No...	21
No...	....	Yes..	No...	Yes..	Yes...	Yes...	(1)	22	13	Yes..	Yes..	No...	22
No...	....	Yes..	No...	Yes..	Yes...	Yes...	(1)	7	21	Yes..	Yes..	No...	23
No...	....	Yes..	No...	Yes..	Yes...	Yes...	(1)	18	28	Yes..	Yes..	No...	24
No...	....	Yes..	No...	Yes..	Yes...	Yes...	(1)	22	46	Yes..	Yes..	No...	25
No...	....	Yes..	No...	Yes..	Yes...	Yes...	8	8	7	Yes..	Yes..	No...	26
No...	....	Yes..	No...	Yes..	Yes...	Yes...	45	27	17	Yes..	Yes..	No...	27
No...	....	Yes..	No...	Yes..	Yes...	Yes...	(1)	11	24	Yes..	Yes..	No...	28
No...	....	Yes..	No...	Yes..	Yes...	Yes...	(1)	8	15	Yes..	Yes..	No...	29
No...	....	Yes..	No...	Yes..	Yes...	No....	(1)	4	16	Yes..	Yes..	No...	30
No...	....	Yes..	No...	Yes..	Yes...	Yes...	30	30	22	Yes..	Yes..	No...	31
No...	....	Yes..	No...	Yes..	Yes...	Yes...	(1)	5	3	Yes..	Yes..	No...	32
No...	....	Yes..	No...	Yes..	Yes...	Yes...	(1)	16	16	No...	No...	No...	33
Yes..	Yes..	Yes..	No...	Yes..	Yes...	Yes...	30	16	6	Yes..	Yes..	No...	34
No...	....	Yes..	No...	Yes..	Yes...	Yes...	(1)	16	16	Yes..	Yes..	No...	35

4 In 1 building, yes; in 1 building, no.
5 Yes, in foundry.

TABLE **V.**—PROVISIONS FOR COMFORT OF EMPLOYEES: WASH ROOM
LUNCH ROOMS, AND

NEW YORK.

Establishment number.	Facilities for washing.			Establishments furnish—		Dressing rooms provided.				Nature of work requires change of clothing for—	
	Separate wash rooms.	Other.	Sufficient.	Towels.	Soap.	Separate for—		Sufficient for—			
						Males.	Females.	Males.	Females.	Males.	Females.
1	No	Sinks	Yes	No	No	No	Yes		No	No	No
2	No	do	No	No	No	No	No			No	No
3	No	do	No	Yes	Yes	Yes	Yes	No	No	No	No
4	No	do	Yes	No	No	Yes	Yes	Yes	Yes	Yes	Yes
5	No	do	No	No	No	No	No			No	No
6	No	do	Yes	Yes	No	No	Yes		Yes	Yes	No
7	No	do	No	Yes	Yes	Yes	Yes	No	No	Yes	Yes
8	Yes	do	Yes	Yes	No	No	Yes		Yes	Yes	No
9	No	do	Yes	Yes	No	No	Yes		Yes	Yes	No
10	No	do	No	No	No	Yes	Yes	Yes	Yes	Yes	No
11	No	do	No	No	No	No	No			No	No
12	Yes	None	Yes	Yes	No	No	Yes		Yes	Yes	No
13	No	Sinks	No	Yes	Yes	Yes	Yes	No	No	Yes	Yes
14	Yes	do	Yes	Yes	Yes	Yes	Yes	Yes	Yes	Yes	Yes
15	Yes	None	Yes	Yes	Yes	Yes	Yes	Yes	Yes	Yes	No
16	Yes	do	Yes	Yes	Yes	Yes	Yes	Yes	Yes	Yes	No
17	No	Sink	Yes	No	No	No	No			Yes	No
18	Yes	None	Yes	Yes	Yes	Yes	Yes	Yes	Yes	No	No
19	Yes	Sinks	Yes	No	No	No	No			Yes	Yes
20	No	do	Yes	No	No	No	No			Yes	No
21	Yes	None	Yes	No	No	Yes	Yes	Yes	Yes	No	No
22	No	Sinks	Yes	No	No	Yes	Yes		Yes	Yes	No
23	No	do	No	Yes	Yes	Yes	Yes	No	No	No	No
24	No	do	Yes	No	No	No	Yes		Yes	No	No
25	No	do	No	No	No	No	No			No	No
26	No	do	Yes	No	Yes	Yes	No			No	No
27	No	Sink	Yes	No	No	No	No			No	No
28	No	do	Yes	No	No	No	Yes		No	No	No
29	No	Sinks	No	No	No	No	No			No	No
30	No	do	Yes	No	No	No	Yes		Yes	No	No
31	No	do	Yes	No	No	No	Yes		Yes	No	No
32	No	Sink	Yes	No	No	No	Yes		Yes	No	No
33	No	Sinks	Yes	Yes	Yes	No	Yes		Yes	No	No
34	Yes	None	Yes	Yes	Yes	Yes	Yes	Yes	Yes	No	No
35	Yes	Sinks	Yes	Yes	Yes	Yes	Yes	Yes	Yes	Yes	Yes
36	No	do	Yes	No	No	No	Yes		Yes	No	No

[1] No urinals.
[2] In 1 building, yes; in 1 building, no.

FACILITIES, DRESSING ROOMS, REST ROOMS, SEATS FOR FEMALES, WATER-CLOSETS—Continued.

NEW YORK.

Rest rooms for females.		Sufficient seats provided for females.	Lunch rooms provided.	Water-closets.									Air of workrooms affected by water-closets.	Establishment number.
Provided.	Sufficient.			Separate for the sexes.	Privacy of approach for—		Number of male employees per urinal.	Number of employees per seat.		Clean for—			
					Males.	Females.		Males.	Females.	Males.	Females.		
No...	....	Yes..	No...	Yes..	Yes...	Yes...	(1)	32	16	Yes..	Yes..	No...	1
No...	....	Yes..	No...	Yes..	Yes...	Yes...	73	24	10	Yes..	Yes..	No...	2
No...	....	Yes..	No...	Yes..	(1)	(2)	(1)	6	12	(2)...	Yes..	No...	3
No...	....	Yes..	No...	Yes..	No....	No....	30	8	19	Yes..	Yes..	No...	4
No...	....	Yes..	No...	Yes..	No....	No....	23	14	22	Yes..	Yes..	No...	5
No...	....	Yes..	No...	Yes..	Yes...	Yes...	(1)	6	7	Yes..	Yes..	No...	6
No...	....	Yes..	No...	Yes..	Yes...	Yes...	7	14	16	Yes..	Yes..	No...	7
No...	....	Yes..	No...	Yes..	Yes...	Yes...	7	4	3	No...	Yes..	No...	8
No...	....	Yes..	No...	Yes..	Yes...	Yes...	(1)	3	6	Yes..	Yes..	No...	9
No...	....	Yes..	No...	Yes..	Yes...	Yes...	45	11	16	Yes..	Yes..	No...	10
No...	....	Yes..	No...	Yes..	No....	No....	18	9	12	Yes..	Yes..	No...	11
No...	....	Yes..	No...	Yes..	Yes...	Yes...	20	20	13	Yes..	Yes..	No...	12
No...	....	Yes..	No...	Yes..	Yes...	Yes...	13	4	6	Yes..	Yes..	No...	13
Yes..	Yes..	Yes..	Yes..	Yes..	Yes...	Yes...	25	20	16	Yes..	Yes..	No...	14
Yes..	Yes..	Yes..	Yes..	Yes..	Yes...	Yes...	14	8	18	Yes..	Yes..	No...	15
No...	....	Yes..	Yes..	Yes..	Yes...	Yes...	11	3	18	Yes..	Yes..	No...	16
No...	....	Yes..	No...	Yes..	Yes...	Yes...	(1)	8	67	Yes..	Yes..	No...	17
No...	....	Yes..	No...	Yes..	Yes...	Yes...	34	11	20	Yes..	Yes..	No...	18
No...	....	Yes..	No...	Yes..	Yes...	Yes...	(1)	20	39	Yes..	Yes..	No...	19
No...	....	Yes..	No...	Yes..	Yes...	Yes...	(1)	13	43	Yes..	Yes..	No...	20
No...	....	Yes..	No...	Yes..	Yes...	Yes...	1	4	18	Yes..	Yes..	No...	21
No...	....	Yes..	Yes..	Yes..	Yes...	Yes...	(1)	23	51	Yes..	Yes..	No...	22
Yes..	Yes..	Yes..	Yes..	Yes..	Yes...	Yes...	24	6	2	Yes..	Yes..	No...	23
No...	....	Yes..	No...	Yes..	Yes...	Yes...	(1)	10	16	Yes..	Yes..	No...	24
No...	....	Yes..	No...	Yes..	Yes...	Yes...	(1)	19	21	Yes..	Yes..	No...	25
No...	....	Yes..	No...	Yes..	Yes...	Yes...	(1)	5	11	Yes..	Yes..	No...	26
No...	....	Yes..	No...	Yes..	No....	No....	(1)	4	6	Yes..	Yes..	No...	27
No...	....	Yes..	No...	Yes..	No....	No....	(1)	9	24	Yes..	Yes..	No...	28
No...	....	Yes..	No...	Yes..	No....	No....	(1)	8	14	No...	No...	No...	29
No...	....	Yes..	No...	Yes..	Yes...	Yes...	38	13	19	Yes..	Yes..	No...	30
No...	....	Yes..	No...	Yes..	Yes...	Yes...	(1)	6	20	Yes..	Yes..	No...	31
No...	....	Yes..	No...	Yes..	No....	Yes...	(1)	3	9	Yes..	Yes..	No...	32
No...	....	Yes..	No...	Yes..	No....	No....	(2)	7	18	Yes..	Yes..	No...	33
No...	....	Yes..	No...	Yes..	Yes...	Yes...	27	(3)	(3)	Yes..	Yes..	No...	34
No...	....	Yes..	No...	Yes..	Yes...	Yes...	27	13	6	Yes..	Yes..	No...	35
No...	....	Yes..	Yes..	Yes..	Yes...	Yes...	7	2	10	Yes..	Yes..	No...	36

[3] Not reported.

TABLE **V.**—PROVISIONS FOR COMFORT OF EMPLOYEES: WASH ROOM
LUNCH ROOMS, AND

NEW JERSEY.

Establishment number.	Facilities for washing.			Establishments furnish—		Dressing rooms provided.				Nature of work requires change of clothing for—	
	Separate wash rooms.	Other.	Sufficient.	Towels.	Soap.	Separate for—		Sufficient for—			
						Males.	Females.	Males.	Females.	Males.	Females.
1	Yes..	None	Yes..	Yes..	Yes..	Yes..	Yes..	Yes..	Yes..	Yes..	Yes..
2	No...	Sinks	Yes..	No...	No...	No...	Yes..		Yes..	No...	No...
3	No...	...do	Yes..	No...	No...	No...	No...			No...	No...
4	No...	...do	Yes..	Yes..	Yes..	No...	Yes..		Yes..	No...	No...
5	Yes..	None	Yes..	Yes..	Yes..	No...	Yes..		Yes..	No...	No...
6	Yes..	Sinks, bathtubs	Yes..	Yes..	Yes..	No...	No...			No...	Yes...
7	Yes..	Sinks	Yes..	No...	No...	No...	No...			No...	No...
8	Yes..	...do	Yes..	No...	No...	No...	No...			No...	No...
9	No...	Sink	Yes..	No...	No...	No...	No...			No...	No...
10	No...	Sinks	Yes..	No...	Yes..	No...	Yes..		Yes..	No...	No...
11	No...	...do	No...	No...	No...	No...	Yes..		No...	No...	Yes...
12	No...	...do	No...	No...	No...	No...	Yes..		No...	No...	Yes...
13	No...	...do	Yes..	No...	No...	No...	Yes..		Yes..	No...	Yes...
14	No...	...do	Yes..	No...	No...	No...	Yes..		Yes..	No...	Yes...
15	Yes..	...do	Yes..	Yes..	Yes..	No...	Yes..		Yes..	No...	Yes...
16	No...	...do	No...	No...	No...	No...	No...			No...	Yes...
17	No...	...do	No...	No...	No...	No...	Yes..		Yes..	No...	Yes...
18	No...	...do	No...	No...	No...	No...	Yes..		Yes..	No...	Yes...
19	No...	...do	No...	No...	No...	No...	No...			No...	Yes...
20	No...	...do	No...	No...	No...	No...	No...			No...	Yes...
21	Yes..	(¹)	Yes..	Yes..	Yes..	Yes..	Yes..	Yes..	Yes..	Yes..	No...
22	Yes..	Sinks	Yes..	No...	No...	No...	Yes..		Yes..	No...	No...
23	Yes..	...do	Yes..	Yes..	Yes..	Yes..	Yes..	Yes..	Yes..	Yes..	No...
24	Yes..	None	Yes..	Yes..	Yes..	No...	No...			No...	No...
25	No...	General wash room	No...	No...	No...	Yes..	Yes..	Yes..	Yes..	No...	No...
26	No...	Sinks	No...	Yes..	Yes..	Yes..	Yes..	Yes..	Yes..	No...	No...
27	Yes..	None	Yes..	No...	Yes..	No...	No...			Yes..	Yes..

¹ No urinals.
² There is no opportunity to use seats because of exacting work and crowded rooms.

FACILITIES, DRESSING ROOMS, REST ROOMS, SEATS FOR FEMALES, WATER-CLOSETS—Continued.

NEW JERSEY.

| Rest rooms for females. | | Sufficient seats provided for the females. | Lunch rooms provided. | Water-closets. | | | | | | | | Air of workrooms affected by water-closets. | Establishment number. |
| Provided. | Sufficient. | | | Separate for the sexes. | Privacy of approach for— | | Number of male employees per urinal. | Number of employees per seat. | | Clean for— | | | |
					Males.	Females.		Males.	Females.	Males.	Females.		
Yes..	Yes..	Yes..	Yes..	Yes..	Yes...	Yes...	15	12	9	Yes..	Yes..	No...	1
No...		Yes..	Yes..	Yes..	Yes...	Yes...	(1)	9	19	Yes..	Yes..	No...	2
No...		Yes..	No...	Yes..	Yes...	Yes...	11	5	38	Yes..	{13 yes 4 no..}	No...	3
Yes..	Yes..	Yes..	Yes..	Yes..	Yes...	Yes...	5	5	39	Yes..	Yes..	No...	4
No...		No...	No...	Yes..	Yes...	Yes...	(1)	10	8	Yes..	Yes..	No...	5
No...		Yes..	Yes..	Yes..	Yes...	Yes...	(1)	5	16	Yes..	Yes..	No...	6
Yes..	Yes..	Yes..	Yes..	Yes..	Yes...	Yes...	(1)	7	14	Yes..	Yes..	No...	7
No...		No...	No...	Yes..	Yes...	Yes...	(1)	25	29	Yes..	Yes..	No...	8
No...		No...	No...	Yes..	Yes...	Yes...	31	10	29	No...	Yes..	No...	9
No...		Yes..	No...	Yes..	Yes...	Yes...	(1)	20	17	{1 yes. 1 no..}	{1 yes 1 no..}	No...	10
No...		No...	No...	Yes..	No....	No....	(1)	12	14	No...	Yes..	Yes..	11
No...		No[3]..	No...	Yes..	Yes..	Yes...	(1)	17	29	No...	Yes..	Yes..	12
No...		No...	No...	Yes..	Yes..	No....	7	22	16	No...	Yes..	No...	13
No...		Yes..	No...	Yes..	No....	No....	(1)	9	27	Yes..	Yes..	Yes..	14
No[3].		Yes..	No...	Yes..	Yes..	Yes...	(1)	11	21	Yes..	Yes..	No...	15
No...		Yes..	No...	Yes..	No....	No....	(1)	40	51	No...	No...	No...	16
No...		Yes..	No...	Yes..	No....	No....	153	31	14	No...	Yes..	No...	17
Yes..	Yes..	Yes..	No...	Yes..	No....	No....	(1)	30	30	No...	Yes..	Yes..	18
No...		No...	No...	Yes..	Yes..	No....	44	19	4	No...	Yes..	No...	19
No...		Yes..	No...	Yes..	No....	No....	114	29	9	No...	Yes..	No...	20
Yes..	Yes..	Yes..	No...	Yes..	Yes..	Yes...	4	2	7	Yes..	Yes..	No...	21
No...		Yes..	No...	Yes..	Yes..	Yes...	(1)	41	7	Yes..	Yes..	No...	22
No...		Yes..	No...	Yes..	Yes..	Yes...	21	4	22	Yes..	Yes..	No...	23
No...		No...	Yes..	Yes..	Yes..	Yes...	162	61	49	Yes..	Yes..	No...	24
No...		Yes..	No...	Yes..	Yes..	Yes...	20	8	17	Yes..	Yes..	No...	25
Yes..	Yes..	No...	Yes..	Yes..	Yes..	Yes...	12	11	14	Yes..	Yes..	No...	26
No...		Yes..	No...	Yes..	Yes..	Yes...	7	15	5	Yes..	Yes..	No...	27

[3] Room with couch for cases of illness.
[4] Shower bath in power department.

TABLE **V.**—PROVISIONS FOR COMFORT OF EMPLOYEES: WASH ROOM LUNCH ROOMS, AND

PENNSYLVANIA.

Establishment number.	Facilities for washing.			Establishments furnish—		Dressing rooms provided.				Nature of work requires change of clothing for—	
	Separate wash rooms.	Other.	Sufficient.			Separate for—		Sufficient for—			
				Towels.	Soap.	Males.	Females.	Males.	Females.	Males.	Females.
1	Yes..	(¹)............	Yes..	Yes..	Yes..	Yes..	Yes..	Yes..	Yes..	No...	Yes..
2	Yes..	Sinks............	Yes..	Yes..	Yes..	No...	Yes..	....	Yes..	No...	Yes..
3	Yes..	......do............	Yes..	Yes..	Yes..	Yes..	Yes..	Yes..	Yes..	No...	Yes..
4	No...	......do............	Yes..	No...	No...	No...	Yes..	....	Yes..	Yes..	Yes..
5	No...	......do............	Yes..	No...	No...	Yes..	Yes..	Yes..	Yes..	No...	No...
6	Yes..	......do............	Yes..	Yes..	Yes..	No...	Yes..	....	Yes..	No...	Yes..
7	Yes..	......do............	Yes..	Yes..	Yes..	No...	No...	....	....	No...	No...
8	Yes..	......do............	Yes..	Yes..	Yes..	No...	No...	....	....	No...	No...
9	Yes..	None............	Yes..	Yes..	Yes..	No...	Yes..	....	Yes..	No...	No...
10	No...	Sinks............	Yes..	No...	Yes..	No...	Yes..	....	Yes..	No...	No...
11	Yes..	......do............	Yes..	No...	No...	No...	Yes..	....	Yes..	No...	Yes..
12	Yes ³.	......do............	Yes..	No...	No...	No...	Yes ⁴.	....	Yes..	No...	Yes..
13	No...	......do............	Yes..	Yes..	Yes..	Yes..	Yes..	Yes..	Yes..	Yes..	Yes..
14	Yes..	......do............	Yes..	Yes..	Yes..	Yes..	Yes..	Yes..	Yes..	Yes..	Yes..
15	Yes..	Sinks and tubs........	Yes..	Yes..	Yes..	Yes..	Yes..	Yes..	Yes..	Yes..	Yes..
16	Yes..	......do............	Yes..	Yes..	Yes..	Yes..	Yes..	Yes..	Yes..	Yes..	Yes..
17	Yes..	None............	Yes..	Yes..	Yes..	Yes..	Yes..	Yes..	Yes..	Yes..	Yes..
18	Yes..	......do............	Yes..	No...	No...	No...	Yes..	....	Yes..	Yes..	Yes..
19	Yes..	Sinks............	Yes..	No...	No...	No...	Yes..	Yes..	Yes..	Yes..	Yes..
20	Yes ³.	Water barrels........	Yes..	No...	No...	No...	Yes..	....	Yes..	Yes..	Yes..
21	Yes..	None............	Yes..	No...	No...	Yes..	Yes..	Yes..	Yes..	Yes..	Yes..
22	Yes..	......do............	Yes..	Yes..	Yes..	Yes..	Yes..	Yes..	Yes..	Yes..	Yes..
23	Yes..	Stationary washbowls	Yes..	Yes..	Yes..	Yes..	Yes..	Yes..	Yes..	Yes..	Yes..
24	No...	Sinks............	Yes..	No...	Yes..	Yes..	Yes..	Yes..	Yes..	Yes..	Yes..
25	No...	......do............	Yes..	No...	Yes..	Yes..	Yes..	Yes..	Yes..	Yes..	Yes..
26	No...	......do............	Yes..	Yes..	Yes..	No...	No...	....	....	Yes..	No...
27	Yes..	Stationary washbowls	Yes..	No...	Yes..	Yes..	Yes..	Yes..	Yes..	Yes..	Yes..
28	Yes..	Sinks............	Yes..	No...	Yes..	Yes..	Yes..	Yes..	Yes..	Yes..	Yes..
29	No...	......do............	Yes..	No...	Yes..	Yes..	Yes..	No...	Yes..	Yes..	No...
30	Yes..	......do............	Yes..	No...	No...	Yes..	Yes..	Yes..	Yes..	Yes..	Yes..
31	Yes..	......do............	Yes..	No...	No...	No...	Yes..	....	Yes..	No...	Yes..
32	Yes..	None............	Yes..	Yes..	Yes..	No...	Yes..	....	Yes..	Yes..	Yes..
33	No...	Sinks............	Yes..	No...	No...	No...	Yes..	....	Yes..	Yes..	Yes..
34	No...	......do............	Yes..	No...	No...	No...	No...	....	....	No...	Yes..
35	Yes..	......do............	Yes..	Yes..	Yes..	No...	Yes..	....	Yes..	No...	No...
36	Yes..	Sink............	Yes..	No...	Yes..	No...	No...	....	....	No...	No...
37	Yes ³.	Sinks............	Yes..	No...	No...	No...	Yes..	....	Yes..	Yes..	Yes..
38	Yes..	None............	Yes..	No...	No...	No...	Yes..	Yes..	Yes..	Yes..	Yes..
39	No...	Sinks............	Yes..	No...	No...	Yes..	Yes..	Yes..	Yes..	Yes..	Yes..
40	Yes..	None............	Yes..	No...	No...	Yes..	Yes..	Yes..	Yes..	No...	Yes..
41	No...	Sinks............	Yes..	No...	No...	No...	No...	....	....	Yes..	Yes..
42	No...	......do............	Yes..	No...	Yes..	No...	No...	....	....	Yes..	Yes..
43	No...	......do............	Yes..	No...	No...	No...	No...	....	....	Yes..	Yes..
44	Yes ³.	......do............	Yes..	No...	Yes..	Yes..	Yes..	Yes..	Yes..	Yes..	Yes..
45	Yes ³.	......do............	Yes..	No...	Yes..	Yes..	Yes..	Yes..	Yes..	Yes..	Yes..
46	Yes..	None............	Yes..	Yes..	Yes..	Yes..	Yes..	Yes..	Yes..	No...	No...
47	Yes..	......do............	Yes..	Yes..	Yes..	Yes..	Yes..	Yes..	Yes..	Yes..	Yes..
48	Yes..	......do............	Yes..	Yes..	Yes..	Yes..	Yes..	Yes..	Yes..	Yes..	No...
49	Yes..	Washstands...........	Yes..	No...	No...	No...	Yes..	Yes..	Yes..	No...	No...
50	Yes..	None............	Yes..	Yes..	Yes..	Yes..	Yes..	Yes..	Yes..	No...	No...

¹ Pool, shower, and tub baths, and washstands, with running water, on each floor.
² No urinals.
³ For females only.

FACILITIES, DRESSING ROOMS, REST ROOMS, SEATS FOR FEMALES, WATER-CLOSETS—Continued.

PENNSYLVANIA.

Rest rooms for females: Provided	Rest rooms for females: Sufficient	Sufficient seats provided for females	Lunch rooms provided	Separate for the sexes	Privacy of approach: Males	Privacy of approach: Females	Number of male employees per urinal	Employees per seat: Males	Employees per seat: Females	Clean for: Males	Clean for: Females	Air of workrooms affected by water-closets	Establishment number
Yes	Yes	Yes	Yes	Yes	Yes	Yes	9	9	18	Yes	Yes	No	1
Yes	Yes	Yes	Yes	Yes	Yes	Yes	[4]	10	19	Yes	Yes	No	2
Yes	Yes	Yes	Yes	Yes	Yes	Yes	30	10	16	Yes	Yes	No	3
No		Yes	No	Yes	Yes	Yes	[4]	6	14	Yes	Yes	No	4
Yes	Yes	Yes	Yes	Yes	Yes	Yes	[4]	3	35	Yes	Yes	No	5
No		Yes	No	Yes	Yes	Yes	[4]	25	44	Yes	Yes	No	6
No		Yes	No	Yes	Yes	Yes	[4]	7	11	Yes	Yes	No	7
No		Yes	No	Yes	Yes	Yes	[4]	1	17	Yes	Yes	No	8
No		Yes	No	Yes	Yes	Yes	97	49	33	No	Yes	No	9
Yes	Yes	Yes	Yes	Yes	Yes	Yes	[4]	14	38	Yes	Yes	No	10
No		Yes	Yes	Yes	Yes	Yes	[4]	5	24	Yes	Yes	No	11
No		Yes	No	Yes	Yes	Yes	52	26	34	Yes	Yes	No	12
No		Yes	No	Yes	Yes	Yes	[4]	9	17	Yes	Yes	No	13
Yes	Yes	Yes	Yes	Yes	Yes	Yes	12	12	9	Yes	Yes	No	14
No		Yes	No	Yes	Yes	Yes	4	4	11	Yes	Yes	No	15
Yes	Yes	Yes	Yes	Yes	Yes	Yes	5	5	9	Yes	Yes	No	16
No		Yes	Yes	Yes	Yes	Yes	4	4	10	Yes	Yes	No	17
No		No	No	Yes	Yes	Yes	[5]	[5]	4	Yes	Yes	No	18
No		No	No	Yes	Yes	Yes	[4]	[5]	19	Yes	Yes	No	19
No		No	No	Yes	[5]	Yes	[5]	[5]	17	[5]	Yes	No	20
Yes	Yes	Yes	Yes	Yes	[5]	Yes	[5]	[5]	8	Yes	Yes	No	21
No		No	Yes	Yes	Yes	{5 yes, 11 no}	[4]	9	9	{5 yes, 9 no}	Yes	No	22
No		Yes	Yes	Yes	Yes	Yes	[4]	4	9	Yes	Yes	No	23
No		Yes	Yes	Yes	Yes	Yes	[4]	10	47	Yes	Yes	No	24
No		Yes	No	Yes	Yes	Yes	[4]	26	13	Yes	Yes	No	25
No		Yes	No	Yes	Yes	Yes	27	18	36	Yes	Yes	No	26
No		Yes	No	Yes	Yes	Yes	[4]	6	10	Yes	Yes	No	27
No		Yes	No	Yes	Yes	Yes	44	11	35	Yes	Yes	No	28
No		Yes	No	Yes	Yes	Yes	[4]	10	30	Yes	Yes	No	29
No		Yes	No	Yes	Yes	Yes	151	19	21	Yes	Yes	No	30
No		Yes	No	Yes	Yes	Yes	[4]	4	38	Yes	Yes	No	31
No		Yes	No	Yes	Yes	Yes	46	23	31	Yes	Yes	No	32
No		Yes	No	Yes	Yes	Yes	[4]	24	19	Yes	Yes	No	33
No		Yes	No	No	No	No	[4]	[6]	[6]	No	No	No	34
Yes	[5]	Yes	Yes	Yes	Yes	Yes	19	19	10	Yes	Yes	No	35
No		Yes	No	Yes	Yes	Yes	[4]	10	4	Yes	Yes	No	36
No		Yes	No	Yes	[5]	Yes	[5]	[5]	12	[5]	Yes	No	37
No		No	No	Yes	Yes	Yes	[5]	[5]	19	Yes	Yes	No	38
No		Yes	No	Yes	Yes	Yes	16	16	29	Yes	Yes	Yes	39
Yes	Yes	Yes	No	Yes	Yes	Yes	17	11	19	Yes	Yes	No	40
No		Yes	No	Yes	Yes	Yes	5	5	30	Yes	Yes	No	41
No		Yes	No	Yes	Yes	Yes	9	9	3	No	Yes	Yes	42
No		No	No	Yes	Yes	Yes	[4]	26	3	Yes	Yes	No	43
No		No	No	Yes	Yes	Yes	202	51	10	No	Yes	Yes	44
No		No	No	Yes	Yes	Yes	[4]	[5]	4	Yes	Yes	No	45
No		Yes	No	Yes	Yes	Yes	[4]	[5]	[4]	Yes	Yes	No	46
No		Yes	No	Yes	Yes	Yes	8	8	5	Yes	Yes	No	47
Yes	Yes	Yes	No	Yes	Yes	Yes	15	18	13	Yes	Yes	No	48
No		Yes	No	Yes	Yes	Yes	7	9	10	Yes	Yes	No	49
Yes	Yes	Yes	No	Yes	Yes	Yes	5	5	2	Yes	Yes	No	50

[4] But without door.
[5] Not reported.
[6] Not separate for sexes; 34 males, 24 females, 3 seats; average, 21 persons per seat.

TABLE V.—PROVISIONS FOR COMFORT OF EMPLOYEES: WASH ROOM LUNCH ROOMS, AND

OHIO.

Establishment number.	Facilities for washing.			Establishments furnish—		Dressing rooms provided.				Nature of work requires change of clothing for—	
	Separate wash rooms.	Other.	Sufficient.			Separate for—		Sufficient for—			
				Towels.	Soap.	Males.	Females.	Males.	Females.	Males.	Females.
1	No...	Sinks...	Yes..	Yes..	Yes..	No...	Yes..		Yes..	No...	No...
2	No...	....do	Yes..	No...	No...	No...	Yes..		Yes..	No...	Yes..
3	No...	....do	No...	No...	No...	No...	Yes..		Yes..	No...	No...
4	Yes.	None	Yes..	No...	No...	Yes..	Yes..	Yes..	Yes..	No...	No...
5	Yes..	Sinks	Yes..	Yes..	Yes..	Yes..	Yes..	Yes..	Yes..	No...	No...
6	Yes..	None	Yes..	Yes..	Yes..	Yes..	Yes..	Yes..	Yes..	No...	No...
7	Yes..	Sinks	Yes..	Yes..	Yes..	(²)....	Yes..		Yes..	(²)....	No...
8	No...	....do	Yes..	Yes..	Yes..	No...	No...			No...	No...
9	Yes..	....do	Yes..	No...	No...	Yes..	Yes..	Yes..	Yes..	No...	No...
10	No...	....do	Yes..	Yes..	Yes..	No...	Yes..		Yes..	No...	No...
11	Yes³.	None	Yes..	Yes..	Yes..	No...	No...			No...	No...
12	No...	Sinks	Yes..	Yes..	Yes..	Yes..	Yes..	Yes..	Yes..	Yes..	Yes..
13	No...	....do	Yes..	Yes..	Yes..	Yes..	Yes..	Yes..	Yes..	Yes..	Yes..
14	No...	....do	Yes..	Yes..	Yes..	Yes..	Yes..	Yes..	Yes..	Yes..	Yes..
15	No...	....do	Yes..	No...	No...	Yes..	Yes..	Yes..	Yes..	Yes..	Yes..
16	No...	....do	Yes..	Yes..	Yes..	Yes..	Yes..	Yes..	Yes..	Yes..	Yes..
17	Yes..	....do	Yes..	Yes..	Yes..	Yes..	Yes..	Yes..	Yes..	Yes..	Yes..
18	Yes..	....do	Yes..	Yes⁴.	Yes⁴.	Yes..	Yes..	Yes..	Yes..	Yes..	Yes..
19	Yes..	None	Yes..	Yes..	Yes..	Yes..	Yes..	Yes..	Yes..	Yes..	Yes..
20	Yes..	Sinks	Yes..	No...	No...	Yes..	Yes..	Yes..	Yes..	Yes..	Yes..
21	No...	....do	Yes..	Yes..	Yes..	Yes..	Yes..	Yes..	Yes..	Yes..	Yes..
22	Yes..	None	Yes..	Yes..	Yes..	Yes..	Yes..	Yes..	Yes..	No...	Yes..
23	No...	Sinks	Yes..	No...	No...	Yes..	Yes..	Yes..	Yes..	No...	Yes..
24	Yes..	None	Yes..	Yes..	Yes..	No...	Yes..		Yes..	Yes..	Yes..
25	No...	Stationary washstands	Yes..	Yes..	No...	Yes..	Yes..	Yes..	Yes..	Yes..	Yes..
26	Yes⁶.	Sinks	Yes..	No...	No...	No...	Yes..		Yes..	No...	Yes..
27	Yes⁶.	....do	Yes..	Yes..	Yes..	No...	Yes..		Yes..	No...	No...
28	No...	None	No...	Yes..	Yes..	No...	No...			No...	No...
29	No...	Sinks	Yes..	Yes..	Yes..	No...	No...			No...	No...
30	Yes..	None	Yes..	Yes..	Yes..	No...	Yes..		Yes..	No...	No...
31	No...	Sinks	Yes..	Yes..	Yes..	No...	No...			No...	No...
32	Yes..	None	Yes..	No...	No...	Yes..	Yes..	Yes..	Yes..	Yes..	Yes..
33	Yes..	Sinks	Yes..	No...	No...	Yes..	Yes..	Yes..	Yes..	Yes..	No...
34	No...	....do	Yes..	No...	No...	Yes..	Yes..	Yes..	Yes..	Yes..	Yes..
35	No...	....do	Yes..	No...	No...	Yes..	Yes..	Yes..	Yes..	Yes..	Yes..
36	No...	....do	Yes..	No...	No...	Yes..	Yes..	Yes..	Yes..	Yes..	Yes..
37	Yes..	None	Yes..	No...	No...	Yes..	Yes..	Yes..	Yes..	Yes..	Yes..
38	Yes..	Sinks	Yes..	No...	No...	Yes..	Yes..	Yes..	Yes..	Yes..	Yes..
39	No...	....do	Yes..	Yes..	Yes..	Yes..	Yes..	Yes..	Yes..	Yes..	Yes..
40	No...	....do	Yes..	Yes..	Yes..	Yes..	Yes..	Yes..	Yes..	Yes..	Yes..
41	No...	....do	Yes..	No...	No...	No...	No...			Yes..	Yes..
42	No...	....do	Yes..	No...	No...	Yes..	Yes..		Yes..	Yes..	Yes..
43	No...	....do	Yes..	No...	No...	Yes..	Yes..		Yes..	Yes..	Yes..
44	No...	None	No...	Yes..	Yes..	No...	Yes..		Yes..	No...	Yes..
45	Yes⁶.	Sinks	Yes..	No...	Yes..	No...	Yes..		Yes..	Yes..	Yes..
46	Yes⁶.	Basins	Yes..	No...	No...	No...	Yes..		Yes..	Yes..	Yes..
47	No...	Sinks	Yes..	No...	No...	No...	Yes..		Yes..	Yes..	Yes..
48	Yes⁶.	....do	Yes..	No...	No...	Yes..	Yes..	Yes..	Yes..	Yes..	Yes..
49	No...	Tanks and running water.	Yes..	No...	Yes..	No...	Yes..		Yes..	Yes..	Yes..
50	Yes..	Sinks	Yes..	No...	Yes..	Yes..	Yes..	Yes..	Yes..	No...	No...
51	No...	Sink	Yes..	No...	No...	Yes..	Yes..		Yes..	No...	No...
52	Yes..	None	No...	No...	No...	Yes..	Yes..		Yes..	Yes..	Yes..
53	No...	Sinks	Yes..	Yes..	No...	No...	No...			No...	No...
54	Yes..	Bowls	Yes..	Yes..	Yes..	Yes..	Yes..	Yes..	Yes..	No...	No...
55	Yes..	Faucets	Yes..	No...	No...	Yes..	Yes..	Yes..	Yes..	No...	No...
56	Yes..	None	Yes..	No...	Yes..	No...	No...			No...	No...
57	Yes..	Faucets	Yes..	No...	No...	No...	No...			No...	No...
58	Yes..	None	Yes..	No...	No...	No...	No...			No...	No...
59	No...	Bowls	Yes..	No...	Yes..	Yes..	Yes..	Yes..	Yes..	No...	Yes..
60	Yes..	Faucets	Yes..	Yes..	Yes..	No...	No...			No...	No...

¹ No urinals.
² No males.
³ Not separate for sexes.
⁴ In one department only.

FACILITIES, DRESSING ROOMS, REST ROOMS, SEATS FOR FEMALES, WATER-CLOSETS—Continued.

OHIO.

Rest rooms for females.		Sufficient seats provided for females.	Lunch rooms provided.	Water-closets.								Air of workrooms affected by water-closets.	Establishment number.
Provided.	Sufficient.			Separate for the sexes.	Privacy of approach for—		Number of male employees per urinal.	Number of employees per seat.		Clean for—			
					Males.	Females.		Males.	Females.	Males.	Females.		
No...		Yes..	No...	Yes..	Yes...	Yes...	(1)	9	39	Yes..	Yes..	No...	1
No...		Yes..	No...	Yes..	Yes...	Yes...	(1)	7	15	Yes..	Yes..	No...	2
No...		Yes..	No...	Yes..	Yes...	Yes...	18	18	100	Yes..	Yes..	No...	3
No...		Yes..	No...	Yes..	Yes...	Yes...	19	5	16	Yes..	Yes..	No...	4
Yes..	Yes..	Yes..	No...	Yes..	Yes...	Yes...	(1)	5	31	Yes..	Yes..	No...	5
Yes..	Yes..	Yes..	No...	Yes..	Yes...	Yes...	37	5	16	Yes..	Yes..	No...	6
No...		Yes..	No...	Yes..	(2).....	Yes...	(1)	(2)	11	(2)...	Yes..	No...	7
No...		Yes..	No...	Yes..	Yes...	Yes...	(1)	33	9	Yes..	Yes..	No...	8
Yes..	Yes..	Yes..	Yes..	Yes..	Yes...	Yes...	(1)	13	31	Yes..	Yes..	No...	9
No...		Yes..	Yes..	Yes..	Yes...	Yes...	(1)	22	12	Yes..	Yes..	No...	10
No...		Yes..	No...	Yes..	No...	No...	(1)	11	21	Yes..	Yes..	No...	11
No...		Yes..	No...	Yes..	Yes...	Yes...	(1)	7	7	Yes..	Yes..	No...	12
No...		Yes..	No...	Yes..	Yes...	Yes...	(1)	5	14	Yes..	Yes..	No...	13
No...		Yes..	No...	Yes..	Yes...	Yes...	(1)	12	20	Yes..	Yes..	No...	14
No...		Yes..	No...	Yes..	Yes...	Yes...	(1)	3	4	Yes..	Yes..	No...	15
No...		Yes..	No...	Yes..	Yes...	Yes...	(1)	15	34	Yes..	Yes..	No...	16
No...		Yes..	No...	Yes..	Yes...	Yes...	(1)	5	21	Yes..	Yes..	No...	17
No...		Yes..	No...	Yes..	Yes...	Yes...	(1)	16	10	Yes..	Yes..	No...	18
No...		Yes..	Yes 5	Yes..	Yes...	Yes...	(1)	16	46	Yes..	Yes..	No...	19
No...		Yes..	No...	Yes..	Yes...	Yes...	(1)	13	5	Yes..	Yes..	No...	20
No...		Yes..	No...	Yes..	Yes...	Yes...	(1)	11	16	Yes..	Yes..	No...	21
No...		No...	No...	Yes..	Yes...	Yes...	(1)	23	10	No...	Yes..	No...	22
No...		Yes..	No...	Yes..	Yes...	Yes...	(1)	14	17	Yes..	Yes..	No...	23
No...		Yes..	No...	Yes..	Yes...	Yes...	(1)	7	22	Yes..	Yes..	No...	24
No...		Yes..	No...	Yes..	Yes...	Yes...	(1)	12	22	Yes..	Yes..	No...	25
No...		Yes..	No...	Yes..	No...	No...	(1)	4	13	Yes..	Yes..	No...	26
Yes..	Yes..	Yes..	Yes 7	Yes..	Yes...	Yes...	(1)	15	26	Yes..	Yes..	No...	27
No...		Yes..	No...	Yes..	Yes...	Yes...	28	14	32	Yes..	Yes..	No...	28
Yes..	Yes..	Yes..	Yes..	Yes..	Yes...	Yes...	39	10	8	Yes..	Yes..	No...	29
Yes..	Yes..	Yes..	Yes..	Yes..	Yes...	Yes...	37	9	14	Yes..	Yes..	No...	30
No...		Yes..	Yes..	Yes..	Yes...	Yes...	9	6	11	Yes..	Yes..	No...	31
No...		Yes..	No...	Yes..	Yes...	Yes...	(1)	(3)	33	Yes..	Yes..	No...	32
No...		Yes..	No...	Yes..	Yes...	Yes...	(1)	10	8	Yes..	Yes..	No...	33
No...		Yes..	No...	Yes..	Yes...	Yes...	(1)	61	23	Yes..	Yes..	No...	34
No...		Yes..	No...	Yes..	Yes...	Yes...	(1)	19	3	Yes..	Yes..	No...	35
No...		Yes..	No...	Yes..	Yes...	Yes...	(1)	8	27	Yes..	Yes..	No...	36
No...		Yes..	No...	Yes..	Yes...	Yes...	(1)	13	12	Yes..	Yes..	No...	37
No...		Yes..	No...	Yes..	Yes...	Yes...	(1)	2	11	Yes..	Yes..	No...	38
No...		Yes..	No...	Yes..	Yes...	Yes...	(1)	6	14	Yes..	Yes..	No...	39
No...		Yes..	No...	Yes..	Yes...	Yes...	(1)	3	13	Yes..	Yes..	No...	40
No...		Yes..	No...	Yes..	Yes...	Yes...	40	40	25	Yes..	Yes..	Yes..	41
No...		Yes..	No...	Yes..	Yes...	Yes...	(1)	20	8	Yes..	Yes..	No...	42
No...		Yes..	No...	Yes..	Yes...	Yes...	(1)	24	8	No...	Yes..	No...	43
No...		Yes..	No...	Yes..	Yes...	Yes...	(1)	25	15	No...	Yes..	No...	44
No...		Yes..	No...	Yes..	Yes...	Yes...	27	11	12	Yes..	Yes..	No...	45
No...		Yes..	No...	Yes..	Yes...	Yes...	91	15	19	Yes..	Yes..	No...	46
No...		Yes..	No...	Yes..	Yes...	Yes...	40	13	25	Yes..	Yes..	No...	47
No...		No...	No...	Yes..	Yes...	Yes...	119	20	18	Yes..	Yes..	No...	48
No...		No...	No...	Yes..	Yes...	Yes...	62	21	10	No...	Yes..	No...	49
Yes..	Yes..	Yes..	No...	Yes..	Yes...	Yes...	(1)	8	(3)	Yes..	Yes..	No...	50
No...		Yes..	No...	Yes..	Yes...	Yes...	(1)	7	12	Yes..	Yes..	No...	51
No...		Yes..	No...	Yes..	Yes...	Yes...	(1)	7	19	Yes..	Yes..	No...	52
No...		Yes..	No...	Yes..	Yes...	Yes...	185	24	27	Yes..	Yes..	No...	53
No...		Yes..	No...	Yes..	Yes...	Yes...	5	4	5	Yes..	Yes..	No...	54
No...		Yes..	No...	Yes..	Yes...	Yes...	11	11	13	Yes..	Yes..	No...	55
No...		Yes..	No...	Yes..	Yes...	Yes...	147	25	14	Yes..	Yes..	No...	56
No...		Yes..	No...	Yes..	Yes...	Yes...	16	16	16	Yes..	Yes..	No...	57
No...		Yes..	No...	Yes..	Yes...	Yes...	54	11	8	Yes..	Yes..	No...	58
No.:		Yes..	No...	Yes..	Yes...	Yes...	8	8	(3)	Yes..	Yes..	No...	59
No...		Yes..	No...	Yes..	Yes...	Yes...	18	18	12	Yes..	Yes..	No...	60

5 For males only.
6 For females only.
7 Coffee, sugar, and cream furnished free, and 1 person employed to care for lunch room.
8 Not reported.

TABLE V.—PROVISIONS FOR COMFORT OF EMPLOYEES: WASH ROOM LUNCH ROOMS, AND

ILLINOIS.

Establishment number.	Facilities for washing.					Dressing rooms provided.				Nature of work requires change of clothing for—	
	Separate wash rooms.	Other.	Sufficient.	Establishments furnish—		Separate for—		Sufficient for—			
				Towels.	Soap.	Males.	Females.	Males.	Females.	Males.	Females.
1	No	Sink	Yes	No	No	Yes	Yes	Yes	Yes	No	No
2	No	....do	Yes	No	No	No	No			No	No
3	Yes	None	Yes	Yes	Yes	No	Yes		Yes	No	Yes
4	Yes	....do	Yes	Yes	Yes	No	Yes		Yes	No	Yes
5	Yes	Sinks	Yes	Yes	Yes	Yes	Yes	Yes	Yes	Yes	Yes
6	No	....do	Yes	Yes	Yes	Yes	Yes	Yes	No	Yes	Yes
7	No	Sink	No	No	No	No	No			No	No
8	Yes	....do	No	Yes	Yes	No	Yes		No	No	No
9	No	....do	No	No	No	No	No			No	No
10	No	Sinks	Yes	No	No	No	No			No	No
11	No	....do	Yes	Yes	Yes	Yes	Yes	Yes	Yes	No	No
12	No	Sink	No	Yes	Yes	Yes	Yes	Yes	Yes	Yes	No
13	No	....do	No	Yes[1]	Yes[1]	No	No			Yes	No
14	Yes	None	Yes	No	No	No	Yes		Yes	No	Yes
15	Yes	Sink	Yes	Yes	Yes	No	Yes		Yes	Yes	Yes
16	Yes	Sinks	Yes	Yes	Yes	Yes	Yes	Yes	Yes	Yes	Yes
17	Yes	Sink	Yes	Yes	Yes	No	Yes		Yes	Yes	Yes
18	Yes	....do	Yes	Yes	Yes	No	Yes		Yes	Yes	Yes
19	Yes	....do	Yes	Yes	Yes	No	No			No	No
20	Yes	None	Yes	Yes	Yes	Yes	Yes	Yes	Yes	Yes	Yes
21	Yes	....do	Yes	Yes	No	Yes	Yes	Yes	Yes	Yes	No
22	No	Sink	No	No	No	Yes	Yes	Yes	Yes	No	No
23	No	....do	No	No	No	Yes	Yes	Yes	No	No	No
24	No	....do	No	No	No	Yes	Yes	Yes	Yes	No	No
25	Yes	None	No	No	No	Yes	Yes	Yes	Yes	No	No
26	No	Sink	Yes	No	No	No	No			No	No
27	Yes	None	Yes	(²)	(²)	No	No			No	No
28	Yes	....do	Yes	No	Yes	No	No			No	No
29	No	Sinks	No	No	No	No	No			No	No
30	No	Sinks and bowls	No	No	No	No	No			Yes	No
31	No	Faucet in yard	No	No	No	No	Yes		No	No	No
32	No	Sink	No	No	Yes	Yes	Yes	Yes	Yes	No	No
33	No	....do	No	No	No	No	No			No	No
34	No	....do	No	No	No	No	No			No	No..
35	Yes	None	Yes	No	No	Yes	Yes	Yes	Yes	No	No
36	No	Sink	Yes	Yes	Yes	No	Yes		Yes	No	No
37	No	Sinks	No	No	Yes	No	Yes		No	Yes	No
38	No	Sinks and pails	No	No	No	No	Yes		No	Yes	Yes
39	No	Sinks	No	No	No	No	Yes		Yes	Yes	Yes
40	No	....do	No	Yes	Yes	Yes	Yes	No	Yes	No	No
41	Yes	None	Yes	Yes	Yes	No	Yes		Yes	No	No
42	No	Sinks	No	Yes	Yes	No	No			No	No
43	No	Sink	No	No	No	No	Yes		No	No	Yes
44	Yes	None	Yes	Yes	Yes	Yes	Yes	Yes	Yes	Yes	No
45	No	Sinks, pans, pails	No	No	No	No	No			No	No
46	No	....do	No	No	No	No	No			No[4]	No
47	No	Pails	No	No	No	No	No			Yes	Yes

1 No urinals.
2 Not reported
3 Insufficient.

FACILITIES, DRESSING ROOMS, REST ROOMS, SEATS FOR FEMALES, WATER-CLOSETS—Continued.

ILLINOIS.

Rest rooms for females.		Sufficient seats provided for females.	Lunch rooms provided.	Water-closets.								Air of work-rooms affected by water-closets.	Establishment number.
Provided.	Sufficient.			Separate for the sexes.	Privacy of approach for—		Number of male employees per urinal.	Number of employees per seat.		Clean for—			
					Males.	Females.		Males.	Females.	Males.	Females.		
No...		Yes..	No...	Yes..	No....	No....	[1]	3	13	Yes..	Yes..	No...	1
No...		Yes..	No...	Yes..	Yes..	Yes...	[1]	9	17	Yes..	Yes..	No...	2
Yes..	Yes..	Yes..	Yes..	Yes..	Yes..	Yes...	35	6	4	Yes..	Yes..	No...	3
No...		No...	No...	Yes..	Yes..	Yes...	[1]	[2]	10	Yes..	Yes..	No...	4
No...		Yes..	No...	Yes..	Yes..	Yes...	[2]	[2]	6	Yes..	Yes..	No...	5
No...		Yes..	No...	Yes..	Yes..	No....	3	3	15	Yes..	Yes..	No...	6
No...		Yes..	No...	Yes..	No....	No....	[1]	26	8	Yes..	Yes..	No...	7
No...		Yes..	Yes..	Yes..	No....	No....	103	39	21	Yes..	Yes..	No...	8
No...		Yes..	No...	Yes..	No....	No....	[1]	25	10	Yes..	Yes..	No...	9
No...		Yes..	No...	Yes..	Yes..	Yes..	68	27	20	No...	No...	No...	10
No...		No...	No...	Yes..	Yes..	Yes...	[1]	5	12	Yes..	Yes..	No...	11
No...		Yes..	No...	Yes..	{4 yes../2 no..}	{4 yes../2 no..}	23	8	25	Yes..	Yes..	No...	12
No...		No...	No...	Yes..	No....	Yes...	[1]	24	39	No...	No...	No...	13
No...		Yes..	No...	Yes..	Yes..	Yes...	4	4	11	Yes..	Yes..	No...	14
No...		Yes..	No...	Yes..	Yes..	Yes...	1	1	6	Yes..	Yes..	No...	15
Yes..	No...	Yes..	Yes..	Yes..	Yes...	Yes...	[2]	[2]	10	Yes..	Yes..	No...	16
No...		Yes..	Yes..	Yes..	Yes..	Yes...	1	1	14	Yes..	Yes..	No...	17
No...		Yes..	Yes..	Yes..	Yes..	Yes...	1	[2]	8	Yes..	Yes..	No...	18
Yes..	Yes..	Yes..	No...	Yes..	Yes..	Yes...	13	13	19	Yes..	Yes..	No...	19
Yes..	Yes..	Yes..	Yes..	Yes..	Yes..	Yes...	14	17	8	Yes..	Yes..	No...	20
No...		No...	No...	Yes..	No....	No....	[1]	7	9	Yes..	Yes..	No...	21
No...		No...	No...	Yes..	No....	No....	[1]	14	16	No...	No...	No...	22
Yes..	No...	Yes..	No...	Yes..	Yes..	Yes...	[1]	16	16	Yes..	Yes..	No...	23
No...		Yes..	No...	Yes..	Yes..	Yes...	[1]	14	17	Yes..	Yes..	No...	24
No...		Yes..	No...	Yes..	No....	No....	[1]	11	19	Yes..	Yes..	No...	25
No...		Yes..	No...	Yes..	Yes..	Yes...	13	13	10	Yes..	Yes..	No...	26
No...		Yes..	No...	Yes..	Yes..	Yes...	12	8	13	Yes..	Yes..	No...	27
No...		Yes..	No...	Yes..	Yes..	Yes...	3	1	9	Yes..	Yes..	No...	28
No...		Yes..	No...	Yes..	No....	No....	[1]	18	19	Yes..	Yes..	No...	29
No...		Yes..	No...	Yes..	No....	Yes...	25	11	18	Yes..	Yes..	No...	30
No...		Yes..	No...	Yes..	No....	No....	[1]	20	15	No...	Yes..	No...	31
No...		Yes..	No...	Yes..	Yes..	Yes...	16	10	15	Yes..	Yes..	No...	32
No...		Yes..	No...	Yes..	No....	No....	[1]	20	20	Yes..	Yes..	No...	33
No...		Yes..	No...	Yes..	No....	No....	[1]	4	24	Yes..	Yes..	Yes..	34
No...		Yes..	No...	Yes..	Yes..	Yes...	11	6	14	Yes..	Yes..	No...	35
No...		Yes..	No...	Yes..	Yes..	No....	16	5	34	Yes..	Yes..	No...	36
No...		Yes..	No...	Yes..	Yes..	Yes...	105	23	13	No...	Yes..	No...	37
No...		Yes..	No...	Yes..	Yes..	Yes...	191	38	29	No...	Yes..	Yes..	38
No...		No...	No...	Yes..	Yes..	Yes...	[1]	[4]	6	No...	Yes..	No...	39
No...		Yes..	No...	Yes..	Yes..	No....	[1]	19	18	Yes..	Yes..	No...	40
No...		Yes..	No...	Yes..	Yes..	Yes...	38	11	7	Yes..	Yes..	No...	41
No...		No...	Yes..	Yes..	No....	No....	47	6	9	No...	No...	No...	42
No...		No...	No...	Yes..	No....	No....	[1]	20	17	No...	No...	No...	43
Yes..	Yes..	Yes..	Yes..	Yes..	Yes..	Yes...	38	5	[2]	Yes..	Yes..	No...	44
No...		No...	No...	[5]...	No....	No....	11	16	9	No...	Yes..	No...	45
No...		Yes..	No...	Yes..	Yes..	No....	5	9	16	No...	No...	No...	46
No...		No...	No...	Yes..	No....	No....	10	19	9	No...	Yes..	No...	47

[4] A trough is provided; no separate seats.
[5] Separate on 2 floors, not separate on 1.
[6] Except 1 man.

TABLE V.—PROVISIONS FOR COMFORT OF EMPLOYEES: WASH ROOM LUNCH ROOMS, AND

INDIANA.

Establishment number.	Facilities for washing.			Establishments furnish—		Dressing rooms provided.				Nature of work requires change of clothing for—	
	Separate wash rooms.	Other.	Sufficient.	Towels.	Soap.	Separate for—		Sufficient for—			
						Males.	Females.	Males.	Females.	Males.	Females.
1	Yes..	Sinks	Yes..	Yes..	Yes..	No...	Yes..	....	Yes..	No...	Yes..
2	No...	Pails	No...	No...	No...	No...	No...			No...	No...
3	No...	Sink	Yes..	No...	No...	Yes..	Yes..	Yes..	Yes..	No...	No...
4	No...	Sinks and water barrels	No...	Yes..	Yes..	Yes..	Yes..	No...	No...	No...	No...
5	Yes³	Sinks	Yes..	Yes..	Yes..	Yes..	Yes..	Yes..	Yes..	No...	No...
6	No...	Sink	No...	No...	No...	No...	No...			No...	No...
7	No...	Spigots	No...	No...	No...	Yes..	Yes..	Yes..	No...	No...	No...
8	No...	Sink	No...	No...	No...	No...	No...			No...	No...
9	No...	....do	No...	No...	No...	No...	Yes..		No...	No...	No...
10	No...	....do	No...	Yes..	Yes..	No...	Yes..		Yes..	No...	No...
11	Yes..	None	Yes..	Yes..	Yes..	Yes..	Yes..	Yes..	Yes..	No...	No...
12	Yes..	....do	Yes..	No...	No...	Yes..	Yes..	Yes..	Yes..	No...	No...
13	Yes..	....do	Yes..	Yes..	Yes..	Yes..	Yes..	Yes..	Yes..	No...	No...
14	No...	Sink	No...	Yes..	Yes..	Yes..	Yes..	Yes..	Yes..	No...	No...
15	No...	Sinks	Yes..	No...	No...	Yes..	Yes..	Yes..	Yes..	Yes..	No...
16	No...	....do	No...	No...	No...	Yes..	Yes..	Yes..	Yes..	Yes..	No...
17	Yes..	....do	No...	No...	No...	No...	No...			No...	No...
18	Yes..	None	Yes..	Yes..	Yes..	Yes..	Yes..	Yes..	Yes..	Yes..	Yes..
19	Yes..	Shower baths for men	Yes..	Yes..	Yes..	Yes..	Yes..	Yes..	Yes..	Yes..	Yes..
20	No...	Sinks	Yes..	Yes..	Yes..	Yes..	Yes..	Yes..	Yes..	Yes..	No...
21	Yes..	None	Yes..	Yes..	No...	No...	No...			No...	No...
22	Yes³	Sinks	Yes..	No...	No...	No...	No...			No...	No...
23	No...	Basins	Yes..	Yes..	Yes..	No...	No...			No...	No...
24	No...	Sinks	Yes..	Yes..	Yes..	No...	No...			No...	No...
25	No...	Sink..	Yes..	Yes..	Yes..	Yes..	Yes..	Yes..	Yes..	No...	No...
26	No...	Basins	Yes..	Yes..	Yes..	Yes..	Yes..	Yes..	Yes..	No..	No.
27	No...	Sinks	No...	No...	No...	No...	No...			No...	No...
28	No...	....do	Yes..	Yes..	Yes..	No...	No...			No...	No...
29	No...	....do	No...	Yes..	Yes..	No...	Yes..		No...	No...	No...
30	Yes³	....do	Yes..	Yes..	Yes..	Yes..	Yes..	Yes..	Yes..	No...	No...
31	Yes..	....do	Yes..	Yes..	Yes..	No...	No...			No...	No...
32	Yes..	None	Yes..	Yes..	Yes..	Yes..	Yes..	Yes..	Yes..	No...	No...
33	No...	Sinks	Yes..	Yes..	Yes..	No...	No...			No...	No...
34	No...	....do	Yes..	Yes..	No...	No...	No...			No...	No...
35	No...	Sink	No...	No...	No...	No...	Yes..	Yes..	No...	No...	No...
36	No...	Sinks	No...	No...	No...	No...	No...			No...	No...
37	No...	Sink and bowls	No...	No...	No...	No...	No...			Yes..	No...
38	Yes..	Basins	Yes..	Yes..	Yes..	No...	No...			No...	No...
39	No...	Sink	Yes..	Yes..	Yes..	No...	No...			No...	No...
40	No...	Sinks for males; basins for females.	No...	No...	Yes..	No...	No...			No...	No...
41	Yes..	Sinks	No...	No...	Yes..	No...	Yes..		Yes..	Yes..	Yes..
42	No...	Pails and trough	No...	No...	No...	No...	No...		....	No...	No...
43	No...	Faucets outside	No...	No...	No...	No...	Yes..		No...	Yes..	Yes..
44	(⁴)	Sinks	No...	No...	Yes..	No...	(⁷)			No...	(⁷)
45	No...	None	No...	No...	No...	No...	Yes..		No...	No...	No...
46	No...	Sinks	No...	No...	No...	No...	No...			Yes..	Yes..
47	No...	Basins	No...	No...	Yes..	No...	No...			No...	Yes..

1 No urinals.
2 A trough is provided; no separate seats.
3 For females only.
4 For males only.

FACILITIES, DRESSING ROOMS, REST ROOMS, SEATS FOR FEMALES, WATER-CLOSETS—Continued.

INDIANA.

Rest rooms for females.		Sufficient seats provided for females.	Lunch rooms provided.	Separate for the sexes.	Privacy of approach for—		Number of male employees per urinal.	Number of employees per seat.		Clean for—		Air of workrooms affected by water-closets.	Establishment number.
Provided.	Sufficient.				Males.	Females.		Males.	Females.	Males.	Females.		
Yes..	Yes..	Yes..	Yes..	Yes..	Yes...	Yes...	(1)	9	26	Yes..	Yes..	No...	1
No...		No...	No...	Yes..	Yes...	Yes...	(1)	(2)	23	No...	No...	No...	2
No...		No...	No...	Yes..	Yes...	Yes...	12	12	4	Yes..	Yes..	No...	3
No...		Yes..	No...	Yes..	Yes...	Yes...	(1)	34	35	No...	No...	No...	4
Yes..	Yes..	Yes..	Yes..	Yes..	Yes...	Yes...	46	15	21	Yes..	Yes..	No...	5
No...		Yes..	No...	Yes..	Yes...	Yes...	72	14	6	Yes..	Yes..	No...	6
No...		Yes..	No...	Yes..	Yes...	Yes...	(1)	15	47	Yes..	Yes..	No...	7
No...		Yes..	No...	Yes..	Yes...	Yes...	(1)	1	62	Yes..	Yes..	No...	8
No...		Yes..	No...	Yes..	Yes...	Yes...	(1)	2	33	Yes..	Yes..	No...	9
No...		Yes..	No...	Yes..	Yes...	Yes...	(1)	3	35	Yes..	Yes..	No...	10
No...		Yes..	Yes..	Yes..	Yes...	Yes...	(1)	1	17	Yes..	Yes..	No...	11
No...		Yes..	Yes..	Yes..	Yes...	Yes...	6	4	3	Yes..	Yes..	No...	12
No...		Yes..	No...	Yes..	Yes...	Yes...	(1)	6	25	Yes..	Yes..	No...	13
No...		Yes..	No...	Yes..	Yes...	Yes...	(1)	5	35	Yes..	Yes..	No...	14
No...		Yes..	No...	Yes..	Yes...	Yes...	8	8	30	Yes..	Yes..	No...	15
No...		Yes..	No...	Yes..	Yes...	Yes...	15	9	33	Yes..	Yes..	No...	16
No...		Yes..	No...	Yes..	Yes...	Yes...	30	15	8	No...	Yes..	No...	17
No...		No...	No...	Yes..	Yes...	Yes...	(1)	22	40	Yes..	Yes..	No...	18
Yes..	Yes..	Yes..	Yes..	Yes..	Yes...	Yes...	(1)	41	10	Yes..	Yes..	No...	19
No...		No...	No...	Yes..	Yes...	Yes...	11	18	22	Yes..	Yes..	No...	20
No...		Yes..	No...	Yes..	Yes...	Yes...	9	8	15	Yes..	Yes..	No...	21
No...		Yes..	Yes⁴.	Yes..	Yes...	Yes...	17	4	10	Yes..	Yes..	No...	22
No...		Yes..	No...	Yes..	No...	No....	45	45	25	Yes..	Yes..	No...	23
No...		Yes..	No...	Yes..	Yes...	Yes...	(1)	5	22	No...	Yes..	No...	24
No...		No...	No...	Yes..	Yes...	Yes...	(1)	10	29	Yes..	Yes..	No...	25
No...		Yes..	Yes..	Yes..	Yes...	Yes...	19	23	17	Yes..	Yes..	No...	26
No...		Yes..	No...	Yes..	Yes...	Yes...	26	26	31	Yes..	Yes..	No...	27
No...		Yes..	No...	Yes..	Yes...	Yes...	6	7	29	Yes..	Yes..	No...	28
No...		Yes..	No...	Yes..	Yes...	Yes...	(1)	18	26	No...	Yes..	No...	29
No...		Yes..	No...	Yes..	Yes...	Yes...	(1)	8	18	Yes..	Yes..	No...	30
No...		Yes..	No...	Yes..	Yes...	Yes...	15	15	18	Yes..	Yes..	No...	31
No...		Yes..	No...	Yes..	Yes...	Yes...	(1)	5	19	Yes..	Yes..	No...	32
No...		Yes..	No...	Yes..	Yes...	Yes...	(1)	11	20	Yes..	Yes..	No...	33
No...		Yes..	No...	Yes..	Yes...	Yes...	(1)	13	33	Yes..	No...	No...	34
No...		Yes..	No...	Yes..	Yes...	Yes...	(1)	19	14	No...	No...	No...	35
No...		Yes..	Yes..	Yes..	Yes...	Yes...	22	22	19	Yes..	Yes..	No...	36
No...		Yes..	No...	Yes..	Yes...	No....	78	33	38	Yes..	Yes..	No...	37
No...		Yes..	No...	Yes..	Yes...	Yes...	28	11	21	Yes..	Yes..	No...	38
No...		Yes..	No...	Yes..	Yes...	Yes...	(1)	1	25	Yes..	Yes..	No...	39
No...		Yes..	No...	Yes..	Yes...	Yes...	(1)	13	23	No...	Yes..	No...	40
No...		No...	No...	Yes..	Yes...	Yes...	378	18	11	Yes..	Yes..	No...	41
No...		Yes..	No...	Yes..	No...	No....	(1)	10	21	Yes..	Yes..	No...	42
No...		No...	No...	Yes..	Yes...	Yes...	268	(5)	24	No...	Yes..	No...	43
(7) ...		(7) ...	No...	(7)...	Yes...	(7)	4	4	(7)	No...	(7) ...	No...	44
No...		No...	No...	Yes..	Yes...	No....	(1)	22	24	Yes..	Yes..	No...	45
No...		Yes..	Yes⁸.	Yes..	No...	No....	79	8	8	No...	Yes..	No...	46
No...		Yes..	No...	Yes..	Yes...	Yes...	6	8	10	Yes..	Yes..	No...	47

⁵ Troughs are provided; no separate seats.
⁶ Not reported.
⁷ No females.
⁸ In 1 department only.

TABLE V.—PROVISIONS FOR COMFORT OF EMPLOYEES: WASH ROOM LUNCH ROOMS, AND

MICHIGAN.

Establishment number.	Facilities for washing.			Establishments furnish—		Dressing rooms provided.				Nature of work requires change of clothing for—	
	Separate wash rooms.	Other.	Sufficient.	Towels.	Soap.	Separate for—		Sufficient for—			
						Males.	Females.	Males.	Females.	Males.	Females.
1	Yes..	None	Yes..	Yes..	Yes..	Yes..	Yes..	Yes..	Yes..	Yes..	No...
2	Yes..	Sinks	No...	No...	No...	Yes..	Yes..	No...	No...	No...	No...
3	No...	...do	Yes..	No...	Yes..	Yes..	Yes..	Yes..	Yes..	No...	No...
4	No...	...do	No...	Yes..	Yes..	Yes..	Yes..	Yes..	Yes..	No...	No...
5	Yes..	...do	Yes..	Yes..	Yes..	Yes..	Yes..	Yes..	Yes..	No...	No...
6	No...	...do	No...	Yes..	No...	Yes..	No...	Yes..		Yes..	No...
7	No...	...do	Yes..	Yes..	Yes..	No...	No...			No...	No...
8	Yes..	...do	No...	Yes..	Yes..	No...	Yes..		No...	Yes..	No...
9	No...	...do	Yes..	No...	No...	Yes..	Yes..	Yes..	Yes..	No...	No...
10	No...	...do	Yes..	Yes..	Yes..	No...	No...			No...	No...
11	No...	...do	Yes..	No...	No...	No...	No...			No...	No...
12	Yes..	None	Yes..	Yes..	Yes..	Yes..	Yes..	Yes..	Yes..	No...	No...
13	No...	Pails	No...	Yes..	Yes..	No...	Yes..		No...	No...	No...
14	Yes..	None	Yes..	No...	Yes..	Yes..	Yes..	Yes..	Yes..	No...	No...
15	No...	Sinks	Yes..	No...	No...	No...	No...			No...	No...
16	Yes¹	...do	No...	No...	Yes..	Yes..	Yes..	Yes..	Yes..	No...	No...
17	No...	...do	No...	No...	Yes..	Yes..	Yes..	Yes..	Yes..	No...	No...
18	No...	...do	Yes..	No...	Yes..	Yes..	Yes..	Yes..	Yes..	Yes..	No...
19	No...	Pans	No...	No...	No...	No...	No...			Yes..	Yes..

WISCONSIN.

Establishment number.	Separate wash rooms.	Other.	Sufficient.	Towels.	Soap.	Separate Males.	Separate Females.	Sufficient Males.	Sufficient Females.	Change Males.	Change Females.
1	Yes..	None	Yes..	Yes..	Yes..	Yes..	Yes..	Yes..	Yes..	No...	No...
2	No...	Sinks	Yes..	No...	No...	No...	Yes..		Yes..	No...	Yes..
3	No...	None	No...	No...	No...	Yes..	Yes..	Yes..	Yes..	Yes..	No...
4	Yes..	...do	Yes..	Yes..	Yes..	Yes..	Yes..	Yes..	Yes..	No...	No...
5	Yes..	...do	Yes..	Yes..	Yes..	Yes..	Yes..	Yes..	Yes..	No...	No...
6	Yes..	...do	Yes..	No...	Yes..	Yes..	Yes..	Yes..	Yes..	Yes..	No...
7	Yes..	...do	Yes..	Yes²	No...	No...	No...			No...	No...
8	No...	Sinks	Yes..	No...	No...	No...	Yes..		Yes..	No...	Yes..
9	No...	...do	Yes..	No...	No...	No...	No...			No...	No...
10	No...	...do	Yes..	No...	No...	No...	Yes..		Yes..	No...	No...
11	No...	Sinks and bowls	Yes..	Yes..	Yes..	Yes..	Yes..	Yes..	Yes..	Yes..	No...
12	No...	None	No...	No...	No...	No...	Yes..		Yes..	Yes..	No...
13	No...	...do	No...	Yes..	Yes..	Yes..	Yes..	Yes..	Yes..	No...	No...
14	No...	Pails	No...	No...	No...	No...	Yes..	No...	Yes..	Yes..	Yes..
15	No...	Bowls	Yes..	Yes..	Yes..	No...	Yes..		Yes..	Yes..	Yes..
16	Yes..	None	Yes..	Yes..	Yes..	No...	No...			No...	No...
17	No...	...do	No...	No...	No...	No...	No...			No...	No...
18	Yes..	...do	Yes..	Yes..	Yes..	No...	Yes..	Yes..		No...	No...
19	No...	...do	No...	No...	No...	No...	No...			No...	No...

¹ No urinals.   ² In 1 of 2 buildings.

FACILITIES, DRESSING ROOMS, REST ROOMS, SEATS FOR FEMALES, WATER-CLOSETS—Continued.

MICHIGAN.

| Rest rooms for females. | | Sufficient seats provided for females. | Lunch rooms provided. | Water-closets. | | | | | | | | Air of workrooms affected by water-closets. | Establishment number. |
| Provided. | Sufficient. | | | Separate for the sexes. | Privacy of approach for— | | Number of male employees per urinal. | Number of employees per seat. | | Clean for— | | | |
					Males.	Females.		Males.	Females.	Males.	Females.		
No...		Yes..	No...	Yes..	Yes...	Yes...	19	14	26	Yes..	Yes..	No...	1
No...		Yes..	No...	Yes..	No...	No...	14	14	5	No...	No...	Yes..	2
No...		Yes..	No...	Yes..	Yes...	Yes...	6	6	13	Yes..	Yes..	No...	3
No..		Yes..	Yes..	Yes..	Yes...	Yes...	(1)	3	23	No...	No...	No...	4
Yes..	Yes.	Yes..	Yes..	Yes..	Yes...	Yes...	50	17	50	Yes..	Yes	No...	5
No...		Yes..	No...	Yes..	No...	No...	(1)	25	18	No...	No...	No...	6
No...		Yes..	No...	Yes..	Yes...	Yes...	45	11	15	Yes..	Yes..	No...	7
No...		Yes..	No...	Yes..	No...	No...	47	47	34	No...	No...	No...	8
No...		Yes..	No...	Yes..	Yes...	Yes...	(1)	3	15	Yes..	Yes..	No...	9
No...		Yes..	No...	Yes..	Yes...	No...	(1)	5	28	Yes..	Yes..	No...	10
No...		Yes..	Yes..	Yes..	Yes...	Yes...	19	9	11	Yes..	Yes..	No...	11
No...		Yes..	Yes..	Yes..	Yes...	Yes...	86	18	14	Yes..	Yes..	No...	12
No...		Yes..	No...	Yes..	No...	Yes...	(1)	23	40	Yes..	Yes..	No...	13
No...		Yes..	No...	Yes..	Yes...	Yes...	50	25	22	Yes..	Yes..	No...	14
No...		Yes..	No...	Yes..	Yes...	Yes...	(1)	14	16	Yes..	Yes..	No ..	15
No...		No...	Yes..	Yes..	Yes...	Yes...	22	11	10	Yes..	Yes..	Yes..	16
No...		Yes..	No...	Yes..	Yes...	Yes...	14	9	21	Yes..	Yes..	No...	17
No...		Yes..	No...	Yes..	Yes...	Yes...	44	18	14	Yes..	Yes..	No...	18
No...		Yes..	No...	Yes..	No...	No...	4	4	7	No...	No...	Yes..	19

WISCONSIN.

No...		Yes..	Yes..	Yes..	Yes...	Yes...	26	9	9	Yes..	Yes..	No...	1
No...		Yes..	No...	Yes..	Yes...	Yes...	(1)	4	14	Yes..	Yes..	No...	2
No...		Yes..	No...	Yes..	Yes...	Yes...	(1)	8	17	Yes..	Yes..	No...	3
No...		No...	No...	Yes..	Yes...	Yes...	(1)	12	18	Yes..	Yes..	No...	4
No...		Yes..	No...	Yes..	Yes...	Yes...	15	5	12	Yes..	Yes..	No...	5
No...		Yes..	No...	Yes..	Yes...	Yes...	8	8	7	Yes..	Yes..	No...	6
No...		Yes..	No...	Yes..	Yes...	Yes...	(1)	25	24	Yes..	Yes..	No...	7
Yes..		Yes..	No...	Yes..	No...	No...	(1)	5	34	Yes..	Yes..	No...	8
Yes..	Yes.	Yes..	No...	Yes..	Yes...	Yes...	122	10	25	Yes..	Yes..	No...	9
No...		Yes..	No...	Yes..	Yes...	Yes...	(1)	4	9	Yes..	Yes..	No...	10
No...		Yes..	Yes..	Yes..	Yes...	Yes...	72	14	17	Yes..	Yes..	No...	11
No...		No...	No...	Yes..	Yes...	Yes...	(1)	(4)	28	Yes..	Yes..	No...	12
No...		Yes..	No...	Yes..	Yes...	Yes...	(1)	19	15	Yes..	Yes..	No...	13
No...		No...	No...	Yes..	No...	Yes...	(1)	16	23	No...	Yes..	No...	14
No...		Yes..	No ..	Yes..	Yes...	Yes...	39	19	11	Yes..	Yes..	No...	15
No...		No...	No...	Yes..	Yes...	Yes...	47	8	8	Yes..	Yes..	No...	16
No...		Yes..	No...	Yes..	Yes...	Yes...	7	9	36	Yes..	Yes..	No...	17
No...		No...	No...	Yes..	Yes...	Yes...	80	13	15	Yes..	Yes..	No...	18
No...		No...	No...	Yes..	Yes...	Yes...	20	10	24	Yes..	Yes..	No...	19

¹ Insufficient. ⁴ Not reported.

TABLE V.—PROVISIONS FOR COMFORT OF EMPLOYEES: WASH ROOM LUNCH ROOMS, AND

MARYLAND.

Establishment number.	Facilities for washing.			Establishments furnish—		Dressing rooms provided.				Nature of work requires change of clothing for—	
	Separate wash rooms.	Other.	Sufficient.			Separate for—		Sufficient for—			
				Towels.	Soap.	Males.	Females.	Males.	Females.	Males.	Females.
1	No	Sinks	Yes	No	No	Yes	Yes	Yes	Yes	Yes	Yes
2	No	...do	Yes	No	No	Yes	Yes	Yes	Yes	Yes	Yes
3	No	Stationary washstands	Yes	Yes	Yes	No	Yes		Yes	Yes	Yes
4	No	Sinks	Yes	No	No	No	Yes		Yes	No	No
5	Yes	None	Yes	No	No	No	No			No	No
6	No	Sinks	Yes	No	No	Yes	Yes	Yes	Yes	No	Yes
7	No	...do	Yes	No	No	No	Yes		Yes	No	Yes
8	No	...do	Yes	No	Yes	No	Yes		Yes	No	Yes
9	No	Sink	No	No	No	No	Yes		Yes	No	No
10	No	...do	No	No	No	No	Yes		Yes	No	No
11	No	Sinks	Yes	No	No	Yes	Yes	Yes	Yes	No	No
12	Yes	None	Yes	No	No	Yes	Yes	Yes	Yes	Yes	Yes
13	No	Sinks	Yes	Yes	Yes	Yes	Yes	Yes	Yes	Yes	Yes
14	Yes	None	Yes	No	Yes	Yes	Yes	Yes	Yes	Yes	Yes
15	No	Sinks	Yes	Yes	Yes	Yes	Yes	Yes	Yes	Yes	Yes
16	No	...do	Yes	No	No	Yes	Yes	Yes	Yes	Yes	Yes
17	No	...do	Yes	No	No	No	Yes		Yes	No	No
18	No	...do	Yes	No	No	No	Yes		Yes	No	No
19	No	...do	Yes	No	No	Yes	Yes	Yes	Yes	No	Yes
20	No	...do	Yes	No	No	No	Yes		Yes	No	Yes
21	No	...do	Yes	No	No	No	No			No	No
22	No	...do	Yes	No	No	No	No			No	No
23	No	...do	Yes	No	No	No	Yes		Yes	No	Yes
24	No	...do	Yes	No	No	No	No			No	No
25	No	...do	No	No	Yes	Yes	Yes	Yes	Yes	Yes	Yes
26	No	...do	Yes	No	No	No	Yes		Yes	No	Yes
27	No	...do	Yes	No	Yes	Yes	Yes	Yes	Yes	Yes	Yes
28	No	...do	Yes	No	No	Yes	Yes	Yes	Yes	Yes	Yes

NORTH CAROLINA.

Establishment number.	Separate wash rooms.	Other.	Sufficient.	Towels.	Soap.	Separate Males.	Separate Females.	Sufficient Males.	Sufficient Females.	Change Males.	Change Females.
1	No	Sinks	Yes	No	No	Yes	Yes	Yes	Yes	No	No
2	No	...do	No	No	No	No	No			No	No
3	No	...do	Yes	No	No	Yes	No			No	No
4	No	None	No	No	No	No	No			No	No
5	No	Sinks	Yes	No	No	No	No			No	No
6	No	Pails out doors	No	No	No	No	No			No	No
7	No	None	No	No	No	No	No			No	No
8	No	Sinks	No	No	No	No	No			No	No
9	No	None	No	No	No	No	No			No	No
10	No	Sink	Yes	No	No	No	No			No	No
11	Yes	Sinks	Yes	No	No	No	No			No	No
12	No	...do	Yes	Yes	Yes	No	Yes		Yes	No	No
13	No	...do	Yes	Yes[5]	Yes[5]	No	No			No	No
14	Yes	None	Yes	No	No	No	No			No	No
15	No	Sink	Yes	No	No	Yes	Yes	Yes	Yes	No	No
16	Yes	Sinks	No	No	No	No	No			No	No
17	No	...do	No	No	No	No	(7)			No	(7)
18	No	...do	Yes	No	No	No	No			No	No
19	No	...do	Yes	No	No	No	No			No	No
20	No	Sinks and tubs	No	No	No	No	No			No	No
21	No	Sinks	Yes	No	No	No	No			No	No
22	No	...do	Yes	No	No	No	No			No	No
23	No	...do	Yes	No	No	No	No			No	No
24	No	...do	Yes	No	No	No	(7)			No	(7)
25	No	...do	No	No	No	No	No			No	No
26	No	...do	Yes	No	No	No	No			No	No
27	No	...do	Yes	No	No	No	No			No	No
28	No	...do	Yes	No	Yes	No	No			No	No

[1] No urinals.
[2] Small room with bed and a few medicines and sick-room utensils.
[3] Coffee is furnished at 2 cents per cup and ham sandwiches at 3 cents apiece.
[4] In 1 of 2 buildings.
[5] In dye room only.
[6] Not reported.

FACILITIES, DRESSING ROOMS, REST ROOMS, SEATS FOR FEMALES, WATER-CLOSETS—Continued.

MARYLAND.

Rest rooms for females.		Sufficient seats provided for females.	Lunch rooms provided.	Water-closets.									Air of work-rooms affected by water-closets.	Establishment number.
Provided.	Sufficient.			Separate for the sexes.	Privacy of approach for—		Number of male employees per urinal.	Number of employees per seat.		Clean for—				
					Males.	Females.		Males.	Females.	Males.	Females.			
No...	....	No...	No...	Yes..	Yes...	Yes...	(1)	16	7	Yes..	Yes..	No...		1
No...	....	No...	No...	Yes..	Yes...	Yes...	(1)	7	16	Yes..	Yes..	No...		2
No...	....	Yes..	No...	Yes..	Yes...	Yes...	(1)	11	12	Yes..	Yes..	No...		3
No...	....	Yes..	No...	Yes..	Yes...	Yes...	25	25	25	Yes..	Yes..	No...		4
No...	....	Yes..	No...	Yes..	Yes...	Yes...	42	3	6	Yes..	Yes..	No...		5
No...	....	Yes..	No...	Yes..	Yes...	Yes...	(1)	5	11	Yes..	Yes..	No...		6
No...	....	Yes..	No...	Yes..	Yes...	Yes...	(1)	16	28	Yes..	Yes..	No...		7
No...	....	Yes..	No...	Yes..	Yes...	Yes...	(1)	15	16	Yes..	Yes..	No...		8
No...	....	Yes..	No...	Yes..	Yes...	Yes...	10	10	12	No...	No...	No...		9
No...	....	Yes..	No...	Yes..	Yes...	Yes...	14	14	27	Yes..	Yes..	No...		10
No...	....	Yes..	No...	Yes..	Yes...	Yes...	(1)	32	42	Yes..	Yes..	No...		11
Yes..	Yes..	Yes..	Yes..	Yes..	Yes...	Yes...	26	11	24	Yes..	Yes..	No...		12
No...	....	Yes..	No...	Yes..	Yes...	Yes...	(1)	8	11	Yes..	Yes..	No...		13
No...	....	Yes..	No...	Yes..	Yes...	Yes...	9	9	5	Yes..	Yes..	No...		14
No...	....	Yes..	No...	Yes..	Yes...	Yes...	(1)	9	3	Yes..	Yes..	No...		15
No...	....	Yes..	No...	Yes..	Yes...	Yes...	(1)	18	38	Yes..	Yes..	No...		16
No...	....	Yes..	No...	Yes..	Yes...	Yes...	(1)	4	20	Yes..	Yes..	No...		17
No...	....	Yes..	No...	Yes..	Yes...	Yes...	(1)	6	5	Yes..	Yes..	No...		18
No...	....	Yes..	No...	Yes..	No...	No...	(1)	9	19	Yes..	Yes..	No...		19
No...	....	Yes..	No...	Yes..	Yes...	Yes...	(1)	6	13	Yes..	Yes..	No...		20
No...	....	Yes..	No...	Yes..	Yes...	Yes...	45	5	33	Yes..	Yes..	No...		21
Yes[2]	No...	Yes..	No[3]	Yes..	Yes...	Yes...	(1)	7	29	Yes..	Yes..	No...		22
Yes[4]	No...	Yes..	No...	Yes..	Yes...	Yes...	(1)	16	26	Yes..	Yes..	No...		23
Yes..	Yes..	Yes..	No...	Yes..	Yes...	Yes...	(1)	14	41	Yes..	Yes..	No...		24
Yes..	Yes..	Yes..	No...	Yes..	Yes...	Yes...	(1)	33	44	Yes..	Yes..	No...		25
No...	....	Yes..	No...	Yes..	Yes...	Yes...	(1)	13	48	Yes..	Yes..	No...		26
No...	....	Yes..	No...	Yes..	Yes...	Yes...	(1)	15	52	Yes..	Yes..	No...		27
Yes..	Yes..	Yes..	Yes..	Yes..	Yes...	Yes...	(1)	12	26	Yes..	Yes..	No...		28

NORTH CAROLINA.

Rest rooms for females.		Sufficient seats provided for females.	Lunch rooms provided.	Water-closets.									Air of work-rooms affected by water-closets.	Establishment number.
Provided.	Sufficient.			Separate for the sexes.	Males.	Females.	Number of male employees per urinal.	Males.	Females.	Males.	Females.			
No...	....	Yes..	No...	Yes..	Yes...	Yes...	46	15	30	Yes..	Yes..	No...		1
Yes..	Yes..	No...	Yes..	Yes..	No...	No...	(1)	7	22	No...	No...	Yes..		2
No...	....	Yes..	No...	Yes..	Yes...	Yes...	(1)	79	36	No...	No...	No...		3
No...	....	No...	No...	Yes..	Yes...	Yes...	(1)	31	20	No...	No...	No...		4
No...	....	No...	No...	Yes..	No...	No...	(1)	15	12	Yes..	Yes..	No...		5
No...	....	No...	No...	Yes..	No...	No...	(1)	34	17	Yes..	Yes..	Yes..		6
No...	....	No...	No...	Yes..	Yes...	Yes...	(1)	10	9	No...	No...	No...		7
No...	....	No...	No...	Yes..	Yes...	Yes...	(1)	27	17	Yes..	Yes..	No...		8
No...	....	No...	No...	Yes..	Yes...	Yes...	(1)	62	32	Yes..	Yes..	No...		9
No...	....	No...	No...	Yes..	{2 yes.. / 1 no...	3 yes... / 1 no...}	52	26	12	{1 yes.. / 2 no..}	Yes..	No...		10
No...	....	No...	No...	Yes..	Yes...	Yes...	28	28	17	{2 yes.. / 1 no..}	Yes..	No...		11
No...	....	Yes..	No...	Yes..	No...	No...	(1)	18	23	Yes..	Yes..	No...		12
No...	....	No...	No...	Yes..	{1 yes.. / 2 no...	1 yes... / 2 no...}	(1)	15	33	Yes..	Yes..	No...		13
(6)	....	No...	No...	Yes..	Yes...	Yes...	(1)	16	75	Yes..	Yes..	No...		14
No...	....	Yes..	No...	Yes..	Yes...	Yes...	12	2	4	Yes..	Yes..	No...		15
No...	....	Yes..	No...	Yes..	No...	No...	257	27	15	Yes..	Yes..	No...		16
(7)	....	(7)...	No...	(7)..	Yes...	(7)...	(1)	22	(7)	Yes..	(7)..	No...		17
No...	....	No...	No...	Yes..	Yes...	Yes...	67	22	22	Yes..	Yes..	No...		18
No...	....	No...	No...	Yes..	No...	No...	49	28	29	Yes..	Yes..	No...		19
No...	....	No...	No...	Yes..	No...	No...	(1)	51	38	Yes..	Yes..	No...		20
No...	....	No...	No...	Yes[8]	No...	No...	(1)	40	18	No...	No...	No...		21
No...	....	No...	No...	Yes..	No...	No...	194	[9]34	[9]45	Yes..	Yes..	No...		22
No...	....	No...	No...	(10)...	No...	No...	(6)	(11)	(11)	No...	No...	No...		23
(7)...	....	No...	No...	(7)...	Yes...	(7)...	(1)	18	(7)	Yes..	(7)..	No...		24
No...	....	No...	No...	Yes..	Yes...	Yes...	(1)	11	8	Yes..	Yes..	No...		25
No...	....	No...	No...	Yes..	Yes...	Yes...	(1)	17	34	Yes..	Yes..	No...		26
No...	....	No...	No...	Yes..	{1 yes.. / 2 no..}	No...	(1)	21	12	Yes..	Yes..	No...		27
No...	....	No...	No...	Yes..	Yes...	Yes...	(1)	3	5	Yes..	Yes..	No...		28

[7] No females.
[8] But used promiscuously at times.
[9] For whites only.
[10] Separate for whites, but not for colored.
[11] Total for all employees, 13; not reported separately by sexes and color.

Table **V.**—PROVISIONS FOR COMFORT OF EMPLOYEES: WASH ROOM
LUNCH ROOMS, AND

GEORGIA.

Establishment number.	Facilities for washing.			Establishments furnish—		Dressing rooms provided.				Nature of work requires change of clothing for—	
	Separate wash rooms.	Other.	Sufficient.			Separate for—		Sufficient for—			
				Towels.	Soap.	Males.	Females.	Males.	Females.	Males.	Females.
1	Yes	None	Yes	Yes	Yes	Yes	Yes	Yes	Yes	Yes	Yes
2	Yes	do	Yes	Yes	Yes	Yes	Yes	Yes	Yes	Yes	Yes
3	Yes	do	Yes	Yes	Yes	Yes	Yes	Yes	Yes	Yes	Yes
4	No	Sinks	Yes	No	No	No	No			No	No
5	No	do	Yes	No	No	No	No			No	No
6	Yes	None	Yes	No	No	No	No			No	No
7	No	Sinks	Yes	No	No	No	No			No	No
8	No	do	Yes	Yes[4]	No	No	No			No	No
9	No	Sinks and basins	Yes	Yes[4]	No	Yes	Yes	Yes	Yes	No	No
10	No	Sinks	Yes	Yes	Yes	No	No			No	No
11	No	do	No	No	No	No	No			No	No
12	Yes	None	Yes	Yes	Yes	Yes	Yes	Yes	Yes	Yes	Yes
13	No	Sinks	Yes	Yes	Yes	Yes	Yes	Yes	Yes	Yes	Yes
14	Yes	None	Yes	Yes	Yes	Yes	Yes	Yes	Yes	Yes	Yes
15	No	Sinks	Yes	Yes	Yes	No	No			No	No
16	Yes	do	Yes	Yes	Yes	No	Yes		(5)	No	No
17	Yes	None	Yes	No	No	No	No		Yes	No	No
18	No	Sink	Yes	Yes	Yes	No	No			No	No
19	No	do	Yes	No	No	No	No			No	No
20	No	None	No	No	No	No	No			No	No
21	No	Sink	Yes	No	No	No	No			No	No
22	No	Sinks	No	Yes	Yes	Yes	Yes	Yes	Yes	Yes	Yes
23	No	do	Yes	Yes	Yes	No	Yes		Yes	No	Yes
24	No	do	No	No	No	No	No			No	No
25	No	None	No	No	No	No	No			No	No
26	No	Sinks	No	No	No	No	No			No	No
27	No	None	No	No	No	No	No			No	No

FLORIDA.

Establishment number.	Separate wash rooms.	Other.	Sufficient.	Towels.	Soap.	Males.	Females.	Males.	Females.	Males.	Females.
1	Yes	None	Yes	No	No	No	No			No	No
2	Yes	do	Yes	No	Yes	No	No			No	No
3	No	Sink	No	No	No	No	No			No	No
4	Yes	do	Yes	No	No	No	No			No	No
5	Yes	do	Yes	Yes	Yes	No	No			No	No
6	No	do	No	No	No	No	No			No	No
7	Yes	None	Yes	No	No	No	No			No	No
8	Yes	do	Yes	No	No	No	No			No	No
9	Yes	do	Yes	No	No	No	No			No	No
10	No	Sink	No	No	No	No	No			No	No
11	No	do	No	No	No	Na	No			No	No
12	Yes	None	Yes	Yes	Yes	No	No			No	No
13	Yes	do	Yes	Yes	Yes	No	No			No	No
14	Yes[6]	Font in yard	No	No	No	No	No			No	No

[1] No urinals.
[2] Establishment furnishes soup and crackers to employees at lunch time; lunch room being planned.
[3] Seats are provided by employees.

FACILITIES, DRESSING ROOMS, REST ROOMS, SEATS FOR FEMALES, WATER-CLOSETS—Continued.

GEORGIA.

Rest rooms for females.		Sufficient seats provided for females.	Lunch rooms provided.	Separate for the sexes.	Water-closets.							Air of work-rooms affected by water-closets.	Establishment number.
					Privacy of approach for—		Number of male employees per urinal.	Number of employees per seat.		Clean for—			
Provided.	Sufficient.				Males.	Females.		Males.	Females.	Males.	Females.		
No		No	No	Yes	No	{1 yes.. 2 no...}	(1)	14	13	Yes	Yes	No	1
No		No	No	Yes	Yes	Yes	(1)	4	11	Yes	Yes	No	2
No		No	No²	Yes	Yes	Yes	(1)	12	7	Yes	Yes	No	3
No		No³	No	Yes	Yes	Yes	(1)	17	12	Yes	Yes	No	4
No		No³	No	Yes	No	No	(1)	34	21	No	No	No	5
No		No³	No	Yes	Yes	Yes	(1)	26	8	Yes	Yes	No	6
No		Yes	No	Yes	Yes	Yes	(1)	8	4	No	No	No	7
No		Yes	No	Yes	Yes	Yes	49	24	13	Yes	Yes	No	8
No		Yes	No	Yes	Yes	Yes	43	22	7	Yes	Yes	No	9
No		No	No	Yes	Yes	Yes	(1)	9	12	Yes	Yes	No	10
No		No	No	Yes	No	No	(1)	30	27	No	No	No	11
No		No	No³	Yes	Yes	Yes	(1)	8	12	Yes	Yes	No	12
No		No	No	Yes	Yes	Yes	(1)	12	19	Yes	Yes	No	13
No		No	No	Yes	Yes	No	(1)	6	31	Yes	Yes	No	14
No		Yes	No	Yes	No	No	28	14	17	Yes	Yes	No	15
No		No	No	Yes	Yes	Yes	(1)	18	27	{1 yes.. 1 no..}	{1 yes.. 1 no..}	No	16
No		No	No	Yes	Yes	Yes	108	54	41	Yes	Yes	No	17
No		Yes	No	Yes	No	No	(1)	17	23	Yes	Yes	No	18
No		Yes	No	Yes	Yes	Yes	(1)	10	20	Yes	Yes	No	19
No		Yes	No	Yes	Yes	Yes	(1)	8	22	No	No	No	20
No		Yes	No	Yes	Yes	Yes	(1)	10	21	Yes	Yes	No	21
No		No	No	Yes	No	No	(1)	11	24	No	No	Yes	22
No		No	No	Yes	No	No	(1)	12	16	No	No	Yes	23
No		No	No	Yes	No	No	(1)	15	13	No	No	Yes	24
No		No	No	Yes	No	No	(1)	9	14	Yes	Yes	No	25
No		No	No	Yes	Yes	No	47	13	11	No	No	No	26
No		No	No	Yes	Yes	No	(1)	9	22	No	Yes	No	27

FLORIDA.

Rest rooms for females.		Sufficient seats provided for females.	Lunch rooms provided.	Separate for the sexes.	Privacy Males.	Privacy Females.	Number of male employees per urinal.	Employees per seat Males.	Females.	Clean Males.	Females.	Air of work-rooms.	Est. number.
No		Yes	No	Yes	Yes	Yes	37	19	13	Yes	Yes	No	1
No		Yes	No	Yes	Yes	Yes	(1)	17	14	No	No	No	2
No		Yes	No	Yes	Yes	Yes	134	27	18	No	Yes	No	3
Yes	Yes	Yes	No	Yes	Yes	Yes	139	70	37	Yes	Yes	No	4
Yes	Yes	Yes	Yes	Yes	Yes	Yes	(1)	45	18	Yes	Yes	No	5
No		Yes	No	Yes	Yes	Yes	(1)	70	35	No	No	No	6
No		Yes	No	Yes	Yes	Yes	14	14	7	Yes	Yes	No	7
No		Yes	No	Yes	Yes	Yes	67	34	61	Yes	Yes	No	8
No		Yes	No	Yes	Yes	Yes	10	51	17	Yes	Yes	No	9
No		Yes	No	Yes	No	No	74	11	8	No	No	No	10
No		Yes	No	Yes	No	Yes	120	48	17	No	No	No	11
No		Yes	No	Yes	Yes	Yes	(1)	13	9	Yes	Yes	No	12
No		Yes	No	Yes	Yes	Yes	278	20	15	No	No	Yes	13
No		Yes	No	Yes	Yes	Yes	102	58	30	Yes	Yes	Yes	14

¹ Use pieces of damaged cloth made in mill.
² Yes, in knitting department; no, in yarn department.
³ For males only.

TABLE **V.**—PROVISIONS FOR COMFORT OF EMPLOYEES: WASH ROOM LUNCH ROOMS, AND

LOUISIANA.

Establishment number.	Facilities for washing.			Establishments furnish—		Dressing rooms provided.				Nature of work requires change of clothing for—	
	Separate wash rooms.	Other.	Sufficient.			Separate for—		Sufficient for—			
				Towels.	Soap.	Males.	Females.	Males.	Females.	Males.	Females.
1	Yes..	None	Yes..	No...	No...	Yes..	Yes..	Yes..	Yes..	Yes..	Yes..
2	Yes..	...do	Yes..	No...	No...	Yes..	Yes..	Yes..	Yes..	Yes..	Yes..
3	Yes..	...do	Yes..	Yes..	Yes..	Yes..	Yes..	Yes..	Yes..	Yes..	Yes..
4	Yes..	...do	Yes..	Yes..	Yes..	Yes..	Yes..	Yes..	Yes..	Yes..	Yes..
5	Yes..	Basins	Yes..	Yes..	Yes..	Yes..	Yes..	Yes..	Yes..	Yes..	Yes..
6	Yes..	None	Yes..	No...	No...	Yes..	Yes..	Yes..	Yes..	Yes..	Yes..
7	No...	...do	No...	No...	No...	No...	No...			Yes..	Yes..
8	Yes [4]	Faucet in yard	No...	Yes..	Yes..	Yes..	Yes..	No...	Yes..	No...	Yes..
9	Yes..	None	No...	No...	No...	Yes..	Yes..	No...	No...	Yes..	Yes..
10	Yes..	Shower baths for men.	Yes..	Yes..	Yes..	No...	Yes..		Yes..	Yes..	No...
11	Yes..	None	Yes..	No...	No...	No...	Yes..		Yes..	No...	No...
12	No...	Basins	Yes..	No...	No...	No...	No...			No...	No...
13	Yes..	Sinks	Yes..	No...	No...	Yes..	Yes..	Yes..	Yes..	No...	No...
14	Yes..	...do	Yes..	No...	No...	Yes..	Yes..	Yes..	Yes..	No...	No...
15	Yes..	Sink	Yes..	No...	No...	No...	Yes..		Yes..	Yes..	Yes..
16	Yes..	Washstands	Yes..	No...	No...	Yes..	Yes..	Yes..	Yes..	Yes..	Yes..
17	No...	Sinks	Yes..	No...	No...	Yes..	Yes..	Yes..	Yes..	Yes..	Yes..
18	No...	Sink	No...	No...	No...	Yes..	Yes..	No...	No...	Yes..	Yes..
19	No...	...do	No...	No...	No...	Yes..	No...	Yes..		Yes..	No...
20	Yes..	None	Yes..	Yes..	Yes..	Yes..	Yes..	Yes..	Yes..	Yes..	Yes..
21	No...	Basins	Yes..	No...	No...	Yes..	Yes..	Yes..	Yes..	No...	No...
22	No...	...do	Yes..	No...	No...	Yes..	Yes..	Yes..	Yes..	No...	No...
23	No...	Sink	No...	No...	Yes..	Yes..	Yes..	Yes..	Yes..	Yes..	Yes..
24	Yes..	None	Yes..	No...	No...	Yes..	Yes..	Yes..	Yes..	Yes..	Yes..
25	Yes..	Stationary washstands	Yes..	Yes..	Yes..	Yes..	Yes..	Yes..	Yes..	No...	No...
26	No...	Basins	No...	Yes..	Yes..	No...	Yes..		Yes..	No...	No...
27	Yes..	...do	Yes..	Yes..	Yes..	No...	Yes..		Yes..	No...	No...
28	Yes..	None	Yes..	Yes..	Yes..	No...	No...			No...	No...
29	Yes..	...do	Yes..	No...	No...	Yes..	Yes..	Yes..	Yes..	Yes..	Yes..

1 Toilets are not marked.
2 No urinals.
3 The establishment furnishes free to employees at lunch time coffee or tea with milk and sugar.
4 For females only.

FACILITIES, DRESSING ROOMS, REST ROOMS, SEATS FOR FEMALES, WATER-CLOSETS—Concluded.

LOUISIANA.

Rest rooms for females.		Sufficient seats provided for females.	Lunch rooms provided.	Water-closets.									Establishment number.
Provided.	Sufficient.			Separate for the sexes.	Privacy of approach for—		Number of male employees per urinal.	Number of employees per seat.		Clean for—		Air of workrooms affected by water-closets.	
					Males.	Females.		Males.	Females.	Males.	Females.		
No...		Yes..	No...	Yes ¹	Yes...	Yes...	42	21	40	Yes..	Yes..	No...	1
No...		Yes..	No...	Yes ¹	Yes...	Yes...	(²)	6	12	Yes..	Yes..	No...	2
No...		Yes..	Yes ³	Yes ¹	Yes...	Yes...	(²)	6	12	Yes..	Yes..	No...	3
No...		Yes..	No...	Yes ¹	Yes...	Yes...	(²)	8	22	Yes..	Yes..	No...	4
No...		Yes..	No...	Yes ¹	Yes...	Yes...	(²)	9	3	Yes..	Yes..	No...	5
No...		Yes..	No...	Yes ¹	Yes...	Yes...	(²)	25	9	Yes..	Yes..	No...	6
No...		No...	No...	Yes..	Yes..	Yes...	(³)	24	33	Yes..	Yes..	No...	7
No...		Yes..	No...	Yes ¹	Yes...	Yes...	45	15	8	No...	Yes..	No...	8
No...		Yes..	No...	Yes ¹	Yes...	Yes...	24	7	4	Yes..	No...	No...	9
Yes..		Yes..	Yes ⁵	Yes..	Yes..	Yes...	(²)	4	25	Yes..	Yes..	No...	10
No...		Yes..	No...	Yes..	Yes..	Yes...	15	15	27	Yes..	Yes..	No...	11
No...		Yes..	No...	Yes..	Yes..	Yes...	(²)	6	6	No...	Yes..	No...	12
No...		Yes..	Yes ⁶	Yes ¹	Yes...	Yes...	120	60	28	Yes..	Yes..	No...	13
No...		Yes..	Yes..	Yes ¹	Yes...	Yes...	14	2	21	Yes..	Yes..	No...	14
No...		No...	No...	Yes ¹	No....	No....	(²)	7	12	Yes..	Yes..	No...	15
No...		No...	No...	Yes ¹	Yes...	Yes...	44	15	8	No...	Yes..	No...	16
No...		Yes..	No...	Yes..	Yes...	Yes...	(²)	9	21	Yes..	Yes..	No...	17
No...		Yes..	No...	Yes..	No....	No....	(²)	19	21	No...	No...	Yes..	18
No...		Yes..	No...	Yes ¹	No....	Yes...	40	20	18	No...	Yes..	Yes..	19
No...		Yes..	No...	Yes ¹	No....	No....	(²)	15	24	Yes..	Yes..	No...	20
No...		Yes..	No...	Yes..	Yes...	Yes...	(²)	19	22	Yes..	Yes..	No...	21
No...		Yes..	No...	Yes ¹	Yes...	Yes...	(²)	2	5	Yes..	Yes..	No...	22
No...		Yes..	No...	Yes..	No....	No....	(²)	5	9	Yes..	Yes..	No...	23
No...		Yes..	No...	Yes..	Yes...	Yes...	21	21	27	Yes..	Yes..	No...	24
No...		Yes..	No...	Yes ¹	Yes...	Yes...	(²)	3	12	Yes..	Yes..	No...	25
No...		Yes..	No...	Yes..	Yes...	Yes...	(²)	(⁷)	16	(⁷)....	Yes..	No...	26
No...		Yes..	No...	Yes ¹	Yes...	Yes...	(²)	4	20	Yes..	Yes..	No...	27
No...		Yes..	No...	Yes..	Yes...	Yes...	(²)	6	6	Yes..	Yes..	No...	28
No...		Yes..	Yes..	Yes ¹	Yes...	Yes...	(²)	7	19	Yes..	Yes..	No...	29

⁴ Lunch furnished for 40 cents per week.
⁶ Lunch furnished for 35 cents per week.
⁵ Men use closets in another building.

Table **VI.**—SANITARY CONDITIONS: CLEANLINESS OF WORKROOMS, SPITTING ON FLOOR, AND DRINKING WATER.

MAINE.

Establishment number.	Workrooms clean.		Conditions of uncleanliness where workrooms are not clean.	Workrooms whitewashed or painted, when.	Spitting on floor.			Fresh, pure drinking water provided.
	Floors.	Walls and ceilings.			Done by employees.	Rule against.	Cuspidors provided.	
1	{4 yes / 1 no}	Yes...	(1)...	No regular period	Yes...	Yes...	No....	Yes.
2	Yes...	Yes...		New building	No...	Yes..	Yes...	Yes.
3	Yes...	Yes...		No regular period	Yes...	Yes...	Yes..	Yes.
4	{2 yes / 3 no}	Yes...	{Accumlated dirt and litter on floors.	...do	Yes...	No...	No....	Yes.
5	Yes...	Yes...		3 years ago	No...	No...	Yes...	Yes.
6	Yes...	Yes...		(1)	No...	No...	Yes...	Yes.
7	{3 yes / 3 no}	No....	Accumulated dirt, etc.	Not since occupancy	No....	Yes...	No....	Yes.
8	Yes...	Yes...		Yearly	No....	Yes...	Yes...	Yes.
9	{2 yes / 3 no}	2 yes / 3 no..	Spattered with materials of manufacture.	Once in 2 years	No....	Yes...	No....	Yes.
10	{3 yes / 4 no}	5 yes / 2 no..	Dusty and spattered with dough and flour	...do	No....	Yes...	No....	Yes.
11	{1 yes / 2 no}	Yes...	Grease and dirt	Not since occupancy	No....	No....	No....	Yes.
12	No....	Yes...	...do	Whitewashed 6 months ago. No regular period.	Yes...	No....	No....	Yes.
13	Yes...	Yes...		7 or 8 years ago	Yes...	Yes...	No....	Yes.
14	No....	No....	Walls grimy, floors covered with paste and rubbish.	Yearly	No....	No....	Yes...	Yes.
15	Yes...	Yes...		No regular period	No....	Yes...	Yes...	Yes.
16	Yes...	Yes...		About 3 years ago	No....	Yes...	Yes..	Yes.
17	{1 yes / 1 no}	Yes...	{Soiled and covered with litterings of manufacture.	Not since occupancy	No....	Yes...	Yes...	Yes.
18	Yes...	Yes...		...do	No....	Yes...	Yes...	Yes.
19	No....	No....	Accumulated dirt	...do	No....	Yes...	Yes...	Yes.
20	Yes...	Yes...		Not within 6 years	Yes...	No....	No....	No.
21	No....	No....	Accumulated dirt	Not within 5 years	Yes...	No....	No....	No.
22	Yes...	No....	...do	...do	Yes...	No....	No....	No.
23	Yes...	Yes...		Not within 2 years	Yes...	No....	No....	No.
24	Yes...	Yes...		Cleaned 2 years ago	Yes...	No....	No....	No.
25	Yes...	Yes...		Not within 3 years	Yes...	No....	No....	Yes.
26	Yes...	{8 yes / 4 no}	Accumulated dirt	Not within 4 or 5 years.	Yes...	No....	No....	No.

MASSACHUSETTS.

Establishment number.	Workrooms clean.		Conditions of uncleanliness where workrooms are not clean.	Workrooms whitewashed or painted, when.	Spitting on floor.			Fresh, pure drinking water provided.
	Floors.	Walls and ceilings.			Done by employees.	Rule against.	Cuspidors provided.	
1	Yes...	Yes...		Once or twice a year	Yes...	No....	No....	Yes.
2	Yes...	Yes...		New building	Yes...	Yes...	Yes..	Yes.
3	Yes...	Yes...		Every 2 years	No....	Yes...	Yes...	Yes.
4	Yes...	Yes...		Every 3 years	No....	Yes...	Yes..	Yes.
5	Yes...	Yes...		Every 2 years	No....	Yes...	Yes...	Yes.
6	Yes...	Yes...		Yearly	No....	Yes...	Yes...	Yes.
7	Yes...	Yes...		Every 2 years	No....	Yes...	Yes...	Yes.
8	Yes...	Yes...		...do	No....	Yes...	Yes...	Yes.
9	Yes...	Yes...		Not for 3 years	No....	Yes...	Yes...	Yes.
10	No....	Yes...	Very dirty; small bits of sugar mashed on floor; dirty water in 1 room.	Not since occupancy	No....	No....	Yes...	Yes.
11	Yes...	Yes...		Every 2 years	No....	Yes...	Yes...	Yes.
12	Yes...	Yes...		Yearly	No....	No....	Yes...	Yes.
13	{6 yes / 1 no}	Yes...	(1)	Every 2 years	No....	Yes...	No....	Yes.
14	{6 yes / 1 no}	Yes...	(1)	...do	No....	No....	No....	Yes.
15	No....	No....	Black soot	Yearly	No....	Yes...	No....	Yes.
16	No....	No....	Blackened with time and steam from candy kettles.	Not for 3 years	No....	No....	Yes...	Yes.

¹ Not reported.

TABLE **VI.**—SANITARY CONDITIONS: CLEANLINESS OF WORKROOMS, SPITTING ON FLOOR, AND DRINKING WATER—Continued.

MASSACHUSETTS—Concluded.

Establishment number.	Workrooms clean.		Conditions of uncleanliness where workrooms are not clean.	Workrooms whitewashed or painted, when.	Spitting on floor.			Fresh, pure drinking-water provided.
	Floors.	Walls and ceilings.			Done by employees.	Rule against.	Cuspidors provided.	
17	Yes...	Yes...		New building..........	No....	Yes...	No....	Yes.
18	Yes...	Yes...		Once in 4 years........	No....	Yes...	No....	Yes.
19	Yes...	Yes...		Constantly.............	No....	Yes...	Yes...	Yes.
20	{22 yes. {2 no...	}Yes...	Cotton lint...........	Yearly...............	Yes...	Yes...	Yes...	Yes.
21	{16 yes. {13 no.	}Yes...	(¹)................	Twice a year..........	Yes...	Yes...	Yes...	Yes.
22	No....	Yes...	(¹)................	Every 2 years........	Yes...	Yes...	Yes...	Yes.
23	No....	Yes...	Dirty dough and drippings from icings.	Yearly...............	No....	Yes...	Yes...	Yes.
24	Yes...	Yes...		New building..........	No....	Yes...	Yes...	Yes.
25	Yes...	{1 no... {8 yes..	}Walls and ceiling spattered.	}When necessary	No....	Yes...	Yes...	Yes.
26	Yes...	Yes...		No regular period.....	No....	Yes...	Yes...	Yes.
27	Yes...	No....	Water stained..........	....do...............	No....	No....	No....	Yes.
28	{3 no.. {2 no...	}Yes...	(¹)................	Not since occupancy...	No....	No....	No....	Yes.
29	Yes...	Yes...		No regular period.....	No....	No....	No....	Yes.
30	Yes...	{4 yes.. {1 no...	}Ceiling unfinished and weather stained.	}....do.............	No....	Yes...	No....	Yes.
31	Yes...	Yes...		Twice a year..........	No....	Yes...	No....	Yes.
32	Yes...	Yes...		15 times a year........	No....	No....	No....	Yes.
33	Yes...	Yes...		Yearly...............	Yes...	Yes...	Yes...	Yes.
34	Yes...	Yes...		Not since painted as new building 7 years ago.	No....	No....	No....	Yes.
35	Yes...	No....	Rough beams and full of dirt.	Not since occupancy...	Yes...	No....	No....	Yes.
36	No....	No....	Dust and litterings of manufacture.	....do.............	Yes...	No....	No....	Yes.
37	{4 yes. {8 no..	{4 yes.. {8 no..	}Accumulated dirt.....	Not for 4 or 5 years......	Yes...	Yes...	No....	Yes.
38	Yes...	No....	....do...........	Not since 1893.........	Yes...	No....	No....	No.
39	Yes...	No....	....do...........	Not for 5 years........	Yes...	No....	No....	No.
40	{3 yes. {5 no..	}No....	....do...........	(¹)................	Yes...	No....	No....	No.
41	Yes...	Yes...		Yearly...............	No....	Yes...	Yes...	Yes.
42	No....	No....	Oily and dirty........	Once this year........	Yes...	No....	No....	No.
43	Yes...	No....	Accumulated dirt.....	Once in 8 years........	Yes...	No....	No....	Yes.
44	Yes...	No....	....do...........	Not for 10 years.......	Yes...	No....	No....	Yes.

RHODE ISLAND.

1	Yes...	Yes...		Papered 5 years ago....	No....	Yes...	Yes...	Yes.
2	Yes...	Yes...		Yearly...............	No....	Yes...	Yes...	Yes.
3	{7 yes. {2 no...	{7 yes. {2 no...	}Grimy and spattered with materials of manufacture.	}....do.............	No....	Yes...	Yes...	Yes.
4	Yes.:.	Yes...		Constantly.............	No....	Yes...	Yes...	Yes.
5	No....	No....	Accumulated dirt.....	Not within 6 years.....	Yes...	Yes...	Yes...	Yes.
6	Yes...	Yes...		Part each year........	Yes...	No....	No....	Yes.
7	Yes...	Yes...		No regular period.....	Yes...	No....	No....	Yes.
8	Yes...	Yes...		....do.............	Yes...	No....	No....	Yes.
9	Yes...	Yes...		Every 2 years........	No....	Yes...	No....	Yes.
10	Yes...	Yes...		No regular period.....	No....	Yes...	Yes...	Yes.
11	Yes...	Yes...		New building..........	No....	Yes...	No....	Yes.
12	{6 yes. {1 no...	{6 yes. {1 no...	}Accumulated dirt.....	}5 years ago..........	Yes...	Yes...	No....	Yes.
13	Yes...	Yes...		2 years ago..........	No....	No....	Yes...	Yes.
14	{1 yes. {1 no...	{1 yes. {1 no..	}Accumulated dirt.....	No regular period.....	Yes...	Yes...	No....	Yes.
15	No...	Yes...	(¹)................	Every 2 or 3 years.....	Yes...	Yes...	Yes...	Yes.
16	Yes...	Yes...		Yearly...............	No....	Yes...	No....	Yes.
17	Yes...	Yes...		....do.............	No....	Yes...	No....	Yes.
18	Yes...	Yes...		....do.............	No....	Yes...	No....	Yes.

¹ Not reported.

TABLE **VI.**—SANITARY CONDITIONS: CLEANLINESS OF WORKROOMS, SPITTING ON FLOOR, AND DRINKING WATER—Continued.

RHODE ISLAND—Concluded.

Establishment number.	Workrooms clean.		Conditions of uncleanliness where workrooms are not clean.	Workrooms whitewashed or painted, when.	Spitting on floor.			Fresh, pure drinking-water provided.
	Floors.	Walls and ceilings.			Done by employees.	Rule against.	Cuspidors provided.	
19	Yes...	Yes...	....	Not since built (1 year)	No....	Yes...	No....	Yes.
20	No....	Yes...	Dirty patches of hardened glue and paste on floors.	Once in 4 years.........	No....	Yes...	Yes...	Yes.
21	Yes...	Yes...	....	Building new..........	No....	No....	No....	Yes.
22	No....	No....	Dusty, littered, and stained with leakage.	Once in 4 years.........	No....	Yes...	No....	Yes.
23	Yes...	Yes...	....	Not since built (2 years)	No....	No....	Yes...	Yes.
24	Yes...	Yes...	....	Twice a year...........	No....	Yes...	No....	Yes.
25	Yes...	Yes...	....	4 years ago............	Yes...	No....	No....	Yes.
26	Yes...	Yes...	....	Ceilings twice a year, walls oftener.	No....	Yes...	Yes...	Yes.
27	Yes...	Yes...	....	Continually............	Yes...	No....	No....	Yes.

CONNECTICUT.

1	Yes...	Yes...	....	2 buildings (28 rooms) yearly; 1 building (4 rooms) never.	Yes...	No....	No....	Yes.
2	Yes...	Yes...	....	When necessary........	No....	Yes...	Yes...	Yes.
3	Yes...	Yes...	....	.....do................	No....	Yes...	No....	Yes.
4	Yes...	{80 yes. {4 no...	Walls spattered with with japan.	2 buildings (59 rooms) when necessary; 1 building (25 rooms) annually.	No....	Yes...	Yes...	Yes.
5	Yes...	Yes...	....	Once in 2 or 3 years.....	No....	Yes...	Yes...	Yes.
6	Yes...	Yes...	....	Yearly.................	No....	No....	Yes...	Yes.
7	Yes...	Yes...	....	Once in 3 years........	No....	Yes...	Yes...	Yes.
8	Yes...	Yes...	....	Yearly.................	No....	Yes...	Yes...	Yes.
9	Yes...	Yes...	....	.....do................	No....	No....	No....	Yes.
10	Yes...	Yes...	....	Twice a year...........	Yes...	No....	No....	Yes.
11	Yes...	Yes...	....	Yearly and when necessary.	Yes...	No....	No....	Yes.
12	Yes...	Yes...	....	When necessary........	Yes...	No....	No....	Yes.
13	No....	No....	Accumulated dust and dirt.	(1)....................	Yes...	Yes...	No....	Yes.
14	Yes...	Yes...	....	Yearly.................	No....	Yes...	Yes...	Yes.
15	Yes...	Yes...	....	.....do................	No....	Yes...	Yes...	Yes.
16	Yes...	Yes...	....	Once in 3 years........	No....	Yes...	Yes...	Yes.
17	Yes...	Yes...	....	When necessary........	No....	Yes...	No....	Yes.
18	Yes...	Yes...	....	.....do................	No....	Yes...	Yes...	Yes.
19	Yes...	Yes...	....	.....do................	Yes...	No....	No....	Yes.
20	Yes...	Yes...	....	Once in 2 years........	No....	Yes...	Yes...	Yes.
21	Yes...	Yes...	....	When necessary........	Yes...	No....	No....	Yes.
22	No....	No....	Walls and stairways not clean. Floors greasy........	Every 2 years..........	Yes...	No....	No....	Yes.
23	No....	Yes...	....	Yearly.................	Yes...	No....	No....	Yes.
24	Yes...	Yes...	....	.....do................	No....	Yes...	No....	Yes.
25	Yes...	Yes...	....	.....do................	No....	Yes...	Yes...	Yes.
26	Yes...	Yes...	....	.....do................	No....	No....	Yes...	Yes.
27	Yes...	Yes...	....	When necessary........	No....	Yes...	Yes...	Yes.
28	Yes...	Yes...	....	Yearly.................	No....	Yes...	Yes...	Yes.
29	Yes...	Yes...	....	When necessary........	No....	No	Yes...	Yes.
30	Yes...	Yes...	....	Every 5 years..........	No....	Yes...	No....	Yes.
31	No....	No....	Walls in forge, press, and buffing rooms very dirty.	(1)....................	Yes...	No....	No....	Yes.
32	Yes...	Yes...	....	Yearly.................	No....	No....	Yes...	Yes.
33	No....	No....	Accumulated dust....	Twice a year...........	No....	Yes...	No....	Yes.
34	Yes...	Yes...	....	Yearly or oftener.......	No....	Yes...	Yes...	Yes.
35	Yes...	Yes...	....	Yearly.................	No....	Yes...	Yes...	Yes.

1 Not reported.

TABLE **VI.**—SANITARY CONDITIONS: CLEANLINESS OF WORKROOMS, SPITTING ON FLOOR, AND DRINKING WATER—Continued.

NEW YORK.

Establishment number.	Workrooms clean.		Conditions of uncleanliness where workrooms are not clean.	Workrooms white-washed or painted, when.	Spitting on floor.			Fresh, pure drinking-water provided.
	Floors.	Walls and ceilings.			Done by employees.	Rule against.	Cuspidors provided.	
1	No	No	Walls of buffing and plating rooms coated with dust and rouge.	Some rooms, not since occupancy.	Yes	No	No	Yes
2	Yes	Yes		When necessary	Yes	No	No	Yes
3	{11 yes, 7 no}	{11 yes, 7 no}	Dirty with licorice and mashed tobacco.	...do	Yes	Yes	Yes	Yes
4	Yes	No	(1)	(1)	No	Yes	No	Yes
5	Yes	Yes		Yearly	No	Yes	Yes	Yes
6	{6 yes, 3 no}	Yes	(1)	When necessary	No	Yes	Yes	Yes
7	No	{12 yes, 7 no}	Dark with smoke	Yearly	No	Yes	Yes	Yes
8	Yes	Yes		Once in 6 or 7 years	No	Yes	Yes	Yes
9	Yes	Yes		Never	No	Yes	No	Yes
10	Yes	Yes		Yearly	No	Yes	Yes	Yes
11	Yes	Yes		When necessary	Yes	No	No	Yes
12	Yes	Yes		Twice a year	No	Yes	Yes	Yes
13	Yes	Yes		...do	No	Yes	Yes	Yes
14	Yes	Yes		When necessary	No	Yes	Yes	Yes
15	Yes	Yes		Monthly	No	Yes	Yes	Yes
16	Yes	Yes		Yearly	No	Yes	Yes	Yes
17	Yes	Yes		Once in 3 years	No	Yes	Yes	Yes
18	Yes	Yes		Yearly	Yes	No	No	Yes
19	Yes	Yes		...do	Yes	No	No	Yes
20	Yes	Yes		...do	No	Yes	Yes	Yes
21	No	No	Accumulated dirt	Not painted for years	No	Yes	No	Yes
22	Yes	Yes		Yearly	Yes	No	Yes	Yes
23	Yes	Yes		When necessary	Yes	No	Yes	Yes
24	Yes	Yes		Once in 2 years	Yes	No	No	Yes
25	Yes	Yes		Once in 2 years or oftener.	Yes	No	No	Yes
26	Yes	Yes		When necessary	Yes	No	No	Yes
27	No	Yes	(1)	(1)	Yes	No	No	Yes
28	Yes	Yes		Yearly	Yes	No	No	Yes
29	Yes	Yes		When necessary	No	No	No	Yes
30	Yes	Yes		...do	No	No	No	Yes
31	Yes	Yes		...do	No	No	No	Yes
32	Yes	Yes		(1)	No	No	Yes	Yes
33	Yes	Yes		When necessary	No	Yes	No	Yes
34	Yes	Yes		Yearly	No	Yes	Yes	Yes
35	Yes	Yes		...do	No	Yes	Yes	Yes
36	Yes	Yes		When necessary	No	Yes	No	Yes

NEW JERSEY.

Establishment number.	Floors.	Walls and ceilings.	Conditions of uncleanliness where workrooms are not clean.	Workrooms white-washed or painted, when.	Done by employees.	Rule against.	Cuspidors provided.	Fresh, pure drinking-water provided.
1	Yes	Yes		Yearly	No	Yes	Yes	Yes
2	Yes	Yes		...do	No	Yes	Yes	Yes
3	Yes	Yes		When necessary	Yes	No	No	Yes
4	Yes	Yes		...do	No	Yes	Yes	Yes
5	Yes	Yes		Yearly	No	Yes	Yes	Yes
6	Yes	Yes		...do	No	Yes	No	Yes
7	Yes	Yes		No regular period	Yes	No	No	Yes
8	Yes	Yes		Yearly	No	Yes	Yes	Yes
9	Yes	Yes		Twice a year	No	Yes	Yes	Yes
10	Yes	Yes		Not within past year	Yes	No	No	Yes
11	No	No	Accumulated dust	Once in 2 years	Yes	No	No	Yes
12	No	Yes	(1)	Yearly	Yes	No	No	Yes
13	Yes	No		...do	Yes	No	No	Yes
14	Yes	No	Accumulated dirt	Once in 3 or 4 years	No	Yes	No	Yes
15	Yes	No		Yearly	No	Yes	Yes	Yes
16	No	No	Dusty from materials of manufacture.	...do	Yes	No	No	Yes
17	Yes	Yes		...do	Yes	No	No	Yes
18	No	No	Dusty from materials of manufacture.	...do	Yes	No	No	Yes
19	Yes	No	Accumulated dust	...do	Yes	No	No	Yes

1 Not reported.

TABLE **VI.**—SANITARY CONDITIONS: CLEANLINESS OF WORKROOMS, SPITTING ON FLOOR, AND DRINKING WATER—Continued.

NEW JERSEY—Concluded.

Establishment number.	Workrooms clean.		Conditions of uncleanliness where workrooms are not clean.	Workrooms whitewashed or painted, when.	Spitting on floor.			Fresh, pure drinking water provided.
	Floors.	Walls and ceilings.			Done by employees.	Rule against.	Cuspidors provided.	
20	No	No	Dusty from materials of manufacture.	Yearly	Yes	No	No	Yes.
21	Yes	Yes		Four times a year	No	Yes	No	Yes.
22	Yes	No	Covered with dust and smoke.	Yearly	Yes	No	No	Yes.
23	Yes	Yes		do	No	Yes	Yes	Yes.
24	Yes	Yes		Twice a year	No	Yes	Yes	Yes.
25	Yes	Yes		Yearly	Yes	No	No	Yes.
26	Yes	Yes		do	Yes	Yes	No	Yes.
27	Yes	Yes		do	Yes	Yes	Yes	Yes.

PENNSYLVANIA.

Establishment number.	Workrooms clean.		Conditions of uncleanliness where workrooms are not clean.	Workrooms whitewashed or painted, when.	Spitting on floor.			Fresh, pure drinking water provided.
	Floors.	Walls and ceilings.			Done by employees.	Rule against.	Cuspidors provided.	
1	Yes	Yes		Twice a year	No	Yes	Yes	Yes.
2	Yes	Yes		Yearly	No	Yes	Yes	Yes.
3	Yes	Yes		do	No	Yes	No	Yes.
4	Yes	Yes		do	Yes	No	No	Yes.
5	Yes	Yes		(1)	No	Yes	Yes	Yes.
6	Yes	Yes		Yearly	No	No	No	Yes.
7	Yes	Yes		do	Yes	Yes	No	Yes.
8	Yes	Yes		do	No	Yes	Yes	Yes.
9	Yes	Yes		do	No	Yes	Yes	Yes.
10	Yes	Yes		do	No	Yes	No	Yes.
11	Yes	Yes		do	No	Yes	Yes	Yes.
12	Yes	Yes		do	Yes	Yes	No	Yes.
13	Yes	Yes		do	No	Yes	No	Yes.
14	Yes	Yes		do	No	Yes	Yes	Yes.
15	Yes	Yes		3 times a year	No	Yes	Yes	Yes.
16	No	Yes	(1)	Twice a year	No	Yes	Yes	Yes.
17	Yes	Yes		Monthly	No	Yes	No	Yes.
18	Yes	No	Soot and other foundry waste.	Not since occupancy	Yes	No	No	Yes.
19	Yes	No	Soot and dirt from work.	do	Yes	No	No	Yes.
20	Yes	Yes		do	Yes	No	No	Yes.
21	Yes	Yes		Once in 2 years	Yes	No	No	Yes.
22	Yes	Yes		Once in 2 months	No	Yes	Yes	Yes.
23	Yes	Yes		Yearly	No	Yes	Yes	Yes.
24	Yes	No	Dingy and dusty	Once in 2 years	No	Yes	Yes	Yes.
25	Yes	Yes		Twice a year	No	Yes	No	Yes.
26	Yes	Yes		Yearly	No	Yes	No	Yes.
27	Yes	Yes		do	No	Yes	Yes	Yes.
28	Yes	Yes		3 times a year	No	Yes	No	Yes.
29	Yes	Yes		Once in 3 months	No	Yes	Yes	Yes.
30	Yes	Yes		Once in 3 years	Yes	Yes	Yes	Yes.
31	Yes	Yes		Yearly	No	Yes	Yes	Yes.
32	Yes	Yes		do	Yes	No	No	Yes.
33	Yes	No	Dirt from operation of machinery.	(1)	Yes	Yes	Yes	Yes.
34	Yes	No	Dirt accumulations of years.	Every 6 or 8 years	Yes	No	No	Yes.
35	Yes	Yes		Yearly	No	Yes	No	Yes.
36	Yes	Yes		Not since occupancy	No	Yes	Yes	Yes.
37	No	No	Floors oily, walls dirty, from operation of machinery.	Every 3 or 4 years	Yes	Yes	No	Yes.
38	Yes	Yes		Yearly	Yes	No	No	Yes.
39	Yes	Yes		Once in 2 years	Yes	No	No	Yes.
40	Yes	Yes		No regular period	Yes	No	No	Yes.
41	Yes	Yes		Once in 2 years	No	Yes	No	Yes.
42	Yes	Yes			Yes	No	No	Yes.
43	No	No	Dust from operations.	(1)	Yes	No	No	Yes.
44	Yes	Yes		Once in 3 years	Yes	No	No	Yes.
45	Yes	Yes		Not since occupancy	Yes	Yes	No	Yes.
46	Yes	Yes		Yearly	No	Yes	Yes	Yes.
47	No	Yes	Dirty and rough	do	No	Yes	No	Yes.
48	Yes	Yes		do	Yes	Yes	No	Yes.
49	Yes	Yes		do	Yes	Yes	No	Yes.
50	Yes	Yes		do	Yes	Yes	Yes	Yes.

1 Not reported.

TABLE **VI.**—SANITARY CONDITIONS: CLEANLINESS OF WORKROOMS, SPITTING ON FLOOR, AND DRINKING WATER—Continued.

OHIO.

Establishment number.	Workrooms clean.		Conditions of uncleanliness where workrooms are not clean.	Workrooms whitewashed or painted, when.	Spitting on floor.			Fresh, pure drinking-water provided.
	Floors.	Walls and ceilings.			Done by employees.	Rule against.	Cuspidors provided.	
1	Yes...	Yes...	....	Once in 2 years........	No....	No....	No....	Yes.
2	Yes...	Yes...	....	Once in 5 years........	No....	Yes...	Yes...	Yes.
3	Yes...	Yes...	....	Yearly.................	No....	Yes...	No....	Yes.
4	Yes...	Yes...	....	...do....	No....	Yes...	No....	Yes.
5	Yes...	Yes...	....	...do....	No....	Yes...	(¹)....	Yes.
6	Yes...	Yes...	....	...do....	No....	Yes...	Yes...	Yes.
7	Yes...	Yes...	....	...do....	No....	Yes...	No....	Yes.
8	No....	No....	Accumulated dirt.....	Once in 3 years........	Yes...	No....	No....	Yes.
9	Yes...	Yes...	....	Yearly.................	No....	Yes...	Yes...	Yes.
10	Yes...	Yes...	....	...do....	No....	Yes...	Yes...	Yes.
11	Yes...	Yes...	....	...do....	No....	Yes...	No....	Yes.
12	Yes...	Yes...	....	...do....	No....	Yes...	Yes...	Yes.
13	Yes...	Yes...	....	Once in 2 years........	No....	Yes...	Yes...	Yes.
14	Yes...	Yes...	....	Yearly.................	No....	Yes...	No....	Yes.
15	Yes...	Yes...	....	...do....	No....	Yes...	Yes...	Yes.
16	Yes...	Yes...	....	...do....	No....	Yes...	Yes...	Yes.
17	Yes...	Yes...	....	...do....	No....	Yes...	Yes...	Yes.
18	Yes...	Yes...	....	...do....	No....	Yes...	Yes...	Yes.
19	Yes...	Yes...	....	....	No....	Yes...	Yes...	Yes.
20	Yes...	Yes...	....	Twice a year...........	No....	Yes...	Yes...	Yes.
21	Yes...	Yes...	....	Yearly.................	No....	Yes...	Yes...	Yes.
22	Yes...	Yes...	....	Twice a year...........	No....	Yes...	Yes...	Yes.
23	Yes...	Yes...	....	Once in 3 years........	Yes...	Yes...	Yes...	Yes.
24	Yes...	Yes...	....	Walls cleaned twice a year.	No....	Yes...	No....	Yes.
25	Yes...	Yes...	....	Not since occupancy (cement walls).	Yes...	No....	No....	Yes.
26	Yes...	Yes...	....	2 years ago............	No....	Yes...	No....	Yes.
27	Yes...	Yes...	....	3 years ago............	Yes...	Yes...	Yes...	Yes.
28	Yes...	Yes...	....	Twice a year...........	No....	No....	No....	Yes.
29	Yes...	Yes...	....	Yearly.................	No....	Yes...	Yes...	Yes.
30	Yes...	Yes...	....	...do....	No....	Yes...	Yes...	Yes.
31	No....	Yes...	(¹).....................	...do....	No....	Yes...	No....	Yes.
32	Yes...	Yes...	....	3 times a year.........	No....	Yes...	No....	Yes.
33	Yes...	Yes...	....	Once in 2 years........	No....	Yes...	Yes...	Yes.
34	Yes...	Yes...	....	Yearly.................	No....	No....	Yes...	Yes.
35	Yes...	Yes...	....	...do....	No....	Yes...	Yes...	Yes.
36	Yes...	Yes...	....	...do....	No....	Yes...	Yes...	Yes.
37	Yes...	Yes...	....	...do....	No....	Yes...	No....	Yes.
38	Yes...	Yes...	....	...do....	No....	Yes...	No....	Yes.
39	Yes...	Yes...	....	Once in 2 years........	No....	Yes...	Yes...	Yes.
40	Yes...	Yes...	....	...do....	No....	Yes...	Yes...	Yes.
41	Yes...	Yes...	....	....	Yes...	Yes...	No....	Yes.
42	Yes...	Yes...	....	3 years ago............	Yes...	No....	No....	Yes.
43	Yes...	No....	Accumulated dust....	No regular period......	Yes...	No....	No....	Yes.
44	Yes...	Yes...	....	When necessary........	Yes...	No....	No....	Yes.
45	Yes...	Yes...	....	Yearly.................	Yes...	No....	No....	Yes.
46	Yes...	Yes...	....	...do....	Yes...	Yes...	No....	Yes.
47	Yes...	Yes...	....	Once in 3 years........	Yes...	No....	No....	Yes.
48	Yes...	Yes...	....	Once in 2 years........	Yes...	No....	No....	Yes.
49	Yes...	Yes...	....	Yearly.................	Yes...	No....	Yes...	Yes.
50	Yes...	Yes...	....	....	No....	Yes...	Yes...	Yes.
51	Yes...	Yes...	....	(¹).....................	No....	Yes...	Yes...	Yes.
52	Yes...	Yes...	....	Cleaned weekly........	No....	No....	Yes...	Yes.
53	Yes...	Yes...	....	Yearly.................	No....	Yes...	Yes...	Yes.
54	Yes...	Yes...	....	...do....	No....	Yes...	Yes...	Yes.
55	Yes...	Yes...	....	...do....	Yes...	No....	No....	Yes.
56	{15 yes. {1 no...	15 yes. 1 no...	}Rag pickers' room } dirty.	}...do....	Yes...	Yes...	No....	Yes.
57	Yes...	Yes...	....	...do....	Yes...	Yes...	No....	Yes.
58	Yes...	Yes...	....	Twice a year...........	Yes...	Yes...	No....	Yes.
59	Yes...	Yes...	....	Yearly.................	Yes...	Yes...	No....	Yes.
60	Yes...	Yes...	....	...do....	Yes...	Yes...	No....	Yes.

¹ Not reported.

TABLE **VI.**—SANITARY CONDITIONS: CLEANLINESS OF WORKROOMS, SPITTING ON FLOOR, AND DRINKING WATER—Continued.

ILLINOIS.

Establishment number.	Workrooms clean. Floors.	Workrooms clean. Walls and ceilings.	Conditions of uncleanliness where workrooms are not clean.	Workrooms whitewashed or painted, when.	Spitting on floor. Done by employees.	Spitting on floor. Rule against.	Spitting on floor. Cuspidors provided.	Fresh, pure drinking-water provided.
1	Yes...	Yes...		When necessary........	No....	No....	No....	Yes.
2	Yes...	Yes...		Yearly................	No....	No....	No....	Yes.
3	Yes...	Yes...		....do................	Yes...	No....	Yes...	Yes.
4	Yes...	No....	(1)...................	No regular period......	No....	Yes...	Yes...	Yes.
5	Yes...	Yes...		New building..........	No....	Yes...	Yes...	Yes.
6	Yes...	Yes...		Once or twice a year...	No....	Yes...	No....	Yes.
7	Yes...	Yes...		Yearly................	No....	Yes...	Yes...	Yes.
8	Yes...	No....	Covered with dust....	Once in 2 years........	No....	Yes...	Yes...	Yes.
9	No....	Yes...	Covered with dust and tobacco.	....do................	Yes...	No....	Yes...	Yes.
10	Yes...	Yes...		No regular period......	Yes...	Yes...	Yes...	Yes.
11	Yes...	Yes...		Once in 2 years........	No....	Yes...	Yes...	Yes.
12	Yes...	Yes...		Yearly................	No....	Yes...	Yes...	Yes.
13	No....	No....	Sticky with material of manufacture, dust, etc.	No regular period......	Yes...	Yes...	Yes...	Yes.
14	No....	Yes...	(1)...................	Twice a year..........	No....	Yes...	Yes...	Yes.
15	Yes...	Yes...		2 or 3 times a year....	Yes...	No....	No....	Yes.
16	Yes...	Yes...		Monthly..............	No....	Yes...	No....	Yes.
17	Yes...	Yes...		....do................	No....	No....	No....	Yes.
18	Yes...	Yes...		2 or 3 times a year....	Yes...	Yes...	No....	Yes.
19	Yes...	Yes...		Yearly................	Yes...	Yes...	No....	Yes.
20	Yes...	Yes...		Frequently............	No....	Yes...	No....	Yes.
21	Yes...	Yes...		Yearly................	No....	Yes...	Yes...	Yes.
22	Yes...	Yes...		....do................	Yes...	Yes...	Yes...	Yes.
23	Yes...	Yes...		....do................	No....	Yes...	Yes...	Yes.
24	Yes...	Yes...		....do................	No....	Yes...	Yes...	Yes.
25	Yes...	Yes...		....do................	No....	Yes...	Yes...	Yes.
26	Yes...	No....	Heavy coating of dust.	Not since occupancy....	Yes...	No....	No....	Yes.
27	Yes...	No....	Dusty and black......	Once in 3 years........	No....	Yes...	No....	Yes.
28	Yes...	Yes...		Twice a year..........	No....	Yes...	No....	Yes.
29	Yes...	Yes...		Once in 2 years........	Yes...	No....	No....	Yes.
30	Yes...	Yes...		Once in 3 years........	Yes...	No....	No....	Yes.
31	Yes...	Yes...		Not since occupancy....	Yes...	No....	No....	Yes.
32	Yes²..	Yes...		No regular period......	Yes...	No....	No....	Yes.
33	Yes...	Yes...		....do................	Yes...	No....	No....	Yes.
34	Yes...	Yes...		....do................	Yes...	No....	No....	Yes.
35	Yes...	Yes...		When necessary........	No....	No....	Yes...	Yes.
36	Yes...	Yes...		Not since occupancy....	Yes...	No....	No....	Yes.
37	No....	No....	Dingy with smoke and dust.	Some parts yearly......	Yes...	No....	No....	Yes.
38	Yes...	Yes...		Once in 2 or 3 years....	Yes...	No....	No....	Yes.
39	Yes...	Yes...		Not since occupancy....	Yes...	No....	No....	Yes.
40	Yes...	Yes...		Yearly................	Yes...	Yes...	No....	Yes.
41	Yes...	Yes...		Once in 3 years........	Yes...	Yes...	Yes...	Yes.
42	Yes...	Yes...		No regular period......	Yes...	No....	No....	Yes.
43	Yes...	No....	Black and dirty.......	Yearly................	Yes...	Yes...	No....	Yes.
44	Yes...	Yes...		....do................	No....	Yes...	No....	Yes.
45	No....	No....	Greasy, dusty, dirty...	Once in 2 or 3 years....	Yes...	No....	No....	Yes.
46	Yes...	{3 yes.. 6 no...}	Greasy and dusty.....	Yearly................	Yes...	No....	No....	Yes.
47	No....	Yes...	(1)...................	Once in 3 or 4 years....	Yes...	No....	No....	Yes.

¹ Not reported.   ² Where women work.

TABLE **VI.**—SANITARY CONDITIONS: CLEANLINESS OF WORKROOMS, SPITTING ON FLOOR, AND DRINKING WATER—Continued.

INDIANA.

Establishment number.	Workrooms clean.		Conditions of uncleanliness where workrooms are not clean.	Workrooms whitewashed or painted, when.	Spitting on floor.			Fresh, pure drinking-water provided.
	Floors.	Walls and ceilings.			Done by employees.	Rule against.	Cuspidors provided.	
1	Yes...	Yes...	....	Yearly..................	No....	No....	Yes...	Yes.
2	Yes...	Yes...	....	Not since built (5 years)	Yes...	No....	No....	Yes.
3	No....	No....	Glass, beer, and mud on floors; walls dusty and steam-soaked.	Yearly..................	Yes...	No....	No....	Yes.
4	Yes...	Yes...	....	...do....................	Yes...	No....	No....	Yes.
5	Yes...	Yes...	....	When necessary.........	No....	Yes...	Yes...	Yes.
6	Yes...	Yes...	....	Once in 2 years........	Yes...	Yes...	Yes...	Yes.
7	Yes...	Yes...	....	When necessary.........	No....	No....	No....	Yes.
8	Yes...	Yes...	....	...do....................	No....	Yes...	Yes...	Yes.
9	Yes...	Yes...	....	...do....................	No....	No....	No....	Yes.
10	Yes...	Yes...	....	No regular period......	No....	No....	No....	Yes.
11	Yes...	Yes...	....	Yearly.................	No....	Yes...	Yes...	Yes.
12	Yes...	Yes...	....	No regular period......	No....	Yes...	Yes...	Yes.
13	No....	Yes...	Littered with candy and trash.	Twice a year..........	No....	No....	No....	Yes.
14	Yes...	Yes...	....	3 times a year.........	No....	Yes...	Yes...	Yes.
15	Yes...	Yes...	....	Yearly.................	No....	Yes...	No....	Yes.
16	No....	No....	Littered with candy; black with dust.	No regular period......	No....	Yes...	Yes...	Yes.
17	Yes...	Yes...	....	Not since occupancy...	Yes...	No....	No....	Yes.
18	Yes...	Yes...	....	Yearly.................	No....	Yes...	No....	Yes.
19	Yes...	{3 yes, 3 no}	}Discolored with smoke	When necessary.........	No....	Yes...	No....	Yes.
20	Yes...	Yes...	....	No regular period......	No....	Yes...	Yes...	Yes.
21	Yes...	Yes...	....	When necessary.........	Yes...	Yes...	Yes...	Yes.
22	Yes...	Yes...	....	Yearly.................	No....	Yes...	Yes...	Yes.
23	Yes...	Yes...	....	...do....................	Yes...	No....	No....	Yes.
24	Yes...	{1 yes, 1 no}	}Discolored with smoke	{1 room once in 2 years; 1 room once in 10 years}	Yes...	Yes...	No....	Yes.
25	Yes...	Yes...	....	Yearly.................	No....	Yes...	No....	Yes.
26	Yes...	Yes...	....	...do....................	Yes...	Yes...	Yes...	Yes.
27	Yes...	Yes...	....	No regular period......	No....	No....	No....	Yes.
28	Yes...	Yes...	....	Yearly.................	No....	No....	No....	Yes.
29	Yes...	Yes...	....	...do....................	Yes...	No....	No....	Yes.
30	Yes...	Yes...	....	When necessary.........	No....	No....	No....	Yes.
31	Yes...	Yes...	....	...do....................	Yes...	Yes...	No....	Yes.
32	Yes...	Yes...	....	...do....................	No....	Yes...	Yes...	Yes.
33	Yes...	Yes...	....	No regular period......	Yes...	No....	No....	Yes.
34	Yes...	Yes...	....	When necessary.........	No....	Yes...	No....	Yes.
35	No....	Yes...	Covered with dust and littered with shells, etc.	Yearly.................	Yes...	No....	No....	Yes.
36	Yes...	Yes...	....	When necessary.........	Yes...	No....	No....	Yes.
37	Yes...	Yes...	....	Once in 2 years........	Yes...	No....	No....	Yes.
38	Yes...	Yes...	....	Yearly.................	No....	Yes...	Yes...	Yes.
39	Yes...	Yes...	....	No regular period......	No....	No....	No....	Yes.
40	Yes...	Yes...	....	Yearly.................	Yes...	Yes...	Yes...	Yes.
41	Yes...	Yes...	....	...do....................	Yes...	No....	No....	Yes.
42	Yes...	Yes...	....	...do....................	Yes...	No....	No....	Yes.
43	Yes...	No....	Blackened by smoke..	Once in 2 or 3 years....	Yes...	No....	No....	Yes.
44	Yes...	Yes...	....	When necessary.........	Yes...	No....	No....	Yes.
45	Yes...	Yes...	....	Yearly.................	Yes...	No....	No....	Yes.
46	Yes...	Yes...	....	{9 rooms twice a year; 8 yearly; 3 once in 2 or 3 years.}	Yes...	Yes...	{11 no, 9 yes}	}Yes.
47	{2 yes, 7 no}	}Yes...	Covered with grease[1]..	When necessary.........	No....	Yes...	Yes...	No.

[1] Walls of spinning room dripping from condensed hot air.

TABLE **VI.**—SANITARY CONDITIONS: CLEANLINESS OF WORKROOMS, SPITTING ON FLOOR, AND DRINKING WATER—Continued.

MICHIGAN.

Establishment number.	Workrooms clean.		Conditions of uncleanliness where workrooms are not clean.	Workrooms whitewashed or painted, when.	Spitting on floor.			Fresh, pure drinking-water provided.
	Floors.	Walls and ceilings.			Done by employees.	Rule against.	Cuspidors provided.	
1	Yes	Yes		Yearly	No	Yes	Yes	Yes
2	Yes	Yes		Once in 2 or 3 years	Yes	Yes	Yes	Yes
3	Yes	Yes		No regular period	No	Yes	Yes	Yes
4	Yes	Yes		Yearly. ●	No	Yes	Yes	Yes
5	Yes	Yes		...do	No	Yes	Yes	Yes
6	No	No	Accumulated filth	No regular period	No	Yes	Yes	Yes
7	Yes	Yes		Once or twice a year	Yes	Yes	No	Yes
8	No	Yes	(1)	Once in 4 or 5 years	Yes	Yes	No	Yes
9	Yes	Yes		When necessary	No	No	No	Yes
10	Yes	Yes		No regular period	No	Yes	No	Yes
11	Yes	Yes		When necessary	No	Yes	No	Yes
12	Yes	Yes		Yearly	Yes	No	No	Yes
13	Yes	Yes		...do	No	No	No	Yes
14	Yes	Yes		...do	No	No	Yes	Yes
15	Yes	Yes		No regular period	No	Yes	Yes	Yes
16	Yes	Yes		Once in 3 years	Yes	Yes	Yes	Yes
17	Yes	Yes		Yearly	No	Yes	Yes	Yes
18	Yes	Yes		...do	Yes	Yes	No	Yes
19	No	No	Covered with grease and lint.	Once in 10 years	Yes	No	No	Yes

WISCONSIN.

Establishment number.	Floors.	Walls and ceilings.	Conditions of uncleanliness.	Whitewashed or painted, when.	Done by employees.	Rule against.	Cuspidors provided.	Drinking-water provided.
1	Yes	Yes		Yearly	No	No	No	Yes
2	Yes	Yes		No regular period	No	Yes	No	Yes
3	Yes	Yes		Once in 2 years	No	Yes	Yes	Yes
4	Yes	Yes		New quarters	No	Yes	No	Yes
5	Yes	Yes		Yearly	No	No	Yes	Yes
6	Yes	Yes		New quarters	No	No	No	Yes
7	Yes	Yes		Yearly	No	No	Yes	Yes
8	Yes	Yes		Once in 2 years	No	No	No	Yes
9	Yes	Yes		No regular period	No	Yes	No	Yes
10	Yes	Yes		...do	Yes	No	No	Yes
11	Yes	Yes		Yearly	Yes	No	No	Yes
12	Yes	{2 yes, 1 no}	Covered with dust	No regular period	No	Yes	{1 no, 2 yes}	Yes
13	Yes	Yes		Once in 3 years	Yes	No	No	Yes
14	Yes	Yes		Once in 2 years	Yes	No	No	Yes
15	Yes	Yes		Once in 2 or 3 years	Yes	No	No	Yes
16	Yes	Yes		Yearly	No	No	Yes	Yes
17	Yes	Yes		...do	No	No	Yes	Yes
18	Yes	Yes		Once in 3 years	No	Yes	Yes	Yes
19	Yes	Yes		...do	No	Yes	No	Yes

MARYLAND.

Establishment number.	Floors.	Walls and ceilings.	Conditions of uncleanliness.	Whitewashed or painted, when.	Done by employees.	Rule against.	Cuspidors provided.	Drinking-water provided.
1	No	No	Spattered with mud from oysters.	Yearly	Yes	No	No	Yes
2	No	Yes	Accumulated dirt	Twice a year	Yes	No	No	Yes
3	Yes	Yes		Three times a year	No	No	No	Yes
4	Yes	Yes		(1)	Yes	No	No	Yes
5	Yes	Yes		Yearly	Yes	No	No	Yes
6	Yes	Yes		...do	Yes	No	No	Yes
7	Yes	Yes		...do	No	Yes	Yes	Yes
8	Yes	Yes		Twice a year	Yes	No	No	Yes
9	No	No	Accumulated dust	When necessary	Yes	Yes	Yes[2]	Yes
10	No	Yes	(1)	Yearly	Yes	Yes	Yes	Yes
11	Yes	No	Accumulated dirt	Once in 2 or 3 years	No	No	No	Yes
12	Yes	Yes		Yearly or oftener	No	Yes	No	Yes
13	Yes	Yes		Yearly	No	Yes	No	Yes
14	Yes	Yes		...do	No	Yes	No	Yes
15	No	{9 yes, 3 no}	Walls spattered with glucose, candy, and smoke.	Once in 3 or 4 years	Yes	Yes	Yes	Yes
16	No	Yes	(1)	Yearly	No	Yes	Yes	Yes

[1] Not reported.   [2] Employees furnish their own cuspidors.

TABLE **VI.**—SANITARY CONDITIONS: CLEANLINESS OF WORKROOMS, SPITTING ON FLOOR, AND DRINKING WATER—Continued.

MARYLAND—Concluded.

Establishment number.	Workrooms clean.		Conditions of uncleanliness where workrooms are not clean.	Workrooms whitewashed or painted, when.	Spitting on floor.			Fresh, pure drinking-water provided.
	Floors.	Walls and ceilings.			Done by employees.	Rule against.	Cuspidors provided.	
17	Yes	Yes		New building	No	Yes	Yes	Yes.
18	Yes	No	Accumulated dirt and smoke.	(1)	No	Yes	No	Yes.
19	Yes	Yes		Yearly	No	Yes	Yes	Yes.
20	Yes	Yes		Once in 2 years	No	No	Yes	Yes.
21	Yes	Yes		When necessary	No	Yes	Yes	Yes.
22	Yes	No	Grimy and dirty	Not in 3 years	No	Yes	Yes	Yes.
23	Yes	Yes		Yearly or oftener	No	Yes	Yes	Yes.
24	Yes	Yes		Twice a year	No	Yes	Yes	Yes.
25	Yes	Yes		When necessary	No	No	No	Yes.
26	Yes	Yes		Yearly	No	Yes	Yes	Yes.
27	Yes	Yes		When necessary	No	Yes	Yes	Yes.
28	{3 no. / 8 yes..} Yes		(1)	3 times a year	No	Yes	Yes	Yes.

NORTH CAROLINA.

Establishment number.	Workrooms clean.		Conditions of uncleanliness where workrooms are not clean.	Workrooms whitewashed or painted, when.	Spitting on floor.			Fresh, pure drinking-water provided.
	Floors.	Walls and ceilings.			Done by employees.	Rule against.	Cuspidors provided.	
1	Yes	Yes		When necessary	Yes	Yes	Yes	Yes.
2	Yes	Yes		Over 3 years ago	Yes	No	No	Yes.
3	Yes	Yes		Once in 2 years	Yes	Yes	Yes	Yes.
4	No	Yes	(1)	Once in 10 years	Yes	No	No	No.
5	Yes			Less than 2 years ago	Yes	No	No	Yes.
6	{6 yes / 5 no} 7 yes / 4 no		Floors littered with cotton waste; walls covered with dust and spattered with oil.	Yearly	Yes	No	No	Yes.
7	{2 yes / 3 no} Yes		Floors littered with greasy waste.	....do	Yes	No	No	Yes.
8	{8 yes / 4 no} 10 yes / 2 no	Grimy and spattered with oil.	3 times a year except 1 room (only twice).	Yes	No	Yes	Yes.
9	{5 no / 2 no} Yes		Floors littered with dust and greasy cotton.	Yearly	Yes	No	Yes	Yes.
10	{2 yes / 4 no} Yes		(1)	Once in about 2 years	Yes	Yes	Yes	Yes.
11	{3 yes / 4 no} 5 yes / 2 no	Accumulated dirt and grease.	....do	Yes	Yes	Yes	Yes.
12	{1 yes / 3 no} 1 yes / 3 no	....do	No regular period	Yes	No	No	Yes.
13	{1 yes / 2 no} 1 yes / 2 no	....do	....do	Yes	Yes	No	Yes.
14	Yes	Yes		....do	No	Yes	Yes	Yes.
15	Yes	Yes		When necessary	No	Yes	Yes	Yes.
16	Yes	Yes		Very often	No	Yes	Yes	Yes.
17	Yes	Yes		Every few weeks	Yes	No	No	No.
18	Yes	Yes		Yearly	No	Yes	Yes	Yes.
19	Yes	Yes		....do	No	Yes	Yes	Yes.
20	No	No	Walls filthy with dust and dirt.	Never	Yes	Yes	Yes	Yes.
21	{2 yes / 2 no} 2 yes / 2 no	Accumulated dirt and stains.		No	Yes	Yes	Yes.
22	Yes	No	Accumulated dirt and stains on walls.	Once in 2 years	Yes	Yes	Yes	Yes.
23	{3 yes / 2 no} No	Ceilings unfinished; walls dirty and stained with age.	....do	Yes	Yes	Yes	Yes.
24	Yes	Yes		(1)	No	Yes	Yes	Yes.
25	{4 yes / 1 no} Yes		Card room floor littered with lint and dust.	Once in 2 years	Yes	No	No	Yes.
26	{7 yes / 2 no} 8 yes / 1 no	Walls and floors covered with dusty lint and oils, grease, etc.	....do	No	Yes	Yes	Yes.
27	{4 yes / 1 no} 4 yes / 1 no	Accumulated wool and cotton lint and waste.	....do	Yes	Yes	Yes	Yes.
28	Yes	Yes		1 year ago	Yes	Yes	No	Yes.

[1] Not reported.

TABLE **VI.**—SANITARY CONDITIONS: CLEANLINESS OF WORKROOMS, SPITTING ON FLOOR, AND DRINKING WATER—Continued.

GEORGIA.

Establishment number.	Workrooms clean.		Conditions of uncleanliness where workrooms are not clean.	Workrooms whitewashed or painted, when.	Spitting on floor.			Fresh, pure drinking-water provided.
	Floors.	Walls and ceilings.			Done by employees.	Rule against.	Cuspidors provided.	
1	{4 yes.. {3 no...	}Yes...	{Spattered with materials of manufacture.	}New building..........	No....	No....	Yes...	Yes.
2	Yes...	Yes...		Yearly................	No....	No....	Yes...	Yes.
3	Yes...	{6 yes.. {2 no...	Spattered with materials of manufacture.	{Not since occupancy (brick walls); woodwork painted yearly.	}Yes...	Yes...	Yes...	Yes.
4	Yes...	Yes...		Once in 2 or 3 years....	Yes...	No....	Yes...	Yes.
5	No....	No....	Accumulated dirt....	(1)........................	Yes...	No....	(2).....	Yes.
6	Yes...	Yes...		When necessary........	Yes...	Yes...	Yes...	Yes.
7	Yes...	Yes...		(1)........................	Yes...	No....	Yes...	Yes.
8	Yes...	Yes...		Whitewashed twice a year; painted once in 2 years.	No....	No....	Yes...	Yes.
9	Yes...	Yes...		Not since occupancy (18 months).	Yes...	No....	Yes...	Yes.
10	Yes...	Yes...		Once in 2 years........	Yes...	No....	Yes...	Yes.
11	Yes...	Yes...		Every few months.....	Yes...	No....	No....	No.
12	Yes...	{2 yes.. {1 no...	Spattered with materials of manufacture.	{Not since occupancy (brick walls); woodwork painted yearly.	}Yes...	Yes...	Yes...	Yes.
13	{2 yes.. {3 no...	{2 yes.. 3 no...	}....do.............	Twice a year..........	No....	Yes...	Yes...	Yes.
14	{2 yes.. {2 no...	}Yes...	....do.............	New building..........	No....	No....	Yes...	Yes.
15	Yes...	Yes...	....do.............	Once in 2 years........	Yes...	Yes...	Yes...	Yes.
16	{6 yes.. {4 no...	{7 yes.. 3 no...	}Accumulated dirt and grease.	}No regular period......	Yes...	No....	No....	Yes.
17	Yes...	Yes...		Once in 2 or 3 years....	Yes...	No....	No....	Yes.
18	{3 yes.. {1 no...	}No.....	{Floors littered, 1 covered with dirt and oil.	}Not since occupancy...	Yes...	No....	No....	Yes.
19	Yes...	Yes...		....do................	Yes...	Yes...	Yes...	Yes.
20	{2 yes.. {1 no...	{2 yes.. 1 no...	}Stained with tobacco juice and oil.	}No regular period......	Yes...	Yes...	No....	Yes.
21	Yes...	Yes...		....do................	Yes...	Yes...	Yes...	Yes.
22	No....	Yes...	Floors covered with dust, paste, and scraps.	Yearly................	Yes...	No....	Yes...	Yes.
23	{2 yes.. {2 no...	}No.....	Accumulated dirt....	Not in 5 years..........	(1).....	(1).....	(1).....	Yes.
24	No....	No....	....do.............	Not for 7 or 8 years.....	Yes...	No....	No....	Yes.
25	No....	No....	....do.............	Not for years..........	Yes...	No....	No....	Yes.
26	Yes...	Yes...		Not in 2 years..........	Yes...	No....	No....	Yes.
27	Yes...	{5 yes.. {2 no...	}Accumulated dirt....	Not for years..........	Yes...	No....	No....	No.

FLORIDA.

1	Yes...	Yes...		New building..........	Yes...	No....	No....	Yes.
2	Yes...	Yes...		Once in 5 years........	Yes...	Yes...	Yes...	Yes.
3	Yes...	Yes...		New building..........	Yes...	No....	Yes...	Yes.
4	Yes...	Yes...		When necessary........	No....	Yes...	Yes...	Yes.
5	Yes...	Yes...		Yearly................	No....	Yes...	Yes...	Yes.
6	No....	No....	Accumulated dirt, scrap, and spit.	....do................	Yes...	No....	Yes...	Yes.
7	Yes...	Yes...		When necessary........	No....	Yes...	Yes...	Yes.
8	Yes...	Yes...		....do................	No....	Yes...	Yes...	Yes.
9	Yes...	Yes...		....do................	No....	Yes...	Yes...	Yes.
10	No....	Yes...	Accumulated dirt, scrap, and spit.	(1)........................	Yes...	No....	No....	Yes.
11	No....	Yes...	(1).................	Not since occupancy...	Yes...	No....	Yes...	Yes.
12	No....	Yes...	Dirty and stained with spit.	When necessary........	Yes...	Yes...	Yes...	Yes.
13	No....	Yes...	Very dirty from dust and spit.	Yearly................	Yes...	No....	Yes...	Yes.
14	Yes...	Yes...		Not since occupancy...	Yes...	No....	Yes...	Yes.

[1] Not reported.　　　　　　　　　[2] In halls only.

TABLE **VI.**—SANITARY CONDITIONS: CLEANLINESS OF WORKROOMS, SPITTING ON FLOOR, AND DRINKING WATER—Concluded.

LOUISIANA.

Establishment number.	Workrooms clean.		Conditions of uncleanliness where workrooms are not clean.	Workrooms whitewashed or painted, when.	Spitting on floor.			Fresh, pure drinking-water provided.
	Floors.	Walls and ceilings.			Done by employees.	Rule against.	Cuspidors provided.	
1	No....	Yes...	Floors covered with lint and dirt.	When necessary........	Yes...	No....	No....	Yes.
2	No....	Yes....	.....do.................	.....do..............	Yes...	No....	No....	Yes.
3	Yes...	Yes....	....	Yearly...............	Yes...	No....	No....	Yes.
4	Yes...	Yes....	....	When necessary........	No....	Yes...	Yes...	Yes.
5	Yes...	Yes....	....	Once in 2 years.........	Yes...	No....	No....	Yes.
6	No....	Yes...	Floors covered with trash and dirt from work.	When necessary........	Yes...	No....	No....	Yes.
7	No....	Yes...	Floor wet and littered with oyster shells.	Not since occupancy...	Yes...	No....	No....	Yes.
8	Yes...	Yes...	....	New building...........	No....	No....	No....	Yes.
9	Yes...	Yes...	....	When necessary........	Yes...	No....	Yes...	Yes.
10	Yes...	Yes...	....	Yearly................	Yes...	No....	No....	Yes.
11	Yes...	Yes...	....	.....do................	Yes...	No....	No....	Yes.
12	Yes...	No....	Stained with smoke and dirt.	(1)...................	No....	No....	No....	Yes.
13	Yes...	Yes...	....	When necessary........	Yes...	No....	No....	Yes.
14	Yes...	Yes...	....	.....do................	Yes...	No....	No....	Yes.
15	Yes...	Yes...	....	Once in 5 years.........	No....	Yes...	No....	Yes.
16	{1 no... / 3 yes..	}Yes...	{Floor in sirup department wet and uncared for.	}When necessary........	Yes...	No....	No....	No.
17	No....	No....	Accumulated dirt.....	(1)..................	Yes...	No....	No....	No.
18	No....	No....	Accumulated dirt and dust.	Yearly...............	Yes...	No....	No....	Yes.
19	Yes...	Yes...	....	3 times a year.........	Yes...	No....	No....	Yes.
20	Yes...	Yes...	....	Once in 2 or 3 years....	No....	Yes...	No....	Yes.
21	Yes...	Yes...	....	When necessary........	Yes...	No....	No....	Yes.
22	Yes...	No....	Dingy and dusty......	Once in 10 years........	No....	No....	No....	Yes.
23	Yes...	Yes...	....	Once in 5 years.........	No....	Yes...	Yes...	Yes.
24	Yes...	Yes...	....	Once in 2 years.........	No....	Yes...	No....	Yes.
25	Yes...	Yes...	....	When necessary........	No....	Yes...	No....	Yes.
26	Yes...	Yes...	....	.....do................	No....	No....	No....	Yes.
27	Yes...	Yes...	....	.....do................	No....	No....	No....	Yes.
28	Yes...	Yes...	....	.....do................	No....	No....	No....	Yes.
29	Yes...	Yes...	....	Yearly...............	No....	Yes...	No....	Yes.

1 Not reported.

TABLE VII.—VENTILATION: FRESH-AIR SUPPLY AND

MAINE.

Establishment number.	Appliances (other than windows and doors) for supplying fresh air.	Cubic feet of air space per person (in rooms which are most crowded).	Injurious or irritating dust in workrooms.	
			Kind.	Occupations affected.
1	None..................	2,000	Leather dust..............	Buffers, trimmers..............
2	Transoms................	1,365	.....do.....	Buffers..............
3	.....do.....	720	None..................	
4	.....do.....	350	Leather dust....	Trimmers and buffers....
5	Air shaft..............	390	Tobacco dust............	Strippers (principally)......
6	None..............	300	.....do.....	Strippers..............
7	.....do.....	465	None..................	
8	.....do.....	600	Starch dust..............	Cream molders..............
9	Blowers for cooling hard candy; pipes carrying refrigerated air into chocolate room.	1,800	.....do.....	Molders..............
10	Rotary fans..............	1,000	Flour dust..............	Men's occupations in bake room.
11	None..............	425	None..................	
12	.....do.....	450	.....do.....	
13	Air pipes and skylights..	671	.....do.....	
14	None..............	2,133	.....do.....	
15	.....do.....	1,800	.....do.....	
16	.....do.....	1,100	.....do.....	
17	.....do.....	1,575	.....do.....	
18	.....do.....	1,400	.....do.....	
19	.....do.....	714	.....do.....	
20	.....do.....	2,887	Lint..............	Carders..............
21	.....do.....	1,536	Dye powders..............	Dye mixers..............
22	.....do.....	1,200	Lint..............	Carders..............
23	.....do.....	2,848	Dust and lint..............	Shearers, dye mixers..............
24	.....do.....	2,285	None..................	
25	.....do.....	2,541	.....do.....	
26	.....do.....	2,744	Lint..............	Carders, picker tenders..........

MASSACHUSETTS.

1	None..................	1,000	Sawdust..................	Sawyers and planers..........
2	.....do.....	2,000	Dust from sandpapering machine and trimmer.	Sandpaper trimmers............
3	.....do.....	1,500	Tobacco dust..............	Cutters, feeders, machinists, and helpers on cigarette machines.
4	.....do.....	1,200	.....do.....	Cutters..............
5	.....do.....	1,000	.....do.....	Cutters, feeders, machinists, and helpers on machines.
6	.....do.....	384	None..............	
7	.....do.....	843	.....do.....	
8	.....do.....	1,008	.....do.....	
9	.....do.....	216	Starch dust..............	Cream molders..............
10	.....do.....	150	.....do.....	.....do.....
11	Ventilators, refrigerating plant.[2]	450	Starch and powdered sugar.	Cream molders, sugar bolters, lozenge makers.
12	None..............	800	Starch dust..............	Cream molders..............
13	.....do.....	480	.....do.....	Cream molders, starch blowers..
14	.....do.....	130	.....do.....	Cream molders..............
15	.....do.....	275	None..............	
16	Refrigerating plant.[2]	300	Starch dust..............	Cream molders..............
17	Intake fans..............	400	.....do.....	.....do.....
18	None..............	190	.....do.....	Molders..............
19	Fans..................	400	Cotton lint..............	Pickers, carders..............
20	Ventilators, fans, skylights, monitor roof.	1,080	Cotton lint and dust......	Openers, pickers, carders, and drawing-room occupations.
21	Fans..................	600	Cotton lint..............	Carders, weavers, drawers, spinners, and spoolers.
22	None..................	914	None..............	
23	Rotary fans..............	1,440	Flour dust..............	Men's occupations in bake room; flour sifters.
24	Monitor roofs, electric fans.	1,740	Sugar and cracker dust....	Sugar tenders, pulverizers, buffers.

[1] Not reported.

REMOVAL OF DUST AND FUMES FROM WORKROOMS.

MAINE.

Injurious or irritating fumes in workrooms.		Appliances for carrying off dust and fumes.		Establishment number.
Kind.	Occupations affected.	Kind.	In good order.	
None		Exhaust fans, hoods	Yes	1
...do		Exhaust fans	Yes	2
...do		Hoods and suction fans	Yes	3
...do		...do	Yes	4
...do		None		5
...do		...do		6
...do		...do		7
...do		...do		8
...do		...do		9
...do		Hoods and flues	Yes	10
Dye fumes	Dyers	None		11
None		...do		12
Fumes of sulphur and phosphorus.	Dippers and wrappers	Suction pipes	Yes	13
Animal glue	Enders, gluers, strippers	None		14
None		...do		15
Animal glue	Hand box-paperers	...do		16
None		...do		17
Animal glue	Glue-machine operators	...do		18
None		...do		19
Aniline dye	Dyehouse occupations	...do		20
...do	...do	Fans	Yes	21
...do	Dyers	None		22
Dye fumes	...do	...do		23
...do	Dyehouse and picker-room occupations.	...do		24
...do	Dyehouse and washer-room occupations.	Fans and hoods	Yes	25
Aniline dye	Dyehouse, picker-room, and finishing-room occupations.	None		26

MASSACHUSETTS.

None		Tube and suction fan	Yes	1
...do		None		2
...do		(¹)		3
...do		None		4
...do		...do		5
...do		...do		6
...do		...do		7
...do		...do		8
...do		...do		9
...do		...do		10
...do		...do		11
...do		...do		12
...do		...do		13
...do		...do		14
...do		...do		15
...do		...do		16
...do		...do		17
...do		...do		18
...do		Humidifiers, electric fans, ventilators.	Yes	19
...do		Hooded vents, rotary fans.	Yes	20
...do		None		21
Gas fumes	Oven tenders, mixers, peelers, and packers.	Flue from oven	Yes	22
None		Rotary fans, hoods on ovens.	Yes	23
...do		Hoods, exhaust fans	Yes	24

¹ In chocolate room.

TABLE **VII.**—VENTILATION: FRESH-AIR SUPPLY AND

MASSACHUSETTS—Concluded.

Establishment number.	Appliances (other than windows and doors) for supplying fresh air.	Cubic feet of air space per person (in rooms which are most crowded).	Injurious or irritating dust in workrooms.	
			Kind.	Occupations affected.
25	Skylights................	450	Flour dust................	Breakers................
26	Fans [1]................	650	None................	
27	Ventilators................	560	....do................	
28	None................	420	....do................	
29	....do................	300	....do.... .	
30	....do................	800	....do................	
31	....do................	250	....do................	
32	....do................	600	....do................	
33	....do................	624	....do................	
34	....do................	1,410	....do................	
35	....do................	750	....do................	
36	....do................	640	....do................	
37	....do................	400	....do................	
38	....do................	2,315	Wool lint................	Card-room hands................
39	....do................	1,969	....do................	Carders................
40	....do.[2]................	3,245	(3).	
41	Fans and ventilators....	1,585	Wool dust and lint........	Sorters, dusters, shearers, dye handlers.
42	None................	1,782	Wool lint................	Carders, dyers................
43	....do................	3,938	None................	
44	....do................	3,237	Lint................	Carders................

RHODE ISLAND.

1	None................	400	None................	
2	....do................	422	Tobacco dust............	Stock handlers (cellarmen)......
3	Air shaft.	833	Starch and dust sugar.....	Starch molders, lozenge makers .
4	Fans and transoms......	1,200	Lint, cotton dust..........	Carding-room hands............
5	Ventilating system with fans.	600	Cotton lint................	....do................
6	None................	2,000	....do................	Pickers, carders, speeders, spinners, doffers, sweepers, slubbers, drawing tenders.
7	Blower system..........	(3)	....do................	Pickers, carders, all occupations except those in cloth room.
8	None................	250	Lint................	Carding and picking room hands.
9	....do................	400	None................	
10	(3)................	1,400	....do................	
11	None................	2,000	....do................	
12	....do................	1,200	Lint................	1 brusher................
13	....do................	2,500	None................	
14	....do................	1,500	....do................	
15	Window ventilators.....	657	....do................	
16	Transoms................	1,575	....do................	
17	Exhaust fans, slanting window ventilators.	636	....do................	
18	Transoms................	532	....do................	
19	....do................	872	....do................	
20	Ventilators................	1,030	....do................	
21	Swinging windows......	1,000	....do................	
22	Roof ventilator..........	1,800	....do................	
23	....do................	3,000	....do................	
24	Skylights................	1,561	Lint................	Carders, spinners, drawers, speeders, twisters, shearers.
25	None................	887	Dust from shears..........	Shearers................
26	Fans in dye house.......	1,193	Lint................	Spinners, carders, drawers, spoolers, twisters, roller coverers.
27	Roof monitors	933	....do................	Carding-room hands............

[1] Used in connection with heating in winter.   [2] Windows nailed.

REMOVAL OF DUST AND FUMES FROM WORKROOMS—Continued.

MASSACHUSETTS—Concluded.

Injurious or irritating fumes in workrooms.		Appliances for carrying off dust and fumes.		Estab-lish-ment num-ber.
Kind.	Occupations affected.	Kind.	In good order.	
None	....	None..................	....	25
.....do.....................	....	.....do..................	....	26
.....do.....................	....	.....do..................	....	27
.....do.....................	....	.....do..................	....	28
.....do.....................	....	.....do..................	....	29
.....do.....................	....	.....do..................	....	30
.....do.....................	....	.....do..................	....	31
.....do.....................	....	.....do..................	....	32
Animal glue.................	Gluers, paperers, labelers, liners, cushioners, finishers.	.....do..................	....	33
.....do.....................	Paperers, toppers, trimmers, band-ers, stayers.	.....do..................	....	34
.....do.....................	Gluers, tenders, paperers, toppers, labelers, finishers, stayers.	.....do..................	....	35
Illuminating gas, animal glue.	Gluers, paperers, toppers, labelers, finishers, lappers.	.....do..................	....	36
Fumes from galvanizing and pickling.	Galvanizers.......................	Exhaust fans..........	Yes...	37
None.......................	....	None..................	....	38
.....do.....................	....	.....do..................	....	39
Fumes from dry finishing...	Dry finishers, burlers, and folders..	.....do..................	....	40
Sulphuric, acetic, tannic, and hydrochloric acid fumes.	Dyers, carbonizers................	Fans and roof ventila-tors.	Yes...	41
Aniline and alizarine dye fumes.	Dyers.............................	None..................	....	42
Aniline dye.................	.....do............................	.....do..................	....	43
Dye fumes..................	Wet finishers, steam pressers, dyers	.....do..................	....	44

RHODE ISLAND.

Kind.	Occupations affected.	Kind.	In good order.	Estab-lish-ment num-ber.
Tobacco....................	Stock handlers....................	None..................	....	1
.....do.....................	.....do...........................	.....do..................	....	2
None.......................	....	.....do..................	....	3
.....do.....................	....	.....do..................	....	4
.....do.....................	....	Humidifiers...........	Yes...	5
.....do.....................	....	Fans, humidifiers.....	Yes...	
.....do.....................	....	Hoods, fans...........	Yes...	7
Aniline dye fumes in dye-house.	Dyers.............................	Fan in dyehouse.......	Yes...	8
None.......................	....	None..................	....	9
.....do.....................	....	.....do..................	....	10
.....do.....................	....	.....do..................	....	11
Lime.......................	Bleachers.........................	.....do..................	....	12
None.......................	....	.....do..................	....	13
.....do.....................	....	.....do..................	....	14
Sulphuric, nitric, and mu-riatic acid.	Colorers..........................	Exhaust fans..........	Yes...	15
None.......................	....	Suction blower........	Yes...	16
Sulphuric and nitric acid, cyanide of potassium.	Colorers, colorers' helpers, polish-ers, platers, melters.	Exhaust blowers, blasts, and hoods.	Yes...	17
.....do.....................	Platers, melters, colorers, colorer's helpers.	Air blasts, exhaust fans, and hoods.	Yes...	18
Muriatic, nitric, and sul-phuric acid.	Colorers and colorers' helpers......	Exhaust shaft and Sturtevant system.	(4)....	19
Animal glue.................	Paperers..........................	None..................	....	20
.....do.....................	.....do...........................	.....do..................	....	21
None.......................	....	(2)...................	(2)...	22
Animal glue.................	Paperers..........................	Roof ventilators.......	Yes...	23
Dye fumes..................	Dyers.............................	Fans in dyehouse......	Yes...	24
Alizarine dye...............	Dyehouse hands...................	Hoods.................	Yes...	25
.....do.....................	Dyers.............................	Fans in dyehouse......	Yes...	26
Aniline and alizarine dye fumes.	.....do............................	None..................	....	27

: Not reported.   4 Sturtevant system, yes; exhaust shaft, no.

TABLE **VII.**—VENTILATION: FRESH-AIR SUPPLY AND

CONNECTICUT.

Es-tab-lish-ment num-ber.	Appliances (other than windows and doors) for supplying fresh air.	Cubic feet of air space per person (in rooms which are most crowded).	Injurious or irritating dust in workrooms.	
			Kind.	Occupations affected.
1	None.....................	1,988	Dust from emery wheels and pouring molten brass.	Buffers, polishers, casters, and helpers.
2	Ventilators.............	540	Tobacco dust..............	Cigar makers....................
3	Ventilator and air shaft.	650	....do.........	....do......................
4	Ventilating fans [1]........	345	Dust from saws and wood turning machines.	Sawyers, buffers, wood turners..
5	None....................	2,184	None......................	
6	....do.....................	430	....do....................	
7	....do.....................	1,609	....do............	
8	....do.....................	460	....do....................	
9	Skylights, suction fan, and pipes.	300	....do....................	
10	None....................	300	Metal dust from tumblers, cotton dust from buffers.	Buffers, tumbling-machine oper-ators.
11	....do.....................	300	None......................	
12	Skylights................	600	....do....................	
13	None....................	1,000	Scale from tumblers........	Tumblers....................
14	....do.....................	1,065	None......................	
15	....do.....................	985	....do....................	
16	....do.....................	1,367	....do....................	
17	....do.....................	1,362	Dust from rolling barrels...	Rolling-barrel operators........
18	Blower in connection with heating plant.	950	None......................	
19	None....................	2,000	....do....................	
20	....do.....................	1,500	....do....................	
21	Ventilators..............	600	....do....................	
22	None....................	450	....do....................	
23	....do.....................	460	....do....................	
24	....do.....................	677	....do....................	
25	....do.....................	672	....do....................	
26	....do.....................	1,000	....do....................	
27	....do.....................	690	....do....................	
28	Ventilators..............	1,067	....do....................	
29	None....................	1,200	....do....................	
30	....do.....................	3,000	....do....................	
31	....do.....................	600	Dust from polishing and buffing wheels.	Polishers and buffers..........
32	....do.....................	380	None......................	
33	Skylights................	1,500	Sulphur....................	Rubber mixers................
34	Ventilators [3]............	800	None......................	
35	Exhaust fans............	825	....do....................	

NEW YORK.

1	None....................	800	Dust from buffing wheel..	Buffers....................
2	....do.....................	700	None......................	
3	None [5]....................	350	....do....................	
4	None....................	280	....do....................	
5	....do.....................	250	....do....................	
6	Suction fan.............	600	....do....................	
7	None....................	120	....do....................	
8	....do.....................	400	....do....................	
9	....do.....................	800	....do....................	
10	....do.....................	600	....do....................	
11	....do.....................	1,000	Cotton lint..............	Carders, winders, **spinners** speeders.
12	....do.....................	3,000	None......................	
13	....do.....................	1,000	....do....................	
14	Skylights and pipe ven-tilators.	1,000	....do....................	
15	Skylights................	1,400	....do....................	
16	Fans....................	600	....do....................	

[1] In 1 of the 3 buildings.　　　[2] Not reported.　　　[3] In 1 of the 2 buildings.

REMOVAL OF DUST AND FUMES FROM WORKROOMS—Continued.

CONNECTICUT.

Injurious or irritating fumes in workrooms.		Appliances for carrying off dust and fumes.		Establishment number.
Kind.	Occupations affected.	Kind.	In good order.	
Steam and gases 'rom plating and lacquering vats; fumes from molten brass.	Platers, dippers, lacquerers, casters, and their helpers.	Exhaust fans	Yes	1
None		Ventilators	Yes	2
....do		Ventilators and air shafts.	Yes	3
Varnish and japan	Platers, japanners, lacquerers	Suction fans and exhaust pipes.	Yes	4
None		Exhaust fans	Yes	5
....do		....do	Yes	6
Gases from plating and lacquering vats.	Platers and lacquerers	....do	Yes	7
None		....do	Yes	8
....do		None		9
....do		Hoods and suction system.	No	10
....do		None		11
....do		....do		12
Gas from japan drier	Japanners	Exhaust fans	No	13
None		....do	Yes	14
....do		None		15
....do		....do		16
....do		Exhaust fans	Yes	17
Fumes from plating and lacquering vats.	Platers and lacquerers, and their helpers.	....do	Yes	18
(¹)	(²)	....do	Yes	19
Gases from plating vats and from tinning and japanning.	Tinners, platers, japanners, and their helpers.	....do	Yes	20
None		None		21
....do		....do		22
Acid fumes	Baggers	....do		23
None		....do		24
....do		....do		25
....do		Blowers and exhaust fans.	Yes	26
....do		Exhaust fans	Yes	27
None		None		28
....do		Exhaust fans	Yes	29
....do		None		30
....do		....do		31
....do		Ventilating fans	Yes	32
Sulphur	Vulcanizers	Exhaust fans	Yes	33
None		Ventilating fans ³	Yes	34
....do		Exhaust fans	Yes	35

NEW YORK.

Acid fumes	Platers and their helpers	None		1
Gas from soldering	Solderers and helpers	None ⁴		2
None		Hoods	Yes	3
....do		None		4
....do		....do		5
....do		....do		6
....do		....do		7
....do		Suction fans	Yes	8
....do		None		9
....do		....do		10
....do		Humidifiers	Yes	11
....do		None		1:
....do		Suction fan and pipes.	Yes	13
....do		None		14
....do		....do		15
....do		....do		16

⁴ Exhaust plant is being installed.   ⁵ Ventilating system is being installed.

TABLE **VII.**—VENTILATION: FRESH-AIR SUPPLY AND

NEW YORK—Concluded.

Establishment number.	Appliances (other than windows and doors) for supplying fresh air.	Cubic feet of air space per person (in rooms which are most crowded).	Injurious or irritating dust in workrooms.	
			Kind.	Occupations affected.
17	None	451	Cotton lint	Knitters and winders
18	....do	600	....do	....do
19	....do	670	None	
20	....do	725	Cotton and wool lint	Sorters, carders, spinners, mixers, etc.
21	....do	600	Cotton lint	Brushers, knitters, winders
22	....do	300	Cotton lint and dust	Pickers, carders, knitters
23	....do	400	Rouge	Grinders, polishers, buffers
24	....do	2,000	None	
25	....do	540	....do	
26	....do	1,000	....do	
27	....do	1,000	....do	
28	....do	1,000	....do	
29	....do	600	....do	
30	....do	4,000	....do	
31	....do	1,000	....do	
32	Window ventilators	3,750	....do	
33	None	2,000	....do	
34	Ventilators in air shaft	600	....do	
35	None	784	....do	
36	....do	780	....do	

NEW JERSEY.

1	Ventilators, suction fans	2,000	None	
2	Ventilators	770	....do	
3	None	200	....do	
4	....do	500	....do	
5	Suction fans	400	....do	
6	None	250	....do	
7	....do	900	Lint	Brushers, carders, pickers
8	....do	1,500	....do	Fleecers
9	....do	600	Cotton lint	Fleecers, knitting machine operators.
10	Ceiling ventilators	500	None	
11	None	1,000	Flour dust	Paste mixers
12	....do	900	Refuse and dust at tube-cutting machine.	Tube cutters
13	....do	4,000	None	
14	....do	1,200	....do	
15	....do	1,000	....do	
16	....do	1,200	Clay and flint dust	Clay mixers, sand blasters, brushers, polishers.
17	....do	1,500	Clay dust	Cleaners
18	....do	1,200	Clay and flint dust	Clay mixers, brushers, dressers
19	....do	1,500	....do	Brushers, stoppers, slip makers
20	....do	1,500	....do	Mixers, brushers, dressers
21	....do	1,000	Soap-powder dust	Packers of soap powder
22	....do	300	Sawdust	Cleaners
23	....do	600	None	
24	Ventilators and suction fans.	4,600	....do	
25	Fans and ventilators	3,400	(1)	
26	....do	5,000	None	
27	Fans in dyehouse	6,000	Carbonizing	Rag sorters

1 For some.

REMOVAL OF DUST AND FUMES FROM WORKROOMS—Continued.

NEW YORK—Concluded.

Injurious or irritating fumes in workrooms.		Appliances for carrying off dust and fumes.		Establishment number.
Kind.	Occupations affected.	Kind.	In good order.	
None		None		17
....do		....do		18
....do		....do		19
Sulphur fumes	Washers and boarders	....do		20
None		....do		21
....do		....do		22
Nitric acid	Polishers, lacquerers	Hoods [1]	Yes	23
None		None		24
....do		....do		25
....do		....do		26
....do		....do		27
....do		....do		28
....do		(1)		29
....do		None		30
....do		....do		31
....do		....do		32
....do		Suction fans	Yes	33
....do		None		34
....do		Suction fans	Yes	35
....do		None		36

NEW JERSEY.

Injurious or irritating fumes in workrooms.		Appliances for carrying off dust and fumes.		Establishment number.
Kind.	Occupations affected.	Kind.	In good order.	
None		None		1
....do		....do		2
....do		....do		3
....do		....do		4
....do		....do		5
....do		....do		6
....do		....do		7
....do		....do		8
....do		....do		9
....do		....do		10
....do		....do		11
....do		....do		12
....do		....do		13
....do		....do		14
....do		Exhaust pipes	Yes	15
....do		None		16
....do		....do		17
....do		....do		18
....do		....do		19
....do		Hood for polishing machine.	Yes	20
....do		None		21
Sulphuric acid	Picklers and scrubbers	Ventilators	Yes	22
None		None		23
....do		Suction fans	Yes	24
....do		None		25
....do		....do		26
....do		Dust collector and fans	Yes	27

[1] Not reported.

TABLE **VII.**—VENTILATION: FRESH-AIR SUPPLY AND

PENNSYLVANIA.

Establishment number.	Appliances (other than windows and doors) for supplying fresh air.	Cubic feet of air space per person (in rooms which are most crowded).	Injurious or irritating dust in workrooms.	
			Kind.	Occupations affected.
1	Ventilators, b l o w e r s, and exhaust fans.	1,000	None	
2	None	1,000	....do	
3	Exhaust fan	1,000	....do	
4	None	800	Sawdust	Sawyers
5	Ventilators	1,500	None	
6	None	500	....do	
7	....do	500	....do	
8	....do	500	....do	
9	....do	750	....do	
10	....do	1,000	....do	
11	....do	1,000	....do	
12	....do	500	Tobacco dust	Preparers (for bunching machines).
13	....do	500	None	
14	....do	900	....do	
15	Exhaust fans and ventilators.	1,300	....do	
16	Draft fans	2,000	....do	
17	Exhaust fans	2,000	....do	
18	None	(¹)	None [2]	
19	....do	700	None	
20	....do	1,200	....do	
21	....do	1,000	....do	
22	Skylight	3,500	Flour dust	Breakers, bag cleaners
23	None	1,000	None	
24	....do	300	....do	
25	Exhaust fans	1,000	....do	
26	None	1,000	....do	
27	....do	400	....do	
28	....do	1,000	....do	
29	....do	1,000	....do	
30	(¹)	700	Lint	Oxidizing and singeing occupations.
31	Ventilators	400	None	
32	None	700	Dust from oxidizing	Oxidizing occupations
33	....do	600	Lint	Fleecing, winding, knitting
34	....do	800	None	
35	Intake and exhaust fans. roof ventilators, and pipes.	1,500	....do	
36	Ventilators	2,500	....do	
37	None	1,000	Iron dust [2]	Polishers [2]
38	....do	1,500	None	
39	....do	900	Paper dust [2]	Cutters and scorers [2]
40	....do	900	Bronze composition	Embossers, bronzers
41	....do	900	None	
42	....do	1,200	Clay and glass dust	Pressers, brushers, dippers, mixers.
43	....do	1,200	....do	Pressers, brushers
44	....do	1,200	None	
45	....do	1,200	....do	
46	....do	Over 500	Metal dust	Polishers, scratchers
47	....do	1,000	None	
48	Belt fans, roof sashes	2,000	....do	
49	Fans in dyehouse	1,500	....do	
50	Fans	1,400	....do	

¹ Not reported.   ² In departments where women are employed.

REMOVAL OF DUST AND FUMES FROM WORKROOMS—Continued.

PENNSYLVANIA.

Injurious or irritating fumes in workrooms.		Appliances for carrying off dust and fumes.		Establishment number.
Kind.	Occupations affected.	Kind.	In good order.	
None.........................	....	None...............	....	1
.....do........		.....do.............	....	2
.....do.........		.....do..........	....	3
.....do.........		Suction fans..........	Yes....	4
.....do.........		None..........	....	5
.....do.........		.....do..........	....	6
.....do.........		.....do..........	....	7
.....do.........		.....do..........	....	8
.....do.........		.....do..........	....	9
.....do.........		.....do..........	....	10
.....do.........		.....do..........	....	11
.....do.........		.....do..........	....	12
.....do.........		.....do..........	....	13
.....do.........		.....do..........	....	14
.....do..,		.....do..........	....	15
.....do.........		.....do..........	....	16
.....do.........		.....do..........	....	17
None [a]..........		.....do..........	....	18
Smoke from coke ovens.....	Core makers.....................	.....do..........	....	19
.....do.........	.....do...............	.....do..........	....	20
Copper, zinc................	Brass-molding occupations........	Canopy over furnace..	Yes....	21
None..........		None..........	....	22
.....do.........		Hoods over ovens.....	Yes....	23
.....do.........		Hoods over ovens, exhaust fans.	Yes....	24
.....do.........		.....do..........	Yes....	25
.....do.........		Hoods over ovens.....	Yes....	26
.....do.........		.....do..........	Yes....	27
.....do.........		.....do..........	Yes....	28
.....do.........		.....do..........	Yes....	29
.....do.........		Power ventilators.....	Yes....	30
.....do.........		None..........	....	31
Gas from oxidizing...........	Oxidizing and pressing occupations.	.....do..........	....	32
None..........		.....do..........	....	33
.....do.........		.....do..........	....	34
Phosphorus..................	Mixers.....................	Exhaust fans..........	Yes....	35
None..........		.....do..........	Yes....	36
.....do.........		Suction fans..........	Yes....	37
.....do.........		None..........	....	38
.....do.........		.....do..........	....	39
.....do.........		.....do..........	....	40
.....do.........		.....do..........	....	41
.....do.........		.....do..........	....	42
.....do.........		.....do..........	....	43
Muriatic acid...............	Picklers	Exhaust chimney.....	Yes....	44
Sulphuric and muriatic acid.	Galvanizers, picklers.............	Suction fan..........	Yes....	45
None..........		Hood on polishing wheel.	Yes....	46
.....do.........		None..........	....	47
Dyeing chemicals............	Dyehouse occupations	Belt fans..............	Yes....	48
.....do.........	.....do.............	Fans in dyehouse.....	Yes....	49
None.		None..........	....	50

[a] To very limited extent.

TABLE **VII.**—VENTILATION: FRESH-AIR SUPPLY AND

OHIO.

Establishment number.	Appliances (other than windows and doors) for supplying fresh air.	Cubic feet of air space per person (in rooms which are most crowded).	Injurious or irritating dust in workrooms.	
			Kind. .	Occupations affected.
1	None	1,000	None	
2	....do	1,000	....do	
3	....do	240	....do	
4	....do	500	....do	
5	....do	1,000	....do	
6	Ventilators	1,000	....do	
7	None	1,000	....do	
8	....do	1,000	....do	
9	....do	1,000	....do	
10	....do	800	....do	
11	....do	1,000	....do	
12	....do	850	....do	
13	....do	800	....do	
14	....do	800	....do	
15	....do	800	....do	
16	Exhaust fans	800	....do	
17	Suction and exhaust fans.	400	....do	
18	None	1,000	....do	
19	....do	600	....do	
20	....do	500	....do	
21	....do	2,000	....do	
22	....do	2,500	....do	
23	Fan	1,500	....do	
24	None	900	....do	
25	....do	1,200	....do	
26	....do	1,500	....do	
27	....do	3,000	Lint	Fleecers.
28	....do	800	None	
29	Roof ventilators, suction fans, and blowers.	1,000	....do	
30	Monitor ventilator and suction fans.	1,000	....do	
31	Roof ventilator and suction fans.	1,500	....do	
32	None	1,000	....do	
33	....do	500	....do	
34	....do	900	....do	
35	....do	800	....do	
36	....do	1,000	....do	
37	....do	1,000	....do	
38	....do	1,000	....do	
39	....do	400	....do	
40	....do	900	....do	
41	....do	1,000	Clay, sand, straw, and lead.	Pressers, brushers, packers
42	....do	1,200	Clay, sand, straw	....do
43	....do	900	Clay, flint, straw	Pressers, brushers, packers, clay mixers.
44	....do	800	Clay, sand, straw	Pressers, brushers, packers
45	....do	1,200	Iron, enamel	Mixers, dippers, scalers, stampers.
46	Drying apparatus	1,500	....do	Mixers, scalers, scrap balers
47	None	1,200	....do	Mixers, dippers, scalers, stampers.
48	....do	1,200	....do	....do
49	....do	1,500	....do	....do
50	....do	1,000	None	
51	....do	1,000	....do	
52	....do	1,000	....do	
53	Suction fans	1,000	....do	
54	Fans	1,500	....do	
55	None	1,000	....do	
56	Fans and roof	800	Rag sorting	Rag sorters, dusters, and carbonizers.
57	Ventilators	1,000	None	
58	Fans	1,000	....do	
59	Fans and ventilators	2,000	....do	
60	None	2,000	....do	

¹ Not all of them.

REMOVAL OF DUST AND FUMES FROM WORKROOMS—Continued.

OHIO.

Injurious or irritating fumes in workrooms.		Appliances for carrying off dust and fumes.		Establishment number.
Kind.	Occupations affected.	Kind.	In good order.	
None........................	....	Suction pipe over circular saw.	Yes...	1
....do........................		Exhaust pipes........	Yes..	2
....do........................		None...............	....	3
....do........................		....do.............	Yes...	4
....do........................		Exhaust pipes........	Yes...	5
....do........................		None...............	....	6
....do........................		....do.............	....	7
....do........................		....do.............	....	8
....do........................		....do.............	....	9
....do........................		....do.............	....	10
....do........................		....do.............	....	11
....do........................		Exhaust fans........	Yes...	12
....do........................		....do.............	Yes...	13
....do........................		....do.............	Yes...	14
....do........................		....do.............	Yes...	15
....do........................		Shafts over kettles....	Yes...	16
....do........................		....do.............	Yes...	17
....do........................		Hoods over ovens......	Yes...	18
....do........................		....do.............	Yes...	19
....do........................		Exhaust fans and hoods over ovens.	Yes...	20
....do........................		Hoods over ovens.....	Yes...	21
....do........................		None...............	....	22
....do........................		....do.............	....	23
....do........................		....do.............	....	24
....do........................		....do.............	....	25
....do........................		....do.............	....	26
....do........................		....do.............	....	27
....do........................		....do.............	....	28
Match composition..........	Mixers................	Exhaust fans........	Yes...	29
None........................		Exhaust fans and pipes.	Yes...	30
Burning matches..........	Plate punchers, composition mixers, fillers, and packers.	Suction fans..........	Yes...	31
None........................		None...............	....	32
●..do........................		....do.............	....	33
....do........................		Exhaust fans..........	Yes...	34
....do........................		None...............	....	35
....do........................		....do.............	....	36
....do........................		Exhaust fans over saw.	Yes...	37
....do........................		Suction pipe over saw.	Yes...	38
....do........................		None...............	....	39
....do........................		Exhaust pipes........	Yes...	40
....do........................		None...............	....	41
....do........................		....do.............	....	42
....do........................		....do.............	....	43
....do........................		....do.............	....	44
Sulphuric acid............	Picklers..............	....do.............	....	45
Muriatic acid............	....do.............	....do.............	....	46
Sulphuric and muriatic acids	Picklers, galvanizers..............	....do.............	....	47
Sulphuric acid............	Picklers..............	....do.............	....	48
....do........................	....do.............	....do.............	....	49
None........................		....do.............	....	50
....do........................		....do.............	....	51
....do........................		Exhaust fan........	Yes...	52
....do........................		....do.............	Yes...	53
....do........................		Fans................	Yes...	54
Dyehouse steam and carbonizing fumes.	Dyehouse and carbonizing room employees.	Fans and ventilators..	Yes...	55
Dye and carbonizing fumes..	Dyers and carbonizers..............	Fans................	(1).....	56
None........................		None...............	....	57
Dye fumes.................	Dyehouse hands..........	Fans and blower......	Yes...	58
Dyeing and carbonizing fumes.	Dyers and carbonizers..............	Fans................	Yes...	59
Carbonizing fumes..........	Carbonizer employees..............	Fans and ventilators..	Yes...	60

TABLE **VII.**—VENTILATION: FRESH-AIR SUPPLY AND

ILLINOIS.

Establishment number.	Appliances (other than windows and doors) for supplying fresh air.	Cubic feet of air space per person (in rooms which are most crowded).	Injurious or irritating dust in workrooms.	
			Kind.	Occupations affected.
1	None	(1)	None	
2	....do	400	....do	
3	Air conduit	2,000	Fiber dust	Openers, preparers, spinners, rope makers.
4	None	1,000	None	
5	....do	1,000	Sugar dust [1]	Chewing-gum makers, kneaders, rollers, cutters.
6	Skylight	1,000	....do.[1]	All in manufacturing department.
7	None	600	Tobacco dust	Cigar makers, strippers, fillers...
8	....do	660	....do	Strippers, selectors, rollers, bunch makers.
9	....do	1,000	....do	Rollers, strippers, bunch makers, stock boy.
10	....do	400	None	
11	....do	1,000	....do	
12	....do	534	....do	
13	....do	220	Starch dust	Starch-room workers
14	Suction fan, pipes, skylights.	500	Particles from buffing, dust from mixture.	Buffers, core makers, patchers, wire cutters, takers-out.
15	Skylights	1,000	Dust from mixture	All in core room.
16	Fans, exhaust pipes, skylights.	400	Dust carried by smoke....	....do
17	Fans, skylights	800	....do	....do
18	....do	400	....do	....do
19	Screen supplied with water, skylights.	350	None	
20	None	6,000	Flour dust	Bag cleaner, breaker
21	....do	1,000	....do	Bakers, mixers, rollers
22	....do	1,000	....do	Mixers
23	....do	600	None	
24	....do	600	....do	
25	Fans	1,540	....do	
26	None	1,000	Metallic dust	Wire workers
27	....do	550	Wool and cotton dust	Knitters and winders
28	....do	2,750	None	
29	....do	600	Wool dust and lint	Carders, sorters, pickers
30	Suction fan	900	None	
31	....do	500	Dust from wood and composition.	Cleaning-machine tenders, levelers, straighteners, etc.
32	None	1,000	None	
33	....do	400	....do	
34	....do	500	....do	
35	....do	1,000	....do	
36	....do	800	....do	
37	....do	250	....do	
38	....do	500	Dust from packing material, enamel, sawdust, etc.	Dippers, burners, **polishers**, packers, putting **ware on** racks.
39	Suction fan	2,500	Dust from enamel	Mixers, burners
40	None	565	None	
41	....do	1,200	....do	
42	....do	1,000	....do	
43	....do	423	Tobacco dust	Sorters, loaders, sweepers, etc...
44	....do	936	....do	Sorters, grinders, cutters
45	....do	1,200	Wool dust and lint	Carders
46	....do	1,426	....do	Carders, pickers, spinners, spoolers, shearers.
47	Sturtevant heating and ventilating system.	1,500	Wool dust	Pickers

[1] Over 1,000.

REMOVAL OF DUST AND FUMES FROM WORKROOMS—Continued.

ILLINOIS.

Injurious or irritating fumes in workrooms.		Appliances for carrying off dust and fumes.		Establishment number.
Kind.	Occupations affected.	Kind.	In good order.	
None....................		None....................	....	1
.....do................		.....do...............	....	2
.....do................		Suction fan in opening department.	Yes...	3
.....do................		None....................	....	4
.....do................		.....do...............	....	5
.....do................		.....do...............	....	6
.....do................		.....do...............	....	7
Tobacco................	Casers....................	.....do...............	....	8
None....................		.....do...............	....	9
Sulphuric and nitric acid....	Employees in gilding and dial departments.	Suction fans...........	Yes...	10
None....................		None....................	....	11
.....do................		.....do...............	....	12
.....do................		.....do...............	....	13
.....do................		Suction fans and pipes.	Yes...	14
Smoke and fumes from ovens	All in core room..............	None....................	....	15
Smoke from oil, resin, etc....	.....do.................	Exhaust pipes........	Yes...	16
Smoke and fumes from oven.	.....do.................	Fans and exhaust pipes.	Yes...	17
.....do................	.....do.................	Fans..................	Yes...	18
None....................		None....................	....	19
.....do................		.....do...............	....	20
.....do................		.....do...............	....	21
Gas.....................	Packers, labelers, bakers, wrappers, etc.	.....do...............	....	22
None....................		.....do...............	....	23
.....do................		.....do...............	....	24
.....do................		.....do...............	....	25
Sulphuric acid..............	Picklers, galvanizers..............	Ventilator in roof......	Yes...	26
None....................		None....................	....	27
.....do................		.....do...............	....	28
Dyes....................	Dyers....................	.....do...............	....	29
.....do................	.....do.................	.....do...............	....	30
Composition..............	Mixers, feeders, kettle tenders, packers, wrappers, etc.	.....do...............	....	31
None....................		.....do...............	....	32
.....do................		.....do...............	....	33
.....do................		.....do...............	....	34
.....do................		.....do...............	....	35
.....do................		.....do...............	....	36
Odors of soap, lye, and perfumes.	All....................	.....do...............	....	37
Pickling acid, paints, japanning materials, etc.	Picklers, polishers, painters, solderers.	.....do...............	....	38
Muriatic acid..............	Picklers....................	.....do...............	....	39
Paint....................	Lithographing, decorating........	.....do...............	....	40
Gas, rosin, solder..........	Solderers....................	.....do...............	....	41
None....................		.....do...............	....	42
Sirup of chemicals..........	Casers, cutters, mixers, sweeteners.	.....do...............	....	43
Ammonia..................	Mixers, packers, labelers, coverers.	.....do...............	....	44
None....................		.....do...............	....	45
Soap and dyes.............	Fullers, washers, dyers..........	.....do...............	....	46
Dye fumes.................	Fullers, scourers, dyers..........	Fans and pipes........	Yes...	47

2 Claimed not to be injurious.

TABLE **VII.**—VENTILATION: FRESH-AIR SUPPLY AND

INDIANA.

Establishment number.	Appliances (other than windows and doors) for supplying fresh air.	Cubic feet of air space per person (in rooms which are most crowded).	Injurious or irritating dust in workrooms.	
			Kind.	Occupations affected.
1	None	1,500	None	
2	....do	750	Sawdust	Sawyers and children helping; laborers.
3	....do	1,000	None	
4	....do	400	Dust from sawing and sandpapering and from emery wheels.	All smith work, sandpaperers...
5	....do	500	Metal dust	Drillers
6	....do	1,000	....do	Polishers
7	....do	400	None	
8	....do	400	....do	
9	....do	500	....do	
10	....do	350	....do	
11	Roof ventilator	520	Tobacco dust	Strippers, rollers, bunch makers, banders.
12	Skylights	500	Steel dust	Grinders
13	None	500	None	
14	....do	542	....do	
15	....do	500	Starch dust	Candy starchers
16	....do	500	....do	....do
17	Skylights	400	None	
18	None	1,800	....do	
19	1 fan on second floor	2,500	....do	
20	None	500	....do	
21	Ventilating fans	1,150	Metal dust	Buffers, lathe hands
22	None	1,000	None	
23	....do	480	Sawdust and sandpaper	Millers, facers
24	....do	600	Cotton lint	Sewers and cutters
25	....do	320	Cotton lint	Glove makers and turners
26	Suction fans	670	None	
27	None	1,000	....do	
28	....do	500	Lint	Pickers, carders, and spinners...
29	....do	250	Sawdust and chemicals	Splint cleaners, mixers
30	....do	500	None	
31	....do	500	....do	
32	....do	3,000	....do	
33	....do	500	....do	
34	1 ventilator on second floor.	900	....do	
35	None	1,000	Shell dust	Cutters, grinders, and machine operators.
36	....do	500	Dust from buffers	Buffers
37	Roof ventilator	1,000	Dust from enamel, coal smoke.	Dippers, brushers
38	Suction fan	550	None	
39	None	400	....do	
40	....do	500	Soda ash	Carton-machine operators, powder packers.
41	Suction pipes	450	Sawdust, sand, enamel dust, smoke.	Sand blasters, dippers, furnace men, polishers, etc.
42	Fans	600	None	
43	None	800	Bran and sawdust	Plate wipers
44	....do	500	Wood dust	Sawyers, planers, turners, sanders.
45	....do	1,000	Lint from wool	Spoolers, spinners, carders, weavers.
46	....do	500	Wool dust and dust from compound lint.	Pickers, sorters, carders, compounders.
47	....do	500	Lint from wool	Spinners and carders.

REMOVAL OF DUST AND FUMES FROM WORKROOMS—Continued.

INDIANA.

Injurious or irritating fumes in workrooms.		Appliances for carrying off dust and fumes.		Establishment number.
Kind.	Occupations affected.	Kind.	In good order.	
None		None		1
....do		....do		2
....do		....do		3
Smoke, odor of paint, turpentine, etc.	All	....do		4
None		....do		5
....do		Exhaust hoods	No	6
Tobacco and rum	All	None		7
Tobacco	Strippers, packers	....do		8
Tobacco and rum	Bunch breakers, rollers, packers	....do		9
None		....do		10
....do		Roof ventilator	Yes	11
Benzine	All	Exhaust hoods	Yes	12
None		None		13
....do		....do		14
....do		....do		15
....do		Exhaust fans	Yes	16
Fumes from baked cores	Coremakers	Roof windows	Yes	17
None		None		18
....do		....do		19
....do		....do		20
Acid fumes	Dippers and platers	Exhaust fans	Yes	21
None		None		22
Wood alcohol	Pasters, steamers	Hoods and exhaust fans	Yes	23
None		None		24
....do		....do		25
....do		....do		26
....do		....do		27
Dye and sulphuric acid	Dyers and carbonizers	Fan in roof	Yes	28
Phosphorus, match composition.	Mixers, wrappers, packers, etc	None		29
None		....do		30
....do		....do		31
....do		....do		32
....do		....do		33
...do		....do		34
....do		Suction fans	Yes	35
Etching mixture	Etchers	None		36
Gold paint	Decorators	Roof ventilators	Yes	37
None		None		38
...do		....do		39
...do		....do		40
Acid fumes	Picklers	Exhaust fans	Yes	41
Tinning solutions and gas	Tin platers, molders, mold handlers, cap washers, etc.	None		42
Lead, tallow, acid, smoke	Plate wipers, tin platers	Hoods and exhaust pipes.	No	43
Paint and varnish	Painters, dippers, truckers	Exhaust pipes	Yes	44
Fumes from dye vat	Dyers, etc	None		45
Benzine, gums, and dyes	Washers, wringers, fullers, grinders, rollers, dyers, felters, etc.	Exhaust pipes	Yes	46
None		None		47

TABLE **VII.**—VENTILATION: FRESH-AIR SUPPLY AND

MICHIGAN.

Establishment number.	Appliances (other than windows and doors) for supplying fresh air.	Cubic feet of air space per person (in rooms which are most crowded).	Injurious or irritating dust in workrooms.	
			Kind.	Occupations affected.
1	Ventilating fans	1,000	None	
2	None	400	....do	
3	....do	(1)	Sawdust	Sawyers and planers
4	....do	660	Tobacco	Rollers, strippers, bunch makers.
5	Ventilating tube	(1)	Starch	Cream-candy makers
6	None	(1)	Starch and flour	....do
7	....do	500	None	
8	Fans	300	Paper and fiber lint, and dust.	Tube winders and cutters
9	None	(1)	None	
10	....do	(1)	....do	
11	Transoms	(1)	Cotton lint and sawdust	Carders, spinners, sawyers
12	Pipes and fans	800	Sawdust	Block removers
13	None	400	None	
14	....do	(1)	....do	
15	....do	(1)	....do	
16	....do	900	Tobacco	All
17	Fans [2]	450	....do	All
18	None	500	Lint and particles of wool.	Carders, spinners, and spoolers.
19	....do	500	Lint from cards	Carders

WISCONSIN.

1	None	500	None	
2	....do	500	....do	
3	Skylights	1,925	....do	
4	None	250	....do	
5	Ventilators	576	....do	
6	None	445	....do	
7	....do	400	....do	
8	Blower system	400	....do	
9	Sturtevant blower system.	1,000	....do	
10	None	1,000	....do	
11	Air pipes, ventilators	1,000	Sawdust	Sawyers, block sorters
12	None	350	Dust from rags	Rag sorters and overlookers
13	....do	324	None	
14	....do	700	Enamel dust, packing hay, dust from mold making.	Dippers, packers
15	....do	500	Bran	Cleaners
16	....do	286	None	
17	....do	285	....do	
18	Overhead ventilators	1,547	....do	
19	Cupolas	954	....do	

MARYLAND.

1	None	500	None	
2	....do	625	....do	
3	....do	692	....do	
4	....do	1,000	....do	
5	Skylights	2,000	....do	
6	None	1,000	....do	
7	....do	650	....do	
8	....do	1,600	....do	
9	....do	700	....do	
10	Exhaust	416	....do	
11	Fans and exhaust	475	....do	

[1] Over 1,000; exact number of cubic feet not reported.

REMOVAL OF DUST AND FUMES FROM WORKROOMS—Continued.

MICHIGAN.

Injurious or irritating fumes in workrooms.		Appliances for carrying off dust and fumes.		Estab-lishment number.
Kind.	Occupations affected.	Kind.	In good order.	
None..........................	....	Exhaust fan.............	Yes...	1
Soldering machines and paints.	Solderers, dippers, painters.......	None......................	....	2
None..........................	....	Hoods and exhaust fans.	Yes...	3
.....do.......................	....	None......................	....	4
.....do.......................	....	.....do...................	....	5
.....do.......................	....	.....do...................	....	6
Steam and odor from irons..	Pressers....................	Exhaust fans and pipes	Yes...	7
Glue..........................	Winders, gluers, and machine hands.	None......................	....	8
None..........................	....	.....do...................	....	9
Dye fumes....................	Dyehouse hands....................	Exhaust fan...........	Yes...	10
Chloride of lime..............	Bleachers............................	Hoods and exhaust fans.	Yes...	11
Match composition...........	Packers, wrappers, machine feeders, etc.	Fans on match machines.	Yes...	12
.....do.......................	All....................................	Fans on shafts.........	Yes...	13
None..........................	....	None......................	....	14
.....do.......................	....	.....do...................	....	15
Tobacco and flavoring materials.	Mixers and soakers................	Dust collectors and exhaust fans.	Yes...	16
None..........................	....	None......................	....	17
Dye fumes....................	Dyers, scourers, fullers..........	Fans and skylights....	Yes...	18
Dye fumes, etc...............	Dyers, scourers, washers, etc......	None......................	....	19

WISCONSIN.

None.......................	....	None......................	....	1
.....do....................	....	.....do...................	....	2
.....do....................	....	.....do...................	....	3
.....do....................	....	.....do...................	....	4
.....do....................	....	.....do...................	....	5
.....do....................	....	.....do...................	....	6
.....do....................	....	.....do...................	....	7
.....do....................	....	.....do...................	....	8
.....do....................	....	.....do...................	....	9
Oils and paint..............	Lacquerers, varnishers, etc........			10
Phosphorus..................	Machine feeders, pickers, packers, wrappers, sweepers, etc.	Exhaust fans...........	Yes...	11
None.......................	....	None......................	....	12
.....do....................	....	.....do...................	....	13
Gas and smoke..............	Burners..............................	.....do...................	....	14
Tinning composition, paint, varnish, tallow, japan, etc.	Painters, strippers, japanners, tinners, solderers, cleaners.	.....do...................	....	15
None.......................	....	.....do...................	....	16
.....do....................	....	.....do...................	....	17
.....do....................	....	.....do...................	....	18
.....do....................	....	.....do...................	....	19

MARYLAND.

None.......................	....	None......................	....	1
.....do....................	....	.....do...................	....	2
.....do....................	....	.....do...................	....	3
Gases from soldering........	Solderers.	.....do...................	....	4
None.......................	....	.....do...................	....	5
.....do....................	....	.....do...................	....	6
.....do....................	....	.....do...................	....	7
.....do....................	....	.....do...................	....	8
Tobacco.....................	Filler driers.......................	.....do...................	....	9
.....do....................	.....do	Ventilator in roof......	Yes...	10
None.......................	....	None......................	....	11

[1] Fans in 1 building; none in 2 buildings.

TABLE **VII.**—VENTILATION: FRESH-AIR SUPPLY AND

MARYLAND—Concluded.

Es-tab-lish-ment num-ber.	Appliances (other than windows and doors) for supplying fresh air.	Cubic feet of air space per person (in rooms which are most crowded).	Injurious or irritating dust in workrooms.	
			Kind.	Occupations affected.
12	Ventilating fan..........	525	Tobacco dust...............	Feeders and helpers on drying machines.
13	Air fan system (hot and cold).	450	None......................	....
14	Ventilating fans..........	450	....do......	
15	.....do...................	450	....do....	
16	Pipes and fans...........	1,400	....do....	
17	None.....................	3,885	....do....	
18	.....do...................	450	....do....	
19	.....do...................	400	....do....	
20	.....do...................	2,000	....do....	
21	Exhaust fans and air shafts.[1]	665	....do....	
22	None.....................	625	....do....	
23	Ventilators[1]............	480	....do....	
24	Fans and window venti-lators.	845	....do....	
25	Ventilators..............	500	....do....	
26	Pressure blower and ventilators.	730	....do....	
27	Pressure blower.........	825	....do....	
28	Ventilating fans..........	600	Tobacco dust...............	Granulating room hands........

NORTH CAROLINA.

1	None.....................	536	None......................	....
2	Skylights................	945	....do....................	....
3	Humidifiers and moni-tors.	2,080	Lint and dust.............	Pickers and carders............
4	Monitors.................	2,213	Lint.....................	Pickers, carders, slubbers, speed-ers, twisters, spinners, spoolers.
5	.....do...................	3,780	.....do..................	Pickers, carders, openers, draw-ers, spinners, spoolers, reelers, twisters.
6	None.....................	1,012	.....do..................	Pickers, carders, openers........
7	.....do...................	1,040	.....do..................	Pickers, carders, etc...........
8	.....do...................	2,000	.....do................:	Pickers, carders, slubbers, speed-ers, drawers, etc.
9	Monitor..................	1,089	.....do..................	Pickers, carders, openers, etc....
10	Fans and humidifiers...	2,200	.....do..................	Picking-room, carding-room, and spinning-room hands.
11	.....do...................	2,400	.....do..................	Picking-room, carding-room, spinning-room and weaving-room hands.
12	None.....................	700	None......................	....
13	Fans in windows........	1,000	....do....................	
14	Monitors.................	(²)	....do....................	
15	None.....................	1,200	....do....................	
16	.....do...................	383	Tobacco dust...............	Granulating-machine operators, etc.
17	.....do...................	594	....do....................	All............................
18	.....do...................	1,000	None......................	
19	.....do...................	1,000	Tobacco dust...............	Butting-machine operators......
20	.....do...................	190	....do....................	Pickers and sorters............
21	.....do...................	500	None......................	
22	.....do...................	325	Tobacco dust...............	Picking-room hands............
23	.....do...................	350	None......................	
24	.....do...................	3,000	....do.,..................	
25	Monitor on dyehouse ...	1,440	Lint, noils, dust...........	Carders, pickers, roving-frame tenders, etc.
26	None.....................	1,170	....do....................	Pickers, openers, carders, etc....
27	.....do...................	2,500	....do....................	.....do........................
28	.....do.,.................	1,500	.....do..................	Pickers, carders, roving-frame tenders, etc.

[1] In 1 building; no appliances in the other.

REMOVAL OF DUST AND FUMES FROM WORKROOMS—Continued.

MARYLAND—Concluded.

Injurious or irritating fumes in workrooms.		Appliances for carrying off dust and fumes.		Establishment number.
Kind.	Occupations affected.	Kind.	In good order.	
None		Ventilating fan	Yes	12
....do		....do	Yes	13
....do		Fans	Yes	14
....do		....do	Yes	15
....do		None		16
....do		Exhaust fan	Yes	17
....do		None		18
....do		....do		19
....do		....do		20
....do		Exhaust fan [1]	Yes	21
....do		None		22
....do		Exhaust fans [1]	Yes	23
....do		Exhaust fans	Yes	24
Steam and chemical fumes	Pressers	....do	Yes	25
Steam and sulphur fumes	Bleachers and blockers	....do	Yes	26
None		....do	Yes	27
....do		Ventilating fans	Yes	28

NORTH CAROLINA.

Injurious or irritating fumes in workrooms.		Appliances for carrying off dust and fumes.		Establishment number.
Kind.	Occupations affected.	Kind.	In good order.	
(²)		None		1
None		....do		2
....do		Fans and flues	Yes	3
....do		None		4
....do		....do		5
Dye fumes	Dyehouse hands	Roof ventilators and monitor skylights.	Yes	6
None		None		7
Dye fumes	Dyehouse hands	Rotary window fans	Yes	8
None		Suction fan and pipes	Yes	9
....do		Humidifiers	Yes	10
....do		Fans and humidifiers	Yes	11
Sulphite of sodium	Dyehouse hands	None		12
Dye fumes	....do	....do		13
Caustic soda and lime	Bleachers and helpers	....do		14
None		....do		15
Tobacco	All	....do		16
....do	....do	....do		17
....do	....do	....do		18
....do	....do	Exhaust pipes	Yes	19
Tobacco and flavorings	....do	None		20
Tobacco	....do	....do		21
Tobacco and flavorings	....do	....do		22
Tobacco	....do	....do		23
None		....do		24
Dye fumes	Dyehouse hands	Vents, fans, monitors	Yes	25
....do	....do	None		26
....do	....do	....do		27
None		Fans and hoods over mixing, opening, and picking machines.	Yes	28

² Not reported.

TABLE **VII.**—VENTILATION: FRESH-AIR SUPPLY AND

GEORGIA.

Establishment number.	Appliances (other than windows and doors) for supplying fresh air.	Cubic feet of air space per person (in rooms which are most crowded).	Injurious or irritating dust in workrooms.	
			Kind.	Occupations affected.
1	Fan.....................	344	Starch dust...............	Cream-candy makers...........
2	Fans and regenerated-air appliances.	1,000	.....do.....................	Starch-molding occupations....
3	Fan.....................	728	.....do.....................	.....do ....
4	Ventilators..............	1,000	Cotton lint................	Carders, weavers.............
5	Fans and ventilators....	1,000	.....do.....................	All ....
6	.....do..................	1,000	None.......................	
7	None....................	1,000	Cotton lint................	Carders, weavers.............
8	.....do..................	4,300	Lint...., ...	Carders.....................
9	.....do..................	4,000	Cotton lint................	.....do.....................
10	Transoms................	3,380	Lint.......................	.....do.....................
11	Monitors................	8,240	Lint and dust.............	Pickers, carders, drawers, slubbers, spinners, etc.
12	None....................	700	None.......................	
13	.....do..................	2,380	.....do.....................	
14	.....do..................	1,000	.....do.....................	
15	Ventilators..............	1,000	.....do.....................	
16	Monitor, ventilators, and fans.	550	Cotton lint................	All in yarn department........
17	Monitor, electric fans, suction fans.	700	.....do.....................	Knitting-machine operators.....
18	Monitor.....	540	None.......................	
19	Fans, roof ventilators...	700	.....do.....................	
20	Ventilators in roof.......	1,000	.....do.....................	
21	Ventilators in roof, fans.	2,000	.....do.....................	
22	None....................	1,400	.....do.....................	
23	Monitors................	2,160	.....do.....................	
24	None....................	1,879	Cotton lint and wool "flying."	Carders, spinners, drawers......
25	.....do..................	909	Cotton lint, wool "flying," and smoke.	Carders, spinners, etc...........
26	.....do..................	3,235	Lint and "flying"........	Carders, spinners, pickers......
27	.....do..................	1,411	.....do.....................	.....do......................

FLORIDA.

1	None....................	5,000	Sawdust...................	Sawyers and planers...........
2	.....do..................	2,600	.....do....................	Sawyers and counters...........
3	.....do..................	1,000	None......................	
4	.....do..................	440	.....do....................	
5	.....do..................	526	.....do....................	
6	.....do..................	375	.....do....................	
7	.....do..................	542	.....do....................	
8	.....do..................	470	.....do....................	
9	.....do..................	345	.....do....................	
10	.....do..................	300	.....do....................	
11	.....do..................	450	.....do....................	
12	.....do..................	640	.....do....................	
13	.....do..................	705	.....do....................	
14	.....do..................	200	.....do....................	

REMOVAL OF DUST AND FUMES FROM WORKROOMS—Continued.

GEORGIA.

Injurious or irritating fumes in workrooms.		Appliances for carrying off dust and fumes.		Establishment number.
Kind.	Occupations affected.	Kind.	In good order.	
None		Ventilators in roof	Yes	1
....do		....do	Yes	2
....do		Skylights and ventilators in roof.	Yes	3
....do		Exhaust fans and humidifiers.	Yes	4
Dyestuffs	Dyers and helpers	None		5
None		Exhaust fans, ventilators, humidifiers.	Yes	6
Dyestuffs	Dyers and helpers	None		7
None		Humidifiers	Yes	8
....do		None		9
....do		....do		10
Dye stuffs	Dyers, extractors, etc	Fans	Yes	11
None		Hoods and ventilators	Yes	12
Coal gas in oven room	Oven and cracker machine occupations.	Hoods at mouth of ovens; monitors over ovens.	Yes	13
None		Hoods at mouth of ovens	Yes	14
Sulphur	Dyers and helpers	None		15
Aniline dyes	Dye-room hands	....do		16
....do	Dyehouse hands	....do		17
None		....do		18
Chlorate of soda, chlorate of potash, dyestuffs.	Dyehouse hands	Ventilators in roof	Yes	19
Caustic soda, oil of vitriol, chloride of lime.	Bleachers	None		20
....do	....do	....do		21
None		....do		22
Fumes of animal glue	Hand paperers, hot glue workers	....do		23
Alizarine dye fumes	Dyehouse hands	....do		24
Sulphur fumes	....do	....do		25
Dye fumes	....do	....do		26
....do	....do	....do		27

FLORIDA.

Injurious or irritating fumes in workrooms.		Appliances for carrying off dust and fumes.		Establishment number.
None		Exhaust fans	Yes	1
....do		....do	Yes	2
....do		None		3
....do		....do		4
....do		....do		5
....do		....do		6
....do		....do		7
....do		....do		8
....do		....do		9
....do		....do		10
....do		....do		11
....do		....do		12
....do		....do		13
....do		....do		14

TABLE **VII.**—VENTILATION: FRESH-AIR SUPPLY

LOUISIANA.

Establishment number.	Appliances (other than windows and doors) for supplying fresh air.	Cubic feet of air space per person (in rooms which are most crowded).	Kind.	Occupations affected.
1	None....................	1,426	Burlap lint................	All......................
2	....do....................	1,625	....do....................	....do....................
3	....do....................	1,605	None....................	
4	....do....................	1,008	Lint......................	Cutters, sewers, turners...
5	....do....................	880	None....................	
6	....do....................	1,520	....do....................	
7	....do....................	2,000	....do....................	
8	....do....................	2,000	....do....................	
9	Skylights...............	(¹)	....do....................	
10	Fans....................	580	....do....................	
11	None....................	1,420	....do....................	
12	....do....................	(¹)	....do....................	
13	Ventilators.............	620	....do....................	
14	....do....................	655	....do....................	
15	Skylights...............	(¹)	....do....................	
16	(²)......................	(²)	....do....................	
17	None....................	1,160	....do....................	
18	....do....................	400	Flour....................	Breakers, mixers, machine ...
19	Skylights...............	1,000	....do....................	Bakers, mixers, sheet mak
20	Stairways...............	625	None....................	
21	None....................	1,204	....do....................	
22	....do....................	3,300	....do....................	
23	....do....................	200	....do....................	
24	Skylights...............	2,500	....do....................	
25	....do....................	1,000	....do....................	
26	None....................	1,500	....do....................	
27	....do....................	800	....do....................	
28	....do....................	900	....do....................	
29	Skylights...............	439	....do....................	

¹ Not reported.

REMOVAL OF DUST AND FUMES FROM WORKROOMS—Concluded.

LOUISIANA.

Injurious or irritating fumes in workrooms.		Appliances for carrying off dust and fumes.		Estab- lish- ment num- ber.
Kind.	Occupations affected.	Kind.	In good order.	
None............	....	None............	....	1
.....do................	....	.....do............	....	2
.....do................	....	Exhaust system........	Yes...	3
.....do................	....	None............	....	4
.....do................	....	Exhaust system........	Yes...	5
.....do................	....	.....do............	Yes...	6
.....do................	....	None............	....	7
.....do................	....	.....do............	....	8
.....do................	....	.....do............	....	9
.....do................	....	.....do............	....	10
.....do................	....	Exhaust fans...........	Yes...	11
.....do................	....	None............	....	12
.....do................	....	Exhaust fans...........	Yes...	13
.....do................	....	Ventilators...........	Yes...	14
.....do................	....	Exhaust fan...........	Yes...	15
.....do................	....	None............	....	16
.....do................	....	Ventilating fans	{1 yes.. {1 no...	17
.....do................	....	None............	....	18
.....do................	....	.....do............	....	19
.....do................	....	.....do............	....	20
.....do................	....	Exhaust fans...........	Yes...	21
.....do................	....	None............	....	22
.....do................	....	.....do............	....	23
.....do................	....	.....do............	....	24
.....do................	....	.....do............	....	25
.....do................	....	.....do............	....	26
.....do................	....	.....do............	....	27
.....do................	....	.....do............	....	28
.....do................	....	Ventilator and ex- haust fans.	Yes...	29

¹ One side of building toward court is entirely open.

APPENDIX A.

LAWS RELATING TO THE EMPLOYMENT OF WOMEN AND CHILDREN, IN FORCE JANUARY 1, 1912.

APPENDIX A.

LAWS RELATING TO THE EMPLOYMENT OF WOMEN AND CHILDREN, IN FORCE JANUARY 1, 1912.

ALABAMA.

CODE OF 1907.

Seats for female employees.

SECTION 6857. Any person owning or controlling a store or shop in which any girl or woman is employed as a clerk or saleswoman, who fails to provide such girl or woman with proper accommodations for sitting and resting when not actively engaged in the work of her employment, or who fails to permit her to do so when not so engaged, or who shall not have in such building, or conveniently thereto, separate water-closets for the use of such girls or women, must, on conviction, be fined not less than fifty dollars nor more than five hundred dollars. Seats to be provided.

Hiring out children to support parents in idleness.

SECTION 7843. The following-described persons are vagrants: Who are vagrants.

*   *   *   *   *   *   *

(12) Any person who has no property sufficient for his support and who is able to work and does not work, but hires out his children or allows them to hire out. *   *   *

SEC. 7844. Vagrancy is a crime, and any person convicted thereof must be fined not more than five hundred dollars, and may also be sentenced to hard labor for the county for not more than twelve months. Penalty.

SEC. 7845. In prosecutions for vagrancy the burden of proof shall not rest upon the State to establish the fact that the defendant has no property sufficient for his support, nor means of a fair, honest, and reputable livelihood, but whenever it shall be established by the proof in any prosecution under this chapter that the defendant *   *   * is able and does not work, but hires out his minor children, or allows them to hire out, then, or in either of such events, a prima facie case of guilt is hereby declared to be established *   *   * and the burden of proof shall be upon the defendant to show that he has sufficient property from which to obtain a support, or sufficient means of maintaining a fair, honest, and reputable livelihood; *   *   * but if the evidence for the defendant is sufficient when considered together with all of the evidence in the case to raise a reasonable doubt as to his guilt he shall be entitled to an acquittal. Proof.

SEC. 7846. The provisions of this chapter shall not apply to persons who are idle because of strikes or lockouts. Exemptions.

ACTS OF 1909.

Employment of children.

(Page 158.)

SECTION 1. No child under twelve years of age, shall be employed, or permitted to work in, or be in, or about any mill, factory, or manufacturing establishment in this State. Age limit.

SEC. 2. No child between the ages of 12 and 16 years shall be employed, or be permitted to work, or be detained in, or about any mill, factory, or manufacturing establishment in this State, unless such child shall attend school for eight weeks in every year of employment, six weeks of which shall be consecutive. School attendance.

Hours of labor.   SEC. 3. No child under the age of 14 years shall be employed, or detained in, or be in, or about any mill, factory, or manufacturing establishment within this State for more than sixty hours in any one week.

Night work.   SEC. 4. No child under 16 years of age shall be employed, or detained in, or be in, or about any mill, factory, or manufacturing establishment within this State between the hours of seven o'clock p. m. and six o'clock a. m., standard time.

SEC. 5. No child over 16 and under 18 years of age, shall be so employed, or detained between said hours for more than eight hours in any one night.

Certificates.   SEC. 6. It shall be unlawful for any person, firm, or corporation, to employ, or detain in, or permit to work in, or be in, or about any mill, factory, or manufacturing establishment any child under 18 years of age, without first requiring said child to present on a blank furnished by the employer, the form of which shall be provided by the inspector, the affidavit of the parent, or guardian, or other person standing in parental relation to such child, stating the date and place of birth of said child.

Filing.   SEC. 7. Such affidavit shall be filed by such employer within ten days after the employment of such child in the office of the judge of probate of said county and shall be numbered and labeled with the name of the child, and a complete index thereof made and preserved as other records in said office. For the services so rendered the judge of probate shall receive from the county treasury ten cents for each such affidavit. A copy of said affidavit shall be forwarded, within ten days after the employment of such child, to the inspector at Montgomery, Alabama.

SEC. 8 (as amended by act, page 546, Acts of 1911). Any person, firm or corporation who violates any of the provisions of this chapter or who knowingly permits any child to be employed, or detained in, or be in, or about his, their, or its mills, factory or manufacturing estab-

Refusing infor-   lishment, contrary to the provisions of this chapter, or who shall fail
mation.   or refuse to furnish the inspector the necessary information upon all such matters as he is required to report upon, and, all such other information as is necessary with reference to the keeping of records in the office of the said inspector, shall be guilty of a misdemeanor, and

Penalty.   upon conviction, shall be punished by a fine of not less than fifty dollars nor more than one hundred dollars for each offense.

Same subject.   SEC. 9. Any person, firm, or corporation who violates any of the provisions of this chapter, or who employs any child, or knowingly permits any child to be employed, or to work in, or about, or be detained in, or be in, or about any mill, factory, or manufacturing establishment contrary to law, or who fails, or refuses to obey promptly every lawful order, or direction given by the inspector under this law, must on conviction be fined not less than fifty dollars, nor more than one hundred dollars, and upon a second conviction for any violation of this law, must be fined not less than one hundred nor more than five hundred dollars, and if a natural person be sentenced to hard labor for not more than six months.

False state-   SEC. 10. Any person, who knowingly makes any false affidavit when
ment.   an affidavit is required under this chapter is guilty of perjury.

Inspection.   SEC. 11 (as amended by act, page 546, Acts of 1911). The State prison inspector, in person or by his chief clerk or deputy inspectors, is charged with the duty of inspecting all mills, factories, and manufacturing establishments wherein women and children work, and he must inspect every such mill, factory or manufacturing establishment at least four times a year, if practicable, without notice of his purpose to do so. He shall thoroughly inspect each manufacturing establishment, and ascertain their sanitary condition, and whether a good supply of fresh drinking water and fresh air and suitable water-closets for the women and girls are provided, separate and apart from those for the use of boys and men, and par icu ar   the ages and conditions of the children employed. at work in, or detained therein and he shall carefully examine all affidavits filed under this law and in connection therewith, the children named therein, and all other matters concerning the operation and condition of the manufacturing establishments in which children work, or are detained. and make written orders requiring correction of defects in, or about the mills, or manufacturing establishment.

SEC. 12. The inspector shall make written report to the governor of **Reports.** every examination of every manufacturing establishment inspected by him, and note every refusal or failure to comply with, or observe the law, in any respect, which reports must be published annually.

SEC. 13. It shall be the duty of the inspector to remove from any **Duty to re-** mill, factory, [or] manufacturing establishment any child found work- **move children.** ing, or detained therein contrary to law, and to remove therefrom any child who is afflicted with any infectious, contagious, or communicable disease. The judgment of the inspector as to the removal of any child shall be final and conclusive.

SEC. 14. It shall be the duty of the inspector to institute prosecutions **Enforcement.** against the owners, operators, managers, and superintendents of any such mill, factory, or manufacturing establishment for every violation of law that they may discover, and to furnish to the solicitor of the circuit, or county the names and addresses of all necessary witnesses.

SEC. 15. The inspector shall have free access at any time to any mill, **Access to** factory, or manufacturing establishment wherein women and children **mills, etc.** work, or are detained, and no person shall refuse to allow the inspector to have free access to a manufacturing establishment and every part thereof.

SEC. 16. No person shall hinder or obstruct the inspector in inspection **Hindering in-** or make any false, or misleading statement to the inspector about the **spector, etc.** establishment, its operation, or condition, or about any person working, or detained therein.

SEC. 17. All persons must have a plainly printed copy of the child- **Law to be** labor law posted up on the office and in every room in which any person **posted.** works in the mill, factory, or manufacturing establishment.

SEC. 18. Any person violating the three preceding sections, must, on **Violations.** conviction, be fined not less than one hundred nor more than five hundred dollars, and on subsequent conviction be fined not less than five hundred dollars, and may be sentenced to hard labor for not more than one year.

SEC. 19. Any owner, or manager of a mill, factory, or manufacturing **Disobeying or-** establishment who disobeys any order of the inspector, [as to] removing **ders.** a child from the mill, factory, or manufacturing establishment; or who permits any child who has been removed by the inspector to return to work therein, or to be in, or about the mill, factory, or manufacturing establishment without the written permission of the inspector, must, on conviction, be fined not less than fifty dollars, nor more than one hundred dollars.

SEC. 20. The inspector of jails and almshouses is authorized to employ **Clerk.** a competent clerk, with the approval of the governor, who shall be authorized to perform the same duties as by law the inspector is authorized to perform, and shall have and exercise the same powers under the direction of the inspector as the inspector has by law. The annual salary of the clerk of the inspector shall be eighteen hundred dollars payable monthly out of the State treasury as clerks in the other departments are paid.

SEC. 21. This chapter shall apply only to manufacturing establish- **Application of** ments engaged in manufacturing, or working in cotton, wool, clothing, **law.** tobacco, printing and binding, glass, or other kind of work that is injurious to health when carried on indoors.

SEC. 22. The inspector and the clerk of the inspector, when traveling **Expenses.** in the performance of their duties hereunder shall be reimbursed their actual traveling expenses when approved by the governor to be paid on the warrant of the State auditor.

ACTS OF 1911.

Employment of children—Schools to be provided.

(Page 247.)

SECTION 1. It shall be the duty of any county board of education **Children em-** or the board of education of any town or city in which there is located **ployed in manu-** one or more manufacturing plants employing fifty or more children **facturing plants.** within the school age, who are required by the child labor law to attend

Location of school for any certain length of time during the year, to locate, or cause to
schools. be located, a public school for the accommodation of the children within
the school age employed by such manufacturing plant, or plants, and
to apportion to the said schools so located such proportion of the school
funds of said district as may be necessary to run the school or schools as
nearly as practicable the same length of time as the other school or
schools of the district are run: *Provided further*, In incorporated cities
or towns in which two or more schools are maintained that one or more
of said schools may be designated by the proper school authorities as
the school for the accommodation of the children within school age
employed in such plant or plants.

Employment of women and children in mines.

(Page 500.)

Employment   SECTION 108. No woman of any age or boy under the age of fourteen
forbidden. shall be employed to work or labor in or about any coal mine in this
State.

ARIZONA.

REVISED STATUTES, 1901.

CIVIL CODE.

Employment of children—School attendance.

Employment   SECTION 2231 (as amended by chapter 67, Acts of 1907). No child
during school under the age of fourteen years shall be employed by any person, per-
hours. sons, company or corporation during the school hours of any school day
of the school term of the public school in the school district where such
child resides, unless such child has been excused from attendance on
instruction, as provided in this section. Every such employer shall require proof that such child has been excused from such attendance, and
shall keep a record of such proof, which shall be open to the inspection
of any peace officer or school trustee of the district. Any employer
employing any child contrary to the provisions of this section shall be
deemed guilty of a misdemeanor, and liable to a fine of not less than
twenty-five ($25.00) dollars, nor more than one hundred ($100.00) dollars,
to be placed to the credit of the school fund of the district. Every parent, guardian, or other person in the Territory of Arizona, having control of any child between the ages of eight and fourteen years (or of any
Age of attend- child of the age of fourteen and under the age of sixteen, who is unable
ance. to read and write in the English language), shall be required to send
such child to a public school or private school taught by a competent
instructor for a period of six schools [sic] months of which twenty school
weeks shall be consecutive, in each school year, said child to begin
attendance on school within two weeks after the opening of school for
Proviso. the admission of pupils: *Provided*, That such parent, guardian, or other
person having control of such child shall be excused from such duty by
the board of trustees of the district whenever it shall be shown to its
satisfaction that one of the following reasons exist [sic] therefor:

1. That such child is taught at home by a competent instructor in
the branches taught in the primary and grammar schools of the Territory.

2. That such child has already completed the grammar school course
prescribed by the Territorial board of education.

3. That such child is in such physical or mental condition (as declared by a competent physician, if required by the board) to render
such attendance inexpedient or impracticable.

4. That circumstances rendering attendance impracticable or dangerous to health, owing to unusual storm, or other sufficient cause,
shall work an exemption from the penalties of this act.

ACTS OF 1907.

CHAPTER 13.—*Employment of women and minors in saloons.*

Employment   SECTION 1. It shall be unlawful for the owner of any saloon within
forbidden. the Territory of Arizona to permit any woman or minor, either for hire
or otherwise, to sing, to recite, to dance, to play on any musical instru-

ment, to give any theatrical or other exhibition, to drink, serve drinks or any other form of refreshment or viands, or to solicit for the purchase of [or] sale thereof; to engage in, or to take part in, any game of chance or amusement, or to loiter in any saloon or in any room or apartment, except the lobby of a legitimate hotel, opening from or into any saloon within the Territory of Arizona.

SEC. 2. Any person who shall violate any provision of this act shall be deemed guilt of a misdemeanor, and upon conviction thereof shall be punished by ɪ fine of not less than fifty dollars, nor more than three hundred dollars, or by imprisonment in the county jail for not less than thirty days or more than one hundred and eighty days, or by both such fine and imprisonment in the discretion of the court. *Penalty.*

ACTS OF 1909.

CHAPTER 100.—*Hours of labor of employees in laundries—Air space.*

SECTION 1. The period of employment of working women and other persons who shall be employed in working in the laundry department in any laundry establishment, shall be eight hours in any one day except when it is necessary to make repairs to prevent the interruption of the ordinary running of the machinery or when a different apportionment of the hours of labor is made for the sole purpose of making a shorter day's work for one day of the week, and in no case shall the hours of labor exceed forty-eight hours in a week. *Eight hours a day's work.*

Every employer shall post in a conspicuous place in every room where such persons are employed a printed notice stating the number of hours work required of them on each day of the week; and the employment of any such person for longer time in any day than that so stated shall be deemed a violation of this section, yunless it appears that such employment is to make up for time lost on some previous day of the same week in consequence of the stopping of machinery upon which such person was employed or depended for employment. *Hours to be posted.*

SEC. 2. There shall be afforded not less than (600) six hundred cubic feet of air to each worker or occupant of any laundry building or room, and every room shall have at least two windows connecting with the external air and so arranged as to provide a cross current of air. *Air space.*

SEC. 3. Any person, body corporate, agent, manager or employer who shall violate any of the provisions of section 1 and 2 of this act shall be guilty of a misdemeanor and on conviction thereof shall be fined in the sum of not less than one hundred ($100) dollars, nor more than three hundred ($300) dollars for each offense, the same to be collected as in other cases where fines are imposed. *Violations.*

ARKANSAS.

DIGEST OF 1904.

Employment of women and children in mines.

SECTION 5343. No person under the age of fourteen years, or female of any age, shall be permitted to enter any mine to work therein; nor shall any boy under the age of sixteen years, unless he can read and write, be allowed to work in any mine, and no owner, agent or operator of any mine operated by a shaft or slope shall place in charge of any engine whereby men are lowered into or hoisted out of the mines, any but an experienced, competent and sober person, not under eighteen years of age, * * *. *Employment forbidden.*

ACTS OF 1907.

ACT No. 456.—*Employment of children—General provisions.*

SECTION 1. From and after the passage of this act no child under twelve years of age shall be employed or allowed to labor in or about any factory or manufacturing establishment within this State under any circumstances: *Provided,* That this act shall not apply to industries *Age limit 12 years.*

engaged in the preservation of fruits or vegetables during the school vacation period.

Fourteen years. SEC. 2. On and after September 1, 1907, no child under fourteen years of age shall be so employed, or allowed to labor unless such child be an orphan and has no other means of support, or unless a widowed mother or an aged or disabled father is dependent upon the labor of such child in which event, before putting such child at such labor, such father shall produce and file in the office of such factory or manufacturing establishment, a certificate from the county clerk of the county in which said factory or manufacturing establishment is located, certifying under his seal of office to the facts required to be shown as herein prescribed: *Provided,* That no county clerk shall issue any such certificate except upon strict proof in writing and under oath, clearly showing the necessary facts: *And provided further,* That no such certificate shall be granted for longer than one year, nor accepted by any employer after one year from the date of such certificate.

Night work. SEC. 3. On and after September 1, 1907, no child under fourteen years of age shall be employed or allowed to labor in or about any factory or manufacturing establishment within this State between the **Hours of labor.** hours of seven p. m. and six a. m., nor for more than sixty (60) hours in any one week, nor more than ten (10) hours in any one day.

School attendance. SEC. 4. On and after September 1, 1907, no child except as heretofore provided, under fourteen years of age, shall be employed or allowed to labor in or about any factory or manufacturing establishment within this State, unless he or she can write his or her name and simple sentences and shall have attended school for twelve weeks of the preceding year, six of which school attendance shall be consecutive; and no such child as aforesaid between the ages of fourteen and eighteen years shall be so employed unless such child shall have attended school for twelve weeks of the preceding year, six weeks of which school attendance shall be consecutive; and at the end of each year, until such child shall have passed the public school age, an affidavit certifying to such attendance, as is required by this section, shall be furnished to the employer by the parent or guardian or person sustaining parental relations to such child.

The provisions of this section shall apply only to children entering such employment at the age of fourteen or less.

Certificates. SEC. 5. It shall be unlawful for any owner, superintendent, agent or any other person acting for or in behalf of any factory or manufacturing establishment to hire or employ any child unless there is first provided and placed on file in the office of such employer an affidavit signed by the parent or guardian or person standing in parental relation thereto, certifying to the age and date of birth of such child, and other facts required in this act.

Any person knowingly furnishing a false affidavit as to the age or as to any other facts required in this act, shall be deemed guilty of a misdemeanor and on conviction thereof shall be punished by a fine of not exceeding one hundred dollars.

List to be open. SEC. 6. The affidavits and certificates required in this act shall be open to inspection by the grand juries or the citizens of any county where such factory or manufacturing establishments are located.

Violations. SEC. 7. Any person or agent, or representative of any firm or corporation, who shall violate any provision of this act shall be deemed guilty of a misdemeanor, and on conviction shall be punished by a fine of not exceeding one hundred dollars. Any parent, guardian or other person standing in parental relation to a child who shall hire or place for employment or labor in or about any factory or manufacturing establishment within this State a child in violation of any provision of this act, shall be deemed guilty of a misdemeanor and on conviction thereof shall be punished by a fine of not exceeding one hundred dollars.

Separate offenses. SEC. 8. Each day during which this act is violated, where the violation is continuous, shall constitute a separate offense.

ACTS OF 1909.

ACT No. 234.—*Employment of children—School attendance.*

SECTION 1. Every parent, guardian or other person in the State of Arkansas, having charge and control of any child between the ages ance required. of (8) and (16) years, shall cause such child to attend regularly some day school, public, private, parochial or parish, not less than one-half of the entire time the public school said child attends is in session, during any one year, or shall provide such child at home with such regular daily instruction during the usual hours as shall be, in the judgment of court or school board having competent jurisdiction, substantially equivalent to at least the instructions given the children of like age and advancement at the day public school in the locality in which said child resides: *Provided*, That every parent, guardian or other Proviso. person in the State of Arkansas, having charge and control of any child between the ages of sixteen and twenty years, who is not actively and regularly and lawfully engaged in some useful employment or service, shall cause said child to attend school as hereinbefore provided for children from 8 to 16 years.

SEC. 3. The board having charge of a public school in a city or Attendance district shall appoint for a period one of year, one or more attend- officers. ance officers to enforce the provisions of this act. * * * The attendance officers shall serve written or printed notices upon the parents or guardians, or persons who have charge and control of any child or children as aforesaid who violate the provisions of this act, and shall, when reasonable doubt exists as to the age of any child, require a properly attested birth certificate or an affidavit stating such child's age, the date of birth and physical characteristics; and shall have the right to visit and enter any office or factory or business house employing children as aforesaid; and the right to require a properly attested certificate of attendance of any child or children at such day school; and power to arrest without warrant, all truants and nonattendants as aforesaid and place them in some public school, unless the parents, guardians, or persons in charge and control of said children, respectively, shall at once place them in some other day school as aforesaid. * * *

SEC. 7. No child between 8 and 16 years of age shall be employed Schooling cer- in any mine, factory, workshop, mercantile establishment, or in any tificate. manner, during the usual school hours while such school is in session, unless the person employing such child shall first procure a certificate from the superintendent or the teacher of the school he or she attended, stating that such child attended school for the period required by law, or has been excused from attendance as provided in section 2 of this act, and it shall be the duty of such superintendent or teacher to furnish such certificate upon application of a parent, guardian, or person having control of such child entitled to same.

SEC. 8. Every owner, superintendent, or officer of any mine, factory, Violations. workshop, or mercantile establishment, and any other person who shall employ any child between 8 and 16 years of age, contrary to the provisions of this act, shall be deemed guilty of a misdemeanor, and upon conviction shall be fined for each offense in a sum not less than ten ($10) dollars, nor more than thirty dollars.

SEC. 9.

* * * * *

Provided, The following counties shall be exempted from the pro- Exemptions. visions of this act: Arkansas, Ashley, Baxter, Boone, Bradley, Calhoun, Clark, Chicot, Cleburne, Columbia, Conway, Crittenden, Cross, Dallas, Desha, Drew, Hempstead, Hot Spring, Howard, Izard, Jefferson, Lafayette, Lee, Lincoln, Little River, Logan, Lonoke, Marion, Miller, Mississippi, Monroe, Montgomery, Ouachita, Perry, Phillips, Pike, Poinsett, Polk, Pope, Pulaski, Saline, Searcy, Woodruff and Yell.

[Act No. 347 enacts for nine counties, including four of those above Special laws. exempted, a compulsory-attendance law for children from eight to fourteen years of age, in the main corresponding in its provisions with those of act No. 234.]

ACTS OF 1911.

ACT No. 231.—*Employment of children—School attendance.*

School attend-
ance required.
SECTION 1. Every parent, guardian or other person in the State of Arkansas, having charge and control of any child between the ages of (8) and (16) years, shall cause such child to attend regularly some day school, public, private, parochial or parish [school], not less than one-half of the entire time the public school said child attends [is] in session during any one year, or shall provide such child at home with such regularly [regular] daily instruction during the usual hours as shall be in the judgment of court or school board having competent jurisdiction, substantially equivalent to at least the instructions given the children of like age and advancement at the day public school in the locality in which said child resides: *Provided,* That every parent, guardian or other person in the State of Arkansas, having charge and control of any child between the ages of sixteen and twenty years, who is not actively and regularly and lawfully engaged in some useful employment or service, shall cause said child to attend school as hereinbefore provided for children from eight to sixteen years.

Unemployed
children.

Exceptions.
SEC. 2. Any child between the ages aforesaid may be excused temporarily from complying with the provisions of this act in whole or in part, if it be shown to the court of competent jurisdiction, or school board of said district * * * that the labor of said child is absolutely necessary for the support of the family, or that said child has completed a common-school course including seven (7) grades, and has certificate of same from the school said child attended. * * *

Enforcement.
SEC. 3. The board having charge of a public school in a city or district shall appoint for a period of one year, one or more attendance officers to enforce the provisions of this act. * * * The attendance officer * * * shall have the right to visit and enter any office or factory or business house employing children as aforesaid; * * *

Counties ex-
cepted.
SEC. 7. * * * *Provided,* The following counties shall be exempted from the provisions of this act: Baxter, Cleburne, Polk, Madison, Franklin, Jefferson, Sebastian, Yell, Independence, Scott, Drew, Little River, Lonoke, Woodruff, Boone, Bradley, Calhoun, Desha, Lafayette, Lincoln, Marion, Monroe, Phillips, Ashley, Dallas, Columbia, Montgomery, Chicot, Hot Spring, Saline, St. Francis, Benton, Lee, Ouachita, Pope, Union, Crittenden, Pulaski, Prairie, Hempstead, Howard.

CALIFORNIA.

CONSTITUTION.

ARTICLE 20.—*Sex no disqualification for employment.*

Sex not a bar.
SECTION 18. No person shall, on account of sex, be disqualified from entering upon or pursuing any lawful business, vocation, or profession.

SIMS' DEERING'S CODES—1906.

CIVIL CODE.

Earnings of minors.

Payment to
minors.
SECTION 212. The wages of a minor employed in service may be paid to him until the parent or guardian entitled thereto gives the employer notice that he claims such wages.

PENAL CODE.

Certain employments of children forbidden.

Mendicant,
acrobatic, etc., oc-
cupations.
SECTION 272. Any person, whether as parent, relative, guardian, employer, or otherwise, having the care, custody, or control of any child under the age of sixteen years, who exhibits, uses, or employs, or in any manner, or under any pretense, sells, apprentices, gives away, lets out, or disposes of any such child to any person, under any

name, title, or pretense, for or in any business, exhibition, or vocation, injurious to the health or dangerous to the life or limb of such child, or in or for the vocation, occupation, service, or purpose of singing, playing on musical instruments, rope or wire walking, dancing, begging, or peddling, or as a gymnast, acrobat, contortionist, or rider, in any place whatsoever, or for or in any obscene, indecent or immoral purposes, exhibition, or practice whatsoever, or for or in any mendicant or wandering business whatsoever, or who causes, procures, or encourages such child to engage therein, is guilty of a misdemeanor, and punishable by a fine of not less than fifty nor more than two hundred and fifty dollars, or by imprisonment in the county jail for a term not exceeding six months, or by both such fine and imprisonment. Nothing in this section contained applies to or affects the employment or use of any such child, as a singer or musician in any church, school, or academy, or the teaching or learning of the science or practice of music; or the employment of any child as a musician at any concert or other musical entertainment, on the written consent of the mayor of the city or president of the board of trustees of the city or town where such concert or entertainment takes place.

This section is constitutional. 86 Pac. Rep. 809.

SEC. 273. Every person who takes, receives, hires, employs, uses, exhibits, or has in custody, any child under the age, and for any of the purposes mentioned in the preceding section, is guilty of a like offense, and punishable by a like punishment as therein provided.   •   *Hiring, etc.*

SEC. 273e. Every telephone, special-delivery company or association, and every o her corporation or person engaged in the delivery of packages, letters, notes, messages, or other matter, and every manager, superintendent, or other agent of such person, corporation, or association, who sends any minor in the employ or under the control of any such person, corporation, association, or agent, to the keeper of any house of prostitution, variety theater, or other place of questionable repute, or to any person connected with, or any inmate of, such house, theater, or other place, or who permits such minor to enter such house, theater, or other place, is guilty of a misdemeanor.   *Sending as messengers.*

SEC. 273f (added by chapter 294, Acts of 1907). Any person, whether as parent, guardian, employer, or otherwise, and any firm or corporation, who as employer or otherwise, shall send, direct, or cause to be sent or directed to any saloon, gambling house, house of prostitution, or other immoral place, any minor under the age of eighteen, is guilty of a misdemeanor.   *Same subject.*

GENERAL LAWS.

ACT No. 1611.—*Employment of children—General provisions.*

(Act approved February 20, 1905, as amended by chapter 456, Acts of 1911.)

SECTION 1. No minor under the age of eighteen shall be employed in laboring in any manufacturing, mechanical, or mercantile establishment, or other place of labor, more than nine hours in one day, except when it is necessary to make repairs to prevent interruption of the ordinary running of the machinery, or when a different apportionment of the hours of labor is made for the sole purpose of making a shorter days' work for one day of the week, and in no case shall the hours of labor exceed fifty-four hours in a week.   *Nine-hour day.*

SEC. 2. No minor under the age of eighteen years shall be employed or permitted to work between the hours of ten o'clock in the evening and five o'clock in the morning. No child under fifteen years of age shall be employed in any mercantile institution, office, laundry, manufacturing establishment, workshop, place of amusement, restaurant, hotel, apartment house, or in the distribution or transmission of merchandise or messages: *Provided,* That the judge of the juvenile court of the county, or city and county, or in any county or city and county in which there is no juvenile court, when any judge of the superior court of the county or city and county in which such child resides shall have authority to issue a   *Night work.*   *Age limit.*   *Children of dependent parents.*

permit to work to any such child over the age of twelve years, upon a sworn statement being made to him by the parent of such child that such child is past the age of twelve years, that the parents or parent of such child are incapacitated for labor, through illness, and after investigation by a probation officer or attendance officer of the city, or city and county, in which such child resides, or in cities and counties where there are no probation or attendance officers, then by such other competent person as the judge may designate for this purpose. The permit so issued shall specify the kind of labor and the time for which it is issued, and shall in no case be issued for a longer period than shall seem necessary to the judge issuing such permit. Such permit shall be kept on file by the person, firm or corporation employing the child therein designated, during the term of said employment, and shall be given up to such child upon his quitting such employment. Such certificate shall be always open to the inspection of the attendance and probation officers of the city and county, city or county, in which the place of employment is situated, or the officers of the State bureau of labor statistics: *And provided,* That the attendance officer of any county, city and county, or school district in which any place of employment, in this section named, is situated, shall have the right and authority, at all times to enter into such place of employment for the purpose of investigating violations of the provisions of this act, or violations of the provisions of an act entitled "An act to enforce the educational rights of children and providing penalties for the violation of the act," approved March 24, 1903, and amended March 20, 1905: *Provided, however,* That if such attendance or probation officer is denied entrance to such place of employment, any magistrate may, upon the filing of an affidavit by such attendance or probation officer setting forth the fact that he had a good cause to believe that the provisions of this act, or the act hereinbefore referred to, are being violated in such place of employment, issue and order directing such attendance or probation officer to enter said place of employment for the purpose of making such investigations: *And provided,* That any such child over the age of twelve years may be employed at any of the occupations mentioned in this act during the regular vacation of the public schools of the city, county, or city and county, in which the place of employment is situated, upon the production of a permit signed by the principal, vice principal of the school, or secretary of the board of school trustees or board of education of the school which such child has attended during the term next preceding any such vacation. Such permit shall contain the name and age of the child to whom it is issued, and the date of the termination of the vacation for which it is issued, and shall be kept on file by the employer during the period of employment, and at the termination of such employment shall be returned to the child to whom it was issued.

Enforcement.

Employment during school time. No minor who is under sixteen years of age shall be employed or permitted to work at any gainful occupation during the hours that the public schools of the city, town or school district in which his place of employment is situated are in session, unless he or she can read English at sight and can write legibly and correctly simple English sentences, or unless he or she is a regular attendant for the then current term at a regularly conducted night school. A certificate of the principal of such school shall be held to be sufficient evidence of such attendance.

Schedule of worktime. SEC. 3. Every person, firm or corporation employing minors under eighteen years of age, in any manufacturing establishment, shall post, and keep posted, in a conspicuous place in every room where such help is employed, a written or printed notice stating the number of hours per day for each day of the week required of such persons. Every person, firm, or corporation, agent or officer of a firm or corporation, employing or permitting minors under sixteen and over fifteen years of age to work in any mercantile institution, office, laundry, manufacturing establishment, workshop, place of amusement, restaurant, hotel, apartment house, or in the distribution or transmission of merchandise or messages, shall keep a record of the names, ages, and places of residence of such minors, and shall have on file a certificate of age and schooling, as provided in this act, for every such minor so employed.

Records.

said record and certificate to be open at all times to the inspection of the school attendance and probation officers of the city and county, city, or county, in which the place of employment is situated, or of the officers of the State bureau of labor statistics.

An age and schooling certificate shall be approved only by the superintendent of schools of the city or city and county, or by a person authorized by him in writing, or where there is no city or city and county superintendent of schools, by a person authorized by the local school trustees: *Provided,* That the superintendent or principal of any school of recognized standing shall have the right to approve an age and schooling certificate, and shall have the same rights and powers as the superintendent of public schools to issue the certificate herein provided, for children attending such schools. The persons authorized to issue age and schooling certificates shall have the authority to administer the oaths necessary for carrying out the provisions of this act, but no fees shall be charged for issuing such certificates. An age and schooling certificate shall not be approved unless satisfactory evidence is furnished by the last school census, the certificate of birth or baptism of such child, the public register of birth of such child, or in some other manner, that such child is of the age stated in such certificate. A duplicate copy of each age and schooling certificate granted under the provisions of this act shall be kept by the person issuing such certificate, such copy to be filed with the county superintendent of schools in the county where the certificate is issued: *Provided,* That all such copies of certificates issued between June 25th and December 25th of any year shall be filed not later than December 31st of such year; and those issued between December 25th and June 25th of the ensuing year shall be filed not later than June 30th of each year. Such certificates shall be substantially in the following form, to wit: {.marginal}Certificates.

AGE AND SCHOOLING CERTIFICATE.

This certifies that I am the (father, mother, or guardian) of (name of the child), and that (he or she) was born at (name of town or city), in the county of (name of county, if known), and State (or country) of (name), on the day (day and year of birth), and is now (number of years and of months) old. {.marginal}Form.

                          Signature, as provided in this act.
Town or city, and date.

There personally appeared before me the above-named (name of person signing) and made oath that the following [foregoing] certificate by (him or her) signed is true to the best of (his or her) knowledge and belief.

I hereby approve the foregoing certificate of (name of child), height (feet and inches), complexion (fair or dark), hair (color), having no sufficient reason to doubt that (he or she) is of the age therein certified, and I hereby certify that (he or she) (can or can not) read English at sight, and (can or can not) write legibly simple sentences in the English language. There is hereto attached a written request from the prospective employer of such child, that an age and schooling certificate be granted to such child.

Signature of the person authorized to sign, with his official character and authority.

Town or city and date.

This certificate belongs to the person in whose behalf it is drawn, and it shall be presented to (him or her) whenever (he or she) leaves the services of the person, firm, or corporation holding the same. The certificate as to the birthplace and age of the minor under sixteen and over fifteen years of age shall be signed by his father, his mother, or his guardian; if a child has no father, mother, or guardian living in the same city or town, his own signature to the certificate may be accepted by the person authorized to approve the same. Every person authorized to sign the certificate prescribed by this act, who knowingly certifies to any false statement therein, is guilty of a misdemeanor, and upon conviction thereof shall be fined not less than five nor more than fifty dollars, or imprisonment not more than thirty days, or by both such fine and imprisonment. The county superintendent {.marginal}Certificate to be returned. {.marginal}Signing.

Report.

of schools of each county shall file with the commissioner of the bureau of labor statistics a report showing the number of age and schooling certificates issued to male and female minors, fifteen years of age, and such other detailed information as the commissioner may require. Said report to be filed during the months of January and July of each year for the preceding six months, ending June 25th and December 25th of each year, and cover certificates issued during said periods and on file in the office of the county superintendent of schools as described in paragraph five of this section.

Unemployed children.

SEC. 3a. *Provided, however,* That no child having a permit to work, as prescribed in section two of this act, and no child having an age and schooling certificate, as described in section three of this act, and no other child, between the ages of fifteen and sixteen years, who, if between the ages of eight and fifteen years, would by law be required to attend school, shall, while the public schools are in session, be and remain idle and unemployed for a period longer than two weeks, but must enroll and attend school: *Provided,* That within one week after any child having such a permit to work or such age and schooling certificate shall have ceased to be employed by any employer, such employer shall, in writing, giving the latest correct address of such child known to such employer, notify, in the case of a child having a permit to work, the judge of the juvenile court in the county of said child's residence or the probation officer of such juvenile court, or in the case of a child having an age and schooling certificate, the county superintendent of schools of such county, that such child is no longer employed by such employer; and such judge of the juvenile court, or such probation officer, or such county superintendent of schools, shall thereupon immediately notify the attendance officer having jurisdiction in the place of such child's residence, giving the said latest correct address of such child, that such child is neither at work nor in school: *And provided, further,* That no such child shall be permitted to cease school attendance, without securing a permit to work, or an age and schooling certificate as provided in this act.

Violations.

SEC. 4. Any person, firm, or corporation, agent, or officer of a firm or corporation that violates or omits to comply with any of the foregoing provisions of this act, or that employs or suffers any minor to be employed in violation thereof, is guilty of a misdemeanor, and shall, upon conviction thereof, be punished by a fine of not less than fifty dollars or more than two hundred dollars, or by imprisonment for not more than sixty days, or by both such fine and imprisonment, for each and every offense. A failure to produce any age and schooling certificate or permit or to post any notice required by this act, shall be prima facie evidence of the illegal employment of any person whose age and schooling certificate or permit is not produced, or whose name is not so posted. Any fine collected under the provisions of this act shall be paid into the school funds of the county, or city, or city and county in which the offense occurred; except such fines imposed and collected as the result of prosecutions by the officer of the bureau of labor statistics. In such cases one-half of the resultant fine or fines shall be paid into the State treasury and credited to the contingent fund of the bureau of labor statistics, and one-half paid into the school funds of the county, or city, or city and county in which the offense occurred.

Exemptions.

SEC. 5. Nothing in this act shall be construed to prohibit the employment of minors at agricultural, horticultural, or viticultural or domestic labor during the time the public schools are not in session, or during other than school hours. Nor shall anything in this act be construed to prohibit any child between the ages of fifteen and eighteen years, who is by any statute or statutes of the State of California, now or hereafter in force, permitted to be employed as an actor, or actress, or performer, in a theatre, or other place of amusement, previous to the hour of ten o'clock p. m., in the presentation of a performance, play or drama, continuing from an earlier hour till after the hour of ten o'clock p. m., from performing his or her part in such presentation as such employee between the hours of ten and twelve o'clock p. m.

Enforcement.

SEC. 6. It shall be the duty of the bureau of labor statistics to enforce the provisions of this act. The commissioner, his deputies, and agents, shall have all powers and authority of sheriffs to make arrests for violations of the provisions of this act.

ACT No. 3574.—*Compulsory school attendance—Employment of children.*

SECTION 1 (as amended by chapter 482, Acts of 1911). Unless excused, as hereinafter provided, each parent, guardian, or other person, in in the State of California, having control or charge of any child between the ages of eight and fifteen years, shall be required to send such child to a public school, during the time in which a public school shall be in session, in the city or city and county or school district in which said child resides: *Provided,* That should it be shown to the satisfaction of the board of education of the city or city and county, or of the board of trustees of the school district, in which such child resides, * * * that any such child between the age of twelve and fifteen has been given a permit to work by the proper judicial officers in accordance with section two of "An act regulating the employment and hours of labor of children, prohibiting the employment of minors under certain ages, prohibiting the employment of certain illiterate minors, providing for the enforcement hereof by the commissioner of the bureau of labor statistics and providing penalties for the violation hereof," approved February 20, 1905 [see act No. 1611, above]; then it shall be the duty of such board of education or board of trustees, upon application of the parent, or guardian, or other person having control or charge of such child, to excuse such child from attendance at school, during the continuance of such * * * condition upon which such excuse is granted; * * *. Attendance required. Exception.

ACTS OF 1909.

CHAPTER 128.—*Employment of children—School attendance.*

SECTION 1. All minors coming within the provisions of an act entitled, "An act regulating the employment and hours of labor of children, prohibiting the employment of minors under certain ages, prohibiting the employment of certain illiterate minors, providing for the enforcement hereof by the commissioner of the bureau of labor statistics and providing penalties for the violation hereof," (approved February 20, 1905) and found employed and at work without the necessary legal authorization as provided for and required in said act, and whose ages are between the maximum and minimum age limits as described in an act entitled, "An act to enforce the educational rights of children and providing penalties for violation of the act," shall be placed or delivered into the custody of the school district authorities of the county, city, or city and county in which they are found illegally at work. Unlawful employment.

SEC. 2. The commissioner of the bureau of labor statistics is hereby authorized, directed and empowered to enforce the provisions of this act. Enforcement.

ACTS OF 1911.

CHAPTER 258.—*Employment of women—Hours of labor—Seats.*

SECTION 1. No female shall be employed in any manufacturing, mechanical or mercantile establishment, laundry, hotel, or restaurant, or telegraph or telephone establishment or office, or by any express or transportation company in this State more than eight hours during any one day or more than forty-eight hours in one week. The hours of work may be so arranged as to permit the employment of females at any time so that they shall not work more than eight hours during the twenty-four hours of one day, or forty-eight hours during any one week: *Provided, however,* That the provisions of this section in relation to the hours of employment shall not apply to nor affect the harvesting, curing, canning or drying of any variety of perishable fruit or vegetables. Eight-hour day. Exceptions.

SEC. 2. Every employer in any manufacturing, mechanical or mercantile establishment, laundry, hotel, or restaurant, or other establishment employing any female, shall provide suitable seats for all female employees, and shall permit them to use such seats when they are not engaged in the active duties of their employment. Seats.

Violations.

SEC. 3. Any employer who shall require any female to work in any of the places mentioned in section one more than the number of hours provided for in this act during any day of twenty-four hours, or who shall fail, neglect, or refuse to so arrange the work of females in his employ so that they shall not work more than the number of hours provided for in this act during any day of twenty-four hours, or who shall fail, neglect, or refuse to provide suitable seats as provided in section two of this act, or who shall permit or suffer any overseer, superintendent, foreman, or other agent of any such employer to violate any of the provisions of this act, shall be guilty of a misdemeanor, and upon conviction thereof shall be fined for each offense not less than fifty dollars nor more than two hundred dollars, or imprisoned in the county jail not less than five nor more than thirty days, or both fined and imprisoned.

CHAPTER 688.—*Children engaged in trade—Night work.*

Night work prohibited.

SECTION 1. It shall be unlawful for any minor under the age of eighteen years to vend and sell goods, engage in, or conduct any business between the hours of ten o'clock in the evening and five o'clock in the morning.

Violations.

SEC. 2. Any person violating any of the provisions of this act shall be guilty of a misdemeanor and shall, upon conviction thereof, be punished by a fine of not more than twenty dollars, or by imprisonment for not more than ten days, or by both such fine and imprisonment for each offense.

COLORADO.

REVISED STATUTES—1908.

Employment of children during school term.

School attendance.

SECTION 530. In all school districts of this State, all parents, guardians and other persons having care of children shall instruct them, or cause them to be instructed, in reading, writing, spelling, English grammar, geography and arithmetic. In such districts, every parent, guardian or other person having charge of any child between the ages of eight (8) and sixteen (16) years, shall send such child to a public, private or parochial school for the entire school year during which the public schools are in session in such districts: *Provided, however,* That

Provisos.

this act shall not apply to children over fourteen (14) years of age where such child shall have completed the eighth grade, or may be eligible to enter any high school in such district, or where its help is necessary for its own or its parents' support, or where for good cause shown it would be for the best interests of such child to be relieved from the provisions of this act: *Provided, further,* That if such child is being sufficiently instructed at home by a person qualified, such child shall not be subject to the provisions of this act: *And provided, further,* That if a reputable physician within the district shall certify in writing that the child's bodily or mental condition does not permit its attendance at school, such child shall be exempt during such period of disability from the requirements of this act. It shall be the duty of the superintendent of the school district, if there be such superintendent, and, if not, then the county superintendent of schools, to hear and determine all applications of children desiring for any of the causes mentioned herein to be exempted from the provisions of this act, and if upon such application such superintendent hearing the same shall be of the opinion that such child is for any reason entitled to be exempted as aforesaid, then such superintendent shall issue a written permit to such child, stating therein his reasons for such exemption. An appeal may be taken from the decision of such superintendent so passing upon such application to the county court of the county in which such district lies, upon such child making such application and filing the same with the clerk or judge of said court within ten days after its refusal by such superintendent, for which no fee to exceed the sum of one dollar shall be charged, and the decision of the county court shall be final. An application for release from the provisions of this act shall not be renewed oftener than once in three months.

Permits.

SEC. 531. No child under the age of 14 years shall be employed by any person, persons, company, or corporations during the school term and while the public schools are in session, unless the parent, guardian or person in charge of such child shall have fully complied with section one [sec. 530] of this act. Every such employer shall require proof of such compliance, and shall make and keep a written record of the proof given, which shall be subject to the inspection of the truant officer, superintendent of schools, or any school director of the district. Any employer employing any child contrary to the provisions of this section, shall be fined not less than twenty-five nor more than one hundred dollars. *Employment during school term.*

SEC. 532. All minors over the age of 14 years and under the age of 16 years who can not read and write the English language, shall attend school at least one-half day of each day, or attend a public night school, or take regular private instruction from some person qualified, in the opinion of the county superintendent of schools, in which such district or the greater portion of the same lies, until such minor obtains a certificate from such superintendent that he or she can read at sight and write legibly, simple sentences in English. Every employer employing or having in employment any such minor shall exact as a condition of employment the school attendance or instruction required by this section, and shall on request of the truant officer, furnish the evidence that such minor is complying with the requirements of this section. Every employer failing to comply with the requirements of this section as to any minor employed by him or in his employ, shall be fined not less than twenty-five dollars, and not more than one hundred dollars: *Provided,* That any employer with the approval or consent of the county superintendent of schools may make provision for the private instruction of minors in his employ. *Illiterates.* *Proviso.*

SEC. 538. Any person who violates any provision of this act, for which a penalty is not herein provided, shall be fined not more than fifty dollars. *Violations.*

SEC. 540. This [act] shall not apply to school districts in which there are not sufficient accomodations in the public schools to seat children compelled to attend under the provisions of this act. *Scope of act.*

SEC. 546. Two week's attendance, at half time or night school, shall be considered within the meaning of the article equivalent to an attendance of one week at a day school. *Half-time or night schools.*

Employment of women and children in coal mines.

SECTION 642. * * * No young person under twelve years of age, or woman or girl of any age, shall be permitted to enter any coal mine to work therein, nor any person under the age of sixteen years, unless he can read and write. *Employment forbidden.*

[See acts of 1911, chapter 95, section 3, for present age limit.]

Seats for female employees.

SECTION 3929. Every person, corporation or company employing females in any manufacturing, mechanical or mercantile establishments in this State, shall provide suitable seats for the use of the females so employed, and shall permit the use of such seats by them when they are not necessarily engaged in the active duties for which they are employed. *Seats to be provided.*

SEC. 3930. Any person, corporation or company violating any of the provisions of this act, shall be punished by fine of not less than ten dollars nor more than thirty dollars for each offense. *Penalty.*

ACTS OF 1911.

Employment of children.

CHAPTER 95.—Employment of children—General provisions.

SECTION 1. No child under the age of fourteen years shall be employed, permitted or suffered to work at any gainable occupation in any theater, concert hall or place of amusement where intoxicating liquors are sold, or in any mercantile institution, store, office or hotel, *Age limit.*

laundry, manufacturing establishment, bowling alley, passenger or freight elevator, factory or workshop, or as a messenger or driver therefor, within this State. That no child under the age of fourteen years shall be employed at any work performed for wages or other compensation, to whomsoever payable, during any portion of any month when the public schools of the town, township, village or city in which he or she resides, are in session, nor be employed in any work before the hour of seven o'clock in the morning, or after the hour of eight o'clock in the evening: *Provided,* That no child shall be allowed to work more than eight hours in any one day.

Employments forbidden are injurious.   The General Assembly of the State of Colorado does hereby declare that all occupations or employments in which children are forbidden to engage by the provisions of this act shall be and hereby declared to be injurious or dangerous to health, life or limb. The employments or occupations permitted under this act, under the sections hereof providing for exemptions shall be considered injurious or dangerous to health, life or limb, unless it shall appear from the evidence produced before the authorities permitted to grant such exemptions that, in their opinion, the injury or danger to health, life or limb has been removed: *Provided, also,* That where conditions are such as to justify granting a permit exempting children from the provisions of this act to take part in concerts and theatrical performances and where such permits have been granted the performances of such children shall be construed to be a part of their training and education.

Exceptions.   Nothing in this act shall be construed to prevent the employment
Permits.   of children in any fruit orchard, garden, field or farm: *Provided,* That any child under fourteen years of age engaging in such employment for persons other than their own parents must first secure a permit from the superintendent of schools in accordance with the provisions of section fifteen of this act. The hours of work during each day, or in any week shall be in compliance with the provisions of this act as to the hours during any day or week when children may be employed.

Prohibited employments.   SEC. 2. It shall be unlawful for any person having the care, custody or control of any child under the age of sixteen years, or apparently under the age of sixteen years, to exhibit, use or employ such child as an actor or performer in any concert hall or room where intoxicating liquors are sold or given away, or in any variety theater, or for any illegal, obscene, indecent or immoral purpose, exhibition or practice whatsoever, or for any business, or in any place, situation or exhibition or vocation injurious to the morals or health, or dangerous to the life or limb of such child, or cause, procure or encourage such child to engage therein. Nothing in this section contained shall apply to or affect the employment or use of any such child as a singer or musician in any church, school or academy, or the teaching or learning the science or practice of music, or in the physical development of its body in any respectable gymnasium or natatorium: *Provided,* That any child may be permitted to take part in any concert or any theatrical exhibition that is being given for profit with the written consent of the authority provided by this act for the granting of permits to children for exemptions from the provisions of this act.

Nothing in this act shall be construed to prevent children taking part in what are known as amateur entertainments or theatricals for charity or not for profit in schools, churches, settlement houses, or boys' or girls' clubs.

Dangerous, etc. occupation.   SEC. 3. It shall be unlawful for any person, firm, or corporation to take, receive, hire or employ any child or children under sixteen years of age in any underground works or mine, in or about the surface workings thereof, or in any smelter, coke oven or to adjust any belt to any machinery, or to operate or assist in operating circular or band saws, wood shapers, wood jointers, planers, sandpaper or wood polishing machinery, emery or polishing wheels used for polishing metal, wood turning or boring machinery, stamping machines in sheet-metal and tinware manufacturing, stamping machines in washer and nut factories, operating corrugating rolls, such as are used in roofing factories, nor shall they be employed in operating any passenger or freight elevators, steam boiler, steam machinery or other steam generating apparatus, or automobiles, wire or iron straightening machinery; nor shall they operate or assist in operating rolling mill machinery punches or shears, washing, grinding or mixing mill or calendary [sic] rolls in rubber manufacturing, nor shall they operate or assist in operating laundry machinery, nor shall children be employed in any capacity in preparing any composition in which dangerous or poisonous acids are used, and they shall not be employed in any capacity in the manufacture of paints, colors or white lead; nor shall they be employed in any capacity whatever in the manufacture of goods for immoral purposes; nor shall females under the age of sixteen years of age be employed in any capacity whatsoever where such employment compels them to remain standing constantly. No female child under ten years of age, shall sell or be permitted or allowed to sell or distribute any newspapers, periodicals or other publication or any article of merchandise or to engage in or carry on any other business or occupation in the streets or alleys of any town or city. Girls.

SEC. 4. It shall be the duty of every person, firm or corporation, agent or manager of any firm or corporation employing minors over 14 years and under 16 years of age in any mercantile institution, store, office, hotel, laundry, manufacturing establishment, bowling alley, theater, concert hall or place of amusement, passenger or freight elevator, factory or workshop or as a messenger or driver therefor, within this State, to keep a register in said mercantile institution, store, office, hotel, laundry, manufacturing establishment, bowling alley, theater, concert hall or place of amusement, factory or workshop in which said minors shall be employed or permitted or suffered to work, in which register shall be recorded the name, age and place of residence of every child employed or suffered or permitted to work there, or as messenger or driver therefor, over the age of fourteen and under the age of 16 years; and it shall be unlawful for any person, firm or corporation agent or manager of any firm or corporation to hire or employ, or permit or suffer to work in any mercantile institution, store, office, hotel, laundry, manufacturing establishment, bowling alley; theater, concert hall or place of amusement, passenger or freight elevator, factory or workshop, or as messenger or driver therefor, any child under the age of 16 years and over 14 years of age, unless there is first produced and placed on file in such mercantile institution, store, office, hotel, laundry, manufacturing establishment, bowling alley, factory or workshop, theater, concert hall or place of amusement, an age and school certificate approved as hereinafter provided. Registers.

SEC. 5. Every person, firm or corporation, employing or permitting or suffering to work five or more children under the age of 16 years and over the age of 14 in any mercantile institution, store, office, laundry, hotel, manufacturing establishment, factory or workshop, shall post and keep posted in a conspicuous place in every room in which such help is employed, or permitted or suffered to work, a list containing the name, age and place of residence of every person under the age of 16 years employed, permitted or suffered to work in such room. List to be posted.

SEC. 6. No child permitted to be employed under this act shall be employed in any mercantile institution, store, office, hotel, laundry, manufacturing establishment, bowling alley, theater, concert hall, or place of amusement, passenger or freight elevator, factory or workshop, or as messenger or driver therefor, unless there is first produced and placed on file in such mercantile institution, store, office, hotel, laundry, manufacturing establishments, bowling alley, theater, concert hall or place of amusement, factory or workshop, and accessible to the State factory inspector, assistant factory inspector or deputy factory inspector, an age and school certificate as hereinafter prescribed; and unless there is kept on file and produced on demand of said inspectors of factories a complete and correct list of all the minors under the age of 16 years so employed who can not read at sight and write legibly simple sentences, unless such child is attending night school as hereinafter provided. Certificates.

SEC. 7. An age and school certificate shall be approved only by the superintendent of schools or by a person authorized by him in writing; or where there is no superintendent of schools, by a person authorized by the school board: *Provided,* That the superintendent or principal of a parochial school shall have the right to approve an age and school certificate, and shall have the same rights and powers as the superin- Issue.

tendent of public schools to administer the oaths therein provided for children attending parochial schools: *Provided further*, That no member of a school board or other person authorized as aforesaid shall have authority to approve such certificates for any child then in or about to enter his own establishment, or the employment of a firm or corporation of which he is a member, officer or employee. The person approving these certificates shall have authority to administer the oath provided herein, but no fee shall be charged therefor. It shall be the duty of the school board or local school authorities to designate a place (connected with their office, when practicable) where certificates shall be issued and recorded, and to establish and maintain the necessary records and clerical service for carrying out provisions of this act.

Proof of age.
SEC. 8. An age and school certificate shall not be approved unless satisfactory evidence is furnished by the last school census, the certificate of birth or baptism of such child, the register of birth of such child with a town or city clerk, or by the records of the public or parochial schools, that such child is of the age stated in the certificate: *Provided*, That in cases arising wherein the above proof is not obtainable, the parent or guardian of the child shall make oath before the juvenile or county court or any officer thereof as to the age of such child, and the court may issue to such child an age certificate as sworn to.

Form of certificates.
SEC. 9. The age and school certificate of a child under 16 years of age shall not be approved and signed until he presents to the person authorized to approve and sign the same a school attendance certificate, as hereinafter prescribed, duly filled out and signed. A duplicate of such age and school certificate shall be filled out and shall be forwarded to the State factory inspectors office. Any explanatory matter may be printed with such certificate, in the discretion of the school board or superintendent of schools. The employment and the age and school certificates shall be separately printed and shall be filled out, signed and held or surrendered as indicated in the following forms:

SCHOOL CERTIFICATE.

(Name of school.)   (City or town and date.)

This certifies (name of minor) of the ....th grade, can read and write legibly simple sentences. This also certifies that according to the records of this school, and in my belief, the said (name of minor) was born at (name of city or town), in (name of county), on the (date) and is now (number of years and months) old.

(Name of parent or guardian.)
(Residence.)

(Signature of teacher) .... grade.
(Name of principal.)

EVENING SCHOOL ATTENDANCE CERTIFICATE.

(Date.)
This certifies that (name of minor) is registered in and regularly attends ...... evening school. This also certifies that according to the records of my school and in my belief the said (name of minor) was born at (name of city or town), on the .... day of (years), and is now (number of years and months) old.

(Name of parent or guardian.)
(Residence.)
(Signature of teacher.)
(Signature of principal.)

AGE AND SCHOOL CERTIFICATE.

This certifies that I am (father, mother, guardian or custodian) of (name of minor), and that (he or she) was born at (name of town or city), in the (name of county, if known) and State and county of ......, ..., on the (day of birth and year of birth) and is now (number of years and months) old.

(Signature of parent, guardian, or custodian.)
(City or town and date.)

There personally appeared before me the above named (name of person signing) and made oath that the foregoing certificate by (him or her) signed is true to the best of (his or her) knowledge. I hereby approve the foregoing certificate of (name of child) height (feet and inches), weight —— complexion (fair or dark), hair (color), having no sufficient reason to doubt that (he or she) is of the age therein certified.

This certificate belongs to (name of child in whose favor it is drawn) and is to be surrendered to (him or her) whenever (he or she) leaves the service of the corporation or employer holding the same; but if not claimed by said child within thirty days from such time it shall be returned to the superintendent of schools, or where there is no superintendent of schools, to the school board. (Signature of person authorized to approve and sign, with official character authority) (town or city and date). **Owner of certificate.**

In the case of a child who cannot read at sight and write legibly simple sentences the certificate shall continue as follows: after the words sentences: "I hereby certify that (he or she) is regularly attending the (name of public or parochial evening school)." This certificate shall continue in force just as long as the regular attendance of said child at said evening school is certified weekly by the teacher and principal of such school. **Illiterates.**

In any city or town in which there is no public or parochial evening school, an age and school certificate shall not be approved for a child under the age of 16 years who can not read at sight and write legibly simple sentences; the certificate of the principal of a public or parochial school shall be prima facie evidence as to the literacy or illiteracy of the child.

SEC. 10. No person shall employ any minor over 14 years of age and under 16 years, and no parent, guardian or custodian shall permit to be employed any such minor under his control who can not read at sight and write legibly simple sentences, while a public evening school is maintained in the town or city in which such minor resides, unless such minor is a regular attendant at such evening school. **Attendance on evening schools.**

SEC. 11. The State inspector of factories, his assistants or deputies, shall visit all mercantile institutions, stores, offices, laundries, manufacturing establishments, bowling alleys, theatres, concert halls or places of amusements, factories or workshops, and all other places where minors are or may be employed in this State, and ascertain whether any minors are employed contrary to the provisions of this act. Inspectors of factories may require that age and school certificates, and all lists of minors employed in such factories, workshops, mercantile institutions and all other places where minors are employed as provided for in this act, shall be produced for their inspection on demand: *And, provided, further,* That upon written complaint to the school board or local school authorities of any city, town, district or municipality, that any minor (whose name shall be given in such complaint) is employed in any mercantile institution, store, office, laundry, manufacturing establishment, bowling alley, theatre, concert hall or place of amusement, passenger or freight elevator, factory or workshop, or as messenger or driver thereof, contrary to the provisions of this act, it shall be the duty of such school board or local school authority to report the same to the State inspector of factories. **Duty of inspectors.**

SEC. 12. No person under the age of 16 years shall be employed or suffered or permitted to work at any gainful occupation more than forty-eight hours in any one week, nor more than eight hours in any one day; or after the hour of 8:00 o'clock in the evening. Every employer shall post in a conspicuous place in every room where such minors are employed a printed notice stating the hours required of them each day of the week, the hours of commencing and stopping work, and the hours when the time or times allowed for dinner or other meals begins and ends. The printed form of such notice shall be furnished by the State inspector of factories, and the employment of any such minor for longer time in any one day so stated shall be deemed a violation of this section. **Hours of labor. Night work.**

dence.

SEC. 13. The presence of any person under the age of 16 years in any manufacturing establishment, factory or workshop shall constitute prima facie evidence of his or her employment therein.

orcement.

SEC. 14. It shall be the special duty of the State factory inspector to enforce the provisions of this act and to prosecute all violations of the same before any magistrate or any court of competent jurisdiction in this State. It shall be the duty of the State factory inspector, assistant State factory inspector and deputy State factory inspectors under the supervision and direction of the State factory inspector, and they are hereby authorized and empowered to visit and inspect, at all reasonable times, and as often as possible, all places covered by this act: *Provided*, That this act shall not be construed to repeal any law of this State imposing duties or responsibilities upon any other officer or person to make inspections or bring prosecutions for the violation of any school law or any other law of this State for the protection of children.

ptions;
s, etc.

SEC. 15. Any child may be exempted from the provisions of this act concerning the employment of children in any concert or theatrical exhibition or performance in any place where intoxicating liquors are not sold, and between the ages of fourteen and sixteen, from any other provisions of this act, except the provisions of section three (3), on the following conditions: Any such child, its parent or person seeking to employ such child shall file an application in writing with the city superintendent of schools if there be any such city superintendent of schools—and if not, then with the county superintendent of schools, or any person deputized by them to receive and act upon such application, stating his or her age, residence, address, school attendance, grade, names of parent, parents or guardian, and in detail the nature of employment sought, the number and character of the performances, the kind of work required and the name of the employer, and such facts as may be required to enable such person to pass intelligently upon such application. Within not less than 48 hours of the filing of such application, it shall be the duty of such officer to hear and determine such application, and if the same shall be granted, such officer granting the same, shall issue a written permit to such child, stating therein his reasons for such permit. If such application is refused, the child or the person making the same for the child shall be entitled upon demand, within 24 hours after such refusal, to be furnished with a written statement of the reasons of such officer for refusing to issue such permit. An appeal may be taken from the decision of such officer so passing upon such application to the county or juvenile court of the county in which such application is made, upon such child, its parent or guardian or any person interested in the protection of such child filing a brief written petition with the clerk of said court, with a copy of such refusal to grant such permit: *Provided*, Such appeal is taken within ten days after the refusal to issue such permit. No fee shall be charged for any such application or on account of any such appeal. No permit shall be granted under the provisions of this section to any child to be employed in any concert or theatrical exhibition or performance unless it shall be made to appear that suitable provisions have been made by the employer of such child for the protection of the moral and physical health and the education of such child. The person passing upon such application or any court before whom such matter may be brought for final determination, may, as a condition to granting such permit, make such reasonable terms and conditions as shall seem necessary and proper for safeguarding the moral and physical health of such child and giving it such educational advantages as may seem to be for its best interests. And it shall be lawful to attach as a condition to any such permit mentioned in this section a written promise of the employer of such child to comply with the terms thereof and a bond or undertaking to the people of the State of Colorado in the penal sum to be fixed by the court, not exceeding two thousand dollars ($2,000), with one or more sureties may be required by the court of such employer conditioned that he will faithfully carry out the terms and conditions upon which such permit may be granted. Permits or copies certified to as correct by the authorities issuing the same granting exemptions from this act for children to appear in any concert or theatrical performance shall be kept on file at the box office of concert halls or theatre in which any such child may appear under such permits. All such permits shall be subject to inspection by the humane society and probation officers and factory inspectors. Any person may apply to the county juvenile court to have the exemption permitted by this act revoked by such court by filing with the clerk of the court a short petition setting up the facts showing that the conditions of the permit granting such exemption have been violated, or that it is not for the best interest of such child to have such permit or exemption. Whereupon, the court shall issue a summons or notice to such child and to at least one of its parents or guardian, if there be such parent or guardian in the county, requiring them to appear before such court within not less than forty-eight hours to show cause why the prayer of such petition should not be granted or such permit or exemption should not be revoked. During that part of the months of June, July and August when the public schools are not in regular session, children over twelve years of age shall be entitled to exemptions from the provisions of this act, permitted by section fifteen, upon complying with the conditions and receiving the permit provided for in said section.

SEC. 16. Whoever, having under his control a child under the age of 16 years, permits such child to be employed in violation of the provisions of this act, shall for each offense be fined not less than five dollars ($5.00) nor more than twenty-five dollars ($25.00), and shall stand committed until such fine and costs are paid. A failure to produce to the inspector of factories, his assistant or deputies, any age and school certificates or lists required by this act, shall constitute a violation of this act, and the person so failing shall, upon conviction, be fined not less than five dollars ($5.00) nor more than fifty dollars ($50.00) for each offense. Every person authorized to sign the certificate prescribed by section 7 of this act, who certifies to any materially false statement therein, shall be guilty of a violation of this act, and upon conviction be fined not less than five dollars ($5.00) nor more than one hundred dollars ($100) for each offense, and shall stand committed until such fine and costs are paid. Any person, firm or corporation, agent or manager, superintendent or foreman of any firm or corporation, whether for himself or for such firm or corporation, or by himself or through subagents or foreman, superintendent or manager, who shall violate or fail to comply with any of the provisions of this act, or shall refuse admittance to premises, or otherwise obstruct the factory inspector, assistant factory inspector or deputy factory inspector in the performance of their duties, as prescribed by this act, shall be deemed guilty of a misdemeanor, and upon conviction thereof shall be fined not less than five dollars ($5.00) nor more than one hundred dollars ($100) for each offense, and shall stand committed until such fine and costs are paid. *[Violations.]*

It is the intention and purpose of this act to extend personal responsibility to the president and general manager of any corporation for violation of this act by any foreman, superintendent or submanager or subagent. *[Who liable.]*

SEC. 17. Any person, agent, firm or corporation who shall be convicted of a second violation of any provision of this act, shall be fined in a sum not less than one hundred dollars ($100), or more than five hundred dollars ($500) or be imprisoned in the county jail for not to exceed ninety (90) days or by both such fine and imprisonment, in the discretion of the court. *[Second offenses.]*

SEC. 19. This act shall not be construed to repeal any part of an act to compel the elementary education of children in school districts of the first and second class, as approved April 12, 1899, and as amended and approved March 7, 1903, [.] * * * *[Construction.]*

Nothing in this act shall be construed to repeal any act or law of this State concerning the dependency or delinquency of children or persons causing, encouraging or contributing thereto.

CONNECTICUT.

GENERAL STATUTES—1902.

Employment of children—Certain employments forbidden.

Acrobatic and immoral occupations. SECTION 1163. Every person who shall exhibit, use, employ, apprentice, give away, let out, or otherwise dispose of any child under the age of twelve years, in or for the vocation, occupation, service, or purpose of rope or wire walking, dancing, skating, bicycling, or peddling, or as a gymnast, contortionist, rider, or acrobat, in any place whatever; or for or in any obscene, indecent, or immoral purpose, exhibition, or practice, whatsoever; or for or in any business, exhibition, or vocation, injurious to the health, or dangerous to the life or limb of such child; or who shall cause, procure, or encourage any such child to engage therein, shall be fined not more than two hundred and fifty dollars, or imprisoned not more than one year, or both. But nothing herein shall prevent the employment of any such child as a singer or musician, in any church or school, or in learning or teaching the science or practice of music.

Employment of children—School attendance.

School attendance. SECTION 2116. All parents and those who have the care of children shall bring them up in some lawful and honest employment, and instruct them or cause them to be instructed in reading, writing, spelling, English grammar, geography, arithemtic, and United States history. Every parent or other person having control of a child over seven or under sixteen years of age shall cause such child to attend a public day school regularly during the hours and terms the public school in the district wherein such child resides is in session, or while the school is in session where provision for the instruction of such child is made according to law, unless the parent or person having control of such child can show that the child is elsewhere receiving regularly thorough instruction during said hours and terms in the studies taught in the public schools. Chil-

Employed children. dren over fourteen years of age shall not be subject to the requirements of this section while lawfully employed at labor at home or elsewhere; but this provision shall not permit such children to be irregular in attendance at school while they are enrolled as scholars, nor exempt any child who is enrolled as a member of a school from any rule concerning irregularity of attendance which has been enacted or may be enacted by the town school committee, board of school visitors, or board of education, having control of the school.

Employment during school time. SEC. 2119. Every person who shall employ a child under fourteen years of age during the hours while the school which such child should attend is in session, and every person who shall authorize or permit on premises under his control any such child to be so employed, shall be fined not more than twenty dollars for every week in which such child is so employed.

False statements. SEC. 2120. Every parent or other person, having control of a child, who shall make any false statement concerning the age of such child with intent to deceive the town clerk or registrar of births, marriages, and deaths of any town, or the teacher of any school, or shall instruct a child to make any such false statement, shall be fined not more than twenty dollars.

Power of visitors. SEC. 2121. The school visitors or the town school committee in every town shall, once or more in every year, examine into the situation of the children employed in all manufacturing establishments, and ascertain whether all the provisions of this chapter are duly observed, and report all violations thereof to the proper prosecuting authority.

Illiterates. SEC. 2147. No person over fourteen and under sixteen years of age, who can not read and write, shall be employed in any town where public evening schools are established unless he can produce every school month of twenty days a certificate from the teacher of an evening school showing that he has attended such school eighteen consecutive evenings in the current school month, and is a regular attendant.

Every person who shall employ a child contrary to the provisions of this section shall be fined not more than fifty dollars, and the State board of education shall enforce the provisions of this section as provided in section 4707 [i. e., through agents appointed by the board].

Employment of children—Elevators.

SECTION 2614. No person, partnership, or corporation shall permit or employ a person under the age of sixteen years to have the care, custody, operation, or management of an elevator. Every person, partnership, or corporation violating any provision of this section shall forfeit not more than twenty-five dollars for each offense. Children under sixteen.

Employment of minors in barrooms, etc.

SECTION 2682. No person having a license under the provisions of this title shall employ any minor as bartender, porter, or in any other capacity, in any saloon where spirituous and intoxicating liquors are kept for sale, and upon such employment the county commissioners shall revoke the license of such person. Every person so licensed employing any minor as aforesaid shall be subject to the penalties of section 2712. [Fine for first offense; fine or imprisonment for subsequent offenses.] Minors not to be employed.

Seats for female employees.

SECTION 4703. Every person, partnership, or corporation, employing females in any mercantile, mechanical, or manufacturing establishment shall furnish and provide suitable seats for the use of all females so employed, and shall permit the use of such seats by said females when they are not necessarily engaged in the active duties for which they are employed. Every person, partnership, or corporation violating any provision of this section shall be fined not more than fifty dollars. Seats to be provided.

ACTS OF 1909.

CHAPTER 220.—*Employment of women and children—Hours of labor.*

SECTION 1. No minor under sixteen years of age, and no woman, shall be employed in laboring in any manufacturing or mechanical establishment more than ten hours in any day, except when it is necessary to make repairs to prevent the interruption of the ordinary running of the machinery, or where a different apportionment of the hours of labor is made for the sole purpose of making a shorter day's work for one day of the week. Every employer in such establishment shall post in a conspicuous place in every room where such persons are employed, a notice, the form of which shall be furnished by the factory inspector, specifically stating the hours of work required of them on each day of the week, and the employment of any such person for a longer time in any day than so stated shall be a violation of this section, unless it appears that such employment is to make up for time lost on some previous day of the same calendar week in consequence of the stopping of machinery upon which such person was employed or dependent for employment; but in no case shall the hours of labor exceed fifty-eight in a calendar week: *Provided,* That in case any employer in such establishment shall, on or before the first day of January of any year, give notice to his employees, by notices posted as hereinbefore provided, that the hours of labor of minors under sixteen years of age and of women employed by him, as aforesaid, shall not exceed fifty-five in any week during the months of June, July, and August of the ensuing calendar year, then said employer may employ such minors and women not to exceed sixty hours in any week during said year, except during said months of June, July, and August. Hours of labor per day in factories, etc.
Schedule to be posted.

SEC. 2 (as amended by chapter 278, Acts of 1911). No minor under sixteen years of age, and no woman, shall be employed in laboring in any mercantile establishment, other than manufacturing or mechanical, more than fifty-eight hours in any calendar week. Every employer in such establishment shall post in a conspicuous place, in Fifty-eight hours per week in mercantile establishments.
Schedules to be posted.

every room where such persons are employed, a notice, the form of which shall be furnished by the factory inspector, stating specifically the hours of work required of such persons on each day of the week, and the employment of any such person for a longer time in any day than so stated shall be a violation of this section: *Provided,* That in **Provisos.** case any employer in such establishment shall, on or before the first day of January of any year, give notice to his employees, by notices posted as hereinbefore provided that the hours of labor of minors under sixteen years of age and of women employed by him, as aforesaid, shall not exceed fifty-five in any calendar week during the months of June, July, and August of the ensuing year, then said employer may employ such minors and women not to exceed sixty hours in any calendar week during said year, except during said months of June, July, and August: *And provided, further,* That any employer in such establishment who shall, during each year, give not less than seven holidays with pay, shall be exempt from the provisions of this section during the period from the seventeenth to the twenty-fifth day of December of each year.

Night work. SEC. 3. No such minor and no woman shall in any event be employed in laboring in any such establishment as is described in section two hereof after ten o'clock in the evening of any day, unless the employer in such establishment shall, on such day, employ two or more shifts or sets of such employees, in which event no one such shift or set of employees shall be employed during more than ten hours of such day.

Enforcement. SEC. 4. It shall be the duty of the factory inspector to examine and inquire into the employment of minors and women in the establishments described in this act, and to investigate all complaints of violations hereof, and to report all cases of such violation to the prosecuting officer having jurisdiction thereof. The factory inspector shall, on or before the first day of December in each year, make a report to the governor of the number of such violations so reported by him, and of the prosecutions instituted thereon.

Violations. SEC. 5. Every person who willfully employs, or has in his employment or under his charge, any person in violation of section one, two, or three of this act, and every parent or guardian who permits any such minor to be so employed, shall be fined not more than twenty dollars for each offense. A certificate of the age of a minor, made as provided in section 4705 of the General Statutes and amendments thereof, shall be conclusive evidence of his age upon the trial of any person other than the parent or guardian for violation of any provision of this act.

Repeal. SEC. 6. * * * Nothing in this act shall be construed as repealing any provision of section 2116 of the General Statutes or any amendments thereto.

ACTS OF 1911.

CHAPTER 101.—*Employment of females in saloons.*

Employment restricted. SECTION 1. Section two of chapter 265 of the Public Acts of 1907 [prescribing who may be licensed to sell intoxicants] is hereby amended by inserting * * * the words "and no female, unless she be the wife or daughter of the proprietor, shall be employed in any capacity in any licensed saloon, except in a hotel of established good reputation in which the county commissioners of the county shall have, in writing, authorized the employment of females," * * *

CHAPTER 119.—*Employment of children—General provisions.*

Age limit. SECTION 1. No child under fourteen years of age shall be employed in any mechanical, mercantile, or manufacturing establishment. Every person, whether acting for himself or as agent for another, who shall employ or authorize or permit to be employed any child in violation of the provisions of this section shall be fined not more than one hundred dollars.

Certificates required. SEC. 2. No child under sixteen years of age shall be employed in any mechanical, mercantile, or manufacturing establishment unless the employer of such child shall have first obtained a certificate, signed by the secretary or an agent of the State board of education, or by a school supervisor, school superintendent, supervising principal, or acting school visitor designated by said board, stating the date of the birth of such child, showing that such child is over fourteen years of age, and stating that such child is able to read with facility, to legibly write simple sentences, and to perform the operations of the fundamental rules of arithmetic with relation both to whole numbers and to fractions, and does not appear to be physically unfit for employment. Such certificate shall be in the form prescribed and upon a blank furnished by the State board of education, and shall be issued in triplicate; and one copy thereof shall be delivered to the parent or guardian of such child, one copy shall be delivered to the employer, and one copy shall be deposited in the office of the State board of education. Copies of such certificate shall be obtainable from the State board of education, upon application, at any time. The copy of such certificate delivered to the parent or guardian of the child may be accepted by the employer as a temporary certificate, good for one week, after which time it shall be returned to the parent or guardian of such child. Every person, whether acting for himself or as agent for another, who shall employ or shall authorize or permit to be employed any child in violation of the provisions of this section, shall be fined not more than one hundred dollars. The secretary or the agent of the State board of education or the school supervisor, school superintendent, supervising principal, or acting school visitor to whom application shall be made for a certificate as provided in this section, shall have power to require all statements of fact offered in support of such application to be made under oath, and such oath may be administered by said secretary, or such agent, school supervisor, school superintendent, supervising principal, or acting school visitor, and said secretary, or any such agent, school supervisor, school superintendent, supervising principal, or acting school visitor may cause any child to be examined by a reputable physician, for the purpose of aiding him in determining whether such child is physically fit for employment, and may charge the expense of such physical examination against the State as a part of his expenses. *Employment without certificate.*

Medical examination.

SEC. 3. Every employer receiving a certificate issued under the provisions of this act shall promptly notify the State board of education, in writing, in the form prescribed and upon a blank furnished by said board, of the time of commencement of the employment of any child thereunder and, whenever such employment terminates before such child attains the age of sixteen years, of the time of the termination of such employment. Every person violating any provision of this section shall be fined not more than ten dollars. *Notices by employers.*

SEC. 4. The provisions of sections two and three of this act shall not apply to employers of children over fourteen years of age in cases in which the employment commenced prior to the date on which this act shall take effect and in which the employer has also complied with the requirements of the statutes in force at the time of the commencement of such employment. *Prior regulations.*

SEC. 5. Every employer or other person having control of any establishment or premises where children under sixteen years of age are employed who shall neglect to have and keep on file the certificate described in section two of this act or to show the same, with a list of the names of such children so employed, to the secretary or an agent of the State board of education, when demanded during the usual business hours, shall be fined not more than one hundred dollars. *Files.*

SEC. 6. The provisions of section 4707 of the General Statutes [relating to enforcement by agents of the State board of education] shall be applicable to sections one, two, and three of this act. * * * *Enforcement.*

CHAPTER 123.—*Employment of children—Age limit in dangerous trades.*

SECTION 1. No child under sixteen years of age shall be employed or permitted to work in operating or assisting in operating any of the following machines: Circular or band saws, wood shapers, wood jointers, planers, sandpaper or wood-polishing machinery; picker machines or machines used in picking wool, cotton, fur, hair, or any upholstery material; paper-lace machines; burnishing machines in any tannery or *Employments forbidden to children under sixteen.*

leather manufactory; job or cylinder printing presses having motor power other than foot; wood turning or boring machinery; stamping machines used in sheet metal and tinware manufacturing or in washer or nut factories; machines used in making corrugating rolls; dough brakes or cracker machinery of any description; wire or iron straightening machinery; rolling mill machinery; power punches or shears; washing, grinding, or mixing machinery; calendar [calender] rolls in rubber manufacturing; or laundering machinery.

Same.

SEC. 2. No child under sixteen years of age shall be employed or permitted to work at adjusting or assisting in adjusting any belt to any machinery, or oiling or assisting in oiling, wiping, or cleaning machinery; or, in any capacity, in preparing any composition in which dangerous or poisonous acids are used; or in soldering; or in the manufacture or packing of paints, dry colors, or red or white lead; or in the manufacture, packing, or storing of powder, dynamite, nitroglycerin, compounds, safety fuses in the raw or unvarnished state, electric fuses for blasting purposes, or other explosives; or in or about any distillery, brewery, or other establishment where malt or alcoholic liquors are manufactured, packed, wrapped, or bottled; and no female under sixteen years of age shall be employed or permitted to work in any capacity requiring such female to stand continuously.

Operating elevators.

SEC. 3. No person under eighteen years of age shall be employed or permitted to have the care, custody, or management of or to operate an elevator, either for freight or passengers, running at a speed of over two hundred feet per minute. Nothing in this section shall be construed as repealing section 2614 of the General Statutes.

Enforcement.

SEC. 4. It shall be the duty of the factory inspector to enforce the provisions of this act, to investigate all complaints of violations thereof, and to report all cases of such violation to the prosecuting officer having jurisdiction. The factory inspector shall, on or before the first day of December in each year, make a report to the governor of the number of such violations found and the number of prosecutions instituted thereon.

Violations.

SEC. 5. Every person, whether acting for himself or as agent for another, who shall employ or authorize or permit to be employed any child in violation of any of the provisions of this act shall be fined not more than one hundred dollars.

DELAWARE.

REVISED CODE—1893.

CHAPTER 127.—*Seats for female employees.*

(Page 932.)

Seats to be provided.

SECTION 1. Every person or corporation employing female employees in any manufacturing, mechanical or mercantile establishments in this State shall provide suitable seats for the use of the female employees so employed, and shall permit the use of such by them when not necessarily engaged in the active duties for which they are employed.

Penalty.

SEC. 2. Any person, firm or corporation violating any of the provisions of this act, shall be punished by a fine of not less than twenty-five dollars ($25) nor more than fifty dollars ($50) for each offense.

CHAPTER 131.—*Employment of children—Certain employments forbidden.*

(Page 954.)

Acrobatic, mendicant, etc., employments.

SECTION 2. Any person having the care, custody, or control of any minor child under the age of fifteen years who shall in any manner sell, apprentice, give away, or otherwise dispose of such minor, or any person who shall take, receive, or employ such child for the vocation or occupation of rope or wire walking or dancing, or as an acrobat or gymnast, or any person who, having the care, custody, or control of any minor child whatsoever, and shall sell, apprentice, give away, or otherwise dispose of such minor, or who shall take, receive, or employ such minor for begging or any obscure [sic], indecent, or illegal exhibition or vocation, or any vocation injurious to the health or dangerous to the life or limb of such child engaged therein, or for the purpose of prostitution, or any person who shall retain, harbor, or employ any minor child in or about any assignation house or brothel, shall be deemed guilty of a misdemeanor, and upon conviction thereof before any justice of the peace or court of record shall be fined not less than twenty dollars nor more than one hundred dollars for each and every offense.

ACTS OF 1897.

CHAPTER 452.—*Factories and workshops—Provisions for female employees—New Castle County.*

SECTION 1 (as amended by chapter 453, Acts of 1897). It shall be the duty of every person or corporation employing female labor to the number of ten or upwards in New Castle County to provide, within three months after the passage of this act, a room or rooms, plainly and appropriately furnished, for such female employees to dress, wash and lunch in, separate and apart from the male employees of such person or corporation, allowing in said separate room or rooms [sic]; *and further*, to provide washing sinks for such female employees, separate and apart from such male employees, allowing one such washing sink to each fifteen of such female employees employed by such person or corporation; *and further*, to provide water-closets for such female employees, separate from those used by such male employees: *Provided*, That nothing in this section shall apply to canning establishments doing business in the rural districts of said county. **Dressing rooms, etc.**

SEC. 2. It shall be the duty of every storekeeper in New Castle County to provide seats for his or her clerks and employees, so that when unemployed such clerks and employees may be seated. **Seats.**

SEC. 3. It shall be the duty of every person or corporation employing female labor to provide such places for such female employees to work in during cold weather as shall be reasonably and comfortably warm. **Workrooms to be warm.**

SEC. 4. It shall be unlawful for any employer of female labor, or any overseer, superintendent, foreman or boss of any such employer of female labor to use toward female employees any abusive, indecent or profane language, or to in any manner abuse, misuse, unnecessarily expose to hardship, or maltreat any such female employee. **Abusive, etc., language forbidden.**

SEC. 5. Any person violating any provision of section 4 of this act shall be deemed guilty of a misdemeanor, and upon conviction thereof shall be fined not less than ten and not exceeding one hundred dollars for each offense; any person or corporation violating any provision of the first, second and third sections of this act shall be deemed guilty of a misdemeanor, and upon conviction thereof shall be fined the sum of ten dollars, and shall be subject to the further penalty of ten dollars for each day thereafter during which such corporation or person shall refuse or neglect to provide the furnished rooms, seats, appliances or furnish the heat therein mentioned. **Penalty.**

SEC. 7. The chief justice of the State of Delaware is hereby authorized and required within sixty days after the passage of this act to appoint a female inspector, whose duty it shall be to visit from time to time all stores, mills, factories and other places of business where female labor is employed and to duly enforce the provisions of this act. Whenever said inspector shall ascertain that the provisions of this act or any of them are being violated by any employer of New Castle County, it shall be the duty of said inspector to serve upon such violator of the provisions of this act written notice that unless such employer shall conform to the requirements of this act, and wholly cease any violation thereof within ten days from the services of such notice, such employer will be prosecuted under the provisions of this act. And it shall further be the duty of said inspector in case of the neglect or failure of such employer, who has received such notice, to conform to the provisions of this act, and to cease all violations thereof within ten days from the said service of notice, to institute the prosecution of such recalcitrant employer or employers under the provisions of this act, by swearing out before any justice of the peace in New Castle County resident **Female inspector.**

in the hundred where said employer may have his, her or its place of business, or in an adjacent hundred, the necessary warrant or complaint and thereupon to assist and enforce the prosecution of the person or corporation so complained of to the full extent of her power, and it shall further be the duty of such inspector in case any prosecutions under the provisions of this act shall be begun or instituted by any other person than such inspector, to aid, further and assist such independent prosecution of such employer to the best of her power, and whenever such independent prosecution of any such employer shall be begun by any person other than said inspector it shall be the duty of the justice of the peace before whom such complaint shall be made to straightway notify by due course of mail the inspector appointed under this act, informing such inspector of the name of the complainant and defendant, of the names of the witnesses indorsed upon said complaint and of the day, hour and place fixed for the hearing of said cause.

Inspector to have access to workrooms. SEC. 8. It shall be the duty of every employer of female labor in New Castle County, whether to the number of ten or upward or less, to permit said inspector to have full and free access at any time during the working noon hours of said employees to the place of business of such employer where such employees are employed, and in case any such employer shall refuse such inspector full and free access to his place of business as aforesaid, or shall in any way hinder or prevent the full performance of her duties of inspection under the provisions of this act, such employer shall be deemed guilty of a misdemeanor, and upon every conviction of such interference with said inspector in the performance of her duties, shall pay a fine to New Castle County of ten dollars, which fine shall be collected in the same manner as the other fines and penalties heretofore provided for in this act.

Terms, etc. SEC. 9 (as amended by chapter 453, Acts of 1897). The inspector appointed under this act shall hold her said office for the term of two years, or until her successor is appointed, and shall receive an annual salary of three hundred dollars, payable quarterly, by warrants upon the county treasury; it shall further be her duty on the first day of August in each year subsequent to the year of her appointment, to *Report.* make a written report to the chief justice of her acts and of all transactions under this statute. The provisions of this act shall apply to and be enforced only in duly incorporated towns and cities in New Castle County.

ACTS OF 1905.

CHAPTER 123.—*Employment of children—General provisions.*

Age limit. SECTION 1 (as amended by chapter 121, Acts of 1909). No child under the age of fourteen years shall be employed or suffered to work at any gainful occupation.

School attendance required. SEC. 2 (as amended by chapter 121, Acts of 1909). No child between the ages of fourteen and sixteen years shall be employed in any factory, workshop or establishment where the manufacture of any kinds of goods whatever is carried on unless such child shall have attended a public school or a school equivalent thereto or a parochial school for not less than one hundred and forty days during the school year previous to his arriving at the age of fourteen years, or within the school year immediately preceding such employment, and unless such child shall be able to read and write simple sentences in the English language, and be familiar with the fundamental operations of arithmetic up to fractions.

Hours of labor. SEC. 3 (as amended by chapter 121, Acts of 1909). No child or children under the age of sixteen years shall be employed in any gainful occupation for a longer period than nine hours a day or fifty-four hours a week or before the hour of seven o'clock in the morning or after the hour of six o'clock in the evening: *And further provided,* That every such child so employed shall be entitled to not less than thirty minutes for mealtime at noon, and every employer shall post in a conspicuous place, where such minor children are employed a printed notice, stating that the maximum work hours required in any one week shall not exceed fifty-four hours. The governor shall immediately after the passage of this bill, appoint by and with the advice and consent of the senate some suitable person, who shall be a resident and citizen of this State, who shall be designated and known by the official title of "Factory and

Workshop Inspector,'' and who shall receive a salary of one thousand dollars per year, payable in equal quarterly installments of two hundred and fifty dollars, and who shall hold office for the term of two years; the said inspector shall be empowered to visit and inspect at all reasonable hours and as often as practicable all factories, workshop's [workshops] and other establishments in this State, where the manufacture or sale of any kind of goods is carried on, and it shall be the duty of the said inspector to enforce the provisions of this act and to prosecute all violations of the same as hereinafter provided, and he shall have the power to demand a certificate of physical fitness from some regularly licensed physician of the State or county in which such establishment is located in the case of a child under sixteen years of age, who may seem physically unable to perform the labor at which such child may be employed, and the said inspector shall have power to prohibit the employment of any such child under the age of sixteen years, who shall be unable to obtain such certificate.

The said factory and workshop inspector is hereby further directed and empowered to inquire into and investigate whether the employers within this act observe its provisions and to examine the sworn statements of the parents or guardians and the certificates of teachers, as required by section 4 of this act, and to thoroughly investigate the truth of the facts therein recited, and after such inquiry, examination and investigation if it appears to the satisfaction of the said factory and workshop inspector that said employers have not observed the provisions of this act or that the said certificates or statements are untrue in whole or in part, he is hereby empowered to deliver to said employer a written notice in the following form, viz: *Enforcement.*

To —— ——

You are hereby notified and directed to discharge from your employ —— within —— days from the receipt of this notice.

—— ——,
Factory and Workshop Inspector.

It shall be unlawful for the employer of any child within the provisions of this act to fail to comply with the terms of said notice.

SEC. 4 (as amended by chapter 121, Acts of 1909). It shall be the duty of every person or corporation employing a child or children within the provisions of this act to keep a register, in which shall be recorded the name, age, day of birth and place of residence of every child under the age of sixteen years so employed by such person or corporation; and such register shall be produced on demand and shown to the factory and workshop inspector. It shall be unlawful for any person or corporation to employ any minor under the age of sixteen years unless there is furnished to said person or corporation a sworn statement made by the parent or guardian of such minor, stating the name, date and place of birth of such minor, and also unless there is furnished to said person or corporation a certificate of the teacher or teachers of said minor child showing that it has attended school, has received the instruction and is qualified as prescribed by section 2 of this act. *Registers.* *Proof of age.* *Schooling certificate.*

It shall be the duty of said person or corporation employing such child to keep on file said affidavit and certificate during such employment, and upon the termination thereof to deliver up said affidavit and certificate to said child upon its request therefor. The sworn statement of the parent or guardian shall be filled out and made in the following form: *Files.*

State of Delaware, *Form of certificate.*
——— County. ss.

Before me —— ——, a notary public for the State of Delaware, personally appears (parent or guardian of child), who being sworn in due form of law, doth depose and say that (he or she) is the (parent or guardian) of (name of minor), who is —— years of age.

That said (minor) was born on the —— day of —— A. D. —— at —— and that the present residence of the said (minor's name) is ——.

Sworn and subscribed before me the —— day of ——, A. D. ——.

—— ——,
Notary Public for the State of Delaware.

The certificate of the teacher or teachers shall be made out in the following form:

Sworn and subscribed before me the —— day of——, A. D. ——.

Notary Public for the State of Delaware.

The certificate of the teacher or teachers shall be made out in the following form:

—— —— 19——.

This is to certify that (minor's name) has attended school in —— Hundred and —— County from —— to —— during the school years of ——.

Total number of days ——.

Total number of nights ——.

and of my personal knowledge (minor's name) is able to read and write simple sentences in the English language, and is familiar with the fundamental operation of arithmetic up to fractions.

—— ——,
Teacher.

It shall be unlawful for any person or corporation to employ a child within the provisions of this act without first receiving and filing said sworn statement of the parent or guardian of such child and said teacher's certificate as hereinabove provided.

Penalty. SEC. 5. Every person, or the officer or officers of any corporation violating the provisions of this act shall be deemed guilty of a misdemeanor and upon conviction thereof shall be fined a sum not less than fifty dollars nor more than one hundred dollars for each and every such offense.

Enforcement. SEC. 6. It shall be the duty of such factory or workshop inspector appointed under the provisions of this act to inspect the sanitary conditions of any factory workshop or other establishment, wherein minors are employed in accordance with the provisions of this act and to make report in writing of his findings to the governor, to the board of health of the city of Wilmington and the State board of health quarterly, or more frequently if he shall deem it necessary.

Canneries, etc. SEC. 7 (as amended by chapter 121, Acts of 1909). The provisions of this act shall not apply to any person or corporation engaged in the canning or preserving of fruits, vegetables or provisions or in the carrying on of any agricultural business "or to any person or persons, firm or corporation, engaged in the manufacture of fruit and berry baskets," or to any person or corporation employing a child or children in domestic service.

DISTRICT OF ALASKA.

ACTS OF U. S. CONGRESS—1898–1899.

CHAPTER 429.—TITLE 2.—*Employment of females and minors in barrooms.*

Employment in barrooms forbidden. SECTION 478. No licensee under a barroom license shall employ, or permit to be employed, or allow any female or minor or person convicted of crime, to sell, give, furnish, or distribute any intoxicating drinks or any admixture thereof, ale, wine, or beer to any person or persons. * * *

DISTRICT OF COLUMBIA.

CODE.

[Approved March 3, 1901; amended January 31 and June 30, 1902.]

Employment of children—Certain employments forbidden.

Acrobatic and mendicant occupations. SECTION 814. * * * Any person, having in his custody or control a child under the age of fourteen years, who shall in any way dispose of it with a view to its being employed as an acrobat, or a gymnast, or a contortionist, or a circus rider, or a ropewalker, or in any exhibition of like dangerous character, or as a beggar, or mendicant, or pauper, or street singer, or street musician; or any person who shall take, receive, hire, employ, use, exhibit, or have in custody any child of the age last named for any of the purposes last enumerated, shall be deemed guilty of a misdemeanor, and, when convicted thereof, shall be subject to punishment by a fine of not more than two hundred and fifty dollars, or by imprisonment for a term not exceeding two years, or both.

ACTS OF 1894-95.

CHAPTER 192.—*Seats for female employees.*

SECTION 1. All persons who employ females in stores, shops, offices, or manufactories as clerks, assistants, operatives, or helpers in any business, trade, or occupation carried on or operated by them in the District of Columbia, shall be required to procure and provide proper and suitable seats for all such females and shall permit the use of such seats, rests, or stools, as may be necessary, and shall not make any rules, regulations, or orders preventing the use of such stools or seats when any such female employees are not actively employed in their work in such business or employment. *Seats to be provided.*

SEC. 2. If any employer of female help in the District of Columbia, shall neglect or refuse to provide seats, as provided in this act, or shall make any rules, orders, or regulations in his shop, store, or other place of business, requiring females to remain standing when not necessarily employed in service or labor therein, he shall be deemed guilty of a misdemeanor, and upon conviction thereof in any court of competent jurisdiction shall be liable to a fine therefor in a sum not to exceed twenty-five dollars, with costs, in the discretion of the court. *Penalty.*

ACTS OF 1905-6.

CHAPTER 3054.—*Employment of children—School attendance.*

SECTION 1. Every parent, guardian, or other person residing in the District of Columbia having charge and control of a child between the ages of eight and fourteen years shall cause such child to be regularly instructed in the elementary branches of knowledge, including reading, writing, English grammar, geography, and arithmetic, and pursuant to this end every such parent, guardian, or other person aforesaid shall cause any child under the charge and control of such person to attend some public, private, or parochial school during the period of each year the public schools in the District are in session, on the customary days and during the customary hours of the school term. No child shall be credited with attendance upon a private or parochial school unless the attendance officer hereinafter provided for receives a certificate of attendance signed by the person in charge of such school. A child between the ages aforesaid may be excused from school attendance or instruction upon presentation of satisfactory evidence to the superintendent of schools that such child is being or has been within said year instructed a like period of time in the branches taught in the public schools, or that such child has acquired these branches of learning, or that the physical or mental condition of such child is such as to render such attendance or instruction inexpedient or impracticable. *Attendance required.*

SEC. 5. Any person who induces or attempts to induce any child to be absent unlawfully from school, or who knowingly employs or harbors while school is in session any child absent unlawfully from school, shall be deemed guilty of a misdemeanor and be punished by a fine of not more than twenty dollars. *Unlawful employment, etc.*

SEC. 6. The officers empowered under this act shall visit any place or establishment where minor children are employed to ascertain whether the provisions of this law are duly complied with, and shall as often as twice a year demand from all employers of such children a list of children employed, with their names and ages. *Enforcement.*

ACTS OF 1907–8.

CHAPTER 209.—*Employment of children—General provisions.*

Age limit.   SECTION 1. No child under fourteen years of age shall be employed or permitted to work in the District of Columbia in any factory, workshop, mercantile establishment, store, business office, telegraph or telephone office, restaurant, hotel, apartment house, club, theater, Employment bowling alley, laundry, bootblack 'stand, or in the distribution or during school transmission of merchandise or messages. No such child shall be time. employed in any work performed for wages or other compensation, to whomsoever payable, during the hours when the public schools of the District of Columbia are in session, nor before the hour of six o'clock in Night work. the morning or after the hour of seven o'clock in the evening: *Provided,* That the provisions of this section shall not apply to children employed Permits, when. in the service of the Senate: *And provided further,* That the judge of the juvenile court of said District may, upon the application of the parent, guardian, or next friend of said child, issue a permit for the employment of any child between the ages of twelve and fourteen years at any occupation or employment not in his judgmen dangerous or injurious to the health or morals of such child, upon evidence satisfactory to him that the labor of such child is necessary for its support, or for the assistance of a disabled, ill, or invalid father or mother, or for the support in whole or in part of a younger brother or sister or a widowed mother. Such permits shall be issued for a definite time, but they shall be revocable at the discretion of the judge by whom they are issued or by his successor in office. Hearings for granting and revoking permits shall be held upon such notice and under such rules and regulations as the judge of said court shall prescribe.

Age and schooling certificate.   SEC. 2. No child under sixteen years of age shall be employed or permitted to work in the District of Columbia in any of the establishments named in section one, unless the person or corporation employing him procures and keeps on file and accessible to the inspectors authorized by this act and the truant officers of the District of Columbia an age and schooling certificate, and keeps two complete lists of all such children employed therein, one on file and one conspicuously posted near the principal entrance of the building in which such children are employed.

Approval.   SEC. 3. An age and schooling certificate shall be approved only by the superintendent of public schools, or by a person authorized by him in writing, who shall have authority to administer the oath provided for therein, but no fee shall be charged therefor.

Evidence.   SEC. 4. No age and schooling certificate shall be approved unless satisfactory evidence is furnished by duly attested transcript of the certificate of birth or baptism of such child, or other religious record, or the register of birth or the affidavit of the parent or guardian or custodian of a child, which affidavit shall be required, however, only in case such last-mentioned transcript of the certificate of birth be not procured and filed, showing the place and date of birth of such child, which affidavit must be taken before the officer issuing the employment certificate, who is hereby authorized and required to administer such oath, and who shall not demand or receive a fee therefor.

Form.   SEC. 5. The age and schooling certificate of a child under sixteen years of age shall be in the following form:

AGE AND SCHOOLING CERTIFICATE.

This certifies that I am the (father, mother, guardian, or custodian) of (name of child) ——— ———, and that (he or she) was born at (name of town or city) ——— in the county (name of county, if known) ——— and State (or country) ——— on the (day and year of birth) ——— **and** is now (number of years and months) ——— old.

Signature of (father, mother, guardian, or custodian).

(Date.)

There personally appeared before me the above-named (name of person signing) ——— ——— and made oath that the foregoing certificate by (him or her) signed is true to the best of (his or her) knowledge and belief. I hereby approve the foregoing certificate of (name of child) —— ——; complexion (fair or dark), ——; hair (color), —— having no sufficient reason to doubt that (he or she) is of the age therein certified, I hereby certify that (he or she) can read at sight and can write legibly simple sentences in the English language, and that (he or she) has reached the normal development of a child of (his or her) age, and is in sound health and is physically able to perform the work which (he or she) intends to do, and that (he or she) has regularly attended the public schools, or a school equivalent thereto, for not less than one hundred and thirty days during the school year previous to applying for such school record, or during the year previous to applying for such school record, and has received during such period instruction in reading, spelling, writing, and arithmetic.

This certificate belongs to (name of child in whose behalf it is drawn) —— —— and is to be surrendered to (him or her) whenever (he or she) leaves the service of the corporation or employer holding the same, but if not claimed by said child within thirty days from such time it shall be returned to the superintendent of schools.

(Signature of person authorized to approve and sign, with official character of authority.)

(Date.)

A duplicate of each age and schooling certificate shall be filled out **Filing.** and kept on file by the superintendent of public schools. Any explanatory matter may be printed with such certificate, in the discretion of said superintendent: *Provided,* That in exceptional cases the judge of the juvenile court, upon the recommendation of the superintendent of public schools, or the person authorized to act for him, may, in writing, waive the necessity of the schooling certificate provided for in this act, and in such cases the age certificate shall entitle the holder to be employed without a violation of this act.

SEC. 6. Whoever employs a child or permits a child to be employed **Violations.** in violation of sections one, two, eight, or nine of this act shall be deemed guilty of a misdemeanor and, for such offense, be fined not more than fifty dollars; and whoever continues to employ any child in violation of any of said sections of this act, after being notified by an inspector authorized by this act, or a truant officer of the District of Columbia, shall for every day thereafter that such employment continues be fined not more than twenty dollars. A failure to produce to an inspector authorized by this act, or a truant officer of the District of Columbia, any age or schooling certificate or list required by this act shall be prima facie evidence of illegal employment of any person whose age and schooling certificate is not produced or whose name is not listed. Any corporation or employer retaining any age and schooling certificate in violation of section five of this act shall be fined not more than twenty dollars. Every person authorized to sign the certificate prescribed by section five of this act who knowingly certifies to any materially false statement therein shall be fined not more than fifty dollars.

SEC. 7. The inspectors authorized by this act and the truant officers **Inspection.** of the District of Columbia shall visit the establishments named in section one and ascertain whether any minors are employed therein contrary to the provisions of this act, and they shall report any cases of such illegal employment to the superintendent of public schools and the corporation counsel of the District of Columbia. The inspectors authorized by this act and the truant officers of the District of Columbia shall require that the age and schooling certificates and lists provided for in this act of minors employed in the establishments named in section one shall be produced for their inspection.

SEC. 8. No minor under sixteen years of age shall be employed, **Hours of labor.** permitted, or suffered to work in any of the establishments named in section one more than eight hours in any one day, or before the **Night work.** hour of six o'clock antemeridian, or after the hour of seven o'clock postmeridian, and in no case shall the number of hours exceed forty-eight in a week.

SEC. 9. Every employer shall post in a conspicuous place in every **Schedule to be** room where such persons are employed a printed notice, stating the **posted.** number of hours required of them on each day of the week, the hours of commencing and stopping work, and the hours when the time or times allowed for dinner or for other meals begin and end The printed form of such notice shall be furnished by the inspectors authorized by this act and the truant officers of the District of Columbia, and the employment of any such person for a longer time in any day than that so stated shall be deemed a violation of this section.

Inspectors. SEC. 10. The Commissioners of the District of Columbia are hereby authorized to appoint two inspectors to carry out the purposes of this act, at a compensation not exceeding one thousand two hundred dollars each per annum.

Street trades. SEC. 11. No male child under ten, and no girl under sixteen years of age shall exercise the trade of boot blacking, or sell or expose or offer for sale any newspapers, magazines, periodicals, or goods, wares, or merchandise of any description whatsoever, upon the streets, roads, or highways, or in any public place within the District of Columbia.

Permits and badges. SEC. 12. From and after July first, nineteen hundred and eight, no male child under sixteen years shall exercise the trade of boot blacking or sell or expose or offer for sale any newspapers, magazines, periodicals or goods, ware or merchandise of any description whatsoever upon the streets, roads, or highways, or in any public place within the District of Columbia unless a permit and badge as hereinafter provided shall have been issued to him by the superintendent of public schools of the District of Columbia, or by a person authorized by him in writing for that purpose upon the application of the parent, guardian, or other person having the custody of the child desiring such a permit and badge, or in case said child has no parent, guardian, or custodian, then on the application of his next friend, being an adult.

Issue. SEC. 13. Such permit and badge shall be issued free of charge to the applicant, but shall not be issued until an age and schooling certificate shall have been issued as provided in this act.

Contents, etc. SEC. 14. Such permit shall state the date and place of birth of the child, the name and address of its parent, guardian, custodian, or next friend, as the case may be, and describe the color of hair and eyes, the height and weight, and any distinguishing facial mark of such child, and shall further state that the age and schooling certificate has been duly examined and filed, and that the child named in such permit has appeared before the officer issuing the permit. The badge furnished by the officer issuing the permit shall bear on its face a number corresponding to the number of the permit and the name of the child. Every such permit, and every such badge on its reverse side, shall be signed in the presence of the officer issuing the same by the child in whose name it is issued. The badge provided for herein shall be worn conspicuously at all times by such child while so working, and all such permits and badges shall expire annually on the first day of January. The color of the badge shall be changed each year. No child to whom such permit and badge are issued shall transfer the same to any other person, nor be engaged in the District of Columbia in any of the trades or occupations mentioned in this section without having conspicuously upon his person such badge, and he shall exhibit the same upon demand to any police or truant officer or to the inspectors in this act provided for.

Sale at night. SEC. 15. No child to whom a permit and badge are issued as provided for in the preceding sections shall sell or expose or offer for sale any newspapers, magazines, or periodicals or goods, wares, or merchandise of any description whatever after ten o'clock in the evening or before six o'clock in the morning.

Theatrical exhibitions. SEC. 16. Nothing in this act contained shall apply to the employment of any child in a theatrical exhibition, provided the written consent of one of the Commissioners of the District of Columbia is first obtained. Such consent shall specify the name of the child, its age, the names and residence of its parents or guardians, together with the place and character of the exhibition.

Jurisdiction. SEC. 17. The juvenile court of the District of Columbia is hereby given jurisdiction in all cases arising under this act.

FLORIDA.

GENERAL STATUTES—1906.

Seats for employees in stores, etc.

SECTION 3235. If any merchant, storekeeper, employer of male or *Seats to be pro-* female clerks, salesmen, cash boys or cash girls, or other assistants, *vided.* in mercantile or other business pursuits, requiring such employees to stand or walk during their active duties, neglect to furnish at their own cost or expense suitable chairs, stools or sliding seats attached to the counters or walls, for the use of such employees when not engaged in their active work, and not required to be on their feet in the proper performance of their several duties; or refuse to permit their said employees to make reasonable use of said seats during business hours, for purposes of necessary rest, and when such use will not interfere with humane or reasonable requirements of their employment, he shall, upon conviction thereof, be punished by a fine of not more than one hundred dollars, or imprisonment not exceeding sixty days.

Certain employments of children forbidden.

SECTION 3237. Whoever takes, receives, hires, employs, uses, exhib- *Acrobatic,* its or in any manner or under any pretense sells, apprentices, gives *mendicant, etc.,* away, lets out or otherwise disposes of to any person any child under *occupations.* the age of fourteen years for or in the vocation, occupation, service or purpose of singing, playing on musical instruments, rope or wire walking, dancing, begging or peddling, or as a contortionist, rider, acrobat, or for or in any obscene, indecent or immoral purpose, exhibition or practice, or for or in any business, exhibition or vocation injurious to the health or dangerous to the life or limbs of such child, or causes or procures, or encourages any such child to engage therein, * * * or has in custody any such child for any of the purposes aforesaid, shall be fined not more than five hundred dollars, or imprisoned not more than six months. Nothing contained in this section shall apply to or affect the employment or use of any such child as a singer or musician in any church, school or academy, or at any amateur concert or entertainment, or in learning the science or practice of music and social dancing.

Employment of children.

SECTION 3728. Whoever hires or employs or causes to be hired or *Consent of pa-* employed any minor, knowing such minor to be under the age of *rents, etc., re-* fifteen years and under the legal control of another, without the con- *quired, when.* sent of those having such legal control, for more than sixty days, shall be punished by imprisonment not exceeding sixty days or by fine not exceeding twenty dollars.

ACTS OF 1907.

CHAPTER 5686.—*Employment of children—General provisions.*

SECTION 1. No child under twelve years of age shall be employed *Age limit in fac-* at any time in any factory or workshop, bowling alley, barroom, beer *tories, etc.* garden, place of amusement where intoxicating liquors are sold, or in or about any mine or quarry.

SEC. 2. No child under twelve years of age shall be employed, *Employment in* required or permitted to work for wages or gain, to whomsoever pay- *vacation.* able, at any occupation at any time, except that during that portion of the year in which there is no public school in the city, town or school district in which such child shall be at the time living, such child may be employed in any store, office, hotel, mercantile establishment, laundry, or other reputable place of work not herein above forbidden: *Provided,* That there shall first be obtained from the county judge of the county or municipal judge of the town or city in which *Certificates.* said store, office, hotel, mercantile establishment, or place of work is located a certificate authorizing such employment. Such certificate shall be issued by said county or municipal judge only upon the affidavit of the parent or guardian or person exercising parental control over said child, stating its age and date of birth, that there is no free public school then in session in the district, city or town where said child lives, and a certificate from a practicing physician that he has examined said child and that said child is, in his opinion, physically able to perform, with reasonable safety to itself, the work for which it is sought to be employed. Whenever it appears that a certificate of a county or municipal judge as herein provided shall have been obtained by a false statement as [to] the age of the child or other material facts, said judge shall revoke said certificate. The judge issuing a certificate shall receive the sum of twenty-five cents therefor, to be paid by the applicant. The certificate of the judge, together with copies of the affidavit of parent or guardian and certificate of the physician, shall be delivered to the employer and kept by him as herein provided: *Provided further*, That nothing herein contained shall be construed to prevent or abridge the right of a parent or guardian to require work from his child in his own vocation and under his supervision and direction.

Hours of labor.   SEC. 3. No child under the age of twelve years shall be employed, required or permitted to work for wages or gain, to whomsoever payable, longer than nine hours in any one day, or more than six days **Nightwork.** in any one week, nor after the hour of nine o'clock at night, nor before the hour of six o'clock in the morning.

Register.   SEC. 4. It shall be the duty of every person, firm or corporation or the agent or manager of any person, firm, or corporation, employing minors under the age of twelve years, wherein by reason of the nature of the employment, or the age of the minor, certificate and affidavits as herein above provided, are required to keep in the place of employment, a register or other convenient book or file for inspection containing all certificates and copies of affidavits and certificates furnished them in compliance with this act, so long as the person furnishing the same shall be in their employ; such register, book or file shall at all times be subject to the free inspection of any city, county or State officer of the county wherein said place of employment is located, or of the city or town marshal, or any member of the police force in whose territory or jurisdiction said place of employment may be located.

Enforcement.   SEC. 5. It shall be the duty of the sheriff in whose county such place of employment may be located, the city or town marshal or police officers within whose territory or jurisdiction such place of employment may be located, to enforce the provisions of this act, and to aid and assist in the prosecution of violations of the same before any court of competent jurisdiction: *Provided*, That nothing herein contained shall abridge or curtail the prosecution for violations of this act in any other way or manner consistent with the enforcement of the criminal laws of this State.

Violations by parents;   SEC. 6. Any parent, guardian or person exercising the parental authority over a child, who knowingly makes a false affidavit to any material fact as herein required, or who suffers or permits a child to be employed or to work in violation of this act or before the provisions hereof to be performed by him have been complied with, shall upon conviction be fined not more than five hundred dollars, or by imprisonment in the county jail not more than ninety days, or by both such fine and imprisonment.

By employers.   SEC. 7. Any person, firm or corporation, or agent or manager of any corporation or firm, who shall violate or fail to comply with any of the provisions of this act, or shall hinder or delay any officer or his agent or deputies in the performance of their duties relative to the enforcement of this act, or refuse or hinder their access to the place of employment of such employer, or fail or refuse to keep for free inspection to such officer, or his agents or deputies, the register, book or file of certificates as herein provided, shall, upon conviction, be fined not more than one thousand dollars, or be imprisoned in the county jail not more than six months, or by both such fine and imprisonment.

Separate violations.   SEC. 8. The performance of the work prohibited herein in any place of employment by a minor for one day shall constitute a violation of this act.

Exceptions.   SEC. 9. Nothing in this act shall be so construed as to apply to household or agricultural work.

GEORGIA.

CODES—1910.

CIVIL CODE.

Hours of labor in factories, etc.

SECTION 3137 (as amended by act, page 65, Acts of 1911). The hours Ten-hour day. of labor required of all persons employed in cotton or woolen manufacturing establishments in this State, except engineers, firemen, watchmen, mechanics, teamsters, yard employees, clerical force, and all help that may be needed to clean up and make necessary repairs or changes in or of machinery, shall not exceed ten hours per day, or the same may be regulated by employers so that the number of hours shall not in aggregate exceed sixty hours per week: *Provided,* That nothing herein contained shall be construed to prevent any of the aforesaid employees from working such time as may be necessary to make up lost time not to Lost time. exceed ten days caused by accidents or other unavoidable circumstances.

SEC. 3138. All contracts made or entered into, whereby a longer time Contracts for for labor than is provided in the foregoing section shall be required of longer day. said employees, shall be absolutely null and void, so far as the same relates to the enforcement of said contracts with said employees, any law, usage, or custom to the contrary notwithstanding.

SEC. 3139. Any cotton or woolen manufacturing establishment that Penalty. shall make or enforce any contract in violation of the foregoing section, with any person as an employee therein, shall be subject to a forfeiture of an amount not less than twenty and not more than five hundred dollars for each and every such violation.

SEC. 3140. Any person with whom said contract is made, or any Who may sue. person having knowledge thereof, shall be competent to institute suit against said cotton or woolen manufacturing establishment: * * *

SEC. 3141. The hours of labor by all persons under twenty-one years Hours of labor of age, in all other manufacturing establishments or machine-shops in of minors. this State, shall be from sunrise until sunset, the usual and customary times for meals being allowed from the same; and any contract made Night work. with such persons or their parents, guardians, or others, whereby a longer time for labor is agreed upon or provided for, shall be null and void, so far as relates to the enforcement of said contracts against such laborers.

Employment of children—Corporal punishment forbidden.

SECTION 3142. No boss or other superior in any manufacturing Punishment of establishment shall inflict corporeal [corporal] punishment upon minor minors. laborers; and the owners of such factory or machine-shop shall be directly liable for all such conduct on the part of their employees; and such minor may sue in his own name for damages for such conduct, and the recovery shall be his own property, and not belong to his parents.

Employment of children in factories—Age limit—Night work.

SECTION 3143. No child under ten years of age shall be employed or Age limit. allowed to labor in or about any factory or manufacturing establishment within the State under any circumstances.

SEC. 3144. On and after January 1, 1907, no child under twelve Limit in 1907. years of age shall be so employed, or allowed to labor, unless such child be an orphan and has no other means of support, or unless a widowed mother or an aged or disabled father is dependent upon the labor of such child, in which event, before putting such child at such labor, such father shall produce and file in the office of such factory or manufacturing establishment a certificate from the ordinary of the county in which such factory or establishment is located, certifying under his seal of office to the facts required to be shown as herein prescribed: *Provided,* That no ordinary shall issue any such certificate except upon strict proof in writing and under oath, clearly showing the necessary facts: *And provided further,* That no such certificate shall be granted for longer than one year, nor accepted by any employer after one year from the date of such certificate.

Night work in 1908.

SEC. 3145. On and after January 1, 1908, no child under fourteen years of age shall be employed or allowed to labor in or about any factory or manufacturing establishment within this State between the hours of seven p. m. and six a. m.

Illiterates.

SEC. 3146. On and after January 1, 1908, no child, except as heretofore provided, under fourteen years of age shall be employed or allowed to labor in or about any factory or manufacturing establishment within this State, unless he or she can write his or her name and simple sen-

School attendance.

tences, and shall have attended school for twelve weeks of the preceding year, six weeks of which school attendance shall be consecutive; and no such child as aforesaid between the ages of fourteen and eighteen years shall be so employed unless such child shall have attended school for twelve weeks of the preceding year, six weeks of which school

Certificates.

attendance shall be consecutive; and at the end of each year, until such child shall have passed the public-school age, an affidavit certifying to such attendance as is required by this section shall be furnished to the employer by the parent or guardian or person sustaining parental relation to such child. The provisions of this section shall apply only to children entering such employment at the age of fourteen years or less.

Affidavits as to age.

SEC. 3147. It shall be unlawful for any owner, superintendent, agent, or any other person acting for or in behalf of any factory or manufacturing establishment to hire or employ any child unless there is first provided and placed on file in the office of such employer an affidavit signed by the parent, guardian, or person standing in parental relation thereto, certifying to the age and date of birth of such child, and other facts required in this article. Any person knowingly furnishing a false affidavit as to the age, or as to any other facts required in this article, shall be guilty of a misdemeanor.

Inspection of list.

SEC. 3148. The affidavit and certificates required in this article shall be open to inspection by the grand juries of any county where such factory or manufacturing establishments are located.

Misdemeanor.

SEC. 3149. Any person or agent, or representative of any firm or corporation, who shall violate any provision of this article, or any parent, guardian, or other person standing in parental relation to a child, who shall hire or place for employment or labor in or about any factory or manufacturing establishment within this State a child in violation of any provision of this article, shall be guilty of a misdemeanor.

PENAL CODE.

Seats for female employees.

Seats to be provided.

SECTION 130. All persons and corporations employing females in manufacturing, mechanical, or mercantile establishments must provide suitable seats, and permit their use by such females when not necessarily engaged in the active duties for which they were employed. Any person who shall fail to comply with the requirements of this section, and the officers of any corporation which shall fail to comply with said requirements, shall be guilty of a misdemeanor.

Employment of children while parents live in idleness.

SECTION 449. Vagrants are—

*　　*　　*　　*　　*　　*　　*

Who are vagrants.

7. All persons who are able to work and do not work, and who have no property or other means of support, but hire out their minor children and live upon their wages.

*　　*　　*　　*　　*　　*　　*

Employment of children—Certain employments forbidden.

SECTION 756. Any person who shall sell, apprentice, give away, let Acrobatic and
mendicant em-
ployments. out, or otherwise dispose of any child under twelve years, to any person, for the vocation, occupation, or service of rope or wire walking, begging, or as a gymnast, contortionist, circus-rider, acrobat, or clown, or for any indecent, obscene, or immoral exhibition, practice, or purpose, shall be guilty of a misdemeanor.

SEC. 757. Whenever a child shall be disposed of in violation of the Receiving chil-
dren. preceding section, the person who, under such selling, apprenticing, or letting out, shall receive and use such child for any of the purposes condemned in said section, shall be guilty of a misdemeanor.

ACTS OF 1910.

Employment of children—Messenger service.

(Page 117.)

SECTION 1. No minor under sixteen years of age shall be employed Night work. in the delivery of messages by any concern or person engaged in the messenger service business, or in the general work of the messenger service between the hours of nine p. m. and six a. m.

SEC. 2. Any person, firm, or corporation, violating the provisions of Violations. this act, or any of them, shall be deemed guilty of a misdemeanor, and upon conviction shall be punished as prescribed in section 1039 of the Penal Code of Georgia, 1895.

HAWAII.

REVISED LAWS—1905.

Employment of children—School attendance.

SECTION 212 (as amended by act No. 150, Acts of 1911). The attend- Attendance re-
quired. ance of all children from six to seventeen years of age, at either a public or private school, is obligatory, * * * provided also, that such attendance shall not be compulsory in the following cases:

* * * * * * *

Fourth. Where any child of not less than the age of thirteen years Exceptions. shall have passed the required examinations of both primary and grammar school grades, as such requirements shall from time to time exist: *Provided,* He shall be suitably employed;

Fifth. When any child of not less than fifteen years of age is suitably employed under the direction of his parent or guardian.

ACTS OF 1907.

ACT No. 119.—*Employment of minors in saloons—Sale of liquor to employees.*

SECTION 30. Licenses shall be subject to the following conditions Conditions of
license. and provisions:

* * * * * * *

(4) That no holder of a license for a saloon business shall employ Minors not to be
employed. any minor in or about the room or place where intoxicating liquors are furnished or sold;

* * * * * * *

IDAHO.

CONSTITUTION.

ARTICLE 13.—*Employment of children in underground mines.*

SECTION 4. The employment of children under the age of fourteen Age limit. (14) years in underground mines is prohibited.

REVISED CODES—1909.

Earnings of minors.

Minor entitled to earnings, when. SECTION 2697. The wages of a minor employed in service may be paid to him, unless within thirty days after the commencement of the service, the parent or guardian entitled thereto gives the employer notice that he claims such wages.

ACTS OF 1911.

CHAPTER 159.—*Employment of children—General provisions.*

Age limit. SECTION 166. No child under fourteen (14) years of age shall be employed, permitted or suffered to work in or in connection with any mine, factory, workshop, mercantile establishment, store, telegraph or telephone office, laundry, restaurant, hotel, apartment house, or in the distribution or transmission of merchandise or messages. It shall

Employment during school hours. be unlawful for any person, firm or corporation to employ any child under fourteen (14) years of age in any such business or service whatever during the hours in which the public schools of the district in which the child resides are in session, or before the hour of six (6)

Night work. o'clock in the morning, or after the hour of nine (9) o'clock in the evening: *Provided,* That any such child over the age of twelve (12) years may be employed at any of the occupations mentioned in this act during the regular vacations of two weeks or more of the public schools of the district in which such child resides.

Illiterates. SEC. 167. No minor who is under sixteen (16) years of age shall be employed or permitted to work at any gainful occupation during the hours that the public schools of the school district in which he resides are in session, unless he can read at sight and write legibly simple sentences in the English language, and has received instructions in spelling, English grammar and geography and is familiar with the fundamental operations of arithmetic up to and including fractions, or has similar attainments in another language.

Register. SEC. 168. Every person, firm, corporation, agent or officer of a firm or corporation employing or permitting minors under sixteen (16) years of age and over fourteen (14) years of age to work in any mine, factory, workshop, mercantile establishment, store, telegraph or telephone office, laundry, restaurant, hotel, apartment house, or on [in] the distribution or transmission of merchandise or messages, shall keep a record of the names, ages, and place of residence of such minors.

Hours of labor. SEC. 169. No person under the age of sixteen (16) years shall be employed or suffered or permitted to work at any gainful occupation more than fifty-four (54) hours in any one (1) week, nor more than nine (9) hours in any one (1) day; nor before the hour of six (6) o'clock in the morning nor after the hour of nine (9) o'clock in the evening.

Penalty. SEC. 170. Whoever employs a child under sixteen (16) years of age, and whoever having under his control a child under such age permits such child to be employed in violation of sections 1 and 2 of this act [Secs. 166, 167, supra] shall, for such offense, be fined not more than fifty dollars ($50), and whoever continues to employ any child in the violation of either of said sections of this act after being notified by a truant officer, probation officer or school authority shall, for every day thereafter that such employment continues, be fined not less than five dollars ($5) nor more than twenty dollars ($20). A failure to produce to a truant officer, policeman, probation officer or school authority, the age record required by this act shall be prima facie evidence of the illegal employment of any person whose age record is not produced. Any parent, guardian or custodian of a minor under sixteen (16) years of age who knowingly swears falsely as to the age of such child for the purpose of obtaining an age record is guilty of perjury.

Dangerous and immoral occupations. SEC. 171. Any person, whether as parent, relative, guardian, employer or otherwise, having the care, custody or control of any child under the age of sixteen (16) years, who exhibits, uses or employes [employs] in any manner or under any pretense, sells, apprentices, gives away, lets out or disposes of such child to any person, under any name, title or pretense, for or in any business, exhibition or vocation, injurious to the health or dangerous to the life or limb of such child, or in or for the vocation, occupation, service or purpose of singing, playing on musical instruments, rope or wire walking, dancing, begging or peddling, or as a gymnast, acrobat, or contortionist, or rider, or in any place whatsoever, or for any obscene, indecent or immoral purpose, exhibition or practice whatsoever, or for or in any mendicant, or wandering business whatsoever, or who causes, procures or encourages such child to engage therein, is guilty of a misdemeanor, and punishable by a fine of not less than fifty dollars ($50) nor more than two hundred and fifty dollars ($250), or by imprisonment in the county jai for a term not exceeding six (6) months or by both such fine and imprisonment. Every person who takes, receives, hires, employs, uses, exhibits, or has in custody any child under the age and for any of the purposes mentioned in this section is guilty of a like offense and punishable by like imprisonment. Nothing in this section contained applies to or affects the employment or use of any such child as a singer or musician in any church, school or academy, or the teaching or learning of the science or practice of music.

SEC. 172. Any person, whether as parent, guardian, employer or otherwise, and any firm or corporation, who as employer or otherwise, shall send, direct, or cause to be sent or directed any minor, to any saloon, gambling house, house of prostitution or other immoral place; or who shall employ any minor to serve intoxicating liquors to customers, or who shall employ a minor in handling intoxicating liquor or packages containing such liquors in a brewery, bottling establishment or other place where such liquors are prepared for sale or offered for sale, shall, for each offense, be punished by a fine of not less than fifty dollars ($50) or imprisonment for not less than two (2) months or by both such fine and imprisonment. *Sending as messengers.* *Employment in saloons, etc.*

SEC. 173. The probation officer, or in counties where there is no probation officer, one or more of the school trustees shall visit the various places of employment mentioned in sections 166 and 172 of this act and ascertain whether any minors are employed therein contrary to the provisions of this act, and they shall bring complaint for offenses under this act to the attention of the prosecuting attorney for prosecution, but nothing herein shall be held to prohibit any reputable citizen from bringing complaint for violations of this act. All offenses under this act shall be prosecuted in the probate court. *Enforcement.*

ILLINOIS.

HURD'S REVISED STATUTES—1905.

CHAPTER 38.—*Employment of children in certain occupations forbidden.*

SECTION 485. It shall be unlawful to hire, use or employ any minor child to sell or give away, or in any manner to distribute, or who, having the care, custody or control of any minor child, to permit such child to sell, give away, or in any manner to distribute any book, magazine, pamphlet, newspaper, story paper or publication coming within the description of matters mentioned in the first section of this act [devoted to the publication, or principally made up of criminal news, police reports, or accounts of criminal deeds, or pictures and stories of deeds of bloodshed, lust or crime], and any person violating any of the provisions of this act shall be guilty of a misdemeanor, and on conviction shall be fined in any sum not exceeding five hundred dollars, or imprisoned in the county jail of the county where the offense has been committed not to exceed six months, or both fine and imprisonment, at the discretion of the court. *Selling obscene, etc., literature.*

SEC. 492. It shall be unlawful for any person having the care, custody or control of any child under the age of fourteen years to exhibit, use or employ, or in any manner, or under any pretense, sell, apprentice, give away, let out or otherwise dispose of any such child to any person in or for the vocation or occupation, service or purpose of singing, playing on musical instruments, rope or wire walking, dancing, begging or peddling, or as a gymnast, contortionist, rider or acrobat in any place *Acrobatic, mendicant, etc., occupations.*

whatsoever, or for any obscene, indecent or immoral purpose, exhibition or practice whatsoever, or for, or in any business, exhibition or vocation injurious to the health, or dangerous to the life or limb of such child, or cause, procure or encourage any such child to engage

Exception.

therein. Nothing in this section contained shall apply to or affect the employment or use of any such child as a singer or musician in any church, school or academy, or in the teaching or learning the science or practice of music.

Unlawful to employ.

Sec. 493. It shall also be unlawful for any person to take, receive, hire, employ, use, exhibit or have in custody any child under the age and for the purposes prohibited in section 42a [492] hereof.

CHAPTER 48.—*Sex no disqualification for employment.*

Sex not a bar.

SECTION 3. No person shall be precluded or debarred from any occupation, profession or employment (except military) on account of sex: *Provided,* That this act shall not be construed to affect the eligibility of any person to an elective office.

Act construed.

SEC. 4. Nothing in this act shall be construed as requiring any female to work on streets or roads, or serve on juries.

CHAPTER 48.—*Employment of children.*

Age limit.

SECTION 20. No child under the age of fourteen years shall be employed, permitted or suffered to work at any gainful occupation in any theater, concert hall or place of amusement where intoxicating liquors are sold or in any mercantile institution, store, office, hotel, laundry, manufacturing establishment, bowling alley, passenger or freight elevator, factory or workshop or as a messenger or driver therefor, within this State. No child under fourteen years of age shall be employed at any work performed for wages or other compensation, to whomsoever payable, during any portion of any month when the public schools of the town, township, village or city in which he or she resides

Night work.

are in session, nor be employed at any work before the hour of seven o'clock in the morning or after the hour of six o'clock in the evening:

Hours of labor.

Provided, That no child shall be allowed to work more than eight hours in any one day.

Register.

SEC. 20a. It shall be the duty of every person, firm or corporation, agent or manager of any firm or corporation employing minors over fourteen years and under sixteen years of age in any mercantile institution, store, office, hotel, laundry, manufacturing establishment, bowling alley, theater, concert hall or place of amusement, passenger or freight elevator, factory or workshop or as messenger or driver therefor, within this State, to keep a register in said mercantile institution, store, office, hotel, laundry, manufacturing establishment, bowling alley, theater, concert hall or place of amusement, factory or workshop in which said minors shall be employed or permitted or suffered to work, in which register shall be recorded the name, age and place of residence of every child employed or suffered or permitted to work therein, or as messenger or driver therefor, over the age of fourteen and under the age of sixteen years; and it shall be unlawful for any person, firm or corporation, agent or manager, of any firm or corporation to hire or employ, or to permit or suffer to work in any mercantile institution, store, office, hotel, laundry, manufacturing establishment, bowling alley, theater, concert hall or place of amusement, passenger or freight elevator, factory or workshop, or as messenger or driver therefor, any child under the age of sixteen years and over fourteen years of age, unless there is first produced and placed on file in such mercantile institution, store, office, hotel, laundry, manufacturing establishment, bowling alley, factory or workshop, theater, concert hall or place of amusement, an age and school certificate approved as hereinafter provided.

List to be posted.

SEC. 20b. Every person, firm or corporation, agent or manager of a corporation employing or permitting or suffering to work five or more children under the age of sixteen years and over the age of fourteen in any mercantile institution, store, office, laundry, hotel, manufacturing establishment, factory or workshop, shall post and keep posted in a conspicuous place in every room in which such help is employed, or permitted or suffered to work a list containing the name, age and place of residence of every person under the age of sixteen years employed, permitted or suffered to work in such room.

SEC. 20c. No child under sixteen years of age and over fourteen years of age shall be employed in any mercantile institution, store, office, hotel, laundry, manufacturing establishment, bowling alley, theater, concert hall, or place of amusement, passenger or freight elevator, factory or workshop, or as messenger or driver therefor, unless there is first produced and placed on file in such mercantile institution, store, office, hotel, laundry, manufacturing establishment, bowling alley, theater, concert hall or place of amusement, factory or workshop, and accessible to the State factory inspector, assistant factory inspector or deputy factory inspector, an age and school certificate as hereinafter prescribed; and unless there is kept on file and produced on demand of said inspectors of factories a complete and correct list of all the minors under the age of sixteen years so employed who can not read at sight and write legibly simple sentences, unless such child is attending night school as hereinafter provided. *Certificate of age, etc.*

SEC. 20d. An age and school certificate shall be approved only by the superintendent of schools or by a person authorized by him in writing; or where there is no superintendent of schools by a person authorized by the school board: *Provided,* That the superintendent or principal of a parochial school shall have the right to approve an age and school certificate and shall have the same rights and powers as the superintendent of public schools to administer the oaths herein provided for children attending parochial schools: *Provided further,* That no member of a school board or other person authorized as aforesaid shall have authority to approve such certificates for any child then in or about to enter his own establishment, or the employment of a firm or corporation of which he is a member, officer or employee. The person approving these certificates shall have authority to administer the oath provided herein, but no fee shall be charged therefor. It shall be the duty of the school board or local school authorities to designate a place (connected with their offices, when practicable) where certificates shall be issued and recorded, and to establish and maintain the necessary records and clerical service for carrying out the provisions of this act. *Who may issue.*

SEC. 20e. An age and school certificate shall not be approved unless satisfactory evidence is furnished by the last school census, the certificate of birth or baptism of such child, the register of birth of such child with a town or city clerk, or by the records of the public or parochial schools, that such child is of the age stated in the certificate: *Provided,* That in cases arising wherein the above proof is not obtainable, the parent or guardian of the child shall make oath before the juvenile or county court as to the age of such child, and the court may issue to said child an age certificate as sworn to. *Evidence.*

SEC. 20f. The age and school certificate of a child under sixteen years of age shall not be approved and signed until he presents to the person authorized to approve and sign the same, a school attendance certificate, as hereinafter prescribed, duly filled out and signed. A duplicate of such age and school certificate shall be filled out and shall be forwarded to the State factory inspector's office. Any explanatory matter may be printed with such certificate in the discretion of the school board or superintendent of schools. The employment and the age and school certificates shall be separately printed and shall be filled out, signed and held or surrendered as indicated in the following forms: *Age and school certificate.*

SCHOOL CERTIFICATE.

(Name of school).   (City or town and date).

This certifies (name of minor) of the ..th grade, can read and write legibly simple sentences. This also certifies that according to the records of this school, and in my belief, the said (name of minor) was born at (name of city or town) in (name of county) on the (date) and is now (number of years and months) old.

(Name of parent or guardian),
(Residence).

(Signature of teacher) ...... grade.
Correct.   (Name of principal).
(Name of school).

EVENING SCHOOL ATTENDANCE CERTIFICATE.

(Date).

This certifies that (name of minor) is registered in and regularly attends the .... evening school.

This also certifies that according to the records of my school and in my belief the said (name of minor) was born at (name of city or town) on the .... day of (year), and is now (number of years and months) old.

(Name of parent or guardian),
(Residence).
(Signature of Teacher).
(Signature of Principal).

AGE AND SCHOOL CERTIFICATE.

This certifies that I am (father, mother, guardian or custodian) of (name of minor), and that (he or she) was born at (name of town or city) in the (name of county, if known) and State or county of ......, on the (day of birth and year of birth) and is now (number of years and months) old.

(Signature of parent, guardian or custodian)
(City or town and date)

There personally appeared before me the above named (name of person signing) and made oath that the foregoing certificate by (him or her) signed is true to the best of (his or her) knowledge. I hereby approve the foregoing certificate of (name of child), height (feet and inches), weight ......, complexion (fair or dark), hair (color), having no sufficient reason to doubt that (he or she) is of the age therein certified.

OWNER OF CERTIFICATE. This certificate belongs to (name of child in whose behalf it is drawn) and is to be surrendered to (him or her) whenever (he or she) leaves the service of the corporation or employer holding the same; but if not claimed by said child within thirty days from such time it shall be returned to the superintendent of schools, or where there is no superintendent of schools, to the school board. (Signature of person authorized to approve and sign, with official character [or] authority.)   (Town or city, and date).

In the case of a child who can not read at sight and write legibly simple sentences, the certificate shall continue as follows, after the word sentences: "I hereby certify that (he or she) is regularly attending the (name of public or parochial evening school)." This certificate shall continue in force just as long as the regular attendance of said child at said evening school is certified weekly by the teacher and principal of said school.

In any city or town in which there is no public or parochial evening school, an age and school certificate shall not be approved for a child under the age of sixteen years who can not read at sight and write legibly simple sentences. When the public or parochial evening schools are not in session an age and school certificate shall not be approved for any child who can not read at sight and write legibly simple sentences. The certificate of the principal of a public or parochial school shall be prima facie evidence as to the literacy or illiteracy of the child.

Illiterates. SEC. 20g. No person shall employ any minor over fourteen years of age and under sixteen years, and no parent, guardian or custodian shall permit to be employed any such minor under his control, who can not read at sight and write legibly simple sentences, while a public evening school is maintained in the town or city in which such minor resides, unless such minor is a regular attendant at such evening school.

tion. SEC. 20h. The State inspector of factories, his assistants or deputies, shall visit all mercantile institutions, stores, offices, laundries, manufacturing establishments, bowling alleys, theaters, concert halls or places of amusement, factories or workshops, and all other places where minors are or may be employed, in this State, and ascertain whether any minors are employed contrary to the provisions of this act. Inspec ors of factories, may require that age and school certificates, and all lists of minors employed in such factories, workshops, mercantile institutions and all other places where minors are employed as provided for in this act, shall be produced for their inspection, on demand.

And provided, further, That upon written complaint to the school board or local school authorities of any city, town, district or municipality, that any minor (whose name shall be given in such complaint) is employed in any mercantile institution, store, office, laundry, manufacturing establishment, bowling alley, theater, concert hall or place of amusement, passenger or freight elevator, factory or workshop, or as messenger or driver therefor, contrary to the provisions of this act, it shall be the duty of such school board or local school authority to report the same to the State inspector of factories.

SEC. 20i. No person under the age of sixteen years shall be employed or suffered or permitted to work at any gainful occupation more than forty-eight hours in any one week, nor more than eight hours in any one day; or before the hours of seven o'clock in the morning or after the hour of seven o'clock in the evening. Every employer shall pos in a conspicuous place in every room where such minors are employed a printed notice stating the hours required of them each day of the week, the hours of commencing and stopping work and the hours when the time or times allowed for dinner or for other meals begins and ends. The printed form of such notice shall be furnished by the State inspector of factories, and the employment of any such minor for longer time in any day so stated shall be deemed a violation of this section. *[margin: Hours of labor. Night work.]*

SEC. 20j. No child under the age of sixteen years shall be employed at sewing belts, or to assist in sewing belts, in any capacity whatever; nor shall any child adjust any belt to any machinery; they shall not oil or assist in oiling, wiping or cleaning machinery; they shall not operate or assist in operating circular or band saws, wood-shapers, wool [wood] jointers, planers. sandpaper or wood-polishing machinery, emery or polishing wheels used for polishing metal, wood-turning or boring machinery, stamping machines in sheet metal and tinware manufacturing, stamping machines in washer and nut factories, operating corrugating rolls, such as are used in roofing factories, nor shall they be employed in operating any passenger or freight elevators, steam boiler, steam machinery, or other steam generating apparatus, or as pin boys in any bowling alleys; they shall not operate or assist in operating, dough brakes, or cracker machinery of any description; wire or iron straightening machinery; nor shall they operate or assist in operating rolling mill machinery, punches or shears, washing, grinding or mixing mill or calender rolls in rubber manufacturing, nor shall they operate or assist in operating laundry machinery; nor shall children be employed in any capacity in preparing any composition in which dangerous or poisonous acids are used, and they shall not be employed in any capacity in the manufacture of paints, colors or white lead; nor shall they be employed in any capacity whatever in operating or assisting to operate any passenger or freight elevator; nor shall they be employed in any capacity whatever in the manufacture of goods for immoral purposes, or any other employment that may be considered dangerous to their lives or limbs, or where their health may be injured or morals depraved; nor in any theater, concert hall, or place of amusement wherein intoxicating liquors are sold; nor shall females under sixteen years of age be employed in any capacity where such employment compels them to remain standing constantly. *[margin: Certain occupations forbidden.]*

SEC. 20k. The presence of any person under the age of sixteen years in any manufacturing establishment, factory or workshop, shall constitute prima facie evidence of his or her employment therein. *[margin: Evidence of employment.]*

SEC. 20l. It shall be the special duty of the State factory inspector to enforce the provisions of this act, and to prosecute all violations of the same before any magistrate or any court of competent jurisdiction in this State.   It shall be the duty of the State factory inspector, assistant State factory inspector and deputy State factory inspectors under the supervision and direction of the State factory inspector, and they are hereby authorized and empowered to visit and inspect, at all reasonable times and as often as possible, all places covered by this act. *[margin: Enforcement.]*

SEC. 20m. Whoever, having under his control a child under the age of sixteen years, permits such child to be employed in violation of the provisions of this act, shall for each offense be fined not less than $5 nor more than $25, and shall stand committed until such fine and costs are paid. *[margin: Violations.]*

A failure to produce to the inspector of factories, his assistants or deputies, any age and school certificates, or lists required by this act, shall constitute a violation of this act, and the person so failing shall, upon conviction, be fined not less than $5 nor more than $50 for each offense. Every person authorized to sign the certificate prescribed by section 7 [20f] of this act, who certifies to any materially false statement therein shall be guilty of a violation of this act, and upon conviction be fined not less than $5 nor more than $100 for each offense, and shall stand committed until such fine and costs are paid.

Any person, firm or corporation, agent or manager, superintendent or foreman of any firm or corporation, whether for himself or for such firm or corporation, or by himself or through subagents or foreman, superintendent or manager, who shall violate or fail to comply with any of the provisions of this act, or shall refuse admittance to premises or otherwise obstruct the factory inspector, assistant factory inspector or deputy factory inspector in the performance of their duties, as prescribed by this act, shall be deemed guilty of a misdemeanor and upon conviction thereof shall be fined not less than $5 nor more than $100 for each offense, and shall stand committed until such fine and costs are paid.

CHAPTER 48.—*Seats for female employees.*

Seats to be provided.
SECTION 36. No person under the age of sixteen years shall be employed or suffered to work for wages at any gainful occupation more than sixty hours in any one week, nor more than ten hours in any one day. All establishments subject to factory inspection, where girls and women are employed, shall provide suitable seats for the use of the girls and women, and they shall be permitted the use of such seats when not necessarily engaged in their active duties.
[See also section 9, Appendix B, page 889.]

CHAPTER 122.—*Employment of children—School attendance.*

Attendance required.
SECTION 313 (as amended by act, page 520, Acts of 1907). Every person having control of any child between the ages of seven (7) and sixteen (16) years, shall annually cause such child to attend some public or private school for the entire time during which the school attended is in session, which period shall not be less than one hundred and ten (110) days of actual teaching: *Provided,* That this act shall not apply in any case where the child has been or is being instructed for a like period of time in each and every year in the elementary branches of education by a person or persons competent to give such instruction, or where the child's physical or mental condition renders his or her attendance impractical or inexpedient, or where the child is excused for temporary absence for cause by the principal or teacher of the school which said child attends, or where the child is between the ages of fourteen (14) and sixteen (16) years and is necessarily and lawfully employed during the hours when the public school is in session.

Penalty.
SEC. 316 (as amended by act, page 520, Acts of 1907). Any person having control of a child, who, with intent to evade the provisions of this act, shall make a false statement concerning the age or the employment of such child or the time such child has attended school, shall for such offense forfeit a sum of not less than three dollars ($3.00) nor more than twenty dollars ($20.00) for the use of the public schools of such city, town, village or district.

ACTS OF 1909.

Hours of labor of female employees.

(Page 212.)

Ten-hour day.
SECTION 1 (as amended by act, page 328, Acts of 1911). No female shall be employed in any mechanical or mercantile establishment, or factory, or laundry, or hotel, or restaurant, or telegraph or telephone establishment or office thereof, or in any place of amusement, or by any person, firm or corporation engaged in any express or transportation or public utility business, or by any common carrier, or in any public

institution, incorporated or unincorporated in this State, more than ten hours during any one day. The hours of work may be so arranged as to permit the employment of females at any time so that they shall not work more than ten hours during the twenty-four hours of any day.

SEC. 2 (as amended by act, page 328, Acts of 1911). Any employer who shall require or permit or suffer any female to work in any of the places mentioned in section 1 of this act more than the number of hours provided for in this act, during any day of twenty-four hours, or who shall fail, neglect or refuse so to arrange the work of females in his employ that they shall not work more than the number of hours provided for in this act, during any one day, or who shall permit or suffer any overseer, superintendent or other agent of any such employer to violate any of the provisions of this act, shall be guilty of a misdemeanor and upon conviction thereof shall be fined for each offense in a sum of not less than $25 or more than $100. *Violations.*

SEC. 3. The State department of factory inspection shall be charged with the duty of enforcing the provisions of this act and prosecuting all violations thereof. *Enforcement.*

SEC. 5 (added by act, page 328, Acts of 1911). Every employer to whom this act shall apply, shall keep a time book or record showing for each day that his establishment is open the hours during which each and every female in his employ, to whom this act applies, is employed. Such time book or record shall be open at all reasonable hours to the inspection of the officials of the factory inspection department. The failure or omission to keep such record, or a false statement contained therein, or any false statement made by any person to an official of the factory inspection department, in reply to any question put in carrying out the provisions of this act, shall be punishable on conviction by a penalty of not more than $25 for each offense. *Record.*

Employment of children—School attendance.

(Page 342.)

SECTION 274. Every person having control of any child between the ages of seven and sixteen years, shall annually cause such child to attend some public or private school for the entire time during which the school attended is in session, which shall not be less than six months of actual teaching: *Provided, however,* That this act shall not apply in case the child has been or is being instructed for a like period in each and every year in the elementary branches of education by a person or persons competent to give such instruction, or in case the child's physical or mental condition renders his or her attendance impracticable or inexpedient, or in case the child is excused for temporary absence for cause by the principal or teacher of the school which said child attends, or in case the child is between the ages of fourteen and sixteen years and is necessarily and lawfully employed during the hours when the public school is in session. For every neglect of the duty prescribed by this section, the person so offending shall forfeit to the use of the public schools of the city, town or district in which such child resides, a sum not less than five dollars nor more than twenty dollars and costs of suit, and shall stand committed until such fine and costs of suit are fully paid. *School attendance required.*

ACTS OF 1911.

Employment of women and children in mines.

(Page 387.)

SECTION 28. No boy under the age of sixteen years, and no woman or girl of any age, shall be permitted to do any manual labor in or about any mine, and before any boy can be permitted to work in any mine he must produce to the mine manager or operator thereof an affidavit from his parent or guardian or next of kin, sworn and subscribed to before a justice of the peace or notary public, that he, the said boy, is sixteen years of age. *Employment forbidden.*

The parent, guardian or next of kin shall submit in connection with said affidavit, a certificate of birth, a baptismal certificate, a passport or other official or religious record of the boy's age or duly attested transcript thereof, which certificate or transcript thereof shall, for the purposes of this act, establish the age of said boy.

Any person swearing falsely in regard to the age of a boy shall be guilty of per ur , and shall be punished as provided in the general statutes of the State pertaining to perjury.

INDIANA.

ANNOTATED STATUTES—1901.

Employment of children—Certain employments forbidden.

Acrobatic, etc., employments. SECTION 2241. Any person having the care, custody or control of any minor child under the age of fifteen years, who shall in any manner sell, apprentice, give away, or otherwise dispose of such child, and any person who shall take, receive or employ such child for the vocation or occupation of rope or wire walking, or as an acrobat, gymnast, contortionist, or rider, and any person who, having the care, custody or control of any minor child shall sell, apprentice, give away or otherwise dispose of such child, or who shall take, receive or employ such child for any obscene, indecent or illegal exhibition or vocation, or any vocation injurious to the health or dangerous to the life or limb of such child engaged therein, or for the purpose of prostitution, and any person who shall retain, harbor or employ any minor child in or about any assignation house or brothel, or in any place where any obscene, indecent or illegal exhibition takes place, shall be guilty of a misdemeanor, and upon conviction thereof before any justice of the peace, mayor, police judge or criminal court shall be fined not less than ten dollars, nor more than one hundred dollars, to which may be added imprisonment not exceeding thirty days.

Mendicant employments. SEC. 2242. Any person having the care, custody or control, lawful or unlawful, of any minor child under the age of eighteen years, who shall apprentice, give away, let out, hire, or otherwise dispose of such minor to any person for the purpose of singing, playing on musical instruments, begging, or for any mendicant business whatever, in the streets, roads or other highways of the State, and whosoever shall take, receive, hire, employ, use or have in custody any such [minor] for the vocation, occupation, calling, service or purpose of singing, playing upon musical instruments or begging upon the streets, roads or other highways of the State, or for any mendicant business whatever, shall be guilty of a misdemeanor, and upon conviction thereof in the manner provided in the first section of this act [sec. 2241], shall be fined not less than five dollars nor more than one hundred dollars, to which may be added imprisonment not exceeding thirty days.

Employment in dance houses, saloons, etc. SEC. 2243. Any person having the care, custody or control of any minor child under the age of fifteen years, who shall in any manner sell, apprentice, give away, or permit such child to sing, dance, act, or in any manner exhibit in any dance house whatever, or in any concert saloon, theater, or place of entertainment where wines or spirituous or malt liquors are sold or given away, or with which any place for the sale of wines or spirituous or malt liquors is directly or indirectly connected by any passage way or entrance, or any proprietor of any dance house whatever, or the proprietor of any such concert saloon, theater or place of entertainment so employing any such child, shall be guilty of a misdemeanor, and upon conviction thereof, * * * shall be fined not less than ten dollars nor more than one hundred dollars for each offense, to which may be added imprisonment not exceeding thirty days.

Employment in mines. SEC. 2244. Any person who shall take, receive, hire or employ any child under twelve years of age in any underground works, or mines, or like place whatsoever, shall be guilty of a misdemeanor, and upon conviction thereof in the manner provided in the first section of this act [sec. 2241], shall be fined not less than five dollars nor more than fifty dollars.

Seats for female employees.

SECTION 2246. Every person or corporation employing women or girls in any business in this State shall provide suitable seats for the use of said employees so employed, and shall permit the use of such seats by them when they are not necessarily engaged in the active duties for the performnce of which they are so employed. Seats to be provided.

SEC. 2247. Any person or persons, or any corporation violating any of the provisions of this act, shall be punished by a fine of not less than ten dollars nor more than thirty dollars for each offense. And it is made the duties of the prosecuting attorneys of the State to enforce the provisions of this act. Penalty.

Employment of children—Hours of labor—Age limit.

SECTION 7087a. No person under sixteen years of age, and no female under eighteen years of age, employed in any manufacturing or mercantile establishment, laundry, renovating works, bakery or printing office, shall be required, permitted or suffered to work therein more than sixty hours in any one week, nor more than ten hours in any one day, unless for the purpose of making a shorter day on the last day of the week; nor more hours in any one week than will make an average of ten hours per day for the whole number of days which such person or such female shall so work during such week; and every person, firm, corporation, or company employing any person under sixteen years of age, or any female under eighteen years of age in any establishment as aforesaid, shall post and keep posted in a conspicuous place in every room where such help is employed a printed notice stating the number of hours of labor per day required of such person for each day of the week, and the number of hours of labor exacted or permitted to be performed by such persons shall not exceed the number of hours of labor so posted as being required. The time of beginning and ending the day's labor shall be the time stated in such notice: *Provided,* That such female under eighteen and persons under sixteen years of age may begin after the time set for beginning and stop before the time set in such notice for the stopping of the day's labor, but they shall not be permitted or required to perform any labor before the time stated on the notices as the time for beginning the day's labor, nor after the time stated upon the notices as the hour of ending the day's labor. Hours of labor of children. Posting notices. Proviso.

SEC. 7087b. No child under fourteen years of age shall be employed in any manufacturing or mercantile establishment, mine, quarry, laundry, renovating works, bakery or printing office within this State. It shall be the duty of every person employing young persons under the age of sixteen years to keep a register, in which shall be recorded the name, birthplace, age and place of residence of every person employed by him under the age of sixteen years; and it shall be unlawful for any proprietor, agent, foreman or other person connected with a manufacturing or mercantile establishment, mine, quarry, laundry, renovating works, bakery or printing office to hire or employ any young person to work therein without there is first provided and placed on file in the office an affidavit made by the parent or guardian, stating the age, date and place of birth of said young person; if such young person have no parent or guardian, then such affidavit shall be made by the young person, which affidavit shall be kept on file by the employer, and said register and affidavit shall be produced for inspection on demand made by the inspector, appointed under this act. There shall be posted conspicuously in every room where young persons are employed, a list of their names, with their ages, respectively. No young person under the age of sixteen years, who is not blind, shall be employed in any establishment aforesaid, who can not read and write simple sentences in the English language, except during the vacation of the public schools in the city or town where such minor lives. The chief inspector of the department of inspection shall have the power to demand a certificate of physical fitness from some regular physician in the case of young persons who may seem physically unable to perform the labor at which they may be employed, and shall have the power to prohibit the employment of any minor that can not obtain such a certificate. Age limit. Register. Illiterates. Physical inspection.

Night work.   SEC. 7087c. No person or corporation, or officer or agent thereof, shall employ any woman or female young person in any capacity for the purpose of manufacturing, between the hours of 10 o'clock at night and 6 o'clock in the morning.

Operating elevators.   SEC. 7087d. No person, company, corporation or association shall employ or permit any young person to have the care, custody, management of or to operate any elevator.

[See also sections 7087i, 7087j, 7087r, Appendix B, pages 902-904.]

ACTS OF 1905.

CHAPTER 50.—*Employment of women and children in mines.*

Employment forbidden.   SECTION 24. No male person under the age of fourteen years or female of any age shall be permitted to enter any mine in this State for the purpose of employment therein, and the parents or guardians of boys shall be required to furnish an affidavit as to the age of said boy or boys when there is any doubt in regard to their age, and in all cases of minors applying for work the operator of any mine shall see that the provisions of this section are not violated.

CHAPTER 169.—*Employment of children—Hours of labor.*

Eight hours a day's work.   SECTION 629. Any person, firm, company, corporation, or association engaged in manufacturing in this State, and permitted by law to employ child labor; or any foreman, clerk, officer, or agent of any such person, firm, corporation or association, who shall employ or keep at work any child under fourteen years of age more than eight hours per day, shall, on conviction, be fined not less than ten dollars nor more than one hundred dollars.

ACTS OF 1911.

CHAPTER 209.—*Employment of children—General provisions.*

Age limit.   SECTION 1. No child under the age of fourteen (14) years shall be employed or permitted to work in any gainful occupation other than farm work or domestic service, excepting that any child between the ages of twelve (12) years and fourteen (14) years may be employed or permitted to work in the business of preserving and canning of fruits and vegetables from the first day of June to the first day of October of each year.

Hours of labor.   SEC. 2. No child under sixteen (16) years of age shall be employed or permitted to work in any gainful occupation other than farm work or domestic service, more than forty-eight (48) hours in any one week, or more than eight (8) hours in any one day, unless the employer shall have first procured the written consent of the parent, legal or natural guardian of said child, but in no event shall any such child work at any gainful occupation other than farm work or domestic service more than fifty-four (54) hours in any one week or nine hours in any one day.

Night work.   SEC. 3. No child under sixteen (16) years of age shall be employed or permitted to work in any gainful occupation other than farm work or domestic service, before the hour of seven (7) in the morning, or after the hour of six (6) in the evening.

Prohibited employments.   SEC. 4. No child under the age of sixteen (16) years shall be employed or permitted to work in any tobacco warehouse, cigar or other factory where tobacco is manufactured or prepared, hotel, theater, or place of amusement; or in any employment where their health may be injured or morals depraved. And no boy under the age of sixteen (16) years and no girl under the age of eighteen (18) years shall be employed or permitted to work in or about any brewery, distillery, saloon, concert hall, or any other establishment where malt or alcoholic liquors are manufactured, packed, wrapped, or bottled; or in dipping, dyeing, or packing matches, or manufacturing, packing or storing gunpowder, dynamite, nitroglycerin or its compounds, fuses or other explosives. Nor shall girls under the age of eighteen (18) years be employed in any capacity where such employment compels them to remain standing constantly.

SEC. 5. No child under the age of sixteen (16) years shall be employed or permitted to operate circular or band saws; wood shapers, wood joiners, planers, stamping machines used in sheet metal or tin work manufacturing, stamping machines in washer or nut factories, and all other stamping machines used in stamping metals; steam boilers; steam machinery; or other steam generating apparatus, dough brakes or cracker machinery of any description, wire or iron straightening machinery, rolling mill machinery, punch or shears, grinding or mixing mills, calendar rolls in rubber manufacturing or laundry machinery, corrugating rolls of the kind used in roofing or washboard manufacturing. *Same subject.*

SEC. 6. Any person who violates any provision of this act or who suffers or permits any child to be employed in violation of its provisions, shall be deemed guilty of a misdemeanor, an [and] on conviction shall be fined not less than five dollars ($5), nor more than two hundred dollars ($200), to which may be added imprisonment for not more than ten (10) days in the county jail, and for a second or subsequent offense he shall be imprisoned in the county jail for not less than ten (10) days nor more than thirty (30) days. *Violations.*

IOWA.

CODE OF 1897 AND SUPPLEMENT OF 1907.

Employment of females in barrooms.

SECTION 2448. * * *.
Subsection 8. No female shall be employed in the place [where intoxicating liquort are sold]. *Employment forbidden.*

Employment of children—General provisions.

SECTION 2477a. No person under fourteen years of age shall be employed with or without wages or compensation in any mine, manufacturing establishment, factory, mill, shop, laundry, slaughterhouse or packing house, or in any store or mercantile establishment where more than eight persons are employed, or in the operation of any freight or passenger elevator. *Age limit. Operating elevators.*

SEC. 2477b. No person under sixteen years of age shall be employed at any work or occupation by which, by reason of its nature or the place of employment, the health of such person may be injured, or his morals depraved, or at any work in which the handling or use of gunpowder, dynamite or other like explosive is required, and no female under sixteen years of age shall be employed in any capacity where the duties of such employment compel her to remain constantly standing. *Dangerous, etc., operations.*

SEC. 2477c. No person under sixteen years of age shall be employed at any of the places or in any of the occupations recited in section 1 [2477a] hereof before the hour of six o'clock in the morning or after the hour of nine o'clock in the evening, and if such person is employed exceeding five hours of each day, a noon intermission of not less than thirty minutes shall be given between the hours of eleven and one o'clock, and such person shall not be employed more than ten hours in any one day, exclusive of the noon intermission, but the provisions of this section shall not apply to persons employed in husking sheds or other places connected with canning factories where vegetables or grain are prepared for canning and in which no machinery is operated. *Night work. Hours of labor.*

SEC. 2777d (as amended by chapter 145, Acts of 1909). Any officer whose duty it is to enforce the provisions of this act shall have authority to demand of employers, proof of age of any child employed in their establishment; such proof shall be an authenticated birth record, and if there is no such record, then a baptismal record fully attested, that will establish the age of the child, and if there is no such record, a school record that will establish the age of the child, attested by a superintendent, principal, or teacher; where no such proof is obtainable, a parents' affidavit, together with ·affidavits made by two dis- *Proof of age.*

interested persons, who are in no way related to either the child or his employers, establishing date of birth may be accepted, and if no such proof is furnished, such child shall forthwith be dismissed from his employment.

False state-ments. SEC. 2477e. Any parent, guardian or other person, who having under his control any person under sixteen years of age causes or permits said person to work or be employed in violation of the provisions of this act, or any person making, certifying to, or causing to be made or certified to, any statement, certificate or other paper for the purpose of procuring the employment of any person in violation of the provisions of this act, or who makes, files, executes or delivers any such statement, certificate or other paper containing any false statement for the purpose of procuring the employment of any person in violation of this act or for the purpose of concealing the violation of this act in such employment, and every person, firm or corporation, or the agent, manager, superintendent, or officer of any person, firm or corporation, whether for himself or such person, firm or corporation, either by himself or acting through any agent, foreman, superintendent or manager, who knowingly employs any person or permits any person to be employed in violation of the provisions of this act, or who shall refuse to allow any authorized officer or person to inspect any place of business under the provisions of this act, if demand is made therefor at any time during business hours, or who shall willfully obstruct such officer or person while making such inspection, or who shall fail to keep posted the lists containing the names of persons employed under six-teen years of age and other information as required by this act, or who shall knowingly insert any false statement in such list, or who violates any other provision of this act, shall be deemed guilty of a misdemeanor, and upon being found guilty thereof, shall be fined not to exceed one hundred dollars or be imprisoned in the county jail not to exceed thirty days.

Enforcement. SEC. 2477f. It shall be the duty of the commissioner of the bureau of labor statistics to enforce the provisions of this act, and such com-missioner and his deputies, factory inspectors, assistants and other persons authorized by him in writing, State mine inspectors, and county attorneys, mayors, chiefs of police and police officers, acting under their written directions, city and town marshals, sheriffs and their deputies within the territories where they exercise their official functions, and any person having authority therefor in writing from the judge of a court of record within the territory over which such judge has jurisdiction, shall have authority to visit any of the places enu-merated in section 1 of this act [2477a], and make an inspection thereof to ascertain if any of the provisions of this act are violated or any person unlawfully employed thereat, and such persons shall not be interfered with or prevented from asking questions of any persons found at the place being inspected by them with reference to the provisions of this act. It shall be the duty of the county attorney to investigate all com-plaints made to him of the violation of this act, and to attend and prosecute at the trial of all cases for its violation upon any information that may be filed within his county.

Earnings of minors.

Payment to minors. SECTION 3191. Where a contract for the personal services of a minor has been made with him alone, and the services are afterwards per-formed, payment therefor made to him, in accordance with the terms of the contract, is a full satisfaction therefor, and the parent or guardian cannot recover a second time.

Seats for female employees.

Seats to be pro-vided. SECTION 4999. All employers of females in any mercantile or manu-facturing business or occupation shall provide and maintain suitable seats when practicable, for the use of such female employees, at or beside the counter or workbench where employed, and permit the use thereof by such employees to such extent as the work engaged in may reasonably admit of.

Any neglect or refusal to comply with the provisions of this section by any employer shall be punished by a fine not exceeding ten dollars.

Employment of women and children.

[See sections 4998–a1, 4998–a2, Appendix B, pages 914, 915.]

KANSAS.

GENERAL STATUTES—1909.

Seats for female employees.

SECTION 4658. The proprietor, manager or person, having charge of any mercantile establishment, store, shop, hotel, restaurant or other place where women or girls are employed as clerks or help therein in this State shall provide chairs, stools or other contrivances for the comfortable use of such female employees, and shall permit the use of the same by such female employees for the preservation of their health and for rest when not actively employed in the discharge of their respective duties. Seats to be provided.

SEC. 4659. Any proprietor, manager or other person violating the preceding section of this act shall be deemed guilty of a misdemeanor, and upon conviction shall be fined in a sum not less than ten dollars nor more than one hundred dollars. Penalty.

Employment of children in mines.

SECTION 4996. No person under twelve years of age shall be allowed to work in any coal mine, nor any minor between the ages of twelve and sixteen years unless he can read and write and furnish a certificate from a school-teacher, which shall be kept on file, showing that he has attended school at least three months during the year; and in all cases of minors applying for work, the agent of such coal mine shall see that the provisions of this section are not violated; and upon conviction of a willful violation of this section of this act, the agent of such coal mine shall be fined in any sum not to exceed fifty dollars for each and every offense. Employment forbidden.

Earnings of minors.

SECTION 5063. When a contract for the personal service of a minor has been made with him alone, and those services are afterwards performed, payment made therefor to such minor in accordance with the terms of the contract is a full satisfaction for those services, and the parent or guardian cannot recover therefor. Payments to minors valid.

Employment of children—General provisions.

SECTION 5094. No child under fourteen years of age shall be at any time employed, permitted or suffered to work in, or in connection with, any factory, workshop, not owned or operated by the parent or parents of the said child, theater or packing-house, or operating elevators, or in or about any mine. It shall be unlawful for any person, firm or corporation to employ any child under fourteen years of age in any business or service whatever during the hours in which the public school is in session in the district in which said child resides. Age limit.

SEC. 5095. It shall be unlawful for children under sixteen years of age, who are employed in the several vocations mentioned in this act, or in the distribution or transmission of merchandise or messages, to be employed before seven o'clock a. m. or after six o'clock p. m., or more than eight hours in any one calendar day, or more than forty-eight hours in any one week. No person under sixteen years of age shall be employed at any occupation nor at any place dangerous or injurious to life, limb, health or morals. Night work.
Hours of labor.
Dangerous, etc. occupations.

SEC. 5096. All persons, firms or corporations employing children in any of the vocations mentioned in this act under sixteen years of age shall be required to first obtain a certificate of the age of such Certificates required.

children, based upon the school census records, the same to be secured where possible from the school superintendent, principal or teacher of the school or other person authorized by the school board to have charge of the school census records in the district or city wherein such children reside. Said certificate shall be issued without charge, and shall be substantially in the following form:

Form.

————————[city], ————————[county], Kan., ————————[date].
This certifies that————————[full name], according to the records of the school census and from all knowledge that I can obtain, was born————————[day], ————————[month], ————————[year], at————————, in————————county, state of————————, and is now———————— years and————————months of age. His (or her) height is———————— [tall—short—medium], weight ———————— [heavy—light— medium], complexion————————[fair or dark], hair————————[color], eyes———————— [color], and he resides at No. ————, ———————— street.
                         (Signature)———————— ————————.
————————————[official school position] of————————
[name of school] school or district No. ————.

When said child's name and age does not appear on the school census enumeration of said city or district, then said firm, person or corporation employing such child shall secure an affidavit from the parent or legal guardian of such child, which statement shall contain the facts and data as set forth in the above certificate, and shall be certified on oath before some officer authorized to administer oaths. Such certificate or affidavit shall be sufficient protection to the employer of any child as to the age of such child, except when such employer has actual knowledge of the falsity of such certificate; and all such certificates shall be kept constantly on file in a convenient place, and shall at all times be open to inspection of the proper authorities, as provided in this act.

Enforcement.   SEC. 5097. It shall be the duty of the State factory inspector, State inspector of mines and their deputies to inspect the certificates hereinabove provided for, to examine children employed in factories, workshops, theaters, elevators, packing-houses and mines, and the vocations mentioned in section 2 of this act [5095] as to their age, and to file complaints in any court of competent jurisdiction to enforce the provisions of this act, and it shall be the duty of the county attorney of the proper county to appear and prosecute all complaints so filed.

Violations.   SEC. 5098. Any person, firm or corporation employing any person or child in violation of any provision of this act, or permitting or conniving at such violation, shall be deemed guilty of a misdemeanor, and upon conviction thereof shall be fined in a sum not less than twenty-five dollars nor more than one hundred dollars, or by imprisonment in the county jail not less than thirty days nor more than ninety days.

Employment of children—Certain employments forbidden.

Acrobatic and mendicant occupations.   SECTION 5136. * * * Any person having in his custody or control a child under the age of fourteen years, who shall in any way dispose of it with a view to its being employed as an acrobat, or a gymnast, or a contortionist, or a circus rider, or a ropewalker, or in any exhibition of like dangerous character, or as a beggar or mendicant, or pauper, or street singer, or street musician; or any person who shall take, receive, hire, employ, use, exhibit, or have in custody any child of the age last named for any of the purposes last enumerated, shall be deemed guilty of a misdemeanor, and when convicted thereof shall be subject to punishment by a fine of not more than two hundred and fty dollars, or by imprisonment for a term not exceeding one year, or both.

Employment of children—School attendance.

School attendance required.   SECTION 7736. Every parent, guardian or other person in the State of Kansas having control or charge of any child or children between the ages of eight and fifteen years, inclusive, shall be required to send such child or children to a public school, or a private, denominational or parochial school taught by a competent instructor, each school year, for such period as said school is in session: *Provided,* That any child of the age of fourteen years or more who is able to read and write the English language, and who is actively and regularly employed for his own support or for the support of those dependent upon him, shall not be required to attend the aforesaid schools for a longer period or term than eight consecutive weeks in any one year: * * *

KENTUCKY.

CONSTITUTION.

Employment of children.

SECTION 243. The general assembly shall, by law, fix the minimum ages at which children may be employed in places dangerous to life or health, or injurious to morals; and shall provide adequate penalties for violations of such law.

Employment of children to be regulated.

STATUTES, 1903.

Employment of children.

SECTION 326. A person who, for gain or reward, employs or causes to be employed, or who exhibits, uses, or who has in his custody for the purpose of exhibiting or employing any child actually or apparently under the age of sixteen years, or any person who, having the care, custody, or control of such child, as parent, relative, guardian, employer, or otherwise, sells, lets out, gives away, or in any way procures or consents, for gain or reward to the employment or exhibition of such child, either, first, in begging or receiving alms, or in any mendicant occupation; second, or (being a female) in peddling or in any wandering occupation; third, or male or female in any indecent or immoral occupation or practice, or in the exhibition of any such child when insane or idiotic; or, fourth, in any practice or exhibition of unusual danger to the life, limb, health, or morals of the child, is guilty of a misdemeanor, and shall, for the first offense, be fined not more than twenty dollars, or confined in the county jail or workhouse, in counties having a workhouse, not more than ninety days, or both so fined and confined within the discretion of the court; and, upon conviction for a second, or any subsequent offense, shall be fined in any sum not exceeding one hundred dollars, or imprisonment in the penitentiary for a term not exceeding one year, or both so fined and confined within the discretion of the jury.

Mendicant, immoral, etc., occupations forbidden.

ACTS OF 1908.

CHAPTER 66.—*Employment of children—Age limit—Inspection of factories.*

SECTION 1. No child under fourteen years of age shall be employed, permitted or suffered to work in or in connection with any factory, workshop, mine, mercantile establishment, store, business office, telegraph office, restaurant, hotel, apartment house or in the distribution or transmission of merchandise or messages. It shall be unlawful for any person, firm or corporation to employ any child under fourteen years of age in any business or service whatever, during any part of the term during which the public schools of the district in which the child resides are in session.

Age limit.

SEC. 2 (as amended by chapter 85, Acts of 1910). No child between fourteen and sixteen years of age shall be employed, permitted or suffered to work in or in connection with any factory, workshop, mine, mercantile establishment, store, business office, telegraph office, restaurant, hotel, apartment house, or in the distribution or transmission of merchandise or messages, unless the person or corporation employing him procures and keeps on file and accessible to the

Certificates.

truant officers of the town or city, and to the labor inspector, an employment certificate as hereinafter prescribed, and keep two complete lists
of all such children employed therein, one on file and one conspicuously posted near the principal entrance of the building in which such
children are employed. On termination of the employment of a child
so registered, and whose certificate is so filed, such certificate shall
forthwith be surrendered by the employer to the child or its parent
File.   or guardian or custodian. The labor inspector may make demands on
an employer in whose establishment a child apparently under the age
of sixteen years is employed or permitted or suffered to work, and
whose employment certificate is not then filed as required by this act,
that such employer shall either furnish him within ten days, evidence
satisfactory to him that such child is in fact over sixteen years of age,
or shall cease to employ, or permit or suffer such child to work therein.
The labor inspector may require from such employer the same evidence of age of such child as is required on the issuance of an employment certificate, and the employer furnishing such evidence shall not
be required to furnish any further evidence of the age of the child.
In case such employer shall fail to produce and deliver to the inspector
within ten days after such demand such evidence of age herein required
of him, and thereafter continue to employ such child, or permit or suffer
such child to work in such establishment, proof of the giving of such
notice and of such failure to produce and file such evidence shall be
prima facie evidence in any prosecution brought for violation of the
provision that such child is under sixteen years of age and is unlawfully
employed.

Who may issue   Sec. 3 (as amended by chapter 85, Acts of 1910). Employment
certificates.   certificates shall be issued only by the superintendent of schools or by
a person authorized by him in writing acting in his name. Where
there is no local superintendent of schools, they shall be issued by the
county superintendent of schools or by a person so authorized by him.

Evidence.   Sec. 4 (as amended by chapter 85, Acts of 1910). The persons authorized to issue employment certificates shall not issue such certificates
until he has received, examined, approved, and filed the following
papers duly executed: (1) The school record of such child properly
filled out and signed as provided herein below. (2) A passport or
duly attested transcript of the certificate of birth or baptism or other
religious record, showing the date and place of birth of such child. A
duly attested transcript of the birth certificate filed according to law
with any officer charged with the duty of recording births, shall be
sufficient evidence of the age of such child. (3) The affidavit of the
parent, guardian or custodian of a child, which shall be required,
however, only in case such last-mentioned transcript of the certificate
of birth be not produced and filed, showing the place and date of birth
of such child; which affidavit must be taken before the officer issuing
employment certificates, who is hereby authorized and required to
administer such oaths, and who shall not demand or receive a fee therefor. Such employment certificate shall not be issued until such child
has personally appeared before and been examined by the officer
issuing the certificates, and until such officer shall, after making
examination, file and sign in his office a statement that the child can
read and legibly write simple sentences in the English language and
that in his opinion the child is fourteen years of age or upwards and has
reached the normal development of a child of its age, and is in sound
health and is physically able to perform the work which it intends to do.
In doubtful cases such physical fitness shall be determined by a medical
officer of the board or department of health, or by the county physician.
Every employment certificate shall be signed in the presence of the
child in whose name it is issued. The superintendent of schools in
any city, town, county, or district, wherever there is one, and where
there is none, then the county superintendent shall, between the first
and tenth days of each month, transmit to the office of the labor in-
Reports.   spector, a report, which report shall give, (1) the name of each child
to whom a certificate has been issued in the previous month, together
with the date of birth of such child; and (2) the name of each child to
whom a certificate has been refused in the previous month, together
with the ground for such refusal. A refusal or failure to transmit such

report by any person charged under this section with the duty of transmitting same to the labor inspector, shall constitute a misdemeanor punishable by a fine of not more than twenty-five nor less than five dollars, to be disposed of as provided in section 18 of this law.

SEC. 5. Such certificate shall state the date and place of birth of the child, and describe the color of the hair and eyes, the height and weight and any distinguishing facial marks of such child, and that the papers required by the preceding section have been duly examined, approved and filed and that the child named in such certificate has appeared before the officer signing the certificate and has been examined. *Description of child.*

SEC. 6. The school record above mentioned shall be signed by the principal or chief teacher of the school which such child has last attended and shall be furnished, on demand, to a child entitled thereto. It shall contain a statement certifying that the child has regularly attended the public schools or schools equivalent thereto or parochial schools for not less than one hundred days during the school year previous to his arriving at the age of fourteen years or during the year previous to applying for such school records, and is able to read and write simple sentences in the English language, and has received during such period instruction in reading, spelling, writing, and geography and is familiar with the fundamental operations of arithmetic up to and including common fractions. Such school record shall also give the age and residence of the child, as shown on the records of the school and the name of its parent, or guardian or custodian: *Provided,* That upon the filing with the person authorized to issue employment certificates of the affidavit of the applicant or of his or her parent, guardian or custodian, showing that diligent effort has been made to obtain the school record hereby required and that it can not be obtained, then the person authorized to issue the certificate may issue such a certificate without having received such school record, but it shall be his duty, in such case, to examine the applicant as to his or her proficiency in each of the studies mentioned in this section; and in such case the employment certificate shall show that such examination was had in lieu of of the filing of the school record. *School record.*

SEC. 7. No person under the age of sixteen years shall be employed or suffered or permitted to work at any gainful occupation more than sixty hours in any one week, not [sic] nor more than ten hours in any one day; or before the hour of seven o'clock in the morning or after the hour of seven in the evening. Every employer shall post in a conspicuous place in every room where such minors are employed a printed notice, stating the hours required of them each day of the week, the hours of commencing and stopping work and the hours when the time or times allowed for dinner or for other meals begin and end. The printed form of such notice shall be furnished by the state labor inspector, and the employment of any minor for longer time in any day so stated shall be deemed a violation of this section. *Hours of labor of children.*

Night work.

SEC. 8 (as amended by chapter 85, Acts of 1910). Whoever employs a child under sixteen years of age, and any parent, guardian, or any adult person under whose care or control a child under such age lives, who permits such child to be employed in violation of section one, two or eight of this act, shall, for such offense, be fined not more than fifty dollars, and whoever continues to employ any child in violation of either of said sections of this act after being notified by a truant officer or a labor inspector thereof, shall for every day thereafter that such employment continues, be fined not less than five nor more than twenty ·dollars. A failure to produce to a truant officer or labor inspector any employment certificate or list required by this act shall be prima facie evidence of the illegal employment of any person whose employment certificate is not produced, or whose name is not so listed. Any corporation or employer retaining employment certificates in violation of section two of this act shall be fined ten dollars. Every person authorized to sign the certificate prescribed by section five of this act, who knowingly certifies to any materially false statement therein shall be fined not more than fifty dollars, nor less than ten dollars. *Violations.*

SEC. 9. Truant officers may visit the factories, workshops, mines, and mercantile establishments in their several towns and cities and *Enforcement.*

ascertain whether any minors are employed therein contrary to the provisions of this act, and they shall report any cases of such illegal employment to the superintendent of schools and to the labor inspector. Labor inspectors and truant officers may require that the employment certificates and lists provided for in this act, of minors employed in such factories, workshops, mines or mercantile establishments, shall be produced for their inspection. Complaints for offenses under this act shall be brought by the labor inspectors.

Certain employments prohibited.

SEC. 10. No child under the age of sixteen years shall be employed at sewing belts, or to assist in sewing belts, in any capacity whatever, nor shall any child adjust any belt to any machinery; they shall not oil or assist in oiling, wiping or cleaning machinery; they shall not operate, or assist in operating circular or band saws, wood shapers, wood joiners, planers, sandpaper or wood-polishing machinery, emery or polishing wheels used for polishing sheet metal, wood turning or boring machinery, stamping machines in sheet metal and tinware manufacturing, stamping machines in washer and nut factories, operating corrugating rolls, such as are used in roofing factories, nor shall they be employed in operating any steam boiler, steam machinery, or other steam generating apparatus, or as a pin boys [sic] in any bowling alley; they shall not operate or assist in operating dough brakes, or cracker machinery of any description, wire or iron straightening machinery, nor shall they operate or assist in operating rolling mill machinery, punches or shears, washing, or grinding or mixing mills, or calendar [sic] rolls in rubber manufacturing, nor shall they operate or assist in operating laundry machinery, nor shall such children be employed in any capacity in preparing any composition in which dangerous or poisonous acids are used, and they shall not be employed in any capacity in the manufacture of paints, colors or white lead, nor shall they be employed in any capacity whatever in operating or assisting to operate any passenger or freight elevator, nor shall they be employed in any capacity whatever in the manufacture of goods for immoral purposes, nor in any theater, concert hall, or place of amusement wherein intoxicating liquors are sold, nor shall females under sixteen years of age be employed in any capacity where such employment compels them to remain standing constantly. Nor shall any child under sixteen years of age be employed at any occupation dangerous or injurious to health or morals, or to lives or limbs, and as to these matters, the decision of the county physician or city health officer, as the case may be, shall be final.

Guards for dangerous machinery.

SEC. 11. It shall be the duty of the owner of any manufacturing establishment, where any person under sixteen years of age is employed, his agents, superintendents or other persons in charge of same, to furnish and supply, when practicable, or cause to be furnished and supplied to him, belt shifters or other safe mechanical contrivance for the purpose of throwing belts on or off pulleys; and, whenever practicable, machinery therein shall be provided with loose belts. All vats, pans, saws, planes, cogs, gearing, belting, set screws and machinery of every description therein, which is palpably dangerous, where practicable, shall be properly guarded; and no person shall remove or make ineffective any safeguard around or attached to any planer, saw, belting, shafting or other machinery, or around any vat or pan, while the same is in use, unless for the purpose of immediately making repairs thereto, and all such safeguards shall be promptly replaced. No person under eighteen years of age shall be allowed to clean machinery while in motion.

Washrooms, etc.

SEC. 12. Suitable and proper wash rooms and water-closets shall be provided in each manufacturing establishment, where any person under sixteen years of age is employed, and such water-closets shall be properly screened and ventilated and be kept at all times in a clean condition; and if girls under sixteen years of age be employed in any such establishment, the water-closet shall have separate approaches and be kept separate and apart from those used by men. All closets shall be kept free from obscene writing and marking. A dressing room shall be provided for such girls when the nature of their work is such as to require any change of clothing.

Seats for female employees.

SEC. 13. Every person, firm, corporation, association, individual or partnership employing girls under sixteen years of age in any manufacturing, mechanical or mercantile industry, laundry, workshop, renovating works, or printing offices in this Commonwealth, shall provide seats for the use of the girls so employed, and shall permit the use of such by them when not necessarily engaged in the active duties for which they are employed.

SEC. 14. The walls and ceilings of each room in every manufacturing establishment where any person under sixteen years of age is employed shall be limewashed or painted, when, in the opinion of the labor inspector, it shall be conducive to the health or cleanliness of the persons working therein. *Walls to be limewashed, etc.*

SEC. 15. Grand juries shall have inquisitorial powers to investigate violations of this act; also shall county judges and circuit judges, and judges of the circuit courts of the State shall specially charge the grand jury at the beginning of each term of the court to investigate violations of this act. *Enforcement.*

SEC. 16. A copy of this act shall be conspicuously posted and kept in each manufacturing establishment, mill, mine or workshop or mercantile or printing establishment, theater, bowling alley, telegraph, telephone or public messenger company or laundry in this Commonwealth. *Law to be posted.*

SEC. 17. Any adult person who violates any of the provisions of this act or who suffers or permits any child to be employed in violation of its provisions, shall be deemed guilty of a misdemeanor, and on conviction, unless otherwise herein expressly provided, shall be punished by a fine of not more than fifty dollars and not less than twenty-five dollars for the first offense, and for each subsequent offense by imprisonment for not more than ninety days and not less than ten days, or by a fine of not less than fifty dollars nor more than two hundred dollars, or by both fine and imprisonment. *Violations.*

LOUISIANA.

REVISED LAWS, 1897.

Employment of women in saloons, etc.

(Page 232. ACT No. 43, Acts of 1894.)

SECTION 1. No owner, proprietor, keeper, lessee or agent, manager or conductor of any concert hall or saloon where spirituous liquors, wines or malt are sold at retail, shall employ or suffer to be employed any female to distribute or appear among the audience or frequenters of such concert hall or saloon for the purpose of distributing or selling or taking orders to be filled, any such spirituous liquors, wines or malt and any person or persons violating the provisions of this act shall be deemed guilty of a misdemeanor, and, on conviction shall be imprisoned in the parish jail not less than thirty days nor more than three months and a fine of not less than fifty nor more than one hundred dollars for each and every offense. *Women not to be employed in concert halls, etc.*

Employment of children in certain occupations forbidden.

(Page 516. ACT No. 59, Acts of 1892.)

SECTION 1. Any person who employs or exhibits or gives away for the purpose of employing or exhibiting a child under fifteen years of age, for the purpose of walking on a wire or rope, or riding or performing as a gymnast, contortionist or acrobat in any circus or theatrical exhibition or in any public place whatsoever or who causes, procures or encourages any such child to engage therein, shall be punished by a fine, by any committing magistrate, of not less than ten dollars, nor more than twenty-five dollars or shall be subject to a term of imprisonment not exceeding thirty days or both at the discretion of the court. *Acrobatic, etc., occupations.*

SEC. 2. No license shall be granted for a theatrical exhibition or public show in which children under fifteen years of age are employed or [as] contortionists, acrobats, or in any feats of gymnast or equestrianism or where in the opinion of the mayor of a city or *Theatrical license refused, when.*

town authorized to grant licenses, such children are employed in such a manner as to corrupt their morals or impair their physical health.

ACTS OF 1900.

Act No. 55.—*Employment of women.*

Seats to be provided.
SECTION 1. Hereafter it shall be unlawful for any person, firm or corporation doing business in the State of Louisiana, where female labor or female clerks are employed, not to maintain seats, chairs or benches which shall be so placed as to be accessible to said employees, for their use during the times when said employees are not actually engaged in the attention to their duties as employees of such firm, person or corporation.

Time for meals.
SEC. 2. Hereafter all persons, firms or corporations doing business at retail in the State of Louisiana where female labor or female clerks are employed, shall be required to give every employee each day, between the hours of ten (10) a. m. and three (3) p. m. not less than thirty (30) minutes for lunch or recreation.

Penalty.
SEC. 3. Whoever shall be found guilty of evading or disobeying any of the provisions of this act, shall be deemed guilty of a misdemeanor, and upon arrest and conviction therefor shall be fined in a sum of not less than twenty-five ($25) dollars nor more than one hundred ($100) dollars, and in default of the payment thereof shall be sentenced to imprisonment for a period not less than five (5) days nor more than six (6) months.

ACTS OF 1904.

Act No. 178.—*Employment of wives and children while men live in idleness.*

Who are vagrants.
SECTION 1. The several municipal corporations throughout the State shall adopt ordinances declaring vagrants, and punishing as such, * * * (all persons able to work who do not work) but who live upon the wages or personal earnings of their wives or of their minor children; * * *

ACTS OF 1908.

Act No. 301.—*Inspection of factories, etc.—Employment of women and children.*

Age limit.
SECTION 1. From and after the passage of this act it shall be unlawful for any person, agent, firm, company, copartnership, or corporation to require or permit or suffer or employ any child under the age of 14 years to labor or work in any mill, factory, mine, packing house, manufacturing establishment, workshop, laundry, millinery or dressmaking store or mercantile establishment in which more than five persons are employed, or in any theater, concert hall, or in or about any place of amusement where intoxicating liquors are made or sold, or in any bowling alley, bootblacking establishment, freight or passenger elevator, or in the transmission or distribution of messages, either telegraph or telephone, or any other messages, or merchandise, or in any other occupation not herein enumerated which may be deemed unhealthful or dangerous. The provisions of this section shall in no way be construed as applying to agricultural or domestic industries. Any violation of this provision shall be punishable by a fine of not less than $25 or more than $50 or by imprisonment in the parish jail (parish prison in New Orleans) for not less than ten days or more than six months, or both, in the discretion of the court.

Certificates.
SEC. 2. The State factory inspector or any factory inspector appointed by the mayor of the city of New Orleans with the consent of the council acting in conjunction with the board of health and school board in the parish shall have full power to issue an age certificate to minors over 14 years and under 16 years of age seeking employment in any part of this State: *Provided, however,* That no person authorized to issue an age certificate as hereafter provided shall have

authority to approve such certificate for any child then in or about to enter his own establishment, or the employment of a firm or corporation of which he is a member, officer or employee.

The person approving these age certificates shall have authority to administer the oath provided therein, but no fee shall be charged therefor. Every person issuing or approving these age certificates shall keep a record of the same, and shall forward to the office of the State factory inspector a duplicate of each certificate issued or approved. All such age certificates shall be subject to review by the State or other factory inspector, and may by him or her be canceled if he or she finds that such certificates have been obtained through fraud, misrepresentation or falsification of facts, and whoever shall obtain or assist in obtaining such age certificates by fraud, misrepresentation or falsification of facts, is hereby declared to be guilty of a misdemeanor, and on conviction before a court of competent jurisdiction shall be fined not less than $10 or more than $50. In such cases the factory inspector shall give written notice to the employer, who shall at once cause the minor affected to be dismissed from employment. Printed forms of the age certificate hereinafter provided shall be furnished by the State factory inspector upon request made by persons authorized to issue them. An age certificate shall not be approved unless satisfactory evidence is furnished by a certificate of birth or baptism of such child, the register of birth of such child with an officer of a city or town designated to keep a register of births, or by the records of the public or parochial school attended by such child, that such child is of the age stated in the certificate, or by a certified copy of their passport from the commissioner of immigration: *Provided,* That in cases where the above proof is not obtainable, the parent, guardian or custodian of the child shall make an oath before the State factory inspector, or any factory inspector, or before a juvenile or district court as to the age of such child, and the State factory inspector, or any factory inspector, or the court, may issue to such child an age certificate as sworn to. A duplicate of such age certificate shall be filled out and shall be forwarded to the office of the State factory inspector. The age certificate shall be printed and shall be filled out, signed and held or surrendered in the following forms:

Records.

Evidence.

Forms.

AGE CERTIFICATES.

This certifies that I am (father, mother, guardian or custodian) of (name of minor) and that (he or she) was born at (name of town or city) in the (name of county if known) and (State or county of ———) on the (date of birth and year of birth) and is now (number of years and months) old.

(Signature of parent, guardian or custodian.)
(City or town and date.)
There personally appeared before me the above-named (name of person signing) and made oath that the foregoing certificate by (him or her) signed, is true to the best of (his or her) knowledge. I hereby approve the foregoing certificate of (name of child), height, (feet and inches,) weight ———, complexion (fair or dark), hair (color), having no sufficient reason to doubt that (he or she) is of the age therein certified.

OWNER OF CERTIFICATE. This certificate belongs to (name of child and in whose behalf it is drawn), and is to be surrendered to (him or her) whenever (he or she) leaves the service of the corporation or employer holding the same, but if not claimed by said child within thirty days from such time, it shall be returned to the office of the State factory inspector for cancellation.

(Signature of person authorized to approve and sign with official character of authority.)
(Town or city and date.)
Such certificate shall be issued without charge. The provisions of this section shall not become operative until 60 days after the promulgation of this act.

SEC. 3. It shall be the duty of the commissioner of labor and industrial statistics and his deputies, and such factory inspectors as will be appointed in incorporated cities and towns by the mayor, with the

Enforcement.

consent of the council, and in parishes, by the police jury, and they are hereby authorized and empowered to visit and inspect, at all reasonable times and as often as possible all places enumerated in section 1 of this act, and to file complaint in any court of competent jurisdiction to enforce the provisions of this act, and it shall be the duty of the parish or district attorney to appear and prosecute all complaints so filed.

Hours of labor. SEC. 4. No child or person under the age of 18 years, and no woman shall be employed in any of the places and industries enumerated in section 1 of this act for a longer period than ten hours per day of [or] 60 hours per week. There shall be one hour allowed each day for dinner, but such dinner time shall not be included as part of the working hours of the day. In case two-thirds of the employees so desire, time for dinner may be reduced at their request to not less than 30 minutes: *Provided*, That this shall not apply to persons working in stores and mercantile establishments on Saturday nights or 20 days before Christmas. Any violation of this provision shall be punishable by a fine of not less than $25 or more than $50, or by imprisonment in the parish jail (parish prison in New Orleans) for not less than ten days or more than six months, or both, in the discretion of the court.

Night work. SEC. 5. No boy under the age of 16 years and no girl under the age of 18 shall be employed at any work before the hour of 6 in the morning or after the hour of 7 at night: *Provided*, That this shall not apply to persons working in stores and mercantile establishments on Saturday nights or during 20 days before Christmas. Any violation of this provision shall be punishable by a fine of not less than $25 nor more than $100, or by imprisonment in the parish jail (parish prison in New Orleans) for not less than ten days nor more than six months, or both, in the discretion of the court.

List of names. SEC. 6. Every person, firm or corporation, agent or manager of a corporation employing or permitting or suffering to work five or more children under the age of 18 years and over the age of 14 in all places of business or establishments or occupations enumerated in section 1 shall post and keep posted in a conspicuous place in every room in which such help is employed or permitted or suffered to work a list containing the names, age and place of residence of every person under the age of 18 years employed, permitted or suffered to work in such room, *Certificates required.* and it shall be unlawful for any person, agent, firm, company, copartnership, corporation or manager of a corporation to require or permit or suffer or employ in any mill, factory, mine or packing house, manufacturing establishment, workshop, store, laundry, millinery, dressmaking or mercantile establishment in which more than five persons are employed, or any theater, concert hall or in or about any place of amusement where intoxicating liquors are made or sold, or in any bowling alley or bootblacking establishment, or in any place where messages are transmitted or distributed, or in any other occupation not herein enumerated which may be deemed unhealthful or dangerous, any child over the age of 14 until an age certificate, approved as hereinabove provided, has been produced and placed on file in any such establishment or place of employment as heretofore mentioned in this section: *Provided, further, however*, That immediately upon the employment of any child in any of the places enumerated in this act the manager, superintendent, owner or agent shall notify in writing, the factory inspector of the employment of said child in the event proper age certificate is not filed, but such establishment or place of employment must procure from said child within five days from employment the age certificate provided for in this act. Any violation of this section shall be punishable by a fine of not less than $25 nor more than $50 or by imprisonment in the parish jail (parish prison in New Orleans) for not less than ten days nor more than six months, or both in the discretion of the court.

False statements. SEC. 7. Any parent or guardian or person or persons having control of or being responsible for the care of any child or person under the age of 16 who shall sign or swear or in any manner make false statement as to the age of said child or person under the age of 16 for the purpose of obtaining employment for said child or young person shall be deemed guilty of an offense for each violation thereof and upon conviction for the same shall be punished by a fine of not less than $10 nor more than $25 or by imprisonment in the parish jail (parish prison in New Orleans) for not less than ten days nor more than thirty days, or both, in the discretion of the court.

SEC. 8. Any child working in or in connection with any of the aforesaid establishments or in the distribution or transmission of merchandise or messages who appears to the inspector to be under the legal age is required to procure from the city or parish physician a certificate as to the physical fitness of said child to perform the work or service he or she is required to do. *Physician's certificate.*

SEC. 9. The presence of any child under 14 years of age in any of the establishments enumerated in section 1, except during the dinner hour, shall constitute prima facie evidence of his or her employment therein. *Presence of child.*

SEC. 10. Any owner, manager, supervisor or employee in any of the aforesaid occupations who shall hide or assist to escape or give warning of the approach of the inspector to any child or young person or woman in said establishments shall be deemed guilty of a misdemeanor and shall be punished by a fine of not less than $5 nor more than $15 or by imprisonment in the parish jail (parish prison in New Orleans) for not less than ten days nor more than thirty days, or both, in the discretion of the court. *Evading inspection.*

SEC. 11. Any person, owner, agent, firm, manager, copartnership or company in charge of any establishment at the time of inspection shall be required to furnish the inspector a true statement of the number of persons employed in such establishment and any person, owner, agent, superintendent, firm, manager, company or copartnership who shall fail or refuse to furnish such statement or willfully understate the number of persons employed shall be deemed guilty of a misdemeanor and upon conviction thereof shall be fined not less than $25 nor more than $100 for each offense or imprisonment for not less than ten nor more than thirty days in the parish jail (parish prison in New Orleans), or both, in the discretion of the court. *Reports by employers.*

SEC. 12. Within one month after the occupancy of any factory, workshop or mill or store or other aforesaid occupation or establishment where children, young persons or women are employed the occupant shall notify the inspector in writing of such occupancy. Failure to do this shall constitute a misdemeanor and shall be punishable by a fine of not less than $10 nor more than $25 or by imprisonment in the parish jail (parish prison in New Orleans) for not less than ten days nor more than thirty days, or both, in the discretion of the court. *Time allowance.*

SEC. 13. Every person who shall employ any female in any factory, mill, warehouse, manufacturing establishment, workshop or store or any other occupation or establishment hereinabove mentioned shall provide suitable seats, chairs or benches for the use of the females so employed, which shall be so placed as to be accessible to said employees and shall permit the use of such seats, chairs or benches by them when they are not necessarily engaged in the active duties for which they are employed, and there shall be provided at least one chair to every three females. Failure to comply with this section shall be punishable by a fine of not less than $25 nor more than $50 or imprisonment in the parish jail (parish prison in New Orleans) for not less than ten days nor more than thirty days, or both, in the discretion of the court. *Seats for females.*

SEC. 14. Every factory, mill, manufacturing establishment, workshop, warehouse, mercantile establishment or store and all other occupations and establishments hereinabove mentioned in which five or more young persons or women are employed and every such institution in which two or more children, young persons or women are employed shall be supplied with proper wash and dressing rooms and kept in a cleanly state and free from effluvia arising from any drain, privy or other nuisance and shall be provided, within reasonable access, with a sufficient number of proper water-closets or privies for the reasonable use of the persons employed and at least one of such closets shall be provided for each twenty-five persons employed and wherever two or more persons and one or more female person[s] *Wash rooms, etc.*

are employed as aforesaid a sufficient number of separate and distinct water-closets, earth closets or privies shall be provided for the use of each sex and plainly so designated, and no person shall be allowed to use any such closet or privy assigned to persons of the other sex, and said closets or privies shall not be locked during working hours. Failure to comply with this section shall be punishable by a fine of not less than $25 nor more than $50 or imprisonment in the parish jail (parish prison in New Orleans) for not less than ten days nor more than thirty days, or both, in the discretion of the court.

Stairways.

Doors to open outwardly.

SEC. 15. Stairways with substantial hand rails shall be provided in factories, mills and manufacturing establishments for the better safety of persons employed in said establishments. The doors of such establishments shall swing outwardly or slide, as ordered by the factory inspector and it shall be neither locked, bolted or fastened during working hours. Failure to comply with this section shall be punishable by a fine of not less than $25 nor more than $50 or imprisonment in the parish jail (parish prison in New Orleans) for not less than ten days nor more than thirty days, or both, in the discretion of the court.

Limewashing, etc.

SEC. 16. Every factory, mill or workshop in this State where women and children are employed shall be limewashed or painted when deemed necessary and ordered by the health authorities. Failure to comply with this section shall be punishable by a fine of not less than $25 nor more than $50 or imprisonment in the parish jail (parish prison in New Orleans) for not less than ten days nor more than thirty days or both, in the discretion of the court.

Cleaning moving machinery.

SEC. 17. No minor or woman shall be required to clean any part of the mill, gearing or machinery in any such establishment in this State while the same is in motion. Failure to comply with this section shall be punishable by a fine of not less than $25 nor more than $50 or imprisonment in the parish jail (parish prison in New Orleans), for not less than ten days nor more than thirty days, or both, in the discretion of the court.

Hatchways, etc.

SEC. 18. The opening of all hatchways, elevators and wellholes upon every floor of every manufacturing, mechanical or mercantile or public buildings where women or children are employed in this State shall be protected by good and sufficient trapdoors of selfclosing hatches or safety catches or good strong guard rails at least three feet high. Failure to comply with this section shall be punishable by a fine of not less than $25 nor more than $50 or imprisonment in the parish jail (parish prison in New Orleans), for not less than ten days nor more than thirty days or both, in the discretion of the court.

Fans for dust producing, etc., machinery.

SEC. 19. In all establishments in this State wherein children, young persons or women are employed where any process is carried on by which dust, or smoke or lint is generated the inspector shall have the power and authority to order that a fan, or fans, or some other dust, or smoke or lint removing or consuming contrivance or contrivances be so placed as to prevent the inhalation of such dust or smoke or lint by the employees: *Provided*, That two mechanical engineers, one chosen by the inspector and the other by the owner or owners of the establishment, shall agree as to the necessity of such fan or fans or other dust or smoke or lint removing or consuming contrivance or contrivances. Upon the failure of said two mechanical engineers to agree, a third mechanical engineer shall be chosen to arbitrate. Failure to comply with this section shall be punishable by a fine of not less than $25 nor more than $50 or imprisonment in the parish jail (parish prison in New Orleans) for not less than ten days nor more than six months or both, in the discretion of the court.

Accidents to be reported.

SEC. 20. All accidents in manufacturing, mechanical or other establishments or places within this State where children, young persons or women are employed which prevent the injured person or persons from returning to work within two weeks after the injury or which result in death shall be reported semiannually by the person in charge of such establishment or place to the inspector. Failure to do this shall be deemed a violation of this section and punishable by a fine of not less than $5 nor more than $10 or imprisonment in the parish jail (parish prison in New Orleans) for not less than twenty-four hours nor more than ten days, or both, in the discretion of the court.

Sec. 21. It shall be the duty of the city or town or parish employing Office for inspector or inspectors to provide a suitable office for same and pay spector. for all necessary expenses incurred in the discharge of the duties of said office.

Sec. 22. There shall be an annual report of inspections made and all Reports. work and expenses in connection with said office forwarded to the commissioner of labor and incorporated towns and cities to the mayor and council of the cities and towns employing said inspector or inspectors.

Sec. 23. In the city of New Orleans, with the consent of the council, New Orleans. [the mayor] shall appoint a factory inspector, who may be either male or female, to see that the regulations of this act are observed and also to prosecute all persons who shall violate the same. Such inspector shall be paid a salary of not more than $750 per annum.

MAINE.

REVISED STATUTES—1903.

Chapter 15.—*Employment of children—School attendance.*

Section 51 (as amended by chapter 113, Acts of 1911). * * * Truant Enforcement of officers, when so directed in writing by the superintendent of schools law. or the superintending school committee of their respective towns, may visit the manufacturing, mechanical, mercantile and other business establishments in their several cities and towns during the hours in which the public schools of such city or town are in session, and ascertain whether any minors under the age of fifteen years are employed therein, and shall report in writing any cases of such employment to the superintendent of schools or the superintending school committee of their city or town, and if employed therein contrary to the provisions of chapter forty, shall also report in writing such illegal employment to the commissioner of labor. The owner, superintendent, overseer or agent of all manufacturing, mechanical, mercantile or other business establishments, upon request, shall produce for the inspection of such truant officers, all certified copies of records of birth and baptism, passports and age and schooling certificates required to be kept on file in such establishments under chapter forty of the Revised Statutes. * * *

Chapter 40.—*Employment of women and children.*

Section 48 (as amended by act 55, Acts of 1911). No female minor Ten-hour day. under eighteen years of age, no male minor under sixteen years of age, and no woman shall be employed in laboring in any manufacturing or mechanical establishment in the State, more than ten hours in any one day, except when it is necessary to make repairs to prevent the interruption of the ordinary running of the machinery, or when a different apportionment of the hours of labor is made for the sole purpose of making a shorter day's work for one day of the week; and in no case shall the hours of labor exceed fifty-eight in a week; and no male per- Fifty-eight son sixteen years of age and over shall be so employed as above, more hours per week. than ten hours a day during minority, unless he voluntarily contracts Boys over 16. to do so with the consent of his parents, or one of them, if any, or guardian, and in such case he shall receive extra compensation for his services: *Provided, however,* That any female of eighteen years of age Girls over 18 or over, may lawfully contract for such labor for any number of hours in excess of ten hours a day, not exceeding six hours in any one week, or sixty hours in any one year, receiving additional compensation therefor; but during her minority, the consent of her parents, or one Exceptions. of them, or guardian, shall be first obtained. Nothing in this section shall apply to any manufacturing establishment or business, the materials and products of which are perishable and require immediate labor thereon, to prevent decay thereof or damage thereto.

Sec. 49. Every employer shall post in a conspicuous place in every Time schedule room where such persons are employed, a notice printed in plain, to be posted. large type, stating the number of hours' work required of them on each day of the week, the exact time for commencing work in the morning,

stopping at noon for dinner, commencing after dinner, and stopping
at night; the form of such printed notice shall be furnished by the
inspector of factories, workshops, mines and quarries, and shall be
approved by the attorney general. And the employment of any such
person for a longer time in any day than that so stated, shall be deemed
a violation of the preceding section, unless it appears that such employment is to make up for time lost on some previous day of the same week,
in consequence of the stopping of machinery upon which such person
was employed or dependent for employment.

Penalty. SEC. 50. Whoever, either for himself, or as superintendent, overseer
or agent of another, employs or has in his employment any person in
violation of the provisions of section forty-eight, and every parent or
guardian who permits any minor to be so employed, shall be punished
by a fine of not less than twenty-five, nor more than fifty dollars for
Certificate. each offense. A certificate of the age of a minor made by him and by
his parent or guardian at the time of his employment, shall be conclusive evidence of his age in behalf of the hirer, upon any prosecution
for a violation of the provisions of section forty-eight. Whoever falsely
makes and utters such a certificate with an intention to evade the
provisions of this chapter relating to the employment of minors, shall
be subject to a fine of one hundred dollars.

Notice of inten- SEC. 51. Any person, firm or corporation engaged in any manufac-
tion to leave em- turing or mechanical business, may contract with adult or minor
ployment, etc. employees to give one week's notice of intention on such employee's
part, to quit such employment under a penalty of forfeiture of one
week's wages. In such case, the employer shall be required to give a
like notice of intention to discharge the employee; and on failure, shall
pay to such employee, a sum equal to one week's wages. No such
forfeiture shall be enforced when the leaving or discharge of the em-
Proviso. ployee is for a reasonable cause: *Provided, however,* That the enforcement of the penalty aforesaid, shall not prevent either party from
recovering damages for a breach of the contract of hire.

Age limit. SEC. 52 (as amended by chapter 257, Acts of 1909). No child under
fourteen years of age shall be employed or allowed to work in or in
connection with any manufacturing or mechanical establishment.
It shall be unlawful for any person, firm or corporation to employ for
wages or hire any child under fourteen years of age in any manufacturing, mechanical, mercantile or other business establishment, or in
any telephone or telegraph office; or in the delivery and transmission
of telephone or telegraph messages during the hours that the public
schools of the town or city in which he resides are in session. Whoever,
either for himself, or as superintendent, overseer or agent of another,
employs or has in his employ any child in violation of the provisions of
this section, and every parent or guardian who allows any child to be so
employed shall be punished by a fine not less than one dollar nor
exceeding fifty dollars for each offense.

Certificate. SEC. 53 (as amended by chapter 257, Acts of 1909). No child over
fourteen years of age and under sixteen years of age shall be employed
or allowed to work in any manufacturing or mechanical establishment
until he, or some one in his behalf, shall have produced and presented
to the owner, superintendent, overseer or agent of such establishment,
a certified copy of the town clerk's record of the birth of such child, or a
certified copy of his baptismal record showing the date of his birth; or
his passport showing the date of his birth; or an age and schooling
certificate duly issued to him as hereinafter provided. No such child
between his fourteenth and fifteenth birthdays shall be employed or
allowed to work in any manufacturing, mechanical, mercantile or
other business establishment, or in any telephone or telegraph office;
or in the delivery and transmission of telephone or telegraph messages
during the hours in which the public schools of the city or town in
which he resides are in session, until he shall have produced and presented to the owner, superintendent, overseer or agent of such establishment an age and schooling certificate duly issued to him as hereinafter provided. No such child between his fifteenth and sixteenth
birthdays shall be employed or allowed to work in any manufacturing
or mechanical establishment during the hours in which the public

schools of the city or town in which he resides are in session, until he shall have produced and presented to the owner, superintendent, overseer or agent of such establishment an age and schooling certificate duly issued to him as hereinafter provided. The employer shall keep on file such birth record, baptismal record, passport or age and schooling certificate in duplicate containing the name of such child, the name of his parents, guardian or custodian, and such data as may be required by the inspector of factories, workshops, mines and quarries. Blank employment certificates, in form approved by the attorney general, shall be furnished by the inspector of factories, workshops, mines and quarries. One of such certificates . **Files.** shall be delivered to such child and the other be immediately forwarded to the office of said inspector of factories, workshops, mines, and quarries, to be kept on file by him. When such child leaves such employment, the employer shall return to such child the copy of the town record, baptismal record, passport or age and schooling certificate furnished by him as aforesaid, and shall immediately notify said inspector that such child has left his employ. The inspector of facto- **Enforcement.** ries, workshops, mines and quarries, or any of his assistants, may demand of any employer or corporation the names of all children under sixteen years of age in his employ in the several cities and towns of the State, and may require that the birth record, baptismal record, passport or age and schooling certificate of such children shall be produced for his inspection, and the failure to produce the same shall be prima facie evidence that the employment of such child is illegal. Whoever, either for himself, or as superintendent, overseer or agent of another, employs or has in his employment any child in violation of the provisions of this section, and every parent or guardian who allows any child to be so employed shall be punished by a fine of not less than one nor more than fifty dollars for each offense.

SEC. 54 (as amended by chapter 118, Acts of 1911). Age and school- **Who issue cer-** ing certificates shall be issued by the superintendent of schools of the **tificates.** city or town in which the child resides, or some person designated or authorized in writing by the school committee, and such age and schooling certificate when duly issued shall excuse such child from attendance at public school; but no person shall issue such certificate to any minor then in or about to enter his employment or the employment of a firm or corporation of which he is a member, stockholder, officer or employee. The person who issues the certificate in accordance with the provisions of this section is hereby empowered to administer the oath provided for therein, but no fee shall be charged therfor [therefor].

SEC. 55 (as amended by chapter 257, Acts of 1909). An age and **Evidence.** schooling certificate shall not be issued until the child applying therefor, or some person in his behalf, shall furnish satisfactory evidence of the age of the child, which evidence shall be a certified copy of the town clerk's record of the birth of said child, or a certified copy of his baptismal record, showing the date of his birth, or a passport showing the date of his birth, or other document satisfactory to the superintendent of schools or the person authorized to issue such age and schooling certificates; nor until such child has demonstrated his ability to read at sight and write simple sentences in the English language, and **Educational** perform simple arithmetical problems involving the fundamental **tests.** processes of addition, substraction, multiplication and division, such educational test to be prepared and furnished by the superintendent of schools or the school committee of each city and town in the State; or has furnished a certificate to that effect signed by any teacher in any of the public schools of the city or town in which such child resides, or by the principal of any approved private school, or a certificate signed by the principal of any evening school in said city or town, to the effect that said child is a regular attendant of said evening school.

SEC. 56 (as amended by chapter 257, Acts of 1909). The form of the **Form of cer-** age and schooling certificate provided for in section fifty-three of this **tificate.** act shall be prepared and furnished to the superintendent of schools or the school committee of the cities and towns by the attorney general, and shall be substantially as follows:

AGE AND SCHOOLING CERTIFICATE, REVISED STATUTES, C. 40, SEC. 53.

This certifies that I am the, [father, mother, guardian or custodian,] of, [name of child], and that he was born at, [name of city or town], in the state, or county, of   on the   day of   in the year and that at, his or her, last birthday he was   years old.
(City or town and date.)
                                   (Signature of parent, guardian or custodian.)

Then personally appeared before me the above named, [name of person signing], and having produced for my inspection the [record passport] of said child, made oath that the foregoing certificate by [him or her], signed is true to the best of [his or her], knowledge and belief. Having no sufficient reason to doubt that he is of the age therein certified, I hereby approve the foregoing certificate of [name of child]; whose signature, written in my presence, appears below; whose height is feet and inches; complexion is [fair or dark]; hair is [color]. I hereby certify that he has satisfactorily demonstrated, [his or her], ability to read at sight and to write legible simple sentences in the English language, and to employ the fundamental principles of arithmetic, according to the test supplied by the local superintendent of public schools; that he has presented us a certificate to that effect signed by the principal a teacher of some public school in said town, or that he has presented a certificate signed by the principal of an evening school in said town to the effect that he, said child is a regular attendant in said evening school.

This certificate belongs to, [name of child], and is to be surrendered to, [him or her], whenever he leaves the service of the employer holding the same, but if not claimed by said minor within thirty days from the time when he leaves such employment, it shall be returned to the superintendent of schools, or to the person by whom it is issued.
Signature of child.

                                   (Signature of person authorized to issue
                                    and approve, with official character or
                                    authority.)
City or town and date.)

Violations. Whoever, being authorized to sign the foregoing age and schooling certificate, or whoever signing any certified copy of a town clerk's record of births, or certified copy of a child's baptismal record, shall knowingly certify to any false statement therein, and any parent or guardian who presents, or who permits or allows any child under his control to present, to any employer, owner, superintendent, overseer or agent as required under section fifty-three, any certified copy of birth or baptismal record, or passport, or age and schooling certificate containing any false statements as to the date of birth or age of such child, knowing them to be false, shall be punished by a fine of not less than twenty-five dollars nor more than fifty dollars for each offense.

Exemptions. SEC. 57 (as amended by chapter 257, Acts of 1909). Nothing in the nine preceding sections shall apply to any manufacturing establishment or business, the materials and products of which are perishable and require immediate labor thereon, to prevent decay thereof or **Proviso.** damage thereto: *Provided, however,* The employment of children therein shall be under the supervision of said inspector who shall on complaint investigate the sanitary conditions, hours of labor and other conditions detrimental to children, and if in his judgment he finds detrimental conditions to exist, he may in conjunction with the municipal officers of the town or city in which the complaint is made, prohibit the employment of children therein until such conditions are removed.

ACTS OF 1905.

CHAPTER 123.—*Employment of children—Certain employments forbidden.*

Mendicant, immoral, etc., occupations. SECTION 9. No person shall employ or cause to be employed, exhibit, use or have in custody, or train for use, employment or exhibition, any child under sixteen years of age, and no parent, guardian or other person, having care, custody and control of such child, shall procure or permit the training, use, employment or exhibition of any such child, in begging or soliciting or receiving alms in any manner or under any pretence, or in any illegal, indecent or immoral exhibition or practice, or in any exhibition of any such child when insane or idiotic, or when possessing any deformity and unnatural physical formation, or in any practice, exhibition or place dangerous or injurious to the life, limb, health or morals of such child. Whoever offends against the provisions of this section shall be punished by a fine not exceeding one hundred dollars or by imprisonment not exceeding sixty days.

ACTS OF 1907.

CHAPTER 4.—*Employment of children on elevators.*

SECTION 1. No person, firm or corporation shall employ or permit any person under fifteen years of age to have the care, custody, management or operation of any elevator, or shall employ a person under eighteen years of age to have the care, custody, management or operation of any elevator running at a speed of over two hundred feet a minute. *Age limit.*

SEC. 2. Whoever violates the provisions of this act shall be punished by a fine not exceeding one hundred dollars and not less than twenty-five dollars for each offense. *Violations.*

ACTS OF 1911.

CHAPTER 26.—*Seats for female employees in stores, etc.*

SECTION 1. The proprietor, manager or person having charge of any merchantile establishment, store, shop, hotel, restaurant or other place where women or girls are employed as clerks or help therein in this State shall provide chairs, stools or other contrivances for the comfortable use of such female employees for the preservation of their health and for rest when not actively employed in the discharge of their respective duties. *Seats to be provided.*

SEC. 2. Any proprietor, manager or other person violating the preceding section of this act shall be deemed guilty of a misdemeanor, and upon conviction shall be fined in a sum not less than ten dollars nor more than one hundred dollars. *Violations.*

CHAPTER 143.—*Employment of women and children.*

SECTION 1. Chapter forty of the Revised Statutes, as amended by chapter forty-six of the Public Laws of Nineteen Hundred and Seven, and chapters seventy and two hundred and fifty-seven of the Public Laws of Nineteen Hundred and Nine, relating to the employment of women and children is hereby amended by striking out the words, "inspector of factories, workshops, mines and quarries," where these words occur, and substituting therefor the words "commissioner of labor." *Commissioner of labor is chief inspector.*

MARYLAND.

PUBLIC GENERAL LAWS—CODE OF 1903.

ARTICLE 27.—*Employment of children—Hours of labor.*

SECTION 217. No child under sixteen years of age shall be employed in laboring more than ten hours a day in any manufacturing business or factory established in any part of the State, or in any mercantile business in the city of Baltimore. *Limit of day's labor.*

SEC. 218 (as amended by chapter 607, Acts of 1910). Any persons who shall so employ a child or suffer or permit such employment shall be guilty of misdemeanor and upon conviction shall be fined not less than one hundred dollars; one-half of which shall be paid to the Maryland State bureau of statistics and information, which is hereby invested with the general duty and power of enforcing this law. *Violations.*

SEC. 219. The word "suffer or permit," includes every act or omission whereby it becomes possible for the child to engage in such labor. *Definition.*

ARTICLE 27.—*Seats for female employees.*

Seats to be pro-
vided.

SECTION 230 (as amended by chapter 287, Acts of 1904). All proprietors or owners of any retaily jobbing or wholesale dry goods store,
notion, millinery or any other business where any female sales people
or other female help are employed for the purpose of serving the public,
shall provide a chair or stool for each one of such female help, in order
that when they are not actively engaged in making sales or taking
stock or in perfoming such other duties as they may have been engaged
to perform, they shall have an opportunity to rest, and they shall not
be forbidden to avail themselves of such opportunity. Any such
owner or proprietor who shall neglect or refuse to obey the provisions
of this section shall be considered to have committed a misdemeanor,
and shall, upon conviction thereof, be fined in an amount not less than
ten dollars nor more than one hundred dollars for the first offense; and
in the event that such proprietor or owner shall continue to disobey
the provisions of this section, he shall be subject to a fine at the rate of
one dollar a day, daily, for every chair or stool he fails to so furnish his
said employees. It shall be the duty of the board or department of
health or health commissioner or commissioners of the cities and towns
in the State to cause this section to be enforced, and whenever any of
its provisions are violated, to cause all violators thereof to be prosecuted,
and for that purpose the health commissioner or commissioners and the
officer or officers of the board of health of every city and town in the
State, or the inspectors thereof, or any other persons designated by such
board of health or health commissioner or commissioners are authorized
and empowered to visit and inspect at all reasonable hours and as often
as shall be practicable and necessary all mercantile establishments in
the city or town in which the office of the said board or department of
health or health commissioner or commissioners is situated, and it shall
be unlawful for any person to interfere with or obstruct any such inspecting official while in performance of his or her duties or to refuse to properly and truthfully answer questions made pertinent by this section
when asked by such inspecting official.

ARTICLE 27.—*Employment of children—Certain employments forbidden.*

Acrobatic and
mendicant occu-
pations.

SECTION 309. Any person having in his custody or control a child
under the age of fourteen years who shall in any way dispose of it with
a view to its being employed as an acrobat, or a gymnast, or a contortionist, or a circus rider, or a ropewalker, or in any exhibition of like
dangerous character, or as a beggar or mendicant, or street singer, or
street musician, and any person who shall take, receive, hire, employ,
use, exhibit or have in custody any child under the age last named for
any of the purposes herein enumerated shall be deemed guilty of a
misdemeanor and when convicted thereof shall be subject to punishment by fine of not more than one hundred dollars, or by imprisonment
for a term not exceeding ninety days in jail, or both.

Employment
in saloons, etc.

SEC. 311. No person shall employ a minor under sixteen years of
age in handling intoxicating liquors, or in handling packages containing intoxicating liquors, in any brewery or bottling establishment where
intoxicating liquors are prepared for sale or offered for sale.

Penalty.

SEC. 312. Whoever violates the provisions of section 311, shall be
guilty of a misdemeanor, and on conviction thereof shall in the discretion of the court be fined a sum not less than ten dollars nor more
than one hundred dollars, or be imprisoned in jail for not less than five
nor more than thirty days, in default of payment of said fine.

Peddling, etc.

SEC. 313. No person engaged in performing upon any musical instrument in, upon or near to any street, lane, alley or highway, or engaged
in selling, vending or disposing of any goods, wares or merchandise in,
upon or near to any street, lane, alley or highway, or engaged in any
business, occupation or calling in, upon or near to any street, lane,
alley or highway, and not having a fixed store, shop or place of business
at which so engaged, shall have in his possession or company while so
engaged, any boy or girl under the age of eight years; and any person
violating the provisions of this section shall be punished by a fine not
exceeding ten dollars for each and every such offense.

ARTICLE 27.—*Employment of women as waiters, etc.*

SECTION 371. It shall not be lawful for any proprietor, lessee or manager of any theater, museum or other place of amusement to employ women or girls as waiters, or to permit them to act in such theater or place of amusement, or among the audience or frequenters of such theater or place of amusement as waiters, or for the purpose or under the pretense of selling, serving, receiving orders or pay for spirituous or malt liquors, wines, lager beer or any other refreshments or merchandise. *Employment in theaters, etc., forbidden.*

ARTICLE 56.—*Employment of minors in barrooms, etc.*

SECTION 97. It shall not be lawful for any person, or for any club or association, or for any corporation now formed or hereafter to be formed, or for any officer, agent or employee of any such club, association or corporation, to hire or employ any minor to sell or dispense anywhere in the State any beer or spirituous or fermented liquors of any kind at retail, where such beer or liquors are to be drunk upon the premises. Any person violating any provision of this section shall upon conviction be fined a sum not exceeding one hundred dollars. *Minors not to be employed.*

ARTICLE 77.—*Employment of children.*

SECTION 160. No proprietor or owner of any mill or factory in Allegany County or the city of Baltimore, other than establishments for manufacturing canned goods, or manager, agent, foreman or other person in charge thereof, shall employ or retain in employment in any such mill or factory any person or persons under sixteen years of age, unless he procures at the time of such employment or retention in employment, and keeps on file and accessible to the attendance officers of said city or county where such minor is employed, a certificate of the principal or head teacher of the school which such child last attended, stating that such child is more than twelve years of age, and a like certificate of the parent or guardian, or other person having control of such child; but the first-named certificate need not be procured if such child has not attended school in this State. He shall require such certificates, shall keep them in his place of business during the time the child is in his employment, and shall show the same during his business hours to any attendance officer who may demand to see them, or either of them; and for each failure to comply with any of the provisions of this section he shall be guilty of a misdemeanor, and shall be fined not exceeding one hundred dollars. Whoever continues to employ any such child under sixteen years of age, in violation of this section, after being notified of such violation by an attendance officer, shall for every day thereafter that such unlawful employment continues be fined not less than five nor more than twenty dollars, in addition to other penalties prescribed by this section for such offenses. A failure to produce on demand to an attendance officer any certificate required by this section shall be prima facie evidence that the child, who is or should have been mentioned in the said certificate, is thus unlawfully employed. *Certificates of age.*

SEC. 161. It shall be the duty of every parent, guardian or other person having control of a child under sixteen years of age, and of every principal or head teacher of said school where such child last attended, to furnish every employer of such child the certificates required by the preceding section. Such certificates, if in substantial conformity with the requirements of that section, shall be prima facie evidence of the facts required to be certified to as therein provided. *Duty of parents, etc.*

SEC. 162. Any parent or guardian or other person having control of a child, or principal or head teacher who shall make any willfully false statement respecting any of the facts required to be certified to as provided in sections 160 and 161 of this subtitle shall be deemed guilty of a misdemeanor, and shall be fined not more than fifty dollars, or to [sic] be imprisoned not more than thirty days, or suffer both fine and imprisonment in the discretion of the court. *False statements.*

SEC. 163. No person shall employ any minor over twelve and less than sixteen years of age, and no parent, guardian or other person *Illiterates.*

having control of a child, shall permit to be employed or retained in employment any such minor under his control, if the said minor can not read at sight and write legibly simple sentences in the English language while a public evening school is maintained in the city or election district or precinct in which such minor resides, unless such minor is a regular attendant at an evening or other school: *Provided,*

Evening schools. That upon presentation by such minor of a certificate signed by a regular practicing physician, and satisfactory to such officer or officers as the school commissioners for such county or city may designate, showing that the physical condition of such minor would render such attendance, in addition to daily labor, prejudicial to health, said officer or officers so designated may issue a permit authorizing the employment of such minor for such period and upon such conditions as said officer or officers so designated as aforesaid may determine. Any person who employs or retains in employment a minor in violation of the provisions of this section shall be deemed guilty of a misdemeanor and be fined for each offense not more than one hundred dollars, which fines shall be paid to the school commissioners for use in supporting evening schools in such city or county. Any parent, guardian or other person having control of a child, who permits to be employed any minor under his control in violation of the provisions of this section, shall be deemed guilty of a misdemeanor and be fined not more than twenty dollars, which fines shall be also paid to the school commissioners for use in supporting evening schools in such city and county.

Attendance officers. SEC. 164. In said city or county where attendance officers may have been appointed. it shall be the duty of the school commissioners to designate an attendance officer, who shall once or more frequently in every year examine into the situation of the children employed in such mills and factories in said city or county, and to ascertain whether all the provisions of this subtitle are duly observed and report all violations thereof to the grand jury of the said city or county.

Powers. SEC. 165. Attendance officers may visit all establishments where minors are employed in said city or county and ascertain whether any minors are employed therein contrary to the provisions of this subtitle. Attendance officers may require that the certificates provided for in this subtitle of minors employed in such establishments shall be produced for their inspection.

Violation. SEC. 166. Any person violating any provision of sections 152–165, where no special provision as to the penalty for such violation is made shall be deemed guilty of a misdemeanor, and be fined not exceeding fifty dollars for each offense. Sections 162–166 are restricted to Baltimore city and Allegany County.

ARTICLE 100.—*Hours of labor—Cotton or woolen manufactures.*

Ten hours a day's work. SECTION 1. No corporation or manufacturing company engaged in manufacturing either cotton or woolen yarns, fabrics or domestics of any kind, incorporated under the laws of this State, and no officer, agent or servant of such named corporation or manufacturing company, and no person or firm owning or operating such corporation or manufacturing company within the limits of this State, and no agent or servant of such firm or person shall require, permit or suffer its, his or their employees in its, his or their service, or under his, its or their control, to work for more than ten hours during each or any day of twenty-four hours for one full day's work and shall make no contract or agreement with such enployees or any of them: *Provided,* That they or he shall [sic] work for more than ten hours for one day's work during each or any day of twenty-four hours and said ten hours shall constitute one full day's work.

Male adult employees SEC. 2. Any such named corporation or manufacturing company within the limits of this State shall be allowed, under the provisions of this section, the privilege of working male employees, over the age of twenty-one years over the limit of ten hours for the express purpose only of making repairs and improvements and getting fires made, steam up and the machinery ready for use in their works, which can not be done during the limits of the ten hours; the extra compensation for all such work to be settled between such corporation and manufacturing companies and the employees: *Provided,* That nothing in this article shall be so construed as to prohibit any employer from making a contract with his male employees, over the age of twenty-one years, to work by the hour for such time as may be agreed upon.

SEC. 3. If any such corporation or manufacturing company within **Penalty.** the limits of this State, or any officer, agent or servant of such corporation or manufacturing company in this State shall do any act in violation of any of the provisions of this article he or they shall be deemed to have been guilty of misdemeanor and shall, on conviction thereof in a court of competent jurisdiction, be fined not less than one hundred dollars for each and every offense so committed, together with the cost of such prosecution, * * *

ARTICLE 100.—*Employment of children—Age limit.*

SECTION 4 (as amended by chapter 192, Acts of 1906). No proprietor, **Age limit.** owner, superintendent, manager, or foreman, or other subordinate or agent of any mill, factory, workshop, office, restaurant, hotel, apartment house, store, telephone or telegraph office, or other establishment or business shall, after the first day of September, in the year 1906, employ for wages or hire, or retain in employment in any such mill, factory, workshop, office, restaurant, hotel, apartment house, store, telephone or telegraph office, or other establishment or business, any person or persons under twelve (12) years of age, except in the counties, from **Exceptions.** June 1st to October 15th, in every year.

SEC. 5 (added by chapter 192, Acts of 1906). No child between the **Permits.** age of twelve (12) and sixteen (16) shall be employed, permitted or suffered to work in any offices, establishment or business mentioned in the preceding section unless the person or corporation employing him or her produces and keeps on file and accessible to the inspectors authorized by this act and the attendance officer of the public schools an employment permit, and keep a complete list of all such children employed thereon on file, and in the case of children employed in factories, workshops, mills or messenger service, a duplicate of said list shall be conspicuously posted near the principal entrance of the building in which such children are employed.

SEC. 6 (added by chapter 192, Acts of 1906). The employment per- **By whom is-** mit for all employments in Baltimore city under the provisions of this **sued.** act shall be issued by the Maryland bureau of statistics and information, and for employment in other cities or in the counties of this State, by any member of the board of health or principal health officer of the city or county in which the employment is sought.

SEC. 7 (added by chapter 192, Acts of 1906). The employment per- **Evidence.** mit shall not be issued unless satisfactory evidence is furnished by duly attested transcript of the certificate of birth or baptism of such child, or other religious records, or the register of birth, or the affidavit of the parent or guardian or custodian of the child, which latter affidavit shall be required, however, only in case it is certified by the proper authorities that the birth certificate showing the place and date of birth of such child is not on record, which affidavit must be taken before the officer issuing the employment permit, who is hereby authorized and required to administer such oath and who shall not demand or receive a fee therefor.

SEC. 8 (added by chapter 192, Acts of 1906). The employment permit shall read as follows:

EMPLOYMENT PERMIT. .

The birth certificate giving the name, date and place of [birth of] **Certificate.** ——— (name of child) is attached hereto. (If there be no birth certificate, then a certificate to that effect, *i. e.,* that there is none from the proper authorities of the city or county where said child was born, shall be attached.) This certifies that I am the ——— father, mother, guardian or custodian of ——— ——— (name of child) and that (he or she) was born at ——— (name of town or city) in the county of ——— (name of county) and State of ———, on the ——— day of ———, in year ———, and is now ——— ——— (number of years and months) old. Signature of (father, mother, guardian or ——— custodian.)
Signature of ——— child.
(Date.)

There personally appeared before me the above-named (name of father, mother, guardian or custodian of) and made oath that the aforegoing certificate by (him or her) signed, is true to the best of (his or her) knowledge and belief.

I hereby approve the foregoing certificate of (name of child), height (feet and inches), eyes (color), complexion (fair or dark), hair (color); having no sufficient reason to doubt that (he or she) is of the age therein certified I hereby certify that (he or she) can read at sight and write legibly simple sentences in the English language, and that (he or she) has reached the normal development of a child of (his or her) age, and is in sound health and is physically able to perform the work which (he or she) intends to do.

This certificate belongs to (name of child in whose behalf it is drawn) and is to be surrendered to (him or her) whenever (he or she) leaves the service of the corporation or employer holding the same; but if not claimed by said child within thirty days from such time it shall be returned to the Maryland bureau of statistics and information (if the employment be in Baltimore city) or the board of health or principal health officer of (if the employment be in any of the counties or other cities outside of Baltimore city.)

Signature of (person authorized to prove and sign with official character or authority.)

Date —— ——.

A duplicate of each employment permit shall be filled out and kept on file by the Maryland bureau of statistics and information or board of health or principal health officer of the county or city outside of Baltimore city, as the case may be.

Penalty.

SEC. 9 (added by chapter 192, Acts of 1906). Whoever employs a child in violation of the provisions of this act, and whoever having under his or her control a child, permits such child to be employed in violation of the provisions of this act, shall for such offense be fined not less than five (5) nor more than fifty ($50) dollars, and whoever continues to employ any child in violation of the provisions of this act, after being notified by an inspector authorized by this act or an attendance officer of the public schools, shall for every day thereafter that such employment continues be fined not less than five (5) nor more than twenty ($20) dollars. A failure to produce to an inspector authorized by this act or an attendance officer of the public schools any employment permit or list required by this act shall be prima facie evidence of illegal employment of any person whose employment permit is not produced, or whose name is not so listed. Any corporation or employer retaining any employment permit in violation of the provisions of this act shall be fined ten ($10) dollars. Every person authorized to sign the employment permit prescribed in this act who knowingly certifies to any materially false statement therein shall be fined not more than fifty ($50) dollars. The chief of the Maryland bureau of statistics and information or any member of the board of health or principal health officer of any county or city outside of Baltimore city is hereby authorized to sign the employment permit mentioned herein and to administer the necessary oath without cost to the applicant.

Enforcement.

SEC. 10 (added by chapter 192, Acts of 1906). The inspectors authorized by this act and the attendance officers of the public schools may visit any office, establishment or place of business contemplated by this act throughout the State of Maryland and city of Baltimore and ascertain whether any minors are employed therein contrary to the provisions of this act, and they shall report any cases of such illegal employment or other violations of this act to the justice of the peace having criminal jurisdiction in the locality where such illegal employment or other violations of this act occur, and which justices of the peace shall have full authority to try and determine all cases arising under this act. Inspectors authorized by this act, and the attendance officers of the public schools may require that the employment permits and lists provided for in this act of minors employed in any such office, establishment or business, shall be produced for their inspection. They shall also be authorized to require a birth certificate or other record evidence of the date of birth of any child, which they have reason to believe is being employed contrary to the provisions of this act, to be produced by either parents, guardian or custodian of said child, and in the absence of such record evidence of the date of birth of such child, they may require an affidavit from either parent, guardian or custodian of such child as to its age, name, place and date of birth.

SEC. 11 (added by chapter 192, Acts of 1906). The chief of the Maryland bureau of statistics and information is hereby authorized to appoint six inspectors to carry out the provisions of this act at a compensation not exceeding nine hundred ($900) dollars each per annum; they shall also be allowed their actual expenses when away from the city of Baltimore in the business of their office; they shall be attached to and be part of the Maryland bureau of statistics and information, and be subject to the order of the chief of said bureau, whose duty it shall be to see that the provisions of this act are enforced.   *Inspectors.*

SEC. 12 (added by chapter 192, Acts of 1906). This act shall not include farm labor.   *Exemption.*

PUBLIC LOCAL LAWS—CODE OF 1888.

ARTICLE 1 (Revision of 1902: chapter 124, Acts of 1902).—*Mine regulations, Allegany and Garrett Counties—Employment of women and children.*

SECTION 209n. * * *

SUBSEC. H. No person under the age of twelve years, or female of any age, shall be permitted to enter any mine to work therein; nor shall any boy under the age of fourteen years, unless he can read and write, be allowed to work in any mine. And the mine boss shall see that this requirement is fully met.   *Employment forbidden.*

ARTICLE 4.—*Seats for female employees—Baltimore.*

SECTION 505 (as amended by chapter 589, Acts of 1900). Every employer of females and mercantile or manufacturing establishment in the city of Baltimore must provide and maintain suitable seats for the use of such employees. A person is deemed not to maintain suitable seats for the use of female employees unless he permits the use thereof by such employees to such extent as may be reasonable for the preservation of health and proper rest, and the question of what is thus reasonable is one for determination by the jury or the court acting as a jury in any prosecution hereunder.   *Seats to be provided.*

SEC. 506 (Revision of 1898: Chapter 123, Acts of 1898). Any violation of the preceding section by any employer shall be deemed a misdemeanor, and shall be punishable by a fine of one hundred and fifty dollars, to be collected as other fines are collected.   *Penalty.*

ACTS OF 1910.

CHAPTER 587.—*Employment of children—Messenger service.*

(Page 66.)

SECTION 1. No telegraph, telephone or messenger company [shall] employ any person under fourteen years of age to call for or deliver any message.   *Age limit.*

SEC. 2. No telegraph, telephone or messenger company shall require or permit any person in its employ under sixteen years of age to call for or deliver any telegram or other message between the hours of eight o'clock p. m. and eight o'clock a. m.   *Night work.*

SEC. 3. No telegraph, telephone or messenger company shall require or permit any minor persons in its employ to call for or deliver any telegram or other message at or to any house of ill repute or questionable character wherein is conducted any business tending to demoralize by example or contact said minor.   *Sending to houses of ill fame, etc.*

SEC. 4. Any company or representative thereof who shall violate the provisions of this bill shall be subject to a fine of not less than one hundred dollars nor more than five hundred dollars, or sixty days in jail or both, at the discretion of the court, for each and every offense   *Violations.*

MASSACHUSETTS.

REVISED LAWS—1902.

CHAPTER 44.—*Employment of children unlawfully absent from school.*

School attendance.

SECTION 1 (as amended by chapter 320, Acts of 1905, and chapter 383, Acts of 1906). Every child between seven and fourteen years of age, and every child under sixteen years of age who can not read at sight and write legibly simple sentences in the English language, shall attend some public day school in the city or town in which he resides during the entire time the public day schools are in session, subject to such exceptions as to children, places of attendance and schools as are provided for in section three of chapter forty-two and sections three, five and six of this chapter [relating to towns having no high school, to attendance and place of residence, and to exclusion on account of contagious diseases]. The superintendent of schools or, if there is no superintendent of schools, the school committee, or teachers acting under authority of said superintendent or committee, may excuse cases of necessary absence. The attendance of a child upon a public day school shall not be required if he has attended for a like period of time a private day school approved by the school committee of such city or town in accordance with the provisions of the following section, or if he has been otherwise instructed for a like period of time in the branches of learning required by law to be taught in the public schools, or if he has already acquired such branches of learning, or if his physical or mental condition is such as to render such attendance inexpedient or impracticable. Every person having under his control a child as described in this section shall cause him to attend school as herein required; and if he fails for five day sessions or ten half-day sessions within any period of six months while under such control to cause such child, whose physical or mental condition is not such as to render his attendance at school harmful or impracticable, so to attend school, he shall, upon complaint by a truant officer and conviction thereof,

Proviso.

be punished by a fine of not more than twenty dollars: *Provided, however,* That no physical or mental condition which is capable of correction, or which renders the child a fit subject for special instruction at public charge in institutions other than the public day schools, shall avail as a defense under the provisions of this section unless it shall be made to appear that the defendant has employed all reasonable measures for the correction of the condition, or the suitable instruction of the child. Whoever induces or attempts to induce a child to absent himself unlawfully from school, or employs or harbors a child who, while school is in session, is absent unlawfully from school shall be punished by a fine of not more than fifty dollars.

CHAPTER 65.—*Employment of children in street trades.*

Who may make regulations.

SECTION 17 (as amended by chapter 419, Acts of 1910). The mayor and aldermen or selectmen may make regulations relative to the exercise of the trade of bootblacking by minors and to the sale by minors of any goods, wares or merchandise, the sale of which is permitted by section 15, and may prohibit such sale or such trade, or may require a minor to obtain from them a license therefor to be issued on terms and conditions prescribed in such regulations: *Provided,* That in the case of persons under the age of fourteen years in the cities of the Commonwealth the foregoing powers shall be vested in and exercised by the

Violations by minors.

school committees of said cities. A minor who sells such articles or exercises such trade without a license if one is required or who violates

By parents, employers, merchants, etc.

the conditions of his license or any of the provisions of said regulations shall be punished by a fine of not more than ten dollars for each offense. Any person who, having a minor under his control, knowingly permits him to violate the provisions of this act, and any person who procures or employs a minor to violate the provisions of this act, and any person who either for himself or as agent of any other person or of any corporation knowingly furnishes or sells to any minor any of the articles above referred to with knowledge that said minor intends to sell said articles in violation of the provisions of this act, and after having received written notice from the school committee that the minor is unlicensed, shall be punished by a fine of not more than two hundred dollars or by imprisonment for not more than six months. Truant and police officers shall enforce the provisions of this chapter.

SEC. 18. A parent or other person who employs a minor under the age of fifteen years in peddling without a license if one is required or who, having the care or custody of such minor, permits him to engage in such employment shall be punished by a fine of not more than two hundred dollars or by imprisonment for not more than six months. *Penalty.*

ACTS OF 1906.

CHAPTER 463.—PART III.—*Street railways—Allowing newsboys on cars.*

SECTION 89. If a street railway company, its agent or servant, allows a child under the age of ten years to enter upon or into any of its cars for the purpose of selling newspapers or other articles therein or offering them for sale, it shall forfeit fifty dollars for each offense, which shall be recovered by any person by an action brought within three months after the offense has been committed. *Newsboys under 10.*

CHAPTER 502.—*Employment of children—Medical inspection.*

SECTION 1 (as amended by chapter 257, Acts of 1910). The school committee of every city and town in the Commonwealth shall appoint one or more school physicians, shall assign one to each public school within its city or town, and shall provide them with all proper facilities for the performance of their duties as prescribed in this act; and shall assign one or more to perform the duty of examining children who apply for health certificates in accordance with this act: *Provided, however,* That in cities wherein the board of health is already maintaining or shall hereafter maintain substantially such medical inspection as this act requires, the board of health shall appoint and assign the school physician. *Duties of school committee.*

SEC. 2 (as amended by chapter 257, Acts of 1910). Every school physician shall make a prompt examination and diagnosis of all children referred to him as hereinafter provided, and such further examination of teachers, janitors and school buildings as in his opinion the protection of the health of the pupils may require. Every school physician who is assigned to perform the duty of examining children who apply for health certificates shall make a prompt examination of every child who wishes to obtain an age and schooling certificate, as provided in section sixty of chapter five hundred and fourteen of the acts of the year nineteen hundred and nine, and who presents to said physician an employment ticket, as provided in said section, and the physician shall certify in writing whether or not in his opinion such child is in sufficiently sound health and physically able to perform the work which the child intends to do. *Duties of school physician.*

ACTS OF 1909.

CHAPTER 514.—*Labor law—Employment of women and children.*

SECTION 17 (as amended by chapter 241, Acts of 1911). * * * "Child" or "minor" shall mean a person under eighteen years of age, except that in regard to the compulsory attendance of illiterate minors at evening schools, the word "minor" shall mean a person under the age of twenty-one years. *Definitions.*

* * * * * * *

"Woman" shall mean a woman eighteen years of age or more.

* * * * * * *

"Young person" shall mean a person of the age of fourteen years and under the age of eighteen years.

SEC. 47. No child and no woman shall be employed in laboring in a mercantile establishment more than fifty-eight hours in a week. Every employer of such persons shall post in a conspicuous place in every room in which they are employed a printed notice stating the *Hours of labor in mercantile establishments.*

number of hours of work which are required of them on each day of
the week, the hours of commencing and stopping such work, and the
time allowed for dinner or other meals. The printed form of such
notice shall be furnished by the chief of the district police and shall
be approved by the attorney general. The employment of any such
person at any time other than as stated in said printed notice shall be
deemed a violation of the provisions of this section. An employer,
superintendent, overseer or other agent of a mercantile establishment
who violates any of the provisions of this section shall be punished by
a fine of not less than fifty nor more than one hundred dollars.

Ten-hour day.   SEC. 48 (as amended by chapter 484, Acts of 1911). No child under
eighteen years of age and no woman shall be employed in laboring in a
manufacturing or mechanical establishment more than ten hours in
any one day, except as hereinafter provided in this section, unless a
different apportionment of the hours of labor is made for the sole purpose
of making a shorter day's work for one day of the week; and in no case
shall the hours of labor exceed fifty-four in a week, except that in
any such establishment where the employment is by seasons, the
number of such hours in any week may exceed fifty-four, but not
Weekly limit. fifty eight. *Provided*, That the total number of such hours in any
year shall not exceed an average of fifty-four hours a week for the
Schedule to be whole year, excluding Sundays and holidays. Every employer shall
posted. post in a conspicuous place in every room in which such persons are
employed a printed notice stating the number of hours' work required
of them on each day of the week, the hours of commencing and stopping
work, and the hours when the time allowed for meals begins and ends
or, in the case of establishments exempted from the provisions of sections thirty-six and thirty-seven, the time, if any, allowed for meals.
The printed forms of such notices shall be provided by the chief of the
district police, after the approval by the attorney general. The employment of such person at any time other than as stated in said printed
notice shall be deemed a violation of the provisions of this section
unless it appears that such employment was to make up time lost on
Stoppage of ma- a previous day of the same week in consequence of the stopping of
chinery. machinery upon which he was employed or dependent for employment; but no stopping of machinery for less than thirty consecutive
minutes shall justify such overtime employment, nor shall such overtime employment be authorized until a written report of the day and
hour of its occurrence and its duration is sent to the chief of the district
police or to an inspector of factories and public buildings.

Violations by SEC. 49. A parent or guardian who permits a minor under his control
parents. to be employed in violation of either of the two preceding sections,
and any person who, either for himself or as superintendent, overseer
or agent for another, employs any person in violation of the provisions
of either of said sections, or fails to post the notice required by either
of the preceding sections, or makes a false report of the stopping of
machinery under the provisions of the preceding section, shall be
punished by a fine of not less than fifty nor more than one hundred
dollars. A certificate of the age of a minor made and sworn to by him
and by his parent or guardian at the time of his employment in a mercantile, manufacturing or mechanical establishment shall be prima facie
evidence of his age in any prosecution under the provisions of this
section.

Night work. SEC. 51. No person, and no agent or officer of a person or corporation,
shall employ a woman or minor in any capacity for the purpose of manufacturing between ten o'clock at night and six o'clock in the morning.
No person, and no agent or officer of a person or corporation engaged in
the manufacture of textile goods, shall employ a woman or a minor
before six o'clock in the morning or after six o'clock in the evening.
Whoever violates the provisions of this section shall be punished by a
fine of not less than twenty nor more than fifty dollars for each offense.

Age limit of SEC. 56. No child under the age of fourteen years, and no child
children. who is over fourteen and under sixteen years of age who does not have
a certificate as required by the four following sections certifying to
the child's ability to read at sight and to write legibly simple sentences
in the English language shall be employed in any factory, workshop
or mercantile establishment. The ability to read at sight and to write

legibly simple sentences in the English language shall be construed as meaning such ability to read and write as is required for admission to the fourth grade of the public schools of the city or town in which such minor lives. No child under the age of fourteen years shall be employed at work performed for wages or other compensation, to whomsoever payable, during the hours when the public schools of the city or town in which he resides are in session, or be employed at work before six o'clock in the morning or after seven o'clock in the evening. But minors to whom the provisions of this section apply shall be permitted to work on Saturdays between the hours of six in the morning and seven in the evening in mercantile establishments. *Employment during school time.*

Night work.

SEC. 57. No child under sixteen years of age shall be employed in a factory, workshop or mercantile establishment unless his employer procures and keeps on file, accessible to the truant officers of the city or town, and to the district police and inspectors of factories and public buildings, an age and schooling certificate and keeps two complete lists of all such minors employed therein, one on file, and one conspicuously posted near the principal entrance of the building in which such children are employed, and also keeps on file and sends to the superintendent of schools, or, if there is no superintendent, to the school committee, a complete list of the names of all minors employed therein who cannot read at sight and write legibly simple sentences in the English language. *Certificates required.*

SEC. 58 (as amended by chapter 269, Acts of 1911). An age and schooling certificate shall be approved only by the superintendent of schools or by a person authorized by him in writing, or, if there is no superintendent of schools, by a person authorized by the school committee; but no member of a school committee or other person authorized as aforesaid shall approve such certificate for any minor then in or about to enter his own employment or the employment of a firm or corporation of which he is a member, officer or employee. The printed form of such age and schooling certificate shall be provided by the chief of the district police. No such certificate shall be approved by any person unless he is satisfied that the minor therein named is able to read at sight and to write legibly simple sentences in the English language, as is required for admission to the fourth grade of the public schools of the city or town in which such minor lives, not until such person has received a certificate signed by a physician, as provided in chapter five hundred and two of the acts of the year nineteen hundred and six and acts passed in amendment thereof, or by a physician appointed by the school committee, stating that said minor has been examined by him and in his opinion is in sufficiently sound health and physically able to perform the work which the minor intends to do: *Provided, however,* That the age and schooling certificate may be approved and issued without a physician's certificate if there shall be on file in connection with the public schools a written record in regard to the child's physical condition made within one year and the person authorized to approve said age and schooling certificate after having examined such record shall certify that in his opinion said minor is in sufficiently sound health and physically able to perform the work which the minor intends to do. The person who approves the certificate may administer the oath provided for therein, but no fee shall be charged therefor. *Who may issue.*

Physician's certificate.

SEC. 59. An age or schooling certificate shall not be approved unless satisfactory evidence is furnished by a certificate of birth or baptism of such minor, or by the register of birth of such minor with a city or town clerk, that such minor is of the age stated in the certificate, except that other evidence, under oath, may be accepted in the case the superintendent or person authorized by the school committee, as provided in the preceding section, decides that neither the certificate of birth or baptism, nor the register of birth is available for the purpose. The certificate of the superintendent of the Lyman School for boys or of the State industrial school for girls given to a child who has been an inmate of such school, shall be sufficient evidence as to the age and ability to read at sight and to write legibly simple sentences in the English language. *Evidence.*

SEC. 60 (as amended by chapter 257, Acts of 1910). The age and schooling certificate of a minor under sixteen years of age shall not be *Employment ticket.*

approved and signed until he presents to the person who is authorized to approve and sign it an employment ticket duly filled out and signed. A duplicate of each age and schooling certificate shall be filled out and shall be kept on file by the school committee. Any explanatory matter may, in the discretion of the school committee or superintendent of schools, be printed with such certificate. The employment ticket and the age and schooling certificate shall be separately printed and shall be filled out, signed and held or surrendered as indicated in the following forms:—

AGE AND SCHOOLING CERTIFICATE, ST. 1909, CH. [514], SEC. [60].

This certifies that I am the [father, mother, guardian or custodian] of [name of minor], and that [he or she] was born at [name of city or town], in the county of [name of county, if known], and state [or country] of ———, on the [day and year of birth], and is now [number of years and months] old.

[Signature of father, mother, guardian, or custodian.]
[City or town and date.]

Then personally appeared before me the above named [name of person signing], and made oath that the foregoing certificate by [him or her] signed is true to the best of [his or her] knowledge and belief. I hereby approve the foregoing certificate of [name of minor], height [feet and inches], complexion [fair or dark], hair [color], having no sufficient reason to doubt that [he or she] is of the age therein certified. I hereby certify and am satisfied that [he or she] can read at sight and can write legibly simple sentences in the English language. I further certify that in my opinion [or in the opinion of ——- ———, the physician by whom said minor has been examined in accordance with section fifty-eight of the above chapter] he [or she] is in sufficiently sound health and physically able to perform the work which he [or she] intends to do.

This certificate belongs to [name of minor in whose behalf it is drawn], and is to be surrendered to [him or her] whenever [he or she] leaves the service of the corporation or employer holding the same; but if not claimed by said minor within thirty days after such time, it shall be returned to the superintendent of schools, or, if there is no superintendent of schools, to the school committee.

[Signature of person authorized to approve and sign, with official character or authority.]
[City or town and date.]

In the case of a minor who cannot read at sight and write legibly simple sentences in the English language, the certificate shall continue as follows, after the word "language":

I hereby certify that [he or she] is regularly attending the [name] ——— ——— public evening school. This certificate shall continue in force only so long as the regular attendance of said minor at the evening school is endorsed weekly by a teacher thereof.

Whoever, being authorized to sign the foregoing certificate, knowingly certifies to any materially false statement therein shall be punished by a fine of not more than fifty dollars.

SEC. 61 (as amended by chapter 249, Acts of 1910). Whoever employs a minor under the age of sixteen years, and whoever procures or, having under his control a minor under such age, permits, such minor to be employed in violation of the provisions of sections fifty-six and fifty-seven of this act, shall for each offense be punished by a fine of not more than three hundred dollars, or by imprisonment for not more than six months, or by both such fine and imprisonment; and whoever continues to employ a minor in violation of the provisions of either of said sections, after being notified thereof by a truant officer or by an inspector of factories and public buildings, shall for every day thereafter while such employment continues be punished by a fine of not less than twenty nor more than one hundred dollars, or by imprisonment for not more than six months; and whoever forges, or procures to be forged, or assists in forging a certificate of birth of such minor, and whoever presents or assists in presenting a forged certificate of birth, to a school committee or to the person authorized by law to receive certificates, for the purpose of fraudulently obtaining the school certificate mentioned in section sixty, shall be punished by a fine of not less than one hundred nor more than five hundred dollars, or by imprisonment for not less than three months nor more than one year, or by both such fine and imprisonment.

Sec. 62. Truant officers may visit the factories, workshops and mercantile establishments in their several cities and towns and ascertain whether any minors are employed therein contrary to the provisions of this act and shall report any cases of such illegal employment to the school committee and to the chief of the district police or to the inspector of factories and public buildings. Inspectors of factories and public buildings shall visit all factories, workshops and mercantile establishments within their respective districts, and ascertain whether any minors are employed therein contrary to the provisions of this act, and shall enter complaint against whoever is found to have violated any of said provisions. An inspector of factories and public buildings who knowingly and willfully violates any provision of this section may be punished by a fine of not more than one hundred dollars. *Enforcement.*

Sec. 63. A truant officer may apprehend and take to school, without a warrant, any minor under the age of sixteen years who is employed in any factory, workshop or mercantile establishment in violation of the provisions of sections fifty-six or fifty-seven of this act, and such truant officer shall forthwith report to the police, district or municipal court or trial justice within whose judicial district the illegal employment occurs, the evidence in his possession relating to the illegal employment of any child so apprehended, and shall make complaint against whomever the court or trial justice may direct. A truant officer who knowingly and willfully violates any provision of this section may be punished by a fine of not more than one hundred dollars for each offense. *Same subject.*

Sec. 64. Inspectors of factories and public buildings, and truant officers may require that the age and schooling certificates and lists of minors who are employed in factories, workshops or mercantile establishments shall be produced for their inspection. A failure to produce to an inspector of factories and public buildings or to a truant officer an age and schooling certificate or list required by law shall be prima facie evidence of the illegal employment of any person whose age and schooling certificate is not produced or whose name is not listed. A corporation or other employer or any agent or officer thereof, who retains an age and schooling certificate in violation of the provisions of said certificate shall be punished by a fine of not less than ten nor more than one hundred dollars. *Lists may be inspected.*

Sec. 65. Police, district and municipal courts and trial justices shall have jurisdiction of offenses arising under the provisions of the four preceding sections. A summons or warrant issued by any such court or justice may be served, at the discretion of the court or magistrate, by an inspector of factories and public buildings, or by a truant officer, or by any officer qualified to serve criminal process. *Jurisdiction.*

Sec. 66. While a public evening school is maintained in the city or town in which any minor resides who is over fourteen years of age and who does not have a certificate signed by the superintendent of schools, or by the school committee, or by some person acting under authority thereof, certifying to his ability to read at sight and write legibly simple sentences in the English language, no person shall employ him, and no parent, guardian or custodian shall permit him to be employed unless he is a regular attendant at such evening school or at a day school; but, upon presentation by him of a certificate signed by a registered practising physician and satisfactory to the superintendent of schools, or, if there is no such superintendent, to the school committee, showing that his physical condition would render such attendance in addition to daily labor prejudicial to his health, said superintendent or school committee shall issue a permit authorizing his employment for such period as said superintendent or school committee may determine. Said superintendent or school committee, or teachers acting under authority thereof, may excuse any absence from such evening school which arises from justifiable cause. Any minor not holding such certificate shall furnish to his employer a record of his school attendance *Illiterates* *Evening schools.*

each week while the evening school is in session, and when said record shows unexcused absences from the sessions, his attendance shall be deemed irregular according to this act. Whoever employs a minor in violation of the provisions of this section shall forfeit not more than one hundred dollars for each offense to the use of the evening schools of such city or town. A parent, guardian or custodian who permits a minor under his control to be employed in violation of the provisions of this section shall forfeit not more than twenty dollars to the use of the evening schools of such city or town.

Time for meals.   SEC. 67. Women and young persons, five or more in number, who are employed in the same factory shall be allowed their meal times at the same hour, except that any such persons who begin work in such factory at a later hour in the morning than other such persons employed therein may be allowed their meal times at a different hour; but no such persons shall be employed during the regular meal hour in tending the machines or doing the work of any other women or young persons in addition to their own.

Continuous employment.   SEC. 68. No woman or young person shall be employed for more than six hours at any one time in a factory or workshop in which five or more such persons are employed without an interval of at least half an hour for a meal; but such person may be so employed for not more than six and one-half hours at one time if such employment ends not later than one o'clock in the afternoon and if he or she is then dismissed from the factory or workshop for the remainder of the day; or for not more than seven and one-half hours at one time if he or she is allowed sufficient opportunity for eating a lunch during the continuance of such employment and if such employment ends not later than two o'clock in the afternoon, and he or she is then dismissed from the factory or workshop for the remainder of the day.

Exemptions.   SEC. 69. The provisions of the two preceding sections shall not apply to iron works, glass works, paper mills, letter press establishments, print works, bleaching works or dyeing works; and the chief of the district police, if it is proved to his satisfaction that in any other class of factories or workshops it is necessary, by reason of the continuous nature of the processes or of special circumstances affecting such class, to exempt it from the provisions of the two preceding sections and that such exemption can be made without injury to the health of the women or young persons affected thereby, may, with the approval of the governor, issue a certificate granting such exemption, public notice whereof shall, without expense to the Commonwealth, be given in the manner directed by said chief.

Working without orders.   SEC. 70. If a minor or a woman shall, without the orders, consent or knowledge of the employer or of a superintendent, overseer or other agent of the employer, labor in a manufacturing or mechanical establishment, factory or workshop during a part of any time allowed for meals in such establishment, factory or workshop, according to the notice required by section forty-eight, and if a copy of such notice was posted in a conspicuous place in the room where such labor was performed with a rule of the establishment, factory or workshop forbidding such minor or woman to labor during such time, then neither the employer nor a superintendent, overseer or other agent of the employer shall be held responsible for such labor.

Penalty.   SEC. 71. Whoever either for himself or as superintendent, overseer or agent violates the provisions of the four preceding sections shall be punished by a fine of not less than fifty nor more than one hundred dollars.

Seats for females.   SEC. 72. A person who employs females in any manufacturing, mechanical or mercantile establishment shall provide suitable seats for their use and shall permit the use of such seats by them when they are not necessarily engaged in the active duties of their employment. Whoever violates the provisions of this section shall be punished by a fine of not less than ten nor more than thirty dollars for each offense.

Children cleaning moving machinery.   SEC. 73. Whoever, either for himself or as superintendent, overseer or agent permits a child under fourteen years of age to clean any part of the machinery in a factory, if it is in motion by the aid of steam, water or other mechanical power, or if it is in dangerous proximity to such moving part, shall be punished by a fine of not less than fifty nor more than one hundred dollars for each offense.

SEC. 74. No elevator for the carriage of freight or passengers shall be operated by or placed in charge of any person under sixteen years of age, and all elevators for the carriage of freight or passengers running at a speed of more than one hundred feet a minute shall be operated by competent persons not less than eighteen years of age and no other person shall operate or have the care or charge of such an elevator. Any person, firm or corporation violating any provision of this section by operating or causing an elevator to be operated or to be taken care or charge of or in any manner contrary to its provisions shall be punished by a fine of not less than twenty-five nor more than one hundred dollars for each offense. *Children operating elevators.*

SEC. 75 (as amended by chapter 404, Acts of 1910). The State board of health may from time to time upon the written application of any citizen of the Commonwealth, or upon its own initiative, after such investigation as it considers necessary determine whether or not any particular trade, process of manufacture or occupation, or any particular method of carrying on such trade, process of manufacture or occupation, is sufficiently injurious to the health of minors under eighteen years of age employed therein to justify their exclusion therefrom, and every decision so rendered shall be conclusive evidence of the facts involved therein, except so far as the same may later be revoked or modified by a subsequent decision of the board. Whoever, after being notified that the state board of health has determined that a particular trade, process of manufacture, occupation or method is injurious as above stated, employs therein a minor under eighteen years of age shall be punished by a fine of not more than two hundred dollars and not less than fifty dollars for each offense, unless prior to the time of such employment such determination shall have been revoked or modified so as not to include the employment complained of. *How trades etc., may be classified.*

SEC. 76. No person shall employ, exhibit or sell, apprentice or give away, a child under fifteen years of age for the purpose of employing or exhibiting him in dancing on the stage, playing on musical instruments, singing, walking on a wire or rope, or riding or performing as a gymnast, contortionist or acrobat in a circus, theatrical exhibition or in any public place, or cause, procure or encourage such child to engage therein; but the provisions of this section shall not prevent the education of children in vocal and instrumental music or dancing or their employment as musicians in a church, chapel, school or school exhibition, or prevent their taking part in any festival, concert or musical exhibition upon the special written permission of the mayor and aldermen of a city or the selectmen of a town. Whoever violates the provisions of this section shall be punished by a fine of not more than two hundred dollars or by imprisonment for not more than six months. *Exhibition, etc., of children.*

SEC. 77. A license shall not be granted for a theatrical exhibition or public show in which children under fifteen years of age are employed as acrobats or contortionists or in any feats of gymnastics or equestrianism, or in which such children who belong to the public schools are employed or allowed to take part as performers on the stage in any capacity, or if, in the opinion of the board authorized to grant licenses, such children are employed in such a manner as to corrupt their morals or impair their health; but the provisions of this section shall not prevent the granting of special permission authorized by the preceding section. *Licenses for shows, etc., to be refused, when.*

ACTS OF 1911.

CHAPTER 229.—*Employment of women before and after childbirth.*

SECTION 1. No woman shall knowingly be employed in laboring in a mercantile, manufacturing or mechanical establishment within two weeks before or four weeks after childbirth. *Employment forbidden, when.*

SEC. 2. The foregoing section shall be included in the notice with regard to the employment of women now required to be posted in mercantile, manufacturing and mechanical establishments, and the provisions thereof shall be enforced by the district police. *Law to be posted.*

SEC. 3. Violations of section one of this act shall be punished by a fine of not exceeding one hundred dollars. *Violations.*

CHAPTER 310.—*Employment of children—Illiterates.*

Age limit. SECTION 1. No illiterate minor between the age of sixteen and twenty-one years shall be employed in a factory, workshop, mechanical or mercantile establishment unless his employer procures and keeps on file, accessible to the truant officers of the city or town and to the district police and inspectors of factories and public buildings, a certificate showing that such minor is sixteen years of age or over. Said certificate shall give the place and date of birth of such minor and his personal description. The printed form of the certificate shall be provided by the chief of the district police and shall be approved by the attorney general.

CHAPTER 313.—*Employment of women and children—Garment workers in mercantile establishments.*

Scope of law extended. SECTION 1. The provisions of section forty-seven of chapter five hundred and fourteen of the Acts of the Year Nineteen Hundred and Nine, relative to the employment of children and women in mercantile establishments, shall also apply to children and women employed in a workshop for the making, altering or repairing of garments: *Provided,* That the workshop is connected with a mercantile establishment where the said garments are sold at retail, and is owned and operated by the proprietor of such mercantile establishment: **Hours of labor.** *And provided, also,* That such children and women shall not be employed more than fifty-six hours in any one week. The provisions of section forty-eight of the said chapter shall not apply to children and women employed as aforesaid.

CHAPTER 629.—*Employment of children—Night messenger service.*

Night work restricted. SECTION 1. Except for the delivery of messages, directly connected with the business of conducting or publishing a newspaper, to a newspaper office or directly between newspaper offices, no person under the age of twenty-one years shall be employed or permitted to work as a messenger for a telegraph, telephone or messenger company in the distribution, transmission or delivery of goods or messages before five o'clock in the morning or after ten o'clock in the evening of any day.

Violations. SEC. 2. Whoever, in violation of the provisions of section one of this act, employs a person under the age of twenty-one years or whoever procures or, having under his control any such person, permits him to be so employed shall for each offense be punished by a fine of not less than fifty nor more than three hundred dollars or by imprisonment for not more than six months, or by both such fine and imprisonment.

Enforcement. SEC. 3. The district police shall enforce the provisions of this act.

MICHIGAN.

CONSTITUTION OF 1909.

ARTICLE V.—*Employment of women and children.*

Power of legislature. SECTION 29. The legislature shall have power to enact laws relative to the hours and conditions under which women and children may be employed.

COMPILED LAWS—1897.

Judgments for wages of female employees—Exemptions—Attorney's fee.

Exemptions limited. SECTION 900. No property, except as exempted by the State constitution, shall be exempt from levy or sale, under an execution, issued upon a judgment obtained before any justice of the peace, for work, labor, or services done or performed by any woman, when such amount does not exceed the sum of twenty-five dollars, exclusive of costs. * * * In addition to all other costs allowed by law, the plaintiff **Attorney's fee.** in any such suit shall recover an attorney's fee of five dollars, * * *.

Employment of females in barrooms, etc.

SECTION 5362. No girl or woman shall be employed to tend bar, serve liquors, to dance or furnish music in any saloon or barroom where spirituous or intoxicating liquors, or malt, brewed or fermented liquors are sold or kept for sale. Employment forbidden.

SEC. 5363. No keeper or proprietor of a saloon where spirituous or intoxicating liquors or malt, brewed or fermented liquors are sold or kept for sale shall permit any girl or woman to tend bar, serve liquors, dance or furnish music for hire in his saloon or barroom: *Provided,* That this act shall not be so construed as to prevent the wife or other females who are bona fide members of the family of a proprietor of a saloon from tending bar or serving liquors in his saloon. Attending bar, etc.
Proviso.

SEC. 5364. Any person who shall violate any of the provisions of this act shall be deemed guilty of a misdemeanor, and upon conviction thereof shall be punished by a fine not to exceed fifty dollars and costs of prosecution, or by imprisonment in the county jail for a term not to exceed thirty days, or by both such fine and imprisonment, in the discretion of the court. Penalty.

ACTS OF 1903.

ACT No. 106.—*Employment of labor—Contracts involving removal from home locality.*

SECTION 1. Any person, company or corporation, or any agent or officer thereof who shall induce another person, by promise of wages or other valuable consideration, to agree to work for the person, company or corporation in whose behalf the offer of inducements is made, at a point away from his or her home locality, shall specify in writing the terms and conditions under which the said work is to be performed, the rate of wages and how, when and where said wages are agreed to be paid, and may furnish a copy of such statement of agreement to the person so induced by the promises therein to agree to work for the person, company or corporation offering said inducements: *Provided,* That it shall be unlawful for any person to make a tender of inducement to go away from the home locality to work, to any child under sixteen years of age unless the written consent of the parents of such child has been first obtained, as well as the consent of the truant officer or county agent of the board of corrections and charities for the locality where said child belongs; and in case such consent is obtained and the child goes abroad under the influence of the inducements so offered, such child under sixteen years of age shall be safely returned to its home at any time when its parents shall request, in writing, such return. Any person or any agent or officer of any corporation who shall, in offering inducements to any person to work for hire at any place apart from his or her home locality, misrepresent any of the conditions of such employment as mentioned above, shall be liable to pay to the person injured by such misrepresentation, the full amount of the damage sustained and shall be further liable to the penalties provided in section three of this act. Contracts to be in writing

Children.

SEC. 3. Every person found guilty of violating the provisions of this act shall be punished by a fine not exceeding twenty-five dollars or by imprisonment of not less than ten nor more than sixty days. Penalty.

ACTS OF 1909.

ACT No. 285.—*Labor law—Employment of women and children.*

SECTION 9 (as amended by act No. 220, Acts of 1911). No male under the age of eighteen years, and no female shall be employed in any factory, mill, warehouse, workshop, clothing, dressmaking or millinery establishment, or any place where the manufacture of any kinds of goods is carried on, or where any goods are prepared for manufacturing, or in any laundry, store, shop, or any other mercantile establishment for a period longer than an average of nine hours a day or fifty-four hours in any week, nor more than ten hours in any one day; and all such Ten-hour day.

Hours per week.

establishments shall keep posted a copy of this section printed in large type, in a conspicuous place; in establishments having a time clock

Act to be *posted.* such copy shall be posted near the time clock. Copies of this section suitable for posting shall be furnished upon the application of any employer by the commissioner of labor: *Provided, however,* That the provisions of this section in relation to the hours of employment shall

Exceptions. not apply to nor affect any person engaged in preserving perishable goods in fruit and vegetable canning establishments. No female under the age of eighteen years shall be employed in any manufacturing establishment between the hours of six o'clock p. m. and six o'clock

Night work. a. m. No child under the age of sixteen years shall be employed in any manufacturing establishment or workshop, mine or messenger service in this State between the hours of six o'clock p. m. and six o'clock a. m. No child under the age of eighteen years shall be employed between the hours of ten o'clock p. m. and five o'clock a. m. in the transmission, distribution or delivery of messages or merchandise.

Employments *forbidden.* SEC. 10 (as amended by act No. 220, Acts of 1911). No child under the age of twenty-one years shall be employed, permitted or suffered to work in any theater, concert hall, or place of amusement where intoxicating

Age limit. liquors are sold. No child under fourteen years of age shall be employed, permitted or suffered to work in or in connection with any mercantile institution, store, office, hotel, laundry, manufacturing establishment, mine, bowling alley, theater, passenger or freight elevator, factory or workshop, telegraph or messenger service within this State. It shall be the duty of every mercantile institution, store, office, hotel, laundry, manufacturing establishment, mine, bowling alley, theater,

Registers. workshop, telegraph or messenger service or any person coming within the provisions of this act to keep a register in which will be recorded the name, birthplace, age and place of residence of every person employed under the age of sixteen years, and it shall be unlawful for any such establishment or person to hire or employ, or permit to be hired or employed or suffered to work, any child under the age of sixteen years without there is first provided and placed on file in the business office

Permits for *children 14 years* *of age.* thereof a permit issued by the superintendent of schools of the school district in which such child resides, or someone duly authorized by him in writing, or, where there is no superintendent of schools, by the county commissioner of schools, or someone duly authorized by him in writing, any of whom shall have power to administer oaths in relation thereto or by the judge of probate of the county wherein such child resides. Such permit shall be returned to the child upon leaving such employ; every limited vacation permit, hereinafter to be described, shall, upon its expiration, be void and of no effect. The said register and permit shall be produced for inspection on demand of any factory inspector appointed under this act; no fee shall be charged for such

Permit as evi- *dence.* permit by any officer by whom it shall be issued. Every employer complying with the provisions of this section shall be at liberty to employ the person so presenting the permit hereinbefore referred to, and is justified in considering and treating such person as of the age shown in such permit and shall not be liable, if it transpires that such person is under the age represented in such permit, to any greater extent than such employer would be liable if such person were of the age represented. The person authorized and required to issue such permit shall not issue the same until he has received, examined, approved and filed the following papers, duly executed.

Proofs of age. (a) The school report of said child properly filled out and signed as hereinafter provided: *Provided, however,* That when such permit is issued during the summer vacation no such record shall be required, but all such permits, called in this act limited vacation permits, shall expire upon the first Monday in September, commonly called Labor Day, shall contain a conspicuous statement of the time at which they shall expire and shall be of a special color distinct from regular permits;

(b) A passport, or duly attested transcript of the record of birth, as kept by any duly authorized public authority, or a record of baptism or other religious record, showing the date and place of birth of such child;

(c) A statement from a physician connected officially with the board or department of health, which shall be required, however, only in case the above-mentioned official or religious record cannot be produced, which statement shall certify that, in the opinion of the physician issuing said statement, the child is fourteen years of age or upwards, is in sound health and physically able to perform the work which it intends to do. Such statement shall also certify to the correct weight and height of said child, and shall be kept on file by the person issuing working permits; such person may, in his discretion, require also an affidavit from the parents or other evidence, as additional proof of age;

(d) A statement by the issuing officer that he has examined said child, that in his opinion the child can read intelligently and write legibly simple sentences in the English language, that in his opinion the child is fourteen years of age or upwards, and has reached the normal development of a child of its age and is in sound health and physically able to perform the work which it intends to do, and that in his opinion the services of the child are essential to the support of itself or its parents. In doubtful cases, such physical fitness shall be determined by a medical officer of the board or department of health. Every such permit shall be signed in the presence of the officer issuing the same by the child in whose name it is issued; and shall state the date and place of birth of the child, and describe the color of the hair and eyes, the height and weight and any distinguishing facial marks of such child, and that the paper required by the preceding sections have [sic] been duly examined, approved and filed, and that the child named in such permit has appeared before the officer signing the same and been examined. The school record required by this article shall be signed by the principal or chief executive officer of the school which such child has attended and shall be furnished on demand to a child entitled thereto. It shall contain a statement certifying that the child has regularly attended the public school or schools equivalent thereto or parochial schools for not less than one hundred days during the school year previous to his arriving at the age of fourteen years during the year previous to applying for such school record, and is able to read intelligently and write legibly simple sentences in the English language, and in the case of the public schools, has passed satisfactorily the work of the school up to and including the work of the fourth grade; in case of schools other than public schools the record shall contain, instead of a statement of the grade passed, a statement that the child has received during the above-mentioned period of a hundred days instructions in reading, writing, spelling, English grammar and geography, and is familiar with the fundamental operations of arithmetic up to and including elementary operations in fractions. Such school board shall also give the age and residence of the child as shown on the records of the school and the name of its parents or guardian or custodian: *Provided*, That in the case of limited vacation permits the school record and all other requirements relating to educational qualifications shall be waived, but all other requirements shall be complied with as prescribed in this section. Every month after the issuance of a permit the child shall report to the person who issued same, either in person or in writing through its parent or guardian, stating that the child is employed, giving the name of employer and the location of the place of employment, and if not employed said child shall be compelled to attend school;

(e) Any person who shall make a false statement, transcript, passport, school certificate, certificate of physical fitness, school record or any other writing required to be made or filed by the provisions of this section shall be deemed guilty of a misdemeanor and shall be punished by a fine of not less than ten nor more than one hundred dollars or imprisonment for not less than ten days nor more than ninety days, or by both such fine and imprisonment in the discretion of the court.

SEC. 11 (as amended by act No. 220, Acts of 1911). No female under the age of twenty-one years and no male under the age of eighteen years shall be allowed to clean machinery while in motion nor employed in or about any distillery, brewery, or any other establishment where malt or alcoholic liquors are manufactured, packed, wrapped or bottled, nor in any hazardous employment, or where their health may be injured or morals depraved, nor shall females be unnecessarily required in any employment to remain standing constantly. No child under the age of sixteen years shall be employed in or about any theater, variety show, moving picture show, burlesque show, or other kind of

[marginal note: Contents of permit.]

[marginal note: Monthly report.]

[marginal note: False statements.]

[marginal note: Employments forbidden.]

Permits for children 16 years of age.

playhouse, music or dance hall, pool room or billiard room: *Provided,* That in all cities in which the department of labor maintains a permanent office, the official in charge thereof shall be authorized and required, under the direction of the commissioner of labor, and in other cities or municipalities the superintendent of schools shall likewise be authorized and required to issue, upon demand, certificates of age to young persons past the age of sixteen years, in accord with the following conditions, to wit: The official authorized to issue such certificate shall not issue the same until he has received, examined, approved and filed the following papers, duly executed:

Proofs of age.

(2) A passport, or duly attested transcript of the record of birth, as kept by any recognized public authority or a record of baptism or other religious record, showing the date and place of birth of such young person:

(b) A statement from a physician connected officially with the board, or department of health, which shall be required, however, only in case the above-mentioned official or religious record can not be produced, which statement shall certify that, in the opinion of the physician issuing said statement, the young person is of the age stated therein. Such statement shall also certify to the correct weight and height of said young person, and shall be kept on file by the official issuing certificates of age; such official may, in his discretion, require also an affidavit from the parent of the young person concerned, or other evidence, as additional proof of age;

(c) A statement by the issuing officer that he has examined said young person, and that in his opinion the young person is of the age stated in said certificate of age. Every such certificate shall be signed, in the presence of the officer issuing same, by the young person in whose name it is issued, and shall state the date and place of birth of said person, and describe the color of the hair and eyes, the height and weight, and any distinguishing facial marks of such person, and that the papers required by the preceding section have been duly received, examined, approved and filed, and that the young person named in such certificate has appeared before the officer and been examined. Every employer complying with the provisions of this section shall be at liberty to employ the person so presenting the certificate hereinbefore referred to, and is justified in considering and treating such person as of the age shown in such certificate and shall not be liable, if it transpire that such person is under the age represented in such certificate, to any greater extent than such employer would be liable if such person were of the age represented;

Exemption.

(d) This act shall not be construed so as to prevent children under sixteen years of age from being employed by traveling theatrical companies whose employment consists of acting a part in the productions of such company.

Seats for female employees.

SEC. 24. All persons who employ females in stores, shops, offices or manufactories, as clerks, assistants, operatives or helpers in any business, trade or occupation carried on or operated by them, shall be required to procure and provide proper and suitable seats for all such females, and shall permit the use of such seats, rests or stools as may be necessary, and shall not make any arbitrary rules, regulations or orders preventing the use of such stools or seats at reasonable times. No employer of female help shall neglect or refuse to provide seats as provided in this act, nor shall make any rules, orders or regulations in their shops, stores or other places of business requiring females to remain standing when not necessarily in service or labor therein.

Women not to be employed in barrooms.

SEC. 25. No person shall employ or permit any girl or woman to act as barkeeper, or to serve liquor, or to furnish music, or for dancing in any saloon or barroom where spirituous or intoxicating liquors, or malt, brewed or fermented liquors are sold or kept for sale.

[See also sections 14, 17, 18 of this act, Appendix B, pp. 956, 957.]

ACTS OF 1911.

ACT No. 198.—*Employment of children—School attendance of poor children.*

SECTION 1. Any truant officer of this State when authorized by the board of education to investigate, and when satisfied that any child within his jurisdiction, required by law to attend school, is unable so to do by reason of the fact that the services of such child are absolutely required for the support of himself or herself, or to assist in the support or care of others legally entitled to his or her services, such person or persons being unable to support or care for themselves, such truant officer shall report the case to the board of education of the school district in which such child may reside, and such board of education shall be authorized to and may in their discretion grant such relief as will enable the child to attend school during the entire school year. In all cases where such relief is necessary the said board of education shall be authorized to, and may in their discretion, furnish to such child the necessary text books free of charge, in addition to such other necessary assistance or support. Children whose services are necessary.

SEC. 2. For the purposes in this act provided such board of education shall pay, during the school year, to the family of such child a sum not to exceed three dollars a week, nor more than six dollars a week for the children of any one family. Said money shall be paid in the same manner and out of the same fund as are the current expenses for the maintenance of public schools. Amount to be allowed.

SEC. 3. It shall be the duty of the truant officer or treasurer of the school board in any district where a child is receiving aid under the provisions of this act to disburse the funds herein provided for, and to investigate the environment of the child, and to make an itemized report monthly to the school board or some officer appointed by the board, of the manner in which such funds were expended: *Provided,* That in cities having a juvenile court such investigation shall be made by such court. Monthly reports.

MINNESOTA.

REVISED LAWS—1905.

Seats for female employees.

SECTION 1802. Every employer of females in any mercantile, manufacturing, hotel, or restaurant business, and every agent in charge of any such business, shall provide and maintain suitable seats in the room where they work, and permit such use thereof by them as may be necessary for the preservation of their health. Seats to be provided.

SEC. 1803. The certificate or testimony of any licensed and practicing physician to the effect that, in his opinion, any person is not complying with the provisions of section 1802 in respect to a specified employee, shall be prima facie evidence of a violation thereof. The labor commissioner, upon information of any such violation, shall forthwith cause the matter to be brought to the attention of the proper authorities, and assist in procuring evidence thereof; but this shall not prevent anyone else from making complaint and furnishing evidence, nor interfere with any State or county officer in the performance of his duty. Evidence of violation.

Earnings of minors—Payment.

SECTION 1812. Any parent or guardian claiming the wages of a minor in service shall so notify his employer, and, if he fail so to do, payment to the minor of wages so earned shall be valid. Payment to minor.

Employment of children in certain occupations forbidden—Overwork.

Acrobatic, mendicant, etc. occupations.　SECTION 4939. Every person who shall employ or cause to be employed, exhibit, or have in his custody for exhibition or employment any minor actually or apparently under the age of eighteen years; and every parent, relative, guardian, employer, or other person having the care, custody, or control of any such minor, who shall sell, let out, give away, or in any way procure or consent to the employment of such minor—

1. As a rope or wire walker, dancer, gymnast, contortionist, rider, or acrobat;

. 2. In begging, receiving alms, or in any mendicant occupation;

. 3. In any indecent or immoral exhibition or practice;

4. In any practice or exhibition dangerous or injurious to life, limb, health, or morals;

5. In labor of any kind outside the family of his residence before 7 o'clock a. m. or after 6 o'clock p. m.; or

6. As a messenger for delivering letters, telegrams, packages, or bundles to any known house of prostitution or assignation—

Shall be guilty of a misdemeanor, and be punished by a fine of not less than fifty dollars, or by imprisonment in the county jail for not less than thirty days, or by both.

Overwork.　SEC. 4940. Every person who shall torture, torment, or cruelly or unlawfully punish any child under the age of sixteen years, or shall compel any such child to labor more than ten hours in any day in a factory, workshop, or mercantile or manufacturing business, or who shall commit any act of cruelty toward such child, shall be guilty of a misdemeanor.

ACTS OF 1907.

CHAPTER 299.—*Employment of children—General provisions.*

Age limit.　SECTION 1. No child, under 14 years of age, shall be employed, permitted or suffered to work at any time, in, or in connection with, any factory, mill or workshop, or in or about any mine; and it shall be unlawful for any person, firm or corporation, to employ any child under 14 years of age in any business or service whatever during any part of the term during which the public schools of the district in which the child resides are in session.

Employment during school term.　SEC. 2. It shall be unlawful for any person, firm or corporation to employ any child over 14 years of age, and under 16 years of age, in any business or service whatever, during any part of the term during which the public schools of the district in which the child resides are in session, unless the employer procures and keeps accessible to the truant officers of the town or city and to the commissioner of labor, assistant commissioner of labor, factory inspectors and assistants, an employment certificate as herein prescribed and a list of all such children employed. On termination of the employment of a child, such certificate shall be forthwith surrendered by the employer to the official who issued the same. The commissioner of labor, assistant commissioner of labor, factory inspectors and assistants, may make demand on an employer when a child apparently under the age of 16 years is employed or permitted or suffered to work and when such employer does not have and. exhibit the certificate as required by this section, that such employer shall either furnish him within 10 days, evidence satisfactory to him that such child is in fact over 16 years of age, or shall cease to employ or permit or suffer such child to continue in his employment. The commissioner of labor, assistant commissioner of labor, factory inspectors and assistants and truant officers may require from such employer the same evidence of age of such child as is required on the issuance of an employment certificate; and the employer furnishing such evidence shall not be required to furnish any further evidence of the age of the child. In case such employer shall fail to produce and deliver within ten days after such demand, such evidence of age herein required of him and shall thereafter continue to employ such child, or permit or suffer such child to continue in his employment, proof of the giving of such notice and such failure to produce such evidence, shall be prima

Certificates.

facie evidence in any prosecution brought for a violation of this section that such child is under 16 years of age; and is unlawfully employed.

SEC. 3. An employment certificate shall be issued only by the superintendent of schools, or by some one authorized by him so to do, or where there is no superintendent of schools, by the chairman of the school board or the chairman of the board of education, or by a person authorized by such chairman: *Provided*, That no superintendent of schools, member of the school board or board of education or other person authorized as aforesaid, shall have authority to issue such certificates for any child then in or about to enter his own employment or the employment of a firm or corporation of which he is a member, officer or employee. By whom issued.

SEC. 4. The person authorized to issue an employment certificate shall not issue such certificate until he has received, examined, approved and retained in his possession for the inspection of the public, the following papers duly executed; (1) The school record of such child, properly filled out and signed as provided in this act. (2) A duly attested transcript of the birth certificate, filed according to law with the officer charged with the duty of recording births which shall be conclusive evidence of the birth of such child. (3) The affidavit of the parent or guardian or custodian of the child, showing the place and date of birth of such child, but such affidavit shall not be required unless the last mentioned transcript of the certificate of birth can not be produced, which affidavit must be taken before the officer issuing the employment certificate, who is hereby authorized and required to administer such oath and shall not demand or receive a fee therefor. Such employment certificate shall not be issued until such child has personally appeared before and been examined by the officer issuing the same and until such officer shall, after making an examination, make and retain for inspection by the public, a statement that, in his opinion, the child is 14 years of age or upward and has reached the normal development of a child of its age, and is in sound health and is physically able to perform the work which it intends to do. In doubtful cases, such physical unfitness shall be determined by the medical officer of the board of [or] department of health. Every such employment certificate shall be signed in the presence of the officer issuing the same, by the child in whose name it is issued: *Provided, however,* That the employment certificate herein provided for shall be issued only to such children as: (1) Those whose pover or that of their families renders it necessary for them to work for their support or that of their families: (2) Those who can produce a school record answering the requirements provided for in section 6 of this act. Issue of certificates.

SEC. 5. Such employment certificate shall state the date and place of birth of the child, and describe the color of the hair and eyes, the height and weight, and any distinguishing facial marks of such child, and that the papers required by the preceding section have been duly examined, approved and retained for inspection by the public, and that the child named in such certificate has appeared before the officer signing the certificate and been examined. Contents of certificates.

SEC. 6. The school record required by this act shall be signed by the principal of the school which the child attends, and if there is no principal, then by the teacher of such child in said school and shall be furnished on demand to a child entitled thereto. It shall contain a statement certifying that the child has regularly attended a parochial or private school as required by law or has been lawfully excused therefrom during the year previous to applying for such school record and is able to read and write simple sentences in the English language, and has received during such period, instruction in reading, spelling, writing, English grammar and geography and is familiar with the fundamental operations of arithmetic, up to and including fractions. Such school record shall also give the age and residence of the child as shown on the record of the school and the name of its parent or guardian or custodian. School record.

SEC. 7. The superintendent of schools and chairman of school boards and of the boards of education, shall transmit between the first and tenth day of each month to the office of the commissioner of labor of the State, a list of the names of the children to whom certificates have Lists to be forwarded.

been issued, and anyone failing to transmit the list herein provided for, shall be guilty of a misdemeanor.

Hours of labor. SEC. 8. No person under the age of 16 years shall be employed, or suffered, or permitted to work at any gainful occupation more than 60 hours in any one week, nor more than 10 hours in any one day; or before the hour of 7 o'clock in the morning or after the hour of 7 o'clock **Night work.** in the evening, except that on Saturday and for 10 days prior to Christmas, such person may be employed until 10 o'clock p. m., but not longer in any day or week than the hours aforesaid. Every employer shall post in a conspicuous place in every room where such minors are employed, a printed notice stating the hours required of them each day of the week, the hours of commencing and stopping work, and the hours when the time or times allowed for dinner or for other meals begin and end. The printed form of such notice shall be furnished by the commissioner of labor of the State, and the employment of any minor for longer time in any day so stated shall be deemed a violation of this section.

Violations. SEC. 9. Whoever employes [employs] a child under 16 years of age, and whoever, having under his control a child under such age, permits such child to be employed in violation of sections 1, 2, or 8 of this act, shall, for such offense, be fined not more than fifty dollars; and whoever continues to employ any child in violation of any of said sections of this act after being notified by a truant officer or the commissioner of labor of the State, shall for every day thereafter, that such employment continues, be fined not less than five dollars nor more than twenty-five dollars. A failure to produce to a truant officer or any official of the labor department, any employment certificate or list required by this act shall be prima facie evidence of the illegal employment of any person whose employment certificate is not produced, or whose name is not so listed. Any corporation or employer retaining employment certificates in violation of section 2 of this act shall be fined ten dollars. Every person authorized to sign the certificate prescribed by section 5 of this act, who knowingly certifies to any materially false statement therein shall be fined not more than fifty dollars.

Enforcement. SEC. 10. Officials of the labor department and the truant officers may visit all factories, mills, workshops, mines, mercantile establishments and all other places where labor is employed and ascertain whether any minors are employed contrary to the provisions of this act, and they shall report any cases of such illegal employment to the school superintendent or to the chairman of the school board or board of education and to the commissioner of labor of the State. Officials of the labor department and truant officers may require that the employment certificates and lists provided for in this act of minors employed, shall be produced for their inspection. Complaints for offenses under this act may be brought by any official of the State labor department, and anyone who shall refuse to allow the visitation in this section provided for, shall be guilty of a misdemeanor.

Occupations prohibited. SEC. 11. No children, under the age of 16 years shall be employed at sewing belts, or to assist in sewing belts, in any capacity whatever; nor shall any children adjust any belt to any machinery; they shall not oil, or assist in oiling, wiping or cleaning machinery; they shall not operate or assist in operating circular or band saws, wood shapers, wood joiners, planers, sandpaper or wood polishing machinery, emery or polishing wheels used for polishing metal, wood turning or boring machinery, stamping machines in sheet metal and tinware manufacturing, stamping machines in washer and nut factories, operating corrugating tools, such as are used in roofing factories, nor shall they be employed in operating any steam boiler, steam machinery or other steam generating apparatus, or as pin boys in any bowling alleys; they shall not operate or assist in operating dough brakes or cracker machinery of any description; wire or iron straightening machinery; nor shall they operate or assist in operating rolling mill machinery, punches or shears, washing, grinding or mixing mill or calender rolls in rubber manufacturing, nor shall they operate or assist in operating laundry machinery; nor shall they be employed in any capacity in preparing any composition in which dangerous or poisonous acids are used, and they shall not be employed in any capacity in the manufacture of paints, colors or white lead; nor shall they be employed in any capacity whatever in operating or assisting to operate any passenger or freight elevator; nor shall they be employed in any capacity whatever in the manufacture of goods for immoral purposes, or any other employment that may be considered dangerous to their lives or limbs, or where their health may be injured or morals depraved; nor in any theater, concert hall, or place of amusement wherein intoxicating liquors are **Saloons, etc.** sold; nor shall females under 16 years of age be employed in any capacity where such employment compels them to remain standing constantly: *Provided,* That in any action brought against an employer of any child under 16 years of age, on account of injuries sustained by the child while so employed, if the employer shall have obtained, and kept on file in like manner as herein provided for employment certificates, an affidavit of the parent or guardian, stating in substance that the child is not less than 16 years of age, such employment shall not be deemed a violation of this act. Any person employing any child in violation of the provisions of this section shall be guilty of a gross misdemeanor.

SEC. 12. In case any child appears to be unable to perform the labor **Physical fitness.** at which he or she is employed, the officials of the labor department or truant officers may require the employer of such child to produce a certificate from some reputable practicing physician of the physical fitness of the child for such work, and a child as to whom such certificate can not be obtained shall not be employed. Any person refusing to produce the certificate herein required upon demand, or who shall employ a child when a certificate has been produced stating that such child is physically unable to work, shall be guilty of a gross misdemeanor.

ACTS OF 1909.

CHAPTER 497.—*Bureau of labor—Women's and children's department.*

SECTION 1. There shall be created in the bureau of labor a woman's **Department** and children's department. **created.**

SEC. 2. There shall be appointed by the commissioner of labor a **Female assist-** competent woman to act as assistant commissioner of labor and such **ant commissioner.** woman factory inspectors as may be necessary to inspect the sanitary and general conditions under which women and children are at work in all factories, workshops, hotels, restaurants, stores and any other places where women and children are employed.

Said assistant commissioner of labor shall collect statistics and render to the next legislature through the commissioner of labor such findings and recommendations as will promote the health and general welfare of the women and children so employed in this State.

CHAPTER 499.—*Employment of women—Hours of labor—Inspection of factories, etc.*

SECTION 1. No female shall be employed in laboring in a mercantile **Hours of labor** establishment more than fifty-eight hours in a week. **in stores.**

Every employer shall post in a conspicuous place in every room in which such persons are employed a printed notice stating the number of hours' work which are required of them on each day of the week, the hours of commencing and stopping such work, and the hour when the time or times allowed for dinner or other meals begin and end.

The printed form of such notice shall be furnished by the commissioner of labor.

The employment of any such person for a longer time in any day than so stated shall be deemed a violation of the provisions of this section.

SEC. 2. No female shall be employed in laboring in a manufacturing **Hours of labor** or mechanical establishment more than ten hours in any one day, **in factories, etc.** except as hereinafter provided in this section, unless a different apportionment of the hours of labor is made for the sole purpose of making a shorter day's work for one day of the week; and in no case shall the hours of labor exceed fifty-eight in a week.

Every employer shall post in a conspicuous place in every room in which such persons are employed a printed notice stating the number of hours' work, and the hours when the time allowed for meals begins and ends.

The printed forms of such notices shall be provided by the commissioner of labor.

Violations. The employment of such person at any time other than as stated in said printed notice shall be deemed a violation of the provisions of this section unless it appears that such employment was to make up time lost on [a] previous day of the same week in consequence of the stopping of machinery upon which he or she was employed or dependent for employment; but no stopping of machinery for less than thirty consecutive minutes shall justify such overtime employment, nor shall overtime employment be authorized until a written report of the day and hour [of] its occurrence and its duration is sent to the commissioner of labor.

Time for meals. SEC. 3. In each factory, workshop, store or mill at least sixty minutes shall be allowed for the noonday meal unless the commissioner of labor shall permit a shorter time.

Such permit must be in writing and conspicuously posted in the main entrance of the factory and may be revoked at any time.

Where employees are required or permitted to work more than one hour after six o'clock in the evening they shall be allowed at least twenty minutes to obtain lunch before beginning to work overtime.

Air space. SEC. 4. No more employees shall be required or permitted to work in a room in a factory than will allow to each of such employees, not less than two hundred and fifty cubic feet of air space; and unless by a written permit of the commissioner of labor, not less than four hundred cubic feet for each employee, so employed.

Ventilation. SEC. 5. The owner, agent, or lessee of a factory shall provide in each workroom thereof, proper and sufficient means of ventilation, and shall maintain proper and sufficient ventilation; if excessive heat be created or if steam, gases, vapors, dust or other impurities that may be injurious to health be generated in the course of the manufacturing process carried on therein the room must be ventilated in such manner as to render them harmless, so far as is practicable; in case of failure the commissioner of labor shall order such ventilation to be provided.

Such owner, agent or lessee shall provide such ventilation within twenty days after the service upon him of such order, and in case of failure, shall forfeit to the people of the State, ten dollars for each day after the expiration of such twenty days, to be recovered by the commissioner of labor.

Sanitation. SEC. 6 (as amended by chapter 184, Acts of 1911). Every factory and workshop in this State where women and children are employed and where dusty work is carried on shall be limewashed or painted at least once in every twelve months.

Every floor of any room in said factory shall be thoroughly cleaned with soap and water at least once in six months and every dressing room and water closet in said factory shall be thoroughly cleaned with soap and water once in every week.

Any employer, superintendent, owner or other agent of any mercantile, manufacturing or mechanical establishment who violates any of the provisions of this chapter shall be guilty of a misdemeanor.

ACTS OF 1911.

CHAPTER 356.—*Employment of children—School attendance.*

SECTION 1. Every child between eight (8) and sixteen (16) years of age shall attend a public school, or a private school, in each year during the entire time the public schools of the district in which the child resides are in session: *Provided,* That in districts where the entire term of school is of unequal length in different schools, such child shall be required to attend school as herein provided during at least the entire time of the shorter term.

Such child may be excused from attendance upon an application of his parent, guardian, or other person having control of such child, to any member of the school board, truant officer, principal, or city superintendent, for the whole or any part of such period, by the school board of the district in which the child resides, upon its being shown to the satisfaction of such board:

* * * * * * *

3. * * * *Provided, first,* That any child fourteen (14) years of age or over, whose help may be required in any permitted occupation in or about the home of his parent or guardian may be excused from attendance between April 1 and November 1 in any year; but this proviso shall not apply to any cities of the first and second class; * * *

The clerk, or any authorized officer of the school board shall issue and keep a record of such excuses, under such rules as the board may from time to time establish.

SEC. 4. Any person who shall refuse or fail to send or keep in school any child or children of whom he has legal charge or control, and who is required by law to attend school, when notified so to do as hereinbefore provided, and any person who induces or attempts to induce any child unlawfully to absent himself from school, or who knowingly harbors or employs while school is in session any child unlawfully absent from school, shall be guilty of a misdemeanor, and shall be punished by a fine of not to exceed fifty (50) dollars, or by imprisonment in the county jail for not more than thirty (30) days.

SEC. 6. The commissioner of labor and his assistants shall assist in the enforcement of the provisions of this act, and shall have authority to examine the excuses granted under this act, to make investigation into the causes for which excuses have been granted, and to revoke and cancel any that may be found to be granted without proper or sufficient cause.

MISSISSIPPI.

CODE OF 1906.

Employment of children—Enticing.

SECTION 1080. Any person who shall persuade, entice, or decoy away from its father or mother, with whom it resides, any child under the age of twenty-one years if a male, or eighteen if a female, being unmarried, for the purpose of employing such child without the consent of its parents, or one of them, shall, upon conviction, be punished by a fine of not more than twenty dollars, or imprisonment in the county jail not more than thirty days, or both. Enticing children.

Hiring out children to support parents in idleness.

SECTION 5055. The following persons are and shall be punished as vagrants, viz.: Who are vagrants.

* * * * * * *

(*m*) All persons who are able to work and do not work, but hire out their minor children or allow them to be hired out, and live upon their wages.

ACTS OF 1908.

CHAPTER 99.—*Employment of children—General provisions.*

SECTION 1. No children under the age of twelve years shall be employed in or permitted to work in any mill, factory or manufacturing establishment in this State. Age limit.

SEC. 2. No child under the age of sixteen years shall be employed or detained in any mill, factory or manufacturing establishment within this State for more than ten hours in any one day, or for more than fifty-eight hours in any one week, or be employed in or detained in any such manufacturing establishment between the hours of 7 p. m. and 6 a. m. Hours of labor. Night work.

SEC. 3. It shall be unlawful for any person, firm or corporation to employ or detain or permit to work in any mill, factory or manfuacturing establishment in this State any child under the age of sixteen years Affidavits.

without first requiring said child to present the affidavit of the parent
or guardian or person standing in parental relation to such child, stating
the place and date of birth of such child, and also stating the last school
attendance of such child and grade of studies pursued, and the name of
school and name of teacher in charge. The employer shall preserve
Register. such affidavit and keep a complete register of all such affidavits showing
all the facts contained therein.

Enforcement. SEC. 4. It is the special duty of the sheriff of the county in which
manufacturing establishments employing child labor are located to
visit, at least once each month, each such manufacturing establishment, and see to the enforcement of this act.

Inspection. SEC. 5. It is the duty of each county health officer to visit, without
notice of his intention to do so, all manufacturing establishments employing child labor within his county, at least twice each year, and
oftener if requested by the sheriff, and to promptly report to the sheriff
any unsanitary condition of the premises, any child or children afflicted
with an infectious, contagious or communicable disease, or whose
physical condition renders such child or children incapacitated to
perform the work required of them; and the sheriff shall promptly remove such child or children from such manufacturing establishment,
and order the premises put in sanitary condition; and the judgment
of the county health officer as to the physical condition of the children
and sanitary condition of the premises shall be final and conclusive.

Investigations. SEC. 6. It shall be the duty of the circuit judge to specially charge
the grand jury to investigate violations of this act.

Refusing infor- SEC. 7. Any officer, manager or superintendent of any manufacturing
mation. establishment in which child labor is employed who shall fail or refuse
to give true and correct information demanded of him by any of the
officers hereinbefore directed to inspect such establishments, or who
shall fail or refuse to obey any lawful order of the sheriff or health officer
of the county in which such establishment is located, for carrying out
purposes of this act, shall be guilty of a misdemeanor, and upon conviction shall be fined not less than ten dollars nor more than one hundred dollars.

Violations. SEC. 8. Any person, firm or corporation, or the superintendent,
manager, or any officer of a manufacturing establishment employing
any child or permitting any child to be employed by or to work in or
to be detained in any mill, factory or manufacturing establishment
in this State contrary to law, shall be guilty of a misdemeanor, and
upon conviction shall be fined not less than fifty dollars nor more than
one hundred dollars, or may be sentenced to the county jail for not less
than ten days nor more than sixty days, or both such fine and imprisonment.

Application of SEC. 9. The provisions of this act shall apply only to manufacturing
act. establishments engaged in manufacturing or working in cotton, wool
or other fabrics, and to manufacturing establishments where children
are employed indoors at work injurious to health, or in operating dangerous machinery.

MISSOURI.

REVISED STATUTES—1909.

Employment of children—General provisions.

Age limit. SECTION 1715 (as amended by act, p. 132, Acts of 1911). No child
under the age of fourteen years shall be employed, permitted or suffered
to work at any gainful occupation within this State, except at agricultural pursuits, and in domestic service.

Hours of labor. SEC. 1716 (as amended by act, p. 132, Acts of 1911). No child under
the age of sixteen years shall be employed, permitted or suffered to
Night work. work at any gainful occupation in this State more than forty-eight
hours in any one week, nor more than eight hours per day; nor before
the hour of seven o'clock in the morning, nor after the hour of seven
Schedule to be o'clock in the evening. Every employer shall post in a conspicuous
posted. place in every room or place where such minors are employed a printed
notice stating the hours of service required of them each day of the

week, the hours of commencing and stopping work, and the hour, or hours, when the time, or times, allowed for meals begin and end. The printed form of such notice shall be furnished by the State factory inspector.

SEC. 1717 (as amended by act, p. 132, Acts of 1911). It shall be the duty of every person, firm or corporation, employing minors over fourteen and under sixteen years of age within this State to keep two complete lists containing the names, ages and places of residence of all such children employed therein, one on file, and one conspicuously posted near the principal entrance of the place or establishment in which such children are employed. *Registers.*

SEC. 1718 (as amended by act, p. 132, Acts of 1911). No child under sixteen years of age, and over fourteen years of age, shall be employed, permitted or suffered to work in this State unless there is first produced and placed on file at the time of employment, and accessible to any factory inspector, and to any school attendance officer, or to any other authorized officer, an employment certificate as hereinafter prescribed. On termination of the employment of any such child, such certificate shall be forthwith surrendered by the employer to the owner thereof, or in the event said certificate is not called for within thirty days, it shall be transmitted by the employer to the person who issued the same. *Employment certificates.*

SEC. 1719 (as amended by act, p. 132, Acts of 1911). An employment certificate shall be issued only by the superintendent of instruction of any board of education in this State, or by a person authorized by him in writing, or, where there is no superintendent of instruction, by a person authorized by the board of directors of any school district in this State. *Who to issue.*

SEC. 1720 (as amended by act, p. 132, Acts of 1911). The person so authorized to issue an employment certificate shall not issue such certificate until he has received, examined, approved and filed the following papers, duly executed: *Proof required.*

1. The school record of such child, properly filled out and signed by the principal or chief executive officer of the school which such child has attended. It shall contain a statement certifying that the child has regularly attended the public schools, or schools equivalent thereto, or parochial schools, and is able to read and write simple sentences in the English language. Such school record shall also give the date of birth and residence of the child, as shown on the record of the school, and the names of its parents, guardian, or custodian.

2. A passport, or duly attested transcript of the certificate of birth, or baptism, or other religious record, showing the date and place of birth of such child.

3. An affidavit of the parent or guardian or custodian of a child (which shall not be accepted, however, unless a passport or certificate of birth, or baptism, or other religious record is not obtainable), showing the date and place of birth of such child. Such affidavit must be taken before the officer issuing the employment certificate, who is hereby authorized and required to administer such oath without demanding or receiving any fee therefor.

SEC. 1721 (as amended by act, p. 132, Acts of 1911). No employment certificate shall be issued until the child in question has personally appeared before and been examined by the officer issuing the certificate, nor until such officer, after making such examination, has signed and filed in his office a statement that the child can read and legibly write simple sentences in the English language, and that in his opinion, the child is fourteen years of age or over, and has reached the normal development of a child of its age, and is in sufficiently sound health and physically able to perform the work it intends to do. Whenever such officer issuing the employment certificate requests it, such normal development, sound health and physical fitness shall be determined by a medical officer of the board or department of health or by a regularly licensed physician. *Issue of certificate.*

SEC. 1722 (as amended by act, p. 132, Acts of 1911). Every such employment certificate shall state the name, sex, residence, the date and place of birth of the child, and describe the color of the hair and eyes, the height and weight, and any distinguishing physical marks of such child, and that the papers required by the preceding sections *Contents.*

have been duly examined, approved and filed, and that the child
named in such certificate has appeared before the officer signing it.
Every such certificate shall be signed in the presence of the officer
issuing it by the child in whose name it is issued. It shall show the
date of its issue. In the event such employment certificate is lost,
duplicates may be issued upon the payment of a fee of 50 cents for
each duplicate, which shall be paid into the general school fund.

Review

SEC. 1723 (as amended by act, p. 132, Acts of 1911). All such employment certificates shall be subject to review by the factory inspector,
or by any of his assistants or deputies, and may by him be cancelled
if he finds such certificate has been obtained through fraud, misrepresentation or falsification of facts. In such cases the factory inspector
shall give written notice to the employer, who shall at once cause the
minor affected to be dismissed from employment. The factory inspector or his assistant or deputy shall also have the power to demand a certificate of physical fitness from some regularly licensed physician in
the case of children who may seem to said inspector physically unable
to perform the labor at which they may be employed; and no such
child shall be employed who can not obtain such a certificate.

SEC. 1724 (as amended by act, p. 132, Acts of 1911). Such employment
certificate shall be printed, the printed form to be furnished by the
State factory inspector, and shall be filled out, signed and held for surrender in the following form:

EMPLOYMENT CERTIFICATE.

Form.

I, ..., (here officer issuing certificate shall insert his name
and official title and by what authority he issues said certificate)
hereby certify that there personally appeared before me ....,
(here insert name of child), and that he, or she, has been duly examined
by me and found by me to be able to read and legibly write simple
sentences in the English language; and I further certify that in my
opinion the said child is fourteen years of age or over and has reached
the normal development of a child of his, or her, age, and is in sufficiently sound health and physically able to perform the work which
he, or she, intends to do, which, according to the statement of the
child, is as follows: ...... (here insert kind of work child states he,
or she, intends to perform).

I further certify that I have received, examined, approved, signed
and filed in my office at ......, (here insert address of officer issuing
certificate), the papers required by the statutes of Missouri pertaining
to the issuance of employment certificates to children over fourteen
years of age.

I further certify that the child in whose name this certificate is
issued, has signed his, or her, name in my presence. His, or her, full
name is ...., (here insert full name of child in whose behalf
certificate is issued). ......(here state whether male or female child);
residence ......; born on the .... day of ...... (month); .... (year),
at ...... (place of birth); color of hair is ......; of eyes is ......;
height, ...; weight, ...; ...... (here insert distinguishing
facial marks).

In the event this certificate is lost, a duplicate may be issued upon
the payment of a fee of 50 cents.

Signed this .... day of ...... (month), ... (year), at ....
(place of issuance).

....,
....,
(Signature and official title of officer issuing certificate.)
....,
....,
(Signature and address of child on whose behalf certificate is issued.)

**Monthly re-
ports.**

SEC. 1725 (as amended by act, p. 132, Acts of 1911). The superintendent of instruction, or other person authorized to issue employment
certificates, shall transmit, between the first and tenth days of each
month, to the office of the factory inspector, upon blanks to be furnished
by him, a list of the names of the children to whom certificates have
been issued. Such list shall give the name of the prospective employer,

if known, and the nature of the occupation the child intends to engage in.

Sec. 1726 (as amended by act, p. 132, Acts of 1911). The presence of any person under the age of sixteen years in any place where labor is employed, shall constitute prima facie evidence of his, or her, employment therein. *Evidence of employment.*

Sec. 1726a (added by act, p. 132, Acts of 1911). No boy under ten, and no girl under sixteen years of age shall sell, or expose, or offer for sale, newspapers, magazines, periodicals, or other merchandise in any street or hotels, railway stations, places of public amusement, places where intoxicating liquors are manufactured or sold or public office building within the State. *Street trades, etc.*

Sec. 1726b (added by act, p. 132, Acts of 1911). No child under the age of sixteen years shall be employed, permitted or suffered to work at any of the following occupations or in any of the following positions: Sewing machine belts in any workshop or factory, or assisting therein in any capacity whatever; adjusting any belt to any machinery; oiling, wiping or cleaning machinery or assisting therein; operating, or assisting in operating circular saws; wood jointers; wood shapers; planers; sandpaper or wood-polishing machinery; picker machines; machines used in picking wool; machines used in picking cotton; machines used in picking hair; machines used in picking upholstering material; paper-lacing machines; leather-burnishing machines; burnishing machines in any tannery or leather manufactory; job or cylinder printing presses, operated by power other than foot power; emery or polishing wheels used for polishing metal; wood-turning or boring machinery; stamping machines used in sheet-metal and tinware manufacturing; stamping machines used in washer and nut factories; corrugating rolls, such as are used in roofing and washboard factories; steam boilers; steam machinery; or other steam generating apparatus; dough brakes; or cracker machinery of any description; wire or strengthening machinery; rolling mill machinery; punches or shears; washing, grinding or mixing mills; calender rolls in rubber manufacturing; laundering machinery. *Occupations forbidden.*

Sec. 1726c (added by act, p. 132, Acts of 1911). No child under the age of sixteen years shall be employed, permitted or suffered to work in any capacity in, about or in connection with the—preparing any composition in which dangerous or poisonous acids or alkalies are used; manufacture of paints, colors or white lead; dipping, drying or packing matches; manufacturing, packing or storing powder, dynamite, nitroglycerine compounds, fuses or other explosives; manufacture of goods for immoral purposes; nor in, about or in connection with any—brewery or other establishment where malt or alcoholic liquors are manufactured, packed, wrapped or bottled; hotel; concert hall; moving picture shows: pool and billiard halls; wholesale drug store; saloon, or place of amusement; nor in operating any automobile, motor car or truck; nor in bowling alleys; nor in any other employment declared by the State factory inspector to be dangerous to lives and limbs, or injurious to the health or morals of children under the age of sixteen. *Same.*

Sec. 1726d (added by act, p. 132, Acts of 1911). The violation of any of the provisions of this act shall be deemed a misdemeanor and every day's violation shall constitute a separate offense, and any person, firm or corporation committing such violation shall be punished by a fine of not more than $100, or by imprisonment in the county jail not exceeding one year, or by both such fine and punishment. *Violations.*

Seats for female employees.

Section 4493. Every person or corporation employing females in any manufacturing, mechanical or mercantile establishment in this State shall provide suitable seats for the use of the females so employed, and permit the use of said seats by them when not engaged in the duties for which they are employed. *Seats to be provided.*

Sec. 4494. A person or corporation violating the provisions of section 4493 of this article shall be punished by a fine of not less than ten dollars nor more than one hundred dollars for each offense. *Penalty.*

[See also sec. 7838, Appendix B, p. 969.]

Employment of females in barrooms.

Women not to be employed. Section 4740. No company, corporation, firm, owner, proprietor, lessee or person owning, conducting or operating any dramshops, saloon or place where spirituous, malt or vinous liquors are sold at retail shall employ or suffer to be employed any female as a servant, bartender, waiter, dancer or singer in said dramshop or place where spirituous, malt, or vinous liquors are sold at retail, and any person violating the provisions of this section shall be deemed guilty of a misdemeanor, and, upon conviction, shall be punished by imprisonment in the county jail not less than three nor more than twelve months, or by fine of not less than fifty nor more than five hundred dollars, or by both such fine and imprisonment; and it shall be the duty of the judge of the court before whom any person is convicted for the violation of the provisions of this section to declare the license of such person for the keeping of a dramshop forfeited and revoked, and enter the same on record; and thereupon it shall be the duty of the clerk of the said court to certify the fact to the authority granting such license, and no such license shall be renewed or again granted to such person until after the expiration of the two years from the day of conviction.

Employment of children—Certain occupations forbidden.

Acrobatic, mendicant, etc., occupations. Section 4741. It shall be unlawful for any person having the care, custody or control of any child under the age of fourteen years to exhibit, use or employ, or in any manner, or under any pretense, sell, apprentice, give away, let out or otherwise dispose of any such child to any person in or for the vocation or occupation, service or purpose of singing, playing on musical instruments, rope or wire walking, dancing, begging or peddling, or as a gymnast, contortionist, rider or acrobat in any place whatsoever, or for any obscene, indecent or immoral purpose, exhibition or practice whatsoever, or for or in any business, exhibition or vocation injurious to the health or dangerous to the life or limb of such child, or cause, procure or encourage any such child to engage therein. Nothing in this section contained shall apply to or affect the employment or use of any such child as a singer or musician in any church, school or academy, or at any respectable entertainment, or the teaching or learning the science or practice of music.

Hiring, etc. Sec. 4742. It shall also be unlawful for any person to take, receive, hire, employ, use, exhibit or have in custody any child under the age and for the purposes prohibited in section 4741 of this article.

Penalty. Sec. 4743. Any person convicted under the provisions of the two preceding sections shall for the first offense be fined not exceeding one hundred dollars, or imprisoned in the county jail not exceeding three months, or both, in the discretion of the court, and, upon conviction for a second or any subsequent offense, shall be fined in any sum not exceeding five hundred dollars, or imprisoned in the penitentiary for a term not exceeding two years, or both, in the discretion of the court.

[See also section 7829, Appendix B, page 969.]

Employment of women—Hours of labor.

Nine-hour day. Section 7815 (as amended by act, p. 311, Acts of 1911). No female shall be employed in any manufacturing or mechanical and mercantile establishments, laundry or workshop, in this State, more than nine hours during any one day, nor more than fifty-four hours during any one week.

Violations. Sec. 7816 (as amended by act, p. 311, Acts of 1911). Any employer or overseer, superintendent, foreman, agent, or any other employee who shall require or permit or suffer any female to work in any of the places mentioned in section 7815 of this act more than the number of hours therein specified, or any employer who permits or suffers any overseer, superintendent, foreman, agent or other employee to require or to permit or to suffer any female to work in any of the places mentioned in section 7815 of this act more than the number of hours therein specified shall be guilty of a misdemeanor, and upon conviction thereof shall be fined for each offense not less than twenty-five dollars nor more than one hundred dollars.

Employment of women and children in mines.

SECTION 8456. * * * No male person under the age of fourteen years, or female of any age, shall be permitted to enter any mine to work therein; nor shall any boy under the age of sixteen years, unless he can read or write, be allowed to work in any mine. Any party or person neglecting or refusing to perform the duties required to be performed by the provisions of this article shall be deemed guilty of a misdemeanor, and punished by a fine, in the discretion of the court trying the same, subject, however, to the limitations as provided by section 8462 of this acticle. Employment of women and children.

Employment of children—School attendance.

SECTION 10896. Every parent, guardian, or other person in the State of Missouri having charge and control of a child between the ages of eight and fourteen years shall cause such child to attend regularly some day school, public, private, parochial or parish not less than three-fourths of the entire time the school which said child attends is in session, or shall provide such child at home with such regular daily instruction during the usual hours as shall be, in the judgment of a court having competent jurisdiction, substantially equivalent at least to the instruction given children of like age at said day school in the locality in which the child resides: *Provided,* That every parent, guardian, or person in the State of Missouri having charge and control of a child between the ages of fourteen and sixteen years, who is not actually and regularly and lawfully engaged in some useful employment or service, shall cause said child to attend regularly some day school as aforesaid. Attendance required.

SEC. 10898. The board having charge of a public school in a city or district of one thousand or more population by the last census shall appoint and remove at pleasure one or more attendance officers to enforce the provisions of sections 10896 to 10905, inclusive, and shall fix the compensation and manner of performance of the duties of said attendance officer, and shall pay them from the public-school funds; and the attendance officer, as aforesaid, * * * shall have the right to visit and enter any office or factory or business house employing children as aforesaid; shall have the right to require a properly attested certificate of the attendance of any child or children at such day school; * * * Enforcement.

SEC. 10906. Every parent, guardian, or other person in any city of the State of Missouri of five hundred thousand inhabitants or over having charge, control or custody of a child between the ages of eight and fourteen years, shall cause such child to attend regularly some day school, public, private, parochial or parish, not less than the entire time the school which said child attends is in session, or shall provide such child at home with such regular daily instructions during the usual hours as shall, in the judgment of a court having competent jurisdiction, be substantially equivalent at least to the instruction given the children of like age at said day school in the locality in which said child resides; and every parent, guardian, or person in the State of Missouri in such cities having charge, control or custody of a child between the ages of fourteen and sixteen years, who is not actually and regularly and lawfully engaged for at least six hours each day in some useful employment or service, shall cause said child to attend regularly some day school as aforesaid. School attendance required, St. Louis.

SEC. 10908. The board having charge of public schools in such city may appoint, and remove at pleasure, one or more attendance officers to enforce the provisions of sections 10906 to 10917, inclusive, and shall fix the compensation and manner of performance of the duties of said attendance officers, and shall pay them from the public school funds; and the attendance officer or officers, as aforesaid, shall have the right * * * to visit and enter any mine, office, factory, workshop, business house, p ace of amusement, or other place in which children are employed lor engaged in any kind of service, or any place or building in which children loiter or idle during school hours; * * * Attendance officers.
Duties.

MONTANA.

CONSTITUTION.

ARTICLE 18.—*Employment of children in mines—Age limit—Hours of labor of employees on public works and in mines, smelters, etc.*

it of sixteen   SECTION 3. It shall be unlawful to employ children under the age of sixteen (16) years of age in underground mines.

REVISED CODES—1907.

Employment of children—School attendance.

ol attend-
equired.   SECTION 965. All parents, guardians and other persons who have care of children, shall instruct them, or cause them to be instructed in reading, spelling, writing, English grammar, geography, physiology and hygiene, and arithmetic. Every parent, guardian or other person having charge of any child between the ages of eight and fourteen years shall send such child to a public, private, or parochial school, for the full time that the school attended is in session, which shall in no case be for less than sixteen weeks during any current year, and said attendance shall begin within the first week of the school term, unless the child is excused from such attendance * * * upon satisfactory showing, either that the bodily or mental condition of the child does not permit of its attendance at school, or that the child is being instructed at home by a person qualified, * * * or that there is no school taught the required length of time within 2½ miles of the residence of such child by the nearest traveled road: *Provided,* That no child shall be refused admission to any public school on account of race or color. * * *

ificates.   SEC. 966. No child under fourteen years of age shall be employed or be in the employment of any person, company or corporation during the school term and while the public schools are in session, unless such child shall present to such person, company or corporation an age and schooling certificate herein provided for. An age and schooling certificate shall be approved only by the superintendent of schools, or by a person authorized by him, in city or other districts having such superintendent, or by the clerk of the board of trustees in village and township districts not having such superintendent, upon a satisfactory proof of the age of such minor and that he has successfully completed the studies enumerated in section 965 of this article; or if between the ages of fourteen and sixteen years, a knowledge of his or her ability to read and write legibly the English language. The age and schooling certificate shall be formulated by the superintendent of public instruction and the same furnished in blank, by the clerk of the board of trustees or the clerk of the district. Every person, company, or corporation employing any child under sixteen years of age, shall exact the age and schooling certificate prescribed in this section, as a condition of employment and shall keep the same on file, and shall upon the request of the truant officer hereinafter provided for, permit him to examine such age and schooling certificate. Any person, company, or corporation, employing any minor contrary to the provisions of this section shall be fined not less than twenty-five nor more than fifty dollars for each and every offense.

srates.   SEC. 967. All minors over the age of fourteen and under the age of sixteen years, who can not read and write the English language shall be required to attend school as provided in section 965, of this article and all the provisions of said section shall apply to said minors: *Provided,* That such attendance shall not be required of such minors after they have secured a certificate from the superintendent of schools in districts having superintendents, or the clerk of the board of trustees in districts not having superintendents, that they can read, and write the English language. No person, company or corporation shall employ any such minor during the time schools are in session, or having such minor in their employ shall immediately cease such employment, upon notice from the truant officer who is hereinafter provided. Every person, company, or corporation violating the provisions of this section shall be fined not less than twenty-five nor more than fifty dollars for each and every offense.

SEC. 968. Every child between the ages of eight and fourteen years, and every child between the ages of fourteen and sixteen years unable to read, and write the English language, or not engaged in some regular employment and who is an habitual truant from school, or who absents itself habitually from school, or who, while in attendance at any public, private, or parochial school, is incorrigible, vicious, or immoral in conduct, or who habitually wanders about the streets and public places during school hours having no business or lawful occupation, shall be deemed a juvenile disorderly person and be subject to the provisions of this act. — *Delinquents.*

SEC. 969. * * * The truant officer shall be vested with police powers, the authority to serve warrants, and have authority to enter workshops, factories, stores and all other places where children may be employed, and do whatever may be necessary, in the way of investigation or otherwise to enforce the provisions of this act; * * * — *Enforcement.*

Employment of children—Enforcement of laws.

SECTION 1660. There is hereby created a State Bureau of Child and Animal protection, for the purpose of enforcing the laws of the State of Montana, pertaining to children and dumb animals which may now or hereafter exist; and to promote the growth of education and sentiment favorable to the protection of children and dumb animals. — *Bureau of child and animal protection.*

SEC. 1664 (as amended by chapter 127, Acts of 1911). The secretary shall have the power to appoint six deputies, one of whom shall have his office in the city of Butte, one in Great Falls, one in Havre, one in Billings, one in Missoula and one in Kalispell. Such deputies shall take and subscribe the same oath required by the principal, and the same shall be of record in the secretary's office. — *Inspectors.*

The deputies shall have the same power and authority as fixed by law in the principal, and shall have a salary of eighteen hundred ($1800) dollars, per annum, payable monthly, out of the public treasury. They shall make full and complete reports every month to said principal showing all their official acts, with names of persons accused and against whom prosecution may have been instituted, and the results thereof. Said deputies may be removed at any time by the secretary, and another appointed to fill the vacancy. All deputies shall have authority to investigate cases reported to said bureau from any section of the State of Montana when called or directed to so do by the secretary of said bureau. — *Reports.*

SEC. 1669. The secretary is hereby vested with authority to make arrests of any person, or persons, violating any provisions of the laws relating to wrongs to children and dumb animals, and is hereby further vested with the authority to enter workshops, factories, stores, mines, mills and smelters, and all other places where children may be employed, and do what may be necessary in the way of investigation, or otherwise, to enforce the laws pertaining to minor children and animals. — *Powers of secretary of bureau.*

Employment of children—Age limit.

SECTION 1746. Any person, company, firm, association, or corporation engaged in business in this State, or any agent, officer, foreman or other employee having control or management of employees, or having the power to hire or discharge employees, who shall knowingly employ or permit to be employed any child under the age of sixteen years, to render or perform any service or labor, whether under contract of employment or otherwise, in, on, or about any mine, mill, smelter, workshop, factory, steam, electric, hydraulic, or compressed air railroad, or passenger or freight elevator, or where any machinery is operated, or for any telegraph, telephone or messenger company, or in any occupation not herein enumerated which is known to be dangerous or unhealthful, or which may be in any way detrimental to the morals of said child, shall be guilty of a misdemeanor and punishable as hereinafter provided. — *Age limit.*

Hiring out chil- SEC. 1747. Any parent, guardian or other person having the care,
dren.   custody or control of any child under the age of sixteen years, who shall
permit, suffer or allow any such child to work or perform service for
any person, company, firm, association or corporation doing business
in this State, or who shall permit or allow any such child over whom
he has·such care, custody or control, to retain such employment as is
prohibited in section 1746 (1) of this act, whether under contract· of
employment or not, shall be guilty of a misdemeanor and punishable
as hereinafter provided.

List.   SEC. 1748. The commissioner of the bureau of agriculture, labor and
industry shall compile and preserve in his office from reports made
to him by the county superintendent of schools, as otherwise provided,
a full and complete list of the name, age, date of birth and sex of each
child, and the names of the parents or guardians of each child under
the age of sixteen years who is now or may hereafter become a resident
of this State, and such list shall be the official record of the age of
children in this State.

Certificate.   SEC. 1749. Upon attaining the age of sixteen years any child may
make application to the commissioner of the bureau of agriculture,
labor and industry for an age certificate, which must be presented to
any employer with whom such child may seek employment. The
employer, if such employment be given, must countersign the certificate, and return the same to the commissioner of said bureau, who shall
Violation.   keep the same on file in his office. Any person, firm, company, association or corporation who employs or permits to be employed in any
occupation prohibited in section 1746 (1) of this act, any child without
such certificate showing the child to be at least sixteen years of age,
shall be guilty of a misdemeanor and punishable as hereinafter provided, should such child prove to be less than sixteen years of age.

Enforcement.   SEC. 1750. To enforce this act the commissioner of the bureau of
agriculture, labor and industry, the bureau of child and animal protection and all county attorneys shall, each upon their own volition,
or upon the sworn complaint of any reputable citizen that this act
is being violated, make prosecutions for such violations.

Penalty.   SEC. 1751. Every person, firm, company, association or corporation
who violates any of the provisions of this act shall be guilty of a misdemeanor, and upon conviction thereof shall be punished by a fine of not
less than twenty-five dollars nor more·than five hundred dollars, or by
imprisonment in the county jail for a period of not less than thirty
days nor more than six months, or by both such fine and imprisonment.

Employment of SEC. 1752. Any person, corporation, stock company or association
children in mines. of persons, owning or operating any underground mine, or any officer,
agent, foreman or boss, having the control or management of employees,
or having the power to hire or discharge employees, who shall employ,
or knowingly permit to be employed, any child under the age of sixteen years, for work or service in any such mine, or the underground
workings thereof, or permit or allow any such child to render or perform
any work or service whatever in such mine, whether under contract
of employment or otherwise, shall be guilty of a misdemeanor and
punishable as hereinafter provided.

Violations by SEC. 1753. Any parent, guardian or other person having the care,
parents.   custody, or control of any child under the age of sixteen years, who
shall permit, suffer, or allow such child to work in any mine having
underground workings, or who shall permit or allow any such child
over whom they may have such care, custody, or control to retain
employment in any such mine, or who, after having knowledge that
any such child has taken employment in any such mine, or is performing work or service therein, whether under contract of employment or not, shall fail forthwith to notify the person or corporation
owning or operating such mine, or some officer, foreman or employee
thereof having the power to hire or discharge employees, of the age of
such child, shall be guilty of a misdemeanor and punishable as hereinafter provided.

Penalty.   SEC. 1754. Any person or corporation violating any of the provisions
of this act shall be guilty of a misdemeanor, and upon conviction thereof
shall be punished by a fine not less than twenty-five ($25) dollars nor

more than. ($500) five hundred dollars, or by imprisonment in the county jail for a period of not less than thirty days nor more than six months, or by both such fine and imprisonment.

Earnings of minors.

SECTION 3757. The wages of a minor employed in service may be paid him until the parent or guardian entitled thereto gives the employer notice that he claims such wages.

Payments valid until notice.

Employment of children—Certain occupations forbidden.

SECTION 8347. Any person, whether as parent, relative, guardian, employer or otherwise, having in his care, custody or control any child under the age of sixteen years, who shall sell, apprentice, give away, let out or otherwise dispose of any such child to any person, under any name, title or pretense, for the vocation, use, occupation, calling, service or purpose of singing, playing on musical instruments, ropewalking, dancing, begging or peddling in any public street or highway, or in any mendicant or wandering business whatever, and any person who shall take, receive, hire, employ, use or have in custody any child for such purposes, or either of them, is guilty of a misdemeanor.

Acrobatic and mendicant occupations.

Employment of children in mines, etc.

SECTION 8349. Every person who receives or employs any child under fourteen years of age in any underground works or mine, or in any similar business, is punishable by a fine not exceeding one thousand dollars. .

Penalty.

NEBRASKA.

COMPILED STATUTES—1901.

Employment of children—School attendance.

SECTION 4853 (as amended by chapter 131, Acts of 1907). In school districts other than city and metropolitan city school districts every person having legal or actual charge or control of any child or children or youth not less than seven nor more than fifteen years of age shall, during each school year between the second Monday of July and the last Monday of June following, cause such child or children or youth to attend the public day schools for a period of not less than twelve weeks, and if the public day school of the school district in which said person or persons having charge or control of such child or children or youth may reside shall be in session during the school year between the second Monday of July and the last Monday of June following more than twelve weeks, then the person having legal control of such child or children or youth shall cause each of them to attend such public day school not less than two-thirds of the entire time that said school shall be in session during the school year as aforesaid; and in no case shall such attendance be for a less period than twelve weeks.

Attendance required.

In city and metropolitan city school districts every person residing within such school district who has legal or actual charge or control of any child or children or youth not less than seven nor more than sixteen years of age shall cause such child or children or youth to attend the public day school for the full period each school year in which the public day schools of such school district are in session.

The portion of this act requiring attendance in public day school shall not apply in any case where the child or youth is, for a time equal to that required by this act, instructed in some private or parochial school; or in any case where the child is instructed at home or elsewhere by a person qualified to give instruction in the studies required to be taught in the public schools; or in any case where the child or youth, being of the age of fourteen years, is legally and regularly employed for his own support or the support of those actually depend-

Exemptions.

ent upon him; or in any case where the child or youth is physically or mentally incapacitated for the work done in the schools; or in any case where the child or youth lives more than two miles from the school by the nearest practicable traveled road, unless free transportation to and from such school is furnished to such child or youth.

In case exemption is claimed on account of mental or physical incapacity, the school authorities shall have the right to employ a physician or physicians who shall have authority to examine such child or youth, and if such physician or physicians shall declare that such child or youth is capable of undertaking the work of the schools, then such child or youth shall not be exempt from the requirements of this act.

In case exemption is claimed and granted on account of a child or youth of the age of fourteen years being legally and regularly employed for his own support or the support of those dependent upon him, such child or youth may, in the discretion of those charged with enforcement of this act, be required to attend a public evening school or some other suitable school for not less than two hours each school day and Evening schools. not less than three days each week for a school year of not less than twenty weeks.

*   *   *   *   *   *   *

Employment of women.

Hours of labor.   Section 6942a. No female shall be employed in any manufacturing, mechanical or mercantile establishment, hotel or restaurant in this State, more than sixty hours during any one week and ten hours shall
Night work.   constitute a day's labor. The hours of each day may be so arranged as to permit the employment of such females at any time from six o'clock a. m. to ten o'clock p. m.; but in no case shall such employment exceed ten hours in any one day.

Schedule to be   Sec. 6942b. Every such employer shall post in a conspicuous place
posted.   in every room where such females are employed, a printed notice, stating the number of hours' work required of them each day of the week the hours of commencing and stopping such work and the hours when the time or times allowed for dinner or for other meals begins and ends. Printed forms of said notice shall be furnished by the deputy labor commissioner, and the form of such notice approved by the attorney general of this State.

Seats.   Sec. 6942c. Every such employer in such establishment, shall provide suitable seats for the females so employed, and shall permit the use of such seats by them when they are not necessarily engaged in the active duties for which they are employed.

Penalty.   Sec. 6942d. Any employer, overseer, superintendent or other agent of any such employer who shall violate any of the provisions of this act, shall be fined for each offense in a sum not less than twenty dollars nor more than fifty dollars; and it is hereby made the duty of the deputy labor commissioner to enforce the provisions of this act: *Provided, however,* That nothing in this act shall be construed to prevent any other person from enforcing its provisions.

ACTS OF 1907.

Chapter 66.—*Employment of children—General provisions.*

Age limit.   Section 1. No child under fourteen years of age shall be employed, permitted or suffered to work in, or in connection with, any theater, concert hall, or place of amusement, or any place where intoxicating liquors are sold, or in any mercantile institution, store, office, hotel, laundry, manufacturing establishment, bowling alley, passenger or freight elevator, factory or workshop, or as a messenger or driver therefor, within this State. It shall be unlawful for any person, firm or corporation to employ any child under fourteen years of age in any business or service whatever during the hours when the public schools of the town, township, village or city in which the child resides are in session.

Certificate.   Sec. 2. No child between fourteen and sixteen years of age shall be employed, permitted or suffered to work in any theater, concert hall, or place of amusement, or in any mercantile institution, store, office, hotel, laundry, manufacturing establishment, bowling alley, passenger or freight elevator, factory, or workshop, or as a messenger or driver therefor within this State, unless the person or corporation employing him procures and keeps on file and accessible to the truant officers of the town- or city, the State commissioner of labor and his deputies, and the members of the State board of inspection, an employment certificate as hereinafter prescribed, and keeps two complete lists of all such children employed therein, one on file and one conspicuously posted near the principal entrance of the building in which such children are employed. Upon the termination of the employment of a child so registered, and whose certificate is so filed, such certificate shall be forthwith transmitted by the employer to the city or county superintendent of schools of the county in which the child resides, and shall be turned over to the child named therein upon demand. Any truant officer, the State commissioner of labor, or his deputies, or any member of the State board of inspection may make demand on any employer in whose place of business a child apparently under the age of sixteen years, is employed or permitted or suffered to work, and whose employment certificate is not then filed as required by this section, that such employer shall either furnish him within ten days, evidence satisfactory to him that such child is in fact over sixteen years of age, or shall cease to employ or permit or suffer such child to work in such place of business. The same evidence of the age of such child may be required from such employer as is required on the issuance of an employment certificate as hereinafter provided; and the employer furnishing such evidence shall not be required to furnish any further evidence of the age of the child. In case such employer shall fail to produce and deliver to the truant officer, the State commissioner of labor, or deputy State commissioner of labor, or member of the State board of inspection, within ten days after demand for the same, such evidence of the age of any child as may be required of him under the provisions of this act, and shall thereafter continue to employ such child or permit or suffer such child to work in such place of business, proof of the giving of such notice and of such failure to produce and file such evidence shall be prima facie evidence, in any prosecution brought for a violation of this section, that such child is under sixteen years of age and is unlawfully employed. *Enforcement.*

SEC. 3. An employment certificate shall be approved only by the superintendent of schools of the school corporation in which the child resides, or by a person authorized by him in writing, or where there is no superintendent of schools, by a person authorized by the school district officers: *Provided,* That no school district officer or other person authorized as aforesaid shall have authority to approve such certificate for any child then in, or about to enter, his own employment, or the employment of a firm or corporation of which he is a member, officer or employee, or in whose business he is interested. The officer or person approving such certificate shall have authority to administer the oath provided for therein or in any investigation or examination necessary for the approval thereof. No fee shall be charged for approving any such certificate nor for administering any oath or rendering any services therein in respect thereto. The board of directors of each school corporation shall establish and maintain proper records where copies of all such certificates and all documents connected therewith shall be filed and preserved and shall provide the necessary clerical service for carrying out the provisions of this act. *Approval of certificates.*

SEC. 4. The person authorized to issue an employment certificate shall not issue such certificate until he has received, examined, approved, and filed the following papers, duly executed: (1) The school record of such child, properly filled out and signed as provided in this act, showing that the child has completed the work of the eighth grade of the public schools, or its equivalent, or is regularly attending night school in compliance with section eight (8) of this act. (2) A passport, or duly attested transcript of the certificate of birth or baptism, or other religious or official record, showing the date and place of birth of such child. A duly attested transcript of the birth certificate filed according to law with a registrar of vital statistics, or other officer charged with *Issue of certificates.*

the duty of recording births, shall be conclusive evidence of the age of such child. (3) The affidavit of the parent, or guardian, or custodian of a child, which shall be required, however, only in case none of the documents mentioned in clause two (2) of this section can be produced and filed, showing the place and date of birth of such child; which affidavit must be taken before the officer issuing the employment certificate. Such employment certificate shall not be issued until such child has personally appeared before, and been examined by, the officer issuing the certificate and until such officer shall, after making such examination, sign and file in his office a statement that the child can read and legibly write simple sentences in the English language and that, in his opinion, the child is fourteen years of age, or upwards, and has reached the normal development of a child of its age, and is in sound health and is physically able to perform the work which it intends

Physical fitness. to do. In doubtful cases such physical fitness shall be determined by a medical officer of the board or department of health, or by a physician provided by the State board of inspection. Whenever the person authorized to issue the employment certificate is in doubt about the age of a child, he may require the party or parties making application for the certificate to appear before the judge of the juvenile court, or county judge, where the question of the age of the child shall be determined and the judgment of the court shall be final and binding upon the person issuing the certificate. Notice of the hearing before the court shall be given to some one of the persons mentioned in section two authorized to demand inspection of employment certificates. Every employment certificate shall be signed in the presence of the officer issuing the same by the child in whose name it is issued.

Contents of certificates.   SEC. 5. Such certificate shall state the date and place of birth of such child and describe the color of the hair and eyes, the height and weight and distinguishing facial marks of such child and that the papers required by the preceding section have been duly examined, approved and filed and that the child named in such certificate has appeared before the officer signing the certificate and been examined.

School record.   SEC. 6. The school record required by section four shall be signed by the teacher and principal of the school which such child has attended and shall be furnished, on demand to a child entitled thereto. It shall contain a statement certifying that the child has regularly attended the public schools, or schools equivalent thereto, or parochial schools for not less than three-fourths of the school year previous to his arriving at the age of fourteen years, or during the year previous to applying for such school record and is able to read and write simple sentences in the English language. It shall also state the amount of work completed by such child, measured by the grade of the public day schools in the city or county. Such school record shall also give the age and residence of the child as shown on the records of the school and the name of its parent, or guardian, or custodian.

Lists to be forwarded.   SEC. 7. The superintendent of schools or the school directors of any village, town, or county, shall transmit between the first and tenth day of each month to the office of the State commissioner of labor a list of the names of the children to whom certificates have been issued.

Evening schools.   SEC. 8. Regular attendance of a child at any public evening school, maintained in any city or village where instruction is given not less than twenty weeks each year and three evenings each week and two hours each evening, shall authorize the issuance of a certificate of employment where the schooling certificate fails to show that the child has completed the work of the eighth grade, required by section six: *Provided*, The schooling certificate and all other certificates are otherwise in due form and the applicant further produces a certificate from the superintendent, or principal, of such public evening school, showing the regular attendance of such child at such evening school: *And provided further*, Every child employed under such certificate shall furnish to his employer a weekly certificate showing regular attendance each week while the evening school is in session. Whoever employs a child in violation of the provisions of this section shall be fined not more than fifty dollars ($50.00) for each offense. A parent, guardian or custodian who permits a child under his control to be employed in violation of the provisions of this section shall be fined not more than twenty dollars ($20.00).

SEC. 9. The age and schooling certificate provided for herein shall be made out upon blank forms furnished by the State commissioner of labor and shall be in the following forms: Forms.

SCHOOL ATTENDANCE CERTIFICATE.

(Name of school) (city or town) NEBRASKA, (date) 190–

This certifies that (name of child) has completed the work of the —th grade, and can read and write legibly simple sentences in the English language.

This also certifies that according to the records of this school and in my belief, the said (name of child) was born at (city or town), in —— county, State of —— on the (date) and is now —— years and —— months old, and has attended said school within the past twelve months the following period ——.

(Name of parent or guardian)

(Residence)

(Signature) —— —— teacher

(Signature) —— —— principal

AGE AND SCHOOLING CERTIFICATE.

(City or town) NEBRASKA, (date) 190–

This certifies that I am the (father, mother, guardian or custodian) of (name of child) and that —— was born at —— in —— county State of —— on the —— and is now —— years and —— months old.

(Signature of father, mother, guardian or custodian).

(Name of city or town) NEBRASKA, (date) 190–

There personally appeared before me the above named (name of person signing) and being sworn testified that the foregoing certificate by (him or her) signed is true to the best of (his or her) knowledge or belief.

I hereby approve the foregoing certificate of (name of child), height —— feet —— inches, weight —— pounds —— ounces, complexion (fair or dark) hair (color) eyes (color) having no sufficient reason to doubt that (he or she) is of the age herein certified.

I hereby certify that (he or she can or can not) read at sight and write legibly simple sentences in the English language, that said child has appeared before me and been personally examined by me; that all certificates and papers required by law have, in due form, been presented to, and approved by, me and the same have been placed on file.

(In case the child is attending school insert here the following:)

I further certify that (he or she) is regularly attending the (name of school).

This certificate shall continue in force only so long as the regular attendance of said child at said school is certified weekly by a teacher thereof.

This certificate belongs to (name of child) and is to be surrendered to the superintendent of schools whenever (he or she) leaves the service of the person, firm or corporation holding the same as employer.

(Signature and official title of person

authorized to approve and sign.)

EVENING SCHOOL ATTENDANCE CERTIFICATE.

This certifies that (name of child) is registered in and regularly attends the —— evening school. This also certifies that according to the records of my school and in my belief (name of child) was born at (name of city or town) on the —— day of —— 1—— and is now —— old.

(Name of parent or guardian)

(Signature of teacher)

(Signature of principal)

Duplicate copies of such certificates shall be retained in all cases by the person or officer issuing the same and kept on file by the superintendent of schools or school district directors of the county in which the same are issued.

Hours of labor.   SEC. 10. No person under the age of sixteen years shall be employed or suffered or permitted to work in any theater, concert hall, or place of amusement, or in any mercantile institution, store, office, hotel, laundry, manufacturing establishment, packing house, bowling alley, passenger or freight elevator, factory, workshop, beet field, or as a messenger or driver therefor, more than forty-eight hours in any one week, nor more than eight hours in any one day, nor before the hour of six o'clock in the morning, nor after the hour of eight o'clock in the even-

Night work.   ing. Every employer shall post in a conspicuous place in every room where such children are employed a printed notice stating the hours required of them each day of the week, the hours of commencing and stopping work, and the hours when the time or times allowed for dinner or for other meals begin and end. The printed form of such notice shall be furnished by the State commissioner of labor.

Violations.   SEC. 11. Whoever employs a child under sixteen years of age and whoever, having under his control a child under such age, permits such child to be employed in violation of section one (1), two (2), ten (10) or twelve (12) of this act shall for each offense be fined not more than fifty dollars ($50.00); and whoever continues to employ any child in violation of either of said sections of this act, after being notified by a truant officer, or a deputy commissioner of labor, or a member of the State board of inspection, shall for every day thereafter that such employment continues be fined not less than five dollars ($5.00) nor more than twenty dollars ($20.00). The failure of an employer of child labor to produce, upon the request of a person authorized to demand the same, any employment certificate or list required by this act, shall be prima facie evidence of the illegal employment of any child whose employment certificate is not produced or whose name is not listed. Any corporation or employer retaining employment certificates in violation of section 2 of this act shall be fined ten dollars ($10.00). Every person authorized or required to sign any certificate or statement prescribed by sections four (4) or five (5) of this act, or who knowingly certifies or makes oath to any material false statement therein or who violates either of said sections, shall be fined not to exceed fifty dollars ($50.00). Every person, firm or corporation, agent or manager, superintendent or foreman of any person, firm or corporation who shall refuse admittance to any officer or person authorized to visit or inspect any premises or place of business under the provisions of this act and to produce all certificates and lists he may have, when demanded, after such person shall have announced his name and the office he holds and the purpose of his visit, or shall otherwise obstruct such officers in the performance of their duties as prescribed by this act, shall be guilty of a misdemeanor and upon conviction, shall be fined in any sum not exceeding fifty dollars ($50.00), or be imprisoned not to exceed thirty days. The presence of a child under sixteen years of age, apparently at work, in any of the places of business enumerated in section one (1) of this act shall be prima facie evidence of

Enforcement.   his employment therein. It shall be the duty of the deputy commissioner of labor and the several truant officers to enforce the provisions of this act and every county attorney, when informed by any officer or person authorized to inspect places where child labor is employed, that any of the provisions of this act have been violated, shall file or cause to be filed information against the person or persons guilty of such offense and cause the arrest and prosecution of the same: *Provided,* That nothing in this act shall prevent any other person from causing the enforcement of the provisions of this act. Truant officers shall visit the places of business enumerated in section one (1) of this act to ascertain whether any children are employed therein contrary to the provisions of this act, and they shall report any cases of such illegal employment to the commissioner of labor and to the county attorney.

Board of inspectors.   SEC. 12. It is hereby made the duty of the governor, immediately upon the passage of this act, to appoint five persons, two, at least, of whom shall be women who shall constitute the board of inspectors and who shall serve without compensation. The term for which such inspectors shall serve is hereby made one, two, three, four and five years, respectively. The appointment shall designate the term for which each inspector is appointed. The governor shall, each year, appoint one person to serve for a period of five years and shall also fill any vacancy on the board. The chairman shall be the executive head of the board and shall reside in the county employing the largest number of children under the age of sixteen years. Any member of the board of inspectors shall have power to demand the examination, by some regularly licensed physician, to be selected by the board, of any child under sixteen years of age who may seem physically unable to perform the labor at which such child may be employed, and no child under sixteen shall be employed who can not obtain a certificate of fitness from such physician.

SEC. 13. No child under the age of sixteen years shall be employed in any work which by reason of the nature of the work, or place of performance, is dangerous to life or limb or in which its health may be injured or its morals may be depraved. Any parent, guardian, or other person, who, having under his control any child, causes or permits said child to work or be employed in violation of this section shall be guilty of a misdemeanor and upon conviction shall be fined not more than fifty dollars ($50.00), or be imprisoned not exceeding ten days. Dangerous, etc., employments.

NEVADA.

ACTS OF 1909.

CHAPTER 158.—*Juvenile court law—Children employed in street trades.*

SECTION 1 (as amended by chapter 197, Acts of 1911). This act shall be known as the "Juvenile Court Law" and shall apply only to children under the age of eighteen years not now or hereafter inmates of a State institution, except as otherwise herein provided. Scope of act.

For the purpose of this act the words "dependent child" and "neglected child" shall mean any child * * * who, while under the age of ten years, is found begging, peddling or selling any article or articles, or singing or playing any musical instrument for gain or giving any public entertainments upon the street, or accompanies or is used in the aid of any person so doing. * * *. Definitions.

ACTS OF 1911.

CHAPTER 133.—*Education—Compulsory school attendance.*

SECTION 203. Each parent, guardian, or other person, in the State of Nevada, having control or charge of any child between the ages of eight and sixteen years shall be required to send such child to a public school during the time in which a public school shall be in session in the school district in which said child resides; but such attendance shall be excused: * * * Attendance required.

4. When satisfactory evidence is presented to the board of trustees that the child's labor is necessary for its own or its parent's support. * * * Exception.

NEW HAMPSHIRE.

PUBLIC STATUTES—1891.

CHAPTER 180.—*Hours of labor of women and children.*

SECTION 14 (as amended by chapter 94, Acts of 1907). No woman and no minor under eighteen years of age shall be employed in a manufacturing or mechanical establishment for more than nine hours and forty minutes in one day except in the following cases: I. To make a shorter day's work for one day in the week. II. To make up time lost on some day in the same week in consequence of the stopping Hours of labor.

of machinery upon which such person was dependent for employment.

III. When it is necessary to make repairs to prevent interruption of the ordinary running of the machinery. In no case shall the hours of labor exceed fifty-eight in one week.

Schedule to be posted. SEC. 15. The proprietors of every such establishment shall keep posted in a conspicuous place in every room where such persons are employed a notice printed in plain, large letters, stating the exact time of beginning and of stopping work in the forenoon and in the afternoon, and the number of hours' *work required of them each day of the week.

Penalty. SEC. 16. If any owner, agent, superintendent, or overseer of any such establishment shall willfully violate the provisions of either of the two preceding sections, he shall be fined not exceeding fifty dollars for each offense.

Certificate. SEC. 17. A certificate of the age of a minor, made by him and by his parents or guardian and presented to the employer at the time the minor is employed, shall be conclusive evidence of his age upon a prosecution for the violation of the provisions of section fourteen.

False statement. SEC. 18. If any person shall make and utter a false certificate in regard to the age of a minor, with intent to evade the provisions of this chapter, he shall be fined twenty-five dollars, or be imprisoned thirty days, or both, for each offense.

Limitation. SEC. 19. * * * Prosecutions under sections sixteen and eighteen shall be barred unless begun within one year after the offense was committed.

CHAPTER 265.—*Employment of children—Certain employments forbidden.*

Acrobatic, etc., occupations. SECTION 3. If any person shall employ or exhibit a child under the age of fourteen years in dancing, playing on musical instruments, singing, walking on a wire or rope, or riding or performing as a gymnast, contortionist, or acrobat in any circus or theatrical exhibition, or in any public place whatsoever, or shall cause, procure, or encourage any such child to engage therein, or if any person having the custody or control of any such child shall permit him to be so employed, such person shall be fined not exceeding one hundred dollars; but nothing in this section shall be construed to prevent the education of children in vocal and instrumental music, or their employment as musicians in any church, chapel, or school, or school exhibition, or to prevent their taking part in any concert or musical exhibition.

Employment to sell obscene, etc., literature. SEC. 7. No person shall in any manner hire, employ, or use any minor to sell, or give away, or in any manner to distribute any such literature, picture, or advertisement [devoted to the publication or illustration of stories or accounts of bloodshed, lust, or crime, or principally made up of police reports and criminal news].

Permitting to sell. SEC. 8. No person having the care or control of a minor child shall permit such child to sell or give away any such reading matter or any such advertisement.

Violations. SEC. 9. If any person shall violate any of the provisions of the three preceding sections, he shall be fined not more than one hundred dollars, or be imprisoned not more than six months, or both.

ACTS OF 1895. •

CHAPTER 16.—*Seats for female employees.*

Seats to be provided. SECTION 1. Every person, firm, or corporation employing females in any manufacturing, mechanical, or mercantile establishment in this State, shall provide suitable seats for the use of the females so employed, and shall permit the use of such seats by them when they are not necessarily engaged in the active duties for which they are employed.

Penalty. SEC. 2. Any person, firm, or corporation violating any of the provisions of this act shall be punished by a fine of not less than ten dollars nor more than.thirty dollars for each offense.

ACTS OF 1903.

CHAPTER 95.—*Employment of women and minors in barrooms—Sale of liquor to employees.*

SECTION 17 (as amended by chapter 49, Acts of 1905). It shall not be lawful

*   *   *   *   *   *   *

2. To permit any girl or woman * * * to sell or serve any liquor on the premises; or to permit any male person under the age of twenty-one years to sell or serve any liquor on the premises, except to bona fide registered guests in their rooms and in dining rooms with meals under licenses of the first class.   *Who may not be employed.*

*   *   *   *   *   *   *

SEC. 27 (as amended by chapter 49, Acts of 1905). The * * * employer of a person who has the habit of drinking intoxicating liquor to excess * * * may give notice in writing, signed by him or her, to any person requesting him not to sell or deliver such liquor to the person having such habit. The notice provided for in this section may be served by any officer duly qualified to serve process or by any individual of lawful age. Such officer or individual shall make return of service of said notice to the clerk of the city or town in which such service is made, giving the name of the party on whom served, the location by street and number, if any, of the place of business of the licensee on whom service is made, and the date and hour of service. An officer making service of such notice shall make his return thereon as upon civil process. An individual making service of such notice shall sign and make oath to the return thereon. The clerk of the city or town in which such service is made shall receive, file and preserve a copy of such notice and return without charge therefor. If the person so notified, at any time within twelve months thereafter, sells or delivers any liquor to the person having such a habit, or permits him to loiter on his premises, the person giving the notice may, in an action of tort, recover of the person notified, not less than one hundred nor more than five hundred dollars, as may be assessed as damages; but an employer who gives such notice shall not recover unless he is injured in his person or property, and a druggist or apothecary shall not be liable hereunder for a sale made upon the prescription of a physician. * * *   *Employers may give notice.*

ACTS OF 1911.

CHAPTER 162.—*Employment of children—General provisions.*

SECTION 1. No child under the age of twelve shall be employed, or permitted or suffered to work, in, about, or in connection with any mill, factory, workshop, quarry, mercantile establishment, tenement house, manufactory or workshop, store, business office, telegraph or telephone office, restaurant, bakery, hotel, barber-shop, apartment house, bootblack stand or parlor, or in the distribution or transmission of merchandise or messages; nor shall any child under the age of fourteen be employed, or permitted or suffered to work, in any of the aforesaid while the public schools are in session in the district in which he resides.   *Age limit.*

SEC. 2. No child under the age of sixteen shall be employed, or permitted or suffered to work, in any establishment named in section 1 during the time in which the public schools are in session in the district in which he resides, unless he can read understandingly and write legibly simple sentences in the English language: *Provided, however,* That if any child shall have reached the age of fourteen and shall have attended an English-taught school regularly for not less than three years and shall then be deemed by the superintendent of schools, or other person authorized to grant employment certificates, to be mentally incapable of learning to read and write legibly the English language in the regular schools, the case may be referred to the state superintendent of public instruction, who, after investiga-   *Work during school time.*

tion either by himself or by his agent, may issue a permit authorizing the employment of such child even though such child may be unable to read understandingly and write legibly simple sentences in the English language.

Inspection.

SEC. 3. Whenever requested by the superintendent of public instruction, the State board of health shall cause to be made an inspection of any factory or other place in which children under the age of sixteen are employed, and may require the discharge of any child or children found employed therein who by reason of physical condition, of unsanitary conditions of employment, or of development below the normal development of children of that age, cannot in their judgment continue to be employed without undue risk to health.

Street trades.

SEC. 4. No boy under ten and no girl under sixteen years of age shall sell or expose or offer for sale newspapers, magazines, periodicals or other merchandise in any street or public p ace. No child shall work as a bootblack in any street or public place unless he is over ten years of age.

Night work of messengers, etc.

SEC. 5. No person under the age of eighteen years shall be employed or permitted to work as a messenger for a telegraph, telephone, or messenger company in the distribution, transmission, or delivery of goods or messages before five o'clock in the morning or after ten o'clock in the evening of any day.

Hours of labor.

SEC. 6. No boy under the age of sixteen years, and no girl under the age of eighteen years, shall be employed, or permitted or suffered to work, at any gainful occupation, other than domestic service or work on a farm, more than fifty-eight hours in any one week, nor more than eleven hours in any one day; nor before the hour of half-past six o'clock in the morning, nor after the hour of seven o'clock in the evening,—except that minors sixteen years of age or over may work in retail stores and telephone exchanges until ten o'clock in the evening.

Night work.

Certificates.

SEC. 7. No child under sixteen years of age shall be employed, or permitted or suffered to work, in, about, or in connection with, any place or establishment named in section 1, unless the person, firm, or corporation employing such child, procures and keeps on file, and accessible to any truant officer, or other authorized inspector, an employment certificate as hereinafter prescribed.

Surrender of certificates.

SEC. 8. On the termination of the employment of a child whose employment certificate is on file, such certificate shall be kept by the employer and surrendered to any authorized inspector on demand.

Who to issue.

SEC. 9. An employment certificate shall be issued only by the superintendent of schools, or where there is no superintendent, by a person authorized by the school board: *Provided, however,* That no person authorized as aforesaid shall have authority to issue such certificate for any child then in or about to enter such person's own employment or the employment of a firm or corporation of which he is a member, officer, or employee; in the city of Manchester the provisions of chapter 205 of the Session Laws of 1905 shall remain in force, but the person appointed under such provisions shall be subject to the terms of this act.

Proof of age, etc.

SEC. 10. The person authorized to issue an employment certificate shall not issue such certificate until he has received, examined, approved, and filed the following papers duly executed: (1) The school record of such child properly filled out and signed, as provided in this act. (2) A passport or duly attested transcript of the certificate of birth or baptism or public record, showing the date and place of birth of such child. (3) A certificate from a medical officer of the local board of health, or from a physician designated by the school board, certifying that the child has reached the normal development of a child of his age, and that he is in sufficiently sound health and physically able to perform the work which he intends to do.

Personal appearance.

SEC. 11. No employment certificate shall be issued until the child in question has personally appeared before and been examined by the person issuing the certificate.

Contents of certificate.

SEC. 12. Every such employment certificate shall state the name, sex, and date and place of birth, of the child, shall describe the color of hair and eyes, the height and weight and any distinguishing facial marks of such child; that all papers required by the preceding sections have been duly examined, approved and filed; that the child named in the certificate has appeared before the person signing the same and been examined; and that such child has been found to be able to read understandingly and write legibly simple sentences in the English language.   Every such certificate shall be signed, in the presence of the person issuing the same, by the child in whose name it is issued, and shall show the date of its issue.

SEC. 13. The school record required by this act shall be signed by the principal or chief executive officer of the school which the child has attended, and shall be furnished on demand to a child entitled thereto.   Such record shall certify that the child has regularly attended the public schools, or private schools lawfully approved as such, for not less than three hundred half-days, as shown by the school register, during the year previous to his arriving at the age of fourteen, or during the year previous to applying for such school record, and that he is able to read understandingly and write legibly simple sentences in the English language.   Such school record shall also give the date of birth and residence of the child as shown on the records of the school and the name of his parent, guardian or custodian. School record.

SEC. 14. The superintendent of schools or other person authorized to issue employment certificates shall keep a record of the same in a book.   Such record shall contain a list of the names of all children to whom certificates are granted, numbered consecutively, together with the date of issue and the signature of the officer issuing the certificate, and such books shall be carefully preserved. Record to be kept.

SEC. 15. All blank forms for records used in the enforcement and administration of this act shall be uniform throughout the State, shall be prescribed by the superintendent of public instruction, and shall be furnished by the State, and methods of keeping the same shall be approved by him as being within the contemplation of this act. Forms.

SEC. 16. The truant officer of each school district shall visit, inspect, and cause to be enforced the provisions of this act in his district, and for this purpose shall have power to serve warrants. Enforcement.

SEC. 17. The superintendent of public instruction shall appoint not exceeding three State inspectors, who shall be paid their necessary expenses and such compensation as the governor and council shall determine, not exceeding $1,200 per annum each, and who shall devote their whole time to their work.   The State inspectors, under the direction of the superintendent of public instruction, shall inspect all factories and other places of employment within the contemplation of this act and all records and methods of enforcement.   They shall have the same power as to enforcement and the serving of warrants as the several truant officers.   The superintendent of public instruction, with the approval of the attorney general, may employ counsel, and provide legal assistance wherever the same may, in his opinion, be necessary for the enforcement of the provisions of this act, and the cost thereof shall be a charge upon the appropriation hereinafter provided. Inspectors.

SEC. 19. An inspector or truant officer shall make demand upon any employer in or about whose place or establishment a child apparently under the age of sixteen years is employed, or permitted or suffered to work, and whose employment certificate is not filed as required by this act, that such employer shall either furnish him within ten days satisfactory evidence that such child is in fact over sixteen years of age, or shall cease to employ, or permit, or suffer such child to work, in such place or establishment.   The inspector shall require from such employer the same evidence of age of such child as is required in the issuance of an employment certificate, and the employer furnishing such evidence shall not be required to furnish any further evidence of the age of the child. Certificate may be demanded.

SEC. 20. Whoever employs any child, and whoever, having under his control as parent, guardian or otherwise, any child, permits or suffers such child to be employed or to work in violation of any of the provisions of this act, shall be fined not less than five nor more than two hundred dollars, or be imprisoned for not less than ten nor more than thirty days, or both, in the discretion of the court. Violations.

49450°—S. Doc. 645, 61-2, vol 19——49

Continued violations.   SEC. 21. Whoever continues to employ any child in violation of any of the provisions of this act, after being notified thereof by an inspector, or truant officer, shall for every day thereafter that such employment continues, be fined not less than five nor more than twenty dollars.

False statements.   SEC. 22. Any person authorized to sign any certificate or paper called for by this act, who certifies to any materially false statement therein, shall be fined not less than five nor more than two hundred dollars, or be imprisoned for not less than five nor more than thirty days, or both, in the discretion of the court.

Refusal to produce certificate.   SEC. 23. Refusal by an employer to produce any employment certificate required by this act shall be prima facie evidence of the illegal employment of any child whose employment certificate is not produced.

Violations by school officers.   SEC. 24. Any superintendent of schools or other person issuing employment certificates, who fails to comply with the provisions of this act shall be fined not less than five nor more than twenty-five dollars.

•

NEW JERSEY.

COMPILED STATUTES—1910.

Employment of children—Certain employments forbidden.

(Page 2816.)

Children under 15 years of age.   SECTION 47. Any person having the care, custody or control of any minor child under the age of fifteen years who shall in any manner sell, apprentice, give away or otherwise dispose of such child, and any person who shall take, receive, or employ such child for the vocation or occupation of rope or wire-walking, or as an acrobat, gymnast, contortionist or rider, and any person having the care, custody or control of any minor child whatsoever who shall sell, apprentice, give away or otherwise dispose of such child, or who shall take, receive or employ such child for any obscene, indecent or illegal exhibition or vocation, or any vocation injurious to the health or dangerous to the life or limb of such child engaged therein, or for the purpose of prostitution, and any person who shall retain, harbor or employ any minor child in or about any assignation-house or brothel, or in any place where any obscene, indecent or illegal exhibition takes place, shall be guilty of a misdemeanor, and upon conviction thereof, before any justice of the peace, magistrate or court of record, shall be fined not less than fifty dollars nor more than one hundred dollars for each offense.

Under 18 years of age.   SEC. 48. Any person having the care, custody or control, lawful or unlawful, or any minor child under the age of eighteen years, who shall use such minor or apprentice, give away, let out, hire or otherwise dispose of such minor to any person for the purpose of singing, playing on a musical instrument, begging, or for any mendicant business whatsoever, in the streets, roads or other highways of this State, and whosoever shall take, receive, hire, employ, use or have in custody any such minor for the vocation, occupation, calling, service or purpose of singing, playing upon musical instruments or begging upon the streets, roads or other highways of the State, or for any mendicant business whatever, shall be guilty of a misdemeanor, and upon conviction thereof, in the manner provided in the first section of this act, shall be fined not less than fifty dollars nor more than one hundred dollars.

Employment in saloons, etc.   SEC. 49. Any person having the care, custody or control of any minor child under the age of fifteen years, who shall in any manner sell, apprentice, give away or permit such child to sing, dance, act or in any manner exhibit in any dance house whatever, or in any concert saloon, theater or place of entertainment where wines or spirituous or malt liquors are sold or given away, or with which any place for the sale of wines or spirituous or malt liquors is directly or indirectly connected by any passageway or entrance, and any proprietor of any dance house whatever, or any such concert saloon, theater or place of entertainment so employing any such child, shall be guilty of a misdemeanor, and upon conviction thereof, in the manner provided in the first section of this act, shall be fined not less than fifty dollars nor more than one hundred dollars for each offense.

SEC. 50. Any person who shall take, receive, hire or employ any child under twelve years of age in any underground works or mine or like place whatsoever, shall be guilty of a misdemeanor, and upon conviction thereof, in the manner provided in the first section of this act, shall be fined not less than ten dollars nor more than fifty dollars. Employment in mines.

Employment of children—General provisions.

(Page 3023.)

SECTION 16. No child under the age of fourteen years shall be employed, allowed or permitted to work in any factory, workshop, mill or place where the manufacture of goods of any kind is carried on; any corporation, firm, individual, parent, parents or custodian of any child who shall violate any of the provisions of this section, shall be liable to a penalty of fifty dollars for each offense. Age limit.

SEC. 17. The word custodian as used in this act shall include any person, organization or society having the legal custody of a child. Definition.

SEC. 18. If at the time of the employment of a child, the proofs of age specified in subdivisions I. and II. of this section, are filed with the corporation, firm or person employing the child, such proofs shall be conclusive evidence of the age of child in a suit against such employer for a violation of section one [16]: *Provided, however,* That correct copies of all papers, certificates, passports and affidavits relating to such employment shall be mailed, postage prepaid, to the department having charge of the enforcement of this act, at Trenton, New Jersey, within twenty-four hours after the same are filed, together with a statement of the legal name of the person, firm or corporation employing such child. Evidence.

I. The parent, parents or custodian shall make and swear to an affidavit before some officer authorized by the law of this State to take affidavits, setting forth the following facts: The name of the child in full; his or her residence, giving street and number; place where and year, month and day when born; name of farther; maiden name of mother; church attended, if any; school last attended and time when, if any, and where the church and school are situated; if child was baptized, name and location of church or parish in which such baptism took place; there must accompany such affidavit a transcript of the record of the child's birth; duly attested by an officer having by law the authority to keep records of birth in the State, county, town or city in which the child was born; if no such birth record can be obtained and the child was baptized, then a certified copy of the baptismal record of the church or parish in which such baptism took place, duly certified as a true copy, under the hand of the person having the custody of such church or parish records, shall accompany the affidavit, and the affidavit shall set forth the age of child at time of baptism. Native - born children.

II. An affidavit to be made by the same persons and containing the same statement of facts as in the case of native born children, with an additional statement that the child named in the affidavit is the same mentioned and described in the passport under which the child was admitted to this country; a true copy of said passport must in all cases be attached to the affidavit. Foreign - born children.

III. The commissioner shall have power to issue permits of employment to children upon the production of evidence of the child's age satisfactory to him: *Provided,* That he shall first be satisfied that the child can not obtain a transcript of birth record, a baptismal certificate or passport, as provided in either subdivision I. or II. Evidence.

SEC. 19. In any suit brought to recover a penalty for violation of section one [16] of this act, a copy of the baptismal record, certified to be a true copy under the hand of the person having the custody of such records for the church or parish in which such child was baptized, shall be prima facie evidence of the child's age (provided, that in case the age of the child is not set forth in the baptismal record, that there shall be other proof showing the age of the child at the time he or she was baptized). Records as evidence.

SEC. 20. The commissioner, assistant or any inspector is hereby empowered to demand of any parent, parents or custodian, proof of the age of a child satisfactory to the commissioner, and such parent, Enforcement.

parents or custodian shall, within five days after such demand is made, furnish to such officer proofs of such child's age; and in event of the failure to procure and furnish such proof of age, such child shall be discharged by his or her employer upon notice in writing signed by the commissioner, and shall not be reemployed until such proof of age shall have been furnished to the commissioner; any person violating the provisions of this section shall be liable to a penalty of fifty dollars for each offense.

False state-ments. SEC. 21. Any one who shall swear falsely to any affidavit or present any certificate or passport which he or she knows to be false, and any person or persons who shall aid, assist or advise the making of a false affidavit or the obtaining of a false certificate or passport, shall be liable to a penalty of fifty dollars for each offense.

Physical fitness. SEC. 22. The commissioner, assistant or the inspectors shall have power to demand a certificate of physical fitness from some regular practicing physician in the case of minors under the age of sixteen years, who, in the judgment of such officer, shall be physically unable to do the work in which such minor is employed, and shall have the power to prohibit the employment of such minor until he or she shall produce a certificate of physical fitness; and any manufacturer or employer who shall retain in his employ a minor after such certificate shall be demanded, shall be liable to a penalty of twenty-five dollars.

Register. SEC. 23. A corporation, firm or person, owning or operating a place coming under the provisions of this act and employing, allowing or permitting minors under the age of sixteen years to work therein, shall keep or cause to be kept in the main office of such place, in the town or city where such place is located, a register in which shall be recorded the names, places of residence and time of employment of all such minors working under certificates, transcripts, passports or affidavits; such registers and certificates, transcripts and affidavits shall be produced for inspection upon demand of the commissioner, assistant or any of the inspectors; truant officers shall have the same right as inspectors to examine such registers and the certificates, transcripts, passports or affidavits, when authorized in writing so to do by the commissioner; any corporation, firm or person failing to keep such register or refusing to permit the person herein authorized to inspect the same or the certificates, transcripts, passports or affidavits, shall be liable to a penalty of fifty dollars for each offense.

Hours per week. SEC. 24. No minor under the age of sixteen years shall be employed, permitted or allowed to work in a place coming under the provisions of this act more than ten hours a day, or fifty-five hours in a week, and between the fourth day of July, in the year nineteen hundred and ten, and the fourth day of July, in the year nineteen hundred and eleven, no minor under the age of fifteen years shall be employed, Night work permitted or allowed to work in a place coming under the provisions of this act between the hours of six o'clock in the evening and six o'clock in the morning, and after the fourth day of July, nineteen hundred and eleven, no minor under the age of sixteen years shall be employed, permitted or allowed to work in a place coming under the provisions of this act between the hours of six o'clock in the evening and six o'clock in the morning. Any corporation, firm or person permitting or allowing any person to work contrary to the provisions of this section shall be liable to a penalty of fifty dollars for each offense.

Affidavits. SEC. 25. Affidavits of the age of children made and filed with the manufacturer before this act takes effect, shall have the same force and effect as the proofs required under subdivisions I. and II. of section three [18], of this act.

Seats for female employees.

(Page 3037.)

Seats to be pro-vided. SECTION 73. Every person or corporation employing female employees in any manufacturing, mechanical or mercantile establishment in this State shall provide suitable seats for the use of the female employees so employed, and shall permit the use of such seats by them when they are not necessarily engaged in the active duties for which they are employed.

SEC. 74. Any person or corporation who shall be guilty of any violation **Penalty.**
of the provisions of this act shall be liable to a penalty of fifty dollars
for each offense: *Provided*, That ten days' notice in writing shall be **Proviso.**
given by any person or persons who may choose to do so, to any person
or persons or corporation violating this act, that they are required to
comply with the provisions of the first section of this act [sec. 73], and
any person or corporation failing to comply therewith upon or before
the expiration of ten days from the date of service of such notice, shall
be liable to the said penalty of fifty dollars for each offense, to be
recovered in an action of debt in any district court in any city or
before any justice of the peace having jurisdiction in civil causes;
* * *

Hours of labor in factories—Employment of women and children.

(Page 3038.)

SECTION 75. * * *, fifty-five hours shall constitute a week's work in **Hours of labor.**
any factory, workshop or establishment where the manufacture of any
goods whatever is carried on; and the periods of employment shall be
from seven o'clock in the forenoon until twelve o'clock noon, and from
one o'clock in the afternoon until six o'clock in the evening of every
working day except Saturday, upon which last named day the period
of employment shall be from seven o'clock in the forenoon until twelve
o'clock noon.

SEC. 76. No person under the age of eighteen years, male or female, **Employment**
and no woman above that age shall be employed in any factory, work- **of women and children.**
shop or manufacturing establishment except during the periods of
employment hereinbefore mentioned: *Provided*, That the provisions **Proviso.**
in this act in relation to the hours of employment shall not apply to or
affect any person engaged in preserving perishable goods in fruit canning
establishments or in any factory engaged in the manufacture of glass.

SEC. 77. The inspector of factories shall investigate any reported **Enforcement.**
violation of the provisions of this act and of the act to which this is a
supplement, after it has been discovered by him or brought to his
notice, * * *

SEC. 78. Any manufacturer or other employer who shall violate any **Penalty.**
of the provisions of this act shall be liable to a penalty of one hundred
dollars for each offense, * * *

Seats for female employees in stores.

(Page 3041.)

SECTION 85. Every individual, firm, or corporation or the managing **Seats to be pro-**
agent of such individual, firm, or corporation, having in his or their **vided.**
employ one or more females engaged in the services and operations
incident to any commercial employment, shall provide and maintain
seats of a suitable kind, conveniently situated at or near the counter,
workbench, or other places where her or their work is ordinarily performed, for the use of such females, who shall be allowed free access to
such seats at all times except when engaged in the discharge of duties
that can not properly be performed in a sitting position.

SEC. 86. It shall be the duty of the commissioner of labor and his **Enforcement.**
authorized deputies to see that the provisions of this act are carried
out in all the mercantile establishments throughout the State in which
female labor is employed, and the said commissioner or one of his
deputies shall thereafter at reasonable intervals examine and inspect
all such mercantile establishments for the purpose of seeing that the
seats as provided for in this act are fully maintained, and that female
employees are permitted to use them freely and without hindrance
according to the spirit of this act.

SEC. 87. Any individual, firm or corporation owning or managing **Violations.**
an establishment to which this act applies, who shall fail to comply
with its requirements within ten days after the date on which notice
to do so has been served by the commissioner of labor or one of his
deputies shall be liable to a penalty of twenty-five dollars (25) for
each offense, and a failure to comply within the period of ten days
(10) with such repetition of the notice as may be necessary, shall each
constitute a separate offense.

Employment of children—School attendance.

(Page 4775.)

School attendance required.

SECTION 153. Every parent, guardian or other person having control of a child between the ages of seven and seventeen years inclusive shall cause such child to regularly attend a day school in which at least the common-school branches of reading, writing, arithmetic, spelling, English grammar and geography are taught by a competent teacher, or receive equivalent instruction elsewhere than at school, unless such child is above the age of fifteen years and has completed the grammar-school course (prescribed by the state board of education), and in addition thereto is regularly and lawfully employed in some useful occupation or service. Such regular attendance shall be during all the days and hours that the public schools are in session in the school district in which the child resides, unless it shall be shown to the satisfaction of the board of education of the school district in which such child resides, that the bodily or mental condition of such child is such as to prevent his or her attendance at school. If such child be under the age of seventeen years and has completed the grammar-school course and is not regularly and lawfully employed in any useful occupation or service, such child shall attend the high

High school.

school or manual-training school in said school district in which such child resides, if there is a high school or manual-training school in said district; if there is no high school or manual-training school in said school district, said child shall be transported to a high school or manual-training school as provided in the act to which this is an amendment. Any child above the age of fourteen years who submits satisfactory evidence to the board of education of the school district in

Necessary employment

which such child resides, that it is necessary that such child should be employed in some occupation or service, may be granted by said board of education a certificate exempting him or her from the provisions of this section, such exemption to continue so long as said child shall be regularly employed as aforesaid.

ACTS OF 1911.

CHAPTER 136.—*Mercantile establishments—Employment of children—Regulations for safety and sanitation.*

Employment during school time.

SECTION 1. No child under the age of fourteen years shall be employed, allowed or permitted to work in any mercantile establishment during any of the hours in which the public schools are in session in the district in which such child resides; any corporation, firm or individual who shall employ, allow or permit to work in any mer

Age limit.

cantile establishment any child under the age of fourteen years during the time prohibited by this section shall incur a penalty of fifty dollars.

Hours of labor.

SEC. 2. No child under the age of sixteen years shall be employed, allowed or permitted to work in or in connection with any mercantile establishment more than fifty-eight hours in any one week, or before seven o'clock in the morning or after seven o'clock in the evening of any day (excepting one day in the week, when such minors may

Night work.

be permitted to work until nine o'clock in the evening). The provisions of this section shall not apply to the employment of such minors between the fifteenth day and the twenty-fifth day of December, inclusive, when such minors may be permitted to work until ten o'clock in the evening; any corporation, firm or individual who shall violate any of the provisions of this section shall be liable to a penalty of fifty dollars.

Enforcement.

SEC. 3. It shall be the duty of the commissioner of labor, the assistant commissioner, or the inspectors of the department of labor, or truant officers or other person empowered by law, to compel the attendance of children at school, and they shall have power to investigate and inspect all mercantile establishments coming under the intent and provisions of this act.

Registers.

SEC. 4. A corporation, firm or person owning or operating a place or places coming under the provisions of this act, and employing, allowing or permitting children actually or apparently under sixteen years of age to work therein, shall keep or cause to be kept in the main office of such place in the town or city in which such place is located, a register or record in which shall be recorded the name, place of residence and time of employment of all such minors employed therein, together with a transcript of the record of birth of such minors duly attested by an officer having by law the authority to keep records of birth in the State, county or city in which such child was born; if no such birth certificate can be obtained, and the child was baptized, then a certified copy of the baptismal record of the church or parish in which such baptism took place, duly certified as a true copy under the hand of the person having the custody of such church or parish records, which shall set forth the age of the child at the time of baptism. In the case of foreign-born children, the same transcript of the record of the birth or baptismal certificate shall be required as is required of a native-born child, in addition to the passport under which such child was admitted to this country, or a true copy of the same. The commissioner of labor shall have power to issue permits of employment to children, **Permits.** upon the production of evidence of the child's age, satisfactory to the commissioner: *Provided,* That he shall first be satisfied that the child cannot obtain a transcript of the birth record or passport or a baptismal certificate as above provided; such registers, certificates and transcripts shall be produced for inspection upon demand of the commissioner, assistant, or any of the inspectors, or any truant officer or other person empowered by law to compel the attendance of children at school; any corporation, firm or person failing to keep such registers, or refusing to permit the persons herein, authorized to inspect the same, or the certificates, transcripts and passports, shall be liable to a penalty of fifty dollars for each offense.

Sec. 5. Anyone who shall swear falsely to any affidavit or present **False state-** any certificate or passport which he or she knows to be false, and any **ments.** person or persons who shall aid, assist or advise the making of a false affidavit or the obtaining of a false certificate or passport, shall be liable to a penalty of fifty dollars for each offense.

Sec. 6. The commissioner of labor, his assistant, or any inspector, or **Inspection.** truant officer, or other person empowered by law to compel the attendance of children at school, is hereby empowered to enter into and inspect at any reasonable time and without notice or request for permission all mercantile establishments coming under the provisions of this act and to demand of any parent, custodian or guardian proof of the age of the child satisfactory to the commissioner, and such parent, parents, custodian or guardians shall, within five days after such demand is made, furnish to such officer proof of such child's age; and in the event of the failure to procure and furnish such proof of age, such child shall be discharged by his or her employer upon notice in writing, signed by the commissioner, and shall not be reemployed until such proof of age shall have been furnished to the commissioner.

Sec. 9. Every mercantile establishment shall contain sufficient, **Water - closets,** suitable, convenient and separate water-closets for each sex, which **etc.** shall be properly screened, ventilated and kept clean; and also, if ordered by the commissioner of labor, a suitable and convenient wash room; the water-closets used by women shall have separate approaches; if women or girls are employed, a dressing-room shall be provided for them when ordered by the commissioner.

CHAPTER 363.—*Employment of children—Messenger service.*

SECTION 1. No person under the age of twenty-one years in cities of **Night work pro-** the first class, and no person under the age of eighteen years in other **hibited.** municipalities, shall be employed or permitted to work as a messenger for or by any telegraph, telephone or messenger corporation, firm or person owning, engaged in or operating the business of distributing, transmitting or delivering goods or messages or in the performance of other service, before five o'clock in the morning or after ten o'clock in the evening of any day: *Provided,* That the commissioner of labor shall have the power to grant permits under extraordinary circumstances for the delivery of telegrams or telephone messages between the hours of ten p. m. and five a. m.

Violations.   SEC. 2. Any such corporation, firm or person engaged in or operating the business of distributing, transmitting or delivering goods or messages as aforesaid, who shall violate any of the provisions of this act, shall be liable to a penalty of one hundred dollars for each offense, to be sued for in an action of debt, for the use of the State as hereinafter provided. Any repetition or repetitions thereof shall each constitute a separate offense.

Enforcement.   SEC. 3. It shall be the duty of the commissioner of labor and his authorized deputies to enforce the provisions of this act, and to examine and inspect, at reasonable intervals, the business and practice of all telegraph, telephone or messenger corporations, firms and persons owning, engaged in or operating the business of distributing, transmitting or delivering goods or messages or in the performance of other service for the purpose of enforcing the provisions of this act.

NEW YORK.

CONSOLIDATED LAWS—1909.

CHAPTER 14.—*Earnings of minors.*

Payment to minors valid, when.   SECTION 72. Where a minor is in the employment of a person other than his parent or guardian, payment to such minor of his wages is valid, unless such parent or guardian notify the employer in writing, within thirty days after the commencement of such service, that such wages are claimed by such parent or guardian, but whenever such notice is given at any time payments to the minor shall not be valid for services rendered thereafter.

CHAPTER 16. (as amended by chapter 140, Acts of 1910).—*Employment of children—School attendance.*

School attendance required.   SECTION 621. 1. Every child within the compulsory school ages, in proper physical and mental condition to attend school, residing in a city or school district having a population of five thousand or more and employing a superintendent of schools, shall regularly attend upon instruction as follows:

(a) Each child between seven and fourteen years of age shall attend the entire time during which the school attended is in session, which period shall not be less than one hundred and sixty days of actual school.

(b) Each child between fourteen and sixteen years of age not regularly and lawfully engaged in any useful employment or service, and to whom an employment certificate has not been duly issued under the provisions of the labor law, shall so attend the entire time during which the school attended is in session.

2. Every such child, residing elsewhere than in a city or school district having a population of five thousand or more and employing a superintendent of schools, shall attend upon instruction as many days annually between the first day of October and the following June as the public school of the district in which such child resides, shall be in session during such period, as follows:

(a) Each child between eight and fourteen years of age.

(b) Each child between fourteen and sixteen years of age not regularly and lawfully engaged in any useful employment or service.

Attendance on night schools.   SEC. 622. Every boy between fourteen and sixteen years of age, in a city of the first class or a city of the second class in possession of an employment certificate duly issued under the provisions of the labor law, who has not completed such course of study as is required for graduation from the elementary public schools of such city, and who does not hold either a certificate of graduation from the public elementary school or the preacademic certificate issued by the Regents or the certificate of the completion of an elementary course issued by by the education department, shall attend the public evening schools of such city, or other evening schools offering an equivalent course of instruction, for not less than six hours each week, for a period of not less than sixteen weeks or upon a trade school a period of eight hours per week for sixteen weeks in each school or calendar year.

SEC. 624. Every person in parental relation to a child within the compulsory school ages and in proper physical and mental condition to attend school, shall cause such child to attend upon instruction, as follows: *Attendance of children under 16.*

1. In cities and school districts having a population of five thousand or above, every child between seven and sixteen years of age as required by section six hundred and twenty-one of this act unless an employment certificate shall have been duly issued to such child under the provisions of the labor law and he is regularly employed thereunder.

2. Elsewhere than in a city or school district having a population of five thousand or above, every child between eight and sixteen years of age, unless such child shall have received an employment certificate duly issued under the provisions of the labor law and is regularly employed thereunder in a factory or mercantile establishment, business or telegraph office, restaurant, hotel, apartment house or in the distribution or transmission of merchandise or messages, or unless such child shall have received the school record certificate issued under section six hundred and thirty of this act and is regularly employed elsewhere than in the factory or mercantile establishment, business or telegraph office, restaurant, hotel, apartment house or in the distribution or transmission of merchandise or messages.

SEC. 625. A violation of section six hundred and twenty-four shall be a misdemeanor, punishable for the first offense by a fine not exceeding five dollars, or five days' imprisonment, and for each subsequent offense by a fine not exceeding fifty dollars, or by imprisonment not exceeding thirty days, or by both such fine and imprisonment. Courts of special session[s] and police magistrates shall, subject to removal as provided in sections fifty-seven and fifty-eight of the code of criminal procedure, have exclusive jurisdiction in the first instance to hear, try and determine charges of violations of this section within their respective jurisdictions. *Violations.*

SEC. 626. It shall be unlawful for any person, firm or corporation: *Unlawful employments.*

1. To employe [employ] any child under fourteen years of age, in any business or service whatever, for any part of the term during which the public schools of the district or city in which the child resides are in session.

2. To employ, elsewhere than in a city of the first class or a city of the second class, in a factory or mercantile establishment, business or telegraph office, restaurant, hotel, apartment house or in the distribution or transmission 'of merchandise or messages, any child between fourteen and sixteen years of age who does not at the time of such employment present an employment certificate duly issued under the provisions of the labor law, or to employ any such child in any other capacity who does not at the time of such employment present a school record certificate as provided in section six hundred and thirty of this chapter.

3. To employ any child between fourteen and sixteen years of age in a city of the first class or a city of the second class who does not, at the time of such employment, present an employment certificate, duly issued under the provisions of the labor law.

SEC. 627. The employer of any child between fourteen and sixteen years of age in a city of the first class or a city of the second class shall keep and shall display in the place where such child is employed, the employment certificate and also his evening school certificate issued by the school authorities of said city or by an authorized representative of such school authorities, certifying that the said boy is regularly in attendance at an evening school of said city as provided in section six hundred and thirty-one of this chapter. *Certificates to be on file.*

SEC. 628. Any person, firm, or corporation, or any officer, manager, superintendent or employee acting therefor, who shall employ any child contrary to the provisions of section six hundred and twenty-six hereof, shall be guilty of a misdemeanor, and the punishment therefor shall be for the first offense a fine of not less than twenty dollars nor more than fifty dollars; for a second, and each subsequent offense, a fine of not less than fifty dollars nor more than two hundred dollars. *Violations.*

SEC. 629. An accurate record of the attendance of all children between seven and sixteen years of age shall be kept by the teacher of every school, showing each day by the year, month, day of the month *School records.*

and day of the week, such attendance, and the number of hours in each day thereof; and each teacher upon whose instruction any such child shall attend elsewhere than at school, shall keep a like record of such attendance. Such record shall, at all times, be open to the attendance officers or other person duly authorized by the school authorities of the city or district, who may inspect or copy the same; and every such teacher shall fully answer all inquiries lawfully made by such authorities, inspectors, or other persons, and a willful neglect or refusal so to answer any such inquiry shall be a misdemeanor.

Contents of certificates. SEC. 630. 1. A school record certificate shall contain a statement certifying that a child has regularly attended the public schools, or schools equivalent thereto, or parochial schools, for not less than one hundred and thirty days during the twelve months next preceding his fourteenth birthday or during the twelve months next preceding his application for such school record, and that he is able to read and write simple sentences in the English language, and has received during such period instruction in reading, writing, spelling, English grammar and geography, and is familiar with the fundamental operations of arithmetic up to to and including fractions. Such record shall also give the date of birth and residence of the child as shown on the school records, and the name of the child's parents, guardian or custodian.

Who may issue. 2. A teacher or superintendent to whom application shall be made for a school record certificate required under the provisions of the labor law shall issue a school record certificate to any child who, after due investigation and examination, may be found to be entitled to the same as follows:

a. In a city of the first class by the principal or chief executive of a school.

b. In all other cities and in school districts having a population of five thousand or more and employing a superintendent of schools, by the superintendent of schools only.

c. In all other school districts by the principal teacher of the school.

d. In each city or school district such certificate shall be furnished on demand to a child entitled thereto or to the board or commissioner of health.

Certificate of attendance at evening school. SEC. 631. The school authorities of a city of the first class or a city of the second class, or officers designated by them, are hereby required to issue to a boy lawfully in attendance at an evening school, an evening school certificate at least once in each month during the months said evening school is in session and at the close of the term of said evening school, provided that said boy has been in attendance upon said evening school for not less than six hours each week for such number of weeks as will, when taken in connection with the number of weeks such evening school shall be in session during the remainder of the current or calendar year, make up a total attendance on the part of said boy in said evening school of not less than six hours per week for a period of not less than sixteen weeks or attendance upon a trade school for at least eight hours per week for not less than sixteen weeks. Such certificate shall state fully the period of time which the boy to whom it is issued was in attendance upon such evening school or trade school.

SEC. 633. * * *

Powers of truant officers. 3. A truant officer in the performance of his duties may enter, during business hours, any factory, mercantile or other establishment within the city or school district in which he is appointed and shall be entitled to examine employment certificates or registry of children employed therein on demand.

Interference with truant officer. SEC. 634. Any person interfering with an attendance officer in the lawful discharge of his duties and any person owning or operating a factory, mercantile or other establishment who shall refuse on demand to exhibit to such attendance officer the registry of the children employed or the employment certificate of such children shall be guilty of a misdemeanor.

CHAPTER 31.—*Seats for female employees.*

Seats to be provided. SECTION 17. Every person employing females in a factory or as waitresses in a hotel or restaurant shall provide and maintain suitable seats for the use of such female employees, and permit the use thereof by such employees to such an extent as may be reasonable for the preservation of their health.

CHAPTER 31.—*Employment of women and children.*

SECTION 70. No child under the age of fourteen years shall be employed, permitted or suffered to work in or in connection with any factory in this State. No child between the ages of fourteen and sixteen years shall be so employed, permitted or suffered to work unless an employment certificate issued as provided in this article shall have been theretofore filed in the office of the employer at the place of employment of such child. *Age limit for children.*

The employment of a child under lawful age is of itself evidence of negligence, where the child is injured on account of such employment. Such a child is not, as a matter of law, chargeable with contributory negligence, nor with the assumption of the risks of his employment. The employer is liable for injuries, though the State makes such employment a misdemeanor. 66 N. E. Rep. 572.

SEC. 71. Such certificate shall be issued by the commissioner of health or the executive officer of the board or department of health of the city, town or village where such child resides, or is to be employed, or by such other officer thereof as may be designated by such board, department or commissioner for that purpose, upon the application of the parent or guardian or custodian of the child desiring such employment. Such officer shall not issue such certificate until he has received, examined, approved and filed the following papers duly executed, viz.: The school record of such child properly filled out and signed as provided in this article; also, evidence of age showing that the child is fourteen years old or upwards, which shall consist of the evidence thereof provided in one of the following subdivisions of this section and which shall be required in the order herein designated as follows: *Issue of certificates.* *Proofs.*

(a) Birth certificate: A duly attested transcript of the birth certificate filed according to law with a registrar of vital statistics or other officer charged with the duty of recording births, which certificate shall be conclusive evidence of the age of such child.

(b) Certificate of graduation: A certificate of graduation duly issued to such child showing that such child is a graduate of a public school of the State of New York or elsewhere, having a course of not less than eight years, or of a school in the State of New York other than a public school, having a substantially equivalent course of study of not less than eight years' duration, in which a record of the attendance of such child has been kept as required by article twenty of the education law: *Provided,* That the record of such school shows such child to be at least fourteen years of age.

(c) Passport or baptismal certificate: A passport or a duly attested transcript of a certificate of baptism showing the date of birth and place of baptism of such child.

(d) Other documentary evidence: In case it shall appear to the satisfaction of the officer to whom application is made, as herein provided, for an employment certificate, that a child for whom such certificate is requested, and who has presented the school record, is in fact over fourteen years of age, and that satisfactory documentary evidence of age can be produced, which does not fall within any of the provisions of the preceding subdivisions of this section, and that none of the papers mentioned in said subdivisions can be produced, then and not otherwise he shall present to the board of health of which he is an officer or agent, for its action thereon, a statement signed by him showing such facts, together with such affidavits or papers as may have been produced before him constituting such evidence of the age of such child, and the board of health, at a regular meeting thereof, may then, by resolution, provide that such evidence of age shall be fully entered on the minutes of such board, and shall be received as sufficient evidence of the age of such child for the purpose of this section.

(e) Physicians' certificates: In cities of the first class only, in case application for the issuance of an employment certificate shall be made to such officer by a child's parent, guardian or custodian who alleges his inability to produce any of the evidence of age specified in the preceding subdivisions of this section, and if the child is apparently at least fourteen years of age, such officer may receive and file an application signed by the parent, guardian or custodian of such child for physicians' certificates. Such application shall contain the alleged age, place and date of birth, and present residence of such child, together with such further facts as may be of assistance in determining the age of such child. Such application shall be filed for not less than ninety days after date of such application for such physicians' certificates, for an examination to be made of the statements contained therein, and in case no facts appear within such period or by such examination tending to discredit or contradict any material statement of such application, then and not otherwise the officer may direct such child to appear thereafter for physical examination before two physicians officially designated by the board of health, and in case such physicians shall certify in writing that they have separately examined such child and that in their opinion such child is at least fourteen years of age such officer shall accept such certificates as sufficient proof of the age of such child for the purposes of this section. In case the opinion of such physicians do not concur, the child shall be examined by a third physician and the concurring opinions shall be conclusive for the purpose of this section as to the age of such child.

Such officer shall require the evidence of age specified in subdivision (a) in preference to that specified in any subsequent subdivision and shall not accept the evidence of age permitted by any subsequent subdivision unless he shall receive and file in addition thereto an affidavit of the parent showing that no evidence of age specified in any preceding subdivision or subdivisions of this section can be produced. Such affidavit shall contain the age, place and date of birth, and present residence of such child, which affidavit must be taken before the officer issuing the employment certificate, who is hereby authorized and required to administer such oath and who shall not demand or receive a fee therefor. Such employment certificate shall not be issued until such child's father has personally appeared before and been examined by the officer issuing the certificate, and until such

Illiterates.
officer shall, after making such examination, sign and file in his office a statement that the child can read and legibly write simple sentences in the English language and that in his opinion the child is fourteen years of age or upwards and has reached the normal development of a child of its age, and is in sound health and is physically able to perform the work which it intends to do. In doubtful cases such physical fitness shall be determined by a medical officer of the board or department of health. Every such employment certificate shall be signed, in the presence of the officer issuing the same, by the child in whose name it is issued.

Certificates to contain what.
SEC. 72. Such certificate shall state the date and place of birth of the child, and describe the color of the hair and eyes, the height and weight and any distinguishing facial marks of such child, and that, the papers required by the preceding section have been duly examined, approved and filed and that the child named in such certificate has appeared before the officer signing the certificate and been examined.

Record.
SEC. 73. The school record required by this article shall be signed by the principal or chief executive officer of the school which such child has attended and shall be furnished, on demand, to a child entitled thereto or to the board, department or commissioner of health. It shall contain a statement certifying that the child has regularly attended the public schools or schools equivalent thereto or parochial schools for not less than one hundred and thirty days during the twelve months next preceding his fourteenth birthday, or during the twelve months next preceding his application for such school record and is able to read and write simple sentences in the English language, and has received during such period instruction in reading, spelling, writing, English grammar and geography and is familiar with the fundamental operations of arithmetic up to and including fractions. Such school record shall also give the date of birth and residence of the child as shown on the records of the school and the name of its parents or guardian or custodian.

Reports of certificates.
SEC. 75. The board or department of health or health commissioner of a city, village or town, shall transmit, between the first and tenth

day of each month, to the office of the commissioner of labor a list of the names of the children to whom certificates have been issued.

SEC. 76. Each person owning or operating a factory and employing *Register.* children therein shall keep or cause to be kept in the office of such factory, a register, in which shall be recorded the name, birthplace, age and place of residence of all children so employed under the age of sixteen years. Such register and the certificate filed in such office shall be produced for inspection upon the demand of the commissioner of labor. On termination of the employment of a child so registered, and whose certificate is so filed, such certificate shall be forthwith surrendered by the employer to the child or its parent or guardian or custodian. The commissioner of labor may make demand on any employer in whose factory a child apparently under the age of sixteen years is employed or permitted or suffered to work, and whose employment certificate is not then filed as required by this article, that such employer shall either furnish him within ten days, evidence satisfactory to him that such child is in fact over sixteen years of age, or shall cease to employ or permit or suffer such child to work in such factory. The commissioner of labor may require from such employer the same evidence of age of such child as is required on the issuance of an employment certificate; and the employer furnishing such evidence shall not be required to furnish any further evidence of the age of the child. A notice embodying such demand may be served on such employer personally or may be sent by mail addressed to him at said factory, and if served by post shall be deemed to have been served at the time when the letter containing the same would be delivered in the ordinary course of the post. When the employer is a corporation such notice may be served either personally upon an officer of such corporation, or by sending it by post addressed to the office or the principal place of business of such corporation. The papers constituting such evidence of age furnished by the employer in response to such demand shall be filled with the commissioner of labor and a material false statement made in any such paper or affidavit by any person, shall be a misdemeanor. In case such employer shall fail to produce and deliver to the commissioner of labor within ten days after such demand such evidence of age herein required by him, and shall thereafter continue to employ such child or permit or suffer such child to work in such factory, proof of the giving of such notice and of such failure to produce and file such evidence shall be prima facie evidence in any prosecution brought for a violation of this article that such child is under sixteen years of age and is unlawfully employed.

SEC. 77. 1. No child under the age of sixteen years shall be em- *Night work of* ployed or permitted to work in or in connection with any factory in this *children.* State before eight o'clock in the morning, or after five o'clock in the evening of any day, or for more than eight hours in any one day, or more than six days in any one week.

2. No male minor under the age of eighteen years shall be employed *Hours of labor.* or permitted to work in any factory in this State more than six days or sixty hours in any one week, or for more than ten hours in any one day, except as hereafter provided; nor between the hours of twelve midnight and four o'clock in the morning.

3. No female minor under the age of twenty-one years and no woman *Night work of* shall be employed or permitted to work in any factory in this State *women.* before six o'clock in the morning, or after nine o'clock in the evening of any day, or more than six days or sixty hours in any one week; nor for more than ten hours in any one day except as hereafter provided.

4. A printed notice, in a form which shall be furnished by the *Notice.* commissioner of labor, stating the number of hours per day for each day of the week required of such persons, and the time when such work shall begin and end, shall be kept posted in a conspicuous place in each room where they are employed. But such persons may begin their work after the time for beginning and stop before the time for ending such work, mentioned in such notice, but they shall not otherwise be employed, permitted or suffered to work in such factory except as stated therein. The terms of such notice shall not be changed after the beginning of labor on the first day of the week without the consent of the commissioner of labor. The presence of such persons

in the factory at any other hours than those stated in the printed notice, or if no such notice be posted, before seven o'clock in the morning or after six o'clock in the evening, shall constitute prima facie evidence of a violation of this section.

Time books.   5. In a factory wherein, owing to the nature of the work, it is practically impossible to fix the hours of labor weekly in advance the commissioner of labor, upon a proper application stating facts showing the necessity therefor, shall grant a permit dispensing with the notice hereinbefore required, upon condition that the daily hours of labor be posted for the information of employees and that a time book in a form to be approved by him, giving the names and addresses of all female employees and the hours worked by each of them in each day, shall be properly and correctly kept, and shall be exhibited to him or any of his subordinates promptly upon demand. Such permit shall be kept posted in such factory as such commissioner may prescribe, and may be revoked by such commissioner at any time for failure to post it or the daily hours of labor or to keep or exhibit such time book as herein provided.

Employment in two or more factories.
Violations.   6. Where a female or male minor is employed in two or more factories or mercantile establishments in the same day or week the total time of employment must not exceed that allowed per day or week in a single factory or mercantile establishment; and any person who shall require or permit a female to work in a factory between the hours of six o'clock in the evening and seven o'clock in the morning in violation of the provisions of this subdivision of this section, with or without knowledge of the previous or other employment, shall be liable for a violation thereof.

The prohibition of night work by adult females is unconstitutional. 81 N. E. Rep. 778.

Work for more than ten hours.   SEC. 78. 1. A female sixteen years of age or upwards and a male between the ages of sixteen and eighteen may be employed in a factory more than ten hours a day:—(a) regularly in not to exceed five days a week, in order to make a short day or a holiday on one of the six working days of the week; (b) irregularly in not to exceed three days a week: *Provided,* That no such person shall be required or permitted to work more than twelve hours in any one day or more than sixty hours in any one week, and that the provisions of the preceding section as to notice or time book be fully complied with.

Proof.   2. In a prosecution for a violation of any provision of this or of the preceding section the burden of proving a permit or exception shall be upon the party claiming it.

Certain employ-ments of children prohibited.   SEC. 93 (as amended by chapter 107, Acts of 1910). No child under the age of sixteen years shall be employed or permitted to work in operating or assisting in operating any of the following machines: Circular or band saws, wood shapers, wood jointers, planers, sand-paper or wood polishing machinery; picker machines or machines used in picking wool, cotton, hair or any upholstery material; paper lace machines; burnishing machines in any tannery or leather manu-factory; job or cylinder printing presses having motive power other than foot; wood turning or boring machinery; drill presses; metal or paper cutting machines; corner staying machines in paper box factories; stamping machines used in sheet metal and tinware manu-facturing or in washer and nut factories; machines used in making corrugating rolls; steam boilers; dough brakes or cracker machinery of any description; wire or iron straightening machinery; rolling mill machinery, power punches or shears; washing, grinding or mixing machinery, calender rolls in rubber manufacturing; or laundering machinery. No child under the age of sixteen years shall be em-ployed or permitted to work at adjusting or assisting in adjusting any belt to any machinery; oiling or assisting in oiling, wiping or cleaning machinery; or in any capacity in preparing any composition in which dangerous or poisonous acids are used; or in the manufac-ture or packing of paints, dry colors, or red or white lead; or in dipping, dyeing [1] or packing matches; or in the manufacture, packing or storing of powder, dynamite, nitroglycerine, compounds, fuses, or other

---

[1] It is possible that *drying* was intended, as drying is an essential and dangerous proc-ess in matchmaking, while *dyeing* is not.

explosives; or in or about any distillery, brewery, or any other establishment where malt or alcoholic liquors are manufactured, packed, wrapped, or bottled; and no female under the age of sixteen shall be employed or permitted to work in any capacity where such employment compels her to remain standing constantly. No child under the age of sixteen years shall be employed or permitted to have the care, custody or management of or to operate an elevator either for freight or passengers. No person under the age of eighteen years shall be employed or permitted to have the care, custody or management of or to operate an elevator either for freight or passengers running at a speed of over two hundred feet a minute. No male person under eighteen years or woman under twenty-one years of age shall be permitted or directed to clean machinery while in motion. No male child under the age of eighteen years, nor any female, shall be employed in any factory in this State in operating or using any emery, tripoli, rouge, corundum, stone, carborundum or any abrasive, or emery polishing or buffing wheel, where articles of the baser metals or of irium are manufactured. Women and children.

SEC. 131. No child under sixteen years of age shall be employed, permitted or suffered to work in or in connection with any mine or quarry in this State. No female shall be employed, permitted or suffered to work in any mine or quarry in this State. Employment in quarries.

CHAPTER 31.—*Employment of women and children in stores, offices, etc.*

SECTION 160. The provisions of this article shall apply to all villages and cities which at the last preceding State enumeration had a population of three thousand or more. Application of law.

SEC. 161 (as amended by chapter 866, Acts of 1911). No child under the age of sixteen years shall be employed, permitted or suffered to work in or in connection with any mercantile establishment, business office, or telegraph office, restaurant, hotel, apartment-house, theater or other place of amusement, bowling alley, barber shop, shoe-polishing establishment, or in the distribution or transmission of merchandise, articles or messages, or in the distribution or sale of articles more than six days or fifty-four hours in any one week, or more than nine hours in any one day, or before eight o'clock in the morning or after seven o'clock in the evening of any day. The foregoing provision shall not apply to any employment prohibited or regulated by section four hundred and eighty-five of the penal law. No female employee between sixteen and twenty-one years of age shall be required, permitted or suffered to work in or in connection with any mercantile establishment more than sixty hours in any one week; or more than ten hours in any one day, unless for the purpose of making a shorter workday of some one day of the week; or before seven o'clock in the morning or after ten o'clock in the evening of any day. This section does not apply to the employment of persons sixteen years of age or upward between the eighteenth day of December and the following twenty-fourth day of December, both inclusive. Not less than forty-five minutes shall be allowed for the noonday meal of the employees of any such establishment. Whenever any employee is employed or permitted to work after seven o'clock in the evening, such employee shall be allowed at least twenty minutes to obtain lunch or supper between five and seven o'clock in the evening. Hours of labor. Night work. Females. Night work. Lunch time.

SEC. 161-a (added by chapter 342, Acts of 1910). In cities of the first or second class no person under the age of twenty-one years shall be employed or permitted to work as a messenger for a telegraph or messenger company in the distribution, transmission or delivery of goods or messages before five o'clock in the morning or after ten o'clock in the evening of any day. Night work of messengers.

SEC. 162 (as amended by chapter 866, Acts of 1911). No child under the age of fourteen years shall be employed or permitted to work in or in connection with any mercantile or other business or establishment specified in the preceding section. No child under the age of sixteen years shall be so employed or permitted to work unless an employment certificate, issued as provided in this article, shall have been theretofore filed in the office of the employer at the place of employment of such child. Age limits. Certificates.

[Sections 163 to 165, inclusive, are identical with sections 71 to 73, pages 779 and 780, above.]

Register. SEC. 167. The owner, manager, or agent of a mercantile or other establishment specified in section one hundred and sixty-one, employing children, shall keep or cause to be kept, in the office of such establishment, a register, in which shall be recorded the name, birthplace, age and place of residence of all children so employed under the age of sixteen years. Such register and the certificates filed in such office shall be produced for inspection, upon the demand of an officer of the board, department or commissioner of health of the town, village or city where such establishment is situated. On termination of the employment of the child so registered and whose certificate is so filed, such certificate shall be forthwith surrendered by the employer to the child or its parent or guardian or custodian. An officer of the board, department or commissioner of health of the town, village or city where a mercantile or other establishment mentioned in this article is situated, may make demand on an employer in whose establishment a child apparently under the age of sixteen years is employed or permitted or suffered to work, and whose employment certificate is not then filed as required by this chapter, that such employer shall either furnish him within ten days, evidence satisfactory to him that such child is in fact over sixteen years of age, or shall cease to employ or permit or suffer such child to work in such establishment. The officer may require from such employer the same evidence of age of such child as is required on the issuance of an employment certificate; and the employer furnishing such evidence shall not be required to furnish any further evidence of the age of the child. A notice embodying such demand may be served on such employer personally or may be sent by mail addressed to him at said establishment, and if served by post shall be deemed to have been served at the time when the letter containing the same would be delivered in the ordinary course of the post. When the employer is a corporation such notice may be served either personally upon an officer of such corporation, or by sending it by post addressed to the office of the principal place of business of such corporation. The papers constituting such evidence of age furnished by the employer in response to such demand shall be filed with the board, department, or commissioner of health and a material false statement made in any such paper or affidavit by any person, shall be a misdemeanor. In case such employer shall fail to produce and deliver to to the officer of the board, department, or commissioner of health within ten days after such demand such evidence of age herein required by him, and shall thereafter continue to employ such child or permit or suffer such child to work in such mercantile or other establishment, proof of the giving of such notice and of such failure to produce and file such evidence shall be prima facie evidence in any prosecution brought for a violation of this article that such child is under sixteen years of age and is unlawfully employed.

Wash-rooms, etc. SEC. 168 (as amended by chapter 866, Acts of 1911). Suitable and proper wash-rooms and water-closets shall be provided in, adjacent to or connected with mercantile establishments. Such rooms and closets shall be so located and arranged as to be easily accessible to the employees of such establishments.

Such water-closets shall be properly screened and ventilated, and, at all times, kept in a clean condition. The water-closets assigned to the female employees of such establishments shall be separate from those assigned to the male employees.

If a mercantile establishment has not provided wash-rooms and water-closets, as required by this section, the board or department of health or health commissioners of the town, village or city where such establishment is situated, unless such establishment is situated in a city of the first class, in which case the commissioner of labor shall cause to be served upon the owner, agent or lessee of the building occupied by such establishment a written notice of the omission and directing such owner, agent or lessee to comply with the provisions of this section respecting such wash-rooms and water-closets.

Such owner shall, within fifteen days after the receipt of such notice, cause such wash-rooms and water-closets to be provided.

SEC. 169. If a lunch room is provided in a mercantile establishment where females are employed, such lunch room shall not be next to or adjoining the water-closets, unless permission is first obtained from the board or department of health or health commissioners of the town, village or city where such mercantile establishment is situated. Such permission shall be granted unless it appears that proper sanitary conditions do not exist, and it may be revoked at any time by the board or department of health or health commissioner, if it appears that such lunch room is kept in a manner or in a part of the building injurious to the health of the employees. *Lunch rooms.*

SEC. 170. Chairs, stools or other suitable seats shall be maintained in mercantile establishments for the use of female employees therein, to the number of at least one seat for every three females employed, and the use thereof by such employees shall be allowed at such times and to such extent as may be necessary for the preservation of their health. If the duties of the female employees, for the use of whom the seats are furnished, are to be principally performed in front of a counter, table, desk or fixture, such seats shall be placed in front thereof; if such duties are to be principally performed behind such counter, table, desk or fixture, such seats shall be placed behind the same. *Seats.*

SEC. 171. Women or children shall not be employed or directed to work in the basement of a mercantile establishment, unless permitted by the board or department of health, or health commissioner of the town, village or city where such mercantile establishment is situated. Such permission shall be granted unless it appears that such basement is not sufficiently lighted and ventilated, and is not in good sanitary condition. *Basements.*

SEC. 172. The board or department of health or health commissioners of a town, village or city affected by this article shall enforce the same and prosecute all violations thereof. Proceedings to prosecute such violations must be begun within thirty days after the alleged offense was committed. All officers and members of such boards, or department, all health commissioners, inspectors, and other persons appointed or designated by such boards, departments or commissioners may visit and inspect at reasonable hours and when practicable and necessary, all mercantile or other establishments herein specified within the town, village or city for which they are appointed. No person shall interfere with or prevent any such officer from making such visitations and inspections, nor shall he be obstructed or injured by force or otherwise while in the performance of his duties. All persons connected with any such mercantile or other establishment herein specified shall properly answer all questions asked by such officer or inspector in reference to any of the provisions of this article. *Enforcement.*

SEC. 173. A copy of this article shall be posted in three conspicuous places in each establishment affected by its provisions. *Law to be posted.*

CHAPTER 31.—*Employment of children—Selling newspapers, etc.*

SECTION 220. No male child under ten, and no girl under sixteen years of age, shall in any city of the first or second class sell or expose or offer for sale newspapers, magazines or periodicals in any street or public place. *Selling newspapers.*

SEC. 221. No male child under fourteen years of age shall sell or expose or offer for sale said articles unless a permit and badge as hereinafter provided shall have been issued to him by the district superintendent of the board of education of the city and school district where said child resides, or by such other officer thereof as may be officially designated by such board for that purpose, on the application of the parent, guardian or other person having the custody of the child desiring such permit and badge, or in case said child has no parent, guardian or custodian then on the application of his next friend, being an adult. Such permit and badge shall not be issued until the officer issuing the same shall have received, examined, approved and placed on file in his office satisfactory proof that such male child is of the age of ten years or upwards, and shall also have received, examined and placed on file the written statement of the principal or chief executive officer of the *Badges.*

school which the child is attending, stating that such child is an attendant at such school, that he is of the normal development of a child of his age and physically fit for such employment, and that said principal or chief executive officer approves the granting of a permit and badge to such child. No such permit or badge shall be valid for any purpose except during the period in which such proof and written statement shall remain on file, nor shall such permit or badge be authority beyond the period fixed therein for its duration. After having received, examined and placed on file such papers the officer shall issue to the child a permit and badge. Principals or chief executive officers of schools in which children under fourteen years are pupils shall keep complete lists of all children in their schools to whom a permit and badge as herein provided have been granted.

Permit to state what. SEC. 222. Such permit shall state the date and place of birth of the child, the name and address of its parent, guardian, custodian or next friend, as the case may be, and describe the color of hair and eyes, the height and weight and any distinguishing facial mark of such child, and shall further state that the papers required by the preceding section have been duly examined and filed; and that the child named in such permit has appeared before the officer issuing the permit. The badge furnished by the officer issuing the permit shall bear on its face a number corresponding to the number of the permit, and the name of the child. Every such permit, and every such badge on its reverse side, shall be signed in the presence of the officer issuing the same by the child in whose name it is issued.

Badge to be worn. Limit. SEC. 223. The badge provided for herein shall be worn conspicuously at all times by such child while so working; and all such permits and badges shall expire annually on the first day of January. The color of the badge shall be changed each year. No child to whom such permit and badge are issued shall transfer the same to any other person nor be engaged in any city of the first or second class as a newsboy, or shall sell or expose or offer for sale newspapers, magazines or periodicals in any street or public place without having conspicuously upon his person such badge, and he shall exhibit the same upon demand at any time to any police, or attendance officer.

Selling at night. SEC. 224. No child to whom a permit and badge are issued as provided for in the preceding sections shall sell or expose or offer for sale any newspapers, magazines or periodicals after ten o'clock in the evening, or before six o'clock in the morning.

Enforcement. SEC. 225. In cities of the first or second class, police officers, and the regular attendance officers appointed by the board of education who are hereby vested with the powers of peace officers for the purpose, shall enforce the provisions of this article.

Violations. SEC. 226. Any child who shall work in any city of the first or second class in any street or public place as a newsboy or who shall sell or expose or offer for sale newspapers, magazines or periodicals in violation of the provisions of this article, shall be arrested and brought before a court or magistrate having jurisdiction to commit a child to an incorporated charitable reformatory or other institution and be dealt with according to law; and if any such child is committed to an institution, it shall when practicable, be committed to an institution governed by persons of the same religious faith as the parents of such child. The permit and badge of any child who violates the provisions of this article may be revoked by the officer issuing the same, upon the recommendation of the principal or chief executive officer of the school which such child is attending, or upon the complaint of any police officer or attendance officer, and such child shall surrender the permit and badge so revoked upon the demand of any attendance officer or police officer charged with the duty of enforcing the provisions of this article. The refusal of any child to surrender such permit and badge, upon such demand, or the sale or offering for sale of newspapers, magazines or periodicals in any street or public place by any child after notice of the revocation of such permit and badge shall be deemed a violation of this article and shall subject the child to the penalties provided for in this section.

CHAPTER 34.—*Employment of women and children in barrooms, etc.*

SECTION 30.   *   *   *   It shall not be lawful for any person, whether   Women not to
having paid such [liquor] tax or not,   be employed.
*   *   *   *   *   *   *

F. To permit any girl or woman, or any minor under the age of
eighteen years, not a member of his family,   *   *   *   to sell or serve
any liquor upon the premises;   *   *   *

CHAPTER 40.—*Employment of children—Certain employments forbidden.*

SECTION 485. A person who employs or causes to be employed, or   Acrobatic, etc.,
who exhibits, uses, or has in custody, or trains for the purpose of the   occupations.
exhibition, use or employment of, any child actually or apparently
under the age of sixteen years; or who having the care, custody or
control of such a child as parent, relative, guardian, employer or otherwise, sells, lets out, gives away, so trains, or in any way procures or
consents to the employment, or to such training, or use, or exhibition
of such child; or who neglects or refuses to restrain such child from
such training, or from engaging or acting:
  1. As a rope or wire walker, gymnast, wrestler, contortionist, rider
or acrobat; or upon any bicycle or similar mechanical vehicle or contrivance; or,
  2. In begging or receiving or soliciting alms in any manner or under
any pretense, or in any mendicant occupation; or in gathering or
picking rags, or collecting cigar stumps, bones or refuse from markets;
or in peddling; or
  3. In singing; or dancing; or playing upon a musical instrument;
or in a theatrical exhibition; or in any wandering occupation; or,
  4. In any illegal, indecent or immoral exhibition or practice; or in
the exhibition of any such child when insane, idiotic, or when presenting the appearance of any deformity or unnatural physical formation
or development; or
  5. In any practice or exhibition or place dangerous or injurious
to the life, limb, health or morals of the child,
  Is guilty of a misdemeanor.
  But this section does not apply to the employment of any child as a   Law does not
singer or musician in a church, school or academy; or in teaching or   apply, where.
learning the science or practice of music; or as a musician in any
concert or in a theatrical exhibition, with the written consent of the
mayor of the city, or the president of the board of trustees of the village
where such concert or exhibition takes place.   Such consent shall not
be given unless forty-eight hours previous notice of the application
shall have been served in writing upon the society mentioned in section
four hundred and ninety one of this chapter [any incorporated society
for the prevention of cruelty to children], if there be one within the
county, and a hearing had thereon if requested, and shall be revocable at the will of the authority giving it.   It shall specify the name
of the child, its age, the names and residence of its parents or guardians,
the nature, time, duration and number of performances permitted,
together with the place and character of the exhibition.   But no such
consent shall be deemed to authorize any violation of the first, second,
fourth or fifth subdivisions of this section.

NORTH CAROLINA.

REVISAL—1905.

Employment of children.

SECTION 3362. If any mill owner, superintendent or other person   Age limit.
acting in behalf of a factory or manufacturing establishment shall
knowingly and willfully employ any child under twelve years of
age to work in any factory or manufacturing establishment, except   Exceptions.

in oyster canning and packing manufactories where said canning and packing manufactories pa for opening or shucking oysters by the gallon or bushel, he shall be guilty of a misdemeanor.

Employment of minors in violation of this section is negligence, which, if followed by injury, gives a cause of action. 53 S. E. Rep. 891.
Illegal employment is negligence per se, and not merely evidence of negligence. The statute is constitutional. 61 S. E. Rep. 525.

Hours of labor.   SEC. 3363. If any mill owner, superintendent, or other person acting in behalf of a factory or manufacturing establishment shall knowingly and willfully require any person under eighteen years of age, except engineers, firemen, machinists, superintendents, overseers, section and yard hands, office men, watchmen or repairers of breakdowns, to work in such factories or establishments a longer period than sixty-six hours in one week, he shall be guilty of a misdemeanor.

Statement as to age.   SEC. 3364. If any parent or person standing in the relation of parent, upon hiring his children to any factory or manufacturing establishment, shall fail to furnish such establishment a written statement of the age of such child or children being so hired, and if any such parent, or person standing in the relation of parent to such child or children shall, in such written statement misstate the age of such child or children being so employed he shall be guilty of a misdemeanor, and upon conviction shall be punished at the discretion of the court.

Contracts of employment—Defrauding minors.

Fraudulent employment of minors.   SECTION 3428a. Whenever any person having a contract with any corporation, company or person for the manufacture or change of any raw material by the piece or pound shall hire and employ any minor to assist in said work upon the faith of and by color of said contract and with intent to cheat and defraud said minor, and shall secure the contract price and shall willfully fail to pay said minor when he shall have performed his part of said contract work, whether done by the day or by the job, the person so offending shall be guilty of a misdemeanor, and upon conviction shall be fined not more than fifty dollars or imprisoned not more than thirty days.

Employment of children—Enticing out of State.

Engaging minor to go out of State.   SECTION 3630. If any person shall employ and carry beyond the limits of this State any minor, or shall induce any minor to go beyond the limits of this State for the purpose of employment without the consent in writing, duly authenticated, of the parent, guardian or other person having authority over such minor, he shall be guilty of a misdemeanor, and on conviction thereof shall be fined not less than five hundred and not more than one thousand dollars for each

Evidence.   offense.   The fact of the employment and going out of the State of a minor, or of the going out of the State by the minor, at the solicitation of the person for the purpose of employment, shall be prima facie evidence of knowledge that the person employed or solicited to go beyond the limits of the State is a minor.

Hiring out children, etc., to support men in idleness.

Who are vagrants.   SECTION 3740. If any person shall come within any of the following classes, he shall be deemed a vagrant, and shall be fined not exceeding fifty dollars or imprisoned not exceeding thirty days.

*   *   *   *   *   *   *

6. All able-bodied men who have no other visible means of support who shall live in idleness upon the wages or earnings of their mother, wife or minor child or children, except male child or children over eighteen years of age.

Employment of children in mines.

Employment of children.   SECTION 4931. No minor under twelve years of age shall be allowed to work in any mine, and in all cases of minors applying for work the agent of such mine shall see that the provisions of this section are not violated; and the inspector may, when doubt exists as to the age of any person found working in any mine, examine under oath such person and his parents, or other witnesses, as to his age.

ACTS OF 1907.

CHAPTER 463.—*Employment of children.*

SECTION 1. No child under twelve years of age shall be employed or worked in any factory or manufacturing establishment within this State: *Provided further,* That after one thousand nine hundred and seven no child between the ages of twelve and thirteen years of age shall be employed or work in a factory except in apprenticeship capacity, and only then after having attended school four months in the preceding twelve months. Age limit.

SEC. 2 (as amended by chapter 85, Acts of 1911). Not exceeding sixty hours shall constitute a week's work in all factories and manufacturing establishments of this State. No person under 18 years of age shall be required to work in such factories or establishments a longer period than sixty hours in one week: *Provided,* That this section shall not apply to engineers, firemen, machinists, superintendents, overseers, section and yard hands, office men, watchmen or repairers of breakdowns. Hours of labor.

SEC. 3. All parents, or persons standing in relation of parent, upon hiring their children to any factory or manufacturing establishment, shall furnish such establishment a written statement of the age of such child or children being so hired, and certificate as to school attendance; and any parent, or person standing in the relation of parent to such child or children, who shall in such written statement misstate the age of such child or children being so employed, or their school attendance, shall be guilty of a misdemeanor, and upon conviction shall be punished at the discretion of the court. Any mill-owner, superintendent or manufacturing establishment, who shall knowingly or willfully violate the provisions of this act shall be guilty of a misdemeanor and upon conviction shall be punished at the discretion of the court. Parents to report age.

SEC. 4. After one thousand nine hundred and seven no boy or girl under fourteen years old shall work in a factory between the hours of eight p. m. and five a. m. Night work.

ACTS OF 1909.

CHAPTER 857.—*Seats for female employees.*

SECTION 1. All persons, firms or corporations who employ females in a store, shop, office or manufacturing establishment, as clerks, operatives or helpers in any business, trade or occupation carried on or operated in the State of North Carolina, shall be required to procure and provide proper and suitable seats for all such females, and shall permit the use of such seats, rests or stools as may be necessary, and shall not make any rules, regulations or orders preventing the use of such seats, stools or rests when any such female employee or employees are not actively employed or engaged in their work in such business or employment. Seats to be provided.

SEC. 2. If any employer of female help in the State of North Carolina shall fail, neglect or refuse to provide seats, as provided in this act, on or before the first day of June, one thousand nine hundred and nine, or shall make any rules, orders or regulations in his or its shop, store or other place of business requiring females to remain standing when not necessarily employed or engaged in service or labor therein, he shall be guilty of a misdemeanor, and upon conviction thereof shall be fined not less than twenty-five dollars nor more than one hundred dollars, in the discretion of the court. Violations.

NORTH DAKOTA.

CONSTITUTION.

Employment of children.

SECTION 209. The labor of children under twelve years of age shall be prohibited in mines, factories and workshops in this State. Age limit.

[See chapter 266, Acts of 1911.]

REVISED CODES—1905.

Earnings of minors.

Payment to minors valid until notice. SECTION 4105. The wages of a minor employed in service may be paid to him or her until the parent or guardian entitled thereto gives the employer notice that he claims such wages.

Employment of women and children—Hours of labor.

Limit of ten hours. SECTION 9440. Every owner, stockholder, overseer, employer, clerk or foreman, of any manufactory, workshop or other place used for mechanical or manufacturing purposes, who, having control, shall compel any woman or any child under eighteen years of age, or permit any child under fourteen years of age, to labor in any day exceeding ten hours, shall be deemed guilty of a misdemeanor, and upon conviction shall be punished by fine not exceeding one hundred and not less than ten dollars.

ACTS OF 1911.

CHAPTER 266.—*Employment of children—General provisions.*

School attendance required. SECTION 232. Every parent, guardian or other person who resides in any school district or city and who has control over any child of or between the ages of eight and fifteen shall send every such child to a public school in each year during the entire time the public schools of such district or city are in session; * * * *Provided,* That such parent, guardian or other person having control of any child shall be excused from such duty by the school board of the district or by the board of education of the city or village whenever it shall be shown to their satisfaction, subject to appeal as provided by law, that one of the following reasons therefor exists:

Proviso.

*   *   *   *   *

Labor necessary. 2. That such child is actually necessary to the support of the family.

*   *   *   *   *

Age limit. SEC. 291. No child under fourteen years of age shall be employed, permitted or suffered to work in or in connection with any mine, factory, workshop, mercantile establishment, store, business office, telegraph office, restaurant, hotel, apartment house or in the distribution or transmission of merchandise or messages. It shall be unlawful for any person, firm or corporation to employ any child under fourteen years of age in any business or service whatever, during the hours when the public schools of the district in which the child resides are in session.

Employment during school term.

Certificates. SEC. 292. No child between fourteen and sixteen years of age shall be employed, permitted or suffered to work in any mine, factory, workshop or mercantile establishment unless the person or corporation employing him procures and keeps on file, and accessible to the superintendent of schools of the city or village, if one is employed, otherwise, to the clerk of the school board or board of education, an employment certificate as hereinafter prescribed, and keeps two complete lists of all such children employed therein, one on file and one conspicuously posted near the principal entrance of the building in which such child is employed. On termination of the employment of a child so registered and whose certificate is so filed, such certificate shall be forthwith surrendered by the employer to the child or its parent, or guardian or custodian. The superintendent of schools or clerk of the school board or board of education, as the case may be, may make demand on an employer in whose factory a child apparently under the age of sixteen years is employed or permitted or suffered to work and whose employment certificate is not then filed as required by this act, that such employer shall either furnish him within ten days evidence satisfactory to him that such child is in fact over sixteen years of age, or shall cease to employ or permit or suffer such child to work in such factory. The superintendent of schools of the city or village or clerk of the school board or board of education may require from such employer

Files.

Enforcement.

the same evidence of age of such child as is required on the issuance of an employment certificate; and the employer furnishing such evidence shall not be required to furnish any further evidence of the age of the child. In case such employer shall fail to produce and deliver to the superintendent of schools of the city or village or the clerk of the school board or board of education, as the case may be, within ten days after such demand, such evidence of age herein required by him, and shall thereafter continue to employ such child or permit or suffer such child to work in such factory, proof of the giving of such notice and of such failure to produce and file such evidence shall be prima facie evidence in any prosecution brought for a violation of this act that such child is under sixteen years of age and is unlawfully employed. *Evidence.*

SEC. 293. The superintendent of schools of the city or village, if one is employed, and if not, then the clerk of the school board or board of education, is hereby authorized to issue an employment certificate in writing, such certificate is to be issued upon the evidence prescribed in section four [294] of this act; *Provided,* That no employment certificate shall be issued for any child then in or about to enter his own employment or the employment of a firm or corporation of which he is a member, officer or employee. *Who may issue certificates.*

SEC. 294. The person authorized to issue employment certificate shall not issue such certificate until he has received, examined, approved and filed the following papers duly executed: *Evidence.*

1. The school record of such child properly filled out and signed as provided in this act.

2. A passport or duly attested transcript of the certificate of birth or baptism or other religious record, showing the date and place of birth of such child. A duly attested transcript of the birth certificate filed according to law with a registrar of vital statistics, or other officer charged with the duty of recording births, shall be conclusive evidence of the age of such child.

3. The affidavit of the parent or guardian or custodian of a child, which shall be required, however, only in case such last mentioned transcript of the certificate of birth be not produced and filed, showing the place and date of birth of such child, which affidavit must be taken before the officer issuing the employment certificate, who is hereby authorized and required to administer such oath, and who shall not demand or receive a fee therefor. Such employment certificate shall not be issued until such child has personally appeared before and been examined by the officer issuing the certificate, and until such officer shall, after making such examination, sign and file in his office a statement that the child can read and legibly write simple sentences in the English language and that in his opinion the child is fourteen years of age or upwards and has reached the normal development of a child of its age, and is in sound health and is physically able to perform the work which it intends to do. In doubtful cases such physical fitness shall be determined by a medical officer of the board or department of health. Every such employment certificate shall be signed, in the presence of the officer issuing the same, by the child in whose name it is issued. *Literacy.*

SEC. 295. Such certificates shall state the date and place of birth of the child and describe the color of the hair and eyes, the height and weight and any distinguishing marks of such child, and that the papers required by the preceding section have been duly examined, approved and filed and that the child named in such certificate has appeared before the officer signing the certificate and been examined. *Description of child.*

SEC. 296. The school record required by this act shall be signed by the principal or chief executive officer of the school which such child has attended and shall be furnished, on demand, to a child entitled thereto. It shall contain a statement certifying that the child has regularly attended the public schools or schools equivalent thereto or parochial schools for not less than one hundred and twenty days during the school year previous to his arriving at the age of fourteen years or during the year previous to applying for such school record and is able to read and write simple sentences in the English language and has received during such period instruction in reading, spelling, writing, English grammar and geography and is familiar with the funda- *School record.*

mental operations of arithmetic up to and including fractions. Such school record shall also give the age and residence of the child as shown on the records of the school and the name of its parent, guardian or custodian.

Hours of labor.

SEC. 297. No persons under the age of sixteen years shall be employed or suffered or permitted to work at any gainful occupation more than forty-eight hours in any one week, nor more than eight hours in any **Night work.** one day; or before the hour of seven o'clock in the morning or after the hour of seven o'clock in the evening. Every employer shall post in a conspicuous place in every room where such minors are employed a printed notice stating the hours required of them each day of the week, the hours of commencing and stopping work and the hours when the time or times allowed for dinner or for other meals begin and end. The printed form of such notice shall be furnished by the superintendent of schools of the city or village, or the clerk of the school board or board of education, and the employment of any minor for longer times in any day so stated shall be deemed a violation of this section.

Enforcement.

SEC. 298. Peace officers may visit mines, factories, workshops and mercantile establishments in their several towns and cities and ascertain whether any minors are employed therein contrary to the provisions of this act; and it shall be their duty to report any cases of such illegal employment to the school board or board of education. Such officer may require that the employment certificates and lists provided for in this act of minors employed in such factories, mines, workshops or mercantile establishments shall be produced for their inspection. Complaints for offenses under this act may be made by such peace officer or by any other person cognizant of the facts.

Employments forbidden.

SEC. 299. No child under the age of sixteen years shall be employed at sewing belts, or to assist in sewing belts, in any capacity whatever; nor shall any child adjust any belt to any machinery, they shall not oil or assist in oiling, wiping or cleaning machinery; they shall not operate or assist in operating circular or band saws, wood shapers, wood-joiners, [jointers] planers, sand-paper or wood polishing machinery, emery or polishing wheels used for polishing metal, wood-turning or boring machinery, stamping machines in sheet metal and tinware manufacturing, stamping machines in washer and nut factories, operating corrugating rolls, such as are used in roofing factories, nor shall they be employed in operating any steam boiler, steam machinery, or other steam generating apparatus, or as pin boys in any bowling alleys; they shall not operate or assist in operating dough brakes, or cracker machinery of any description; wire or iron straightening machinery; nor shall they operate or assist in operating rolling mill machinery, punches or shears, washing, grinding or mixing mill or calender rolls in rubber manufacturing; nor shall they operate or assist in operating laundry machinery; nor shall children be employed in any capacity in preparing any composition in which dangerous or poisonous acids are used, and they shall not be employed in any capacity in the manufacture of paints, colors, or white lead; nor shall they be employed in any capacity whatever in operating or assisting to operate any passenger or freight elevator; nor shall they be employed in any capacity whatever in the manufacture of goods for immoral purposes, or any other employment that may be considered dangerous to their lives or limbs, or where their health may be injured or morals depraved; nor in any theater, concert hall, or place of amusement wherein intoxicating liquors are sold; nor shall females under sixteen years of age be employed in any capacity where such employment compels them to remain standing constantly.

Violations.

SEC. 300. Each owner, superintendent, manager or overseer of any mine, factory, workshop or mercantile establishment, and any other person who shall employ any child contrary to the provisions of this act or who shall in any manner violate the provisions thereof, shall be deemed guilty of a misdemeanor, and upon conviction thereof shall be fined for each offense in a sum not less than twenty dollars nor more than fifty dollars and costs. Each person authorized to sign a certificate as prescribed in the preceding section who certifies to any material false statement therein shall be deemed guilty of a misdemeanor, and upon conviction thereof, shall be fined not less than twenty dollars nor more than fifty dollars and costs.

OHIO.

GENERAL CODE—1910.

Employment of children in mines.

SECTION 944 (as amended by act, p. 52, Acts of 1910). The owner, lessee or agent of a mine shall not employ, or permit to work therein, any boy under fourteen years of age; nor employ, or permit to work therein, any boy under fifteen years of age during a term of the public schools, in the district in which he resides.

Employment forbidden.

*   *   *   *   *

Employment of women—Seats, etc.

SECTION 1008 (as amended by act, p. 488, Acts of 1911). Every person, partnership or corporation employing females in any factory, workshop, business office, telephone or telegraph office, restaurant, bakery, millinery or dressmaking establishment, mercantile or other establishments shall provide a suitable seat for the use of each female so employed, and shall permit the use of such seats when such female employees are not necessarily engaged in the active duties for which they are employed and when the use thereof will not actually and necessarily interfere with the proper discharge of the duties of such employees, such seat to be constructed, where practicable, with an automatic back support and so adjusted as to be a fixture but not obstruct employees in the performance of duty, and shall further provide a suitable lunch room, separate and apart from the workroom, and in establishments where lunch rooms are provided, female employees shall be entitled to no less than thirty minutes for meal time: *Provided,* That in any establishment aforesaid in which it is found impracticable to provide a suitable lunch room, as aforesaid, female employees shall be entitled to no less than one hour for mealtime during which hour they shall be permitted to leave the establishment. Females over eighteen years of age shall not be employed or permitted or suffered to work in or in connection with any factory, workshop, telephone or telegraph office, millinery or dressmaking establishment, restaurant or in the distributing or transmission of messages more than ten hours in any one day, or more than fifty-four hours in any one week, but meal time shall not be included as a part of the work hours of the week or day: *Provided, however,* That no restriction as to the hours of labor shall apply to canneries or establishments engaged in preparing for use perishable goods.

Seats to be provided.

Lunch rooms.

Time for meals.

Hours of labor.

Exception.

SEC. 1009 (as amended by act, p. 488, Acts of 1911). The owner or person having charge of the building wherein any female is employed shall provide in each establishment on the same floor or the floor immediately above or immediately below the floor where such employee works, suitable and separate toilet and dressing rooms and water-closets, properly ventilated, for the exclusive use of such employees. Such toilet and dressing rooms and water-closets shall be situated together, with one water-closet for every twenty-five females or less, and where there are more than twenty-five females employed, additional water-closets shall be provided in the same ratio; no toilet or dressing room or water-closet shall be placed in the basement or cellar unless females are actually and regularly employed therein, and unless such basement or cellar is properly ventilated.

Toilet rooms.

SEC. 1010 (as amended by act, p. 488, Acts of 1911). In cities, towns and villages not provided with water works and sewage, closets in the same ratio as above mentioned in section 1009 shall be placed on the outside of such building, at a distance not to exceed fifty and not less than twenty feet from such building, with suitable and separate toilet and dressing rooms in such building, or such building may be provided with a dry closet system at the same ratio provided in section 1009, all closets to be supplied with disinfectants and kept in good sanitary condition at all times.

Location of toilet rooms.

SEC. 1011 (as amended by act, p. 488, Acts of 1911). Any person, partnership or corporation or agent thereof, who shall violate any of the provisions of this act, shall upon conviction be fined not less than

Violations.

twenty-five dollars, nor more than two hundred dollars. It shall be the duty of the chief inspector of workshops and factories to see that the provisions of this act are enforced. * * *

Employment of children—Enforcement of laws.

Power of inspectors. SECTION 6246. A child working in or in connection with a factory, workshop, business office, telephone or telegraph office, restaurant, bakery, hotel, apartment house, mercantile or other establishment or in the distribution or transmission of merchandise or messages, who appears to the inspector of workshops and factories to be under the legal age, or refuses to give such inspector his or her name, age and place of residence, shall be forthwith conducted by such inspector to the office of the judge of the juvenile or probate court for examination. If such inspector is in doubt as to the physical fitness of a boy under sixteen years of age, or a girl under eighteen years of age found working in or in connection with any of such establishments, or in the distribution or transmission of merchandise or messages, he shall require a certificate signed by a medical officer of the board of health certifying that such child is of sound health and physically able to perform the work or service such child is required to do. Such certificate shall be signed by the child in whose name it is issued in the presence of the officer issuing it, and such examination shall be made and certificate issued without expense to said child.

Female visitors. SEC. 6247. The chief inspector of workshops and factories, with the approval of the governor, shall designate eight female visitors and make such rules and regulations for their direction and guidance as shall secure uniformity of action and proceedings throughout the State. Such visitors shall receive like compensation as the district inspectors of workshops and factories, payable in a like manner. The necessary traveling expenses incurred by such visitors shall be paid in a like manner and subject to like limitations as is provided by law for such district inspectors.

Duties of visitors. SEC. 6248. Such visitors, as provided in the next preceding section, shall visit all shops and factories in their respective districts in which women or children are employed, including mercantile establishments, as often as possible, to see that the provisions and requirements of the laws relating to the employment of women and children are strictly observed and carried out. They shall carefully inspect the sanitary condition of and examine the system of sewage in connection with such shops, factories and establishments, the situations and conditions of water-closets or urinals in and about such shops, factories and establishments for the use of women or children and also the system of heating, lighting and ventilating all rooms therein, and the means of exit therefrom in case of fire or other disaster; and also all belting, shafting, gearing, elevators, drums and machinery in and about such shops, factories and establishments and see that they are not located so as to be dangerous to such women or children when engaged in their ordinary duties, and as far as practicable, are securely guarded and that every vat, pan or structure filled with molten metal or hot liquid is surrounded with proper safeguards for preventing accident or injury to women or children employed therein; and that such shops, factories and establishments are in proper sanitary condition and adequately provided with means of escape in case of fire or other disaster.

Same subject. SEC. 6249. Such visitors may enter all shops, factories and mercantile establishments, including public institutions of the State which have shops and factories or either, at any reasonable time for the purpose of making the inspection provided in the next preceding section. If they find upon such inspection, that any of the provisions of law relating to buildings, factories or the employment of women or children are being violated or that the heating, lighting, ventilating or sanitary arrangements for women and children of a shop, factory or mercantile establishment are such as to be injurious to the health of such women or children employed or residing therein, they shall notify the chief inspector of workshops and factories, who may notify the owner, proprietor or agent of such shop, factory or mercantile establishment, as provided by law, and may proceed to prosecute such violation of law.

Employment of children—General provisions.

SECTION 7762. All parents, guardians and other persons who have care of children, shall instruct them, or cause them to be instructed in reading, spelling, writing, English grammar, geography and arithmetic. Instruction required.

SEC. 7763 (as amended by act, p. 310, Acts of 1910). Every parent, guardian or other person having charge of any child between the ages of eight and fourteen years must send such child to a public, private or parochial school, for the full time that the school attended is in session, which shall in no case be for less than twenty-eight weeks. Such attendance must begin within the first week of the school term, unless the child is excused therefrom by the superintendent of the public schools, in city or other districts having such superintendent, or by the clerk of the board of education in village, special and township districts, not having a superintendent, or by the principal of the private or parochial school upon satisfactory showing, either that the bodily or mental condition of the child does not permit of its attendance at school, or that the child is being instructed at home by a person qualified, in the opinion of such superintendent, or clerk as the case may be, to teach the branches named in the next preceding section. School attendance.

SEC. 7764. In case such superintendent, principal or clerk refuses to excuse a child from attendance at school, an appeal may be taken from such decision to the probate judge of the county, upon the giving of a bond, within ten days thereafter, to the approval of such judge, to pay the costs of the appeal. His decision in the matter shall be final. All children between the ages of fourteen and sixteen years, not engaged in some regular employment, shall attend school for the full term the schools of the district in which they reside are in session during the school year, unless excused for the reasons above named. Appeals. Children 14 to 16 years of age.

SEC. 7765 (as amended by act, p. 310, Acts of 1910). No child under sixteen years of age shall be employed or be in the employment of any person, company or corporation during the school-term and while the public schools are in session, unless such child presents to such person, company or corporation an age and schooling certificate herein provided for as a condition of employment, who shall keep the same on file for inspection by the truant officer or officers of the department of workshops and factories. Employment certificates required, when.

SEC. 7766 (as amended by act, p. 310, Acts of 1910). An age and schooling certificate shall be approved only by the superintendent of schools, or by a person authorized by him, in city or other districts having such superintendent, or by the clerk of the board of education in village, special and township districts not having such a superintendent, upon satisfactory proof that such child is over fourteen years of age, and that such child has been examined and passed a satisfactory fifth grade test in the studies enumerated in section seventy-seven hundred and sixty-two: *Provided*, That residents of other States who work in Ohio must qualify as aforesaid with the proper school authority in the school district in which the establishment is located, as a condition of employment or service, and that the employment contemplated by the child is not prohibited by any law regulating the employment of children under sixteen years of age. Every such age and schooling certificate shall be signed in the presence of the officer issuing the same, by the child in whose name it is issued. The age and schooling certificate must be formulated by the State commissioner of common schools and furnished, in blank, by the clerk of the board of education. Any child between fourteen and sixteen years of age, who shall cease to work for any cause whatever shall report the fact and cause at once to the superintendent of schools, or by person authorized by him, in city or other districts having such superintendent, or to the clerk of the board of education in village, township or special districts not having such superintendent; said child shall be required to return to school within two weeks, provided other employment is not secured within such time: *Provided*, That should a child in the opinion of the superintendent or person authorized by him in cities and districts having such superintendent or the clerk of the board of education in village, township, or special districts lose his employment by reason of persistent, willful misconduct or continuous inconstancy, he may be placed in school until the close of the current school year. The superintend- Who to issue. Child stopping work. Evidence.

ent of schools, or the person authorized by him to issue age and schooling certificates, shall not issue such certificate until he has received, examined and approved and filed the following papers duly executed: (1) The written pledge or promise of the person, partnership or corporation to legally employ the child, also the written agreement to return to the superintendent of schools or to the person authorized by the superintendent of schools to issue such certificate, the age and schooling certificate of the child, within two days from date of the child's withdrawal or dismissal from the service of the person, partnership or corporation, giving the reason for such withdrawal or dismissal; (2) the school record of such child properly filled out and signed by the principal or other person in charge of the school which such child last attended, giving the name, age, address, standing in studies enumerated in section seven thousand seven hundred and sixty-two and number of weeks attendance in school during the year previous to applying for such school record, and general conduct; (3) a passport or duly attested transcript of the certificate of birth or baptism or other religious record, showing the date and place of birth of such child; a duly attested transcript of the birth certificate filed according to law with a registrar of vital statistics, or other officer charged with the duty of recording births, shall be conclusive evidence of the age of the child; or the affidavit of the parent or guardian or custodian of the child applying for an age and schooling certificate showing the place and date of birth of such child, which affidavit must be taken before the officer issuing the age and schooling certificate, who is hereby authorized and required to administer such oath, and who shall not receive or demand a fee therefor; (4) when a reasonable doubt exists in the mind of the superintendent or the person authorized by him that the child has not reached the normal development of a child of its age and is not in sound health and physically able to perform the work which it intends to do, he shall require of the parent or guardian a certificate from the board of health showing that the child is able to perform the work he is to be employed at.

Educational test. SEC. 7767 (as amended by act, p. 310, Acts of 1910). All minors over the age of fourteen and under the age of sixteen years, who have not passed a satisfactory fifth grade test in the studies enumerated in section seventy-seven hundred and sixty-two, shall attend school as provided in section seventy-seven hundred and sixty-three, and all the provisions thereof shall apply to such minors.

In case the board of education of any school district establishes part time day schools for the instruction of youth over fourteen years of age who are engaged in regular employment, such board of education is authorized to require all youth who have not satisfactorily completed the eighth grade of the elementary schools, to continue their schooling until they are sixteen years of age: *Provided, however,* That such youth if they have been granted age and schooling certificates and are regularly employed, shall be required to attend school not to exceed eight hours a week between the hours of 8 a. m. and 5 p. m. during the school term. All youth between fourteen and sixteen years of age, who are not employed, shall be required to attend school the full time.

Enforcement. SEC. 7770 (as amended by act, p. 310, Acts of 1910). The truant officer and assistants shall be vested with police powers, the authority to serve warrants, and have authority to enter workshops, factories, stores and all other places where children are employed, and do whatever may be necessary, in the way of investigation or otherwise, to enforce this act. He also may take into custody any you h between eight and fourteen years of age, or between fourteen and sixteen years of age when not regularly employed who is not attending school, and shall conduct such youth to the school he has been attending, or which he rightfully should attend.

Same subject. SEC. 7771 (as amended by act, p. 310, Acts of 1910). The truant officer shall institute proceedings against any officer, parent, guardian, person, partnership or corporation violating any provisions of this chapter, and otherwise discharge the duties described therein, and perform such other services as the superintendent of schools or the board of education may deem necessary to preserve the morals and secure the good conduct of school children, and to enforce the provisions of this chapter. The truant officer shall keep on file the name, address and record of all children between the ages of fourteen and sixteen to whom age and schooling certificates have been granted who desire employment, and manufacturers, employers or other persons requiring help of legal age shall have access to such files. The truant officer shall coooperate with the department of workshops and factories in enforcing the conditions and requirements of the child labor laws of Ohio, furnishing upon request such data as he has collected in his reports of children from eight to sixteen years of age and also concerning employers, to the department of workshops and factories and to the state commissioner of schools. He must keep a record of his transactions for the inspection and information of the superintendent of schools and the board of education; and make daily reports to the superintendent during the school term in districts having them, and to the clerk of the board of education in districts not having superintendents as often as required by him. Suitable blanks for the use of the truant officer shall be provided by the clerk of the board of education.

SEC. 7777. When a truant officer is satisfied that a child, compelled to attend school by the provisions of this chapter, is unable to do so because absolutely required to work at home or elsewhere in order to support itself or help to support or care for others legally entitled to its services who are unable to support or care for themselves, such officer must report the case to the president of the board of education. Thereupon he shall furnish text books free of charge, and such other relief as may be necessary to enable the child to attend school for the time each year required by law. The expenses incident to furnishing books and relief must be paid from the contingent funds of the school district. Such child shall not be considered or declared a pauper by reason of the acceptance of the relief herein provided for. If the child, or its parents or guardian, refuses or neglects to take advantage of the provisions thus made for its instruction, it may be committed to a children's home or a juvenile reformatory, * * * *   {Indigent children.}

Employment of children—Certain employments forbidden.

SECTION 12968. Whoever takes, receives, hires, employs, uses, exhibits, sells, apprentices, gives away, lets out or otherwise disposes of a child, under the age of fourteen years for or in the vocation, occupation, service or purpose of singing, playing on musical instruments, rope or wire walking, dancing, begging or peddling or as a gymnast, contortionist, rider or acrobat, or for an obscene, indecent or immoral purpose, exhibition or practice, or for or in a business exhibition or vocation injurious to the health or dangerous to the life or limb of such child, or causes, procures or encourages such child to engage therein, or causes or permits such child to suffer, or inflicts upon it unjustifiable physical pain or mental suffering, or has such child in custody for any of such purposes, shall be fined not more than two hundred dollars or imprisoned not more than six months, or both.   {Acrobatic, mendicant, etc., occupations.}

SEC. 12969 (as amended by act, page 413, Acts of 1911). Section 12968 of the general code shall not apply to or affect the taking part without remuneration of such child with the consent of its parents or guardian in a church, or any school or academy, or at a concert or entertainment given for charitable purposes, or by a church or any school, academy, charitable, eleemosynary or religious institution.   {Exemption.}

SEC. 12972. Whoever willfully causes or permits the life or limb of a child under the age of sixteen years to be endangered, its health to be injured or its morals to become depraved, from and while actually in his employ, or willfully permits such child to be placed in such a position or engage in employment whereby its life or limb is in danger, its health likely to be injured or its morals likely to be impaired or depraved, shall be fined not less than ten dollars nor more than fifty dollars or imprisoned not less than thirty days nor more than ninety days.   {Penalty.}

SEC. 12973. The State inspector of workshops and factories shall enforce the provisions of the next preceding section.   {Enforcement.}

Employment of children—Violations of statutes.

Failure to require certificate.   SECTION 12975 (as amended by act, p. 310, Acts of 1910). Whoever employs a minor under sixteen years of age before exacting from such minor the age and schooling certificate provided by law, or fails to keep such certificate on file, or who fails to return to the superintendent of schools or the person authorized by him such certificate within two days from such minor's withdrawal or dismissal from his services as provided in section seventy-seven hundred and sixty or to permit a truant officer, upon request therefor, to examine such certificate, shall be fined not less than twenty-five dollars nor more than fifty dollars.

Illiterates.   SEC. 12976. Whoever employs, during the time a public, private or parochial school is in session in the school district in which such minor resides, a minor over the age of fourteen and under the age of sixteen years who cannot read and write the English language as provided by law; or whoever, employing such minor, fails forthwith to cease such employment upon notice from a truant officer as provided by law, shall be fined not less than twenty-five dollars nor more than fifty dollars.

Retaining wages.   SEC. 12989. Whoever, being a person, officer or agent of a company or corporation doing business in this State, retains or withholds from a minor in his employ the wages or compensation, or a part thereof, agreed to be paid and due such minor for work performed or services rendered, because of presumed negligence or failure to comply with rules, breakage of machinery or alleged incompetence to produce work or perform labor according to any standard of merit, shall be fined not more than two hundred dollars or imprisoned in the county jail not more than six months, or both.

Accepting guarantees, etc.   SEC. 12990. Whoever, being a person, officer or agent of a company or corporation, receives a guarantee, bonus, money deposit or other form of security to obtain or secure employment for a minor or to insure faithful performance of labor, guarantee strict observance of rules or make good losses which may be charged to such minor's incompetence, negligence or inability, shall be fined not more than two hundred dollars or imprisoned in the county jail not more than six months, or both.

Employment without agreement as to wages.   SEC. 12991. Whoever, being a person, officer or agent of a company or corporation, gives employment to a minor, without agreeing with him as to the wages or compensation he shall receive for each day, week, month or year, or per piece, for work performed and without furnishing such minor with written evidence of such agreement and, on or before each pay-day, with a statement of the earnings due and the amount thereof to be paid to him or changes the wages or compensation of a minor without giving him notice thereof at least twenty-four hours previous to its going into effect, when a written agreement thereof shall be given to such minor as for an original employment, shall be fined not more than two hundred dollars or imprisoned in the county jail not more than six months, or both.

Enforcement.   SEC. 12992. The inspector of workshops and factories shall enforce the provisions of the next three preceding sections.

Employing child under 14.   SEC. 12993. Whoever, having charge or management of a factory, workshop, business office, telephone or telegraph office, restaurant, bakery, hotel, apartment house, mercantile or other establishment, employs or permits a child under the age of fourteen years to work in or in connection with such establishment, or in the distribution or transmission of merchandise or messages, shall be fined not less than twenty-five dollars nor more than fifty dollars.

Children 14 to 16 years of age.   SEC. 12994. Whoever, having charge or management of such establishment as provided in the next preceding section, employs or permits a child between fourteen and sixteen years of age to work in or in connection with such establishment, or in the distribution or transmission of merchandise or messages, without first procuring from the proper authority the age and schooling certificate provided by law, shall be fined not less than twenty-five dollars nor more than fifty dollars.

Certificates to be on file.   SEC. 12995. The certificate mentioned in the next preceding section shall be filed in the office of such establishment and shall be produced for inspection upon request therefor by the chief or district inspector of workshops and factories or a truant officer and shall be returned forthwith to the superintendent of schools or other person legally issuing it, by the person in charge or manager of such establishment upon the termination of the employment of such minor.

SEC. 12996. Whoever, having charge or management of such establishment, as provided in section twelve thousand nine hundred and ninety-three, employs or permits a boy under sixteen years of age or a girl under eighteen years of age to work in or in connection with such establishment or in the distribution or transmission of merchandise or messages, for more than forty-eight hours in one week, more than eight hours in one day, before the hour of seven o'clock in the morning or after the hour of six o'clock in the evening, shall be fined not less than twenty-five dollars nor more than fifty dollars. `Hours o flabor.`

SEC. 12997. A boy or girl employed as provided in the next preceding section, shall be entitled to not less than thirty minutes for meal time which shall not be included as a part of the work hours of the day or week. `Meal time.`

SEC. 12998. Whoever, having charge or management of an establishment, as provided in section twelve thousand nine hundred and ninety-three, or his agent, fails to keep a correct record containing the name, birthplace, date of birth and place of residence of each boy between fourteen and sixteen years of age and each girl between fourteen and eighteen years of age, or fails to post in a conspicuous place in each room where such boy or girl works, a printed notice stating the maximum number of work hours for each day and week, shall be fined not less than twenty-five dollars nor more than fifty dollars. `Records to be kept.`

SEC. 12999. The notice provided in the next preceding section shall be formulated by the chief inspector of workshops and factories, approved by the attorney general and furnished by such inspector upon application therefor. `Notice.`

SEC. 13000. Failure to produce for lawful inspection the age and schooling certificate as provided by law, or the record as provided in section twelve thousand nine hundred and ninety-eight, shall be prima facie evidence of the illegal employment or service of the child whose certificate is not so produced or whose record is not so correctly kept. `Evidence.`

SEC. 13001. Whoever employs or permits a child under sixteen years of age to work at the occupation of sewing or assisting in sewing machine belts in a workshop or factory in any capacity; adjusting a belt to machinery; oiling or assisting in oiling, wiping or cleaning machinery; operating or assisting in operating circular or band saws, wood-shapers, wood-jointers, planers, sand-paper or wood-polishing machinery, job or cylinder printing presses operated by power other than foot, emery or polishing wheels used for polishing metal, wood-turning or boring machinery, stamping machines used in sheet metal and tinware manufacturing, stamping machines in washer and nut factories, corrugating rolls, such as are used in roofing and washboard factories, steam boilers, steam machinery, or other steam generating apparatus, dough brakes or cracker machinery of any description, wire or iron straightening machinery, rolling mill machinery, punches or shears, washing, grinding or mixing mills; calender rolls in rubber manufacturing, laundry machinery, or passenger or freight elevators, shall be fined not less than twenty-five dollars nor more than fifty dollars. `Employment at dangerous machinery.`

SEC. 13002. Whoever employs or permits a child under sixteen years of age to work in any capacity in the preparation of a compound in which dangerous or poisonous acids are used; in the manufacture of paints, colors or white lead; in the manufacturing, packing or storing of powder, dynamite, nitro-glycerine compounds, fuses or other explosives, or in dipping, dyeing or packing matches, shall be fined not less than twenty-five dollars nor more than fifty dollars. `Acids, etc.`

SEC. 13003. Whoever employs or permits a child under sixteen years of age to work at the manufacture of goods for immoral purposes, or in or about a distillery, brewery, or other establishment where malt or alcoholic liquor is manufactured, packed, wrapped or bottled, or in a hotel, theater, concert hall, drug store, saloon or place of amusement where intoxicating liquor is sold, or in assorting, manufacturing or packing tobacco, or as a pin boy in a bowling alley, shall be fined not less than twenty-five dollars nor more than fifty dollars. `Immoral and other hurtful employments.`

Employments not enumerated.
SEC. 13004. Whoever employes [employs] or permits a child under sixteen years of age to work at any employment, other than those mentioned in the next three preceding sections, that may be considered dangerous to its life or limbs, or where its health may be injured or its morals depraved, shall be fined not less than twenty-five dollars nor more than fifty dollars.

Requiring girls to stand constantly.
SEC. 13005. Whoever employes [employs] or permits a girl under the age of sixteen years to work at an employment which compels her to remain standing constantly, shall be fined not less than twenty-five dollars nor more than fifty dollars.

Hindering inspection.
SEC. 13006. Whoever prevents a female visitor, as provided by law, from entering, at reasonable hours, a shop, factory, or mercantile establishment for the purpose of making a lawful inspection thereof, shall be fined not less than twenty-five dollars nor more than fifty dollars.

OKLAHOMA.

CONSTITUTION.

ARTICLE XXIII.—*Employment of children.*

Age limit for children.
SECTION 3. The employment of children, under the age of fifteen years in any occupation, injurious to health or morals or especially hazardous to life or limb, is hereby prohibited.

Women and children in mines.
SEC. 4. Boys under the age of sixteen years, and women and girls, shall not be employed, underground, in the operation of mines; and, except in cases of emergency, eight hours shall constitute a day's work underground in all mines of the State.

STATUTES OF 1893.

Employment of women and children—Hours of labor.

Ten hours a day's labor.
PARAGRAPH 2550. Every owner, stockholder, overseer, employer, clerk or foreman, of any manufactory, workshop, or other place used for mechanical or manufacturing purposes, who, having control, shall compel any woman or any child under eighteen years of age, or permit any child under fourteen years of age, to labor in any day exceeding ten hours, shall be deemed guilty of a misdemeanor, and upon conviction, shall be punished by fine not exceeding one hundred and not less than ten dollars.

Earnings of minors.

Payment to minors valid, when.
PARAGRAPH 3562. The wages of a minor employed in service may be paid to him or her until the parent or guardian entitled thereto gives the employer notice that he claims such wages.

ACTS OF 1907–8.

ARTICLE V.—*Seats for female employees.*

(Page 499.)

Seats required.
SECTION 17. The proprietor, manager or person having charge of any mercantile establishment, store shop, hotel, restaurant or other place where women or girls are employed as clerk in this State, shall provide chairs, stools or other contrivances for the comfortable use of such female employees, and shall permit the use of the same by such female employees for the preservation of their health and for rest when not actually employed in the discharge of their respective duties.

ACTS OF 1909.

Employment of children.

(Page 629.)

Age limit.
SECTION 1. No child under the age of fourteen years shall be employed or permitted or suffered to work in any factory, factory workshop, theater, bowling alley, pool hall, steam laundry or in any occupation injurious to health or morals or especially hazardous to life or

limb. It shall be the duty of the commissioner of labor upon investigation by himself or the agents of his department, or upon comp aint of the commissioner of charities and corrections, or the board of health, to determine what occupations are injurious to health or morals or especially hazardous to life or limb, and to notify employers in such occupations of his decision, which decision shall be final until such occupation or occupations shall be defined by law as safe for health, morals, life and limb. Dangerous, etc., occupations.

SEC. 2. No child under the age of sixteen years shall be employed, permitted or suffered to work at any of the following occuaptions: Oiling or assisting in oiling, operating, wiping or cleaning any dangerous machinery, or adjusting any belt to any such machinery, while in motion; operating, or assisting in operating, circular or band saws; steam boilers, steam machinery, or other steam-generating apparatus; rolling-mill machinery, punches or shears; washing, grinding or mixing mills; passenger or freight elevators; preparing any composition in which dangerous or poisonous acids are used; manufacturing of paints, colors or white lead; where there are acids, dyes, lyes, gases, glass dust or other dust or lint in such quantities as to be injurious to health; dipping, dyeing ([1]) or packing matches; manufacturing, packing or storing powder, dynamite, nitroglycerine compounds, fuses or other explosives; manufacture of goods for immoral purposes; nor shall females under the age of sixteen years be employed in any capacity where such employment compels them to remain standing constantly. Employments prohibited.

SEC. 3. No child under the age of sixteen years and no girl or woman shall be employed or permitted or suffered to work under ground in any mine or quarry. Employment in mines.

SEC. 4. No girl under the age of sixteen years shall, in any city, sell, or expose or offer for sale newspapers, magazines or periodicals in any street or out-of-doors public place. Girls not to sell papers.

SEC. 5. No child under the age of sixteen years shall be employed or permitted or suffered to work in any of the occupations specified in section one of this act unless such child is able to read and write simple sentences in the English language, or shall have attended some school during the preceding year for the time that attendance is compulsory under the laws. Literacy test.

SEC. 6. No child under the age of sixteen years shall be employed or permitted or suffered to work in any gainful occupation, except agriculture or domestic service, more than eight hours in any one day, allowing one hour each day for noonday meal and rest, or more than forty-eight hours in any one week. During the time that a child is at work at such occupation, the employer must provide suitable seats and permit their use so far as the nature of the work allows. Hours of labor. Seats.

SEC. 7. No boy under the age of sixteen years and no girl under the age of eighteen shall be employed or permitted or suffered to work in any of the occupations mentioned in section one of this act between the hours of six o'clock p. m. and seven o'clock a. m. Night work.

SEC. 8. Before any child under the age of sixteen years shall be employed in any occupation specified in section one of this act, it shall be the duty of the parent or guardian of such child to procure and furnish the employer of such child an age and schooling certificate as hereinafter provided by this act. Certificates.

It shall be the duty of every person, firm or corporation of such establishments as are specified in section one of this act, or employers in such occupations, to keep on file for the inspection of factory inspectors, truant officers, or other persons charged with the administration of this act, such age and schooling certificate, for every child under sixteen years of age employed in such occupation, and to keep on file and to post conspicuously in every room where such children are employed a register, with a complete list of children under sixteen years of age so employed, together with the age of each child as set forth in the age and schooling certificate opposite the name of such child, and also to keep on file and to post conspicuously in such place or establishment, in such form as the factory inspector may prescribe, Files. Schedule to be posted.

---

[1] It is possible that *drying* was intended, as drying is an essential and dangerous process in matchmaking, while *dyeing* is not.

the time of opening and closing of such factory or other establishment, the number of hours of labor required or permitted in such establishment, the hours of commencing and stopping work, and the time allowed for meals, and if there be two or more shifts in such establishment the number of hours in each shift during which the employees are required or permitted to work. On termination of the employment of a child so registered, and whose certificate is so filed, such certificate shall be forthwith surrendered by the employer to the **Enforcement.** child or its parent or guardian or custodian. The inspector of factories, truant officer or other person charged with the administration of this act, may make demand on an employer in whose factory or establishment a child apparently under the age of sixteen years is employed or permitted or suffered to work, and whose employment certificate is not then filed as required by this section, that such employer shall either furnish him, within ten days, evidence satisfactory to him that such child is in fact over sixteen years of age, or shall cease to employ or permit or suffer such child to work in such factory or establishment. Such officer may require from such employer the same evidence of age of such child as is required on the issuance of an employment certificate; and the employer furnishing such evidence shall not be required to furnish any further evidence of the age of the child. In case such employer shall fail to produce and deliver to such officer, within ten days after such demand, such evidence of age herein required by him, and shall thereafter continue to employ such child to work in such factory or establishment, proof of the giving such notice and of such failure to produce and file such evidence shall be prima facie evidence in any prosecution brought for a violation of this provision of this act that such child is under sixteen years of age and is unlawfully employed.

Who approves certificates. SEC. 9. The age and schooling certificate shall be approved only by the county superintendent of public instruction, or other school official designated by him, who shall, for the purpose of this act, be empowered to administer an oath.

Evidence. SEC. 10. The age and schooling certificate shall not be approved unless satisfactory evidence is furnished by the last school census, or certificate of birth, or the register of the city or county, or an affidavit of the date of such birth by a legally registered physician residing therein, stating the time of birth of such child, or the school record of such child, in the public or other school, setting forth the age of such child: *Provided,* That in cases where such evidence can not be obtained and the child appears to be in good health, and of normal size, of not less than sixty inches in height and weighing not less than eighty pounds, the parent or guardian of such child may make affidavit stating the age, place and time of birth of such child, or if the child shall have no parent or guardian, such affidavit may be made by the child. The affidavits required by this section must be taken before the officer issuing the employment certificate, who is hereby authorized and required to administer such oath, and who shall not demand or receive a fee therefor. The employment certificate shall not be issued until such child has further personally appeared before the officer issuing the same and he is satisfied that such child is physically able to perform the work which it intends to do. In doubtful cases such physical fitness shall be determined by a medical officer of the board or department of health. Every employment certificate shall be signed, in the presence of the officer issuing the same, by the child in whose name it is issued.

Certificate of school attendance. SEC. 11. The age and schooling certificate shall not be approved until the parent or guardian of such child shall present a school attendance certificate as hereinafter prescribed by this act. A duplicate of such age and schooling certificate shall be filled out and sent by the school officer, before whom the same is made, to the commissioner of labor. The blank forms for school attendance certificate and for the age and schooling certificate shall be supplied to the county superintendents of public instruction by the State superintendent of public instruction as hereinafter indicated:

SCHOOL ATTENDANCE CERTIFICATE.

....(Name of school)

....(City and county)

....(Date)

This certifies that (name of child) can read and write simple sentences in the English language and that according to the records of this school and in my belief is now (number of years and months) old, and has attended school during the full school term of the preceding year.

....(Name of parent or guardian)

....(Residence)

(Signature of teacher)..

AGE AND SCHOOLING CERTIFICATE.

This certifies that I am (father, mother or guardian) of (name of child) and that he (or she) was born at —— (town or city) —— (county) —— (State or county [country]) on the (day, month and year of birth) and is now (number of years and months old).

...................................(Signature of parent or guardian)

....(Date)

....(City or town or county)

Personally appeared before me the above-mentioned (name of person signing) and made oath that the foregoing certificate is true to the best of his (or her) knowledge and belief.

I hereby approve the foregoing certificate of (name of child), height (feet and inches), weight (pounds), complexion (fair or dark), hair (color), eyes (color), having no sufficient reason to doubt that he (or she) is of the age therein certified.

OWNER OF CERTIFICATE.

This certificate belongs to —— —— (name of child) and is to be surrendered to him (or her) whenever he (or she) leaves the service of the employer holding the same, but if not claimed by said child within thirty days after leaving said service, shall be sent to the commissioner of labor.

—— ——

(Signature of officer, with name of city, town or county, and date.)

SEC. 12. Any person, firm or corporation violating any of the provisions of this act shall be punished by a fine of not less than ten dollars nor more than fifty dollars, or imprisonment for not less than ten nor more than thirty days, or by both such fine and imprisonment. The employment of any child under sixteen years of age, without a certificate as herein prescribed, or the employment of any child under sixteen years of age or any girl or woman underground in any mine or quarry, or the signing of any false statement as to the age of any child, or the making of any false statement in an affidavit of an employer, shall be prima facie evidence of guilt. It shall be the duty of the commissioner of labor to see that the provisions of this act are enforced, with the exception of section three shall be enforced by the mine inspector or under his direction. *Violations.*

OREGON.

ACTS OF 1903.

(Page 79. Amended by chapter 138, Acts of 1911.)

Age limit.   SECTION 2. No child under fourteen years of age shall be employed, permitted, or suffered to work in, or in connection with, any factory, workshop, mercantile establishment, store, business office, restaurant, bakery, hotel, or apartment house. No child under the age of sixteen shall be employed, permitted or suffered to work in the telegraph, telephone, or public messenger service.

Employment during school time.   SEC. 3. No child under the age of fourteen years shall be employed in any work, or labor in any form, for wages or other compensation to whomsoever payable, during the term when the public schools of the town, district, or city in which he or she resides are in session.

School attendance required.   SEC. 4. Attendance at school shall be compulsory upon all children between the ages of nine and fourteen years in all cities, towns, and villages of the State of Oregon during the whole of the school term in the city, town or village in which the child resides, and upon all children in such cities, towns and villages between the ages of fourteen and sixteen years who are not legally employed in some lawful work.

Night work.   SEC. 5. No child under sixteen years of age shall be employed at any work before the hour of seven in the morning, or after the hour of six at night, nor employed for longer than 10 hours for any one day, nor more than six days in any one week; and every such child, under sixteen years of age, shall be entitled to not less than thirty minutes for meal time at noon, but such meal time shall not be included as part of the work hours of the day; and every employer shall post in a conspicuous place where such minors are employed, a printed notice stating the maximum work hours required in one week, and in every day of the week from such minors.

Certificate to be on file.   SEC. 6. No child under sixteen years of age shall be employed, permitted or suffered to work in any employment enumerated in section 2 unless the person or corporation employing him procures and keeps on file and accessible to the school authorities of the district where such child resides, and to the police and board of inspectors of child labor an age and schooling certificate as hereinafter prescribed, and keep a complete list of all such children employed therein.

Who may issue.   SEC. 7. An age and schooling certificate shall be executed, issued and approved only by the secretary of the board of inspection of child labor, or by a person authorized by him or her in writing: *Provided*, That no person authorized as aforesaid shall have authority to approve such certificate for any child then in or about to enter his own employment, or the employment of a firm or corporation of which he is a member, officer or employee. The person approving the certificate shall have authority to administer the oath provided for therein, but no fees shall be charged therefor, but in case of the loss of such certificate a certified cop may be furnished, for which a fee of fifty cents may be charged. y

Evidence of age.   SEC. 8. An age and schooling certificate shall not be approved unless satisfactory evidence is furnished by the last school census, the passport, the duly attested transcript of the certificate of birth or baptism of such child or other religious record, or the register of birth of such child with a town or city, that such child is of the age stated in the certificate.

Duplicate copy.   SEC. 9. A duplicate of each age and schooling certificate shall be filled out and kept on file by the secretary of the board of inspection of child labor. Any explanatory matter may be printed with such certificate in the discretion of the secretary. The age and schooling certificate shall be printed and shall be filled out, signed and held or surrendered as indicated in the following form:

AGE AND SCHOOLING CERTIFICATE.

Form.   This certifies that I am the (father, mother, guardian or custodian) of (name of child) ...., and that (he or she) was born at (name of town or city) ......, in the county of (name of county, if known), and

State (or country) of ...... on the (day and year of birth) ....,
and is now (number of years and months) .... old.

(Signature of father, mother, guardian or custodian.)
(Town or city and date.)
Then personally appeared before me the above named (name of person
signing), ..., and made oath that the foregoing certificate by
(him or her) signed is true to the best of (his or her) knowledge and
belief. I hereby approve the foregoing certificate of (name of child)
.... height (feet and inches) .... eyes (color) ......,
complexion (fair or dark), hair (color), having no sufficient reason to
doubt that (he or she) is of the age therein certified. I hereby certify
that (he or she) can read at sight and (can or cannot) write legibly simple
sentences in the English language, and that (he or she) has reached the
normal development of a child of (his or her) age, and is in sound health
and is physically able to perform the work which (he or she) intends to
do, and that (he or she) has regularly attended the public schools or a
school equivalent thereto, for not less than 160 days during the school
year previous to arriving at the age of 14 years, or during the school year
previous to applying for such school record, and has received during
such period instruction in reading, spelling, writing, English grammar,
and geography, and is familiar with the fundamental operations of
arithmetic to and including fractions.
This certificate belongs to (name of child in whose behalf it is drawn)
...., and is to be surrendered to (her or him) whenever (he or
she) leaves the service of the corporation or employer holding the same,
but if not claimed by said child within thirty days from such time it
shall be returned to the secretary of the board of inspectors of child
labor.

....
(Signature of person authorized to approve and sign, with official
character or authority.)
(Town or city and date.)

SEC. 10. A failure to produce to the school authorities of the district **Evidence of il-legal employ-ment.**
where such child resides and to the police and to the board of inspectors
of child labor any age and schooling certificate or list required by this
act shall be prima facie evidence of the illegal employment of any person whose age and schooling certificate is not produced or whose name
is not so listed. Any corporation or employer retaining any age and
schooling certificate in violation of section 5, of this act shall be fined
$10. Every person authorized to sign the certificate prescribed by
section 5 of this act who knowingly certifies to any material false statement therein shall be guilty of a misdemeanor and upon conviction
thereof shall be fined not less than $5 and not more than $50.

The board of inspectors of child labor or any one or more of them or **Enforcement.**
any one authorized by such board in writing may visit the factories,
workshops and mercantile establishments in their several towns and
cities and ascertain whether any minors are employed therein contrary
to the provisions of this act, and they shall report any cases of such
illegal employment to the proper school authorities and to the district
attorney of the county. The board of inspectors of child labor may
require that the age and schooling certificates and lists provided for by
this act, of minors employed in such factories, workshops, or mercantile establishments, shall be produced for their inspection. Complaints
for offenses under this act shall be brought by the board of inspectors
of child labor to the attention of the proper district attorney and offenses
hereunder shall be prosecuted by such district attorney.

SEC. 11. Any person or corporation who shall employ a minor contrary **Violations by employers.**
to the provisions of this act, or who shall violate any of the provisions
thereof, shall be guilty of a misdemeanor and upon conviction shall be
fined in a sum of not less than $10 nor more than $25 for the first offense,
nor less than $25 nor more than $50 for the second offense, and be imprisoned for not less than ten nor more than 30 days for the third and
each succeeding offense.

SEC. 12. Any parent or guardian who shall violate any of the pro- **By parents.**
visions of this act or allow any child under their custody or control to

be employed contrary to the provisions of this act shall be guilty of a misdemeanor, and upon conviction thereof shall be fined not less than $5 and not more than $25.

Vacation employment. SEC. 13. The board of inspectors of child labor may in its discretion allow children between the ages of twelve and fourteen to be employed in any suitable work during any school vacation extending over a term of two weeks and may issue permits therefor. It shall be the duty of such board to exercise careful discretion as to the character of such employment and its effect on the physical and moral well-being of the child.

Board not compensated. SEC. 14. The board of inspectors of child labor of the State of Oregon, heretofore appointed such board under the provisions of the act of which this is amendatory, and now serving are hereby appointed a board of inspectors of child labor of the State of Oregon, and shall serve without **Secretary.** compensation, except that the secretary of such board of inspectors who shall be a member of such board, shall be allowed a yearly salary not exceeding one thousand five hundred dollars. The term for which such inspectors shall serve shall be one, two, three, four and five years, respectively, from the time of their original appointment, the terms to remain as already determined by lot under said original act, and upon the expiration of the term of any one of said inspectors the governor shall appoint his or her successor to serve for a term of five years. Appointments shall be so made that three at least of said inspectors shall always be women.

Night messenger service. SEC. 15. No person under the age of eighteen years shall be employed or permitted to work as a messenger for a telegraph or messenger company or any one engaged in such a business in the distribution, transmission or delivery of goods or messages before five o'clock in the morning or after ten o'clock in the evening of any day.

Employment of women.

(Page 148. Amended by chapter 200, Acts of 1907.)

Ten hours a day's work. SECTION 1 (as amended by chapter 138, Acts of 1909). No female shall be employed in any manufacturing, mechanical, or mercantile establishment, laundry, hotel or restaurant, or telegraph or telephone establishment or office, or by any express or transportation company in this State more than ten hours during any one day or more than sixty hours in one week. The hours of work may be so arranged as to permit the employment of females at any time so that they shall not work more than ten hours during the twenty-four hours of one day, or sixty hours during any one week.

Seats to be provided SEC. 2. Every employer in any manufacturing, mechanical or mercantile establishment, laundry, hotel or restaurant, or other establishment employing any female, shall provide suitable seats for all female employees, and shall permit them to use such seats when they are not engaged in the active duties of their employment.

Violations. SEC. 3. Any employer who shall require any female to work in any of the places mentioned in section 1 more than the number of hours provided for in this act during any day of twenty-four hours, or who shall fail, neglect or refuse to so arrange the work of females in his employ so that they shall not work more than the number of hours provided for in this act during any day of twenty-four hours, or who shall fail, neglect or refuse to provide suitable seats, as provided in section 2 of this act, or who shall permit or suffer any overseer, superintendent, or other agent of any such employer to violate any of the provisions of this act, shall be guilty of a misdemeanor, and upon conviction thereof shall be fined for each offense not less than $25 nor more than $100.

ACTS OF 1909.

CHAPTER 54.—*Employment of children—Operators of elevators.*

Age limit. SECTION 1. No person, firm, or corporation shall employ or allow any person under the age of eighteen (18) years to run, operate, or have charge of, any elevator used for the purpose of carrying either persons or property.

SEC. 2. Any person, either for himself or as manager, agent, or officer Violation. of any corporation, who is guilty of violating any of the provisions of this act shall be deemed guilty of a misdemeanor, and upon conviction thereof shall be punished by a fine of not less than $10 nor more than $100, or by imprisonment in the county jail not less than thirty days nor more than six months, or by both such fine and imprisonment.

PENNSYLVANIA.

BRIGHTLY'S PURDON'S DIGEST—1895.

Seats for female employees.

(Page 902.)

SECTION 1. Every person, firm, association, individual, partnership Seats to be provided. or corporation employing female employees in any manufacturing, mechanical or mercantile establishment in this State, shall provide suitable seats for the use of the female employees so employed, and shall permit the use of such by them when they are not necessarily engaged in the active duties for which they are employed.

SEC. 2. Any person, firm, association, individual, partnership or cor- Penalty. poration violating any of the provisions of this act shall, upon conviction thereof before any magistrate, alderman or justice of the peace, be sentenced to pay a fine of not less than twenty-five nor more than fifty dollars, to be paid into the treasury of the proper county, and costs for each offense, and any [sic] failure to pay the same shall be committed to the proper jail until discharged according to law.

Employment of children.

(Page 1015.)

SECTION 9. Any person having the care, custody or control, lawful or Mendicant occupations forbidden. unlawful, for [of] any minor child under the age of eighteen years, who shall use such minor or apprentice, give away, let out, hire or otherwise dispose of such minor, to any person, for the purpose of singing, playing on musical instruments, begging, or for any mendicant business whatsoever, in the streets, roads or other highways of this Commonwealth, and whosoever shall take, receive, hire, employ, use or have in custody, any such minor, for the vocation, occupation, calling, service or purpose of singing, playing upon musical instruments or begging, upon the street, roads or other highways of the Commonwealth, or for any mendicant business whatever, shall be guilty of a misdemeanor, and upon conviction thereof * * * shall be fined not less than fifty dollars nor more than one hundred dollars.

SEC. 10. Any person having the care, custody or control of any minor Employment in dance houses, saloons, etc. child under the age of fifteen years, who shall in any manner sell, apprentice, give away or permit such child to sing, dance, act, or in any manner exhibit, in any dance house whatever, or in any concert saloon, theatre or place of entertainment, where wines or spirituous or malt liquors are sold or given away, or with which any place for the sale of wines or spirituous or malt liquors is directly or indirectly connected, by any passageway or entrance, and any proprietor of any dance house whatever, or any such concert saloon, theatre or place of entertainment, so employing any such child, shall be guilty of a misdemeanor, and upon conviction thereof * * * shall be fined not less than fifty dollars nor more than one hundred dollars for each offense.

SEC. 11. Any person having the care, custody or control of any Acrobatic etc., employments. minor child under the age of fifteen years, who shall in any manner sell, apprentice, give away or otherwise dispose of such child, and any person who shall take, receive or employ such child for the vocation or occupation of rope or wire walking, or as an acrobat, gymnast, contortionist or rider, and any person who, having the care, custody or control of any minor child whatsoever, shall sell, apprentice, give away or otherwise dispose of such child, or who shall take, receive or employ such child, for any obscene, indecent or illegal exhibition or vocation, or any vocation injurious to the health or dangerous to the life or limb of such child engaged therein, or for the purpose of prostitution, and any person who shall retain, harbor or employ any minor child in or about any assignation house or brothel, or in any place where any obscene, indecent or illegal exhibition takes place, shall be guilty of a misdemeanor, and upon conviction thereof before any justice of the peace, magistrate or court of record, shall be fined not less than fifty dollars nor more than one hundred dollars for each offense.

Minor under 14 not to run elevator   SEC. 12. No person, firm or corporation shall employ or permit any minor under the age of fourteen years to have the care, custody, management or operation of any elevator. Any person, firm or corporation, employing any minor under the age of fourteen years to operate, manage or otherwise have the care or custody of an elevator, shall be guilty of a misdemeanor, and upon conviction thereof, shall be sentenced to pay a fine of not less than twenty-five dollars nor more than one hundred dollars.

Women and children in mines.   SEC. 14 (as amended by act No. 266, Acts of 1903). No boy under the age of sixteen years, and no woman or girl of any age, shall be employed or permitted to be in any mine for the purpose of employment therein. Nor shall a boy under the age of fourteen years, or a woman or girl of any age, be employed of [or] permitted to be in or about the outside structures or workings of a colliery for the purpose of employment:

Proviso.   *But it is provided, however,* That this prohibition shall not affect the employment of a boy or female, of suitable age, in an office or in the performance of clerical work at a colliery.

Certificate of age.   SEC. 15. When an employer is in doubt as to the age of any boy or youth applying for employment in or about a mine or colliery, he shall demand and receive proof of the said lawful employment age of such boy or youth, by certificate from the parent or guardian, before said boy or youth shall be employed.

What are violations.   SEC. 16. If any person or persons contravene or fail to comply with the provisions of this act [secs. 14 to 16] in respect to the employment of boys, young male persons or females, or if he or they shall connive with or permit others to contravene or fail to comply with said provisions, or if a parent or guardian of a boy or young male person make or give a false certificate of the age of such boy or young male person, or knowingly do or perform any other act for the purpose of securing employment for a boy or young male person under the lawful employment age and in contravention of the provisions of this act, he or they shall be guilty of an offense against this act.

Employment of women and children in anthracite mines.

(Page 1349.)

Oiling machinery by children.   SECTION 88. No person under fifteen (15) years of age shall be appointed to oil the machinery, and no person shall oil dangerous parts of such machinery while it is in motion.

Employment forbidden.   SEC. 112 (as amended by act No. 266, Acts of 1903). No boy under the age of sixteen years, and no woman or girl of any age, shall be employed or permitted to be in any mine for the purpose of employment therein. Nor shall a boy under the age of fourteen years, or a woman or girl of any age, be employed or permitted to be in or about the outside structures or workings of a colliery for purpose of employment; but it is provided, however, that this prohibition shall not affect the employment of a boy or female, of suitable age, in an office or in the performance of clerical work at a colliery.

Certificate of age.   SEC. 113. When an employer is in doubt as to the age of any boy or youth applying for employment in or about a mine or colliery, he shall demand and receive proof of the said lawful employment age of such boy or youth, by certificate from the parent or guardian, before said boy or youth shall be employed.

Violations.   SEC. 114. If any person or persons contravene or fail to comply with the provisions of this act in respect to the employment of boys, young male persons or females, or if he or they shall connive with or permit others to contravene or fail to comply with said provisions, or if a parent or guardian of a boy or young male person make or give a false certificate of the age of such boy or young male person, or knowingly do or perform any other act for the purpose of securing employment for a boy or young male person under the lawful employment age and in contravention of the provisions of this act, he or they shall be guilty of an offense against this act.

BRIGHTLY'S DIGEST—1903.

Employment of women and children in bakeries.

(Page 62.)

SECTION 1. No employee shall be required, permitted or suffered to work in a biscuit, bread or cake bakery, [or] confectionery establishment more than six (6) days in any one week, said week to commence on Sunday not before six o'clock post meridian, and to terminate at the corresponding time on Saturday of the same week. No person under the age of eighteen (18) years shall be employed in any bakehouse between the hours of nine (9) o'clock at night and five (5) in the morning. Excepted from this rule shall be the time on Sunday for setting the sponges for the night's work following. *Hours of labor.* *Night work of minors.*

The week may begin on Sunday any time after 6 p. m. and close at the same hour on Saturday of the same week. 19 Co. C. Rep. 476.
The provision as to the limit of a week's labor is meaningless and absurd, and no indictment upon it can be sustained. 20 Co. C. Rep. 476.

SEC. 13. No minor male or female, or adult woman, shall be employed at labor or detained in any biscuit, bread, pie or cake bakery, pretzel or macaroni establishment, for a longer period than twelve hours in any one day, nor for a longer period than sixty hours in any one week. *Women and children.*

Employment of children—School attendance.

(Page 143.)

SECTION 128 (as amended by act No. 237, Acts of 1907). Every parent, guardian, or other person in this Commonwealth having control or charge of a child, or children, between the ages of eight and sixteen years, shall be required to send such child, or children, to a day school in which the common English branches are taught, and such child or children shall attend such school continuously during the entire time in which the public school in their respective districts shall be in session, unless such child or children shall be excused from such attendance by the board of the school district in which the parent, guardian or other person resides, upon the presentation to said board of satisfactory evidence showing such child or children are prevented from attendance upon school or application to study by mental, physical or other urgent reasons. But the term "urgent reasons" shall be strictly construed, and shall not permit of irregular attendance: *Provided,* That the school board in each district shall have power, at its June meeting, to reduce the period of compulsory attendance to not less than seventy per centum (70 per centum) of the school term in such district, in which case the board must, at that date, fix the time for compulsory attendance to begin. This act shall not apply to any child between the ages of fourteen and sixteen years, who can read and write the English language intelligently, and is regularly engaged in any useful employment or service. A certificate of age, and ability to read and write the English language intelligently, shall be issued by the superintendent of schools, notary public, justice of the peace, or any other person duly authorized to administer oaths, in cities and boroughs, and by the secretary of the school board in rural districts: *Provided,* That in case there be no public school in session within two miles, by the nearest traveled road, of any person within the school district, he or she shall not be liable to the provisions of this act: *Provided,* That this act shall not apply to any child that has been or is being otherwise instructed in English in the common branches of learning, for a like period of time, by any legally qualified governess or private teacher in a family: *And provided, further,* That any teacher or principal of any private school or educational institution shall report nonattendance, as provided in sec- *School attendance required.* *Literates.*

tion five (5) of this act [sec. 132]: *Provided, further,* That any person
employing a child, or children, shall furnish, on or before the third
Employers to Monday of the school term, and quarterly thereafter, to the superin-
furnish lists. tendent of schools, to the secretary of the board of school directors or
controllers, of the district in which such child or children reside, the
name, age, place of résidence, and name of parent or guardian, of every
person under the age of sixteen years in his employ at the time of said
report: *And provided, also,* That the certificate of any principal or
teacher of a private school, or of any institution for the education of
children, in which the common English branches are taught, setting
forth that the work of said school is in compliance with the provisions
of this act, shall be sufficient and satisfactory evidence thereof, and
the principal or teacher of said school or institution shall have the power
to excuse any child or children for nonattendance during temporary
periods, in accordance with the provisions of this act.

Violations. SEC. 129 (as amended by act No. 241, Acts of 1907). * * * Any
person, firm, or corporation who shall employ, or have in his or their
employ, any child not in attendance at school as provided in section
one (1) of this act [sec. 128], shall be guilty of a misdemeanor, and,
upon conviction thereof before a justice of the peace, magistrate, or
alderman, shall be fined in the sum of ten dollars for the first offense,
and in the sum of thirty dollars for each subsequent offense: *Provided,*
Upon conviction, the defendant or defendants may appeal to the court
of quarter sessions of the peace of the proper county, within five days,
upon entering into recognizance with one surety for the amount of
the fines and costs. The fines provided for by this act shall, when
collected, be paid over by the officers collecting the same, into the
school treasury of the respective districts, for the use of the said school
district of the city, borough, or township in which such principal,
or teacher, or person in parental relation, convicted, resides; or in
cases of conviction for employing or having in employ any child not
in attendance at school, as provided in section one (1) of this act,
for the use of the said school district of the city, borough, or township
in which such child is employed; to be applied and accounted for by
such treasurers in the same way as other moneys raised for school
purposes. Such fines shall be collected by a process of law similar
to the collection of other fines.

Attendance of- SEC. 130 (as amended by act No. 241, Acts of 1907). The board of
ficers. school directors or school controllers shall in cities, and may in all
other school districts, employ one or more persons, to be known as
attendance officers, * * * Such attendance officers shall have
authority to enter any place wherein any gainful occupation is carried
on, to ascertain whether any child or children not in attendance at
school, as provided in section one (1) of this act [sec. 128], are employed
therein; and, in pursuance of such authority, such officers shall have
the right to inspect any employment certificates, notices, registers,
or other lists required by law to be kept on file or to be posted therein.
Any owner, superintendent, lessee, or other person in charge of any
place wherein any gainful occupation is carried on, who shall refuse
admittance to an attendance officer, or opportunity to an attendance
officer for inspecting freely any child or children employed therein,
or who shall refuse to permit inspection by an attendance officer of
any employment certificate, notice, registers, and other lists required
by law to be filed or to be posted therein, shall be guilty of a misdemeanor, and, upon conviction thereof, shall be fined in a sum not
less than twenty-five dollars nor more than fifty dollars. Such attendance officers shall have authority to dismiss from employment, in
any such place wherein any gainful occupation is carried on, any
child or children not in attendance at school as provided in section
one (1) of this act [sec. 128] and employed therein, and dismissal to
take effect at the end of working hours upon the day upon which
such dismissal is ordered: *Provided,* That any child who shall be
aggrieved by the order of dismissal of such attendance officer shall
have the right of appeal, forthwith, to the county, city, or borough
common school superintendent of the district wherein such child was
employed, or his deputy duly authorized by him to hear such appeals,
whose duty it shall be forthwith to hear and decide such appeal: *Pro-*

vided, further, That such child who shall be aggrieved by the decision, upon such appeal, of a county, city, or borough common school superintendent, or his deputy aforesaid, shall have the right of appeal to the court of quarter sessions of the peace of the county wherein such child was employed, which court is authorized to hear and decide such appeal, and whose decision shall be final. * * *

SEC. 132 (as amended by act No. 241, Acts of 1907). * * * In all cases of the violation, by any person, firm, or corporation, or of any owner, superintendent, lessee, or other person, in charge of any place wherein any gainful occupation is carried on, of any of the provisions of this act, the superintendent of schools, or the secretary of the board of directors or controllers, or attendance officer if there be one, of the school district within which the offense is alleged to have been committed, in the name of the school district, shall proceed against the offending parties in accordance with the provisions of this act: *Provided,* That if the costs of prosecution can not be collected from such offending parties defendant, said costs may be paid out of the district funds, upon a proper voucher approved by the board of directors or controllers. **[Enforcement.]**

ACTS OF 1905.

ACT No. 226.—*Employment of women and children—Inspection of factories.*

SECTION 1. The term "establishment" where used for the purpose of this act, shall mean any place within this Commonwealth other than where domestic, coal mining or farm labor is employed; where men, women or children are engaged, and paid a salary or wages, by any person, firm or corporation, and where such men, women or children are employees, in the general acceptance of the term. **[Definition.]**

SEC. 2. No child under fourteen years of age shall be employed in any establishment. **[Age limit.]**

SEC. 3. No minor under sixteen, and no female, shall be employed in any establishment for a longer period than sixty hours in any one week, nor for a longer period than twelve hours in any one day. No minor under sixteen shall be employed in any establishment between the hours of nine postmeridian and six antemeridian: *Provided,* That where the material in process of manufacture requires the application of manual labor for an extended period after nine o'clock postmeridian, to prevent waste or destruction of said material, male minors over fourteen years of age, and who have not been employed in or about such establishment between the hours of six antemeridian and nine postmeridian, may be employed, for not more than nine consecutive hours in any one day, after nine postmeridian: *And provided further,* That in establishments where night work is hereby permitted to prevent waste or destruction, and where the nature of the employment requires two or more working shifts in the twenty-four hours, males over fourteen years of age may be employed, partly by day and partly by night: *Provided,* Said employment does not exceed nine consecutive hours: *And provided further,* That retail mercantile establishments shall be exempt from the provisions of this section on Saturday of each week, and during a period of twenty days beginning with the fifth day of December and ending with the twenty-fourth day of the same month: *Provided,* That during the said twenty days preceding the twenty-fourth day of December, the working hours shall not exceed ten hours per day, or sixty hours per week. **[Hours of labor.] [Night work.] [Proviso.]**

A provision of law limiting the hours of labor of adult females is within the police power of the State, and does not interfere with their constitutional rights, nor is it class legislation. 15 Superior Ct. 5.

SEC. 4. No minor under sixteen years of age shall be permitted to clean or oil machinery while in motion, or to operate, or otherwise have the care or custody of, any elevator or lift. **[Cleaning moving machinery.]**

SEC. 5. It shall be unlawful for the owner, superintendent, lessee, or other person in charge of any establishment where persons are employed for wages or salary, to employ any child between the ages of fourteen and sixteen years, unless there is first provided, and placed on file in the office of the establishment where said child is employed, **[Certificates.]**

a certificate in the form provided by the chief factory inspector, which certificate shall be uniform throughout the State. It shall be the duty of the factory inspector or any of his office force, the deputy factory inspectors, or of the city or borough common school superintendents within their various jurisdictions, or of the principal teacher of the common schools in localities not under the jurisdiction of any city or borough superintendent, or of their respective duly authorized deputies, to issue the employment certificate hereinafter prescribed. No principal teacher shall be authorized to issue said employment certificate within any district over which a superintendent has jurisdiction. The district of such city or borough superintendent or principal teacher shall be the same as that in which the child seeking an employment certificate resides.

Contents. SEC. 6. The employment certificate shall state the name, age, date, place of birth, and description (including color of eyes, hair and complexion) of said child, its residence, and the residence of its parent, guardian or custodian, and the ability of said child to read and write simple sentences in the English language, that it has complied with the educational laws of the Commonwealth, and is physically able to perform the work to be required of it.

Proof of age, etc. *Provided,* That before any such certificate of employment is issued, the person authorized to issue the same shall first demand and obtain of the parent, guardian or custodian of said child an affidavit, sworn to before any officer authorized to administer oaths, made by him or her, stating the age, date and place of birth of said child; and shall further demand and obtain a certificate of said child's birth, as kept by any public authority, or, transcript of the record of its birth, baptism or circumcision, as kept by any religious denomination, or, in the case of a foreign-born child (if such evidence of age be lacking), a true copy of the passenger manifest, passport or official record filed at the office of the commissioner of immigration at the port of arrival, as corroborative evidence of the truth of the facts set forth in the affidavit; and shall note in his statement, as aforesaid, the character of such record and by what public or religious authority the same is issued: *Provided, however,* That where no such transcript of public or religious record, or passenger manifest, passport or official record, as aforesaid, of said child's age is obtainable, the same may be substituted by a statement signed by the principal teacher of the last school which said child attended, certifying that said child has received instruction in reading, spelling, writing, English grammar, and geography, and is familiar with the fundamental operations of arithmetic, and has completed the course of study in the common schools prescribed for the first five years, or a course of study in other schools equivalent thereto. At the time of the issue of the employment certificate, the person so issuing the same shall make one copy thereof, which copy shall be filed, within ten days from the date of its issue, in the office of the common school superintendent in the district in which the child holding the certificate resides; and in districts not having such a superintendent, the said copy shall be filed in the office of the chief factory inspector, and shall be subject to the inspection of the public. The certificate of the registration of birth, baptism or circumcision, or, in the case of a foreign born child, the copy of passenger manifest, passport or official record, as hereinbefore prescribed, or, in the absence of such transcripts, the statement of the principal teacher, certifying that such child has received instruction as prescribed, as well as the affidavit of the parent, guardian or custodian, shall be filed with a copy of said employment certificate. The certificate when issued shall be the property of the said child, who shall be entitled to a surrender of the certificate to him or her by the employer whenever said child shall leave the service of any employer holding the certificate.

Seats for females SEC. 7. Every person, firm or corporation employing girls or adult women, in any establishment, shall provide suitable seats for their use, and shall permit such use when the employees are not necessarily engaged in active duties.

Wash rooms. SEC. 8. Every person, firm or corporation employing males and females in the same establishment, shall provide for such employees suitable and proper wash and dressing rooms, and water-closets for males and females; and the water-closets, wash and dressing rooms used by females shall not adjoin those used by males, but shall be built entirely away from them, and shall be properly screened and ventilated; and all water-closets shall at all times be kept in a clean and sanitary condition.

SEC. 9. Not less than one hour shall be allowed for the noonday meal in any establishment. But the chief factory inspector may, for good cause, reduce the time for the noonday meal in establishments where all the other provisions of this act are observed, which entail duties upon the part of employers. *Time for meals.*

SEC. 10. Every person, firm or corporation employing men, women or children, in any establishment, shall post and keep posted in a conspicuous place, in every room where such help is employed, a printed copy of the factory laws, a printed notice stating the number of hours per day for each day of the week required of such persons; and in every room where children under sixteen years of age are employed, a list of their names, with their ages. *Law, etc., to be posted*

ACTS OF 1909.

ACT No. 34.—*Employment of children as messengers—Sending to immoral resorts.*

SECTION 1. Any person, firm, company or corporation, having authority over a minor, who knowingly takes or sends, or causes or permits such minor to be sent, to any house of prostitution or assignation, or other immoral place of resort or amusement, shall be guilty of a misdemeanor, and, on conviction thereof, shall be sentenced to pay a fine not exceeding one thousand dollars, or to undergo an imprisonment not exceeding one year, or both, at the discretion of the court. *Sending to immoral resorts forbidden.*

ACT No. 182.—*Employment of children—General provisions.*

SECTION 1. From and after the passage of this act, no minor under the age of eighteen years, except as hereinafter provided shall be employed, permitted, or suffered to work, in, about, or for any factory, workshop, rolling mill, sawmill, quarry, laundry, store; mercantile, printing, or binding establishment; dock, wharf; vessel or boat engaged in lake or river navigation or commerce, railroad, in the erection or repair of electric wires, business office, telegraph office, telephone office, stable, garage, hotel, resturant, [restaurant] bootblack stand, or in the transmission of newspapers, messages, or merchandise. *Children under eighteen.*

SEC. 2 (as amended by act, p. 832, Acts of 1911). Male minors over the age of eighteen years may be employed in any and all kinds of legal employment, within the Commonwealth; but all minors under the age of eighteen years shall not be employed in or about blast furnaces, docks, wharves, quarries; in the outside erection and repair of electric wires; in the running or management of elevators, lifts, or hoisting machines; in oiling hazardous and dangerous machinery, in motion; at switch tending, gate tending, track repairing; as brakemen, firemen, engineers, motormen, conductors, upon railroads; as pilots, firemen, or engineers upon boats or vessels engaged in the transportation of passengers or merchandise; in or about establishments wherein nitroglycerin, dynamite, dualin, guncotton, gunpowder, or other high or dangerous explosive, is manufactured, compounded or stored. *Employments prohibited.*

SEC. 3. Minors over the age of sixteen years may be employed in or about establishments for the manufacture or preparation of white lead, red lead, paints, phosphorus, phosphorus matches, poisonous acids, or for the manufacture or stripping of tobacco or cigars: *Provided,* That where it is proved to the satisfaction of the chief factory inspector that the danger or menace to the health or safety of minors employed in any establishment or industry named in this section has been removed, or that employment in some part or parts of said industry is not dangerous, or a menace to the health or safety of minors employed therein, that in such case minors under the age of sixteen years, and not under the age of fourteen years, who can read and write the English language intelligently, and are physically qualified, may be therein employed. *Children over sixteen.*

Children over fourteen. SEC. 4. Minors over the age of fourteen years, who can read and write the English language intelligently, and are physically qualified, may be employed in or for mercantile establishments, stores; telegraph, telephone, or other business offices; hotels, restaurants; or in any factory, workshop, rolling mills, or other establishment having proper sanitation; or in any factory, workshop, rolling mills, or other establishment having proper sanitation and proper ventilation, and in which power machinery is not used, or, if used, that the same, and all other dangerous appliances used, are kept securely and proper safeguarded; rules and regulations for the same to be prescribed and provided by the chief factory inspector.

Hours of labor. SEC. 5. No male minor under the age of sixteen years, and no female under the age of eighteen years, shall be employed, permitted, or suffered to work, in or about or for any establishment, place of business, or industry, named in sections three and four of this act, for a longer period than ten hours in any one day, except when a different apportionment of the hours of labor is made for the sole purpose of making a shorter workday for one day in the week; nor shall a less period than forty-five minutes be allowed for the midday meal; and in no case shall the hours

Night work. of labor exceed fifty-eight in any one week. No male minor under the age of sixteen years, and no female under the age of eighteen years, shall be employed or permitted to work between the hours of nine postmeridian and six antemeridian.

Nine-hour day, when. SEC. 6. Where the usual process of manufacture, or the nature of the business named in section four of this act, is of a kind that customarily necessitates a continuous day and night employment, male minors, not under the age of fourteen years, may be employed day or night, or partly by day and partly by night; but said employment shall not exceed nine hours during any twenty-four hours for minors under the age of sixteen years. A violation of any of the provisions of this section shall be deemed to be in contravention of this act.

Certificates required. SEC. 7. No minor under the age of sixteen years shall be employed in or about or for any establishment or industry named in sections three and four of this act, unless the employer of said minor procures and keeps on file, and accessible to the deputy factory inspectors, the employment certificate as hereinafter provided, issued to said minor, and keeps two complete lists of all minors under the age of sixteen

Files. years employed in or for his or her establishment; one of said lists to be kept on file in the office of the employer, and one to be conspicuously posted in each of the several departments in or for which minors are employed. Said employment certificate, when issued, shall be the property of the minor named therein, who shall be entitled to a surrender of said certificate to him or her by the employer whenever said minor shall leave the service of any employer holding said certificate.

How certificate st o beIssued. SEC. 8. The employment certificate required by the provisions of this act shall be issued as follows:

In school districts having a district superintendent or supervising principal, by such superintendent or supervising principal; in school districts having no superintendent or supervising principal, but having one or more principals of schools, by such principals, each principal to issue the certificate to minors residing within the territory belonging to the school over which he has supervision; in school districts, or parts of districts, having no district superintendent or principal, by the secretary of the board of school directors for that district: *Provided,* That any district superintendent, supervising principal, principal of schools, or secretary of the board of school directors, hereby directed to issue such certificates, may authorize and deputize, in writing, such persons as they may see proper to act in their place and stead for the purpose of issuing such certificates. Any of the hereinbefore mentioned officials, authorized to issue employment certificates, before doing so shall demand, and if possible obtain, a birth certificate, or baptismal certificate, or passport, or other official or religious record of the minor's age, or a duly attested transcript thereof; and, in the event that none of these is obtainable, may accept, in lieu thereof, a record of the age as given on the register of a school the minor has attended; or, in the absence of such record, may accept the affidavit of the minor's parent or guardian, or other person, which affidavit he is empowered to administer: *Provided*, That the powers and duties conferred by this section on the superintendents, supervising principa s, principal, or secretary of a board of school directors, be and the same are conferred upon superintendents, supervising principals, principal, teachers, or secretaries of any private academy, parochial or denominational school, in all cases where the applicant for an employment certificate is, or recently has been, an attendant pupil in a private academy, parochial or denominational school, and is not a pupil in a public school: *And provided further*, That whenever in any school district an employment certificate is issued by any persons other than the public school official hereinbefore directed to issue such certificates in said district, said persons shall, on or before the third day of each month, file with the aforementioned public school official, in said district, true copies of all employment certificates so issued.

SEC. 9. The employment certificate provided by this act for the use of a minor between fourteen and sixteen years of age shall be in the following form: Form.

This certifies that (name and residence of minor) is aged —— years —— months —— days; whose complexion is ——, hair is ——, and eyes are ——; is able to read and write the English language intelligently, and may be employed at labor in any of the following establishments, businesses, and industries: The manufacture or the preparation of white lead, red lead, paints, phosphorus, phosphorus matches, poisonous acids, tobacco or cigars, in which industries minors between fourteen and sixteen years of age may be employed, only when their labor is performed in such part or parts of such industries as are not dangerous or a menace to their health and safety,—and mercantile establishments, stores; telephone, telegraph or other business offices; hotels, restaurants; or in any factory, workshop, or other establishment having proper sanitation and proper ventilation, and in which power machinery is not used, or, if used, that the same, and all other dangerous appliance used, are kept securely and properly safeguarded.

This certificate is a legal warrant for the employment of the minor named hereon, in any of the above-named establishments, businesses and industries, under the provisions of an act approved —— one thousand nine hundred and nine.

(Signature of person who issued certificate, official title and official address.)

(Signature of minor to whom issued.)

SEC. 10. The blank exployment certificate shall be prepared by the superintendent of public instruction, in accordance with the form prescribed in this act; the same to be printed in accordance with the laws regulating printing and binding, under the supervision of the superintendent of public printing and binding. The superintendent of public instruction shall also supply the aforesaid certificates to all persons authorized to issue the same. Who to furnish.

SEC. 11. Any person or persons violating any of the provisions of this act shall be deemed guilty of a misdemeanor, and, upon conviction, shall be punished, for a first offense, by a fine of not less than ten dollars or more than twenty-five dollars, or ten days imprisonment in the county jail, or either or both, at the discretion of the court; and for a second offense, shall be punished by a fine of not more than fifty dollars, and ninety days imprisonment in a county jail, or either or both, at the discretion of the court. It shall be the duty of the chief factory inspector to carry out the provisions of this act, and prosecutions for violations thereof shall be instituted by the chief factory inspector. Violations.

ACT No. 210.—*Employment of children in coal mines and breakers.*

SECTION 1 (as amended by act, page 983, Acts of 1911). No minor under the age of fourteen years shall be employed, permitted or suffered to work in, about, or for any coal breaker or washery, or in or about the outside workings of any coal mine. Age limit.

SEC. 2 (as amended by act, page 537, Acts of 1911). No minor under the age of sixteen years shall be employed, permitted, or suffered to Hours of labor.

work, in or about or for any establishment or industry named in section one of this act, for a longer period than ten hours in any one day, except when a different apportionment of the hours of labor is made for the sole purpose of making a shorter workday for one day in the week; nor shall a less period than thirty minutes be allowed for the midday meal; and in no case shall the hours of labor exceed fifty-eight in any one week. No minor under the age of sixteen years shall be employed or permitted to work between the hours of nine postmeridian and six antemeridian.

Night work.

SEC. 3 (as amended by act, page 983, Acts of 1911). No minor under the age of sixteen years shall be employed, permitted or suffered to work, inside any coal mine, and no minor under the age of sixteen years shall be employed in or about or for any establishment or industry named in section one of this act, unless the employer of said minor procures and keeps on file, and accessible to the mine inspector, the employment certificate as hereinafter provided, issued to said minor, and keeps two complete lists of all minors under the age of sixteen years employed in or for his or her establishment; one of said lists to be kept on file in the office of the employer, and one to be conspicuously posted in each of the several departments in or for which minors are employed. Said employment certificate, when issued, shall be the property of the minor named therein, who shall be entitled to a surrender of said certificate to him or her by the employer whenever said minor shall leave the service of any employer holding said certificate. In case a minor, who is employed or permitted to work in or about or for any establishment or industry named in section one of this act, as being sixteen years of age or over, appears to the chief of the department of mines or any mine inspector to be under the age of sixteen years, said chief of the department of mines or mine inspector shall make written demand that the employer of said minor shall procure and keep on file in the office of said establishment, subject to inspection, the same evidence that said minor is in fact sixteen years of age or over as is required as evidence of age for the issuance of the employment certificates hereinafter provided for; and the employer furnishing such evidence shall not be required to furnish any further evidence of the age of said minor. In case the evidence of age, for which demand is so made, be not filed as hereinbefore required, within thirty days after said demand, the employer shall cease to employ the minor named in said demand or to permit said minor to work: *Provided, however,* That said employer, by thus ceasing to employ or permit said minor to work, shall not be relieved from any of the penalties provided in this act for the employment of a minor under the age of sixteen years without the filing for such minor of the employment certificate hereinbefore required.

Work inside mines.

Lists.

Minor apparently under sixteen.

SEC. 4. The employment certificates required by the provisions of this act shall be issued as follows:—

How certificate is to be issued.

In school districts having a district superintendent or supervising principal, by such superintendent or supervising principal; in school districts having no superintendent or supervising principal, but having one or more principals of schools, by such principals, each principal to issue the certificate to minors residing within the territory belonging to the school over which he has supervision; in school districts, or parts of districts, having no district superintendent or principal, by the secretary of the board of school directors for that district: *Provided,* That any district superintendent, supervising principal of schools, or secretary of the board of school directors, hereby directed to issue such certificates, may authorize and deputize, in writing, such persons as they may see proper, to act in their place and stead for the purpose of issuing such certificates. Any of the hereinbefore mentioned officials, authorized to issue employment certificates, before doing so shall demand, and if possible obtain, a birth certificate, or baptismal certificate, or passport, or any other official or religious record of the minor's age, or duly attested transcript thereof; or, in the event that none of these is obtainable, may accept, in lieu thereof, the record age as given on the register of a school the minor has attended; or, in the absence of such record, may accept the affidavit of the minor's parent, guardian, or other person, which affidavit he is empowered to administer: *Provided,* That the powers and duties conferred by this

Evidence.

section on the superintendents, supervising principa s, principal, or secretary of a board of school directors, be and the same are conferred upon superintendents, supervising principals, principal, teachers, or secretaries of any private academy, parochial or denominational schools, in all cases where the applicant for an employment certificate is, or recently has been, an attendant pupi in a private academy, parochial or denominational school, and is not a pupil in a public school: *And provided further*, That whenever in any school district an employment certificate is issued by any persons other than the public school official hereinbefore directed to issue such certificates in said district, said persons shall, on or before the third day of each month, file with the aforementioned public school official, in said district, true copies of all employment certificates so issued.

SEC. 5 (as amended by act, p. 983, Acts of 1911). The employment certificate provided by this act for the use of a minor between fourteen and sixteen years of age shall be in the following form:

This certifies that (name and residence of minor) is aged ...... Form of certificate. years .... months .... days; whose complexion is ......, hair is ...... and eyes are ......; is able to read and write the English language intelligently, and may be employed at labor in any coal breaker, washery or other outside workings of a coal mine.

This certificate is a legal warrant for the employment of the minor hereon, in any of the above-named establishments and industries, under the provisions of an act approved .... one thousand nine hundred and nine, as amended by an act approved .... one thousand nine hundred and eleven.

(Signature of person who issued certificate, official title and official address.)

(Signature of minor to whom issued.)...... ....

(Date.)

SEC. 6. The blank employment certificates shall be prepared by the superintendent of public instruction, in accordance with the form prescribed in this act; the same to be printed in accordance with the laws regulating printing and binding, under the supervision of the superintendent of public printing and binding. The superintendent of public instruction shall also supply the aforesaid certificates to all persons authorized to issue the same. *Who to furnish.*

SEC. 7. Any person or persons violating any of the provisions of this act shall be deemed guilty of a misdemeanor, and, upon conviction, shall be punished, for a first offense, by a fine of not less than ten dollars or more than twenty-five dollars, or ten days imprisonment in the county jail, or either or both, at the discretion of the court; and, for a second offense, shall be punished by a fine of not more than fifty dollars, and ninety days imprisonment in a county jail, or either or both, at the discretion of the court. *Violations.*

It shall be the duty of the chief of the department of mines to carry out the provisions of this act, and prosecutions for violations thereof shall be instituted either [sic] by the chief of the department of mines. *Enforcement.*

ACTS OF 1911.

Employment of children—School attendance.

(Page 309.)

SECTION 1416. The provisions of this act requiring regular attendance shall not apply to any child, between the ages of fourteen and sixteen years, who can read and write intelligently and is regularly engaged in any useful and lawful employment or service during the time the public schools are in session, and who holds an employment certificate issued according to law. *Exempt children.*

SECTION 1419. Every person, firm, association, or corporation in this Commonwealth accepting service from, or employing, a child or children, between the ages of fourteen and sixteen years, during the hours when the public schools are in session, shall, on or before the first day of September in each year, and quarterly thereafter, during the period of compulsory attendance, furnish to the superintend- *Employers to furnish names.*

ent of schools, supervising principal, or secretary of the board of school directors of the district in which such child or children reside, the name, age, place of residence, and name of parent or guardian, of every such child in his or its employ or service. Such reports shall be made upon blanks to be furnished by the superintendent of public instruction at the expense of the Commonwealth.

List to be posted.

Sec. 1420. Every person, firm, association, or corporation in this Commonwealth accepting service from, or employing, a child or children, between the ages of fourteen and sixteen years, during the hours when the public schools are in session, and during the period of compulsory attendance in any school district, shall make a true and correct list of all such children, giving their names, ages, places of residence, names of parents or guardians, the dates of and names of the persons issuing the employment certificates, and the time of beginning and ending of service with him or it, which list shall be clearly written or printed and kept publicly posted at the place of employment of such child, where the same may be inspected by any member of the board of school directors or the secretary thereof, by the district superintendent, the supervising principal, or the attendance officer of any school district, at any time during business hours.

Children under fourteen.

Sec. 1421. No person in this Commonwealth, either for himself or for any firm, association, or corporation, shall, during the term of compulsory attendance as fixed by the board of school directors in any school district, and during the hours the public schools are in session, accept service from, engage, or employ any child or children between eight and fourteen years of age; nor shall he accept service from, engage, or employ any child or children between the ages of fourteen and

Under sixteen.

sixteen years, unless such child shall first furnish and deliver to such employer an employment certificate issued according to law.

Violations.

Sec. 1422. Any person or persons accepting service from, or engaging or employing, any child between eight and fourteen years of age during the term of compulsory attendance, and while the public schools are in session, or accepting service from, engaging, or employing any child during the same period of time, between the ages of fourteen and sixteen years, without being first furnished by such child with an employment certificate, or failing to furnish to the district superintendent of schools, supervising principal, attendance officer, or secretary of the board of schools directors the information required by this act concerning the children employed by him or them, or shall fail to post for inspection at the place of employment of such children the list of children engaged by him or them, as required by the provisions of this act, shall be deemed guilty of a misdemeanor, and upon conviction shall be punished for a first offense by a fine of not less than ten dollars ($10) or more than twenty-five dollars ($25) or ten days' imprisonment in the county jail, or either or both, at the discretion of the court, and for a subsequent offense shall be punished by a fine of not less than twenty dollars ($20) or more than fifty dollars ($50), or ninety days' imprisonment in the county jail, or either or both, at the discretion of the court.

Employment of women and children in bituminous mines.

(Page 756.)

Article XVIII.

Employment of women and children.

Section 1. No boy under the age of fourteen years, and no woman or girl of any age, shall be employed, permitted or suffered to work in or about any mine, and no boy under the age of eighteen years shall be permitted to mine or load coal in any room, entry, or other working place, unless in company with an experienced person over eighteen years of age.

Employment certificates.

No boy under the age of sixteen years shall be employed in or about any mine, unless during the entire period that said boy is so employed there is on file in the office of said mine, and accessible to the inspector, an employment certificate issued by the city, borough, township, or county superintendent of public schools, or by the secretary of the school board of the township, borough, or city, or by a principal of a parochial school, or by such superintendent's, secretary's, or principal's duly appointed deputy or assistant reciting the age of said boy as it appears on any record that the person who issues said certificate has reason to believe to be true and correct, or, if such record of age be lacking, reciting the age of said boy according to an affidavit taken by his parent, guardian, or custodian, and attached to said certificate, and said certificate and the affidavit, if any, shall for the purposes of this act be conclusive evidence of the age of said boy.

Nothing in this section shall be held to forbid the employment of a girl between the ages of fourteen and sixteen years in the office of a mine: *Provided,* That, during the entire period of said employment, there is in like manner on file for said girl, in said office, an employment certificate of the character hereinbefore provided for as a prerequisite to the employment of boys under the age of sixteen years inside any mine. Girls in offices.

Sec. 2. Any superintendent or mine foreman who fails to comply with the provisions of this article shall be deemed guilty of a misdemeanor, and it shall be the duty of the inspector, or any other person who knows that the superintendent or mine foreman has violated any of the provisions of this article, to prosecute said superintendent or said mine foreman in accordance with section two of article twenty-six of this act; and any person who shall falsely certify or swear to the age of any boy or girl, in the certificate and affidavit described and required by section one of this article, shall be deemed guilty of a misdemeanor. Noncompliance by superintendent and foreman. False certificate.

PORTO RICO.

REVISED STATUTES AND CODES—1902.

Revised Statutes.

Employment of children.

Section 166. No child of either sex, under sixteen years shall be compelled to work in agricultural factories and manufacturing establishments over six hours per day, three in the morning and three in the afternoon. All persons who shall violate this provision shall be fined in a sum of from five to fifteen dollars, or imprisonment not to exceed thirty days for each offense. Limit of day's labor.

Sec. 167. No foreman, teacher or other person having under his charge the work, care or education of a minor under sixteen years of age, shall resort to inhumane treatment to compel such minor to work or to study. Any violation of the provisions hereof shall be punished with a fine of from five to fifteen dollars or imprisonment not to exceed thirty days for each offense. Compulsion to labor.

Penal Code.

Employment of children—Certain employments forbidden.

Section 265. Any person, whether as parent, relative, guardian, employer or otherwise, having in his care, custody, or control any child under the age of twelve years, who shall sell, apprentice, give away, let out, or otherwise dispose of any such child to any person, under any name, title, or pretense, for the vocation, use, occupation, calling, [or] service of begging, or peddling, in any public street or highway, or in any mendicant or wandering business whatsoever, and any person who shall take, receive, hire, or employ, use, or have in custody any child for such purposes, or either of them, is guilty of a misdemeanor. Begging and peddling.

Civil Code.

Earnings of minors.

Section 225. Property acquired by an unemancipated child by labor or industry, or for any valuable consideration, belongs to the said child, but the usufruct thereof belongs to the parents having potestas over him whilst he lives in their company; but if the child, Usufruct belongs to parents, when.

with the consent of his parents, lives independently, he shall be deemed emancipated for all effects as regards the said property, and he shall be the full owner and have the usufruct and administration thereof.

RHODE ISLAND.

GENERAL LAWS—1909.

CHAPTER 72.—Employment of children—School attendance.

School attendance required.

SECTION 1. Every child who has completed seven years of life and has not completed fifteen years of life, unless he has completed in the public schools the elementary studies taught in the first eight years of school attendance, exclusive of kindergarten instruction, provided for in the course of study adopted by the school committee of the city or town wherein such child resides, or unless he shall have completed fourteen years of life and shall be lawfully employed at labor or at service or engaged in business, shall regularly attend some public day-school during all the days and hours that the public schools are in session in the city or town, wherein he resides; and every person having under his control a child as above described in this section, shall cause such child to attend school as required by the above-stated provisions of this section, and for every neglect of such duty the person having control of such child shall be fined not exceeding twenty dollars: * * *

Enforcement.

SEC. 4. The truant officers may visit any places or establishments where such minor children as are described in the preceding sections of this chapter are employed, to ascertain whether the provisions of this chapter are duly complied with, and may as often as twice in every year demand from all employers of such children a report containing the names of all children who have not completed sixteen years of life that are employed by them, such report to give the names, ages, and residences of all such children; and all employers of such children shall, upon request, produce for the inspection of the truant officer the certificates prescribed in chapter seventy-eight; and for any refusal to make such reports as are above provided for, or for any refusal to produce the above-mentioned certificates, any employer of such children shall be fined not exceeding ten dollars.

CHAPTER 78.—Employment of children—General provisions.

Age limit.

SECTION 1 (as amended by chapter 533, Acts of 1910). No child under fourteen years of age shall be employed or permitted or suffered to work in any factory, manufacturing or business establishment within this State, and no child under sixteen years of age shall be employed or permitted or suffered to work in any factory or manufacturing or business establishment within this State between the hours of eight o'clock

Night work.

in the afternoon of any day and six o'clock in the forenoon of the following day. No child under sixteen years of age shall be employed or permitted or suffered to work in any factory or manufacturing or business establishment unless said child shall present to the person or corporation employing him or her an age and employment certificate, given by or under the direction of the school committee of the city or

Certificates.

town in which said child resides. Such certificate shall state (a) the name of said child, (b) the date and place of birth of said child, (c) the height, color of eyes and hair, and complexion of said child, (d) the name and place of residence of the person having control of said child, and such certificate shall certify (1) that said child has completed fourteen years of age, (2) that said child is able to read at sight and write legibly simple sentences in the English language, and (3) that there is reason to believe that said child is healthy and physically able to perform the work which he or she intends to do. The statements contained in such certificate in regard to the name, date and place of birth of said child, shall be substantiated by a duly attested copy of the birth certificate, baptismal certificate, or passport of such child. All such certificates issued on or after the first day of January, A. D., 1911, shall be uniform throughout the State, and in the following form, or such substantially similar form as may be approved by the secretary of the State board of education:

AGE AND EMPLOYMENT CERTIFICATE.

This certifies that I am the (father, mother, guardian, or custodian) Form.
and have control of (name of child), whose signature appears below, and
that (he or she) was born at (name of town or city), in the county of
———, and State (or country) of ———, on the (day) of (month),
A. D. ———, and is now (number of years and months) old.

(Signature of child.) (Signature of person having control of said
child and his or her residence.)

(Town or city and date).

I hereby approve the foregoing certificate of (name of child); whose
height is (feet and inches); eyes are (color); hair is (color), and complexion is (fair or dark).

I certify that said (name of child) is able to read at sight and write
legibly simple sentences in the English language, and that I have reason
to believe that said (name of child) has completed fourteen years of age,
is of the age therein certified, and is healthy and physically able to
perform the work which (he or she) intends to do.

This certificate belongs to (name of child), and is to be surrendered
to (him or her) whenever (he or she) leaves the service of the person
or corporation holding the same; but if not claimed by said child
within two weeks from such time it shall be returned to the school
committee which issued it, or to such person as such committee shall
designate.

(Signature of person authorized to approve and sign, with official
character or authority.)

(Town or city and date.)

In case it appears to the satisfaction of the school committee, or person authorized to give such certificate, that neither the birth certificate,
baptismal certificate, nor passport of such child can be produced, the
age and employment certificate may be granted on other evidence
satisfactory to the secretary of the State board of education.

All certificates required by this chapter relating to the qualification
of children employed in any factory or manufacturing or business
establishment coming under the provisions of this chapter shall be kept
by the employer at the place where such child is employed, and shall be
shown to the factory inspectors provided for by this chapter, or either
or any of them, on demand by said inspector or inspectors; and the
proprietor or manager of any such factory or manufacturing or business
establishment who shall fail to produce or shall refuse to show to any
factory inspector any such certificate when demand is made therefor
shall be deemed guilty of a misdemeanor, and on conviction thereof
shall be punished by a fine of not less than ten nor more than fifty
dollars.

Whenever any factory inspector shall have reason to doubt the accu- Investigations
racy of any statement made in any such certificate concerning the age in case of doubt.
or other qualifications of any child employed thereunder, such inspector shall demand such certificate of the employer of such child, and
upon receiving the same shall give such employer a receipt therefor.
If after investigation such inspector shall find that such certificate
should not have been issued to said child under the provisions of this
law, then he shall deliver such certificate to the person who issued it,
and shall order it to be canceled, and shall forthwith notify the said
employer that such child must not be longer employed. Every employer or proprietor or manager of any factory or manufacturing or
business establishment who shall continue to employ such child after
receiving such notice from any factory inspector shall be deemed
guilty of a misdemeanor, and on conviction thereof shall be subject to
the penalty imposed by section 12 of this chapter.

Whenever any factory inspector shall have reason to doubt that any
child employed in any factory, or manufacturing or business establishment, and not provided with an age and employment certificate, has
reached the age of sixteen years, such factory inspector shall make
demand on such child's employer that such employer shall either
furnish him within ten days a certificate of age issued by the same
authority and based on the same evidence required for the issuance of
age and employment certificates, or shall cease to employ such child

or permit or suffer such child to work in such factory or manufacturing or business establishment. In case such employer shall fail to deliver such certificate to the factory inspector, within ten days after such demand, and shall thereafter continue to employ such child, or permit or suffer such child to work in such factory or manufacturing or business establishment, such employer shall be deemed guilty of a misdemeanor, and on conviction thereof shall be subject to the penalty imposed by section 12 of this chapter, and proof of the making of such demand and of failure to deliver such certificate shall be prima facie evidence, in any prosecution brought for a violation of this provision, that such child is under 16 years of age and is unlawfully employed.

Certificatet o be returned. When any child employed under the provisions of this section leaves his or her employment, the person or corporation by whom such child has been employed shall, on demand by said child, deliver to him or her the certificate on the authority of which such child has been employed, unless such certificate has been canceled as hereinbefore provided, or if such certificate is not demanded by such child, shall, within two weeks after said child has left the employment of said person or corporation, send said certificate to the school committee which issued it, or to such person as the school committee may designate. The school committee of each town, or such person as the school committee may designate to issue the certificate provided for in this section, shall keep on file a copy of each certificate granted, together with the evidence on which such certificate was granted.

Application law. SEC. 2. Every person, firm, or corporation doing business within this State employing five or more persons, or employing any child under sixteen years of age, shall be subject to the provisions of this chapter, whatever shall be the business conducted by said person, firm, or corporation: *Provided, however,* That the provisions of this chapter shall not apply to children employed in household service or in agricultural pursuits: *And provided, further,* That said provisions shall not apply to the employment of children in the vocation, occupation, or service of rope or wire walking, or as gymnasts, wrestlers, contortionists, equestrian performers, or acrobats, riders upon bicycles or mechanical contrivances, or in any dancing, theatrical, or musical exhibition, but the employment of children in any vocation, occupation, or service enumerated in this proviso shall continue to be governed by the provisions of the General Laws, chapter one hundred thirty-nine.

Violations. SEC. 12. Any person or corporation who employs a child under sixteen years of age without the certificate required by section one of this chapter, or who makes a false statement in regard to any part required by such certificate or who violates any of the provisions of this chapter, or who suffers or permits any child or woman to be employed in violation of its provisions, shall be deemed guilty of a misdemeanor, and, on conviction, shall be punished by a fine of not more than five hundred dollars: *Provided, however,* That this section shall not apply to that portion of section one of this chapter which fixes the penalty for the refusal to show to the inspector any certificate provided for in that section.

[See also sections 6 and 8, Appendix B, page 1063.]

CHAPTER 139.—*Employment of children in certain occupations forbidden.*

Acrobatic, mendicant, etc., occupations. SECTION 4. Every person having the custody or control of any child under the age of sixteen years, who shall exhibit, use or employ, or shall in any manner or under any pretense sell, apprentice or give away, let out or otherwise dispose of any such child to any person for or in the vocation, occupation, service or purpose of rope or wire walking, or as a gymnast, wrestler, contortionist, equestrian performer, acrobat, or rider upon any bicycle or mechanical contrivance, or in any dancing, theatrical or musical exhibition unless it be in connection with churches, schools, or private instruction in dancing or music or unless it be under the auspices of a Rhode Island society incorporated, or organized without incorporation, for a purpose authorized by section eleven of chapter two hundred twelve, or unless it be with the written consent, previously obtained and revocable at will, of the mayor of the city or the president of the town council where such child is to be employed; or for in gathering or picking rags, or collecting cigar stumps, bones, or refuse from markets, or in begging, or in any mendicant or wandering occupation, or in peddling in places injurious to the morals of such child; * * * or in any illegal, obscene, indecent, or immoral purpose, exhibition or practice whatsoever; or for or in any business, exhibition or vocation injurious to the health or morals, or dangerous to the life or limb of such child, or who shall cause, procure or encourage any such child to engage therein, or who after being notified by an officer mentioned in section six of this chapter to restrain such child from engaging therein, shall neglect or refuse to do so, shall be held guilty of a misdemeanor and shall, for every such offense, be imprisoned not exceeding one year or be fined not exceeding two hundred [and] fifty dollars, or be both fined and imprisoned as aforesaid, and shall forfeit any right which he may have to the custody of such child.

SEC. 5. Every person who shall take, receive, hire or employ, exhibit, or have in custody, or who shall cause to be taken, hired or employed, exhibited, or held in custody, any child under the age of sixteen years, for any of the purposes prohibited in the preceding section, shall be held guilty of a misdemeanor, and shall be punished for every such offense in the manner provided in said section. *Hiring for prohibited purposes.*

SEC. 6. The town sergeant of any town, the chief of police of any city, or the general agent or agents of the Rhode Island Society for the Prevention of Cruelty to Children may enter any place where any child may be held, detained or employed in violation of this chapter, and without process of law seize and detain such child and hold him as a witness to testify upon the trial of any person charged with violating the provisions of this chapter; * * * *Enforcement.*

CHAPTER 249.—*Employment of women and children.*

SECTION 22 (as amended by chapter 384, Acts of 1909). No minor under sixteen years of age, and no woman, shall be employed in laboring in any manufacturing or mechanical establishment more than fifty-six hours in any one week; and in no case shall the hours of labor exceed ten hours in any one day, excepting when it is necessary to make repairs to prevent the interruption of the ordinary running of the machinery, or when a different apportionment of the hours of labor is made for the sole purpose of making a shorter day's work for one day of the week. *Hours of labor.*

Every employer shall post in a conspicuous place in every room where such persons are employed a printed notice stating the number of hours required of them on each day of the week; and the employment of any such person for a longer time in any day than so stated shall be deemed a violation of this section, unless it appears that such employment is to make up for time lost on some previous day of the same week in consequence of the stopping of the machinery upon which such person was employed or dependent for employment: *Provided,* That the provisions of this section shall not be construed to enlarge or impair any restriction placed upon the employment of any minor mentioned in chapter 64. *Schedule to be posted.*

SEC. 23. Every person who willfully employs, or has in his employment or under his charge any person, in violation of the provisions of the preceding section, and every parent or guardian who permits any such minor to be so employed, shall be fined not exceeding twenty dollars for each offense. A certificate of the age of a minor, made by him or by his parent or guardian, at the time of his employment in a manufacturing establishment, shall be conclusive evidence of his age upon any trial of any person other than the parent or guardian for a violation of the preceding section. *Penalty.*

SEC. 24. Labor performed in any manufacturing establishment, and all mechanical labor, during the period of ten hours in any one day, shall be considered a legal day's work, unless otherwise agreed by the parties to the contract for the same, or unless for the purposes, and subject to all restrictions, mentioned in section twenty-two of this chapter. *Ten hours a day's labor*

CHAPTER 302.—*Earnings of wives and children exempt.*

Exemption from attachment.

SECTION 5. The following goods and property shall be exempt from attachment on any warrant of distress or on any other writ, original, mesne, or judicial:

*   *   *   *   *   *

13. The salary and wages of the wife and of the minor children of any debtor.

ACTS OF 1911.

CHAPTER 653.—*Employment of children—certificates.*

Exemption

SECTION 1. The requirement of chapter 533 of the Public Laws, passed at the January session, A. D. 1910, respecting the ability of the child to read at sight and to write legibly simple sentences in the English language, shall not apply to children holding certificates lawfully issued prior to January 1, A. D. 1911.

SOUTH CAROLINA.

CODE 1902.

CIVIL CODE.

Earnings of minors.

Consent of parents required.

SECTION 2694 (as amended by act No. 451, Acts of 1908). If any person shall hire or employ any minor, or person under the age of twenty-one years, without the knowledge and consent of the parents or guardian of such minor, such person shall pay to said parents or guardian the full value of the labor of said minor from and after notice from the parents or guardians that payment of such service shall be made to him or them, as the case may be: *Provided,* This section shall not apply to cases where the parents or guardian fails or refuses to furnish the minor a home and support, in which cases the minor shall have the right to make contracts in regard to his own labor and enforce same in his own name and for his own benefit, and the employer shall be responsible to the minor only in such cases.

Proviso.

CRIMINAL CODE.

Seats for female employees.

Seats to be provided.

SECTION 333 (as amended by act No. 93, Acts of 1911). It shall be the duty of all employers of females in any mercantile establishment, or any place where goods or wares or merchandise are offered for sale, to provide and maintain chairs or stools, or other suitable seats, for the use of such female employees, to the number of one seat for every three females employed, and to permit the use of such seats by such employees, at reasonable times, to such an extent as may be requisite for the preservation of their health. And such employees shall be permitted to use same, as above set forth, in front of the counter, table, desk or any fixture when the female employee for the use of whom said seat shall be kept and maintained is principally engaged in front of said counter, table, desk or fixture; and behind such counter, table, desk or fixture when the female employee for the use of whom said seat shall be kept and maintained is principally engaged behind said counter, table, desk or fixture.

Penalty.

Any person who violates or omits to comply with any of the foregoing provisions of this section, or who suffers or permits any woman to stand, in violation of its provisions, shall be guilty of a misdemeanor, and, on conviction, shall be punished by a fine of not less than twenty dollars nor more than one hundred dollars for each offense.

Enforcement

The commissioner of agriculture, commerce and industries, and the State factory inspectors are hereby charged with the enforcement of the provisions of this law, and said commissioner is hereby empowered, from time to time whenever he may deem it necessary, to employ female inspectors for the purpose of collecting evidence. The sum of $300, if so much be necessary, shall annually be appropriated for the purpose of compensating such female inspectors. * * *

ACTS OF 1903.

Act No. 74.—*Employment of children.*

Section 1 (as amended by act No. 18, Acts of 1911). From and after Age limit
the first day of May, 1903, no child under the age of ten years shall
be employed in any factory, mine, or textile manufacturing establishment of this State; that from and after the first day of May, 1904, no
child under the age of eleven years shall be employed in any factory,
mine or textile establishment of this State; that from and after the
first day day of May, 1905, no child under the age of twelve years shall
be employed in any mine, factory or textile establishment of this
State.

Sec. 2 (as amended by act No. 18, Acts of 1911). From and after Night work
May 1st, 1903, no child under the age of sixteen years shall be permitted to work between the hours of eight o'clock p. m. and six o'clock
in the morning in any factory, mine or textile manufactory of this State:
Provided, That no children under the age of sixteen, whose employment
is permissible under the provisions of this act, may be permitted to
work after the hours of eight p. m. in order to make up lost time which
has occurred from some temporary shut down of the mill, on account
of accident or breaking down in the machinery, which has caused loss
of time: *Provided, however,* That under no circumstances shall a child
below the age of sixteen work later than the hour of nine p. m.

Sec. 3. Any owner, superintendent, manager or overseer of any Violations by
factory, mine or textile manufacturing establishment, or any other employers.
person in charge thereof or connected therewith, who shall knowingly
employ any child contrary to the provisions of this act, shall be guilty
of a misdemeanor, and for every such offense shall, upon conviction
thereof, be fined not less than ten dollars nor more than fifty dollars,
or be imprisoned not longer than thirty days, at the discretion of the
court.

Sec. 4. Any parent, guardian or other person having under his By parents, etc.
or her control any child, who consents, suffers or permits the employment of his or her child or ward under the ages as above provided, or
who knowingly or willfully misrepresents the age of such child or
ward to any of the persons named in section 3 of this act, in order to
obtain employment for such child or ward, shall be deemed guilty of
a misdemeanor, and for every such offense shall, upon conviction
thereof, be fined not less than ten dollars nor more than fifty dollars,
or be imprisoned not longer than thirty days, in the discretion of the
court.

Sec. 5 (as amended by act No. 18, Acts of 1911.) In the employment Statement of
of any child under the age of fourteen years in any factory, mine or age by parent, etc.
textile manufacturing establishment, the owner or superintendent of
such factory, mine or textile manufacturing establishment shall require
of the parent, guardian or person standing in loco parentis of such
child a sworn statement, made in duplicate, in which shall be recorded
the name, birthplace, age and place of residence of every such child
under 14 years of age, the original of which statement shall be produced
for inspection on the demand of [the] commissioner of agriculture, commerce and industries, or his agents or inspectors, and the duplicate of
which shall be forwarded to the commissioner at his office at Columbia;
the commissioner shall thereupon issue permit for employment. The
commissioner shall prescribe and furnish forms under registered num- Permit.
bers for these statements and duplicates, and shall prescribe regulations
for the keeping of proper records of the children employed in the
State under the laws of the State; and any person knowingly furnishing
a false statement of the age of such child or children, shall be guilty of False state-
a misdemeanor, and for every such offense shall, upon conviction, be ments.
fined not less than ten dollars nor more than fifty dollars, or be imprisoned not longer than thirty days, in the discretion of the court. The
commissioner shall likewise prescribe proper forms and regulations for
the employment of children provided for in any other act, making such
forms and regulations compatible with those provided for in this section.

ACTS OF 1907.

ACT NO. 233.—Hours of labor of employees in cotton and woolen mills.

Limi of ten hours.　SECTION 1. Ten hours a day, or sixty hours a week, shall constitute the hours for working for all operatives and employees in cotton and woolen manufacturing establishments engaged in the manufacture of yarns, cloth, hosiery and other products for merchandise except mechanics, engineers, firemen, watchmen, teamsters, yard employees and clerical force. All contracts for longer hours of work other than herein provided in said manufacturing establishments shall be, and the same are hereby, declared null and void; and any person entering into or enforcing such contracts shall be deemed guilty of a misdemeanor, in each and every instance, and on conviction in a court of competent jurisdiction shall be fined a sum of money not less than $25 nor more

Proviso.　than $100, or imprisonment not exceeding thirty days: *Provided*, That nothing herein contained shall be construed as forbidding or preventing any such manufacturing company from making up lost time, to the extent of sixty hours per annum, where such lost time has been caused by accident or other unavoidable cause.

ACTS OF 1909.

ACT NO. 4.—Employment of children.

Cleaning moving machinery.　SECTION 13. It shall be the duty of each corporation or other employer to place in one or more conspicuous places in each room of the factory in which any children under fourteen years of age are employed a notice or notices to the effect that said children are forbidden to clean any gears, cams or pulleys, or to clean in dangerous proximity thereto, while the same are in motion by aid of steam, water, electricity or other mechanical power; and no such employer, or its officers, superintendents, overseers or agents shall knowingly or willfully permit or consent to such children so cleaning the said moving parts; and any officer, superintendent, overseer or agent violating the provisions of this act shall be punished by a fine of not less than fifty nor more than one hundred dollars for each offense.

Statements as to age, etc.　SEC. 14. Every person, firm or corporation employing children shall procure from the parent, guardian, or person in custody of said child or children, a signed statement in which shall be recorded the name, birthplace, age and place of residence of every such child under fourteen years of age, and the same shall be produced for inspection on demand of the commissioner or his agents or inspectors.

ACTS OF 1911.

No. 83.—Hours of labor of female employees—Mercantile establishments.

Sixty hours per week.　SECTION 1. From and after the passage of this act the hours of labor of women employed in mercantile establishments in this State shall be limited to sixty hours per week, not to exceed twelve hours in any one

Night work　day, and that such female employees shall not be required to work later than the hour of ten o'clock p. m. The enforcement of this law is placed in the hands of the commissioner and inspectors.

Violations　SEC. 2. Any employer or employers of female labor in mercantile establishments who shall violate the provisions of this act shall be deemed guilty of a misdemeanor and shall be punished by a fine of not less than $10 nor more than $40, or imprisonment of not less than ten days nor exceeding thirty days.

SOUTH DAKOTA.

REVISED CODES—1903.

POLITICAL CODE.

Employment of children in mines.

Employment of children.　SECTION 145. All corporations or individuals working mines in South Dakota who shall employ, or permit to be employed, in such mines any children under fourteen years of age shall be deemed guilty of a

misdemeanor and on conviction thereof shall be punished by a fine
not exceeding one thousand dollars.

Employment of minors in barrooms.

SECTION 2844 (as amended by chapter 165, Acts of 1903). * * * Sale to employ-
it shall also be unlawful for any person to whom any license may be ees may be forbid-
granted to employ any person under twenty-one (21) years of age as Employing mi-
a bartender or in any other capacity in connection with the place or nors.
room where intoxicating liquors are sold.

CIVIL CODE.

Earnings of minors.

SECTION 124. The wages of a minor employed in service may be Wages may be
paid to him or her until the parent or guardian entitled thereto gives paid to minor,
the employer notice that he claims such wages.

PENAL CODE.

Hours of labor of women and children.

SECTION 764. Every owner, stockholder, overseer, employer, clerk Limit of ten
or foreman, of any manufactory, workshop or other place used for hours.
mechanical or manufacturing purposes, who, having control, shall
compel any woman or any child under eighteen years of age, or permit
any child under fourteen ears of age, to labor in any day exceeding
ten hours, shall be deemed guilty of a misdemeanor, and upon conviction, shall be punished by fine not exceeding one hundred and not less
than ten dollars.

ACTS OF 1907.

CHAPTER 135.—Employment of children—Age limit.

SECTION 150. No child under the age of fifteen years shall be em- Age limit.
ployed, permitted or suffered to work at any gainful occupation in any
mine, hotel, laundry, manufacturing establishment, factory, passenger
or freight elevator [,] bowling alley, or in any saloon, theater, concert
hall or place of amusement where intoxicating liquors are sold, or as
messenger or driver thereof, or in any other manner in work performed for wages or other compensation, to whomsoever payable, during
any portion of any month during the hours when the public schools of
any district in which he or she resides are in session.

Every owner, superintendent or overseer of any mine, factory, Violations.
workshop, mercantile establishment, or any other person who shall
employ any child under fifteen years of age contrary to the provisions
of this article shall be deemed guilty of a misdemeanor, and for every
offense shall upon conviction thereof be fined not less than $10 nor
more than $50 and costs.

Any person having the control of a child or who may have children
in his employ, who with the intent to evade the provisions of this
article shall make a willfully false statement concerning the age of such
child or in regard to facts covered by any other provision of this article,
shall for such an offense be fined in any sum not less than $10 nor
more than $50 for the use of the public school corporation.

TENNESSEE.

SHANNON'S SUPPLEMENT OF 1904.

Provisions for female employees—Water-closets.

(CHAPTER 98, Acts of 1897. Supplement, p. 472.)

SECTION 1. All persons hiring or employing female help in any Water-closets to
manufacturing or mercantile business or establishment, shall provide be provided.
separate privies or water-closets for such female help.

SEC. 2. No male person shall enter such separate privies or water- Males excluded.
closets except for the purpose of repairing or cleaning the same.

SEC. 3. A violation of the foregoing sections shall be a misdemeanor, Penalty.
punishable by a fine of not less than two or more than ten dollars.

ACTS OF 1905.

CHAPTER 171.—*Seats for female employees in stores, etc.*

Seats to be provided.

SECTION 1. All proprietors or owners of any retail, jobbing, or wholesale dry goods store, or dealers in notions, millinery, or any other business where any female help are employed for the purpose of serving the public in the capacity of clerks or sales ladies, shall provide a chair or stool for each one of such female help or clerks, in order that during such periods as they are not actively engaged in making sales or taking stock or performing other duties of their employment, they may have an opportunity to be seated and to rest.

Violation.

SEC. 2. Any proprietor, owner, or dealer, mentioned in section 1 of this act, who shall undertake by any direction or order to prohibit or prevent any one of such female help or clerks to use the seats provided for in the foregoing section shall be guilty of a misdemeanor, and, upon conviction, shall be fined as provided in the next section of this act.

Penalty.

SEC. 3. Any owner, proprietor, or dealer, mentioned in the foregoing sections, who shall neglect or refuse to obey and observe the provisions of this act shall be guilty of a misdemeanor, and upon conviction thereof, shall be fined in an amount not less than ten dollars and not exceeding one hundred dollars for the first offense, and in the event said owner or proprietor shall continue to disobey said act he shall be subjected to a fine at the rate of one dollar daily for every chair he fails to furnish his said employees, and for every violation of section 2 of this act such owner, proprietor, or dealer shall, upon conviction, be fined not less than ten dollars and not exceeding one hundred dollars for each and every violation.

ACTS OF 1907.

CHAPTER 256.—*Hiring out children to support parents in idleness.*

Who are vagrants.

SECTION 1. The following persons are and shall be defined and punished as vagrants, viz.:

*   *   *   *   *   *

(n) All persons who, though able to work, fail to do so, but hire out their minor children, or allow them to be hired out, and subsist upon their wages.

*   *   *   *   *   *   *

CHAPTER 308.—*Employment of women and children—Hours of labor.*

Limit in 1908.

SECTION 1. Commencing January 1, 1908, it shall be unlawful for any person, firm, or corporation to employ in any manufacturing establishment in this State any female, or any child under the age of sixteen years, more than sixty-two (62) hours in any one week.

In 1909.

SEC. 2. Commencing January 1, 1909, it shall be unlawful for any person, firm, or corporation to employ in any manufacturing establishment in this State any female, or any child under the age of sixteen years, more than sixty-one (61) hours in any one week.

In 1910 and thereafter.

SEC. 3. Commencing January 1, 1910, it shall be unlawful for any person, firm, or corporation to employ in any manufacturing establishment in this State any female, or any child under the age of sixteen years, more than sixty (60) hours in any one week.

Violation.

SEC. 4. Every violation of this act is hereby declared to be a misdemeanor punishable by a fine of not less than twenty-five ($25) dollars and not more than one hundred ($100) dollars for each offense.

ACTS OF 1909.

CHAPTER 163.—*Employment of children—School attendance.*

School attendance required.

SECTION 1. Every parent, guardian, or other person in this State having control or charge of a child or children between the ages of eight and sixteen years shall send such child or children to a public school or to some other school for at least sixteen weeks or eighty days of not less than four hours each of each year, or as long as the public school of the city or district in which such child resides shall be in session, in case the session shall be less than sixteen weeks during the year, unless such attendance, in whole or in part, is excused by the district or city school directors or other officers having control of the public school in written exemption showing on whose application granted and the period and reasons for which the exemption was granted. Exemption.

SEC. 2. No such exemption from school attendance shall be granted unless such child has completed the primary school course and attained proficiency in all the subjects or branches thereof, or unless such child has been or is being instructed for not less than sixteen weeks in the year or in some private, parochial, or tutorial school or at home by competent and reliable teachers, or unless it appear from the competent medical or other positive and satisfactory testimony that the child is or was in such condition physically or mentally as to prevent its attendance at school, or its application to study for the period of exemption, or unless, because of sickness or extreme poverty, the wages, time, or labor of such child or children are essentially necessary for the support of a destitute parent, or brother, or sister in such indigent family to prevent them from becoming objects of charity: *Provided,* That if any such child or children is of a family in extreme poverty and destitution, as aforesaid, the commissioner of the poor of the county may make an allowance or appropriation to reimburse the family or indigent child for the loss of time, work, or wages during school attendance, and to furnish such child or children necessary clothing so as to enable such child or children to attend school for the time required without exemption on account of poverty and destitution aforesaid, which sum shall be paid by the commissioners out of any funds at their disposal or by the county upon the recommendation of such payment by said commissioners of the poor: *Provided, further,* That the district directors and city boards or other officers having control of the public schools of the districts and cities may, with the consent of the county or city superintendent of schools, buy and furnish with the school funds for any such child who is of a family in extreme poverty and destitution all necessary textbooks for use under the direction of the teacher in the schoolroom during school hours by such indigent child or children and no others, which books shall be delivered by the teacher to the district directors or the city boards of education at the close of the school, or when the necessity thereof terminates: *Provided, further,* That the occasional absence from such attendance by any such child between the ages of eight and sixteen years, not amounting to more than two unexcused absences in four consecutive weeks, reckoned in periods of four weeks from the beginning of the school term, shall not be unlawful. Exemption not granted, when. Allowances. Textbooks.

SEC. 3. The attendance of sixteen weeks or eighty days required shall begin with the opening of the school session for the year, and shall be consecutive, except for holidays, vacation, detention by sickness, and other necessary and unavoidable causes, and such intermissions of such attendance shall not be counted as part of the sixteen weeks required: *Provided,* That any responsible principal or teacher of any school shall have power to exempt any such child for temporary absence on account of unusual storm, bad weather, or high waters, death in the child's family, providential hindrance, unforeseen and unavoidable accidents, and for the observance of religious festivals and holidays: *Provided further,* That the provisions of this act shall not apply in cases where the home of the parent or other custodian of a child or children between the said ages of eight and sixteen years is more than two and one-half miles from the nearest public school by the shortest road. Attendance at beginning of school.

SEC. 5. During the period of the year that the public schools of any district or city of this State are in operation it shall be a misdemeanor, punishable by fine, for any person, firm, or corporation to hire or use the services of any child between the ages of eight and sixteen years, unless such child shall first have attended school during the year then current for the length of time required by this act, or unless such child has been excused from school attendance in the manner allowed and prescribed by this act, and a violation of this provision shall subject the Employing children unlaw fully absent from school.

offender to a fine of ten dollars ($10) for each offense, collectable [collectible] in an action in the name of the State before any court of competent jurisdiction, and payable to the county trustee for the benefit of the public school of the district or [sic] in which the offense was committed.

Enforcement. SEC. 8. It shall be the duty of the district, county, and city school boards having control of the public schools in the districts and cities, through the clerk or secretary, as their agent or other school officer designated by the respective boards, to enforce the payment and collection of all fines for the violation of this act incurred by employers, parents, and others within respective districts and cities, and for this purpose to institute all necessary suits therefor in the name of the State before any court having competent jurisdiction, * * *

Application of law. [This act applies to Cocke County only. The legislature of 1909 passed laws embodying similar provisions, applicable to the following counties: Anderson (age limit, 8 to 14 years), Blount, Carter, Cumberland, Hancock, Hardin, Jefferson, Johnson, Marion, Monroe, Roane, and Sevier.]

ACTS OF 1911.

CHAPTER 57.—Employment of children—Age limit.

Age limit. SECTION 1. It shall be unlawful for any proprietor, foreman, owner, or other person to employ, permit, or suffer to work any child less than fourteen years of age in, about, or in connection with any mill, factory, workshop, laundry, telegraph or telephone office, or in the distribution or transmission of merchandise or messages.

Employment during school time. SEC. 2. It shall be unlawful for any proprietor, foreman, owner, or other person to employ, permit, or suffer to work any child under fourteen years of age in any business or service whatever which interferes with the child's attendance at school, except in agricultural or domestic service, during any part of the term the public schools of the district in which the child resides are in session.

Occupations forbidden. SEC. 3. No child under the age of sixteen years shall be employed, permitted, or suffered to work at any of the following occupations or in any of the following positions: Repairing machine belts, while in motion, in any workshop or factory, or assisting therein in any capacity whatever; adjusting any belt to any machinery; oiling or cleaning machinery or assisting therein; operating or assisting in operating circular or band saws, wood shapers, wood jointers, planers, sandpaper or wood-polishing machinery; picker machines, machines used in picking wool, machines used in picking cotton, machines used in picking hair, machines used in picking any upholstering material; paper-lacing machines, leather-burnishing machines in any tannery or leather manufactory; job or cylinder printing presses operated by power other than foot power, emery or polishing wheels used for polishing metal, wood-turning or boring machinery, stamping machines used in sheet metal and tinware manufacturing, stamping machines in washer and nut factories, corregating [corrugating] rolls, such as are used in roofing and washboard factories; steam boilers, steam machinery or other steam generating apparatus, dough brakes or crackery machinery of any description; wire or iron straightening machinery, rolling mill machinery, punches or shears; washing, grinding, or mixing mills; calender rolls in rubber manufacturing; laundering machinery; dipping, drying, or packing matches; or in mines or quarries.

SEC. 4. It shall be unlawful for any proprietor, foreman, owner, or other person to employ any child under eighteen years of age as a messenger for a telegraph or messenger company in the distribution, transmission, or delivery of goods or messages before five o'clock in the morning or after ten o'clock in the evening of any day.

Statements of age on file. SEC. 5. It shall be unlawful for any proprietor, foreman, owner, or other person to employ, permit, or suffer to work any child between the ages of fourteen and sixteen years in, about, or in connection with any place or establishment named in section 1, unless said proprietor, foreman, owner, or other person keep on file and accessible to the shop and factory inspector a sworn statement made by the parent or guardian or any person acting as guardian of such child, setting forth the place and date of birth of such child, and whoever shall make false statement as to the age of such child in such sworn statement shall be deemed guilty of perjury.

SEC. 6. Whoever employs any child and whoever having under his control as parent, guardian, or otherwise any child, permits or suffers such child to be employed or to work in violation of any of the provisions of this act shall be deemed guilty of a misdemeanor, and upon conviction shall be fined not less than twenty-five dollars nor more than two hundred and fifty dollars, in the discretion of the court. *Violations.*

TEXAS.

ACTS OF 1907.

CHAPTER 138.—*Employment of women and minors in saloons.*

SECTION 19. Every retail liquor dealer or malt liquor dealer, * * * who shall have in his employ about his place of business, * * * any minor * * * shall be guilty of a misdemeanor, and upon conviction therefor shall be punished by a fine of not less than ten dollars nor more than two hundred dollars, or by imprisonment in the county jail for not longer than sixty days, or by both such fine and imprisonment. *Employment of minors;*

SEC. 25., No retail liquor dealer or retail malt dealer shall employ or suffer to be employed, any female as a servant, bartender or waitress, other than a member of his own family, in his place of business, * * * and any person violating the provisions of this section shall be deemed guilty of a misdemeanor and upon conviction shall be punished by imprisonment in the county jail for not more than twelve months or by a fine of not exceeding five hundred dollars, or both such fine and imprisonment. *Of females.*

ACTS OF 1909.

CHAPTER 59.—*Hiring out children to support parents in idleness.*

SECTION 1. The following persons are and shall be punished as vagrants, viz:

* * * * * *

(n) All persons who are able to work and do not work, but hire out their minor children or allow them to [be] hired out and live upon their wages, being without other means of support. *Who are vagrants.*

ACTS OF 1911.

CHAPTER 46.—*Employment of children—Age limit.*

SECTION 1. Any person, or any agent, or any employee of any person, firm or corporation who shall hereafter employ any child under the age of fifteen years to labor in or about any manufacturing or other establishment using dangerous machinery, or about the machinery in any mill or factory, or in any distillery, brewery, or to labor in any capacity in the manufacture of goods for immoral purposes, or where their health may be impaired or morals debased, or shall send any such child to any disorderly house, bawdy house, or assignation house, or having the control of such child, shall permit him or her to go to any such house, shall be deemed guilty of a misdemeanor, and, upon conviction, shall be fined not less than fifty dollars nor more than two hundred dollars, and each day the provisions of this act are violated shall constitute a separate offense. *Age limit.* *Dangerous or immoral employments.*

SEC. 1a. Such person, firm or corporation, or any agent thereof, shall give free access at all times to the commissioner of labor statistics of the State of Texas, and his deputies, for the inspection of their premises and of the methods employed, to insure compliance with the provisions of the foregoing section. *Inspection.*

SEC. 2. Any person, agent, or any employee of any person, firm or corporation, who shall hereafter employ any child under the age of 17 years to labor in or about any quarry or mine shall be punished as provided for in section 1 of this act. *Age limit in mines.*

Inspection to be allowed.
SEC. 2a. Such person, firm or corporation, or any agent thereof, shall give free access at all time to the commissioner of labor statistics of the State of Texas, and his deputies, for the inspection of their premises and of the methods employed, to insure compliance with the provisions of the foregoing section.

UTAH.

CONSTITUTION.

ARTICLE 16.—*Employment of labor—Women and children.*

Employment in mines forbidden.
SECTION 3. The legislature shall prohibit: (1) The employment of women, or of children under the age of fourteen years, in underground mines.

* * * ● * * * *

COMPILED LAWS—1907.

Employment of women and children.

Employment in mines and smelters.
SECTION 1338. It shall be unlawful for any person, firm, or corporation to employ any child under fourteen years of age, or any female, to work in any mine or smelter in the State of Utah. Any person, firm, or corporation who shall violate any of the provisions of this section shall be deemed guilty of a misdemeanor.

Seats for female employees in stores, etc.
SEC. 1339. The proprietor, manager, or person having charge of any store, shop, hotel, restaurant, or other place where women or girls are employed as clerks or help therein, shall provide chairs, stools, or other contrivances where such clerks or help may rest when not employed in the discharge of their respective duties. Any person who shall violate any of the provisions of this section shall be guilty of a misdemeanor.

Earnings of minors.

Payments to, minors valid, when.
SECTION 1544. When a contract for the personal services of a minor has been made with him alone, and those services are afterward performed, payment made therefor to such minor in accordance with the terms of the contract is a full satisfaction for those services, and the parent or guardian cannot recover therefor a second time.

ACTS OF 1911.

CHAPTER 106.—*Employment of women and children in barrooms, etc.— Sale of intoxicants near labor camps.*

Employment of minors.
SECTION 23. No holder of a license for the sale at retail of intoxicating liquors shall employ any person under the age of twenty-one years to serve such liquors to be drunk on the premises.

Employment of minors.
SEC. 24. No person, partnership or corporation shall employ a minor under the age of twenty-one years in handling intoxicating liquors or packages containing such liquors in a brewery or bottling establishment, in which such liquors are prepared for sale or offered for sale.

Employment of females.
SEC. 28. The licensed premises shall be conducted in a quiet, orderly manner; * * * no female shall be employed in the place; * * *

CHAPTER 133.—*Hours of labor of women.*

Fifty-four hours per week.
SECTION 1. No female shall be employed in any manufacturing, mechanical, or mercantile establishment, laundry, hotel, or restaurant, or telegraph or telephone establishment, hospital or office, or by any express or transportation company in this State, more than nine hours during any one day, or more than fifty-four hours in any one week, except in cases of emergency in hospitals and in cases of emergency or where life or property is in imminent danger or where materials are liable to spoil by the enforcement of this act.

Sec. 2. Any person or persons, corporation or other association en- Violations. gaged in conducting or operating any of the business institutions or enterprises set forth in the foregoing section, requiring or employing any female to work longer than the period of nine hours constituting a day's labor, except as above provided, or more than fifty-four hours in any one week shall be guilty of a misdemeanor, and, upon conviction thereof shall be fined not less than twenty-five dollars nor more than one hundred dollars, and costs of prosecution.

CHAPTER 144.—*Employment of children—General provisions.*

SECTION 1. No child under the age of fourteen years shall be Age limit. employed, permitted or suffered to work in any capacity in, about or in connection with the preparing of any composition in which dangerous or poisonous acids are used—manufacture of paints, colors or white Dangerous, etc., lead; manufacturing, packing or storing powder, dynamite, nitro- employments. glycerin compounds, fuses or other explosives; manufacture of goods for immoral purposes; nor in any quarry, any mine, coal breaker, laundry, tobacco warehouse, cigar factory, or other factory where tobacco is manufactured or prepared; distillery, brewery or any other establishment where malt or alcoholic liquors are manufactured, packed, wrapped or bottled; theatre, concert hall, nor saloon, nor in operating any automobile, motor car or truck; in the running or management of elevators, lifts or hoisting machines; nor in bowling alleys, nor in any other employment declared by the State board of health to be dangerous to lives or limbs, or injurious to the health or morals of children under the age of fourteen.

SEC. 2. An employment certificate shall be issued only by the super- Certificates. intendent of schools or by a person authorized by him in writing, or, where there is no superintendent of schools, by a person authorized by the school board: *Provided,* That no member of a school board or other person authorized as aforesaid shall have the authority to issue such certificate for any child then in or about to enter such person's own employment or the employment of a firm or corporation of which he is a member, officer or employee: *Provided,* That no such certificate shall be issued until the person issuing the same shall have received, examined and approved the school record of such child.

SEC. 3. No employment certificate shall be issued until the child in Issue. question has personally appeared before and been examined by the officer issuing the certificate, nor until such officer, after making such examination, has signed and filed in his office a statement that the child can read and legibly write simple sentences in the English language.

SEC. 4. The school record required by this act shall be signed by the School records. principal or chief executive officer of the school which such child has attended, and shall be furnished on demand to a child entitled thereto.

It shall contain a statement certifying that the child has attended the public schools or parochial schools equivalent thereto for not less than one hundred days during the year previous to his arriving at the age of fourteen years, or during the year previous to applying for such school record, and is able to read and write simple sentences in the English language.

SEC. 5. Any authorized inspector or the truant officer shall make Power of in- demand on any employer in or about whose place or establishment a spectors. child apparently under the age of fourteen years is employed or permitted or suffered to work, and require such employer to furnish him within ten days satisfactory evidence that such child is in fact over fourteen years of age, or shall cease to employ or permit or suffer such child to work in such factory.

SEC. 6. No female under the age of twenty-one years shall be Employment employed, permitted or suffered to work in, about or in connection with of females in sa- any restaurant, resort or place of amusement where alcoholic liquors loons, etc. are manufactured or dispensed.

SEC. 7. In cities of the first or second class no person under the age Messengers. of twenty-one years shall be employed or permitted to work as a messenger for a telegraph or a messenger company in the distribution, transmission or delivery of goods or messages before 5 o'clock in the morning Night work.

Immoral resorts.

or after 9 o'clock in the evening of the day. And no person under the age of twenty-one years shall be permitted to deliver messages or goods to, or required to visit, in the course of any employment, any house of ill repute, or saloon, or gambling house, or other places of objectionable character which have been disapproved by the juvenile court.

Hours of labor for children.

SEC. 8. No boy under the age of fourteen years and no girl under the age of sixteen years shall be employed, permitted or suffered to work at any gainful occupation other than domestic service, fruit or vegetable packing or work on a farm more than fifty-four hours in any one week.

Street trades.

SEC. 9. No male child under twelve and no girl under sixteen years of age shall, in any city of the first or second class, sell or expose or offer for sale newspapers, magazines, periodicals or other articles in any street or public place. No child shall work as a bootblack in any street or public place unless he is over twelve years of age.

Permits for street trades.

SEC. 10. No male child under sixteen years of age shall sell or expose or offer for sale in any street or public place any of the articles mentioned in section 9 or work as a bootblack therein, unless a permit as hereinafter provided shall have been issued to him by the superintendent of schools or by a person authorized by him in writing, or, where there is no superintendent of schools, by a person authorized by the school board on the application of the parent, guardian or other person having the custody of the child desiring such permit or in case said child has no parent, guardian or custodian, then on the application of his next friend, being an adult. Such permit shall not be issued until the officer issuing the same shall have received, examined, approved and placed on file in his office satisfactory proof that such male child is of the age of twelve years or upwards, and shall also have received, examined and placed on file the written statement of the principal or chief executive officer of the school which the child is attending, stating that such child is an attendant at such school, that he is of the normal development of a child of his age and physically fit for such employment, and that said principal or chief executive officer approves the granting of a permit to such child.

Contents of permit.

SEC. 11. Such permit shall state the name and address of its parent, guardian, custodian or next friend, as the case may be, and shall describe the color of the hair and eyes, the height and weight and any distinguishing facial mark of such child.

Night work.

SEC. 12. No child to whom a permit is issued as provided for in section 10 of this act shall work as a bootblack, sell or expose or offer for sale any newspapers, magazines, periodicals or other merchandise in any street or public place after 9 o'clock in the evening.

Evidence.

SEC. 13. In case any employer shall fail to produce and deliver to an authorized inspector or truant officer, within ten days after demand made pursuant to section 2 of this act, the evidence of age therein required, and shall thereafter continue to employ such child or permit or suffer such child to work in such place or establishment, proof of the giving of such notice and of such failure to produce and file such evidence shall be prima facie evidence of the illegal employment of such child in any prosecution brought therefor.

Violations.

SEC. 14. Whoever employs any child, and whoever having under his control as a parent, guardian or otherwise, any child, permits or suffers such child to be employed or to work in violation of any of the provisions of this act, shall for such offense be fined not less than twenty-five dollars nor more than two hundred dollars, or be imprisoned for not less than ten days nor more than thirty days, or both, in the discretion of the court.

Jurisdiction of courts.

SEC. 15. The juvenile court or courts of like jurisdiction of the State of Utah is [are] hereby given jurisdiction in all cases arising under this act.

VERMONT.

` PUBLIC STATUTES, 1906.

Employment of children—General provisions.

Employment during school time.

SECTION 1044 (as amended by act No. 69, Acts of 1910). A child under sixteen years of age who has not completed the course of study of nine years prepared for the elementary schools by the superintendent of education shall not, unless excused in writing by the town or union superintendent of schools, or by the chairman of the prudential committee in the case of an incorporated district, be employed in work connected with railroading, mining, manufacturing or quarrying, or be employed in a hotel or bowling alley, or in delivering messages, except during vacations and before and after school, unless said child deposits with his employer a certificate from said superintendent, or chairman of the prudential committee, to the effect that he is eligible to employment in accordance with the provisions of this chapter; and no child under sixteen years of age shall be employed after eight o'clock **Night work.** at night in any of the occupations or industries herein enumerated. In case said child has been in attendance upon a private or parochial school, such superintendent or chairman of the prudential committee may examine said child for the purpose of determining his eligibility to employment in accordance with this section. ·

SEC. 1045 (as amended by act No. 69, Acts of 1910). The town **Enforcement.** superintendent, union superintendent, or the chairman of the prudential committee, may inquire of the owner or superintendent of a mill, factory, quarry, workshop, hotel, bowling alley, or railroad office, shop or yards, as to the employment of children therein, may call for the production of certificates deposited with such owner or superintendent, and satisfy himself that the requirements of law have been complied with.

SEC. 1046 (as amended by act No. 70, Acts of 1910). No child **Age limit.** under fourteen years of age shall be employed, permitted or suffered to work for any railroad company or in, about or in connection with any mill, factory, quarry or workshop, wherein are employed exceeding ten persons. No child under the age of twelve years shall be employed by or permitted to work in, about or in connection with any mill, factory, quarry, workshop, or in delivering messages for a corporation or company or in any mercantile establishment, store, business office, restaurant, bakery or hotel.

SEC. 1047. No person having a child under his control shall allow **Acts of parents** him to be employed contrary to the provisions of this chapter. **etc.**

SEC. 1048 (as amended by act No. 70, Acts of 1910). A person who **Violations.** violates a provision of chapter 50 [sections 1044–1050] of the Public Statutes or of this act shall be fined not less than five dollars nor more than two hundred dollars for each offense, and upon a second conviction, may be so fined or imprisoned for not more than six months.

Employment of women and children in barrooms.

SECTION 5130. Licenses shall be subject to the following conditions: **Employment**
      *   *   *   *   * **forbidden.**
That no female, or person under the age of twenty-one, shall be employed in such barroom.   *   *   *   ●
    *   *   *   *   ●

ACTS OF 1910.

No. 69.—Employment of children—Certificate.

SECTION 4. Any person having control of a child * * * **seeking** **Evidence of age.** an employment certificate for such child, shall, when required by the town or union superintendent, or by the school board of an incorporated district, furnish evidence of the age of such child.

No. 70.—Employment of children.

SECTION 2. No child under the age of sixteen years shall be em- **Occupations** ployed, permitted or suffered to work at any of the following occupa- **forbidden.** tions or in any of the following positions: Sewing machine belts in any workshop or factory, or assisting therein in any capacity whatever; adjusting any belt to any machinery; oiling, wiping or cleaning machinery or assisting therein; operating circular or band saws, wood shapers, wood jointers, planers, sandpaper or wood-polishing machinery, picker machines, machines used in picking wool, machines used in picking

persons so convicted of the custody of such child, and thereafter such child shall be deemed in the custody of the court, and thereupon such proceedings shall be had as to the commitment, custody, care, and education of such child as are provided for in section five of this act [for vagrant or destitute children].

(7) A person convicted under any of the provisions of this act shall be deemed guilty of a misdemeanor and shall be punished by fine not exceeding two hundred dollars or by imprisonment in jail not exceeding twelve months or both.

(8) In this act the word "person" shall be construed to include corporations, partnerships, companies, and associations, as well as individuals.

ACTS OF 1908.

CHAPTER 301.—*Employment of children—Age limit.*

Age limit.

SECTION 1. On and after March first, nineteen hundred and nine, no child under the age of thirteen years, and on and after March first, nineteen hundred and ten, no child under the age of fourteen years, shall be employed, permitted or suffered to work in any factory, workshop, mercantile establishment, or mine in this Commonwealth: *Pro-*

Orphans, etc.

vided, This act shall not exclude any child over the age of twelve, who is an orphan, or who for any other reason is dependent on its own labor for support, nor any child or children whose parent or parents are invalids, and solely dependent upon the labor of such child or children

Certificate.

for support; in either of which cases a certificate shall be obtained from the circuit court of the county, or corporation court of the city, or the judge thereof in vacation, or from the mayor of the city or town, or a justice of the peace of the magisterial district, as the case may be, in which such child or children reside, setting forth the fact that a necessity exists, and authorizing the employment of said child or children, and a copy of such permit shall be forwarded to the commissioner of labor within ten days from the granting thereof, by the clerk of the court in which, or the officer by whom such permit was granted.

Violations.

Any owner, superintendent, overseer, foreman or manager, who shall knowingly employ or permit any child to be employed contrary to the provisions of this act, in any factory, workshop, mercantile establishment, or mine, with which he is connected, and any parent or guardian, who allows any such employment of his child or ward, shall upon conviction of such offense, be fined not less than twenty-five dollars nor more than one hundred dollars: *Provided,* That as to fruit and vegetable canneries, and as to stores in the country and in towns of less than two thousand population, and country workshops not in the suburbs of a city, the law shall remain as if this act had not been passed. But nothing in this act shall prevent a parent from working his or her child in any factory, workshop, mercantile establishment, or mine, or other place owned or operated by said parent.

Any employment contrary to the provisions of this act shall be prima facie evidence of guilt, both as to the employer and the parent or guardian of the child so employed.

Repeal.

SEC. 2. All acts and parts of acts that are or may be in conflict with the operation of this act on and after March the first, nineteen hundred and nine, are to that extent hereby repealed, said repeal to take effect as of March the first, nineteen hundred and nine.

WASHINGTON.

CODES AND STATUTES—1909.

Employment of children—Certain occupations forbidden—Age limit.

Mendicant, etc., occupations.

SECTION 2446. Every person who shall employ, or cause to be employed, exhibit or have in his custody for exhibition or employment any minor actually or apparently under the age of eighteen years; and every parent, relative, guardian, employer or other person having the care, custody, or control of any such minor, who shall in any way procure or consent to the employment of such minor—

(1) In begging, receiving alms, or in any mendicant occupation; or,
(2) In any indecent or immoral exhibition or practice; or,
(3) In any practice or exhibition dangerous or injurious to life, limb, health or morals; or,
(4) As a messenger for delivering letters, telegrams, packages or bundles, to any known house of prostitution or assignation;

Shall be guilty of a misdemeanor.

SEC. 2447. Every person who shall employ, and every parent, guardian or other person having the care, custody or control of such child, who shall permit to be employed, by another, any male child under the age of fourteen years or any female child under the age of sixteen years at any labor whatever, in or in connection with any store, shop, factory, mine or any inside employment not connected with farm or house work, without the written permit thereto of a judge of a superior court of the county wherein such child may live, shall be guilty of a misdemeanor. *Permits required, when.*

Employment of children—School attendance.

SECTION 4714. All parents, guardians and other persons in this State having or who may hereafter have immediate custody of any child between eight and fifteen years of age (being between the eighth and fifteenth birthdays), or of any child between fifteen and sixteen years of age (being between the fifteenth and sixteenth birthdays) not regularly and lawfully engaged in some useful and remunerative occupation, shall cause suchychild to attend the public school of the district, in which the child resides, for the full time when such school may be in session or to attend a private school for the same time, unless the superintendent of the schools of the district in which the child resides, if there be such superintendent, and in all other cases the county superintendents of common schools, shall have excused such child from such attendance because the child is physically or mentally unable to attend school or has already attained a reasonable proficiency in the branches required by law to be taught in the first eight grades of the public schools of this State as provided by the course of study of such school, or for some other sufficient reason. Proof of absence from public schools or approved private school shall be prima facie evidence of a violation of this section. *School attendance required.*

SEC. 4715. No child under the age of fifteen years shall be employed for any purpose by any corporation, person or association of persons in this State during the hours which the public schools of the district in which such child resides are in session, unless the said child shall present a certificate from a school superintendent as provided for in section 4714, excusing the said child from attendance in the public schools and setting forth the reason for such excuse, the residence and age of the child, and the time for which such excuse is given. Every owner, superintendent, or overseer of any establishment, corporation, company or person employing any such child shall keep such certificate on file so long as such child is employed by him, her or it. The form of said certificate shall be furnished by the superintendent of public instruction. Proof that any child under fifteen years of age is employed during any part of the period in which public schools of the district are in session, shall be deemed prima facie evidence of a violation of this section. *Employment during school hours.* *Certificates.*

SEC. 4716. Any person violating any of the provisions of either of the two preceding sections shall be fined not more than twenty-five dollars. Attendance officers shall make complaint for violation of the provisions of this act, to a justice of the peace or to a judge of the superior court. *Violations.*

SEC. 4717. * * * The attendance officer shall be vested with police powers, the authority to make arrests and serve all legal processes contemplated by this act, and shall have authority to enter all stores, mills, shops, or other places in which children may be employed, for the purpose of making such investigations as may be necessary for the enforcement of this act. * * * The attendance officer shall insti- *Enforcement.*

tute proceedings against any officer, parent, guardian, person, company or corporation violating any provisions of this act, and shall otherwise discharge the duties prescribed in this act, and shall perform such other services as the superintendent of schools or the board of directors may deem necessary. * * *

Earnings of minors.

Payments to minors valid, when.

SECTION 5295. When a contract for the personal services of a minor has been made with him alone, and those services are afterwards performed, payment made therefor to such minor in accordance with the terms of the contract is a full satisfaction for those services, and the parents or guardian cannot recover therefor.

Hours of labor of children in bakeries.

Night work of children.

SECTION 5490. No employer shall require, permit or suffer any person under sixteen years of age to work in his bakeshop between the hours of 8 o'clock in the evening and 5 o'clock in the morning.

Employment of women in saloons.

Employment of females forbidden.

SECTION 6285. No female person shall be employed in any capacity in any saloon, beer hall, barroom, theater, or place of amusement, where intoxicating liquors are sold as a beverage, and any person or corporation convicted of so employing, or of participating in so employing, any such female person shall be fined not less than five hundred dollars; and any person so convicted may be imprisoned in the county jail for a period of not less than six months.

Employment of women and children.

Seats to be provided.

SECTION 6566. It shall be the duty of every agent, proprietor, superintendent, or employer of female help in stores, offices, or schools, within the State of Washington, to provide for each and every such employee a chair, stool, or seat, upon which such female worker or workers shall be allowed to rest when their duties will permit, or when such rest shall or does not interfere with a faithful discharge of their incumbent duties. A violation of any of the provisions of this section shall be deemed a misdemeanor, and upon conviction thereof by any court of competent jurisdiction shall subject the person offending to a fine of not less than ten dollars nor more than fifty dollars.

Sex not a bar.

SEC. 6569. * * * every avenue of employment shall be open to women; and any business, vocation, profession, and calling followed and pursued by men may be followed and pursued by women, and no person shall be disqualified from engaging in or pursuing any business, vocation, profession, calling, or employment on account of sex: Proviso. *Provided,* That this section shall not be construed so as to permit women to hold public office.

Messenger service.

SEC. 6570. No person under the age of nineteen years shall be employed as a public messenger by any person, telegraph company, telephone company, or messenger company in any city of the first class in this State, nor shall any child of either sex under Factory, etc., labor. the age of fourteen years be hired out to labor in any factory, mill, workshop or store at any time: *Provided,* That any superior court judge may issue a permit for the employment of any child between the ages of twelve and fourteen years at any occupation, not in his judgment, dangerous or injurious to the health or morals of such child, upon evidence satisfactory to him, that the labor of such child is necessary for its support or for the assistance of any parent: *And provided further,* That the judge of the juvenile court may issue permits for the employment of any male child over fourteen years of age, as messenger by telegraph, telephone and messenger companies subject to such limitations and conditions as may be imposed by said court. All permits herein provided for shall be issued for a definite time and shall be revocable at the discretion of the judge by whom issued.

SEC. 6571. Any employer, or any overseer, superintendent, or **Violations.** agent of such person, telegraph company, telephone company or messenger company who shall violate any of the provisions of the preceding section shall, upon conviction thereof, be fined for each offense not less than ten dollars nor more than five hundred dollars, or be imprisoned in the county jail not to exceed six months, or by both such fine and imprisonment.

Employment of women and children at mines.

SECTION 7388. No boy under the age of sixteen years and no **Employment** female of any age shall be employed or permitted to be in any **forbidden.** mine for the purpose of employment therein, nor shall a boy under the age of fourteen years be employed or permitted to be in or about the outside structures or workings of a colliery for the purpose of employment: *Provided,* That this prohibition shall not affect the employment of boys of suitable age in an office or in the performance of clerical work at the colliery. When an employer is in doubt as to the age of any boy applying for employment in or about a mine or colliery, he shall demand and receive proof of the age of such boy by certificate from the parents or guardian of such boy before he shall be employed.

ACTS OF 1911.

CHAPTER 37.—*Employment of women—Hours of labor—Seats.*

SECTION 1. No female shall be employed in any mechanical or **Eight-hour day.** mercantile establishment, laundry, hotel or restaurant in this State more than eight hours during any day. The hours of work may be so arranged as to permit the employment of females at any time so that they shall not work more than eight hours during the twenty-four: *Provided, however,* That the provisions of **Exemptions.** this section in relation to the hours of employment shall not apply to, nor affect, females employed in harvesting, packing, curing, canning or drying any variety of perishable fruit or vegetable, nor to females employed in canning fish or shellfish. If it shall be adjudicated that the foregoing proviso and exception shall be unconstitutional and invalid for any reason, an adjudication of invalidity of said proviso or of any part of this act shall not affect the validity of the act as a whole or any other part thereof.

SEC. 2. Every employer in establishments where females are **Seats.** employed shall provide suitable seats for them and shall permit the use of such seats by them when they are not engaged in the active duties for which they are employed, and every such employer shall keep posted in an open and conspicuous place in each room where such females are at work a copy of this act printed in such form and style as may be prescribed by the commissioner of labor.

SEC. 3. Any employer, overseer, superintendent or other agent **Violations.** of any such employer who shall violate any of the provisions of this act, shall, upon conviction thereof be fine for each offense in a sum not less than ten dollars nor more than one hundred dollars.

WEST VIRGINIA.

CODE—EDITION OF 1899.

APPENDIX.

Employment of children.

(Act, page 1055, as amended by chapter 60, Acts of 1911.)

SECTION 1. No child under the age of fourteen years shall be **Age limit.** employed, permitted or suffered to work in, about or in connection with any factory, mill, workshop or manufacturing establishment. It shall be unlawful for any person, firm, or corporation without written permission from the State commissioner of labor or county superintendent of free schools to employ any child under fourteen years of age in any business or service whatever during the hours when the public schools of the district in which the said child resides are actually in session.

Certificates required. SEC. 2. No child under the age of sixteen shall be employed, permitted or suffered to work in, about or in connection with any of the establishments or occupations named in section one of this act, unless the person, firm or corporation employing such child procures and keeps on file, accessible to any truant officer, inspector or factories or authorized agent of the humane society, an employment certificate as hereinafter prescribed. On termination of employment of a child whose employment certificate is on file, such certificate shall be forthwith returned by the employers to the person who issued the same.

Who to issue. The employment certificate shall be issued only by the superintendent of schools, or by persons authorized by him in writing, or where there is no superintendent of schools, then by a person authorized by the local school board: *Provided,* That no member of a school board or other person authorized, as aforesaid, shall have authority to issue such certificates to any child then in or about to enter such person's own employment or the employment of a firm or corporation of which he is a member, officer or employee.

Evidence. The person authorized to issue an employment certificate shall not issue such certificate until he has received, examined and approved and filed the following papers duly executed:

1. The school record of such child properly filled out and signed.
2. A passport or duly attested transcript of the school census record, showing the date and place of birth of such child.
3. The affidavit of the parent or guardian or custodian of such child (which shall be required, however, only in case no one of the above mentioned proofs of age is obtainable), showing the date and place of birth of such child. Such affidavit must be taken before the officer issuing the employment certificate, who is hereby authorized and required to administer such oath without demanding or receiving any fee therefor.

No employment certificate shall be issued until the child in question has personally appeared before the officer issuing the certificate nor until such officer has satisfied himself that the child can read and write legibly simple sentences in the English language, and that the child is fourteen years of age or upwards and has reached the normal development of a child of its age, and is in sufficiently sound health and physically able to perform the work it intends to do, which shall be stated. In all cases of doubt such development, health and physical fitness shall be determined by a medical officer of the board or department of health, or by a physician appointed by the school board.

Contents of certificate. Every such employment certificate shall state the race, residence, sex, and the date and place of birth of the child, and that the papers required by the preceding sections have been duly examined, approved and filed. Every such certificate shall be signed in the presence of the officer issuing the same, by the child in whose name it is issued, and it shall show the date of its issue; the school record required by the act shall be signed by the principal or other chief executive officer of the school which such child has attended and shall be furnished on demand to a child entitled thereto. It shall contain a statement certifying that the child is able to read and legibly write simple sentences in the English language, and has received instruction equivalent to that given in the first four grades of the common schools Such school record shall also give the date of birth and residence of the child as shown on the records of the school. The employment certificate provided for must be formulated by the State superintendent of free schools and furnished in blank by the clerk of the local school board.

Sec. 3. Whoever, whether he be the employer, parent, guardian or custodian of any child, employs, permits or suffers such child to be employed or to work in violation of any of the provisions of this act, shall be deemed guilty of a misdemeanor and upon conviction thereof shall be fined not less than ten dollars nor more than fifty dollars for each and every offense. *Violations.*

Sec. 4. It shall be the duty of the prosecuting attorney to enforce the provisions of this act and to, prosecute any person, firm or corporation charged with violation of the same, before any magistrate or court of competent jurisdiction in this State; and it shall be the duty of the truant officers, inspectors of factories and authorized agents of the humane society to expose all violations of this act to the prosecuting attorney. All fines collected for violations of this act shall be paid into the building fund of the school district or independent district in which the offense is committed. *Enforcement.*

ACTS OF 1901.

CHAPTER 14.—*Employment of children—Certain employments forbidden.*

SECTION 2. Any person having the care, custody, or control of any minor child under the age of fifteen years, who shall in any manner sell, apprentice, give away, or otherwise dispose of such child, or any person who shall take, receive or employ such child for the vocation or occupation of rope or wire walking or as an acrobat, gymnast, contortionist or rider, and any person who, having the care, custody, or control of any minor child whatsoever, shall sell, apprentice, give away or otherwise dispose of such child, or who shall take, receive or employ such child for any obscene, indecent or illegal exhibition or vocation, or any vocation injurious to the health, or dangerous to the life or limb, of such child engaged therein, or for the purpose of prostitution, and any person who shall retain, harbor, or employ any minor child in or about any assignation house or brothel, or any place where any obscene, indecent or illegal, exhibition takes place, shall be guilty of a misdemeanor, and shall be fined not less than five dollars, nor more than one hundred dollars, for each offense. *Acrobatic and immoral occupations.*

SEC. 3. Any person having the care, custody, or control, lawful or unlawful, of any minor child under the age of eighteen years, who shall use such minor, or apprentice, give away, let out, hire or otherwise dispose of, such minor child to any person, for the purpose of singing, playing on musical instruments, begging or for any mendicant business whatsoever in the streets, roads, or other highways of this State, and whosoever shall take, receive, hire, employ, use or have in custody, any minor for the vocation, occupation, calling, service or purpose of singing, playing upon musical instruments or begging upon the streets, roads or other highways of this State, or for any mendicant business whatever, shall be guilty of a misdemeanor and shall be fined not less than five dollars nor more than one hundred dollars. *Mendicant employments.*

SEC. 4. Any person having the care, custody, or control of any minor child under the age of fifteen years, who shall in any manner sell, apprentice, give away or permit such child to sing, dance, act, or in any manner exhibit it in any dance house, concert saloon, theater or place of entertainment where wines or spirituous or malt liquors are sold or given away, or with which any place for the sale of wines or spirituous or malt liquors is directly or indirectly connected by any passageway or entrance, and any proprietor of any dance house whatever, or any such concert saloon, theater, or place of entertainment, so employing any such child, shall be guilty of a misdemeanor, and shall be fined not less than five dollars nor more than one hundred dollars for each offense. *Employment in saloons, etc.*

CHAPTER 19.—*Seats for female employees.*

Seats to be provided.

SECTION 4. In every manufacturing, mechanical, mercantile and other establishments, in this State, wherein females are employed, there shall be provided, and conveniently located, seats sufficient to comfortably seat such females; and during such times as such females are not necessarily required by their duties to be upon their feet, they shall be allowed to occupy the seats provided.

[See also Appendix B, page 1087.] •

CHAPTER 78.—*Employment of women and children in mines.*

Employment forbidden.

SECTION 17. No boy under fourteen years of age, nor female person of any age shall be permitted to work in any coal mine, and in all cases of doubt, the parents or guardians of such boys shall furnish affidavits of their ages; any operator, agent or mine foreman who shall knowingly violate the provisions of this section or any person knowingly making a false statement as to the age of any boy under fourteen years of age, applying for work in any coal mine shall, upon conviction, be fined not less than ten nor more than five hundred dollars, or be imprisoned in the county jail not less than ten nor more than ninety days, in the discretion of the court.

WISCONSIN.

ANNOTATED STATUTES OF 1898—SUPPLEMENT OF 1906—ACTS OF 1907, 1909, 1911.[1]

Unlawful employment of children.

Enforcement of laws.

SECTION 439ca. Any truant officer within this State shall have power to visit factories, workshops, mercantile establishments and other places of employment in their respective localities and ascertain whether any minors are employed therein contrary to law. They may require that the age and school certificates and lists of minors who are employed in such factories, workshops, mercantile establishments and other places of employment, shall be produced for their inspection, and they shall report all cases of such illegal employment to the school authorities of their respective cities, towns, villages or districts and to the commissioner of labor, State factory inspector or any assistant factory inspector. Such truant officer shall receive no compensation from the State for performing such services.

Employment of women and children.

Limit of day's labor.

SECTION 1728. In all manufactories, workshops and other places used for mechanical or manufacturing purposes the time of labor of children under the age of eighteen years and of women employed therein shall not exceed eight hours in one day; and any employer, stockholder, director, officer, overseer, clerk or foreman who shall compel any woman or any such child to labor exceeding

Age limit.

eight hours in any one day, or who shall permit any child under fourteen years of age to labor more than ten hours in any one day in any such place, if he shall have control over such child sufficient to prevent it, or who shall employ at manual labor any child under twelve years of age in any factory or workshop where more than three persons are employed, or who shall employ any child of twelve and under fourteen years of age in any such factory or workshop for more than seven months in any one year shall be punished by fine not less than five nor more than fifty dollars for each such offense.

Certificates required.

SEC. 1728a. 1. No child between the ages of fourteen and sixteen years shall be employed, required, suffered or permitted to work at any time in any factory or workshop, store, hotel, res-

---

[1] All statutes amended or created by acts of 1907, 1909, and 1911 appear in their proper places as of the Annotated Statutes, serially numbered.

taurant, bakery, mercantile establishment, laundry, telegraph, telephone or public messenger service, or the delivery of any merchandise or at any gainful occupation, or employment, directly or indirectly, unless there is first obtained from the commissioner of labor, State factory inspector or any assistant factory inspector or from the judge of the county court or municipal court or from the judge of a juvenile court where such child resides, a written permit authorizing the employment of such child within such time or times as the said commissioner of labor, State factory inspector, any assistant factory inspector, county judge, municipal judge, or judge of a juvenile court may fix: *Providing*, That such times shall not conflict with those designated in subsection 1, of section 1728c, and that no officer herein mentioned shall have power to delegate the duty of granting permits to any subordinate officer or other person.

2. No child under the age of sixteen years shall be employed, **Employments prohibited.** required, suffered or permitted to work at adjusting any belt or in oiling or assisting in oiling, wiping or cleaning any machinery when the same is in motion or in operating or assisting in operating or taking material from any circular [circular] or band saw, or any crosscut saw or slasher or other cutting or pressing machine, from which material is taken from behind, wood-shaper, wood-jointer, planer, sandpaper or wood-polishing machine, picker machine, carding machine or machines used in picking wool, cotton, hair or any upholstering material, cylinder or job presses, dough brakes or cracker machinery of any description, laundry machinery, emery or polishing wheel for polishing metal or wood turning machine or stamping machine in sheet-metal and tinware manufacturing, or boring or drill presses or stamping machine in washer and nut factory, stamping machine in lace, paper and leather manufacturing, corrugating rolls in roofing or washboard factories, burnishing machines in any tannery or leather manufactory, wire or iron straightening machinery, rolling mill machinery, punchers or shears or washing, grinding or mixing mill of calendar [sic] rolls in rubber manufacturing, nor shall any such child be employed at or assist in sewing belts in any capacity, or in the manufacture of paints, colors or white lead, or in the manufacture of any composition in which dangerous or poisonous acids are used, or occupation causing dust, in injurious quantities, or in the manufacture or preparing of compositions of dangerous or poisonous dyes, or in the manufacture or preparing of compositions with dangerous or poisonous gases, or in the manufacture or preparation of compositions of lye, or in which the quantity thereof is injurious to health, or on scaffolding or on a ladder or in heavy work in the building trades, or in the manufacture of any goods for immoral purposes, nor in any tobacco warehouse, cigar or other factory where tobacco is manufactured or prepared or as pin boys in bowling alleys, or in any theater or concert hall, or in operating any steam boiler or steam generating apparatus, or in any other employment dangerous to life or limb, injurious to the health or depraving to the morals of such child; nor shall any female child under sixteen years of age be employed in any capacity where such employment compels her to remain constantly.

3. No child under the age of fourteen years shall be employed, **Age limit.** required, suffered or permitted to work at any time in any factory, manufacturing establishment or workshop, store, hotel, restaurant or bakery, mercantile establishment, laundry, telegraph, telephone or public messenger service, delivery or merchandise or at any gainful occupation or employment, directly or indirectly, except as provided in this section.

4. No child under the age of fourteen years shall be employed, **Vacation employment.** required, permitted or suffered to work at any gainful occupation or employment at any time except that during the vacation of the public or equivalent school in the town, district or city where any child between the ages of twelve and fourteen years resides, it

may be employed in any store, office, mercantile establishment, warehouse, telegraph, telephone or public messenger service in the town, district or city where it resides and not elsewhere: *Provided*, That it shall have first obtained a permit in the same manner and under the same conditions set forth for employment during the regular session of the school, except that for such vacation permit no proof of educational qualification shall be necessary.

Records.

5. The said commissioner of labor, State factory inspector, any assistant factory inspector, county judge, municipal judge, or judge of a juvenile court shall keep a record, stating the name. date and place of birth and place of school attended by any such child, and the county judge, municipal judge or judge of a juvenile court shall report when so requested by the commissioner of labor or State factory inspector, the number of permits issued by him from time to time as hereinbefore provided.

Proof.

6. When the commissioner of labor, State factory inspector, any assistant factory inspector, county judge, municipal judge or judge of a juvenile court has reason to doubt the age of any child who applied for such permit the commissioner of labor, State factory inspector, any assistant factory inspector, county judge, municipal judge or judge of a juvenile court shall demand proof of such child's age, by the production of a verified baptismal certificate or a duly attested birth certificate, or in case such certificates can not be secured, by the record of age stated in the first school of enrollment of such child, and if such proof does not exist or can not be secured then by the production of such other proof as may be satisfactory to said commissioner of labor, State factory inspector, any assistant factory inspector, county judge, municipal judge or judge of a juvenile court and no permit shall be issued unless proof of such child's age is filed with the said commissioner of labor, State factory inspector, county judge, municipal judge or judge of a juvenile court. Whenever it appears that a permit has been obtained by a wrong or false statement as to any child's age, the commissioner, State factory inspector, any assistant factory inspector, county judge, municipal judge or judge of a juvenile court of the county where such child resides shall revoke such permit.

Public performances.

SEC. 1728a–1. No child under sixteen years of age shall be employed, required, suffered or permitted to play on any musical instrument, or to sing or perform in a circus, theatrical or musical exhibition, concert or festival, or in any public place, unless there is first obtained from the commissioner of labor, State factory inspector, or assistant factory inspector, county judge, municipal judge or the judge of a juvenile court where the child resides, if such child is a resident of this State, and by a county judge. municipal judge, or judge of a juvenile court of this State if such child is not a resident of the State, a written permit authorizing the appearance of such child at such places, at times as the said commissioner of labor, State factory inspector or any assistant factory inspector, county judge, municipal judge or judge of a juvenile court may fix: *Provided*, That it appears to the satisfaction of such commissioner of labor, State factory inspector or any assistant factory inspector, county judge, municipal judge, or judge of a juvenile court, that the appearance of such child shall not be detrimental to its morals, health, safety, welfare of [or] opportunities for education equivalent to that of the common schools: *Provided, also*, That a child under fourteen years of age shall be accompanied by a parent or guardian, approved by the said commissioner of labor, State factory inspector or any assistant factory inspector, county judge, municipal judge or judge of a juvenile court. But the provisions of this section shall not prevent the education of children in music or their employment as musicians, or participants, in a church, chapel, school or school exhibition or any home-talent exhibition given by people of the local community.

SEC. 1728a–2. No child under sixteen years of age shall be *Saloons, etc.* employed, permitted or suffered to work in or about any store, brewery, distillery, bottling establishment, hotel, barroom, saloon, saloon dining room or restaurant, or any place in connection with a saloon or similar place of any name, or in or about any dance hall, bowling alley, pool room, beer garden or similar place of any name in which strong, spirituous or malt liquors are made, bottled, sold or given away.

SEC. 1728a–3. 1. The permit required by section 1728a of the *Contents of permits.* Statutes shall state the name, the date and place of birth of the child, and describe the color of hair and eyes, the height and weight, and by distinguishing facial marks of such child, and that the papers required in subsection 2 hereof have been duly examined, approved and filed.

2. The following evidence, records and papers shall be filed before such permit is issued:

(1) Evidence showing that such child is fourteen years of age *Evidence of* in one of the following forms: *age, etc.*

(a) A duly attested transcript of the birth certificate, filed as prescribed by law with the register of vital statistics, or other officer charged with the duty of recording births.

(b) A certificate of a person in charge of a public school in the State or elsewhere, having a course of not less than eight years, or of a school in the State other than a public school, having a substantially equivalent course of study of not less than eight years' duration, in which school a record of the attendance of such child has been kept, showing that such child is a graduate of such school, and that according to the records kept in such school, such child is at least fourteen years of age; or

(c) A passport or a duly attested transcript of a certificate of baptism, showing the date and place of baptism of such child.

(d) If such proof does not exist or can not be secured as provided in subdivisions (a), (b) or (c), of subdivision (1) hereof, then such proof as may be satisfactory to the official issuing such permit may be filed in lieu thereof.

(2) A certificate of the superintendent of schools or the prin- *Literacy.* cipal of the school last attended by the child, or in the absence of both of the aforementioned persons, a certificate of the clerk of the school board, showing that such child is more than fourteen years of age, and stating also the date of the birth of such child, and the number of years it has attended school. Such certificate shall contain the further statement that such child has attended the public school, or some other school having a substantially equivalent course, as required by law, within the twelve months next preceding the date of such certificate, or next preceding the fourteenth birthday of such child; that such child is able to read and write simple sentences in the English language, and is familiar with the fundamental operations in arithmetic up to and including fractions, and that it has received during such one-year period, instructions in spelling, reading, writing, English grammar and geography; or in lieu of such statement relative to its educational attainments, that such child has passed successfully the fifth grade in the public school, or in some school having a substantially equivalent course, or that it has attended school for at least seven years. It shall be the duty of such superintendent, principal or clerk to issue certificate upon receipt of any application in behalf of any child entitled thereto.

(3) A letter written on such regular letterhead or other busi- *Statement by* ness paper used by the person, stating the intention of such per- *employer.* son, firm or corporation to employ such child, and signed by such person, firm or corporation, or by some one duly authorized by them.

SEC. 1728a–4. 1. For the purposes of [sections 1728a to 1728j, *Complaints.* inclusive,] the commissioner of labor, factory inspector, any assistant factory inspector, truant officer, any police officer or any private citizen may make complaint of the violation of any provisions of [sections 1728a to 1728j, inclusive.]

Investigation.   2. When complaint is made by truant officer, police officer or any private citizen to the commissioner of labor, State factory inspector or any assistant factory inspector, the commissioner of labor shall investigate or cause to be investigated such complaint, and if pursuant to any such investigation, a violation of any of the provisions of this act shall be found, the commissioner of labor shall prosecute or cause to be prosecuted any such violation.

Delivery of messages at night.   SEC. 1728a–5. In cities of the first, second or third class no person under the age of twenty-one years shall be employed or permitted to work as a messenger for a telegraph or messenger company in the distribution, transmission or delivery of messages or goods before six o'clock in the morning and after eight o'clock in the evening of any day.

Statements as to employment.   SEC. 1728a–6. 1. Every person, firm or corporation, agent or manager of any firm or corporation, employing minors in any factory or workshop, store, office, hotel, mercantile establishment, laundry, telegraph, telephone or public messenger service within this State, in addition to filing the certificate of intention to employ with the commissioner of labor, State factory inspector or any assistant factory inspector, shall file with the officer signing such permit, a statement of actual employment of such minor, the date of employment, and that the necessary permit has been duly received and filed, shall keep said permits on file in the same place where such minor is employed, and subject at all times to the inspection of the commissioner of labor, State factory inspector or assistant factory inspector, and shall post a list of said employees with said information at or near the principal entrance to the factory, or other building where such children are employed: *It is further provided,* That upon the termination of employment of any minor, said employer shall return within twenty-four hours the permit for employment of such minor to the person and place, designated by the commissioner of labor, with a statement of reasons for the termination of said employment.

Special inspection.   2. Every person, firm or corporation, desiring to become the employer of children under the age of eighteen years, shall file with the commissioner of labor a statement of this fact, in order that a special inspection of his factory, workshop, bowling alley, store, hotel or mercantile establishment, restaurant, bakery, laundry, telegraph, telephone or public messenger service may be made or caused to be made by the commissioner of labor.

Certificates.   SEC. 1728a–11. No person shall employ a minor over fourteen years of age in any city, village or town in which a public evening school or continuation school, for the industry in which the minor is to work, is maintained, unless he receives and places on file a written permit issued by the commissioner of labor, State factory inspector or any assistant factory inspector, or from the judge of a juvenile court where such child resides, authorizing the employment of the minor, as provided in section 1728b of the Statutes, and certifying either to his ability to read at sight and write legibly simple sentences in the English language, or that he is a regular attendant at the public evening school or continuation school.

Acts of parents.   SEC. 1728a–12. No parent, guardian or custodian shall permit a minor over fourteen years of age who has not the certificate referred to in section 1728a–11 to be employed.

Weekly statements.   SEC. 1728a–13. Any minor over fourteen years of age, required by section 1728a–11 to attend an evening school or continuation school, shall furnish to his employer each week during its session a record showing that he is a regular attendant at the evening school or continuation school. The employer shall file all records of attendance with the minor's permit to work, and no minor, subject to [sections 1728a–11 to 1728a–17, inclusive,] shall be employed unless the records of attendance or absence for valid cause during the previous week be on file.

SEC. 1728a–14. Upon presentation by a minor of a certificate signed by a registered practicing physician, showing that his physical condition, or the distance necessary to be traveled, would render the required school attendance, in addition to his daily labor, prejudicial to his health, the commissioner of labor, State factory inspector or any assistant factory inspector, may issue a permit authorizing his employment for such period as he may determine. *Physician's certificate.*

SEC. 1728a–15. No permit issued under section 1728a shall excuse any minor from attendance at evening school, or evening continuation school. *Evening schools.*

SEC. 1728a–16. Any person, firm or corporation, agent or manager of any corporation, who whether for himself or for such firm or corporation, or by himself or through agents, servants or foremen, shall violate or fail to comply with any of the provisions of sections 1728a–11 to 1728a–14, inclusive, of the Statutes, shall be deemed guilty of a misdemeanor, and upon conviction thereof, shall be fined not less than ten nor more than one hundred dollars for each offense. Any corporation which by its agents, officers or servants shall violate or fail to comply with any of the provisions of [sections 1728a–11 to 1728a–15, inclusive], shall.be liable to the same penalty which may be recovered against such corporation in action for debt or assumpsit, brought before any court of competent jurisdiction. *Violations.*

SEC. 1728b. 1. Every person, firm or corporation, agent or manager of any firm or corporation employing minors in any factory or workshop, store, office, hotel, restaurant, bakery, mercantile establishment, laundry, telegraph, telephone or public messenger service within this State shall keep a register in the place where such minor is employed, and subject at all times to the inspection of any factory inspector, or assistant factory inspector, or truant officer, in which register shall be recorded the name, age, date of birth and place of residence, of every child employed, permitted or suffered to work therein, under the age of sixteen years. *Registers.*

2. No person, firm or corporation, agent or manager of any firm or corporation shall hire or employ, permit or suffer to work in any mercantile establishment, factory or workshop, store, office, hotel, restaurant, bakery, laundry, telegraph, telephone or public messenger service, any child under sixteen years of age, unless there is first provided and placed on file in such mercantile establishment, factory, workshop, store, office, hotel, restaurant, bakery, laundry, telegraph, telephone or public messenger service office, a permit granted by the commissioner of labor, State factory inspector, or any assistant factory inspector, or county judge, municipal judge or judge of a juvenile court of the county where such child resides. *Permit required.*

SEC. 1728c. 1. No child under the age of sixteen years, shall be employed, required, permitted or suffered to work at any gainful occupation for more than forty-eight hours in any one week, nor more than eight hours in any one day, or before the hour of seven o'clock in the morning, or after the hour of six o'clock in the evening, nor more than six days in any one week. A lunch period of not less than thirty minutes shall be allowed during each day: *Provided,* Nothing in [sections 1728a–to 1728j, inclusive,] shall be construed to interfere with the employment of children as provided in sections 1728a–1 and 1728u of the Statutes. *Hours of labor.* *Night work.* *Time for meals.*

2. Each employer shall post in a conspicuous place in each of the several departments in or for which minors are employed, a list on a printed form furnished by the bureau of labor and industrial statistics or factory inspection department, stating the names, ages and the hours required of each child during each day of the week, the hours of commencing and stopping work, and the hours when the time or times allowed for dinner or other meals begin and end. *List to be posted.*

Evening schools.   SEC. 1728c–1. 1. Whenever any evening school, continuation classes, industrial school or commercial school, shall be established in any town, village or city in this State for minors between the ages of fourteen and sixteen, working under permit as now provided by law, every such child, residing within any town, village or city in which any such school is established, shall attend such school not less than five hours per week for six months each year, until such child becomes sixteen years of age, and every employer shall allow *all minor employees over fourteen and under sixteen years of age a reduction in hours of work of not less than the number of hours the minor is by this section required to attend school.

2. The total number of hours spent by such minors at work and in the before-mentioned schools shall together not exceed the total number of hours of work for which minors over fourteen and under sixteen years of age ma by law be employed, except when the minor shall attend school ŋ greater number of hours than is required by law, in which case the total number of hours may be increased by the excess of the hours of school atendance [attendance] over the minimum prescribed by law.

3. Employers shall allow the reduction in hours of work at the time when the classes which the minor is by law required to attend, are held whenever the working time and the class time coincide.

4. Any violation of this section shall be punished as is provided in the case of a violation of section 172Sa of the Statutes.

Prosecution.   SEC. 1728d. 1. It shall be the duty of the commissioner of labor, the factory inspector and every assistant factory inspector to enforce all the provisions of the Statutes regulating or relative to child labor, and to prosecute violations of the same before any justice of the peace or other court of competent jurisdiction in this State. It shall be the duty of the said commissioner of labor and every factory inspector and assistant factory inspector and truant officers, and they are hereby authorized and empowered to visit and inspect, at all reasonable times, and as often as possible, all places covered by [sections 1728a to 1728j, inclusive.] The factory inspector and assistant factory inspector shall have the power of truant officers to enforce all legal requirements relating to school attendance. .

Jurisdiction.   2. The justices of the peace in the various counties of the State of Wisconsin shall have criminal jurisdiction of actions brought for violations of all statutes regulating or relative to child labor, notwithstanding any statute depriving such justices of the peace in any county of such jurisdiction. Nothing contained herein, however, shall deprive the municipal courts and other courts of record of concurrent jurisdiction, nor shall anything contained herein be construed to give justices of the peace in cities of the first class jurisdiction of such actions.

Physical unfit-ness.   SEC. 1728e. 1. The commissioner of labor, the factory inspector or assistant factory inspectors, or county judge, municipal judge or judge of a juvenile court, may refuse to grant permits in the case of children who may seem physically unable to perform the labor at which they may be employed.

Permits in du-plicate.   2. All permits provided for under [sections 1728a to 1728j, inclusive,] shall be issued upon blanks furnished by the commissioner of labor and shall be made out in duplicate. One of such duplicates shall be forthwith returned to the commissioner of labor, together with a detailed statement of the character and substance of the evidence offered prior to the issuance of such permit. Such statement so forwarded shall be upon blanks furnished by the commissioner of labor and shall contain such details as to such evidence, and shall fully reveal its character and substance as indicated in such blank.

Revocation.   3. Whenever it shall appear to the commissioner of labor that any permit has been improperly or illegally issued, or that the physical or moral welfare of such child would be best served by the revocation of the permit he may forthwith, without notice, revoke the same, and shall by registered mail notify the person employing such child and the child holding such permit of such revocation.

4. Nothing contained in [section 1728a to 1728j, inclusive,] shall be construed to forbid any child from being employed in agricultural pursuits, nor to require a permit to be obtained for such child. Farm labor.

SEC. 1728f. 1. No child under the age of eighteen years shall be employed in or about any blast furnaces, docks, wharves, in the outside erection and repair of electric wires; in the running or management of elevators, lifts or hoisting machines; in oiling or cleaning hazardous or dangerous machinery in motion; switch tending, gate tending or track repairing; as brakeman, fireman, engineer, motor man, conductor, telegraph operator, upon railroads; as pilot, fireman or engineer upon boats and vessels engaged in the transportation of passengers or merchandise; in or about establishments where nitroglycerin, dynamite, dualin, guncotton, gunpowder or other high or dangerous explosive is manufactured, compounded or stored; or in dipping, dyeing or packing matches; or in any factory in operating or using any emery, tripoli, rouge, corundum, stone carborundum or any abrasive or emery polishing or buffing wheel, where articles of the baser materials or of iridium are manufactured. Children under 18.

2. No minor under the age of eighteen, nor any female, shall be employed in or about any mine or quarry.

SEC. 1728g. The words "manufacturing establishment," the word "factory" or the word "workshop," as used in [sections 1728a to 1728j, inclusive,] shall each be construed to mean any place where goods or products are manufactured or repaired, dyed, cleaned or assorted, stored or packed, in whole or in part, for sale, for wages, or directly or indirectly, for gain or profit. Definitions.

SEC. 1728h. 1. Any person, firm or corporation, agent or manager of any firm or corporation who, whether for himself or for such firm or corporation, or by himself or through agents, servants or foreman violates or fails to comply with any of the provisions of sections 1728a, 1728b, 1728c, 1728d, 1728e, 1728f, 1728g, 1728h, 1728i, 1728a-1, 1728a-2, 1728a-3, 1728a-4, 1728a-5 or 1728a-6, or hinders or delays the commissioner of labor, the factory inspector or assistant factory inspectors, or truant officers, or any or either of them, in the performance of their duties or refuses to admit or locks out any such officer from any place required to be inspected by said sections, shall be deemed guilty of a misdemeanor, and upon conviction thereof, shall be fined not less than twenty-five dollars nor more than one hundred dollars for each offense, or imprisoned in the county jail not longer than thirty days. Violations.

2. Any corporation which, by its agents, officers or servants violates or fails to comply with any of the provisions of [the sections specified in subsection 1] shall be liable to the above penalties, which may be recovered against such corporations in action for debt or assumpsit brought before any justice of the peace or other court of competent jurisdiction.

3. Any person, being the owner or lessee of any opera house, theater or moving picture house, or any similar place of any name, or having in whole or in part, the management or control thereof, shall be responsible for any violation of [sections 1728a to 1728j, inclusive,] on the premises, of such opera house, theater or moving picture house or similar place of any name.

4. Any person, firm or corporation, agent or manager of any corporation who, whether for himself or for such firm or corporation, or by himself or through agents, servants or foreman fails to return the employment permit of any child in violation of section 1728a-6, shall be liable in action to such child whose permit is not returned, for two dollars for each day during which such failure continues.

5. The failure of any person, firm or corporation, agent or manager of any firm or corporation, to produce for inspection to the commissioner of labor, factory inspector or any assistant

factory inspector, truant officers, the employment permit herein-before described, shall be prima facie evidence of illegal employ-ment of minor before any justice of the peace or other court of competent jurisdiction. The presence of any minor in any factory, workshop, place of employment or in or about any mine, or the presence of any minor at any time other than those on the posted hours of labor, as hereinbefore provided, or in any establishment employed at any work listed as dangerouse [sic] or forbidden employments, shall be prima facie evidence of the employment of such child.

Acts of parents.   SEC. 1728i. Any parent or guardian, who suffers or permits a child to be employed, at any gainful occupation, directly or in-directly, or suffered or permitted to work in violation of [sec-tions 1728a to 1728j, inclusive,] shall be guilty of a misdemeanor, and upon conviction thereof, shall be fined not less than five nor more than twenty-five dollars or by imprisonment in the county jail for not longer than thirty days.

Evidence.   SEC. 1728j. When in any proceeding in any court under this section [act] there is any doubt as to the age of any child, a veri-fied baptismal certificate or a duly attested birth certificate shall be produced and filed with the court. In case such certificates cannot be secured, upon proof of such fact, the record of age stated in the first school enrollment of such child shall be ad-missible as evidence thereof.

Girls not to be employed as mes-sengers.   SEC. 1728k. No female under eighteen years of age shall be em-ployed as a messenger by any telegraph or telephone company, firm or corporation or by any company, firm, corporation or indi-vidual engaged in similar business.

Whoever violates the provisions of this act [section] shall be punished by a fine of not less than twenty-five dollars nor more than two hundred dollars or by imprisonment for not more than six months.

Seats for fe-males to be pro-vided.   SEC. 1728l. Every person or corporation employing females in any manufacturing, mechanical or mercantile establishment in the State of Wisconsin shall provide suitable seats for the fe-males so employed, and shall permit the use of such seats by them when they are not necessarily engaged in the active duties for which they are employed.

Any person or corporation who shall violate the provisions of this act [section] shall, upon conviction thereof, be considered guilty of a misdemeanor and shall be punished by a fine of not less than ten dollars, nor more than thirty dollars for each and every offense.

Licenses for the-atrical, etc., per-formances with-held, when.   SEC. 1728o. No license shall be granted for a theatrical exhi-bition or public show in which children under fifteen years of age are employed as acrobats, contortionists or in any feats of gym-nastics or equestrianism, when in the opinion of the board of offi-cers authorized to grant licenses such children are employed in such manner as to corrupt their morals or impair their physical health.

Any person who shall violate any of the provisions of this act shall, upon conviction, be fined in a sum not exceeding one hun-dred dollars.

Definition.   SEC. 1728p. The term "street trade," as used in [sections 1728p to 1728za, inclusive,] shall mean any business or occupation in which any street, alley, court, square or other public place is used for the sale, display or offering for sale of any articles, goods or merchandise. No boy under the age of twelve years, and no girl under the age of eighteen years, shall in any city of the first class distribute, sell or expose or offer for sale newspapers, magazines or periodicals in any street or public place.

Age of news-boys and girls.

Boys in street trades.   SEC. 1728q. No boy under fourteen years of age, shall, in any city of the first class, work at any time, or be employed or per-mitted to work at any time, as a bootblack or in any other street trade, or shall sell or offer any goods or merchandise for sale or distribute handbills or circulars or any other articles, except newspapers, magazines or periodicals as hereinafter provided.

SEC. 1728r. No girl under eighteen years of age shall, in any city Girls. of the first class, work at any time, or be employed or permitted to work at any time, as a bootblack or at any other street trades or in the sale or distribution of handbills or circulars or any other articles upon the street or from house to house.

SEC. 1728s. No boy under sixteen years of age shall, in any Permits and badges. city of the first class, distribute, sell or expose or offer for sale any newspapers, magazines or periodicals in any street or public place or work as a bootblack, or in any other street or public trade or sell or offer for sale or distribute any handbills or other articles unless he complies with all the legal requirements concerning school attendance, and unless a permit and badge, as hereinafter provided, shall have been issued to him by the State factory inspector. No such permit and badge shall be issued until the officer issuing the same shall have received an application in writing therefor, signed by the parent or guardian or other person having the custody of the child, desiring such permit and badge, and until such officer shall have received, examined and placed on file the written statement of the principal or chief executive officer of the public, private or parochial school, which the said child is attending, stating that such child is an attendant at such school with the grade such child shall have attained, and provided that no such permit and badge shall be issued, unless such officer issuing it is satisfied that such child is mentall[y] and physically able to do such work besides his regular school work as required by law.

SEC. 1728t. Before any such permit is issued, the State factory Evidence inspector, shall demand and be furnished with proof of such child's age by the production of a verified baptismal certificate or a duly attested birth certificate or, in case such certificate can not be secured, by the record of age stated in the first school enrollment of such child. Whenever it appears that a permit was obtained by wrong or false statements as to any child's age, the officer who granted such permit shall forthwith revoke the same. After having received, examined and placed on file such papers, the officer shall issue to the child a permit and badge. The principal or chief executive officer of schools in which children under fourteen years of age are pupils, shall keep a complete list of all children in their school to whom a permit and badge has been issued, as herein provided.

SEC. 1728u. Such permit shall state the place and date of birth Permit to state, what. of the child, the name and address of its parent, guardian, custodian or next friend, as the case may be, and describe the color of hair and eyes, the height and weight and any distinguishing facial marks of such child, and shall further state that the papers required by the preceding section have been duly examined and filed; and that the child named in such permit has appeared before the officer issuing the permit. The badge furnished by the officer issuing the permit shall bear on its face a number corresponding to the number of the permit, and the name of the child. Every such permit, and every such badge on its reverse side, shall be signed in the presence of the officer issuing the same by the child in whose name it is issued. *Provided*, That in case of carrier boys Carriers. working on salary for newspaper publishers delivering papers, a card of identification shall be issued to such carriers by the factory inspector, which they shall carry on their person, and exhibit to any officer authorized under sections 1728p to 1728za, inclusive, who may accost them for a disclosure of their right to serve as such carriers.

SEC. 1728v. The badge provided for herein shall be such as the Badges. State factory inspector shall designate and shall be worn conspicuously in sight at all times in such position as may be designated by the said factory inspector by such child while so working. No child to whom such permit and badge or identification card are issued shall transfer the same to any other person.

SEC. 1728w. No boy under fourteen years of age shall, in any Night work. city of the first class, sell, expose or offer for sale any newspapers, magazines or periodicals after the hour of six-thirty o'clock in the evening, between the first day of October and the first day of

Work during school hours. April, nor after seven-thirty o'clock in the evening between the first day of April and the first day of October, or before five o'clock in the morning; and no child under sixteen years of age shall distribute, sell, expose or offer for sale any newspapers, magazines or periodicals or shall work as a bootblack or in any street or public trades or distribute hand bills or shall be employed or permitted to work in the distribution or sale or exposing or offering for sale of any newspapers, magazines or periodicals or as a bootblack or in other street or public trades or in the distribution of hand bills during the hours when the public schools

Proviso. of the city where such child shall reside are in session. *Provided,* That any boy between the ages of fourteen and sixteen years, who is complying and shall continue to comply with all the legal requirements concerning school attendance, and who is mentally and physically able to do such delivery besides his regular school work, shall be authorized to deliver newspapers between the hours of four and six in the morning.

Enforcement. SEC. 1728x. The commissioner of labor or any factory inspector acting under his direction shall enforce the provisions of sections 1728p to 1728za, inclusive, and he is hereby vested with all powers requisite therefor.

Revocation of permit. SEC. 1728y. The permit of any child, who in any city of the first class distributes, sells or offers for sale any newspapers, magazines or periodicals in any street or public place or works as a bootblack or in any other street trade, or sells or offers for sale or distributes any handbills or other articles in violation of the provisions of sections 1728p to 1728za, inclusive, or who becomes delinquent or fails to comply with all the legal requirements concerning school attendance, shall forthwith be revoked for a period of six months and his badge taken from said child. The refusal of any child to surrender such permit, and the distribution, sale or offering for sale of newspapers, magazines or periodicals or any goods or merchandise, or the working by such child as a bootblack or in any other street or public trade, or in distributing handbills or other articles, after notice, by any officer authorized to grant permits under this law of the revocation of such permit and a demand for the return of the badge, shall be deemed a violation of this act. The permit of said child may also be revoked by the officer who issued such permit, and the badge taken from such child, upon the complaint of any police officer or other attendance officer or probation officer of a juvenile court and such child shall surrender his permit and badge upon the demand of any police officer, truancy or other attendance officer or probation officer of a juvenile court or other officer charged with the

Second violations. duty of enforcing this act. In case of a second violation of this act by any child, he shall be brought before the juvenile court, if there shall be any juvenile court in the city where such child resides or, if not, before any court or magistrate having jurisdiction of offenses committed by minors and be dealt with according to law.

Violations. SEC. 1728z. Any parent or other person who employs a minor under the age of sixteen years in peddling without a license or who, having the care or custody of such minor, suffers or permits the child to engage in such employment, or to violate sections 1728p to 1728za, inclusive, shall be punished by a fine not to exceed one-hundred dollars nor less than twenty-five dollars, or by his commitment to the county jail for not more than sixty days or less than ten days.

Certificates required. SEC. 1728za. Providing that no badge shall be issued for a boy selling papers between the ages of twelve and sixteen years by the State factory inspector, except upon certificate of the principal of either public, parochial or other private school attended by said boy, stating and setting forth that said boy is a

Loitering forbidden. regular attendant upon said school. No boy under the age of sixteen years shall be permitted by any newspaper publisher or printer or persons having for sale newspapers or periodicals of any character, to loiter or remain around any salesroom, assembly room, circulation room or office for the sale of newspapers, between the hours of nine in the forenoon and three in the afternoon, on days when school is in session. Any newspaper publisher, printer, circulation agent or seller of newspapers shall upon conviction for permitting newsboys to loiter or hang around any assembly room, circulation room, salesroom or office where papers are distributed or sold, shall be punished by a fine not to exceed one hundred dollars nor less than twenty-five dollars, or by commitment to the county jail for not more than sixty days or less than ten days.

SEC. 1728–1. 1. No female shall be employed or be permitted to work in any manufacturing, mechanical or mercantile establishment, laundry or restaurant, or confectionery store, or telegraph or telephone office or exchange, or by any express or transportation company, in this State, more than ten hours during any one day, or more than fifty-five hours in any one week. The hours may be so arranged as to permit the employment of females at any time, but they shall not work more than ten hours during the twenty-four hours of any one day, nor more than fifty-five hours during one week. If, however, any part of a female's daily employment is performed between the hours of eight o'clock p. m. and six o'clock a. m. of the following day, all the employment shall be considered night work, and no such female so employed at night work shall be employed or permitted to work thereat more than eight hours in any twenty-four hours, nor more than forty-eight hours during one week. If any such female is employed not more than one night in the week (after eight o'clock as herein provided), then such female may be permitted to work fifty-five hours in any such week: *Provided*, That at least one hour for dinner be allowed each female during her working period, but no part of such hour shall be considered as a part of the permitted period of daily employment. *(Ten-hour day.)* *(Night work.)*

2. Every employer shall post in a conspicuous place in every room, where such females are employed, a printed notice stating the hours of commencing and stopping such work, the time allowed for dinner or other meals, and the maximum number of hours any female employee is permitted to work in any one day. *(Schedule.)*

3. The employment of any female in any such place or establishment, as defined in subsection 1, of this section, at any time other than those of the posted hours of labor, as hereinbefore provided for, shall be prima facie evidence of a violation of this act. *(Evidence.)*

4. Any person violating any provision of this section shall be deemed guilty of a misdemeanor, and upon conviction thereof, shall be punished by a fine of not less than five nor more than one hundred dollars. *(Violations.)*

Employment of children—Certain employments forbidden.

SEC. 4587a. Any person having the care, custody or control of any child under the age of fourteen years who shall exhibit, use or employ, or in any manner or under any pretense sell, apprentice, give away, let out or otherwise dispose of such child to any person for any obscene, indecent or immoral purpose, exhibition or practice, or for any business, exhibition or vocation injurious to the health or dangerous to the life or limb of such child, or who shall cause, procure or encourage any such child to engage therein, and any person who shall take, receive, hire, employ, use, exhibit or have in custody any such child for any such purpose shall be punished by imprisonment in the county jail not exceeding six months or by fine of not more than one hundred dollars, or by both imprisonment and fine. *(Obscene and immoral employments.)*

WYOMING.

CONSTITUTION.

ARTICLE 9.—Mine regulations—Employment of women and children.

Employment forbidden.

SECTION 3. No boy under the age of fourteen years and no woman or girl of any age shall be employed or permitted to be in or about any coal, iron or other dangerous mines for the purpose of employment therein: *Provided, however,* This provision shall not affect the employment of a boy or female of suitable age in an office or in the performance of clerical work at such mine or colliery.

COMPILED STATUTES—1910.

Employment of children.

Acrobatic and mendicant occupations.

SECTION 3101. It shall be unlawful for any person having the care, custody or control of any child under the age of fourteen years to exhibit, use or employ, or in any manner, or under any pretense, sell, apprentice, give away, let out or otherwise dispose of any such child to any person, in or for the vocation or occupation, service or purpose of singing, playing on musical instruments, dancing, rope or wire walking, begging or peddling, or as a gymnast, contortionist, rider or acrobat, in any place whatsoever; or as an actor or performer in any concert hall or room where intoxicating liquors are sold or given away, or in any variety theater, or for any illegal, obscene, indecent or immoral purpose, exhibition or practice whatsoever; or for or in any business exhibition or vocation, injurious to the health or dangerous to the life or limb of such child, or cause, procure or encourage such child to engage therein. Nothing in this section contained shall apply to or affect the employment or use of any child as a singer or musician in any church, school or academy, or at any respectable entertainment, or the teaching or learning the science or practice of music. It shall be unlawful for any person to take, receive, hire, employ, use, exhibit or have in custody any child, under the age, and for the purposes prohibited in this section.

Employment of women and children in mines.

SEC. 3107. Any person who shall take, receive, hire or employ, either in his or her own behalf, or as the agent, servant or employee of any person, persons, association of persons, copartnership, company, corporation, any boy or male child under the age of fourteen years, or any woman or girl of any age, or shall allow or permit the said persons to be in or about any coal, iron or other dangerous mine, or underground works or dangerous place whatsoever in this State, for the purpose of employment therein or thereabouts, shall be fined not less than twenty-five dollars, nor more than one hundred dollars to which may be added imprisonment in the county jail not more than six months; *Provided, however,* That the provisions of this section shall not affect or apply to the employment of a boy or female of suitable age in an office, or in the performance of clerical work at such mine, colliery or place.

Proviso.

Seats for female employees.

Seats to be provided.

SEC. 5815. Every person or corporation employing females in any manufacturing, mechanical or mercantile establishment in the State of Wyoming shall provide suitable seats for females so employed, and shall permit the use of such seats by them when they are not necessarily engaged in the active duties for which they are employed. Any person or corporation who shall violate the provisions of this section shall upon conviction thereof, be considered guilty of a misdemeanor and shall be punished by a fine of not less than ten dollars, nor more than thirty dollars for each and every offense.

Penalty.

APPENDIX B.

LAWS RELATING TO THE REGULATION AND INSPECTION OF FACTORIES AND WORKSHOPS, IN FORCE JANUARY 1, 1912.

APPENDIX B.

LAWS RELATING TO THE REGULATION AND INSPECTION OF FACTORIES AND WORKSHOPS, IN FORCE JANUARY 1, 1912.

ALABAMA.

CODE OF 1907.

Fire escapes on factories, etc.

SECTION 7095. Any owner, proprietor, or manager of any * * * manufacturing building, which is more than two stories high, now erected, who shall fail for six months after the adoption of this Code to have securely fixed and conveniently arranged so as to be accessible to persons * * * working in, or occupying such building, in case of fire in such building, good and sufficient fire escapes or ladders for each story of said building, shall be guilty of a misdemeanor, and, on conviction, shall be fined not less than fifty nor more than five hundred dollars, and may be imprisoned in the county jail, or sentenced to hard labor for the county, for not more than six months, for each day so continued. *Fire escapes to be provided.*

SEC. 7096. Any owner, proprietor, or manager of any * * * manufacturing building erected hereafter who shall fail to erect with such building such fire escapes as are required in the preceding section, shall, on conviction, be fined not less than fifty nor more than five hundred dollars, and may be imprisoned in the county jail, or sentenced to hard labor for the county, for not more than six months. *Violation.*

Inspection of cotton mills, etc.[1]

SECTION 7212. There is created the office of inspector of jails, almshouses, cotton mills, or factories; the officer or inspector shall be a practicing physician in good standing, learned in the science of sanitation and hygiene, and shall reside at Montgomery and have an office in the capitol. *Inspector.*

SEC. 7213. The inspector shall be appointed by the governor and shall hold office for a term of four years from the date of his appointment, and until his successor is appointed and qualified. *Appointment.*

SEC. 7214. The salary of the inspector shall be twenty-four hundred dollars annually, and in addition to his salary he shall be paid his necessary traveling expenses, to be paid as the salaries of the State officers are paid. *Salary.*

SEC. 7215. The following are the general duties of the inspector: *Duties.*
* * * * * * *

(5) To visit at least four times each year, and oftener when ordered by the governor so to do, each and every cotton mill or factory in this State, and to thoroughly inspect the same for the purpose of ascertaining their sanitary condition, the ages and condition of the children employed therein, and all other matters concerning the operation and condition of said mills or factories as to which the laws of this State prescribe any rules or regulations.

---

[1] See Acts of 1909, p. 158; Appendix A, p. 655.

(6) To make reports to the governor of the result of each such inspection.

(7) To institute prosecutions against the owners and operators of such mills or factories for the violation of any of the rules or regulations prescribed by any law of this State relating to the conditions or operations of such mills or factories or the employment of children therein.

Refusing to give information.

SEC. 7217. Any sheriff or other keeper of jails or members of commissioners court or board of revenue, or keeper or manager of any almshouse, cotton mill, or factory, or any person or persons charged with the management of any almshouse, cotton mill, or factory who shall willfully refuse or fail to give the inspector the information called for by him, and any such officer or other person who, when summoned by the inspector to come before him and testify concerning any matter upon which the inspector is required to report, shall willfully refuse or fail to attend and testify, shall be deemed guilty of a misdemeanor, and, upon conviction, shall be fined not less than twenty-five nor more than one hundred dollars.

ARIZONA.

ACTS OF 1909.

CHAPTER 100.—*Laundries—Air space, etc.*

[See Appendix A, p. 659.]

ARKANSAS.

ACTS OF 1911.

ACT No. 472.—*Commissioner of health—Sanitation of factories, etc.*

Inspection.

SECTION 8. The commissioner [of health] shall have power and authority to investigate the sanitary conditions of schools, mills, mines, railroads, * * * and to prescribe and enforce such measures of sanitation of them as may be deemed advisable. * * *

CALIFORNIA.

CODES OF 1906—GENERAL LAWS.

ACT No. 1098.—*Inspection of factories and workshops.*

[This act (chapter 5, Acts of 1889) was declared unconstitutional by the supreme court of the State on account of certain provisions in section 4, and for this reason was omitted from Sims' Edition of the General Laws, and from the Twenty-second Annual Report of the U. S. Commissioner of Labor. The action of the legislature in amending the law, eliminating the invalid provisions, indicates that it is regarded as valid as amended. It is therefore reproduced in full in its amended form.]

Sanitation.

SECTION 1. Every factory, workshop, mercantile or other establishment, in which five or more persons are employed, shall be kept in a cleanly state and free from the effluvia arising from any drain, privy, or other nuisance, and shall be provided, within reasonable access, with a sufficient number of water-closets or privies for the use of the persons employed therein. Whenever the persons employed as aforesaid are of different sexes, a sufficient number of separate and distinct water-closets or privies shall be provided for the use of each sex, which shall be plainly so designated, and no person shall be allowed to use any water-closet or privy assigned to persons of the other sex.

Ventilation.

SEC. 2. Every factory or workshop in which five or more persons are employed shall be so ventilated while work is carried on therein that the air shall not become so exhausted as to be injurious to the health of the persons employed therein, and shall also be so ventilated as to render harmless, as far as practicable, all the gases, vapors, dust, or other impurities generated in the course of the manufacturing process or handicraft carried on therein, that may be injurious to health.

SEC. 3. No basement, cellar, underground apartment, or other place which the commissioner of the bureau of labor statistics shall condemn as unhealthy and unsuitable, shall be used as a workshop, factory, or place of business in which any person or persons shall be employed. Use of cellars, etc.

SEC. 4 (as amended by chapter 52, Acts of 1909). In any factory, workshop, or other establishment where a work or process is carried on by which dust, filaments, or injurious gases are produced or generated, that are liable to be inhaled by persons employed therein, the person, firm or corporation, by whose authority the said work or process is carried on, shall cause to be provided and used in said factory, workshop or other establishment, exhaust fans or blowers with pipes and hoods extending therefrom to each machine, contrivance or apparatus by which dust, filaments or injurious gases are produced or generated. The said fans and blowers, and the said pipes and hoods, all to be properly fitted and adjusted, and of power and dimensions sufficient to effectually prevent the dust, filaments, or injurious gases produced or generated by the above said machines, contrivances or apparatuses, from escaping into the atmosphere of the room or rooms of said factory, workshop or other establishment where persons are employed. Fans, blowers, etc., to be installed.

SEC. 5 (as amended by chapter 12, Acts of 1903). Every person, firm, or corporation employing females in any manufacturing, mechanical, or mercantile establishment shall provide suitable seats for the use of the females so employed, and shall provide such seats to the number of at least one-third the number of females so employed; and shall permit the use of such seats by them when they are not necessarily engaged in the active duties for which they are employed. Seats for female employees.

SEC. 6 (as amended by chapter 176, Acts of 1901). Any person or corporation violating any of the provisions of this act is guilty of a misdemeanor, and upon conviction thereof shall be punished by a fine of not less than fifty dollars nor more than three hundred dollars, or by imprisonment in the county jail for not less than thirty days nor more than ninety days, or by both such fine and imprisonment, for each offense. Violations.

SEC. 7. It shall be the duty of the commissioner of the bureau of labor statistics to enforce the provisions of this act. Enforcement.

ACTS OF 1909.

CHAPTER 104.—*Inspection of factories, etc.—Manufacture of food products.*

SECTION 1. Every building, room, basement or cellar, occupied, or used as a bakery, confectionery, cannery, packing house, slaughterhouse, restaurant, hotel, grocery, meat market, or other place or apartment, used for the production, preparation for sale, manufacture, packing, storage, sale or distribution of any food, shall be properly lighted, drained, plumbed and ventilated, and conducted with strict regard to the influence of such conditions upon the health of the operatives, employees, clerks or other persons therein employed, and the purity and wholesomeness of the food therein produced, kept, handled or sold; and for the purpose of this act the term "food" shall include all articles used for food, drink, confectionery or condiment, whether simple or compound, and all substances and ingredients used in the preparation thereof. Sanitation required.

SEC. 2. The floors, side walls, ceilings, furniture, receptacles, utensils, implements and machinery of every establishment or Floors, utensils, etc., to be clean.

place where food is manufactured, packed, stored, sold or distributed, shall at no time be kept in an unclean, unhealthful or unsanitary condition; and for the purposes of this act, unclean, unhealthful and unsanitary conditions shall be deemed to exist if food in the process of manufacture, preparation, packing, storing, sale or distribution is not securely protected from flies, dust, dirt, unsanitary conditions, and as far as may be necessary, by all reasonable means from all other foreign or injurious contamination; and if the refuse, dirt, and, the waste products subject to decomposition and fermentation incident to the manufacture, preparation, packing, storing, selling and distributing of food, are not removed daily; and if all trucks, trays, boxes, baskets, buckets, and other receptacles, chutes, platforms, racks, tables, shelves, and all knives, saws, cleavers, and all other utensils, receptacles, and machinery, used in moving, handling, cutting, chopping, mixing, canning, and all other processes used in the preparation of food, are not thoroughly cleaned daily; and if the clothing of operatives, employees, clerks, and other persons therein employed, is unclean, or if they dress or undress, or leave or store their clothing therein.

Construction of walls and ceilings. SEC. 3. The side walls and ceilings of every bakery, confectionery, hotel and restaurant kitchen, shall be well plastered, or ceiled, with metal or lumber, or shall be oil painted or kept well limewashed, or otherwise kept in a good sanitary condition and all interior woodwork of every bakery, confectionery, hotel and restaurant kitchen, shall be kept well oiled or painted with oil paint, and be kept washed clean with soap and water or otherwise kept in a good sanitary condition; and every building, room, basement or cellar, occupied or used for the preparation, manufacture, packing, storage, sale or distribution of food, shall have an impermeable floor, made of cement or tile laid in cement, brick, wood or other suitable, nonabsorbent material which can be flushed and washed clean with water.

Floors.

Screens. SEC. 4. The doors, windows and other openings of every food producing or distributing establishment, where practicable, shall be fitted with stationary or self-closing screen doors and wire window screens, of not coarser than fourteen-mesh wire gauze.

Toilet rooms, etc. SEC. 5. Every building, room, basement or cellar, occupied or used for the preparation, manufacture, packing, canning, sale or distribution of food, shall have convenient toilet or toilet rooms, separate and apart from the room or rooms where the process of production, manufacture, packing, canning, selling or distributing, is conducted. The floors of such toilet rooms shall be of cement, tile laid in cement, wood, brick or other nonabsorbent material, and shall be washed and scoured daily. Such toilets shall be furnished with separate ventilating pipes or flues, discharging into soil pipes, or on the outside of the building in which they are situated. Lavatories and wash rooms shall be adjacent to toilet rooms, and shall be supplied with soap, running water and towels, and shall be maintained in a clean and sanitary condition. Operatives, employees, clerks and all persons who handle the material from which food is prepared, or the finished product, before beginning work and immediately after visiting a toilet or lavatory shall wash their hands and arms thoroughly in clean water.

Cuspidors. SEC. 6. Cuspidors, for the use of operatives, employees, clerks and other persons, shall be provided, and each cuspidor shall be emptied and washed out daily with disinfectant solution and not less than five ounces of such solution shall be left in each cuspidor while in use. No operative, employee, clerk or other person, shall expectorate or discharge any substance from his nose or or mouth, on the floor or interior side wall of any building, room, basement, or cellar where the production, manufacture, packing, storing, preparation or sale of any food product is conducted.

Sleeping in workrooms. SEC. 7. No person shall be allowed to, nor shall he, reside or sleep in any room of a bake shop, public dining room, hotel or restaurant kitchen, confectionery, or other place where food is prepared, produced, manufactured, served or sold.

SEC. 8. No employer shall require, permit or suffer any person to work, nor shall any person work, in a building, room, basement, cellar, place or vehicle, occupied or used for the production, preparation, manufacture, packing, storage, sale, distribution or transportation of food, who is afflicted or affected with any venereal disease, smallpox, diphtheria, scarlet fever, yellow fever, tuberculosis, consumption, bubonic plague, Asiatic cholera, leprosy, trachoma, typhoid fever, epidemic dysentery, measles, mumps, German measles, whooping cough, chicken pox, or any other infectious or contagious disease. *Contagious or infectious diseases.*

SEC. 9. The members of the State board of health, inspectors and agents appointed by said board, and all local health officers and inspectors, shall have full power at all times to enter every building, room, basement, cellar, or any place occupied or used, or suspected of being occupied or used, for the production, manufacture, preparation, storage, sale or distribution of food, and to inspect the premises and all utensils, implements, receptacles, fixtures, furniture and machinery used as aforesaid, and if, upon inspection, any such building, room, basement, cellar, or any such place, vehicle, employer, operative, employee, clerk, driver, or other person, is found to be in violation or violating any of the provisions of this act, or if the production, preparation, manufacture, packing, storing, sale or distribution of food is being conducted in a manner detrimental to the health of the employees or operatives or to the character or quality of the food therein being produced, manufactured, packed, stored, sold, distributed or conveyed, the officer or inspector making the examination shall at once make a written report of the same to the district attorney of the county who shall prosecute all persons violating any of the provisions of this act, and also to the State board of health. The State board of health, from time to time, as in its discretion it may determine, may publish such reports in its monthly bulletin. *Enforcement.*

SEC. 10. All buildings, rooms, basements, cellars, and other places and things, kept, maintained or operated, or which are, in violation of the provisions of this act or any of them, and all food produced, prepared, manufactured, packed, stored, kept, sold, distributed or transported, in violation of the provisions of this act or any of them, are hereby declared to be public nuisances, dangerous to health. Such nuisances may be abated or enjoined, in an action brought for that purpose by the local or State board of health, or they may be summarily abated in the manner provided by law for the summary abatement of public nuisances dangerous to health. *What are nuisances.*

SEC. 11. Any person, firm or corporation, whether as principal or agent, employer or employee, who violates any of the provisions of this act shall be guilty of a misdemeanor, and each day that conditions or actions, in violation of this act, shall continue, shall be deemed to be a separate and distinct offense, and for each offense, upon conviction, he shall be punished by a fine of not less than twenty-five dollars, nor more than five hundred dollars, or shall be imprisoned in the county jail for a term not exceeding six months, or by both such fines and imprisonment. *Violations.*

COLORADO.

REVISED STATUTES—1908.

Inspection of steam boilers.

SECTION 6309 (as amended by chapter 86, Acts of 1911). The governor of the State of Colorado shall, by and with the advice and consent of the senate, on or before April 1, 1911, appoint one chief and three deputies, inspectors of steam boilers. The person so appointed shall be well qualified from practical experi- *Inspectors.*

ence in the use and construction of boilers, engines, generators, superheaters and their appurtenances used for the generating of steam for power, steaming or hearing [heating] purposes, to enable him to judge of their safety for use as such, and shall be neither directly or indirectly interested in the manufacture, ownership or sale thereof. The duty of said inspector shall be to inspect steam boilers throughout the State as hereinafter specified and directed. The inspector shall hold office for the term of two years from the date of his appointment and until his successor shall have been appointed and qualified. Before entering upon the duties of his office such inspector shall give a bond, with good and sufficient surety, in the sum of five thousand [dollars] ($5,000) for the faithful performance of his duties, said bond to be approved by the Attorney General and deposited with the Secretary of State. Said inspector shall receive an annual salary of two thousand five hundred dollars ($2,500), and mileage at the rate of ten cents per mile for each mile necessarily traveled by him in the performances of his duties: *Provided*, Said inspector shall not receive mileage in excess of the sum of six hundred dollars ($600.00)

Deputies. in any one year. The deputy inspectors shall have had not less than five years' actual practical experience in the operation of steam engines, steam boilers and steam machinery. Such deputy inspectors shall each receive as compensation for their services the sum of one thousand eight hundred dollars ($1,800.00) per annum, and mileage at the rate of ten cents per mile for each mile necessarily traveled by them in the performance of their duties: *Provided*, None of said deputy inspectors shall receive mileage in excess of the sum of six hundred dollars ($600.00) each in any one year. Said inspector may also employ a clerk at an annual salary not exceeding one thousand dollars ($1,000.00).

Annual inspections. SEC. 6310. The inspector shall devote his time and attention to the duties of the office. He shall carefully inspect and test every stationary boiler and steam generatoring [generating] apparatus under pressure used for stationary power, as provided by this act, including all attachments and connections, located within the State of Colorado, once annually, and shall give the owner of any such boiler five days' notice of the time when he will make such in-

Proviso. spection: *Provided*, That any owner or user of any steam boiler in this State who may desire to insure such boiler in any reputable insurance company, and who shall desire to have an inspection made for the purpose of said insurance, may give to said State steam boiler inspector ten days' notice, in writing, of the time of such contemplated insurance inspection, and it shall thereupon be the duty of said State steam boiler inspector to cause the annual State inspection, by this act provided, to be made at the same time that said examination for insurance is made; he shall examine into and report to the governor the cause of any boiler explosion that may occur within the State; he shall keep in his office a complete and accurate record of the names of owners or users of steam boilers inspected, giving a full description of the same, the amount of pressure allowed, the date when last tested, and shall make an annual report to the governor.

Boilers to be reported. SEC. 6311. It shall be the duty of every owner or user of steam boiler or boilers, in use or to be used in any part of this State within thirty days after the passage of this act, and once a year thereafter, at such convenient times and in such manner and form as may be determined by rules and regulations to be made therefor by the inspector, to report to said inspector the location of such steam boiler or boilers, and all apparatus and appliances connected therewith, and the strength and security of such boiler

Test. shall be tested by hydrostatic pressure, each boiler being tested one-third greater than the ordinary working steam pressure used, and to a pressure demanded by the owner; and the certificate of inspection herein provided shall state the maximum pressure at which such boiler may be worked. If at any time the inspector shall find a boiler which, in his judgment, is unsafe after inspecting the same, he shall condemn its future use. All boilers to be

tested by hydrostatic pressure shall be filled with water by the owners or users, and they shall furnish the necessary labor required to work and handle the pumps in applying the test, which pumps shall be furnished by the inspector if necessary. All certificates shall be for one year, unless sooner revoked for cause.

SEC. 6312. The owners or users of steam boilers, or engineers in charge of same, shall not allow a greater pressure in any boiler than is stated in the certificate of inspection granted by the inspector. No person or persons shall use or cause to be used for generating steam any boiler that has been condemned as unsafe by the inspector. Before the owner, owners or users of any steam boiler or boilers shall have said boilers placed in position, he or they shall notify the inspector, who shall, within ten days from the date of receiving such notification, examine the same and satisfy himself that the construction, material, bracing and all other parts of such boiler or boilers are such as to assure the safety of the same. Any person or persons violating any of the provisions of this section shall be deemed guilty of a misdemeanor, and, upon conviction thereof, shall be punished by a fine in any sum not exceeding one thousand (1,000) dollars, or by imprisonment for a period not exceeding two years, or by both such fine and imprisonment. *Pressure limited. Condemned boilers. Installation of boilers.*

SEC. 6313. There shall be paid for the inspection of each boiler, according to the provisions of this act, the sum of five (5) dollars, to be paid by the owner, user or agent of the same, occupying the buildings in which it may be situated, and the inspector shall receipt for the same. In case the owner, user or agent of any such boiler or boilers shall fail to report the location of such boiler or boilers to the inspector, as aforesaid, he shall be liable to pay a penalty of fifty (50) dollars, and in case the owner, user or agent of any such boiler or boilers shall fail to have the same ready for inspection as aforesaid, he shall be liable to pay the fees and expenses of the inspector incurred in the inspection of any such boiler, and a penalty of ten (10) dollars in addition thereto; fees, expenses and penalty in all such cases may be sued for and recovered in any court of record, by and in the name of the people of the State of Colorado, in any county of the State, and it shall be the duty of the district attorney of the district wherein such county may be situated to prosecute all such suits. *Fees. Failure to report,*

SEC. 6315. The secretary of state shall provide a suitable office for said inspector, properly furnished and supplied with such tools, apparatus and stationery as may be required. *Office, etc.*

SEC. 6316. The inspector of steam boilers provided for in this act shall for every failure to perform his duties as herein directed be deemed guilty of a misdemeanor, and, upon conviction thereof, shall be punished by a fine in a sum not less than one hundred (100) dollars nor more than one thousand (1,000) dollars, or be imprisoned for a period of not less than two months nor greater than one year, or by both such fine and imprisonment. *Neglect of duty.*

SEC. 6317. The provisions of this act shall not apply to cities where city boiler inspectors are appointed, under the provisions of the ordinances of said city. *Exception.*

ACTS OF 1911.

CHAPTER 132.—*Inspection of factories and workshops.*

SECTION 1. There is hereby established a separate and distinct department to be known as the Department of Factory Inspection of the State of Colorado, which department shall be charged with the inspection of all factories, mills, workshops, bakeries, laundries, stores, hotels, boarding or bunk houses, or any kind of an establishment wherein laborers are employed or machinery used, for the purpose of protecting said employees or guests against damages arising from imperfect or dangerous machinery, or hazardous and unhealthy occupation and regulating sanitary conditions under which guests are protected or. laborers are em- *Department of factory inspection.*

ployed by providing individual towels in place of roller towels in hotel wash rooms, and nine-foot top sheets for beds, which sheets shall be provided not later than September 1, 1911.

*   *   *   *   *

Guards for dangerous machinery. SEC. 2. Any person, firm, corporation or association operating a factory, mill, workshop, bakery, laundry, store, hotel or any kind of an establishment wherein laborers are employed, or machinery used shall provide and maintain in use belt shifters or other mechanical contrivance for the purpose of throwing on or off belts or pulleys while running, where the same are practicable with due regard to the nature and purpose of said belts and the dangers to employees therefrom; also reasonable safeguards for all vats, pans, trimmers, cut-offs, gang edger and other saws, planers, cogs, gearings, beltings, shafting, coupling, set screws, line rollers, conveyors, manglers in laundries, and machinery of other or similar description, which it is practicable to guard, and which can be effectively guarded with due regard to the ordinary use of such machinery and appliances, and the dangers to employees therefrom, and with which the employees of any such factory, mill, or workshop are liable to come in contact while in the performance of their duties; and if any machinery, or any part thereof, is in a defective condition, and its operation would be extrahazardous because of such defect, or if any machinery is not safeguarded as provided in this act, the use thereof is prohibited, and a notice to that effect shall be attached thereto by the employer immediately upon receiving notice of such defect or lack of safeguard, and such notice shall not be removed until said defect has been remedied or the machine safeguarded as herein provided.

Ventilation. SEC. 3. Any person, firm, corporation or association operating a factory, mill, workshop, bakery, laundry, store, hotel, or any kind of an establishment wherein laborers are employed, or machinery used and manual labor is exercised by the way of trade for the purpose of gain within an enclosed room (private houses in which the employees live excepted) shall be provided in each workroom thereof with good sufficient ventilation and kept in a clean and sanitary state, and shall be so ventilated as to render harmless, so far as practicable, all gases, vapors, dust or other impurities, generated in the course of the manufacturing or laboring process carried on therein; and if any factory, mill, workshop, bakery, laundry, store, hotel, or any kind of an establishment wherein laborers are employed or machinery used in any enclosed rooms thereof by which dust is generated and inhaled to an injurious extent by the persons employed therein, conveyors, receptacles or exhaust fans, or other mechanical means shall be provided and maintained for the purpose of carrying off or receiving and collecting such dust.

Hoistways, etc. SEC. 4. The openings of all hoistways, hatchways, elevators and wellholes and stairways in factories, mills, workshops, bakeries, laundries, stores, hotels, or any kind of an establishment wherein laborers are employed, or machinery used, shall be protected by good and sufficient trap doors, hatches, fences, gates or other safeguards, and all due diligence shall be used to keep all such means of protection closed, except when it is necessary to have the same opened that the same may be used.

Inspection. SEC. 5. It shall be the duty of the chief factory inspector, by himself or his duly appointed deputy, to examine as soon as may be after the passage of this act, and thereafter annually, and from time to time, all factories, mills, workshops, bakeries, stores, hotels, or any kind of an establishment wherein laborers are employed or machinery used or appliances therein contained to which the provisions of this act are applicable, for the purpose of determining whether they do conform to such provisions, and to granting or refusing certificates of approval, as hereinafter provided.

Notices by employees. SEC. 6. Any employee of any person, firm, corporation or association operating a factory, mill, workshop, bakery, laundry, store, hotel, or any kind of an establishment wherein laborers are employed or machinery used shall notify his employer of any defect in, or failure to guard the machinery, appliances, ways, works or plants, on which or in or about which he is working, when any such defect or failure to guard shall come to the knowledge of any said employee, and if such employer shall fail to remedy such defect then said employee may complain in writing to the chief factory inspector of any such alleged defect in or failure to guard the machinery, appliances, ways, works, and plants, or any alleged violation by such person, firm, corporation or association, of any of the provisions of this act, in the machinery and appliances and premises used by such person, firm, corporation or association and with or about which said employee is working and upon receiving such complaint it shall be the duty of the chief factory inspector, by himself or his deputy, to forthwith make an inspection of the machinery and appliances complained of.

SEC. 7. Whenever upon any examination or reexamination of any factory, mill, workshop, bakery, laundry, store, hotel, or any kind of an establishment wherein laborers are employed, or machinery used to which the provisions of this act are applicable, the property so examined and the machinery and appliances therein conform in the judgment of said chief factory inspector to the requirements of this act, he shall thereupon issue to the owner, lessee or operator of any such storehouse, factory, mill, workshop, bakery, laundry, hotel, or any kind of an establishment wherein laborers are employed or machinery used a certificate to that effect, and such certificate shall be prima facie evidence as long as it continues in force of compliance on part of the person, firm, corporation or association to whom it is issued, with the provisions of this act. Such certificate may be revoked by said chief factory inspector at any time upon written notice to the person, firm, corporation or association holding the same whenever in his opinion after reexamination, condition and circumstances have so changed as to justify the revocation thereof. A copy of said certificate shall be kept posted in a conspicuous place on every floor of all factories, mills, workshops, bakeries, laundries, stores, hotels, or any kind of an establishment wherein laborers are employed or machinery used to which the provisions of this act are applicable. If, in the judgment of the said chief factory inspector, such factory, mill, workshop, bakery, laundry, store, hotel, or any kind of an establishment wherein laborers are employed or machinery is used does not conform to the requirements of this act he shall forthwith personally or by mail serve on the person, firm, corporation or association operating or using such machinery or appliances or occupying such premises a written statement of the requirements of said chief factory inspector, before he will issue a certificate as hereinbefore provided for; and upon said requirements being complied with within a period of thirty days after said written statement has been served as aforesaid the said chief factory inspector shall forthwith issue such certificate; but if the person, firm, or corporation operating or using said machinery and appliances or occupying such premises shall consider the requirements of said chief factory inspector unreasonable and impracticable or unnecessarily expensive, he may within ten days after the requirements of said chief factory inspector have been served upon him, appeal therefrom or from any part thereof to three arbitrators to whom shall be submitted the matters and things in dispute, and their findings shall be binding upon said applicant and upon the chief factory inspector. Such appeal shall be in writing, addressed to the chief factory inspector and shall set forth the objections to his requirements, or any part thereof, and shall mention the name of one person who will serve as a representative of said applicant calling for arbitration. Immediately upon the receipt of such notice of appeal, it shall be the duty of the chief factory inspector to appoint a competent person as arbitrator resident in the county

Marginal notes: Certificates of inspection. Revocation. Posting. Orders. Appeals. Arbitration.

from which such appeal comes, and to notify such person so selected, and also the party appealing, stating the cause of the arbitration, and the place, date and time of meeting. These two arbitrators shall select the third within five days and within ten days thereafter, give a hearing on the matters of said appeal, and the finding of those arbitrators by a majority vote shall be reported to the chief factory inspector and to the applicant and shall be binding upon each. The expense of such arbitration shall be borne by the party calling for the arbitration; and if said arbitrators sustain the requirements of said chief factory inspector or any part thereof, said applicant shall within thirty days comply with the findings of said arbitrators, and thereupon said chief factory inspector shall issue a certificate as hereinbefore provided (in section 5 of this act); but if said arbitrators shall sustain such appeal or any part thereof, the same shall be binding upon said chief factory inspector and any such person, firm, corporation or association shall within thirty days after the finding of the board of arbitrators, comply with the requirements of the chief factory inspector, as amended by said arbitrators, if so amended as herein provided for, and thereupon said chief factory [inspector] shall forthwith issue to any such person, firm, corporation or association, his certificate as provided for in section five of this act: *Provided*, That in case such arbitrators shall decide against such chief factory inspector, the cost of such arbitration shall be paid out of the funds for such purposes. In case the chief factory inspector is sustained in part by the arbitrators, the cost of arbitration shall be divided equitably, in proportion to that decision, the appellant paying such share as the arbitrators may deem fair, the rest to be paid out of said fund.

Provisions in
case of fire. SEC. 8. In all factories, mills, workshops, offices, bakeries, laundries, stores, hotels, or any other buildings in which people are employed at manual or other labor, proper and sufficient means of escape in case of fire shall be provided by more than one way of egress, and such means of escape shall at all times be kept free from any obstruction; in good repair and ready for use; and at night, or where lights are necessary in the daytime, a red light shall be provided with the words inscribed thereon "Fire
Doors to open
outward. escape." All doors leading into or to such factories, workshops, offices, bakeries, mills, laundries, stores, hotels, or other buildings in which people are employed at manual or other labor, shall be so constructed as to open outward when practicable, and shall not be locked, bolted or fastened during working hours as to prevent free egress. Proper and substantial handrails shall be provided
Stairways. on all stairways and in factories, hotels, mills and workshops and other buildings where people are employed at manual or other labor. And in all factories, laundries, mills and workshops in which females are employed the stairs regularly used by them shall be properly screened at the sides and bottom: *And be it further provided*, That hotels, boarding or bunk houses of more than one story shall have a hemp rope in each room of not less than three-quarters (¾) inch in thickness, the same to be firmly attached to wall in such manner that it may be thrown out of the window instantly to allow persons in case of fire, etc., to descend to the ground. The rope must have a knot tied in it at spaces of not more than eighteen (18) inches apart; the ropes to be placed in every room·above the second floor: *Provided*, That any rope, ladder or device for the protection of guests may be used upon approval by the chief factory inspector.

·Fire escapes. SEC. 9. In any factory, mill, workshop, office, bakery, laundry, store, hotel, or other building of three or more stories in height, [where] proper and sufficient means of escape in case of fire are not provided as required by preceding section of this act, the owner or occupant of said building upon notice by the chief factory inspector or any deputy factory inspector employed in the bureau of labor statistics shall construct one or more fire escapes as the same may be found necessary and sufficient. Said fire escape or fire escapes, shall be provided on the outside of such factories, mills, workshops, offices, bakeries, laundries, stores, hotels, or other buildings, connecting with each floor above the first, well fastened and secured and of sufficient strength. Each of such fire escapes shall have landings or balconies not less than six feet in length and three in width, guarded by iron railings not less than three feet in height and embracing at least two windows at each story, and connecting with the interior by easily accessible and unobstructed openings; and the balconies or landings shall be connected by iron stairs not less than 24 inches wide, and the steps to be not less than eight inches tread, placed at not more than an angle of forty-five degrees slant, and protected by well secured handrails on both sides, with a twelve-inch wide drop ladder from the lower platform reaching to the ground. Any fire escape so constructed shall be sufficient. Any other plan for style of fire escapes shall be sufficient if approved by the chief factory inspector, but if not so approved the said chief factory inspector or one of the deputy fatcory [factory] inspectors may notify the owner, proprietor or lessee of such factory, mill, workshop, office, bakery, laundry, store, hotel, or other building in which factory or workshop is conducted, or the agent or the superintendent, or either of them, in writing, that any such style of fire escape is not sufficient and he may issue an order in writing requiring one or more fire escapes as he shall deem necessary and sufficient and to be provided for such factory, mill, workshop, office, bakery, laundry, store, hotel or other buildings in which people are employed at manual or other labor at such location and of such plan and style as shall be specified in such written order. Within thirty days after the service of such order the number of fire escapes required in such order for such factory, mill, workshop, office, bakery, laundry, store, hotel, or other building, shall be provided therefor, each of which will be either of the plan and style and in accordance with the specifications in said order required or the plan and style in this section above described and declared sufficient.

The windows and doors of each fire escape shall be located as far as possible consistent with accessibility from the stairways and elevators, hatchways or openings, and the ladder thereof shall extend to the roof.

Stationery [stationary] stairs or ladders shall be provided on the inside of each such factory, mill, workshop, office, bakery, laundry, store, hotel or other buildings where people are employed at manual or other labor from the upper story to the roof as a means of escape in case of fire. *Ladders to roof.*

Sec. 10. Every factory, workshop, office, bakery, laundry, store, hotel, or other building in which four or more persons are employed shall be provided within reasonable access with a sufficient number of water-closets, earth closets or privies, for the reasonable use of the persons therein; and whenever male or female persons are employed as aforesaid together, water-closets, earth closets or privies separate and apart shall be provided for the use of each sex and plainly so designated, and no person shall be allowed to use such closets or privy assigned to the other sex. Such closets shall be properly screened and ventilated and at all times kept in a clean and good sanitary condition. *Water-closets.*

In factories, laundries, mills, and workshops and in all other places where the labor performed by the operator is of such character that it becomes desirable or necessary to change the clothing wholly or in part before leaving the building at the close of the day's toil, separate dressing rooms shall be provided for women and girls whenever so required by the factory inspector. It shall be the duty of every occupant, whether owner or lessee of any premises so used as to come within the provisions of this act to carry out the same and to make all the changes and additions necessary therefor. In case such changes are made upon the order of the chief factory inspector or of a factory inspector by the lessee of the premises he may at any *Dressing rooms.*

time within thirty (30) days after the completion thereof bring an action before any justice of the peace, county or district court, having competent jurisdiction against any person having an interest in such premises and may recover such portion of the expense of making such changes and in addition as the court adjudges should justly and equitably be borne by such defendant.

Damages.

Evidence.

SEC. 11. In all actions brought to recover damages for personal injuries or death caused by reason of the violation of any of the provisions of this act, it shall be sufficient for the plaintiff to prove in the first instance, in order to establish the liability of the defendant, that the death or injury complained of resulted in consequence of the failure of the person owning or operating the manufacturing establishment where such death, or injury occurred to provide said establishment with safeguards as required by this act, or that the failure to provide such safeguards directly contributed to such death or injury.

Definitions.

Manufacturing establishments, as those words are used in this act, shall mean and include all smelters, oil refineries, cement works, mills of every kind, machine and repair shops, and in addition to the foregoing, any other kind or character of manufacturing establishment, of any nature or description whatsoever, wherein any natural product or other articles or materials of any kind, in a raw or unfinished or incomplete state or condition, are converted into a new or improved or different form.

Wherever the expression occurs in this act in substantially the followings words: " Every person owning or operating any manufacturing establishment," or where language similar to that is used, the word " person " in that connection shall be held and construed to mean any person or persons, partnership, corporation, receiver, trust, trustee, or any other person or combination of persons, either natural or artificial, by whatever name he or they may be called.

Powers of factory inspector.

SEC. 12. The chief factory inspector or any employee of the department of factory inspection shall have power to enter any factory, mill, workshop, office, bakery, laundry, store, hotel, or any public or private works where labor is employed or machinery used. Any person, persons, firm, copartnership, corporation, trust, trustee, their agent, or agents, who shall refuse to allow an inspector or employee of the said department to enter or who shall violate any of the provisions of this act, shall be deemed guilty of a misdemeanor, and upon conviction thereof before any court of competent jurisdiction shall be punished by a fine of not less than fifty ($50) dollars nor more than one hundred ($100) dollars or be imprisoned in the county jail not to exceed ninety (90) days for each and every offense.

CONNECTICUT.

GENERAL STATUTES—1902.

Inspection of bakeries.[1]

Construction and sanitation of rooms.

SECTION 2569 (as amended by chapter 147, Acts of 1909). Every building or room occupied as a bakery shall be drained and plumbed in a manner conducive to its healthful and sanitary condition, and constructed with air shafts and windows or ventilating pipes sufficient to insure ventilation, as the factory inspector shall direct. Every bakery shall be provided with a wash room and water-closet apart from the bake room and rooms where the manufacturing of food products is conducted; no water-closet, earth closet, privy, or ash pit shall be within or communicate directly with a bakery. Rooms used for the manufacture of flour and meal food shall be at least eight feet in height; the side walls of such rooms shall be plastered or wainscoted, the ceiling plastered or

---

[1] See also chapter 120, Acts of 1909, page 876.

ceiled with lumber or metal, and, if required by the factory inspector, shall be whitewashed at least once in three months; the furniture, utensils, and floor of such rooms shall be kept in healthful sanitary condition. The manufactured flour or meal food products shall be kept in dry, clean, and airy rooms. The sleeping Sleeping rooms. rooms for persons employed in a bakery shall be separate from the rooms where food products are manufactured or stored. No person, firm, or corporatioi. shall operate a bakery without having obtained from the factory inspector a certificate of inspection de- Certificates of scribing the building used as a bakery and stating that the same inspection. complies with the laws of this State relating to bakeries, which certificate shall be kept posted by the owner or operator of such bakery in a conspicuous place in the shop described in such certificate or in the salesroom connected therewith. Such certificate may be revoked by said inspector, for cause, and when revoked said inspector shall cite the person operating such bakery, or, in the case of a corporation, the manager, to appear before him within ten days thereafter to show cause why such certificate should not remain revoked. No person, firm, or corporation shall open a New bakeries. new bakery without having given at least ten days' notice to the factory inspector of his intention to open such bakery, which notice shall contain a description of the building proposed to be used as such bakery and shall give its location. Upon receipt of such notice said inspector shall examine the premises, and if found to comply with the provisions of the statutes relating to bakeries he shall issue such certificate of inspection.

SEC. 2570. No employer shall permit any person to work in his Contagious diseases. bakeshop who is affected with pulmonary tuberculosis, scrofulous, or venereal disease, or with a communicable skin affection, and every employer shall maintain himself and his employees in a clean and sanitary condition while engaged in the manufacture. handling, or sale of such food products.

SEC. 2571. The owner, agent, or lessee of any property used as a Notice to be bakery shall, within thirty days after the service of notice upon complied with. him of an order issued by the factory inspector, comply therewith, or cease to use or allow the use of such premises as a bake shop; such notice shall be in writing and may be served upon such owner, agent, or lessee, either personally or by mail, and a notice by registered letter, mailed to the last known address of such owner, agent, or lessee, shall be sufficient service.

SEC. 2572. Every person who violates any provision of sections Violations. 2569, 2570 or 2571, or who fails to comply with an order of the factory inspector, shall be fined not more than fifty dollars for tht first offense, not more than one hundred dollars or imprisoned not more than ten days for the second offense, and not more than two hundred dollars and imprisoned not more than thirty days for each subsequent offense.

Fire escapes on factories, etc.[1]

SECTION 2628 (as amended by chapter 239, Acts of 1911). Exits required. Every story above the first story of a building used as a * * * workshop, manufactory, or store in which more than ten persons are employed above the first story, shall be provided with more than one way of egress, by stairways on the inside or fire escapes on the outside of such buildings. Said stairways and fire escapes shall be so constructed, in such number, of such size, and in such locations as to give, in the opinion of the officer charged with the enforcement of this act, safe, adequate, and convenient means of exit, in view of the number of persons who may need to use such stairway or fire escape, shall, at all times be kept free from obstruction and shall be accessible from each room in every story above the first story.

SEC. 2629 (as amended by chapter 239, Acts of 1911). If any Fire escapes. building · specified in section 2628, or any workshop, manufactory, hotel, boarding house, tenement house, or other building used, in whole or in part, for any of the purposes therein

[1] See also chapter 239, Acts of 1911, page 876.

specified, or in which more than six persons shall be employed above the third story, shall be more than three stories in height, it shall be provided with at least one fire escape, of iron or other incombustible material, on the outside of said building; and if such building shall be more than one hundred and fifty feet in length it shall be provided with one such fire escape for every one hundred and fifty feet, or fractional part thereof exceeding fifty feet, and such fire escape shall be conveniently accessible from each story of said building; and if such building be a tenement house the fire escapes shall be directly accessible from each apartment, without passing through any public hall.

Regulation and inspection of factories, etc.

Duty of inspector. SECTION. 4515. The inspector shall, as often as practicable, examine all buildings and places where machinery is used, and may enter such buildings and places at all proper times for the purposes of inspection. He shall, on or before the first of December in each year, make a report to the governor of the condition, as respects safety to life and health, of the factories, buildings, and places visited by him.

Lightning, etc. SEC. 4516. All factories and buildings where machinery is used shall be well lighted, ventilated, and kept as clean as the nature **Safety appli-** of the business will permit. The belting, shafting, gearing, ma-**ances.** chinery, and drums, of all factories and buildings where machinery is used, when so placed as, in the opinion of the inspector, to be dangerous to the persons employed therein while engaged in their ordinary duties, shall, as far as practicable, be securely guarded. No machinery other than steam engines in a factory shall be cleaned while running after notice forbidding the same is given by the inspector to the owners or operators of the factory.

Colored win- SEC. 4518. Every person, firm, or corporation using stained, **dows.** painted, or corrugated glass in factory windows, where the same is injurious to the eyes of the workmen therein, shall remove the same upon the order of the factory inspector.

Water-closets. SEC. 4519. Every person or corporation managing or operating any factory, or owning or controlling the use of any other building where more than five persons are employed, shall provide and keep in good sanitary condition suitable water-closet accommodations for the use of the persons employed.

Enforcement. SEC. 4520. The inspector shall enforce the provisions of this chapter by giving proper orders or notices to the persons or corporations owning, operating, or managing the factories or buildings inspected by him, and shall make complaint to the State's attorneys of all violations of this chapter.

Buffing, grind- SEC. 4521. Whenever the inspector, on complaint of any person, **ing, etc.** shall find it necessary, for the preservation of the health of the employees in any manufacturing establishment, factory, or mill in which is carried on the business of buffing, polishing, or grinding metals, or any operations in which an excessive amount of dust is generated, that such dust should be removed from the atmosphere of the rooms or apartments used for that purpose, he shall, in writing, direct the person, or corporation owning, occupying, or carrying on business in such premises, within three months from the date of said order, to introduce and operate such appliances or devices as may be necessary to remove, so far as the nature of the business will permit, such excessive dust or foreign matter: *Provided,* That such appliances or devices do not restrict or interfere with the aforesaid business or operations.

Violations. SEC. 4522 (as amended by chapter 53, Acts of 1903). Every owner, lessee, or occupant of a factory, or building included within the provisions of this chapter, or owning or controlling the use of any room in such building, shall for the violation of any provision of sections 4516, 4517, 4518, 4519, or 4521, or for obstructing or hindering the inspector of factories or his deputies in carrying out the duties imposed on them by law, be fined not more than fifty dollars; but no prosecution shall be brought for any such violation until four weeks after notice has been given by the inspector to such owner, lessee, or occupant of any changes necessary to be made to comply with the provisions of said sections, and not then, if, in the meantime, such changes have been made in accordance with such notification. Nothing herein shall limit the right of a person injured to bring an action to recover damages.

SEC. 4523. The orders and notices given by the inspector under this chapter shall be written or printed, signed by him officially, and may be served by himself or any proper officer or indifferent person, by leaving an attested copy thereof with or at the usual place of abode of the person upon whom service is to be made; and the notice, properly indorsed with the doings of the person or officer serving the same, shall be returned to the office of the town clerk of the town in which is located the factory, building, or business to which such notice appertains, where it shall be kept on file. Such notice, or copies thereof duly certified by the town clerk, shall be prima facie evidence that notice was given as therein appears. Notice to one member of a firm shall be notice to every member thereof, and notice to the president, secretary, or treasurer of a corporation shall be notice to such corporation. The fees for serving such orders and notices, unless served by the inspector, shall be the same as for the service of process in civil actions, and shall be included in the necessary expenses of the inspector.. *Notices*

SEC. 4524. Any person, firm, or corporation aggrieved by any order of the factory inspector may appeal to the superior court in the county where the person, firm or corporation owns, leases, or occupies the factory or building to which said order relates, within four weeks after notice of such order shall be given. Said appeal shall operate as a supersedeas, shall be made in writing, and shall contain a brief statement of the facts and reasons of appeal and a citation to the inspector to appear before said court, and said court or a judge thereof may direct the time of appearance and the manner of service. Said court may review the doings of the factory inspector, confirm, change, or set them aside, and make such orders in the premises, including orders as to costs, as it may find to be proper and equitable. *Appeals.*

SEC. 4527. The inspector shall, as often as practicable, examine all buildings, apartments, rooms, and places in any tenement or dwelling house used for residential purposes and used in whole or in part by others than the immediate members of the family therein, for the manufacture of artificial flowers, purses, cigars, cigarettes, or any articles of wearing apparel intended for sale. *Sweat shops.*

SEC. 4528. The persons engaged in the manufacture of such goods in such premises, within thirty days after beginning such manufacture, shall notify said inspector of the location of said workrooms, the nature of the work there carried on, and the number of persons therein employed. *Notice of use.*

SEC. 4529. The person operating said workrooms shall keep the same at all times in a clean and sanitary condition, properly lighted, ventilated, and fit for the occupancy of the persons engaged in work therein. The inspector or any of his special agents shall notify the owner of such premises, and the person using the same for the purposes set forth in section 4527 to provide ample means for lighting or ventilating such workrooms, and to put the same in a clean, sanitary, and fit condition for occupancy for said work; and if said notification be not complied with in thirty days after the service of such notice, said inspector or any of his special agents shall cause complaint to be made to the proper prosecuting authority. *Sanitation, etc.*

SEC. 4530. Every person, firm, or corporation owning, using, or occupying any workroom for the purposes specified in section 4527 shall, for the violation of any provision of sections 4528 or 4529, be fined not more than five hundred dollars. *Violations*

[See also section 4703, Appendix A, page 677.]

Inspection of steam boilers.

Inspector.

SECTION 4890. The governor shall appoint, in each congressional district, a suitable person to inspect steam boilers used for manufacturing, heating, and mechanical purposes, who shall hold office for three years. Said inspector shall, as often as once in each year, carefully inspect every such boiler in his district, and, if he finds such boiler to be in good order, and free from weakness and material defects, he shall give a certificate of inspection to the per-

Inspection by company's inspectors.

son using the same; but any company incorporated by any State of the United States, for the purpose of making inspection of steam boilers, and that maintains a corps of steam boiler inspectors, and has complied with the insurance laws of this State, may issue certificates of inspection in lieu of those issued by the inspectors appointed by the governor: *Provided,* A policy of insurance is issued covering loss or damage to person or property arising from the explosion of the boiler or boilers so inspected; and the boilers on which such certificates have been issued shall be exempt from inspection by the steam boiler inspectors of the State.

Notice of defects.

SEC. 4891. If said inspector finds any boiler out of order, materially weak, or defective, he shall advise its owner, lessee, or user as to its necessary repairs, and if such repairs are not made, he may call in the inspector from an adjoining district, and if they agree that such boiler is not in proper condition, they shall give written notice to its owner, lessee, or user not to use it until such repairs are made as said inspectors shall specify, or if they are of the opinion that it is utterly worthless, or that its use will endanger the public safety, they shall forbid its use.

Act does not apply, when.

SEC. 4892. The provisions of section 4890 and 4891 shall not apply to any city or town having a system of boiler inspection, unless accepted and adopted by it.

Violation.

SEC. 4894. Every person who shall neglect or refuse to have any steam boiler used by him inspected, or shall suffer it to carry a greater pressure of steam than is allowed by the certificate of the inspector, shall be fined not more than two hundred dollars.

Use of condemned boiler.

SEC. 4895. Every person who shall use any steam boiler after its use is forbidden by the inspectors shall be fined not more than one thousand dollars, or imprisoned not more than six months, or both.

False certificates.

SEC. 4896. Every inspector who shall willfully and knowingly falsely certify to the condition of any boiler inspected by him, or who shall issue a certificate without having made a careful inspection, as provided in section 4890, shall be fined not more than five hundred dollars, or imprisoned not more than six months, or both.

Exemptions.

SEC. 4897. The provisions of this chapter shall not apply to the boilers of locomotive engines or to boilers used exclusively for heating private residences.

Intemperance, etc., of operators.

SEC. 4898. Whenever in the opinion of the inspectors any person operating a steam boiler, subject by law to their inspection, shall, by reason of intemperate habits or for any other cause, be incompetent to safely operate such boiler, said inspector shall order the discharge of such person, and serve written notice to that effect upon his employer. If at the expiration of thirty days from the serving of such notice such employer shall have failed to comply with the requirements thereof, he shall be fined not more than one hundred dollars.

ACTS OF 1903.

CHAPTER 97.—*Inspector of factories, etc.*

Inspector.

SECTION 1. The governor shall, with the consent of the senate, on or before the fifteenth day of May, A. D. 1903, and before the first day of May quadrennially thereafter, appoint a factory inspector, who shall hold office for four years and until his successor is appointed and qualified. The governor may remove the inspector for cause. Said factory inspector shall receive an annual salary of twenty-five hundred dollars and necessary expenses.

Sec. 2. The inspector shall examine all elevators, whether in *Elevators, etc., to be inspected.* factories, mercantile establishments, storehouses, workhouses, dwellings, or other buildings, and may order hoistways, hatchways, elevator wells, and wellholes to be protected by trapdoors, self-closing hatches, safety catches, or other safeguards as will insure the safety of all persons therein. Due diligence shall be used to keep such trapdoors closed at all times, except when in actual use by an occupant of the building having the use and control of the same. All elevator cabs or cars, whether used for freight or passengers, shall be provided with some suitable mechanical device, if considered necessary by said inspector, whereby the cab or car will be securely held in the event of accident to the shipper rope or hoisting machinery, or from any similar cause, and said mechanical device shall at all times be kept in good working order.

Sec. 3 (as amended by chapter 241, Acts of 1907). The in- *Deputies.* spector may from time to time appoint deputies to assist him in the performance of his duties. Such deputies shall have the same power and authority as the inspector, subject to his approval. Each of said deputies shall receive a compensation of five dollars per day for actual services, and his or her necessary expenses incident to the performance of the duties of his or her office. The total amount expended under this section shall not exceed in any one year nine thousand dollars, which shall be paid upon proper vouchers by the deputies, signed by the inspector.

ACTS OF 1905.

Chapter 140.—*Inspection of factories—Toilet rooms in foundries.*

Section 1. The factory inspector shall have power and author- *Power of factory inspector.* ity by order to that effect to require the proprietor of any foundry in this State in which ten or more men are employed, and situated in a locality where there is such system for the disposal of sewage as to make such order practicable, to provide for the use of such employes a toilet room of such suitable dimensions as such inspector may determine, containing wash bowls or sinks connected with running water, with facilities for heating the same, such room to be directly connected with such foundry building, properly heated, ventilated, and protected from the dust of said foundry.

Sec. 2. Any person, company, or corporation failing to comply *Violations.* with such order shall be fined not more than fifty dollars, in each prosecution for such neglect or refusal to obey such order.

ACTS OF 1907.

Chapter 241.—*Factory inspectors—Female deputy.*

Section 1. The factory inspector shall, in addition to the deputy *Advisory commission.* factory inspectors provided for by chapter 97 of the Public Acts of 1903, appoint, from time to time, on the recommendation of an advisory commission of three women appointed by the governor for that purpose as specified in section five of this act, a female *Female deputy.* deputy factory inspector, who shall hold office until her successor is appointed and qualified, unless removed by said factory inspector for cause. Said female deputy factory inspector shall receive the compensation for services and expenses provided by section three of chapter 97 of the Public Acts of 1903 as amended by this act.

Sec. 2. Said female deputy factory inspector shall inquire into *Duties.* the enforcement of the laws regulating the employment of women and girls in any manufacturing, mechanical, or mercantile establishment, investigate the conditions relating to the health and welfare of women and girls employed in such establishments, and report thereon to the factory inspector: *Provided, however,* That she shall have no power or authority over and no duty concerning any machinery, appliances, or fixtures except sanitary fixtures.

Powers.

SEC. 3. Said female deputy factory inspector shall have the same power and authority as the factory inspector, except as to machinery, appliances, and fixtures, subject to his approval, and shall serve under the direction of said factory inspector in all respects as other deputy inspectors.

Commission

SEC. 5. The governor shall, on or before the first day of August, 1907, appoint three women, no two of whom shall be residents of the same town, who shall constitute an advisory commission for the appointment of a female deputy factory inspector and shall serve for two, four, and six years respectively; and biennially thereafter the governor shall appoint one member of said commission to serve for the term of six years. It shall be the duty of said commission to recommend to the factory inspector some woman for appointment as female deputy factory inspector, such recommendation to be made on or before October 1, 1907, and thereafter whenever a vacancy shall occur in said office.

ACTS OF 1909.

CHAPTER 10.—*Fire escapes on factories, etc.*

Enforcement.

SECTION 1 (as amended by chapter 239, Acts of 1911). The factory inspector shall have power to enforce the provisions of sections 2628 and 2629 of the General Statutes as amended by this act so far as concerns workshops and manufactories and may order fire escapes erected thereon whenever deemed by him to be necessary; and any owner, agent, or lessee neglecting or refusing to comply with such order shall be subject to the penalties prescribed in section 2633 of the general statutes.

CHAPTER 120.—*Inspection of bakeries, etc.—Tuberculosis, etc., employees.*

Law extended.

SECTION 14. The provisions of sections 2569, 2570, 2571, and 2572 of the General Statutes relating to bakeshops shall apply to all confectionery, candy, and ice cream factories, macaroni factories, and all other factories for the preparation of foodstuffs, tobacco, and cigars. In any factory of the above-named classes where the factory inspector shall have cause to suspect that an operative or employee has any disease enumerated in the statutes thereto pertaining, he shall have authority to cause an examination to be made of such suspected case by a physician.

Posters.

SEC. 15. It shall be the duty of the factory inspector to cause to be posted, in prominent places in factories and shops, such posters as may be supplied to him for that purpose by the board of directors.

ACTS OF 1911.

CHAPTER 239.—*Fire escapes on factories, etc.*

Damages for injuries.

SECTION 4. In all cases in which any person shall suffer injury or in which the death of any person shall ensue in consequence of the failure of the owner of any building to provide the same with fire escapes or stairways, as required by the provisions of this act [amending sections 2628, 2629, G. S.], or in consequence of the failure of such owner to comply with any order of the factory inspector, made in conformity to the provisions of this act, such owner shall be liable to any person so injured for damages for such injury; and in case of death such owner shall be liable in damages for the injury caused by the death of such person. · It shall be no defense to any action for the recovery of such damages that the person injured, or whose death ensued as aforesaid, had knowledge that such building was not provided with fire escapes or stairways as required by the provisions of this act, or that such person continued to work in or to occupy such building with such knowledge.

SEC. 5. The owner of any building, or in case such owner be non compos mentis or a minor, the guardian of such owner, or in case such owner be nonresident, the agent of such owner having charge of such property, who shall neglect or fail to comply with the foregoing provisions of this act shall be fined not less than one hundred dollars nor more than five hundred dollars. In case there shall be several owners of any building the use of which shall be continued in violation of the provisions of this act, all such owners jointly, or any one of them, shall be liable to such fine. *(Violations.)*

DELAWARE.

REVISED CODE—1893.

CHAPTER 127.—*Fire escapes on factories, etc.*

(Page 929.)

SECTION 1. The owner or owners of any building * * * being more than two stories in height and which shall be used in the third or any higher story, in whole or in part as a * * * factory or workshop, or as a tenement house * * * shall be required to furnish such building with sufficient permanent fire escapes from the third and all higher stories, and which escapes shall be kept and maintained in good order. Such fire escapes may be by means of stairways or ladders outside the building, or by stairways in a separate tower or structure furnished with safe and easy communication with such building: *Provided,* That this act shall not apply to any building whatever that is already supplied with two or more independent stairways leading from the highest story to the ground floor, if said stairways shall not be nearer to each other at any point than a distance of sixty feet. *(Fire escapes to be provided for certain buildings.)*

SEC. 2. It shall be the duty of the chief engineer of the fire department in any city, town or borough where there may be such officers, or if there be no such officer therein, then of the mayor or chief officer thereof, and in all other places of the clerk of the school district wherein any such building is located to examine such fire escapes as to their suitableness and sufficiency, whether as to quality, location or number. If upon such examination such escapes be found to be sufficient and suitable, the person examining shall give the owner of such building or some one of them, if more than one, a certificate stating such examination and his approval, which certificate shall be good for two years, at the expiration of which time another examination shall be had and a like certificate given. Such certificate of approval shall be evidence of sufficient compliance with the requirements of this act and shall protect such owner from any penalty herein prescribed during the time for which it may have been given. The fee for such examination shall be one dollar. *(Inspection.)*

SEC. 4. Every owner of any such building as is specified in this act, whether an individual or a body corporate, who shall fail to comply with the provisions thereof shall be deemed guilty of a misdemeanor and be liable to indictment, and upon conviction shall forfeit and pay to the State a fine not exceeding two hundred dollars, and in case of a corporation, payment of the fine may be enforced by a writ of fieri facias to be issued out of the court where such conviction was had on the judgment thereof and continued by venditioni exponas as upon judgments in the superior court. *(Penalty.)*

ACTS OF 1897.

CHAPTER 452.—*Factories and workshops—Provisions for female employees—New Castle County.*

[See Appendix A, page 681.]

878 • LABOR LAWS AND FACTORY CONDITIONS.

DISTRICT OF COLUMBIA.

ACTS OF U. S. CONGRESS, 1886-87.

CHAPTER 390.—*Elevators.*

Commissioners
to regulate.

SECTION 1. The Commissioners of the District of Columbia * * * are hereby, authorized and directed to make and publish such orders as may be necessary to regulate the construction, repair, and operation of all elevators within the District of Columbia, and prescribe such means of security as may be found necessary to protect life and limb.

Penalty.

SEC. 2. Any person or persons, or corporations, who shall neglect or refuse to comply with the orders made pursuant to this act, shall, upon conviction thereof in the police court of the District of Columbia, * * * be fined not less than ten dollars nor more than one hundred dollars for each offense.

ACTS OF 1897-98.

CHAPTER 8.—*Factories and workshops—Water-closets.*

Water-closets to
be provided.

SECTION 9. Every building in said District * * * where persons are employed or intended to be employed in any trade or business, shall be provided with sufficient and suitable privy accommodations, having regard to the number of persons employed in or in attendance at such building; and also where persons of both sexes are employed or intended to be employed, or in attendance, with sufficient, suitable, and separate privy accommodations for persons of each sex. It shall be unlawful for any owner or agent to put any person or persons in possession of any building, or any part thereof, not provided with privy accommodations as aforesaid, except a watchman for the purpose of guarding such building or part thereof.

ACTS OF 1905-6.

CHAPTER 957.—*Fire escapes on factories, etc.*

Fire escapes required.

SECTION 2 (as amended by chapter 2566, Acts of 1906-7). It shall be the duty of the owner entitled to the beneficial use, rental, or control of any building already erected, or which may hereafter be erected, in which ten or more persons are employed at the same time in any of the stories above the second story, except three-story buildings used exclusively as stores or for office purposes, and having at least two stairways from the ground floor each three or more feet wide and separated from each other by a distance of at least thirty feet, from one of which stairways shall be easy access to the roof, to provide and cause to be erected and affixed thereto a sufficient number of * * * fire escapes, [of such material, type, and construction as the Commissioners of the District of Columbia may determine] the location and number of the same to be determined by the said Commissioners, and to keep the hallways and stairways in every such building as is used and occupied at night properly lighted, to the satisfaction of the Commissioners of the District of Columbia, from sunset to sunrise.

Signs, lights,
etc.

SEC. 3 (as amended by chapter 2566, Acts of 1906-7). It shall be the duty of the owner entitled to the beneficial use, rental, or control of * * * any building in which ten or more persons are employed, as set forth in section two of this act where fire escapes are required, also to provide, install, and maintain therein proper and sufficient guide signs, guide lights, exit lights, hall and stairway lights, fire hose, and fire extinguishers in such location and numbers and of such type and character as the Commissioners of the District of Columbia may determine.

SEC. 5 (as amended by chapter 2566, Acts of 1906-7). Each elevator shaft and stairway extending to the basement of the buildings heretofore mentioned shall terminate in a fireproof compartment or inclosure, separating the elevator shaft and stairs from other parts of the basement, and no opening shall be made or maintained in such compartment or inclosure unless the same be provided with fireproof doors. * * * Elevator shafts.

SEC. 6. It shall be unlawful to obstruct any hall, passageway, corridor, or stairway in any building mentioned in this act with baggage, trunks, furniture, cans, or with any other thing whatsoever. Obstructions.

SEC. 7. No door or window leading to any fire escape shall be covered or obstructed by any fixed grating or barrier, and no person shall at any time place any incumbrance or obstacle upon any fire escape or upon any platform, ladder, or stairway leading to or from any fire escape. Same.

SEC. 8. No license shall be issued to any person to conduct any business for which a license is required in any building mentioned in this act until such building has been provided and equipped with a sufficient number of fire escapes and other appliances required by this act. Licenses refused, when.

SEC. 9. Any person failing or neglecting to provide fire escapes, alarm gongs, guide signs, fire hose, fire extinguishers, or other appliances required by this act, after notice from the Commissioners of the District of Columbia so to do, shall, upon conviction thereof, be punished by a fine of not less than ten dollars nor more than one hundred dollars, and shall be punished by a further fine of five dollars for each day that he fails to comply with the notice aforesaid. Any person violating any other provision of this act shall be punished, upon conviction thereof, by a fine of not less than ten dollars nor more than one hundred dollars for each offense. Violations.

SEC. 10. The said notice requiring the erection of fire escapes and other appliances mentioned in this act shall specify the character and number of fire escapes or other appliances to be provided, the location of the same, and the time within which said fire escapes or other appliances shall be provided, and in no case shall more than ninety days be allowed for compliance with said notice unless the Commissioners of the District of Columbia shall, in their discretion, deem it necessary to extend their time. Contents of notice.

SEC. 11 (as amended by chapter 2566, Acts of 1906-7). Said notice shall be deemed to have been served if delivered to the person to be notified, or if left with any adult person at the usual residence or place of business of the person to be notified in the District of Columbia, or if no such residence or place of business can be found in said District by reasonable search, if left with any adult person at the office of any agent of the person to be notified: *Provided,* Such agent has any authority or duty with reference to the building to which said notice relates, or if no such office can be found in said District by reasonable search if forwarded by registered mail to the last known address of the person to be notified and not returned by the Post-Office authorities, or if no address be known or can by reasonable diligence be ascertained, or if any notice forwarded as authorized by the preceding clause of this section be returned by the Post-office authorities, if published on ten consecutive days in a daily newspaper published in the District of Columbia, or if by reason of an outstanding unrecorded transfer of title the name of the owner in fact can not be ascertained beyond a reasonable doubt, if served on the owner of record in the manner hereinbefore in this section provided. Any notice to a corporation shall, for the purposes of this act, be deemed to have been served on such corporation if served on the president, secretary, treasurer, general manager, or any principal officer of such corporation in the manner hereinbefore provided for the service of notices on natural persons holding property in their own right, and notice to a foreign corporation shall, for the purposes of this act, be deemed to have been served if served on any agent of such corporation personally, or if left with any person of suit- Service of notice.

able age and discretion residing at the usual residence or employed at the usual place of business of such agent in the District of

Noncompliance. Columbia: *Provided,* That in case of failure or refusal of the owner entitled to the beneficial use, rental, or control of any buildings specified in this act, to comply with the requirements of the notice provided for in section ten, then, and in that event, the Commissioners are hereby empowered and it is their duty to cause such erection of fire escapes and other appliances mentioned in the notice provided for, and they are hereby author ized to assess the costs thereof as a tax against the buildings on which they are erected and the ground on which the same stands, and to issue tax-lien certificates against such building and grounds for the amount of such assessments, bearing interest at the rate of ten per centum per annum, which certificates may be turned over by the Commissioners to the contractor for doing the work.

Enforcement. SEC. 12. The supreme court of the District of Columbia, in term time or in vacation, may, upon a petition of the District of Columbia, filed by its said Commissioners, issue an injunction to restrain the use or occupation of any building in the District of Columbia in violation of any of the provisions of this act.

GEORGIA.

CODE—1910.

Fire escapes on factories, etc.

What buildings to have fire escapes. SECTION 3151. Owners of every building more than two stories in height, not including the basement, used in the third or higher stories, in whole or in part, as factory or workshop, shall provide more than one way of egress from each story of said building, above the second story, by stairways on the inside or outside of said building, and such stairways shall be, as nearly as may be practicable, at apposite [opposite] ends of each story, and so constructed that, in case of fire, the ground can be readily reached

Landings. from the third and higher stories. Stairways on the outside of said buildings shall have suitable railed landings at each story above the first, and shall connect with each of said stories by doors or windows opening outwardly, and such doors, windows, and land-

Doors to open ings shall be kept at all times clear of obstructions. All the main
outwardly. doors of such buildings, both inside and outside, shall open outwardly, and each story shall be amply supplied with means for extinguishing fires.

Inspection. SEC. 3152. The municipal authorities of the town or city where such building is situated, or the ordinary of the county if the building is situated outside of any town or city, shall require the fire marshal or chief officer of the fire department, and if there is no fire marshal nor chief fireman, then some other suitable official, to examine such buildings at least once a year, and report in writing to said municipal authorities, or said ordinary, that said requirements have or have not been complied with. If not complied with, the municipal authorities or the ordinary, as the case may be, shall notify in writing the owner of such building to provide needful alterations or additions.

Who to make SEC. 3154. The owners of buildings referred to in this article
alterations. shall make all alterations or additions necessary to comply with the requirements of this article. Examinations and reports shall be made during the month of December of each year.

ACTS OF 1911.

Commissioner of commerce and labor—Inspection of factories, etc.

(Page 133.)

Law enforce- SEC. 4. Said commissioner shall make investigation concerning
ment. the operation of the various laws relating to the safety of the

life and limb of employees, especially those concerning the employment of child labor, and of women, and he shall take legal steps looking to the proper enforcement and due observance of such laws.

HAWAII.

REVISED LAWS—1905.

Regulations of laundries.

SECTION 1063. The superintendent of public works may cause to be built and erected in the district of Kona, Island of Oahu, a sufficient number of laundries and washhouses, and to let the same to persons applying therefor at such rents, and upon such terms as the said superintendent shall deem advisable. And in like manner to designate and use for such purposes buildings already erected. Laundries, etc. to be erected.

SEC. 1065. Such laundries and washhouses when erected shall be under the supervision and control of the board of health. Board of health.

SEC. 1066 (as amended by act No. 111, Acts of 1907). Every person who shall carry on the business of laundry keeping or washing for hire, within the limits of the city of Honolulu, except in such buildings as shall be provided for such purpose, in accordance with the provisions of section 1063, or in such buildings as may be approved and designated for such purpose by the board of health, shall upon conviction be liable to a fine not to exceed ten dollars for each and every day during which he shall so carry on such business, and in default of payment of such fine shall be imprisoned until such fine is paid. Use of other buildings.

SEC. 1375. The treasurer with the approval of the governor may issue to any person, partnership or corporation a license to erect, maintain and operate a steam laundry within the district of Kona, Island of Oahu, upon such conditions as to location and otherwise as shall be set forth in the license. Laundries to be licensed.

SEC. 1376. Said license shall not be issued except upon the certificate of the board of health, setting forth that an agent of said board has examined the location at which it is proposed to operate said steam laundry, and that the same is suitable for the purpose. Inspection.

SEC. 1377. The annual fee for said license shall be fifty dollars. Fee.

SEC. 1378. Said steam laundries shall be subject to such regulations as to sanitation as may be prescribed from time to time by the board of health. Regulations.

IDAHO.

REVISED CODES—1909.

Fire escapes on factories, etc.

SECTION 1550. It is hereby made the duty of every person, firm or corporation, or his or its agents, officers or trustees, owning or having the management or control of any * * * factory or other structure over two stories in height to provide and furnish such building with safe and suitable metallic, iron or fireproof ladders of sufficient strength, and to permanently and securely attach the same to the outside or outer walls of such buildings, in such manner and in such position as to be adjacent to the windows, and convenient and easy of access to the occupants of such buildings in case of fire. Factories more than two stories in height.

SEC. 1551. Such metallic, iron or fireproof ladders must connect with each floor above the first, and be well fastened and secure and of sufficient strength and must extend from the first story to the upper stories of such building or to the cornice thereof. Ladders.

SEC. 1553. Any person, firm or corporation, or his or its agents, officers or trustees, who shall fail to comply with the provisions of Violation.

this chapter, shall be guilty of a misdemeanor, and, on conviction thereof, shall be punishable by imprisonment in the county jail for not less than three, nor more than six, months, or by a fine of not less than two hundred dollars, nor more than three hundred dollars, or by both such fine and imprisonment.

ILLINOIS.

HURD'S REVISED STATUTES—1905.

CHAPTER 48.—*Factories and workshops—Inspection.*

Sewing, etc., in living rooms.

SECTION 21. No room or rooms, apartment or apartments in any tenement or dwelling house used for eating or sleeping purposes, shall be used for the manufacture, in whole or in part, of coats, vests, trousers, knee pants, overalls, cloaks, shirts, ladies' waists, purses, feathers, artificial flowers or cigars, except by the immediate members of the family living therein. Every such workshop shall be kept in a cleanly state, and shall be subject to the provisions of this act; and each of said articles made, altered, re-

Inspection.

paired or finished in any of such workshops shall be subject to inspection and examination, as hereinafter provided, for the purpose of ascertaining whether said articles, or any of them, or any part thereof, are in a cleanly condition and free from vermin and any matter of an infectious and contagious nature; and every person so occupying or having control of any workshop as aforesaid, shall within fourteen days from the taking effect of this act, or from the time of beginning of work in any workshop as aforesaid, notify the board of health of the location of such workshop, the nature of the work there carried on, and the number of persons therein employed.

Infectious diseases, etc.

SEC. 22. If the board of health of any city or said State inspector finds evidence of infectious or contagious diseases present in any workshop, or in goods manufactured, or in process of manufacture therein, and if said board or inspector shall find said shop in an unhealthy condition, or the clothing and materials used therein to be unfit for use, said board or inspector shall issue such order or orders as the public health may require, and the board of health are hereby enjoined to condemn and destroy all such infectious and contagious articles.

Importation of sweatshop manufactures.

SEC. 23. Whenever it shall be reported to said inspector or to the board of health, or either of them, that coats, vests, trousers, knee pants, overalls, cloaks, shirts, ladies' waists, purses, feathers, artificial flowers or cigars are being transported to this State, having been previously manufactured in whole or part under unhealthy conditions, said inspector shall examine said goods and the condition of their manufacture, and if upon such examination said goods, or any of them, are found to contain vermin, or to have been [made] in improper places or under unhealthy conditions, he shall make report thereof to the board of health, or inspector, which board or inspector shall thereupon make such order or orders as the public health shall require, and the board of health are hereby empowered to condemn and destroy all such articles.

List of names, etc.

SEC. 26. Every person, firm or corporation, agent or manager of a corporation employing any female in any manufacturing establishment, factory or workshop, shall post and keep posted, in a conspicuous place in every room where such help is employed, a printed notice stating the hours for each day of the week between which work is required of such persons, and in every room where children under sixteen years of age are employed a list of their names, ages and place of residence.

Definitions.

SEC. 27. The words "manufacturing establishment," "factory" or "workshop," wherever used in this act, shall be construed to mean any place where goods or products are manufactured or repaired, cleaned, or sorted, in whole, or in part, for sale, or for wages. Whenever any house, room or place is used for the purpose of carrying on any process of making, altering, repairing or finishing for sale, or for wages any coats, vests, trousers, knee-pants, overalls, cloaks, shirts, ladies' waists, purses, feathers, artificial flowers or cigars, or any wearing apparel of any kind whatsoever, intended for sale, it shall within the meaning of this act be deemed a workshop for the purposes of inspection. And it shall be the duty of every person, firm or corporation to keep a complete list of all such workshops in his, their or its employ, and such list shall be produced for inspection on demand by the board of health or any of the officers thereof, or by the State inspector, assistant inspector, or any of the deputies appointed under this act.

SEC. 28. Any person, firm or corporation who fails to comply with any provision of this act shall be deemed guilty of a misdemeanor and on conviction thereof shall be fined not less than three dollars, nor more than one hundred dollars for each offense. *Violations.*

SEC. 29 (as amended by act, page 326, Acts of 1911). 1. There is hereby created and established a separate and distinct department of the State government to be known as the "Illinois Department of Factory Inspection." *Department of factory inspection.*

2. The governor shall, upon the taking effect of this act, appoint a chief State factory inspector, whose duty it shall be to exercise general supervision over the department of factory inspection and all of its inspectors, and secure the enforcement of all laws now in force or hereafter enacted relating to the inspection of factories, mercantile establishments, mills, workshops and commercial institutions in this State, and to perform such other duties as are now or may hereafter be prescribed by law to be performed by the factory inspector. The salary of such chief State factory inspector shall be three thousand dollars ($3,000.00) per annum and his term of office shall be four (4) years. *Chief inspector.*

The governor shall appoint, upon the taking effect of this act, an assistant chief factory inspector at a salary of two thousand two hundred and fifty [dollars] ($2,250.00) per annum; one physician at a salary of fifteen hundred dollars ($1,500.00) per annum; and thirty (30) deputy factory inspectors, who shall receive a salary of twelve hundred dollars ($1,200.00) per annum, and an attorney for said department at a salary of fifteen hundred dollars ($1,500.00) per annum. *Assistants.*

The duties of the assistant chief factory inspector, medical, expert and deputy inspectors, as herein provided, shall be the same as those now or hereafter imposed by law upon the chief State factory inspector and the assistant chief factory inspector and the deputy factory inspectors, and they shall be subject to the supervision and direction of the chief State factory inspector in the discharge of such duties. Said chief State factory inspector and the other inspectors provided for herein shall visit and inspect, at all reasonable hours, as often as practicable, the factories, mercantile establishments, mills, workshops and commercial institutions in this State, where goods, wares and merchandise are manufactured, stored, purchased or sold at wholesale or retail. *Duties.*

And the chief State factory inspector shall report in writing to the governor on the thirtieth (30th) day of June annually, the result of his inspections and investigations, together with such other information and recommendations as he may deem proper. And said inspectors shall make a special investigation into the conditions of labor in this State, or into any alleged abuses in connection therewith, whenever the governor shall direct, and report the results of the same to the governor.

It shall be the duty of the said inspectors to enforce the provisions of this act, and perform such other duties as now are or shall hereafter be prescribed by law, and to prosecute all violations of law relating to the inspection of factories, mercantile establishments, mills, workshops and commercial institutions in this State before any magistrate or in any court of competent jurisdiction in this State.

And it shall be the duty of the State's attorney of the proper county, upon request of the chief State factory inspector or his deputies, to prosecute any violation of law which it is made the duty of the factory inspectors to enforce. And it shall be the duty of the attorney for such department to prosecute, when requested by the chief State factory inspector, any infractions or violations of law which is now or may be hereafter made the duty of the factory inspector to enforce.

Districts.

Said chief factory inspector shall, by written order filed with the governor, divide the State into inspection districts, due regard being had to the number of establishments and the amount of work required to be performed in each district. And he shall assign to each district a deputy inspector who shall have charge of the inspection in the district to which he is assigned, under the supervision of the chief State factory inspector. The chief State factory inspector may at any time, when in his discretion the good of the service requires, change a deputy inspector from one district to another, or reassign the districts of the State among the several deputy inspectors under his charge. He may at any time, when the conditions are changed, or in his discretion the good of the service requires, by a like order filed with the governor, redivide the State into inspection districts, changing the territory embraced within the several districts as to him may seem advisable.

CHAPTER 48.—*Factories and workshops—Use of blowers upon metal-polishing machinery.*

Blowers for emery wheels, etc.

SECTION 43. All persons, companies or corporations operating any factory or workshop, where emery wheels or emery belts of any description are used, either solid emery, leather, leather covered, felt, canvas, linen, paper, cotton, or wheels or belts rolled or coated with emery or corundum, or cotton wheels used as buffs, shall provide the same with blowers, or similar apparatus, which shall be placed over, besides or under such wheels or belts in such a manner as to protect the person or persons using the same from the particles of the dust produced and caused thereby, and to carry away the dust arising from or thrown off by such wheels or belts while in operation, directly to the outside of the building, or to some receptable [receptacle] placed so as to receive and confine

Provisos.

such dust: *Provided*, That grinding machines upon which water is used at the point of the grinding contact shall be exempt from the provisions of this act: *And provided*, This act shall not apply to small shops employing not more than one man in such work.

Hoods or hoppers.

SEC. 44. It shall be the duty of any person, company or corporation operating any such factory or workshop to provide or construct such appliances, apparatus, machinery or other things necessary to carry out the purpose of this act, as set forth in the preceding section, as follows: Each and every such wheel shall be fitted with a sheet of [or] cast-iron hood or hopper of such form and so applied to such wheel or wheels that the dust or refuse therefrom will fall from such wheels, or will be thrown into such hood or hopper by centrifugal force and be carried off by the current of air into a suction pipe attached to same [said] hood or hopper.

Suction pipes.

SEC. 45. Each and every such wheel six inches or less in diameter shall be provided with a three-inch suction pipe; wheels six inches to twenty-four inches in diameter with four-inch such suction pipe; wheels from twenty-four inches to thirty-six inches in diameter with five-inch suction pipe; and all wheels larger in diameter than those stated above shall be provided each with a suction pipe, not less than six inches in diameter. The suction pipe from each wheel, so specified, must be full size to the main trunk suction pipe, and the main suction pipe to which smaller pipes are attached, shall, in its diameter and capacity, be equal to the combined area of such smaller pipes attached to the same, and the discharge pipe from the exhaust fan, connected with such suction pipe or pipes, shall be as large or larger than the suction pipe.

SEC. 46. It shall be the duty of any person, company or corporation operating any such factory or workshop to provide the necessary fans or blowers to be connected with such pipe or pipes, as above set forth, which shall be run at a rate of speed as will produce a velocity of air in such suction or discharge pipes of at least nine thousand feet per minute to an equivalent suction of [or] pressure of air equal to raising a column of water not less than five inches in a U-shaped tube. All branch pipes must enter the main trunk pipe at an angle of forty-five degrees or less, the main suction or trunk pipe shall be below the emery or buffing wheels, and as close to the same as possible, and to be either upon the floor or beneath the floor on which the machines are placed to which such wheels are attached. All bends, turns or elbows in such pipes must be made with easy, smooth surfaces, having a radius in the throat of not less than two diameters of the pipe on which they are connected. Fans. etc.

SEC. 47. It shall be the duty of any factory inspector, sheriff, constable or prosecuting attorney of any county in this State in which any such factory or workshop is situated, upon receiving notice in writing signed by any person having knowledge of such facts, accompanied by the sum of one dollar as compensation for his services, that such factory or workshop is not provided with such appliances as herein provided for, to visit any such factory or workshop and inspect the same, and for such purpose, they are hereby authorized to enter any factory or workshop in this State during working hours, and upon ascertaining the facts that the proprietors or managers of such factory or workshops have failed to comply with the provisions of this act to make complaint of the same in writing before a justice of the peace or police magistrate having jurisdiction, who shall thereupon issue his warrant, directed to the owner, manager or director, in such factory or workshop, who shall be thereupon proceeded against for the violation of this act and [as] hereinafter mentioned, and it is made the duty of the prosecuting attorney to prosecute all cases under this act. Investigation of complaints.

SEC. 48. Any such person or persons or company, or managers, or directors of any such company or corporation who shall have the charge or management of such factory or workshop, who shall fail to comply with the provisions of this act, shall be deemed guilty of a misdemeanor and upon conviction thereof before any court of competent jurisdiction shall be punished by a fine of not less than twenty-five dollars, and not exceeding one hundred dollars. Penalty.

CHAPTER 55a.—*Fire escapes on factories, etc.*

SECTION. 1. * * * all buildings in this State which are four or more stories in height, excepting such as are used for private residences exclusively, but including flats and apartment buildings, shall be provided with one or more metallic ladder or stair fire escapes attached to the outer walls thereof and extending from, or suitably near the ground, to the uppermost story thereof, and provided with platforms of such forms and dimensions, and in such proximity to one or more windows of each story above the first, as to render access to such ladder or stairs from each such story easy and safe; the number, location, material and construction of such escapes to be subject to the approval of the board of supervisors in counties under township organization, and a board of county commissioners in counties not under township organization, except in villages, towns and cities organized under any general or special law of this State, such approval shall be had by the corporate authorities of such villages, towns and cities: *Provided, however,* That all buildings more than two stories in height, used for manufacturing purposes or for hotels, dormitories, schools, seminaries, hospitals or asylums, shall have at least one Fire escapes on certain buildings.

such fire escape for every fifty (50) persons for which working, sleeping or living accommodations are provided above the second stories of said buildings; * * *

New buildings. Sec. 2. All buildings of the number of stories and used for the purposes set forth in section one (1) of this act, which shall be hereafter erected within this State, shall upon or before their completion each be provided with fire escapes of the kind and number, and in the manner set forth in said section 1 of this act.

Enforcement. Sec. 3. The boards of supervisors and commissioners, and in villages, towns and cities, the corporate authorities thereof, as aforesaid, shall direct the sheriff of their respective counties to serve a written notice in behalf of the people of the State of Illinois, upon the owner or owners, trustees, lessee or occupant of any building within their county, not provided with fire escapes in accordance with the requirements of this act commanding such owners, trustees, lessee or occupant, or either of them, to place or cause to be placed upon such building such fire escape or escapes within thirty (30) days after the service of such notice. And the grand juries of the several counties of this State may also, during any term, visit or hear testimony relating to any building or buildings within their respective counties, for the purpose of ascertaining whether it or they are provided with fire escapes in accordance with the requirements of this act, and submit the result of their inquiry, together with any recommendations they may desire to make, to the circuit court, except in Cook County, and to the criminal court of Cook County, and said court may thereupon, if it find from the report of said grand jury that said building or buildings is [not] or are not provided with a fire escape or escapes in accordance with this act, cause the sheriff to serve a notice or notices upon the owner, trustees, lessee or occupant of such building or buildings.

Penalty. Sec. 4. Any such owner or owners, trustees, lessee or occupant, or either of them, so served with notice as aforesaid, who shall not within thirty (30) days after the service of such notice upon him or them, place or cause to be placed such fire escape or escapes upon such building as required by this act and the terms of such notice, shall be subject to a fine of not less than twenty-five (25) nor more than two hundred (200) dollars, and, to a further fine of fifty (50) dollars for each additional week of neglect to comply with such notice.

Complaints. Sec. 6. Any person may at any time make complaint in writing to the board of supervisors or commissioners or corporate authorities whose duty it is hereunder to enforce this law, that such escape or escapes are needed or are unsafe or insufficient, and it shall be the duty of such board of supervisors or commissioners or corporate authorities to at once inspect such building and escape or escapes and cause the sheriff to notify the owner, occupant or party in control, to immediately take such steps as to overcome the cause of complaint, and any officer, officers or persons failing to comply with this act, upon such complaint being made, shall be fined upon conviction, for each offense, not less than five dollars nor more than one hundred dollars, in any court of competent jurisdiction.

Negligence of officers.

ACTS OF 1907.

Inspection of factories—Butterine and ice cream factories.

(Page 309.)

Sanitation. Section 1. All buildings or rooms occupied by butterine and ice cream manufacturers shall be drained and plumbed in a manner conducive to the proper and healthful sanitary condition thereof, and shall be constructed with air shafts, windows and ventilating pipes sufficient to insure ventilation. The factory inspector shall direct the proper drainage, plumbing and ventilation of such rooms or buildings. No cellar or basement now used for the manufacture of butterine or ice cream shall be so occupied or used unless the proprietor shall comply with the sanitary provisions of this act.

SEC. 2. Every room used for the manufacture of butterine and ice cream shall be at least eight feet in height, and shall have, if deemed necessary by the factory inspector, an impermeable floor, constructed of cement, or of tiles laid in cement, or an additional flooring of wood, properly saturated with linseed oil. The side walls of such room shall be plastered and wainscoted. The factory inspector may require the side walls and ceiling to be white-washed at least once in three months. He may also require the woodwork of such walls to be painted. The furniture and utensils shall be so arranged as to be readily cleansed, and not prevent the proper cleaning of any part of the room. The manufactured butterine and ice cream shall be kept in dry and airy rooms, so arranged that the floors, shelves and all other facilities for storing the same can be properly cleaned. No domestic animal shall be allowed to remain in a room where butterine or ice cream is manufactured or stored, and no water closets or ash pit shall be within or connected with the rooms used in the manufacture of butterine or ice cream. *Construction.* *Storage, etc.*

SEC. 3. The State factory inspector shall cause such manufactories to be inspected. If it be found, upon such inspection, that the manufactories so inspected are constructed and conducted in compliance with the provisions of this act, the factory inspector shall issue a certificate to the persons owning or conducting such manufactories. *Inspection.*

SEC. 4. If, in the opinion of the State factory inspector, alterations are required in or upon premises occupied and used as butterine and ice cream manufactories, in order to comply with the provisions of this act, a written notice shall be served by him upon the owner, agent or lessee of such premises, either personally or by mail, requiring such alterations to be made within sixty days after such service, and such alterations shall be made accordingly. *Alterations.*

SEC. 5. Any person who violates any of the provisions of this act, or refuses to comply with any of the requirements as provided herein, of the factory inspector or his deputy, who are hereby charged with the enforcement of this act, shall be guilty of a misdemeanor, and, on conviction shall be punished by a fine of not less than fifty dollars ($50) nor more than two hundred dollars ($200), nor more than five hundred dollars ($500) for the second offense, or imprisonment for not more than thirty days, and for a third offense by a fine of not less than five hundred dollars ($500) nor more than sixty (60) days imprisonment, or both. *Violations.*

ACTS OF 1909.

Inspection of factories and workshops.

(Page 202.)

SECTION 1. All power driven machinery, including all saws, planers, wood shapers, jointers, sandpaper machines, iron mangles, emery wheels, ovens, furnaces, forges and rollers of metal; all projecting set screws on moving parts; all drums, cogs, gearing, belting, shafting, tables, fly wheels, flying shuttles and hydro-extractors; all laundry machinery, mill gearing and machinery of every description; all systems of electrical wiring or transmission; all dynamos and other electrical apparatus and appliances; all vats or pans, and all receptacles containing molten metal or hot or corrosive fluids in any factory, mercantile establishment, mill or workshop, shall be so located wherever possible, as not to be dangerous to employees or shall be properly enclosed, fenced or otherwise protected. All dangerous places in or about mercantile establishments, factories, mills or workshops, near to which any employee is obliged to pass, or to be employed shall, where practicable, be properly enclosed, fenced or otherwise guarded. No machine in any factory, mercantile establishment, mill or work- *Guards for dangerous machinery.*

shop, shall be used when the same is known to be dangerously defective, and no repairs shall be made to the active mechanism or operative part of any machine when the machine is in motion.

Removing guards. SEC. 2. No person shall remove or make ineffective any safeguard required by this act, during the active use or operation of the guarded machine or device, except for the purpose of immediately making repairs thereto, and all such safeguards so removed shall be promptly replaced.

Cut-offs. SEC. 3. In every factory, mercantile establishment, mill or workshop, effective means shall be provided for immediately disconnecting the power, so that in case of need or accident, any particular machine, group of machines, room or department, can be promptly and effectively shut down.

Pulleys. a. Where machines require to be started and stopped frequently, they shall, whenever practicable, be provided with tight and loose pulleys, clutch or other effective disengaging device. When provided with tight and loose pulleys, the shifting of the belt shall be accomplished by the use of a belt shifter, placed within easy reach of the operator. When a clutch, or other disengaging device is used, an effective means for throwing such device into or out of engagement shall be provided, and shall be placed within easy reach of the operator.

Switches. b. Where machines are direct connected with the prime mover, (electric motor, steam, gas or gasoline engine, or other source of power), a switch, throttle, or other power controlling device shall be furnished and shall be placed within easy reach of the operator, or his coworker.

Same. c. Where machines are arranged in groups, rooms or departments, and power is supplied by a prime mover, located within the confines of such group, room or department, a switch, throttle, or other power controlling device shall be furnished, and shall be placed within easy reach of the operators affected, so that all shafting, transmitting machinery and machines of such group, room or department, can be simultaneously shut down.

Friction clutches. d. Where machines are arranged in groups, rooms or departments, and are supplied by power through the use of main or line shafts, receiving power from some prime mover, located without the group, room or department, the power receiving wheel of such main or line shaft, shall, wherever possible, be provided with a friction clutch, or other effective power disengaging device, with suitable means for operating the clutch, or power disengaging device, and these means shall be placed within the confines of such group, room or department, and within easy reach of the employees or operatives affected, so that all machines, shafting and other transmission machinery within such group, room or department, can be simultaneously shut down. In addition to such safeguard, communication, consisting of speaking tubes, electric bells, electric colored lights, or other approved and ffective means, shall be provided in all cases covered by this paragraph between each such group, room or department, and the room in which the engineer, or prime mover, is located, so that in case of need or accident, the motive power of such group, room or department can be promptly stopped or controlled.

Hoistways, etc., to be guarded. SEC. 4. All hoistways, hatchways, elevator wells and wheel holes in factories, mercantile establishments, mills or workshops, shall be securely fenced, inclosed or otherwise safely protected, and due diligence shall be used to keep all such means of protection closed, except when it is necessary to have the same open, in order that the said hatchways, elevators or hoisting apparatus may be used. All elevator cabs or cars, whether used for freight or passengers, shall be provided with some device, whereby the car or cab may be held in the event of accident to the shipper rope or hoisting machinery or controlling apparatus.

Defects to be remedied. SEC. 5. If any elevator, machine, electrical apparatus or system of wiring, or any part or parts thereof, in any factory, mercantile establishment, mill or workshop, are in an unsafe condition, or are not properly guarded, where reasonable to guard the same, the owner or lessee, or his agent, superintendent or other person in charge thereof, shall, upon notice from the chief State factory inspector, or the assistant chief State factory inspector, remedy such unsafe condition within a reasonable time after receiving such notice.

SEC. 6. No employee of any factory, mercantile establishment, mill or workshop, shall operate or tamper with any machine or appliance with which such employee is not familiar and which is in no way connected with the regular and reasonable necessary duties of his employment, unless it be by and with the direct or reasonably implied command, request, or direction of the master or representative or agent. *Unskilled employees.*

SEC. 7. The traversing carriage of any self-acting machine must not be allowed to run out within a distance of eighteen (18) inches from any fixed structure, not being part of the machine, if the space over which it runs out is a space through which any employee is liable to pass, whether in the course of his employment or otherwise. *Traversing machinery.*

SEC. 8. No employee shall take or be allowed to take food into any room or apartment in any factory, mercantile establishment, mill or workshop, where white lead, arsenic or other poisonous substances or injurious or noxious fumes, dusts or gases under harmful conditions are present, as the result of the business conducted by such factories, mercantile establishments, mills or workshops, and notice to this effect shall be posted in each room or apartment. Employees shall not remain in any such room or apartment during the time allowed for meals, and suitable provision shall be made and maintained by the employer, when practicable, for enabling the employees to take their meals elsewhere in such establishments: *Provided, however,* That this section shall not apply to such employees whose presence during meal hours may be necessary for the proper conduct of such business. *Food not to be taken into certain factories.*

SEC. 9. Every person, firm or corporation employing females in any factory, mercantile establishment, mill or workshop in this State, shall provide a reasonable number of suitable seats for the use of such female employee[s], and shall permit the use of such seats by them when they are not necessarily engaged in the active duties for which they are employed, and shall permit the use of such seats at all times when such use would not actually and necessarily interfere with the proper discharge of the duties of such employees, and where practicable, such seats shall be made a permanent fixture and may be so constructed or adjusted that when said seats are not in use, they will not obstruct such female employee, when engaged in the performance of her duties. *Seats for females.*

SEC. 10. In every factory, mercantile establishment, mill or workshop, where one or more persons are employed, adequate measures shall be taken for securing and maintaining a reasonable, and as far as possible, equable temperature, consistent with the reasonable requirements of the manufacturing process. No unnecessary humidity which would jeopardize the health of employees shall be permitted. *Temperature, etc., of workrooms.*

SEC. 11. In every room or apartment of any factory, mercantile establishment, mill or workshop, where one or more persons are employed, at least 500 cubic feet of air space shall be provided for each and every person employed therein, and fresh air, to the amount specified in this act, shall be supplied in such a manner as not to create injurious drafts, nor cause the temperature of any such room or apartment to fall materially below the average temperature maintained: *Provided,* Where lights are used which do not consume oxygen, 250 cubic feet of air space shall be deemed sufficient. All rooms or apartments of any factory, mercantile establishment, mill or workshop, having at least 2,000 cubic feet of air space for each and every person employed in each room or apartment, and having outside windows and doors whose area is at least one-eighth of the total floor area, shall not *Air space and ventilation.*

be required to have artificial means of ventilation; but all such rooms or apartments shall be properly aired before beginning work for the day and during the meal hours. All such rooms, or apartments, having less than 2,000 cubic feet of air space, but more than 500 cubic feet of air space, for each and every person employed therein, and which have outside windows, and doors whose area is at least one-eighth of the floor area, shall be provided with artificial means of ventilation, which shall be in operation when the outside temperature requires the windows to be kept closed, and which shall supply during each working hour at least 1,500 cubic feet of fresh air for each and every person employed therein. All such rooms or apartments, having less than 500 cubic feet of air space for each and every person employed therein, all rooms or apartments having no outside windows or doors, and all rooms or apartments having less than 2,000 cubic feet of air space for each and every person employed therein, and in which the outside window and door area is less than one-eighth of the floor area, shall be provided with artificial means of ventilation, which will supply during each working hour throughout the year, at least 1,800 cubic feet of fresh air for each and every person employed therein: *Provided*, That the provisions of the preceding portions of this section shall not apply to storage rooms or vaults: *And provided further*, That the preceding portions of this section shall not apply to those rooms or apartments in which manufacturing processes are carried on which from their peculiar nature would be materially interfered with by the provisions of this section. No part of the fresh air supply required by this section shall be taken from any cellar or basement.

The following terms of this section shall be interpreted to mean: The air space available for each person is the total interior volume of a room, expressed in cubic feet, without any deductions for machinery contained therein, divided by the average number of persons employed therein.

Outside windows and doors are those connecting directly with the outside air; the window and door area is the total area of the windows and doors of all outside openings; and the floor area is the total floor area of each room.

Ventilation.

SEC. 12. All factories, mercantile establishments, mills or workshops shall be kept free from gas or effluvia arising from any sewer, drain, privy or other nuisance on the premises. All poisonous or noxious fumes or gases arising from any process, and all dust of a character injurious to the health of the persons employed, which is created in the course of a manufacturing process, within such factory, mill or workshop, shall be removed, as far as practicable, by either ventilating or exhaust devices.

Rooms to be cleaned daily.

SEC. 13. All decomposed, fetid or putrescent matter, and all refuse, waste and sweepings of any factory, mercantile establishment, mill or workshop, shall be removed and disposed of, at least once each day, and in such a manner as not to cause a nuisance; and all cleaning shall be done, as far as possible, outside of working hours; but if done during working hours, shall be done in such a manner as to avoid the unnecessary raising of dust or noxious odors. In every factory, mill or workshop, in which any process is carried on which makes the floors wet, the floor shall be constructed and maintained with due regard to the health of employees, and gratings or dry standing rooms shall be provided if practicable, at points where employees are regularly stationed, and adequate means shall be provided for drainage, and for preventing seepage or leakage to the floors below.

Fire escapes.

SEC. 14. In all factories, mercantile establishments, mills or workshops, sufficient and reasonable means of escape in case of fire shall be provided, by more than one means of egress, and such means of escape shall at all times be kept free from any obstruction and shall be kept in good repair and ready for use, and shall be plainly marked as such.

Doors.

SEC. 15. All doors used by employees as entrances to or exits from any factory, mercantile establishment, mill or workshop, of a height of two stories or over, shall open outward, slide or roll, and shall be so constructed as to be easily and immediately opened from within in case of fire or other emergency.

SEC. 16. Proper and substantial hand rails shall be provided on all stairways in factories, mercantile establishments, mills or workshops, and the treads on all stairways shall be so constructed as to furnish a firm and safe foothold. Stairways.

SEC. 17. In all factories, mercantile establishments, mills or workshops, a proper light shall be kept burning by the owner or lessee in all main passageways, main hallways, at all main stairs, main stair landings and shafts, and in front of all passenger or freight elevators, upon the entrance floors and upon the other floors, on every work day of the year, from the time that the building is opened for use until the time when the influx of natural light shall make artificial light unnecessary: *Provided,* That when two or more tenants occupy different floors in one building, such elevator shafts need be lighted only on the floors occupied and used by employees. Lights in hall-
ways, etc.

SEC. 18. No floor space or any workroom in any factory, mercantile establishment, mill or workshop, shall be so overloaded with machinery or other material as thereby to cause serious risk to or endanger the life or limb of any employee, nor shall there be permitted in any such establishment a load in excess of the safe sustaining power of the floors and walls thereof. Overloading
floors.

SEC. 19. In all factories, mercantile establishments, mills or workshops, machines must not be placed so closely together as to be a serious menace to those that have to pass between them. Passageways must be of ample [width] and head room and must be kept well lighted and free from obstructions. Passageways
between machin-
ery.

SEC. 20. Every factory, mercantile establishment, mill or workshop shall be provided with a sufficient number of water-closets, earth closets or privies, within reasonable access of the persons employed therein, and such water-closets, earth closets or privies shall be supplied in the proportion of at least one (1) to every thirty (30) male persons and one (1) to every twenty-five (25) female persons; and whenever both male and female persons are employed, said water-closets and privies shall be provided separate and apart for the use of each sex, and plainly marked by which sex they are to be used; and no person or persons shall be allowed to use the closets or privies assigned to the opposite sex; and such water-closets or privies shall be constructed in an approved manner and properly enclosed, and at all times kept in a clean and sanitary condition. The closets or privies, where practicable, shall be located so that they shall have direct ventilation with the outside air; where it is impracticable to locate the closet[s] or privies so as to have direct ventilation with the outside air, they shall be placed in an enclosure, and every such closet or privy, shall be properly and effectively disinfected and separately ventilated, and shall be properly lighted by artificial light, except when the influx of natural light makes artificial light unnecessary: *Provided,* That nothing in this section shall be construed to prevent any city, town or village, by appropriate ordinance or regulation, from prohibiting the construction, use or maintenance in such city, town or village, of any kind of earth closets, or privies, which may be considered a nuisance or detrimental to the public health. Water-closets.

SEC. 21. In all factories, mercantile establishments, mills or workshops, adequate washing facilities shall be provided for the employees, where necessary, and in such case in all factories, mills and workshops not less than one spigot, basin or receptacle shall be provided for each thirty (30) employees, and in mercantile establishments, not less than one spigot, basin or receptacle shall be provided for each fifty (50) employees. Where the labor performed by the employee is of such a character as to make customary or necessary a change of clothing by the employees, there shall be provided sanitary and suitable dressing room or rooms, and both such dressing rooms and washing facilities shall be sepa- Wash rooms.

rately maintained for each sex : *Provided,* That nothing in this act shall be construed as abrogating or repealing any provision of section 5 of an act entitled "An act to provide for the licensing of plumbers, and to supervise and inspect plumbing," approved June 10, 1897, and in force July 1, 1897, or the provisions of any local ordinance or regulation of any city, town or village, requiring approved and sufficient methods of sanitation, light, heat, drainage or ventilation of an equal or superior standard to that required in this act.

Duty of employers, etc. SEC. 22. It shall be the duty of every person, firm or corporation to which the provisions of this act may apply, to carry out the same, and make all the changes and additions necessary therefor, and in every way to comply with all the provisions of this act, and it shall be the duty of the owner of the building in which is located any such factory, mercantile establishment, mill or workshop, to permit any alterations or additions to such building as may be necessary to comply with the provisions of this act.

Changes to be made. SEC. 23. Whenever, by the provisions of this act, it is made the duty of any person, firm or corporation within this State, to make or install any alterations, additions or changes, the same shall be made and installed in conformity with the provisions of this act, and completed within a reasonable time after notification by the chief State factory inspector or his deputy.

Reports of accidents. SEC. 24. It shall be the duty of the owner or lessee, or superintendent or person in charge of any factory, mercantile establishment, mill or workshop in this State, to send to the chief State factory inspector, in writing, an immediate report of all accidents or injuries resulting in death. It shall also be the duty of the person in charge of such factory, mercantile establishment, mill or workshop, to report between the 15th and 25th of each month, all accidents or injuries occurring during the previous calendar month, which entailed a loss to the person injured of fifteen (15) consecutive days' time or more. All reports shall state the cause and character of the injury, character of employment and the age and sex of the person injured. No statement contained in any such report shall be admissible in evidence in any action arising out of the death or accident therein reported: *Provided,* That any such employer who shall make the reports of accidents, required by this act, shall not be required to make such reports to any other State officer, board or commission.

Enforcement. SEC. 25. It shall be the duty of the chief State factory inspector, and of the assistant chief State factory inspector, and deputy factory inspectors, under the direction and supervision of the chief State factory inspector, to enforce the provisions of this act, and to prosecute all violations of the same before any magistrate or any court of competent jurisdiction in this State, and for that purpose they and each of them are hereby empowered to visit and inspect, at all reasonable times, all such factories, mercantile establishments, mills and workshops in this State: *Provided,* That whenever any secret process is used in any factory, mercantile establishment, mill or workshop, the owner shall, whenever asked by the chief State factory inspector or the assistant chief State factory inspector, file with him an affidavit that the owner has in all respects complied with the provisions of this act, and such affidavit shall be accepted in lieu of inspection of any room or apartment in which such secret process is carried on.

Notices In enforcement of the provisions of this act, the chief State factory inspector, and the assistant chief State factory inspector, and the deputy factory inspectors, under the direction and supervision of the chief State factory inspector, shall give proper notice in regard to any violation of this act to the persons owning, operating or managing any such factory, mercantile establishment, mill or workshop. Such notice shall be written or printed and signed officially by the chief State factory inspector, or the assistant chief State factory inspector, and said notice may be served by delivering the same to the person upon whom service is to be had, or by leaving at his usual place of abode, or business, an exact copy thereof, or by sending a copy thereof to such person by mail.

When general changes relative to the location and spacing of machinery or to ventilation have been made and such changes comply with the provisions of this act, such arrangements, conditions remaining the same, shall not be disturbed by any requirement of the chief State factory inspector or his deputies within the period of twelve (12) months.

SEC. 26. Any person, firm or corporation who shall, or any agent, manager or superintendent of any person, firm or corporation, who, for himself or for such person, firm or corporation, shall violate any of the provisions of this act, or who omits or fails to comply with any of the foregoing requirements of this act, or who disregards any notice of the chief State factory inspector, or of the assistant chief State factory inspector, when said notice is given in accordance with the provisions of this act; or who obstructs or interferes with any examination or investigation being made by a State factory inspector, under this act, or any employee in any such factory, mercantile establishment, mill or workshop who shall remove or interfere with any guard or protective or sanitary device, required by the provisions of this act, except as hereinbefore provided, or who shall violate any of the other provisions of this act, shall be deemed guilty of a misdemeanor, and on conviction thereof, shall be punished for the first offense by a fine of not less than ten dollars ($10) nor more than fifty [dollars] ($50); and upon conviction of the second or subsequent offense, shall be fined not less than twenty-five [dollars] ($25) nor more than two hundred dollars ($200); and in each case shall stand committed until such fine and costs are paid unless otherwise discharged by due process of law. *Violations.*

SEC. 27. Whenever any inspection of machinery, ways, means, instruments or appliances in, on, about or connected with any factory, mill, mercantile establishment or workshop is required to be made by the ordinances of any city, town or village of a standard equal to that of this act and the inspection required by such ordinances has been made, then and in every such case such inspection shall be accepted by the chief State factory inspector, the assistant chief State factory inspector and the deputy factory inspectors as a compliance in that respect with the provisions of this act; and it shall be the duty of the person for whom such inspection has been made to furnish the chief State factory inspector, or his assistant or deputies, with a copy of the report of inspection made under such ordinances. *City ordinances.*

SEC. 28. The provisions of this act relating to sanitation and ventilation shall not be held to apply to such rooms or apartments of any factory, mercantile establishment, mill or workshop, which are being operated under the supervision of the Federal Government, by virtue of an act of Congress entitled, "An act making appropriations for the Department of Agriculture for the fiscal year ending June thirtieth, nineteen hundred and seven," approved June 30, 1906, or any amendment thereof; nor shall any other of the provisions of this act so apply respecting matters and conditions over which the Federal Government now exercises or shall hereafter exercise jurisdiction. *Establishments under Federal supervision.*

SEC. 29. The following terms used in this act shall have the following meaning: The term "factory" means any premises wherein electricity, steam, water or other mechanical power is used to move or work any machinery employed in preparing, manufacturing or finishing, or any process incident to the manufacturing of any article or part of any article; or the altering, repairing, ornamenting or the adapting for sale of any article. The term "mill or workshop" shall include any premises, room or apartment not being a factory as above defined, wherein any labor is exercised by way of trade or for the purpose of gain in or incidental to any process of making, altering, preparing, cleaning, repairing, ornamenting, finishing or adapting for sale any article or part of any article, and to which or over which building, premises, room or *Definitions.*

apartment, the employer of the person employed or working therein has the right of access or control : *Provided, however,* That a private house or private room in which manual or other labor is performed by a family dwelling therein, or by any of them for the exclusive use of the members of such family is not a factory, mill or workshop, within this definition. The term " mercantile establishment " shall include all concerns or places where goods, ware[s] or merchandise are purchased or sold, either at wholesale or retail.

Law to be printed. SEC. 30. Copies of this act shall be printed in English and such other languages as may be necessary to disseminate a general knowledge of the provisions herein set forth and shall be supplied by the chief State factory inspector on application.

Notice to be posted. SEC. 31. For the purpose of disseminating a general knowledge of the provisions of this act among employees, the chief State factory inspector shall have prepared a notice covering the salient features of this act, which may be in the following form :

NOTICE TO OWNERS AND EMPLOYEES OF MERCANTILE ESTABLISHMENTS, FACTORIES, MILLS AND WORKSHOPS.

This notice must be posted in a conspicuous place, in every office and workroom of this establishment. The object of this notice is to promote the health, comfort and safety of employees, and requires their attention and cooperation.

1. All machinery when in operation is dangerous, and should be considered so by the operator. It should be so protected as to offer the least possible chance for injury to those who operate it.

2. All machinery must be daily inspected by the operator, and upon discovery of any defects, notice of the same shall be given at once to anyone in authority, and the machine not used until repaired.

3. All set screws or other dangerous projections on revolving machinery shall be countersunk or otherwise guarded when possible.

4. Means shall be provided and placed within convenient reach for promptly stopping any machine, group of machines, shafting or other power transmitting machinery.

5. Machines must not be placed so closely together as to be a serious menace to those who have to pass between them. Passageways must be of ample width and head room, and must be kept well lighted and free from obstructions.

6. All hatchways, elevator wells or other openings in floors shall be properly enclosed or guarded.

7. The premises must be kept in a clean and sanitary condition.

8. Ample and separate toilet facilities for each sex shall be provided, and toilet rooms must be kept clean, well ventilated and well lighted.

9. Food must not be taken into any workroom where white lead, arsenic or other poisonous subtsances or gases are present under harmful conditions.

10. Proper and sufficient means of escape, in case of fire, shall be provided, and shall be kept free from obstructions.

11. Poisonous and noxious fumes or gases, and dust injurious to health, arising from any process, shall be removed, as far as practicable.

12. All employees are strictly prohibited from attempting to operate, experiment or tamper with machines or appliances with which they are not familiar and which are in no way connected with their regular duties. All employees are prohibited from jumping on or off moving cars, elevators, machines or appliances not under their immediate charge or control. All employees are prohibited from carrying to their place of work acids, chemicals or explosives of any kind which are liable to endanger life or property.

13. Reports must be sent to the office of the State factory inspector, as provided by law, and immediate notice of the death of

any employee resulting from accident or injuries must be sent to the same office.

The notice shall be printed on cardboard of suitable character, and the type used shall be such as to make it easily legible. In addition to English, this notice shall be printed in such other languages as may be necessary to make it intelligible to employees. Copies shall be supplied by the chief State factory inspector on application, and must be posted in a conspicuous place in every office and workroom of every establishment covered by the provisions of this act.

ACTS OF 1911.

Factory, etc., regulations—Gas safety appliances.

(Page 146.)

SECTION 1. It shall be the duty of the fire marshal or such other officer or officers as are or may be charged with the duty of fire protection in each town, village or city in the State of Illinois, to require the owner, agent or person in charge of each public building, factory, store, hotel, theater, tenement or other building, except private residences in each of said towns, villages or cities, in which gas is used for illuminating or heating or other purposes, to equip said building or buildings with an automatic gas cock, valve or appliance by means of which, in case of fire, accident or other necessity, the supply of gas may be shut off from said building or buildings, without requiring firemen or other persons to enter within said building or buildings for said purpose. *Buildings affected.* *Appliance required.*

SEC. 2. All such safety cocks, valves, or appliances, as herein provided for, shall be of such design and quality of workmanship as to be reasonably certain to perform the work required to be done thereby and shall be approved by, and installed under the supervision and control of the duly authorized officer or officers charged with the duty of fire protection in said town, village or city in which said gas cocks, valves or devices are required to be installed; and when thus installed in any building, shall continue to be and remain under their supervision and control: *Provided, however,* That in all cases where the total volume of gas led into any building or buildings is not more than the average volume delivered through a three-fourths inch pipe, then all such buildings shall be exempt from the requirements herein named, unless the conditions under which the gas is used are such as to endanger life or property to the same extent as the larger average volume carried by pipes of the next larger size, then in all such cases, at the discretion of said duly authorized officer or officers, all such buildings may be required to be equipped as provided for herein. *Standard for appliances.* *What buildings exempt.*

SEC. 3. From and after the time of taking effect of this act any owner, agent or person in control of any building or buildings within the requirements hereof, who shall fail, neglect or refuse to equip said building or buildings or to comply with the requirements set forth herein, shall be served with legal notice by the officer or officers duly charged with the fire protection of same to comply therewith within thirty days, and if at the expiration of the time specified in said notice said building or buildings are not equipped as provided for herein, then said owner, agent or person in control shall be guilty of a misdemeanor and upon conviction thereof shall be punished by a fine of not less than ten (10) nor more than fifty dollars ($50) for each offense. And upon such conviction [of] such owner, agent or person in control of any building or buildings, it shall be unlawful for any person, firm or corporation or company to supply gas to such building or buildings for a longer period of time than thirty (30) days next succeeding said conviction, until such building or buildings have been equipped as provided herein. *Violations.*

SEC. 4. When any such device is installed and approved, it shall be unlawful for any unauthorized persons to willfully disturb, de- *Injuring appliances.*

stroy, meddle or tamper with any such device in any way, and upon conviction thereof, shall be punished by a fine of not less than fifty dollars ($50) for each offense.

Factory regulations—Use of polishing wheels in basements, etc.

(Page 314.)

<table>
<tr><td>Employment in basements, etc., prohibited.</td><td>SECTION 1. No person shall be employed to operate any emery wheels or emery belts of any description, either leather, leather. covered, felt, canvas paper, cotton, or wheels or belts rolled or coated with emery, corundom [sic] or cotton, or wheels used as buffs, in any basement so-called, or in any room lying wholly or partly beneath the surface of the ground.</td></tr>
<tr><td>Violations.</td><td>SEC. 2. Any person, company, corporation or manager or director of any such company or corporation who shall fail to comply with the provisions of section (1) of this act shall be deemed guilty of a misdemeanor and upon conviction thereof, before any court of competent jurisdiction, shall be punished by a fine of not less than twenty-five (25) dollars and not more than two hundred dollars ($200).</td></tr>
</table>

Occupational diseases—Preventive regulations—Reports.

(Page 330.)

<table>
<tr><td>Preventive devices.</td><td>SECTION 1. Every employer of labor in this State, engaged in carrying on any work or process which may produce any illness or disease peculiar to the work or process carried on, or which subjects the employees to the danger of illness or disease incident to such work or process, to which employees are not ordinarily exposed in other lines of employment, shall, for the protection of all employees engaged in such work or process, adopt and provide reasonable and approved devices, means or methods for the prevention of such industrial or occupational diseases as are incident to such work or process.</td></tr>
<tr><td>Working clothing, etc., to be provided, when.</td><td>SEC. 2. Every employer in this State engaged in the carrying on of any process of manufacture or labor in which sugar of lead, white lead, lead chromate, litharge [litharge], red lead, arsenate of lead, or paris green are employed, used or handled, or the manufacture of brass or the smelting of lead or zinc, which processes and employments are hereby declared to be especially dangerous to the health of the employees engaged in any process of manufacture or labor in which poisonous chemicals, minerals or other substances are used or handled by the employees therein in harmful quantities or under harmful conditions, shall provide for and place at the diposal of the employees engaged in any such process or manufacture and shall maintain in good condition and without cost to the employees, proper working clothing to be kept and used exclusively for such employees while at work, and all employees therein shall be required at all times while they are at work to use and wear such clothing; and in all processes of manufacture or labor referred to in this section which are unnecessarily productive of noxious or poisonous dusts, adequate and approved respirators shall be furnished and maintained by the employer in good condition and without cost to the employees, and such employees shall use such respirators at all times while engaged in any work necessarily productive of noxious or poisonous dusts.</td></tr>
<tr><td>Medical examinations.</td><td>SEC. 3. Every employer engaged in carrying on any process or manufacture referred to in section 2 of this act, shall, as often as once every calendar month, cause all employees who come into direct contact with the poisonous agencies or injurious processes referred to in section 2 of this act, to be examined by a competent licensed physician for the purpose of ascertaining if there exists in any employee any industrial or occupational disease or illness, or any disease or illness due or incident to the character of the work in which the employee is engaged.</td></tr>
</table>

SEC. 4. It is hereby made the duty of any licensed physician Physicians to make reports. who shall make the physical examination of employees under the provisions óf section 3 of this act, to make an immediate report thereof to the State board of health of the State of Illinois upon blanks to be furnished by said board upon request, and if on such disease or illness is found, the physician shall so report, and if any such disease is found, the report shall state the name, address, sex and age of such employee and the name of such employer, and the nature of the disease or illness with which the employee is afflicted, and the probable extent and duration thereof, and the last place of employment: *Provided*, That the failure of any such physician to receive the blanks of the State board of health for the making of such report, shall not excuse such physician from making the report as herein provided.

SEC. 5. The secretary of the State board of health shall, imme- Reports to department of factory inspection. diately upon receipt of any report from any physician in accordance with the provisions of section 4 of this act, transmit a copy thereof to the Illinois Department of Factory Inspection.

SEC. 6. Every employer engaged in carrying on any process Dressing and wash rooms. or manufacture referred to in section 2 of this act, shall provide, separate and apart from the workshop in which such employees are engaged, a dressing room and lavatory for the use of such employees who are exposed to poisonous or injurious dusts, fumes and gases, and such lavatory shall be kept and maintained in a clean and wholesome manner and provided with a sufficient number of basins or spigots, with adequate washing facilities, including hot and cold water, clean towels and soap and shower bath, and the dressing rooms shall be furnished with clothes presses or compartments, so that the ordinary street clothes of such employees shall be kept separate and apart from their working clothes.

SEC. 7. No employee shall take or be allowed to take any food Taking food. or drink of any kind into any room or apartment in which any process or manufacture referred to in section 2 of this act is carried on, or in which poisonous substances or injurious or noxious fumes, dusts or gases are present as the result of such work or process being carried on in such room or apartment, and the employees shall not remain in any such room or apartment during the time allowed for meals, and suitable provision shall be made and maintained by the employer for enabling the employees to take their meals elsewhere in such place of employment, and a sufficient number of sanitary closed receptacles containing wholesome drinking water shall be provided and maintained for the use of the employees within reasonable access and without cost to them.

SEC. 8. All employers engaged in carrying on any process or Ventilation. manufacture referred to in section 2 of this act, shall provide and maintain adequate devices for carrying off all poisonous or injurious fumes from any furnaces which may be employed in any such process or manufacture, and shall also provide and maintain adequate facilities for carrying off all injurious dust, and the floors in any room or apartment where such work or process is carried on shall, so far as practicable, be kept and maintained in a smooth and hard condition, and no sweeping shall be permitted during working hours except where the floors in such workshop are dampened so as to prevent the raising of dust; and all ore, slag, dross and fume shall be kept in some room or apartment separate from the working rooms occupied by the employees, and where practicable, all mixing and weighing of such ore. slag, dross or fume shall be done in such separate room or apartment, and all such material shall, so far as practicable, be dampened before being handled or transported by employees.

SEC. 9. When any flues are used in any such process or manu- Cleaning flues, etc. facture referred to in section 2 of this act, and such flues are being cleaned out or emptied, the employer shall in every case provide and maintain a sufficient and adequate means or device, such as canvas bags or other practical device, or by dampening the dust, or some other sufficient method for catching and collecting the dust and preventing it from unreasonably fouling or polluting the air in which the employees are obliged to work, and, wherever practicable, the dust occasioned in any process or manufacture referred to in section 2 of this act, and any polishing or finishing therein, shall be dampened or wet down, and every reasonable precaution shall be adopted by the employer to prevent the unnecessary creation or raising of dust, and all floors shall be washed or scrubbed at least once every working-day; and such parts of the work or process as are especially dangerous to the employees, on account of poisonous fumes, dust and gases, shall, where practicable, be carried on in separate rooms and under cover of some suitable and sufficient device to remove the danger to the health of such employee, as far as may be reasonably consistent with the•manufacturing process, and the fixtures and tools employed in any such process of manufacture, shall be thoroughly washed and cleaned at reasonable intervals.

Hoods and fans. SEC. 10. All hoppers or chutes or similar devices used in the course of any process or manufacture referred to in section 2 of this act shall, where practicable, be provided with a hood or covering, and an adequate and sufficient apparatus or other proper **Receptacles.** device for the purpose of drawing away from the employees noxious, poisonous or injurious dusts, and preventing the employees from coming into unnecessary contact therewith; and all conveyances or receptacles used for the transportation about or the storage in any place where any such process or manufacture referred to in section 2 of this act is carried on, shall be properly covered or dampened in such way as to protect the health of the employees, and no refuse of a dangerous character incident to the work or process carried on in any such place shall be allowed to unnecessarily accumulate on the floors thereof.

Enforcement. SEC. 11. It shall be the duty of the State department of factory inspection to enforce the provisions of this act and to prosecute all violations of the same before any magistrate or any court of competent jurisdiction in this State, and for that purpose such department and its inspectors are empowered to visit and inspect at all reasonable times all places of employment covered by the provisions of this act. In the enforcement of the provisions hereof the department of factory inspection shall give proper notice in regard to any violation of this act to any employer of labor violating it, and directing the installment of any approved device, means or method reasonably necessary, in his judgment, to protect the health of the employees therein, and such notice shall be written or printed and shall be signed officially by the chief State factory inspector or the assistant chief State factory inspector, and said notice may be served by delivering the same to the person upon whom service is to be had, or by leaving at his usual place of abode or business an exact copy thereof, or by sending a copy thereof to such person by registered mail, and upon receipt of such notice calling the attention of the employer to such violation, he shall immediately comply with all the provisions of this act.

Inspectors may give orders. SEC. 12. If any occupational or industrial disease or illness or any disease or illness peculiar to the work or process carried on shall be found in any place of employment in this State by the inspectors of the State department of factory inspection, or called to their attention by the State board of health, which disease or illness shall be caused in whole or in part, in the opinion of the inspector, by a disregard by the employer of the provisions of this act, or a failure on the part of the employer to adopt reasonable appliances, devices, means or methods which are known to be reasonably adequate and sufficient to prevent the contraction or continuation of any such disease or illness, it shall be the duty of the department of factory inspection to immediately notify the employer in such place of employment, in the manner provided in section 12 of this act, to install adequate and approved appliances, devices, means or methods to prevent the contracting and continuance of any such disease or illness and to comply with all the provisions of this act.

SEC. 13. For the purpose of disseminating a general knowledge of the provisions of this act and of the dangers to the health of employees in any work or process covered by the provisions of this act, the employer shall post in a conspicuous place in every room or apartment in which any such work or process is carried on, appropriate notices of the known dangers to the health of any such employees arising from such work or process, and simple instructions as to any known means of avoiding, so far as possible, the injurious consequences thereof, and the chief State factory inspector shall, upon request, have prepared a notice covering the salient features of this act, and furnish a reasonable number of copies thereof to employers in this State, covered by the provisions of this act, which notice shall be posted by every such employer in a conspicuous place in every room or apartment in such place of employment. The notices required by this section shall be printed on cardboard of suitable character and the type used shall be such as to make them easily legible, and in addition to English they shall be printed in such other language or languages as may be necessary to make them intelligible to the employees. *Act to be posted.*

SEC. 14. Any person, firm or corporation who shall, personally or through any agent, violate any of the provisions of this act, or who omits or fails to comply with any of its requirements, or who obstructs or interferes with any examination or investigation being made by the State department of factory inspection in accordance with the provisions of this act, or any employee who shall violate any of the provisions of this act shall be deemed guilty of a misdemeanor and on conviction thereof shall be punished for the first offense by a fine of not less than ten dollars ($10) or more than one hundred dollars ($100), and upon conviction of the second or subsequent offenses, shall be fined not less than fifty dollars ($50) or more than two hundred dollars ($200), and in each case shall stand committed until such fine and costs are paid, unless otherwise discharged by due process of law. *Violations.*

SEC. 15. For any injury to the health of any employee proximately caused by any willful violation of this act or willful failure to comply with any of its provisions, a right of action shall accrue to the party whose health has been so injured, for any direct damages sustained thereby; and in case of the loss of life by reason of such willful violation or willful failure as aforesaid, a right of action shall accrue to the widow of such deceased person, his lineal heirs or adopted children, or to any other person or persons who were, before such loss of life, dependent for support upon such deceased person, for a like recovery of damages for the injury sustained by reason of such loss of life, not to exceed the sum of ten thousand dollars: *Provided,* That every such action for damages in case of death shall be commenced within one year after the death of such employee. *Damages.*

SEC. 16. The invalidity of any portion of this act shall not affect the validity of any other portion thereof which can be given effect without such invalid part. *Invalidity of part of act.*

Factory regulations—Bakeries, confectioneries, etc.

(Page 528.)

SECTION 1. Every building, room, basement, inclosure or premises, occupied, used or maintained as a bakery, confectionery, cannery, packing house, slaughterhouse, creamery, cheese factory, restaurant, hotel, grocery, meat market, or as a factory shop, warehouse, any public or place or manufacturing establishment used for the preparation, manufacture, packing, storage, sale or distribution of any food as defined by statute, which is intended for sale, shall be properly and adequately lighted, drained, plumbed and ventilated, and shall be conducted with strict regard *Sanitation.*

to the influence of such conditions upon the health of the operatives, employees, clerks, or other persons therein employed, and the purity and wholesomeness of the food therein produced, prepared, manufactured, packed, stored, sold or distributed.

Walls and ceilings.   SEC. 3. The side walls and ceilings of every bakery, confectionery, creamery, cheese factory, and hotel or restaurant kitchen shall be so constructed that they can be easily kept clean; and every building, room, basement or inclosure occupied or used for the preparation, manufacture, packing, storage, sale or distribution of food shall have an impermeable floor made of cement or tile laid in cement, brick, wood or other suitable material which can be flushed and washed clean with water.

Toilet rooms, etc.   SEC. 5. Every such building, room, basement, inclosure, or premises occupied, used or maintained for the production, preparation, manufacture, canning, packing, storage, sale or distribution of such food, shall have adequate and convenient toilet rooms, lavatory or lavatories. The toilet rooms shall be separate and apart from the room or rooms where the process of production, preparation, manufacture, packing, storing, canning, selling and distributing is conducted. The floors of such toilet rooms shall be of cement, tile, wood, brick or other nonabsorbent material, and shall be washed and scoured daily. Such toilet or toilets shall be furnished with separate ventilating flues and pipes discharging into soil pipes or shall be on the outside of and well removed from the building. Lavatories and wash rooms shall be adjacent to toilet rooms, or when the toilet is outside of the building the wash room shall be near the exit to the toilet and shall be supplied with soap, running water and towels and shall be maintained in a sanitary condition.

Violations.   SEC. 6. If any such building, room, basement, inclosure or premises occupied, used or maintained for the purposes aforesaid, or if the floors, side walls, ceilings, furniture, receptacles, implements, appliances or machinery of any such establishment, shall be constructed, kept, maintained, or permitted to remain in a condition contrary to any of the requirements or provisions of the preceding five (5) sections of this act, the same is hereby declared a nuisance, and any toilet, toilet room, lavatory or wash room as aforesaid, which shall be constructed, kept, maintained or permitted to remain in a condition contrary to the requirements or provisions of section five (5) of this act, is hereby declared a nuisance; and any car, truck, or vehicle used in the moving or transportation of any food product as aforesaid, which shall be kept or permitted to remain in an unclean, unhealthful or insanitary condition is hereby declared a nuisance. Whoever unlawfully maintains, or allows or permits to exist a nuisance as herein defined shall be guilty of a misdemeanor, and, on conviction thereof, shall be punished as herein provided.

Cuspidors.   SEC. 7. Every person, firm or corporation operating or maintaining an establishment or place where food is produced, prepared, manufactured, packed, stored, sold or distributed shall provide the necessary cuspidors for the use of the operatives, employees, clerks, and other persons, and each cuspidor shall be thoroughly emptied and washed out daily with water or a disinfectant solution, and five ounces thereof shall be left in each cuspidor while it is in use. Whoever fails to observe the provisions of this section shall be guilty of a misdemeanor, and punished as hereinafter provided.

Duties of employees.   SEC. 8. No operative, employee, or other persons shall expectorate on the food or on the utensils or on the floors or side walls of any building, room, basement or cellar where the production, preparation, manufacture, packing, storing or sale of any such food is conducted. Operatives, employees, clerks, and all other persons who handle the material from which such food is prepared or the finished product, before beginning work, or after visiting toilet or toilets, shall wash their hands thoroughly in clean water. Whoever fails to observe or violates the provisions of this section shall be guilty of a misdemeanor and punished by a fine of not more than twenty-five dollars.

SEC. 9. It shall be unlawful for any person to sleep, or to allow **Sleeping in workrooms, etc.** or permit any person to sleep in any work room of a bake shop, kitchen, dining room, confectionery, creamery, cheese factory, or any place where food is prepared for sale, served or sold, unless all foods therein handled are at all times in hermetically sealed packages.

SEC. 10. It shall be unlawful for any employer to require, suffer **Contagious or infectious diseases.** or permit any person who is affected with any contagious or venereal disease to work, or for any person so affected to work in a building, room, basement, inclosure, premises or vehicle occupied or used for the production, preparation, manufacture, packing, storage, sale, distribution, or transportation of food.

SEC. 11. It shall be the duty of the State food commissioner **Enforcement.** and those appointed by him to enforce this act, and for that purpose the State food commissioner and his appointees shall have full power at all times to enter every such building, room, basement, inclosure or premises occupied or used or suspected of being occupied or used for the production, preparation or manufacture for sale, or the storage, sale, distribution or transportation of such food, to inspect the premises and all utensils, fixtures, furniture and machinery used as aforesaid ; * * *

INDIANA.

ANNOTATED STATUTES—REVISION OF 1901.

Factories and workshops—Inspection, etc.

SECTION 7087e. It shall be the duty of the owner or lessee of any **Safety appliances for elevators, etc.** manufacturing or mercantile establishment, laundry, renovating works, bakery or printing office, where there is an elevator, hoisting shaft or wellhole, to cause the same to be properly and substantially inclosed or secured, if in the opinion of the chief inspector it is necessary, to protect the lives or limbs of those employed in such establishment. It shall also be the duty of the owner, agent or lessee of each of such establishments to provide, or cause to be provided, if in the opinion of the chief inspector, the safety of persons in or about the premises should require it, such proper trap or automatic doors so fastened in or at all elevator ways as to form a substantial surface when closed, and so constructed as to open and close by the action of the elevator in its passage, either ascending or descending, but the requirements of this section shall not apply to passenger elevators that are closed on all sides. The chief inspector shall inspect the cables, gearing or other apparatus of elevators in the establishments above enumerated and require that the same be kept in safe condition with proper safety devices whereby the cabs or cars will be securely held in event of accident to the cable or rope or hoisting machinery, or from any similar cause.

SEC. 7087f. Proper and substantial handrails shall be provided **Handrails, etc., on stairways.** on all stairways in all establishments above enumerated, and where, in the opinion of the chief inspector it is necessary, the steps of said stairs in all such establishments shall be substantially covered with rubber, securely fastened thereon, for the better safety of persons employed in said establishments. The stairs shall be properly screened at the sides and bottom. All **Doors to open outwardly.** doors leading in or to such establishments aforesaid shall be so constructed as to open outwardly where practicable, and shall be neither locked, bolted nor fastened during working hours.

SEC. 7087g. In every manufacturing or other establishment, **Communication with engine room.** where the machinery used is propelled by steam, communication shall be provided between each room where such machinery is placed and the room where the engineer is stationed, by means of speaking tubes, electric bells or appliances that may control the motive power, or such other means as shall be satisfactory to the chief inspector : *Provided,* That in the opinion of the inspector such communication is necessary.

Accidents.   SEC. 7087h. It shall be the duty of the owner, agent, superintendent or other person having charge of any manufacturing or mercantile establishment, mine, quarry, laundry, renovating works, bakery or printing office within this State, or of any floor or part thereof, to report in writing to the chief inspector all accidents or injury done to any person in such premises within forty-eight hours of the time of the accident, stating as fully as possible the extent and cause of such injury, and the place where the injured person is sent, with such other information relative thereto as may be required by the chief inspector. The chief inspector is hereby authorized and empowered to fully investigate the causes of such accident, and to require such reasonable precautions to be taken as will, in his judgment, prevent the recurrence of similar accidents.

Guards, etc., for machinery.   SEC. 7087i. It shall be the duty of the owner of any aforesaid establishment, or his agent, superintendent or other person in charge of the same, to furnish and supply, or cause to be furnished and supplied therein, in the discretion of the chief inspector, where machinery is used, belt shifters or other safe mechanical contrivances for the purpose of throwing on or off belts or pulleys; and whenever possible, machinery therein shall be provided with loose pulleys; all vats, pans, saws, planers, cogs, gearing, belting, shafting, set screws and machinery of every description therein shall be properly guarded, and no person shall remove or make ineffective any safeguard around or attached to any planer, saw, belting, shafting or other machinery, or around any vat or pan, while the same is in use, unless for the purpose of immediately making repairs thereto, and all such safeguards shall be promptly replaced. By attaching thereto a notice to that effect, the use of any machinery may be prohibited by the chief inspector should such machinery be regarded as dangerous. Such notice must be signed by the chief inspector, and shall only be removed after the required safeguards are provided, and the unsafe or dangerous machine shall not be used in the meantime.

Exhaust fans.   Exhaust fans of sufficient power shall be provided for the purpose of carrying off dust from emery wheels and grindstones and dust-creating machinery from establishments where used. No person **Cleaning machinery in motion.** under sixteen years of age, and no female under eighteen years of age, shall be allowed to clean machinery while in motion.

Wash rooms, etc.   SEC. 7087j. A suitable and proper wash room and water-closets shall be provided by the owner, agent or lessee in each establishment above enumerated, and such water-closets shall be properly screened and ventilated and kept at all times in a clean condition, with not less than one seat for each twenty-five persons, and one seat for each fraction thereof above ten, employed in such establishment; and if women and girls are employed in any such establishment, the water-closets used by them shall have separate approaches and be separated and apart from those used by the men. All water-closets shall be kept free of obscene writing and marking. A dressing room shall be provided for women and girls, when required by the chief inspector, in any establishment aforesaid in which women and girls are employed; and the employer **Seats for female employees.** of such women and girls shall provide a suitable seat for the use of each female employee placed conveniently where she works, and shall permit the use of the same when she is not necessarily engaged in the active duties for which she is employed, and such seats shall be constructed or adjusted where practicable so as to be a fixture and not obstruct such female when actually engaged in the performance of such duties when such seat can not be used.

Time for noonday meal.   SEC. 1087k. Not less than sixty minutes shall be allowed for the noonday meal in any aforesaid establishment in this State. The chief inspector shall have the power to issue written permits in special cases, allowing shorter mealtime at noon, and such permit must be conspicuously posted in the main entrance of the establishment, and such permit may be revoked at any time the chief inspector deems necessary, and shall only be given where good cause can be shown.

SEC. 70871. The walls and ceilings of each room in every establishment aforesaid, shall be limewashed or painted, when in the opinion of the chief inspector it shall be conducive to the health or cleanliness of the persons working therein. *Walls to be limewashed, etc.*

SEC. 7087m. The chief inspector, or other competent person designated for such purpose by the chief inspector, shall inspect any building used as aforesaid, or anything attached thereto, located therein, or connected therewith which has been represented to be unsafe or dangerous to life or limb. If it appears upon such inspection that the building or anything attached thereto, located therein, or connected therewith, is unsafe or dangerous to life or limb, the chief inspector shall order the same to be removed or rendered safe and secure, and if such notification be not complied with within a reasonable time, he shall prosecute whoever may be responsible for such delinquency. *Inspection.*

SEC. 7087n. No room or rooms, apartment or apartments in any tenement or dwelling house shall be used for the manufacture of coats, vests, trousers, knee pants, overalls, cloaks, furs, fur trimmings, fur garments, shirts, purses, feathers, artificial flowers or cigars, for sale, excepting by the immediate members of the family living therein. No person, firm or corporation shall hire or employ any person to work in any one room or rooms, apartment or apartments, in any tenement or dwelling house, or building in the rear of a tenement or dwelling house at making, in whole or in part, any vests, coats, trousers, knee pants, fur, fur trimmings, shirts, purses, feathers, artificial flowers or cigars, for sale, without obtaining first a written permit from the chief inspector, which permit may be revoked at any time the health of the community, or of those employed therein, may require it, and which permit shall not be granted until an inspection of such premises is made by the chief inspector or a deputy inspector, and the maximum number of persons allowed to be employed therein shall be stated in such permit. Such permit shall be framed and posted in a conspicuous place in the room, or in any one of the rooms to which it relates. *Sweat shops.*

SEC. 7087o. No less than two hundred and fifty cubic feet of air space shall be allowed for each person in any workroom where persons are employed during the hours between six o'clock in the morning and six o'clock in the evening, and not less than four hundred cubic feet of air space shall be provided for each person in any workroom where persons are employed between six o'clock in the evening and six o'clock in the morning. By a written permit the chief inspector may allow persons to be employed in a room where there are less than four hundred cubic feet, but not less than two hundred and fifty cubic feet of air space for each person employed between six o'clock in the evening and six o'clock in the morning: *Provided,* Such room is lighted by electricity at all times during such hours while persons are employed therein. There shall be sufficient means of ventilation provided in each workroom of every manufacturing or mercantile establishment, laundry, renovating works, bakery or printing office within this State, and the chief inspector shall notify the owner in writing to provide, or cause to be provided, ample and proper means of ventilation for such workroom, and shall prosecute such owner, agent or lessee if such notification be not complied with within twenty days of the service of such notice. *Air space.* *Ventilation.*

SEC. 7087p. Proprietors, agents or managers of any manufacturing or mercantile establishment, mine or quarry, laundry, renovating works, bakery or printing office, are prohibited from discriminating against any person or persons, or class of labor seeking work, by posting notices or otherwise. *Discrimination in employment.*

SEC. 7087q. It shall be unlawful for notaries public and other officers to receive more than ten cents for the preparing and certifying to a "certificate of parent or guardian," provided for in this act. *Notaries' fees.*

SEC. 7087r. The language used in this act shall be interpreted to have the following meaning: The word "person" means any in- *Definitions.*

dividual, corporation, partnership, company, or association. The word "child" means a person under the age of fourteen years. The words "young person" means [mean] a person of the age of fourteen years and under the age of eighteen years. The word "woman" means a female of the age of eighteen years and upwards. The words "manufacturing or mercantile establishment, mine, quarry, laundry, renovating works, bakery or printing office" means [mean] any mill, factory, workshop, store, place of trade, or other establishment where goods, wares or merchandise are manufactured or offered for sale, or any mine or quarry where coal and stone are mined and quarried for the market, and persons are employed for hire.

Inspectors to be appointed. SEC. 7087s. For the purpose of carrying out the provisions of this act, a department of inspection is hereby created, and the governor shall by and with the advice and consent of the senate, appoint a chief inspector to have charge of said department. Said inspector shall hold and continue in office after the expiration of his term of office until his successor shall have been appointed and qualified. The term of office of the chief inspector

Salaries, etc. shall be for four years. The annual salary of such chief inspector shall be one thousand eight hundred dollars ($1,800) and actual expenses when absent from home in the discharge of his official duties. Said chief inspector shall, by and with the consent of the governor, appoint a sufficient number of deputies to enforce the provisions of this act, not to exceed five (5) one of which shall be a chief deputy inspector, whose salary shall be one thousand five hundred dollars ($1,500) per annum and actual expenses when absent from home in the discharge of his official duties. The salaries of such other deputies as may be appointed shall be one thousand dollars ($1,000). each per annum and actual expenses when absent from home in the discharge of their official duties. But said actual expenses for the department of inspection shall in no year exceed the sum of three thousand dollars ($3,000), and the duties of the deputy inspectors shall be such as shall be assigned them by the chief inspector. Said chief inspector shall also employ a stenographer at a salary not to exceed six hundred dollars ($600) per annum. The salary and actual expenses of said deputy inspectors and stenographer shall be paid monthly as due, on voucher duly attested before some officer authorized to administer oaths, and approved and signed by the chief inspector, and the salary and actual expenses of the chief inspector shall be paid in monthly installments, out of the treasury of the State, upon warrants of the auditor of state, and the total annual appropriations of ten thousand nine hundred dollars ($10,900) for such payments aforesaid, is hereby made out of any moneys in the State treasury not otherwise appropriated: *Provided*, That the auditor of state shall issue no warrant, except upon itemized bills, sworn to, and presented by the chief inspector provided for in this act.

Record, reports, etc. SEC. 7087u. The chief inspector shall keep a record of all inspections and examinations made by his department, and copies of all notices and orders made by him, and, at the close of his term of office, transfer the books containing the same to his successor. He shall make an annual report of his doings as such inspector to the governor at the close of each fiscal year, and cause the same to be printed, at the expense of the State, not later than the first day of January next ensuing, in such numbers as the governor may approve. Such inspector and deputy inspectors shall have power as notaries public to administer oaths and take affidavits in matters connected with the enforcement of the provisions of this act.

Duties SEC. 7087v. It shall be the duty of the chief inspector to cause this act to be enforced, and to cause all violators of the same to be prosecuted, and for that purpose he is empowered to visit and inspect at all reasonable hours, and as often as shall be practicable and necessary, all manufacturing or other establishments to which this bill relates. It shall be the duty of the chief inspector to examine into all violations of laws made for the benefit or protection of labor and to prosecute all violations thereof. It shall be unlawful for any person to interfere with, obstruct or hinder said chief inspector or deputy inspectors while in the performance of his or their duties, or to refuse to properly answer questions asked by him or them with reference to any of the provisions hereof.

SEC. 7087w. It shall be the duty of the chief inspector to supply all blanks necessary to make reports to his office, as required in this act, and be furnished [to furnish] copies of this act, which shall be conspicuously posted or hung, and kept posted or hung, in each workroom of every manufacturing or other establishment to which it relates, in the State, by the proprietor or occupant thereof. *Furnishing blanks, etc.*

SEC. 7087x. The prosecuting attorney of any county of this State is hereby required upon request of the chief inspector, or of any other person of full age, to commence and prosecute to a termination before any court of competent jurisdiction, in the name of the State, actions or proceedings against any person or persons reported to him to have violated the provisions of this act. *Prosecuting attorney.*

SEC. 7087y. Any person who violates or omits to comply with any of the provisions of this act, or who refuses to comply with the orders of the chief inspector, properly made under the provisions of this act, or who suffers or permits any young person or child to be employed in violation of its provisions, shall be deemed guilty of a misdemeanor, and on conviction shall be fined not more than fifty dollars for the first offense, and not more than one hundred dollars for the second offense, to which may be added imprisonment for not more than ten days, and for the third offense a fine of not less than two hundred and fifty dollars and not more than thirty days' imprisonment in the county jail. *Violations.*

SEC. 7087z. Any person, company, corporation or association aggrieved by any order of the chief inspector may appeal to the circuit court in the county where the person, firm or corporation owns, leases or occupies the factory or buildings in relation to which said order relates, within ten days after notice of such order shall have been given. Said appeal shall operate as a supersedeas, shall be made in writing, and contain a brief statement of the facts and reasons for such appeal and a citation for the chief inspector to appear before said court, and said court or any judge thereof may direct the time of appearance and manner of service. Said court may review the doings of the chief inspector, may examine the question in issue, and may confirm, change or set aside the doings of the chief inspector, in this particular case, and may make such orders in the premises, including orders as to costs, as it may find to be proper and equitable. *Appeals.*

SEC. 7087a1. In case of an appeal from any order of the chief inspector the prosecuting attorney of the circuit court shall appear as counsel for the State to sustain and defend such orders, and in case such order be sustained on such appeal, a fee of twenty-five dollars shall be taxed against the appellant as the prosecuting attorney's fee, which fee shall be taxed as costs in the case. *Counsel, fees, etc.*

ACTS OF 1903.

CHAPTER 246.—*Inspection of steam boilers.*

SECTION 1. It shall be the duty of every person, firm or corporation owning or using or causing to be used any steam boiler for generating steam to be applied to machinery in all industrial institutions subject to inspection by the department of inspection, shall [to] provide them with a full complement of gauge cocks, some visible means of indicating the water level, one steam gauge, one fusible plug properly inserted, one safety valve, all to be kept in good working order (the area of said valve, if known as a pop valve, shall be in the ratio of one square inch of area to three square feet of grate surface), a lever and ball safety valve *Equipment.*

in the ratio of one square inch of area to two square feet of grate surface: *Provided*, That fusible plugs shall be required only in boilers having crown sheets.

Inspection. SEC. 2. The owner, agent, manager, or lessee of any boiler or boilers described in section 1 of this act, of 10 or more horsepower, shall cause such boiler or boilers to be inspected, internally, once in six months by a practical boiler maker of not less than five years' experience; or a practical steam engineer who has had not less than ten years' experience with steam boilers carrying not less than seventy (70) pounds pressure per square inch; or by a boiler inspector of any company doing business under the laws of the State, who shall furnish to the owner, agent, or lessee of such boiler a certificate of inspection stating the kind and showing the condition of said boiler, the connections and maximum pressure to be carried by said boiler; such certificate to be retained in the office of said establishment and to be shown to the chief inspector of the department of inspection or his deputy when required.

Steam gauges. SEC. 3. Every boiler house in which a boiler, or nest, or battery of boilers is placed shall be provided with a steam gauge or gauges, properly connected with the boilers, and where the engine is in a separate room, or more than forty feet distant from the gauge or nearest boiler, shall have another gauge attached to the steam pipe, so the engineer can readily ascertain the pressure carried. The safety valves of steam boilers subject to inspection under this act shall be loaded to sustain only the maximum pressure allowed by said certificate of inspection.

Enforcement. SEC. 4. The prosecuting attorney of any county of this State is hereby required upon request of the chief inspector of the department of inspection, his deputy or any other person of full age, to commence and prosecute to a termination before any court of competent jurisdiction, in the name of the State, actions or proceedings against any person, firm or corporation reported to him to have violated the provisions of this act.

Penalty. SEC. 5. It shall be unlawful for any person, firm or corporation to knowingly operate any aforesaid boilers except as provided for in this act, and for the violation of section 1 or 3 a fine of not less than ten dollars ($10) nor more than twenty-five dollars ($25) shall be assessed for each offense. Each day such violation or violations continue shall constitute a separate offense. Any person, firm or corporation knowingly failing to comply with section 2 of this act, or any order issued by the department of inspection in accordance therewith, shall be fined not less than twenty-five dollars ($25) nor more than one hundred dollars ($100).

ACTS OF 1909.

CHAPTER 118.—*Fire escapes on factories, etc.*

Provisions required. SECTION 1. * * * Every building in which persons are employed above the second story in a factory, workshop, or mercantile or other establishment, * * * and every factory, workshop, mercantile or other establishment of more than two stories in height, shall be provided with proper ways of egress or means of escape from fire, sufficient for the use of all persons * * * employed, * * * in such buildings, and such ways of egress and means of escape shall be kept free from obstruction, in good repair and ready for use at all times, and all rooms above the second story in such building shall be provided with more than one way of egress or escape from fire, placed as near as practicable at opposite ends of the room and leading to fire escape [s] on the outside of such building or to stairways on the inside, provided with proper railings. All outside doors subject to the provisions of this section shall open outward, and all windows open outward or upward. * * * The certificate of the fire chief of the city where said building is located, certifying that the provisions of this act have been complied with, shall be prima facie evidence of a compliance with such requirements.

SEC. 2. In addition to the foregoing means of escape from fire, all such buildings as are enumerated in section 1 of this act as are more than two stories in height shall have one or more fire escapes on the outside of said building, as may be directed by the fire chief aforesaid, except in such cases as the said fire chief may deem such fire escape to be unnecessary in consequence of adequate provisions having been already made for the [sic] safety in event of fire, and in such cases of exemption the said fire chief shall give the owner, lessee or occupant of said building a written certificate to that effect and his reasons therefor, and such fire escapes as are provided for in this section shall be constructed according to specifications issued by [the] State department of inspection and accepted by the chief inspector, or approved by the fire chief, and shall be connected with each floor above the first, well fastened and secured by extending the bolts or fastenings entirely through the walls, and of sufficient strength, each of which fire escapes shall have landings or balconies guarded by iron railings not less than three feet in height and embracing one or more windows at each story and connecting with the interior by easily accessible and unobstructed openings; and all the balconies or landings shall be connected by iron stairs, placed at a slant of not more than forty-five degrees, protected by a well-secured handrail on both sides, with a sixteen-inch wide drop ladder from the lower platform, reaching to the ground; * * * iron stairs shall extend to a ground landing, and no telegraph, telephone, electric-light poles, trees or wire, signs or other obstructions shall interfere with the construction and use of any fire escape. *(margin: Fire escapes on certain buildings.)* *(margin: Construction)*

SEC. 3. Any other plan or style of fire escape shall be sufficient if approved by the chief inspector, but if not so approved the chief inspector may notify the owner, propietor or lessee of such establishment or of the building in which such establishment is conducted, or the agent or superintendent, * * * or either of them, in writing that any such plan or style of fire escape is not sufficient, and may by an order in writing, served in like manner, require one or more fire escapes as he shall deem necessary and sufficient to be provided for such establishment at such location, and [of] such plan and style as shall be specified in such written order. Within twenty days after the service of such order the number of fire escapes required in such order for such establishment shall be provided therefor, each of which shall be of the plan and style in accordance with the specifications in said order required. The windows or doors to each fire escape shall be of sufficient size and be located, as far as possible, consistent with accessibility from the stairways and elevators, hatchways or openings, and the ladder thereof shall extend to the roof. Stationary stairs or ladders shall be provided on the inside of such establishment from the upper story to the roof as a means of escape in case of fire. *(margin: Other types.)*

SEC. 7. It is hereby made the duty of the chief inspector or his deputies or their assistants in every city or town where there are fire companies, and every township trustee in townships where there are buildings coming under the provisions of this act and where there are no fire chiefs in said townships, to see that the provisions of this act are enforced, and for this purpose they or their assistants or deputies shall have free access at all hours to all buildings embraced herein. * * * *(margin: Enforcement.)*

SEC. 9. In all places where there is no fire chief the trustee of the township wherein any such buidings are situated, as in this act provided and described. shall do and perform all the duties otherwise required of said fire chiefs, and be subject to all penalties provided in this act. *(margin: Same.)*

CHAPTER 163—*Inspection of factories, etc.—Manufacture of food products.*

Sanitation.

SECTION 1. Every building, room, basement, or cellar occupied or used as a bakery, confectionery, cannery, packing house, slaughterhouse, dairy, creamery, cheese factory, restaurant, hotel, grocery, meat market or other place or apartment used for the preparation for sale, manufacture, packing, storage, sale or distribution of any food, shall be properly lighted, drained, plumped and ventilated and conducted with strict regard to the influence of such condition upon the health of the operatives, employees, clerks or other persons therein employed and the purity and wholesomeness of the food therein produced; and for the purpose of this act the term "food" as used herein, shall include all articles used for food, drink, confectionery or condiment, whether simple, mixed or compound and all substances or ingredients used in the preparation thereof.

Floors, furniture, etc., to be clean.

SEC. 2. The floors, sidewalks, ceilings, furniture, receptacles, implements and machinery of every establishment or place where food is manufactured, packed, stored, sold or distributed, and all cars, trucks and vehicles used in the transportation of food products, shall at no time be kept in an unclean, unhealthful or unsanitary condition, and for the purpose of this act, unclean, unhealthful or unsanitary conditions shall be deemed to exist if food in the process of manufacture, preparation, packing, storing, sale, distribution or transportation is not securely protected from flies, dust, dirt, and, as far as may be necessary, by all reasonable means from all other foreign or injurious contamination; and if the refuse, dirt and the waste products subject to decomposition and fermentation incident to the manufacture, preparation, packing, storing, selling, distributing and transporting of food, are not removed daily; and if all trucks, trays, boxes, baskets, buckets and other receptacles, chutes, platforms, racks, tables, shelves and all knives, saws, cleavers and other utensils and machinery used in moving, handling, cutting, chopping, mixing, canning and all other processes are not thoroughly cleaned daily, and if the clothing of operatives, employees, clerks or other persons therein employed is unclean.

Construction of rooms.

SEC. 3. The side walls and ceilings of every bakery, confectionery, creamery, cheese factory, hotel and restaurant kitchen, shall be well plastered, wainscoted or ceiled with metal or lumber and shall be oil painted or kept well limewashed, and all interior woodwork in every bakery, confectionery, creamery, cheese factory, hotel and restaurant kitchen, shall be kept well oiled or painted with oil paints and be kept washed clean with soap and water; and every building, room, basement or cellar occupied or used for the preparation, manufacture, packing, storage, sale or distribution of food, shall have an impermeable floor made of cement or tile laid in cement, brick, wood or other suitable nonabsorbent material which can be flushed and washed clean with water.

Windows and doors to be screened.

SEC. 4. The doors, windows and other openings of every food producing or distributing establishment during the fly season shall be fitted with self-closing screen doors and wire window screens of not coarser than 14-mesh wire gauze.

Toilet rooms.

SEC. 5. Every building, room, basement or cellar occupied or used for the preparation, manufacture, packing, canning, sale or distribution of food, shall have convenient toilet or toilet rooms separate and apart from the room or rooms where the process of production, manufacture, packing, canning, selling or distributing is conducted. The floors of such toilet rooms shall be of cement, tile, wood, brick or other nonabsorbent material and shall be washed and scoured daily. Such toilet or toilets shall be furnished with separate ventilating flues or pipes, discharging into soil pipes, or on the outside of the building in which they are situated. Lavatories and wash rooms shall be adjacent to toilet rooms and shall be supplied with soap, running water and towels, and shall be maintained in a sanitary condition. Operatives, employees, clerks and all persons who handle the material from which food is prepared, or the finished product, before beginning work or after visiting toilet or toilets, shall wash their hands and arms thoroughly in clean water.

SEC. 6. Cuspidors for the use of operatives, employees, clerks or other persons shall be provided whenever necessary, and each cuspidor shall be thoroughly emptied and washed out daily with disinfectant solution and five ounces of such solution shall be left in each cuspidor while it is in use. No operative, employee, or other person shall expectorate on the floor or side walls of any building, room, basement or cellar where the production, manufacture, packing, storing, preparation, or sale of any food is conducted. *Cuspidors.*

SEC. 7. No person or persons shall be allowed to live or sleep in any workroom of a bake shop, kitchen, dining room, confectionery, creamery, cheese factory, or place where food is prepared for sale, served or sold. *Sleeping in workrooms.*

SEC. 8. No employer shall require, permit or suffer any person to work, nor shall any person work, in a building, room, basement, cellar or vehicle occupied or used for the production, preparation, manufacture, packing, storage, sale, distribution and transportation of food, who is affected with any venereal disease, smallpox, diphtheria, scarlet fever, yellow fever, tuberculosis, or consumption, bubonic plague, Asiatic cholera, leprosy, trachoma, typhoid fever, epidemic dysentery, measles, mumps, German measles, whooping cough, chicken pox or any other infectious or contagious disease. *Contagious and infectious diseases.*

SEC. 9. It shall be the duty of the State board of health to enforce this act, and for that purpose the State, county, city and town health officers shall be food inspectors subordinate to the State board of health. The State food and drug commissioner, the food inspectors of the State board of health, the State, county, city and town health officers shall have full power at all times to enter every building, room, basement, or cellar occupied or used or suspected of being occupied or used for the production for sale, manufacture for sale, storage, sale, distribution or transportation of food, and to inspect the premises and all utensils, fixtures, furniture and machinery used as aforesaid, and if upon inspection any food producing or distributing establishment, conveyance, employer, operative, employee, clerk, driver or other person is found to be violating any of the provisions of this act, or if the production, preparation, manufacture, packing, storing, sale, distribution or transportation of food is being conducted in a manner detrimental to the health of the employees and operatives or to the character or quality of the food therein being produced, manufactured, packed, stored, sold, distributed or conveyed, the officer or inspector making the examination or inspection shall furnish evidence of said violation to the prosecuting attorney of the county or circuit wherein such violations occur, who shall prosecute all persons violating any of the provisions of this act, or said inspector shall report such conditions and violations to the State food and drug commissioner, who shall issue an order to the person or persons in authority at the aforesaid establishment to abate the condition or violation or to make such improvements as may be necessary to abate them, within a period of five days or such reasonable time as may be required in which to abate them. Such order shall be in writing and the person receiving the order shall have the power of appeal from the order and instructions, and may within five days from the issuance of the order appear in person or by attorney before the State food and drug commissioner to give reason why such order or instructions should not be obeyed. *Enforcement.*

SEC. 10. Any person who violates any of the provisions of this act or who refuses to comply with any lawful orders or requirements of the State food and drug commissioner duly made in writ- *Violations.*

ing as provided in section 9 of this act, shall be guilty of a misdemeanor and on conviction shall be punished for the first offense by a fine of not less than $10 nor more than $50; for the second offense by a fine of not less than $50 nor more than $100, and for the third and subsequent offense by a fine of $200 and imprisonment in the county jail for not less than 30 nor more than 90 days, and each day after the expiration of the time limit for abating unsanitary conditions and completing improvements to abate such conditions as ordered by the State food and drug commissioner, shall constitute a distinct and separate offense.

ACTS OF 1911.

CHAPTER 226.—*State bureau of inspection.*

Bureau created.   SECTION 1. There shall be and is hereby created a bureau to be known as the State bureau of inspection. The governor shall appoint a chief inspector to have charge of said bureau, who shall hold his office for a period of four years, and until his successor is appointed and qualified. The annual salary of said chief inspector shall be four thousand ($4,000) dollars, and the actual expenses when absent from his office in the discharge of his official duties. Said chief inspector shall, before entering upon his official duties, execute to the State of Indiana a bond in the sum of three thousand ($3,000) dollars, with good and sufficient surety conditioned for the faithful performance of the duties of said office and the proper expenditure of all moneys that may come into his hands as such chief inspector, which bond shall be subject to the approval of the governor and filed in his office.

SEC. 2. Said bureau of inspection shall consist of the following departments:

Departments.   First. Department of inspection of buildings, factories and workshops;

Second. Department of inspection of mines and mining;

Third. Department of inspection of boilers.

The governor shall also appoint the following deputy inspectors: Inspector of buildings, factories and workshops; inspector of boilers, and an inspector of mines and mining.

Said deputy inspectors shall hold their office for a term of four years and until their successors are appointed and qualified. The salaries of said deputies shall be two thousand ($2,000) dollars, per annum, and actual traveling expenses when absent from home in the discharge of their official duties. Each deputy inspector shall, before entering upon his official duties, execute to the State

Bonds.   of Indiana, a bond in the sum of one thousand ($1,000) dollars, with good and sufficient surety, conditioned for the faithful performance of duties of said office. Said chief inspector and each of said deputies may employ a stenographer at a salary of nine

Assistants.   hundred ($900) dollars, per annum. For the purpose of carrying out the provisions of this act each deputy inspector, by and with the consent of the chief inspector, may appoint three assistants at a salary of twelve hundred ($1,200) dollars, per annum, and actual expenses when away from home in the discharge of official duties. The salary and actual expenses of said deputy inspectors, assistants and stenographers shall be paid monthly as due, on voucher duly attested before some officer authorized to administer oaths, and approved and signed by the chief inspector; and the salary and actual expenses of the chief inspector shall be paid in monthly installments, out of the treasury of the State, upon warrants of the auditor of State. With the consent of the governor each of said deputies may appoint two additional assistants at the annual salary above provided for. The chief inspector may appoint a license clerk at an annual salary of twelve hundred ($1,200) dollars and a bookkeeper for such department at an annual salary of one thousand ($1,000) dollars. No one shall be appointed deputy or assistant deputy inspector who has not had

at least ten years' practical experience in the line of employment
to which he is assigned as inspector.

SEC. 3. Said deputy inspector of buildings, factories and work-   Powers and duties.
shops, and said deputy inspector of mines and mining, shall have
all the powers and perform all the duties now conferred by law
upon the chief inspector of factories, and inspector of mines, and
labor commissioners respectively, which offices are by this act
hereby abolished.

SEC. 4. The inspector of boilers shall make or cause to be made,   Inspection of
an inspection of every stationary boiler at least once every year,   boilers.
and such inspection shall determine whether such boilers are
safe, and whether the laws of the State relating to boilers are
complied with, and shall perform all duties in relation to the inspection of boilers, now performed by the chief inspector of the
department of inspection.

SEC. 5. Said assistant inspectors shall make inspection and per-   Duties of as-
form such duties as may be assigned them by the chief inspector,   sistants.
and the deputy inspector of the department to which they belong,
and after making each inspection file a written report of such   Reports.
inspection with said chief inspector, setting forth the character of
such inspection. Said deputy inspectors in making inspections
shall likewise make a report to said chief inspector.

SEC. 6. The chief inspector shall submit to each person, firm   Blanks to be
or corporation, subject to the provisions of this act, a blank   furnished.
form upon which such person, firm or corporation shall report to
the chief inspector the following information, and such other facts
as may be required by the chief inspector:

1. Officers.
2. Character and location of the business.
3. Number of persons employed; males, females.
4. Description of buildings and equipments, number of floors,
elevators, boilers and fire escapes.

SEC. 7. Every person, firm or corporation operating any busi-   License fee.
ness, regularly employing five or more persons, shall annually pay
to the chief inspector the sum of one ($1) dollar as a license fee
and upon the receipt thereof, the chief inspector shall give to such
person, firm or corporation a certificate showing the license fee
has been paid: *Provided*, That the provisions of this section shall   Certificate.
not apply to agriculture or domestic service. Within thirty (30)
days after his appointment and annually thereafter, the chief
inspector shall cause to be published in a paper published in the
county seat of each county of the State a notice setting forth the
provisions of this section. Any person, firm or corporation sub-   Violations.
ject to the provisions of this act failing or refusing to comply with
the provisions of this section within sixty days thereafter shall
be guilty of a misdemeanor and on conviction shall be subject to
a fine of twenty-five ($25.00) dollars.

SEC. 10. Nothing contained in the provisions of this act shall   Act supple-
affect, amend, repeal or alter in any way the present inspection   mental.
laws of this State, except as herein set forth, but this act shall be
deemed additional and supplemental thereto.

IOWA.

CODE OF 1897 AND SUPPLEMENT OF 1907.

Bureau of labor statistics—Inspection, etc., of factories.

SECTION 2469. The bureau of labor statistics shall be under the   Commissioner.
control of a commissioner, biennially appointed by the governor by
and with the advice and consent of the executive council, whose
term of office shall commence on the first day of April in each odd-
numbered year and continue for two years, and until his successor
is appointed and qualified. He may be removed for cause by the
governor, with the advice of the executive council, record thereof
being made in his office; any vacancy shall be filled in the same

manner as the original appointment. He shall give bonds in the sum of two thousand dollars with sureties to be approved by the governor, conditioned for the faithful discharge of the duties of his office, and take the oath prescribed by law. He shall have an office in the capitol, safely keep all records, papers, documents, correspondence, and other property pertaining to or coming into his hands by virtue of his office, and deliver the same to his successor, except as hereinafter provided. * * *

Duties. SEC. 24˜0. The duties of said commissioner shall be to collect, assort, systematize and present in biennial reports to the governor statistical details relating to all departments of labor in the State, especially in its relations to the commercial, social, educational and sanitary conditions of the laboring classes, the means of escape from, and the protection of life and health in factories, the employment of children, the number of hours of labor exacted from them and from women and to the permanent prosperity of the mechanical, manufacturing and productive industries of the State; and he shall, as fully as practicable, collect such information and reliable reports from each county in the State, the amount and condition of the mechanical and manufacturing interests, the value and location of the various manufacturing and coal productions of the State, * * * and in said biennial report he shall give a statement of the business of the bureau since the last regular report, and shall compile and publish therein such information as may be considered of value to the industrial interests of the State, the number of laborers and mechanics employed, the number of apprentices in each trade, with the nativity of such laborers, mechanics' and apprentices' wages earned, the savings from the same, with age and sex of laborers employed, the number and character of accidents, the sanitary condition of institutions where labor is employed, the restrictions, if any, which are put upon apprentices when indentured, the proportion of married laborers and mechanics who live in rented houses, with the average annual rental, and the value of property owned by laborers and mechanics; and he shall include in such report what progress has been made with schools now in operation for the instruction of students in the mechanic arts, and what systems have been found most practical, with details thereof. Such report shall not contain more than six hundred printed pages, and shall be of the number, and distributed in the manner, provided by law. He shall make a report to the governor during the year 1906, and biennially thereafter. * * *

Witnesses. SEC. 2471. The commissioner of the bureau of labor statistics shall have power to issue subpœnas, administer oaths and take testimony in all matters relating to the duties herein required by said bureau, said testimony to be taken in some suitable place in the vicinity to which testimony is applicable. Witnesses subpœnaed and testifying before the commissioner of the bureau shall be paid the same fees as witnesses before a justice's court, such payment to be made out of the general funds of the State on voucher by the commissioner, but such expense for witnesses shall not exceed one hundred dollars annually. Any person duly subpœnaed under the provisions of this section, who shall willfully neglect or refuse to attend or testify at the time and place named in the subpœna, shall be deemed guilty of a misdemeanor, and, upon conviction thereof before any court of competent jurisdiction, shall be punished by a fine not exceeding fifty dollars and costs of prosecution, or by imprisonment in the county jail not exceeding thirty days: *Provided, however,* That no witness shall be compelled to go outside the county in which he resides to testify.

May enter premises. SEC. 2472. The commissioner of the bureau of labor statistics shall have the power, upon the complaint of two or more persons, or upon his failure to otherwise obtain information in accordance with the provisions of this chapter, to enter any factory or mill, workshop, mine, store, business house, public or private work, when the same is open or in operation, upon a request being made in writing, for the purpose of gathering facts and statistics such as are contemplated by this chapter, and to examine into the **Inspection.** methods of protection from danger to employees, and the sanitary conditions in and around such buildings and places, and make a record thereof. If the commissioner shall learn of any violation of, or neglect to comply with the law in respect to the employment of children, or in respect to fire escapes, or the safety of employees, or for the preservation of health, he shall give written notice to the owner or person in charge of such factory or building, of such offense or neglect, and if the same is not remedied within sixty days after service of such notice, such officer shall give the county **Notice.** attorney of the county in which such factory or building is situated, written notice of the facts, whereupon that officer shall immediately institute the proper proceedings against the person guilty of such offense or neglect. And any owner or occupant of such factory **Hindering em-** or mill, workshop, mine, store, business house, public or private **ployees of bureau.** work, or any agent or employee of such owner or occupant, who shall refuse to allow any officer or employee of said bureau to so enter, or who shall hinder him, or in any way deter him from collecting information, shall be deemed guilty of a misdemeanor, and, upon conviction thereof before any court of competent jurisdiction, shall be punished by a fine of not exceeding one hundred dollars and costs of prosecution, or by imprisonment in the county jail not exceeding thirty days.

SEC. 2473. The expressions "factory," "mill," "workshop," **Definition.** "mine," "store," "business house," and "public or private work," as used in this chapter, shall be construed to mean any factory, mill, workshop, mine, store, business house, public or private work, where five or more wage-earners are employed for a certain stipulated compensation.

SEC. 2474. It shall be the duty of every owner, operator or **Reports to bu-** manager of every factory, mill, workshop, mine, store, business **reau.** house, public or private work, or any other establishment where labor is employed as herein provided, to make to the bureau, upon blanks furnished by said bureau, such reports and returns as said bureau may require for the purpose of compiling such labor statistics as are contemplated in this chapter; and the owner, operator or business manager shall make such reports or returns within sixty days from the receipt of blanks furnished by the commissioner, and shall certify under oath to the correctness of the same. Any owner, operator or manager of such factory, mill, workshop, mine, store, business house, public or private work, as herein stated, who shall neglect or refuse to furnish to the commissioner of labor such reports or returns as may be required by the following blank, shall be deemed guilty of a misdemeanor, and upon conviction thereof, shall be punished by a fine not exceeding one hundred dollars and cost of prosecution, or imprisoned in the county jail not exceeding thirty days.

BLANK.

Name of firm or corporation?_____ Number of hands employed during year ending December thirty-first?_____ Males? _____ Females?_____ Apprentices?_____ Total amount of wages paid during the year ending December thirty-first? $____ Total amount of wages paid previous year? $____ Any general increase or reduction of wages during the past year? If so, what per cent of increase or reduction?_____ Cause of increase or reduction?_____ Any increase or decrease of business during past year?____ What means are provided for the escape of employees in case of fire?_____ What measures are taken to prevent accidents to employees from machinery?_____ How are buildings ventilated?_____ Are separate water-closets and wash rooms provided for the different sexes?_____ Number of weeks during past year business was run on full time with full force?_____ Number of weeks during past year business was run on short time or with reduced force?_____ Number of weeks during past year business was suspended?_____ Number of

strikes during year ending December thirty-first?____ Number
involved?_____ Alleged cause?_____ Result?_____ How many
days did strike continue, and what was loss of wages in consequence thereof?_____ Was any property destroyed, and, if
so, its value?_____

Information confidential.   SEC. 2475. In the reports of the commissioner no use shall be
made of names of individuals, firms or corporations supplying the
information called for by sections twenty-four hundred and
seventy and twenty-four hundred and seventy-one of this chapter,
such information being deemed confidential and not for the purpose of disclosing personal affairs; and any officer or employee of
the bureau of labor statistics violating this provision shall be
deemed guilty of a misdemeanor, and, upon conviction thereof,
shall be fined in a sum not exceeding five hundred dollars and
costs of prosecution, or by imprisonment in the county jail not exceeding one year.   •

Reports to be preserved.   SEC. 2476. No report or return made to said bureau in accordance with the provisions of this chapter, and no schedule,
record or document gathered or returned by its officers or employees, shall be destroyed within two years of the collection or
receipt thereof. At the expiration of two years all records, schedules or papers accumulating in said bureau during said period
that may be considered of no value by the commissioner may be
destroyed, provided the authority of the executive council be first
obtained for such destruction.

Salaries.   SEC. 2477 (as amended by chapter 144, Acts of 1909). The commissioner of the bureau of labor statistics shall receive a salary
of eighteen hundred dollars per annum and shall be allowed a
deputy at a salary of fifteen hundred dollars per annum payable
monthly; he shall also be allowed one factory inspector at a salary
of one hundred dollars per month, and if, in the opinion of the executive council, it is deemed necessary, one additional factory inspector may be employed at a salary of one hundred dollars per
month, one office clerk at a salary of sixty-five dollars per month.
Appointment of inspector. The appointment by the commissioner of such factory inspector
shall be subject to the approval of the executive council. Said
commissioner shall be allowed necessary postage. stationery and
office expenses; the said salaries and expenses shall be paid as the
salaries and expenses of other State officers are provided for. The
commissioner or any officer or employee of the bureau of labor
statistics shall be allowed, in addition to his salary, his actual and
necessary traveling expenses while in the performance of his
duties, said expenses to be audited by the executive council and
paid out of the general fund of the State upon a voucher verified
by the commissioner or his deputy; but the total of the expense
for the officers and employees of said bureau, other than the
salaries of the commissioner, his deputy, the factory inspector and
clerk, shall not exceed two thousand dollars per annum.

Factories-and workshops—Inspection, etc.

Toilet rooms.   SECTION 4999–a1 (as amended by chapter 171, Acts of 1911).
Every manufacturing establishment. workshop or hotel in which
five or more persons are employed, shall be provided with a sufficient number of water-closets, earth closets or privies for the
reasonable use of the persons employed therein, which shall be
properly screened and ventilated and kept at all times in a clean
condition; and free from all obscene writing or marking; and
such .water-closets or privies shall be supplied in the proportion
of at least one, (1), to every twenty, (20), employees; and if
women or girls are employed in such establishment, the water-
closets, earth closets or privies used by them shall have separate
approaches and be separate and apart from those used by the men.
In factories, mercantile establishments, mills and workshops,
adequate washing facilities shall be provided for all employees;
and when the labor performed by the employees is of such
character as to require or make necessary ·a change of clothing,

wholly or in part, by the employees, there shall be provided a dressing-room, or rooms, lockers for keeping clothing and suitable washing facilities separate for each sex, and no person, or persons, shall be allowed to use the facilities assigned to the opposite sex; a sufficient supply of water suitable for drinking purposes shall be provided. *Drinking water.*

SEC. 4999–a2. It shall be the duty of the owner, agent, superintendent or other person having charge of any manufacturing or other establishment where machinery is used, to furnish and supply or cause to be furnished and supplied therein, belt shifters or other safe mechanical contrivances for the purpose of throwing belts on and off pulleys, and, wherever possible, machinery therein shall be provided with loose pulleys; all saws, planers, cogs, gearing, belting, shafting, set screws and machinery of every description therein shall be properly guarded. No person under sixteen years of age, and no female under eighteen years of age shall be permitted or directed to clean machinery while in motion. Children under sixteen years of age shall not be permitted to operate or assist in operating dangerous machinery of any kind. *Safety appliances. Cleaning machinery in motion Employment of children.*

SEC. 4999–a3 (as amended by chapter 219, Acts of 1909). In all cases where the property, works, machinery, or appliances of an employer are defective or out of repair, and where it is the duty of the employer from the character of the place, work, machinery or appliances to furnish reasonably safe machinery, appliances or place to work, the employee shall not be deemed to have assumed the risk, by continuing in the prosecution of the work, growing out of any defect as aforesaid, of which the employee may have had knowledge when the employer had knowledge of such defect, except when in the usual and ordinary course of his employment it is the duty of such employee to make the repairs, or remedy the defects. Nor shall the employee under such conditions be deemed to have waived the negligence, if any, unless the danger be imminent and to such extent that a reasonably prudent person would not have continued in the prosecution of the work; but this statute shall not be construed so as to include such risks as are incident to the employment. And no contract which restricts liability hereunder shall be legal or binding. *Defective appliances. Assumption of risks. Waiver. Contracts.*

SEC. 4999–a4. All persons, companies or corporations operating any factory or workshop where emery wheels or emery belts of any description, or tumbling barrels used for rumbling or polishing castings, are used, shall provide the same with blowers and pipes of sufficient capacity, placed in such manner as to protect the person or persons using same from the particles of dust produced or caused thereby, and to carry away said particles of dust arising from or thrown off such wheels, belts or tumbling barrels while in operation, directly to the outside of the building, or to some receptacle place[d] so as to receive or confine such particles or dust: *Provided, however,* That grinding machines upon which water is used at the point of grinding contact, and small emery wheels which are used temporarily for tool grinding. are not included within the provisions of this section, and the shops employing not more than one man at such work may, in the discretion of the commissioner of the bureau of labor of the State, be exempt from the provisions hereof. *Blowers for polishing machines, etc.*

SEC. 4999–a5 (as amended by chapter 172, Acts of 1911). It shall be the duty of the commissioner of the bureau of labor of the State, and the mayor, and chief of police of every city or town, to enforce the provisions of the foregoing sections. Any person, whether acting for himself or for another or for a copartnership, joint stock company or corporation, having charge or management of any manufacturing establishment, workshop or hotel, who shall fail to comply with the provisions of said sections, within thirty days after being notified in writing to do so, by any one of said officers whose duty it may be to enforce the provisions of said sections. shall be punished by a fine not exceeding **one** hundred dollars or by imprisonment in the county jail not exceeding thirty days. *Enforcement.*

Removing guards. Whenever any person, in any manufacturing or other establishment wherein machinery is used and wherein or whereon guards or safety appliances have been provided, shall remove such guards or safety appliances from any machine or other equipment or shall so adjust such guards or safety appliances as to destroy their purpose of preventing bodily injuries, excepting whenever it becomes necessary to remove some or all of the guards, including springs or pressure bars that may properly come under this act, to enable the employee operating said machine to perform certain special work that can not be performed with guard, it shall be the duty of said employee or employer to immediately replace them after said work has been completed. Any person, who may neglect or refuse to comply with the provisions of this act, shall

Penalty. be punished by a fine of not less than five, ($5.00), dollars, or more than one hundred, ($100.00) dollars, or by imprisonment in the county jail not to exceed thirty, (30), days.

Fire escapes required. SEC. 4999–a6. The owners, proprietors and lessees of all buildings, structures or enclosures of three or more stories in height, now constructed or hereafter to be erected, shall provide for and equip said buildings and structures with such protection against fire and means of escape from such buildings as shall hereafter be set forth in this bill.

On what buildings. SEC. 4999–a7. The buildings, structures and inclosures contemplated in this act shall be classified as follows:

First. Hotels, office buildings or lodging rooms of three or more stories in height.

*   *   *   *   *

Fifth. Manufactories, warehouses and buildings of all character of three or more stories in height, not specified in the foregoing sections.

Number, etc., required. SEC. 4999–a8. Each twenty-five hundred (2500) superficial feet of area, or fractional part thereof, covered by buildings or structures specified under classification one, of section 2, of this act [4999–a6], shall be provided with one ladder fire escape of steel or wrought-iron construction, attached to the outer wall thereof, and provided with platforms of steel or wrought iron construction of such size and dimensions and such proximity to one or more windows of each story above the first with all doors leading thereto of half glass locked in such manner as to render access to such ladder from each story easy and safe, and with red lights to designate location of escapes[,] said ladder to start about five feet from the ground and extend above the roof, or a drop ladder may be hung at the second story in such a manner that it can be easily lowered in case of necessity: *Provided, however,* That where such buildings shall be occupied by more than twenty (20) persons, the said building shall as a substitute for one ladder be provided with one stairway of steel or wrought iron construction with above-described platforms, accessible from each story with a drop or counterbalance stairway from the second-story balcony to the ground, or a stationary stairway may be carried down to within five feet from the ground. * * * Each five thousand (5,000) superficial feet of area, or fractional part thereof covered by buildings under classification 6, [5] section 2 of this act, shall be provided with at least one above-described ladder, and platforms at each story, if not more than twenty (20) persons be employed in the same. If more than twenty (20) persons be employed, then there shall be at least two of the above-described ladders, and platforms attached, or one such stairway, and platforms of sufficient size at each story, and if more than forty (40) persons be employed in said building, then there shall be at least two, or such number of the above-described outside stairways as the chief of fire department, or the mayor of any city or town where no such chief of fire department exists, may from time to time determine. * * *

SEC. 4999–a9. In buildings under all above classification[s] signs indicating location of fire escapes shall be posted at all entrances to elevators, stairway landings and in all rooms. Signs.

SEC. 4999–a10 (as amended by chapter 173, Acts of 1911). It is hereby made the duty of commissioner of the bureau of labor statistics, the chief of fire department, or the mayor of each city or town where no such chief of fire department exists, or the chairman of the board of supervisors, in case such building is not within the corporate limits of any city or town, to adopt uniform specifications for fire escapes hereinbefore provided, and keep such specifications on file in their respective offices, and to serve or cause to be served a written notice in behalf of the State of Iowa upon the owner or owners, or their agents or lessees, of buildings within this State not provided with fire escapes in accordance with the provisions of this act, commanding such owner, owners, or agents or either of them, to place or cause to be placed upon said buildings, such fire escape or fire escapes as are provided in this act within sixty days after service of such notice, pursuant to the specifications established. Any such owner, owners' agents, trustees and lessees or either or any of them so served with notice as aforesaid, who shall not within sixty days after the service of said notice upon him or them, place or cause to be placed such fire escape or fire escapes upon such buildings as required by this act and the terms of said notice, shall be subject to a fine not less than fifty ($50) dollars, and not more than one hundred ($100) dollars, and shall be subject to a further fine of twenty-five ($25) dollars for each additional week of neglect to comply with such notice. Enforcement.

Any owner, agent, trustee or leasee having charge of any building that is not equipped as provided in section forty-nine hundred and ninety-nine–a9 (4999–a9) of the Supplement to the Code, 1907, as amended, who shall refuse or neglect to comply with the provisions of said section, shall be punished by a fine of not less than twenty-five ($25) dollars and not to exceed one hundred ($100) dollars.

SEC. 4999–a11. All fire escapes erected under the provisions of this act shall be subject to inspection and approval or rejection in writing, by the person named in section 4 [5, see sec. 4999–a10] of this act who has caused such written notice to be served. Inspection.

SEC. 4999–a13. It shall be unlawful for any person to establish or operate any dye works, pantorium, or cleaning works, in which gasoline, benzine, naphtha, or other explosive or dangerous fluids are used for the purpose of cleaning or renovating wearing apparel or other fabrics, in any building any part of which is used as a residence or lodging house. Use of explosive fluids, etc.

SEC. 4999–a14. Any person convicted of violating the provisions of the foregoing section shall be fined in a sum not exceeding fifty ($50) nor less than ten ($10) dollars. Penalty.

Inspection, etc., of steam boilers.

SECTION 5026. Any person owning or operating steam boilers in this State shall provide the same with steam gauge, safety valve etc., and water gauge, and keep the same in good order. Any person neglecting so to do shall be fined not less than fifty nor more than five hundred dollars. Steam gauges, etc., to be provided.

KANSAS.

GENERAL STATUTES—1909.

Inspection of factories, etc.—Fire escapes—Safety appliances.

SECTION 4676. Every person owning or operating any manufacturing establishment which may contain any elevator, hoisting-shaft or wellhole shall cause the same to be properly and substan- Elevator shafts.

tially inclosed or secured, in order to protect the lives or limbs of those employed in such establishment.

Stairways

SEC. 4677. Proper and substantial handrails shall be provided in all stairways in manufacturing establishments. The stairs shall be properly secured at the sides and ends, and all doors leading into such establishments shall be so constructed as to open outwardly, and shall be neither locked, bolted nor fastened during working hours.

Fire escapes.

SEC. 4678. In all manufacturing establishments three or more stories high, at least one fire escape, and as many more as may be reasonably necessary, shall be provided on the outside of said establishment, connecting with each floor above the first, well fastened and secured, and of sufficient strength. Each of said fire escapes shall have landings or balconies not less than six feet in length and three feet in width, guarded by iron railings not less than three feet in height, and embracing at least two windows at each story, and connecting with the interior by easily accessible and unobstructed openings, and the balconies or landings shall be connected by iron stairs not less than eighteen inches wide, the steps not to be less than six inches tread, placed at a proper slant, and protected by a well-secured handrail on each side, with twelve-inch drop ladder from the lower platform reaching to the ground.

Belt shifters, guards, etc.

SEC. 4679. Every person owning or operating any manufacturing establishment in which machinery is used shall furnish and supply for use therein belt shifters, or other safe mechanical contrivance, for the purpose of throwing on or off belts or pulleys; and wherever it is practicable machinery shall be operated with loose pulleys. All vats, pans, saws, planers, cog gearing, belting, shafting, set screws and machinery of every description used in a manufacturing establishment shall, where practicable, be properly and safely guarded, for the purpose of preventing or avoiding the death of or injury to the persons employed or laboring in any such establishment; and it is hereby made the duty of all persons owning or operating manufacturing establishments to provide and keep the same furnished with safeguards as herein specified.

Action for injuries.

SEC. 4680. If any person employed or laboring in any manufacturing establishment shall be killed or injured in any case wherein the absence of any of the safeguards or precautions required by the act shall directly contribute to such death or injury, the personal representatives of the person so killed, or the person himself, in case of injury only, may maintain an action against the person owning or operating such manufacturing establishment for the recovery of all proper damages. In cases where the action is brought by the personal representative of the deceased, said action shall be governed in all respects not herein provided for by the provisions of the statutes now in force which authorize and regulate the bringing of actions to recover damages in cases where the death of one is caused by the wrongful act or omission of another: *Provided*, Action shall be commenced in the county where the accident occurred.

Failure to provide appliances.

SEC. 4681. In all actions brought under and by virtue of the provisions of this act, it shall be sufficient for the plaintiff to prove in the first instance, in order to establish the liability of the defendant, that the death or injury complained of resulted in consequence of the failure of the person owning or operating the manufacturing establishment where such death or injury occurred to provide said establishment with safeguards as required by this act, or that the failure to provide such safeguard directly contributed to such death or injury.

Definition.

SEC. 4682. Manufacturing establishments, as those words are used in this act, shall mean and include all smelters, oil refineries, cement works, mills of every kind, machine and repair shops, and, in addition to the foregoing, any other kind or character of manufacturing establishment, of any nature or description whatsoever, wherein any natural products or other articles or materials of any kind, in a raw or unfinished or incomplete state or condition, are converted into a new or improved or different form.

SEC. 4683. Wherever the expression occurs in this act in substantially the following words: "Every person owning or operating any manufacturing establishment," or where language similar to that is used, the word "person" in that connection shall be held and construed to mean any person or persons, partnership, corporation, receiver, trust, trustee, or any other person or combination of persons, either natural or artificial, by whatever name he or they may be called. *Person defined.*

Commissioner of labor—Inspection of factories, etc.

SECTION 8017. It shall be the duty of the commissioner to collect, assort, arrange and present in annual reports to the governor, to be by him biennially transmitted to the legislature, statistical details relating to all departments of labor and industrial pursuits in the State; to the subjects of cooperaion, srikes, and other labor difficulties; to trade unions and other labor organizations and their effect upon labor and capital; to other matters relating to the commercial, industrial, social, educational, moral and sanitary conditions prevailing within the State; and the exploitation of such other subjects as will tend to promote the permanent prosperity of the respective industries of the State. It shall also be the duty of the commissioner of the bureau to cause to be enforced all laws regulating the employment of children, minors, and women; all laws established for the protection of health, lives and limbs of operators in workshops and factories, on railroads, and other places; and all laws enacted for the protection of the working classes now in force or that may hereafter be enacted. In its annual report the bureau shall also give an account of all proceedings which have been taken in accordance with the provisions of this act, or any of the other laws herein referred to, and in addition thereto such remarks, suggestions and recommendations as the commissioner may deem necessary for the information of the legislature. *Duties of commissioner.*

SEC. 8018. The commissioner is hereby authorized to furnish and deliver a written or printed list of interrogatories to any person, company, or the proper officer of any corporation operating within the State, and require full and complete answers to be made thereto, and returned under oath. The commissioners [commissioner] shall have a seal, and have power to take and preserve testimony, to issue subpœnas and administer oaths, and examine witnesses under oath in all matters relating to the duties herein required by said bureau, such testimony to be taken in some suitable place in the vicinity to which the testimony is applicable. Witnesses subpœnaed and testifying before the commissioner of said bureau shall be paid the same fees as witnesses before the district court; such payment to be made from the incidental fund of the bureau. Any person duly subpœnaed under the provisions of this act who shall willfully neglect or refuse to attend, or refuse to answer any question propounded to him concerning the subject of such examination as provided in this act, or if any person to whom a written or printed list of interrogatories has been furnished by said commissioner shall neglect or refuse to answer and return the same under oath, such person or persons shall be deemed guilty of a misdemeanor, and upon complaint of the commissioner before a court of competent jurisdiction, and upon conviction thereof, such person or persons shall be fined in a sum not less than twenty-five dollars nor more than one hundred dollars, or by imprisonment in the county jail not exceeding ninety days, or by both such fine and imprisonment: *Provided, however,* That no witness shall be compelled to go outside of the county in which he resides to testify. In the report of said bureau no use shall be made of the names of individuals, firms or corporations supplying the information called for by this act, unless by written permission, such information being deemed confidential and not for the *Powers of commissioner.*

purpose of disclosing personal affairs; and any officer, agent or employee of the bureau violating this provision shall forfeit a sum not exceeding five hundred dollars, or be imprisoned not more than one year.

Inspection of factories, etc

SEC. 8019. The commissioner, as State factory inspector, shall have power to enter any factory or mill, workshop, private works or State institutions which have shops or factories, when the same are open or in operation, for the purpose of gathering facts and statistics such as are contemplated by this act, and to examine into the methods of protection from danger to employees and the sanitary conditions in and around such buildings and places, and to make a record thereof of such inspection. If the commissioner as State factory inspector shall find upon such inspection that the heating, lighting, ventilation or sanitary arrangement of any workshops or factories is such as to be injurious to the health of the persons employed or residing therein, or that the means of egress in case of fire or other disaster are not sufficient, or that the belting, shafting, gearing, elevators, drums, saws, cogs and machinery in such workshops and factories are located or are in a condition so as to be dangerous to employees, and not sufficiently guarded, or that the vats, pans, or any other structures, filled with molten metal or hot liquid, are not surrounded with proper safeguards for preventing accidents or injury to those employed at or near them, he shall notify in writing the owner, proprietor or agents of such workshops or factories to make, within thirty days, the alterations or additions by him deemed necessary for the safety and protection of the employees; and if such alterations or additions are not made within thirty days from the date of such written notice, or within such time as said alterations or additions can be made with proper diligence upon the part of such proprietors, owners, or agents, said proprietors, owners or agents so notified shall be deemed guilty of a misdemeanor, and upon complaint of the commissioner as State factory inspector before a court of competent jurisdiction, and upon conviction thereof shall be fined in a sum not less than twenty-five dollars nor more than two hundred dollars, or by imprisonment not more than ninety days, or by both such fine and imprisonment.

Definitions.

SEC. 8020. The following expressions used in this act shall have the following meanings: The expression "person" means an individual, corporation, partnership, company, or association. The expression "children" means minor persons under the age of fourteen years. The expression "minor" means a male person under the age of twenty-one years, or a female person under the age of eighteen years. The expression "women" means female persons of eighteen years of age and upward. The expression "factory" means any premises where steam, water or other mechanical power is used in aid of any manufacturing process there carried on. The expression "workshop" means any premises, room, or place, not being a factory as above defined, wherein any manual labor is exercised by way of trade, or for the purpose of gain in or incidental to any process of making, altering, repairing, ornamenting, finishing or adapting for sale any article or part of an article, and to which or over which premises, room or place the employer of the person or persons working therein has the right of access or control: *Provided, however,* That the exercise of such manual labor in a private house, or a private room by the family dwelling therein, or by any of them, or in case a majority of persons therein employed are members of such family, shall not of itself constitute such house or room a workshop within this definition. The aforesaid expressions shall have the meanings above defined for them respectively in all laws of this State relating to the employment of labor, unless a different meaning is plainly required by the context.

Information to be furnished.

SEC. 8021. All State, county, township and city officers are hereby directed to furnish said commissioner, upon his request, such statistical or other information contemplated by this act as shall be in their possession as such officers.

Sec. 8022. The annual reports of the bureau of labor and in- Reports.
dustry provided for in this act shall be printed in the same
manner and under the same regulations as the report of the
executive officers of the State: *Provided*, Not less than three
thousand nor more than ten thousand copies of the report shall be
printed and distributed annually, as the judgment of the commissioner may deem best: *And provided further*, That said report
shall not contain more than six hundred pages. The blanks and
other stationery required in accordance with the provisions of
this act shall be furnished by the secretary of state upon the
requisition of the commissioner of said bureau, and paid for from
the printing fund of the State.

Sec. 8023. In addition to the assistant commissioner provided Special agents,
for by section 2 of this act [sec. 8016], the commissioner shall etc.
appoint a stenographer for the bureau, and he may also employ
special agents and such other assistants as may be necessary in
the discharge of the official duties of said bureau. Such special
agents and other assistants shall be paid for the services rendered
such compensation as the commissioner may deem proper, but no
such agents or assistants shall be paid more than three dollars
per day in addition to necessary traveling expenses.

KENTUCKY.

STATUTES—1903.

*Bureau of agriculture, labor, and statistics—Inspection of fac-
tories, etc.*

Section 33a. 1. In the bureau of agriculture, labor and statistics Labor inspec-
there shall be appointed by the commissioner, with the approval of tor.
the governor, a labor inspector, and one assistant labor inspector,
who shall be men having practical knowledge of factories, machine or work shops, and who shall be under the supervision of
the commissioner.

2. It shall be the duty of the labor inspector to visit and inspect Duties.
the various factories, machine and work shops in this State, and
under the direction of the commissioner to report to the Commonwealth's attorney and county attorney of the county or district,
where such factory, machine or work shop is located, any violation or infraction of laws enacted for the protection of women,
children and other persons laboring in such places.

3. It shall be the duty of every owner, manager and agent of Access to fac-
any factory, machine or workshop where laborers are employed, tories, etc.
to admit the labor inspectors during reasonable hours and while
the same is open, for the purpose of making an inspection of same,
and any person who shall refuse to admit such inspectors in violation of the provisions of this section shall be fined not to exceed
one hundred dollars, or to be imprisoned in jail not more than six
months, or both be so fined and imprisoned in the discretion of the
jury.

4. It shall further be the duty of the labor inspector to collect Collection of
statistics concerning labor wherever and however employed in statistics.
this State, and report the same to the commissioner at such times
as he may direct. It shall be the duty of the owner, officers,
manager, or agent, of any factory, machine or work shop where
laborers are employed, to furnish upon demand of the labor inspectors statistical information concerning the number and sex of
laborers employed, the compensation of each, the amount and kind.
of labor performed by such laborers, and such other reasonable
information as may be required by the commissioner: *Provided*, Provisos.
That no person shall be required to furnish the labor inspectors
information concerning the private conduct or condition of his
affairs, or the affairs of the firm or concern he represents, touch-
ing matters not contemplated in the provisions of this act: *And,
provided, further,* That no labor inspector, for the purpose of

gathering statistics, shall interfere or detain from work any laborer while on duty during working hours.

Report on labor.   5. The commissioner shall make a separate report biennially to the legislature on or before the second Monday in January, on the subject of labor, and include such recommendations as may be deemed proper, together with an account of the work done by the labor inspectors, and the expenses incurred in by them. The number of copies of such reports shall not be less than one thousand nor more than three thousand, in the discretion of the commissioner.

Interference with strikes, etc.   7. Neither the labor inspector nor assistant labor inspector shall take any part, interfere, or become involved in any strike or similar labor difficulty, other than the performance of his duty as prescribed by law, upon penalty of forfeiting his office.

Salaries.   8. The labor inspector and assistant labor inspector shall receive annual salaries of twelve hundred dollars and one thousand dollars, respectively, and their actual necessary traveling expenses while in the performance of their duties to be paid out of the fund appropriated for the bureau. Said labor inspectors shall make reports of expenses as directed by the commissioner, who shall approve the same when proper and certify same for payment as other expenses of said bureau are now allowed and paid.

Act construed.   9. Nothing in this act shall be construed to conflict with the powers and duties of the State mine inspectors as now prescribed by law. The words factory, machine and work shop, shall not be construed to mean a newspaper or printing office.

Information to be furnished.   Sec. 34. The auditor of public accounts, assessors of the several counties, and all other officers of the State and counties, shall furnish the commissioner with such information within their power as he may require in regard to the matters connected with the bureau; and as a further means of procuring information, the commissioner shall put himself in communication with the different agricultural, horticultural and labor societies, manufacturing and mining companies, and such other organizations or persons in or out of the State, as he may deem proper.

Fire escapes on factories, etc.

Fire escapes to be erected.   Section 1830. All buildings of three or more stories in height, in every city of more than ten thousand inhabitants as enumerated by the last United States census, excepting private residences and store and ware houses in which not more than twenty persons are employed, shall be provided with one or more permanent metallic ladders or fire escapes, extending from the first story to the upper stories of such building, and above the roof and on the outer walls thereof, in such location, numbers and character of construction as the chief of fire department or chief fire officer of each such city may determine. The said chief of the fire department or chief fire officer shall examine the building and serve, either in person or by deputy, a notice, in writing, upon the owner, agent, lessee or occupant of such building, by leaving at his or her residence or place of business a copy of such notice, setting forth the number, kind, construction and location of the ladder or ladders required, and directing that the work shall be completed not later than thirty days from the filing of the notice.

By whom.   Sec. 1831. If the owner of the building fails to take steps looking to the compliance of the specifications of the said notice, then the agent, lessee or occupant, who is jointly liable for the violation of the provisions of this act, must have the work performed at his own expense, and for which a lien on the building and grounds is hereby declared to exist after record in the office of the county clerk.

Violations.   Sec. 1832. Any owner, agent, lessee or occupant of such building violating any of the provisions of this act shall be fined not less than fifty dollars nor more than two hundred and fifty dollars for each thirty days the building may be unprovided with the ladder or fire escapes, recoverable on motion before any court of competent jurisdiction.

ACTS OF 1908.

CHAPTER 66.—*Regulation and inspection of factories.*

[See Appendix A, page 700.]

LOUISIANA.

CONSTITUTION.

Who may be officers—Factory inspectors.

ARTICLE 210 (as amended, 1906). No person shall be eligible to any office, State, judicial, parochial, municipal, or ward, who is not a citizen of this State and a duly qualified elector of the State, judicial district, parish, municipality or ward, wherein the functions of said office are to be performed. And whenever any officer, State, judicial, parochial, municipal or ward, may change his residence from this State, or from the district, parish, municipality or ward in which he holds such office, the same shall thereby be vacated, any declaration of retention of domicile to the contrary notwithstanding. But the appointment or election to office of either male or female persons is allowed, to serve as factory inspectors as provided for by an act entitled "An act to regulate the employment of children, young persons and women in certain cases, and to provide penalties for violations of the provisions of this act," adopted by the general assembly at its session of the year 1906. *Electors eligible.* *Exception.*

. REVISED LAWS—1897.

Fire escapes on factories, etc.

(Page 754. Act No. 97, Acts of 1888.)

SECTION 1. All buildings, except such as are used for private residences exclusively, in the city of New Orleans, of four or more stories in height, shall be provided with one or more metallic ladders or metallic fire escapes, including from the first story to the upper stories of such buildings, and above the roof and on the outer walls thereof, in such location and numbers and of such material and construction as the mayor, chief engineer of the fire department of their respective districts, the city surveyor and chairman of the fire committee of the city council and commissioner of public buildings, or a majority of them may from time to time determine; after such determination shall have been made as aforesaid, the chief engineer of the fire department of said city may at any time, by a notice in writing served upon the owner or agent of any such building by leaving with such owner or agent, or at his residence or place of business, a copy of such notice, require such owner or agent to cause such building within thirty days after the service of such notice [sic], require such owner or agent to cause such metallic ladder or fire escape to be placed upon such building, within thirty days after the service of such notice: *Provided, however,* That all buildings more than two stories in height, used for manufacturing purposes, shall have one metallic ladder for every twenty-five persons, or less, employed above the second story. *What buildings to have fire escapes.* *Notice.* *Number.*

SEC. 2. In case such owner, or agent, so served with notice as aforesaid shall not, within thirty days after the service of such notice upon him, place, or cause to be placed, such metallic ladder or fire escape upon such building, as required by this article and the terms of such notice, he shall be subject to a fine of not less than twenty-five nor more than two hundred and fifty dollars, and to a further fine of twenty-five dollars for each week of such neglect to comply with such notice after the service of the same. The fines imposed for violation of this act shall be collected by any court of competent jurisdiction. *Penalty.*

Enforcement.   SEC. 3. It is hereby made the duty of the parties herein designated to execute the provisions of this act.

ACTS OF 1908.

ACT No. 73.—*Inspection of factories, etc.—Doors to open outwardly.*

Doors to open outwardly.   SECTION 1. All the doors for ingress and egress to * * * factories with more than twenty employees * * * shall be so swung as to open outwardly from the * * * workshops; but such doors may be hung on double-jointed hinges, so as to open with equal ease outwardly or inwardly.

Allowance of time.   SEC. 2. The provisions of this act shall apply to all buildings and houses within its terms, erected after its passage, from the date it becomes in force. As to all such buildings and houses heretofore erected, said provisions shall be applied from and after the expiration of six months from the date when this act became operative.

Violations.   SEC. 3. * * * The owner of any * * * factory, failing to comply with the provisions of this act or to have same complied with as relates * * * to such building or buildings owned by them, shall be guilty of a misdemeanor and upon conviction shall be fined not less than ten dollars nor more than one hundred dollars, and upon failure to pay such fine and costs shall be imprisoned in the parish jail for a period not exceeding (90) ninety days.

Sliding doors.   SEC. 4. *Provided*, That this act shall not apply to factories, cotton-seed-oil mills and other like establishments where the doors for the purpose of protection against fire, are so arranged as to slide back and forth on rollers.   •

ACT No. 301.—*Regulation and inspection of factories, etc.*

[See Appendix A, page 714.]

MAINE.

REVISED STATUTES—1903.

CHAPTER 22.—*Inspection of steam boilers.*

Safety plugs.   SECTION 22. No person or corporation shall manufacture, sell, use or cause to be used, except as hereinafter provided, any steam boiler in the State unless it is provided with a fusible safety plug, made of lead for boilers carrying steam pressure above fifty pounds per square inch, and of tin for boilers carrying steam pressure of fifty pounds and less per square inch, and said safety plug shall be not less than one-half inch in diameter, and shall be placed in the roof of the fire box when a fire box is used, and in all cases shall be placed in the part of the boiler fully exposed to the action of the fire, and as near the surface line of the water as good judgment shall dictate, excepting in cases of upright tubular boilers, when the upper tube sheet is placed above the surface line of the water, which class of boilers shall be exempted from the provisions of this section.

Violations.   SEC. 23. If any person without just and proper cause removes from the boiler the safety plug, or substitutes any material more capable of resisting the action of the fire, or if any person or corporation uses or causes to be used, for six consecutive days, or manufactures or sells a steam boiler of a class not exempted from the provisions of the preceding section, unprovided with such safety fusible plug, such offender shall be fined not exceeding one thousand dollars.

CHAPTER 28.—*Factories and workshops—Inspection, etc.*

Doors opening outwardly.   SECTION 37. Every building intended temporarily or permanently for public use, * * * shall have all inner doors, intended for egress, open outwards. The outer doors of all such buildings shall be kept open when the same are used by the public, unless they open outwards; but fly doors opening both ways may be kept closed.

SEC. 38 (as amended by chapter 194, Acts of 1909). * * * Every building in which any trade, manufacture or business is carried on, requiring the presence of workmen above the first story, * * * shall at all times be provided with proper egresses or other means of escape from fire sufficient for the use of all persons * * * employed * * * therein. These egresses and means of escape shall be kept unobstructed, in good repair and ready for use, the sufficiency thereof to be determined as provided in the following section. *Egress in case of fire.*

SEC. 39. In towns or parts of towns having no organized fire department, the municipal officers shall annually make careful inspection of the precautions and safeguards provided in compliance with the foregoing requirements, and pass upon their sufficiency as to arrangement and number, and upon their state of repair; and direct such alterations, additions and repairs as they adjudge necessary. In towns, cities and villages having an organized fire department, the duties aforesaid shall be discharged by the board of fire engineers. *Inspection.*

SEC. 40. Such municipal officers or fire engineers shall give written notice to the occupant of such building, also to the owner thereof, if known, of their determination as to the sufficiency of said precautions and safeguards, specifying in said notice any alteration, addition or repair which they require. Sixty days are allowed for compliance with such notice and order. *Notice.*

SEC. 41. Any owner or occupant who neglects to comply with such order, within the time so allowed, forfeits fifty dollars, besides five dollars for every day's continuance of such neglect; and the building or part of a building so occupied shall be deemed a common nuisance, without any other evidence than proof of its use; and the keeper shall be punished accordingly. Said officers may forbid the use of such building for any public purpose until their order has been complied with. And if the owner or occupant of said building lets or uses the same in violation of such order, he forfeits not less than twenty nor more than fifty dollars for each offense. *Penalty.*

SEC. 42. Whenever the municipal officers or engineers upon inspection, find that proper safeguards and precautions for escape in case of fire, or of alarm, have been provided, they shall give to the occupant of such building a certificate, under their hands, of such fact; which shall be valid for one year only from its date; * * * Such officers shall return to the clerk's office of their town, monthly, a list of such certificates by them issued, which the clerk shall record in a suitable book. *Certificate.*

SEC. 43. Every person receiving such certificate shall keep the same posted in such building. Such annual certificate, so posted. is prima facie evidence of the inspection of such building, and of the presence of such suitable safeguards and precaution. Every occupant of such building who neglects or refuses to procure such certificate, or to post the same as aforesaid, forfeits ten dollars for every week that he so neglects and refuses. *Evidence.*

SEC. 44. Every municipal officer or fire engineer who refuses or neglects to perform the duties imposed upon him by the seven preceding sections forfeits fifty dollars. *Penalty.*

SEC. 46 (added by chapter 156, Acts of 1911). Should it come to the notice of the State factory inspector or his deputy, or should complaint be made to such State factory inspector or his deputy by any citizen of the State, of the failure of any of the above-named officers to comply with any of the provisions of this act, the State factory inspector or his deputy shall at once proceed to investigate such complaint, and if sufficient evidence can be obtained, he shall at once file a complaint against such officer with the county attorney, who shall prosecute the same under the provisions of this act. *Negligence of inspectors.*

ACTS OF 1911.

CHAPTER 65.—*Commissioner of labor—Inspection of factories, etc.*

Inspection of factories, etc.

SECTION 4. The commissioner as State factory inspector and any authorized agent of the labor department shall have power to enter any factory or mill, workshop, private works or State institutions which have shops or factories, when the same are open or in operation, for the purpose of gathering facts and statistics such as are contemplated by this act, and to examine into the methods of protection from danger to employees and the sanitary conditions in and around such buildings and places, and to make a record thereof of such inspection. And if any person, or persons, shall refuse to allow the commissioner, or any authorized agent of the labor department, to so enter, or shall refuse to give the information so desired by said commissioner or authorized agent, then said person or persons, shall be deemed guilty of a misdemeanor, and, upon conviction thereof, before any court of competent jurisdiction, shall be punished by a fine not to exceed one hundred dollars, or by imprisonment for not more than ninety days, or both such fine and imprisonment in the discretion of the court. If the commissioner as State factory inspector, or any authorized agent of the department of labor, shall find upon such

Defective conditions.

inspection that the heating, lighting, ventilation or sanitary arrangement of any workshops or factories is such as to be injurious to the health of the persons employed or residing therein or that the means of egress in case of fire or other disaster are not sufficient, or that the belting, shafting, gearing, elevators, drums, saws, cogs and machinery in such workshops and factories are located or are in a condition so as to be dangerous to employees and not sufficiently guarded, or that vats, pans, or any other structures, filled with molten metal or hot liquids, are not surrounded with proper safeguards for preventing accidents or injury to those employed at or near them, he shall notify, in writing, the owner, proprietor or agent of such workshops or factories to make, within thirty days, the alterations ar [or] additions by him deemed necessary for the safety and protection of the employees; and if such alterations or additions are not made within thirty days from the date of such written notice, or within such time as said alterations or additions can be made with proper diligence upon the part of such proprietors, owners or agents, said proprietors, owners or agents so notified shall be deemed guilty of a misdemeanor, and upon complaint of the commissioner as State factory inspector before a court of competent jurisdiction, and upon conviction thereof, shall be fined in a sum not less than twenty-five dollars nor more than two hundred dollars, or by imprisonment not more than thirty days, or by both such fine and imprisonment.

Definitions.

SEC. 5. The following expressions used in this act shall have the following meanings: The expression "person" means an individual, corporation, partnership, company or association. The expression "factory" means any premises where steam, water or other mechanical power is used in aid of any manufacturing process there carried on. The expression "workshop" means any premises, room or place, not being a factory as above defined, wherein any manual labor is exercised by way of trade, or for the purpose of gain in or incidental to any process of making, altering, repairing, ornamenting, finishing or adapting for sale any article or part, of an article, and to which or over which premises, room or place the employer of the person or persons working therein has the right of access or control: *Provided, however,* That the exercise of such manual labor in a private house, or a private room by the family dwelling therein, or by any of them, or in case a majority of persons therein employed are members of such family, shall not of itself constitute such house or room a workshop within this definition. The aforesaid expressions shall have the meanings above defined for them respectively in all laws of this State relating to the employment of labor, unless a different meaning is plainly required by the context.

SEC. 6. All State, county, city and town officers are hereby directed to furnish said commissioner, upon his request, such statistical or other information contemplated by this act as shall be in their possession as such officers. Municipal affairs.

SEC. 7. In addition to the deputy commissioner provided for by section one of this act, the commissioner shall appoint a stenographer for the department of labor; he shall also employ a woman factory inspector, and he may also employ special agents and such other assistants, as may be necessary in the discharge of the official duties of said department of labor; such special agents and other assistants shall be paid for the services rendered such compensation as the commissioner may deem proper, but no such agents or assistants shall be paid more than three dollars per day in addition to necessary traveling expenses, said agents and assistants shall work under the supervision and direction of the commissioner of labor. Assistants.

SEC. 8. The salary of said commissioner shall be sixteen hundred dollars per year, and that of his deputy, thirteen hundred dollars per year, together with all necessary traveling expenses. The salary of the stenographer shall be six hundred dollars per year. All such salaries and other expenses provided for in this act, shall be audited the same as salaries and expenses of other State departments and shall be payable upon proper vouchers certified by the commissioner: *Provided,* That the amount thereof, exclusive of the salaries provided for by this section, shall not exceed for any two years the sum of nine thousand dollars, making the total annual appropriation for this department of labor for all purposes, eight thousand dollars: *Provided, however,* That any unexpended balance to the credit of the department of labor at the close of any year in which the legislature regularly meets shall be carried over and made available for use in the following year. Salaries, etc.

SEC. 11. All authority heretofore vested in the commissioner of the bureau of industrial and labor statistics as such, and the inspector of factories, workshops, mines and quarries as such, are hereby vested in the commissioner of labor and industry and State factory inspector as provided for in this act. Authority of commissioner.

MARYLAND.

PUBLIC GENERAL LAWS—CODE OF 1903.

ARTICLE 27.—*Factories and workshops—Inspection, etc.*

SECTION 234. All factories, manufacturing establishments or workshops in this State shall be kept in a cleanly condition and free from effluvia arising from any drain, privy or other nuisance; and no factory, manufacturing establishment or workshop shall be so overcrowded while work is carried on therein as to be injurious to the health of the persons employed therein; and every such factory, manufacturing establishment or workshop shall be well and sufficiently lighted and ventilated in such a manner as to render harmless, as far as practicable, all the gases, vapors, dust or other impurities generated in the course of the manufacturing process or handicraft carried on therein, which may be injurious to health. Sanitation.

SEC. 235. Any person, firm or corporation managing or conducting any factory, manufacturing establishment or workshop in this State, who shall neglect any of the requirements of the preceding section, or do or permit to be done in the factory, manufacturing establishment or workshop conducted or managed by him, her, them or it, any act contrary to the provisions of said section, shall be guilty of a misdemeanor, and shall upon conviction thereof in Penalty.

a court of competent jurisdiction, be fined one hundred and fifty dollars for each offense so committed.

Manufacture of clothing, etc., in unhealthful surroundings. SEC. 236. If any individual or body corporate engaged in the manufacture or sale of clothing or of any other article whereby disease may be transmitted shall with reasonable means of knowledge, by purchase, contract or otherwise, directly or indirectly, cause or permit any garments, or such other articles as aforesaid, to be manufactured or made up, in whole or in part, or any work to be done thereupon within this State and in a place or under circumstances involving danger to the public health, such individual or corporation, upon conviction in any court of competent jurisdiction shall be fined not less than ten dollars nor more than one hundred dollars for each garment manufactured, made up or worked upon.

Endangering public health. SEC. 237. If any individual or the officer of any corporation shall so as as [sic] aforesaid cause or permit any garment or other articles in the next preceding section mentioned to be manufactured, made up or worked upon in a place or under circumstances involving danger to the public health, with the knowledge that it will or may be thus dealt with, he shall, upon conviction in any court of competent jurisdiction, be imprisoned not less than sixty days nor more than one year, and may be further fined not exceeding one thousand dollars, in the discretion of the court.

Term construed. SEC. 238. Any room or apartment which shall not contain at least 400 cubic feet of clear space for each person habitually laboring in or occupying the same, or wherein the thermometer shall habitually stand, during the hours of labor, at or above 80 degrees Fahrenheit, before the first day of May or after the first day of October of any year, or wherein any person suffering from a contagious, infectious or otherwise dangerous disease or malady, shall sleep, labor or remain, or wherein, if of less superficial area than 500 square feet, any artificial light shall be habitually used between the hours of 8 a. m. and 4 p. m., or from which the debris of manufacture and all other dirt or rubbish shall not be removed at least once in every twenty-four hours, or which shall be pronounced ill ventilated or otherwise unhealthy by any officer or board having legal authority so to do, shall be deemed a place involving danger to the public health, as mentioned in the two preceding sections.

Use of living room as work room. SEC. 240. No room or apartment in any tenement or dwelling house shall be used except by the immediate members of the family living therein, which shall be limited to a husband and wife, their children, or the children of either, for the manufacture of coats, vests, trousers, knee pants, overalls, cloaks, hats, caps, suspenders, jerseys, blouses, waists, waistbands, underwear, neckwear, furs, fur trimmings, fur garments, shirts, purses, feathers, artificial flowers, cigarettes, or cigars. No room or apartment in any tenement or dwelling house shall be used by any family or **Permit.** part of family until a permit shall first have been obtained from the chief of the bureau of industrial statistics, stating the maximum number of persons allowed to be employed therein. Such **Inspection.** permit shall not be granted until an inspection of such premises has been made by the inspector or his assistant, named by the chief of the bureau of industrial statistics, and such permit may be revoked by the said chief of the bureau of industrial statistics at any time the health of the community or those employed or **Number of employees.** living therein may require it. No person, firm or corporation shall work in, or hire or employ any person to work in any room or apartment in any building, rear building, or building in the rear of a tenement or dwelling house, at making in whole or in part any of the articles mentioned in this section, without first obtaining a written permit from the chief of the bureau of industrial statistics stating the maximum number of persons allowed to be employed therein. Such permit shall not be granted until an inspection of such premises has been made by the factory inspector or his assistant, named by the chief of the bureau of industrial statistics, and such permit may be revoked by the chief of the bureau of industrial statistics at any time the health of the community or of those so employed may require it. All families, persons, firms or corporations now engaged in such manufacture in such tenement or dwelling house or other building, shall apply for said permit on or before July 1, 1902, and annually thereafter at the same date. The said permit shall be posted in a conspicuous place in the room, or one of the rooms to which it relates. *Permit to be posted.*

Every person, firm or corporation contracting for the manufacture of any of the articles mentioned in this section, or giving out the incomplete materials from which they or any of them are to be made, or to be wholly or partially finished, or employing persons in any tenement or dwelling house, or other building, to make, wholly or partly finish, the articles mentioned in this section, shall keep a written register of the names and addresses of all persons to whom such work is given to be made, or with whom they may have contracted to do the same. Such register shall be produced for inspection, and a copy thereof shall be furnished on demand made by the chief of the bureau of industrial statistics or one of his deputies. *Register.*

SEC. 241. The chief of the bureau of industrial statistics, or his assistant, or any inspector, shall have authority to enter any room in any tenement or dwelling house, workshop, manufacturing establishment, mill, factory or place where any goods are manufactured, for the purpose of inspection. The person, firm or corporation owning or controlling or managing such places shall furnish access to and information in regard to such places to the said chief of the bureau of industrial statistics or his deputies at any and all reasonable times while work is being carried on. *Right to inspect.*

SEC. 242. The chief of the bureau of industrial statistics shall appoint two deputies as assistants, whose duty it shall be to make such inspections of the tenements, dwelling houses, factories, workshops, mills and such other places as he may designate and to do such other work as the said chief of the bureau of industrial statistics shall designate. *Duties.*

SEC. 243. Any person, firm or corporation who shall in any manner violate the provisions of sections 240, 241 and 242, or who shall refuse to give such information and access to the chief of the bureau of industrial statistics or his deputies, or secure such permit as provided, shall, upon conviction in any court of competent jurisdiction, be fined not less than five dollars nor more than one hundred dollars, or imprisoned not less than ten days nor more than one year, or both, in the discretion of the court; such fines to be collected as all other fines are collected by law. *Violations.*

PUBLIC LOCAL LAWS—CODE 1888.

ARTICLE 4 (REVISION OF 1898: CHAPTER 123, ACTS OF 1898).—*Factories and workshops—Oil—Fire escapes—Baltimore.*

SECTION 280. * * * It shall not be lawful for any person, agent, owner or proprietor of any sweat shop or factory where four or more persons are employed, to use any coal oil, gasoline, or any other explosive or inflammable compound for the purpose of lighting or heating in any form; and any person, agent, owner or proprietor violating this provision shall be guilty of a misdemeanor, and on conviction thereof, be fined by the court before which such conviction is had, for every violation, the sum of one hundred dollars and costs, and stand committed until such fine and costs be paid. The owner or owners of any such house or building used as a sweat shop or factory where four or more persons are employed as garment workers, on other than the first floor of such house or building, shall provide fire escapes for the same; and if any owner or owners of any house or building so used, fail to make or provide a fire escape, such owner or owners shall pay a fine of two hundred dollars, to be recovered as other fines in this State, or imprisonment in the city jail for sixty days, or both fine and imprisonment, in the discretion of the court. *Use of coal oil, etc., forbidden.* *Fire escapes.*

ARTICLE 4 (REVISION OF 1898: CHAPTER 123, ACTS OF 1898).—*Inspection of steam boilers—Baltimore.*

nspectors.

SECTION 572. The governor shall biennially appoint two suitable persons who are well skilled in the construction and use of steam engines and boilers, and in application of steam thereto, whose duty it shall be to inspect steam boilers in the city of Baltimore, as hereinafter specified and directed; said inspectors before enter· ing on their duties, shall make oath before a justice of the peace, * * * that they are not, and will not during their term of office, be connected with, or interested in the manufacture of steam boilers, engines or machinery applicable thereto, * * *

istricts.

SEC. 573. The city of Baltimore is divided into two districts, which shall be known as the first and second steam boiler inspection districts; * * *

ffice, notices,
·

SEC. 574. The inspectors, before entering on the discharge of their duties, shall provide themselves with an office in a central part of said city, also with the necessary apparatus and appliances for the testing of steam boilers; and they shall give notice for three successive days, through the two daily papers having the largest circulation in said city, of the time and manner in which they shall receive the reports of the locations of steam boilers.

wners to re-
t.

SEC. 575. Every owner or renter using a steam boiler in said city, shall, within ten days after the publication of the aforesaid notice, report to the inspector of the district the location of such boiler, under a penalty of fifty dollars for each day a boiler is used and neglected to be reported.

otice to pre-
e inspection.

SEC. 576. The inspector of each district shall give six days' notice in writing to each owner or renter of a steam boiler, or the engineer or person in charge, of the time when he will inspect such boiler; and such owner or renter shall have such boiler ready for inspection, in compliance with the requirements of said notice, and shall furnish such assistance as the inspector may require, under a penalty of fifty dollars for such failure or neglect, and a further penalty of fifty dollars for each day any such boiler is used without a certificate of inspection.

nnual inspec-
·

SEC. 577. It shall be the duty of each inspector, once at least in every year, to inspect all stationary steam boilers of three horsepower and upwards, used within the limits of his district, subjecting them to a hydrostatic test of at least twenty-five per cent in excess of the steam pressure allowed, and satisfy himself, by a thorough external and internal examination, (if possible) with a hammer, that the boilers are free from danger from corrosion or other defects, are well made of good material, the openings for the passage of water and steam, respectively, and all pipes and tubes exposed to heat are of proper dimensions, and free from obstruction; that the flues and tubes, if any, are circular in form, the furnaces in proper shape, and the fire line of the furnaces is at least two inches below the minimum water line of the boilers; and shall also satisfy himself that the safety valves are of suitable dimensions, sufficient in number and well arranged, and that the weights are properly adjusted so as to allow no greater pressure in the boiler than the amount prescribed in the certificate of inspection; that there is a sufficient number of gauge cocks, a steam gauge, a coupling cock in suitable position for attaching the hydrostatic test, that means for blowing out are provided, so as to thoroughly remove the mud and sediment from all parts of the boilers when they are under the pressure of steam, and that fusible metals are properly inserted so as to fuse by the heat of the furnaces when the water in the boilers shall fall below the prescribed limits, and that adequate and certain provision is made for an ample supply of water at all times; when the inspection is completed and the inspector approves the boiler, he shall make and subscribe a certificate of inspection, stating the condition of the boiler, the number of years or months it has been in use, and the pressure of steam allowed; and no greater pressure than that allowed by the certificate shall be applied to such boiler. In limiting pressure, whenever the boiler under test will, with safety, bear the same, the limit desired by the owner shall be the one certified; and such certificate of inspection shall be framed under glass, and kept in some conspicuous place on the premises where said boiler referred to is used; and if the inspector shall deliver or cause to be delivered to the owner or renter of any boiler a certificate of inspection without having first subjected the said boiler to the tests as herein provided, he shall forfeit his bond, and upon conviction shall be removed from office by the governor.

SEC. 578. In addition to the annual inspection, it shall be the duty of the inspector to examine all boilers within the limits of their respective districts once at least in every three months, and if deemed necessary, apply the hydrostatic test; and if on such examination the inspector shall find evidence of deterioration in strength, he shall revoke the certificate and issue another, assigning a lower rate of pressure; and if the defect be of such character as to make the boiler dangerous, the inspector shall notify the owner or renter in writing, stating in the notice what is required, and order the use of the boiler discontinued until the necessary repairs are made; and if he considers it beyond repair, he shall condemn it; and if the owner or renter shall refuse or neglect to comply with the requirements of the inspector, and shall, contrary thereto, and while the same remains unreversed, use the boiler, he shall be liable to a penalty of not less than one hundred dollars for each day such boiler is used, and in addition thereto shall be liable for any damage to persons or property which shall occur from any defects, as stated in the notice of the inspector. *Quarterly inspection.* *Compliance with orders.*

SEC. 579. Any owner or renter of a boiler, who shall consider himself aggrieved by the action of the inspector, under the provisions of the preceding section, may, within ten days after such inspection, notify the inspector of the fact, and demand a re-examination of the said boiler; the owner or renter shall select a practical engineer, who, with the inspector, shall select a third person, skilled in the manufacture and use of steam boilers, which said two persons, after taking an oath as reviewers, shall, together with the inspector, carefully examine the said boiler, and the decision of any two of these shall be final; should the decision of the inspector be sustained, the said owner or renter shall pay the expense of such review; but should it be reversed, the inspector shall restore the certificate, and the expense of the review shall be paid by the State; such reviewers shall receive five dollars for each day or part of a day they are engaged in making such review. *Appeal from orders, etc.*

SEC. 580. Any person erecting or using a steam boiler without having the same inspected by the inspector of the district in which the said boiler is located, shall pay a fine of one hundred dollars, and fifty dollars for each day any such boiler is used without being inspected; and any person who shall alter or change a steam gauge or weight on a safety valve for the purpose of carrying a greater pressure of steam on a boiler than that allowed by the certificate of inspection, shall be liable to a fine of five hundred dollars; and any owner or renter of a steam boiler who shall neglect or refuse to place his certificate of inspection on the premises, as prescribed in section 577 hereof, shall pay a fine of five dollars for each day's refusal or neglect. *Use without inspection, etc.*

SEC. 581. The inspector shall have power to examine the engineers and assistants in charge of boilers, and if any engineer or assistant is found incompetent or addicted to intemperance, the inspector shall notify the owner or renter, and withdraw the certificate of inspection until such engineer or assistant is displaced. *Examination of engineers.*

SEC. 583. It shall be the duty of each inspector to keep a correct record of the locations of all boilers in his district, when each boiler was inspected, the condition of the same at the time of inspection, the instructions given to the engineers in charge, the certificates issued, and the amount of steam pressure allowed in each certificate, and the boilers condemned or ordered to be re- *Record.*

paired; also a correct account of all money received or paid out; and they shall report the same annually to the State comptroller.

Inspection for insurance.

SEC. 586. Every steam boiler insurance company doing business in this State shall have a resident inspector, whose duty it shall be to make inspections of steam boilers submitted for insurance to such steam boiler insurance company; and any owner or renter of a steam boiler who has the same insured in a steam boiler insurance company doing business in this State, in compliance with the laws thereof, and having a resident inspector and an established system of inspection, must immediately after the first annual inspection in each year by such resident inspector of such steam-boiler insurance company, present to the State inspector of the district in which the said steam boilers are located, the certificate of inspection of the said company; and the said company shall be charged and chargeable with a fee of one dollar for each and every boiler so inspected and insured, which shall be paid to the State inspector with such certificate: *Provided*, That when there is more than one steam boiler belonging to the same owner or renter so insured, then the fee so chargeable to the insurance company shall be one dollar per boiler for the first five, and one dollar for each additional five or fraction thereof over and above the first five; and upon the acceptance of the provisions of this section by the owner or renter of said steam boiler, the said owner or renter shall be exempted from the requirements of this subdivision of this article.

ACTS OF 1894.

CHAPTER 202.—*Factories and workshops—Ventilating apparatus—Carroll County.*

Ventilating fans, etc., in mills for grinding stone.

SECTION 1. Every person or corporation owning or controlling any mill for grinding flint or any other kind of stone by the cylinder or dry process, in Carroll County, shall be required to furnish and equip said mill with the most improved fans, ventilators and other appliances for the removal from said mill of the dust made therein by conducting said business, and to provide for the use of each person employed in said mill, the most approved apparatus for the protection of said person so employed, from inhaling said dust, and to keep in repair and renew said apparatus from time to time as may be necessary, free of cost to said person so employed; and any such person or corporation failing to comply with the requirements of this act shall be guilty of a misdemeanor, and upon indictment and conviction, shall be subject to a fine of not less than five hundred dollars for each and every offense.

Duty of employees.

SEC. 2. Every person employed in any such mill for grinding flint or other stone, as specified in the preceding section, shall use and wear the apparatus provided for his protection as above specified, during the entire time he is at work in any part of said mill where there is any dust, and any such person so employed, who shall fail to comply with this requirement, shall be guilty of a misdemeanor, and upon indictment and conviction, shall be subject to a fine of not less than five dollars for each and every offense.

Inspection.

SEC. 3. It shall be the duty of the constable of said county, at least twice in every year, to inspect all such mills which may be located within the districts for which the said constables are appointed, respectively, and to report to the next grand jury for said county any violations of any of the requirements of this act which they may discover or which may come to their knowledge.

ACTS OF 1910.

CHAPTER 724.—*Inspection of factories and workshops—Floors of shirt factories to be sprinkled.*

(Page 139.)

Sprinkling required.

SECTION 1. The proprietors or managers of shirt factories in the State of Maryland are hereby required to sprinkle the floors of said factories every morning with water, and any proprietor or manager failing to comply with the provisions of this act shall be deemed guilty of a misdemeanor and upon conviction shall be fined the sum of ten dollars, and cost of prosecution, for each and every offense, one-half of said fine to go to the informer, balance to be paid into the treasury of the State.

MASSACHUSETTS.

REVISED LAWS—1902.

CHAPTER 75.—*Regulation and inspection of bakeries.*

SECTION 28. All buildings which are occupied as biscuit, bread or cake bakeries shall be properly drained and plumbed. They shall be provided with a proper wash room and water-closets, having ventilation apart from the bake room or rooms where food products are manufactured; and no water-closet, earth closet, privy or ash pit shall be within or communicate directly with the bake room of any bakery. *Sanitation.*

SEC. 29. Every room which is used for the manufacture of flour or meal food products shall, if required by the board of health, have an impermeable floor constructed of cement or of tiles laid in cement, and an additional floor of wood properly saturated with linseed oil. The walls and ceiling of such rooms shall be plastered or wainscoted, and, if required by the board of health, shall be whitewashed at least once in three months. The furniture and utensils therein shall be so arranged that they and the floor may at all times be kept clean and in good sanitary condition. *Construction of workrooms.*

SEC. 30. The sleeping places for persons who are employed in a bakery shall be separate from the rooms in which flour or meal food products are manufactured or stored. *Sleeping places.*

SEC. 32. The owner, agent or lessee of any property affected by the provisions of sections twenty-eight and twenty-nine shall, within sixty days after service of notice requiring any alterations to be made on such property, comply therewith. Such notice shall be in writing, and may be served upon such owner, agent or lessee personally or by mail directed to his last known address. *Time for alterations.*

SEC. 33. Whoever violates the provisions of the five preceding sections, or refuses to comply with any requirement of the board of health authorized therein, shall, for the first offense, be punished by a fine of not less than twenty nor more than fifty dollars; for the second offense, by a fine not less than fifty nor more than one hundred dollars or by imprisonment for not more than ten days; for the third offense, by a fine of not less than two hundred and fifty dollars or by imprisonment for not more than thirty days or by both such fine and imprisonment. *Penalties.*

SEC. 34 (as amended by chapter 403, Acts of 1902). The board of health of a city or town may make such further regulations as the public health may require, and shall cause such regulations, together with the six preceding sections, to be printed and posted in all such bakeries and places of business. *Added regulations.*

CHAPTER 104.—*Factories and workshops—Inspection, etc.*

SECTION 1. Every city, except Boston, and every town which accepts the provisions of this section or has accepted the corresponding provisions of earlier laws may, for the prevention of fire and the preservation of life, by ordinances or by-laws not inconsistent with law and applicable throughout the whole or any defined part of its territory, regulate the inspection, materials, construction, alteration and use of buildings and other structures within its limits, except such as are owned or occupied by the United States or by the Commonwealth and except bridges, quays and wharves, and may prescribe penalties not exceeding one hundred dollars for each violation of such ordinances or by-laws. *Power of towns, etc., to inspect.*

Who are inspectors.   SEC. 14. The words "inspector of factories and public buildings," as used in this chapter, shall mean a member of the inspection department of the district police.

[See chapter 537, Acts of 1907, page 943.]

Buildings to be examined.   SEC. 15. The inspectors of factories and public buildings shall from time to time examine all buildings within their respective districts which are subject to the provisions of this chapter. If, in the judgment of any such inspector, such building conforms to the requirements of this chapter, he shall issue to the owner, lessee or occupant thereof, or any portion thereof used in the manner described in section twenty-five, a certificate to that effect, specifying the number of persons for whom the egresses and means of escape from fire are sufficient. Such certificate shall not continue in force for more than five years after its date, but so long as it continues in force it shall be conclusive evidence of a compliance by the person to whom it is issued with the provisions of this chapter. It shall be void if a greater number of persons than is therein specified are * * * employed * * * within such building or portion thereof, or if such building is used for any purposes materially different from those for which it was used at the time of the granting thereof, or if its interior arrangement is materially altered, or if any egresses or means of escape from fire in such building at the time of granting such certificate are rendered unavailable or materially changed. Such certificate may be revoked by such inspector at any time upon written notice to the holder thereof or to the occupant of the premises for which it was granted, and shall be so revoked if, in the opinion of such inspector, the conditions have so changed that the existing egresses and means of escape are not proper and sufficient. A copy of said certificate shall be kept posted in a conspicuous place upon each story of such building by the occupant of the premises covered thereby.

Certificate.

Alterations, change of use, etc.

Filing application.   SEC. 16. Upon application to an inspector for a certificate under the provisions of this chapter, he shall issue to the applicant an acknowledgment of such application, which for ninety days pending the granting or refusal of such certificate, shall have the same effect as such certificate, and such acknowledgment may be renewed by him with the same effect for a further period, not exceeding ninety days, and may be further renewed by the chief of the district police, until such times as such certificates shall be granted or refused.

Notice of changes.   SEC. 17. If any change in the use or otherwise shall be made upon premises for which such certificate has been issued which would render the certificate void according to the provisions of section fifteen, the person who makes such change shall forthwith give written notice thereof to an inspector for the district or to the chief of the district police.

Notice of failure to conform.   SEC. 18. If an inspector finds that any building or portion thereof which is subject to the provisions of this chapter fails to conform thereto, or if any change is made therein which would render a certificate void according to the provisions of section fifteen, he shall give notice in writing to the owner, lessee, occupant or agent in charge thereof, specifying such additional egresses and means of escape from fire as in his opinion may be necessary to conform to the provisions of this chapter and to obtain a certificate as aforesaid.

Appeals.   SEC. 19. Whoever is aggrieved by the order, requirement or direction of an inspector given under the provisions of this chapter may, within ten days after the service thereof, apply to the superior court for the county in which the building to which such order, requirement or direction relates is situated for an injunction to restrain its enforcement; and after such notice as said court shall order to all parties interested, a hearing may be had before said court at such early and convenient time and place as shall be fixed by said order; or the court may appoint three disinterested persons skilled in the subject-matter of the controversy, to ex-

amine the matter and hear the parties; and the decision of said
court, or the decision, in writing and under oath, of the majority
of said experts, filed in the office of the clerk of courts in said
county within ten days after such hearing, may alter, annul or
affirm such order, requirement or direction. Such decision or a
certified copy thereof shall have the same authority, force and
effect as the original order, requirement or direction of the inspector. If such decision annuls or alters such order, requirement
or direction, the court shall also enjoin the said inspector from
enforcing it, and in every such case the certificate required by
section fifteen shall thereupon be issued by said court or by said
experts.

SEC. 22. No building * * * more than two stories in height Plans of build-
which is designed to be used above the second story, in whole or ings to be filed.
in part, as a factory, workshop or mercantile or other establishment and has accommodations for ten or more employees above
said story, * * * shall be erected until a copy of the plans
thereof has been deposited with the inspector of factories and
public buildings for the district in which it is to be erected by the
person causing its erection, or by the architect thereof. Such plans
shall include the method of ventilation provided therefor and a
copy of such portion of the specifications thereof as the inspector
may require. Such building shall not be so erected without sufficient egresses and other means of escape from fire, properly located
and constructed. The certificate of the inspector, indorsed with
the approval of the chief of the district police, shall be conclusive
evidence of a compliance with the provisions of this chapter unless, after it is granted, a change is made in the plans or specifications of such egresses and means of escape without a new certificate therefor. Such inspector may require that proper fire stops
shall be provided in the floors, walls and partitions of such building, and may make such further requirements as may be necessary
or proper to prevent the spread of fire therein or its communication from any steam boiler or heating apparatus.

SEC. 23. No wooden flue or air duct for heating or ventilating Wooden flues,
purposes shall be placed in any building which is subject to the etc., forbidden.
provisions of sections twenty-four and twenty-five and no pipe for
conveying hot air or steam in such building shall be placed or remain within one inch of any woodwork, unless protected to the
satisfaction of said inspector by suitable guards or casings of
incombustible material.

SEC. 24. Whoever erects or constructs a building, or an architect Penalty.
or other persons who draws plans or specifications or superintends
the erection or construction of a building, in violation of the provisions of this chapter, shall be punished by a fine of not less than
fifty nor more than one thousand dollars.

SEC. 25 (as amended by chapter 503, Acts of 1907). A building Fire escapes,
* * * in which ten or more persons are employed above the etc.
second story in a factory, workshop, mercantile and other establishment, * * * and a factory, workshop, mercantile or other
establishment the owner, lessee or occupant of which is notified in
writing by an inspector of factories and public buildings that
the provisions of this chapter are deemed by him applicable
thereto shall be provided with proper egresses or other means of
escape from fire, sufficient for the use of all persons * * * employed * * * therein; but no owner, lessee or occupant of
such building shall be deemed to have violated this provision
unless he has been notified in writing by such inspector what additional egresses or means of escape from fire are necessary and has
neglected or refused to supply the same. The egresses and means
of escape shall be kept unobstructed, in good repair and ready for
use, and every such egress shall be provided with a sign having on
it the word "Exit" in letters not less than five inches in height
and so as plainly to indicate to persons within the building the
location of such egresses. Stairways on the outside of a building
shall have suitable railed landings at each story above the first,
accessible at each story from doors or windows, and such land-

ings, doors and windows shall be kept clear of ice, snow and other obstructions. * * * If the inspector so directs in writing, women or children shall not be employed in a factory, workshop, mercantile or other establishment, in a room above the second story from which there is only one egress, and all doors and windows in any building which is subject to the provisions of this section shall open outwardly, and every room above the second story in any such building, in which ten or more persons are employed, shall be provided with more than one egress by stairways or by such other way or device, approved in writing by the inspector, as the owner may elect, on the inside or outside of the building, placed as near as practicable at each end of the room. The certificate of the inspector shall be conclusive evidence of a compliance with such requirements.

Fire extinguishers.   SEC. 26. Each story above the second story of a building which is subject to the provisions of the preceding section shall be supplied with means of extinguishing fire, consisting of pails of water or other portable apparatus or of a hose attached to a suitable water supply and capable of reaching any part of such story; and such appliances shall be kept at all times ready for use and in good condition.

Safety devices on elevators.   SEC. 27. Elevator cabs or cars, whether used for freight or passengers, shall be provided with a suitable mechanical device by which they will be securely held in the event of an accident to the shipper rope or hoisting machinery, or any similar accident, and they shall be guarded and equipped with some attachment or device fastened to the elevator cab or car, elevator well, or floor of the building, which shall prevent any person from being caught between the floor of the cab or car and the floor of the building while attempting to enter or leave the elevator. Elevators used for carrying freight shall be equipped with a suitable device which shall act as a danger signal to warn people of the approach of the elevator.

Construction.   Elevator wells hereafter built shall be so constructed that that part of the inside surface of the well which comes in front of the opening or door of the cab or car shall be flush with the cab or car, and the door opening from said elevator well into the building shall be placed not more than two inches back from the face of said well, so as to allow no space for a foothold between the car and well door of the building. All the above construction work and devices shall be approved by the inspectors of factories and public buildings, except that in the city of Boston they shall be approved by the building commissioner, and in other cities by the inspector of buildings; but, upon the approval of said commissioner, or inspector or buildings, or inspector of factories and public buildings, any elevator may be used without any or all of such appliances or devices if the nature of the business is such that the necessity for the same will not warrant the expense.

Notice of unsafe elevators.   SEC. 28 (as amended by chapter 455, Acts of 1911). If an elevator which is used for freight or passengers is, in the judgment of the inspector of factories and public buildings, or of the inspector of buildings of a city or town, unsafe or dangerous to use or has not been constructed in the manner required by law, said inspector shall immediately post conspicuously upon the entrance to or door of the cab or car of such elevator a notice of its dangerous condition and shall prohibit its use until made safe to his satisfaction. No person shall, without authority from said inspector, remove such notice or operate such elevator while the notice is posted as aforesaid. The provisions of this section shall not apply to the city of Boston.

Use of explosive compounds.   SEC. 47. Explosives or inflammable compounds shall not be used in any factory in such place or manner as to obstruct or render hazardous the egress of operatives in case of fire.

Cotenant may provide fire escape.   SEC. 48. If a building which is subject to the provisions of this chapter is owned, leased or occupied, jointly or in severalty, any owner, lessee or occupant may affix to any part of the outside wall of such building any means of egress or of escape from fire specified and described by an inspector as above provided, notwithstanding the objection of any other such owner, lessee or occupant; and such means of egress or of escape may project over the highway.

SEC. 49. A license which is required by law, ordinance or by-law to authorize any premises to be used for any purpose specified in section twenty-five shall not be granted until a certificate for such building or portion thereof shall first have been obtained from an inspector as above provided, and, when issued, shall not continue in force after the expiration of such certificate. *Certificate to precede license.*

SEC. 50. The owner, lessee or occupant of a theater, factory, workshop or manufacturing establishment, or whoever owns any building or room mentioned in and subject to the provisions of sections fifteen, seventeen, twenty-two, twenty-three, twenty-five, twenty-six, thirty-six and thirty-seven, or controls the use thereof, shall cause the provisions thereof to be observed, and such person or corporation shall be liable to any person injured for all damages caused by a violation of the provisions of this chapter. No criminal prosecution shall be commenced for such violation until four weeks after notice in writing to such person or corporation has been given by an inspector of factories and public buildings of any changes necessary to be made to conform to the provisions of said sections, nor if such changes shall have been made in accordance with such notice. Notice to one member of a firm or to the clerk or treasurer of a corporation or to the person in charge of the premises shall be sufficient notice hereunder to all members of such firm or to such corporation owning, leasing, or controlling the premises. Such notice may be served personally or sent by mail. *Who liable.* *Allowance of time.* *What constitutes notice.*

SEC. 53. Sections fifteen to eighteen, inclusive, twenty-two to twenty-six, inclusive, * * * .forty-eight to fifty-one, inclusive, * * * shall not apply to the city of Boston. *Exceptions as to Boston.*

SEC. 55. Whoever, being the owner, lessee or occupant of any building or room described in section twenty-two violates the provisions of sections fifteen to eighteen, inclusive, twenty-two to twenty-six, inclusive, thirty-six, thirty-seven, forty-eight and forty-nine, shall be punished by a fine of not less than fifty nor more than one thousand dollars. *Penalty.*

SEC. 56. Whoever violates any provision of this chapter for which no other penalty is specifically prescribed shall be punished by a fine of not more than one hundred dollars. *General penalty.*

CHAPTER 108.—*Factories and workshops—Inspectors.*

SECTION 8 (as amended by chapter 413, Acts of 1907). The members of the inspection department of the district police shall, except as otherwise provided in chapters one hundred and four, one hundred and five and one hundred and six, enforce the provisions thereof and all other provisions of law relative to the employment of women and minors in manufacturing, mechanical and mercantile establishments, the employment of children, young persons or women in factories or workshops, the lighting and the ventilation of factories or workshops, the keeping of them clean, and the securing of proper sanitary provisions therein, and the making of clothing in unsanitary conditions. For such purposes, said inspectors may enter all buildings and parts thereof which are subject to the provisions of said chapters and examine the methods of protection from accident, the means of escape from fire. the sanitary provisions, the lighting and the means of ventilation, and may make investigations as to the employment of children, young persons and women. *District police as inspectors.* *Duties.* *May enter buildings.*

[See chapter 537, Acts of 1907, page 943.]

ACTS OF 1904.

CHAPTER 430.—*Inspectors of factories, etc.*

SECTION 1. The governor is hereby authorized and requested to appoint two additional members of the district police force, who *Additional inspectors.*

shall be employed as additional inspectors of factories and public buildings. The terms of office, salaries, powers and duties of said additional members shall be the same as those of the district police force already appointed. The said appointments may be made without giving to veterans the preference required by sections twenty-one and twenty-two of chapter 19 of the Revised Laws.

[See chapter 537, Acts of 1907, page 943.]

ACTS OF 1906.

CHAPTER 521.—*Inspection of steam boilers—Chief inspector.*

Appointment. SECTION 1. The governor is hereby authorized to appoint, as hereinafter provided, one of the members of the boiler inspection department of the district police as chief inspector of said boiler inspection department. Said chief inspector shall have supervision over the members of said boiler inspection department in order to secure uniform enforcement throughout the Commonwealth of all acts relative to the inspection of boilers and the examination of engineers and firemen. Said chief inspector shall receive an annual salary of two thousand dollars and his actual and necessary traveling expenses.

Examinations. SEC. 2. As soon as practicable after the passage of this act the civil service commissioners shall hold an examination to determine the qualifications of applicants for the position of said chief inspector. The commissioners shall certify to the governor the names of the three persons receiving the highest percentage on such examination, and the percentage obtained by each, and the governor shall appoint one of said three persons as chief inspector of the boiler inspection department.

CHAPTER 522.—*Inspection of steam boilers—Inspector.*

Additional inspectors. SECTION 1. The governor is hereby authorized and directed to appoint five additional members of the inspection department of the district police, who shall be not above forty-five years of age. Said age limit shall apply to all new appointments to said boiler inspection department, but shall not apply to any reappointment thereto. They shall be detailed for the inspection of boilers, and shall receive the same compensation now received by the present inspectors of boilers. The governor is also hereby authorized to appoint one clerk, at an annual salary of eight hundred dollars, to serve in the said department, and four additional clerks, at an annual salary of six hundred dollars each, to serve at branch offices in the said department.

ACTS OF 1907.

CHAPTER 451·—*Inspectors of boilers.*

Additional inspectors. SECTION 1. The governor is hereby authorized and directed to appoint five additional members of the boiler inspection department of the district police, who shall be licensed engineers having not less than five years' experience, and who shall be not above forty-five years of age. The said age limit shall apply hereafter to all new appointments in said boiler inspection department, but shall not apply to any reappointment therein. The said five additional members shall be detailed for the inspection of boilers and the examination of engineers and firemen, and shall receive the same compensation now received by the present inspectors of boilers. * * *

CHAPTER 465.—*Inspection of steam boilers.*

What boilers to be inspected. SECTION 1 (as amended by chapter 393, Acts of 1909). All steam boilers and their appurtenances, except boilers of railroad locomotives, motor road vehicles, boilers in private residences, boilers in public buildings and in apartment houses used solely for heating, and carrying pressures not exceeding fifteen pounds per square inch, and having less than four square feet of grate surface, boilers of not more than three horsepower, boilers used for horticultural and agricultural purposes exclusively, and boilers under the jurisdiction of the United States, shall be thoroughly inspected internally and externally at intervals of not over one year, and shall not be operated at pressures in excess of the safe working pressure stated in the certificate of inspection hereinafter mentioned, which pressure is to be ascertained by rules established by the board of boiler rules, to be appointed as hereinafter provided; and shall be equipped with such appliances to insure safety of operation as shall be prescribed by said board. All such boilers installed after January first, nineteen hundred and eight, shall be so inspected when installed. A boiler in this Commonwealth at the time of the passage of this act, which does not conform to the rules of construction formulated by the board of boiler rules may be installed after a thorough internal and external inspection and hydrostatic pressure test by a member of the boiler inspection department of the district police, or by an inspector holding a certificate of competency as an inspector of steam boilers, as provided by section six of chapter four hundred and sixty-five of the acts of the year nineteen hundred and seven, and employed by the company insuring the boiler. The pressure allowed on such boilers is to be ascertained by rules formulated by the board of boiler rules. No certificate of inspection shall be granted on any boiler installed after May first, nineteen hundred and eight, which does not conform to the rules formulated by the board of boiler rules. *Boilers not conforming to standard.*

SEC. 2. Whoever owns, or uses or causes to be used, any such boiler, unless the same is under the periodically guaranteed inspection of insurance companies authorized to insure boilers in this Commonwealth, shall annually report to the chief of the district police the location of such boiler. *Duty of owners, etc.*

SEC. 3. All such boilers shall also be inspected externally at least once each year when in operation, and it shall be the duty of the inspector to observe the pressure of steam carried, and the general condition of each boiler, and to ascertain if the safety valve, and the appliances for indicating the pressure of steam and level of water in the boiler, are in proper working order. No person shall remove or tamper with any safety appliance prescribed by the board of boiler rules, and no person shall in any manner load the safety valve to a greater pressure than that allowed by the certificate of inspection. *Annual inspections.*

SEC. 4. The inspection of boilers and appurtenances shall be made by the boiler inspection department of the district police, under the supervision of the chief inspector of boilers, or by inspectors of such insurance companies as have complied with the laws of the Commonwealth and are authorized to insure steam boilers. Inspectors of boilers in the boiler inspection department hereafter appointed shall not be subject to the rules of the civil service commission requiring members of the district police to be of a certain height and weight, but shall be appointed solely on the basis of their ability and competency properly and thoroughly to inspect steam boilers. *Who may inspect.*

SEC. 5. No person shall act as an inspector of boilers which are under the periodically guaranteed inspection of companies that have complied with the laws of this Commonwealth, unless he holds a certificate of competency as hereinafter provided. *Certificates required.*

SEC. 6. Whoever desires to act as an inspector of boilers, as specified in section five, shall make application upon blanks to be furnished by the chief of the district police. Three members of the boiler inspection department shall act as a board of examiners. The application shall show the total experience of the applicant and shall be accompanied by a letter of request for his examination from the boiler insurance company by whom he is or is to be employed. Willful falsification in the matter of any statement *Applications.*

contained in the application shall be deemed sufficient cause for
Examination. the revocation of said certificate at any time. The applicant shall
be examined as to his knowledge of the construction, installation,
maintenance and repair of steam boilers and their appendages.
and, if found competent, he shall receive a certificate of competency to inspect steam boilers for the boiler insurance company
by whom he is or is to be employed, and the certificate shall continue in force during his employment by said company, unless revoked for incompetency or untrustworthiness. When a person
ceases to be employed as an inspector by a boiler insurance company the insurance company shall notify the chief of the district
police of the matter, giving the reasons therefor. A period of
ninety days shall elapse between the dates of examinations, except
in the case of an appeal as hereinafter provided. The certificate
of competency shall be revoked for the incompetence or untrustworthiness of the holder thereof, and shall remain revoked until
a new certificate is issued. If a certificate is lost by fire or other
cause a new certificate shall be issued in its place, upon satisfactory proof of such loss, without reexamination.

Appeals.   Sec. 7. A person who is refused a certificate of competency, or
whose certificate is revoked, may appeal from such decision to the
chief of the district police, who shall grant a rehearing of the
case by a board of five examiners, no one of whom shall have
acted as an examiner in the former instance, whose decision shall
be final if approved by the chief of the district police. The applicant shall have the privilege of having one representative of the
boiler insurance company by whom he is or is to be employed
present during an examination or the hearing of an appeal.

Unlawful in- Sec. 8. Any steam boiler insurance company which issues a
spections. certificate of inspection signed by an inspector who does not hold
a certificate of competency may have its authority to insure steam
boilers revoked by the commissioner of insurance for the Commonwealth. Any person in the employ of a steam boiler insurance
company who applies for a certificate of competency as an inspector of boilers before this act takes effect shall be authorized to
inspect boilers until his application is passed upon by the proper
authority.

Reports.   Sec. 9. The inspectors of the boiler inspection department of the
district police shall make reports of all inspections and shall make
such recommendations to the chief inspector of boilers as they
may deem expedient.

Reports of in- Sec. 10. Every insurance company authorized to insure steam
surance com- boilers within the Commonwealth shall forward to the chief in-
panies. spector of boilers, within fourteen days after each internal and
external inspection of boilers herein required to be inspected, reports of all boilers so inspected by it. Such reports shall be made
on blanks furnished by the chief inspector of boilers, and shall
contain all orders made by the company regarding the boilers so
inspected.

Boilers rejected. Sec. 11. Every boiler insurance company shall report immediately to the chief inspector of boilers the name of the owner or
user and the location of every boiler herein required to be inspected, upon which they have canceled or refused insurance,
giving the reasons for so doing.

Heating plants. Sec. 12. Boilers and their appurtenances used exclusively for
heating purposes, but which are not herein required to be inspected, shall be provided with such appliances to insure safety
as shall be prescribed by the board of boiler rules, and it shall be
the duty of the boiler inspection department to inspect such boilers
upon application of the owner.

Owner to pre- Sec. 13. The owner or user of a boiler herein required to be
pare boiler. inspected which is not insured by a boiler insurance company,
shall, after due notice, prepare the boiler for internal and external inspection, at the appointed time, by drawing the water
from the boiler and removing the manhole and hand-hole plates.
The boiler inspection department shall give the owner at least
fourteen days' notice to prepare boilers for this inspection, but
shall not be required to give notice of external inspection.

SEC. 14. The owner or user of a boiler inspected by the boiler Fee. inspection department shall pay to the inspector five dollars for each boiler internally and externally inspected, and two dollars for each visit for external inspection. The inspector shall give receipts for the same, and shall pay all sums so received to the chief inspector of boilers, who shall pay the same to the treasurer of the Commonwealth.

SEC. 15. If, upon inspection the inspector finds the boiler to be Certificate of inspection. in safe working order, with the fittings necessary to safety, and properly set up, he shall issue to the owner or user thereof a certificate of inspection stating the maximum pressure at which the boiler may be operated, as ascertained by the rules established by the board of boiler rules, and thereupon such owner or user may operate the boiler mentioned in the certificate. If the inspector finds that the boiler is not in safe working condition, or is not provided with fittings necessary to safety, or if the fittings are improperly arranged, he shall withhold his certificate until the boiler and its fittings are put in a condition to insure safety of operation, and the owner or user shall not operate the boiler, or cause it to be operated, until such certificate has been granted.

SEC. 16. Every boiler which has been inspected by the boiler Marking. inspection department shall be numbered either by stamping the number upon the boiler or by attaching a numbered metal tag by a seal or otherwise to the boiler or its fittings. No person except a member of the boiler inspection department shall deface or remove any such number or tag.

SEC. 17. Insurance companies engaged in the business of inspecting and insuring steam boilers shall, after each internal Certificates issued by companies. and external inspection, if they deem the boiler to be in safe working condition, issue a certificate of inspection stating the maximum pressure at which the boiler may be operated. This maximum pressure shall be determined under the rules established by the board of boiler rules.

SEC. 18 (as amended by chapter 563, Acts of 1908). No insurance company shall issue a policy of insurance on a steam boiler Limit. for a longer period than three years. If a boiler is insured which has not previously been inspected externally and internally and a certificate of inspection issued, the company so insuring shall forthwith notify the chief of the boiler inspection department of the district police to that effect, and shall inspect such boiler internally and externally within one month after the insurance is effected. No insurance shall be effected on any boiler installed after May first, nineteen hundred and eight, which does not conform to the rules formulated by the board of boiler rules.

SEC. 19. The certificate of inspection issued by the boiler inspection department, or by an insurance company, shall state Certificate to state what. the name of the owner or user, the location, size and number of the boiler, the date of inspection and the maximum pressure at which the boiler may be operated, under the signature of the person who made the inspection, and shall also contain such quotations from the statutes as shall be deemed necessary by the board of boiler rules, and shall so be placed as to be easily read in the engine room or boiler room of the plant where the boiler is located, except that the certificate of inspection for a portable boiler shall be kept on the premises and shall be accessible at all times.

SEC. 20. No person shall use, or cause to be used, a steam boiler, Safety plugs. excepting boilers upon motor road vehicles, steam fire engines, boilers in private residences, or boilers under the jurisdiction of the United States, unless it is provided with a fusible safety plug made of lead or some other equally fusible material, as specified by the rules to be established by the board of boiler rules.

SEC. 21. The owner or user of any boiler herein required to be Notice of defects. inspected shall immediately notify the boiler inspection department, if the boiler is being operated under the inspection of that department, or the insurance company, if it is being operated under its inspection, in case a defect affecting the safety of the boiler is discovered.

Operation to cease, when.
SEC. 22. If the insurance on any boiler herein required to be inspected expires, or is canceled because the insurers deem it unsafe to continue the operation of the boiler, the owner or user shall cease to operate it until it has been put in a safe condition, satisfactory to the insurers, or has been inspected by the boiler inspection department and a certificate of inspection has been issued.

Hydrostatic test.
SEC. 23. If, in the judgment of the inspector or of the insurance company, it is advisable to apply a hydrostatic pressure test to a boiler, the owner or user shall prepare the boiler for such test, as directed by the inspector or by the insurance company.

Board of boiler rules.
SEC. 24. The governor, within thirty days after the passage of this act, with the consent of the council, shall appoint a board of five persons, to be known as the board of boiler rules, of whom the last four shall be appointed to serve as follows: Two for a term of two years each and two for a term of three years each. At the expiration of their terms of office their successors shall be appointed for terms of three years each. The members of the board, other than the chairman hereinafter designated, shall receive for their services the first year in office the sum of five hundred dollars each. Thereafter they shall receive as compensation for their services and reimbursement for their expenses such amount as the governor and council shall order, not exceeding in the aggregate in any one year the sum of one thousand dollars. The board shall be constituted as follows: The chief inspector of the boiler inspection department of the district police, who shall be its chairman; one member representing the boiler using interests; one member representing the boiler manufacturing interests; one member representing the boiler insurance interests; and one member who is an operating engineer.

Clerk.
SEC. 25. The chief inspector of boilers of the boiler inspection department of the district police shall appoint a clerk, who shall be a stenographer, and who shall also act as secretary of the board of boiler rules, and whose salary shall be twelve hundred dollars a year.

Expenses.
The necessary expenses of the board, including those of the secretary of the board, incurred in the discharge of their duty during the first year, shall be paid out of the treasury of the Commonwealth, but shall not exceed the sum of fifteen hundred dollars for that year. The attorney-general of the Commonwealth shall furnish all needed assistance to the board in the framing of the rules hereinafter provided for.

Rules.
SEC. 26 (as amended by chapter 393, Acts of 1909). It shall be the duty of the board of boiler rules to formulate rules for the construction, installation and inspection of steam boilers, and for ascertaining the safe working pressure to be carried on said boilers, to prescribe tests, if they deem it necessary, to ascertain the qualities of materials used in the construction of boilers; to formulate rules regulating the construction and sizes of safety -valves for boilers of different sizes and pressures, the construction, use and location of fusible safety plugs, appliances for indicating the pressure of steam and the level of water in the boiler, and such other appliances as the board may deem necessary to safety in operating steam boilers; and to make a standard form of certificate of inspection.

Meetings.
The board of boiler rules shall hold public hearings on the first Thursday in May and November of each year, and at such other times as the board may determine, on petitions for changes in the rules formulated by said board. If the board, after any such hearing, shall deem it advisable to make changes in said rules, it shall appoint a day for a further hearing, and shall give notice thereof and of the changes proposed by advertising in at least one newspaper in each of the cities of Boston, Worcester, Springfield, Fall River, Lowell and Lynn, at least ten days before said hearing. If the board on its own initiative contemplates changes in said rules, like notice and a hearing shall be given and held before the

adoption thereof. Changes made in the rules which affect the construction of new boilers shall take effect six months after the approval of the same by the governor: *Provided, however,* That the board may, upon request, permit the application of such change in, or additions to, rules, to boilers manufactured or installed during said six months. When a person desires to manufacture a special type of boiler the design of which is not covered by the rules formulated by the board of boiler rules, he shall submit drawings and specifications of such boiler to said board, which, if it approves, shall permit the construction of the same.

SEC. 27. The rules so formulated shall be submitted to the governor for his approval, and when approved shall have the force of law, and shall be printed and furnished to those requesting them by the boiler inspection department. Governor to approve.

SEC. 28 (as amended by chapter 393, Acts of 1909). The boiler inspection department of the district police shall enforce the provisions of the preceding sections, and such rules as shall be promulgated by the board of boiler rules with the approval of the governor. Whoever violates any provision of this act or of the said rules shall be punished by a fine of not less than twenty nor more than five hundred dollars or by imprisonment for not more than six months, or by both such fine and imprisonment. A trial justice shall have jurisdiction of complaints for violation of the provisions of this act, and in such cases may impose a fine of not more than fifty dollars. All members of the boiler inspection department of the district police shall have authority in the pursuance of their duty to enter any premises on which a boiler is situated, and any person who hinders or prevents or attempts to prevent any member of the boiler inspection department from so entering shall be liable to the penalty specified in this section. Enforcement.

The provisions of this act relative to the inspection and operation of boilers within the Commonwealth shall not be held to apply to steam fire engines brought into the Commonwealth for temporary use in times of emergency, for the purpose of checking conflagrations. Steam fire engines.

CHAPTER 537.—*Inspection of factories and workshops—Inspectors of health.*

SECTION 1. The State board of health shall, as soon as may be after the passage of this act, divide the Commonwealth into not more than fifteen districts, to be known as health districts, in such manner as it may deem necessary or proper for carrying out the purposes of this act. Districts.

SEC. 2. After the division aforesaid has been made, the governor, with the advice and consent of the council, shall appoint in each health district one practical and discreet person, learned in the science of medicine and hygiene, to be State inspector of health in that district. Every nomination for such office shall be made at least seven days prior to the appointment. The said State inspectors of health shall hold their offices for a period of five years from the time of their respective appointments, but shall be liable to removal from office by the governor and council at any time. Inspectors.

SEC. 3. Every State inspector of health * * · * shall inform himself concerning the health of all minors employed in factories within his district, and, whenever he may deem it advisable or necessary, he shall call the ill health or physical unfitness of any minor to the attention of his or her parents or employers and of the State board of health. Duties.

SEC. 5. The State inspectors of health shall, under the direction of the State board of health and in place of the inspection department of the district police, enforce the provisions of section forty-one of chapter one hundred and four of the Revised Laws so far as said section provides that factories shall be well ventilated and kept clean, sections forty-one, forty-four and forty-seven to sixty-one, inclusive, of chapter one hundred and six of the Revised Enforcement of inspection laws in factories.

Laws, chapter three hundred and twenty-two of the Acts of the year nineteen hundred and two, chapter four hundred and seventy-five of the Acts of the year nineteen hundred and three, chapter two hundred and thirty-eight of the Acts of the year nineteen hundred and five, and chapter two hundred and fifty of the Acts of the year nineteen hundred and six; and the powers and duties heretofore conferred and imposed upon the members of said inspection department of the district police by section eight of chapter one hundred and eight of the Revised Laws in respect to the foregoing sections and acts, and in respect to all acts in amendment thereof or in addition thereto, and in respect to any other laws, are hereby conferred and imposed upon said State inspectors of health or such other officers as the State board of health may from time to time appoint: *Provided, however,* That neither said board of health nor any inspector thereof shall have authority to require structural alterations to be made in buildings, but shall report the necessity therefor to the inspection department of the district police. Wherever in said provisions of law the words "inspector" or "inspectors of factories and public buildings," "inspection department of the district police," "inspector" or "inspectors of the district police," "district police," "factory inspector" or "inspectors," and "member" or "members of the district police" occur, they shall be taken to mean State inspector or inspectors of health. Wherever the words "chief of the district police" occur, they shall be taken to mean the State board of health.

Salaries.

SEC. 6. The governor, with the advice and consent of the council, shall establish the salaries of said State inspectors of health, having regard in each district to the extent of territory, the number of inhabitants, the character of the business there carried on, and the amount of time likely to be required for the proper discharge of the duties. The salaries thus established shall be paid from the treasury of the Commonwealth monthly.

Same.

SEC. 7. There may be expended out of the treasury of the Commonwealth annually, for the purposes specified in this act, for salaries, a sum not exceeding twenty-five thousand dollars, and for other expenses, a sum not exceeding five thousand dollars.

Experts.

SEC. 8. For the purpose of carrying out the provisions of this act the State board of health may employ from time to time experts in sanitation.

ACTS OF 1908.

CHAPTER 325.—*Inspection of factories, etc.—Pure water for humidifying.*

Water to be pure.

SECTION 1. The water used for humidifying purposes by any person, firm or corporation operating a factory or workshop, shall be of such a degree of purity as not to give rise to any impure or foul odors, and shall be so used as not to be injurious to the health of persons employed in such factories or workshops.

Violations.

SEC. 2. Any person, firm or corporation violating any provision of this act shall, upon conviction thereof, be punished by a fine of not less than ten nor more than one thousand dollars.

Enforcement.

SEC. 3. The state inspectors of health shall, under the direction of the state board of health, enforce the provisions of this act.

CHAPTER 375.—*Factory inspectors—Age of eligibility.*

Age of fifty years.

SECTION 1. A person who is not above the age of fifty years, if otherwise qualified, shall be eligible for appointment as an inspector of factories and public buildings, as a member of the inspection department of the district police.

CHAPTE 389.—*Inspectors of factories, etc.—Powers and duties.*

Inspectors may enter factories, etc.

SECTION 1 (as amended by chapter 354, Acts of 1909). The chief of the district police, the deputy chief of the inspection department of the district police, and the inspectors of factories and public buildings may, in the performance of their duty in enforcing the laws of the Commonwealth, enter any building, structure or inclosure, or any part thereof, and examine the methods of prevention of fire, means of exit, and means of protection against accident, and may make investigations as to the employment of children, young persons and women, except concerning health and the influence of occupation upon health. They may, except in the city of Boston, enter any public building, public or private institution, schoolhouse, church, theater, public hall, place of assemblage, or place of public resort, and make such investigations and order such structural or other changes, in said buildings, as are necessary relative to the construction, occupation, heating, ventilating and the sanitary condition and appliances of the same.

SEC. 2. Any person who hinders or prevents or attempts to prevent any member of the inspection department of the district police from entering any building, structure or inclosure or part thereof specified in the preceding section shall be liable to a penalty of not less than fifty nor more than one hundred dollars. _Hindering inspectors._

SEC 3. Trial justices, police, municipal and district courts shall have concurrent jurisdiction with the superior court to enforce the provisions of this act.

CHAPTER 487.—*Inspection of factories—Appeals from orders of inspectors.*

SECTION 1. Whoever is aggrieved by the order, requirement, or direction of an inspector of factories and public buildings may, within ten days after the service thereof, appeal to a judge of the superior court for the county in which the building to which such order, requirement or direction relates is situated, for an order forbidding its enforcement; and after such notice as said court shall order to all parties interested, a hearing may be had before said court at such early and convenient time and place as shall be fixed by said order; or the court may appoint three disinterested persons, skilled in the subject-matter of the controversy, to examine the matter and hear the parties; and the decision of said court, or the decision, in writing and under oath, of the majority of said experts, filed in the office of the clerk of courts in said county within ten days after such hearing may alter, annul or affirm such order, requirement or direction. Such decision or a certified copy thereof shall have the same authority, force and effect as the original order, requirement or direction of the inspector. If such decision annuls or alters such order, requirement or direction of the inspector, the court shall also order the said inspector not to enforce his order, requirement or direction, and in every case the certificate required by law shall thereupon be issued by said court or by said experts. _Appeal._

SEC. 2. The court may award reasonable compensation to experts appointed under the provisions of the preceding section which, if the order, requirement or direction of the inspector is altered or annulled, shall be paid by the county in which the application for an order of the court was made; otherwise by the applicant. If the order, requirement or direction of the inspector is affirmed by the court or the experts, costs shall be taxed against the applicant for the order of the court, as in civil cases, and shall be paid into the treasury of the county in which the application for such order of the court was made. _Experts to be compensated._

ACTS OF 1909.

CHAPTER 514.—*Inspection, etc., of factories—General provisions.*

SECTION 17 (as amended by chapter 241, Acts of 1911). The following words and phrases as used in all laws relative to the em- _Definitions of terms used._

ployment of labor shall, unless a different meaning is plainly required by the context, have the following meanings:

"Bleaching works" shall mean any premises in which the process of bleaching yarn or cloth of any material is carried on.

"Child" or "minor" shall mean a person under eighteen years of age, except that in regard to the compulsory attendance of illiterate minors at evening schools, the word minor shall mean a person under the age of twenty-one years.

"Dyeing works" shall mean any premises in which the process of dyeing yarn or cloth of any material is carried on.

"Factory" shall mean any premises where steam, water or other mechanical power is used in aid of any manufacturing process there carried on.

"Glass works" shall mean any premises in which the manufacture of glass is carried on.

"Iron works" shall mean a mill, forge or other premises in or upon which any process is carried on for converting iron into malleable iron, steel or tin plate, or for otherwise making or converting steel.

"Letterpress establishments" shall mean any premises in which the process of letterpress printing is carried on.

"Manufacturing establishments" shall mean any premises, room or place used for the purpose of making, altering, repairing, ornamenting, finishing or adapting for sale any article or part of an article.

"Mechanical establishments" shall mean any premises, other than a factory as above defined, in which machinery is employed in connection with any work or process carried on therein.

"Mercantile establishments" shall mean any premises used for the purposes of trade in the purchase or sale of any goods or merchandise, and any premises used for the purposes of a restaurant or for publicly providing and serving meals.

"Paper mills" shall mean any premises in which the manufacture of paper is carried on.

"Person" shall mean an individual, corporation, partnership, company or association.

"Print works" shall mean any premises in which is carried on the process of printing figures, patterns or designs upon cotton, linen, woolen, worsted or silken yarn or cloth, or upon any woven or felted fabric which is not paper.

"Public building" shall mean any building or premises used as a public or private institution, church, theater, public hall, place of public entertainment, resort or assemblage.

"Schoolhouse" shall mean any building or premises in which public or private instruction is afforded to not less than ten pupils at one time.

"Women" shall mean a woman eighteen years of age or over.

"Workshop" shall mean any premises, room or place, which is not a factory as above defined, wherein manual labor is exercised by way of trade or for purposes of gain in or incidental to a process of making, altering, repairing, ornamenting, finishing or adapting for sale any article or part of an article, and to which or over which premises, room or place the employer of the persons working therein has the right of access or control; but the exercise of such manual labor in a private house or private room by the family dwelling therein or by any of them or if a majority of the persons therein employed are members of such family, shall not of itself constitute such house or room a workshop within this definition.

"Young person" shall mean a person of the age of fourteen years and under the age of eighteen years.

Pure drinking water to be supplied. SEC. 78. All manufacturing establishments within this commonwealth shall provide fresh and pure drinking water to which their employees shall have access during working hours. Any person, firm, association or corporation owning, in whole or in part, managing, controlling or superintending any manufacturing establishment in which the provisions of this section are violated shall, upon complaint of the State inspectors of health, of the board of health of the city or town, or of the selectmen of the town in which the establishment is located be punished by a fine of one hundred dollars for each offence.

SEC. 79. Every factory in which five or more persons are employed, and every factory, workshop, mercantile or other establishment or office in which two or more children or women are employed, shall be kept clean and free from effluvia arising from any drain, privy or nuisance, and shall be provided, within reasonable access, with a sufficient number of proper water-closets, earth closets or privies; and wherever two or more males and two or more females are employed together, a sufficient number of separate water-closets, earth closets or privies shall be provided for the use of each sex, and plainly so designated; and no person shall be allowed to use a closet or privy which is provided for persons of the other sex. *Sanitation.*

SEC. 80 (as amended by chapter 259, Acts of 1910). The owner, lessee or occupant of any premises which are used as described in the preceding section shall make the changes necessary to conform thereto. If such changes are made upon the order of a State inspector of health, by the occupant or lessee of the premises, he may, within thirty days after the completion thereof bring an action against any other person who has an interest in such premises, and may recover such proportion of the expense of making such changes as the court adjudges should justly and equitably be borne by the defendant. *Who to make changes.*

SEC. 81. If it appears to a State inspector of health that any act, neglect or fault in relation to any drain, water-closet, earth closet, privy, ash pit, water supply, nuisance or other matter in a factory or workshop included under the provisions of section seventy-nine, is punishable or remediable under the provisions of chapter seventy-five of the Revised Laws or any other law relative to the preservation of the public health, but not under the provisions of this chapter, he shall give notice in writing thereof to the board of health of the city or town in which such factory or workshop is situated, and such board of health shall thereupon inquire into the subject of the notice and enforce the laws relative thereto. *Board of health to act when.*

SEC. 82 (as amended by chapter 259, Acts of 1910). A criminal prosecution shall not be instituted against a person for a violation of the provisions of sections seventy-nine and eighty until four weeks after notice in writing by a state inspector of health of the changes necessary to be made to comply with the provisions of said sections has been sent by mail or delivered to such person, nor if such changes shall have been made in accordance with such notice. A notice shall be sufficient under the provisions of this section if given to one member of a firm, or to the clerk, cashier, secretary, agent or any other officer who has charge of the business of a corporation, or to its attorney; and in case of a foreign corporation, to the officer who has the charge of such factory or workshop; and such officer shall be personally liable for the amount of any fine if a judgment against the corporation is returned unsatisfied. *Allowance o time.* *Notice.*

SEC. 83. A factory in which five or more persons and a workshop in which five or more women or young persons are employed shall, while work is carried on therein, be so ventilated that the air shall not become so impure as to be injurious to the health of the persons employed therein and so that all gases, vapors, dust or other impurities injurious to health, which are generated in the course of the manufacturing process or handicraft carried on therein shall, so far as practicable, be rendered harmless. *Ventilation.*

SEC. 84. If, in a workshop, or factory which is within the provisions of the preceding section, any process is carried on by which dust is caused which may be inhaled to an injurious extent by the persons employed therein, and it appears to a state inspector of health that such inhalation would be substantially diminished without unreasonable expense by the use of a fan or by other *Use of fans, etc.*

mechanical means, such fan or other mechanical means, if he so directs, shall be provided, maintained and used.

Allowance of time.
SEC. 85. A criminal prosecution shall not be instituted for any violation of the provisions of the two preceding sections unless such employer neglects, for four weeks after the receipt of a notice in writing, to make such changes in his factory or workshop as shall be ordered by a State inspector of health.

Blowers for emery wheels, etc.
SEC. 86. Any person, firm or corporation operating a factory or workshop in which emery wheels or belts or buffing wheels or belts injurious to the health of employees are used shall provide such wheels and belts with a hood or hopper connected with suction pipes, and with fans or blowers, in accordance with the provisions hereinafter contained, which apparatus shall be so placed and operated as to protect any person using such wheel or belt from the particles or dust produced by its operation, and to convey the particles or dust either outside of the building or to some receptacle so placed as to receive and confine such particles or dust.

Hoods and pipes.
SEC. 87. Every such wheel shall be fitted with a sheet iron or cast-iron hood or hopper of such form and so placed that the particles or dust produced by the operation of the wheel or of any belt connected therewith shall fall or will be thrown into such hood or hopper by centrifugal force; and the fans or blowers shall be of such size and shall be run at such speed as will produce a volume and velocity of air in the suction and discharge pipes sufficient effectually to convey all particles or dust from the hood or hopper through the suction pipes and so outside of the building or to a receptacle as aforesaid. The suction pipes and connections shall be suitable and efficacious, and such as shall be approved by the State inspector of health.

Exemptions.
SEC. 88. The two preceding sections shall not apply to grinding machines upon which water is used at the point of grinding contact, nor to solid emery wheels used in sawmills or in planing mills or in other woodworking establishments, nor to any emery wheel six inches or less in diameter used in establishments where the principal business is not emery wheel grinding.

Enforcement.
SEC. 89. State inspectors of health, upon receipt of notice in writing, signed by any person having knowledge of the facts, that any factory or workshop as aforesaid is not provided with the apparatus prescribed in sections eighty-six and eighty-seven of this act shall visit and inspect such factory or workshop, and for that purpose they are authorized to enter any such factory or workshop during working hours; and if they ascertain, in the foregoing or in any other manner, that the owner, proprietor or manager thereof has failed to comply with the provisions of said sections, they shall make complaint to a court or judge having jurisdiction, and cause such owner, proprietor or manager to be prosecuted; and it is made the duty of the district attorney to prosecute all cases arising under this section or sections eighty-six and eighty-seven of this act.

Violations.
SEC. 90. Whoever fails to comply with any provision of the four preceding sections shall, for the first offence be punished by a fine of not less than twenty-five nor more than one hundred dollars, and, for a second offence he shall be punished by the fine aforesaid or by imprisonment in jail for not more than sixty days or by both such fine and imprisonment.

Speaking tubes, etc., to engine rooms.
SEC. 91. In every manufacturing establishment in which the machinery is propelled by steam, communication shall be provided between each room in which such machinery is placed and the room in which the engineer is stationed by means of speaking tubes, electric bells or appliances to control the motive power, or such other means as shall be satisfactory to the inspectors of factories and public buildings, if in the opinion of the inspectors such communication is necessary. Whoever, being the occupant or controlling the use of any such manufacturing establishment, violates the provisions of this section shall forfeit to the Commonwealth not less than twenty-five nor more than one hundred dollars,

SEC. 92. No prosecution for a violation of the provisions of the preceding section shall be commenced until four weeks after notice in writing by an inspector has been sent by mail to such person, firm or corporation of any changes necessary to be made to comply with the provisions of said section, nor if such changes shall have been made in accordance with such notice. *Allowance of time.*

SEC. 93. No outside or inside doors of any building in which operatives are employed shall be so locked, bolted or otherwise fastened during the hours of labor as to prevent free egress. The owner, lessee or occupant of any such building shall, five days after receiving notice in writing from an inspector of factories and public buildings, comply with the provisions of this section. *Doors not to be locked.*

SEC. 94. The belting, shafting, gearing and drums of all factories, if so placed as, in the opinion of the inspectors of factories and public buildings, to be dangerous to employees therein while engaged in their ordinary duties, shall be as far as practicable securely guarded. No machinery except steam engines in a factory shall be cleaned while running if objection in writing is made by one of said inspectors. All factories and workshops shall be well lighted, well ventilated and kept clean, and this requirement shall be enforced by the state inspectors of health. *Guards for dangerous machinery.*

SEC. 95. The owner of a cotton factory which shall have been erected subsequently to the twenty-eighth day of May in the year eighteen hundred and ninety-six, in which there is any traversing carriage of a self-acting mule installed, or of any cotton factory erected previously to such date in which hereafter such traversing carriage is installed, who permits such carriage to travel within twelve inches of any pillar, column, pier or fixed structure, shall be punished by a fine of not less than twenty nor more than fifty dollars for each offence. *Space near traversing machinery.*

SEC. 96. The openings of hoistways, hatchways, elevators and well holes upon every floor of a factory or mercantile or public building shall be protected by sufficient trapdoors or self-closing hatches and safety catches, or such other safeguards as the inspectors of factories and public buildings direct; and due diligence shall be used to keep such trapdoors closed at all times, except when in actual use by the occupant of the building who has the use and control of the same. *Hoistways, etc., to be guarded.*

SEC. 97. If, in the erection of an iron or steel framed building the spaces between the girders or floor beams of any floor are not filled or covered by the permanent construction of said floors before another story is added to the building, a close plank flooring shall be placed and maintained over such spaces, from the time when the beams or girders are placed in position until said permanent construction is applied; but openings, protected by a strong hand railing not less than four feet high, may be left through said floors for the passage of workmen or material. *Protection of employees on buildings.*

SEC. 98. In the construction of any iron or steel framed building having a clear story of twenty-five feet elevation or more, a staging with a close plank flooring shall be placed under the whole extent of the beams, girders or trusses of such story upon which iron or steel workers are working, and not more than ten feet below the under side of such beams, girders and trusses. *Same.*

SEC. 99. Inspectors of factories and public buildings shall enforce the provisions of the two preceding sections, and whoever violates any provision thereof shall be punished by a fine of not less than fifty nor more than five hundred dollars for each offence. *Enforcement.*

SEC. 100. Explosive or inflammable compounds shall not be used in any factory in such place or manner as to obstruct or render hazardous the egress of operatives in case of fire. *Explosives, etc., in factories.*

SEC. 101. Any person, firm or corporation owning, managing or operating factories in this Commonwealth in which looms are employed shall equip the looms with such guards or other devices as will prevent injury to employees from shuttles falling or being thrown from the looms. Such guards or devices shall be made of such material and placed in such manner as shall be approved by the inspection department of the district police, who are hereby *Shuttle guards.*

directed to enforce the provisions of this section. Whoever violates any provision of this section shall be punished by a fine of not more than one hundred dollars for every week during which such violation continues.

Toilet rooms in foundries. SEC. 102. The proprietor of every foundry engaged in the casting of iron, brass, steel or other metal, and employing ten or more men, shall establish and maintain, except in cities or towns in which it would be impracticable by reason of the absence of public or private sewerage or of any running water system, a toilet room of suitable size and condition for the men to change their clothes therein, and provided with washbowls, sinks or other suitable set appliances connected with running hot and cold water, and also a water-closet connected with running water and separated from the said toilet room. The said water-closet and toilet room shall be connected directly with the foundry building, properly heated, ventilated and protected, so far as may be reasonably practicable, from the dust of the foundry. Whoever fails to comply with the provisions of this section, after being requested so to do by a State inspector of health, shall be punished by a fine of not more than fifty dollars for each offence.

Cuspidors. SEC. 103. Suitable receptacles for expectoration shall be provided in all factories and workshops by the proprietors thereof, the same to be of such form and construction and of such number as shall be satisfactory to the board of health of the city or town in which the factory or workshop is situated.

Medical and surgical supplies. SEC. 104. Every person, firm or corporation operating a factory or shop in which machinery is used for any manufacturing or other purpose except for elevators, or for heating or hoisting apparatus, shall at all times keep and maintain, free of expense to the employees, such a medical and surgical chest as shall be required by the board of health of the city or town where such machinery is used, containing plasters, bandages, absorbent cotton, gauze, and all other necessary medicines, instruments and other appliances for the treatment of persons injured or taken ill upon the premises. A person, firm or corporation violating any provision of this section shall be punished by a fine of not less than five dollars nor more than five hundred dollars for every week during which such violation continues.

Manufactures in tenements.

Sweat shops to be licensed. SECTION 106. A room or apartment in a tenement or dwelling house shall not be used for the purpose of making, altering, repairing or finishing therein coats, vests, trousers or wearing apparel of any description, except by the members of the family dwelling therein; and a family which desires to make, alter, repair or finish coats, vests, trousers or wearing apparel of any description in a room or apartment in a tenement or dwelling house shall first procure a license therefor from a State inspector of health, which shall be approved by the State board of health. A license may be applied for by, and issued to, any member of a family which desires to do such work. No person, partnership or corporation shall hire, employ or contract with a member of a family which does not hold a license therefor to make, alter, repair or finish garments or articles of wearing apparel as aforesaid, in any room or apartment in a tenement or dwelling house as aforesaid. Every room or apartment in which garments or articles of wearing apparel are made, altered, repaired or finished shall be kept in a cleanly condition and shall be subject to the inspection and examination of the State inspectors of health for the purpose of ascertaining whether said room or apartment or said garments or articles of wearing apparel or any parts thereof are clean and free from vermin and from infectious or contagious matter. A room or apartment in a tenement or dwelling house which is not used for living or sleeping purposes, and which is not connected with a room or apartment used for living or sleeping purposes and which has a separate and distinct entrance from the outside shall not be subject to the provisions of this section, nor shall the provisions of this section prevent the employment of a tailor or seamstress by any person or family for the making of wearing apparel for the use of such person or family. Every person, firm or corporation hiring, employing or contracting with a member of a family holding a license under this section for the making, altering, repairing or finishing of garments or wearing apparel to be done outside the premises of such person, firm or corporation, shall keep a register of the names and addresses plainly written in English of the persons so hired, employed or contracted with, and shall forward a copy of such register once a month to the State board of health. *Register of employees.*

SEC. 107. If an inspector finds evidence of infectious or contagious disease or of vermin present in a workshop or in a room or apartment in a tenement or dwelling house in which garments or articles of wearing apparel are made, altered or repaired, or in goods manufactured or in process of manufacture therein, he shall report the same to the State board of health, who shall then notify the local board of health to examine said workshop, room or apartment and the materials used therein; and if the board of health finds that said workshop or tenement or dwelling house is in an unhealthy condition, and that the clothing and materials used therein are unfit for use, it shall issue such orders as the public safety may require. *Infectious diseases, etc.*

SEC. 108. Whoever sells or exposes for sale coats, vests, trousers or wearing apparel of any description which have been made in a tenement or dwelling house in which the family dwelling therein has not procured a license, as required by section one hundred and six, shall have affixed to each of said garments a tag or label not less than two inches in length and one inch in width, upon which shall be legibly printed or written the words "tenement-made" and the name of the State and the city or town in which the garment was made. *Tag to be affixed, when.*

SEC. 109. No person shall sell or expose for sale any of said garments without a tag or label as aforesaid affixed thereto, nor willfully remove, alter or destroy such tag or label upon any of said garments when exposed for sale, nor sell or expose for sale any of said garments with a false or fraudulent label affixed thereto. *Sale of tenement-made articles.*

SEC. 110. If it is reported to said inspector or to the State board of health that ready-made coats, vests, trousers, overcoats or other garments are being shipped to this Commonwealth, having been manufactured under unhealthy conditions, said inspector shall examine said goods and the condition of their manufacture, and if they are found to contain vermin or to have been made in improper places or under unhealthy conditions, he shall so report to the state board of health, which shall thereupon make such orders as the public safety may require. *Inspection of clothing brought into the State.*

SEC. 111. Whoever violates any of the provisions of the five preceding sections shall be punished by a fine of not less than fifty nor more than five hundred dollars. *Violations.*

ACTS OF 1910.

CHAPTER 543.—*Inspection of factories and workshops—Humidity.*

SECTION 1. In every weaving and spinning department in a textile factory wherein water is introduced for humidifying purposes there shall be provided, maintained and kept in correct working order, for the purpose of recording and regulating the humidity of the atmosphere and the temperature, at least one set of standardized wet and dry bulb thermometers, and, if required by a State inspector of health, two sets of such thermometers, and the following regulations shall be observed in the use of the thermometers: (a) The thermometers shall be placed as directed or sanc- *Thermometers required.*

tioned by a State inspector of health, and shall be plainly visible to the workers. (b) The occupier or manager or person for the time being in charge of the weaving or spinning department in question shall read the thermometers thrice in the day, namely, between seven and eight o'clock in the forenoon, between ten and eleven o'clock in the forenoon and between three and four o'clock, except in rooms which are lighted by gas, and then between four and five o'clock, in the afternoon of every day on which any persons are employed in any weaving or spinning department, and he shall record the readings of each thermometer in such department at each of the said times upon a form provided for the purpose, which, together with the regulations relating thereto, shall be furnished by the State board of health. The records of the readings shall not be destroyed until they have first been seen by the State inspector of health in whose district the factory is situated, and then not without his knowledge and consent.

Other apparatus. SEC. 2. Section one shall not apply to textile factories already equipped with, or which become equipped with, such a number and type of standardized self-registering hygrometers, or psychrometers, or hygrometric system, as meet the approval of the State board of health : *Provided*, That the manner of using the same is approved by the State inspector of health in whose district the factory is situated :. *And provided*, That the records of the readings from the said hygrometers, or hygrometric system installed, are not destroyed without the knowledge and consent of said inspector.

Same subject. SEC. 3. Section one shall not apply to textile factories the occupier or manager or person in charge of which makes use of the sling hygrometer with the express purpose of quickly and accurately determining the actual moisture and temperature of a weaving or spinning department as frequently and in such a manner as is approved by the State inspector of health in whose district the factory is situated : *And provided*, That the records of the readings from the use of the said hygrometer are not destroyed without the knowledge and permission of said inspector.

Scale. SEC. 4. No owner, occupier or manager or person for the time being in charge of a textile factory shall permit the relative humidity in a weaving or spinning department in the textile factory under his control to exceed the following limits:

I Dry bulb thermometer readings (degrees Fahr.).	II Wet bulb thermometer readings (degrees Fahr.).	III Percentage of humidity.	I Dry bulb thermometer readings (degrees Fahr.).	II Wet bulb thermometer readings (degrees Fahr.).	III Percentage of humidity.
60	58	88	78	73.5	77
61	59	88	79	74.5	77.5
62	60	88	80	75.5	77.5
63	61	88	81	76	76
64	62	88	82	76.5	74
65	63	88	83	77.5	74
66	64	88	84	78	72
67	65	88	85	79	72
68	66	88	86	80	72
69	67	88	87	80.5	71
70	68	88	88	81.5	71
71	68.5	85.5	89	82.5	71
72	69	84	90	83	69
73	70	84	91	83.5	68
74	70.5	81.5	92	84.5	68
75	71.5	81.5	93	85.5	68
76	72	79	94	86	66
77	73	79	95	87	66

Pure water to be used. SEC. 5. Water used for humidifying purposes in a textile factory shall be taken either from a public supply of drinking water, or from some other source of pure water, or from a supply of water which, although in the opinion of the State board of health not suitable for drinking purposes is sufficiently free from impurities as not to be dangerous to the health of employees when used for humidifying purposes; and all ducts for the introduction or distribution of humidified air shall be kept clean.

Sec. 6. This act shall be enforced by the State inspectors of health under the supervision of the state board of health. Whoever fails to comply with the provisions contained herein after being requested so to do by a State inspector of health shall be fined not more than fifty dollars for each offence. Enforcement.

ACTS OF 1911.

Chapter 584.—*Fines of weavers for imperfect work.*

Section 1. No employer shall impose a fine upon an employee engaged at weaving for imperfections that may arise during the process of weaving. Fines forbidden.

Sec. 2. Any employer who violates the provisions of this act shall be punished by a fine not exceeding one hundred dollars for the first offense, and not exceeding three hundred dollars for any subsequent offense. Violations.

Chapter 603.—*Factory regulations—Lighting—Occupational diseases.*

Section 1. The State inspectors of health, or such other officers as the State board of health may from time to time appoint, shall, when obtaining information concerning the proper lighting of factories, workshops and other industrial establishments, make such investigation concerning the eye and vision in their relation to diseases of occupation, including injuries to the eyes of the employees, and to the pathological effects which are produced or promoted by the circumstances under which the various occupations are carried on, as, in the opinion of said board is practicable, and the board shall from time to time issue such printed matter containing suggestions to employers and employees for the protection of the eyes of the employees as it may deem advisable. Investigation.
Injuries to eyes.

Sec. 2. If it appears to an inspector of health, or other officer appointed by said board, that in any factory, workshop or other industrial establishment, from the nature of the work or of the machinery used in connection therewith, or of other circumstances, there is danger of injury to the eyes of employees engaged in such work, and that the danger of injury may be decreased or prevented by any mechanical device or other practicable means, he shall, if said board so directs, order in writing that such device or other means shall be provided therein; and it shall be the duty of the proprietors and managers of the factory, workshop or other industrial establishment to comply with the order. Changes may be required.

Sec. 3. Any person, firm or corporation violating any provisions of this act shall be subject to a fine of not less than five nor more than two hundred dollars for every week during which such violation continues: *Provided, however,* That a criminal prosecution for any violation hereof shall not be begun unless such person, firm or corporation shall, for a period of four weeks after the receipt of an order in writing from a State inspector of health or other officer, as provided in the preceding section, neglect to comply therewith. Violations.

Chapter 620.—*Inspectors of steam boilers—Appointment.*

Section 1. The governor is hereby authorized and directed to appoint five additional members of the boiler inspection department of the district police, who shall be not above forty-five years of age; and this age limit shall apply hereafter to all appointments to the said department. The said five additional members shall be detailed for the inspection of boilers and the examination Additional inspectors.
Age limit.

Examinations. of engineers and firemen, and shall receive the same compensation now received by the present inspectors of boilers. The civil service commissioners shall hold an examination for the said appointments, and no person shall hereafter be eligible to take the civil service examination for appointment as an inspector of boilers, unless he holds a first class engineer's license granted by the boiler inspection department of this commonwealth.

MICHIGAN.

ACTS OF 1903.

ACT No. 87.—*Inspection of factories—Duty to make improvements.*

Owner to make improvements. SECTION 1. Whenever fire escapes, elevator protection or repairs, water-closets and other permanent improvements to buildings are ordered by factory or deputy factory inspectors under the provisions of act one hundred thirteen, Session Laws of nineteen hundred one, said improvements shall be made by the owner of the building or premises where such improvements are ordered: Proviso. *Provided,* That nothing in this section shall be construed to interfere with any contract between owner and tenant whereby the tenant agrees to make such improvements when ordered by factory or deputy factory inspectors.

Tenant may deduct cost. SEC. 2. Whenever the owner of any building or premises, as mentioned in section one of this act, is a nonresident of this State, the tenant shall make such improvements and may deduct the cost thereof from the amount of rent for use of said premises.

ACT OF 1909.

ACT No. 285.—*Department of labor—Employment of women and children—Inspection of factories and workshops—Mine regulations.*

Commissioner to be appointed. SECTION 1. The governor is hereby authorized and empowered to appoint within thirty days after the passage of this act, and every second year thereafter, by and with the advice and consent of the senate, and also within thirty days after the occurrence of any vacancy in the office, a suitable person, who shall be a citizen of this State, as commissioner of labor, who shall hold his office until his successor be appointed and qualified. The title of such officer shall be "commissioner of labor," and the term of office of such commissioner shall be for a period of two years after such appointment. Such commissioner shall keep an office in the city · of Lansing, and shall appoint a deputy, whose term of office shall continue during the pleasure of such commissioner. The commissioner may appoint such deputy factory inspectors and assistants from time to time as shall be necessary for the transaction of the business of his office.

Duties. SEC. 2. The duties of such department shall be to collect in the manner herein provided, assort, systematize, print and present to the governor, on or before the first day of April, nineteen hundred and ten, and annually thereafter, statistical details relating to all departments of labor in this State, including the penal institutions thereof, particularly concerning the hours of labor, the number of employees and sex·thereof, the daily wages earned, and savings, the number and character of accidents, the conditions of all manufacturing establishments, hotels, stores, and workshops where labor is employed, with such other matter relating to the industrial, social, educational, moral and sanitary conditions of the · laboring classes and the productive industries of the State, including the names of firms, companies or corporations, where located, the kind of goods produced or manufactured, the time operated each year, the number of employees, male or female, the number engaged in clerical work and the number engaged in manual labor, with a classification of the number of each sex engaged in each occupation and the average daily wages paid each. The commissioner of labor is authorized to appoint special agents to represent the department, with authority to visit firms and establishments and to collect such statistics, and perform such other duties as may be required, with like power as is conferred on said commissioner. The commissioner of labor and all appointees connected with the department, when so directed by said commissioner, shall have full authority to visit and inspect all manufacturing establishments, workshops, hotels, stores and all places where labor is employed, at any reasonable hour, and shall have authority to gather such statistics as may be deemed necessary by the commissioner: *Provided,* That the commissioner of labor or any one connected with his office shall not publish, make public nor give to any individual or to the public the individual statistics obtained from any manufacturing establishment, but all such statistics may be published in connection with other similar statistics and given to the public in aggregates and averages.

SEC. 3. Such department or any member thereof shall have full power to examine witnesses on oath, compel the attendance of witnesses, the giving of testimony and the production of papers while acting in any part of this State, and witnesses may be summoned by such department or any member thereof, by its process in the same manner, and pay the same fees as are allowed to witnesses attending in the circuit court of any county. Any person duly subpœnaed under the provisions of this section, who shall willfully neglect to attend or testify at the place named in the subpœna served for such purpose, shall be guilty of a misdemeanor, and on conviction before any court of competent jurisdiction may be punished by a fine not exceeding fifty dollars or imprisonment in the county jail not exceeding thirty days, or both such fine and imprisonment in the discretion of the court: *Provided,* That no witness shall be compelled to go outside of the county in which he or she resides to testify. *Witnesses.*

SEC. 5. Said department may collect the information called for in section two of this act, or such information as shall by the commissioner be considered essential to perfect the work of the department, from the several State, county, city, village and township officers, and from the officers of prisons, penal and reformatory institutions, or by means of special canvassers under the direction of the commissioner, and it shall be the duty of all such officers to furnish upon the written or printed request of the commissioner such information as shall be considered necessary for the department upon blanks furnished by said department. *Officials to furnish information.*

SEC. 6. It shall be the duty of the several supervisors of the townships, and the supervisor and assessor of the wards of cities in this State, at the time of assessing the property thereof, to obtain the facts and information determined upon by said department, as provided in section five of this act, in accordance with the terms, conditions and requirements of said blanks, and to return said blanks properly filled and duly certified to by such officer without delay to the commissioner of labor at Lansing. *Township, etc., officers.*

SEC. 7. The commissioner or his deputy and deputy factory inspectors shall have the power to enter any factory, workshop, hotel or store when open or in operation, for the purpose of gathering facts and statistics relating to hours of labor, wages, industrial, economic and sanitary conditions or matters; and if the owner or occupant or his or her agent or agents shall refuse to allow the officers of said department to so enter, or shall refuse to give the information so desired by said commisioner or deputy factory inspectors, then said owner or occupant or his or her agent shall be deemed guilty of a misdemeanor, and upon conviction thereof before any court of competent jurisdiction shall be punished by a fine not to exceed one hundred dollars or by imprisonment for not more than ninety days or both such fine and imprisonment in the discretion of the court. *Access to factories, etc.*

False state-
ments.

SEC. 8. Any person who shall willfully and intentionally testify falsely before said commissioner or any authorized deputy shall be deemed guilty of a felony, and on conviction thereof shall be punished by imprisonment in the State prison for a period not exceeding five years, and any person who shall refuse to testify before said commissioner or before any deputy thereof shall on conviction thereof be deemed guilty of a misdemeanor, and shall be punished by a fine not exceeding one hundred dollars or imprisonment not exceeding sixty days or both in the discretion of the court: *Provided*, That no person or corporation shall be required to answer any question that shall be an improper subject of inquiry or foreign to the object of this act.

Hoistways, etc.,
to be guarded.

SEC. 12. It shall be the duty of the owner, agent or lessee of any manufacturing establishment where hoisting shafts or wellholes are used, to cause the same to be properly enclosed and secured. It shall be the duty of the owner, agent or lessee to provide or cause to be provided at all elevator openings in any manufacturing establishment, workshop, hotel or store, proper trap or automatic doors or automatic gates so constructed as to open and close by the action of elevators either ascending or descending. The deputy factory inspector shall inspect the cables, gearing or other

Elevators.

apparatus of elevators in manufacturing establishments, workshops, hotels and stores at least once in each year, and more frequently if necessary, and require that the same be kept in a safe condition, and shall have power to condemn any elevator if in his opinion the same be unsafe, and stop the operation of such elevator until the same be put in safe condition.

Fire escapes.

SEC. 13 (as amended by act No. 251, Acts of 1911). * * * Factory inspectors shall have power to order fire escapes on all manufacturing establishments, * * * and office buildings two or more stories in height, if in the opinion of the factory inspector it be necessary to insure the safety of persons in such places; said fire escape or means of egress, or as many thereof as may be deemed sufficient by the inspector, shall be provided, and where it is necessary to provide fire escapes on the outside of such building they shall consist of landings and balconies at each floor above the first, to be built according to specifications provided by the factory inspector. * * * Factory inspectors shall in writing notify the owner, agent or lessee of such manufacturing establishments, * * * and office buildings of the required location and specifications of such escapes as may be ordered and as to all failures to comply with the provisions of this act. Any person, firm or corporation, * * * who shall violate or cause to be violated any of the provisions of this section, or who shall fail or refuse to erect or cause to be erected any fire escape ordered by any factory inspector, under authority of this section, shall be deemed guilty of a misdemeanor, and upon conviction shall be fined not less than one hundred dollars nor more than one thousand dollars, or imprisoned for not less than three months nor more than one year, or by both such fine and imprisonment in the discretion of the court.

Stairways.

SEC. 14. Stairways with substantial hand rails shall be provided in manufacturing establishments, and where in the opinion of the factory inspector it be necessary, the steps of such stairs in all such establishments shall be substantially covered with rubber securely fastened thereon, for the better safety of persons employed in said establishments. The stairs shall be properly screened at sides and bottom where females are employed, and where practicable the doors of such establishments shall swing

Doors.

outwardly or slide, as ordered by said factory inspector, and shall be neither locked, bolted nor fastened during working hours.

Guards for dan-
gerous machin-
ery.

SEC. 15. It shall be the duty of the owner of any factory, storehouse or warehouse, or his agent, superintendent or other person in charge of the same, to furnish or supply, or cause to be furnished or supplied, in the discretion of the factory inspector, where machinery is in use, proper shifters or other mechanical contrivances for the purpose of throwing belts on or off pulleys.

All gearing or belting shall be provided with proper safeguards, and whenever possible machinery shall be provided with loose pulleys. · All vats, saws, pans, planers, cogs, set screws, gearing and machinery of every description shall be properly guarded when deemed necessary by the factory inspector.

SEC. 16. Exhaust fans shall be provided for the purpose of carrying off dust from emery wheels and grindstones, and dust-creating machinery, wherever deemed necessary by the factory inspector.   *Emery wheels.*

SEC. 17. Every manufacturing establishment, workshop, hotel or store in which five or more persons are employed, and every institution in which two or more children, young persons or women are employed, shall be supplied with proper wash and dressing rooms, and kept in a cleanly state and free from effluvia arising from any drain, privy or other nuisance, and shall be provided within reasonable access with a sufficient number of proper water-closets, earth closets or privies for the reasonable use of persons employed therein, at least one of such closets for each twenty-five persons employed; and whenever two or more persons and one or more female persons are employed as aforesaid, a sufficient number of separate and distinct water-closets, earth closets or privies shall be provided for the use of each sex, and plainly so designated, and no person shall be allowed to use any such closet or privy assigned to persons of the other sex. In all hotels where sleeping rooms are provided for female help such rooms shall have proper heat and ventilation.   *Toilet rooms.*

SEC. 18. The commissioner of labor shall be the chief factory inspector, and the deputy commissioner of labor and deputy factory inspectors shall be factory inspectors in the meaning of this act. At least two of such deputy factory inspectors shall be women. Said factory inspectors are hereby empowered to visit and inspect at all reasonable hours, as often as practicable or required, the factories, workshops and other manufacturing establishments in this State where the manufacture of goods is carried on, and all hotels where any person or persons are employed, also all stores in this State. · Deputy factory inspectors shall report to the commissioner of labor at such time and manner as he may require. It shall also be the duty of the factory inspectors to enforce all the provisions of this act and to prosecute all violations of the same before a magistrate or in a court of competent jurisdiction in this State.   *Inspectors.*

SEC. 19. Deputy factory inspectors shall return to the commissioner of labor, as he may require, detailed reports of the results of all inspections, together with statistics gathered, and said commissioner shall keep on file in his office at Lansing a record of all reports so returned. A copy of the report on such inspection and of any order in reference thereto shall·be served by the factory inspector on the superintendent, owner or manager of each building, establishment or workshop inspected. Service of such order shall be accepted and a duplicate thereof signed by such superintendent, owner or manager. If the superintendent, owner or manager of whom such signature is demanded shall refuse to so sign such acceptance of service, an affidavit by the inspector showing the facts of such service, demand of signature and refusal shall be sufficient evidence of service when duly filed; but such superintendent, owner or manager shall not thereby be released from any criminal liability attending his refusal under this act. Deputy factory inspectors and special canvassers shall have the same power to administer oaths as is now given to notaries public, in cases where persons desire to verify documents connected with the proper enforcement of this act.   *Reports.*   *Owners to sign.*

SEC. 20. For the purpose of carrying out the provisions of this act, the commissioner of labor is hereby authorized and required to cause at least an annual inspection of all manufacturing establishments, factories. hotels, workshops and stores. Such inspection may be made by the commissioner of labor, the deputy commissioner of labor, deputy factory inspectors, or such other person   *Annual inspections.*

as may be appointed by the commissioner of labor for the purpose of making such inspection. Such persons shall be under the control and direction of the commissioner of labor. All compensation for services and expenses provided for in this act shall be paid by the State treasurer upon the warrant of the auditor general and audited by the auditor general : *Provided*, That the commissioner of labor shall present to the governor on or before the first day of April of each year, a report of such inspection, with such recommendations as may **í**n his judgment be necessary.

Enforcement. SEC. 21. The prosecuting attorney of any county of this State is hereby authorized and shall, upon the complaint on oath of the commissioner of labor or any factory inspector, prosecute to termination before any court of competent jurisdiction, in the name of the people of the State, actions or proceedings against any person or persons reported to him to have violated any of the provisions of this act. •

Manufactures—Tenements.

Permits for sweat shops. SECTION 22. No room or apartment in any tenement or dwelling house shall be used for the manufacture of coats, vests, trousers, knee pants, overalls, skirts, dresses, cloaks, hats, caps, suspenders, jerseys, blouses, waists, waistbands, underwear, neckwear, furs, fur trimming, fur garments, shirts, hosiery, purses, feathers, artificial flowers, cigarettes or cigars, and no person, firm or corporation shall hire or employ any persons to work in any room, apartment or in any building or parts of buildings, at making in whole or in part any of the articles mentioned in this section, without first obtaining a written permit from the factory inspector or one of his deputies, stating the maximum number of persons allowed to be employed therein and that the building or part of building intended to be used for such work or business is thoroughly cleaned, sanitary and fit for occupancy for such work or business. Such permit shall not be granted until an inspection of such premises is made by the factory inspector or one of his deputies. Said permit may be revoked by the factory inspector at any time the health of the community or of those so employed may require it. It shall be framed and posted in a conspicuous place in the room, or in one of the rooms to which it relates. Every person, firm, company or corporation contracting for the manufacture of any of the articles mentioned in this section, or giving out the incomplete material from which they or any of them are to be made, or to be wholly or partially finished, shall, before contracting for the manufacture of any of said articles, or giving out said material from which they or any of them are to be made, require the production by such contractor, person or persons of said permit from the factory inspector, as required in this section, and shall keep a written register of the names and addresses of all persons to whom such work is given to be made, or with whom they may have contracted to do the same. Such register shall be produced for inspection and a copy thereof shall be furnished on demand by the factory inspector or one of his deputies : *Provided*, That nothing in this section shall be so construed as to prevent the employment of a seamstress by any family for manufacturing articles

Workrooms. for such family use. None of the work mentioned in this section shall be done in any room or apartment used for living or sleeping purposes, or which is connected with the room or rooms used for such purposes, and which has not a separate and distinct outside entrance for use of others than members of the family dwelling

Air space. therein. Not less than two hundred and fifty cubic feet of air space shall be allowed for each person employed, and all work rooms shall be provided with sufficient means of light, heat and ventilation as may be prescribed by the chief factory inspector. It shall be the duty of local boards of health, health officers and physicians to report within twenty-four hours to the deputy factory inspector in their respective districts each and every case of contagious or infectious disease coming officially to their knowledge,

The chief factory inspector or any duly appointed deputy factory inspector shall have power to seize and take charge of all articles found that are being made or partially made, finished, cleaned or repaired in unhealthy or insanitary places where there are contagious or infectious diseases, in violation of the law, and may proceed to disinfect, condemn or destroy the same as in the opinion of the local board of health officer, the public health or safety may require. Whenever it is reported to the chief factory inspector or to the State board of health, or to either of them, that any of the articles named in this section are being or have been shipped into this State, having previously been manufactured in whole or in part under unhealthy conditions, said chief factory inspector shall examine said goods and the condition of their manufacture, and if upon such examination said goods or any of them are found to contain vermin or to have been made in improper places or under unhealthy conditions, he shall make report thereof to the State board of health, which board shall thereupon make such order or orders as the public health and safety may require: *Provided*, That in stores where goods are manufactured, altered or repaired, work rooms shall be provided with proper heat, light and ventilation, as prescribed in this section. *Infected, etc., articles.*

Sec. 23. Factory inspectors shall have power to order all improvements herein specified, such as the repairing of elevators, the installment of wash and dressing rooms and water-closets. When such improvements are found necessary orders for same shall be served on the owner of the building or premises: *Provided*, That whenever the owner of such buildings or premises as mentioned in this act be a nonresident of this State said order may be made on his resident agent or the tenant of such buildings or premises. If the tenant be required to make such improvements he may deduct the cost thereof from the amount of rent for use of such buildings or premises. *Changes in buildings.*

Inspection of factories and workshops.

Section 26. All entrances to foundries shall be constructed and maintained so as to minimize drafts. All passage ways in foundries, now in operation or hereafter to be built, shall be constructed and maintained of sufficient width to make them reasonably safe for the workmen, and no unnecessary obstruction shall be allowed in such passage ways during the hours of casting. Whenever a foundry is so constructed or operated that smoke, steam, dust or noxious gases are not promptly carried off by the general ventilation, exhaust fans shall be provided. No salamanders or open fire places shall be used, unless ample provision be made for conveying the gases arising therefrom directly from the building. Foundries shall be reasonably well lighted throughout working hours, and reasonably well heated during the cold and inclement weather. Hot water shall be kept available for washing purposes during the season in which artificial heating is necessary. When it is thought necessary and advisable by a State factory inspector, facilities shall be provided for drying the clothing of persons employed therein. All pits around furnaces in any such foundry shall be covered with substantial iron gratings. All stairways around such furnaces shall be constructed of iron. There shall be kept on hand at all times in every foundry a reasonable supply of limewater, sweet oil, vaseline, bandages and absorbent cotton for use by the workmen in case of burns or accident. It is hereby made the duty of each and every State factory inspector to enforce the provisions of this section. Any place or establishment where metal castings or cores are made shall be deemed a foundry within the meaning of this act. *Arrangement of foundries.* *Ventilation.* *Wash, etc., rooms.*

Sec. 27. All persons, companies or corporations operating any factory or workshop, where wheels or emery belts of any description are in general use, either leather, leather covered, felt, canvas, paper, cotton, or wheels or belts rolled or coated with emery or corundum, or cotton wheels used as buffs, shall provide the same *Blowers for emery wheels.*

with fans or blowers or similar apparatus, which shall be placed in
such a position or manner as to protect the person or persons using
the same from the particles of dust produced and caused thereby,
and to carry the dust arising from, or thrown off by such wheels
or belts while in operation, directly to the outside of the building
or to some other receptacle placed so as to receive and confine
such dust: *Provided*, That grinding machines upon which water is
used at the point of grinding contact shall be exempt from the conditions of this act: *Provided further*, That this act shall not apply
to solid emery wheels used in sawmills or planing mills or other
wood-working establishments.

Hoods.   SEC. 28. It shall be the duty of any person, company or corporation operating any such factory or workshop to provide or construct such appliances, apparatus, machinery or other things
necessary to carry out the purposes of this act, as set forth in the
preceding section, as follows: Each and every such wheel shall be
fitted with a sheet or cast iron hood or hopper of such form and so
applied to such wheel or wheels that the dust or refuse therefrom
will fall from such wheels or will be thrown into such hood or
hopper by centrifugal force and be carried off by the current of
air into a suction pipe attached to such hood or hopper.

Pipes.   SEC. 29. Each and every such wheel six inches or less in diameter shall be provided with a three-inch suction pipe, wheels
six inches to twenty-four inches in diameter with four-inch suction pipes, wheels from twenty-four inches to thirty-six inches
in diameter with five-inch suction pipes, and all wheels larger in
diameter than those stated above shall be provided each with a
suction pipe not less than six inches in diameter. The suction
pipe from each wheel so specified must be full size to the main
trunk suction pipe, and the said main suction pipe to which
smaller pipes are attached shall, in its diameter and capacity, be
equal to the combined areas of such smaller pipes attached to the
same, and the discharge pipe from the exhaust fan connected with
such suction pipe or pipes shall be as large or larger than the
suction pipe.

Speed of fans.   SEC. 30. It shall be the duty of any person, company or corporation operating any such factory or workshop, to provide the necessary fans or blowers to be connected with such pipe or pipes, as
above set forth, which shall be run at such rate of speed as will
produce a velocity of air in such suction or discharge pipes of at
least nine thousand feet per minute or an equivalent suction or
pressure of air equal to raising a column of water not less than
five inches high in an U-shaped tube. All branch pipes must enter
the main trunk pipe at an angle of forty-five degrees or less.
The main suction or trunk pipe shall be below the polishing or
buffing wheels and as close to the same as possible, and be either
upon the floor or beneath the floor on which the machines are
placed to which such wheels are attached. All bends, turns or
elbows in such pipes must be made with easy smooth surfaces
having a radius in the throat of not less than two inches diameter,
of the pipe on which they are connected.

Enforcement.   SEC. 31. It shall be the duty of any factory inspector, sheriff,
constable or prosecuting attorney of any county in this State, in
which any such factory or workshop is situated, upon receiving
notice in writing, signed by any person or persons having knowledge of such facts, that such factory or workshop is not provided
with such appliances as herein provided for, to visit any such
factory or workshop and inspect the same, and for such purpose
they are hereby authorized to enter any factory or workshop in
this State during working hours, and upon ascertaining the facts
that the proprietors or managers of such factories or workshops
have failed to comply with the provisions of this act, to make
complaint of the same in writing before a justice of the peace or
police magistrate having jurisdiction, who shall thereupon issue
his warrant directed to the owner, manager or director of such
factory or workshop, who shall be thereupon proceeded against
for the violation of this act as hereinafter mentioned, and it is

made the duty of the prosecuting attorney to prosecute all cases under this act. No person shall be employed to operate any of the wheels, buffers or belts mentioned in this act in any basement, so-called, or in any room lying wholly or partly beneath the surface of the ground, unless such workroom shall be provided with sufficient means of light, heat and ventilation as shall be prescribed by the State factory inspector. No female shall be employed in operating or using any of the wheels or belts specified in this section. Basements.

SEC. 32. All persons, companies or corporations operating any upholstering or mattress establishments or other establishments, factory or place where hair, moss, tow or cotton is used for filling, shall provide the same with hair-picking machines when ordered by the commissioner, deputy commissioner of labor or deputy factory inspector, which shall be placed in such a position or manner as to carry away the dust arising from or thrown off by such machines while in operation directly to the outside of the building or to some other receptacle established so as to receive and confine such dust, and the same shall be placed within such establishment, place or factory within three months after having been ordered to be so placed by the commissioner, deputy commissioner of labor or deputy factory inspector. Hair-picking machines.

SEC. 33. All stationary steam boilers operated or used, or caused to be operated or used, by any person, firm or corporation within the State of Michigan, shall, whenever so ordered by the chief factory inspector or any of his duly authorized deputies, have upon them some device which will sound an alarm for the purpose of calling the attention of the engineer, fireman or person in charge of any such boiler to the depth of the water in the boiler before the same reaches the danger point: *Provided,* That the kind of device or alarm used shall be approved by the chief factory inspector of the State; and he or any of the duly authorized deputies shall be authorized to enter upon the premises of any person, firm or corporation within this State for the purpose of inspecting any stationary steam boiler so used or operated. Low-water alarms on steam boilers.

SEC. 34. It shall be unlawful for any person, firm or corporation to operate any stationary steam boiler without its having a low-water alarm attached thereto, after the chief factory inspector or any duly authorized deputy has ordered the same to be used as specified in this act. Operating boilers without alarms.

MINNESOTA.

REVISED LAWS—1905.

Regulation and inspection of factories, etc.

SECTION 1813 (as amended by chapter 288, Acts of 1911). All saws, planers, wood shapers, jointers, sand-papering machines, and ironing mangles; all set screws, drums and machinery, including belts, shafting, cables, and fly wheels; all electrical dynamos and other dangerous electrical apparatus and appliances; and all vats, pans, or other receptacles containing molten metal or boiling liquid, in any factory, mill, or workshop, shall be so located as not to be dangerous to workmen, or, as far as practicable, shall be fenced or otherwise protected. Every dangerous place in or about factories, mills, workshops, and engineering work, near to which any employee is obliged to pass or to be employed, shall be securely fenced, enclosed, or otherwise protected. No grindstone, emery wheel, or machine in any factory, mill, or workshop shall be used when the same is known to be cracked or otherwise defective. If a machine or any part thereof is in a dangerous condition or is not properly guarded, the use thereof may be prohibited by the commissioner of labor or his assistants and a notice to that effect shall be attached thereto. Such notice shall not be removed until the machine is made safe and the required Guards for dangerous machinery.

safeguard provided, and in the meantime such unsafe or dangerous machinery shall not be used.

Belt shifters, etc.
SEC. 1814 (as amended by chapter 288, Acts of 1911). Every owner of a factory, mill or workshop where machinery is in use shall furnish or cause to be furnished, wherever practicable, belt shifters or other safe mechanical contrivances for the purpose of throwing on or off belts or pulleys; and, whenever practicable, machinery shall be provided with loose pulleys. Exhaust fans of sufficient power shall be provided for carrying off dust from emery wheels, grindstones and other dust creating machinery. Where the machinery is propelled by steam, communication shall be provided between each workroom in which machinery is placed and the room in which the engineer is stationed by means of speaking tubes, electric bells, telephone or appliances that may control the motive power.

Hoistways.
SEC. 1815 (as amended by chapter 288, Acts of 1911). Every hoisting apparatus used in the construction of any building, every hoistway, hatchway, elevator well, and wheel hole in any factory, mill, workshop, storehouse[,] wareroom, or store, shall be securely protected on each floor by a metal barrier at least four feet high, which shall be kept closed except when necessarily opened for use. Every elevator car used for either freight or passengers shall be provided with some suitable mechanical device by which it can be securely held in the event of accident to the rope or hoisting machinery.

Fire escapes.
SEC. 1816 (as amended by chapter 288, Acts of 1911). Every building in which laborers are employed shall be provided with sufficient means of escape in case of fire, by more than one way of egress, each of which shall be at all times free from obstruction and ready for immediate use, and every such egress shall be provided with a sign having on it the word " exit " in letters not less than five inches in height and so as plainly to indicate to persons within the building the location of such egresses. Every door leading in or to any such building shall be so constructed as to open outward, when possible, and shall not be so fastened during working hours as to prevent free egress. Substantial hand rails shall be provided on all stairways in every such building; and, where females are employed, the stairs regularly used by them shall be properly screened at the sides and bottom. When in the opinion of the factory inspectors it is necessary, the steps of said stairs shall be substantially covered with rubber, securely fastened thereon, for the better safety of persons employed in such buildings.

Same subject.
SEC. 1817 (as amended by chapter 288, Acts of 1911). If any such building where persons are employed be more than two stories high, it shall be the duty of the owner of such building (unless otherwise provided by lease,) to provide at least one fire escape, and as many more as the labor commissioner may require. Every such fire escape shall be on the outside of the building, connecting on each floor above the first with at least two openings; shall be well fastened and secured, with landings not less than six feet in length and three in width, guarded by an iron railing not less than three feet in height. Such landings shall be connected by iron stairs, not less than two feet wide, and with steps of not less than six inches tread, placed at an angle of not more than forty-five degrees, and protected by a well-secured hand rail on both sides, with an automatic drop ladder, two feet wide, reaching from the lower platform to the ground. Such fire escape shall be sufficient if constructed on any other plan approved by the labor bureau. The openings to each fire escape shall be as far as practicable from the stairways and elevator shafts, and the ladder of each fire escape shall extend to the roof. Stationary stairs or ladders shall also be provided on the inside from the upper story to the roof. Every factory, mill, and workshop more than two stories high shall also be provided with inside and outside standpipes, and with hose connected therewith, as required in the case

of hotels of the same height, and with one chemical fire extinguisher on each floor, always ready for use.

SEC. 1818 (as amended by chapter 288, Acts of 1911). Every build- *Ventilation.* ing in which labor is employed shall be kept clean and free from effluvia arising from any sewer, drain, or privy, be properly ventilated; and provided with privies for the separate use of male and *Toilet rooms,* female employees, to the number of at least one of such closets *etc.* for each twenty-five persons employed, properly screened, and at all times kept in a sanitary condition. Whenever the labor performed is such as to require a change of clothing, separate dressing rooms shall be provided for the sexes. Suitable receptacles for sputum shall be provided by the employers, the same to be of such form and construction and of such number as shall be satisfactory to the state board of health, or the commissioner of labor and his assistants.

SEC. 1819. Every bakery and confectionery establishment shall *Bakeries, etc.* be of good workmanship, well drained, and constructed and plumbed according to established sanitary principles. Every room used for the manufacture, storage, or sale of bread or other food products shall be light, dry, and airy. The floors and walls of every room used for the manufacture of such food products shall be so constructed as to exclude rats and other vermin, be at all times free from moisture, and kept in good repair. Its floors shall have a smooth surface, constructed of wood, cement, or tile laid in cement, save that, when it is more than four feet below the level of the street or adjacent ground, it shall never be constructed of wood. Its walls and ceilings shall be whitewashed at least once in three months, and the floors, utensils, and furniture of such room, and of every room used for the storage or sale of such food products, shall be so arranged as to be easily kept clean, and, together with the wagons used for its delivery, shall be kept in a clean and sanitary condition. No water-closet, earth closet, privy, ash pit, or sleeping room for workmen shall be in, or communicate directly with, any bake room or with the kitchen of any hotel or public restaurant.

SEC. 1820. No employee in any factory, mill, workshop, or upon any engineering work, nor any other person, by permission or otherwise, shall remove, displace, or destroy any guard for danger- *Removing* ous machinery, or other safety device, which the employer shall *guards.* have provided under the requirements of this chapter or any other law, save under rules established by the employer therefor.

SEC. 1821. Whenever any accident to an employee, resulting in *Accidents to be* death or requiring the aid of a surgeon, occurs in connection with *reported.* any factory, mill, workshop, or any engineering work, the employer, superintendent, or agent in charge, within ten days thereafter, shall furnish the labor commissioner with written notice thereof, stating as fully as possible the time and place of its occurrence, the name and residence of the person killed or injured, and, in case of injury, the place to which he has been removed.

SEC. 1824 (as amended by chapter 288, Acts of 1911). Every person who violates or fails to comply with any requirement of *Violations.* this chapter, or disregards any order, notice, or direction of any member or employee of the labor bureau made in accordance with its provisions, or who obstructs or interferes with any inspection being made pursuant thereto, or who removes any notice from a machine stating that such machine is dangerous and unsafe, or who operates any such machine while such notice is attached and such machine is still unguarded and unsafe, shall be guilty of a misdemeanor, the minimum penalty whereof shall be a fine of twenty-five dollars, or imprisonment for fifteen days. But whenever notice is required before prosecution, no criminal proceeding shall be commenced until thirty days after such notice, nor then, if within such time the requirements of the notice have been met: *Provided,* That if such requirement be to put a water-closet or privy in sanitary condition, where the only defect is due to carelessness in its management, or to put an elevator in safe condition, only forty-eight hours shall be allowed. In case of application to the court to restrain, the time aforesaid shall not begin to run until the decision thereon.

Inspection of steam boilers.

Inspectors.   SECTION 2168. In the month of January in every odd-numbered year the governor shall appoint a board of inspectors, consisting of one resident of each senatorial district, except that where there is more than one senatorial district in any county there shall be but one inspector in such county. Such inspector shall inspect all steam boilers in use in the State, not subject to inspection under the laws of the United States and not hereinafter excepted, and examine and grant certificates of license to steam engineers intrusted with the management of steam boilers, except those in heating plants in private residences. They shall examine and license all masters and pilots on inland waters of the State, as nearly as may be according to the regulations provided by the laws of the United States. Each shall hold office for the term of two years, commencing February 1, unless sooner removed by the **Reports.** governor. Annually on or before January 31 each shall render a report to the secretary of state, containing a detailed statement of the number of inspections made and licenses issued, the amount of fees received therefor, and the amount of disbursements of their offices. The secretary of state shall include in his biennial report a summary of such report.

Qualifications.   SEC. 2169. Every boiler inspector shall be a man of good moral character, and qualified by experience in the construction of steam boilers, and shall have had at least ten years' actual experience in operating steam engines and boilers. He shall not be directly or indirectly interested in the manufacture or sale of boilers or steam machinery, or in any patented article required or generally used in the construction of engines or boilers.

Deputies.   SEC. 2170. Each boiler inspector may appoint one or more deputies, who shall possess the same qualifications and have the same authority as are prescribed for inspectors in section 2169. Each such deputy, before entering upon the duties of his office, shall take and subscribe the oath required by law, and file the same with the secretary of state.

Board to make rules.   SEC. 2171. In February of each year said inspectors shall meet as a board, at the capitol in St. Paul, and establish regulations for the inspection of vessels and boilers, and for the performance of their other duties. * * *

Inspection of steam boilers, etc.   SEC. 2175. Such inspectors shall inspect all steam boilers and steam generators before the same shall be used, and all such boilers at least once each year thereafter. They shall subject all boilers to hydrostatic pressure or hammer test, and ascertain by a thorough internal and external examination that they are well made and of good and suitable material; that the openings for the passage of water and steam respectively, and all pipes and tubes exposed to heat, are of proper dimensions and free from obstructions; that the flues are circular in form; that the arrangements for delivering the feed water are such that the boilers can not be injured thereby; and that such boilers and their steam connections may be safely used without danger to life or property. They shall also ascertain that the safety valves are of suitable dimensions, sufficient in number, and properly arranged, and that the safety valve weights are so adjusted as to allow no greater pressure in the boilers than the amount prescribed by the inspector's certificate; that there is a sufficient number of gauge cocks, properly inserted, to indicate the amount of water, and suitable gauges that will correctly record the pressure of steam; and that the fusible metals are properly inserted so as to fuse by the heat of the furnace whenever the water in the boiler falls below its prescribed limit; and that provisions are made for an ample supply of water to feed the boilers at all times, so that in high-pressure boilers the water shall not be less than three inches above the top of the fire surface; and that means for blowing out are provided, so as to thoroughly remove the mud and sediment from all parts when under pressure of steam. *Tests.*

SEC. 2176. In subjecting high-pressure boilers to the hydrostatic test, the inspector shall assume one hundred and twenty-five pounds to the square inch as the maximum working pressure allowable for new boilers forty-two inches in diameter, double riveted, and made in the best manner, of plates one-fourth of an inch thick and of good material; but he shall rate the working power of all high-pressure boilers according to their strength compared with this standard, and in all cases the test applied shall exceed the working power allowed in the ratio of one hundred and sixty-five to one hundred and ten. In subjecting low-pressure boilers to hydrostatic tests, he shall allow as a working power for each new boiler a pressure of only three-fourths the number of pounds to which it has been so subjected. If any inspector is of opinion that any boiler will not safely allow so high a working pressure, he may, for reasons specially stated in his certificate, fix the pressure at less than the test pressure. No boiler or steam pipe, nor any of the connections therewith, which are made wholly or partly of bad material, or of cast iron, or which are unsafe from any cause, shall be approved. But this shall not be construed to prevent the use of any boiler or steam generator not constructed of riveted iron or steel plates, when the inspector is satisfied by evidence that such boiler or generator is equal in strength to, and as safe from explosion as, boilers of the best quality, constructed of riveted steel or iron plates.

SEC. 2177. Every person who shall construct a boiler or steam pipe or iron or steel plates known to be faulty or imperfect, or shall drift any rivet hole to make it come fair, or who shall deliver any such boiler for use, knowing it to be imperfect in its flues, flanging, riveting, bracing, or in any other of its parts, shall be guilty of a gross misdemeanor, and punished by a fine of two hundred dollars, one-half of which shall be paid to the informer. *Faulty construction.*

SEC. 2178. In addition to the annual inspection, the inspectors at any time, when in their opinion such examinaton shall be necessary, shall examine all boilers which have become unsafe, and notify the owners or operators of any defect, and what repairs are necessary; and such a boiler shall not thereafter be used until so repaired. Every person operating any such boiler who fails to comply with the inspector's requirements shall be guilty of a misdemeanor, and also liable for damages to persons or property resulting therefrom. *Special inspections.*

SEC. 2179. Every steam boiler shall be provided with a fusible plug, of good banca tin, inserted in the flues, crown sheet, or other parts of the boiler most exposed to the heat of the furnace when the water falls below the prescribed limits. *Fusible plugs.*

SEC. 2180. Every owner or manager of a steam boiler shall allow inspectors full access to the same, and every engineer operating the same shall assist the inspector in his examination and point out any known defect in the boilers or machinery in his charge. No person shall be intrusted with the operation of any steam boiler or steam machinery who has not received a license so to act, which license shall be renewed biennially. Every person who shall violate any provision of this section shall be guilty of a misdemeanor, and punished by a fine of not less than ten dollars nor more than fifty dollars. *Access to boilers.*

SEC. 2183. In making the inspection of boilers, machinery, or steam vessels, the inspectors may act jointly or separately, but shall in all cases verify the certificate of inspection. * * * *False certificates.*

SEC. 2184. After examination and tests, if the inspector shall find any steam boiler or generator safe and suitable for use, he shall deliver to the secretary of state a verified certificate, in such form as the board of inspectors shall prescribe, containing a specification of the tests applied and the working power allowed, a copy of which the inspector shall furnish to the owner of the boiler or generator, who shall post and keep the same in a con- *Certificate to be posted.*

spicuous place on or near such boiler or generator. The inspector shall be entitled to a fee of three dollars for the inspection of each single boiler and its steam connections, and two dollars for each additional boiler when connected and inspected at the same time, payable on delivery of the certificate. The fee for an engineer's license, and for each biennial renewal, shall be one dollar, which shall accompany the application.

ACTS OF 1909.

CHAPTER 289.—*Inspection of factories and workshops—Use of basements, etc.*

Basements, etc., not to be used, when.

SECTION 1. No basement, cellar, underground apartments, or other place which the commissioner of labor shall condemn as unhealthy and unsuitable shall be used as a workship [workshop], factory or place of business in which any person or persons shall be employed.

Violations.

SEC. 2. Any person, firm or corporation violating any of the provisions of this act shall be guilty of a misdemeanor and, upon conviction thereof, shall be punished by a fine of not more than one hundred ($100) dollars, nor less, nor less [sic] than twenty-five ($25) dollars, or by imprisonment for not more than ninety (90) days, nor less than thirty (30) days, or by both such fine and imprisonment, for each offense.

CHAPTER 497.—*Bureau of labor—Women's and children's department.*

Department created.

SECTION 1. There shall be created in the bureau of labor a woman's and children's department.

Female assistant commissioner.

SEC. 2. There shall be appointed by the commissioner of labor a competent woman to act as assistant commissioner of labor and such woman factory inspectors as may be necessary to inspect the sanitary and general conditions under which women and children are at work in all factories, workshops, hotels, restaurants, stores and any other places where women and children are employed.

Said assistant commissioner of labor shall collect statistics and render to the next legislature through the commissioner of labor such findings and recommendations as will promote the health and general welfare of the women and children so employed in this State.

CHAPTER 499.—*Ventilation and sanitation of factories.*

[See Appendix A, p. 747.]

MISSISSIPPI.

CODE OF 1906.

Factories and workshops—Doors to swing outwardly.

Doors to open outwardly.

SECTION 2272. All the doors for ingress and egress to * * * factories with more than twenty employees * * * shall be so swung as to open outwardly from the * * * workshops; but such doors may be hung on double-jointed hinges, so as to open with equal ease outwardly or inwardly.

Penalty.

SEC. 2277. Any architect, carpenter, or builder, or the owner or other person, who may hereafter erect or cause to be erected, or aid in erecting, any hotel or other house or structure for the construction of which provisions are made in this chapter, who shall refuse or fail to comply, in the erection or construction thereof, with such provisions, shall be guilty of a misdemeanor, and, on conviction, shall be punished by a fine not exceeding five hundred dollars.

Sec. 2278. Every day's omission or failure by any person to do **Separate of fenses.** whatever under the provisions of this chapter is required to be done or provided, shall be considered and treated as a separate offense.

MISSOURI.

REVISED STATUTES—1909.

Inspector of factories.

· Section 7823. * * * the governor of the State, with the **Inspector to be appointed.** advice and consent of the senate, shall appoint a competent person to serve as factory inspector, who shall hold office for four years from the date of his appointment, or until his successor is appointed and qualified. The factory inspector may appoint, from time to time, two assistant factory inspectors and seven deputy **Assistants, etc.** factory inspectors, two of whom may be women, who may be removed by him at any time for just cause. Before entering upon his official duties, the inspector shall make oath to support the constitution and faithfully demean himself in office; he shall also execute a bond to the State of Missouri, in such sum as the governor may prescribe, with two or more solvent sureties, to be approved by the governor, conditioned upon his faithful performance of the duties imposed upon him by this article.

Sec. 7824. The State factory inspector may divide the State into **Districts.** districts, assign one or more deputy inspectors to each district, and may, at his discretion, change or transfer them from one district to another. It shall be the duty of the factory inspector, his assistants or deputy inspectors, to make not less than two inspections during each year of all factories, warehouses, freight depots, machine shops, laundries, tenement, workshops, bake shops, hotels, restaurants, bowling alleys, theaters, concert halls or places of public amusement, and other manufacturing, mechanical and mercantile establishments and workshops, in all cities having a population of ten thousand inhabitants or more. The last inspection shall be completed on or before the first day of October of each year, and the factory inspector shall enforce all laws relating to the inspection of the establishments enumerated heretofore in this section, and prosecute all persons for violating the same. Any municipal ordinance relating to said establishments or their inspection, shall be enforced by the factory inspector. The factory inspector, his assistants and deputy inspectors, may administer oaths and take affidavits in matters concerning the enforcement of the various inspection laws relating to these establishments.

Sec. 7825. The inspector provided for in this article shall be **Fees.** entitled to demand and receive from the owner, superintendent, manager or other person in charge of every establishment inspected, as provided for by law, the following fee for each inspection made in accordance with the provisions of this article: For the inspection of every building or shop in which three or less persons are employed or found at work, the sum of fifty cents; for the inspection of every building or shop in which more than three or not exceeding twenty-five persons are employed, the sum of one dollar; for the inspection of every building or shop in which more than twenty-five and less than sixty persons are employed, the sum of two dollars, and in every building or shop in which more than sixty persons are employed, an additional fee of one dollar shall be charged and collected for every fifty additional persons employed, or any additional fraction thereof, and the fee herein provided for shall be due immediately upon completion of the inspection. The owner, superintendent, manager or other person in **Duties of owners, etc.** charge of any establishment at the time of inspection shall be required to furnish the inspector making the inspection a true statement of the number of persons employed in such establishment at the time of inspection, and any owner, superintendent, manager or other person in charge who shall fail or refuse to furnish such

statement, or understate the number of persons employed in such
establishment at the time of inspection, shall be deemed guilty of
a misdemeanor, and, upon conviction thereof, shall be fined not

Refusing ad-
mission.
less than twenty-five dollars nor more than one hundred dollars
for each offense. Any person, firm or corporation, agent or manager, superintendent or foreman of any firm or corporation,
whether acting for himself or for such firm or corporation, or by
himself or through subagents or foreman, superintendent or manager, who shall refuse or attempt to prevent the admission of any
inspector authorized by this article, upon or within the premises
or buildings of any such establishments or place included in this
article, at any reasonable business hour, or during working hours
of the persons employed therein or thereat, or shall in any manner
interfere with the performance of the official duties of such inspector, or shall neglect or refuse to pay the inspection fee upon
the completion of such inspection, shall be deemed guilty of a misdemeanor, and, upon conviction thereof, shall be fined not less
than twenty-five dollars nor more than one hundred dollars for
each offense: *Provided*, That the owner or manager of any establishment inspected shall not be required to pay for more than
two such inspections between the first day of October of one year
and thirtieth day of September of the next year, unless, through
noncompliance with the written orders of the inspector, additional
inspections are made necessary.

Salaries.
SEC. 7826. All fees received by the factory inspector under the
provisions of this article, shall be paid into the State treasury on
or before the last day of each month to be placed to the credit of
the " factory inspection fund." The factory inspector shall receive
an annual salary of two thousand dollars; the two assistant factory inspectors shall receive an annual salary of one thousand four
hundred dollars each, and the deputy factory inspectors shall each
receive a salary of one hundred dollars per month for the time
actually employed; and the factory inspector, assistant factory inspectors and deputy factory inspectors shall further receive actual
necessary expenses incurred in the discharge of their duties, to
be paid monthly upon a warrant of the State auditor, issued upon

Offices.
vouchers therefor. The factory inspector shall establish and maintain an office in the city of St. Louis, and also an office in the city
of Kansas City. The offices herein provided for in St. Louis and
Kansas City shall each be in charge of one of said assistant factory inspectors. Each of said assistant factory inspectors shall devote his entire time to the discharge of the duties of the office in
the city for which he is appointed. The persons appointed assistant factory inspectors under this article shall possess all the qualifications now required of city officers by the charters of the respective cities in which their said offices are located: *Provided*,
That no salary or expense shall be paid for the factory inspector
or assistant or deputy factory inspectors or clerks in excess of the
receipts from the fees paid into the factory inspection fund; *And*,
provided further, That the salary of the factory inspector and his
assistants, and all expenses for traveling, office rent, printing, stationery, postage and other items of expenditure, shall be limited
for the biennial term of two years to an amount not exceeding
thirty-five thousand dollars, and all money remaining in said factory inspection fund at the close of each biennial term, after the
payment of the salaries and expenses herein provided for, shall
be transferred to the general revenue fund.

Regulation and inspection of factories.

Belting, etc., to
be guarded.
SECTION 7828. The belting, shafting, machines, machinery, gearing and drums, in all manufacturing, mechanical and other establishments in this State, when so placed as to be dangerous to persons employed therein or thereabout while engaged in their ordinary duties, shall be safely and securely guarded when possible;
if not possible, then notice of its danger shall be conspicuously
posted in such establishments.

SEC. 7829. No minor or woman shall be required to clean any *Women and children cleaning moving machinery, etc.* part of the mill, gearing or machinery while it is in motion in such establishment, nor shall any minor under the age of sixteen years be required to work between the fixed and traversing or the traversing parts of any machine while it is in motion by the action of steam, water, electricity or other mechanical power; and no woman shall be required to work between the fixed and traversing or the traversing parts of any such machine, except the machine being operated by her.

SEC. 7830. The openings of all hatchways, elevators and well-holes upon every floor of every manufacturing, mechanical or mercantile or public building in this State shall be protected by *Hatchways, etc., to be guarded.* good and sufficient trapdoors or self-closing hatches or safety catches, or strong guard rails at least three feet high, and all due diligence shall be used to keep such trapdoors closed at all times, except when in actual use by the occupant of the building having the use and control of the same.

SEC. 7831. All manufacturing, mechanical, mercantile or other *Fire escapes.* establishments in this State, of two or more stories in height, in which twenty or more persons are employed above the first floor thereof, shall be provided with at least one or more outside iron fire escapes. For every twenty persons employed on every floor above the second floor of such establishment, there shall be one rope or portable fire escape, and each story shall be amply supplied with means for extinguishing fire.

SEC. 7832. In all such establishments the main doors, both in-side and outside, shall open outwardly, when the inspector, in *Doors to open outwardly.* writing so directs; and no outside or inside door of any building wherein labor is employed shall be so locked, bolted or otherwise fastened during the hours of labor as to prevent egress.

SEC. 7833. Every factory and workshop in this State where *Limewash or paint to be used.* women and children are employed, and where dusty work is car-ried on, shall be limewashed or painted at least once in every twelve months.

SEC. 7834. No explosive or inflammable compound shall be used *Placing explo-sives near egress.* in any establishment in this State where labor is employed, in such place or manner as to obstruct or render hazardous the egress of operatives in case of fire.

SEC. 7835. In every factory, workshop or other establishment in *Wash rooms for women.* this State where girls or women are employed, where unclean work of any kind has to be performed, suitable places shall be provided for such girls or women to wash and dress, and stairs in use by female employees shall in all such establishments be prop-erly screened.

SEC. 7836. Separate water-closets shall be provided for the use *Water-closets.* of employees of either sex in manufacturing, mechanical, mercan-tile and other establishments in this State where persons of both sexes are employed.

SEC. 7837. All manufacturing, mechanical, mercantile and other *Ventilation.* establishments in this State shall be so ventilated as to render harmless all impurities, as near as may be.

SEC. 7838. In every manufacturing, mechanical, mercantile and *Seats for female employees.* other establishment in this State wherein girls or women are em-ployed, there shall be provided and conveniently located seats suffi-cient to comfortably seat such girls or women, and during such times as such girls or women are not necessarily required by their duties to be upon their feet, they shall be allowed to occupy the seats provided.

SEC. 7839. Every person, firm or corporation using any polish- *Hoods and blowers for dust-producing ma-chinery, etc.* ing wheel or machine of any character which generates dust smoke or poisonous gases in its operation, shall provide each and every such wheel or machine with a hood, which shall be con-nected with a blower or suction fan of sufficient power to carry off said dust, smoke and gases and prevent its inhalation by those employed about said wheel or machine; and any violation of this section is hereby declared to be a misdemeanor, and a person, firm or corporation so violating this section shall, upon conviction, be punished by a fine of not less than one hundred dollars nor more than five hundred dollars for each and every offense. It shall be the duty of the factory inspector and his deputies to see that this sec ion is enforced and to prosecute any violations thereof.

Exhaust fans or smoke, etc. Sec. 7840. In all establishments in this State wherein labor is employed, where any process is carried on by which dust or smoke is generated, the factory inspector and his deputies shall have the power and authority to order that a fan or some other contrivance be put in to prevent the inhalation of such dust or smoke by employees.

Overcrowding. Sec. 7841. Where, in the opinion of the inspector, any establishment wherein labor is employed is so overcrowded with employees as to endanger health or safety, the factory inspector, when supported in his opinion by the opinion of some reputable physician, shall be authorized and empowered to prohibit such overcrowding.

What are violations. Sec. 7842. Whenever the factory inspector, or assistant inspector, finds that the heating, lighting, ventilating or sanitary arrangements of any establishment where labor is employed is such as to be dangerous to the health or safety of empoyees therein or thereat, or the means of egress, in case of fire or other disaster, are not sufficient, or that the building, or any part thereof, is unsafe, or that the belting, shafting, gearing, elevators, drums or other machinery are located so as to be dangerous to empoyees, and not sufficiently guarded, or that the vats, pans, ladles or structures filled with molten or hot liquid, or any furnace, be not sufficiently surrounded with proper safeguards, or the platforms, passageways and other arrangements around, in or about any railroad yard or switch be such as to probably lead to injury or accident to those employed in, around or about any such establishment or place, the factory inspector or assistant inspector shall at once notify the person or persons in charge of such establishment or place to make the alterations or additions necessary within thirty days; and if such alterations or additions be not made within thirty days from the date of such notice, or within such time as said alterations could be made with proper diligence, then such failure to make such alterations shall be deemed a violation of this article.

Notice to inspector. Sec. 7845. Within one month after the occupancy of any factory, workshop or mill, the occupant shall notify the inspector, in writing, of such occupancy.

Penalty. Sec. 7846. Any person or persons, firm or corporation, being the owner, agent, lessee or occupant of any manufacturing, mechanical, mercantile or other establishment, business or calling in this State to which this article applies, or any employee therein or thereat, who shall violate, or aid or abet in violating, any of the proyisions of this article, shall be deemed guilty of a misdemeanor, and, upon conviction in any court of competent jurisdiction in this State, be fined for the first offense not less than twenty-five dollars nor more than two hundred dollars, and for each subsequent offense, not less than one hundred dollars nor more than five hundred dollars, and, in default of payment of such fine and costs, shall be committed to the common jail. of the county or city in which the offense was committed until such fine and costs are fully paid.

Officers and agents of corporations. Sec. 7847. When any of the provisions of this article are violated by a corporation, proceedings may be had against any of the officers or agents of such corporation who in any way participated in such violation by the corporation of which they are the officers or agents, and, upon conviction, such officers or agents shall be subject to the same penalty as in case of individuals so offending.

Violation of other laws. Sec. 7851. In case of an offense which is a violation of both this article and of some other law of this State, then the inspector or assistant inspector may elect under which law he will prosecute; but where an offense is in violation of some other law of this State in relation to the protection of employees, but is not covered by this article, then it shall be the duty of the inspector or assistant inspector to prosecute for all such offenses under the law violated.

SEC. 7852. All assistant inspectors appointed in accordance with the provisions of this article shall have the same authority as that vested in the State inspector, and, as far as consistent, their duties shall be the same as defined for the State inspector. *Powers of assistant inspectors.*

Sweatshops.

SECTION 7853. No room or apartment in any tenement or dwelling house shall be used by more than three persons, not immediate members of the family living therein, for the manufacture of any wearing apparel, purses, feathers, artificial flowers or other goods for male or female wear. Every person, firm or corporation contracting for the manufacture of any of the articles mentioned in this section, or giving out the complete material from which they are to be made, or to be wholly or partially finished, shall keep a register of the names and addresses of all person to whom such work is given to be made or with whom they have contracted to do the same. Such register shall be produced for the inspection, and a copy thereof shall be furnished to, the factory inspector on demand. *Manufactures in tenements.*

SEC. 7854. No person, firm or corporation shall knowingly sell or expose for sale any of the articles mentioned herein when such articles were made in violation of this article; and the factory inspector, his deputy or any officer appointed to enforce the provisions of this article, who shall find any such articles made in violation of the provisions of this article, or who shall find that the articles herein mentioned are made under unclean or unhealthy conditions, shall conspicuously affix thereto a label containing the words " tenement made" or " made under unhealthy conditions," as the case may be, printed in plain letters on a tag not less than two inches in length, and it shall be unlawful to remove such tag, except by the permission of the factory inspector or the officer under whose direction such label was affixed. *Certain goods to be labeled.*

SEC. 7855. Any person, firm or corporation engaged in the manufacture or sale of the articles herein mentioned who shall violate or who shall fail to comply with the provisions of this article, shall be deemed guilty of a misdemeanor, and on conviction, shall be punished by a fine of not less than ten nor more than fifty dollars, or by imprisonment in the county jail for a period of not more than ten days, or by both such fine and imprisonment. *Penalty.*

Sanitation, etc., of factories.

SECTION 7856. Every person employing five or more persons in a factory, or employing children, young persons or women, five or more in number, in a workshop, shall keep such factory or workshop in a cleanly state and free from effluvia from any drain, privy or other nuisance. *Sanitation required.*

SEC. 7857. Every person employing five or more persons in a factory, or employing children, young persons or women, five or more in number, in a workshop, shall provide, with reasonable access, a sufficient number of proper water-closets, earth closets or privies, for the reasonable use of all persons so employed; and wherever male and female persons are employed in the same factory or workshop, a sufficient number of separate and distinct water-closets, earth closets or privies shall be provided for the use of each sex, and shall be plainly designated; and no person shall be allowed to use any such closet or privy assigned to persons of the other sex. *Water - closets, etc.*

SEC. 7858. Every factory in which five or more persons are employed, and every workshop in which children, young persons or women, five or more in number, are employed, shall be so ventilated while work is carried on therein that the air shall not become so exhausted as to be injurious to the health of the persons employed therein, and shall also be so ventilated as to render harmless, so far as is practicable, all the gases, vapors, dust or *Ventilation.*

other impurities generated in the course of the manufacturing process or handicraft carried on therein that may be injurious to health.

Exhaust fans.   SEC. 7859. If, in a factory or workshop included in section 7858 of this article, any process is carried on by which dust is generated and inhaled to an injurious extent by the persons employed therein, and it appears to an inspector of factories that such inhalation could be to a great extent prevented by the use of a fan or other mechanical means, and that the same could be provided without excessive expense, such inspector may direct a fan, or other mechanical means of a proper construction, to be provided within a reasonable time; and such fan or other mechanical means shall be so provided, maintained and used.

Penalty.   SEC. 7860. Any person employing labor in a factory or workshop, and violating any provision of this article, shall be deemed guilty of a misdemeanor, and punished by a fine of not less than fifty nor more than two hundred dollars; but no criminal prosecution shall be made for such violation until four weeks after notice in writing by an inspector of factories of the changes necessary to be made to comply with the provisions of this article has been sent by mail or delivered to such person, nor then, if in the meantime such changes have been made in accordance with such notification. A notice shall be a sufficient notice under this article to all the members of a firm, company or corporation, when given to one member of such firm or company, or to the clerk, cashier, secretary, agent or any other officer having charge of the business of such corporation, or to its attorney; and in case of a foreign corporation, notice to the officer having charge of such factory or workshop shall be sufficient.

Definitions.   SEC. 7861. The following expressions used in this article shall have the following meanings: The expression "person" means any individual, corporation, partnership, company or association. The expression "child" means a person under the age of fourteen years. The expression "young person" means a person of the age of fourteen years and under the age of eighteen years. The expression "woman" means a woman of the age of eighteen years and upward. The expression "factory" means any premises where steam, water or other mechanical power is used in aid of any manufacturing process there carried on. The expression "workshop" means any premises, room or place, not being a factory as above defined, wherein any manual labor is exercised by way of trade, or for purposes of gain, in or incidental to any process of making, altering, repairing, ornamenting, finishing or adapting for sale any article or part of an article, and to which or over which premises, room or place the employer of the persons working therein has the right of access or control: *Provided, however,* That the exercise of manual labor in a private house or room by a family dwelling therein, shall not in itself constitute such house or room a workshop within this definition.

Fire escapes on factories, etc.

What buildings to have fire escapes.   SECTION 10666. It shall be the duty of the owner, proprietor, lessee or keeper of every * * * factory, office building, except fireproof office buildings, in which all structural parts are wholly of brick, stone, tile, concrete, reinforced concrete, iron, steel, or incombustible material, and which are not used for lodging purposes, in the state of Missouri, * * * which has a height of three or more stories, to provide said structure with stair fire escapes attached to the exterior of said building and by staircases located in the interior of said building. The fire escapes shall commence at the sill of the second story window, and run to the upper sill of the upper story, with an iron ladder from the upper story to the roof. The fire escape shall extend downward from said second story to within nine feet of the ground, pavement or sidewalk. * * * In no case shall a fire escape run past a window where it is practicable to avoid it. All fire escapes required by this article must be of the kind known as stationary fire escapes. All buildings heretofore erected shall be made to conform to the provisions of this article.

SEC. 10667. When fire escapes are to be attached to buildings within a city, they shall be constructed under the supervision of and subject to the approval of the commissioner or superintendent of public buildings within such city, and if there be no such office within such city, they shall be subject to the approval of the chief of the fire department of such city. Whenever a fire escape attached to any building located within a city shall, upon inspection by the commissioner or superintendent of public buildings, or chief of the fire department of such city, be found in an unsafe and dangerous condition, the owner, lessee, proprietor or keeper of said building shall forthwith rebuild or repair same or replace same in safe condition, upon written notice of such commissioner or superintendent. When fire escapes are to be attached to buildings not within the limits of any city, they shall be subject to the approval of the sheriff of the county in which such building is located. And should such fire escape, through age or otherwise, be or become unsafe or dangerous, the same shall be repaired and placed in safe condition, upon written notice by said sheriff to the person in charge of such building. All fire escapes shall have proper and safe balconies for each story thereof, surrounded on the sides with wire bank and pipe rail not less than three feet in height with openings from the building to said balconies. Whenever a stair fire escape is to be constructed, the stairway shall where practicable, be of an angle of not more than fifty-five degrees and constructed so as to be placed on a blank wall. The stair fire escape shall be provided with one or more landings in each story, and inclosed on the sides with wire bank and pipe rail not less than three feet in height and running on the same angle as the stairs.

SEC. 10668. The number of fire escapes to be attached to any one building as required in this article shall, when the building is located within a city, be determined by the commissioner or superintendent of public buildings within such city, and if there be no such officer in such city, then by the chief of the fire department of such city: *Provided, however,* That all buildings of nonfireproof construction three or more stories in height used for manufacturing purposes, * * * shall have not less than one fire escape for every fifty persons or fraction thereof for whom working * * * accommodations are provided above the second story * * *.

SEC. 10669. All buildings hereafter erected in this State which shall come within the provisions of this article shall, upon or before their completion, be provided with fire escapes of the kind and number and in the manner set forth in this article, and any violation of this section shall constitute a misdemeanor on the part of the owner of such building, punishable as provided in section ten thousand six hundred and seventy.

SEC. 10670. The owner, proprietor, lessee or manager of a building which, under the terms of this article, is required to have one or more fire escapes, who shall neglect or refuse for the period of sixty days after this article takes effect to comply with its provisions, shall be deemed guilty of a misdemeanor, and on conviction shall be fined not less than fifty nor more than two hundred dollars, or by imprisonment in the county or city jail not more than three months, or by both fine and imprisonment, and each day shall be deemed a separate offense.

SEC. 10678. All the doors for ingress and egress to and from all * * * factories with more than twenty employees, * * * which shall hereafter be erected, * * * shall be so hung as to open outwardly from the * · * workshops of such buildings or places: *Provided,* That said doors may be hung on double-jointed hinges so as to open with equal ease outwardly and inwardly.

Marginal notes:
Inspection.
Construction.
Number.
Violation a misdemeanor.
Penalty.
Doors to open outward.

Penalty.

SEC. 10679. Any architect, superintendent or other person or persons or body corporate, who may have charge of the erection, or may have the control or custody of any of the said buildings or places of resort mentioned in the preceding section, who shall refuse or fail to comply with the provisions of said section within six months from the passage of this article, in case of said buildings or places aforesaid which have been heretofore erected, and before the completion or occupation for said purposes of any of said buildings or places now in process of erection, shall, on proof of such refusal or failure before any court of competent jurisdiction, be adjudged to be guilty of a misdemeanor, and be punished by a fine of not less than one hundred nor more than one thousand dollars, which said fine shall be collected as is now provided by law for the collection of fines in such cases, and when collected shall be paid into and become a part of the public school fund of the county, city or incorporated town in which said misdemeanor was committed.

ACTS OF 1911.

Factory regulations—Bakeries, etc.

(Page 258.)

Sanitation.

SECTION 1. Every building, room, basement, or cellar occupied or used as a bakery, confectionery, cannery, packing house, slaughterhouse, restaurant, hotel, dining car, grocery, meat market, dairy, creamery, butter factory, cheese factory, or other place or apartment used for the preparation for sale, manufacture, packing, storage, sale or distribution of any food, shall be properly lighted, drained, plumbed and ventilated and conducted with strict regard to the influence of such condition upon the health of the operatives, employees, clerks or other persons therein employed, and the purity and wholesomeness of the food therein produced; and for the purpose of this act the term, "food," as used herein, shall include all articles used for food, drink, confectionery, condiment, whether simple, mixed or compound, and all substances or ingredients used in the preparation thereof.

Same.

SEC. 3. The ceilings of every bakery, confectionery, hotel and restaurant kitchen shall be well plastered, wainscoted or ceiled with metal or lumber and shall be oil painted or kept well lime washed and all interior woodwork in every bakery, confectionery, hotel, dining car, and restaurant kitchen shall be kept well oiled or painted with oil paints, and be kept washed clean with soap and water; and every building, room, basement or cellar, occupied or used for the preparation, manufacture, packing, storage, sale or distribution of food, shall have an impermeable floor made of cement or tile laid in cement, brick, wood or other suitable nonabsorbent material which can be flushed and washed clean with water.

Toilet rooms.

SEC. 5. Every building, room, basement or cellar, occupied or used for the preparation, manufacture, packing, canning, sale or distribution of food, shall have convenient toilet or toilet rooms, separate and apart from the room or rooms where the process of production, manufacture, packing, canning, selling or distributing is conducted. The floors of such toilet rooms shall be of cement, tile, wood, brick or other nonabsorbent material and shall be furnished with separate ventilating flush or pipes, discharging into soil pipes, or on outside of the building in which they are situated.

Wash rooms.

Lavatories and wash rooms shall be adjacent to toilet rooms, and shall be supplied with soap, running water and towels, and shall be maintained in a sanitary condition. Operatives, employees, clerks and all other persons, who handle the material from which food is prepared, or the finished product, before beginning work or after visiting toilets, shall wash their hands and arms thoroughly with soap and clean water.

Cuspidors.

SEC. 6. Cuspidors for the use of operatives, employees, clerks or other persons shall be provided whenever necessary, and each cuspidor shall be thoroughly emptied and washed out daily with disinfectant solution and five ounces of such a solution shall be left in each cuspidor while it is in use. No operative, employee or other person shall expectorate on the floor or sidewalks of any building, room, basement or cellar where the production, manufacture, packing, storing, preparation or sale of any food is conducted.

Sec. 7. No person or persons shall be allowed to live or sleep in any room of a bakeshop, kitchen, dining room, confectionery or place where food is prepared, served or sold. Sleeping, etc., in workrooms.

Sec. 8. No employer shall require, permit or suffer any person to work, nor shall any person work, in a building, room, basement, cellar or vehicle occupied or used for the production, preparation, manufacture, packing, storage, sale, distribution and transportation of food, who is affected with any venereal disease, smallpox, diphtheria, scarlet fever, yellow fever, tuberculosis or consumption, bubonic plague, Asiatic cholera, eczema or other skin diseases, leprosy, eye disease, typhoid fever (epidemic), epidemic dysentery, measles, mumps, German measles (Rothein), whooping cough, chicken pox or any other infectious disease. Contagious and infectious diseases.

Sec. 9. The State [food] and drug commissioner and his assistants or agents by him appointed, the State, county, city and town health officers shall have full power at any time to enter and inspect every building, room, basement or cellar, occupied or used, or suspected of being used, for the production for sale, manufacture for sale, storage, sale, distribution or transportation of food and all utensils, fixtures, furniture and machinery used as aforesaid, and if upon inspection any food producing or distributing establishment, conveyance, employer, operative, employee, clerk, driver or other person is found to be violating any of the provisions of this act, or if the production, cooking, preparation, manufacture, packing, storing, sale, distribution or transportation of food is being conducted in a manner detrimental to the health of the employees and operatives and the character or quality of the food therein being produced, manufactured, packed, stored, sold, distributed or conveyed, the officer or inspector, making the examination or inspection, shall furnish evidence of said violation to the prosecuting attorney of the county in which the violation occurs, and it shall be the duty of all prosecuting attorneys to represent and prosecute, in behalf of the people, when called upon by the food and drug commissioner to do so, all such cases of offense[s] arising under the provision of this act. When complaint is made by the said food and drug commissioner, security for costs shall not be required of the complainant in any case at any time of the prosecution or trial. Inspection.

MONTANA.

REVISED CODES—1907.

Commissioner of agriculture, labor, and industry—Inspection of factories, etc.

Section 284. The commissioner shall have the power to administer oaths, have and use a seal, with power, to examine witnesses under oath to take depositions or cause the same to be taken by anyone authorized to take depositions, and said commissioner may deputize any male citizen over the age of twenty-one years to serve subpœnas upon witnesses who shall be summoned in the same manner as witnesses before the district court, and any person or owner, operator, or lessee of any mine, factory, workshop, smelter, mill, warehouse, elevator, foundry, machine shop or other establishment, any agent or employee of such owner, operator, manager or lessee, who shall refuse to said commissioner admission therein for the purpose of inspecting, or who shall when requested by him willfully neglect or refuse to furnish to him any statistics or other information relating to his lawful Powers.

duties, which may be in their possession or under their control, or who shall willfully neglect or refuse for thirty days to answer questions by circular or by personal application, or who shall knowingly answer such questions untruthfully or who shall refuse to obey any such subpœnas and give testimony according to the provisions of this act, shall for every such willful neglect or refusal be guilty of a misdemeanor, and upon conviction thereof shall be punished by a fine not, less than fifty nor more than one hundred dollars: *Provided*, That no witness shall be compelled to answer questions respecting his private affairs nor ,to go outside of his own county to give testimony.

Inspection of steam boilers.

Inspector of boilers.

SECTION 1639. There must be appointed by the governor, by and with the advice and consent of the senate, one inspector of boilers, whose duty it is to inspect all steam boilers now in use in the State, not subject to inspection under the laws of the United States, and to examine and grant licenses to steam engineers intrusted with the care and management of steam boilers and steam machinery. The salary of the inspector of boilers is twenty-four hundred dollars per year, and his term of office is four years, unless sooner removed by the governor. The inspector of boilers must execute an official bond in the sum of five thousand dollars.

Qualifications.

SEC. 1640. No person is eligible to hold the office of inspector of boilers and steam machinery who has not had at least five years of actual practice in the operations of steam engines, steam boilers and steam machinery, or who is directly or indirectly interested in the manufacture or sale of boilers or steam machinery, or any patented article required to be sold or in general use in the construction of steam boilers or steam engines.

Assistant inspectors.

SEC. 1641 (as amended by chapter 10, Acts of 1911). There shall be three assistant inspectors of boilers, each of whom shall be called assistant inspector of boilers. Such assistant inspectors must be persons who have had at least four years practical experience in the operation of steam engines and boilers and must be persons of temperate habits and good character and qualified to perform the duties of their office. They shall be appointed by the governor, by and with the advice and consent of the senate, and be subject to removal at the will of the governor. The salary of each assistant inspector shall be $2100.00 per year. Each assistant inspector must execute an official bond in the sum of $2500.00.

There shall be a clerk to the State boiler inspector to be appointed by the governor who shall also perform the duties of clerk of the State quartz mine inspector and clerk of the State coal mine inspector. The salary of the clerk to the boiler inspector shall be $1500.00 per year and the clerk must execute an official bond in the sum of $2000.00.

Rules to be adopted.

SEC. 1642. The inspector of boilers must have his office at the seat of government, and must adopt rules as nearly uniform as possible for the inspection of steam boilers, and prescribe the nature and extent of the examination of applicants for licenses and adopt such rules for the issuing thereof as are required by the provisions of this article, and must adopt such rules as he may deem necessary to carry into effect the provisions of this article, and distribute copies of such rules among the engineers, superintendents of mines and mining companies of the State, and all persons having charge or control of steam machinery.

Inspection of boilers, etc.

SEC. 1643. The inspector of boilers must inspect all steam boilers and steam generators before the same are used, except in the case of new boilers, which must be inspected within ninety days after they are put in use, unless accompanied by a certificate that such boiler has been inspected by a regular State inspector, and all boilers must be inspected at least once in every year. And the inspector of boilers must subject all boilers to hydrostatic pressure, and satisfy himself by a thorough internal and external examination, that the boilers are well made and of good and suitable materials; that the openings for the passage of water and steam, respectively, and all pipes and tubes exposed to heat are of the proper dimensions and free from obstructions; that the flues are circular in form; that the fire line of the furnace is at least two inches below prescribed minimum water line of the boilers; that the arrangement for delivering the feed water is such that the boilers can not be injured thereby, and that such boilers and their steam connections may be safely employed without danger to life.

SEC. 1644. He must also satisfy himself that the safety valves *Safety valves.* are of suitable dimensions, sufficient in number and area, and properly arranged, and that the safety valve weights are properly adjusted, so as to allow no greater pressure in the boilers than the amount prescribed by the inspection certificate; that there are a sufficient number of gauge cocks properly inserted to indicate the amount of water, and suitable gauges that will correctly record the pressure of steam; and adequate and certain provisions for an ample supply to feed the boilers at all times, and that suitable means for blowing out are provided, so as to thoroughly remove the mud and sediment from all parts of the boilers when they are under pressure of steam. In subjecting boilers to the hydrostatic *Maximum pres-* test, the inspector must assume one hundred and twenty-five *sure.* pounds to the square inch as the maximum pressure allowable as a working pressure for new boilers of forty-two inches in diameter, made in the best manner, of plates one-fourth of an inch thick, and of good material; but the inspector must rate the working power of all high-pressure boilers according to their strength as compared with this standard, and in all cases the test applied must exceed the working pressure allowed, in the ratio of one hundred to seventy-five. Should the inspector be of the opinion that any boiler, by reason of its construction, or material, will not safely allow so high a working pressure, or will allow a greater working pressure than is herein provided, he may, for reasons to be stated specifically in his certificate, fix the pressure of such boiler at more or less than three-fourths of the test pressure, as the case may be.

SEC. 1645. No boiler or steam pipe, nor any of the connections *Use of bad ma-* thereto must be approved which is made in whole or in part of *terial, etc.* bad material, or is unsafe from any cause. Nothing herein shall be construed to prevent the use of any boiler or steam generator which may not be constructed of riveted iron or steel plates, when the inspector has satisfactory evidence that such boiler or steam generator is equal in strength to and as safe from explosion as boilers of the best quality, constructed of iron or steel plates. In any case where for good cause the inspector is unable to make any such inspection or examination of any steam boiler, it is the duty of the assistant inspector to proceed and act in accordance with the requirements of this article as fully as the inspector is empowered to do.

SEC. 1646. In addition to the annual inspection, it is the duty of *Additional in-* the inspector, or of the assistant inspector, to examine at proper *spections.* times, when in their opinion such examination is necessary, all such boilers as shall have become unsafe from any cause, and to notify the owner or the person using such boilers of any defect and what repairs are necessary to render them safe.

SEC. 1647. It is the duty of the owners or managers of steam *Access to boil-* boilers to allow the inspectors free access to the same, and the *ers.* engineer operating the same must assist the inspectors in their examinations and point out any defects they may know in the boilers or machinery in their charge. Any engineer not complying with this section shall have his license revoked or be suspended.

SEC. 1651. In making the inspection of boilers and machinery *Inspections* herein provided for, the inspectors may act jointly or separately; *may be joint or* but the inspector or assistant inspector, making such inspection, *separate.* must in all cases subscribe ond [and] make oath to the certificate of inspection, and report such action. Any inspector or assistant *False certificate.*

inspector who willfully and falsely certifies regarding any steam boilers or their attachments, or grants a license to any person to act as engineer, contrary to the provisions of this article, is punishable under the provisions of section 8446, of the Penal Code.

Application of law.

SEC. 1655. This article does not apply to locomotives in Montana, nor to boilers used for heating purposes in private residences, nor to any boiler having a capacity of only five horsepower or less; nor are locomotive engineers or persons operating any of the engines or boilers herein exempted from the operation of this article, required to procure licenses from the inspector or assistant inspectors. It shall be the duty of the owner or user of any traction engine or boiler on wheels, other than locomotives, to notify the inspector of the location of such boiler on or before the first day of June in each year. Any owner or user of such engine or boiler failing to so notify the inspector shall be punished by a fine of not less than twenty-five dollars nor more than one hundred dollars.

Selling boilers.

SEC. 1659. Any person who offers for sale within this State a boiler subject to the provisions of this article, which has been in use and is out of service, or who brings into the State and places in service any such boiler which has heretofore been in use in any other State, without first notifying the boiler inspector, and having such boiler inspected, and securing from the inspector a certificate of such inspection, shall be punished by a fine of not less than one hundred dollars nor more than five hundred dollars for each offense.

Penalty.

SEC. 8468. Every person who violates any of the provisions of * * * [sections 1639 to 1659, inclusive] of the Political Code, relating to boiler inspection, except as otherwise provided, is guilty of a misdemeanor.

NEBRASKA.

COMPILED STATUTES—1901.

Bureau of labor census and industrial statistics.

Bureau created.

SECTION 3310. There is hereby created a bureau of labor census and industrial statistics, with headquarters in the capitol building, for which stationery, postage, expressage, printing, and facilities for transacting business shall be furnished the same as for other executive departments.

Commissioner.

SEC. 3311. The governor of this State is hereby made commissioner of said bureau.

Deputy commissioner.

SEC. 3312. Said commissioner shall have the power to appoint a deputy at a salary of fifteen hundred dollars per annum, who, when acting for or instead of said commissioner, shall have and may exercise equal power and authority subject to the approval of the commissioner.

Duties.

SEC. 3313. The duties of said commissioner shall be to collect, collate, and publish statistics and facts relative to manufacturers, industrial classes, and material resources of the State, and especially to examine into the relations between labor and capital, the means of escape from fire and protection of life and health in factories and workshops, mines and other places of industries, the employment of illegal child labor, the exaction of unlawful hours of labor from any employee, the educational, sanitary, moral, and financial condition of laborers and artisans, the cost of food, fuel, clothing, and building material, the causes of strikes and lockouts, as well as kindred subjects and matters pertaining to the welfare of industrial interests and classes.

Powers.

SEC. 3314. The commissioner or his deputy shall have power to enter any factory or workshop in which labor is employed, for the purpose of gathering facts and statistics, or of examining the means for escape from fire, and the provisions for the health and safety of operatives in such factory or workshop. He may also post in such factory or workshop the laws now, or hereafter to be, made in respect to child labor, fire escapes, hours of labor, or others pertaining to the health or safety of employees; and if the owner, manager or agent shall remove or destroy the same he shall, upon conviction thereof, be fined in any sum not to exceed fifty dollars for each offense. And in case the officer of the bureau shall discover any violation of, or neglect to comply with, said laws, he shall notify the owner or occupant of said workshop or factory in writing of the offense or neglect, and if such offense or neglect is not corrected within thirty days after the service of notice aforesaid, he shall lodge formal complaint with the attorney of the county in which the offense is committed or the neglect occurs, whereupon said officer shall proceed against the offender according to law.

SEC. 3317. The said commissioner shall have power to prescribe *Reports from employers* blank forms and transmit them to employers, which shall be filled out clearly and completely under oath, by the person or persons to whom they are sent, with the facts, statistics, and statements asked for, and returned to him within such reasonable time as he may fix. In case any owner or occupant, or his agent, shall refuse *Refusing access.* to admit any officer of the said bureau to his workshop or factory, when open or in operation, he shall forfeit the sum of ten dollars for each and every offense, and if he shall, through his agent or otherwise, neglect, fail, or refuse to fill out the said blank forms, and verify and return them as required, he shall forfeit the sum of ten dollars for each and every day said blanks may be so delayed beyond the time fixed by the commissioners for their return. The forfeits named and provided in this act shall be sued for in the name of the State by the county attorney of the respective county where such offense is committed, upon the complaint of any officer of said bureau, or any citizen, and shall be paid into the school fund.

CHAPTER 68.—*Inspection of factories, etc.—Manufacture of food products.*

SECTION 1. Every building, room, basement or cellar occupied *Sanitation.* or used as a bakery, confectionery, cannery, packing house, slaughterhouse, dairy, creamery, cheese factory, restaurant, hotel, grocery, meat market or other place or apartment used for the preparation for sale, manufacture, packing, storage, sale, or distribution of any food, shall be properly lighted, drained, plumbed and ventilated and conducted with strict regard to the influence of such condition upon the health of the operatives, employees, clerks or other persons therein employed and the purity and wholesomeness of the food therein produced; and for the purpose of this act the term "food" as used herein shall include all articles used for food, drink, confectionery, or condiment whether simple, mixed or compound and all substances or ingredients used in the preparation thereof.

SEC. 2. The floors, side walls, ceilings, furniture, recepticles. *Floors, walls,* [receptacles], implements and machinery of every establishment *etc.* or place where food is manufactured, packed, stored, sold or distributed, and all cars, trucks and vehicles used in the transportation of food products, shall at no time be kept in an unclean, unhealthy and unsanitary condition, and for the purpose of this act, unclean, unhealthful and unsanitary conditions shall be deemed to exist if food in the process of manufacture, preparation, packing, storing, sale, distribution or transportation [transportation], is not securely protected from flies, dust, dirt and, as for [far] as may be necessary by all reasonable means from all other foreign or injurious contamination; and if the refuse, dirt and the waste products subject to decomposition and fermentation incident to the manufacture, preparation, packing, storing, selling, distributing and transporting of food, are not removed daily; and if all trucks, trays, boxes, baskets, buckets and other receptacles, chutes, platforms, racks, tables, shelves and all knives, saws, cleavers and other utensils and machinery used in moving, handling, cutting, chopping, mixing, canning and all other

processes are not thoroughly cleaned daily, and if the clothing of
operatives, employees, clerks or other persons therein employed is
unclean.

Construction, painting, etc.   SEC. 3. The side walls and ceilings of every bakery, confectionery, creamery, cheese factory, hotel and restaurant kitchen, shall
be brick, cement, plastered, wainscoated [wainscoted] or ceiled
with metal or lumber, and shall be oil painted or kept well limewashed, and all interior woodwork in every bakery, confectionery,
creamery, cheese factory, hotel and restaurant kitchen, shall be
kept well oiled or painted with oil paints or lime wash and be
kept clean and every building, room, basement, or cellar occupied
or used for the preparation, manufacture, packing, storage, sale
Floors.   or distribution of food, shall have an impermeable floor made of
cement or tile laid in cement, brick, wood or other suitable nonabsorbent material which can be flushed and washed clean with
water.

Screens.   SEC. 4. The doors, windows and other openings of every food
producing or distributing establishment during the fly season shall
be fitted with self-closing screen doors and wire window screens
of not coarser than 14-mesh wire gauze.

Toilet rooms, etc.   SEC. 5. Every building, room, basement or cellar occupied or
used for the preparation, manufacture, packing, canning, sale or
distribution of food, shall have a convenient toilet or toilet rooms
separate and apart from the room or rooms where the process
of production, manufacture, packing, canning, selling or distributing is conducted. The floors of such toilet rooms shall be of
cement, tile, wood, brick or other nonabsorbent material and shall
be kept in a thoroughly cleanly and sanitary condition. Such
toilet or toilets shall be furnished with separate ventilating flues
or pipes, discharging into soil pipes, on or outside of the building
in which they are situated. Lavoratories [lavatories] and wash
rooms shall be supplied with soap, water and towels, and shall
be maintained in a sanitary condition. Operatives, employees,
clerks, and all other persons who handle the material from which
food is prepared, or the finished product, before beginning work
or after visiting toilet or toilets, shall wash their hands and arms
thoroughly in clean water.

Cuspidors.   SEC. 6. Cuspidors for the use of operatives, employees, clerks
or other persons shall be provided whenever necessary, and each
cuspidor shall be thoroughly emptied and washed out daily with
disinfectant solution and five ounces of such a solution shall be
left in each cuspidor while it is in use. No operative, employee,
or other person shall expectorate on the floor or side walls of any
building, room, basement, or cellar where the production, manufacture, packing, storing, preparation, or sale of any food is
conducted.

Sleeping rooms.   SEC. 7. No person or persons shall be allowed to live or sleep
in any room of a bakeshop, kitchen, dining room, confectionery,
creamery, cheese factory, or place where food is prepared, served
or sold.

Diseased employees.   SEC. 8. No employer shall require, permit or suffer any person
to work, nor shall any person work in a building, room, basement,
cellar, or vehicle occupied or used for the production, preparation,
manufacture, packing, storage, sale, distribution and transportation of food who is affected with with [sic] any veneral [venereal]
disease, smallpox, diphteria, [diphtheria], scarlet fever, yellow
fever, tuberculosis, or consumption, bubonic plague, Asiatic cholera, leprosy, trachoma, typhoid fever, (epidemic), epidemic dysentery, measles, mumps, German measles, (Rothein,) whooping
cough, chicken pox or any other infectious or contagious disease.

Enforcement.   SEC. 9. The State food, drug and dairy inspector or deputy inspector or agent of the said inspector shall have full power at all
times to enter and inspect every building, room, basement, or cellar occupied or used for the production for sale, manufacture for
sale, storage, sale, distribution or transportation of food and all
utensils, fixtures, furniture and machinery used as aforesaid
[aforesaid], and if upon inspection any food producing or distrib-

uting establishment, conveyance, employer, operative, employee, clerk, driver or other person is found to be violating any of the provisions of this act, or if the production, preparation, manufacture, packing, storing, sale, distribution or transportation of food is being conducted in a manenr [manner] detrimental to the health of the employees and operatives and the character or quality of the food therein being produced, manufactured, packed, stored, sold, distributed, or conveyed, the officer or inspector making the examination or inspection shall furnish evidence of said violation to the county attorney who shall prosecute all persons violating any of the provisions of this act, or shall report such conditions and violations to the State food, drug and dairy inspector, who shall issue an order to the person or persons in authority at the aforesaid establishment to abate the condition or violation or make such improvements as may be necessary to abate them, within the period of five days or such reasonable time as may be required in which to abate them. Such order shall be in writing and the person receiving the order shall have the power of appeal from the order and instructions, and may within five days from the issuance of the order appear in person or by attorney before the State food, drug and dairy commissioner to give reason why such order or instruction should not be obeyed.

SEC. 10. Any person who violates any of the provisions of this act or who refuses to comply with any lawful orders or requirements of the State food, drug and dairy commissioner duly made in writing as provided in section 9 of this act, shall be guilty of a misdemeanor and on conviction shall be punished for the first offense by a fine of not less than $10 nor more than $50; for the second offense by a fine of not less than $50 nor more than $100 and for the third and subsequent offense by a fine of $200 and imprisonment in the county jail for not less than 30 days nor more than 90 days and each day after the expiration of the time limit for abating unsanitary conditions and completing improvements to abate such conditions as ordered by the State food commissioner shall constitute a distinct and separate offense. *Violations.*

ACTS OF 1911.

CHAPTER 56.—*Fire escapes on factories, etc.*

SECTION 1. After the passage and approval of this act, * * * every building * * * more than two stories high and containing above the ground floor * * * work rooms, * * * all or any of which rooms are designed for occupancy by fifteen or more persons, shall be provided with one or more fireproof stairways, chutes or toboggans constructed on the outside thereof, placed in such position and as many in number as may be designated by the commissioner of labor, or his deputy commissioner of labor. Such fireproof stairways, chutes or toboggans shall connect the cornice with the top of the first story of such building by a wrought iron or steel platform, properly surrounded with a wrought iron or steel railing; said platform to be constructed on a level with the floor of each story so connected, and of sufficient length to permit access to the same from not less than two windows of each story—said platform shall be so constructed as to be of convenient access from the interior of the building, commodious in size and form and of sufficient strength to be safe for the purpose of ascent and descent, * * * further, that all buildings more than two stories in height used for manufacturing purposes, mercantile establishments, * * * where twenty-five or more persons congregate at any one time, there shall be placed one automatic metallic fire escape or device for every twenty-five persons, for which working, * * * accommodations are provided above the second floor of said building, material, design and location of such escapes to be subject to the approval of the deputy commissioner of labor. * * * *What buildings to have fire escapes.* *Construction.*

Inspection.

SEC. 2. For the purpose of carrying out the provisions of this act the commissioner of labor is hereby authorized and required when it shall come to his notice that there is any building in this State where the provisions of this bill are being violated, to inspect such building. Such inspection may be by the commissioner of labor, deputy commissioner of labor or such other person as may be appointed by the deputy commissioner of labor for the purpose of making such inspection.

Such persons shall be under control and direction of the deputy commissioner of labor and are especially charged with the duties imposed, and shall receive such compensation as shall be fixed by the deputy commissioner of labor, not to exceed three dollars a day, together with all necessary expenses. All compensation for services and expenses provided for in this act shall be paid by the State treasurer out of the general appropriation for the bureau of labor census and industrial statistics, upon the warrant of the State auditor: *Provided*, That the deputy commissioner of labor in charge shall present to the governor, on or before the fifteenth day of December of each year, a report of such inspection with such recommendation as may be necessary.

Violations.

SEC. 3. Any owner, lessee, or occupant who shall fail to place or cause to be placed upon such building such fire escape or escapes as required by this act, shall be guilty of a misdemeanor and upon conviction thereof shall be fined in any sum not less than twenty-five nor more than one hundred dollars and shall stand committed to the county jail until such fine is paid.

Prosecutions.

SEC. 4. The county attorney of each county in this State is hereby authorized and required upon the complaint on oath of the deputy commissioner of labor or other person, to prosecute to termination before any court of competent jurisdiction, in the name of the people of the State of Nebraska a proper action or proceeding against any person or persons violating the provisions of this act.

CHAPTER 67.—*Factory regulations—Sanitation.*

Water-closets, etc

SECTION 1. Every factory, mill, or workshop, mercantile or mechanical establishment or other building where eight or more persons are employed, shall be provided within reasonable access, with a sufficient number of water-closets, earth closets, or privies for the reasonable use of the persons employed therein, and whenever male or female persons are employed as aforesaid together, water-closets, earth closets or privies separate and apart, shall be provided for the use of each sex, and plainly so designated, and no person shall be allowed to use such closet or privy assigned to the other sex. Such closets shall be properly enclosed and ventilated and at all times kept in a clean and good sanitary condition. When the number employed is more than twenty of either sex, there shall be provided an additional closet for such sex up to the number of forty, and above that number in the same ratio. The labor commissioner, his deputy or any member of the State board of inspectors, may require such changes in the placing of such closets as he may deem necessary and may require other changes which may serve the best interests of morals and sanitation.

Dressing rooms.

SEC. 2. In factories, mills or workshops, mercantile or mechanical establishments or other places where the labor performed by the operator is of such a character that it becomes desirable or necessary to change the clothing, wholly or in part, before leaving the building at the close of the day's work, separate dressing rooms shall be provided for females whenever so required by the labor commissioner, his deputy or any member of the State board of inspectors. It shall be the duty of every occupant, whether owner or lessee of any such premises used as specified by this act, to make all the changes and additions thereto. In case such changes are made upon the order of the commissioner of labor, or any factory inspector to the lessee of the premises, the lessee may at any time within thirty days after the completion thereof, bring an action against any person or corporation or partnership having interest in such premises, and may recover such proportion of expenses of making such changes and additions as the court adjudges should justly and equitably be borne by such defendant.

SEC. 3. If in any of the aforesaid places, any process is carried on, by which dust or fumes is caused, which may be inhaled by the persons employed therein, or if the air should become exhausted or impure, there shall be provided a fan or such other mechanical device, as will substantially carry away all such dust or fumes or other impurities. *Ventilation.*

SEC. 4. All of the aforesaid places shall be kept clean and free from effluvia arising from any drain, privy or nuisance, and shall be ventilated and kept in a sanitary condition. The labor commissioner, his deputy or any memer of the State board of inspectors may require such changes or additions to be made in any of the aforesaid places as will promote the best measures of sanitation. *Sanitation.*

SEC. 5. All persons, companies or corporations operating any factory or workshop where grinding machines or grinding wheels, emery wheels or emery belts of any description are used either solid emery, leather, leather covered, felt, canvas, linen, paper, cotton, or wheels or belts rolled or coated with emery or corundum or cotton wheels used as buffs, shall, when deemed necessary, by the labor commissioner, his deputy or any member of the State board of inspectors, provide such wheels or belts with blowers or similar apparatus, which shall be placed over, beside or under such wheels or belts in such manner as to protect the person or persons using the same from the particles of the dust produced and caused thereby, and to carry away the dust arising from or thrown off by such wheels or belts while in operation, directly to the outside of the building or to some receptacle placed so as to receive and confine such dust: *Provided*, That grinding machines upon which water is used at the point of grinding contact and other wheels used for tool grinding shall be exempt from the provisions of this act. *Grinding and polishing machines.*

SEC. 6. No emery wheels or grindstones in any factory, mill or workshop, shall be used when the same is known to the person using the same to be cracked or otherwise defective, nor operated at a greater speed than indicated or guaranteed by the manufacturer of such emery wheel or grindstone. *Cracked wheels.*

SEC. 7. It shall be the duty of any person, company or corporation operating any such factory or workshop to provide or construct such appliances, apparatus, machinery or other things necessary to carry out the purpose of this act, as set forth in the preceding section, as follows: Each and every such wheel shall be fitted with a sheet or cast iron hood or hopper, of such form and so applied to such wheel or wheels that the dust or refuse therefrom will fall from such wheels, or will be thrown into such hood or hopper by centrifugal force, and be carried off by the current of air into a suction pipe attached to same hood or hopper. *Apparatus to be provided.*

SEC. 8. Each and every such wheel six inches or less in diameter shall be provided with a three-inch suction pipe; wheels six inches to twenty-four inches in diameter, with four inch suction pipe; wheels from twenty-four inches to thirty-six inches in diameter, with five inch suction pipe; and all wheels larger in diameter than those stated above shall be provided each with a suction pipe not less than six inches in diameter. The suction pipe from each wheel, so specified, must be full size as [to] the main trunk suction pipe, and the main suction pipe to which smaller pipes are attached shall, in its diameter and capacity, be equal to the combined area of such smaller pipes attached to the same, and the discharge pipe from the exhaust fan connected with the suction pipe or pipes shall be as large, or larger than the suction pipe. *Suction pipes.*

Guards for dangerous machinery. SEC. 9. It shall be the duty of any person, company or corporation operating any factory, mill, workshop, mercantile or mechanical establishment to provide or construct such guards and protection as will protect all employees against injury from all belting, shafting, gearing, elevators, drums, saws, cogs, or any vessel filled with molten metal or hot liquid shall be properly protected by placing guards, boxing or screens to prevent all such and they shall also furnish and supply therein belt shifters or other safe mechanical contrivance, for the purpose of throwing on or off belts or pulleys.

Accidents to be reported. SEC. 10. It shall be the duty of the owners or superintendents of all factories, workshops, mills, or mechanical establishments, to report in writing to the labor commissioner or his deputy, all fatal accidents within forty-eight hours after their occurrence; and all accidents which prevent the injured person or persons from returning to work within two weeks after the injury shall within one week after the expiration of such two weeks, be reported in writing by the person in charge of such establishment or place to the said labor commissioner or his deputy, stating as fully as possible the cause of such accidents.

Existing appliances. SEC. 11. The provisions of section 8, shall not apply to existing mills, factories or workshops which, at the time of the passage of this act, have an appliance or appliances designed and used for the purpose of removing such dust from the polishing room, and which said appliance or appliances substantially effect such design.

Damages. SEC. 12. For an injury to a person occasioned by any violation of this act, by the failure to comply with any of its provisions, a right of action shall accrue to the party injured, for any direct damages sustained thereby; and in case of loss of life by reason of such violation or failure, as aforesaid, a right of action shall accrue to the heirs of the person so killed. The fact that any employee, servant or other person shall continue to work during the time such owner has failed to comply with the provisions of **Risks not assumed.** this act shall not be considered as an assumption of the risk of such employment by such employee, servant or other person and shall not in any case bar recovery of damages for the failure of such owner, to comply with the provisions of this act. In all actions brought to recover damages for injuries caused by failure to comply with the terms and provisions of this act the owner, **Liability for noncompliance.** shall in all cases be liable in damages for all injuries caused through a failure to comply with this act. The owner shall in all cases be held liable for the failure or neglect of any superintendent, foreman, or other agent, employed by them, or either of them, to comply with the provisions of this act.

Enforcement SEC. 13. It shall be the duty of the deputy labor commissioner and every factory inspector of this State, or his deputies to enter any factory or workshop in this State during working hours, and upon ascertaining the facts that the proprietors or managers of such factory or workshops have failed to comply with the provisions of this act, to make complaint of the same in writing before a justice of the peace or police magistrate having jurisdiction, who shall thereupon issue his warrant, direct to the owner, manager or director, in such factory or workshop, who shall be thereupon proceeded against for the violation of this act as hereinafter mentioned, and it is made the duty of the prosecuting attorney to prosecute all cases under this act.

Violations. SEC. 14. Any owner, lessee, or any person or corporation having charge of any of the aforesaid buildings or places or any such person or persons or company, or managers, superintendents or directors of any such company or corporation, who shall have the charge or management of such factory or workshop or places aforesaid, who shall fail to comply with the provisions of this act, shall be deemed guilty of a misdemeanor, and upon conviction thereof before any court of competent jurisdiction shall be punished by a fine of not less than ten dollars and not exceeding one hundred dollars.

NEVADA.

ACTS OF 1903.

CHAPTER 13.—*Inspection of factories—Safety appliances.*

SECTION 1. It shall be unlawful for any person, company or cor- *Set screws to*
poration, after the first day of July, nineteen hundred and three, *be countersunk.*
to construct or place any shaft or shafting with collars, sleeves or
pulleys over two feet in diameter attached or secured to such
shaft by set screws projecting above the hub of such collars,
sleeves or pulleys. In all such cases where set screws are used,
the heads thereof shall be countersunk below the surface of the
hub of the collar, sleeve or pulley in which they are placed.

SEC. 2. Any person or corporation who shall, after the first day *Penalty.*
of July, 1903, fail or refuse to comply with the requirements of
this act, when constructing or changing any machinery, shall be
guilty of a misdemeanor, and upon conviction thereof shall be
fined not less than one hundred nor more than five hundred
dollars.

SEC. 3. Nothing contained in this act, shall be so construed as *Liability.*
to prevent recovery in a suit for damages, for injuries sustained
by the party so injured or his heirs or administrators.

NEW HAMPSHIRE.

ACTS OF 1907.

CHAPTER 137.—*Fire escapes.*

SECTION 1 (as amended by chapter 43, Acts of 1911). No build- *Construction.*
ing three or more stories in height, any part of which is used or
occupied above the second story as a * * * factory shall be
let, leased or occupied for such purposes unless provided with a
steel or wrought-iron balcony and stairway fire-escape built and
attached to the outer wall in such manner and place as to render
egress from said building easy and safe. If said building be of a
length greater than one hundred and fifty feet it shall be provided
with one additional such fire escape for every additional one
hundred and fifty feet or fractional part thereof: *Provided,* That
any other metal fire escape may be so attached if approved by the
building inspector, chief of the fire department or board of selectmen. The provisions of this section shall not apply to any such
building as is at the time of the passage of this amendment sufficiently equipped with a steel or wrought-iron balcony and ladder
fire escape until such time as said fire escape becomes insecure or
is removed; nor shall the provisions of this section apply to any
such factory building as shall be adequately equipped with an
approved sprinkler system and stairways inclosed with walls of
fireproof material, or other means of exit duly approved in writing by said officers.

SEC. 2 (as amended by chapter 164, Acts of 1909). Such fire *Construction.*
escapes shall reach within eight feet of the ground and the location of the exits thereto shall be designated by red lights during *Exits.*
such hours of the night as the building is occupied for the purposes designated in section 1 of this act.

SEC. 3 (as amended by chapter 164, Acts of 1909). If any person *Violations.*
shall violate any of the provisions of this act, he shall be fined
not exceeding five hundred dollars or imprisoned not exceeding
six months, or both, and it shall be the duty of said officers to
enforce the provisions of this act.

ACTS OF 1911.

CHAPTER 30.—*Factory regulations—Provisions for accidents.*

SECTION 1. Every person, firm or corporation operating a fac- *Medical, etc.,*
tory or shop in which power machinery is used for any manufac- *supplies.*

turing purpose and in which three or more persons are employed, or for any purpose except for elevators, or for heating or hoisting apparatus, shall at all times keep and maintain, free of expense to the employees, such a medical and surgical chest as shall be required by the local board of health of any city or town where such machinery is used, containing plasters, bandages, absorbent cotton, gauze, and all other necessary medicines, instruments and other appliances for the treatment of persons injured or taken ill upon the premises.

Violations.   SEC. 2. Any person, firm or corporation violating this act shall be subject to a fine of not less than five dollars nor more than five hundred dollars for every week during which such violation contiuues.

NEW JERSEY.

COMPILED STATUTES—1910.

Regulation of bakeries, etc.

(Page 2577.)

Rooms to be lighted, ventilated, etc.   SECTION 51. Every building, room, basement or cellar occupied or used as a bakery, confectionery, cannery, packing house, slaughterhouse, dairy, creamery, cheese factory, restaurant, hotel, grocery, meat market, or other place or apartment used for the production, manufacture, preparation, packing, storage, or distribution of food intended for sale or distribution, shall be properly lighted, drained, plumbed and ventilated, and the operations car-

Basements, etc. ried on in such building, room, basement or cellar shall be conducted in such a manner that the purity and wholesomeness of the food therein produced, manufactured, prepared, packed, stored, sold or distributed shall not be impaired.

Cleanliness and sanitation.   SEC. 52. The floors, side walls, ceilings, furniture, receptacles, implements and machinery of every establishment, or place where food intended for distribution or sale is produced, manufactured, prepared, packed, stored, sold or distributed, and all cars, trucks and vehicles used in the transportation of such food products shall at no time be kept in an unclean or unsanitary condition. * * * The clothing worn by all operatives, employees, clerks and and [sic] other persons while engaged in work in any of the places where food intended for sale or distribution is produced, manufactured, prepared, packed, stored, sold, distributed or transported shall be in a clean condition at all times. No person shall transport any such food in such a manner that the purity or wholesomeness thereof shall be in any wise impaired.

Walls.   SEC. 53. The side walls of every bakery, confectionery, creamery, cheese factory, hotel or restaurant kitchen shall be well plastered, wainscoted or ceiled with metal or lumber, and shall be oil painted, or kept well limewashed, and all interior woodwork in every bakery, confectionery, creamery, cheese factory, hotel or restaurant kitchen shall be kept well oiled or painted with oil paint, and shall be kept washed clean with soap and water; and every building, room, basement or cellar occupied or used for the preparation, manufacture, packing, storage, sale or distribution of food intended for distribution or sale in which food is exposed

Floors.   shall have a tight floor made of cement, or of tile laid in cement, brick, wood, or other suitable material which can be flushed or washed clean with water.

Rules for workmen.   SEC. 54. All operatives, employees, clerks, or other persons who handle the material from which food intended for distribution or sale is prepared, or the finished product, before beginning work and after visiting the toilet, shall wash their hands and arms thoroughly with clean water and soap, and every owner or manager of any place in which food is produced, manufactured, prepared, packed, stored, distributed or sold shall provide adequate facilities for such washing, and it shall be the duty of every such

owner or manager to take all reasonable means to compel all operatives, employees, clerks, or other persons handling the material from which such food is prepared, or the finished product, to perform such washing as aforesaid. All toilets, lavatories and wash rooms shall be separate and apart from the room or rooms where any processes incident to the production, manufacture, preparation, packing, storage, sale or distribution of such, food are carried on, and such toilets, lavatories and wash rooms shall, at all times, be kept in a clean and sanitary condition. *Toilets, etc.*

SEC. 55. Cuspidors for the use of operatives, employees, clerks, or other persons, shall be provided wherever necessary, and each cuspidor shall be emptied and thoroughly washed out daily with a disinfectant solution, and at least five ounces of such disinfectant solution shall be left in each cuspidor while the same is in use. No operative, employee, clerk, or other persons shall expectorate anywhere in any building, room, basement or cellar where the production, manufacture, preparation, packing, storage, sale or distribution of any food intended for sale or distribution is conducted, except in cuspidors provided for that purpose. *Cuspidors.*

SEC. 56. No person or persons shall be allowed to live or sleep in any room where food intended for sale or distribution is produced, manufactured, packed, distributed or sold. *Sleeping in workrooms.*

SEC. 57. No employer shall require, permit or allow any person to work, nor shall any person work in any building, room, basement, cellar or vehicle, occupied or used for the production, preparation, manufacture, packing, storage, sale, distribution or transportation of food intended for sale or distribution who is affected with any communicable disease. *Diseased employees.*

SEC. 59. Any person who violates any of the provisions of this act, or refuses, neglects or fails to comply with any lawful order or requirement of the state board of health or of any local boards of health, duly made in writing, * * *   shall be liable to a penalty not exceeding fifty dollars for the first offense, one hundred dollars for the second offense, and two hundred dollars for the third and each subsequent offense; such penalties to be recovered by an action of debt in the name of the State board of health or local board of health, as the case may be, in the manner prescribed for the recovery of penalties in the act to which this is a supplement. *Violations.*

SEC. 60. When any person shall violate any of the provisions of this act, or shall refuse to comply with any orders duly made in writing, * * * each day upon which such violation occurs shall be deemed to constitute a distinct and separate violation, and each day elapsing after the expiration of the time limit fixed for the compliance with the said order in writing shall be deemed to constitute a distinct and separate offense. *Each day a violation.*

SEC. 61. The State board of health shall make uniform rules and regulations for the carrying out of the provisions of this act, which said rules and regulations shall apply to all boards and persons entrusted with the enforcement of the provisions of this act. *Enforcement.*

SEC. 62. An abstract of this law shall be prepared and furnished upon request by the board of health to every corporation, firm or person in this State who is affected thereby, and every person engaged in the production, manufacture, preparation, packing, storing, distribution, or transportation of food intended for sale or distribution to whom a copy of such abstract is sent or delivered shall post such abstract of this law, and keep it posted, in plain view in such place that it can be easily read by the employees or operatives in coming in or going from the place where the aforesaid business of such person is conducted. *Abstract of law to be posted.*

Regulation and inspection of factories.

(Page 3026.)

SECTION 26. The openings of all hoistways, hatchways, elevators and wellholes upon every floor of any place coming under the pro- *Hoistways, etc., to be guarded.*

visions of this act, shall be protected by good and sufficient trapdoors or self-closing hatches and safety catches, or strong guardrails at least three feet high, and shall be kept closed and protected at all times except when in actual use by the occupant of the building having the use and control of the same.

Belt shifters, guards, etc.

SEC. 28. The owner or person in charge of any of the places coming under the provisions of this act, where machinery is used, shall provide, in the discretion of the commissioner, belt shifters or other mechanical contrivances for the purpose of throwing on or off belts or pulleys; whenever practicable, all machinery shall be provided with loose pulleys, all vats, pans, saws, planers, cogs, gearing, belting, shafting, set screws, drums and machinery of every description shall be properly guarded; no person shall remove or make ineffective any safeguard around or attached to such machinery, vats or pans while the same are in use, unless for the purpose of immediately making repairs thereto, and all such safeguards so removed shall be promptly replaced; if the machinery, or any part thereof, or any vat, pan or vessel containing molten metal or hot liquid is in a dangerous condition or is not properly guarded, the use thereof may be prohibited by the commissioner, and a notice to that effect shall be attached thereto; such notice shall not be removed until the machinery is made safe and the required safeguards are provided; and in the meantime such unsafe or dangerous machinery, vats, pans, or vessels containing molten metal or hot liquid shall not be used; when, in the opinion of the commissioner, it is necessary, the halls leading to workrooms shall be provided with proper lighting facilities.

Blowers for emery wheels, etc.

SEC. 29. All corporations, firms or persons conducting a manufacturing business in any of the places coming under the provisions of this act, where emery wheels or emery belts of any description are used, either solid emery, leather, leather covered, felt, canvas, linen, paper, cotton, or wheels, or belts rolled or coated with emery or corundum, or cotton wheels used as buffs, shall provide the same with blowers or similar apparatus, which shall be placed over, beside or under wheels or belts in such a manner as to protect the person or persons using the same from the particles of the dust produced and caused thereby, and to carry away the dust arising from or thrown off by such wheels or belts while in operation, directly to the outside of· the building, or to some receptacle placed so as to receive and confine such dust: *Provided,* That grinding machines upon which water is used at the point of the grinding contact and small emery wheels that are used temporarily for tool grinding in small shops employing not more than three persons at such work, shall be exempt from the provisions of this section if so ordered by the commissioner.   ·

Construction.

SEC. 30. It shall be the duty of any person, firm or corporation conducting such manufacturing business, to provide or construct such appliances, apparatus, machinery or other things necessary to carry out the purpose of this act, as set forth above, as follows: Each and every such wheel shall be fitted with a sheet or cast-iron hood or hopper of such form and so applied to such wheel or wheels that the dust or refuse therefrom will fall from such wheels or will be thrown into such hood or hopper by centrifugal force and be carried off by a current of air into a suction pipe attached to some hood or hopper.

Same subject.

SEC. 31. Each and every such wheel six inches or less in diameter shall be provided with a round suction pipe three inches in diameter; wheels six inches to twenty-four inches in diameter, with round suction pipe five inches in diameter; and all wheels larger in diameter than those stated above shall be provided each with a round suction pipe not less than six inches in diameter; the suction pipe from each wheel so specified must be full size to the main trunk suction pipe, and the main suction pipe to which smaller pipes are attached shall in its diameter and capacity be equal to the combined area of such smaller pipes attached to the same. and the discharge pipe from the exhaust fan connected with such suction pipe or pipes shall be as large or larger than the suction pipe.

SEC. 32. It shall be the duty of any person, firm or corporation. operating any such place to provide the necessary fans or blowers to be connected with such pipe or pipes, as set forth in this act, which shall be run at the rate of speed such as will produce a pressure of air in such suction or discharge pipes sufficient to raise a column of water not less than five inches in a U-shaped tube; all branch pipes must enter the main trunk pipe at an angle of forty-five degrees or less; the main suction or trunk pipe shall be below the emery or buffing wheels and as close to the same as possible, and shall be either upon or beneath the floor on which the machines are placed to which such wheels are attached; all bends, turns or elbows in such pipes must be made with easy, smooth surfaces, having a radius in the throat of not less than two diameters of the pipe on which they are connected. *Air pressure, etc.*

SEC. 33. It shall be the duty of the commissioner to make orders in writing for the carrying into effect the provisions of sections fourteen, fifteen, sixteen and seventeen. *Enforcement.*

SEC. 34. Not less than two hundred and fifty cubic feet of air space shall be provided for each employee or operative at work in a room in a place within the meaning this act between the hours of six o'clock in the morning and six o'clock in the evening. and not less than four hundred cubic feet of air space for each employee so employed between the hours of six o'clock in the evening and six o'clock in the morning: *Provided,* In all cases where the amount of air space provided does not exceed the amount above fixed, that such room is lighted by electricity during all hours that artificial lights are necessary and persons are employed therein, unless a written permit shall be obtained from the commissioner. *Air space.*

SEC. 35. The owner, agent or lessee of a place coming under the provisions of this act, or employer, shall provide in each workroom thereof proper and sufficient means of ventilation; in case of failure the commissioner shall order such ventilation to be provided; such owner, agent, lessee or employer shall provide such ventilation within twenty days after the service upon him of such order in writing, and in case of failure shall be liable to a fine of ten dollars for each day after the expiration of the time given by such order to make the change. *Ventilation.*

SEC. 36. No minor under sixteen years of age shall be required. allowed or permitted to clean any part of the gearing or machinery in any place coming under the provisions of this act, while the same is in motion, or to work between the fixed or traversing parts of any machinery while it is in motion by the action of steam, water or other mechanical power. *Minors cleaning machinery.*

SEC. 37. Every corporation, firm or person having or keeping in his place or its place or manufactory coming under the provisions of this act, any explosive or inflammable compound, shall keep or store such explosive or inflammable compound in such factory, mill, workshop or place in such way as not to obstruct or render hazardous the egress of employees or operatives in case of fire. *Explosives.*

SEC. 38. Every factory, workshop or mill shall contain sufficient, suitable, convenient and separate water-closets for each sex, which shall be properly screened, ventilated and kept clean; and also a suitable and convenient washroom; the water-closets used by women shall have separate approaches; if women or girls are employed, a dressing room shall be provided for them when ordered by the commissioner. *Water-closets.*

SEC. 39. Factories and workshops in which women and children are employed, and where dusty work is carried on, shall be limewashed or painted at least once in every twelve months. *Lime washing.*

SEC. 40. An abstract of this law shall be prepared and furnished upon request by the commissioner to every corporation, firm or person in this State who is affected thereby, and every manufacturer to whom a copy of such abstract is sent or delivered shall *Law to be posted.*

post such abstract of this law and keep it posted in plain view in such place that it can be easily read by the employees or operatives in coming in or going out from said factory, workshop or mill.

Hindering commissioner.   SEC. 41. No person shall interfere with, delay, obstruct or hinder by force or otherwise, the commissioner, the assistant commissioner or inspectors, while in the performance of their duties, or refuse to answer in writing or otherwise, questions asked by such officers relating to the matters coming under the provisions of this act; no person shall impersonate an officer of the department or forge his certificate of authority.

Forfeitures to be reciprocal.   SEC. 42. Any person, firm or corporation engaged in manufacturing which requires from persons in his or its employ, under penalty of forfeiture of a part of the wages earned by them, a notice of intention to leave such employ, shall be liable to the payment of a like forfeiture if he or it discharges without similar notice a person in such employ, unless in case of a general suspension of labor in his or its factory, mill or place where the manufacture of goods of any kind is carried on.

Accidents   SEC. 43. All accidents that prevent the injured person or persons from returning to work within two weeks, or which result in death, shall be reported in writing to the department, at Trenton, New Jersey, within twenty-four hours after the expiration of four weeks or after the death of such person injured, as the same may be; such notice may be sent by mail, postage prepaid.

Name of firm to be furnished.   SEC. 44. Every corporation, firm or person shall within one month after he, they or it shall begin to occupy a factory, workshop, mill or place where the manufacture of goods of any kind is carried on, notify in writing the department, at Trenton, New Jersey, of such occupancy, giving the legal title of such corporation and name of agent upon whom service of a summons can be made, and in case of a firm, the individual names of the members of the firm or the legal title of the concern so occupying such factory or workshop.

Powers of commissioner.   SEC. 45. For the purpose of carrying into effect the provisions of sections * * * [26 to 32, 34, 36 to 39 and 41 to 43] the commissioner shall be and he is hereby authorized to make such orders in writing for the protection and safety of employees and operatives and the enforcement of this act in places coming under the provisions of this act, as in his judgment shall seem necessary to carry into effect the provisions of such sections; such order shall be in writing, signed by the commissioner, and shall specify what shall be done and within what time; any corporation, firm or person violating any of the provisions of [the above-mentioned] sections * * * shall, for each offense, be liable to a penalty of fifty dollars.

Manufacture in tenements.   SEC. 46. No room or rooms, apartment or apartments, in any tenement or dwelling house, shall be used for the manufacture of coats, vests, trousers, knee pants, overalls, cloaks, furs, fur trimmings, fur garments, shirts, purses, feathers, artificial flowers or cigars, except by the immediate members of the family living therein; no person, firm or corporation shall hire or employ any person to work in any room or rooms, apartment of apartments, in any tenement or dwelling house, at making, in whole or in part, any coats, vests, trousers, knee pants, overalls, cloaks, furs, artificial flowers or cigars, unless such person, firm or corporation first shall have obtained a written permit from the commissioner; which permit may be revoked by the commissioner at any time that the health of the community or of those employed as aforesaid may, in his judgment, require it, and that such permit shall not be granted until due and satisfactory inspection of the premises affected shall have been made by the said commissioner, assistant, or an inspector; such permit shall be framed and posted in a conspicuous place in the main room of the place to which it relates, shall be duly numbered and shall state the number of persons allowed to be employed therein.

Violations.   SEC. 47. Any person, firm or corporation being the owner, lessee or occupant of the place to which the preceding section relates, shall, for the violation of any of the provisions therein, be liable to a penalty of one hundred dollars for each offense.

SEC. 48. This act shall not apply to a private house or private room used for manufacturing purposes by the family dwelling therein. *Exemptions.*

SEC. 60. For the purpose of carrying into effect and enforcing the provisions of this act, there shall be and hereby is established a department to be known as the department of labor; the department shall have its main office in Trenton, and shall consist of a commissioner, an assistant commissioner and eleven inspectors; the governor shall, immediately after the passage of this act, with the advice and consent of the senate, appoint some suitable person who shall be a resident and citizen of this State, as head of the said department, at a salary of thirty-five hundred dollars per year, to be paid monthly, whose term of office shall be three years and until his successor is appointed, and whose title shall be commissioner of labor; the commissioner shall, with the approval of the governor, appoint the assistant commissioner, who shall be an experienced machinist; he shall receive a salary of two thousand dollars per year, to be paid monthly; the governor shall appoint eleven suitable persons as inspectors, two of whom shall be women, whose salary shall be one thousand five hundred dollars per year each, to be paid monthly; the terms of office of the assistant and the inspectors shall be three years unless sooner removed by the commissioner; the assistant and the inspectors shall each be furnished with certificates of authority by the secretary of state, and they shall produce the same if so required by any manufacturer; the commissioner shall have the power, out of the appropriation made for the purpose of carrying on the work of the department, to purchase badges for the assistant, the inspectors and himself; the commissioner may divide the State into districts, assign inspectors to such districts, and may, in his discretion, transfer them from one district to another; the commissioner, assistant and inspectors may administer oaths and take affidavits in matters relating to the enforcement of this act; the commissioner shall have the right to employ such department clerks for carrying on the work of the department as may, in his judgment, be necessary; such clerks shall receive such salaries as the commissioner, with the approval of the governor, shall fix, to be paid by the treasurer on warrant of the comptroller in equal monthly installments; when the work of the department shall necessitate the employment of additional inspectors, the commissioner shall have the power to employ such inspectors at such compensation and for such length of time as he may deem necessary, and such extra inspectors shall have the same rights, powers and privileges as the inspectors appointed by the governor; all salaries and expenses incurred by the commissioner, assistant and all inspectors, in the discharge of their duties, and all salaries and expenses necessary to carry out the provisions of this act, shall be paid from the funds of the State, out of the moneys appropriated for that purpose, by the treasurer, upon warrant of the comptroller, upon presentation of proper vouchers for the same, approved by the commissioner; it shall be the duty of the commissioner to enforce the provisions of this act and to exercise supervision and control over the assistant and the inspectors, and to cause inspections to be made of the factories, mills, workshops. and places where the manufacture of goods of any kind is carried on, by the assistant and the inspectors, as often as practicable, and to make a report of the work of the department to the governor of the State on or before the thirty-first day of October in each year; to prosecute violations of the provisions of this act in any district court, recorders' courts of cities and before any justice of the peace having due jurisdiction, or in any other court of competent jurisdiction in this State; the commissioner, the assistant commissioner and the inspectors shall have the right at all reasonable hours to enter and inspect factories, mills, workshops and places, where the manufacture of goods of any kind is carried on, and

Department of labor.

Inspectors.

Clerks.

Duties.

each inspector shall make a report in writing of such inspections to the commissioner at least once in each week; inspectors shall make out a list of minors discharged, with the name of child in full, residence, street and number, name of place from which such minor was discharged and date of discharge; he shall send or deliver within twenty-four hours, such list to the principal of the public school in the district where the minor resides, or to the truant officer having such school district in charge; every deputy inspector shall devote at least eight hours of every working day except public holidays, and four hours on Saturdays, to the discharge of his or her duties as such deputy inspector, unless prevented by illness or other disability, and no deputy inspector shall engage in any business, occupation or employment during his or her term of office that will in any way interfere with or prevent the full and faithful performance of such duties.

Additional inspectors. SEC. 61. In addition to the inspectors provided by the act to which this is a supplement, and the amendments and supplements thereto, the governor shall, immediately after the passage of this act, appoint two suitable persons as inspectors, one of whom shall be a woman, whose salary, powers and duties and term of office, shall be the same as the inspectors already provided for.

Bakeries, etc, are factories. SEC. 62. For the purposes of this act and the act to which it is a supplement [inspection of factories act] biscuits, pies, bread, crackers, cakes and confectionery shall be interpreted to be goods, and places wherein the same are made or manufactured shall be held and considered as places where goods are manufactured; the word bakery in this act shall include all buildings, rooms or places where biscuits, pies, bread, crackers, cakes and confectionery are made or manufactured, and the provisions of this act, or any supplement thereof or amendment thereto, shall be enforced by the department of labor, and it shall be the duty of the officers of that department to enforce the provisions of this act; all suits brought for violations of any of the provisions of this act shall be brought in the manner and under the same restrictions as is provided for bringing suits under the act to which this is a supplement.

Hours of labor. SEC. 63. No employee shall be required, permitted or suffered to work in any bakery more than sixty hours in any one week, or more than ten hours in any one day, unless for the purpose of making a shorter work day on the last day of the week, nor more hours in any one week than will make an average of ten hours per day for the whole number of days in which such employee shall so work during such week, but it shall be lawful, in cases of emergency, for an employer to permit any employee to work an additional time, not exceeding two hours per day, such extra work to be remunerated at the rate of weekly wages paid to such employee for his week of sixty hours; no employee in any bakery **Witnesses** shall be discharged by his employer for having made any truthful statement as a witness in a court, or to the commissioner, assistant commissioner of labor, or any inspector in pursuance of this act, or any act amendatory hereof or supplementary hereto.

Sanitation SEC. 64 (as amended by chapter 327, Acts of 1911). All buildings or rooms where goods are manufactured or made shall be drained and plumbed in a manner that will conduce to the proper and healthful sanitary conditions thereof, and shall have air shafts, windows or ventilating pipes sufficient to insure ventilation, and all the doors, windows and other openings shall be thoroughly screened so as to prevent the entrance of flies or other insects between the first day of April and the thirty-first day of October; expectorating is prohibited within the buildings or rooms except into a proper receptacle; no person or corporation shall hereafter engage or continue in the business of making or manufacturing biscuit, pies, bread, crackers, cakes or confectionery for **License.** the purpose of distribution or sale, unless he shall first obtain from the commissioner of labor of this State a license so to do. The applicant for any such license shall state in his application the location of the place or places at which he intends to engage in such business and such license shall not be issued unless the said commissioner is satified that such place or places conform to all the requirements of this act. Such license shall specify the place or places at which such business is authorized to be carried on, and shall not authorize the engaging in such business at any other place or places. When it shall be made to appear to the said commissioner that any place at which such business is carried on under a license as aforesaid is not kept in accordance with or does not conform to the requirements of this act, said commissioner may revoke the license of the person engaging in such business at such place. No person whose license to engage in such business has been revoked, shall engage in such business in this State until he has procured a new license in accordance with the terms of this act. Any applicant for any such license shall pay to the commissioner of labor a license fee of one dollar, which fee shall be returned to such applicant, in case the license is not granted; no cellar, basement or place which is below the street level shall hereafter be used and occupied as a place in which to manufacture biscuits, pies, bread, crackers, cakes or confectionery, except where the same was used for the purpose at the time of the passage of the act to which this act is an amendment: *Provided*, That this act shall not prevent the use for the manufacture of confectionery of any cellar, basement or place which shall, after due inspection and examination by inspectors of the department of labor, be certified to by the commissioner of labor as sanitary in all respects and proper to be occupied for such purposes, which certificate may be revoked at any time; * * *. Use of basements, etc.

SEC. 65. Every room used for a bakery shall be at least eight feet in height and shall have, if required by the said commissioner or assistant commissioner, an impermeable floor, constructed of wood properly saturated with linseed oil; the side walls of such rooms shall be plastered or wainscoted, except where brick walls are shown, and if required by the said commissioner or assistant commissioner, shall be whitewashed at least once in three months; the furniture and utensils in such rooms shall be so arranged that the furniture and floor may at all times be kept in a proper and healthful, sanitary and clean condition; the commissioner shall have the power to order that any bakery shall be cleaned in such manner as he shall direct; no domestic animal, except cats, shall be allowed to remain in a room used as a bakery. Same subject.

SEC. 66. Biscuits, pies, bread, crackers, cake and confectionery, after the same are made or manufactured, shall be kept in dry and airy rooms; the floors, shelves, pans, trays and every kind of appliances used for storing the same shall be so arranged that they can be easily and thoroughly cleaned. Storage rooms.

SEC. 67. Whoever shall conduct a place covered by the provisions of this act shall provide a proper wash room and water-closet or closet separate and apart from the room or rooms in which the manufacture of the goods is carried on; no water-closet, earth closet or privy shall be within or communicate directly with the room in which goods covered by the provisions of this act are made or manufactured. Wash rooms, etc.

SEC. 68. Sleeping places for persons employed in a bakery shall be kept separate from the room or rooms used for the bakery, and the commissioner or assistant commissioner or an inspector may inspect such sleeping places, if they are on the same premises as the bakery, and order them cleaned or changed, in compliance with sanitary principles. Sleeping places.

SEC. 69. The commissioner of labor shall be required to enforce compliance with all the provisions of this act, and for that purpose it shall be his duty to have all bakeries visited and inspected at least once in six months; and whenever a complaint in writing, signed by any employee in any such bakery or by any officer or representative of any labor union in the county wherein the same is located, shall be received by the said commissioner, stating that any provision of this act is being violated in any bakery, it shall be the duty of the said commissioner forthwith to have the said Enforcement.

bakery concerning which complaint is made visited and inspected. The visit or inspection shall be made in the presence of those then working or employed in said bakery, and during the usual hours of employment therein. All bakeries shall be kept at all times in a clean and sanitary condition. If on inspection the commissioner of labor find any bakery to be so unclean, ill drained or ill venti-

Unclean, etc., lated as to be unsanitary, he may, after not less than forty-
bakeries. eight hours' notice in writing, to be served by affixing the notice on the inside of the main entrance door of said bakery,· order the person found in charge thereof immediately to cease operating it until it be properly cleaned, drained or ventilated. If such bakery be thereupon continued in operation, or be thereafter operated before it be properly cleaned, drained or ventilated, the commissioner of labor may, after first making and filing in the public records of his office a written order stating the reasons therefor, at once and without further notice fasten up and seal the oven or other cooking apparatus of said bakery, and affix to all materials, receptacles, tools and instruments found therein, labels or conspicuous signs bearing the word "unclean." No one but the commissioner of labor shall remove any such seal, label or sign, and he may refuse to remove it until such bakery be properly cleaned, drained or ventilated.

Night work by   SEC. 70. No person under the age of eighteen years shall be em-
children. ployed, allowed, permitted or required to work in any bakery between the hours of seven o'clock in the afternoon and seven o'clock in the forenoon following.

Notices.   SEC. 71. All notices given under or pursuant to this act, or any act supplementary thereof or mandatory [amendatory] thereto, shall be in writing, signed by the commissioner of labor, and may be served upon the owner or proprietor of the place wherein such violation occurred either by delivering the same to him in person or by sending it to him by mail at his last known post-office address, wth [with] postage prepaid; if his post-office address is not known, then the said notice may be mailed to the address of the bakery or place wherein such violation shall have been committed; the notice providing for the doing of any act or the abating of anything forbidden by this act shall fix the time within which such act shall be done or such thing abated, and if the order shall not be obeyed within the time therein fixed the person so failing to obey shall be liable to the penalty herein fixed for the violation hereof.

Violations.   SEC. 72. Any person violating any of the provisions of this act, or any owner or proprietor who fails to obey any order of this act, shall be liable to a penalty of fifty dollars for the first offense and one hundred dollars for each subsequent offense.

ACTS OF 1911.

CHAPTER 206.—*Factory, etc., regulations—Foundries.*

Entrances.   SECTION 1. All entrances to foundries shall be constructed and maintained so as to minimize drafts. All passageways in foundries, now in operation or hereafter to be built shall be constructed and maintained of sufficient width to make them reasonably safe for the workmen, and no unnecessary obstruction shall be allowed

Ventilation. in such passageways during the hours of casting. Whenever a foundry is so constructed or operated that smoke, steam, dust or noxious gases are not promptly carried off by the general ventila-

Sanitation. tion, exhaust fans shall be provided. Foundries shall be reasonably well lighted throughout the working hours and reasonably well heated during the cold and inclement weather. Hot water shall be kept available for washing purposes during the season in which artificial heating is necessary. When it is thought necessary and advisable by a State factory inspector, facilities shall be

Guards. provided for drying the clothing of persons employed therein. All pits around furnaces in any such brass factory shall be covered

Provisions for with substantial iron gratings. All stairways around such fur-
accidents. naces shall be constructed of iron. There shall be kept on hand

at all times in every foundry a reasonable supply of limewater, sweet oil, vaseline, bandages and absorbent cotton for use by the workmen in case of burns or accident. It is hereby made the duty of each and every State factory inspector to enforce the provisions of this act.

SEC. 2. Any place or establishment where metal castings or cores are made shall be deemed a foundry within the meaning of this act. *Definition.*

CHAPTER 210.—*Factory, etc., regulations—Inspectors.*

SECTION 1. In addition to the inspectors provided by the act to which this is a supplement, and the amendments and supplements thereto, the Commissioner of Labor shall, immediately after the passage of this act, appoint six suitable persons as inspectors, whose salary, powers, duties and term of office shall be the same as the inspectors already provided for. *Additional inspectors.*

SEC. 2. All inspectors of the Department of Labor, appointed under this act, or the act to which this act is a supplement, shall hereafter be appointed by the Commissioner of Labor, and all inspectors, including those referred to in paragraph one, shall be appointed, hold their offices and perform their duties subject to the provisions of an act entitled "An act regulating the employment, tenure and discharge of certain officers and employees of this State, and of the various counties and municipalities thereof, and providing for a civil service commission, and defining its powers and duties," approved April tenth, one thousand nine hundred and eight, and amendments thereof and supplements thereto. *Civil service.*

CHAPTER 214.—*Factory, etc., regulations—Fire escapes.*

manufacture of goods of any kind is carried on shall hereafter, *Exits.*

SECTION 1. Every factory, workshop, mill or place where the under the supervision and direction of the commissioner of labor, be provided with ample and proper ways and means of egress or escape in emergency arising from fire or otherwise, sufficient for the use of all persons therein, and as well shall be protected, so far as practicable, against the origin and spread of fire.

SEC. 2. Buildings two stories in height used for any purpose as stated in paragraph one at the time this act becomes effective, shall have at least two means of egress from the second story thereof, placed as far as possible at opposite ends of the room or building. Such egress may be provided by inside stairways or outside fire escapes, or both, and doors communicating therewith, as the said commissioner shall direct. Buildings more than two stories in height used for any purpose as stated in paragraph one at the time this act becomes effective, shall have at least two means of egress communicating with each story thereof, one of which shall be an inside stairway and one an outside fire escape. The said commissioner shall have power to order the construction of a second inside stairway and additional outside fire escapes, doors and windows as in his judgment are necessary to furnish proper and adequate protection to the inmates of such building. *Two ways of egress.* *Fire escapes.*

SEC. 3. All such fire escapes, stairways, doors and windows shall be located at such places in or on said building, and shall include as many stories and doors thereon as the commissioner shall direct. All such stairways, fire escapes, doors and windows added by order of the commissioner shall conform to the requirements and standards established by this act for new buildings. The commissioner is hereby given authority to order such changes in existing stairways, fire escapes and elevator shafts, doors and windows as may in his judgment be necessary to establish them as safe and proper means of egress. Any existing fire escape or stairway which in the judgment of the commissioner cannot be made safe and proper by alteration shall be condemned, removed and replaced as the commissioner shall direct. *Location.* *Type.*

truction of
buildings.

SEC. 4. No building shall hereafter be erected, nor any building not now used for factory purposes be adopted for such use, nor any addition be constructed, more than two stories in height, unless the plans and specifications, as to stairways, elevator shafts, fire escapes and doors and winows, ventilation and sanitation therefor be first submitted to and approved by the commissioner upon the advice of the department of charities and corrections. With such plans and specifications shall be submitted an estimated number of employes to be engaged upon each story or separated subdivision of any story of the proposed building. Such buildings two stories in height shall conform to the provisions of paragraph two.

Irways and
scapes.

SEC. 5. Buildings referred to in paragraph four, more than two stories in height, shall be equipped with one or more inside stairways and one or more outside fire escapes, the number, location and construction thereof to be approved by the commissioner. All stairways and elevator shafts in such buildings shall be enclosed in walls of fireproof or fire-resisting material, which shall run from the foundations to and through the roof; the stairways shall be constructed as nearly as possible of fireproof or fire-resisting material, and all entrances thereto shall be protected by doors of fireproof or fire-resisting material. The commissioner of labor may require that proper fire-stops shall be provided in the floors, walls and partitions of such buildings, and may make such further requirements as may be necessary or proper to prevent the origin or spread of fire therein.

rm of fire es-
.

SEC. 6. The fire escape shall be constructed according to specifications to be issued or approved by the commissioner of labor, and shall, as near as practicable, conform to the requirements of this act; and shall consist of outside iron balconies, and stairways at each floor above the first, connecting said balconies to the ground, except in the case of a fire escape over a public highway, or private driveway, when balanced stairs shall connect the lowest balcony to the ground in a manner hereinafter specified; the stairways shall be placed at a slope no steeper than forty-five degrees, or as near as possible thereto, and shall be, where practicable, on the straight run type similar to a flight of stairs; the balcony on the top floor shall be provided with a gooseneck ladder leading from said balcony to and above the roof, when ordered by the commissioner. Fire escapes may project into the public highway to a distance not greater than four feet six inches beyond the building line. The balconies shall not be less than four feet wide in the clear, when one balcony is placed directly above another, and three feet when the escape is constructed on the straight run plan, taking in at each story above the ground floor at least one door of each part of building separated by inside walls; they shall be not more than one foot below the door sills, and extend in front of and not less than nine inches beyond each door; there shall be a landing not less than twenty-four inches square at the head and foot of each stairway; the stairway wellhole on each platform shall be of a size sufficient to provide a clear headway, and shall be protected by a railing similar to that provided for balance of platform. All entrances to fire escape platforms shall be made by means of doors, which must be cut down to the level of the floor, except when some other construction is specified by the commissioner of labor. The doors shall open in the manner designated by the commissioner of labor. All doors or windows opening onto a fire escape or directly under a fire escape shall be metal-covered and all glass used therein shall be wire glass.

conies.

SEC. 7. The floors of balconies shall be of wrought iron slats not less than two inches by three-eighths inch refined flat wrought iron placed not more than one inch apart, and well secured and riveted at each intersection with three-eighths inch rivets, the iron runners not less than one and three-quarters inch by one and three-quarters inch by one-quarter inch gusset plate placed at point of bracket one-quarter inch thick. Brackets to be riveted together with one-half inch rivets driven hot concentric with sections. riveted together in such a manner that the holes are completely filled, and rivets must be well rounded; wall connections to be provided with one fifteen-sixteenths inch hole. For frame buildings to have feet turned down two inches on lower flange of angle with eleven-sixteenths inch hole in same. For brick, stone or cement buildings to extend in wall one and one-half inches. The openings for stairways in all balconies shall not be less than twenty-four inches wide, and such openings shall have no covers of any kind; the platforms of balconies shall be constructed and erected to safely sustain in all their parts a safe load of not less than eighty pounds per square foot, utilizing a ratio of four to one between the safe working load and the ultimate strength of all parts.

SEC. 8. All balcony rails shall in no case be less than three feet Balcony rails. above the floor of balcony, and shall extend around the entire platform, and in all cases shall go through the wall at each end and be worked out to three-quarters inch both sides and be properly secured by nuts with washers at least four inches square and three-eighths inch thick, and no top rail shall be connected at angles by gray cast iron. The top rail of balconies shall be one three-quarters inch by one-half inch of wrought iron, or one three-quarters inch angle iron at least three-sixteenths of an inch thick, or a three run three-quarters inch inside diameter wrought iron pipe railing, all pipe railings to be continuous. The bottom rails shall in no case be more than eight inches above the floor of balcony, and shall be of one one-half inch by three-eighths inch wrought iron, or of one one-half inch angle iron at least three-sixteenths of an inch thick, all leaded or cemented into the wall; the standard or filling-in bars shall not be less than five-eighths inch round or square wrought iron well riveted to the top and bottom rails, and shall be placed not more than six inches apart, and the lower rail of the platform shall be riveted or bolted to the frame of platform in such a manner as approved by the commissioner. of labor. Where the three run pipe-rail is adopted for the balcony railing no additional filling-in bars will be required.

SEC. 9. The stairway shall be constructed and erected to fully Stairways. sustain all parts and carry a safe load of not less than one hundred pounds per square foot, utilizing a ratio of four to one between the safe working load and the ultimate strength of all parts, with the exception of the tread which must safely stand at said ratio a concentrated load of two hundred pounds. The treads shall be not less than seven inches wide in the clear, and the rising of each step not more than nine inches; the treads shall be constructed of two pieces of one one-quarter inch by one one-quarter inch by three-sixteenths inch angles and one piece of two one-half inch by three-sixteenths inch flat riveted on each end with five-sixteenths inch rivets to one one-quarter inch by three-sixteenths inch angles. Each step will have one piece of one inch by one inch by one-eighth inch angle riveted to each of the side angles forming the step and a two one-half inch by three-sixteenths inch slat between same with five-sixteenths inch countersunk rivets on top, such stiffener to be located in the center of steps. The stairs shall be not less than twenty-four inches wide between inside of strings, and there shall remain a clear passageway between the stairway and wall. The strings shall be not less than six inches by one-quarter inch flat wrought refined iron. Stairways to be connected to platforms by two one three-quarter inch by three-eighths inch flat wrought iron hooks, one on each side, both secured by two half-inch bolts. The stairs shall have a hand rail of not less than three-quarters inch inside diameter round wrought iron pipe, to be of double run pattern, railing to connect at top and bottom to platform; posts to be not less than thirty-six inches in a vertical line from top to step to top run of railing. All posts to be of three-quarter inch inside diameter wrought iron, pipe to be spaced at intervals not greater than six feet and all fittings to be standard malleable iron; said pipe posts to be secured to the stairway runners by seven-sixteenths inch U bolts. The pipe posts must not be flattened where connection is made to stair runners, but must extend to bottom of said runners in its full and original shape.

Brackets SEC. 10. Brackets shall be placed not more than four feet apart, and shall extend across full width of balcony and on new buildings shall be set as walls are being built.

Landings. SEC. 11. Proper balanced stairways of a cantilever type or such other style as may be approved by the commissioner of labor reaching to a safe landing place below on the ground, shall be provided from the lower balcony of any fire escape over a public highway or private driveway in place of a stairway and when the floor of such balcony is more than sixteen feet above the sidewalk or ground, a suitable landing platform shall be provided; such platform shall be located not more than ten feet above the ground and shall be connected with the balcony above by means of a stairway constructed as this act requires for stairways between balconies; such platform shall not be less than three feet in width and four feet long and provided with railings as before specified for balconies, and the ground shall be reached in the manner specified for lower balconies not more than sixteen feet in height or by such other method as may be approved by the commissioner of labor; the gooseneck ladder shall be securely bolted through the wall of the building and the strings shall extend at least thirty inches above the roof and return down and be secured to same; there shall be a space of not less than fourteen inches between such ladder and the outer rail of balconies.

Painting. SEC. 12. All the parts of such fire escapes shall receive not less than two coats of paint, one in the shop and one after erection, and shall be painted thereafter at least once in each year.

Enforcement. SEC. 13. The commissioner shall have power to enforce the provisions of this act by order in writing served upon the owner or owners of any building coming within the operation of this act, specifying the directions to be executed and the time limited for the completion thereof. Any person, firm or corporation failing or neglecting to comply with the terms of such order within the time therein limited, or any extension thereof granted by the said commissioner, shall be liable to a penalty of one hundred dollars for such failure and to a further penalty of ten dollars for each day that shall elapse after the expiration of the time limit until compliance is made with the terms of such order. If the order is not complied with within the time limited, in addition to the foregoing penalty, the commissioner shall forthwith cause the said building to be closed for manufacturing purposes until such order is complied with. The commissioner shall give the owner of such building twenty-four hours' notice, in writing, of a closing order, and then shall post on the doors of such building a notice that such building has been closed for manufacturing purposes pending compliance with an order of the department of labor. If the said building shall be used for any manufacturing purpose until such order shall have been revoked by the said commissioner upon compliance with said order, the owner of such building shall be liable to a penalty of one thousand dollars.

For violation of any mandatory portion of this act, if an order of the commissioner with reference thereto have not been issued, the owner of such building shall be liable to a penalty of one hundred dollars.

Minimum requirements. SEC. 14. The provisions of this act shall be construed as furnishing minimum requirements for the guidance of said commissioner of labor; he may multiply or add such requirements as in his judgment are necessary and proper in each particular instance, and the orders of the said commissioner shall be construed as the minimum requirements in each particular case. No municipality shall issue orders or permits in derogation thereof, but any municipality may require, in addition thereto, such precautions or devices as are not inconsistent with the provisions of this act, but the muncipality shall be responsible for the enforcement of the orders issued under its authority.

SEC. 15. All installation of fire escapes or stairways shall be made with reference to the maximum number of persons to be employed upon each story of any building or separate subdivision thereof, a statement of which number shall be posted by the owner upon the wall of each story or separated subdivision thereof, so as to be visible at all times. Under no circumstances shall this number, when once ascertained and installation of fire escapes and stairways be made with reference thereto, be exceeded, except by permission of the commissioner. *Number of employees to be considered.*

SEC. 16. In all buildings not detached, a stairway running from the top floor to the roof by means of a bulkhead may be ordered by the commissioner. *Stairway to roof.*

No partitions which interfere with established means of egress shall be erected unless by approval of the commissioner. *Partitions.*

Pails of water and sand shall be provided and located as ordered by the commissioner. *Water, etc.*

A suitable disposition shall be made of all inflammable articles and suitable waste cans or barrels shall be provided for the proper handling of sweepings, oily waste or other combustible material, as directed by the commissioner. *Waste.*

Such doors and hand rails may be required on stairways as may be approved by the commissioner. *Doors and hand rails.*

No fire escapes shall be constructed without the approval of the commissioner of labor, unless specifically required by municipal authorities. *Approval.*

Doors leading to fire escapes shall be clearly indicated by signs posted or painted on the walls above or at the side of such doors. The approaches to such doors shall be kept free and unobstructed at all times. *Signs.*

A fire tower approved by the commissioner may be substituted for an inside stairway or outside fire escape. *Tower.*

All exit doors throughout the building shall open outward, or be sliding doors, and if kept closed during working hours, shall be fastened only in such manner as to be capable of ready and immediate opening from the inside. *Doors to open outward.*

SEC. 17. Factory buildings more than two stories in height shall be equipped with a system of fire alarm, with sufficiently large gongs, located on each floor of the factory building, or within each separate room where more than one factory is located on a single floor. *Fire alarm.*

'The system shall be so installed as to permit the sounding of all the alarm gongs within a single building whenever the alarm is sounded in any one portion thereof. The means of sounding these alarms shall be placed within easy access of all the operatives within the specified factory or room, and shall be plainly labeled. This system of fire alarms is not to be used for any purpose other than in case of a fire or fire drill, and it shall be the duty of the person in charge of any factory or section of a factory wherein a fire originates immediately to cause an alarm to be sounded.

SEC. 18. A fire drill sufficient to enable the operatives of a factory immediately and rapidly to leave a building shall be maintained in every factory building more than two stories in height, and shall be practiced at least once in every calendar month. A demonstration of this fire drill shall be given upon the request of a representative either of the department of labor, or of the fire department of the municipality to which the factory is located. The chief of each fire department shall advise the commissioner of labor of any violation of the requirements of this law coming to his knowledge. *Fire drill.*

CHAPTER 273.—*Factory, etc., regulations—Time for meals.*

SECTION 1. Every corporation, firm or person owning or operating any place coming under the provisions of the act to which this act is a supplement, [ch. 64, Acts of 1904], shall give all *One-half hour to be allowed.*

operatives and employees at least one-half hour for their midday meal, after being continuously employed for a period of not more than six hours, on any workday except Saturday.

Fixing time.   SEC. 2. The period for such meal shall be fixed by every such employer, having in view the health and physical welfare of such operatives and employees in all such factories, workshops, mills and places where the manufacture of goods of any kind is carried on; if any such place is operated at night, or in eight-hour shifts, such meal period shall be fixed as aforesaid for such operatives and employees at such time as may be consistent with the mutual interests of such employer and operatives and employees.

Notice to be posted.   SEC. 3. Notice of the hours within which such operatives may obtain such meals shall be plainly printed and kept posted in a conspicuous place in all workrooms where any such employees or operatives are engaged.

Violations.   SEC. 4. Any such owner or employer, violating any of the provisions of this act shall be liable to a penalty of one hundred dollars for the first offense and of two hundred dollars for each subsequent offense.

NEW YORK.

CONSOLIDATED LAWS—1909.

CHAPTER 28. Article 10a (added by chapter 451, Acts of 1911).— *State fire marshal—Fire escapes.*

Office created.   SECTION 350. The office of State fire marshal is hereby established. The governor is hereby authorized and empowered to appoint, within thirty days after this act shall take effect, by and with the advice and consent of the senate, a suitable person who shall be a citizen of this State, as State fire marshal, who shall hold the office for a period of five years or until his successor is appointed and qualified. The office of the State fire marshal shall be located in the capitol in the city of Albany. He shall receive an annual salary of seven thousand dollars and shall be paid, in addition, his actual and necessary expenses incurred in the performance of the duties of his office. He shall devote his whole time to the duties of his office. Whenever there shall be a vacancy in the office of State fire marshal, the governor shall fill the vacancy for the unexpired term in the manner provided in this section. The State fire marshal and his deputies shall take and subscribe and file in the office of the secretary of state the constitutional oath within fifteen days from time of notice of their appointment respectively.

Duties of fire marshal.   SEC. 351. It shall be the duty of the State fire marshal to enforce all laws and ordinances of the State, and the several counties, cities and political subdivisions thereof, except in cities having over one million inhabitants, as follows:

1. The prevention of fires;
2. The storage, sale or use of combustibles and explosives;
3. The installation and maintenance of automatic or other fire-alarm systems and fire-extinguishing equipment;
4. The inspection of steam boilers;
5. The construction, maintenance and regulation of fire escapes;
6. The means and adequacy of exit, in case of fire, from factories, asylums, hospitals, churches, schools, halls, theaters, amphitheaters and all other places in which numbers of persons work, live, or congregate from time to time for any purpose;
7. The suppression of arson and investigation of the cause, origin and circumstances of fires.

Deputies.   SEC. 352. The State fire marshal shall appoint a first deputy fire marshal, who shall receive an annual salary of five thousand dollars, and a second deputy fire marshal who shall receive an annual salary of three thousand dollars. Each such deputy shall also be paid his actual and necessary expenses incurred in the performance of the duties of his office. The State fire marshal shall also appoint a secretary and such other clerks and assistants as shall be needed in the performance of the duties of his office. In case of the absence of the State fire marshal, or his inability from any cause to discharge the duties of his office, such duties shall devolve upon the first deputy State fire marshal; and in case of the absence of the State fire marshal and the first deputy State fire marshal, or their inability from any cause to discharge the duties and powers of their office, such duties and powers shall devolve upon the second deputy State fire marshal.

SEC. 353. All municipal fire marshals in those municipalities having such officers, and, where no such officer exists, the chief of the fire department of every incorporated city or village in which a fire department is established, the president or like senior officer of each incorporated village in which no fire department exists, and the clerk of each organized town without the limits of any incorporated village or city, shall be, by virtue of such office so held by them, assistants to the State fire marshal and subject to the duties and obligations imposed by this article and shall be subject to the directions of the State fire marshal in the execution of the provisions hereof. *Municipal fire marshals, where.*

Immediately upon taking office the State fire marshal shall prepare instructions to the assistants designated herein and forms for their use in the reports required by this article and cause them to be printed and sent, together with a copy of this article, to each such officer located in this State. *Instructions.*

SEC. 355. The State fire marshal, his deputies or assistants, upon the complaint of any person or whenever he or they shall deem it necessary shall inspect all buildings and premises within their jurisdiction. Whenever any of said officers shall find any building or other structure which, for want of repairs, lack of or insufficient fire escapes, automatic or other fire-alarm apparatus or fire-extinguishing equipment, or by reason of age or dilapidated condition or for any other cause, is especially liable to fire and which is so situated as to endanger other property, and whenever such officer shall find in any building combustible or explosive matter or inflammable conditions dangerous to the safety of such buildings he or they shall order the same to be removed or remedied, and such order shall forthwith be complied with by the owner of occupant of such premises or buildings. If such order is made by any deputy or assistant to the State fire marshal such owner or occupant may, within twenty-four hours, appeal to the State fire marshal, who shall, within ten days, review such order and file his decision thereon, and unless by his authority the order is revoked or modified it shall remain in full force and be obeyed by such owner or occupant. *Inspection of buildings.*

Any owner or occupant failing to comply with such order within ten days after said appeal shall have been determined, or, if no appeal is taken, then within ten days after the service of the said order, shall be liable to a penalty of fifty dollars for each day's neglect thereafter. The service of any such order shall be made upon the occupant of the premises to whom it is directed by either delivering a true copy of same to such occupant personally or by delivering the same to and leaving it with any person in charge of the premises, or in case no such person is found upon the premises by affixing a copy thereof in a conspicuous place on the door to the entrance of the said premises; whenever it may be necessary to serve such an order upon the owner of premises, such order may be served either by delivering to and leaving with the said person a true copy of the said order, or, if such owner is absent from the jurisdiction of the officer making the order, by mailing such copy to the owner's last known post-office address. *Orders to be complied with.*

The penalty herein provided may be recovered in an action brought in any court of the county where such property is located, in the name of the people of the State, under the direction of the State fire marshal or any of his assistants herein designated, by the legally constituted law officer of the city, village or town where such property is located or by an attorney specially designated therefor by the attorney general.

The State fire marshal shall also cause to be inspected all boilers in buildings and all other places where same are used for the generation of steam, except where a certificate has been filed certifying that such boilers have been inspected by a duly authorized insurance company. A fee of five dollars shall be charged the owner or lessee of each boiler inspected by the inspector of the office of the State fire marshal.

Law applies, where.
SEC. 2. This act shall not apply to cities having more than one million inhabitants, which maintains a municipal fire marshal except that such municipal fire marshal shall prepare and forward such reports as to fires, et cetera, which the State fire marshal may require.

CHAPTER 31.—*Regulation and inspection of factories, etc.*

Department of labor.
SECTION 42 (as amended by chapter 514, Acts of 1910). The department of labor shall be divided into five bureaus as follows: Factory inspection, labor statistics, mediation and arbitration, industries and immigration, and mercantile inspection.

Powers of commissioner, etc.
SEC. 43 (as amended by chapter 514, Acts of 1910). 1. The commissioner of labor, his deputies and their assistants and each special agent, deputy factory inspector, chief investigator, special investigators, mercantile inspector, or deputy mercantile inspectors may administer oaths and take affidavits in matters relating to the provisions of this chapter.

2. No person shall interfere with, obstruct or hinder by force or otherwise the commissioner of labor, his deputies, their assistants or the special agents, deputy factory inspectors, chief investigator, special investigators, the mercantile inspector, or deputy mercantile inspectors while in the performance of their duties, or refuse to properly answer questions asked by such officers pertaining to the provisions of this chapter, or refuse them admittance to any place where and when labor is being performed which is affected by the provisions of this chapter.

3. All notices, orders and directions of deputies, assistants, special agents, deputy factory inspectors, chief investigators, special investigators, the mercantile inspector, or deputy mercantile inspectors given in accordance with this chapter are subject to the approval of the commissioner of labor. And all acts, notices, orders, permits and directions by any provisions of this chapter directed to be performed or given by the factory inspector, chairman of the board of mediation and arbitration, chief investigator, special investigators, mercantile inspector or other officer of the department of labor may be performed or given by and in the name of the commissioner of labor and by any officer of the department thereunto duly authorized by such commissioner in the name of such commissioner.

4. The commissioner of labor may procure and cause to be used badges for himself and his subordinates in the department of labor while in the performance of their duties.

Bureau continued.
SEC. 55. There shall continue to be a bureau of labor statistics, which shall be under the immediate charge of a chief statistician, but subject to the direction and supervision of the commissioner of labor.

Duties and powers.
SEC. 56. The commissioner of labor shall collect, assort, systematize and present in annual reports to the legislature, statistical details in relation to all departments of labor in the State, especially in relation to the commercial, industrial, social and sanitary condition of working men and to the productive industries of the state. He may subpœna witnesses, take and hear testimony, take or cause to be taken depositions and administer oaths.

Duties of owners, etc., of establishments.
SEC. 57. The owner, operator, manager or lessee of any mine, factory, workshop, warehouse, elevator, foundry, machine shop or other manufacturing establishment, or any agent, superintendent, subordinate, or employee thereof, and any person employing or directing any labor affected by the provisions of this chapter, shall, when requested by the commissioner of labor, furnish any

information in his possession or under his control which the commissioner is authorized to require, and shall admit him to any place where labor is carried on which is affected by the provisions of this chapter for the purpose of inspection. All statistics furnished to the commissioner of labor, pursuant to this article, may be destroyed by such commissioner after the expiration of two years from the time of the receipt thereof. A person refusing to admit such commissioner, or a person authorized by him, to any such establishment, or to furnish him any information requested, or who refuses to answer or untruthfully answers questions put to him by such commissioner, in a circular or otherwise, shall forfeit to the people of the State the sum of one hundred dollars for each refusal or untruthful answer given, to be sued for and recovered by the commissioner in his name of office. The amount so recovered shall be paid in to the state treasury.

SEC. 60 (as amended by chapter 729, Acts of 1911). There shall continue to be a bureau of factory inspection. The first deputy commissioner of labor shall be the chief factory inspector of the state and in immediate charge of this bureau, but subject to the direction and supervision of the commissioner of labor. *Chief inspector.*

SEC. 61 (as amended by chapter 729, Acts of 1911). The commissioner of labor may appoint from time to time not more than eighty-five persons as factory inspectors, not more than fifteen of whom shall be women, and who may be removed by him at any time. The factory inspectors may be divided into five grades, but not more than thirty shall be of the third grade, and not more than eight shall be of the fourth grade and not more than one shall be of the fifth grade. Each inspector of the first grade shall receive an annual salary of one thousand dollars, each of the second grade an annual salary of one thousand two hundred dollars and each of the third grade an annual salary of one thousand five hundred dollars. There shall be after October first, nineteen hundred and eleven, no further appointments in the first grade and no vacancies in the first grade shall be filled. There may be at any time not to exceed fifty persons in the second grade. Each inspector of the fourth grade shall receive an annual salary of two thousand five hundred dollars. Each inspector of the fifth grade shall receive an annual salary of three thousand five hundred dollars. Each inspector of the fifth grade shall be a mechanical engineer. *Inspectors.*

SEC. 62 (as amended by chapter 729, Acts of 1911). 1. The commissioner of labor shall from time to time divide the State into districts, assign one factory inspector of the fourth grade to each district as supervising inspector, and may in his discretion transfer them from one district to another; he may assign any factory inspector to inspect any special class or classes of factories or to enforce any special provisions of this chapter; and he may assign any one or more of them to act as clerks in any office of the department. *Districts.*

2. The commissioner of labor may authorize any deputy commissioner or assistant and any special agent or inspector in the department of labor to act as a deputy factory inspector with the full power and authority thereof. *Who may act as deputies.*

3. The commissioner of labor, the first deputy commissioner of labor and his assistant or assistants and every factory inspector may in the discharge of his duties enter any place, building or room where and when any labor is being performed which is affected by the provisions of this chapter and may enter any factory whenever he may have reasonable cause to believe that any such labor is being performed therein. *Access to buildings.*

4. The commissioner of labor shall visit and inspect or cause to be visited and inspected the factories, during reasonable hours, as often as practicable, and shall cause the provisions of this chapter to be enforced therein. *Inspections.*

5. Any lawful municipal ordinance, by-law or regulation relating to factories, in addition to the provisions of this chapter and not in conflict therewith, may be observed and enforced by the commissioner of labor. *Municipal ordinances.*

Annual reports.   SEC. 63. The commissioner of labor shall make an annual report
to the legislature of the operation of this bureau.

Act to be   SEC. 68. A copy or abstract of the provisions of this chapter
posted.   applicable thereto, to be prepared and furnished by the commissioner of labor, shall be kept posted by the employer in a conspicuous place on each floor of every factory where persons are employed who are affected by the provisions thereof.

Elevator ways   SEC. 79. If, in the opinion of•the commissioner of labor, it is
etc., to be guard-   necessary to protect the life or limbs of factory employees, the
ed.   owner, agent or lessee of such factory where an elevator, hoisting
shafts or wellhole is used, shall cause, upon written notice from
the commissioner of labor, the same to be properly and substantially inclosed, secured or guarded, and shall provide such proper
traps or automatic doors so fastened in or at all elevator ways,
except passenger elevators inclosed on all sides, as to form a
substantial surface when clôsed and so constructed as to open and
close by action of the elevator in its passage either ascending or
descending. The commissioner of labor may inspect the cable,
gearing or other apparatus of elevators in factories and require
them to be kept in a safe condition.

Stairways.   SEC. 80 (as amended by chapter 461, Acts of 1910). Proper and
substantial hand rails shall be provided on all stairways in factories. The steps of such stairs shall be covered with rubber,
securely fastened thereon, if in the opinion of the commissioner of
labor the safety of employees would be promoted thereby. The

Locking, etc.,   stairs shall be properly screened at the sides and bottom. All
of doors and win-   doors leading in or to any such factory shall be so constructed as
dows.   to open outwardly where practicable, and shall not be locked,
bolted or fastened during working hours. No door, window or
other opening on any floor of any such factory shall be obstructed
by stationary metal bars, grating,·or wire mesh. Any metal bars,
grating, or wire mesh provided for any such doors, windows or
openings, shall be so constructed as to be readily movable or
removable from the interior in such a manner as to afford the free
and unobstructed use of such doors, windows or openings for
purposes of egress, in case of need.

Belt shifters.   SEC. 81 (as·amended by chapter 106, Acts of 1910). The owner
or person in charge of a factory where machinery is used, shall
provide, in the discretion of the commissioner of labor, belt shifters
or other mechanical contrivances for the purpose of throwing on
or off belts on pulleys. Whenever practicable, all machinery shall
be provided with loose pulleys. All vats, pans, saws, planers, cogs,
gearing, belting, shafting, set-screws and machinery, of every
description shall be properly guarded. No person shall remove or
make ineffective any safeguard around or attached to machinery,
vats or pans, while the same are in use, unless for the purpose of

Guards.   immediately making repairs thereto, and all such safeguards so
removed shall be promptly replaced. All grinding, polishing or
buffing wheels used in the course of the manufacture of articles

Exhaust fans.   of the baser metals shall be equipped with proper hoods and pipes
and such pipes shall be connected to an exhaust fan of sufficient
capacity and power to remove all matter thrown off such wheels in
the course of their use. Such fan shall be kept running constantly
while such grinding, polishing or buffing wheels are in operation;
except that in case of wet grinding it is unnecessary to comply
with this provision. All machinery creating dust or impurities
shall be equipped with proper hoods and pipes and such pipes shall
be connected to an exhaust fan of sufficient capacity and power to
remove such dust or impurities; such fan shall be kept running
constantly while such machinery is in use; except where, in case
of woodworking machinery, the commissioner of labor, after first
making and filing in the public records of his office a written statement of the reasons therefor, shall decide that it is unnecessary
for the health and welfare of the operatives. If a machine or·any
part thereof is in a dangerous condition or is not properly guarded,
the use thereof may be prohibited by the commissioner of labor
and a notice to that effect shall be attached thereto. Such notice

shall not be removed until the machine is made safe and the required safeguards are provided, and in the meantime such unsafe or dangerous machinery shall not be used. When in the opinion of the commissioner of labor it is necessary, the workrooms, halls and stairs leading to the workrooms shall be properly lighted, and in cities of the first class, if deemed necessary by the commissioner of labor, a proper light shall be kept burning by the owner or lessee in the public hallways near the stairs upon the entrance floor and upon the other floors on every work day in the year, from the time when the building is opened for use in the morning until the time it is closed in the evening, except at times when the influx of natural light shall make artificial light unnecessary. Such lights shall be independent of the motive power of such factory. **Lighting.**

SEC. 82. Such fire escapes as may be deemed necessary by the commissioner of labor shall be provided on the outside of every factory in this State consisting of three or more stories in height. Each escape shall connect with each floor above the first, and shall be of sufficient strength, well fastened and secured, and shall have landings or balconies not less than six feet in length and three feet in width, guarded by iron railings not less than three feet in height, embracing at least two windows at each story and connected with the interior by easily accessible and unobstructed openings. The balconies or landings shall be connected by iron stairs, not less than eighteen inches wide, with steps, of not less than six inches tread, placed at a proper slant and protected by a well-secured hand rail on both sides, and shall have a drop ladder not less than twelve inches wide reaching from the lower platform to the ground. **Fire escapes.**

The windows or doors to the landing or balcony of each fire escape shall be of sufficient size and located as far as possible, consistent with accessibility from the stairways and elevator hatchways or openings, and a ladder from such fire escapes shall extend to the roof. Stationary stairs or ladders shall be provided on the inside of every factory from the upper story to the roof, as a means of escape in case of fire.

SEC. 83 (as amended by chapter 461, Acts of 1910). Any other plan or style of fire escape shall be sufficient if approved in writing by the commissioner of labor. If there is no fire escape, or the fire escape in use is not approved by the commissioner of labor, he may, by a written order served upon the owner, proprietor or lessee of any factory, or the agent or superintendent thereof, or either of them, require one or more fire escapes to be provided therefor, at such locations and of such plan and style as shall be specified in such order. Within twenty days after the service of such order, the number of fire escapes required therein shall be provided, each of which shall be of the plan and style specified in the order, or of the plan and style described in the preceding section. If any of the doors, windows or other openings of any floor of any factory is obstructed by any form of stationary metal bars, gratings, or wire mesh, or if any metal obstruction or protective device for any such door, window or opening is not approved by the commissioner of labor, he shall, by a written order served upon the owner, proprietor or lessee of any factory, or the agent or superintendent thereof, or either of them, require such stationary bars, grating, mesh or other stationary obstruction shall be removed. Immediately after the service of such order, the said stationary bars, grating or other obstruction shall be removed. **Same subject.**

SEC. 84 (as amended by chapter 114, Acts of 1910). The walls and ceilings of each workroom in a factory shall be limewashed or painted, when in the opinion of the commissioner of labor, it will be conducive to the health or cleanliness of the persons working therein. Floors shall be maintained in a safe condition and shall be kept clean and sanitary at all times. No person shall spit or expectorate upon the walls, floors, or stairs of any building used in whole or in part for factory purposes. Sanitary **Walls.** **Floors.** **Expectoration.**

cuspidors shall be provided, in the. discretion of the commissioner of labor, in every workroom in a factory in such numbers as the commissioner of labor may determine. Such cuspidors shall

Waste and ref
use. be thoroughly cleaned daily. Suitable receptacles shall be provided and used for the storage of waste and refuse; such receptacles shall be maintained in a sanitary condition.

Air space. SEC. 85. No more employees shall be required or permitted to work in a room in a factory between the hours of six o'clock in the morning and six o'clock in the evening than will allow to each of such employees, not less than two hundred and fifty cubic feet of air space; and, unless by a written permit of the commissioner of labor, not less than four hundred cubic feet for each employee, so employed between the hours of six o'clock in the evening and six o'clock in the morning, provided such room is lighted by electricity at all times during such hours, while persons are employed therein.

Ventilation. SEC. 86. The owner, agent or lessee of a factory shall provide, in each workroom thereof, proper and sufficient means of ventilation, and shall maintain proper and sufficient ventilation; if excessive heat be created or if steam, gases, vapors, dust or other impurities that may be injurious to health be generated in the course of the manufacturing process carried on therein the room must be ventilated in such a manner as to render them harmless, so far as is practiable; in case of failure the commissioner of labor shall order such ventilation to be provided. Such owner. agent or lessee shall provide such ventilation within twenty days after the service upon him of such order, and in case of failure. shall forfeit to the people of the State, ten dollars for each day after the expiration of such twenty days, to be recovered by the commissioner of labor.

Accidents to be
reported. SEC. 87. The person in charge of any factory shall report in writing to the commissioner of labor all deaths, accidents or injuries sustained by any person therein or on the premises, within forty-eight hours after the time of the accident, death or injury, stating as fully as possible the cause of the death or the extent and cause of the injury, and the place where the injured person has been sent, with such other or further information relative thereto as may be required by the said commissioner, who may investigate the causes thereof and require such precautions to be taken as will prevent the recurrence of similar happenings. No statement contained in any such report shall be admissible in evidence in any action arising out of the death or accident therein reported.

D r i n k i n g
water. SEC. 88 (as amended by chapter 229, Acts of 1910). In every factory there shall be provided at all times, for the use of employees, a sufficient supply of clean and pure drinking water. Such. water shall be supplied through proper pipe connections with water mains through which is conveyed the water used for domestic purposes, or, from a spring or well or body of pure water; if such drinking water be placed in receptacles in the factory, such receptacles shall be properly covered to prevent contamination

Wash rooms. and shall be thoroughly cleaned at frequent intervals. In every factory there shall be provided and maintained for the use of employees, suitable and convenient wash rooms, adequately equipped with sinks and proper water service. Where females are employed, dressing or emergency rooms shall be provided for their use; each such room shall have at least one window opening to the outer air and shall be inclosed by means of solid partitions or

Drying rooms. walls. In brass and iron foundries suitable provision shall be made and maintained for drying the working clothes of persons

Water-closets. employed therein. In every factory there shall be provided suitable and convenient water-closets for each sex, in such number as the commissioner of labor may determine. Such water-closets shall be properly screened, lighted, ventilated and kept clean and sanitary; the inclosure of each closet shall be kept clean and sanitary and free from all obscene writing or marking. The water-closets used by the females shall be entirely separated from those used by males and the entrances thereto shall be effectively screened. The water-closets shall be maintained inside the factory whenever practicable and in all cases, when required by the commissioner of labor.

SEC. 89. In each factory at least sixty minutes shall be allowed for the noon-day meal, unless the commissioner of labor shall permit a shorter time. Such permit must be in writing and conspicuously posted in the main entrance of the factory, and may be revoked at any time. Where employees are required or permitted to work overtime for more than one hour after six o'clock in the evening, they shall be allowed at least twenty minutes to obtain a lunch, before beginning to work overtime. *Time for meals.*

SEC. 90. The commissioner of labor, or other competent person designated by him, upon request, shall examine any factory outside of the cities of New York and Brooklyn, to determine whether it is in a safe condition. If it appears to him to be unsafe, he shall immediately notify the owner, agent or lessee thereof, specifying the defects, and require such repairs and improvements to be made as he may deem necessary. If the owner, agent or lessee shall fail to comply with such requirement, he shall forfeit to the people of the State the sum of fifty dollars, to be recovered by the commissioner of labor in his name of office. *Inspections.*

SEC. 91. All boilers used for generating steam or heat for factory purposes shall be kept in good order, and the owner, agent, manager or lessee of such factory shall have such boilers inspected by a competent person approved by the commissioner of labor once in six months, and shall file a certificate showing the result thereof in such factory office and a duplicate thereof in the office of the commissioner of labor. Each boiler or nest of boilers used for generating steam or heat for factory purposes shall be provided with a proper safety-valve and with steam and water gauges, to show, respectively, the pressure of steam and the height of water in the boilers. Every boiler house in which a boiler or nest of boilers is placed, shall be provided with a steam gauge properly conected with the boilers, and another steam gauge shall be attached to the steam pipe in the engine house, and so placed that the engineer or fireman can readily ascertain the pressure carried. Nothing in this section shall apply to boilers in factories which are regularly inspected by competent inspectors acting under the authority of local laws or ordinances. *Boilers.*

SEC. 92. A shop, room or building where one or more persons are employed in doing public laundry work by way of trade or for purposes of gain is a factory within the meaning of this chapter, and shall be subject to the visitation and inspection of the commissioner of labor and the provisions of this chapter in the same manner as any other factory. No such public laundry work shall be done in a room used for sleeping or living room. All such laundries shall be kept in a clean condition and free from vermin and all impurities of an infectious or contagious nature. This . section shall not apply to any female engaged in doing custom laundry work at her home for a regular family trade. *Laundries.*

[For section 93, see Appendix A, p. 782.]

SEC. 94. A tenant-factory within the meaning of the term as used in this chapter is a building, separate parts of which are occupied and used by different persons, companies or corporations, and one or more of which parts is so used as to constitute in law a factory. The owner, whether or not he is also one of the occupants, instead of the respective lessees or tenants, shall be responsible for the observance and punishable for the nonobservance of the following provisions of this article, anything in any lease to the contrary notwithstanding,—namely, the provisions of sections seventy-nine, eighty, eighty-two, eighty-three, eighty-six, ninety, and ninety-one, and the provisions of section eighty-one with respect to the ligting of halls and stairways; except that the lessees or tenants also shall be responsible for the observance and punishable *Tenant factories.*

for the nonobservance of the provisions of sections seventy-nine, eighty, eighty-six and ninety-one within their respective holdings. The owner of every tenant-factory shall provide each separate factory therein with water-closets in accordance with the provisions of section eighty-eight, and with proper and sufficient water and plumbing pipes and a proper and sufficient supply of water to enable the tenant or lessee thereof to comply with all the provisions of said section. But as an alternative to providing water-closets within each factory as aforesaid, the owner may provide in the public hallways or other parts of the premises used in common, where they will be at all times readily and conveniently accessible to all persons employed on the premises not provided for in accordance with section eighty-eight, separate water-closets for each sex, of sufficient numbers to accommodate all such persons. Such owner shall keep all water-closets located as last specified at all times provided with proper fastenings, and properly screened, lighted, ventilated, clean, sanitary and free from all obscene writing or marking. Outdoor water-closets shall only be permitted where the commissioner of labor shall decide that they are necessary or preferable, and they shall then be provided in all respects in accordance with his directions. The owner of every tenant-factory shall keep the entire building well drained and the plumbing thereof in a clean and sanitary condition; and shall keep the cellar, basement, yards, areaways, vacant rooms and spaces, and all parts and places used in common in a clean, sanitary and safe condition, and shall keep such parts thereof as may reasonably be required by the commissioner of labor properly lighted at all hours or times when said building is in use for factory purposes. The term "owner" as used in this article shall be construed to mean the owner or owners of the freehold of the premises, or the lessee or joint lessees of the whole thereof, or his, her or their agent in charge of the property. The lessee or tenant of any part of a tenant-factory shall permit the owner, his agents and servants, to enter and remain upon the demised premises whenever and so long as may be necessary to comply with the provisions of law, the responsibility for which is by this section placed upon the owner; and his failure or refusal so to do shall be a cause for dispossessing said tenant by summary proceedings to recover possession of real property, as provided in the code of civil procedure. And whenever by the terms of a lease any lessee or tenant shall have agreed to comply with or carry out any of such provisions, his failure or refusal so to do shall be a cause for dispossessing said tenant by summary proceedings aforesaid. Except as in this article otherwise provided the person or persons, company or corporation conducting or operating a factory whether as owner or lessee of the whole or of a part of the building in which the same is situated or otherwise, shall be responsible for the observance and punishable for the nonobservance of the provisions of this article, anything in any lease or agreement to the contrary notwithstanding.

Contagious diseases. SEC. 95. If the commissioner of labor finds evidence of contagious disease present in any tenant-factory in which any of the articles enumerated in section one hundred hereof are manufactured, altered, repaired or finished he shall affix to any such articles exposed to such contagion a label containing the word "unclean" and shall notify the local board of health, who may disinfect such articles and thereupon remove such label. If the commissioner of labor finds any of the articles specified in said section in any workroom or factory in a tenant-factory which is foul, unclean or unsanitary, he may, after first making and filing in the public records of his office a written order stating the reasons therefor, affix to such articles a label containing the word "unclean." No one but the commissioner of labor shall remove any label so affixed; and he may refuse to remove it until such articles shall have been removed from such factory and cleaned, or until such room or rooms shall have been cleaned or made sanitary.

Manufactures in tenements.

SECTION 100. 1. No tenement-house nor any part thereof shall be used for the purpose of manufacturing, altering, repairing or finishing therein, any coats, vests, knee-pants, trousers, overalls, cloaks, hats, caps, suspenders, jerseys, blouses, dresses, waists, waistbands, underwear, neckwear, furs, fur trimmings, fur garments, skirts, shirts, aprons, purses, pocket-books, slippers. paper boxes, paper bags, feathers, artificial flowers, cigarettes, cigars, umbrellas, or articles of rubber, nor for the purpose of manufacturing, preparing or packing macaroni, spaghetti, ice cream, ices, candy, confectionery, nuts or preserves, without a license therefor as provided in this article. But nothing herein contained shall apply to collars, cuffs, shirts or shirt waists made of cotton or linen fabrics that are subjected to the laundrying process before being offered for sale. *License required.*

2. Application for such a license shall be made to the commissioner of labor by the owner of such tenement-house. or by his duly authorized agent. Such application shall describe the house by street number or otherwise, as the case may be, in such manner as will enable the commissioner of labor easily to find the same; it shall also state the number of apartments in such house; it shall contain the full name and address of the owner of the said house, and shall be in such form as the commissioner of labor may determine. Blank applications shall be prepared and furnished by the commissioner of labor. *Applications.*

3. Upon receipt of such application the commissioner of labor shall consult the records of the local health department or board, or other appropriate local authority charged with the duty of sanitary inspection of such houses; if such records show the presence of any infectious, contagious or communicable disease, or the existence of any uncomplied-with orders or violations which indicate the presence of unsanitary conditions in such house, the commissioner of labor may, without making an inspection of the building, deny such application for a license, and may continue to deny such application until such time as the records of said department, board or other local authority show that the said tenement-house is free from the presence of infectious, contagious or communicable disease, and from all unsanitary conditions. Before, however, any such license is granted, an inspection of the building sought to be licensed must be made by the commissioner of labor, and a statement must be filed by him as a matter of public record, to the effect that the records of the local health department or board or other appropriate authority charged with the duty of sanitary inspection of such houses show the existence of no infectious, contagious or communicable disease nor of any unsanitary conditions in the said house; such statement must be dated and signed in ink with the full name of the employee responsible therefor. A similar statement similarly signed, showing the results of the inspection of the said building, must also be filed in the office of the commissioner of labor before any license is granted. If the commissioner of labor ascertain that such building is free from infectious, contagious or communicable disease, that there are no defects of plumbing that will permit the free entrance of sewer air, that such building is in a clean and proper sanitary condition and that the articles specified in this section may be manufactured therein under clean and healthful conditions, he shall grant a license permitting the use of such building, for the purpose of manufacturing, altering, repairing or finishing such articles. *Investigations.*

4. Such license may be revoked by the commissioner of labor if the health of the community or of the employees requires it, or if the owner of the said tenement-house, or his duly authorized agent, fails to compy with the orders of the commissioner of labor within ten days after the receipt of such orders, or if it appears that the building to which such license relates is not in a healthy *Revocation of license.*

and proper sanitary condition. In every case where a license is revoked or denied by the commissioner of labor the reasons therefor shall be stated in writing, and the records of such revocation or denial shall be deemed public records. Where a license is revoked, before such tenement-house can again be used for the purposes specified in this section, a new license must be obtained, as if no license had previously existed.

Sanitation.   5. Every tenement-house and all the parts thereof in which any of the articles named in this section are manufactured, altered, repaired or finished shall be kept in a clean and sanitary condition and shall be subject to inspection and examination by the commissioner of labor, for the purpose of ascertaining whether said garments or articles, or part or parts thereof, are clean and fee from vermin and every matter of an infectious or contagious

Inspections.   nature. An inspection shall be made by the commissioner of labor of each licensed tenement-house not less than once in every six months, to determine its sanitary condition, and shall include all parts of such house and the plumbing thereof. Before making such inspection the commissioner of labor may consult the records of the local department or board charged with the duty of sanitary inspection of tenement-houses, to determine the frequency of orders issued by such department or board in relation to the said tenement-house, since the last inspection of such building was made by the commissioner of labor. Whenever the commissioner of labor finds any unsanitary condition in a tenement-house for which a license has been issued as provided in this section, he shall at once issue an order to the owner thereof directing him to remedy such condition forthwith. Whenever the commissioner of labor finds any of the articles specified in this section manufactured, altered, repaired or finished, or in process thereof, in a room or apartment of a tenement-house, and such room or apartment is in a filthy condition, he shall notify tenants thereof to immediately clean the same, and to maintain it in a cleanly condition at all times; where the commissioner of labor finds such room or apartment to be habitually kept in a filthy condition, he may in his discretion cause to be affixed to the entrance door of such apartment a placard calling attention to such facts and prohibiting the manufacture, alteration, repair or finishing of said articles therein. No person, except the commissioner of labor, shall remove or deface any such placard so affixed.

Infectious, etc.,   6. None of the articles specified in this section shall be manu-
diseases.   factured, altered, repaired or finished in any room or apartment of a tenement-house where there is or has been a case of infectious, contagious or communicable disease in such room or apartment, until such time as the local department or board of health shall certify to the commissioner of labor that such disease has terminated and that said room or apartment has been properly disinfected, if disinfection after such disease is required by the local ordinances, or by the rules or regulations of such department or board. None of the articles specified in this section shall be manu-

Basement   factured, altered, repaired or finished in a part of a cellar or base-
rooms.   ment of a tenement-house, which is more than one-half of its height below the level of the curb or ground outside of or adjoin-

Unlicensed   ing the same. No person shall hire, employ or contract with any
rooms.   person to manufacture, alter, repair or finish any of the articles named in this section in any room or apartment in any tenement-house not having a license therefor issued as aforesaid. None of the articles specified in this section shall be manufactured, altered, repaired or finished in any room or apartment of a tenement-house unless said room or apartment shall be well lighted and ventilated

Air space.   and shall contain at least five hundred cubic feet of air space for every person working therein, or by any person other than the members of the family living therein; except that in licensed tenement-houses persons not members of the family may be employed in apartments on the ground floor or second floor, used only for shops of dressmakers who deal solely in the custom trade direct to the consumer, provided that such apartments shall be in the opinion of the commissioner of labor in the highest degree sanitary, well lighted, well ventilated and plumbed, and provided further that the whole number of persons therein shall not exceed one to each one thousand cubic feet of air space, and that there shall be no children under fourteen years of age living or working therein; before any such room or apartment can be so used a special permit therefor shall be issued by the commissioner of labor, a copy of which shall be entered in his public records with a statement of the reasons therefor.

Nothing in this section contained shall prevent the employment of a tailor or seamstress by any person or family for the purpose of making, altering, repairing or finishing any article of wearing apparel for the use of such person or family. Nor shall this section apply to a house if the only work therein on the articles herein specified be carried on in a shop on the main or ground floor thereof with a separate entrance to the street, unconnected with living rooms and entirely separate from the rest of the building by closed partitions without any openings whatsoever and not used for sleeping or cooking. *Exemptions.*

SEC. 101. Persons contracting for the manufacturing, altering, repairing or finishing of any of the articles mentioned in section one hundred of this article or giving out material from which they or any part of them are to be manufactured, altered, repaired or finished, shall keep a register of the names and addresses plainly written in English of the persons to whom such articles or materials are given to be so manufactured, altered, repaired or finished or with whom they have contracted to do the same. It shall be incumbent upon all persons contracting for the manufacturing, altering, repairing or finishing of any of the articles specified in section one hundred of this article or giving out material from which they or any part of them are to be manufactured, altered, repaired or finished, before giving out the same to ascertain from the office of the commissioner of labor whether the tenement-house in which such articles or materials are to be manufactured, altered, repaired or finished, is licensed as provided in this article, and also to ascertain from the local department or board of health the names and addresses of all persons then sick of any infectious, contagious or communicable disease, and residing in tenement-houses; and none of the said articles nor any material from which they or any part of them are to be manufactured, altered, repaired or finished shall be given out or sent to any person residing in a tenement-house that is not licensed as provided in this article, or to any person residing in a room or apartment in which there exists any infectious, contagious or communicable disease. The register mentioned in this section shall be subject to inspection by the commissioner of labor, and a copy thereof shall be furnished on his demand as well as such other information as he may require. *Register.*

SEC. 102. Articles manufactured, altered, repaired or finished contrary to the provisions of section one hundred of this chapter shall not be sold or exposed for sale by any person. The commissioner of labor may conspicuously affix to any such article found to be unlawfully manufactured, altered, repaired or finished, a label containing the words "tenement made" printed in small pica capital letters on a tag not less than four inches in length, or may seize and hold such article until the same shall be disinfected or cleaned at the owner's expense. The commissioner of labor shall notify the person stated by the person in possession of said article to be the owner thereof, that he has so labeled or seized it. No person except the commissioner of labor shall remove or deface any tag or label so affixed. Unless the owner or person entitled to the possession of an article so seized shall provide for the disinfection or cleaning thereof within one month thereafter it may be destroyed. *Articles not to be sold, when.* *Labels.*

SEC. 103. If the commissioner of labor finds evidence of disease present in a workshop or in a room or apartment in a tenement-house or dwelling house in which any of the articles named in *Infected articles.*

section one hundred of this chapter are manufactured, altered, repaired or finished or in process thereof, he shall affix to such articles the label prescribed in the preceding section, and immediately report to the local board of health, who shall disinfect such articles, if necessary, and thereupon remove such label. If the commissioner of labor finds that infectious or contagious diseases exist in a workshop, room or apartment of a tenement or dwelling house in which any of the articles specified in section one hundred of this chapter are being manufactured, altered, repaired or finished, or that articles manufactured or in process of manufacture therein are infected or that goods used therein are unfit for use, he shall report to the local board of health. The local health department or board in every city, town and village whenever there is any infectious, contagious or communicable disease in a tenement-house shall cause an inspection of such tenement-house to be made within forty-eight hours. If any of the articles specified in section one hundred of this chapter are found to be manufactured, altered, repaired or finished, or in process thereof in an apartment in which such disease exists, such order as the public health may require, and shall at once report such facts to the commissioner of labor, furnishing such further information as he may require. Such board may condemn and destroy all such infected article or articles manufactured or in the process of manufacture under unclean or unhealthful conditions. The local health department or board or other appropriate authority charged with the duty of sanitary inspection of such houses in every city, town and village shall, when so requested by the commissioner of labor, furnish copies of its records as to the presence of infectious, contagious or communicable disease, or of unsanitary conditions in said houses; and shall furnish such other information as may be necessary to enable the commissioner of labor to carry out the provisions of this article.

ds to be la-
when. SEC. 104. Whenever it is reported to the commissioner of labor that any of the articles named in section one hundred of this chapter are being shipped into this State, having previously been manufactured in whole or in part under unclean, unsanitary or unhealthy conditions, said commissioner shall examine said articles and the conditions of their manufacture, and if upon such examination said goods or any part of them are found to contain vermin or to have been manufactured in improper places or under unhealthy conditions, he shall forthwith affix to them the tag or label hereinbefore described and report to the local board of health, which board shall thereupon make such order or orders as the public safety may require.

y of own-
l agents. SEC. 105. The owner or agent of a tenement-house or dwelling house shall not permit the use thereof for the manufacture, repair, alteration or finishing of any of the articles mentioned in this article contrary to its provisions. If a room or apartment in such tenement-house or dwelling house be so unlawfully used, the commissioner of labor shall serve a notice thereof upon such owner or agent. Unless such owner or agent shall cause such unlawful manufacture to be discontinued within ten days after the service of such notice, or within fifteen days thereafter institutes and faithfully prosecutes proceedings for the dispossession of the occupant of a tenement-house, or dweling house, who unlawfully manufactures, repairs, alters or finishes such articles therein, he shall be deemed guilty of a violation of this article, as if he, himself, was engaged in such unawful manufacture, repair, alteration or finishing. The unlawful manufacture, repair, alteration or finishing of any of such articles by the occupant of a room or apartment of a tenement-house or dwelling shall be a cause for dispossessing such occupant by summary proceedings to recover possession of real property, as provided in the Code of Civil Procedure.

CHAPTER 31.—*Regulation of bakeries, etc.*

SECTION 111 (as amended by chapter 637, Acts of 1911). All buildings or rooms, except kitchens in hotels and private residences, used or occupied for the purpose of making, preparing or baking bread, biscuits, pastry, cakes, doughnuts, crullers, noodles, macaroni or spaghetti, to be sold or consumed on or off the premises, shall for the purpose of this act be deemed bakeries. The commissioner of labor shall have the same powers with respect to the machinery, safety devices and sanitary conditions in hotel bakeries that he has with respect thereto in bakeries as defined by this chapter. The term cellar when used in this article shall mean a room or part of a building which is more than one-half its height below the level of the curb or ground adjoining the building (excluding area ways). The term owner as used in this article shall be construed to mean the owner or owners of the freehold of the premises, or the lessee or joint lessees of the whole thereof, or his, her or their agent in charge of the property. The term occupier shall be construed to mean the person, firm or corporation in actual possession of the premises, who either himself makes, prepares or bakes any of the articles mentioned in this section, or hires or employs others to do it for him. Bakeries are factories within the meaning of this chapter, and subject to all the provisions of article six hereof. *Scope of law.* *Definitions.*

SEC. 112 (as amended by chapter 637, Acts of 1911). All bakeries shall be provided with proper and sufficient drainage and with suitable sinks, supplied with clean running water, for the purpose of washing and keeping clean the utensils and apparatus used therein. All bakeries shall be provided with windows, or if deemed necessary by the commissioner of labor, with ventilating hoods and pipes over ovens and ash pits, or with other mechanical means, to so ventilate same as to render harmless to the persons working therein, any steam, gases, vapors, dust, excessive heat or any impurities that may be generated or released by or in the process of making, preparing or baking in said bakeries. Every bakery shall be at least eight feet in height measured from the surface of the finished floor to the under side of the ceiling, and shall have a flooring of even, smooth cement, or of tiles laid in cement, or a wooden floor, so laid and constructed as to be free from cracks, holes and interstices, except that any cellar or basement less than eight feet in height which was used for a bakery on the second day of May, eighteen hundred and ninety-five, need not be altered to conform to this provision with respect to height; the side walls and ceiling shall be either plastered, ceiled or wainscoted. The furniture, troughs and utensils shall be so arranged and constructed as not to prevent their cleaning or the cleaning of every part of the bakery. Every bakery shall be provided with a sufficient number of water-closets, and such water-closets shall be separate and apart from and unconnected with the bake room or rooms where food products are stored or sold. *Sanitation and construction.*

SEC. 113 (as amended by chapter 637, Acts of 1911). All floors, walls, stairs, shelves, furniture, utensils, yards, area ways, plumbing, drains and sewers, in or in connection with bakeries in bakery water-closets and wash rooms, in rooms where raw materials are stored, and in rooms where the manufactured product is stored, shall at all times be kept in good repair, and maintained in a clean and sanitary condition, free from all kinds of vermin. All interior woodwork, walls and ceilings shall be painted or limewashed once every three months, where so required by the commissioner of labor. Proper sanitary receptacles shall be provided and used for storing coal, ashes, refuse and garbage. Receptacles for refuse and garbage shall have their contents removed from bakeries daily and shall be maintained in a cleanly and sanitary condition at all times; the use of tobacco in any form in a bakery or room where raw materials or manufactured product of such bakery is stored is prohibited. No person shall sleep, or be per- *Maintenance.* *Refuse.* *Use of tobacco.* *Sleeping, etc.*

mitted, allowed or suffered to sleep in a bakery, in a room where
raw materials are stored, or in rooms where the manufactured
product is stored or sold, and no domestic animals or birds,
except cats, shall be allowed to remain in any such rooms.

Inspection.   SEC. 114 (as amended by chapter 637, Acts of 1911). It shall be
the duty of the owner of a building wherein a bakery is located
to comply with all the provisions of section one hundred and
twelve of this article, and of the occupier to comply with all the
provisions of section one hundred and thirteen of this article,
unless by the terms of a valid lease the responsibility for compliance therewith has been undertaken by the other party to the
lease, and a duplicate original lease, containing such obligation,
shall have been previously filed in the office of the commissioner
of labor, in which event the party assuming the responsibility
shall be responsible for such compliance. The commissioner of
labor may, in his discretion, apply any or all of the provisions of
this article to a factory located in a cellar wherein any food product is manufactured: *Provided*, That basements or cellars used as
confectionery or ice cream manufacturing shops shall not be
required to conform to the requirement as to height of rooms.
Such establishments shall be not less than seven feet in height,
except that any cellar or basement so used before October first,
nineteen hundred and six, which is more than six feet in height
need not be altered to conform to this provision. If on inspection
the commissioner of labor find a bakery or any part thereof to
be so unclean, ill drained or ill ventilated as to be unsanitary, he
may, after not less than forty-eight hours' notice in writing, to be
served by affixing the notice on the inside of the main entrance
door of said bakery, order the person found in charge thereof
immediately to cease operating it until it shall be properly cleaned,
drained or ventilated. If such bakery be thereupon continued in

Closing bakery. operation or be thereafter operated before it be properly cleaned,
drained or ventilated, the commissioner of labor may, after first
making and filing in the public records of his office a written order
stating the reasons therefor, at once and without further notice
fasten up and seal the oven or other cooking apparatus of said
bakery, and affix to all materials, receptacles, tools and instruments found therein, labels or conspicuous signs bearing the word
" unclean." No one but the commissioner of labor shall remove
any such seal, label or sign, and he may refuse to remove it until
such bakery be properly cleaned, drained or ventilated.

CHAPTER 37.—*Inspectors of public works—Employment in department of labor.*

Transfer of in-   SECTION 3. * * * During such periods of the year as in
spectors.   the judgment of the superintendent of public works, the services
of the inspectors provided to be appointed by this article shall
not be needed in the administration of the provisions of this
article, he may, upon request of the commissioner of labor, for
temporary periods, transfer such inspectors to the department of
labor, and during the periods in which said inspectors are so
transferred, they shall be subject to the jurisdiction of the commissioner of labor and subject to detail by him as experts in the
administration of the labor law. * * *

ACTS OF 1901.

CHAPTER 466.—AMENDING THE CHARTER OF GREATER NEW YORK.

CHAPTER 8.—*Inspection of steam boilers—New York City.*

Boilers to be re-   SECTION 342. Every owner, agent or lessee of a steam boiler or
ported.   boilers in use in the city of New York shall annually, and at such
convenient times and in such manner and in such form as may,
by rules and regulations to be made therefor by the police com-

missioner be provided, report to the said department the location
of each steam boiler or boilers, and thereupon, and as soon thereafter as practicable, the sanitary company or such member or
members thereof as may be competent for the duty herein described, and may be detailed for such duty by the police commis-   Inspection.
sioner shall proceed to inspect such steam boilers, and all apparatus and appliances connected therewith; but no person shall be
detailed for such duty except he be a practical engineer, and the
strength and security of each boiler shall be tested by atmospheric
and hydrostatic pressure and the strength and security of each
boiler or boilers so tested shall have, under the control of said
sanitary company, such attachments, apparatus and appliances as
may be necessary for the limitation of pressure, locked and secured in like manner as may be from time to time adopted by the
United States inspectors of steam boilers or the Secretary of the
Treasury, according to act of Congress, passed July twenty-fifth,
eighteen hundred and sixty-six; and they shall limit the pressure
of steam to be applied to or upon such boiler, certifying each inspection and such limit of pressure to the owner of the boiler inspected, and also to the engineer in charge of same, and no greater
amount of steam or pressure than that certified in the case of any
boiler shall be applied thereto. In limiting the amount of pressure, wherever the boiler under test will bear the same, the limit
desired by the owner of the boiler shall be the one certified.
Every owner, agent or lessee of a steam boiler or boilers in use
in the city of New York shall, for the inspection and testing of
such or each of such boilers, as provided for in this act, and upon
receiving from the police department a certificate setting forth   Certificate.
the location of the boiler inspected, the date of such inspection, the
persons by whom the inspection was made, and the limit of steam
pressure which shall be applied to or upon such boiler or each of
such boilers, pay annually to the police commissioner for each
boiler, for the use of the police pension fund, the sum of two dol-   Fee.
lars, such certificate to continue in force for one year from the
granting thereof when it shall expire, unless sooner revoked or
suspended. Such certificate may be renewed upon the payment
of a like sum and like conditions, to be applied to a like purpose.
It shall not be lawful for any person or persons, corporation or
corporations, to have used or operated within the city of New
York any steam boiler or boilers except for heating purposes and
for railway locomotives, without having first had such boiler or
boilers inspected or tested and procured for such boiler or each
of such boilers so used or operated the certificate herein provided
for. The superintendent and inspectors of boilers, in the employ
of the police department, in the city of Brooklyn, and the boiler
inspectors in Long Island City, shall continue to discharge the
duties heretofore devolved upon them, subject, however, to removal for cause, or when they are no longer needed.

SEC. 343. It shall not be lawful for any person or persons to   Engineer's cer-
operate or use any steam boiler to generate steam except for rail-   tificate required.
way locomotive engines, and for heating purposes in private dwell-
ings, and boilers carrying not over ten pounds of steam and not
over ten horsepower, or to act as engineer for such purposes in
the city of New York without having a certificate of qualification
therefor from practical engineers detailed as such by the police
department, such certificate to be countersigned by the officer in
command of the sanitary company of the police department of
the city of New York and to continue in force one year, unless
sooner revoked or suspended. Such certificate may be revoked or
suspended at any time by the police commissioner upon the report of any two practical engineers, detailed as provided in this
section, stating the grounds upon which such certificate should
be revoked or suspended. Where such certificate shall have been
revoked, as provided in this section, a like certificate shall not
in any case be issued to the same person within six months from
the date of the revocation of the former certificate held by such
person.

Records.

SEC. 344. A correct record in proper form shall be kept and preserved of all inspections of steam boilers made under the direction of the police board, and of the amount of steam or pressure allowed in each case, and in cases where any steam boiler or the apparatus or appliances connected therewith shall be deemed by the department, after inspection, to be insecure or dangerous, the department may prescribe such changes and alterations as may render such boilers, apparatus and appliances secure and devoid of danger. And in the meantime, and until such changes and alterations are made and such appliances attached, such boiler, apparatus and appliances may be taken under the control of the police department and all persons prevented from using the same, and in cases deemed necessary, the appliances, apparatus or attachment for the limitation of pressure may be taken under the control of the said police department.

Exceeding authorized pressure.

SEC. 345. It shall not be lawful for any person or persons to apply or cause to be applied to any steam boiler a higher pressure of steam than that limited for the same in accordance with the provisions of this chapter and any person violating the provisions

Failing to report.

of the last preceding section shall be guilty of a misdemeanor. In case any owner of any steam boiler in the said city shall fail or omit to have the same reported for inspection, as provided by law, such boiler may be taken under the control of the police department and all persons prevented from using the same until it can be satisfactorily tested, as hereinbefore provided for, and the owner shall, in such case, be charged with the expense of so testing it.

NORTH CAROLINA.

ACTS OF 1909.

CHAPTER 637.—*Fire escapes on factories, etc.*

Doors to open outward.

SECTION 3. All doors for ingress and egress * * * of all * * * factories with more than twenty employees * *. * which shall hereafter be erected, together with all those heretofore erected and which are still in use as such buildings * * * shall be so hung as to open outwardly from the * * * workshops of such buildings or places: *Provided,* That said doors may be hung on double hinges, so as to open with equal ease outwardly or inwardly.

Fire escapes.

SEC. 4. All factories, manufactories, establishments or workshops of three or more stories in height, in which thirty or more people are employed above the first floor thereof, shall be provided with one or (if the proper officials shall deem necessary) more outside fire escapes, not less than six feet in length and three feet in width, properly and safely constructed, guarded by iron railings not less than three feet in length and taking in at least one door and one window or two windows at each story and connected with the interior by easily accessible and unobstructed openings; and the said fire escapes shall connect by iron stairs not less than twenty-four inches wide, the steps to be not less than six inches tread, placed at not more than an angle of forty-five degrees slant and protected by a well-secured hand rail on both sides, with a twelve-inch wide drop ladder from the lowest platform reaching

Other provisions.

to the ground; that no outside fire escapes shall be required where there are already sufficient inside stairways; that for every twenty people employed on any floor above the second floor of every factory and workshop there shall be one rope or portable fire escape, and that each story shall be amply supplied with means for extinguishing fires; that all the main doors, both inside and outside, in factories, except fire doors, shall open outwardly when the proper official shall so direct, and that no outside or inside door of any building wherein operatives are employed shall be so locked, bolted or otherwise fastened during the hours of labor as to prevent egress.

SEC. 5. * * * every building in which twenty or more persons are employed above the second story in a factory, workshop or mercantile or other establishment, the owner or agent of the owner of which said buildings is notified in writing by the insurance commissioner or any one of his deputies, shall be provided with proper ways of egress or other means of escape .from fire sufficient for the use of all persons * * * employed * * * in such building or buildings, and such ways of egress and means of escape shall be kept free from obstructions, in good repair and ready for use. Every room above the second story in any such building in which twenty or more persons are employed shall be provided with more than one way of egress by stairways on the inside or outside of the building. All doors in any building subject to the provisions of this act shall open outwardly, if the insurance commissioner or one or his deputies shall direct in writing. *Means of egress.*

SEC. 6. The insurance commissioner is charged with the execution of this law, and the said commissioner or chief of the fire department are hereby vested with all privileges, duties and obligations placed upon them in section four, chapter fifty-eight, Public Laws of one thousand eight hundred and ninety-nine, in regard to the inspection of buildings for the purpose of enforcing the provisions of this act in regard to the buildings and requirements herein, and any owner or occupant of premises failing to comply with the provisions of this act in accordance with the orders of the authorities above specified shall be guilty of a misdemeanor and punished by a fine of not less than ten dollars nor more than fifty dollars for each day's neglect: *Provided, however,* That if any owner or lessee of any building referred to in this act shall deem himself aggrieved by any ruling or order of any chief of fire department or local inspector, he may within twenty-four hours appeal to the insurance commissioner, and the cause of complaint shall at once be investigated by the direction of said commissioner, and unless by his authority the order or ruling is revoked it shall remain in full force and effect and be forthwith complied with by said owner or lessee. *Enforcement.* *Violations.*

ACTS OF 1911.

CHAPTER 57.—*Factory regulations—Provisions for accidents.*

SECTION 1. Every person, firm, or corporation operating a factory or shop employing over twenty-five laborers, in which machinery is used for any manufacturing purpose, or for any purpose except for elevation or for heating or hoisting apparatus, shall at all times keep and maintain free of expense to the employees a medical or surgical chest which shall contain two porcelain pans, two tourniquets, gauze, absorbent cotton, adhesive plasters, bandages, antiseptic soap, one bottle of carbolic acid with directions on bottle, one bottle antiseptic tablets, one pair of scissors, one folding stretcher, all of which shall not cost to exceed ten dollars, for the treatment of persons injured or taken ill upon the premises. *Medical, etc., supplies required.*

SEC. 2. Any person, firm or corporation violating this act shall be subject to a fine of not less than five dollars or more than twenty-five dollars for every week during which such violation continues. *Violations.*

NORTH DAKOTA.

REVISED CODES—1905.

POLITICAL CODE.

Factories and workshops—Fire escapes—Doors to open outward.

SECTION 2175. The owners and proprietors of all hotels, factories, public halls, offices and other buildings in this State, over *Fire escapes to be provided.*

two stories in height, are required to provide safe and suitable fire escapes from all rooms above the second story of such hotel or other building, and· when rooms have no outside windows there shall be affixed to the window in the hallway leading from such room at least three fire escapes in each window as herein directed. Such fire escape shall consist of at least one good cotton rope not less than one inch in diameter, to be securely and permanently· fastened with iron rings or bolts·at a point immediately outside or inside of at least one window in each room above the second story; and such rope shall be of sufficient length to reach to the

Proviso.   ground: *Provided,* That if the owner or proprietor of any such buildings shall provide good and sufficient iron ladders extending from each of the windows herein mentioned, and from points immediately adjacent to each of such windows, to the ground, securely and permanently fastened to such building, or shall have the fire escape ladder in each of the rooms and hall windows aforesaid, of sufficient length to reach from such windows to the ground, he will be deemed to have complied with the requirements of this section.

Penalty.   SEC. 2176. Any person violating any of the provisions of the last section shall be punished by a fine of not less than twenty-five dollars for each room in such hotel or other building not provided with fire escapes as aforesaid.

Doors to open outward.   SEC. 2177. All doors of ingress and egress in all buildings used for * * * factories, * * * wherein numbers of persons are employed * * * shall be so constructed as to open and swing outward, and doorways shall not be less than four feet in width, with proper landings and stairways of at least equal width.

Who to make changes.   SEC. 2178. It shall be the duty of all persons owning or having charge of such buildings, * * * to comply with the provisions of the last section * * *.

Penalty.   SEC. 2179. Any person failing to comply with the provisions of * * * [section 2177], or who shall build, maintain or permit to be used any such building contrary to the provisions hereof shall be deemed guilty of a misdemeanor.

OHIO.

GENERAL CODE—1910.

Regulation and inspection of factories and workshops—Inspectors.

Chief inspector.   SECTION 979. The governor, with the advice and consent of the senate, shall appoint a chief inspector of workshops and factories, who shall hold his office for a term of four years from the first day of May following his appointment and until his successor is appointed and qualified. He shall have an office in the state-house in which the records of the department shall be kept.

Qualifications and duties.   SEC. 980. The chief inspector of workshops and factories shall be a competent and practical mechanic, and shall give his whole time and attention to the duties of his office. He shall enforce the provisions of this chapter and the laws relating to workshops, factories and public buildings, prosecute violations thereof and perform such other duties as are required of him by law.

Bond.   SEC. 981. Before entering upon the discharge of the duties of his office, the chief inspector of workshops and factories shall give a bond to the State in the sum of five thousand dollars with two or more sureties approved by the governor conditioned for the faithful discharge of the duties of his office. Such bond with the approval of the governor and the oath of office indorsed thereon shall be deposited with the secretary of state and kept in his office.

Assistant inspectors.   SEC. 982 (as amended by act, page 456, Acts of 1911). With the approval of the governor, the chief inspector of workshops and factories shall appoint a first assistant chief inspector of workshops and factories, and a second assistant chief inspector of workshops and factories, each of whom shall give his whole time and attention to the duties of his office. The first assistant chief inspector of workshops and factories shall be a competent and practical architect, and the second assistant chief inspector of workshops and factories shall have a practical knowledge of architecture and of heating and ventilating. Such first and second assistant chief inspectors of workshops and factories shall carefully examine the plans and specifications, for the construction, addition or alteration of buildings named in section one thousand and thirty-one of this chapter, and perform such other duties as the chief inspector directs. In addition to their respective salaries, the first and second assistant chief inspectors of workshops and factories shall each be allowed his necessary traveling expenses incurred in the discharge of his official duties.

SEC. 983. Before entering on the discharge of the duties of his office, he shall give bond to the State in the sum of two thousand dollars, with two or more sureties, approved by the governor, conditioned for the faithful discharge of the duties of his office. Such bond, with the approval of the governor and the oath of office indorsed thereon, shall be deposited with the secretary of state and kept in his office. *Bonds of assistants.*

SEC. 984. With the approval of the governor, the chief inspector of workshops and factories shall appoint twenty-five district inspectors of workshops and factories, each of whom shall hold his office for a term of three years from the first day of May after his appointment and until his successor is appointed and qualified. *District inspectors.*

SEC. 985. Each district inspector of workshops and factories shall be a competent and practical mechanic, and must devote his whole time and attention to the duties of his office. Ten of such inspectors shall have knowledge of building construction, and one shall be a skilled and experienced person who is thoroughly conversant with the manufacture and use of powder, dynamite, nitroglycerin, fuses and other explosives and their compounds. *Qualifications.*

SEC. 986. Each district inspector shall give a bond to the State in the sum of two thousand dollars with two or more sureties approved by the governor conditioned for the faithful discharge of the duties of his office. Such bond with the approval of the governor and the oath of office indorsed thereon shall be deposited with the secretary of state and kept in his office. *Bonds.*

SEC. 987. The chief inspector of workshops and factories shall divide the State into districts, make such assignments of district inspectors therein, and prescribe such rules and regulations for their government as the service may require. Twelve district inspectors shall be assigned especially to the inspection of shops and factories, two to the inspection of bakeries, and the district inspector skilled in the manufacture and use of explosives to the inspection of buildings in which such explosives are manufactured or stored. *Districts.*

SEC. 988. Each district inspector of workshops and factories shall visit the shops and factories of the district assigned him as often as practicable, see that the laws relating to workshops and factories are enforced, and perform such other duties pertaining to the department of workshops and factories as the chief inspector directs. *Duties of district inspectors.*

SEC. 989. Each district inspector of workshops and factories assigned to a district for the inspection of shops and factories therein, shall carefully inspect the sanitary conditions, system of sewerage, situation and condition of water-closets, system of heating, lighting and ventilating rooms where persons are employed at labor, and the means of exit in case of fire or other disaster, within or connected with such shops and factories. He shall examine the belting, shafting, gearing, elevators, drums and machinery in and about such shops and factories, and see that they are not so located as to be dangerous to employees when engaged in their ordinary duties, and, so far as practicable, securely guarded. He shall see that each vat, pan or structure filled with molten metal or hot liquid is surrounded by proper safeguards for preventing accident or injury to persons employed at or near them. *Same subject.*

Bakeries.

SEC. 990. Each inspector of workshops and factories assigned to a district for the inspection of bakeries therein, shall visit each bakery in his district as often as practicable, see that the laws relating to workshops and factories and the laws relating to bakeries are strictly enforced, and perform such other duties pertaining to the department of workshops and factories as the chief inspector directs.

Manufacture of explosives.

SEC. 991. The district inspector of workshops and factories assigned to the inspection of buildings wherein explosives are manufactured or stored, shall inspect all manufacturing establishments in the State wherein powder, dynamite, nitroglycerine, compounds, fuses or other explosives are manufactured, all magazines or storehouses wherein such explosives are stored, and perform such other duties connected with the department of workshops and factories as the chief inspector of workshops and factories directs.

Same subject.

SEC. 992. The district inspector of workshops and factories assigned to the inspection of buildings in which explosives are manufactured or stored shall inspect the process of manufacture and the handling and storing of such explosives, and may order such changes or additions in or about such manufactories, magazines or storehouses, as he deems necessary for the safety of the employees and the public. If such manufactory, magazine or storehouse is in such close proximity to a residence or dwelling as to cause accident in case of explosion, he may cause the explosives to be removed to a place of safety. With the advice of the chief inspector, the inspector of explosives may provide such rules and regulations as he deems necessary, which, with the laws relating thereto, and to the duties of the inspector of workshops and factories and district inspectors, shall be applicable to the places of manufacturing, sale and storage of such explosives.

Traveling expenses.

SEC. 993. The necessary traveling expenses of the chief inspector of workshops and factories and each district inspector, incurred in the discharge of his official duties shall be paid by the State.

Entering factories, etc.

SEC. 994. For the purpose of an inspection or examination required of him by law, the chief inspector of workshops and factories, and each district inspector at reasonable hours may enter a shop or factory, a State institution having a shop or factory, a bakery, or a building in which powder or other explosives are manufactured or stored.

Power as to oaths.

SEC. 995. In the performance of his duties pertaining to his office, the chief inspector of workshops and factories and each district inspector shall have the authority of a notary public to administer oaths and take affidavits.

Notice of alterations.

SEC. 996 (as amended by act, page 360, Acts of 1911). If the chief inspector of workshops and factories or a district inspector finds that the heating, lighting, ventilation or sanitary arrangements of a shop or factory are injurious to the health of persons employed or residing therein, that the means of egress therefrom in case of fire or other disaster is not sufficient, that efficient means for extinguishing fires is not provided on each floor, that the belting, shafting, gearing, elevators, drums and machinery therein are so located as to be dangerous to employees and not safely guarded, or that the vats, pans or structures filled with molten metal or hot liquid are not surrounded by proper safeguards for preventing accident or injury to persons employed at or near them, or that there is danger from explosives in a building in which explosives are manufactured or stored, he shall notify the owner, proprietor or agent of such shop or factory or building by personally serving a notice in writing, or mailing it to his last known address, to make the necessary alterations or additions. Said notice shall describe the alterations and additions which shall be installed therein and the time in which each alteration or addition therein required shall be made and each appliance installed.

Changes to be made.

SEC. 997 (as amended by act, page 360, Acts of 1911). Upon receipt of the notice provided in the next preceding section, the owner, proprietor, or agent of a shop or factory shall make the necessary alterations or additions to such shop or factory or install the appliances therein required within the time designated therein.

SEC. 998 (as amended by act, page 360, Acts of 1911). Whoever being notified by the chief inspector of workshops and factories or a district inspector to make alterations or additions to a shop or factory or to install appliances therein fails or refuses to comply with any requirement of such notice within the time therein designated as provided in the preceding two sections or the provisions of section 1000 of the General Code shall be fined not less than fifty ($50) dollars nor more than one hundred ($100) dollars for each day after the expiration of the time so designated until such alterations and additions have been made. Such failure or refusal shall constitute a single offense and the amount of the fine imposed under these sections shall be dependent upon the number of days as herein provided. *Failure to comply.*

Any person who has been convicted and fined under the provisions of the next two preceding sections or the provisions of section 1000 of the General Code may be prosecuted and convicted from time to time under these sections until the alterations and additions have been made or the appliances installed as required in such order; if convicted in such subsequent prosecution, the amount of the fine shall be computed upon the number of days intervening between the date of the former conviction and the filing of the subsequent affidavit. *Continuing offenses.*

SEC. 999. Proof of the failure of the proprietor of a shop or factory to make alterations or furnish the safeguards ordered by the chief inspector of workshops and factories or a district inspector within the time designated shall be deemed prima facie evidence of negligence and render such proprietor liable for injury sustained by reason of a failure to make such alterations or furnish such safeguards. *Failure to obey orders.*

SEC. 1000. Upon an examination as provided by law, if it is found necessary to cut through the walls or floors of a shop or factory to provide stairways on the inside or outside for additional exits in case of fire or other disaster; if found necessary to make changes in or additions to a shop or factory for ventilation, sewerage, water-closets or plumbing, for additional means of lighting by windows or skylights, for efficient safety-guards at elevator openings, for the guarding of hatchways, for hoisting apparatus in floors or outside, for the repair of elevators or gearing, for the repair of walls, roofs, ceilings, stairways or doors, or, if found necessary to make any other improvement needful for the health or safety of the employees or persons occupying a shop or factory, the chief inspector of workshops and factories shall require the owner or agent of the building in which such shop or factory is situated, to provide the necessary fire escapes, changes, additions or improvements, if·they are of permanent character and will become the property of the owner of the building in which such shop or factory is located. Notice thereof must be given in writing to such owner or agent, which may be mailed to his last known address. Such time may be allowed for compliance therewith as the chief inspector of workshops and factories deems necessary. *Ordering changes.*

SEC. 1001. Each district inspector of workshops and factories shall make a record of shops and factories in his district, showing the date when an examination was made, the condition in which the shop or factory was found and what changes were ordered. The record shall also show the number of shops and factories in the district, the number of men, women and·children employed in each, and such other facts and information concerning the condition of such shops and factories as the chief inspector deems necessary. Each week this record shall be filed in the office of the chief inspector, and so much of it as is of public interest, included in his annual report. *Records.*

laition.   SEC. 1002. The term "shops and factories" as used in this chapter shall include the following: manufacturing, mechanical, electrical, mercantile, art and laundering establishments, printing, telegraph and telephone offices, railroad depots, hotels, memorial buildings, tenement and department houses.

ration may eined.   SEC. 1002-1 (added by act, page 360, Acts of 1911). If the alterations and additions required in the notice provided for in sections 996 and 1000 are not made within the time therein designated or if the appliances that are required are not installed within the time designated, the use of the building within which the shop or factory is located for shop and factory purposes as defined in section 1002, shall be deemed a public nuisance. After the expiration of the time prescribed in such notice the chief inspector of workshops and factories may in writing inform the attorney general of the fact that such notice has been given and that the person to whom it was directed has not complied therewith. On receipt thereof, the attorney general shall bring suit in the name of the State in the court of common pleas of the county where such shop or factory is located to enjoin the continued operation of such shop or factory until the requirements of such notice are complied with. In such action it shall be sufficient to serve the summons upon the person to whom the notice prescribed in sections 996 or 1000 was sent, and such summons may be served in any county of the State. The court may issue a temporary restraining order without notice to the defendant in such action. Upon final hearing thereof, if the court is satisfied that the requirements of the notice by the chief inspec[t]or of workshops and factories or the district inspector to the defendant was not unreasonable or arbitrary, it shall issue an order enjoining the defendant from the continued operation of such shop or factory or from permitting the use of such building for shop or factory purposes until compliance therewith. Such injunction shall continue operative until the court is satisfied that the requirements of such notice have been substantially complied with and the court shall have and exercise with respect to the enforcement of such injunctions all the powers vested in it in other similar cases. Both the plaintiff and defendant in such action shall have the same rights of appeal and error as are provided by law in other injunction cases.

Idents to be ed.   SEC. 1003. Every manufacturer of the State shall forward by mail to the chief inspector of workshops and factories a report of each serious accident resulting in bodily injury to a person which occurs in his establishment, giving particulars thereof as fully as can be ascertained upon blanks furnished by the chief inspector of workshops and factories. If death results from an accident to an employee, the report shall contain the name, sex, age and employment of the deceased, whether married, the number of persons, if any, deprived of support in consequence thereof, and the cause of the accident, if known. If the accident has caused bodily injury of such nature as prevents the person injured from returning to his or her employment within six or more days after the occurrence of the accident, the report shall state the cause of the injury, if known, the name, sex, age and employment of the disabled person, the nature and extent of the injuries received, the duration of continuous disability, the loss of time and wages therefrom, and if possible the expenses incurred thereby.

ations.   SEC. 1004. A manufacturer who fails to comply with the requirements of the preceding section in case of death by accident within seven days thereafter, or in case of injury by accident, within thirty days thereafter, shall be fined not less than ten dollars nor more than fifty dollars.

ition.   SEC. 1005. The term "manufacturer" as used in the preceding two sections shall include a person who as owner, manager, lessee, assignee, receiver, contractor, or as agent makes or causes to be made, or deals in any kind of goods or merchandise or who controls or operates a street railway or laundering establishment, or who is engaged in the construction of buildings, bridges or other structures, or in loading or unloading vessels or cars, moving heavy materials, or operating dangerous machinery, or engaged in the manufacture or use of explosives.

SEC. 1006. In tenement houses, apartments, manufactories, mills, shops, stores, churches, hotels, halls for public meetings, lecture rooms, restaurants, public library rooms, business offices of professional men and others doing business for or with the public, all public buildings and other rooms or places of public resort or use, whether for the transaction of business or social enjoyment, the owners, directors, trustees, lessees, managers, controllers or proprietors thereof shall provide and maintain for all stairs or stairways for ingress or egress, a substantial handrail extending from the top to the bottom thereof, and firmly fastened to the wall or other support or partition at the side of such stairs. Such handrail shall be constructed of wood not less than one and one-half inches wide and two and one-half inches thick or of iron not less than one and one-half inches in diameter. `Stairways.`

SEC. 1007. Whoever owns or has in charge such stairs or stairways as directors, trustees, lessees, managers or proprietors and neglects or refuses to provide and maintain in good repair the hand-rail provided in the preceding section shall be fined not less than ten dollars nor more than one hundred dollars and be liable to any person injured because of the want of such rail and for any injury or damages to a person resulting from a defective rail. `Violations.`

SEC. 1012. All bakeries shall be drained and plumbed in a sanitary manner and provided with such air shafts, windows or ventilating pipes, as the chief inspector of workshops and factories or a district inspector directs. No cellar or basement shall be used as a bakery. `Sanitation of bakeries.`

SEC. 1013. Each bakery shall be provided with a suitable wash room and water-closet apart from the bake room where manufacturing of food products is conducted. No water-closet, earthcloset, privy or ash pit shall be in or communicate directly with a bake shop or any bakery for a hotel or public restaurant. `Water-closets, etc.`

SEC. 1014. Each room used for the manufacture of flour and meal food products shall be at least eight feet in height. Sidewalls of such a room shall be plastered or wainscoted and the ceiling plastered or ceiled with lumber or metal. If required by the inspector of workshops and factories, such sidewalls and ceilings must be whitewashed or painted at least once in three months. The furniture, utensils and machinery of each room shall be so arranged as to be easily moved and the furniture and floor kept thoroughly cleaned and in a sanitary condition. `Construction, etc., of rooms.`

SEC. 1016. The sleeping places for persons employed in a bakery shall be kept separate from a room in which flour and meal products are manufactured or stored. The chief inspector of workshops and factories or a district inspector may inspect such sleeping places, if they are on the same premises as the bakery, and order them cleaned and changed in compliance with sanitary principles. `Sleeping places.`

SEC. 1017. If, on inspection of a bakery, it is found that the provisions herein relating to bakeries have been complied with, the chief inspector of workshops and factories may issue a certificate to the owner or operator of such bakery that is being conducted in accordance with such provisions. `Certificates.`

SEC 1018. If an order has been issued by the inspector to improve the condition of a bakery, such certificate shall not be issued until such order has been complied with. `Changes to be complied with.`

SEC. 1019. Whoever violates any provisions herein relating to bakeries or refuses to comply with a requirement of the chief inspector of workshops and factories or a district inspector made as provided herein shall be fined not less than twenty dollars nor more than fifty dollars, and not less than fifty dollars nor more than two hundred dollars, or imprisoned not more than ten days, for each succeeding offense. `Violations.`

SEC. 1020. No dwelling or building or room or apartment thereof in or connected with a tenement, dwelling or other building `Manufactures in tenements.`

shall be used, except by the members of the family living therein, for carrying on any process of making wearing apparel or goods for wear, use or adornment, or for manufacturing cigars, cigarettes or tobacco goods in any form, if such wearing apparel or other goods are to be exposed for sale or sold by a manufacturer, wholesaler or jobber or by a retailer, unless such room or apartment is made to conform to the requirements and regulations herein provided.

Workrooms.   SEC. 1021. Each room or apartment used for the purposes named in the preceding section, except by the immediate members of the family living therein, shall be regarded as a shop or factory and shall be separate from and have no door, window or other opening into a living or sleeping room of a tenement or dwelling. No such shop or factory shall be used for living or sleeping purposes or contain any bed, bedding or cooking utensils, or other utensils, except those required to carry on the work therein. Each such shop or factory shall have a direct entrance from the outside, and, if above the first floor, have a separate and distinct stairway leading thereto, and be well and sufficiently lighted, heated and ventilated.

Water-closets.   SEC. 1022. A shop or factory used for the purposes named in the preceding two sections shall have suitable closet arrangements for each sex employed therein. When there are ten or more persons and three or more to the number of twenty-five are of either sex, a separate and distinct water-closet, either inside the building with adequate plumbing and connections, or on the outside at least twenty feet from the building, shall be provided for each sex. When the number employed is more than twenty-five of either sex, there shall be provided an additional water-closet for each sex up to the number of fifty persons and above that number in the same ratio. Such closets shall be kept exclusively for the use of employees or employers in such shop or factory.

Each room a shop.   SEC. 1023. If more than one room is used under the direction of one employer for the purposes named in the preceding three sections, such rooms shall be regarded as one shop or factory. Each

Cleanliness.   shop or factory shall be kept in a clean and wholesome condition, stairways and premises within the radius of thirty feet shall be kept clean, and closets regularly disinfected and supplied with disinfectants. The chief inspector of workshops and factories or a district inspector may require necessary changes or the cleaning, painting or whitewashing necessary to insure absolute freedom from odor, filth, vermin, decaying matter or any other thing liable to impair health or breed infectious or contagious diseases. Such inspector shall prevent the operation of such shops and factories, if they do not conform to the provisions of the preceding sections, and cause the arrest and prosecution of the persons operating them.

Work not to be given out, when.   SEC. 1024. No person, firm or corporation shall give work to or contract with a person to make goods used for wearing apparel or adornment or to manufacture tobacco, after receiving notice from the chief inspector of workshops and factories or a district inspector that such person has not complied with the provisions of law relating to rooms in which such goods are manufactured. The notice shall remain in force until such person has complied with the provisions of law. Each person, firm or corporation shall obtain and keep a record of all persons to whom work is given or with whom it is contracted for or from whom such goods or tobacco is purchased, which record must include their names and addresses, and be open to the inspection of the chief inspector of workshops and factories or a district inspector.

Sale, etc., of goods.   SEC. 1025. No person or corporation shall receive, handle or convey to others, or sell, hold in stock or expose for sale the goods named in the preceding section, unless such goods are made under the sanitary conditions prescribed herein, but this does not include the making of garments or other goods for another by personal order, which will be received for wear or use direct from the maker's hands.

SEC. 1026. Whoever, being a person, firm or corporation, violates any provision of the preceding two sections shall be fined not less than fifty dollars nor more than one hundred dollars or imprisoned not less than thirty days nor more than sixty days, or both, which fine shall be collected by the court and paid into the State treasury to the credit of the general revenue fund.

SEC. 1027 (as amended by act, page 428, Acts of 1911). The Guards for dangerous machinery, etc. owners and operators of shops and factories shall make suitable provisions to prevent injury to persons who use or come in contact with machinery therein or any part thereof as follows:

1. They shall case or box all shafting operating horizontally near floors, or perpendicularly or otherwise between, from or through floors or traversing near floors, or when operating near a passageway or directly over the heads of the employees.

2. They shall enclose with substantial railings or casing all exposed cogwheels, flywheels, band wheels, main belts, transmitting power from engine to dynamo, or other kind of machinery and all openings through floors, through or in which such wheels or belts may operate.

3. They shall cover, cut off or countersink keys, bolts, set screws and all parts of wheels, shafting or other revolving machinery projecting unevenly beyond the surface of such revolving machinery.

4. They shall case in all unused openings of elevators and elevator shafts and place automatic gates or floor doors on each floor where entrance to the elevator carriage is obtained. They shall keep such gates or doors in good repair and examine frequently and keep in sound condition the ropes, gearing and other parts of elevators.

5. They shall close stair openings on each floor, except where access to stairs is obtained, and rail such stairs between floors.

6. They shall light the hallways, rooms, approaches to rooms, basements and other places wherein sufficient daylight is not obtainable.

7. They shall guard all saws, wood-cutting, wood-shaping and all other dangerous machinery.

8. They shall provide shifters for shifting belts, and poles and other appliances for removing, replacing and repairing belts or single pulleys.

9. They shall adjust with handrailing, runways and staging used for oiling and other purposes when more than five feet from floors.

10. They shall provide countershafting in each room separate from the engine-room, with tight and loose pulleys and other suitable appliances for disconnecting machinery when in operation.

11. They shall provide emery wheels or belts of solid emery, Blowers for emery wheels, etc. leather, leather covered, felt, canvas, linen, paper, cotton or wheels or belts, rolled or coated with emery or corundum, or cotton wheels used as buffs, with blowers or similar apparatus placed over, beside or under such wheels or belts in such a manner as to protect the person or persons using them from particles of dust produced and caused thereby.

12. They shall provide each emery wheel with a sheet or cast iron hood or hopper of such form and so applied to it that the dust or refuse therefrom will fall from such wheels or will be thrown into such hood or hopper by centrifugal force and be carried off by the current of air into a suction pipe attached to such hood or hopper.

13. They shall provide an emery wheel six inches or less in diameter with a three-inch suction pipe, and emery wheel six inches to twenty-four inches in diameter with a four-inch suction pipe; an emery wheel twenty-four inches to thirty-six inches in diameter with a five-inch suction pipe and every emery wheel larger than those provided for with a suction pipe not less than six inches in diameter. Such suction pipe shall be full-sized to the main trunk suction pipe, and the main suction pipe to which smaller pipes are attached shall be equal in its diameter and capac-

ity to the combined area of the smaller.pipes attached to it. The
discharge pipe from the exhaust fan connected with pipe or pipes
shall be as large or larger than the suction pipe.

14. They shall provide necessary fans or blowers connected
with suction pipes, which shall be run at a rate of speed sufficient
to produce a velocity of air in such suction or discharge pipes of
at least nine thousand feet per minute to an equivalent suction or
pressure of air equal to raising a volume of water not less than
five inches in a U-shaped tube. All branch suction pipes must
enter the main pipe at an angle of forty-five degrees or less; the
main suction or trunk pipe shall be below the emery or buffing
wheels and as close to them as possible and be either upon the
floor or beneath the floor on which the machinery to which such
wheels are attached are placed. All bends, turns or elbows in
such suction pipes must be made with easy smooth surfaces having a radius in the throat of not less than two diameters of the
pipe on which they are connected.

Uses of water.   15. Nothing in this section regarding blowers, hoods, hoppers,
or suction pipes shall apply to emery wheels upon which water is
used at the point of grinding contact, small emery wheels used
temporarily for tool grinding or small shops employing not more
than one man at work upon an emery wheel, which does not create
dust enough in the opinion of the chief inspector of workshops
and factories or a district inspector to be injurious to its operator.

Employment of females.   No female shall be employed in operating, assisting to operate, or
using any of the wheels or belts specified in the preceding four
subdivisions of this section.

Violations.   SEC. 1028. Whoever, being a person, firm or corporation, fails
to comply with any provision of the preceding section, or fails to
comply with such orders for changes as are issued by the chief
inspector, within thirty days thereafter shall be fined not less
than fifty dollars nor more than two hundred dollars for each
offense. * * * In prosecutions for violations of this section.
by or under the direction of the chief inspector, such inspector
shall not be required to give security for costs or adjudged to
pay any costs. In cases where the accused is acquitted, the costs
shall be paid from the treasury of the county in which such proceedings were brought.

Means of egress.   SEC. 1028-1 (added by act, page 360, Acts of 1911). The owners
of buildings wherein shops or factories are operated shall make
suitable provisions for the safe and speedy egress therefrom in
case of fire or other disaster of persons employed in such shop or
factory or residing therein or who may be invited any time there-
into as follows:

1. They shall provide on each floor or basement of each section
of such building separated from other sections or parts thereof by
fire walls, or not so separated, and in which a shop or factory is
operated, excepting only rooms on such floors or basements used
only for storage purposes, two separate and distinct means of
egress placed at opposite ends of the section or building and
located as far apart as possible. Such means of egress shall be
either an inclosed fireproof stairway running continuously from
each floor on which such shop or factory is operated to the grade
line and opening directly to the outside of the building; or a
standard fire escape leading from such floors to the grade line or
a convenient and safe distance above grade line; or a self-closing
door leading directly to the next adjoining section of the same
building containing a stairway, or a door opening directly upon a
street, alley or open court.

2. They shall provide substantial handrails on each side of all
stairways.

3. They shall provide on each floor on which a shop or factory
is operated doors or other means of egress therefrom to such fire
escapes or inside stairways, which said doors or other means of
egress must swing outward and toward the natural means of
egress, and if capable of being locked or latched, the same must
be operated from the inside.

4. They shall provide signs over all doors as exits and over all openings or passageways leading to exits which shall be clearly marked with the word "Exit" in plain block letters not less than six inches high; such signs shall be so placed that they may be seen from any part of the room, if possible.

5. They shall so arrange and hang doors and windows or other means of egress to fire escapes or fireproof stairways that when open they shall not obstruct or close off any of the passageway or in any way interfere with the use of fire escapes or other means of egress.

SEC. 1028-2 (added by act, page 360, Acts of 1911). The owners and operators of manufacturing, mechanical, electrical, mercantile, art and laundering establishments, printing, telegraph and telephone offices, and railroad depots shall observe the following rules and regulations for the safety of persons employed or assembled therein: *Rules for safety.*

1. The number of persons at any time employed or permitted to work or to be assembled therein shall at no time be such as to provide fewer than the following number of square feet of floor space for each person:

If the establishment, office or depot is in a basement there shall be ten square feet to a person; if on the first or grade floor, eight square feet to a person; if on the second floor, ten square feet to a person; if on the third floor, fifteen square feet to a person; if on the fourth floor, twenty square feet to a person; if on the fifth floor, thirty square feet to a person; if on the sixth floor, forty square feet to a person; if on the seventh floor, sixty square feet to a person; if on the eighth floor, eighty square feet to a person; if on the ninth floor, one hundred square feet to a person; if on or above the tenth floor, one hundred and twenty-five square feet to a person.

2. The number of persons employed or permitted to work or assemble therein shall at no time be greater than one hundred persons for each three feet of exit space, but this ratio may be decreased where highly inflammable materials are manufactured, sold or stored, by order of the chief inspector of workshops and factories, a district inspector thereof, or the chief of any fire department having authority in the premises.

3. Each floor on which any establishment mentioned in this section is located shall be provided with standpipe with one and one-half inch hose not more than seventy-five feet in length so located that any part of the floor may be reached by a stream of water expelled therefrom, and where water supply is not available, fire extinguishers or barrels of salt water with round bottom buckets may be substituted.

4. The floors of all such establishments shall be swept at least once a day, and the sweepings therefrom removed from every room thereof.

5. No door or other means of egress shall be locked, barred or bolted during the time when such shop or factory is operated.

6. Such owners or operators shall provide passageways or aisles equal in width to such doors or exits and leading to the same from all parts of the floor on which the shop or factory is operated, and shall keep such passageways or aisles at all times clear of all obstructions.

In computing the number of persons who may be employed or assembled in any such establishment, the portion of the floor space occupied by counters, cases and fixtures, or from which the public is excluded, shall be deemed and regarded as floor space.

SEC. 1028-3 (added by act, page 360, Acts of 1911). Whoever violates any of the provisions of the preceding sections shall be fined not less than one hundred ($100) dollars nor more than one thousand ($1,000) dollars. *Violations.*

SEC. 1029. The chief inspector of workshops and factories, or a district inspector, if he deems it advisable, may paste upon a machine, device, elevator, utensil, structure or machinery, or part thereof, a notice stating that it or a part thereof does not conform *Notice as to dangerous machinery.*

to the provisions of the second preceding section, and that operators or employees are liable to injury by operating it. Such notice shall designate and describe the alteration or other change necessary to be made in order to secure safety of operation, date of inspection, and time allowed for such alteration or change. After the pasting of such notice on a machine, it shall not be used or operated until the changes or alterations indicated in the notice have been made to the satisfaction of the chief inspector or district inspector.

Violations.

SEC. 1030. Whoever, being the owner or operator of a shop or factory, violates any provision of the preceding section shall be fined for the first offense not less than twenty-five dollars, nor more than one hundred dollars, and for each subsequent offense not less than fifty dollars nor more than five hundred dollars.

Steam boilers.

SEC. 1054. All stationary steam boilers used or operated by a person, firm or corporation shall be equipped by such person, firm or corporation with a low water safety alarm column which shall sound an alarm for the purpose of calling the attention of the engineer, fireman or person in charge to the depth of the water in the boiler, before it reaches the danger point. Such low water safety alarm column shall be capable of being easily tested and shall be so connected with the boiler that the low water alarm will be sounded when there is not less than two inches of water over the highest point of the tubes or crown sheets.

Penalty.

SEC. 1055. Whoever, being a person, member of a firm or officer of a corporation, violates or refuses or neglects to comply with any provision of the preceding section shall be fined not less than twenty-five dollars nor more than fifty dollars or imprisoned in the county jail not less than thirty days nor more than ninety days, or both.

Fire escapes on factories, etc.

Exits required.

SECTION 4658. If a factory, workshop, tenement house, inn or public house is more than two stories high, the owner or agent of the owner shall provide convenient exits from the different upper stories thereof, which shall be easily accessible in case of fire, and the owner or person having control of an inn or public house where travelers or boarders are lodged above the second story thereof, shall also provide a good rope or other life line for each sleeping room for guests above such story.

Life-saving devices.

SEC. 4659. The owner or agent of the owner of a factory, workshop, tenement house, inn, or public house, if it is more than three stories high, in addition to the provisions governing three-story buildings, shall provide a life-saving device or net, which shall be approved by the fire chief of the city, or village in which such building is situated, or if such building is situated outside of the city or village, such life-saving device or net shall be approved by the State inspector of workshops and factories. Such life-saving device or net shall be kept on the first floor at or near the entrance of the building.

Enforcement.

SEC. 4660. The mayor of each municipality shall require the owner or agent of the owner of such factory, workshop, tenement house, or inn or public house, within the meaning of the preceding two sections to comply with the requirements of such section within sixty days from the serving of a notice by the mayor so to do, unless such owner or agent for owner shall have previously complied with the requirements of such sections. Whoever being such owner or agent of owner fails to comply with the requirements of the preceding three sections within the time specified in such notice, shall forfeit not less than fifty nor more than three hundred dollars for each month he so fails, to be recovered in the name of and for the use of such municipality in an action in the police court or other competent tribunal. Such owner or agent for owner may also be held for civil damages to the party injured.

SEC. 4661. The mayor of each municipality, personally, or by the Inspections. marshal or chief of police thereof, or other proper person whom the mayor appoints acting under his direction, as inspector of fire-escapes shall carefully examine such factories, workshops, tenement houses, inns or public houses once in each year, and report all violations of the preceding five sections to the council thereof, and thereupon proceedings shall be commenced against the person so offending. The mayor, marshal, or chief of police, or persons appointed by the mayor to act as inspector of fire escapes, shall be entitled to receive for such notices and examination, such fees as the council may by ordinance provide.

Manufacture, etc., of explosives.

SECTION 5903. A person, partnership or corporation manufac- Scope of law. turing, handling, or storing gunpowder, blasting powder, dynamite, nyalite, jovite, masurite, fulminates, nitroglycerine, any nitro-explosive compound, chlorate of potash explosive compound, picric acid explosive compound, or other explosive substance, shall file with the chief inspector of workshops and factories, upon blanks furnished by him upon application, a complete statement of the Applications of manufacturers. location of such factory, storehouse or magazine owned or controlled by such person, partnership or corporation, together with the kind and character of the explosive substance or substances manufactured, handled or stored and intended to be manufactured, handled or stored thereat, the quantity stored or kept on hand, and the quantity intended to be stored or kept on hand, the number of persons employed at each factory, storehouse or magazine and the number of persons intended to be employed thereat, and the distance which such factory, storehouse or magazine is located or will be located from the nearest factory, workshop, mercantile or other establishment, occupied dwelling, church, schoolhouse, building in which people are accustomed to assemble, railroad or public highway.

SEC. 5904. Such statement, when filed, shall be submitted by the Certificates granted, when. chief inspector of workshops and factories, for examination, correction and investigation, to the district inspector of explosives, who shall make a personal examination of each such factory, storehouse or magazine. If it is found to be located at a safe distance from the nearest factory, workshop, mercantile or other establishment, occupied dwelling, church, schoolhouse, building in which people are accustomed to assemble, railroad or public highway, and so planned and managed as to insure as great safety as is consistent with the nature of the business, and if the facts required in such statement are fully set out therein, and found to be true, such inspector shall grant a certificate approving the plans and location of such factory, storehouse or magazine as set forth in such statement.

SEC. 5905. Such certificate shall remain good and in force from Term of certificate. the date of issue, except when otherwise ordered for cause by the chief inspector of workshops and factories, and shall be void and a new statement and certificate shall be required of such person, partnership or corporation, whenever any change is made in the manufacture, handling or storing of such explosives as to the location of a factory, storehouse or magazine, or as to the kind or character of explosives manufactured, handled or stored, or whenever the number of men employed or the amount of explosives manufactured, handled or stored becomes greater than the number or amount designated in the last statement made to the chief inspector of workshops and factories.

SEC. 5906. A person, partnership or corporation shall not manu- Bonds facture such explosives or store more than one hundred pounds thereof without giving bond in the sum of five thousand dollars in each county in which such explosives are manufactured or stored, to the county commissioners of such county, with such surety or sureties as is approved by the judge of the probate or common pleas court of such county, conditioned for the payment of all damages that may be caused to persons or property by reason of an explosion of any of such substances and without filing with the chief inspector of workshops and factories, a sworn statement that such bond has been approved and filed.

Exemptions.

SEC. 5907. This chapter shall not apply to persons, partnerships or corporations storing not more than twenty-five pounds of gunpowder or blasting powder in any one place at one time nor to the manufacturing or storing of drugs. The chief inspector of workshops and factories and the district inspector of explosives shall enforce the provisions of this chapter.

Enforcement.

ACTS OF 1911.

Inspection of steam boilers—State board.

(Page 494.)

Board of boiler rules.

SECTION 1. There is hereby established, in the office of the chief examiner of steam engineers, a department to be known as the board of boiler rules, to consist of the chief examiner of steam engineers, who shall be chairman of the board, and four members to be appointed by the governor, with the advice and consent of the senate, within thirty days after the passage of this act, one member to be appointed for the term of one year, one member for two years, one member for three years, and one member for four years, and, as their terms expire, the governor shall appoint a member for four years. Vacancies shall be filled by appointment by the governor for the unexpired term. One of the persons so appointed shall be an employee of the boiler using interests; one shall be an employee of the boiler manufacturing interests; one shall be an employee of the boiler insurance interests; and one shall be an operating engineer; or the governor, if he deems the same advisable, may make such appointments from any class of citizens.

Inspection exemptions.

SEC. 2. On and after January 1, 1912, all steam boilers and their appurtenances, except boilers of railroad locomotives, portable boilers used in pumping, heating, steaming and drilling, in the open field, for water, gas and oil, and portable boilers used for agricultural purposes, and in construction of and repairs to public roads, railroad and bridges, boilers on automobiles, boilers of steam fire engines brought into the State for temporary use in times of emergency for the purpose of checking conflagrations, boilers carrying pressures of less than fifteen pounds per square inch, which are equipped with safety devices approved by the board of boiler rules, and boilers under the jurisdiction of the United States, shall be thoroughly inspected, internally and externally, and under operating conditions at intervals of not more than one year, and shall not be operated at pressures in excess of the safe working pressure stated in the certificate of inspection hereinafter mentioned. And shall be equipped with such appliances as to insure safety of operation as shall be prescribed by the board of boiler rules.

Rules to be formulated.

SEC. 3. It shall be the duty of the board of boiler rules to formulate rules for the construction, installation, inspection and operation of steam boilers, and for ascertaining the safe working pressure to be carried on such boilers, to prescribe tests, if it is deemed necessary, to ascertain the qualities of materials used in the construction of boilers, to formulate rules regulating the construction and sizes of safety valves for boilers of different sizes and pressures, for the construction, use, and location of fusible plugs, appliances for indicating the pressure of steam and level of water in the boiler, and such other appliances as the board may deem necessary to safety in operating steam boilers, to make a standard form of certificate of inspection, and to examine applicants for certificate as boiler inspectors as hereinafter provided.

SEC. 4. The board of boiler rules shall hold examinations and public hearings on complaints and recommendations in the city of Columbus on the second Wednesday in February, May, August, and November, of each year, and at such other times as it may determine. *Meetings.*

SEC. 5. If the board, after any hearings, shall deem it advisable to make changes in its rules, it shall appoint a day for a further hearing, and shall give notice thereof, and of the changes proposed, by advertisement in at least one newspaper in each of the cities of Cleveland, Cincinnati, Columbus, Toledo, Dayton, and Youngstown, at least ten days before such hearing. If the board, on its own initiative, contemplates changes in its rules, like notice and a hearing shall be given and held before the adoption thereof. *Special hearings.*

SEC. 6. Changes in the rules which affect the construction of new boilers shall take effect six months after the approval of the same by the governor: *Provided, however,* That the board may, upon request, permit the application of such changes in, or additions to, rules, to boilers manufactured or installed during the said six months. *Changes take effect, when.*

SEC. 7. When a person desires to manufacture a special type of boiler, the design of which is not covered by the rules formulated by the board of boiler rules, he shall submit drawings and specifications of such boiler to said board, who may permit the installation of the same in the State of Ohio. *Special types.*

SEC. 8. All rules formulated by the board of boiler rules shall be submitted to, and subject to, the approval of the governor, and when so approved shall be printed and furnished to those requesting them. *Rules to be approved.*

SEC. 9. In addition to the duties heretofore imposed upon him by law, the chief examiner of steam engineers shall be the head of the department of the board of boiler rules and chief inspector of steam boilers. He shall appoint an assistant chief inspector of steam boilers, and such other inspectors, under conditions hereinafter provided, as he may deem necessary, together with such number of clerks, one of whom shall act as the clerk of the board of boiler rules, as may be approved by the governor; and he may incur such other expenses as may be necessary to an efficient administration of said department. * * * All appointments shall be subject to the approval of the governor. *Chief examiner*

SEC. 10. The chief inspector of steam boilers shall give a bond payable to the State in the sum of five thousand dollars, with surety to be approved by the governor, conditioned upon the faithful performance of his duty. Like bonds shall be given in the sum of two thousand dollars to be approved in the same manner by the assistant chief inspector and by each general inspector of steam boilers. *Bond.*

SEC. 11. Applications for examination as an inspector of steam boilers shall be in writing, accompanied by a fee of ten dollars, upon a blank to be furnished by the chief inspector of steam boilers, stating the school education of the applicant, a list of his employers, his period of employment and the position held with each. He shall also submit a letter from one or more of his previous employers certifying to his character and experience. Applications shall be rejected which contain any willful falsification, or untruthful statements. Such applicant, if the board of boiler rules deem his history and experience sufficient, shall be examined by the board at its next regular meeting, by a written examination dealing with the construction, installation, operation, maintenance and repair of steam boilers and their appurtenances, and the applicant shall be accepted or rejected on the merits of his application and examination. A rejected applicant shall be entitled, after the expiration of ninety days, and upon payment of an examination fee of ten dollars, to another examination. *Applications for examination.*

Upon a favorable report by the board of boiler rules, of the result of an examination, to the chief inspector of steam boilers, he shall immediately issue to the successful applicant a certificate to that effect. *Examinations.*

Inspectors.

Sec. 12. The chief inspector of steam boilers may, with the consent of the governor, appoint from the holders of certificates provided for in section 11, not to exceed ten general inspectors.

Any company authorized to insure boilers against explosion in this State may designate from holders of such certificates persons to inspect the boilers covered by such company's policies, and the chief inspector of steam boilers shall issue to such persons commissions authorizing them to act as special inspectors. Such special inspectors shall be compensated by the company designating them, and the fee provided for in section 20 shall not be collected by such special inspectors.

The chief inspector of steam boilers shall issue to each of such appointees, a commission to the effect that the holder thereof is authorized to inspect steam boilers for the State of Ohio.

No person shall be authorized to act for the State, either as a general inspector or a special inspector, unless he holds a certificate of having passed the examination as herein provided, and also that he holds a commission from the chief inspector of steam boilers to represent the State in that capacity.

Revocation of certificate.

Sec. 13. A commission shall be revoked by the chief inspector of steam boilers for the incompetence or untrustworthiness of the holder thereof, or for willful falsification of any matter or statement contained in his application, or in a report of any inspection. A person whose commission is revoked may appeal from the revocation to the board of boiler rules which shall at its next regular meeting, hear the appeal and either set aside or affirm the revocation, and its decision shall be final. The person whose commission has been revoked shall be entitled to be present in person and by counsel on the hearing of the appeal. If a certificate or commission is lost or destroyed a new certificate or commission shall be issued in its place without another examination.

Inspections.

Sec. 14. The owner or user of a boiler required to be inspected shall, after due notice, prepare the boiler for internal and external inspection at the appointed time, by drawing the water from the boiler and removing the manhole and hand-hole plates and thoroughly cleaning the boiler and its setting. The chief inspector of steam boilers shall give such owner or user at least fourteen days' notice to prepare the boiler for this inspection, but shall not be required to give notice for inspection under operating conditions. It shall be the duty of the inspector when making inspection under operating conditions to observe the pressure of steam carried, the general condition of each boiler, to ascertain if the safety valve and the appliances for indicating the pressure of steam and the level of water in the boiler are in proper working order. No person shall remove or tamper with any safety appliance prescribed by the board of boiler rules, and no person shall in any manner load the safety valve to a greater pressure than that allowed by the certificate of inspection. If in the judgment of the inspector it is advisable to apply a hydrostatic pressure test to the boiler, the owner or user shall prepare the boiler for such test, as directed by the inspector.

Certificate of inspection.

Sec. 15. If, upon inspection, the inspector finds the boiler to be in safe working order, with the fittings necessary to safety, and properly set up, upon his report to the chief inspector of steam boilers, the chief inspector shall issue to the owner or user thereof, a certificate of inspection stating the maximum pressure at which the boiler may be operated, as ascertained by the rules established by the board of boiler rules, and thereupon such owner or user may operate the boiler mentioned in the certificate. If the inspector finds that the boiler is not in safe working condition, or is not provided with the fittings necessary to safety, or if the fittings are improperly arranged, he shall immediately notify the owner or user and person in charge of the boiler and shall report the same to the chief inspector of steam boilers, and shall withdraw or withhold such certificate until the boiler and its fittings are put in condition to insure safety of operation, and the owner or user shall not operate the boiler, or cause it to be operated until such certificate has been granted.

If the owner or user of any boiler disagrees with the inspector as to the necessity for shutting down a boiler or for making repairs or alterations in it, or taking any other measures for safety that may be requested by an inspector, the owner or user may appeal from the decision of the inspector to the chief inspector of steam boilers, who may, after such other inspection by a general inspector or special inspector, as the chief inspector may deem necessary, decide the issue and his decision shall be final.

Nothing in the act and no inspection or report by any inspector shall relieve the owner or user of a steam boiler of the duty of using due care himself in the inspection, operation and repair of said boiler or of any liability for damages for his failure to inspect or repair or operate said boiler safely. **Owner's duty.**

SEC. 16. The certificate of inspection shall state the name of the owner or user, the location, size and number of each boiler, the date of inspection, and the maximum pressure at which the boiler may be operated, the name of the person that made the inspection, and of the chief inspector of steam boilers, and shall also contain such quotations from the statutes as shall be deemed necessary by the board of boiler rules, and shall be so placed as to be easily read in the engine-room or boiler room of the plant where the boiler is located, except that the certificate of inspection for a portable boiler shall be kept on the premises and shall be accessible at all times. **Contents of certificate.**

The owner or user of a boiler herein required to be inspected shall pay to the chief inspector of steam boilers the sum of fifty cents for each certificate issued.

SEC. 17. Each boiler which has been inspected shall be numbered either by stamping the number on the boiler or by attaching a numbered metal tag by a seal or otherwise to the boiler or its fittings. No person except an inspector shall deface or remove any such number or tag. **Boilers to be numbered.**

SEC. 18. All such boilers installed after January 1, 1912, shall be inspected when installed. A boiler installed in this State prior to July 1, 1912, which does not conform to the rules of construction formulated by the board of boiler rules, may be used after a thorough internal and external inspection, and if the inspector deems it necessary, a hydrostatic test, and after a certificate has been issued by the chief inspector. The pressure allowed on such boilers is to be ascertained by rules formulated by the board of boiler rules. No certificate of inspection shall be granted on any boiler installed after July 1, 1912, which does not conform to the rules formulated by the board of boiler rules. **New boilers.**

SEC. 19. The owner or user of any stationary boiler herein required to be inspected, who moves the same, shall report to the chief inspector of steam boilers the new location of said boiler, and the boiler shall be inspected before it is again operated. The owner or user of any boiler herein required to be inspected shall immediately notify the chief inspector of steam boilers in case a defect affecting the safety of the boiler is discovered. **Moving boilers.**

SEC. 20. The owner or user of a boiler herein required to be inspected shall pay to the inspector upon inspection five dollars for each boiler internally and externally inspected, and two dollars for each boiler inspected while in operation. The inspectors shall give receipts for the same, and when the fee is collected by a general inspector the same shall be forwarded, with his report of the inspection, to the chief inspector of steam boilers: *Provided, however,* That not more than eight dollars shall be collected in any one year on each such boiler, unless additional inspections are requested by the owner or user of same, or unless the boiler has been inspected and a certificate has been refused, or unless an additional inspection is required because of the change of location of a stationary boiler. **Fee.**

SEC. 21. The inspection of boilers and their appurtenances shall be made by the inspectors mentioned herein under the supervision **Duty of chief inspector.**

of the chief inspector of steam boilers, and it shall be the duty of the chief inspector to enforce the provisions of this act and of such rules as shall be promulgated by the board of boiler rules that have been approved by the governor.

Violations.   SEC. 23. Whoever being the owner, or operator of any steam boiler, herein required to be inspected, operates the same in violation of any rule promulgated by the board of boiler rules, and approved by the governor, or without having the same inspected and a certificate issued therefor as provided in this act, or who hinders or prevents a duly qualified inspector from entering any premises in or on which a steam boiler is situated for the purpose of inspection, shall be fined not less than twenty dollars nor more than five hundred dollars, or imprisoned not to exceed six months, or both.

OKLAHOMA.

ACTS OF 1907–8.

Fire escapes on factories.

(Page 427.)

Fire escapes required.   SECTION 1. * * * all building[s] more than two stories in height, used for manufacturing purposes, * * * shall have at least one fire escape for every thirty persons for which working * * * accommodations are provided above the second stories of said buildings, * * *

Enforcement.   SEC. 5. It shall be the duty of the chief of the fire department in all cities and towns to visit all public buildings, hotels, lodging houses and buildings described in section one hereof, and which have and maintain fire escapes, at least once every three months, and to investigate whether the provisions of this act are duly observed, and to report all violations of the same to the city or prosecuting attorney for prosecution. In cities or towns not having a chief of fire department, it shall be the duty of the marshal to perform the duties imposed by this section.

Regulation and inspection of factories.

(Page 499.)

ARTICLE V.

Factory inspector.   SECTION 1. The governor shall, upon the recommendation of the commissioner of labor, by and with the consent of the senate, appoint a factory inspector, whose duty it shall be to exercise general supervision over the department of factory inspection, under the direction of the commissioner of labor. The salary of the factory inspector shall be fifteen hundred dollars per annum and he shall serve during the term of the governor. It shall be

Duties.   the duty of the factory inspector to visit and inspect at all reasonable hours, not less than once in each year, the factories, workshops, machine shops, foundries, laundries, manufacturing establishments in the State, and such other places where labor is employed as the commissioner of labor may designate and shall make special investigation into the conditions of labor or into any alleged abuses in connection therewith, and shall perform such other duties as now or shall hereafter be prescribed by law. Said inspector shall, under the direction of the commissioner of labor, collect, assort, systematize and compile, statistical details and information relating to all departments of labor in the State. He shall report in writing to the commissioner of labor on the fifteenth day of May and the first day of November of each year, and at such other times as the commissioner of labor may require, the result of his inspection and investigation together with such other information and recommendation as he may deem proper.

It shall be the duty of the county attorney of the proper county upon the request of the state factory inspector, to prosecute any violation of law which it is made the duty of the factory inspector to enforce. In addition to the salary provided herein for the factory inspector he shall be allowed his actual and necessary traveling expenses incurred in performance of his duties in carrying out the provisions of this article.

SEC. 2. The superintendent of the state board of health, the labor commissioner, and the factory inspector shall formulate, publish and enforce such rules as they may deem necessary for the sanitary regulations of manufacturing institutions, factories and workshops in this State. *Rules to be formulated.*

SEC. 5. Every person, firm, or corporation, agent, or manager of a corporation employing any female in any manufacturing establishment, factory or workshop shall post and keep posted in a conspicuous place in every room where such help is employed, a printed or written notice, stating the hours of each day of the week between which work is required of such person, and every room where children under sixteen years of age are employed, a list of their names, ages and place[s] of residence. *Hours of labor to be posted, when.*

SEC. 6. The words, "manufacturing establishments" "factory" or "workshop" whenever used in this act shall be construed to mean any place where goods or products are manufactured or repaired, cleaned or sorted in whole or in part, for sale or for wages. *Definition.*

SEC. 7. The owner or person in charge of a factory or any institution where machinery is used shall be provided with belt shifters or other mechanical contrivances for the purpose of throwing on or off belts on pulleys whenever practicable. All machines shall be provided with loose pulleys and all vats, pans, plainers [planers], cogs, gearings, belting, shafting, set screws and machinery of every description shall be properly guarded. No person shall remove or make ineffective any safeguard around or attached to any machinery, vats, or pans, while the same are in use, unless for the purposes of immediately making repairs thereto and all such safeguards so removed shall be promptly replaced. If a machine or any part thereof is not properly guarded, the use thereof may be prohibited by the factory inspector or deputy factory inspector, and notice to that effect shall be attached thereto, such notice shall not be removed until the machine is made safe and the required safeguards are provided, and in the meantime such unsafe or dangerous machinery shall not be used. *Guards for dangerous machinery.*

SEC. 8. If in the opinion of the factory inspector, it is necessary to protect life or limbs of factory employee or employees in any other institution, the owner, agent, or lessee of such factory or institution where any elevator, hoisting shaft or wellhole is used, shall cause, upon written notice from the factory inspector, the same to be properly and substantially enclosed, secured or guarded, and shall provide such proper traps or automatic doors so fastened in or at all elevator ways except passenger elevators enclosed on all sides, as to form a substantial surface when closed or so constructed as to open and close by the action of the elevator in its passage whether ascending or descending. The factory inspector may inspect the cable gearing or other apparatus of all elevators in factories and require them to be kept in a safe condition. No child under the age of fifteen years shall be employed or permitted to have the care, custody or management of or to operate an elevator in a factory or in any other institution where a freight elevator is operated. *Elevator shafts, etc.*

SEC. 9. When in the opinion of the factory inspector, it is necessary, the workrooms, halls and stairs leading to workrooms shall be properly lighted. *Lighting halls.*

SEC. 10. Proper and substantial handrails shall be provided on all stairways in factories. The stairs shall be properly screened at the sides and bottom and all doors in or to such factory shall be so constructed as to open outwardly and shall not be locked or bolted or fastened during working hours. *Stairways.*

Toilet rooms.   SEC. 11. There shall be provided in every factory, manufacturing establishment or workshop, where men and women are employed, separate toilet and wash rooms.

Fire escapes.   SEC. 12. Such fire escapes as may be deemed necessary by the factory inspector shall be provided on the outside of every factory in this State, consisting of two or more stories in height. Each escape shall connect with each floor above the first, and shall be of sufficient strength, well-fastened and secured, and shall have landings and balconies not less than six feet in length, and three feet in height, embracing at least two windows at each story, and connecting with the interior by easily accessible and unobstructed openings. The balconies or landings shall be connected by iron stairs not less than eighteen inches wide, with steps not less than six inches tread, placed at a proper slant and protected by well-secured handrails on both sides, and shall have a drop ladder not less than twelve inches wide, reaching from the lower platform to the ground. The windows or doors to the landing or balcony of each fire escape shall be of sufficient size and located as far as possible, consistent with accessibility from the stairways and elevator hatchways and openings and a ladder from such fire escape shall extend to the roof. Stationary stairs or ladders shall be provided on the inside of every factory from the upper story as means of escape in case of fire.

Accidents to be reported.   SEC. 13. The person in charge of any factory, shall report in writing to the factory inspector all accidents or injuries sustained by any person therein, immediately after the time of the accident, stating as fully as possible the extent and cause of the injury and the place where the injured person had been sent, with such other information relative thereto as may be required by the factory inspector, who may investigate the cause of such accident or injury and order precautions to be taken as will in his judgment prevent the recurrence of similar accidents.

Reports by owners of establishments.   SEC. 14. The owner, superintendent, manager or other person in charge of any establishment at the time of inspection shall be required to furnish the inspector making the inspection a true statement of the number of persons employed in such establishment, and any owner, superintendent manager or other person in charge who shall fail or refuse to furnish such statement or understate the number of persons employed in such establishment at the time of such inspection shall be fined not less than twenty-five dollars nor more than one hundred dollars for each offense. Any person, firm or corporation, agent or manager, superintendent or foreman of any firm or corporation, whether acting for himself or for such firm or corporation, or by himself through subagents or foreman, superintendent or manager, who shall refuse or attempt to prevent the admission of any inspector authorized by this act, upon or within the premises or buildings of any such establishment or place included in this act, at any reasonable business hours of the persons employed therein or thereat or shall in any manner interfere with the performance of the official duties of such inspector, shall be deemed guilty of a misdemeanor and upon conviction thereof shall be fined not less than ten dollars nor more than one hundred dollars for each offense.

Reports by employers.   SEC. 15. It shall be the duty of every owner or operator or lessee of any factory, foundry or machine shop or other manufacturing establishment, railroads, street railways, interurban railways, elevated railways or commercial and industrial institutions and other mechanical manufacturing institutions doing business in this State, subject to the provisions of this act, to report annually on or before the first day of March, to the commissioner of labor, the name of the firm or corporation and the number of members, male or female constituting the same; where located, capital invested in grounds, building and machinery; class and value of goods manufactured; aggregate value of material use[d]; total number of days in operation; amount paid yearly for rent, taxes and insurance; total amount paid in wages; total number of employees, male and female, number engaged in clerical and manual labor, with detailed classification of the number and sex of employees engaged in each class, and children employed under the age of sixteen years, and average daily wages paid in each.

SEC. 16. The commissioner of labor is hereby authorized to furnish suitable blanks to the owner, operator, manager or lessee of any factory, workshop, elevator, foundry, machine shop or any other mechanical or manufacturing establishment, to enable said owner, operator, manager or lessee to intelligently comply with the provisions of the preceding section of this article. *Blanks.*

SEC. 17. The proprietor, manager or person having charge of any mercantile establishment, store shop, hotel, restaurant or other place where women or girls are employed as clerks in this State, shall provide chairs, stools or other contrivances for the comfortable use of such female employees, and shall permit the use of the same by such female employees for the preservation of their health and for rest when not actually employed in the discharge of their respective duties. *Seats for female employees.*

SEC. 18. Any person, firm or corporation who fails to comply with any of the provisions of this article, except as otherwise provided, shall be deemed guilty of a misdemeanor, and on conviction thereof shall be fined in a sum not less than ten dollars nor more than one hundred dollars for each offense. *Violations.*

ACTS OF 1911.

CHAPTER 125.—*Factory, etc., regulations—Sanitation.*

SECTION 1. Every room or building occupied as a bakery or confectionery, canning, packing, pickling or preserving establishment, or for the manufacture of any food product, shall be drained and plumbed in a manner conductive [conducive] to its healthful and sanitary condition, and constructed with air shafts and windows or ventilating pipes sufficient to insure ventilation, as the factory inspector shall direct. No cellar or basement shall hereafter be used as a bakery, and no cellar occupied by a bakery on or before the passage of this act, when once closed, shall be again opened for such use. Every bakery shall be provided with a wash room and a water-closet apart from the bake room and rooms where the manufacturing of such food products is conducted; no water-closet, earth closet or privy shall be within, or communicate directly with, a bakeshop. Rooms used for the manufacture of flour or meal food shall be at least eight feet in height. The side walls of such rooms shall be plastered or wainscoted, the ceiling plastered or ceiled with lumber or metal, and, if required by the factory inspector, shall be whitewashed at least once in three months; the furniture, utensils and floor of such room shall be kept in a healthful sanitary condition. The manufactured flour or meal products shall be kept in dry, clean and airy rooms. The sleeping places for persons employed in a bakery shall be separate from the rooms where food products are manufactured or stored. *Drainage and ventilation.* *Use of basements.* *Wash-rooms, etc.* *Sleeping places.*

SEC. 2. No employer shall permit any person to work in his bakeshop or other institution in which foodstuffs are manufactured who is affected with pulmonary tuberculosis, scrofulous or venal [venereal] diseases, or with a communicable skin affection, and every employer shall maintain himself and his employees in a clean and sanitary condition while engaged in the manufacture, handling or sale of such food products. Every owner, agent or lessee of any establishment where food products are manufactured shall provide cuspidors or vessels to be used for expectoration purposes by employees; chairs shall also be furnished, and employees are hereby prohibited from sitting on any dough boards or tables used for the purpose of manufacturing, in any way whatever, any food products. *Infectious and contagious diseases.* *Cuspidors.*

SEC. 3. The owner, agent or lessee of any property used as a bakery or in manufacturing foodstuff[s], shall within thirty days after the service of notice upon him of an order issued by the factory inspector, comply therewith, or cease to use or allow the *Time for compliance.*

use of such premises as a bakeshop. Such notice shall be in writing and may be served upon such owner, agent or lessee either personally or by mail, and a notice of registered letter, mailed to the last known address of such owner, agent or lessee shall be sufficient service. A copy of the foregoing sections shall be conspicuously posted in each workroom of every establishment affected by the provision of this act.

Ventilation. SEC. 4. There shall be sufficient means of ventilation provided in each workroom of every manufacturing or mercantile establishment, laundry, renovating works, bakery or printing office within this State, and the factory inspector shall notify the owner, agent or lessee, in writing, to provide, or cause to be provided, ample and proper means of ventilation for such workroom, and shall prosecute such owner, agent or lessee if such notification be not complied with within the time specified by the factory inspector, after service of such notice.•

Enforcement. SEC. 5. The chief factory inspector, and deputy factory inspector, are hereby empowered to act as police officers with full power to arrest and detain any person found violating any of the provisions of this act, or any laws pertaining to factory inspection or parts thereof, or against whom there is found any evidence of a previous violation of such laws: *Provided, however,* That no such person shall'be detained for any period of time longer than twenty-four hours without warrant or the filing of a charge against him in a court of competent jurisdiction.

Repairs, etc., SEC. 6. If, in the opinion of the factory inspector, or deputy **may be required.** factory inspector, any building being used as a manufacturing establishment or workshop is in an unsafe or dilapidated condition, thereby endangering human life or property, he shall immediately notify the owner, agent or lessee thereof, specifying the defect, and require such repairs and improvements to be made as he may deem necessary, and the owner of said premises shall immediately repair or correct such defects.

Duty of owner. SEC. 7. Every owner or person in charge of any manufacturing establishment, factory or workshop, shall comply with any order issued by the factory inspector, or deputy factory inspector, within the time specified by such inspector, and notify the department of labor upon affidavit when such order has been complied with.

Violations. SEC. 8. Any person, firm or corporation who fails to comply with any provisions of this act except as otherwise provided, shall be deemed guilty of a misdemeanor and on conviction thereof shall be fined in a sum not less than ten dollars ($10) nor more than one hundred dollars ($100), for each offense.

OREGON.

ACTS OF 1903.

Bureau of labor statistics and factory inspection.

(Page 205.)

Bureau estab- SECTION 1. There is hereby established a separate and distinct **lished.** department in this State, to be known as the "Bureau of Labor Statistics and Inspector of Factories and Workshops," to be in charge and under control of a commissioner of the bureau of labor statistics, which office is hereby created.

Commissioner. SEC. 3. At the general election in the year 1906, there shall be elected, as other State officers are elected, a citizen of the State of Oregon, who has been a resident of the State over five years, to fill the office of commissioner of labor statistics and inspector of factories and workshops, whose term of office shall be four years. and until his successor shall be elected and qualified. At the general election every fourth year thereafter, there shall be elected a commissioner of labor statistics and inspector of workshops and factories, whose term of office shall be four years, and until his successor is elected and has qualified.

SEC. 4. It shall be the duty of such officer to cause to be enforced all the laws regulating the employment of children, minors, and women; all laws established for the protection of the health, lives, and limbs of operatives in workshops, factories, mills, and other places, and all laws enacted for the protection of the working classes; laws which declare it to be a misdemeanor on the part of the employees [employers] to require as a condition of employment the surrender of any rights of citizenship; laws regulating and prescribing the qualifications of persons in trade and handcrafts, and similar laws now in force or hereafter to be enacted. It shall also be the duty of the officers to collect, assort, arrange, and present, in biennial reports to the legislature, on or before the first Monday in January, statistical details relating to all the departments of labor in the State; to the subject of corporations, strikes, or other labor difficulties; to trade unions and other labor organizations, and their effect upon labor or capital; the number and condition of the Japanese and Chinese in the State, their social and sanitary habits; number of married, and of single; the number employed, and the nature of their employment; the average wages per day at each employment, and the gross amount yearly; the amount expended by them in rent, food, and clothing, and in what proportion such amounts are expended for foreign and home productions, respectively; to what extent their employment comes in competition with the white industrial classes of the State; and to such other matters relating to the commercial, industrial, social, educational, moral, and sanitary conditions of the laboring classes, and the permanent prosperity of the respective industries of the State as the bureau may be able to gather. In its biennial report the bureau shall also give account of all the proceedings of its officers which have been taken in accordance with the provisions of this act, herein referred to, including a statement of all violations of law which have been observed, and the preceedings [proceedings] under the same, and shall join with such amounts [accounts] and such remarks, suggestions and recommendations as the commissioner may deem necessary.

SEC. 5. It shall be the duty of every owner, operator, or manager of every factory, workshop, mill, or other establishment, excepting mines, where labor is employed, to make to the bureau, upon blanks furnished by said bureau, such reports and returns as the said bureau may require, for the purpose of compiling such labor statistics as are authorized by this act, and the owner or business manager shall make such reports and returns within the time prescribed therefor by said commissioner, and shall certify to the correctness of the same. In the report of said bureau no use shall be made of the names of individuals, firms, or corporations supplying the information called for by this section; such information shall be deemed confidential, and not for the purpose of disclosing personal affairs. Any officer, agent, or employee of said bureau violating this provision shall be guilty of a misdemeanor, and shall be fined in a sum not exceeding $500, or be imprisoned for not more than one year in the county jail.

SEC. 6. Said commissioner shall have the power to issue subpœnas, administer oaths, and take testimony in all matters relating to the duties herein required by such bureau, and such testimony to be taken in some suitable place in the vicinity to which testimony is applicable. Witnesses subpœnaed and testifying before any officer of the said bureau shall be paid the same fees as witnesses before a circuit court, such payment to be made from the fund appropriated for the use of the bureau, and in the manner provided in section 10 of this act for the payment of other expenses of the bureau. Any person duly subpœnaed under the provisions of this section, who shall willfully neglect or refuse to attend, or testify, at the time and place named in the subpœna, shall be guilty of a misdemeanor, and, upon conviction thereof be-

Marginal notes: Duties. Reports. Reports from factories, etc. Powers of commissioner.

fore any court of competent jurisdiction, shall be punished by a fine of not less than $25 or more than $100, or by imprisonment in the county jail not exceeding thirty days.

Same subject.   SEC. 7. Said commissioner of the bureau of labor shall have power to enter any factory, mill, office, workshop, or public or private works, at any reasonable time, for the purpose of gathering facts and statistics, such as are contemplated by this act; and **Inspection.** to examine into the methods of protection from danger to employees, and the sanitary conditions in and around such buildings and places, and make a record thereof; and any owner or occupant of said factory, mill, office, or workshop, or public or private works, or his agent, or agents, who shall refuse to allow an inspector or employee of said bureau to enter shall be guilty of a misdemeanor, and, upon conviction thereof, before any court of competent jurisdiction, shall be punished by a fine of not less than $25 nor more than $100, or be imprisoned in the county jail not to exceed ninety days for each and every offense.

Schedules, etc., to be destroyed.   SEC. 8. At the expiration of two years all records, schedules, and papers accumulating in said bureau that may be considered of no value by the commissioner may be destroyed: *Provided,* The authority of the governor be first obtained for such destruction.

Publication of reports.   SEC. 9. The biennial reports of said commissioner, provided for in section 4 of this act, shall be printed in the same manner, and under the same regulations, as the reports of the executive officers of the State: *Provided,* That no less than four hundred and eighty copies of the report shall be distributed as the judgment of the commissioner may deem best. The blanks and stationery required by the bureau of labor statistics, in accordance with the provisions of this act, shall be furnished by the secretary of state and shall be paid for from the printing fund of the State.

Bond.   SEC. 10 (as amended by chapter 92, Acts of 1909). * * * Said commissioner shall, before entering upon the duties of his office, execute a bond to the State of Oregon, in the sum of $3,000, conditioned upon the faithful, honest, and impartial performance of his duties under this act, which bond shall be approved by the secretary of state and filed in his office. Such commissioner shall include in his biennial report to the governor and legislature an itemized statement of the expense of the bureau incurred by him.

ACTS OF 1907.

CHAPTER 158.—*Inspection of factories and workshops.*

Belt shifters, guards, etc.   SECTION 1. Any person, firm, corporation or association operating a factory, mill or workshop where machinery is used, shall provide and maintain in use belt shifters or other mechanical contrivances for the purpose of throwing on or off belts or pulleys while running, where the same are practicable with due regard to the nature and purpose of said belts and the dangers to employees therefrom; also 'reasonable safeguards for all vats, pans, trimmers, cut-off, gang edger, and other saws, planers, cogs, gearings, belting, shafting, coupling, set screw, live rollers, conveyors, mangles in laundries, and machinery of other or similar descriptions, which it is practicable to guard, and which can be effectively guarded with due regard to the ordinary use of such machinery and appliances, and the dangers to employees therefrom, and with which the employees of any such factory, mill or workshop are liable to come in contact while in the performance of their duties; and if any machine, or any part thereof, is in a defective condition and its operation would be extra hazardous because of such defect, or if any machine is not safeguarded as provided in this act, the use thereof is prohibited, and a notice to that effect shall be attached thereto by the employer immediately on receiving notice of such defect or lack of safeguard, and such notice shall not be removed until said defect has been remedied or the machine safeguarded as herein provided.

SEC. 2. Every factory, mill or workshop where machinery is *Ventilation.* used and manual labor is exercised by the way of trade for the purposes of gain within an enclosed room (private houses in which the employees live, excepted) shall be provided in each workroom thereof with good and sufficient ventilation and kept in a cleanly and sanitary state, and shall be so ventilated as to render harmless, so far as practicable, all gases, vapors, dust, or other impurities, generated in the course of the manufacturing or laboring process carried on therein; and if in any factory, mill or workshop any process is carried on in any enclosed room thereof, by which dust is generated and inhaled to an injurious extent by the persons employed therein, conveyors, receptacles or exhaust fans, or other mechanical means, shall be provided and maintained for the purpose of carrying off or receiving and collecting such dust.

SEC. 3. The openings of all hoistways, hatchways, elevators, and *Hoistways, etc.* wellholes and stairways in factories, mills, workshops, storehouses, warerooms, or stores, shall be protected, where practicable, by good and sufficient trapdoors, hatches, fences, gates or other safeguards, and all due diligence shall be used to keep all such means of protection closed, except when it is necessary to have the same open that the same may be used.

SEC. 4. It shall be the duty of the labor commissioner, by him- *Annual inspec-* self or his duly appointed deputy, to examine as soon as may be *tions.* after the passage of this act, and thereafter annually and from time to time, all factories, mills, workshops, storehouses, warerooms, stores, and buildings and the machinery and appliances therein contained to which the provisions of this act are applicable for the purpose of determining whether they do conform to such provisions, and of granting or refusing certificates of approval, as hereinafter provided.

SEC. 5. Any person. firm, corporation, or association carrying on *Requests for in-* business to which the provisions of this act are applicable, shall *spection.* have the right to make written request to said labor commissioner to inspect any factory, mill, or workshop, and the machinery therein used, and any storehouse, wareroom or store, which said applicant is operating, occupying or using, and to issue his certificate of approval thereof; and said labor commissioner. by himself or his deputy, shall forthwith make said inspection. Upon receiving such application the labor commissioner shall issue to the person making the same an acknowledgment that such certificate has been applied for, and thirty days after such acknowledgment by said labor commissioner, and pending the granting of such certificate, such acknowledgment shall have the same effect as such certificate, till the granting of such certificate by said labor commissioner.

SEC. 6. Any employee of any person, firm, corporation or associa- *Duty of em-* tion shall notify his employer of any defect in or failure to guard *ployees.* the machinery, appliances. ways, works, and plants, with which or in or about which he is working, when any such defect or failure to guard shall come to the knowledge of any said employee, and if said employer shall fail to remedy such defects then said employee may complain in writing to the labor commissioner of any such alleged defects in or failure to guard the machinery, appliances, ways, works, and plants, or any alleged violation by such person, firm, corporation or association, of any of the provisions of this act, in the machinery and appliances and premises used by such person, firm, corporation or association, and with or about which such employee is working, and upon receiving such complaint, it shall be the duty of the labor commissioner, by himself, or his deputy, to forthwith make an inspection of the machinery and appliances complained of.

SEC. 7 (as amended by chapter 130, Acts of 1909). Whenever *Certificate of in-* upon any examination or reexamination of any factory, mill, or *spection.* workship, store or building, or the machinery or appliances therein to. which the provisions of this act are applicable, the property so examined and the machinery and appliances therein conform, in the judgment of said labor commissioner, to the requirements of this act, he shall thereupon issue to the owner, lessee, or operator of such factory, mill or workshop, or to the owner, lessee or occupant of any such storehouse, wareroom or store, a certificate to that effect, and such certificate shall be prima facie evidence as long as it continues in force of compliance, on the part of the person, firm, corporation, or association to whom it is issued, with the provisions of this act. Such certificates may be revoked by said labor commissioner at any time upon written notice to the person, firm, corporation, or association holding the same, whenever in his opinion, after reexamination, conditions and circum-

Copy to bestances have so changed as to justify the revocation thereof. A
posted.copy of said certificate shall be kept posted in a conspicuous place on every floor of all factories, mills, workshops, storehouses, warerooms or stores to which the provisions of this act are applicable.

Notice of de-   SEC 7a (added by chapter 130, Acts of 1909). If, in the judgment
fects.of said labor commissioner, such factory, mill or workshop, or the machinery and appliances therein contained, or such storehouse, wareroom or store does not conform to the requirements of this act, he shall forthwith, personally or by mail, serve on the person, firm, corporation or association operating or using such machinery or appliances, or occupying such premises, a written statement of the requirements of said labor commissioner, before he will issue a certificate as hereinbefore provided for; and upon said requirements being complied with, within a period of thirty days after said requirements have been served as aforesaid, the said labor commissioner shall forthwith issue such certificate; but if the person, firm, or corporation operating or using said machinery and appliances, or occupying such premises, shall consider the requirements of said labor commissioner unreasonable and impracticable or unnecessarily expensive, he may, within ten days after the requirements of said labor commissioner have been

Appeals.served upon him, appeal therefrom or from any part thereof, to three arbitrators, to whom shall be submitted the matters and things in dispute, and their findings shall be binding upon said applicant and upon the labor commissioner.

Arbitration of   SEC. 7b (added by chapter 130, Acts of 1909). Such appeals
appeal.shall be in writing, addressed to the labor commissioner, and shall set forth the objection to his requirements, or any part thereof, and shall mention the name of one person who will serve as the representative of said applicant calling for arbitration. Immediately upon receipt of such notice of appeal, it shall be the duty of the labor commissioner to appoint a competent person as arbitrator, resident in the county from which such appeal comes, and to notify such person so selected, and also the party appealing, stating the cause for arbitration, and the place, date and time of meeting. These two arbitrators shall select a third, and as soon thereafter as practicable, give a hearing on the matters of said appeal, and the findings of these arbitrators, by a majority vote, shall be reported to the labor commissioner, and to the applicant, and shall be binding upon each. The expense of such arbitration shall be borne by the party calling for the arbitration; and if

Findings.said arbitrators sustain the requirements of said labor commissioner or any part thereof, said applicant shall, within thirty days, comply with the findings of said arbitrators, and thereupon said labor commissioner shall issue his certificate as hereinbefore provided (in section 4 of this act); but if said arbitrators shall sustain such appeal or any part thereof, the same shall be binding upon said labor commissioner; and any such person, firm, corporation or association shall, within thirty days after the findings of the board of arbitrators, comply with the requirements of the labor commissioner, as amended by said arbitrators, if so amended as herein provided for, and thereupon said labor commissioner shall forthwith issue to any such person, firm, corporation or association his certificate as provided for in section 4 of this act.

Sec. 7c (as amended by chapter 48, Acts of 1911). The labor *Fee to be paid.* commissioner shall not issue any certificate of inspection to any person, firm, corporation or association who has not paid for that year the inspection fee herein provided for. Every person, firm, corporation and association being the owner, operator, lessee or occupant of any factory, mill, workshop, storehouse, wareroom or store coming within the provisions of this act shall pay to the state treasurer, and take his receipt therefor, an annual inspection fee, determined as follows: For each place of business operated by him and which may be inspected under the provisions of this act in which are employed two persons or less, $2; not less than three nor more than seven persons, $5; not less than eight nor more than twenty persons, $10; not less than twenty-one nor more than forty persons, $15; more than forty persons, $20. Any person, firm, corporation or association whose factory, mill, workshop, storehouse, wareroom or store, etc., which, on account of the nature of the business, is not operated more than four months during the year shall not be required to pay more than $10, regardless of the number of persons employed: *Provided, however,* The provisions of this act shall not apply to plants of any kind which use not to exceed two horse power.

Sec. 7d (added by chapter 130, Acts of 1909). The payment of *Fee a debt.* such annual inspection fee by every such person, firm, corporation, and association shall constitute an obligation in favor of the State and shall be a debt due and owing by every ·such person, firm, corporation and association to the State from and after the time of the first inspection, herein provided for and annually thereafter, and shall be enforced in the same manner that other debts are collected by the State.

Sec. 7e (as amended by chapter 48, Acts of 1911). The State *Fee covers one* treasurer shall issue his receipt for all moneys so received. Upon *year's inspec-* presentation of said receipt to said labor commissioner and com- *tions.* pliance with the requirements of the labor commissioner and the provisions of this act, he shall forthwith issue said certificate as in this act provided. Said fee shall entitle the person, firm, corporation, or association paying the same, to any and every inspection of any factory, mill, workshop, storehouse, wareroom, or store, and the machinery and appliances contained in any such premises, owned or operated by the party paying said fee, that may be necessary, for a period of one year subsequent to the time when its payment becomes due, and all moneys collected for licenses and fines, under the provisions of this act, shall be paid into the State treasury, and be converted into a special factory inspection fund: *Provided, however,* That all sums in excess of three thousand dollars ($3,000) remaining in said fund at the end of each fiscal year shall be transferred to the general fund.

Sec. 8. Any person, firm, corporation or association who violates *Violations.* or omits to comply with any of the foregoing requirements or provisions of this act, and such violation or omission shall be the approximate cause of any injury to any employee, shall be liable in damages to any employee who sustains injuries by reason thereof: *Provided,* The amount of damages which any one person *Liability.* may recover in an action for or [on] account of injuries received by reason of any alleged violation of any of the provisions of this act, is hereby expressly limited to the sum of $7,500.

Sec. 9. No action for the recovery of compensation for injury *Action.* under this act shall be maintained unless notice of the time, place and cause of injury is given to the employer within six months, and the action is commenced within one year from the occurrence of the accident causing the injury. The notice required by this section shall be in writing, signed by the person injured, or by some one in his behalf; but if from mental or physical incapacity it is impossible for the person injured to give the notice within the time provided in this section, he may give the same within ninety days after such incapacity is removed; and in case of his death without having given the notice because of mental or physical incapacity, his executor or administrator may give such notice within thirty days after his appointment.

Penalty.   Sec. 10. Any person, firm, corporation or association who violates or fails to comply with any of the provisions of this act
shall be deemed guilty of a misdemeanor, and upon conviction
thereof shall be punished by a fine of not less than $25.00 nor
more than $100.00.

Law to be   Sec. 11. A copy of this act, together with the name and address
posted.   ·of the labor commissioner, printed in a legible manner, shall be
kept posted in a conspicuous plaꞓe on each floor of every factory,
mill, workshop, storehouse, wareroom or store, and at the office
of every public and private work to which the provisions of this
act are applicable. The labor commissioners shall supply such
operators, owners, lessees or occupants with a sufficient number of
said copies to enable such persons to comply with this section.

Definition.   Sec. 12. Wherever in this act the term labor commissioner or
commissioner of·labor is used, it shall be understood to mean the
Commissioner of Labor Statistics and Inspector of Factories and
Workshops.

<h1 style="text-align:center">PENNSYLVANIA.</h1>

<h2 style="text-align:center">BRIGHTLY'S PURDON'S DIGEST—1895.</h2>

Factories and workshops—Inspection, etc.

(Page 865.)

Inspector.   Section 14. The governor shall, immediately after the passage
of this act, appoint, with the advice and consent of the senate,
a factory inspector, at a salary of three thousand dollars per year,
whose term of office shall be three years, at the expiration of

Duties.   which the governor shall appoint his successor. The said inspector
shall be empowered to visit and inspect at all reasonable hours
and as often as practicable. the factories, workshops and other
establishments in the the State employing women and children. It
shall also be the duties of said inspector to enforce the provisions
of this act and to prosecute all violations of the same before any
magistrate or any court of competent jurisdiction in the State. It

Reports.   shall be the duty of the factory inspector to report to the governor,
on or before the thirtieth day of November of each year, the names
of factories inspected, the number of hands employed in each, the
maximum number of hours' work performed each week. Of these
reports five thousand shall be published. five hundred of which
shall be furnished to the governor, two thousand to the house of
representatives, one thousand to the senate, and fifteen hundred
to the factory inspector's department.

Expenses.   Sec. 15. All necessary expenses incurred by said inspector in the
discharge of his duty shall be paid from the funds of the State,
upon the presentation of proper vouchers for the same: *Provided*,
That not more than four thousand dollars shall be expended by
him therefor in any one year.

Hoisting shafts, Sec. 16. It shall be the duty of the owner, agent or lessee of·
etc.   any such factory, manufacturing or mercantile establishment,
where hoisting shafts or wellholes are used, to cause the same to
be properly and substantially enclosed or secured, if, in the opinion of the inspector, it is necessary to protect the life or limbs of
those employed in such establishments. It shall be the duty of
the owners, agent' or lessee, to provide, or cause to be provided,
such proper trap or automatic doors so fastened in or at all elevator ways as to form a substantial surface when closed, and so
constructed as to open and close by action of the elevator in its
passage either ascending or descending.

Belt shifters, Sec. 17. It shall also be the duty of the owner of such factory,
etc.   mercantile industry or manufacturing establishment, or his agent,
superintendent or other person in charge of the same, to furnish
and supply, or cause to be furnished and supplied, in the discretion of the inspector, where dangerous machinery is in use,
automatic shifters, or other mechanical contrivances, for the pur-

pose of throwing on or off belts or pulleys. And no minor under Cleaning mov- sixteen years of age shall be allowed to clean machinery while in ing machinery. motion. All gearing and belting shall be provided with proper safeguard.

SEC. 18. It shall be the duty of the owner or superintendent to Accidents. report, in writing, to the factory inspector all accidents or serious injury done to any person employed in such factory within twenty-four hours after the accident occurs, stating as fully as possible the cause of such injury.

SEC. 19. A suitable and proper wash and dressing room and Wash rooms, water-closets shall be provided for females, where employed, and etc. the water-closets used by females shall not adjoin those used by males, but shall be built entirely away from them, and shall be properly screened and ventilated and at all times kept in a clean condition.

SEC. 20. Not less than forty-five minutes shall be allowed for Time for meals the noonday meal in any manufacturing establishment in this State. The factory inspector, his assistant or any of his deputies, shall have power to issue permits in special cases, allowing a shorter mealtime at noon, and such permit must be conspicuously posted in the main entrance of the establishment, and such permit may be revoked at any time the inspector deems necessary, and shall only be given where good cause can be shown.

SEC. 21. If the inspector of factories find that the heating, light- Defective con- ing, ventilation or sanitary arrangement of any shop, or factory, ditions. is such as to be injurious to the health of persons employed therein, or that the means of egress in case of fire or other disaster is not sufficient or in accordance with all the requirements of law, or that the belting, shafting, gearing, elevators, drums and machinery, in shops and factories are located so as to be dangerous to employees and not sufficiently guarded, or that the vats, pans or structures filled with molten metal or hot liquid are not surrounded with proper safeguards for preventing accident or injury to those employed at or near them, he shall notify the pro- Notice of al- prietor of such factory or workshop to make the alterations or terations. additions necessary within sixty days, and any factory requiring exits or other safeguards provided for in fire-escape law in case of fire, the same shall be erected by order of factory inspector regardless [of] the exemption granted by any board of county commissioners, fire marshals or other authorities, and if such alterations and additions are not made within sixty days from the date of such notice, or within such time as said alterations can be made with proper diligence upon the part of such proprietors, said proprietors or agents shall be deemed guilty of violating the provisions of this act.

SEC. 22. The factory inspector, now or hereafter appointed un- Deputy inspec- der and by virtue of the provisions of this law, is hereby author- tors. ized to appoint such number of persons as in his judgment may be deemed necessary, not exceeding twelve, five of whom shall be females, who shall be known as deputy factory inspectors, either or any one or more of whom may be appointed to act as clerk in the main office, and whose duties it shall be to enforce the provisions of this act and of the several acts relating to factories and manufacturing establishments. The powers of said deputies shall be the same as the powers of the factory inspector, subject to the supervision and direction of the factory inspector.

SEC. 23. The traveling expenses of each of said deputies shall Expenses, etc. be approved by the inspector and audited by the auditor-general of the State before payment, and said deputy inspectors shall have an annual salary of twelve hundred dollars, to be paid monthly by the treasurer of the State out of any moneys not otherwise appropriated.

SEC. 24. Said factory inspector shall have power to divide the Inspection dis- State into districts and to assign one of said deputies to each dis- tricts. trict, and may transfer any of the deputies to other districts in

Removal of deputies. o f case the best interests of the State require it. The inspector shall have the power of removing any of the deputy inspectors at any time.

Office. SEC. 25. An office shall be furnished in the capitol, as soon as practicable, which shall be set apart for the use of the factory inspector. The factory inspector and his deputies shall have the

Power to administer oaths. same power to administer oaths or affirmations as is now given to notaries public in cases where persons desire to verify documents connected with the proper enforcement of this act.

Penalty. SEC. 26. Any person who violates any of the provisions of this act, or who suffers or permits any child or female to be employed in violation of its provisions, shall be deemed guilty of a misdemeanor, and on conviction, shall be punished by a fine of not more than five hundred dollars.

Copy of act to be posted. SEC. 27. A printed copy of this act shall be furnished by the inspector for each workroom of every factory, manufacturing or mercantile house, where persons are employed who are affected by the provisions of this act, and it shall be the duty of the employer of the people employed therein to post and keep posted said printed copy of the law in each room.

[The attorney-general has decided that this act does not apply to factories wherein men only are employed.]

Fire escapes on factories, etc.

(Page 914.)

Chains and ropes to be provided on certain buildings. SECTION 1. In addition to the means of escape required in secction one [now secs. 10 to 14, below], of the act to which this is a supplement, it shall be the duty of the owner or owners, in fee or for life, of every building constructed more than two stories high and used or intended to be used as a hotel, factory, manufactory, workshop, * * * and of the trustee or trustees of every estate, association, society, * * * owning or using any building constructed more than two stories high and used, or intended to be used, for any of said purposes, * * * to provide and cause to be securely affixed to a bolt through the wall over the window head, inside of at least one window in each room on the third floor, and in each room on each higher floor, of every such building, a chain at least ten feet in length, with a rope at least one inch in diameter, securely attached thereto, of sufficient length to extend to the ground, or such other appliances as may be approved by the board of fire commissioners of any city or county having a board of fire commissioners, or by the county commissioners of any county where there is no board of fire commissioners.

When floor is not subdivided. SEC. 2. When the third floor or any higher floor of any such building is not subdivided into rooms, then at least six windows of each of such floors shall be provided with such chains and ropes, or such other appliances as may be approved by any board of fire commissioners, or by the county commissioners of any county where no board of fire commissioners shall exist.

Rooms with more than three windows. SEC. 3. Whenever any room on the third floor, or on any higher floor of any such building, shall contain more than three windows, then at least one window out of every three windows in every such room, shall be provided with such chain and rope, or other such appliances as may be approved by any board of fire commissioners, or by the county commissioners of any county having no board of fire commissioners.

Position of ropes. SEC. 4. Each of such ropes shall be coiled and kept in an unlocked box, in an unobstructed place, near the inside sill of the window to which such rope is attached.

Hallways to be lighted. SEC. 5. In all hotels, factories, manufactories, workshops, * * * the hallways and stairways shall be promptly lighted at night, and at the head and foot of each flight of stairs, and at the intersection of all hallways with main corridors, shall be kept

during the night, a red light, and one or more proper alarms or   Alarms.
gongs, capable of being heard throughout the building, shall always remain easy of access and ready for use in each of said
buildings, to give notice to the inmates in case of fire.

SEC. 6. Every keeper of such hotel, factory, manufactory, work-   Notices to be
shop, * * * shall keep posted in a conspicuous place in every   posted.
sleeping room, a notice descriptive of such means of escape.

SEC. 7. The board of fire commissioners, and county commis-   Location of
sioners of any county having no board of fire commissioners, shall   chains, etc.
have the right to designate the location of the chains and ropes or
other such appliance, in conformity with this act, to be attached
to any building under the provisions of this act [secs. 1 to 9], and
shall grant certificates of approval to every person, firm, corporation, trustees, * * * complying with the requirements of this
act; which certificates shall relieve the party or parties to whom
the same shall be issued from the liabilities, fines, damages and
imprisonment imposed by this act.

SEC. 9. Every person, corporation, trustee, * * * neglecting   Penalty.
or refusing to comply with the requirements of the first section of
this act, shall be liable to a fine not exceeding three hundred dollars, to be collected as fines are now by law collectible, and shall
also be deemed guilty of a misdemeanor, punishable by imprisonment for not less than one month, nor more than twelve months.
And in case of fire occurring in any such building not provided
with the chains and ropes, or such other appliances as may be required by any board of fire commissioners, or by the county commissioners of any county where no board of fire commissioners
shall exist, in accordance with the requirements with [of] the
first section of this act, the person, persons, trustee, trustees, corporation, * * * who or which, neglected or refused to provide such building with the chains and ropes, or such other appliances as aforesaid, shall be liable in an action for damages in case   Damages.
of death or personal injury being caused in consequence of such
fire breaking out in said building, and such action may be maintained by any person or persons now authorized by law to sue in
other cases for injuries caused by neglect of duty.

SEC. 10 (as amended by act No. 204, Acts of 1897). All the fol-   Fire escapes to
lowing described buildings within this Commonwealth, to wit: be provided.
* * * every storehouse, factory, manufactory or workshop of
any kind in which employees or operatives are usually employed
at work in the third or any higher story, * * * shall be provided with a permanent, safe, external means of escape therefrom
in case of fire, independent of all internal stairways; the number
and location of such escapes to be governed by the size of the
building and the number of its inmates, and arranged in such a
way as to make them readily accessible, safe and adequate for
the escape of said inmates.

SEC. 11 (as amended by act No. 204, Acts of 1897). Such es-   Description.
capes to consist of outside open iron stairway of not more than
forty-five degrees slant, with steps not less than six inches in
width and twenty-four inches in length.

SEC. 12 (as amended by act No. 204, Acts of 1897). And all of   Two escapes to
said buildings, capable of accommodating from one hundred to   be provided,
five hundred or more persons as operatives, * * * shall be   when.
provided with two such stairways, and more than two stairways
if such be necessary to secure the speedy and safe escape of said
inmates in case the internal stairways are cut off by fire or
smoke.

SEC. 13 (as amended by act No. 204, Acts of 1897). And it shall   Duty of own-
be the duty of the owner or owners in fee [or] for life, of every   ers, etc.
such building, and of the trustee or trustees of every estate, association, society, * * * owning or using any such building,
* * * to provide and cause to be securely affixed outside of
every such building such permanent, external, unenclosed fire
escape.

SEC. 14 (as amended by act No. 204, Acts of 1897). Nothing   Erection of
herein contained shall prohibit any person whose duty it is under   other escapes.

this act to erect fire escapes from selecting and erecting any other and different device, design or instrument, being a permanent, safe, external means of escape, subject to the inspection and approval of the constituted authorities for that purpose.

Inspection.   SEC. 15. It shall be the duty of the board·of fire commissioners, in conjunction with the fire marshall of the district, where such commissioners and fire marshal are elected or appointed, to first examine and test such fire escape or escapes, and, after [if] upon trial said fire escape or escapes should prove to be in accordance with the requirements of section one of this act [secs. 10 to 14, above], then the said fire marshal, in connection with the fire commissioners, or a majority of them, shall grant a certificate approving said fire escape, thereby relieving the party or parties to whom such certificate is issued from the liabilities of fines, damages and imprisonment imposed by this act: *Provided, further,* That in counties where no such fire marshal or fire commissioners exist, then the county commissioners in each said county shall be the board of examiners, and shall grant certificates of approval when escapes are erected in accordance with the requirements of section one of this act [secs. 10 to 14, above].

Penalty.   SEC. 16. Every person, corporation, trustee, * * * neglecting or refusing to comply with the requirements of section one of this act [secs. 10 to 14, above], in erecting said fire escape or escapes, shall be liable to a fine not exceeding three hundred dollars, and also be deemed guilty of a misdemeanor punishable by imprisonment for not less than one month or more than two months. And in case of fire occurring in any of said buildings in the absence of such fire escape or escapes, approved by certificate of said officials, the said person or corporations shall be liable in an action for damages in case of death or personal injuries sustained in consequence of such fire breaking out in said building, and shall also be deemed guilty of a misdemeanor punishable by imprisonment for not less than six months nor more than twelve months; and such action for damages may be maintained by any person now authorized by law to sue, as in other cases of similar injuries.

Escapes now in use.   SEC. 17. Nothing in this act shall interfere with fire escapes now in use, approved by the proper authorities.

Coal mines—Guards for dangerous machinery.

(Page 1348.)

Guards for machinery.   SECTION 84. All machinery used in or about the mines and collieries, and especially in breakers, such as engines, rollers, wheels, screens, shafting and belting, shall be protected by covering or railing so as to prevent persons from inadvertently walking against or falling upon the same.

Factories, workshops, etc.—Safeguards against fire—Philadelphia.

(Page 1449.)

Stairway.   SECTION 235. All buildings to be hereafter erected or altered to be used as a schoolhouse, church, public building, hall, place of assembly or resort, tenement house, hotel, lodging house, factory or workshop more than two stories in height, shall have at least one stairway, accessible from each apartment, which shall be inclosed with brick walls or partitions made of incombustible materials and shall have no interior openings other than the doors of the apartments from which it is an exit.

Fire escape.   SEC. 236. All stores to be hereafter erected or altered to the extent of twenty-five per centum of the assessed valuation, when more than three stories in height, and in which any one of the stories above the second shall have a clear floor space of not less than four thousand square feet, shall be provided with a tower fire escape, enclosed in incombustible material adjoining one of its fronts, and such fire escape from the first to the second story may be a spiral staircase. Such fire escape shall be held and taken as a fire escape under the terms of the act approved June eleventh, one thousand eight hundred and seventy-nine, entitled "An act to provide for the better security of life and limb in cases of fire in hotels and other buildings," and the several supplements and amendments thereto. And in the case of such stores in which the clear floor space of any story above the second shall be over ten thousand square feet, the board of fire escapes may require one or more additional tower fire escapes as above described. And all mills, more than two stories high, of the floor area per story of three thousand square feet or more, shall have such brick enclosed fire escape or escapes as shall be approved by the board of fire escapes.

SEC. 237. No obstruction shall be placed upon any way of egress from any building. *Obstructions.*

SEC. 238. No explosives or inflammable compound or combustile material shall be stored or placed under any stairway of any building, or be used in any such place or manner as to obstruct or render egress hazardous in case of fire. *Storing explosives.*

SEC. 240. In any store or building, in the city of Philadelphia, in which there shall exist or be placed, any hoistway, hatchway, elevator or wellhole, or in which there shall be made an opening through the floor, the same shall be properly protected or covered, by a good and sufficient trapdoor, or such other appliances as may be necessary to secure the same from being or becoming dangerous to life or limb, and on the completion of the business of each day the said trapdoor or other appliances shall be safely closed by the occupant having the use and control of the same; any violation of the provisions of this act shall subject the offender or offenders to a fine of fifty dollars, for each offense, to be recovered, with cost of suit, in an action of debt, in any court having cognizance thereof, by, to and for the use of the Philadelphia Association for the Relief of Disabled Firemen. *Trapdoors for hoistways.*

SEC. 241. In any hoistway, elevator or wellhole not inclosed in walls of brick or other fireproof materials, the openings through and upon each floor shall be provided with and protected by a substantial guard or gate, or with good and sufficient automatic trapdoors to close the same. Outside windows or openings of every elevator shaft shall have such sign or device to indicate the existence of the said shaft as shall be approved by the bureau of fire. No passenger elevator shall be operated, unless a certificate, signed by some reputable elevator builder that the elevator is safe and in good order, has been furnished within six months and is posted in the car at the entrance. *Guards.* *Certificate.*

Inspection of steam boilers—Philadelphia.

(Page 1460.)

SECTION 351. There shall be an inspector of steam engines and boilers in and for the city of Philadelphia, who shall be nominated by the mayor and confirmed by select council. The mayor shall appoint an advisory commission, consisting of five persons, either practically engaged in the manufacture of steam engines and boilers, or scientific experts familiar with their management, who shall give their written consent to serve on such commission without compensation, and perform the duties as hereinafter provided. Whenever the mayor shall have appointed all the members of the said commission as aforesaid, he shall call them together at such time and place as he may select, for the purpose of organization and the adoption of such by-laws as to them may seem useful. The mayor is hereby authorized to have suitable accommodations provided for the use of said commission, and to furnish them with the requisite stationery and the services of a competent clerk. To this commission the mayor shall refer for examination such person or persons as he may consider suitable *Inspector.*

candidates for the office of inspector of steam engines and boilers, and the said commission shall inquire into the qualifications of such candidates without unnecessary delay, and report the result thereof to the mayor. In case the commission shall not report upon said candidate or candidates within thirty days from the time they have received notice of reference, or shall not have reported satisfactory reasons for longer delay, the mayor may discharge said commission and appoint another in its place. No appointment of inspector shall be confirmed by select council until the nominee shall have been reported by the aforesaid commission as qualified for the position. Whenever an appointment of inspector shall have been confirmed by select council, the duties of the advisory commission shall cease and determine, and all books, papers, and records shall be deposited in the mayor's office for the use of any subsequent commission.

Duty of Inspector. SEC. 352. It shall be the duty of the inspector to carefully examine and inspect all stationary steam engines and steam boilers, erected or in use at the time this goes into effect; and thereafter no stationary steam engine or steam boiler shall be ereced and put into use and operation in the city of Philadelphia, without being first inspected and certified to be competent and safe, under the hand and seal of the officer created by this act; and he shall furnish to the owner, proprietor or other person using

Certificate. such engine or steam boiler, a certificate under his hand and the seal of his office that it has been so inspected and found to be competent and safe; he shall, from time to time, and as often as he may deem expedient, examine all or any such engines or steam boilers in use or operation, and for such purpose, he, together with his assistants, may enter upon any premises and require the removal of any part of the building, fixtures or machinery, and he shall note in a book, to be kept for that purpose, the result of every such examination; and he shall, at least once in every year, make such examination, and give certificate of the result thereof, whenever required.

Operating engine without certificate. SEC. 355. If any person shall maintain or keep in use or operation, or shall put in use or operation, any stationary steam engine or steam boiler, within the said city of Philadelphia, without having first received a certificate that the same has been found to be safe and competent, as is hereinbefore provided for, or shall put or keep in use or operation any such stationary steam engine or steam boiler, within the said city after notice from the said inspector, that the same is not competent and safe, he or she so offending shall be deemed guilty of a misdemeanor, and upon conviction in the said court of quarter sessions for the said county, shall be sentenced to pay a fine not exceeding five thousand dollars, and to undergo imprisonment in the jail of said county, either with or without labor, as the court may direct, for a term not exceeding two years; and each and every such person shall be liable for all damages that may accrue, directly or indirectly to any person or persons whatever.

BRIGHTLY'S DIGEST, 1893–1903.

Regulation and inspection of bakeries.

(Page 62.)

Hours of labor. SECTION 1. No employee shall be required, permitted or suffered to work in a biscuit, bread or cake bakery, [or] confectionery establishment more than six (6) days in any one week, said week to commence on Sunday not before six o'clock post meridian, and to terminate at the corresponding time on Saturday of the same week. No person under the age of eighteen (18) years shall be employed in any bakehouse between the hours of nine (9) o'clock at night and five (5) in the morning. Excepted from this rule shall be the time on Sunday for setting the sponges for the night's work following.

SEC. 13. No minor male or female, adult woman, shall be employed at labor or detained in any biscuit, bread, pie or cake bakery, pretzel or macaroni establishment, for a longer period than twelve hours in any one day, nor for a longer period than sixty hours in any one week. Women and children.

SEC. 14. All buildings or rooms occupied as a biscuit, bread, pretzel, pie or cake bakery, or macaroni establishment, shall be drained and plumbed in the manner directed by the rules and regulations governing the house drainage and plumbing, as prescribed by law, and all rooms used for the purpose aforesaid shall be ventilated by means of air shafts, windows or ventilating pipes, so as to insure a free circulation of fresh air. No cellar, or basement, not now used for a bakery, shall hereafter be occupied and used as a bakery unless the proprietor shall have previously complied with the sanitary provisions of this act [secs. 13 to 23]. Sanitation.

SEC. 15. Every room used for the manufacture of flour or meal food products shall have a tight floor, constructed of cement, wood, or tiles, laid in cement. The inside walls shall be plastered, or painted with oil paint, three (3) coats, or be limewashed. When painted, shall be renewed at least once in every five years, and shall be washed with hot water and soap at least once in every three (3) months; when limewashed, the lime washing shall be renewed at least once in every three (3) months. The furniture and utensils in such room shall be so arranged that the furniture and floor may at all times be kept in a thoroughly sanitary and clean condition. No domestic or pet animal shall be allowed in a room used as a biscuit, bread, pie, or cake bakery, or in any room in such bakery where flour or meal food products are stored. Same subject.

SEC. 17. Every such bakery shall be provided with a wash room and water-closet, or closets, apart from the bake room or rooms, where the manufacture of such food products is conducted, and no water-closet, earth closet, privy, or ash pit, shall be within or communicate directly with the bake room of any bakery. Wash rooms, etc.

SEC. 18. The sleeping room or rooms, for persons employed in bakeries, shall be kept separate and apart from the room or rooms where flour or meal food products are manufactured or stored. And such sleeping places, when they are on the same floor as the bakery, shall be inspected in order to maintain them in a condition of cleanliness. Sleeping rooms.

SEC. 19. No employer shall, knowingly, require, permit or suffer, any person to work in his bakeshop who is affected with consumption of the lungs, or with scrofulous diseases, or with any veneral diseases, or with any communicable skin affection; and every employer is hereby required to maintain himself and his employees in a clean condition while engaged in the manufacture, handling or sale of such food products, and it is hereby made the duty of the board of health to enforce the provisions of this section. Contagious diseases.

SEC. 20. The factory inspector is authorized to issue a certificate of satisfactory inspection to a person conducting a bakery, where such bakery is conducted in compliance with all the provisions of this Act [secs. 13 to 23]. Inspection.

SEC. 21. The owner, agent or lessee of any property * * * shall make the alterations or additions necessary, within such time as said alterations can be made with proper diligence upon the part of such proprietors, and notice to the last known address of such owner, agent or lessee, shall be deemed sufficient for the purpose of this act [secs. 13 to 23]. Alterations.

SEC. 22. A copy of this act shall be conspicuously posted and kept posted in each workroom of every bread, cake, or pie bakery, or confectionery establishment, in this State. Law to be posted.

SEC. 23. Any person who violates any of the provisions of this act [secs. 13 to 23], or refuses to comply with any requirements, as provided herein, of the factory inspector or his deputy, who are hereby charged with the enforcement of this act, excepting section seven [sec. 19], shall be guilty of a misdemeanor, and on conviction before any justice of the peace, magistrate, alderman, mayor or burgess, shall be punished by a fine of not less than Violations.

twenty nor more than fifty ($50) dollars, for the first offense; and not less than fifty ($50) [dollars] nor more than one hundred ($100) dollars, for a second offense, or imprisonment for not more than ten (10) days; and for a third offense, by a fine of not less than two hundred and fifty ($250) dollars and [not] more than thirty (30) days' imprisonment.

Fire escapes on factories, etc.—Cities of the first class.

(Page 525.)

What build- SECTION 89. All buildings of the first, second and third classes,
ings to have fire hereafter erected or altered to be used as * * * stores,
escapes. offices, manufactories, workshops, [or] mills * * * shall have,
in addition to the main stairs or other means of egress, a tower
fire escape, or escapes, as set forth in the following schedule:

BUILDINGS OF THE FIRST CLASS.

One tower fire escape.		Two tower fire escppes [escapes].
Number of stories in height.	Maximum area per floor in square feet.	Area per floor in square feet.
3 or 4	20,000	Over 20,000 to 25,000.
5	15,000	Over 15,000 to 25,000.
6	12,000	Over 12,000 to 25,000.
7	10,000	Over 10,000 to 22,000.
8	9,000	Over 9,000 to 20,000.
9	8,000	Over 8,000 to 18,000.
10	7,500	Over 7,500 to 17,000.
11	7,000	Over 7,000 to 16,000.
12	6,500	Over 6,500 to 15,000.

BUILDINGS OF THE SECOND AND THIRD CLASSES.

Onr [one] tower fire escape.		Two tower fire escapes.
Number of stories in height.	Maximum area per floor in square feet.	Area per floor in square feet.
3	10,000	Over 10,000 to 15,000.
4	6,000	Over 6,000 to 12,000.
5	4,500	Over 4,500 to 10,000.
6	3,500	Over 3,500 to 8,000.

Additional es- SEC. 90. If the total floor space above the second floor exceeds
capes. the number of square feet as set forth in the above schedule,
there may be required, in addition to the above mentioned number of fire escapes, as many additional tower fire escapes as the
chief of the bureau of building inspection may determine.

Location, etc. SEC. 91. The location and construction of all stairways and
tower fire escapes shall be determined and approved by the chief
of the bureau of building inspection.

Buildings ex- SEC. 92. *Provided*, That this section does not apply to office
empt. buildings of the first class, nor to buildings less than three stories
high, and buildings of greater number of stories in height than
two, in which the stories above the second story are not occupied
by persons: *Provided*, That in store buildings, in which tower
fire escapes in the first story would interfere with the bulk win-

dows, the said tower may stop at the second floor and that an exterior, continuous balcony be provided at the second floor level, with drop ladders.

SEC. 93. [In] All buildings used as stores, department stores, or buildings of any kind in which people assemble in the basement of said stores or buildings, there shall be provided safe means of egress from the basement, leading directly to the street, the proper location of such places of egress to be determined by the chief of the bureau of building inspection. Basement rooms.

SEC. 94. In this act the term "height" of a building, means the vertical distance of the highest point of the roof, in the case of flat roofs; and for high-pitched roofs, the average of the height of the gable above the mean grade of the curbs of all the streets, or the mean grade of the natural ground adjoining the building, if the said grade or ground is not below the grade of the curb. Definition.

Inspection of factories, etc.—Fire escapes, etc.—Cities of the second class.

(Page 581.)

SECTION 199. All buildings [in cities of the second class] to be hereafter erected or altered to be used as a * * * factory or workshop, more than two stories in height, shall have at least one stairway accessible from each department, which shall be enclosed wtih [with] brick walls, or partitions made of incombustible materials, and shall have no interior openings, other than the doors of the apartments from which it is an exit. All stores to be hereafter erected or altered to the extent of twenty-five per centum of the assessed valuation, when more than three stories in height, and in which any one of the stories above the second shall have a clear floor space of not less than four thousand square feet, may be provided with a tower fire escape, enclosed in incombustible material, adjoining one of its fronts, and such fire escape from the first to the second story may be a spiral staircase. Such fire escape shall be held and taken as a fire escape under the terms of the act, approved June eleventh, one thousand eight hundred and seventy-nine, entitled "An act to provide for the better security of life and limb in cases of fire in hotels and other buildings," and the several supplements and amendments thereto; and in the case of such stores in which the clear floor space of any story above the second shall be over ten thousand square feet, the said bureau [bureau of building inspection] may require one or more additional tower fire escapes as above described; and all mills more than two stories high of the floor area per story of three thousand square feet, or more, shall have such brick enclosed fire escape, or escapes as shall be approved by the director of the department of public safety. No obstruction shall be placed upon any way of egress from any building. No explosive or inflammable compound or combustible material shall be stored or placed under any stairway of any building, or to be used in any such place or manner as to obstruct or render egress hazardous in case of fire. Stairways.

Fire escape.

SEC. 200. In any hoistway, elevator or wellhole not enclosed in walls of brick or other fireproof materials, the openings through and upon each floor shall be provided with, and protected by, a substantial guard or gate, or with good and sufficient automatic trapdoors to close the same. Outside windows or openings of every elevator shaft shall have such sign or device to indicate the existence of the said shaft, as shall be approved by the said director of the department of public safety. No passenger elevator shall be operated unless a certificate signed by some reputable elevator builder that the elevator is safe and in good order has been furnished within six months, and is posted in the car at the entrance, and such further examinations and certificates shall be made and furnished as the director of the department of public safety may require. Hoistways to be guarded.

Certificates for elevators.

Factories and workshops—Sweat shops.

(Page 825.)

Manufactures in tenements.   SECTION 1. No room or apartment in any tenement or dwelling house shall be used for the manufacture of coats, vests, trousers, knee pants, overalls, skirts, dresses, cloaks, hats, caps, suspenders, jerseys, blouses, waists, waistbands, underwear, neckwear, furs, fur trimming, fur garments, shirts, hosiery, purses, feathers, arti-. ficial flowers, cigarettes or cigars, and no person, firm or corporation shall hire or employ and [any] person to work in any room, apartment, or in any building or parts of building, at making in whole or in part any of the articles mentioned in this section Permit required.   without first obtaining a written permit from the factory inspector, or one of his deputies, stating the maximum number of persons allowed to be employed therein, and that the building or part of building intended to be used for such work or business is thoroughly clean, sanitary and fit for occupancy for such work or business. Such permit shall not be granted until an inspection of such premises is made by the factory inspector or one of his deputies. Said permit may be revoked by the factory inspector at any time the health of the community or of those so employed may require it. It shall be framed and posted in a conspicuous place in the room, or in one of the rooms to which it relates. Every person, firm, company or corporation contracting for the manufacture of any of the articles mentioned in this section, or giving out the incomplete material from which they or any of them are to be made, or to be wholly or partly finished shall, before contracting for the manufacture of any of said articles or giving out said material from which they or any of them are to be made, require the production by such contractor, person or persons of said permit from the factory inspector as required in this section, and Register.   shall keep a written register of the names and addresses of all persons to whom such work is given to be made, or with whom they may have contracted to do the same. Such register shall be produced for inspection and a copy thereof shall be furnished on demand made by the factory inspector or one of his deputies: *Providing,* That nothing in this section shall be so construed as to prevent the employment of a seamstress by any family for manufacturing articles for such family['s] use.

Air space.   SEC. 2. Not less than two hundred and fifty cubic feet of air space shall be allowed for each and every person in any workroom where persons are employed at such labor as hereinbefore de-Ventilation.   scribed. There shall be sufficient means of ventilation provided in each workroom of every such establishment, and said workroom or rooms in said establishment shall be kept thoroughly clean, sanitary and fit for occupancy for such work or business. The factory inspector and deputy factory inspector, under the direction of the factory inspector, shall notify the owner, agent or lessee in writing to provide, or cause to be provided, ample and proper means for ventilating such workroom or rooms, and to Sanitary requirements, etc.   put said workroom or rooms in a thoroughly clean, sanitary and fit condition for occupancy for such work or business, and shall prosecute such owner, agent or lessee if such notification be not complied with within ten days of the service of such notice; and any factory or shop under this act requiring exits or other safeguards provided for in the fire-escape law, the same shall be erected and located by order of [the] factory inspector regardless of the exemption granted by any board or [of] county commissioners, fire marshals or other authorities, and if such alterations and additions are not made within sixty days from the date of such notice, or within such time as said alterations can be made with proper diligence upon the part of such proprietors, said proprietors or agents shall be deemed guilty of violating the provisions of this act.

Copy of law to be posted.   SEC. 3. A printed copy of this act shall be furnished by the inspector for each workroom of every factory, manufacturing or mercantile house where persons [are] employed who are affected by the provisions of this act, and it shall be the duty of the employer of the person[s] employed therein to post and keep posted said printed copy of the law in each room.

SEC. 4. Any person who violates any of the provisions of this act, or refuses to comply with any requirements of the factory inspector or a deputy factory inspector, as provided herein, shall be guilty of a misdemeanor, and on conviction shall be punished by a fine of not less than twenty dollars nor more than fifty dollars for the first offense, and not less than fifty dollars nor more than one hundred dollars for a second offense, or imprisonment for not more than ten days; and for a third effense [offense], by a fine of not less than two hundred and fifty dollars and not more than thirty days' imprisonment. In all such cases the hearing shall be conducted by the alderman or justice of the peace before whom information is lodged, and after full hearing of parties in interest the alderman or justice of the peace shall impose the fine herein provided, which shall be final unless an appeal be taken to the court of quarter sessions within twenty days from the date of the imposition of the fine as herein provided. And it shall also be lawful for the factory inspector or any of his deputies, and each and every one of them are hereby authorized and empowered to seize, take charge of, condemn and destroy any or all clothing found that is being made, or partially made, or manufactured in unhealthy or unsanitary places, or where there are contagious or infectious diseases, in violation of the provisions of this act of assembly. *Penalty.*

ACTS OF 1905.

ACT No. 226.—*Regulation and inspection of factories.*

SECTION 11. The owner or person in charge of an establishment where machinery is used shall provide belt shifters or other mechanical contrivances for the purpose of throwing on or off belts or pulleys. Whenever practicable, all machinery shall be provided with loose pulleys. All vats, pans, saws, planers, cogs, gearing, belting, shafting, set screws, grindstones, emery wheels, fly wheels, and machinery of every description shall be properly guarded. The floor space of no working room in any establishment shall be so crowded with machinery as thereby to cause risk to the life or limb of an employee; nor shall there be in any establishment machinery in excess of the sustaining power of the floors and walls thereof. No person shall remove or make ineffective any safeguard around or attached to machinery, vats or pans while the same are in use, except for the purpose of immediately making repairs thereto, and all such safeguards so removed shall be properly replaced. Exhaust fans of sufficient power, or other sufficient devices, shall be provided for the purpose of carrying off poisonous fumes and gases, and dust from emery wheels, grindstones and other machinery creating dust. If a machine or any part thereof is in a dangerous condition, or is not properly guarded, the use thereof may be prohibited by the chief factory inspector or by his deputy, and a notice to that effect shall be attached thereto. Such notice shall not be removed until the machinery is made safe and the required safeguards are provided, and in the meantime such unsafe or dangerous machinery shall not be used. *Belt shifters, guards, etc.*

Fans.

SEC. 12. The owner, agent, lessee, superintendent, or other person having charge or managerial control of any establishment, hotel, hospital, apartment house or other building, where elevators, hoisting shafts, lifts or wellholes are used, shall cause the same to be properly and substantially inclosed, secured or guarded; and shall provide such proper traps or automatic doors, so fastened in or at all elevator ways, except elevators inclosed on all sides, as to form a substantial surface when closed, and so constructed as to open and close by action of the elevator in its passage, either ascending or descending. The cable, gearing *Elevator wells, etc.*

or other apparatus of elevators, hoisters, or lifts, shall be kept in a safe condition: *Provided*, That the provisions of this section shall not apply to cities of the first and second classes.

space.

Sec. 13. The owner, agent, lessee, or other person having charge or managerial control of any establishment, shall provide or cause to be provided not less than two hundred and fifty cubic feet of air space for each and every person in every workroom in said establishment, where persons are employed, and shall provide that all workrooms, halls and stairways in said establishment be kept in a clean and sanitary condition and properly lighted.

n u factures ements.

Sec. 14. No person, firm or corporation engaged in the manufacture or sale of clothing or other wearing apparel, cigars or cigarettes, shall bargain or contract with any person, firm or corporation for the manufacture, or partial manufacture, of any of said articles or goods where the same are to be made in any kitchen, living room or bedroom in any tenement house or dwelling house, except where the persons bargaining or contracting to make or partially make any of the aforesaid articles or goods are resident members of the family, residing in such tenement house or dwelling house where the said articles or goods are to be made or partially made, and who have furnished the person, firm or corporation engaged in the manufacture or sale of said articles or goods, and with whom the bargain or contract is to be made, a certificate from the board of health, of the city or town in which such tenement house or dwelling house is situated, that the same is free from any infectious or contagious disease; which certificate may be revoked by the board of health whenever the exigencies of the case shall require: *Provided*, That the term "family" in this section shall include only the parents and their children, or the children of either.

section re-

Sec. 15. No person, firm or corporation engaged in the manufacture or sale of any of the articles or goods enumerated in section fourteen of this act, shall bargain or contract with any person, firm or corporation for the manufacture, or partial manufacture, of any of the said articles or goods in any workshop, not part of a tenement or dwelling house, unless the said workshop shall have been inspected by the chief factory inspector or by one of his deputies, and who shall have issued a printed permit to the person in charge of such workshop, stating that the same is in a clean and safe and sanitary condition, and fixing the maximum limit to the number of persons who may be employed therein; the permit to be posted and kept posted in a conspicuous place in such workshop: *Provided*, That this section shall not apply to any workshop wherein the aforesaid articles or goods are manufactured for the general trade, and are to be sold and delivered in or upon the premises, and are not manufactured, or partially manufactured, under a bargain or contract with any person, firm or corporation employed in the manufacture and sale of the article aforesaid.

its can- when.

Sec. 16. Whenever the sanitary conditions of any workshop, as defined in section fifteen, is dangerous to the health and safety of the employees therein or to the public, the chief factory inspector or his deputy shall cancel the permit aforesaid, and shall order that the workshop be vacated until the provisions of this act shall have been complied with and the workshop restored to proper sanitary condition.

eries.

Sec. 17. All persons, firms and corporations engaged in the manufacture or baking of bread, cakes, crackers, pastry, pretzels or macaroni, for public sale, shall keep their room or rooms for baking, mixing, storing, or sale of flour or other grain products separate and apart from any sleeping room, water-closet, urinal, defective drain or sewer pipe, and shall not permit the harboring of any domestic animal therein. The floors of all baking, mixing, storing and sales rooms shall be kept clean and tightly joined and free from crevices, and the walls and ceilings shall be painted, kalsomined or whitewashed as often as twice in each year and oftener if, in the opinion of the chief factory inspector or his deputy, the safety of the employees or the public shall require.

SEC. 18. When the foregoing provisions of section seventeen are complied with, the chief factory inspector or his deputy shall issue to the owner or person in charge of such bake shop a permit, stating that the same is in a clean and sanitary condition; which permit shall be posted and kept posted in the office or sales room of the bake shop, aforesaid; but when any of the foregoing provisions of section seventeen are not being complied with in any bake shop, the chief factory inspector or his deputy shall issue to the person in charge, or his representative, a written order to comply with the law aforesaid, within ten days; or he may order the closing of any such bake shop until the order shall have been complied with, should the safety of the employees, or the public, in his opinion, so require. Permits.

SEC. 19. All boilers used for generating steam or heat in any establishment shall be kept in good order, and the owner, agent or lessee of such establishment shall have said boilers inspected, by a casualty company in which said boilers are insured, or by any other competent person approved by the chief factory inspector, once in twelve months, and shall file a certificate showing the result thereof, in the office of such establishment, and shall send a duplicate thereof to the department of factory inspection. Each boiler or nest of boilers used for generating steam or heat in any establishment shall be provided with a proper safety valve and with steam and water gauges, to show, respectively, the pressure of steam and the height of water in the boilers. Every boiler house, in which a boiler or nest of boilers is placed, shall be provided with a steam gauge properly connected with the boilers, and another steam gauge shall be attached to the steam pipe in the engine house, and so placed that the engineer or fireman can readily ascertain the pressure carried. Nothing in this section shall apply to boilers which are regularly inspected by competent inspectors, acting under local laws and ordinances. Boilers to be inspected.

SEC. 20. It shall be the duty of the owner or superintendent of any establishment to report, in writing, to the chief factory inspector every serious accident or serious injury done to any person in his or her employ, where such accident or serious injury occurred in or about the premises where employed, within twenty-four hours after the accident or injury occurs, stating as fully as possible the cause of such accident or injury; and in all fatal and serious accidents the chief factory inspector or his deputy may subpœna witnesses, administer oaths, and do whatever may be necessary in order to make a thorough and complete investigation of the same: *Provided however,* That the provisions of this section shall not be construed as interfering with the duties of coroners, under existing laws. Accidents.

SEC. 21. It shall be the duty of the owner, superintendent, assistant or person in charge of any establishment to furnish, from time to time, to the chief factory inspector or his deputy any information required by the provisions of this act, and the chief factory inspector and his deputies shall have authority to inspect any such establishment, at any time, for the purpose of enforcing the provisions of this act. Duty of owner, etc.

SEC. 22. Wherever the law makes it the duty of the owner, lessee, or other person in charge of any building, or room or rooms in any building, to erect and maintain fire escapes, or appliances for the extinguishment of fire, or for proper and sufficient exits in case of fire or panic, the chief factory inspector or his deputy shall inspect all said buildings, or the room or rooms in said buildings, and notify the owners, lessees, or other persons in charge of same, to comply with said law. And all fire escapes, exits and fire extinguishing appliances shall be provided and located by order of the chief factory inspector or his deputy, and shall be subject to the approval of the chief factory inspector or Fire escapes, etc.

his deputy: *Provided*, That the provisions of this section shall not apply to cities of the first and second classes.

Violations.　SEC. 23. Any person who violates any of the provisions of the foregoing sections of the act, or who suffers any female, minor or a child to be employed in or about his or her establishment, in violation of any of the provisions of the foregoing sections of this act, or who, being authorized to administer oaths, shall violate any of the provisions of sections five and six of this act, shall be deemed guilty of a misdemeanor, and, on conviction, shall be punished by a fine of not less than twenty-five dollars and not more than five hundred dollars, or an imprisonment in the county jail for a term not less than ten days nor more than sixty days, for each and every such violation. In all cases the prosecution shall be instituted, in the name of the Commonwealth, by the deputy factory inspector of the district where the offense is alleged to have been committed, and the hearing shall be conducted by the alderman, justice of the peace or other committing magistrate before whom the information is lodged. After full hearing of the parties in interest, the alderman, justice of the peace or other committing magistrate shall, if the evidence warrants it, impose the penalty herein provided, which shall be final to the party against whom the penalty is imposed, unless the party upon whom the penalty is imposed shall furnish good and sufficient bail for his or her appearance at the next term of the court of quarter sessions of the county wherein the offense is alleged to have been committed.

Duty of chief inspector.　SEC. 25. The chief factory inspector shall prepare the form of the employment certificate for children, and the permits, blanks, orders and notices required by this act; the same to be printed in accordance with the laws regulating printing and publishing, under the supervision of the superintendent of public printing and binding. He shall also divide the State into inspection districts, and assign one of the deputy factory inspectors to each district, and may transfer any of the said inspectors from one district to another, and make such rules and regulations governing their employment as the best interests of the service shall require. And he, the deputy factory inspector, and those employed in the office of the chief factory inspector, shall have the same power to administer oaths or affirmations as is now given to notaries public, in all cases where any person desires to verify documents necessary and incident to the issuing of employment certificates for children.

Report.　SEC. 26. After the first day of January in each year, the chief factory inspector shall compile or cause to be compiled a succinct statistical and narrative report, to be addressed to the governor of the Commonwealth, of the work of his department for the year ending December thirty-first.

Officials.　SEC. 27. To more effectually secure the observance of the provisions of this act and the fire escape laws, the governor shall appoint, by and with the advice and consent of the senate, a chief factory inspector, for a term of four years, at a salary of five thousand dollars per annum; and who shall appoint a chief clerk, at a salary of two thousand dollars per annum; a statistician, at a salary of eighteen hundred dollars per annum; an assistant clerk, at a salary of fourteen hundred dollars per annum; a messenger, who shall be a typewriter, at a salary of twelve hundred dollars per annum, and thirty-nine deputy factory inspectors, five of whom shall be women, at a salary of twelve hundred dollars each, per annum, and their necessary traveling expenses; the chief factory inspector and his appointees, aforesaid, to constitute the department of factory inspection.

[The appropriation act of 1907 (Acts of 1907, page 777) increased the number of deputy factory inspectors to forty-one. As to salary, see act, page 911, Acts of 1911, page 1061 of this volume.]

ACTS OF 1909.

Act No. 233.—*Fire escapes on factories, etc.*

Section 1. * * * every building in which persons are usually *Fire escapes to* employed above the second story, in a factory, workshop, or mer- *be provided.* cantile establishment; * * * shall be provided with proper ways of egress, or means of escape from fire, sufficient for the use of all persons * * * employed * * * therein; and such ways of egress and means of escape shall be kept free from obstruction, in good repair, and ready for use, at all times; and all rooms above the second story in said buildings shall be provided with more than one way of egress, or escape from fire, which shall be placed as near as practical at opposite ends or sides of the room, and leading to fire escapes on the outside of such buildings or to stairways on the inside. Where any of said buildings is designated for the use or occupancy of fifty or more persons, the external doors of the same shall open outward, and be so constructed or arranged as to afford, when open, an unobstructed external passageway of not less than five feet in the clear, and shall have landings, inside of the external doorways, of dimensions not less than four feet between the external doors and the adjoining stairways, said landings to be of a width not less than the stairway approaches thereto.

Sec. 3. In addition to the foregoing means of escape from fire, *Outside fire es-* all such buildings as are enumerated in section one of this act *capes.* that are more than two stories in height, * * * shall have one or more fire escapes on the outside of said buildings, as may be directed by the chief factory inspector or a deputy factory inspector, except in such cases as he may deem such fire escape to be unnecessary, in consequence of adequate provision having been already made for safety in event of fire or panic; and in such cases of exemption, the said chief factory inspector or a deputy factory inspector shall give the owner, lessee, or occupant of said building a certificate to that effect, and his reason therefor.

And such fire escapes as are provided for in this section shall *Construction.* be of wrought iron, constructed according to specifications to be issued or approved by the department of factory inspection, and shall be connected with each floor above the first, firmly fastened and secured, and of sufficient strength to sustain a weight of not less than four hundred pounds per step, on a safety factor of four; each of which fire escapes shall have landings or balconies at each story, capable of sustaining a weight of not less than eighty pounds per square foot, guarded by railings, not less than three feet in height, and embracing one or more windows or doors at each story, and connecting with the interior by easily accessible and unobstructed openings; and all the balconies or landings shall be connected by external iron stairways, placed at a slant of not more than forty-five degrees, protected by well-secured hand rails; the stairway steps to be not less than six inches in width and twenty-four inches in length. Fire escapes now in use and hereafter erected must be painted once a year, and be kept in safe condition and up to the standard requirements of this section.

Sec. 6. The owner or owners of any of the buildings mentioned *Violations.* in the foregoing provisions of this act, who shall willfully fail or refuse to comply with the provisions of this act, or who shall willfully fail or refuse to observe the orders for the enforcement of this act, issued to said owner or owners by the chief factory inspector or deputy factory inspector, shall be deemed guilty of a misdemeanor, and, on conviction thereof, shall be punished by a fine of five hundred dollars, or six months imprisonment, or either or both, in the discretion of the court. And in case of *Liability of* fire occurring in any of said buildings, in the absence of such *negligent owners.* doorways, landings, exits, fire escapes or fire preventives, as provided for in this act, the owner or owners aforesaid shall be liable for damages, in case of death or personal injury, the result of fire or panic in any of said buildings; and such action for damages may be maintained by any person now authorized by law to sue, as in other case of loss by death or injuries.

ACTS OF 1911.

Factory regulation—Foundries.

(Page 673.)

Wash rooms.   SECTION 1. Every person, firm, or corporation, being the owner or lessee of any foundry for the casting of iron, steel, brass, or other metal, wherein ten or more men shall be employed, shall cause to be established and maintained in a place conveniently accessible, and connected with said foundry in a manner that access thereto can be had without exposure to the open air, a toilet room of suitable size, wherein said employees may change their clothes; such toilet room shall be provided with washbowls, sinks, or other suitable fixed appliances, duly connected and supplied with running hot and cold water. There shall also be established and maintained, separate from said toilet room, a suitable water-closet.

Access.   SEC. 2. The said toilet room and the said water-closet shall be connected with the foundry building in such a way that access thereto may be had without exposure to the open air, and shall be properly heated, ventilated, cleaned, and protected, so far as reasonably practicable, from the dust of such foundry.

Violations.   SEC. 3. Any person, firm, or corporation who or which shall violate any of the provisions of this act shall be guilty of a misdemeanor, and upon conviction thereof before any magistrate, alderman, or justice of the peace, shall be sentenced to a fine not exceeding one hundred dollars.

Factory regulations—Fire drills.

(Page 677.)

Fire drills monthly.   SECTION 1. In all factories and industrial establishments where women or girls are employed, and where fire escapes, appliances for the extinguishment of fires, or proper and sufficient exits in case of fires or panic, either or all, are required by law to be maintained, fire drills shall be periodically conducted, not less than once a month, by the person or persons in charge, under rules and regulations to be promulgated, in cities of the first and second classes, by the fire marshal, and, elsewhere in the Commonwealth, by the chief factory inspector, in which the persons employed in such factories or establishments shall be instructed in, and made thoroughly familiar with, the use of the said fire escapes, appliances, and exits; which said drills shall include the actual use of the same, and the complete removal of the persons, in an expeditious and orderly manner, by means of such fire escapes and exits, from the building to a place of safety on the ground outside.

Enforcement.   SEC. 2. The fire marshal and his assistants in cities of the first and second classes, and the chief factory inspector and several deputy inspectors elsewhere in the Commonwealth, are hereby required to see that the provisions of this act are faithfully carried out.

Violations.   SEC. 3. Any person who violates or fails to comply with the provisions of this act shall be guilty of a misdemeanor, and on conviction shall be sentenced to pay a fine of not less than twenty-five dollars ($25) nor more than five hundred dollars ($500), and to undergo imprisonment in the county jail for not less than ten days nor more than sixty days, either or both.

Fire escapes on factories.

(Page 705.)

SECTION 12. The fire marshal, his chief assistant and inspectors, Inspection. may examine all buildings upon which any fire escapes may be erected, shall see that it is kept in good order and repair, and no person shall at any time, place any incumbrance of any kind whatsoever upon any of said fire escapes or passageways constructed or intended for the escape of persons from the premises in case of fire. Any owner or occupant of buildings or premises, failing to comply with the orders of the authorities above specified, shall be deemed guilty of keeping and maintaining a nuisance detrimental to life and property, and on conviction before any magistrate be fined twenty-five dollars, or, in default of such payment, imprisoned in the county prison not more than thirty days.

Factory inspectors—salary.

(Page 911.)

SECTION 1. From and after June first, Anno Domini one thou- Increase of salsand nine hundred and eleven, the compensation of the deputy ary. factory inspectors shall be fifteen hundred dollars per annum, and their traveling expenses.

PHILIPPINE ISLANDS.

ACTS OF 1908.

ACT No. 1868.—*Bureau of labor.*

SECTION 1. There is hereby established in the department of Bureau estab. commerce and police a bureau which shall be known as the lished. bureau of labor.

SEC. 2. The purpose of this bureau shall be:

(a) To see to the proper enforcement of all existing laws and Purposes: those which shall be enacted hereafter with reference to labor Law enforce- and capital in the Philippine Islands, and to promote the enact- ment. ment of all other legislation which shall tend to establish the material, social, intellectual, and moral improvement of workers;

(b) To acquire, collect, compile, systematize, and submit from Statistics. time to time reports to the secretary of commerce and police, statistical data relative to the hours and wages of labor, the number of workers in each trade or occupation employed and unemployed, their place of birth, age, sex, civil status, and moral and mental culture; the estimated number of families of married workers, houses rented by them, and annual rental; property owned by them, the value of such property; the cost of living, the amount of labor required, the estimated number of persons dependent on their daily wages, the probable changes in all the persons employed, the condition of shops, factories, railways, tramways, industrial and commercial establishments, and all other places or temples of labor, whether public or private, including the penal institutions of these islands, with respect to the safety of life and health of workers; the means adopted to avoid accidents or make reparation therefor; the number of accidents which take place, their causes and the action taken in each case; conditions and certainty of the payment of wages; the business of savings banks with the working classes; corporations, strikes, suspensions of work, and other labor difficulties, their causes and the remedies adopted in each case; mutual benefit associations, workers' insurance societies, associations for the collection of statistics and cooperative production and other labor organizations, and their effects on labor and capital; private employment, complaint, defense, and consultation agencies for laborers; their conditions and effects and other matters relative to the commercial, industrial, social, educational, moral, and sanitary condition of the working classes and the permanent prosperity of the various industries of the Islands; and in the case of laborers born in foreign countries, the date of their arrival and the length of their stay in these Islands;

Inspection of factories, etc. (c) To inspect all shops, factories, railways, tramways, vessels, industrial and commercial establishments, and all other places or centers of labor, whether public or private, and to take the proper legal steps to prevent the exposure of the health or lives of laborers, and to aid and assist by all proper legal means laborers and workers in securing just compensation for their labor, and the indemnity prescribed by law for injuries resulting from accidents when engaged in the performance of their duties.

Arbitration of disputes. (d) To secure the settlement of differences between employer and laborer and to avert strikes and lockouts by inducing all parties to the controversy to submit their differences to arbitration.

Establishment of free employment offices. (e) To organize in such towns in the Philippine Islands as it may deem necessary or advisable one or more free employment agencies.

Powers. SEC. 3. By and with the approval of the governor general, the director of labor shall have power to administer oaths, to issue subpoenas and subpoenas duces tecum, and to receive and take affidavits and the testimony of witnesses and experts, when making investigations authorized by this act.

Officers. SEC. 4. The bureau of labor shall have one chief and one assistant chief, who shall be appointed by the governor general, by and with the consent of the Philippine Commission, and who shall be known respectively as the director of labor and the assistant director of labor. The director of labor shall exercise the powers and perform the duties herein imposed upon the bureau of labor. The assistant director of labor shall perform the duties of the director of labor during the absence or disability of the latter and such other duties as may be required of him by the director of labor. The salary of the director of labor shall be seven thousand pesos and that of the assistant director of labor four thousand pesos per annum.

PORTO RICO.

ACTS OF 1910.

No. 33.—*Provisions in case of accident—Cane mills.*

Resident physician. SECTION 1. Owners of sugar centrales located at a distance of over four kilometers from a township are hereby directed to keep during the grinding season, a dispensary and a physician or minor surgeon who shall remain in the centrale during working hours, in order to urgently lend assistance to persons in cases of accidents to them.

RHODE ISLAND.

GENERAL LAWS—1909.

CHAPTER 78.—*Regulation and inspection of factories and workshops.*

Inspectors. SECTION 3 (as amended by chapter 576, enacted 1910). The governor shall, upon the passage of this act, and in the month of January of every third year hereafter, appoint, with the advice and consent of the senate, one chief and four assistant factory inspectors, one of whom shall be a woman, whose term of office shall be three years and until their successors shall be so appointed and qualified. * * * Any vacancy which may occur in said offices when the senate is not in session shall be filled by the governor until the next session thereof, when he shall, with the advice and consent of the senate, appoint some person to fill such vacancy for the remainder of the term. Said inspector shall be empowered to visit and inspect, at all reasonable hours and as often as practicable, the factories, workshops, and other establishments in this State subject to the provisions of this chapter, and shall report to the general assembly of this State at its January session in each year, including in said reports the names of the factories, the number of such hands employed, and the number of hours of work performed in each week. It shall also be the duty of said inspectors to enforce the provisions of this chapter and prosecute all violations of the same before any court of competent jurisdiction in the State.

The name and residence of any child found working without the certificate provided for in section one of this chapter shall be reported by the chief inspector to the school committee in the city or town where such child resides. Said inspectors shall devote their whole time and attention to the duties of their respective offices, under the direction of the chief inspector. The annual salary of the chief inspector shall be two thousand dollars; and each of the assistant inspectors, fifteen hundred dollars.

SEC. 4 (as amended by chapter 576, Acts of 1910). All necessary expenses incurred by such inspectors in the discharge of their duty shall be paid by the general treasurer out of any funds in the treasury not otherwise appropriated, upon the presentation of proper vouchers for the same approved by the governor: *Provided*, That not more than twenty-three hundred dollars in the aggregate shall be expended by said inspectors for such expenses in any one year. Expenses.

SEC. 5 (as amended by chapter 701, Acts of 1911). It shall be the duty of the owner, agent or lessee of any factory, manufacturing or mercantile establishment, where hoisting shafts or well holes are used, to cause the same to be properly and substantially enclosed or secured if, in the opinion of the inspectors, it is necessary to protect the life or limbs of those employed in such establishments. The owner, agent or lessee of any factory, manufacturing or mercantile establishment shall enclose or cause to be enclosed all freight elevator ways on all sides thereof, and shall provide or cause to be provided an entrance or entrances thereto by means of an automatic or semiautomatic gate or gates, not less than six feet in height, sliding vertically upward and so constructed as to close by the action of the elevator on leaving each floor. Guards required for hoisting ways, etc.

SEC. 6. No minor under sixteen years of age shall be allowed to clean machinery while in motion, unless the same is necessary and is approved by said inspectors as not dangerous. All belting and gearing shall be provided with proper safeguard[s]. Minor cleaning moving machinery.

SEC. 7. It shall be the duty of the owners or superintendent to report in writing to the factory inspectors all fatal accidents within forty-eight hours after their occurrence; and all accidents which prevent the injured person or persons from returning to work within two weeks after the injury shall, within one week after the expiration of such two weeks, be reported in writing by the person in charge of such establishment or place to the said inspectors, stating as fully as possible the cause of such accidents. Accidents.

SEC. 8. Water-closets, earth closets or privies shall be provided in all places where women and children are employed, in such manner as shall, in the judgment of said inspectors, meet the demands of health and propriety. Separate dressing rooms for women and girls shall be provided in all establishments where such are deemed a necessity by said factory inspectors; and in every manufacturing, mechanical or mercantile establishment in which women and girls are employed, there shall be provided, conveniently located, seats for such women and girls, and they shall be permitted to use them when their duties do not require their standing. Water-closets, etc. Seats for female employees.

Defective conditions. SEC. 9. If the factory inspectors, or either one of them, find that the heating, lighting, ventilation or sanitary arrangement of any shop or factory is such as to be injurious to the health of the persons employed therein, or that the means of egress in case of fire or other disaster is not sufficient, or in accordance with all the requirements of law, or that the belting, shafting, gearing, elevators, drums and machinery in shops and factories are located so as to be dangerous to employees, and not sufficiently guarded, or that the vats, pans or structures filled with molten metal or hot liquid are not surrounded with proper safeguards for preventing accident or injury to those employed at or near them, either **Notice.** or both shall notify the proprietor of such factory or workshop to make the alterations or additions necessary within ninety days; and if such alterations or additions are not made within ninety days from the day of such notice, or within such time as such alterations can be made with proper diligence upon the part of said proprietors, said proprietors or agents shall be deemed guilty of violating the provisions of this chapter, subject, however, to the right of appeal as hereinafter provided.

Appeal from inspectors' orders. SEC. 10. Any person who is aggrieved by any order of said inspectors may appeal therefrom to the district court of the judicial district in which the building which is the subject of the order is situated, by filing his reasons of appeal within seven days after the date of the order appealed from, and by giving notice thereof to the inspector who made the order within forty-eight hours after filing said reasons of appeal; and said court shall proceed to hear the said appeal at its first session after such notice shall have been given, and shall approve, modify, or revoke said order as it may deem right, subject, however, to the right of a jury trial after decision * * * And any such decision of said court from which a jury trial is not claimed shall be final and conclusive.

Power of inspectors. SEC. 11. The State shall provide a suitable office for the use of said factory inspectors; and said factory inspectors shall have the power to administer oaths or affirmations in cases where persons desire to verify documents connected with the proper enforcement of this chapter.

Violations. SEC. 12. Any person or corporation who employs a child under sixteen years of age without the certificate required by section one of this chapter, or who makes a false statement in regard to any part required by such certificate or who violates any of the provisions of this chapter, or who suffers or permits any child or woman to be employed in violation of its provisions, shall be deemed guilty of a misdemeanor and, on conviction, shall be punished by a fine of not more than five hundred dollars: *Provided, however*, That this section shall not apply to that portion of section one of this chapter which fixes the penalty for the refusal to show to the inspector any certificate provided for in that section.

Copy of act to be posted. SEC. 13. A printed copy of this chapter shall be posted by the inspectors in each workroom of every factory, manufacturing or mercantile establishment where persons are employed who are affected by the provisions of this chapter.

Surety for costs. SEC. 14. The inspectors created by section three of this chapter shall not be required to give surety nor personal recognizance for costs.

Enforcement of law as to hours of labor. SEC. 15. The factory inspectors shall, in addition to their duties otherwise provided, enforce the provisions of section twenty-two, chapter two hundred forty-nine [see page 823] and may prosecute all violations of the same before any court of competent jurisdiction in the State.

Drinking water to be provided. SEC. 16. All manufacturing establishments in this State shall provide fresh drinking water, of good quality, to which their employees shall have access during working hours.

Violation. SEC. 17. Any corporation, association, firm or person owning, in whole or in part, managing, controlling, or superintending any manufacturing establishment in which the provision of the preceding section is violated shall, upon complaint of the board of health of the city or town, or the town council of the town, in which the establishment is located, be liable to a fine of one hundred dollars for each offense.

SEC. 18 (added by chapter 576, Acts of 1910). Said chief [factory] inspector or any assistant factory inspector required by him, shall have charge of the inspection of bakeries, confectioneries, and ice cream manufactories, and any premises upon which bread or other products of flour or meal are baked or mixed or prepared for baking or for sale as food, in this State. Said inspector shall have charge of the inspection of cooked and prepared foods and food stuffs displayed or offered for sale in any store, market, restaurant, lunch cart or lunch counter, or other place of public display which are liable to become detrimental to public health through exposure to and contact with flies, animals, insects, dust, and germs, and he shall have the authority to require that all foods of this description shall be kept in tight wooden or glass cases or cupboards, or under glass, earthen, or tin covers, or in cases or cans, or wrapped in paraffin paper, or protected in such a manner that no dust or animals can come in contact with said foods while thus offered for sale. He is also authorized to require that said foods, when carried through any street, private way, or public place, shall be protected in a similar manner. All candies, confectionery, dried or preserved fruits, dates, figs, cut fruits, cut melons, cracked nuts, or nut meats shall be protected as provided above, when offered for sale, and any such inspectors so acting, whether one or more of such inspectors, or whether acting at the same or different times, shall for such purposes be designated as a State inspector of bakeries and foods. Such inspector shall not be pecuniarily interested, directly or indirectly, in the manufacture or sale of any article or commodity used in any business included in the provisions of this act, and shall not give certificates or written opinions to a maker or vender of any such article or commodity.

Duties of inspectors as to bakeries, etc.

Markets, restaurants, etc.

SEC. 19 (added by chapter 576, Acts of 1910). No person, copartnership, or corporation shall carry on the business of a public bakery, confectionery, or ice cream manufactory, or place where bread or other products of flour or meal are baked or mixed or prepared for baking or for sale as food, until such premises are inspected by said State inspector. If such premises be found to conform to the provisions of this act, said inspector shall issue a certificate to the owner or operator of such bakery, confectionery, or ice cream manufactory, or place where flour or meal food products are baked or mixed or prepared for baking or for sale as food.

Bakeries to be inspected.

SEC. 20 (added by chapter 576, Acts of 1910). All buildings or rooms used or occupied as biscuit, bread, macaroni, spaghetti, pie or cake bakeries, ice cream or confectionery manufactories, or where flour or meal food products are baked or mixed or prepared for baking or for sale as food, shall be drained and plumbed in a manner conducive to the proper and healthful sanitary condition thereof, and shall be constructed with air shafts, windows, or ventilating pipes sufficient to insure adequate and proper ventilation. No cellar, basement, or place which is below the street level shall hereafter be used or occupied for the purposes mentioned in this section: *Provided*, That the same may be so used or occupied by the present occupant only.

Sanitary requirements.

SEC. 21 (added by chapter 576, Acts of 1910). Every room used for the purposes included in this act shall have, if deemed necessary by such inspector, an impermeable floor constructed of cement, or of tiles laid in cement, or of wood or other suitable nonabsorbent material which can be flushed and washed clean with water. Such inspector shall require said premises to be kept at all times in a sanitary condition; he may also require the woodwork of such walls to be well oiled, varnished, or painted. The furniture and utensils shall be so arranged as to be readily cleansed and not prevent the proper cleaning of any part of the room.

Same subject.

The manufactured flour or meal food products shall be kept in dry and airy rooms, so arranged that the floors, shelves, and all other facilities for storing the same can be properly cleaned.

No domestic animals except cats shall be allowed to remain in
a room used as a biscuit, bread, pie, or cake bakery, or any room
in such bakery where flour or meal products are stored or kept.

Wash rooms,
water-closets, etc.
SEC. 22 (added by chapter 576, Acts of 1910). Every such
bakery, confectionery, or ice cream manufactory, or place where
flour or meal food products are baked or mixed or prepared for
baking or for sale as food, shall be provided with a proper wash
room and water-closet, or water-closets, apart from the bake-
rooms or rooms where the manufacture of such food products is
conducted, and they shall be maintained in a sanitary condition;
no water-closet, earth closet, privy, or receptacle for garbage shall
be within or connect directly with the bake room of any bakery or
room where ice cream or confectionery is manufactured. Operatives, employees, clerks, and all persons who handle the material
from which food is prepared, or the finished product, before beginning work, or after visiting toilet or toilets, shall wash their
hands and arms thoroughly in clean water.

Sleeping in
workrooms.
No person shall sleep in a room occupied as a bake room
Sleeping places for the persons employed in the bakery shall be
separate from the rooms where flour or meal food products are
manufactured or stored. If the sleeping places are on the same
floor where such products are manufactured, stored, or sold, such
inspector may inspect and order them put in a proper sanitary
condition.

Stables.
SEC. 23 (added by chapter 576, Acts of 1910). No bakery, confectionery, or ice cream manufactory, or place where flour or meal
food products are baked or mixed or prepared for baking or for
sale as food, shall be conducted in a room adjoining a stable, unless separated from such stable by a wall or partition without any
door or other opening between such stable and such bakery, confectionery, or manufactory, or place where flour or meal food
products are baked or mixed or prepared for baking or for sale
as food; and no material used therein shall be kept in a stable.

Use of tobacco
SEC. 25 (added by chapter 576, Acts of 1910). Smoking, snuffing,
or chewing of tobacco, or spitting on floor in working rooms in
such bakery, confectionery, or manufactory, or place where flour
or meal food products are baked or mixed or prepared for baking
or for sale as food, is strictly forbidden.

Infectious and
contagious dis-
eases.
SEC. 26 (added by chapter 576, Acts of 1910). No employer in
any bakery, confectionery, or ice cream manufactory, or place
where flour or meal food products are baked or mixed or prepared
for baking or for sale as food, shall require, permit, or suffer any
persons to work, nor shall any person work, in a building, room,
basement, cellar, or vehicle occupied or used for the production,
preparation, manufacture, packing, storage, sale, distribution, and
transportation of food, who is affected with any venereal disease,
smallpox, diphtheria, scarlet fever, yellow fever, tuberculosis or
consumption, bubonic plague, Asiatic cholera, leprosy, trachoma,
typhoid fever, epidemic dysentery, measles, mumps, German
measles, whooping cough, chicken pox, or any other infectious or
contagious disease.

Semiannual in-
spections.
SEC. 28 (added by chapter 576, Acts of 1910). Bakeries, confectioneries, and ice cream manufactories, or places where flour or
meal food products are baked or mixed or prepared for baking or
for sale as food, shall be kept at all times in a clean and sanitary
condition, and shall be inspected by said inspector at least twice
each year. If on inspection said inspector finds any bakery, confectionery, or ice cream manufactory, or place where flour or meal
food products are baked or mixed or prepared for baking or for
sale as food, to be so unclean, ill-drained, or ill-ventilated as to be
unsanitary, he may, after such reasonable time, to be fixed by
said inspector, not less than five days, by notice in writing, to be
served by affixing the notice on the inside of the main entrance
door of said bakery, confectionery, or ice cream manufactory, or
place where flour or meal food products are baked or mixed or
prepared for baking or for sale as food, order the person found

in charge thereof immediately to cease operating it until it be properly cleaned, drained, or ventilated.

SEC. 29 (added by chapter 576, Acts of 1910). Any person who **Appeals.** is aggrieved by any order or requirement of said State inspector may appeal therefrom in the same manner in all respects, and with the same rights and liabilities, as provided in section 10 of this chapter.

SEC. 30 (added by chapter 576, Acts of 1910). Any person who **Violations.** violates any of the provisions of said sections nineteen to twenty-eight, both inclusive, of this chapter, or who refuses to comply with any lawful requirement of the authority vested with the enforcement of such sections, as provided therein, shall be guilty of a misdemeanor, and on conviction shall be punished by a fine of not less than twenty or more than fifty dollars for a first offense, and for a second offense by a fine of not less than fifty or more than one hundred dollars or by imprisonment for not more than ten days, and for a third offense by a fine of not less than one hundred or more than two hundred and fifty dollars or by imprisonment for not more than thirty days, or by both such fine and imprisonment.

SEC. 31 (added by chapter 576, Acts of 1910). Such inspector **Enforcement.** shall be empowered to visit and inspect all parts of stores, bakeries, confectioneries, and storerooms and places where ice cream, flour and meal food products are manufactured, and all stores, markets, restaurants, lunch carts or lunch counters, and other places where food is kept for sale, at any and all reasonable times, and as often as practicable. Such inspector shall promptly enforce the provisions of this act, and shall prosecute all violations of the same before any court of competent jurisdiction in the State. The attorney general shall act as his legal adviser in all matters pertaining to his official duties. He shall cause copies of this act to be printed and kept posted in all bakeries, confectioneries, and manufactories of ice cream, flour and meal food products, and all places where such business is carried on. Any mutilation of such printed matter shall be punished as provided in the preceding section. Such inspector shall not be required to give surety, nor furnish recognizance for costs, in any prosecution or proceeding under this act.

CHAPTER 117.—*Factory regulations—Foundries.*

SECTION 1. Every foundry in this State employing ten or more **Wash rooms to be provided.** men shall provide suitable toilet rooms, containing washbowls or sinks, provided with water. water-closets, and a room wherein the men may change their clothes, said rooms to be within the building used for said foundry, and shall be protected from the weather, heated and ventilated.

SEC. 2. Any person or corporation failing to comply with section **Violations.** 1 of this chapter shall be deemed guilty of a misdemeanor, and upon conviction thereof shall be fined not less than fifty nor more than one hundred dollars, one-half thereof to the use of the complainant, one-half thereof to the use of the State.

CHAPTER 129.—*Fire escapes on factories, etc.*

SECTION 1. Every building three or more stories in height, now **Fire escapes to be provided.** or hereafter used wholly or in part as a * * * factory or workshop in which employees are usually working in the third or any higher story thereof, and every building used for office purposes three or more stories in height, shall be provided by the owner or owners thereof either with proper and sufficient, strong and durable metallic fire escapes upon the external walls, sufficient in number, which fire escapes shall extend from the highest occupied story to the top of the first story of said building, or with proper and sufficient incombustible stairs and stairways at opposite ends of the building, extending from the highest occupied story to the ground; said stairs and stairways shall be connected by open passageways of suitable width; said fire escapes, stairs and stairways to be suitable and sufficient to afford to persons within said building proper egress from said building in case of fire therein, and to be kept in repair by said owner or owners.

Inspectors. SEC. 2. The town councils of the several towns throughout the State, and the mayors of the several cities, except in the city of Providence, shall annually in the month of January elect an inspector of buildings, who shall be paid such amount for his services as shall be determined by the town or city council electing him.

Duty of inspectors. SEC. 3. It shall be the duty of the inspectors of buildings of the city of Providence and of the other cities and towns, from time to time as may be necessary, to make a careful and thorough inspection of all buildings in the city or town for which they shall be elected, which in their opinion might, by reason of the height thereof, character or number of stairways, number of persons ordinarily therein or at work therein, nature of use of said buildings, nature of the industries or occupations carried on therein, or for any other reason, be specially dangerous to persons therein in case of conflagration in said buildings.

Buildings may be exempted. SEC. 5. Said inspectors of buildings shall have power within their respective towns and cities, upon the application in writing of any owner or owners of any building in said town or city, setting forth specific, just and true reasons why said building should be exempted from the provisions of this chapter, to exempt by written certificate, setting forth the reasons therefor, any building from the provisions of this chapter, whenever in the opinion of said inspector said building, by reason of location, special features of construction, or for any other reason, does not require said fire escapes or said stairs and stairways: *Provided, however,* That such written application, together with a duly certified copy of such certificate of exemption, shall by said inspector be deposited with the city or town clerk for said city or town, to be kept on file by said city or town clerk: *And provided further,* That such exemption may at any time be revoked by the inspector of buildings of said city or town upon thirty days' notice in writing to the owner or owners of said building.

Certificate of inspection. SEC. 6. Whenever the inspector of buildings for any city or town shall upon inspection be satisfied that any building in said town or city is provided with fire escapes or with stairs and stairways, in accordance with the provisions of this chapter, he shall upon request of any owner of said building give to such owner a certificate to that effect, and shall deposit a certified copy thereof in the office of the city or town clerk for said city or town, to be kept on file by said city or town clerk. Such certificate, including any unexpired certificate heretofore issued, shall exempt the owners of said building from all civil and criminal liability under this chapter until revoked as hereinafter provided: *Provided, however,* That such certificate may be at any time revoked by the inspector of buildings for said town or city, by notice in writing to such owner to whom said certificate may have been issued, and by filing a copy of said notice of revocation with the said city or town clerk, to be by said city or town clerk kept on file: *And provided further,* That in case said building shall be materially changed or altered in form or use, then such certificate shall be utterly void and of no effect. It shall be the duty of the several city and town clerks to receive and keep on file the notices and certificats provided for in this chapter.

Owners may enter leased premises. SEC. 7. The owner or owners of any building or premises under lease, and their servants and agents, may enter upon such leased building or premises for the public welfare, for the purpose of making said building conform with the provisions of this chapter, and may remain thereon during such time as may reasonably be required for the performance of such work as may be necessary to effect said purpose, interfering with the lessee no more than may be necessary.

SEC. 8. In all cases in which any person shall suffer injury or **Damages.** in which the death of any person shall ensue in consequence of the failure of the owner or owners of any building to provide the same with fire escapes or stairs and stairways, as required by the provisions of this chapter, or in consequence of the failure of said owner or owners to comply with the written notice and requirement of any inspector of buildings, when made in conformity to the provisions of this chapter, such owner or owners shall be jointly and severally liable, to any person so injured, in an action of trespass on the case for damages for such injury; and in case of death such owner or owners shall be jointly and severally liable in damages for the injury caused by the death of such person, to be recovered, by action of trespass on the case, in the same manner and for the benefit of the same persons as is provided in sections fourteen and fifteen of chapter two hundred eighty three; which action, when the owners are nonresidents, may be commenced by attachment. It shall be no defense to said action that the person injured or whose death ensued as aforesaid, had knowledge that any such building was not provided with fire escapes or stairs and stairways as required by the provisions of this chapter, or that such person continued to work in or to occupy said building with said knowledge.

SEC. 9. The owner or owners of any building, or in case such **Penalty.** owners, or any of them, be non compos mentis, or a minor, the guardian of any such owner, or in case such owners, or any of them, be nonresident, the agent of any such owner having charge of such property, who shall neglect or fail to comply with the foregoing provisions of this chapter shall be fined not less than one hundred dollars nor more than five hundred dollars. In case there shall be several owners of any building which shall be continued in violation of said provisions of this chapter, proceedings may be had against any or all of them jointly, or against any one of them, for the recovery of such fine.

SEC. 10. The mayor of each of the cities in the State shall, in **Board of appeal.** the month of April, in the year nineteen hundred and nine, and in the month of April in each third year thereafter, appoint three competent men, two of whom at least shall be architects or master mechanics, as a board of appeal from the actions or decisions of the inspector of buildings in such city, as hereinafter provided, to hold their office for three years, and until others are appointed and qualified in their stead; and any two members of such board for the time being shall form a quorum for the transaction of its business; and any vacancy, from any cause, may be filled by the mayor at any time, or from time to time, as occasion may require. And in the several towns of the State, the town council shall constitute such board of appeal from the inspector of buildings of the town.

SEC. 11. Any person aggrieved by the refusal of the inspector **Appeal from ruling of inspector.** of buildings to give his certificate of exemption under section five, or his certificate of compliance with the provisions of this chapter under section six, of this chapter, may appeal therefrom to such board of appeal, in the city or town of such inspector, by filing with such inspector, within three days thereafter, written notice of such appeal, and by filing with the city or town clerk, within three days after such notice, his reasons of appeal in writing, specifying the subject matter of such appeal, and paying to the clerk fifty cents for filing the same.

SEC. 12. Upon the filing of such reasons of appeal, the clerk **Proceedings in appeal.** shall enter the name of the appellant, with a general description of the building and its location referred to therein, in a book to be by him kept for that purpose; and shall thereupon, pursuant to such general rules as may be adopted by the board of appeal regulating their proceedings, or, in the absence of such rules, by his special order, of which special order he shall immediately give notice to the members of the board, fix a time and place for hearing such appeal, and shall indorse the same in writing upon such reasons of appeal; and the parties thereto and the inspector shall be bound to take notice thereof. And at the time and place so fixed, or at any adjournment thereof, such board of appeal, after hearing such of the parties as see fit to attend, and their allegations and evidence, and after inspecting the premises, shall make their determination in respect thereof in writing, to be filed with such clerk; and such determination shall be final, and the clerk's certificate of such determination shall have the same effect, for all purposes of this chapter, as if given by such inspector at the time of the application to him for the same. And if such appeal shall be from the inspector's refusal to give his certificate of exemption or compliance aforesaid, and such board of appeal shall concur in such refusal, they shall then also determine what they require to be done to entitle the appellant to such certificate; and upon the appellant's compliance with such requirement, such certificate shall be issued to him by such inspector.

Neglect to give certificate.

SEC. 13. The inspector's neglect to give his certificate, and file a copy of the same with the city or town clerk within three days after application or request made to him as provided in sections five and six of this chapter, shall be deemed a refusal to give the same for the purposes of such appellate proceedings:

Compensation of board.

SEC. 14. Said board of appeal shall be paid by the city or town such compensation for their services as shall be fixed by ordinance of the city or town council. And the appellant in each case who fails to obtain relief upon his appeal shall pay to the city or town such reasonable costs and charges thereof as the board of appeal shall tax or determine against him. Nothing contained in this chapter shall be construed to relieve any person or any corporation from any liability now existing by virtue of the provisions of this chapter, during the pendency of any appeal, unless said board of appeal shall reverse the decision of said inspector.

CHAPTER 129.—*Factory regulations—Elevators.*

Automatic signals.

SECTION 15. Every elevator used for conveying persons or goods from one story to another of any building, the well of which elevator is not so protected as to be inaccessible from without while the elevator is moving, shall have attached to it some suitable appliance which shall give automatically, at all times, on every floor of said building which it approaches, a distinct, audible warning signal that said elevator is in motion.

Hoistways to be guarded.

SEC. 16 (as amended by chapter 549, acts of 1910). All hoistway and elevator openings through floors where there is no shaft shall be protected by sufficient railings, gates, trapdoors, or other mechanical devices equivalent thereto, and the same shall be kept closed in the nighttime or when not in use. On and after July 1,

Egress from elevators.

1911, any passenger elevator which is not constructed so as to allow egress of persons from such elevator in any position in which it might be stopped, by accident or otherwise, shall be constructed or arranged so that the roof or the top of such elevator, or a sufficient portion thereof to allow egress of persons therefrom, may be conveniently opened from the inside; and no such elevator shall be thereafter used or operated which shall not be so constructed or arranged. Every passenger elevator except plunger elevators shall be provided with some safety arrangement to prevent falling, and every passenger elevator shall be fitted with some suitable device to prevent the elevator car from being started until the door or doors opening into the elevator shaft

Age of operators.

are closed; and no person under the age of eighteen years shall take charge of or operate any passenger elevator. It shall be

Inspection.

the duty of every inspector of buildings, elected or empowered under the provisions of this chapter, to inspect all elevators in every building within his jurisdiction; and it shall be the duty of the factory inspectors, appointed or empowered by law, to inspect all elevators in every building within their jurisdiction in any city or town where there is no inspector of buildings; and it shall be the duty of said inspectors of buildings and said factory inspectors to notify the lessee and owner, or some one of the owners, of every building in which an elevator shall be used or operated contrary to the provisions of this and the preceding section, of such violation and require the lessee and owner, or some one of the owners of said building, within thirty days after the receipt of such notice, to comply with the provisions of said sections, and it shall be the duty of said lessee and owner, or owners, to comply with such requirement. The owner or owners of any building or Owner may make alterations. premises under lease, and their servants and agents, may enter upon such leased building or premises for the public welfare, with the purpose of making said building comply with the provisions of this and the preceding section, and may remain thereon during such time as may reasonably be required for the performance of such work as may be necessary to effect said purpose, interfering with the lessee no more than may be necessary. In all cases in which any Negligence. person shall suffer injury, or in which the death of any person shall ensue, in consequence of the failure of the lessee or owner or owners of any building to comply with the provisions of this and the preceding section, or in consequence of the failure of said lessee or owner or owners to comply with the written notice and requirement of any inspector of buildings or factory inspector, when made in conformity to the provisions of this and the preceding section, such lessee and owner or owners shall be jointly Damages. and severally liable to any person so injured, in an action of trespass on the case, for damages for such injury; and in case of death such lessee and owner or owners shall be jointly and severally liable in damages for the injury caused by the death of such person, to be recovered by action of trespass on the case in the same manner and for the benefit of the same persons as is provided in sections fourteen and fifteen of chapter two hundred and eighty-three; which action, when the lessee and the owner are nonresidents, may be commenced by attachment. It shall be no defense to said action that the person injured, or whose death ensues as aforesaid, had knowledge that any elevator was being operated in said building contrary to the provisions of this and the preceding section, or that such person continued to ride in said elevator with said knowledge. The lessee or owner or owners of Penalty. any building, or, in case such lessee or owner, or any of them, be non compos mentis or a minor, the guardian of any such lessee or owner, or, in case such lessee or owner, or any of them, be a nonresident, the agent of any such lessee or owner, having charge of such property, who shall neglect or fail to comply with the provisions of this and the preceding section, shall be fined not less than five dollars and not more than ten dollars for each day that an elevator shall be used or operated in said building contrary to the provisions of this and the preceding section. In case there shall be several such lessees or owners or agents in charge of any building in which an elevator shall be used or operated contrary to the provisions of this and the preceding section, proceedings may be had against any or all of them jointly, or against any one of them, for the recovery of such fine.

Chapter 131.—*Factories and workshops—Fire escapes, etc.*

Section 7. * * * All buildings used as factories, laundries, Exits required. or workshops, in whole or in part, in which buildings severally twenty-five or more persons are employed, shall have the doors or windows of or to any exit or fire escape so arranged as to swing outward. All factories, laundries, workshops, or rooms in any building where the entrance thereto is from a corridor or hallway, and in which factories, laundries, workshops, or rooms, severally, twenty-five, or more persons are employed, shall have the doors of entrance thereto so arranged as to swing outward. If any such door or window of such factory, laundry, workshop Doors to open outwardly. or room shall be locked or fastened during working hours the lock or fastening shall be such, and kept in such condition, that the same can be easily and quickly unlocked or unfastened by any person from the inside.

Who to make changes
SEC. 8. It shall be the duty of the owner or owners of every such building, or, in case the lessee or lessees thereof shall be required under the terms of his or their lease, the duty of such lessee or lessees, to comply with the structural and fixture requirements specified in this act. * * *

Enforcement.
SEC. 9. In every city or town, the inspector of buildings, and any assistant inspector of buildings, any member of the board of police commissioners, the chief of police, any member of the board of fire commissioners if any, the chief of the fire department, and any person charged hereunder with the enforcement of the provisions hereof, shall be at all reasonable times admitted free of charge into all parts of every * * * factory, laundry, or shop included within the provisions hereof, to ascertain whether the requirements of this act are complied with.

Violations.
SEC. 10. Any person, whose duty it is to comply with any of the provisions of this act, who shall neglect or refuse to comply with the same, shall be fined not exceeding one hundred dollars for each offense, and every day of such neglect or failure shall constitute a separate offense. The supreme court and the superior court within their respective jurisdictions shall have power to issue any extraordinary writs, or to proceed according to the course of equity, or both, to secure the fulfillment and execution of the provisions hereof. If any such remedy or proceeding is sought or brought in the superior court, it shall be in the court for the county in which the building is located.

Enforcement.
SEC. 11. It shall be the duty of the inspector of buildings of each city or town to enforce the structural and fixture requirements of this act. In any city or town, where there is no such inspector, it shall be the duty of each of the factory inspectors, and such person or persons as may be appointed for the purpose by any city or town council, to enforce the same.

SOUTH CAROLINA.

ACTS OF 1909.

ACT No. 4.—*Regulation and inspection of factories, etc.*

Inspectors.
SECTION 9. Said commissioner [of agriculture, commerce and industries] may employ two inspectors, who shall be appointed by the commissioner at a salary of ten hundred dollars each per annum and necessary traveling expenses, not to exceed two hundred dollars each in any one year, to assist him in the discharge of the duties imposed by this act. The inspectors shall be under the supervision and control of the commissioner.

May enter buildings.
SEC. 10. The commissioner, his agents and inspectors, may enter all buildings and parts thereof which are subject to the provisions of this act and examine the methods of protection from accidents, the means of escape from fire, the sanitary provisions and the means of ventilation, and may make investigations as to the employment of children and women.

Water-closets, etc.
SEC. 11. Every factory, mercantile or other establishment or office where two or more males and two or more females are employed together, shall be provided with a sufficient number of separate water-closets, earth closets or privies, for the use of each sex, and plainly so designated; and no person shall be allowed to use a closet or privy which is provided for persons of other sex. Such water-closets, earth closets or privies, shall be kept clean and free from disagreeable odors.

Violations.
SEC. 12. Whoever violates the provisions of section 11 shall be punished by a fine of not less than ten (10) nor more than thirty (30) dollars.

Inspections.
SEC. 15. The inspectors appointed under this act are hereby empowered to visit and inspect, at reasonable hours, and as often

as practicable, the factories, workshops and other establishments in this State referred to in this act, and shall report to the commissioner the result of their inspections. They shall enforce the provisions of this act and prosecute all violations of the same.

SEC. 16. All blanks and forms required by the commissioner under this act shall be furnished by the comptroller general. *Blanks.*

SEC. 17. Inspectors provided for in this act shall keep and furnish to the comptroller general and commissioner itemized statements of necessary expenses incurred in enforcing this act. And all the money paid out under this act shall be on a warrant of the comptroller general. *Expenses.*

SOUTH DAKOTA.

REVISED CODES.

Exhaust fans, etc., in smelting and reducing works.

SECTION 2583. Any person or persons, corporations or companies operating smelters or dry crushing reduction works are hereby required to put in their respective works exhaust fans and dust chambers or some other contrivance for the removal of all gases, fumes, dust and other impurities that accumulate, at all times in the operation of such works. *Gases, etc., to be removed.*

SEC. 2584. Any person or persons, corporations or companies that shall fail to provide all reasonable safeguards for the protection of life and health of their employees by not putting in their respective works such appliances as provided in the preceding section shall be guilty of a misdemeanor and upon conviction thereof shall be fined in a sum not exceeding one thousand dollars nor less than five hundred dollars for each offense. *Penalty.*

SEC. 2585. Proof of the failure of any such person or persons, corporation or company to comply with the provisions of section 2584 shall be prima facie evidence of negligence on the part of any person or persons, corporation or company. *Evidence.*

SEC. 2586. The State mine inspector is hereby empowered and compelled to visit such works at least once every month to see that the provisions of section 2583 are enforced. *Enforcement.*

TENNESSEE.

SHANNON'S CODE OF 1896 AND SUPPLEMENT OF 1904.

Factories and workshops—Inspection, etc.

(Chapter 401, Acts of 1899; chapter 67, Acts of 1901. Supplement, p. 470.)

SECTION 1. The governor, with the consent and advice of the senate, shall appoint an officer to be known as a shop and factory inspector, who shall hold his office for a term of two years, or until his successor shall be appointed and qualified: *Provided,* That he may be removed at any time by the governor for cause. *Factory inspector.*

SEC. 2. It shall be the duty of the shop and factory inspector to inspect all workshops and factories where machinery is used at least once every six months, and he shall have authority to enter such workshops or factories at all proper times for the purposes of such inspection. He shall, on or before the first day of January of each year, make a report to the governor of the condition as respects safety to life and health of workshops and factories visited by him, and said report shall be printed for the use of the general assembly at its regular sessions. The expense of printing said report shall be paid out of the general appropriation for printing the reports of State officers. *Duties.*

SEC. 3. All workshops and factories where machinery is used shall be well ventilated and kept as clean as the nature of the busi- *Ventilation, safety appliances, etc.*

ness will permit. The belting, shafting, gearing, machinery, and drums of all workshops and factories where machinery is used, when so placed as in the opinion of the shop and factory inspector to be dangerous to persons employed therein while engaged in their ordinary duties, shall, as far as practicable, be securely guarded.

Protection of hatchways, etc. SEC. 4. The shop and factory inspector may order the opening[s] of all hatchways, elevator wells, and wheel holes, upon every floor of any workshop or factory where machinery is used, to be protected by good trapdoors, self-closing hatches, or safety catches or other safeguards such as will insure the safety of the employees in such workshop or factory when engaged in their ordinary duties.

Water-closets. SEC. 5. Every person, firm, or corporation running or operating any workshop or factory where fifteen or more persons are employed at labor, shall provide separate water-closets for males and females, and keep the same in good sanitary condition.

Enforcement. SEC. 6. It shall be the duty of the shop and factory inspector to enforce the provisions of this act by giving proper notices to the person, firm, or corporation operating or running workshops or factories inspected by him, and also to make complaint to the attorneys general of the respective districts of all violations of this act.

Penalty. SEC. 7. Any person, firm, or corporation operating or running any workshop or factory where machinery is used, upon conviction of a violation of this act, shall be fined not less than twenty-five dollars ($25) nor more than one hundred dollars ($100) for each offense: *Provided,* No action shall be taken until after four weeks' notice shall have been given by the shop and factory inspector to any firm, person, or corporation operating or running a workshop or factory of the changes necessary to be made, and not then if in the meantime said changes have been made.

Notices. SEC. 8. The orders or notices given by the shop and factory inspector shall be written or printed, and signed by him officially, and served by himself or by leaving an attested copy thereof at the usual place of business of the person upon whom service is to be made, and a copy of the same shall be filed in the office of the county court clerk of the county in which the workshop or factory is located, and such copy shall be prima facie evidence that notice was given.

Salary. SEC. 9. The salary of said inspector shall be $1,200 per annum, payable monthly on warrant of comptroller, as other salaries are paid.

(Chapter 98, Acts of 1897. Supplement, p. 472.)

Water-closets. SECTION 1. All persons hiring or employing female help in any manufacturing or mercantile business or establishment, shall provide separate privies or water-closets for such female help.

Males excluded. SEC. 2. No male person shall enter such separate privies or water-closets except for the purpose of repairing or cleaning the same.

Penalty. SEC. 3. A violation of the foregoing sections shall be a misdemeanor, punishable by a fine of not less than two or more than ten dollars.

[See chapter 159, Acts of 1905.]

ACTS OF 1905.

CHAPTER 159.—*Inspection of bakeries.*

Bakeries as workshops. SECTION 1. Chapter 401, of the Acts of 1899 [relating to the inspection of factories, etc., above], is hereby amended to make the word "workshop," whenever the same shall appear therein, include bakeries, whether the same be run by machinery or not.

ACTS OF 1909.

CHAPTER 124.—*Factory inspector—Powers.*

SECTION 1. Police powers and authority are hereby conferred upon and vested in the factory inspector, and he shall have full power and authority to enforce all the labor laws of the State, with the exception of the mining laws, by making arrests for the violation of such laws in the same manner as officers of the State empowered by law to make arrests for violation of the laws of the State now have and possess. *Enforcement of laws.*

CHAPTER 473.—*Inspection of factories, etc.—Manufacture of food products.*

SECTION 1. Every building, room, basement, or cellar occupied or used as a bakery, confectionery, cannery, packing house, slaughterhouse, dairy, creamery, cheese factory, restaurant, hotel, grocery, meat market, or other place or apartment used for the preparation for sale, manufacture, packing, storage, sale, or distribution of any food shall be properly lighted, drained, plumbed, and ventilated and conducted with strict regard to the influence of such condition upon the health of the operatives, employees, clerks, or other persons therein employed and the purity and wholesomeness of the food therein produced; and for the purpose of this act the term "food," as used herein, shall include all articles used for food, drink, confectionery, or condiment, whether simple, mixed, or compound, and all substances or ingredients used in the preparation thereof. *Lighting, ventilation, etc.*

SEC. 3. The side walls and ceilings of every bakery, confectionery, creamery, cheese factory, hotel, and restaurant kitchen shall be well plastered, wainscoted, or ceiled with metal or lumber, and shall be oil painted or kept well limewashed, and all interior woodwork in every bakery, confectionery, creamery, cheese factory, hotel and restaurant kitchen shall be kept washed clean with soap and water; and every building, room, basement, or cellar occupied or used for the preparation, manufacture, packing, storage, sale, or distribution of food shall have an impermeable floor made of cement, or tile laid in cement, brick, wood, or other suitable nonabsorbent material which can be flushed and washed clean with water. *Walls.* *Floors.*

SEC. 4. The doors, windows, and other openings of every food producing or distributing establishment during the fly season shall be fitted with self-closing screen doors and wire window screens of not coarser than fourteen-mesh wire gauze. *Screens.*

SEC. 5. Every building, room, basement, or cellar occupied or used for the preparation, manufacture, packing, canning, sale, or distribution of food shall have convenient toilet or toilet rooms separate and apart from the room or rooms where the process of production, manufacture, packing, canning, selling, or distributing is conducted. The floors of such toilet rooms shall be of cement, tile, wood, brick, or any other nonabsorbent material, and shall be washed and scoured daily. Such toilet or toilets shall be furnished with separate ventilating flues or pipes discharging into soil pipes, or on the outside of the building in which they are situated. Lavatories and wash rooms shall be adjacent to toilet rooms, and shall be supplied with soap, running water, and towels, and shall be maintained in a sanitary condition. Operatives, clerks, and all persons who handle the material from which food is prepared, or the finished product, before beginning work or after visiting toilet or toilets, shall wash their hands and arms thoroughly in clean water. *Toilet rooms.*

SEC. 6. Cuspidors, for use of operatives, employees, clerks, or other persons, shall be provided whenever necessary, and each cuspidor shall be thoroughly emptied and washed out daily with disinfectant solution, and five ounces of such solution shall be left in each cuspidor while it is in use. *Cuspidors.*

No operative, employee, or other person shall expectorate on floors or side walls of any building, room, basement, or cellar where the production, manufacture, packing, storing, preparation, or sale of any food is conducted.

Living or sleeping in rooms.   SEC. 7. No person or persons shall be allowed to live or sleep in any room of a bake shop, kitchen, dining room, confectionery, creamery, cheese factory, or place where food is prepared for sale, served, or sold.

Diseased employees.   SEC. 8. No employer shall require, permit, or suffer any person to work, nor shall any person work in a building, room, basement, cellar, or vehicle occupied or used for the production, preparation, manufacture, packing, storage, sale, distribution, and transportation of food who is affected with any venereal disease, smallpox, diphtheria, scarlet fever, yellow fever, tuberculosis (or consumption), bubonic plague, Asiatic cholera, leprosy, trachoma, typhoid fever, epidemic dysentery, measles, mumps, German measles, whooping cough, chicken pox, or any other infectious or contagious disease.

Enforcement.   SEC. 9. The pure food and drug inspector or other legal agent of the State board of health shall have full power at all times to enter every building, room, basement, or cellar occupied or used or suspected of being used for the production for sale, manufacture for sale, storage, sale, distribution, or transportation of food, and to inspect the premises and all utensils, fixtures, furniture, and machinery used as aforesaid; and if, upon inspection, any food producing or distributing establishment, conveyance, employer, operative, employee, clerk, driver, or other person is found to be violating any of the provisions of this act, or if the production, preparation, manufacture, packing, storing, sale, distribution, or transportation is being conducted in a manner detrimental to the health of the employees and operatives or to the character or quality of the food therein being produced, manufactured, packed, stored, sold, distributed, or conveyed, the officer or inspector making the examination or inspection shall report such conditions and violations to the pure food and drug inspector, who shall issue an order to the person or persons in authority at the aforesaid establishment to abate the condition or violation or make such improvements as may be necessary to abate them, within the period of five days or such reasonable time as may be required in which to abate them. Such order shall be in writing, and the person receiving the order may, within five days from the issuance of the order, appear in person or by attorney before the pure food and drug inspector to give reason why such instruction should not be obeyed.

Violations.   SEC. 10. Any person who violates any of the provisions of this act or who refuses to comply with any lawful orders or requirements of the State pure food and drug inspector duly made in writing as provided in section 9 of this act shall be guilty of a misdemeanor, and, on conviction, shall be punished for the first offense by a fine of not less than $10 nor more than $50; for the second offense, by a fine of not less than $50 nor more than $100; and for the third and subsequent offense, by a fine of $200 and imprisonment in the county workhouse for not less than thirty nor more than ninety days, and each day after the expiration of the time limit for abating unsanitary conditions and completing improvements to abate such conditions as ordered by the State pure food and drug inspector shall constitute a distinct and separate offense, and in case of any violation of this act, the State board of health, or its duly authorized agent, shall act as prosecutor in the court having criminal jurisdiction of said offense. The grand juries of the several counties of this State shall have inquisitorial power over said offenses, and the judges of the several criminal courts and circuit courts having criminal jurisdiction shall especially charge this law to the grand juries of the several counties of the State.

ACTS OF 1911.

CHAPTER 30.—*Inspector of factories, etc.*

SECTION 1. The salary of the shop and factory inspector shall be fifteen hundred dollars ($1,500) per annum, payable monthly on the warrant of the comptroller, as other salaries are paid, and the sum of five hundred dollars ($500) per annum, or as much thereof as may be necessary, is hereby appropriated for the expenses of said shop and factory inspector incurred in the actual performance of his official duties, said expenses to be itemized, evidenced by vouchers, and sworn to. *Salary.* *Expenses.*

SEC. 2. The shop and factory inspector, in addition to the annual reports now required of him, shall make additional monthly reports to the governor of the inspections made by him, and other official duties performed during the preceding month. *Monthly reports.*

VERMONT.

PUBLIC STATUTES—1906.

Fire escapes on factories, etc.

SECTION 5512. The owner or lessee of a building, factory, mill or workshop more than two stories high, in which persons are employed above the second story, shall provide suitable ladders or other safe fire escapes for the safety of patrons and occupants of such buildings. *Fire escapes required.*

SEC. 5513. An owner, keeper or lessee of a place mentioned * * * who fails to comply with a provision thereof [in this act] shall be fined not more than four hundred dollars nor less than twenty-five dollars. *Penalty.*

Smoking in factories, etc.

SECTION 5515. A person who smokes a pipe, cigar or cigarette in a mill, factory, barn, stable or other outbuilding belonging to or occupied by another person, in which a notice containing this section, prohibiting such smoking, signed by the owner, agent or occupant of the same is posted conspicuously near the main entrance thereof, shall be fined not more than five dollars. *Smoking an offense, when.*

VIRGINIA.

CODE—1904.

Fire escapes on factories, etc.

SECTION 1067a. It shall be the duty of the owner or owners of all factories, workshops, * * * in this State of over three stories in height, * * * to provide for the safe exit of the occupants thereof in case of fire by the erection or construction of fire escapes of the most approved modern design. The character and design of said fire escapes shall, in cities and towns, be selected by the council of said cities and towns; and where the buildings are not located in cities or towns, by the board of supervisors of the county. Any owner or owners of such buildings shall have the right to require the council of the city or town in which said buildings are located, or in the counties the board designated by this act, to make such selection of said fire escapes as is provided by this act; and in case of their failure or refusal they shall be compellable by mandamus. Any owner or owners of such buildings who shall fail to comply with * * * this act * * * shall be deemed guilty of a misdemeanor, and upon conviction shall be fined not less than twenty-five dollars nor more than one hundred dollars for each month they shall fail to provide such fire escapes. *Fire escapes to be provided.*

ACTS OF 1908.

CHAPTER 228.—*Inspection of factories—Respiratory shields.*

Shields to be furnished at cost. SECTION 1. Every owner or agent of a peanut cleaning establishment operated for the purpose of cleaning peanuts, and every owner or agent operating a cotton factory in this Commonwealth [shall] be, and the same are hereby required to furnish each employee or operative employed in any such peanut cleaning establishment or cotton factory, who may wish to use the same, a suitable sponge shield to protect such operative or employee from inhaling the dust and floating particles in the air while employed in such peanut cleaning establishment or cotton factory. Said shield to be supplied by the owner or agent of said peanut cleaning establishment or cotton factory at actual cost and to be paid for by each operative or employee.

Violations. SEC. 2. Any owner or agent of said peanut cleaning establishment or cotton factory who shall fail to provide such shield upon application after a reasonable time shall be subject to a fine of not less than one dollar nor more than five dollars, and every day's failure to comply with such request shall constitute a separate offense.

ACTS OF 1910.

CHAPTER 6.—*Inspection and regulation of laundries.*

Laundries and washhouses to be inspected. SECTION 1. The boards of health of the respective cities of the State of Virginia (where such cities have such boards of health) shall supervise all laundries or public washhouses within any city of the State of Virginia and shall not permit the employment, by any public laundry or public washhouse, of any person suffering with an infectious or contagious disease; nor allow any person to sleep in such public laundry or public washhouse or in any room adjoining and opening into such public laundry or public washhouse, and every room in such laundry or washhouse that is used for the purpose of washing or drying clothes, shall be properly ventilated and drained and shall be used for no purposes other than that specified. The floors of all rooms used for the purpose of washing clothes shall, if required by the regulations of the local board of health, be made of cement or other mineral substance, and shall be arranged so as to be easily drained. A public laundry or public washhouse within the meaning of this section shall be any place within any city of the State of Virginia, licensed to conduct a laundry in any of its branches. Any person, firm or corporation violating any of the provisions of this section shall be deemed guilty of a misdemeanor and shall be fined not less than fifty dollars nor more than one hundred dollars for each offense.

Scope of law. Any person, firm or corporation conducting a public laundry or public washhouse within a distance of a half mile of the city limits of any city of the State of Virginia shall be subject to the provisions of this act.

Nothing in this section shall be construed to prevent the washing of clothes in any private residence where no license to do washing is required.

CHAPTER 14.—*Inspection of factories and workshops—Toilets, etc.*

Sanitary provisions required. SECTION 1. Every factory, in which five or more persons are employed, and every factory, workshop, mercantile or other establishment or office, in which two or more children, under eighteen years of age, or women are employed, shall be kept clean and free from effluvia arising from any drain, privy or nuisance, and shall be provided with a sufficient number of proper water-closets, earth closets or privies, and reasonable access shall be afforded thereto; and whenever two or more males and two or more females are employed together, a sufficient number of separate water-closets, earth closets or privies shall be provided for the use of each sex, and plainly so designated; and no person shall be allowed to use a closet or privy which is provided for persons of the other sex: *Provided,* In mercantile establishments and offices the provisions of this section shall not apply so far as toilets are concerned, if separate toilets are within reasonable access.

SEC. 2. The owner, lessee or occupant of any premises which are used as described in the preceding section shall make the changes necessary to conform thereto. If such changes are made upon the order of the commissioner of labor by the occupant or lessee of the premises, he may, within thirty days after the completion thereof, bring an action against any other person who has an interest in such premises, and may recover such proportion of the expense of making such changes as the court may adjudge should be equitably borne by such other interested party defendant. *[margin: Changes to be made.]*

SEC. 3. If it appears to the commissioner of labor that any act, neglect or fault in relation to any drain, water-closet, earth closet, privy, ash pit, water supply, nuisance or other matter in a factory or workshop included under the provisions of section one is punishable or remediable under any law relative to the preservation of the public health, but not under the provisions of this chapter, he shall give notice in writing thereof to the board of health of the city or county in which such factory or workshop is situated, or to the State health commissioner, and such board of health or State health commissioner shall thereupon inquire into the subject of the notice and enforce the laws relative thereto. *[margin: Inspectors' orders.]*

SEC. 4. A criminal prosecution shall not be instituted against a person for a violation of the provisions of sections one and two until four weeks after notice in writing by the commissioner of labor of the changes necessary to be made to comply with the provisions of said sections has been sent by mail or delivered to such person, nor if such changes shall have been made in accordance with such notice. A notice shall be sufficient under the provisions of this section if given to one member of a firm, or to the clerk, cashier, secretary, agent or any other officer who has charge of the business of a corporation, or to its attorney; and in case of a foreign corporation, to the officer who has charge of such factory or workshop; and such officer shall be personally liable for the amount of any fine if a judgment against the corporation is returned unsatisfied. *[margin: Prosecutions.]*

SEC. 5. Any person, firm or corporation who shall violate the provisions of this act shall be deemed guilty of a misdemeanor, and upon conviction thereof, be subject to a fine of not less than five nor more than twenty-five dollars, and each day of such violation may constitute a separate offense. *[margin: Violations.]*

WASHINGTON.

CONSTITUTION.

ARTICLE 2.—*Protection of employees—Life and health.*

SECTION 35. The legislature shall pass necessary laws for the protection of persons working in mines, factories, and other employments dangerous to life or deleterious to health, and fix pains and penalties for the enforcement of the same. *[margin: Protective laws to be passed.]*

CODES AND STATUTES—1909.

Regulation of bakeries.

SECTION 5482 All buildings or rooms occupied as biscuit, bread or cake bakeries shall be drained or plumbed in a manner conducive to the proper healthful and sanitary condition thereof, and constructed with air shafts and windows or ventilating pipes *[margin: Ventilation, etc.]*

sufficient to insure ventilation as the commissioner of labor shall direct, and no cellar or basement, not now used as a bakery, shall hereafter be used and occupied as a bakery and a cellar or basement heretofore occupied as a bakery shall, when once closed, not be reopened for use as a bakery.

Wash rooms.　SEC. 5483. Every such bakery shall be provided with a proper wash room and water-closet, or closets, apart from the bake room or rooms where the manufacturing of such products is conducted; and no water-closet, earth closet, privy or ash pit shall be within or communicate directly with a bake shop.

Construction of rooms.　SEC. 5484. Every room used for the manufacture of flour or meal food shall be at least eight feet in height, the side walls of such room shall be plastered or wainscoted, the ceiling plastered or ceiled with lumber or metal, and if required by the commissioner of labor, shall be whitewashed at least once in three months; the furniture and utensils of such room shall be so arranged as to be easily moved in order that the furniture and floor may at all times be kept in proper healthful sanitary condition.

Sleeping places.　SEC. 5486. The sleeping places for persons employed in a bakery shall be kept separate from the room or rooms where flour or meal food products are manufactured or stored.

Inspection.　SEC. 5487. After an inspection of a bakery has been made by the commissioner of labor and it is found to conform to the provisions of this chapter, said commissioner shall issue a certificate to the owner or operator of such bakery, that it is conducted in compliance with all the provisions of this chapter, but where orders are issued by said commissioner to improve the condition of a bakery, no such certificate shall be issued until such order and the provisions of this chapter have been complied with.

Alterations.　SEC. 5488. The owner, agent or lessee of any property affected by the provisions of this chapter, shall, within thirty days after the service of notice upon him, of an order issued by the commissioner of labor requiring any alterations to be made in or upon such premises, comply therewith, or cease to use or allow the use of such premises as a bake shop; such notice shall be in writing Notice. and may be served upon such owner, agent, or lessee, either personally or by mail, and a notice by registered letter, postage prepaid, mailed to the last known address of such owner, agent, or lessee shall be deemed sufficient for the purposes of this chapter.

Contagious diseases.　SEC. 5489. No employer shall require, permit or suffer any person to work in his bake shop who is affected with tuberculosis, or with scrofulous diseases, or with any venereal disease, or with any communicable skin affection or contagious disease and no person so affected shall work or remain in a bake shop. Every employer is hereby required to maintain himself and his employees in a clean and sanitary condition while engaged in the manufacture, handling or sale of such food products.

Night work of children.　SEC. 5490. No employer shall require, permit or suffer any person under sixteen years of age to work in his bake shop between the hours of 8 o'clock in the evening and 5 o'clock in the morning.

Violations.　SEC. 5491. Any person who violates the provisions of this chapter or refuses to comply with the requirements of the commissioner of labor, as provided herein, shall be guilty of a misdemeanor, and on conviction thereof before any court of competent jurisdiction, shall be fined not less than twenty-five nor more than fifty dollars or imprisoned not more than ten days for the first offense; and shall be fined not less than fifty nor more than one hundred dollars and imprisoned not less than ten nor more than thirty days for each offense after the first.

Inspection of factories, etc.—Bureau of labor.

Commissioner.　SECTION 6550. A commissioner of labor shall be appointed by the governor, and said commissioner of labor, by and with the consent of the governor, shall have power to appoint and employ such assistants as may be necessary to discharge the duties of said commissioner of labor; and said commissioner of labor, together with the inspector of coal mines, shall constitute a bureau of labor. On the first Monday in April in 1897, and every four years thereafter, the governor shall appoint a suitable person to act as commissioner of labor, and as factory, mill and railroad inspector, who shall hold office until his successor is appointed and qualified.

SEC. 6551. The salary of the commissioner of labor, provided for in this act shall be twenty-four hundred (2,400) dollars per annum, and he shall be allowed his actual and necessary traveling expenses; and any assistant of said commissioner of labor shall be paid for each full day service rendered by him, such compensation as the commissioner of labor may deem proper, but no such assistant shall be paid to exceed four ($4) dollars per day, and his actual and necessary traveling expenses. Salaries.

SEC. 6552. The commissioner of labor shall appoint one female as assistant commissioner of labor and such female assistant shall have charge, under the direction of the commissioner of labor, of the enforcement of all laws relating to the health, sanitary conditions, surroundings, hours of labor and all other laws affecting the employment of female wage earners. She shall receive a salary of twelve hundred dollars per annum and shall be allowed her actual and necessary expenses in the performance of her duties as such assistant. Such salary and expenses to be paid in the same manner as other expenses of the office of commissioner of labor. Female assistant to be appointed.

SEC. 6553. It shall be the duty of such officer and employees of the said bureau to cause to be enforced all laws regulating the employment of children, minors and women, all laws established for the protection of the health, lives and limbs of operators in workshops, factories, mills and mines, on railroads and other places, and all laws enacted for the protection of the working classes, and declaim it a misdemeanor on the part of the employers to require as a condition of employment the surrender of any rights of citizenship, laws regulating and prescribing the qualifications of persons in trades and handicrafts, and similar laws now in force or hereafter to be enacted. It shall also be the duty of officers and employees of the bureau to collect, assort, arrange and present in biennial reports to the legislature, on or before the first Monday in January, statistical details relating to all departments of labor in the State; to the subjects of corporations, strikes or other labor difficulties; to trade unions and other labor organizations and their effect upon labor and capital; and to such other matters relating to the commercial, industrial, social, educational, moral and sanitary conditions of the laboring classes, and the permanent prosperity of the respective industries of the State as the bureau may be able to gather. In its biennial report the bureau shall also give account of all proceedings of its officers and employees which have been taken in accordance with the provisions of this act or of any other acts herein referred to, including a statement of all violations of law which have been observed, and the proceedings under the same, and shall join with such accounts and such remarks, suggestions and recommendations as the commissioner may deem necessary. Duties.

SEC. 6554. It shall be the duty of every owner, operator or manager of every factory, workshop, mill, mine or other establishment where labor is employed, to make to the bureau, upon blanks furnished by said bureau, such reports and returns as the said bureau may require, for the purpose of compiling such labor statistics as are authorized by this act, and the owner or business manager shall make such reports and returns within the time prescribed therefor by the commissioner of labor, and shall certify to the correctness of the same. In the reports of said bureau no use shall be made of the names of individuals, firms or corporations supplying the information called for by this section, such information being deemed confidential, and not for the purpose of disclosing personal affairs, and any officer, agent or employee of said bureau violating this provision shall be fined in the sum not ex- Duties of owners of factories, etc.

ceeding five hundred dollars, or be imprisoned for not more than one year.

Powers of commissioner.   SEC. 6555. The commissioner of [or] the bureau of labor shall have the power to issue subpœnas, administer oaths and take testimony in all matters relating to the duties herein required by such bureau, such testimony to be taken in some suitable place in the **Witnesses.** [vicinity] to which testimony is applicable. Witnesses subpœnaed and testifying before any officer of the said bureau shall be paid the same fees as witnesses before a superior court, such payment to be made from the contingent fund of the bureau. Any person duly subpœnaed under provisions of this section [who] shall willfully neglect or refuse to attend or testify at the time and place named in the subpœna, shall be guilty of a misdemeanor, and, upon conviction thereof, before any court of competent jurisdiction, shall be punished by a fine not less than twenty-five dollars or more than one hundred dollars, or by imprisonment in the county jail not exceeding thirty days.

Access to premises.   SEC. 6556. The commissioner of labor, the coal mine inspector or any employee of the bureau of labor, shall have power to enter any factory, mill, mine, office, workshop or public or private works at any time for the purpose of gathering facts and statistics such as are contemplated by this chapter, and to examine into the methods of protection from danger to employees, and the sanitary conditions in and around such buildings and places and make a record thereof, and any owner or occupant of said factory, mill, mine, office or workshop, or public or private works, or his agent or agents, who shall refuse to allow an inspector or employee of the said bureau to enter, shall be deemed guilty of a misdemeanor, and, upon conviction thereof, before any court of competent jurisdiction, shall be punished by a fine of not less than twenty-five dollars nor more than one hundred dollars, or be imprisoned in the county jail not to exceed ninety days, for each and every offense.

Returns, etc., to be preserved.   SEC. 6557. No report or return made to the said bureau in accordance with the provisions of this chapter, and no schedule, record or documents gathered or returned by the commissioner or inspector [shall be destroyed within two years of the receipt or collection], thereof, such reports, schedules and documents being declared public documents. At the expiration of the period of two years above referred to in this section, all records, schedules and papers accumulating in the said bureau that may be considered of no value by the commissioner may be destroyed: *Provided,* The authority of the governor be first obtained for such destruction.

Reports.   SEC. 6558. The biennial reports of the bureau of labor, provided for by section 6553, shall be printed in the same manner and under the same regulations as the reports of the executive officers of the State: *Provided,* That not less than five hundred copies of the report shall be distributed, as the judgment of the commissioner may deem best. The blanks and other stationery required by the bureau of labor in accordance with the provisions of this act shall be furnished by the secretary of the State, and shall be paid for from the printing fund of the State.

Consolidation of duties.   SEC. 6559. All the powers and duties heretofore exercised by the assistant commissioner of labor and the factory, mill and railway inspector are hereby devolved on the commissioner of labor.

Regulation, etc., of factories and workshops.

Belt shifters, guards, etc.   SECTION 6587. Any person, firm, corporation or association operating a factory, mill or workshop where machinery is used shall provide and maintain in use, belt shifters or other mechanical contrivances for the purpose of throwing on or off belts on pulleys while running, where the same are practicable with due regard to the nature and purpose of said belts and the dangers to employees therefrom ; also reasonable safeguards for all vats, pans, trimmers, cut-off, gang edger, and other saws, planers, cogs, gearings, belting, shafting, coupling, set screws, live rollers, conveyors, mangles in laundries and machinery of other or similar description, which it is practicable to guard, and which can be effectively guarded with due regard to the ordinary use of such machinery and appliances, and the dangers to employees therefrom, and with which the employees of any such factory, mill or workshop are liable to come in contact while in the performance of their duties; and if any machine or any part thereof, is in a defective condition, and its operation would be extra hazardous because of such defect, or if any machine is not safeguarded as provided in this act, the use thereof is prohibited, and a notice to that effect shall be attached thereto by the employer or inspector immediately on receiving notice of such defect or lack of safeguard, and such notice shall not be removed until said defect has been remedied or the machine safeguarded as herein provided.

SEC. 6588. Every factory, mill or workshop where machinery is used and manual labor is exercised by the way of trade for the purposes of gain within an inclosed room (private houses in which the employees live, excepted) shall be provided in each workroom thereof with good and sufficient ventilation and kept in a cleanly and sanitary state, and shall be so ventilated as to render harmless, so far as practicable, all gases, vapors, dust or other impurities, generated in the course of the manufacturing or laboring process carried on therein; and if in any factory, mill or workshop, any process is carried on in any inclosed room thereof, by which dust is generated and inhaled to an injurious extent by the persons employed therein, conveyors, receptacles or exhaust fans, or other mechanical means, shall be provided and maintained for the purpose of carrying off or receiving and collecting such dust. *Ventilation.*

SEC. 6589. The openings of all hoistways, hatchways, elevators and wellholes and stairways in factories, mills, workshops, storehouses, warerooms or stores, shall be protected where practicable, by good and sufficient trapdoors, hatches, fences, gates or other safeguards, and all due diligence shall be used to keep all such means of protection closed, except when it is necessary to have the same open that the same may be used. *Hoistways, etc.*

SEC. 6590. It shall be the duty of the commissioner of labor, by himself or his duly appointed deputy, to examine as soon as may be after the passage of this act, and thereafter annually and from time to time, all factories, mills, workshops, storehouses, warerooms, stores and buildings and the machinery and appliances therein contained to which the provisions of this chapter are applicable for the purpose of determining whether they do conform to such provisions, and of granting or refusing certificates of approval, whether requested to do so or not. *Annual inspections.*

SEC. 6591. Any person, firm, corporation or association carrying on business to which the provisions of this act are applicable, shall have the right to make written request to said commissioner of labor to inspect any factory, mill or workshop, and the machinery therein used, and any storehouse, wareroom or store, which said applicant is operating, occupying or using, and to issue his certificate of approval thereof; and said commissioner of labor by himself, or his deputy, shall forthwith make said inspection. Upon receiving such application, the commissioner of labor shall issue to the person making the same, an acknowledgment that such certificate has been applied for, and thirty days after such acknowledgment, by said commissioner of labor, and pending the granting of such certificate, such acknowledgment shall have the same effect as such certificate, till the granting of such certificate by said commissioner of labor: *Provided,* Said applicant has not been notified by an inspector what alterations or repairs are necessary: *Provided,* The commissioner of labor by himself or deputy shall make such examination annually whether requested to do so or not. *Requests for inspection.*

SEC. 6592. Any employee of any person, firm, corporation or association shall notify his employer of any defect in, or failure to guard the machinery, appliances, ways, works and plants, with which or in about which he is working, when any such defect or failure to guard shall come to the knowledge of any said em- *Employees to give notice of defects.*

ployee, and if said employer shall fail to remedy such defects then said employee may complain in writing to the commissioner of labor of any such alleged defects in or failure to guard the machinery appliances, ways, works and plants, or any alleged violation by such person, firm, corporation or association, of any of the provisions of this chapter, in the machinery and appliances and premises used by such person, firm, corporation or association, and with or about which such employee is working, and upon receiving such complaint, it shall be the duty of the commissioner of labor, by himself or his deputy, to forthwith make an inspection of the machinery and appliances complained of.

Certificates. SEC. 6593. Whenever upon examination or reexamination of any factory, mill or workshop, store or building, or the machinery or appliances therein to which the provisions of this chapter are applicable, the property so examined and the machinery and appliances therein conform in the judgment of said commissioner of labor to the requirements of this chapter, he shall thereupon issue to the owner, lessee or operator of such factory, mill or workshop or to the owner, lessee or occupant of any such storehouse, wareroom or store, a certificate to that effect, and such certificate shall be prima facie evidence as long as it continues in force of compliance on the part of the person, firm, corporation or association to whom it is issued, with the provisions of this act. Such certificate may be revoked by said commissioner of labor at any time upon written notice to the person, firm, corporation or association holding the same, whenever in his opinion after reexamination, conditions and circumstances have so changed as to justify the revocation thereof. A copy of said certificate shall be kept posted in a conspicuous place on every floor of all factories, mills, workshops, storehouses, warerooms or store to which the **Defective con-** provisions of this act are applicable. If, in the judgment of said **ditions.** commissioner of labor, such factory, mill or workshop, or the machinery and appliances therein contained, or such storehouse, wareroom or store does not conform to the requirements of this act, he shall forthwith, personally or by mail, serve on the person, firm, corporation or association operating or using such machinery or appliances, or occupying such premises, a written statement of the requirements of said commissioner of labor before he will issue a certificate as hereinbefore provided for; said requirements shall be complied with, within a period of thirty days after said requirements have been served as aforesaid and thereupon the said commissioner of labor shall forthwith issue such certificate; but if the person, firm or corporation operating or using said machinery and appliances or occupying such premises shall consider the requirements of said commissioner of labor unreasonable and impracticable or unnecessarily expensive, he may within ten days after the requirements of said commissioner of labor have been served upon him appeal therefrom or from any part thereof, to three arbitrators to whom shall be submitted the mat-**Appeals.** ter and things in dispute, and their findings shall be binding upon said applicant and upon the commissioner of labor. Such appeal shall be in writing, addressed to the commissioner of labor and shall set forth the objections to his requirements, or any part **Arbitration.** thereof, and shall mention the name of one person who will serve as the representative of said applicant calling for arbitration. Immediately upon the receipt of such notice of appeal, it shall be the duty of the commissioner of labor to appoint a competent person as arbitrator resident in the county from which such appeal comes, and to notify such person so selected, and also the party appealing, stating the cause of the arbitration, and the place, date and time of meeting. These two arbitrators shall select the third, and as soon thereafter as practicable, give a hearing on the matters of said appeal, and the findings of these arbitrators by a majority vote, shall be reported to the commissioner of labor, and to the applicant, and shall be binding upon each. The expense of such arbitration shall be borne by the party calling for the arbitration; and if said arbitrators sustain the requirements of said commissioner of labor or any part thereof, said applicant shall within thirty days, comply with the findings of said arbitrators, and thereupon said commissioner of labor shall issue his certificate as hereinbefore provided (in section 6590), but if said arbitrators shall sustain such appeal or any part thereof, the same shall be binding upon said commissioner of labor; and any such person, firm, corporation or association shall within thirty days, after the finding of the board of arbitrators, comply with the requirements of the commissioner of labor, as amended by said arbitrators, if so amended as herein provided for, and thereupon said commissioner of labor shall forthwith issue to any such person, firm, corporation or association, his certificate as provided for in section 6590 : *Provided, however,* That before any certificate shall **Fees.** be issued by said commissioner of labor as provided for in this act, the person, firm, corporation or association which has complied with the provisions of this act, shall pay to the commissioner of labor of the State of Washington, an annual fee of ten dollars (*provided*, That any person, firm, corporation or association, employing not to exceed five persons in said factory, mill or workshop shall pay a fee of five dollars), and take his receipt therefor : *It is further provided,* That the withholding of such certificate shall not excuse such person, firm, corporation or association from obtaining the same and paying the required inspection fee, and the person, firm, corporation or association inspected shall likewise be civilly liable for such inspection fee.

Upon presentation of said receipt to said commissioner of labor, or his deputy, he shall forthwith issue said certificate as in this chapter provided. Said fee shall entitle the person, firm, corporation or association paying the same, to any and every inspection of any factory, mill, workshop, storehouse, wareroom or store, and the machinery and appliances contained therein, owned and operated by the party paying said fee, that may be necessary, for a period of one year subsequent to its payment; and all moneys collected for licenses and fines, under the provisions of this act, shall be paid into the State treasury and be converted into a special factory inspection fund, from which special fund shall be paid the deputy factory inspectors required to enforce the provisions of this chapter. Said deputy factory inspectors shall be paid from the special factory inspection fund, upon the presentation of vouchers properly signed by the labor commissioner in the same manner in which other employees of the State are paid.

SEC. 6597. Any person, firm, corporation or association who vio- **Violations.** lates or fails to comply with any of the provisions of this chapter or to pay for and obtain the certificate of inspection shall be deemed guilty of a misdemeanor, and upon conviction thereof shall be punished by a fine of not less than twenty-five dollars nor more than one hundred dollars.

SEC. 6598. A copy of this chapter, together with the name and **Act to be** address of the commissioner of labor, printed in a legible manner. **posted.** shall be kept posted in a conspicuous place on each floor of every factory, mill, workshop, storehouse, wareroom or store, and at the office of every public and private work to which the provisions of this chapter are applicable, upon the same being supplied to the operators, owners, lessee, or occupants, of such places with sufficent copies thereof by the commissioner of labor.

WEST VIRGINIA.

CODE—1899.

APPENDIX.—*Inspection of factories, etc.—Bureau of Labor.*

(Page 1057.)

SECTION 1. There * * * is hereby created a State bureau of **Bureau created.** labor, to be under the control and management of a commissioner to be known as the State commissioner of labor, who is to be appointed as hereinafter provided.

Commissioner. SEC. 2. The governor shall, with the advice and consent of the senate, appoint a competent person, who is identified with the labor interests of the State, to be State commissioner of labor, who shall hold his office * * * for a term of four years and until his successor is appointed and qualified. * * *

Salary, etc. SEC. 3. The commissioner of labor * * * shall receive an annual salary of $1,200 for his services. The commissioner of labor is hereby authorized to employ such assistance and incur such expenses as may be necessary to carry into effect the pur- poses of this act; but such assistance and expenses shall not exceed $1.200.

Duties. SEC. 4. It shall be the duty of the commissioner of labor to col- lect, compile and present to the governor, in annual report, statis- tical details relating to all departments of labor and the industrial interests of the State, especially in relation to the financial, social, educational and sanitary condition of the laboring classes, and all statistical information that may tend to increase the prosperity of the productive industries of the State. He shall, once at least in each year, visit and inspect the principal factories and workshops of the State; and shall, upon complaint and request of any three or more reputable citizens, visit and inspect any place where labor is employed and make true report of the result of his inspection.

Powers. SEC. 5. The commissioner of labor shall have power, in the dis- charge of his duties, to enter and inspect any public institution of the State and any factory, workshop or other place where labor is

Answers to in- employed. He may furnish a written or printed list of interroga-
quiries. tories, asking information essential to a proper discharge of his duties, to any person, company or corporation employing labor, and require full and complete answers thereto. And if any person, or the officers of any company or corporation shall neglect or re- fuse to answer, within a reasonable time, any proper question pro- pounded to him by the commissioner of labor; or if any person or the officers of any company or corporation to whom a list of inter- rogatories has been furnished, shall neglect or refuse to fully and truthfully answer and return the same, such person or such officer of such company or corporation shall be deemed guilty of a misde- meanor. The commissioner of labor shall report to the prosecut- ing attorney of the proper county all such violations of this act; whereupon said prosecuting attorney shall proceed against the persons guilty thereof, as in other cases of misdemeanor; and any person or any officer of any company or corporation, convicted in such proceedings shall be fined not less than ten dollars nor more than fifty dollars, or shall be confined in the county jail not less than ten nor more than ninety days, or shall be both fined and imprisoned within the above limits.

Duty of officers. SEC. 6. All State, county, district and city officers shall furnish the commissioner of labor, upon his request, all statistical infor- mation relating to labor, which may be in their possession as such officers. The commissioner of labor shall report to the governor. on or before the first day of December in each year, all the statis- tics he has collected and compiled, with such suggestions as he may deem advisable as to legislation tending to promote and in- crease the prosperity of the industrial establishments of the State, and to protect the lives and health and to promote the prosperity of the persons employed therein.

ACTS OF 1901.

CHAPTER 19.—*Factories and workshops—Inspection, etc.*

Guards for ma- SECTION 1. In all manufacturing, mechanical and other estab-
chinery. lishments, in this State, where the machinery, belting, shafting, gearing, drums and elevators, are so arranged and placed as to be dangerous to persons employed therein, while engaged in their ordinary duties, shall be safely and securely guarded when pos- sible, and if not possible, the notices of the danger shall be con-

spicuously posted in such establishments, and no minor or female of any age shall be permitted to clean any of the mill gearing or machinery in such establishments while the same is in motion. *Cleaning moving machinery.*

SEC. 2. The opening of all hatchways, elevators and wellholes, upon each floor of every manufacturing, mechanical, mercantile or public building in this State, shall be protected by good and sufficient trapdoors, self-closing hatches, or strong guard rails at least three feet high. All due vigilence shall be used to keep such trapdoors closed at all times, except when in actual use. *Hatchways, etc.*

SEC. 3. In every factory, workshop or establishment, in this State, where females are employed, where unclean work of any kind has to be performed, suitable places shall be provided for such females to wash and to change clothing, and stairs. in use by females shall, in all such establishments, be properly screened, and separate water-closets shall be provided for the use of employees of either sex, in all manufacturing, mechanical, mercantile and other establishments in this State where persons of both sexes are employed. *Wash rooms, etc.*

SEC. 4. In every manufacturing, mechanical, mercantile and other establishments, in this State, wherein females are employed, there shall be provided, and conveniently located, seats sufficient to comfortably seat such females; and during such times as such females are not necessarily required by their duties to be upon their feet, they shall be allowed to occupy the seats provided. *Seats for female employees.*

SEC. 5. And all establishments, to which this act applies, must be kept in a clean condition; the sanitary and hygienic regulations shall be such as will not endanger or be injurious to the lives or health of the employees employed therein. *Sanitation.*

SEC. 6. Any person or persons, firm or corporation of any manufacturing, mechanical, mercantile or other establishments, business or calling, in this State, to which this act applies, who shall violate any of the provisions of this act shall be deemed guilty of a misdemeanor, and upon conviction, in any court of competent jurisdiction in this State, shall be fined not less than twenty dollars nor more than one hundred dollars, and in default of payment of such fine shall be imprisoned until such fine and costs are fully paid. *Penalty.*

SEC. 7. It shall be the duty of the commissioner of labor or his assistant to enforce the provisions of this act, and to prosecute all violations of the same before any magistrate or court of competent jurisdiction in this State. *Enforcement.*

ACTS OF 1905.

CHAPTER 76.—*Fire escapes on factories.*

SECTION 1. Every building or structure in this State of three or more stories in height, used as a factory or workshop, and in which ten or more persons are employed above the first story, or any hotel three or more stories in height, or any other building of more than three stories in height occupied or used as a tenement house, shall be provided with one or more suitable and substantial metallic fire escapes or ladders, reaching from the top of the first story to the cornice, and placed on the outside of the building. At each story above the first there shall be one or more metallic balconies substantially attached to the building and to the fire escape. Such fire escapes and balconies shall be in number, size, capacity, design and location as shall be necessary to furnish reasonable means of escape to all persons employed in the building in case of fire. *What buildings to have fire escapes.*

SEC. 2. It shall be the duty of the owner of every such building to equip the same as hereinbefore provided, within six months after the passage of this act. And thereafter no building as is described in the first section shall be used as a factory or workshop in which ten or more persons are employed above the first story, or a hotel three or more stories in height, until the same is so equipped. The word " owner " as used in this section *Duty of owner* shall include the person in whom is vested the legal title to the building.

SEC. 3. It shall be the duty of the mayor, the sergeant or chief of police, and the fire marshal of every city, town or village, annually to inspect every such building therein as described in the first section. They shall make inspection of any such building at any other time that they deem proper, and shall promptly make inspection of any such building whenever complaint thereof may be made to them in writing by any person. They shall serve written notice upon the owner, or his agent, of every such building not so provided with adequate fire escapes to provide the same within thirty days thereafter. It shall be the duty of the owner of such building to comply with such notice and to provide such adequate fire escapes within thirty days thereafter.

Violations.

SEC. 4. Any such owner violating any of the provisions of this act shall be subject to a fine of not less than one hundred dollars ($100), nor more than two hundred dollars, ($200), which may be recovered before any justice or court having jurisdiction. Each week of failure to comply with the notice mentioned in section three shall be deemed a separate and distinct offense. And in addition, if any such owner shall fail for the space of sixty days after the receipt of such notice to provide adequate fire escapes the building may be declared a nuisance in the manner prescribed in section twenty-eight of chapter forty-seven of the Code of West Virginia. If any officer shall fail to perform any duty required of him by this act, or shall violate any of its provisions, he shall be fined not less than twenty-five dollars, ($25), nor more than fifty dollars, ($50), to be recovered before any justice or court having jurisdiction.

WISCONSIN.

ANNOTATED STATUTES OF 1898—SUPPLEMENT OF 1906— ACTS OF 1907, 1909, 1911.[1]

Factory inspectors.

Assistants.

SECTION 1021d. The commissioner may appoint a deputy, who, when acting for or instead of the commissioner, shall have equal authority with him. He may also appoint a clerk, a clerk and typewriter operator, a factory inspector, an assistant factory inspector and a clerk and janitor. The factory inspector shall be a resident of Milwaukee, and he and the assistant inspector shall perform their duties under the direction of the commissioner. * * *

The commissioner of labor and industrial statistics shall have power to appoint ten suitable persons as assistant factory inspectors who shall perform their duties under his direction and who may be removed by him for cause.

The factory inspector or assistant factory inspector having inspected any factory or mercantile establishment under his jurisdiction shall, at the time such inspection is made, issue a certificate or statement as to how the factory laws were complied with at the time of his inspection.

Each of the said assistant factory inspectors shall be paid a salary at the rate of one thousand dollars per annum together with necessary traveling expenses to be paid out of money in the general fund not otherwise appropriated.

Female inspector.

The commissioner of labor and industrial statistics shall have power to appoint one assistant factory inspector in addition to those now authorized by law who shall be a woman and who shall perform her duties under his direction and who may be removed by him for cause.

Said additional assistant factory inspector shall be paid a salary at the rate of one thousand dollars per annum, together

<hr />

[1] All acts amended or created by the Acts of 1907, 1909, and 1911 appear in their proper places as of the Annotated Statutes, serially numbered.

with necessary traveling expenses to be paid out of money in the general fund not otherwise appropriated.

[The salary of assistant factory inspectors was fixed at one thousand .two hundred dollars per annum by an amendment of 1907 to A. S., section 170.]

Sec. 1021t. The commissioner of labor and industrial statistics Extra assistis authorized to employ, for his office, such extra assistants as he ants. may from time to time deem necessary and fix their compensation : *Provided*, That the compensation so fixed by said commissioner of labor and industrial statistics, shall not exceed the amount fixed by law for similar services : *And, provided further*, That the total amount expended for such extra assistants shall be paid out of moneys in the general fund not otherwise appropriated, and shall not in any one year, exceed two thousand five hundred dollars.

Regulation and inspection of factories, etc.

Section 1416–4a. 1. It shall be the duty of the owner and occu- Duty of owned pant, and every person in charge of any * * * factory, work- ers, etc. shop * * * to keep the same in a clean and sanitary condition. In order to promote the general health, whenever ordered by the local health department or board, it shall be the duty of every such person to furnish and place in an efficient manner, in every such building, a reasonable number of cuspidors, as required Cuspidors. or prescribed by the order of said health department or board, and to thoroughly cleanse and disinfect the same daily, except when such building is closed to the public or is not in ordinary use.

2. The type of cuspidors to be used and a reasonable system, method or manner of cleansing and disinfecting the same may be prescribed by the local health department or board : *Provided,* That any cuspidors and system so prescribed shall be reasonably inexpensive, and shall be such as to fulfill the requirements of the highest sanitary efficiency.

3. The powers and duties conferred upon all local health de- Local boards o partments or boards by this section shall be in addition to all health. powers and duties already conferred upon such boards, and this section shall not be construed as lessening or abrogating such powers and duties in any manner.

4. Any person violating any of the provisions of this section Violations. shall be deemed guilty of a misdemeanor, and upon conviction thereof, shall be punished by a fine of not less than five nor more than one hundred dollars.

Sec. 1418m. 1. Spitting * * * upon the floor of any Spitting on * * * store, factory, or of any building which is used in com- floors. mon by the public, * * * is hereby forbidden.

2. The corporations or persons owning or having the manage- Notice. ment or control of any such building, store, factory, * * * are hereby required to keep permanently posted in each of said places a sufficient number of notices forbidding spitting upon the floors and calling attention to the provisions of this section.

3. The corporations or persons owning or having the manage- Cuspidors. ment or control of such buildings, stores, factories, * * * are hereby required to provide sufficient and proper receptacles for expectoration, and also to provide for the cleansing and disinfection of said receptacles at least once every twenty-four hours.

4. Any violation of any of the provisions of this section or Violations. failure or neglect to comply with said provisions, shall be punished by a fine not exceeding two hundred dollars, or by imprisonment in the county jail not more than six months, or by both fine and imprisonment.

Sec. 1636j. No person or corporation shall employ and put to Overcrowding. work in any factory, workshop or other place where labor is performed, or in any part of any such place, a larger number of persons than can be kept at work there without doing violence to the laws of health. The local board of health shall have power to

determine any question arising under this provision, and its
written determination shall be conclusive upon all parties to any
action or proceeding under the same. The owner or manager of
every place where persons are employed to perform labor shall
surround every stationary vat, pan or other vessel into which
molten metal or hot liquids are poured or kept with proper safeguards for the protection of his employees, and all saws, belting,
shafting, gearing, hoists, fly wheels, elevators, any revolving appliances, and drums therein which are so located as to be dangerous to employees in the discharge of their duty shall be securely
guarded or fenced. Any person or corporation which shall neglect
for thirty days after the receipt of written notice from the State
factory inspector to provide a suitable place for the persons employed by him to work in or who shall fail to make and maintain
such safeguards as this section requires and as said inspector shall
specify, shall forfeit not to exceed twenty-five dollars for each
offense, and every day's neglect or failure, after a conviction hereunder, shall constitute a separate offense.

Guards for ma-
chinery, etc.

SEC. 1636jj. 1. In any action brought by an employee or his legal
representative to recover for personal injuries, if it appear that
the injury was caused by the negligent omission of his employer
to guard or protect his machinery or appliances, or the premises
or place where said employee was employed, in the manner required in the foregoing section, the fact that such employee continued in said employment with knowledge of such omission, shall
not operate as a defense.

Actions for in-
juries.

2. The duty to guard or protect the machinery or appliances, or
the premises or place where said employee was employed, in the
manner required in the foregoing section, as well as the duty of
maintaining the same after installation, shall be absolute. The
exercise of ordinary care on the part of the employer shall not be
deemed a compliance with such duties.

Statutory duty
absolute.

3. The commission may conduct any member of such investigations contemporaneously through different agents, and may delegate to such agent the taking of all testimony bearing upon any
investigation or hearing. The decision of the commission shall be
based upon its examination of all testimony and records. The
recommendations made by such agents shall be advisory only and
shall not preclude the taking of further testimony if the commission so order nor further investigation.

SEC. 2394-66. 1. The commission shall have authority to direct
any deputy who is a citizen to act as special prosecutor in any
action, proceeding, investigation, hearing or trial relating to the
matters within its jurisdiction.

Special prose-
cutors.

2. Upon the request of the commission, the attorney general or
district attorney of the county in which any investigation, hearing
or trial had under the provisions of sections 2394–41 to 2394–71,
inclusive, is pending, shall aid therein and prosecute under the
supervision of the commission, all necessary actions or proceedings for the enforcement of said sections and all other laws of
this State relating to the protection of life, health, safety and
welfare, and for the punishment of all violations thereof.

SEC. 2394–67. A substantial compliance with the requirements of
sections 2394–41 to 2394–71, inclusive, shall be sufficient to give
effect to the orders of the commission, and they shall not be
declared inoperative, illegal or void for any omission of a technical
nature in respect thereto.

Sufficient com-
pliance.

SEC. 2394–68. 1. Any employer or other person in interest being
dissatisfied with any order of the commission may commence an
action in the circuit court for Dane County against the commission as defendant to vacate and set aside any such order on the
ground that the order is unlawful, or that any such order is unreasonable, in which action the complaint shall be served with the
summons.

Actions to va-
cate orders.

2. The answer of the commission to the complaint shall be
served and filed within ten days after service of the complaint,

whereupon said action shall be at issue and stand ready for trial upon ten days' notice to either party.

3. All such actions shall have precedence over any civil cause of a different nature pending in such court, and the circuit court shall always be deemed open for the trial thereof, and the same shall be tried and determined as other civil actions.

4. No injunction shall issue suspending or staying any order of the commission, except upon application to the circuit court or the presiding judge thereof, notice to the commission and hearing.

SEC. 2394–69. 1. If upon trial of such action it shall appear that all issues arising in such action have not theretofore been presented to the commission in the petition filed as provided in section 2394–57, or that the commission has not theretofore had an ample opportunity to hear and determine any of the issues raised in such action, or has for any reason, not in fact heard and determined the issues raised, the court shall, before proceeding to render judgment, unless the parties to such action stipulate to the contrary, transmit to the commission a full statement of such issue or issues not adequately considered, and shall stay further proceedings in such action for fifteen days from the date of such transmission, and may thereafter grant such further stays as may be necessary. *Reference to commission.*

2. Upon the receipt of such statement, the commission shall consider the issues not theretofore considered, and may alter, modify, amend or rescind its order complained of in said action, and shall report its action thereon to said court within ten days from the receipt of the statement from the court for further hearing and consideraion.

3. The court shall thereupon order such amendment or other proceeding as may be necessary to raise the issues as changed by such modification of the order as may have been made by the commission upon the hearing, if any such modification has in fact been made, and shall proceed with such action.

SEC. 2394–70. If any employer, employee or other person shall violate any provisions of sections 2394–41 to 2394–55, inclusive, of the Statutes, or shall do any act herein prohibited in sections 2394–41 to 2394–71, inclusive, or shall fail or refuse to perform any duty lawfully enjoined, within the time prescribed by the commission, for which no penalty has been specifically provided, or shall fail, neglect or refuse to obey any lawful order given or made by the commission, or any judgment or decree made by any court in connection with the provisions of sections 2394–41 to 2394–71, for each such violation, failure or refusal, such employer or other person shall forfeit and pay into the State treasury a sum not less than ten dollars nor more than one hundred dollars for each such offense. *Violations.*

SEC. 2394–71. A sum sufficient to carry out the provisions of sections 2394–41 to 2394–71, inclusive, not exceeding seventy-five thousand dollars, is appropriated annually out of any money in the treasury not otherwise appropriated. *Appropriation.*

SEC. 1636–4.

* * * * * * *

2. There shall be provided and kept connected with * * * every factory, workshop or other structure, three or more stories high, in which ten or more persons may be employed above the ground floor, at any kind of labor, one or more good and substantial metallic or fireproof stairs or stairways, ready for use at all times, reaching from the cornice to the top of the first story and attached to the ouside thereof in such reasonable position and number as to afford reasonable safe and convenient means of egress and escape in case of fire. *Fireproof stairways required.*

3. All fire-escape stairways shall be placed at an angle not more than forty-five degrees, shall have attached thereto a wrought iron handrail, not less than three feet in height; be constructed with steps not less than six inches in width, nor less than twenty-two inches in length, and with a rise of not more *Construction.*

than eight inches, and constructed of sufficient strength, and in all other respects shall afford an accessible and safe exit and escape in case of fire, for all occupants of the building that may at any time be dependent thereon. Such stairs shall rest upon and be securely bolted to wrought iron balcony, that shall be located at each floor above the first, access to be provided to such balcony from at least two windows. Such balcony shall rest upon and be securely bolted to wrought iron brackets, the upper arm of which shall go through the wall and be securely fastened with nut and washer, and the lower end of which shall be let into the wall and be securely fastened in place. Such balcony shall not be less than three feet four inches wide, and shall be provided with a wrought iron railing not less than two feet nine inches high, and in all cases the ends of said railing shall be securely fastened to the building. No balcony railing shall be connected at angles by cast iron. All said fire-escape stairs shall be of such strength and construction as will sustain a load of at least one hundred and fifty pounds per step; and all said fire-escape balconies shall sustain a load of eighty pounds per square foot. There shall be afforded at all times free and unobstructed passageway to such fire escape The balcony on the top floor shall be provided with a goose-neck ladder leading to and above the roof, also to be placed at an angle of forty-five degrees. The lowest balcony shall be provided with a permanent balance stairway reaching to the ground.

Existing provisions. 4. Nothing in this section shall be construed to require existing iron ladders or other fire escapes to be replaced by iron stairs or stairways, but no existing ladder shall be replaced except by iron stairs or stairways. Nor shall anything in this section prohibit the use of such spiral or chute fire escapes, as may be approved by the State factory inspector or commissioner of labor.

Standpipes. 5. In all cities and villages where there is a water supply, either from waterworks, fire engines or pumping station, there shall be attached to such fire escapes, except on structures equipped with automatic sprinklers, a three-inch wrought iron standpipe extending from a point within five feet from the ground to a point three feet above the roof or cornice, and on the roof shall be attached a two and one-half inch angle hose valve with male hose connection and a double or Siamese " Y " female hose connection at the base of the pipe, the threads of which shall conform to the size and pattern used by the fire department where the structure is located.

Violations by architects. 6. Any architect, who shall fail to specify fire escapes as herein provided in plans for such buildings as are herein enumerated, or any person, firm or corporation, who shall move into or occupy any new building (or any old building having once been vacated) without such building or buildings being equipped with fire escapes as herein provided, shall be deemed guilty of a misdemeanor, and upon conviction thereof, shall be fined not less than one hundred dollars, or six months in the county jail, or both such fine and imprisonment.

* * * * * * *

Lights. 8. All hallways and stairways in all * * * factories and workshops, when used at night, shall be kept lighted at the head and foot of each flight of stairs and at the intersection of all corridors. Such light shall be so placed and arranged as to designate the direction of fire escapes, which three escapes shall be designated by red lights. One or more gongs or alarms, capable of being heard throughout the building, shall be placed and remain easy of access and ready for use in said * * * factories and workshops to give notice to occupants of said places in case of fire. A notice descriptive of the means of escape shall be posted in conspicuous places in every factory and workshop * * *.

Violations. 9. Any such person or corporation, who shall fail for three months after the receipt of notice in writing, stating the substance of the provisions of this section, from such chief, marshal or inspector to provide and keep such means of escape or such stand-pipe, shall be deemed guilty of a misdemeanor, and upon conviction thereof, shall be punished by a fine not exceeding one hundred dollars or by imprisonment in the county jail not more than thirty days.

SEC. 1636–5. The inside walls or casings of every elevator used for the conveyance of passengers to and from the upper stories of any such building as is [described] within the preceding section, shall be constructed of fireproof material throughout. *Elevator shafts.*

SEC. 1636–7. It shall be the duty of the commissioner of labor, factory inspector, assistant factory inspector, chief or marshal of the fire department of every city or village to enforce the provisions of the foregoing sections. Any person who shall fail to comply with the provisions of said sections within ninety days after being notified in writing to do so by either of said officers whose duty it may be to give notice, shall be punished according to law. Said commissioner of labor, factory inspector, assistant factory inspector, chief or marshal upon receiving notice or obtaining knowledge that any person within his jurisdiction has not so complied with said provisions, shall file a written statement to that effect with the proper district attorney, which, being done, he shall prosecute such person. *Enforcement.*

SEC. 1636–8. The owner, tenant or other person in charge of any building within either of the four next preceding sections, who shall fail or neglect, after a written notice has been given him in accordance with the next preceding section, to comply with any of the provisions of said sections, which are applicable to the building owned, leased or in his charge, shall be deemed guilty of a misdemeanor and be punished by a fine not exceeding one thousand dollars or by imprisonment in the county jail not longer than ninety days. *Penalty.*

SEC. 1636–31. Every factory, mill, or workshop, mercantile or mechanical establishment or other building where eight or more persons are employed, shall be provided within reasonable access with a sufficient number of water-closets, earth closets, or privies for the reasonable use of the persons employed therein, and whenever male and female persons are employed as aforesaid together, water-closets, earth closets or privies separate and apart, shall be provided for the use of each sex, and plainly so designated, and no person shall be allowed to use such closet or privy assigned to the other sex. Such closet shall be properly enclosed and ventilated and at all times kept in a clean and good sanitary condition. When the number employed is more than twenty of either sex, there shall be provided an additional closet for such sex up to the number of forty, and above that number in the same ratio. The commissioner of labor or any factory inspector may require such changes in the placing of such closets as he may deem necessary and may require other changes which may serve the best interest of morals and sanitation. *Water - closets, etc.*

SEC. 1636–32. In factories, mills or workshops, mercantile or mechanical establishments or other places where the labor performed by the operator is of such a character that it becomes desirable or necessary to change the clothing, wholly or in part, before leaving the building at the close of the day's work, separate dressing rooms shall be provided for females whenever so required by the commissioner of labor or any factory inspector. It shall be the duty of every occupant, whether owner or lessee of any such premises used as specified by this act, to make all the changes and additions thereto. In case such changes are made upon the order of the commissioner of labor, or any factory inspector to the lessee of the premises, the lessee may at any time within thirty days after the completion thereof, bring an action against any person or corporation or partnerships having interest in such premises, and may recover such proportion of expenses of making such changes and additions as the court adjudges should justly and equitably be borne by such defendant. *Dressing rooms.*

Windows.

SEC. 1636–32 1. In factories, mills, workshops, mercantile or mechanical establishments, the windows shall be so arranged that they will permit of the sufficient circulation of fresh air from the outside of the building during working hours, and shall be so constructed as to prevent direct drafts striking the employees working therein. Where the circulation of fresh air can not be satisfactorily secured through an arrangement of the windows, any system of ventilation may be installed that will keep the air therein free from substances and qualities injurious to the health or comfort of the employees, if approved by the bureau of labor and industrial statistics.

Ventilation system.

Inspection.

SEC. 1636–32 m. Every factory inspector and every assistant factory inspector charged with the inspection of factories, mills, workshops, mercantile or mechanical establishments, shall investigate the system of ventilation in every plant inspected, and wherever same is not found to comply with the provisions of this act, written notice thereof shall be given to the owner or owners thereof, or to the officer or officers, if said factories, mills, workshops, mercantile or mechanical establishments be corporations. Whenever the owner or owners of said factories, mills, workshops, mercantile or mechanical establishments, or officer or officers of said plants do not take steps to remedy the system of ventilation, after written notice of defects thereof has been given in accordance with the provisions of this act, said owner or owners thereof, or the officer or officers thereof shall be punished by a fine not less than twenty-five dollars, nor more than five hundred dollars, or by imprisonment not less than thirty days, nor more than six months, or by both such fine and imprisonment.

Enforcement.

SEC. 1636–32 n. It shall be the duty of the district attorney of every county in this State to prosecute all violations of this act upon complaint of any factory inspector or deputy.

Sanitation of bakeries, etc.

SEC. 1636–61 1. All buildings occupied for bakeries and confectionery establishments, and all buildings or rooms connected with, or part of such bakeries or confectionery establishments and used for storage of goods that are intended to be used in the preparation of the products of such establishments or for storage of the products of such establishments shall be well drained, and all plumbing therein, if any, shall be constructed in accordance with well established sanitary principles and of good workmanship; and the rooms thereof used for the manufacture, storage, or sale of bread and other food products, or for the storage of goods that are intended to be used in the preparation of such bread and other food products, shall be light, dry, and airy. * * *

Location of water-closets, etc.

2. No water-closet, earth closet, privy, urinal or ash pit shall be within the bake room or any other room used in the manufacture of bread or other food products in any bakery or confectionery establishment. All water-closets, urinals, or privies connected with, part of, or within any building used as a bakery or confectionery shall be so arranged that gases or odors out of said closets, urinals, or privies connected with, part of, or within any closets, urinals, or privies cannot enter into any room used in the production or storage of food in any bakery or confectionery, and such closets, privies, or urinals shall be equipped with efficient natural or mechanical means of removing all odors or gases into the outer air.

Toilet rooms.

SEC. 1636–62. 1. All bakeries and confectioneries shall be provided with ample toilet facilities apart from the utensils used in the preparation of said foods to enable the workmen employed therein to keep their persons clean. Said bakeries and confectioneries shall also be provided with a separate place to enable the workmen to change their clothes and keep the same in a proper condition. * * * The air within such bakery or confectionery establishment shall at all times be kept pure and free from noxious odors and harmful gases.

2. No room used as a bakery or confectionery shall be used as a habitation or sleeping place by any person, and such rooms

used as bakeries or confectioneries shall not be used for any purpose except those incidental to the manufacture, storage, or sale of the products of such bakery or confectionery establishments.

3. All persons engaged in the manufacture of bread or other food products in bakery or confectionery establishments shall provide themselves with caps and slippers or shoes and an external suit of washable material, and wear these garments while engaged in the preparation, packing, or handling of food in or about bakeries or confectioneries, said garments to be used for that purpose only and to be kept at all times in a clean condition. — Clothing.

4. No food shall be prepared, handled, or cared for in any unclean manner or near any filthy object in any bakery or confectionery establishment, nor by any person wearing filthy clothing, nor by any person afflicted with a loathsome or venereal disease. * * * No person shall befoul any room or any utensil used in the preparation of food in any bakery or confectionery establishment. — Cleanliness. Diseased persons.

* * * * *

SEC. 1636–63. After the passage of this act no new bakery or confectionery establishment shall be established or operated in a room the floor of which is more than five feet below the level of the street, sidewalk or adjacent ground, nor in any room the ceiling of which is less than eight feet high from the floor and no bake shop nor confectionery shall be reopened in such a room where the same has not been used for a period over six months. — Basements.

SEC. 1636–64 (as amended by chapter No. 446, Acts of 1911). No person shall work or be employed in or about any bakery or confectionery establishment for the manufacture of food products during the time in which a case of contagious or infectious disease exists in the house in which such person resides, and not thereafter until such house has been properly disinfected: *Provided*, That such persons may be employed if the local board of health issue a certificate in writing that no danger of pubic [public] contagion or infection would result from the employment of said person in such establishment. — Contagious, etc., diseases.

SEC. 1636–65. It shall be the duty of the State bureau of labor and boards of health, both State and local, to see that the provisions of this act are enforced and the commissioner of labor shall appoint a proper and competent person to act as bakery inspector for two years, who shall perform his duties under the direction of the said commissioner. The State factory inspector or any assistant State factory inspector shall have the same power as the bakery inspector. The said bakery inspector shall receive a salary of $1,000 per annum together with necessary traveling expenses, to be paid out of the general fund not otherwise appropriated. — Enforcement.

No building, room or apartment shall be used for the purpose of establishing a bakery or confectionery establishment for the manufacture of bread and other food products, unless a license is secured as provided in this act. Application for a license shall be made to the commissioner of labor and industrial statistics by any person, firm or corporation desiring to establish or conduct a bakery or confectionery for the manufacture of bread and other food products. Such application shall be made in such form as the commissioner of labor may determine. Blank applications shall be prepared and furnished by the commissioner of labor. — License.

If the commissioner of labor and industrial statistics or bakery inspector, ascertain that such building, room or apartment is in clean and proper sanitary condition, and otherwise conforms to all provisions of this act, and that bread and other food products may be manufactured therein under clean and sanitary conditions, he shall grant a license permitting the use of such building, room or apartment for the purpose of making bread and other food products. The license so issued shall be revoked ipso facto upon a second conviction of any violation or failure to comply with any of the provisions of this act.

Inspector. SEC. 1636-66. It shall be the duty of the State bureau of labor and boards of health, both State and local, to see that the provisions of this act are enforced and the commissioner of labor shall appoint a proper and competent person to act as bakery inspector for two years, who shall perform his duties under the direction of the said commissioner. The State factory inspector or any assistant State factory inspector shall have the same power as the bakery inspector. The said bakery inspector shall receive a salary of twelve hundred dollars per annum and necessary expenses incurred in the performance of his official duties, to be paid out of the general fund not otherwise appropriated.

Violations. SEC. 1636-67. Any person who shall engage in or continue in the operation of a bakery or confectionery establishment after this act shall take effect without first procuring a license so to do, as provided by this act, shall be deemed guilty of a misdemeanor, and shall be punished by a fine of not less than twenty dollars nor more than one hundred dollars, or by imprisonment in the county jail for not more than ninety days, or both. Any person who violates or fails to comply with any other provision of this act after thirty days notice in writing has been served upon, or sent through registered mail to, the owner, manager or officer operating such establishment, by an officer or inspector of the bureau of labor or some officer or agent of the board of health, of any change necessary to be made to comply with the provisions of this act, shall be deemed guilty of a misdemeanor, and shall be punished by a fine of not less than twenty dollars nor more than one hundred dollars, or by imprisonment in the county jail for not more than ninety days, or both: *Provided, however*, That nothing in this section shall be so construed as to prevent immediate prosecution, without notice, for any violation of the provisions of subdivision 2 of section 1636-61 as created by this act.

Factories and workshops—Sweat shops.

License required. SECTION 1636-71. No room or apartment in any tenement or dwelling house or in a building situated in the rear of any tenement or dwelling house, shall be used for the purpose of manufacturing, altering, repairing or finishing therein, for wages or for sale, any coats, vests, knee pants, trousers, overalls, cloaks, hats, caps, suspenders, jerseys, blouses, dresses, waists, waist bands, underwear, neckwear, knit goods of all kinds, furs, fur trimmings, fur garments, skirts, shirts, purses, feathers, cigarettes, cigars or unbrellas, unless a license is secured therefor as provided in this act.

Applications. Application for such a license shall be made to the commissioner of labor and industrial statistics by any family or a member thereof or any person, firm or corporation, desiring to manufacture, alter, repair or finish any such articles in any room or apartment in any tenement or dwelling house or by any person, firm or corporation desiring to perform such work in any building in the rear of any tenement or dwelling house. Such application shall describe the room or apartment, shall specify the number of persons to be employed therein, and shall be in such form as the commissioner of labor and industrial statistics may determine. Blank applications shall be prepared and furnished by the commissioner of labor and industrial statistics. Before any such license is granted, an inspection of the room, apartment, or building sought to be licensed, must be made by the commissioner of labor and industrial statistics, factory inspector or assistant factory inspector.

If the commissioner of labor and industrial statistics, factory inspector, or assistant factory inspector, ascertain that such room, apartment or building, is in a clean and proper sanitary condition, and that the articles specified in this section may be manufactured therein under clean and healthful condition[s], he shall grant a license permitting the use of such room, apartment or building for the purpose of manufacturing, altering, repairing or finishing such articles. Each license shall state the maximum number of persons who may be employed in the room or rooms to which such license relates.

The number of persons to be so employed shall be determined **Air space.** by the number of cubic feet of air space contained in each room or apartment mentioned in such license, allowing not less than two hundred and fifty cubic feet for each person employed between the hours of six o'clock in the morning and six o'clock in the evening, and unless by a special written permit of the commissioner of labor and industrial statistics, factory inspector, or assistant factory inspector, not less than four hundred cubic feet for each person employed therein between the hours of six in the evening and six in the morning, but no such permit shall be issued unless such room or apartment has suitable light at all times during such hours, while such persons are employed therein.

Such license must be posted in a conspicuous place in the room or apartment to which it relates. It may be revoked by the commissioner of labor and industrial statistics, factory inspector or assistant factory inspector, if the health of the community or of the employees requires it, or if it appears that the rooms or apartments, to which such license relates, are not in a healthy and proper sanitary condition.

Every room or apartment in which any of the articles named **Sanitation.** in this section are manufactured, altered, repaired or finished, shall be kept in a clean and sanitary condition and shall be subject to inspection and examination by the commissioner of labor and industrial statistics, factory inspector, or assistant factory inspector, for the purpose of ascertaining whether said garments or articles or any part or parts thereof are clean and free from vermin and every matter of infectious or contagious nature.

No person, firm or corporation, shall hire, employ or contract with any member of a family or any person, firm or corporation not holding a license therefor, to manufacture, alter, repair or finish any of the articles named in this section in any room or apartment in any tenement or dwelling house or in any room or apartment in any building, situated in the rear of a tenement or dwelling house as aforesaid; and no person, firm or corporation shall receive, handle or convey to others or sell, hold in stock or expose for sale, any goods mentioned in this section unless made under the sanitary conditions and in accordance with this act.

This section shall not prevent the employment of a tailor or seamstress by any person or family for the purpose of making, altering, repairing or finishing any article of wearing apparel for such person or for family use.

Sec. 1636–72. Whenever the commissioner of labor and industrial **Revocation of** statistics, factory inspector or assistant factory inspector in his **license.** judgment revokes or refuses to grant a license to any person or persons because of the unhealthy or unsanitary conditions in or surrounding the place where any of the aforesaid goods are or are to be manufactured, the person or persons aggrieved by such decision may appeal to the board of health of such city, village or town wherein said license was refused or revoked. The board of health after receiving a written notice of the appeal from the person or persons aggrieved, shall immediately investigate the conditions and surroundings of the place wherein any of the goods are or are to be manufactured as mentioned in the aforesaid, [sic] and if they find that a license can be granted without injuring or impairing the public health, then such finding shall be immediately reported in writing to the commissioner of labor and industrial statistics who shall thereupon grant such license.

Sec. 1636–73. The commissioner of labor and industrial statistics, **Separation of** factory inspector or assistant factory inspector, may when he **workrooms from** deems it necessary, require that all rooms or apartments used for **living rooms.** the purpose of manufacturing, altering, repairing or finishing therein, any of the aforesaid goods or articles as mentioned in section 1 [sec. 1636–71] shall be separate from and have no door, window or other opening into any living or sleeping room or **any** tenement or dwelling and that no such rooms or apartments shall be used at any time for sleeping purposes and shall contain no bed, bedding or cooking utensils. He may further require or direct a separate outside entrance to the room or apartments where the work is carried on, and if such work is carried on above the first floor, then there may be directed a separate and distinct stairway leading thereto and every such room or apartment shall be well and sufficiently lighted, heated and ventilated by ordinary, or if necessary, by mechanical appliance.

Water-closets.   He may also require suitable closet arrangements for each sex employed as follows: Where there are ten or more persons and three or more to the number of twenty are of either sex, a separate and distinct water-closet, either inside the building with adequate plumbing connections or on the outside. at least twenty feet from the building, shall be provided for each sex. When the number employed is more than twenty-five of either sex, there shall be provided an additional water-closet for such sex up to the number of fifty persons, and above that number in the same ratio, and all such closets shall be kept strictly and exclusively for the use of the employees and employer and [or] employers. All closets shall be regularly disinfected and the commissioner of labor and industrial statistics, factory inspector or assistant factory inspector may require all other necessary changes or any process of cleaning, painting or whitewashing which they may deem necessary, before the issuing of the license.

Register.   SEC. 1636–74. Any person, firm or corporation, by themselves or by their agents or managers, contracting for the manufacturing, altering, repairing or finishing of any of the articles mentioned in section 1 [sec. 1636–71] of this act, or giving out material from which they or any part of them are to be manufactured, altered, repaired or finished, shall keep a register of the names and addresses, plainly written in English, of the persons to whom such articles or materials are given to be so manufactured, altered, repaired or finished or with whom they have contracted to do the same. Such register shall be subject to inspection on demand, by the commissioner of labor and industrial statistics, factory inspector or assistant factory inspector, and a copy thereof shall be furnished at his request.

Infectious diseases.   SEC. 1636–75. If the commissioner of labor and industrial statistics, factory inspector or assistant factory inspector find that infectious or contagious diseases exist in a workshop, room or apartment of a tenement or dwelling house or of a building in the rear thereof in which any of the articles specified in section 1 [sec. 1636–71] of this act are being manufactured, altered, repaired or finished or that articles manufactured or in process of manufacture therein are infected or that goods used therein are unfit for use, he shall report to the local board of health, and such board shall issue such order as the public health may require. Such board may condemn and destroy all such infectious article or articles manufactured or in the process of manufacture under unclean or unhealthful conditions.

Owner not to permit unlawful use.   SEC. 1636–76. The owner, lessee or agent of a tenement or dwelling house or of a building in the rear of a tenement or dwelling house shall not permit the use thereof for the manufacture, repair, alteration or finishing of any of the articles mentioned in this act contrary to its provisions. If a room or apartment in such tenement or dwelling house or in a building in the rear of a tenement or dwelling house be so unlawfully used, the commissioner of labor and industrial statistics, factory inspector, or assistant factory inspector, shall serve a notice thereof upon such owner, lessee or agent. Unless such owner, lessee or agent shall cause such unlawful manufacture to be discontinued within thirty days after the service of such notice or within fifteen days thereafter, institutes and faithfully prosecutes proceedings for the dispossession of the occupant of a tenement or dwelling house or of a building in the rear of a tenement or dwelling house who unlawfully manufactures, repairs, alters or finishes such articles in any room or apartment therein, he shall be deemed guilty of a violation of this act as if he himself was engaged in such unlawful manufacture, repair, alteration or finishing.

SEC. 1636–77. Any person, firm or corporation, agent or manager of any corporation who whether for himself or for such firm or corporation or by himself or through agents, servants or foremen shall violate any of the provisions of this act shall upon conviction thereof be fined in any sum not less than twenty dollars nor more than one hundred dollars for each offense, or imprisoned not less than twenty or more than sixty days or both, and in all prosecutions brought by or under the direction of the commissioner of labor and industrial statistics for the violation of this act, he shall not be held to give security for costs or adjudged to pay any costs but in all cases where the accused be acquitted or is found to be indigent, the costs shall be paid out of the county treasury of the county in which the proceedings are brought the same as the costs in all other cases of misdemeanor. *Penalty.*

Cigar factories.

SECTION 1636–101. No shop or place wherein cigars are manufactured shall be located below the ground floor. *Location.*

SEC. 1636–102. Each employee in any shop or place wherein cigars are manufactured, shall, while actually employed, be allowed to use twenty square feet of surface space, unobstructed to the ceiling. *Surface space.*

SEC. 1636–103. Every room wherein cigars are manufactured shall contain at least seven hundred cubic feet of air space. It shall in every part be not less than eight feet in height, from floor to ceiling, every window shall have not less than twelve square feet on superficial area, and the entire area of window surface shall be not less than twelve per cent of the floor space of such room. *Air space.*

SEC. 1636–104. Every room in which cigars are manufactured while work is carried on shall be so ventilated that the air shall not become impure and injurious to the health of the persons employed therein, and it shall wherever necessary, by the means of air shafts or other ventilation, be so changed as to render harmless all gases, dust and other impurities generated in the process of manufacturing cigars. All windows are to be kept open for thirty minutes before working hours and for thirty minutes after working hours. *Ventilation.*

SEC. 1636–105. Every such shop or place in which one or more persons are employed and every such factory in which five or more persons are employed, shall be kept clean. The dust must be removed from work tables and floors once every day, the floors scrubbed at least once a week and one cuspidor provided for every two employees. *Cleanliness.*

SEC. 1636–106. No person under eighteen years of age shall be employed or permitted to work in a cigar shop or a cigar factory at manufacturing cigars for longer than eight hours a day or forty-eight hours a week. *Hours of labor of minors.*

SEC. 1636–107. Where men and women are employed there shall be separate dressing rooms and water-closets for the different sexes. *Dressing rooms, etc.*

SEC. 1636–108. Any person violating any provision of this act shall be punished by fine not exceeding twenty-five dollars and no less than ten dollars for the first offense, and by fine not exceeding fifty dollars, and no less than twenty-five dollars for the second and each following offense. *Penalty.*

SEC. 1636–109. The factory inspector shall have full power and it shall be his duty to enforce all the provisions of this act, but no prosecution shall be instituted for any violations of sections 2, 3 and 4 [1636–102 to 1636–104] unless the employer or manufacturer, or the firm has been notified by a notice sent in a registered letter for at least four weeks prior to a prosecution, requiring the necessary changes in the factory or workshop, and such request has not been complied with. *Enforcement.*

Wood-sawing machinery.

Guards required. SECTION 1636–136. No person, firm or corporation shall offer or expose for sale any machine for the purpose of sawing wood unles [unless] the said machine shall be provided with reasonable safety devices for the protection from accidents from saws, gears, knuckles, belts, set screws or other dangerous parts.

Not to be detached while in use. SEC. 1636–137. It shall be unlawful for any person, firm or corporation owning such machine to use, operate or permit to be used or operated any such machine while the safety devices or guards are detached.

Violations. SEC. 1636–138. Any such person, firm or corporation who shall violate any of the provisions of this act shall be punished by a fine of not less than twenty dollars nor more than one hundred dollars for each offense.

Enforcement. SEC. 1636–139. Upon complaint to the commissioner of labor, factory inspector or assistant inspector, it shall be his duty to enforce the provisions of this act.

Inspection, etc., of factories and workshops.

SECTION 2394–41. The following terms as used in sections 2394–41 to 2394–71 of the Statutes, shall be construed as follows:

Definitions. (1) The phrase "place of employment" shall mean and include every place, whether indoors or out or underground and the premises appurtenant thereto where either temporary or permanently any industry, trade or business is carried on, or where any process or operation, directly or indirectly related to any industry, trade or business, is carried on, and where any person is directly or indirectly, employed by another for direct or indirect gain or profit, but shall not include any place where persons are employed in private domestic service or agricultural pursuits which do not involve the use of mechanical power.

(2) The term "employment" shall mean and include any trade, occupation or process of manufacture, or any method of carrying on such trade, occupation, or process of manufacture in which any person may be engaged, except in such private domestic service or agricultural pursuits as do not involve the use of mechanical power.

(3) The term "employer" shall mean and include every person, firm, corporation, agent, manager, representative or other person having control or custody of any employment, place of employment or of any employee.

(4) The term "employee" shall mean and include every person who may be required or directed by any employer, in consideration of direct or indirect gain or profit, to engage in any employment, or to go or work or be at any time in any place of employment.

(5) The term "frequenter" shall mean and include every person, other than an employee, who may go in or be in a place of employment under circumstances which render him other than a trespasser.

(6) The term "deputy" shall mean and include any person employed by the industrial commission designated as such deputy by the commission, who shall possess special, technical, scientific, managerial or personal abilities or qualities in matters within the jurisdiction of the industrial commission, and who may be engaged in the performance of duties under the direction of the commission, calling for the exercise of such abilities or qualities.

(7) The term "order" shall mean and include any decision, rule, regulation, direction, requirement or standard of the commission, or any other determination arrived at or decision made by such commission.

(8) The term "general order" shall mean and include such order as applies generally throughout the State to all persons, employments or places of employment, or all persons, employ-

ments, or places of employment of a class under the jurisdiction of the commission. All other orders of the commission shall be considered special orders.

(9) The term "local order" shall mean and include any ordinance, order, rule or determination of any common council, board of aldermen, board of trustees, or the village board, of any village or city, or the board of health of any municipality, or an order or direction of any official of such municipality, upon any matter over which the industrial commission has jurisdiction.

(10) The term "welfare" shall mean and include comfort, decency and moral well-being.

(11) The term "safe" and "safety" as applied to an employment or a place of employment shall mean such freedom from danger to the life, health or safety of employees or frequenters as the nature of the employment will reasonably permit.

SEC. 2394–42. There is hereby created a board which shall be known as the "Industrial Commission of Wisconsin." Within thirty days after the passage of this act the governor, by and with the advise [sic] and consent of the senate, shall appoint a member who shall serve two years, another who shall serve four years, and another who shall serve six years. Thereafter each member shall be appointed and confirmed for terms of six years each. Vacancies shall be filled in the same manner for unexpired terms. Each member of the board, before entering upon the duties of his office, shall take the oath prescribed by the constitution. A majority of the board shall constitute a quorum for the exercise of the powers or authority conferred upon it. In case of a vacancy the remaining two members of the board shall exercise all the powers and authority of the board until such vacancy is filled. Each member of the board shall receive an annual salary of five thousand dollars, and actual expenses necessarily incurred in the performance of his duties, which shall be in full for all services performed under sections 2394–41 to 2394–71, inclusive. This board shall supersede and perform all of the duties of the industrial accident board provided in sections 2394–1 to 2394–40, inclusive. *Board created.*

SEC. 2394–43. Within thirty days after the passage and publication of this act, such commission shall meet at the State capitol and organize in the manner provided for the organization of the industrial accident board in section 2394–13 of the Statutes. A majority of said commissioners shall constitute a quorum to transact business. No vacancy shall impair the right of the remaining commissioners to exercise all the powers of the commission. *Organization.*

SEC. 2394–44. The commission shall keep its office at the capitol and shall be provided by the superintendent of public property with suitable rooms, necessary furniture, stationery, books, periodicals, maps, instruments and other necessary supplies. The commission may, however, hold sessions at any place other than the capitol when the convenience of the commission and the parties interested so requires. *Office.*

SEC. 2394–45. The commissioners and employees of the commission shall be entitled to receive from the State their actual necessary expenses while traveling on the business of the commission, either within or without the State of Wisconsin. Such expenditure shall be presented in an account verified by the person who incurred the expenses, approved by the chairman of the commission and shall be audited and paid as are the expenses of employees and members of other State commissions. *Expenses.*

SEC. 2394–46. The commission shall be known collectively as the "Industrial Commission of Wisconsin" and in that name may sue and be sued. It shall have a seal for the authentication of its orders and proceedings, upon which shall be inscribed the words "Industrial Commission—Wisconsin—Seal." *Title.*

SEC. 2394–47. When public interest requires, the employees of either the industrial commission or those of the industrial acci- *Employees.*

dent board may be required to perform service in whole or in
part for either such board or commission.

Safe condi- SEC. 2394-48. Every employer shall furnish employment which
tions. shall be safe for the employees therein and shall furnish a place
of employment which shall be safe for employees therein and for
frequenters thereof and shall furnish and use safety devices and
safeguards, and shall adopt and use methods and processes reasonably adequate to render such employment and place of employment safe, and shall do every 6ther thing reasonably necessary to
protect the life, health, safety and welfare of such employees and
frequenters.

Same. SEC. 2394-49. 1. No employer shall require, permit or suffer any
employee to go or be in any employment or place of employment
which is not safe, and no such employer shall fail to furnish,
provide and use safety devices and safeguards, or fail to adopt
and use methods and processes reasonably adequate to render
such employment and place of employment safe, and no such employer shall fail or neglect to do every other thing reasonably
necessary to protect the life, health, safety or welfare of such
employees and frequenters; and no such employer or other person
shall hereafter construct or occupy or maintain any place of employment that is not safe.

Removing 2. No employee shall remove, displace, damage, destroy or carry
guards, etc. off any safety device or safeguard furnished and provided for use
in any employment or place of employment, nor interfere in any
way with the use thereof by any other person, nor shall any such
employee interfere with the use of any method or process adopted
for the protection of any employee in such employment or place
of employment or frequenter of such place of employment, nor fail
or neglect to do every other thing reasonably necessary to protect
the life, health, safety or welfare of such employees or frequenters.

Information SEC. 2394-50. 1. Every employer shall furnish to the commission
from employers. all information required by it to carry into effect the provisions
of sections 2394-1 to 2394-71, inclusive, and shall make specific
answers to all questions submitted by the commission relative
thereto.

2. Any employer receiving from the commission any blanks calling for information required by it to carry into effect the provisions of sections 2394-41 to 2394-71, inclusive, with directions to
fill the same, shall cause the same to be properly filled out so as
to answer fully and correctly each question therein propounded,
and in case he is unable to answer any question, he shall give a
good and sufficient reason for such failure; and said answer shall
be verified under oath by the employer, or by the president, secretary or other managing officer of the corporation, if the employer
is a corporation, and returned to the commission at its office within
the period fixed by the commission.

3. Any commissioner or deputy of the commission may enter any
place of employment for the purpose of collecting facts and statistics, examining the provisions made for the health, safety and
welfare of the employees therein and bringing to the attention of
every employer any law, or any order of the commission, and any
failure on the part of such employer to comply therewith. No
employer shall refuse to admit any commissioner or deputy of the
commission to his place of employment.

Powers of com- SEC. 2394-51. The industrial commission is vested with the
mission power and jurisdiction to have such supervision of every employment and place of employment in this State as may be necessary
adequately to enforce and administer all laws and all lawful
orders requiring such employment and place of employment to be
safe, and requiring the protection of the life, health, safety and
welfare of every employee in such employment or place of employment and every frequenter of such place of employment.

Duties. SEC. 2394-52. It shall also be the duty of the industrial commission, and it shall have power, jurisdiction and authority:

Administra- (1) To employ, promote and remove deputies, clerks and other
tion. assistants as needed, to fix their compensation, and to assign to

them their duties; to appoint advisors who shall, without compensation, assist the industrial commission in the execution of its duties; to retain and to assign to their duties any or all the officers, subordinates and clerks of the bureau of labor and industrial statistics, of the State factory inspectors' department, and of the free employment offices, the bakery inspector, woman factory inspector, and secretary of the State board of arbitration: *Provided*, That the number of employees of said commission shall not be increased to exceed the number now employed in the bureau of labor and industrial statistics, except upon the certificate of the governor, to be filed with the secretary of state before any such additional employee shall be appointed, certifying that any such additional employee is necessary to the work of this commission, and approving the amount of salary to be paid to any such additional employee. The deputies employed by the commission shall not be exempt from the operation of sections 990–1 to 990–32, inclusive, of the Statutes.

(2) To administer and enforce the laws relating to child labor, laundries, stores, employment of females, licensed occupations, school attendance, bakeries, employment offices, intelligence offices and bureaus, manufacture of cigars, sweatshops, corn shredders, wood-sawing machines, fire escapes, and means of egress from buildings, scaffolds, hoists, ladders and other matters relating to the erection, repair, alteration or painting of buildings and structures, and all other laws protecting the life, health, safety and welfare of employees in employments and places of employment and frequenters of places of employment. *Enforcement of laws.*

(3) To investigate, ascertain, declare and prescribe what safety devices, safeguards or other means or methods of protection are best adapted to render the employees of every employment and place of employment and frequenters of every place of employment safe, and to protect their welfare as required by law or lawful orders, and to establish and maintain museums of safety and hygiene in which shall be exhibited safety devices, safeguards and other means and methods for the protection of life, health, safety and welfare of employees. *Inspection.*

(4) To ascertain and fix such reasonable standards and to prescribe, modify and enforce such reasonable orders for the adoption of safety devices, safeguards and other means or methods of protection to be as nearly uniform as possible, as may be necessary to carry out all laws and lawful orders relative to the protection of the life, health, safety and welfare of employees in employments and places of employment or frequenters of places of employment. *Fixing standards.*

(5) To ascertain, fix and order such reasonable standards or the construction, repair and maintenance of places of employment as shall render them safe.

(6) To investigate, ascertain and determine such reasonable classifications of persons, employments and places of employment as shall be necessary to carry out the purposes of sections 2394–41 to 2394–71, inclusive. *Classifying employments.*

(7) To adopt reasonable and proper rules and regulations relative to the exercise of its powers and authorities and proper rules to govern its proceedings and to regulate the mode and manner of all investigations and hearings; such rules and regulations shall not be effective until ten days after their publication. A copy of such rules and regulations shall be delivered to every citizen making application therefor, and a copy delivered with every notice of hearing. *Rules.*

*   *   *   *   *   *

SEC. 2394–53. 1. Upon petition, after January 1, 1912, by any person that any employment or place of employment is not safe or is injurious to the welfare of any employee or frequenter, the commission shall proceed with or without notice, to make such investigation as may be necessary to determine the matter complained of. *Investigations.*

2. After such hearing as may be necessary, the commission may enter such order relative thereto as may be necessary to render such employment or place of employment safe and not injurious to the welfare of the employees therein or frequenters thereof.

3. Whenever the commission shall learn that any employment or place of employment is not safe or is injurious to the welfare of any employee or frequenter it may of its own motion, summarily investigate the same, with or without notice, and enter such order as may be necessary relative thereto.

Powers, etc., transferred.
SEC. 2394–54. 1. All duties, liabilities, authority, powers and privileges heretofore or hereafter conferred and imposed by law upon the commissioner of labor and industrial statistics, deputy commissioner of labor and industrial statistics, factory inspector, woman factory inspector, assistant factory inspectors and bakery inspector, are hereby imposed and conferred upon the industrial commission and its deputies.

Reference of laws.
2. All laws relating or referring to the commissioner of labor and industrial statistics, and the deputy commissioner of labor and industrial statistics, except those laws relating or referring to their appoinment and qualification and to their membership or service on the industrial accident board and all laws relating or referring to the factory inspector, the woman factory inspector, assistant factory inspectors and the bakery inspector, shall apply to and be deemed to relate and refer to the industrial commission, so far as the said laws are applicable.

Orders.
SEC. 2394–55. All orders of the industrial commission in comformity with law shall be in force, and shall be prima facie lawful; and all such orders shall be valid and in force, and prima facie reasonable and lawful until they are found otherwise in an action brought for that purpose, pursuant of the provisions of section 2394–69 of the Statutes, or until altered or revoked by the commission.

Orders take effect, when.
SEC. 2394–56. 1. All general orders shall take effect within thirty days after their publication in the official State papers. Special orders shall take effect as therein directed.

2. The commission shall, upon application of any employer, grant such time as may be reasonably necessary for compliance with any order.

3. Any person may petition the commission for an extension of time, which the commission shall grant if it finds such an extension of time necessary.

Hearings.
SEC. 2394–57. 1. Any employer or other person interested either because of ownership in or occupation of any property affected by any such order, or otherwise, may petition for a hearing on the reasonableness of any order of the commission in the manner provided in sections 2394–41 to 2394–71, inclusive.

2. Such petition for hearing shall be by verified petition filed with the commission, setting out specifically and in full detail the order upon which a hearing is desired and every reason why such order is unreasonable, and every issue to be considered by the commission on the hearing. The petioner shall be deemed to have finally waived all objections to any irregularities and illegalities in the order upon which a hearing is sought other than those set forth in the petition. All hearings of the commission shall be open to the public.

3. Upon receipt of such petition, if the issues ·raised in such petition have theretofore been adequately considered, the commission shall determine the same by confirming without hearing its previous determination, or if such hearing is necessary to determine the issues raised, the commission shall order a hearing thereon and consider and determine the matter or matters in question at such times as shall be prescribed. Notice of the time and place of such hearing shall be given to the petitioner and to such other persons as the commission may find directly interested in such decision.

4. Upon such investigation, if it shall be found that the order complained of is unjust or unreasonable the commission shall substitute therefor such other order as shall be just and reasonable.

5. Whenever at the time of the final determination upon such hearing it shall·be found that further time is reasonably necessary for compliance with the order of the commission, the commission shall grant such time as may be reasonably necessary for such compliance.

SEC. 2394-58. 1. Nothing contained in this act shall be construed to deprive the common council, the board of alderman, the board of trustees or the village board of any village or city, or the board of health of any municipality of any power or jurisdiction over or relative to any place of employment: *Provided*, That, whenever the industrial commission shall, by an order, fix a standard of safety or any hygienic condition for employment or places of employment, such order shall, upon the filing by the commission of a copy thereof with the clerk of the village or city to which it may apply, be held to amend or modify any similar conflicting local order in any particular matters governed by said order. Thereafter no local officer shall make or enforce any order contrary thereto. Local authorities.

2. Any person affected by any local order in conflict with an order of the commission, may in the manner provided in section 2394-57 of the Statutes, petition the industrial commission for a hearing on the ground that such local order is unreasonable and in conflict with the order of the commission. The petition for such hearing shall conform to the requirements set forth for a petition in said section 2394-57 of the Statutes.

3. Upon receipt of such petition the commission shall order a hearing thereon, to consider and determine the issues raised by such appeal, such hearing to be held in the village, city or municipality where the local order appealed from was made. Notice of the time and place of such hearing·shall be given to the petitioner and such other persons as the commission may find directly interested in such decision, including the clerk of the municipality or town which such appeal comes. If upon such investigation it shall be found that the local order appealed from is unreasonable and in conflict with the order of the commission, the commission may modify its order and shall substitute for the local order appealed from such order as shall be reasonable and legal in the premises, and thereafter the said local order shall, in such particulars, be void and of no effect.

SEC. 2394-59. 1. No action, proceeding or suit to set aside, vacate or amend any order of the commission or to enjoin the enforcement thereof, shall be brought unless the plaintiff shall have applied to the commission for a hearing thereon at the time and as provided in section 2394-57 of the Statutes, and in the petition therefor shall have raised every issue raised in such action. Action to set aside orders.

2. Every order of the commission shall, in every prosecution for violation thereof, be conclusively presumed to be just, reasonable and lawful, unless prior to the institution of prosecution for such violation an action shall have been brought to vacate and set aside such order, as provided in section 2394-68 of the Statutes.

SEC. 2394-60. Every day during which any person, persons, corporation or any officer, agent or employee thereof, shall fail to observe and comply with any order of the commission or to perform any duty enjoined by sections 2394-41 to 2394-71, inclusive, shall constitute a separate and distinct violation of such order, or of said section as the case may be. Separate offenses.

SEC. 2394-61. Each of the commissioners for the purposes mentioned in sections 2394-41 to 2394-71, inclusive, shall have power to administer oaths, certify to official acts, issue subpœnas, compel the attendance of witnesses, and the production of papers, books, accounts, documents and testimony. In case of failure of any person to comply with any order of the commission or any subpœna lawfully issued or on the refusal of any witness to Powers of commissioners.

testify to any matter regarding which he may be lawfully interrogated, it shall be the duty of the circuit court of any county, or the judge thereof, on application of a commissioner to compel obedience by attachment proceedings for contempt, as in the case of disobedience of the requirements of a subpœna issued from such court, or a refusal to testify therein.

Witnesses.   SEC. 2394-62. Each witness who shall appear before the commission by its order shall receive for his attendance the fees and mileage now provided for witnesses in civil cases in courts of record, which shall be audited and paid by the State in the same manner as other expenses are audited and paid, upon the presentation of properly verified vouchers approved by the chairman of the commission. But no witness subpœnaed at the instance of parties other than the commission shall be entitled to compensation from the State for attendance or travel unless the commission shall certify that his testimony was material to the matter investigated.

Depositions.   SEC. 2394-63. The commission or any party may in any investigation cause the depositions of witnesses residing within or without the State to be taken in the manner prescribed by law for like depositions in civil actions in circuit courts.

Records.   SEC. 2394-64. A full and complete record shall be kept of all proceedings had before the commission on any investigation and all testimony shall be taken down by the stenographer appointed by the commission.

Deputies.   SEC. 2394-65. 1. For the purpose of making any investigation with regard to any employment or place of employment the commission shall have power to appoint, by an order in writing, any member of the commission, any deputy who is a citizen of the State, or any other competent person as an agent whose duties shall be prescribed in such order.

2. In the discharge of his duties such agent shall have every power whatsoever of an inquisitorial nature granted in this act to the commission, and the same powers as a court commissioner with regard to the taking of depositions; and all powers granted by law to a court commissioner relative to depositions are hereby granted to such agent.

Provisions in case of fire.

Doors to open outward.   SECTION 4390. Every building now or hereafter used, in whole or in part, as a * * * factory or workshop, * * * or office building, must be provided with exits having doors that open or swing outward, whether such doors are outer doors or open upon vestibules or stairways, and when storm doors are used at the entrance of any such building, either inside or outside, said storm doors shall have a glass therein, not less than fifteen inches square, and such doors through which employees must pass to gain access to the outside of the building, in which they are em-
Not to be locked. ployed, must remain unlocked during working hours. Any owner, tenant, corporation, person or persons in charge of any of the above named buildings, who shall fail to comply with this section, or any architect who shall prepare plans for any building which is required by this section to be provided with such doors. without providing in such plans for the same, shall be punished by a fine of not exceeding five hundred dollars, or by imprisonment in the county jail not longer than ninety days. * * *

Fire escapes.   SEC. 4390a. Every person or corporation owning, occupying or controlling any factory, workshop or structure three or more stories high, except such as are included in the next preceding section, in which twenty-five or more persons are employed at any kind of labor, shall provide and keep connected with the same one or more good and substantial metallic or fireproof ladders, stairs or stairways, ready for use at all times, reaching from the cornice to the top of the first story, and placed on the outside thereof in such position and number as may be designated by the chief of the fire department or fire marshal of the city or village in which such structure is situated, or by the State factory inspector, and at each story above the first a wrought iron balcony in connection with such ladder, such balcony to be substantially attached to the structure, and of such length as to permit of access to it from two or more windows on each story, and of sufficient size to furnish reasonable means of escape to the persons employed therein from each and every floor or story above the first; and in all cities and villages where there is a water supply, either from waterworks, fire engines or pumping station, there shall be attached to such fire escape, except on structures equipped with automatic sprinklers, a three-inch wrought iron standpipe **Standpipes.** extending from a point within five feet from the ground to a point three feet above the roof or cornice, and on the roof shall be attached a two and one-half inch angle hose valve, with male hose connection and a double or Siamese " Y " female hose connection at the base of the pipe, the threads of which shall conform to the size and pattern used by the fire department where the structure is located. Any such person or corporation who shall fail, for three months after the receipt of notice in writing, stating the substance of the provisions of this section, from such chief, marshal or inspector to provide and keep such means of escape or such standpipe shall be punished by fine not exceeding one hundred dollars.

INDEX.

A.

S.

O